GUNSLINGER GIRL

OMNIBUS COLLECTION 2

Vol. 4-6

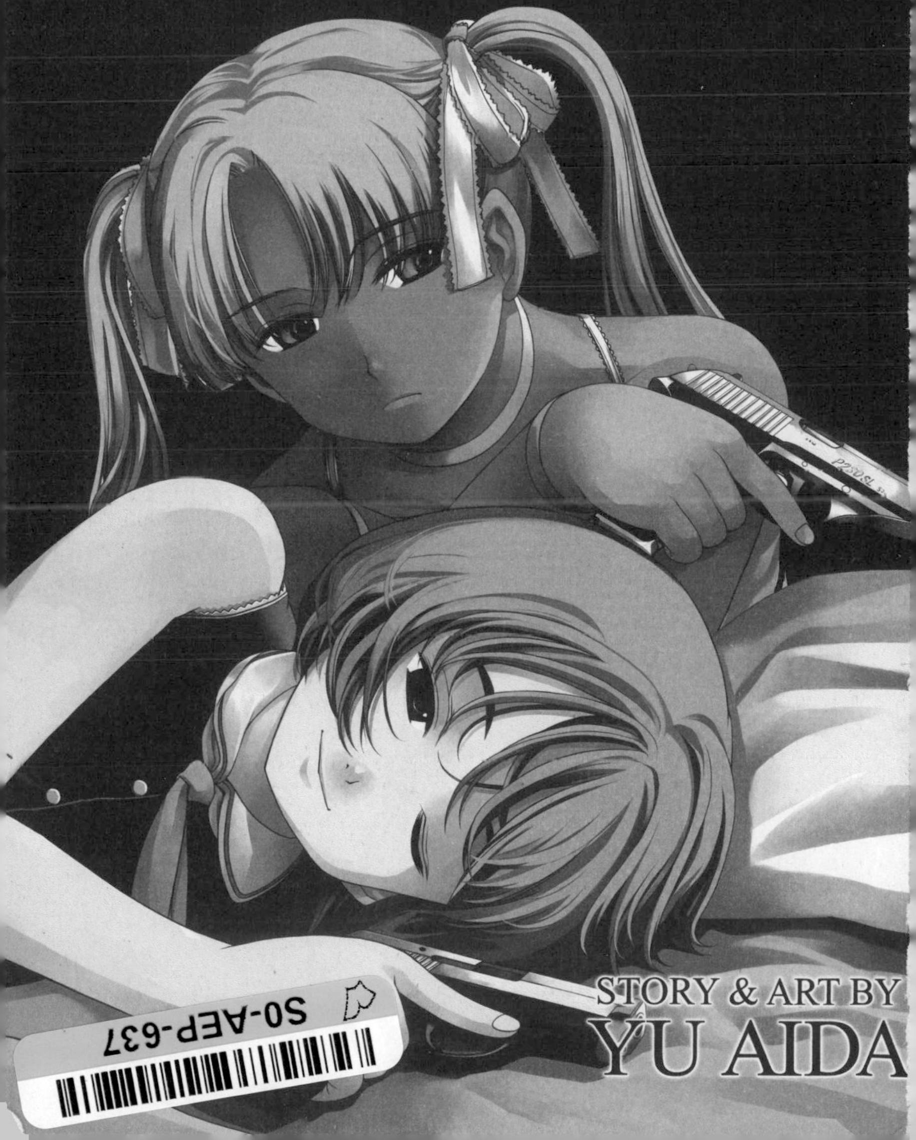

STORY & ART BY
YU AIDA

GUNSLINGERGIRL

OMNIBUS COLLECTION 2

Vol. **4-6**

STORY & ART BY
YU AIDA

STAFF CREDITS

translation	**Adrienne Beck**
adaptation	**Janet Houck**
retouch & lettering	**Roland Amago**
cover design	**Nicky Lim**
layout	**Bambi Eloriaga-Amago**
copy editor	**Shanti Whitesides**
editor	**Adam Arnold**
publisher	**Jason DeAngelis**
	Seven Seas Entertainment

GUNSLINGER GIRL OMNIBUS COLLECTION 2
Content originally published as Gunslinger Girl Vol. 4-6.
Copyright © Yu Aida 2004-2006
First published in 2004-2006 by Media Works Inc., Tokyo, Japan.
English translation rights arranged with ASCII MEDIA WORKS.

Visit us online at www.gomanga.com.

ISBN: 978-1-934876-97-8

Printed in Canada

First Printing: May 2011

10 9 8 7 6 5 4 3 2 1

C O N T E N T S

Vol. 4-6

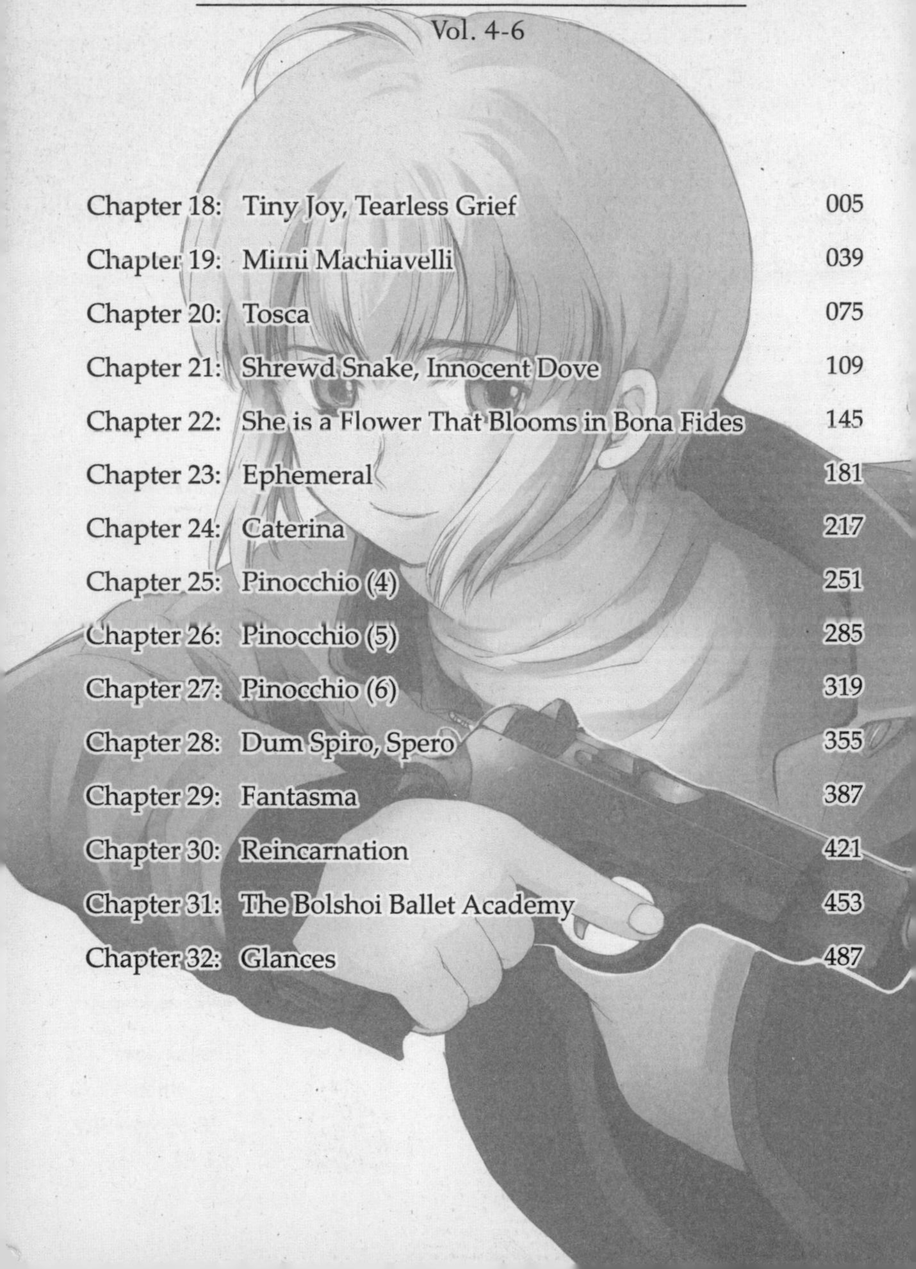

CAST OF CHARACTERS

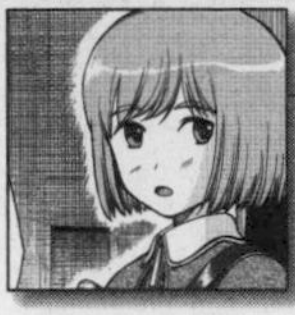

HENRIETTA

The only survivor of a slaughtered family of six. Thanks to her "conditioning" when she was converted into a cyborg, she is blindly in love with her handler, Jose.

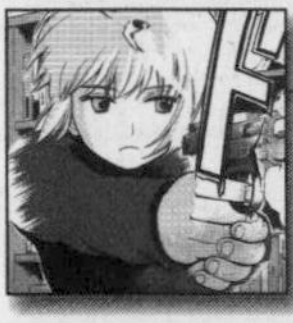

RICO

Former quadriplegic. Innocent and cheerful, even the most common everyday things bring her much joy. Her handler is Jean.

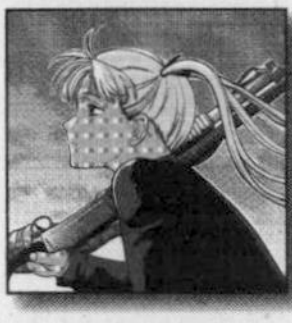

TRIELA

Smart and responsible, she is an "older sister" figure for the other cyborgs. She was defeated only once, when she faced the hitman "Pinocchio" in his Montalcino home.

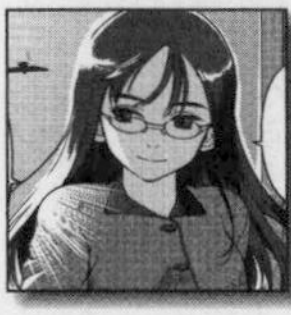

CLAES

Triela's roommate. When her handler Raballo was killed, she became the Agency's "guinea pig" cyborg. All cyborg developments are first tested on her.

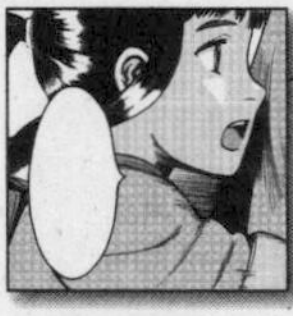

ANGELICA

The first prototype cyborg. She was the first to start displaying side effects to the cyborg conversion process, and has an acute dependency on the "drug" used. Her handler is Marco.

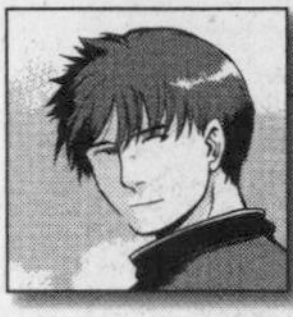

JOSE

Ex-military. Generally, he is very kind to Henrietta, but he is beginning to find himself disturbed at how much he unconsciously imposes his late sister's image onto her.

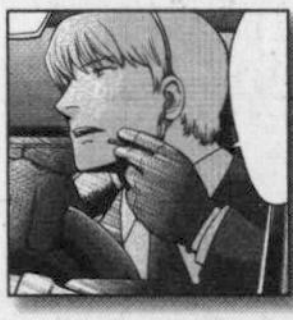

JEAN

Jose's older brother. Very serious-minded and business-like. He is the cyborg handlers' leader and field commander for Section 2 operations.

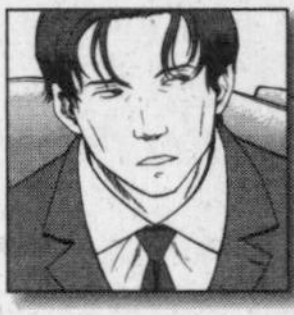

HILSHIRE

German. Former detective with Europol. He tries very hard to be kind to Triela, but has difficulty in figuring out what kind of distance there should be in their relationship.

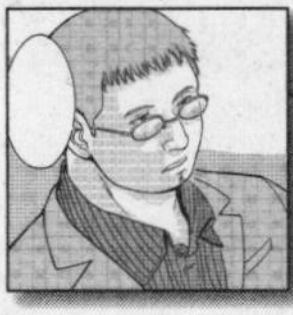

MARCO

Ex-military special forces. When he was discharged due to an injury, he took up a job with the Agency. He has trouble dealing with feelings of helplessness and frustration as he watches Angelica's condition deteriorate day by day.

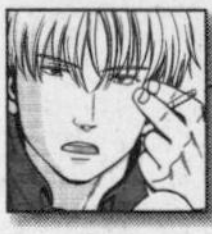

PINOCCHIO

A naturally gifted killer. He is guarding Franco and Franca on Cristiano's orders.

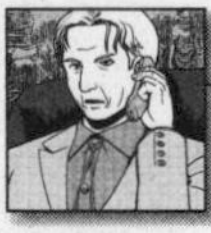

CRISTIANO

Conservative leader of the Milan Group, a part of Padania's Five Republics Faction. He raised Pinocchio.

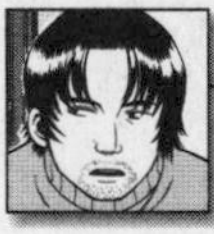

FRANCO

Professional bomb-maker. Franca's partner.

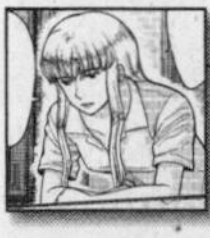

FRANCA

Five Republics Faction terrorist. Following her own cause, she is a freelance activist and bomb-maker. Currently partnered with Franco.

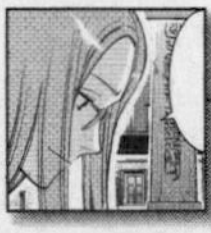

PATRICIA

Marco's ex-fiancée. She works for a publishing company.

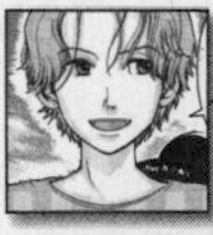

PRISCILLA

Agent for Section 2. Her main responsibilities center around data analysis.

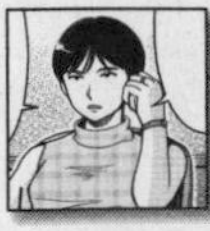

FERRO

Agent for Section 2. She serves as the lead for all regular agents and as an assistant to the cyborg handlers.

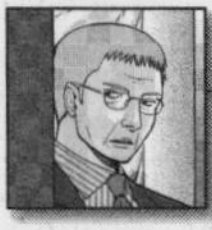

LORENZO

Section 2 chief. Formerly employed with the Ministry of State.

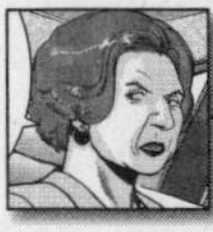

MONICA MARIA PETRIS

Director of both Section 1 and 2.

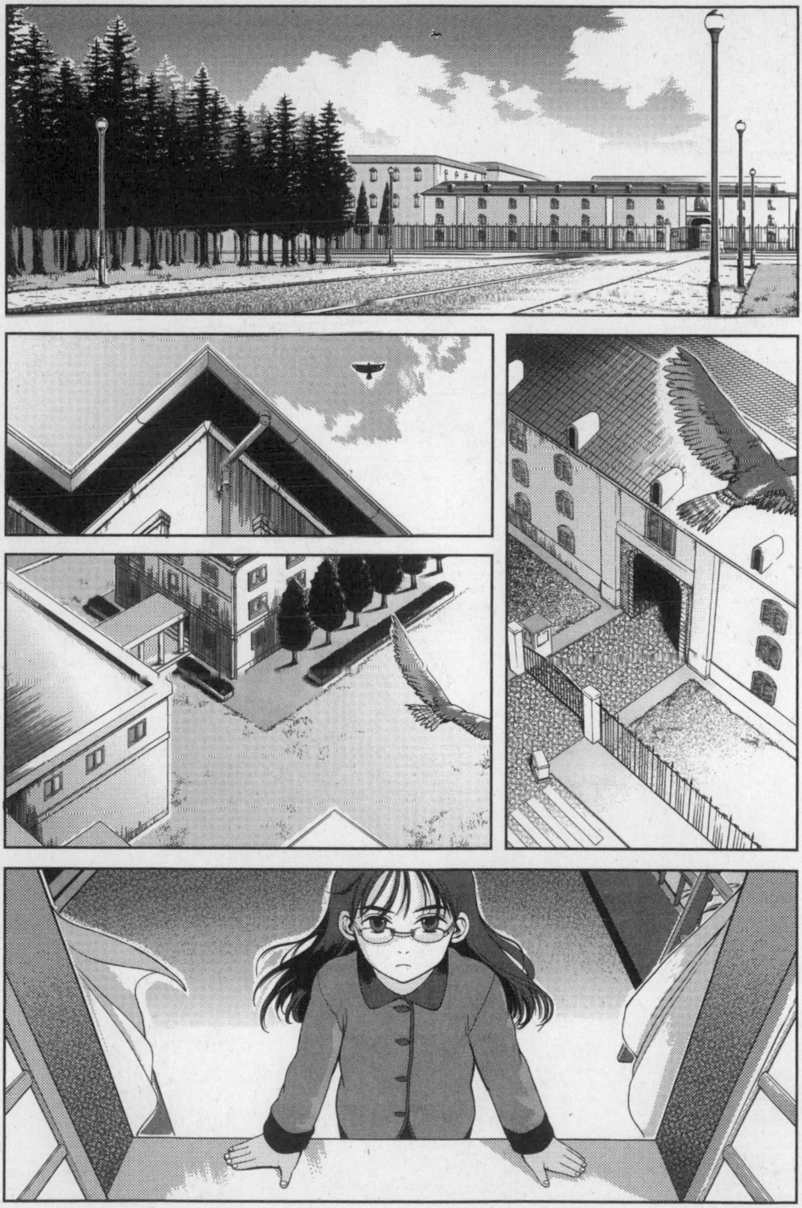

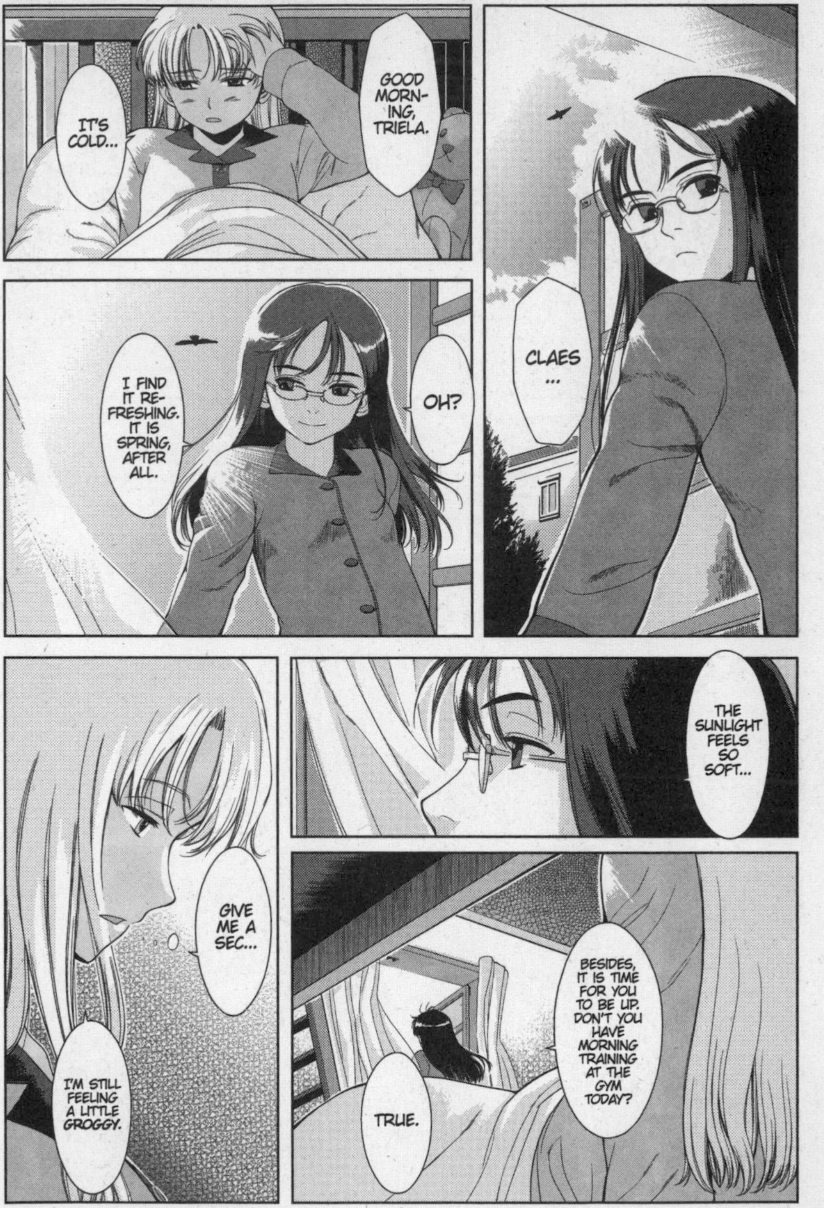
CLAES ...
GOOD MORNING, TRIELA.
IT'S COLD...
OH?
I FIND IT REFRESHING. IT IS SPRING, AFTER ALL.
THE SUNLIGHT FEELS SO SOFT...
BESIDES, IT IS TIME FOR YOU TO BE UP. DON'T YOU HAVE MORNING TRAINING AT THE GYM TODAY?
TRUE.
GIVE ME A SEC...
I'M STILL FEELING A LITTLE GROGGY.

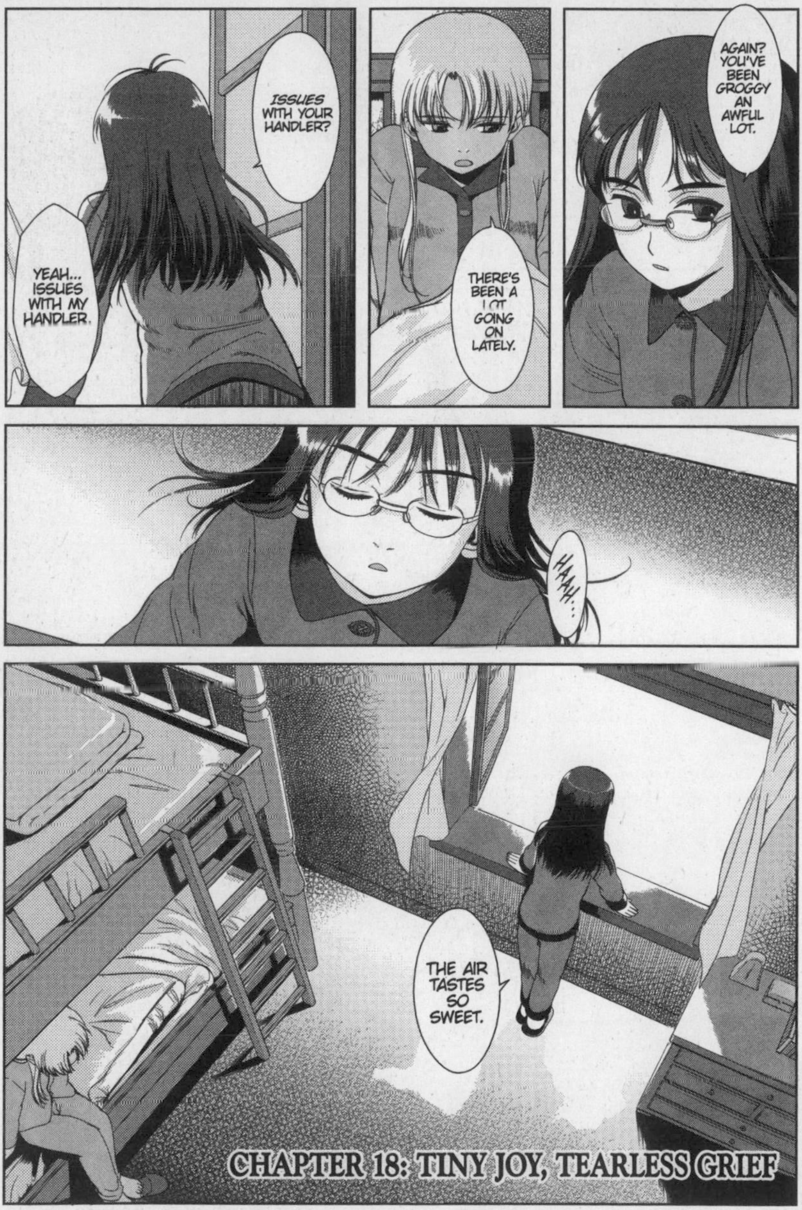
AGAIN? YOU'VE BEEN GROGGY AN AWFUL LOT.
THERE'S BEEN A LOT GOING ON LATELY.
ISSUES WITH YOUR HANDLER?
YEAH... ISSUES WITH MY HANDLER.
HAAH...
THE AIR TASTES SO SWEET.

CHAPTER 18: TINY JOY, TEARLESS GRIEF

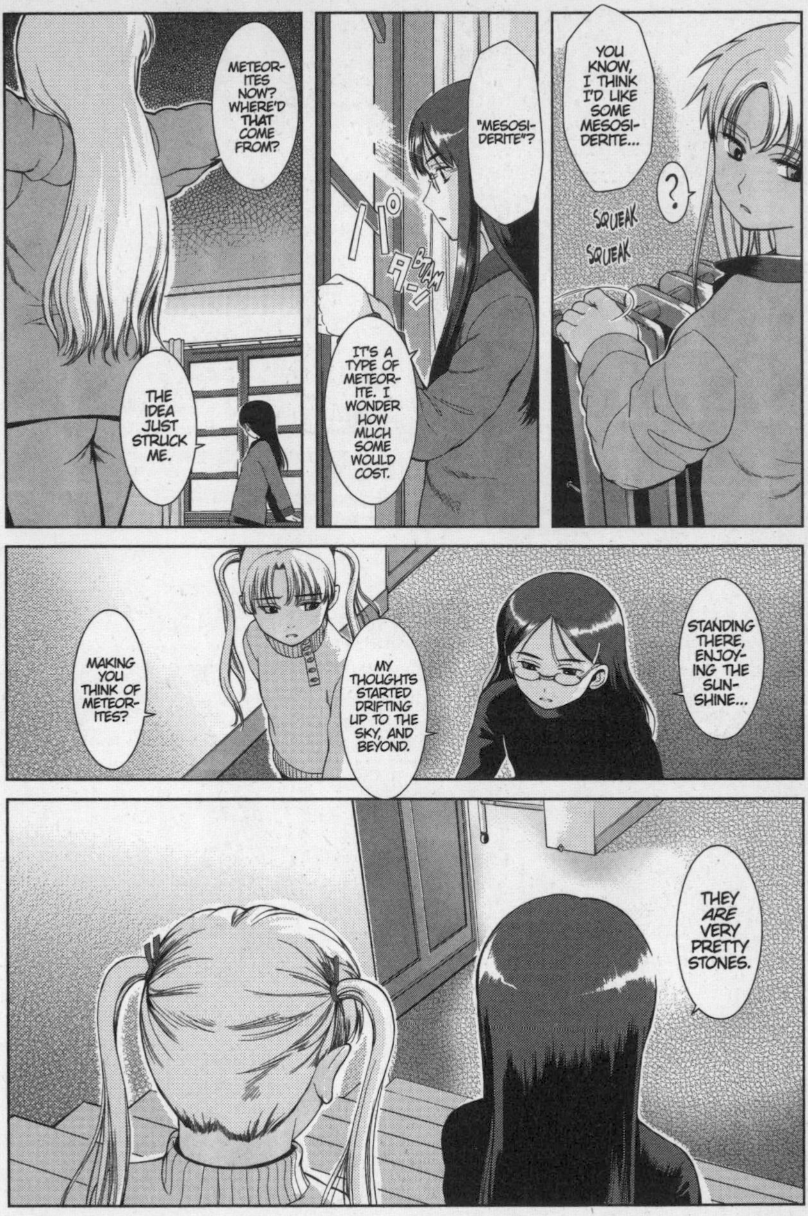
YOU KNOW, I THINK I'D LIKE SOME MESOSIDERITE...
?
SQUEAK
SQUEAK
"MESOSIDERITE"?
BLAM
IT'S A TYPE OF METEORITE. I WONDER HOW MUCH SOME WOULD COST.
METEORITES NOW? WHERE'D THAT COME FROM?
THE IDEA JUST STRUCK ME.
STANDING THERE, ENJOYING THE SUNSHINE...
MY THOUGHTS STARTED DRIFTING UP TO THE SKY, AND BEYOND.
MAKING YOU THINK OF METEORITES?
THEY ARE VERY PRETTY STONES.

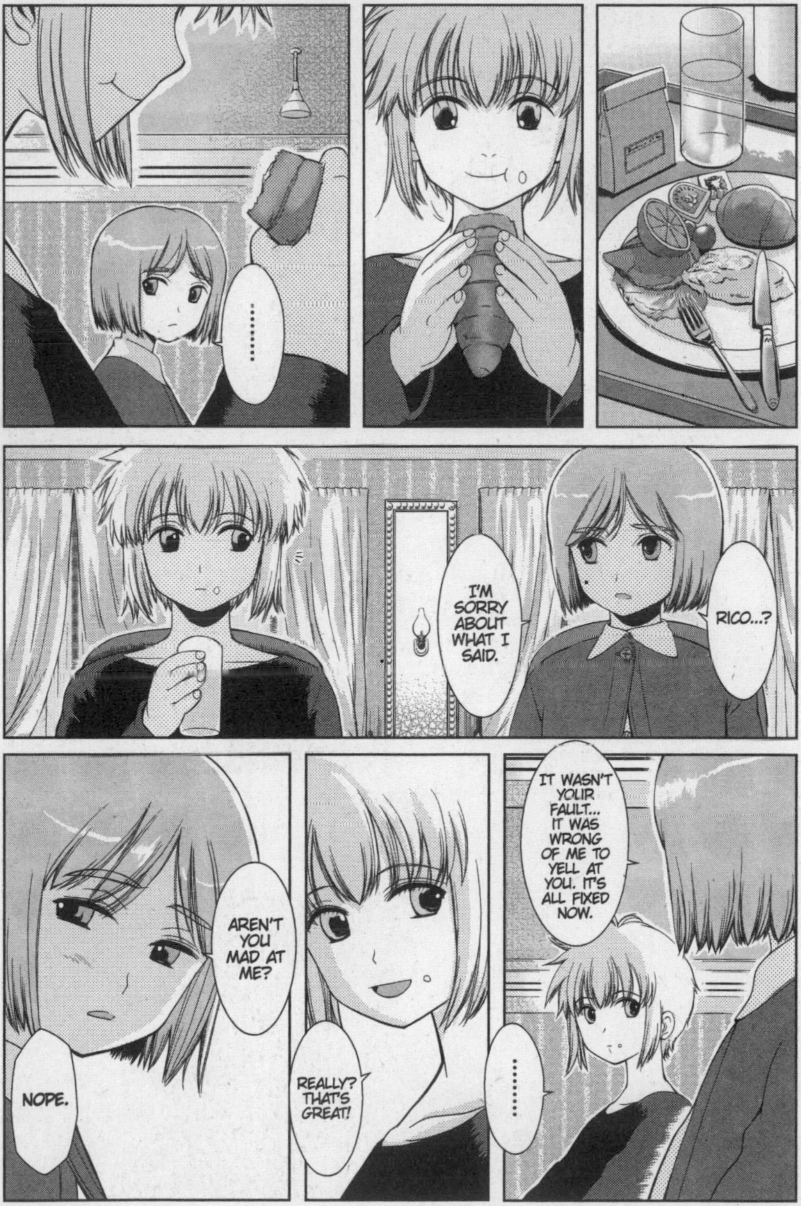
......
RICO...?
I'M SORRY ABOUT WHAT I SAID.
IT WASN'T YOUR FAULT... IT WAS WRONG OF ME TO YELL AT YOU. IT'S ALL FIXED NOW.
......
REALLY? THAT'S GREAT!
AREN'T YOU MAD AT ME?
NOPE.

YOU'RE STILL HERE WITH ME, RIGHT?
AND YOU'RE GOING TO STAY WITH ME, RIGHT? SO WHY SHOULD I BE MAD?
?
SQUEEZE
HEE HEE HEE!
SHAKE SHAKE
YOU SHOULD HAVE THEM BUY YOU SOME.
BUY SOME WHAT?
THAT SPACE ROCK YOU MENTIONED.

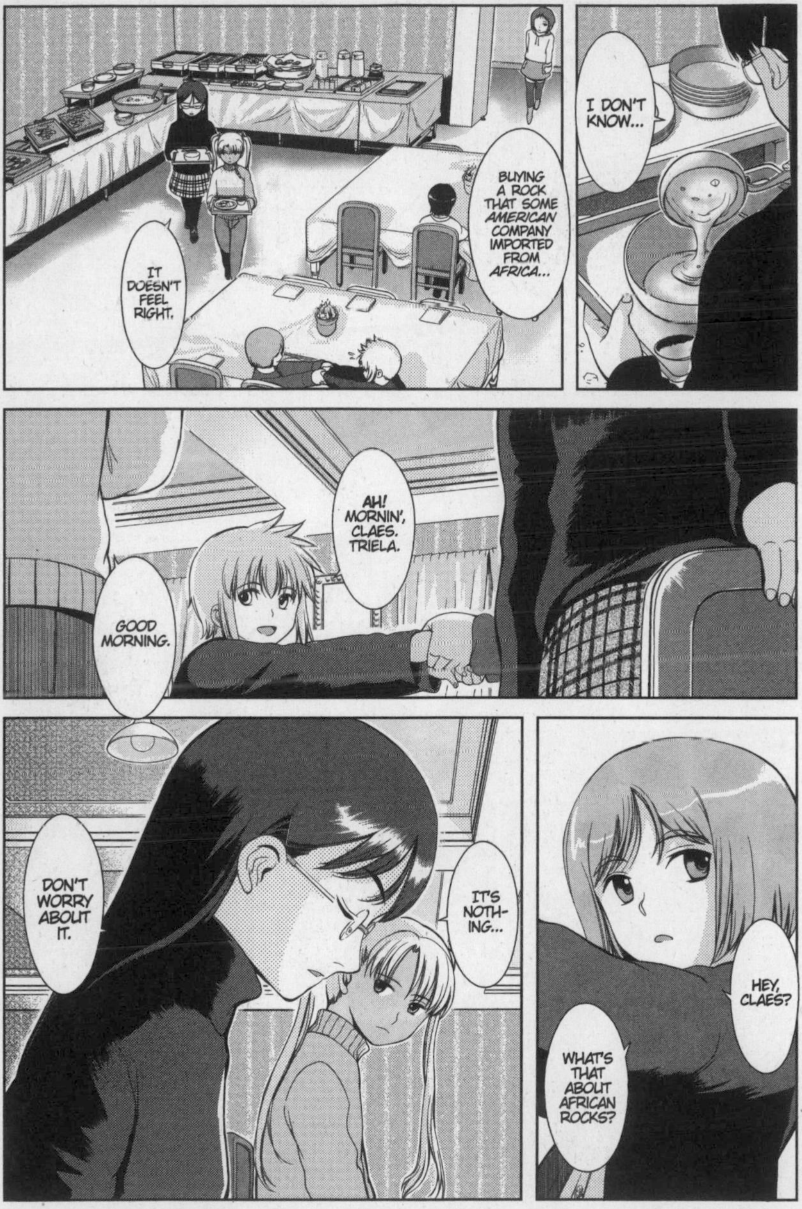
I DON'T KNOW...
BUYING A ROCK THAT SOME AMERICAN COMPANY IMPORTED FROM AFRICA...
IT DOESN'T FEEL RIGHT.
AH! MORNIN', CLAES. TRIELA.
GOOD MORNING.
HEY, CLAES?
WHAT'S THAT ABOUT AFRICAN ROCKS?
IT'S NOTHING...
DON'T WORRY ABOUT IT.

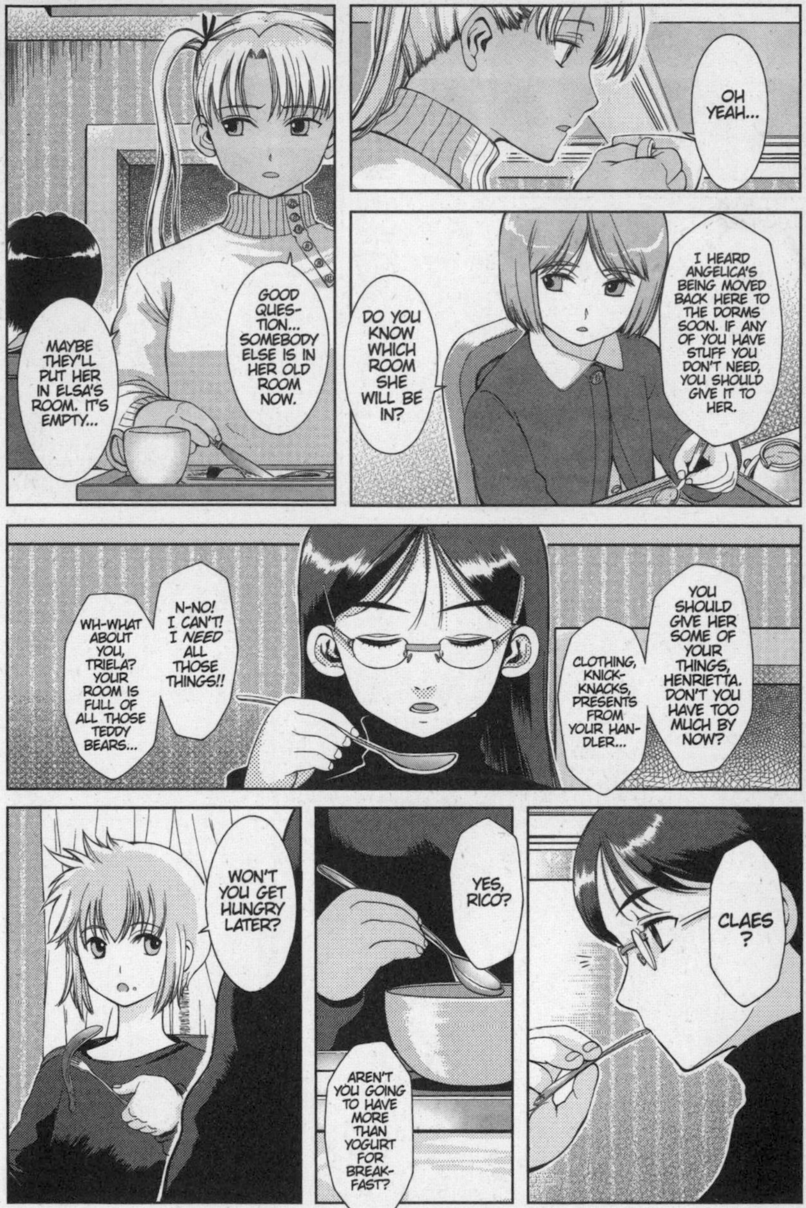
OH YEAH...
I HEARD ANGELICA'S BEING MOVED BACK HERE TO THE DORMS SOON. IF ANY OF YOU HAVE STUFF YOU DON'T NEED, YOU SHOULD GIVE IT TO HER.
DO YOU KNOW WHICH ROOM SHE WILL BE IN?
GOOD QUES-TION... SOMEBODY ELSE IS IN HER OLD ROOM NOW.
MAYBE THEY'LL PUT HER IN ELSA'S ROOM. IT'S EMPTY...
YOU SHOULD GIVE HER SOME OF YOUR THINGS, HENRIETTA. DON'T YOU HAVE TOO MUCH BY NOW?
CLOTHING, KNICK-KNACKS, PRESENTS FROM YOUR HAN-DLER...
N-NO! I CAN'T! I *NEED* ALL THOSE THINGS!!
WH-WHAT ABOUT YOU, TRIELA? YOUR ROOM IS FULL OF ALL THOSE TEDDY BEARS...
CLAES?
YES, RICO?
AREN'T YOU GOING TO HAVE MORE THAN YOGURT FOR BREAK-FAST?
WON'T YOU GET HUNGRY LATER?

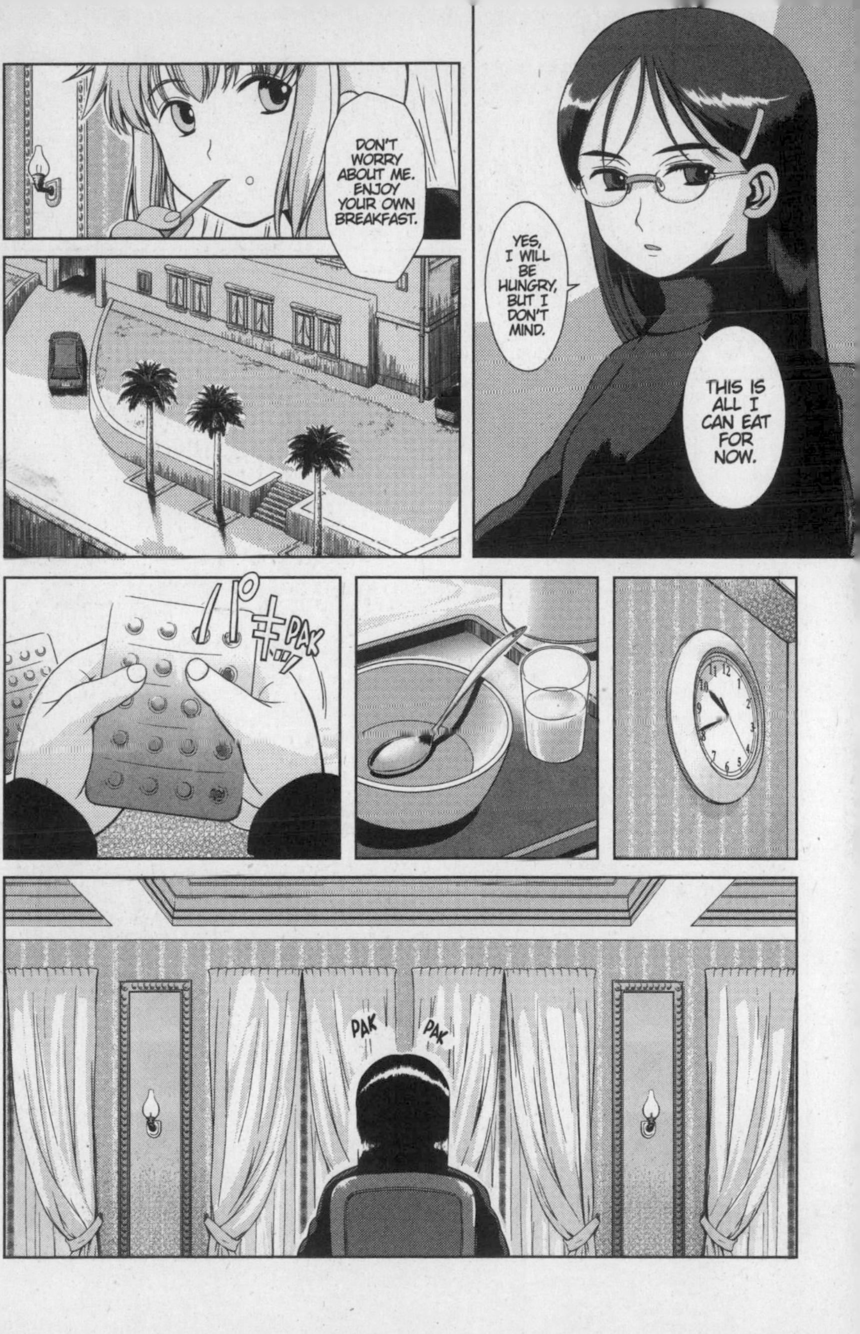
YES, I WILL BE HUNGRY, BUT I DON'T MIND.
THIS IS ALL I CAN EAT FOR NOW.
DON'T WORRY ABOUT ME. ENJOY YOUR OWN BREAKFAST.
パキッ PAK
PAK
PAK

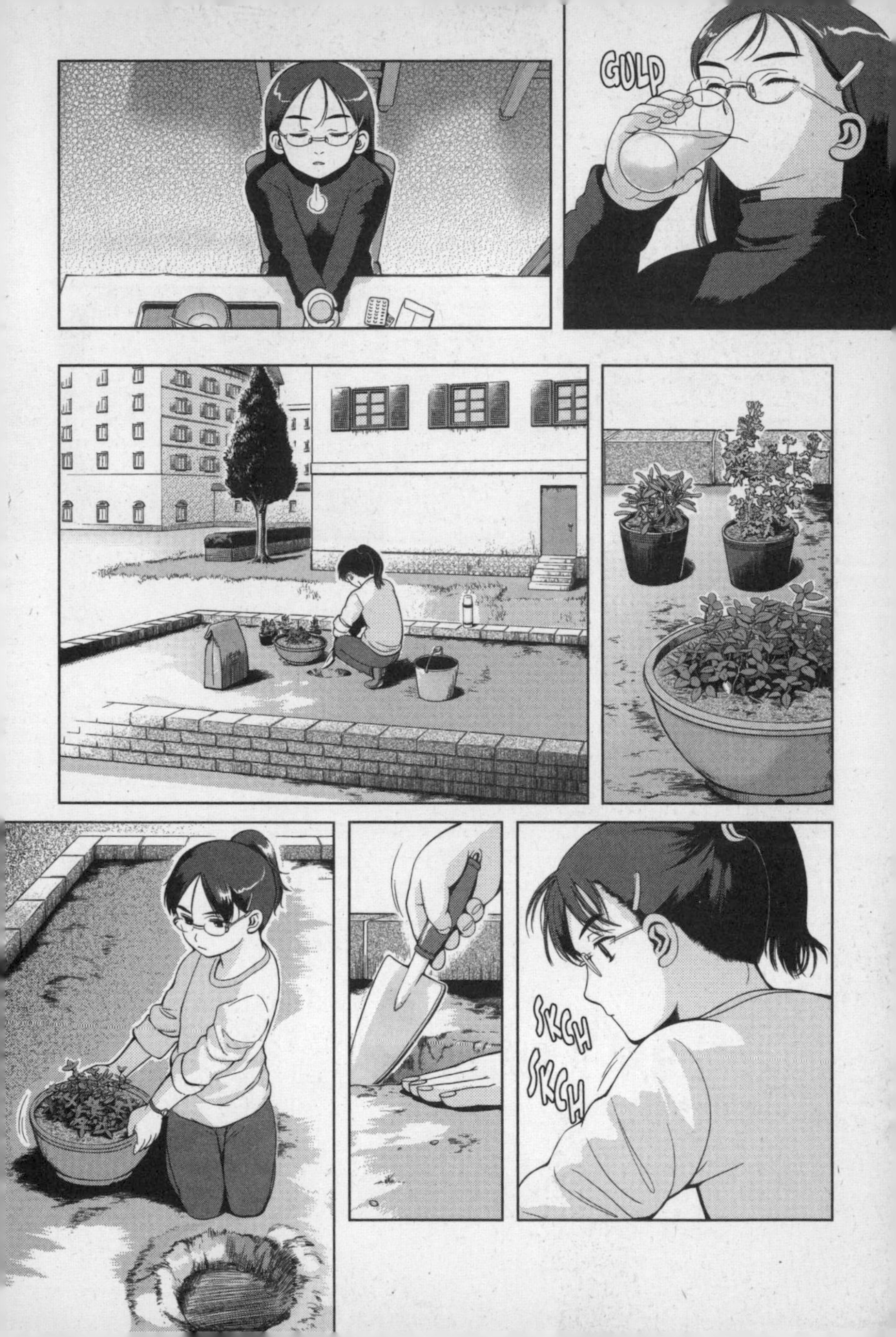
GULP
SKCH
SKCH

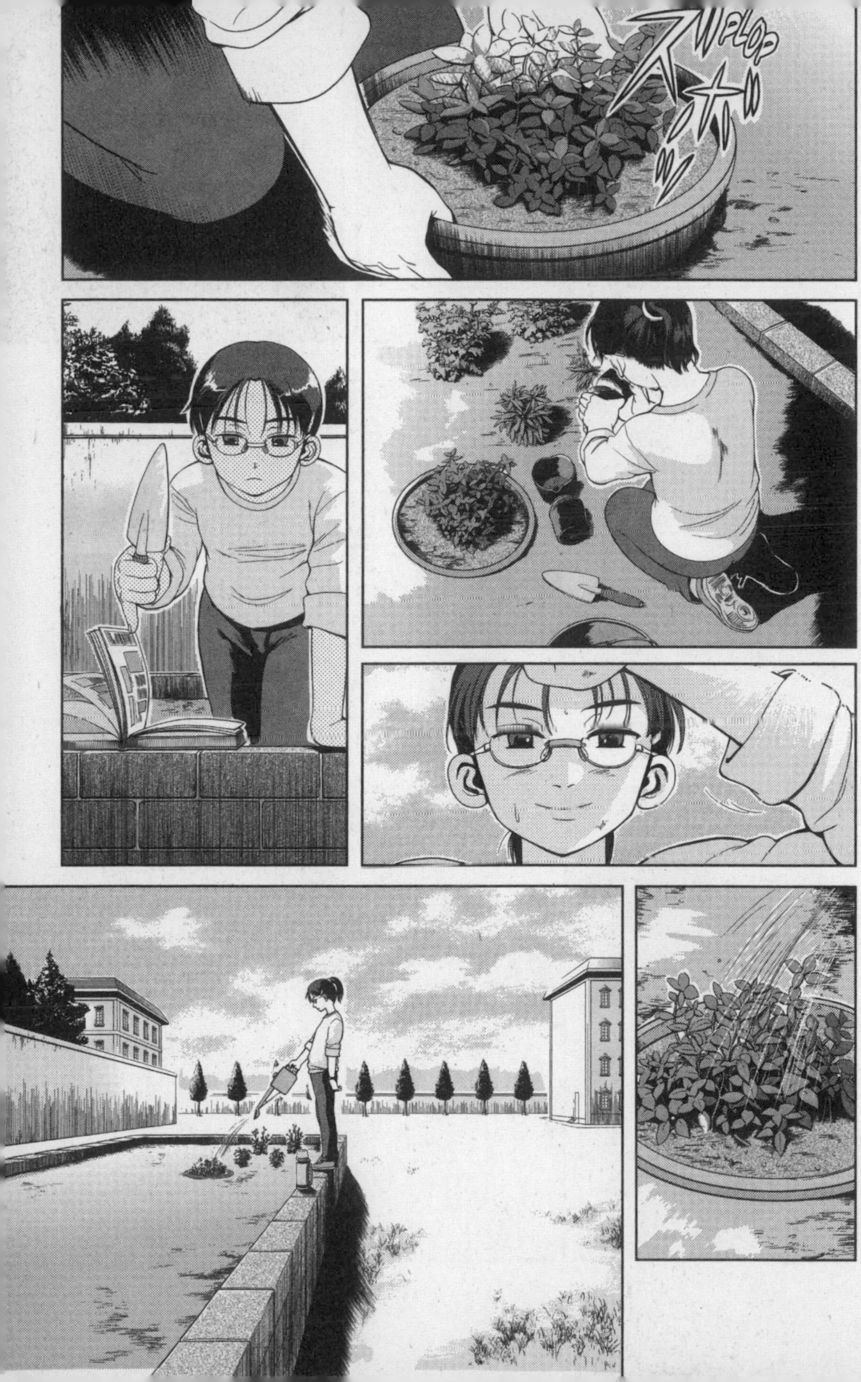
PLOP

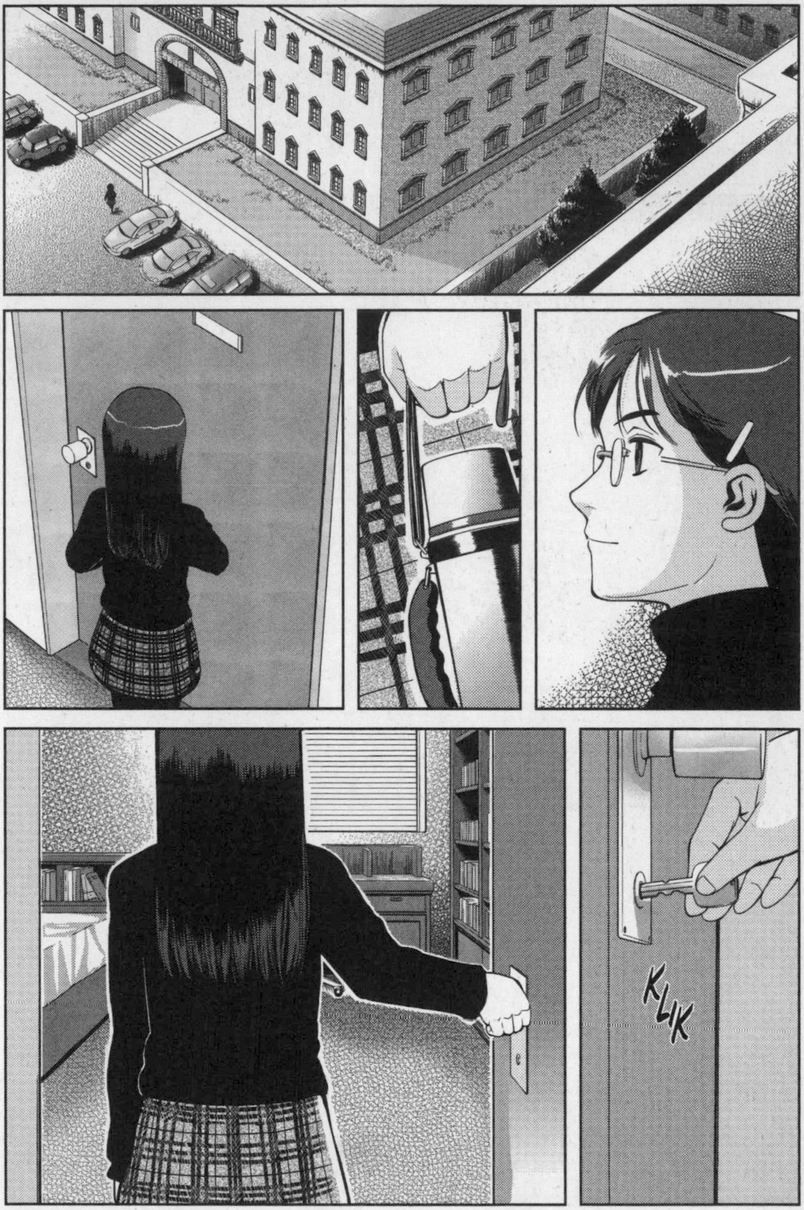
KLIK

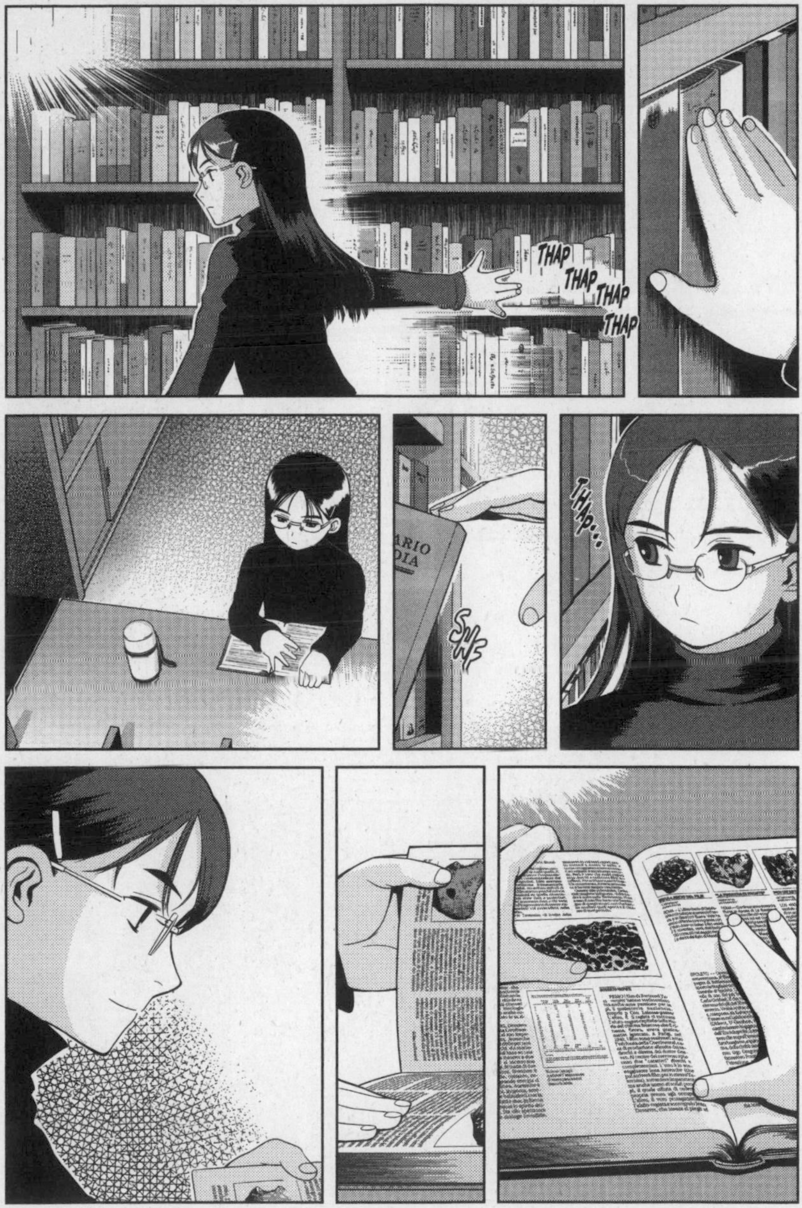
THAP
THAP
THAP
THAP
THAP...
ARIO
DIA
SHF

·········

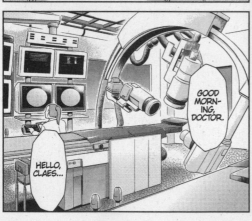

GOOD MORN- ING, DOCTOR.

HELLO, CLAES...

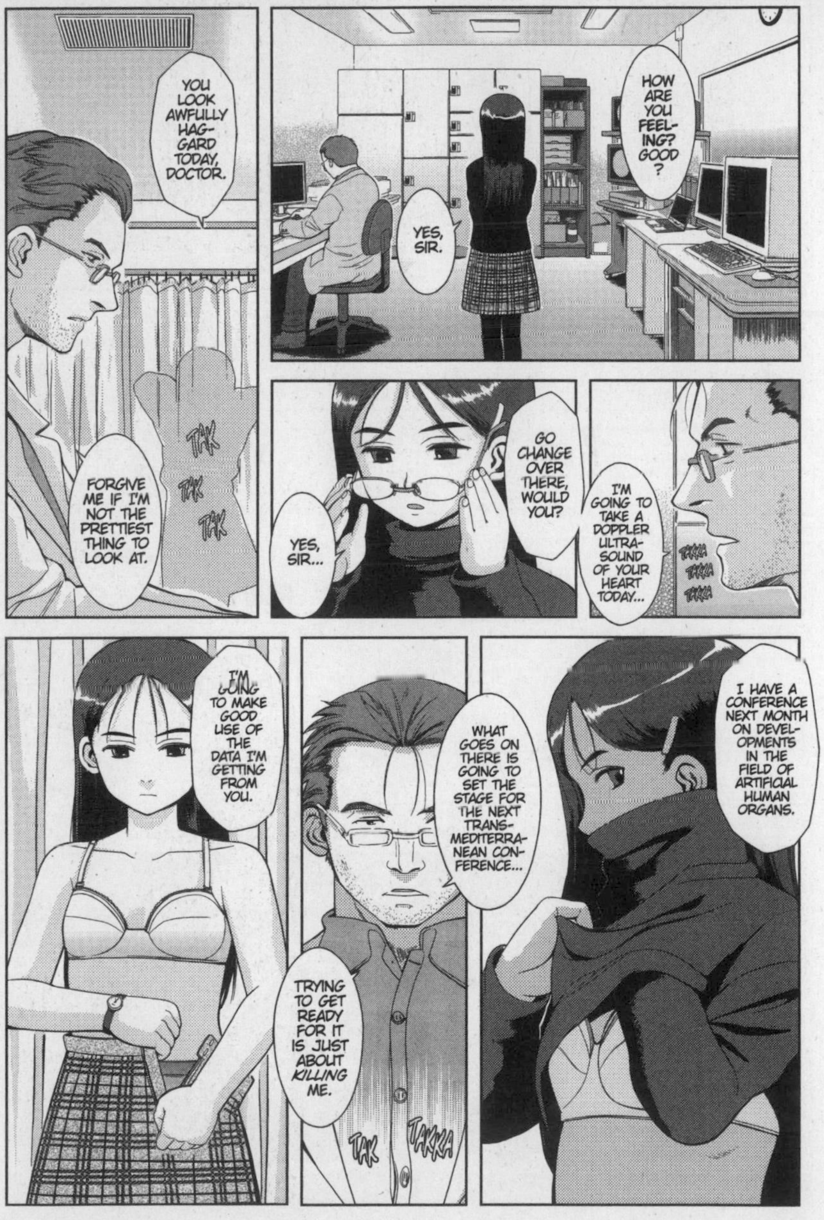
HOW ARE YOU FEELING? GOOD?
YES, SIR.
I'M GOING TO TAKE A DOPPLER ULTRASOUND OF YOUR HEART TODAY...
TAKKA TAKKA TAKKA
GO CHANGE OVER THERE, WOULD YOU?
YES, SIR...
YOU LOOK AWFULLY HAGGARD TODAY, DOCTOR.
TAK TAK TAK
FORGIVE ME IF I'M NOT THE PRETTIEST THING TO LOOK AT.
I HAVE A CONFERENCE NEXT MONTH ON DEVELOPMENTS IN THE FIELD OF ARTIFICIAL HUMAN ORGANS.
WHAT GOES ON THERE IS GOING TO SET THE STAGE FOR THE NEXT TRANS-MEDITERRANEAN CONFERENCE...
TRYING TO GET READY FOR IT IS JUST ABOUT *KILLING* ME.
TAKKA TAK
I'M GOING TO MAKE GOOD USE OF THE DATA I'M GETTING FROM YOU.

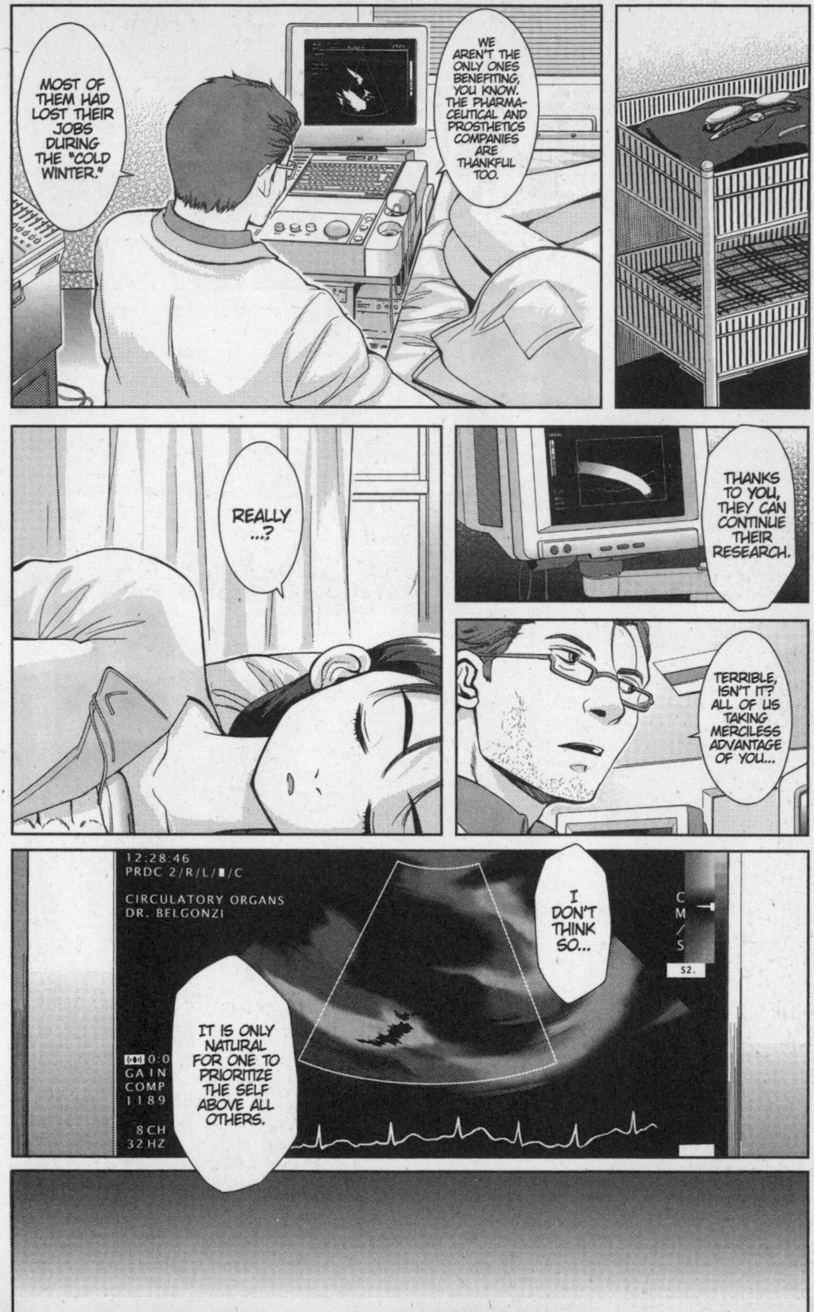

WE AREN'T THE ONLY ONES BENEFITING, YOU KNOW. THE PHARMA-CEUTICAL AND PROSTHETICS COMPANIES ARE THANKFUL TOO.
MOST OF THEM HAD LOST THEIR JOBS DURING THE "COLD WINTER."
THANKS TO YOU, THEY CAN CONTINUE THEIR RESEARCH.
TERRIBLE, ISN'T IT? ALL OF US TAKING MERCILESS ADVANTAGE OF YOU...
REALLY ...?
I DON'T THINK SO...
12:28:46
PRDC 2/R/L/■/C
CIRCULATORY ORGANS
DR. BELGONZI
CM/S
52.
IT IS ONLY NATURAL FOR ONE TO PRIORITIZE THE SELF ABOVE ALL OTHERS.
0:0
GAIN
COMP
1189
8CH
32HZ

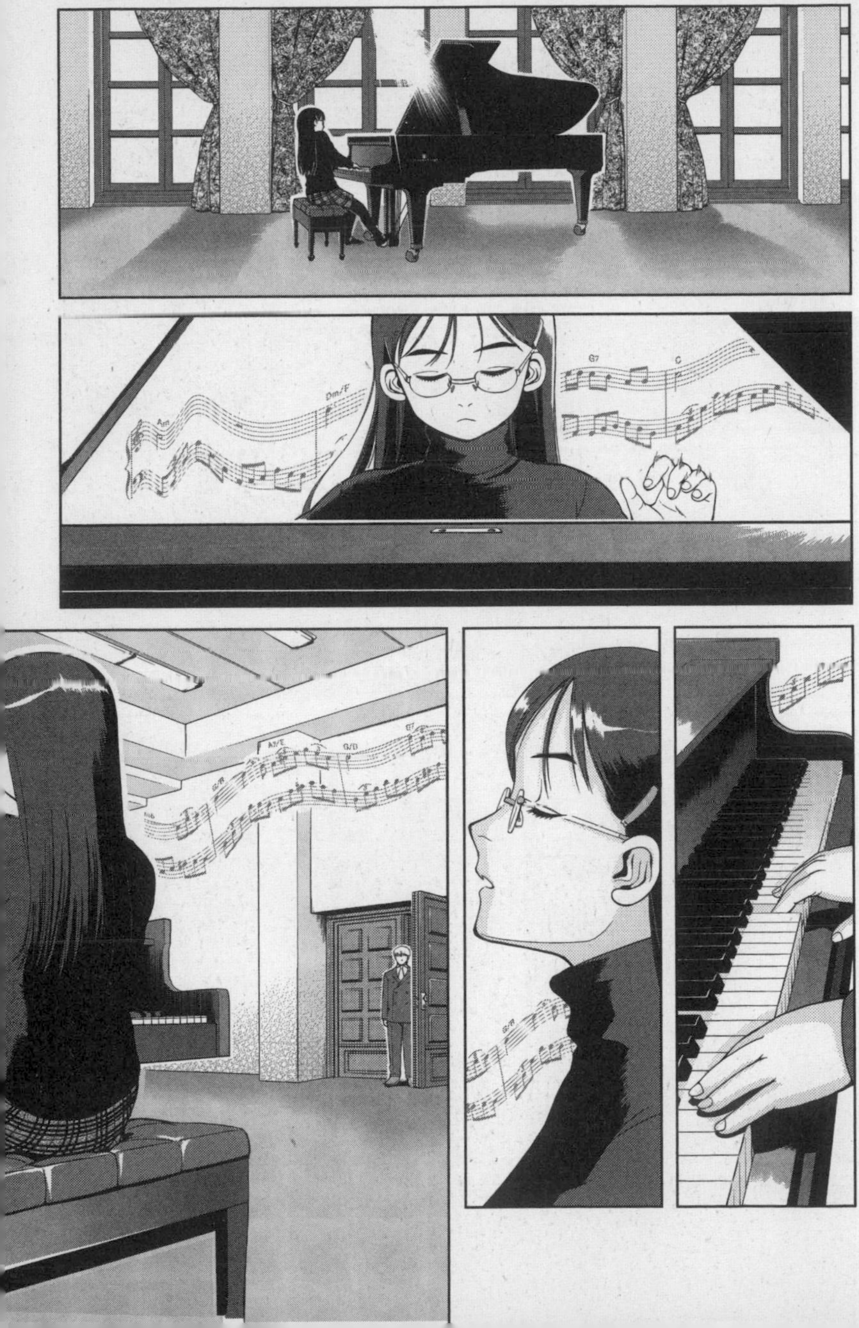
G7
C
Dm/F
Am

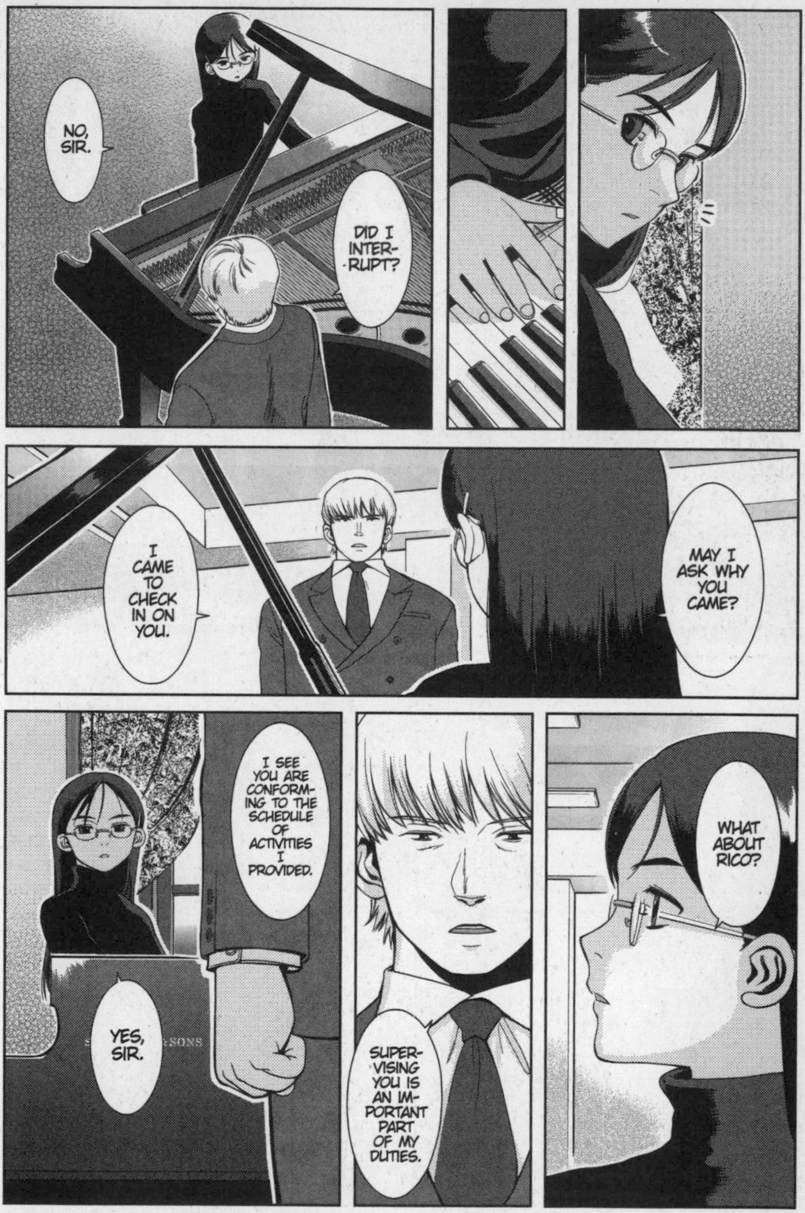
DID I INTER-RUPT?
NO, SIR.
MAY I ASK WHY YOU CAME?
I CAME TO CHECK IN ON YOU.
WHAT ABOUT RICO?
SUPER-VISING YOU IS AN IM-PORTANT PART OF MY DUTIES.
I SEE YOU ARE CONFORM-ING TO THE SCHEDULE OF ACTIVITIES I PROVIDED.
YES, SIR.

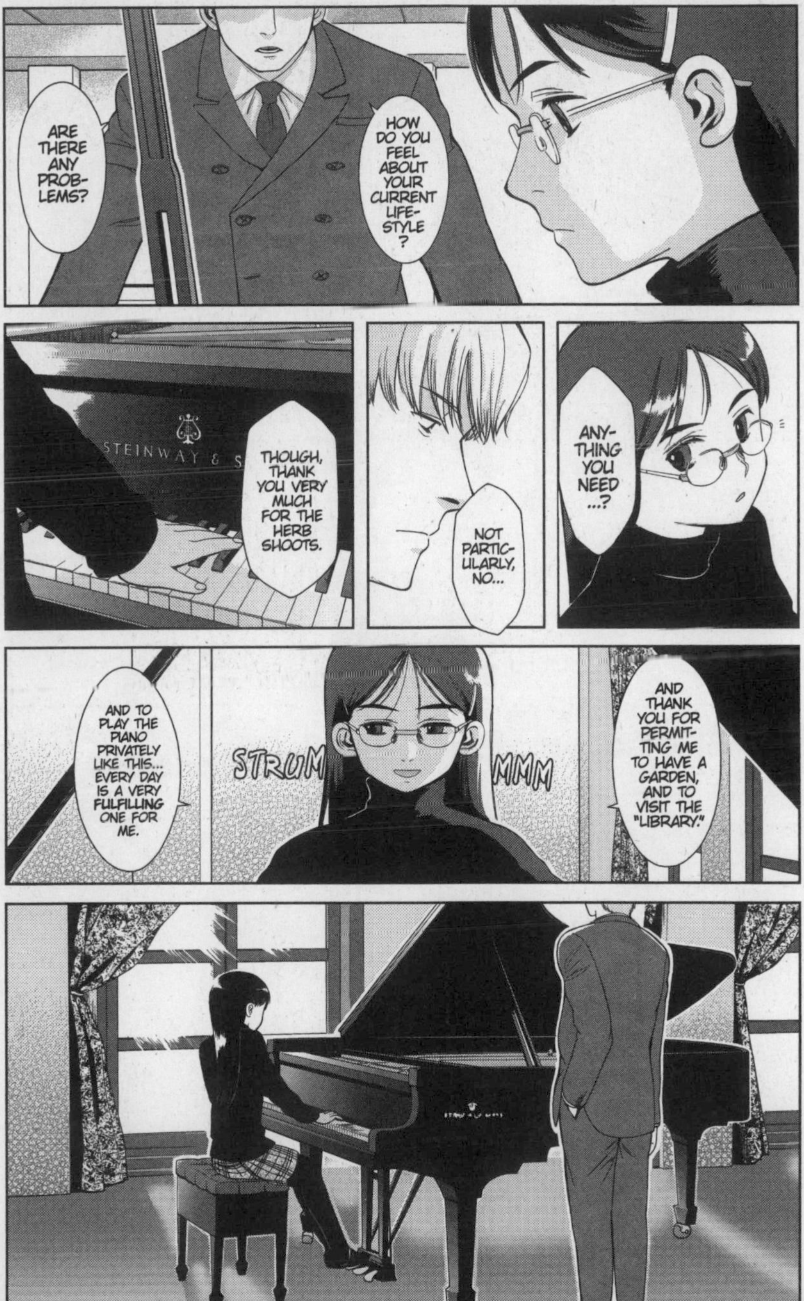
HOW DO YOU FEEL ABOUT YOUR CURRENT LIFESTYLE?
ARE THERE ANY PROBLEMS?
ANYTHING YOU NEED...?
NOT PARTICULARLY, NO...
STEINWAY & S
THOUGH, THANK YOU VERY MUCH FOR THE HERB SHOOTS.
AND THANK YOU FOR PERMITTING ME TO HAVE A GARDEN, AND TO VISIT THE "LIBRARY."
STRUMMMM
AND TO PLAY THE PIANO PRIVATELY LIKE THIS... EVERY DAY IS A VERY FULFILLING ONE FOR ME.

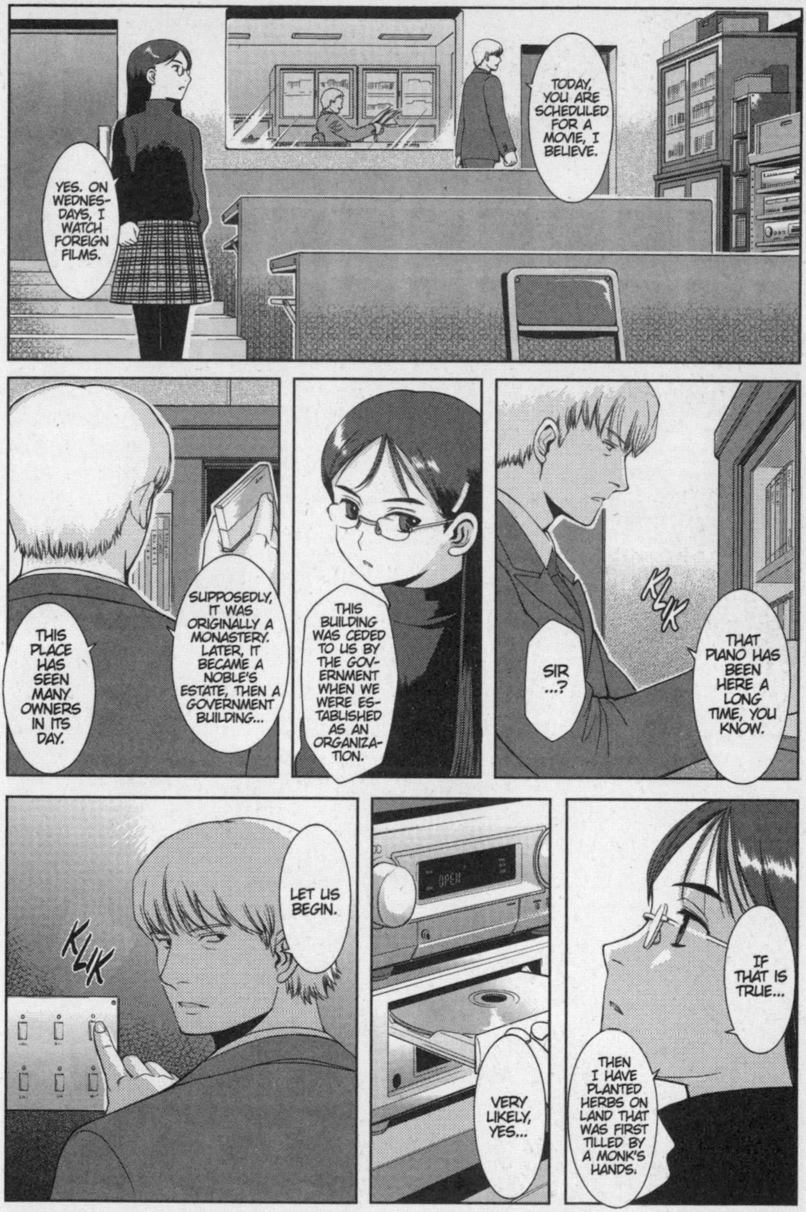
TODAY, YOU ARE SCHEDULED FOR A MOVIE, I BELIEVE.
YES. ON WEDNES-DAYS, I WATCH FOREIGN FILMS.
THAT PIANO HAS BEEN HERE A LONG TIME, YOU KNOW.
KLIK
SIR ...?
THIS BUILDING WAS CEDED TO US BY THE GOVERNMENT WHEN WE WERE ESTABLISHED AS AN ORGANIZA-TION.
SUPPOSEDLY, IT WAS ORIGINALLY A MONASTERY. LATER, IT BECAME A NOBLE'S ESTATE, THEN A GOVERNMENT BUILDING...
THIS PLACE HAS SEEN MANY OWNERS IN ITS DAY.
IF THAT IS TRUE...
THEN I HAVE PLANTED HERBS ON LAND THAT WAS FIRST TILLED BY A MONK'S HANDS.
OPEN
VERY LIKELY, YES...
LET US BEGIN.
KLIK

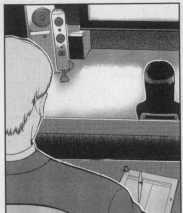
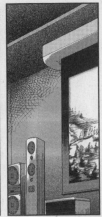

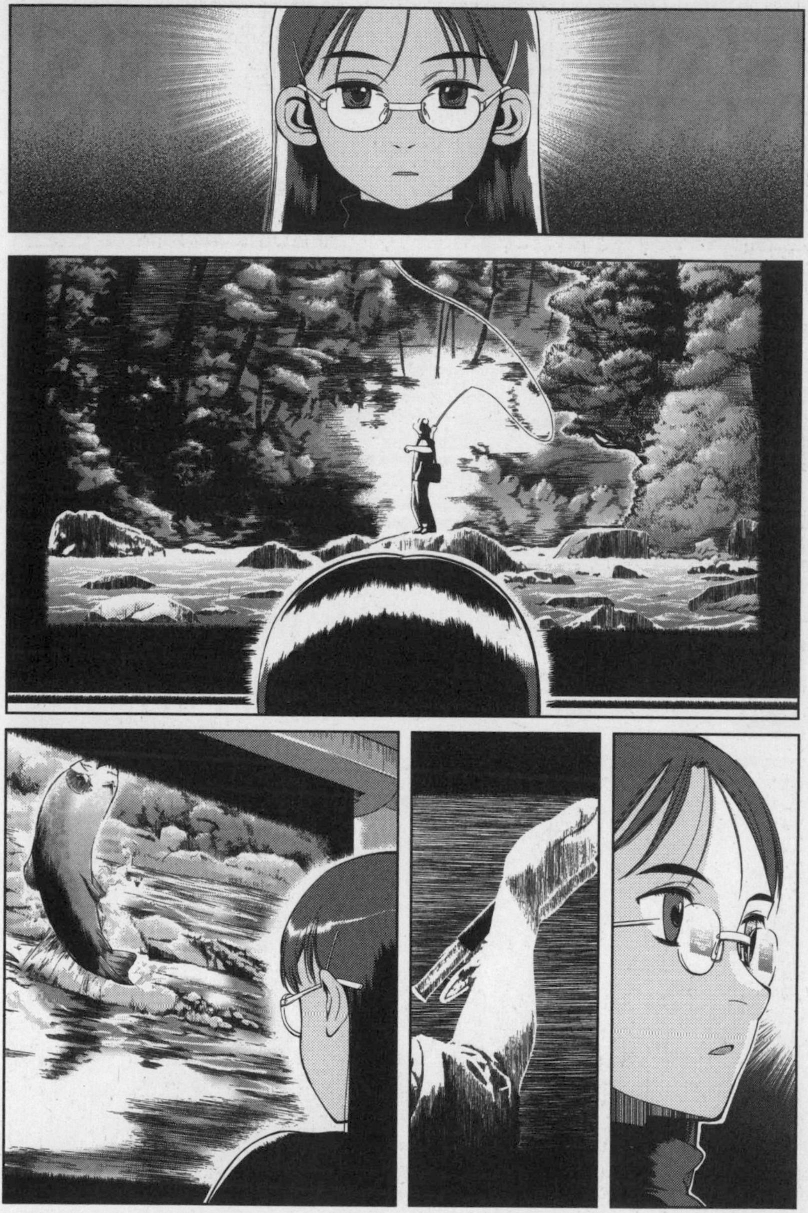

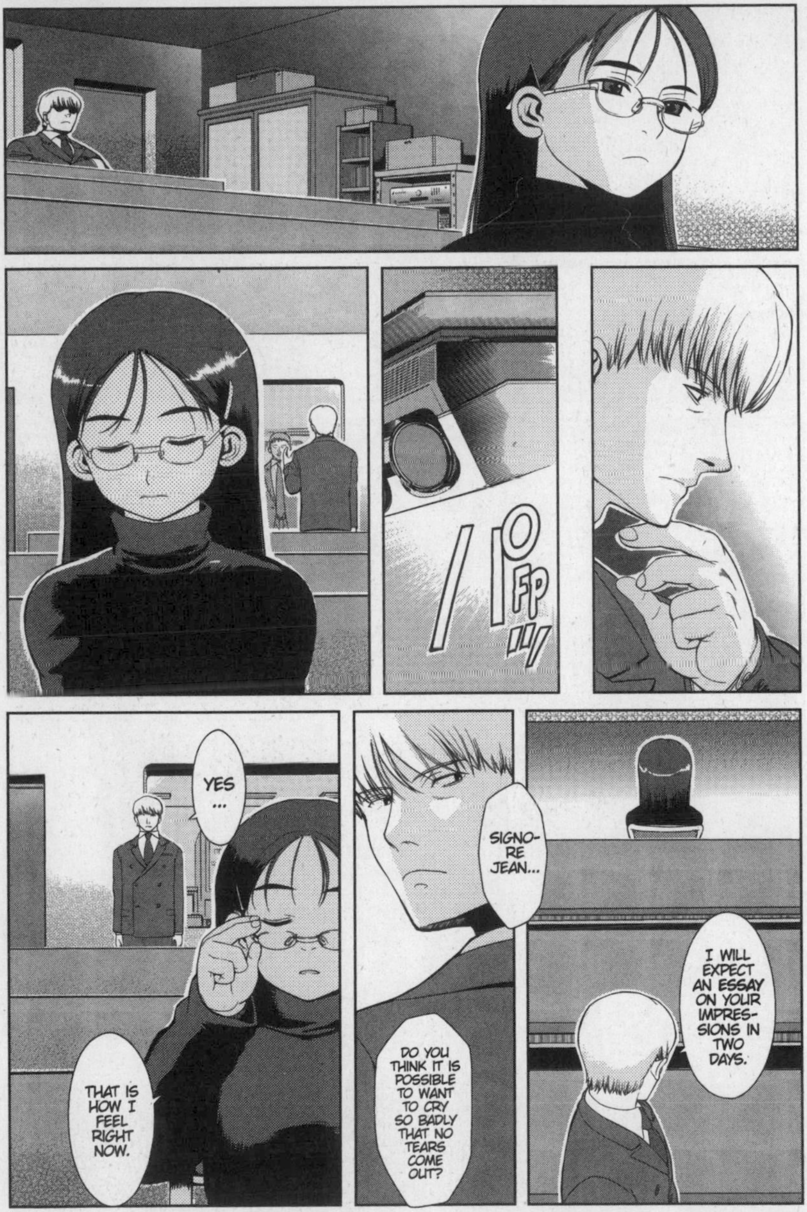
I WILL EXPECT AN ESSAY ON YOUR IMPRESSIONS IN TWO DAYS.
SIGNORE JEAN...
DO YOU THINK IT IS POSSIBLE TO WANT TO CRY SO BADLY THAT NO TEARS COME OUT?
YES ...
THAT IS HOW I FEEL RIGHT NOW.

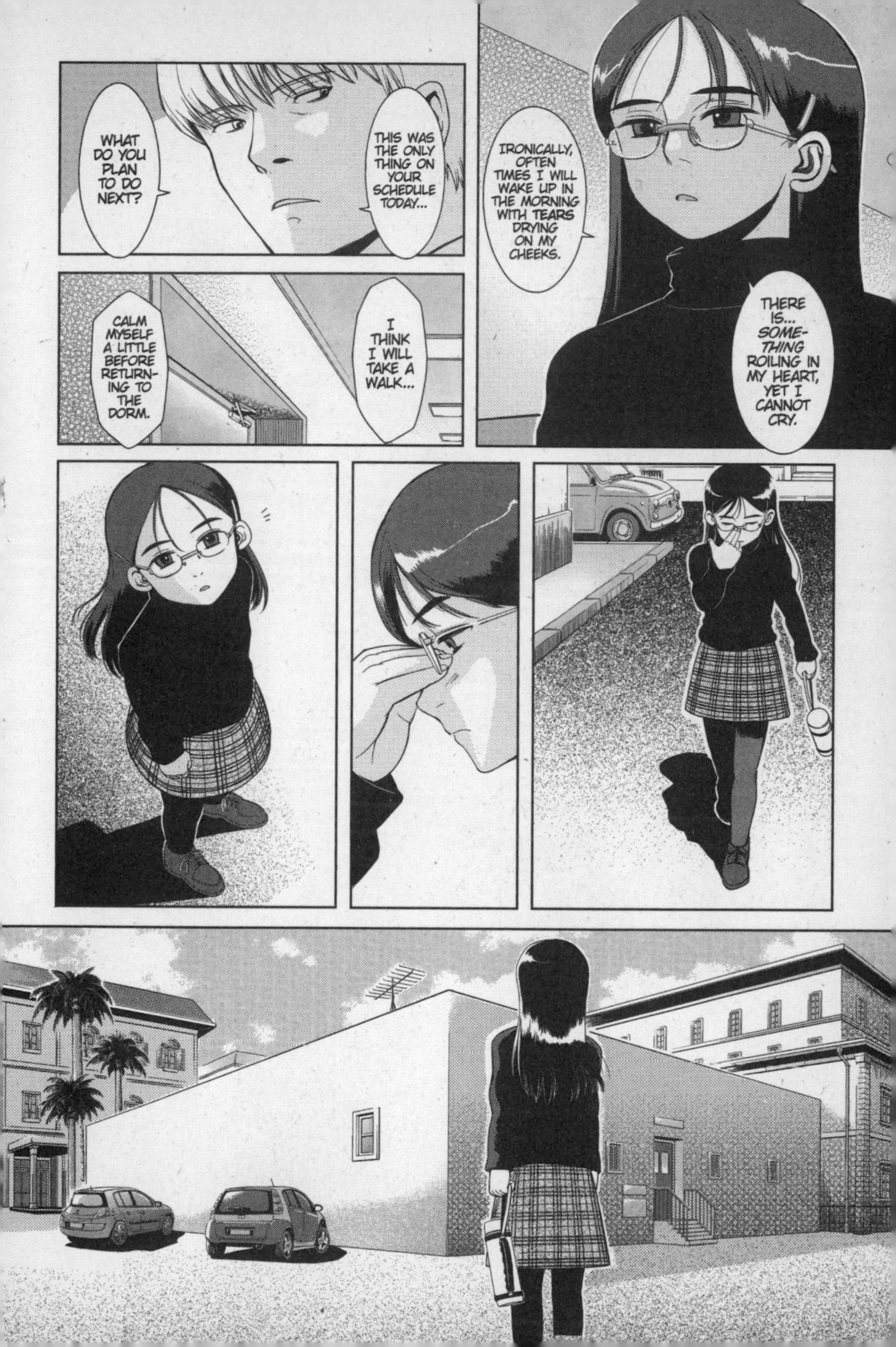
IRONICALLY, OFTEN TIMES I WILL WAKE UP IN THE MORNING WITH TEARS DRYING ON MY CHEEKS.
THERE IS... SOME-THING ROILING IN MY HEART, YET I CANNOT CRY.
THIS WAS THE ONLY THING ON YOUR SCHEDULE TODAY...
WHAT DO YOU PLAN TO DO NEXT?
I THINK I WILL TAKE A WALK...
CALM MYSELF A LITTLE BEFORE RETURN-ING TO THE DORM.

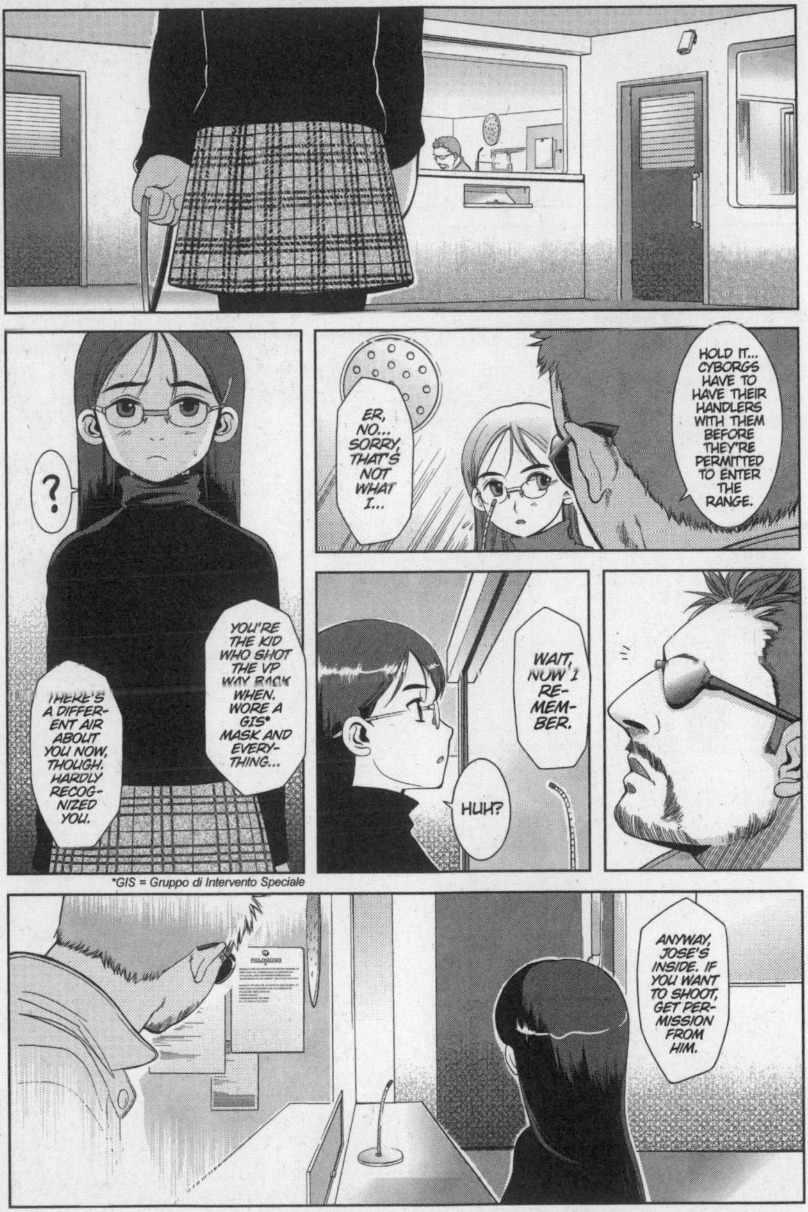
HOLD IT... CYBORGS HAVE TO HAVE THEIR HANDLERS WITH THEM BEFORE THEY'RE PERMITTED TO ENTER THE RANGE.
ER, NO... SORRY, THAT'S NOT WHAT I...
WAIT, NOW I REMEMBER.
HUH?
?
YOU'RE THE KID WHO SHOT THE VP WAY BACK WHEN. WORE A GIS* MASK AND EVERYTHING...
THERE'S A DIFFERENT AIR ABOUT YOU NOW, THOUGH. HARDLY RECOGNIZED YOU.
ANYWAY, JOSE'S INSIDE. IF YOU WANT TO SHOOT, GET PERMISSION FROM HIM.

*GIS = Gruppo di Intervento Speciale

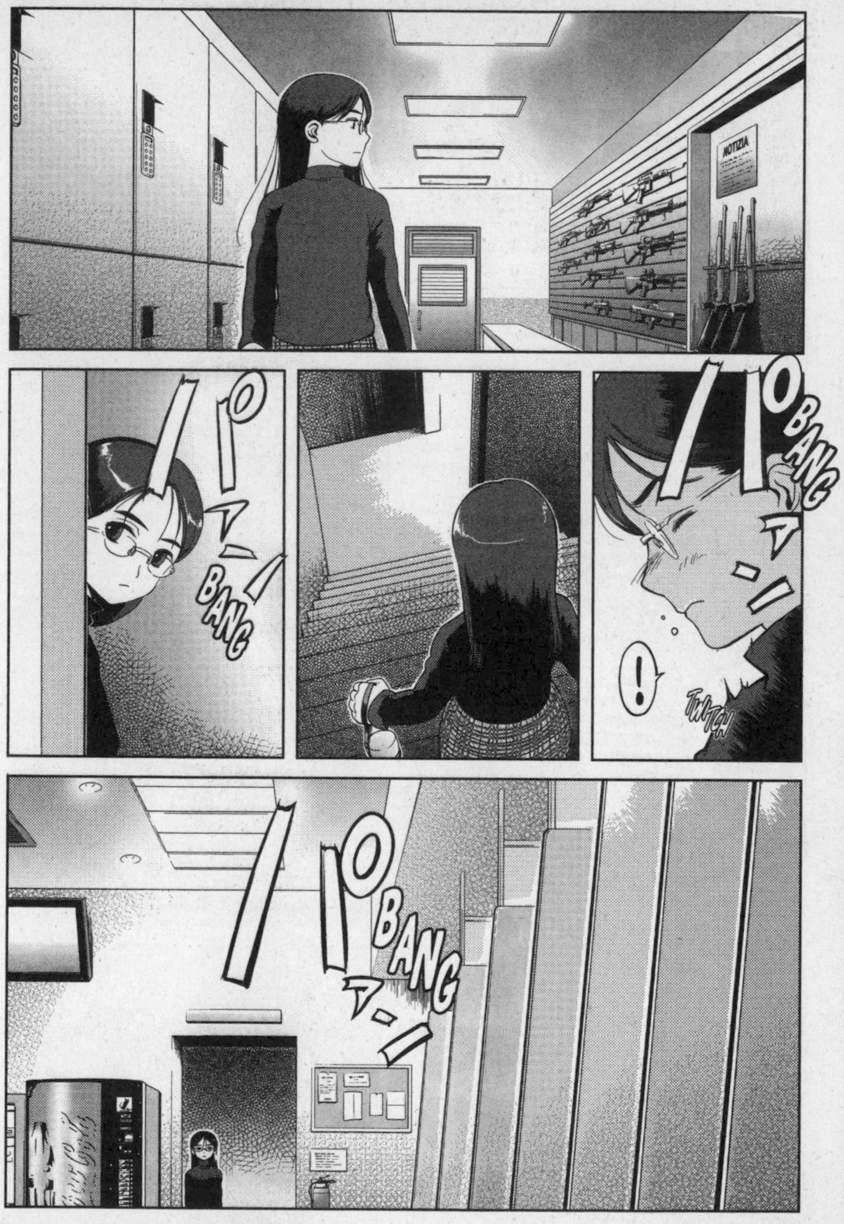

NOTIZIA
BANG
!
TWITCH
BANG
BANG

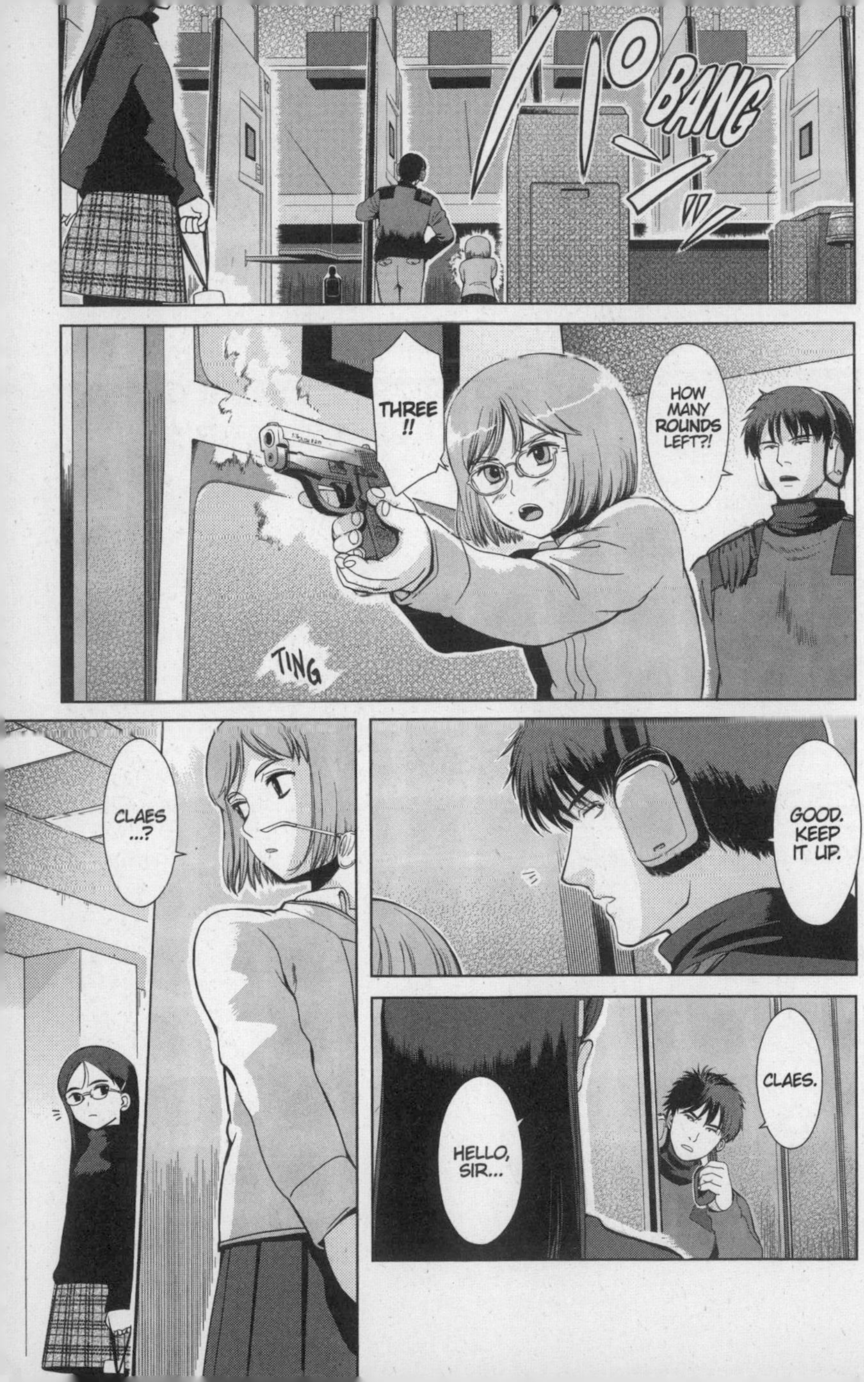
BANG
HOW MANY ROUNDS LEFT?!
THREE !!
TING
GOOD. KEEP IT UP.
CLAES.
HELLO, SIR...
CLAES ...?

JUST OBSERV- ING.

WHAT ARE YOU DOING HERE?

HENRI- ETTA, GO BRING IN THE TARGET.

DON'T FORGET TO TAKE OUT THE MAG- AZINE AND EMPTY THE CHAMBER FIRST.

YES, SIR.

....

IT'S BEEN SO LONG SINCE I'VE HEARD A GUNSHOT. I JUMPED A LITTLE.

SORRY, SIR...

I'LL GO BACK TO THE DORM.

?

CLAES, YOU *SHOULDN'T* BE IN HERE.

SigSauer P239 STAINLESS SIGARMS INC EXETER-NH-USA

SHAK

SHK

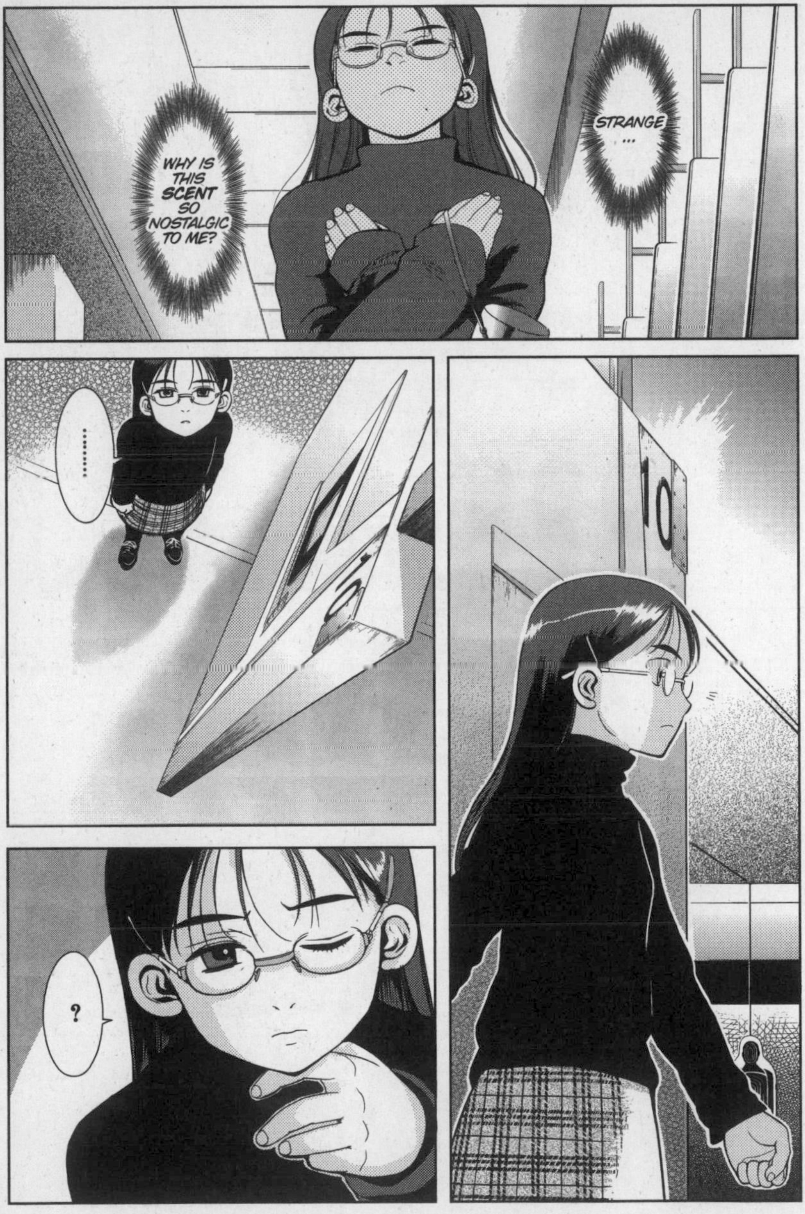
STRANGE ...
WHY IS THIS SCENT SO NOSTALGIC TO ME?
....
?

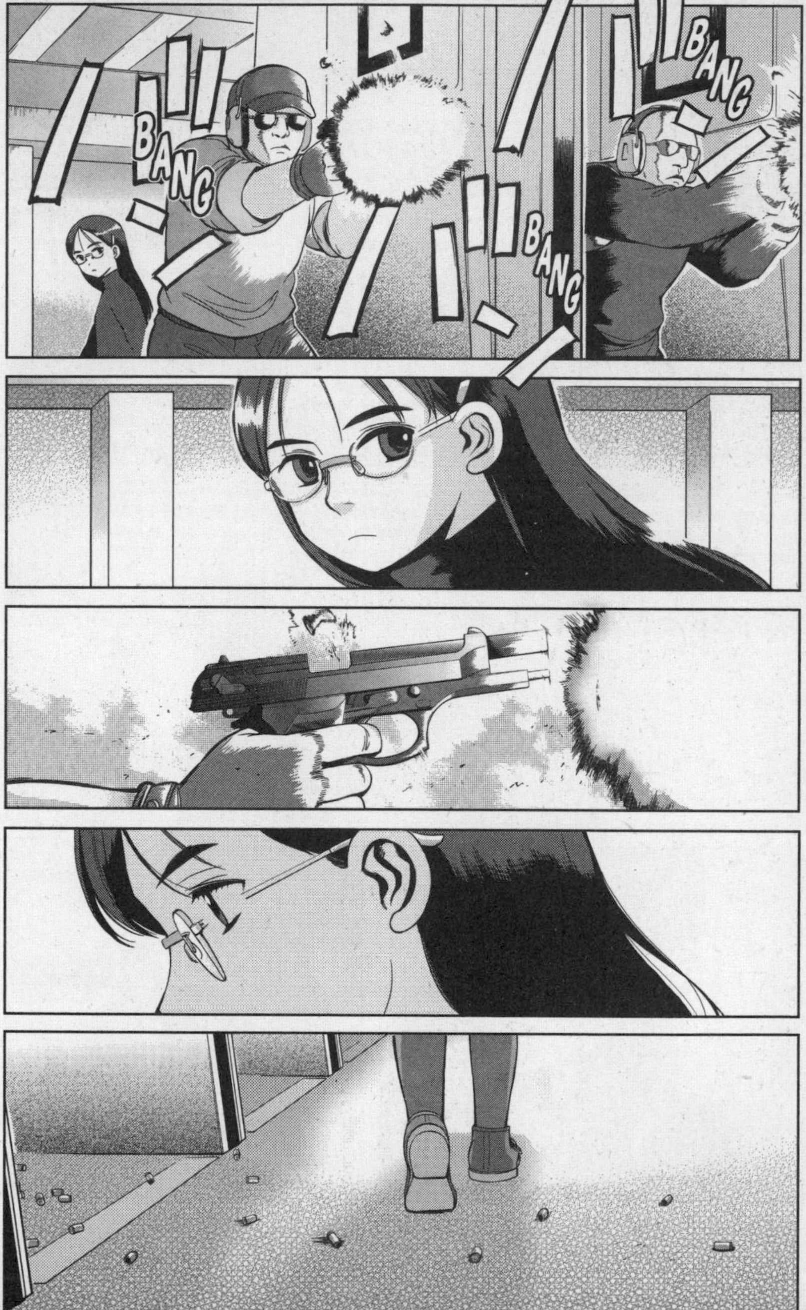
BANG
BANG
BANG

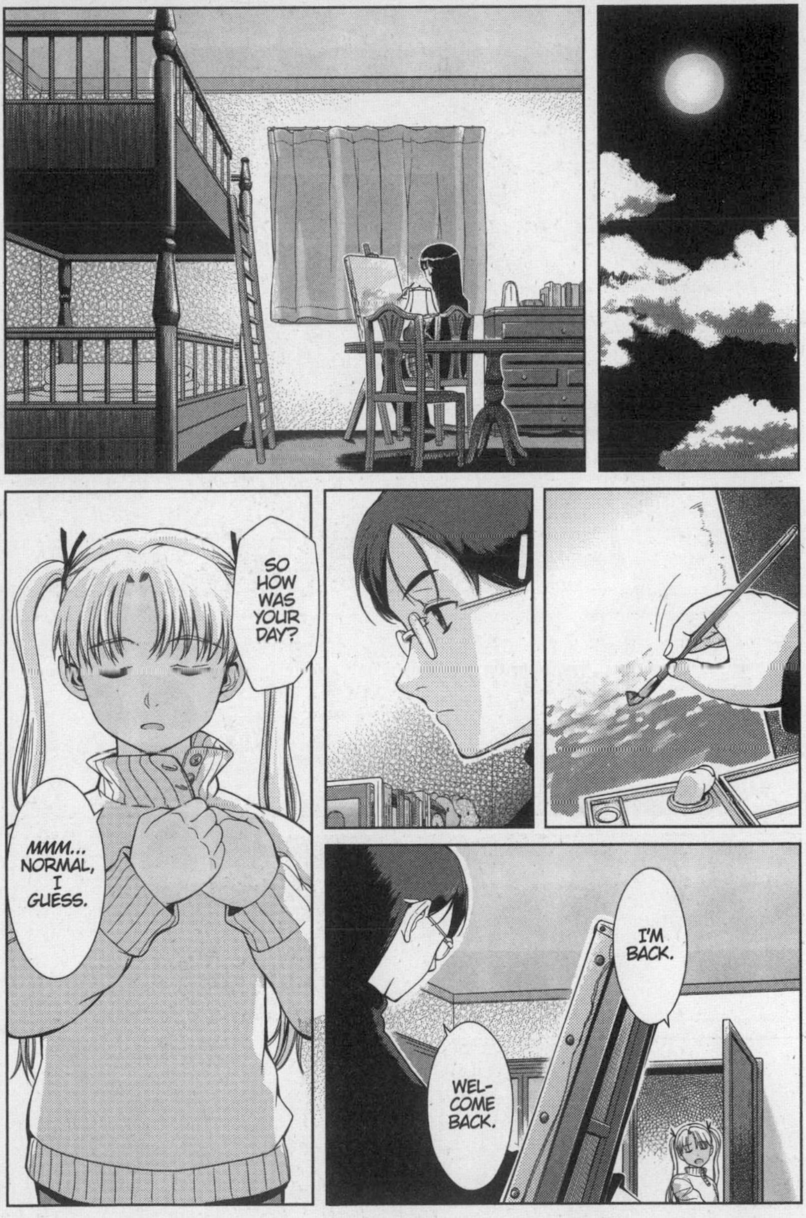
I'M BACK.
WEL-COME BACK.
SO HOW WAS YOUR DAY?
MMM... NORMAL, I GUESS.

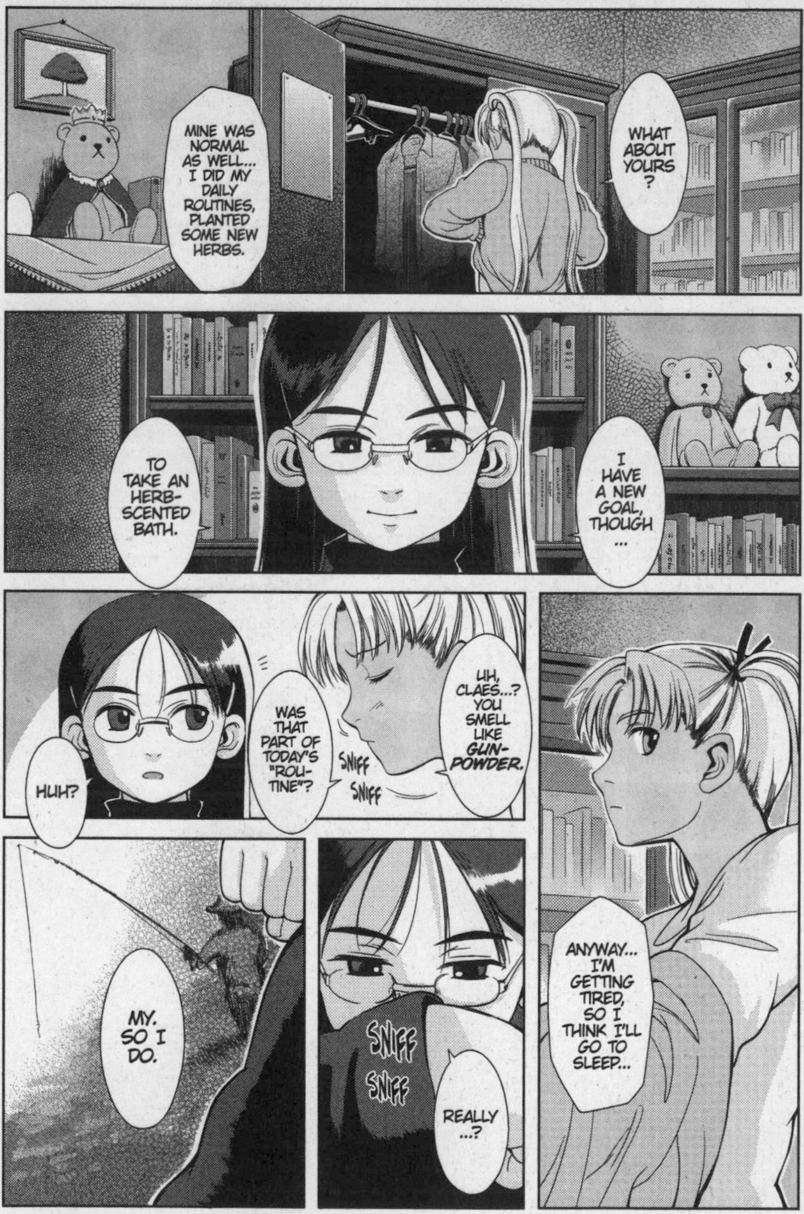
WHAT ABOUT YOURS?
MINE WAS NORMAL AS WELL... I DID MY DAILY ROUTINES, PLANTED SOME NEW HERBS.
I HAVE A NEW GOAL, THOUGH...
TO TAKE AN HERB-SCENTED BATH.
ANYWAY... I'M GETTING TIRED, SO I THINK I'LL GO TO SLEEP...
UH, CLAES...? YOU SMELL LIKE GUN-POWDER.
SNIFF
SNIFF
WAS THAT PART OF TODAY'S "ROU-TINE"?
HUH?
SNIFF
SNIFF
REALLY...?
MY. SO I DO.

GUNSLINGERGIRL.

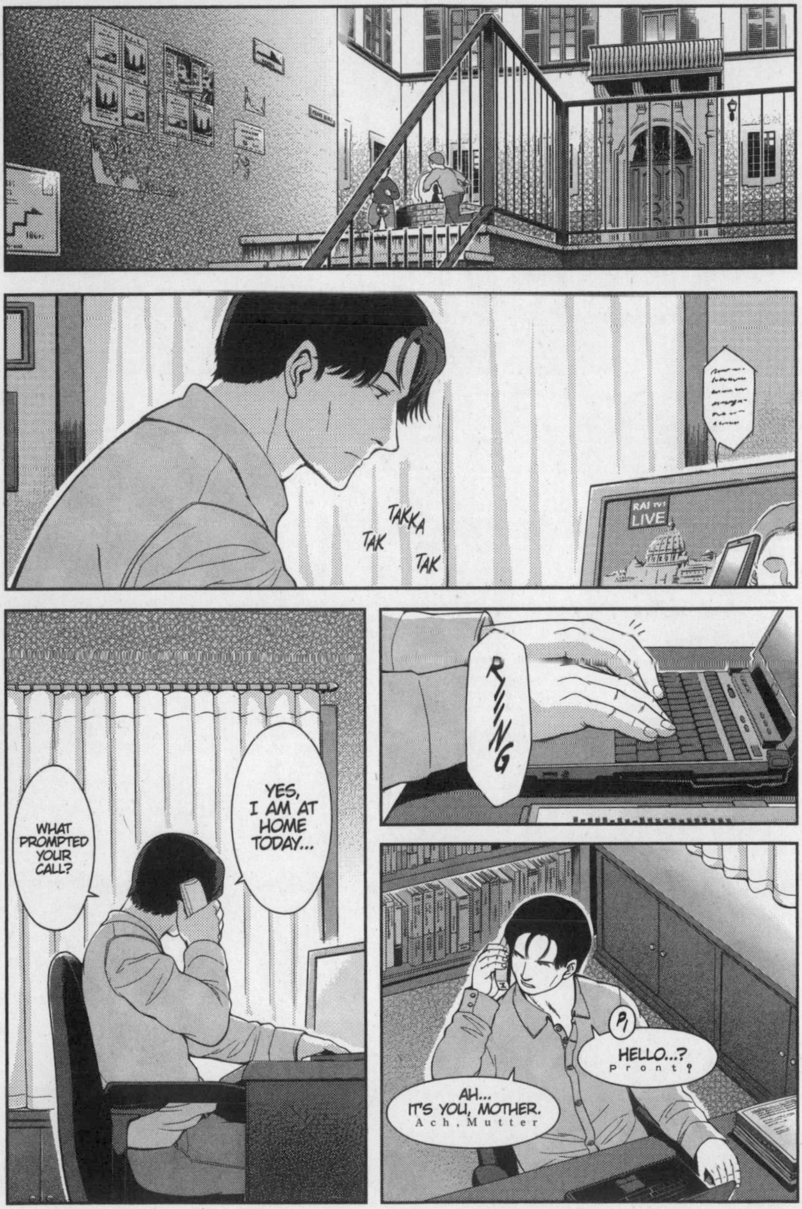
TAKKA
TAK
TAK
RAI TV1
LIVE
RING
PI
HELLO...? Pront?
AH... IT'S YOU, MOTHER. Ach, Mutter
YES, I AM AT HOME TODAY...
WHAT PROMPTED YOUR CALL?

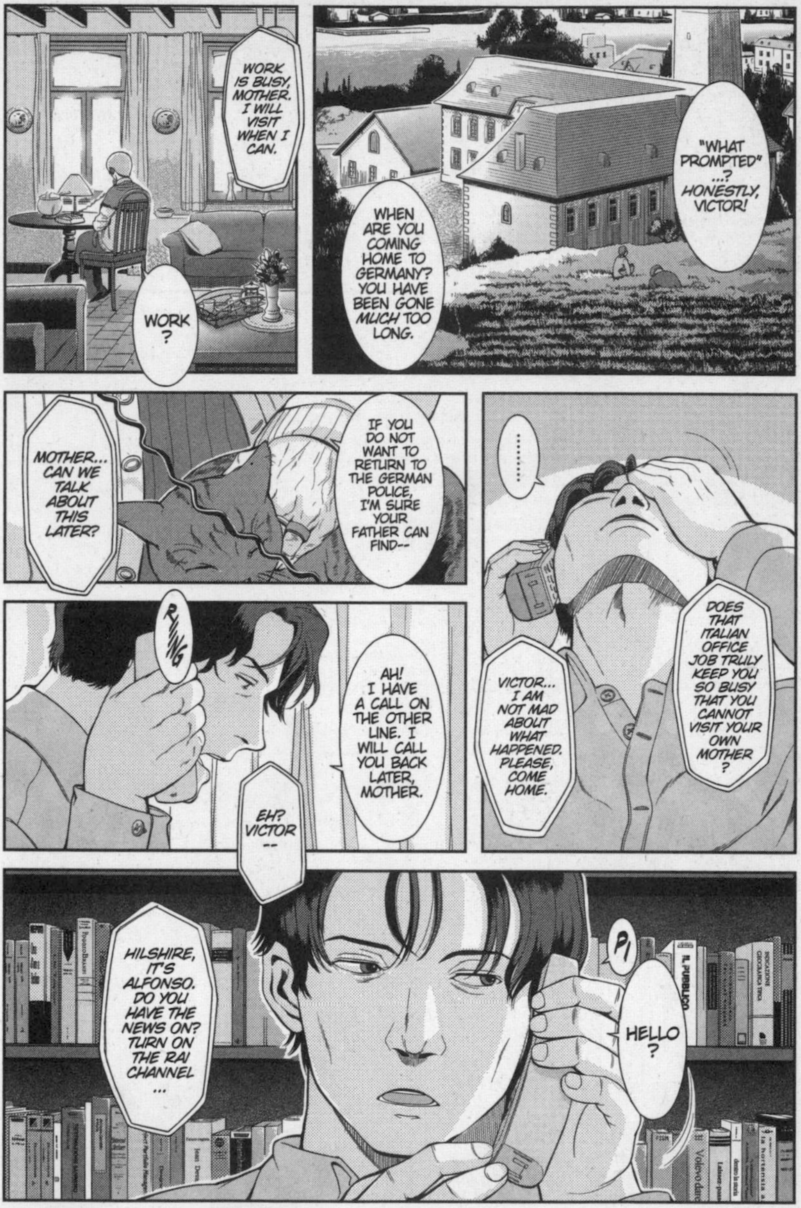
"WHAT PROMPTED" ...? HONESTLY, VICTOR!
WHEN ARE YOU COMING HOME TO GERMANY? YOU HAVE BEEN GONE MUCH TOO LONG.
WORK IS BUSY, MOTHER. I WILL VISIT WHEN I CAN.
WORK ?
......
DOES THAT ITALIAN OFFICE JOB TRULY KEEP YOU SO BUSY THAT YOU CANNOT VISIT YOUR OWN MOTHER ?
VICTOR... I AM NOT MAD ABOUT WHAT HAPPENED. PLEASE, COME HOME.
IF YOU DO NOT WANT TO RETURN TO THE GERMAN POLICE, I'M SURE YOUR FATHER CAN FIND--
MOTHER... CAN WE TALK ABOUT THIS LATER?
RING
AH! I HAVE A CALL ON THE OTHER LINE. I WILL CALL YOU BACK LATER, MOTHER.
EH? VICTOR --
PI
HELLO ?
HILSHIRE, IT'S ALFONSO. DO YOU HAVE THE NEWS ON? TURN ON THE RAI CHANNEL ...

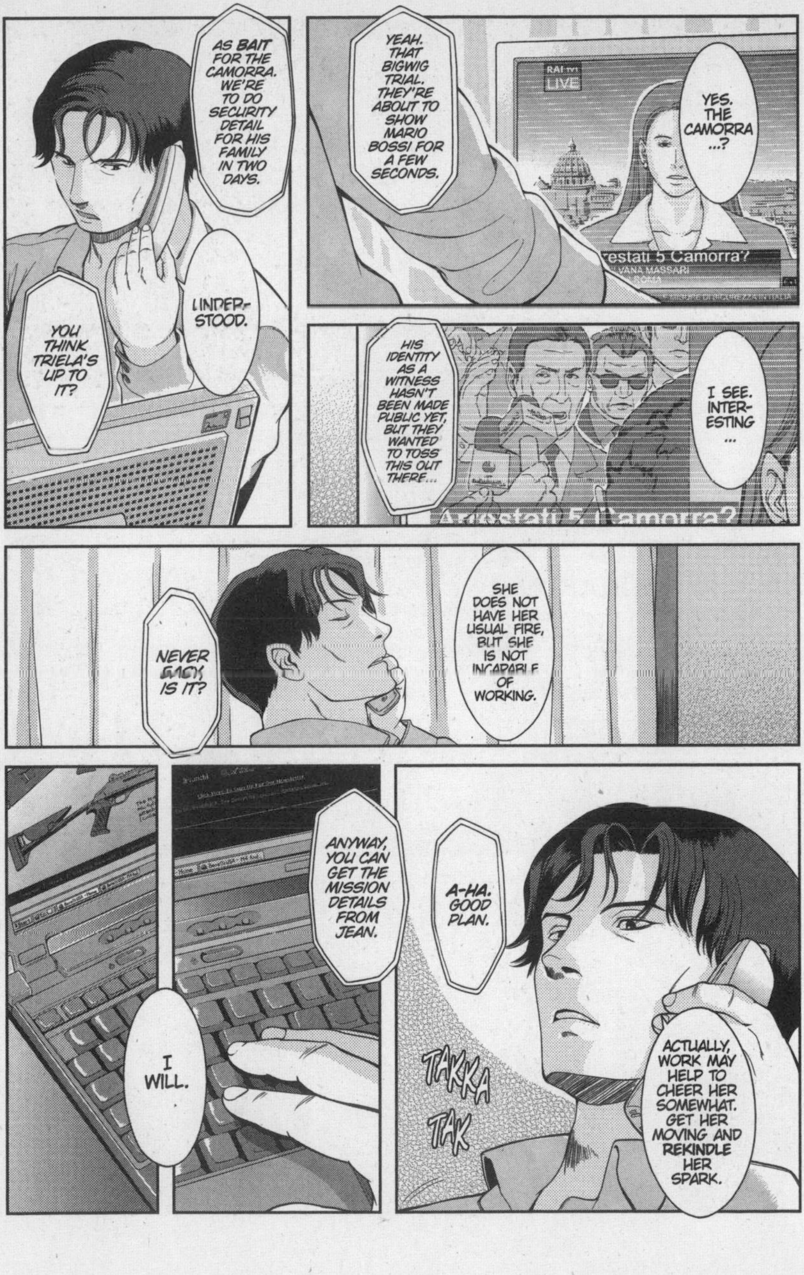
YES. THE CAMORRA ...?
YEAH. THAT BIGWIG TRIAL. THEY'RE ABOUT TO SHOW MARIO BOSSI FOR A FEW SECONDS.
I SEE. INTERESTING ...
HIS IDENTITY AS A WITNESS HASN'T BEEN MADE PUBLIC YET, BUT THEY WANTED TO TOSS THIS OUT THERE...
AS BAIT FOR THE CAMORRA. WE'RE TO DO SECURITY DETAIL FOR HIS FAMILY IN TWO DAYS.
UNDERSTOOD.
YOU THINK TRIELA'S UP TO IT?
SHE DOES NOT HAVE HER USUAL FIRE, BUT SHE IS NOT INCAPABLE OF WORKING.
NEVER EASY IS IT?
ACTUALLY, WORK MAY HELP TO CHEER HER SOMEWHAT. GET HER MOVING AND REKINDLE HER SPARK.
A-HA. GOOD PLAN.
TAKKA TAK
ANYWAY, YOU CAN GET THE MISSION DETAILS FROM JEAN.
I WILL.

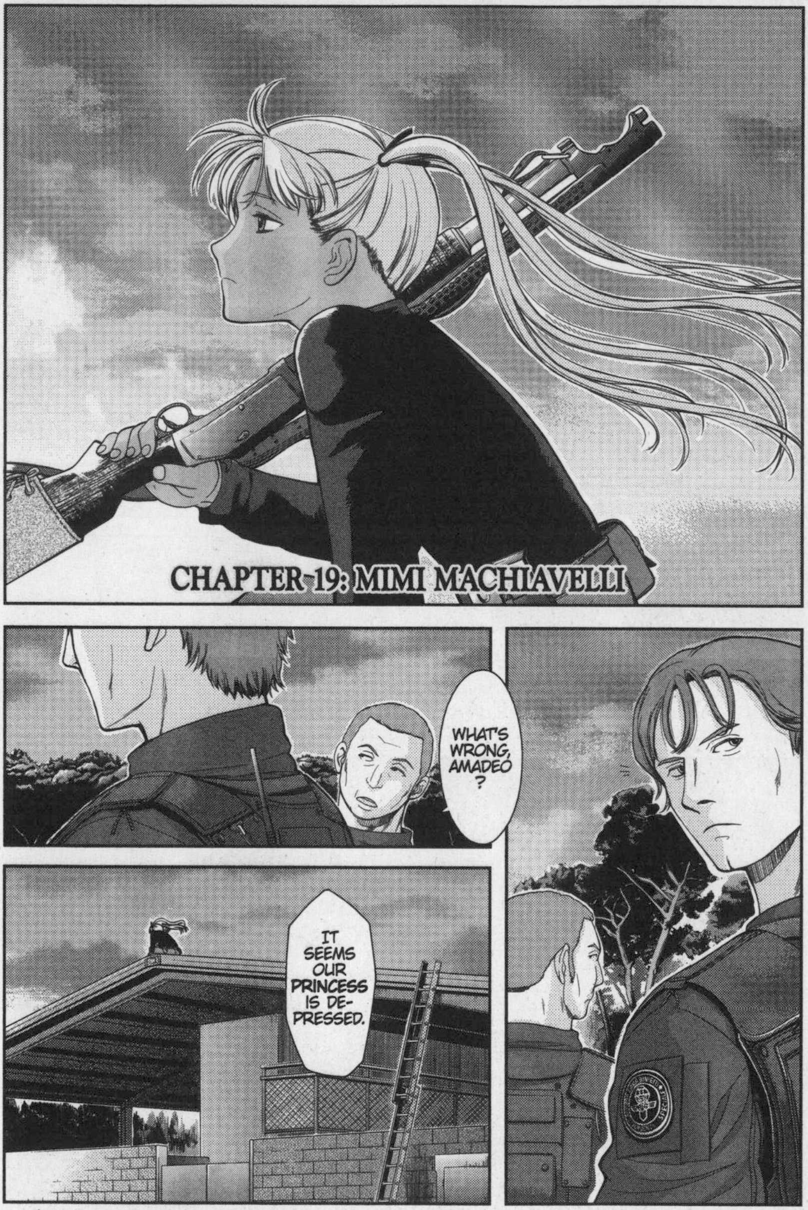
CHAPTER 19: MIMI MACHIAVELLI
WHAT'S WRONG, AMADEO?
IT SEEMS OUR PRINCESS IS DE-PRESSED.

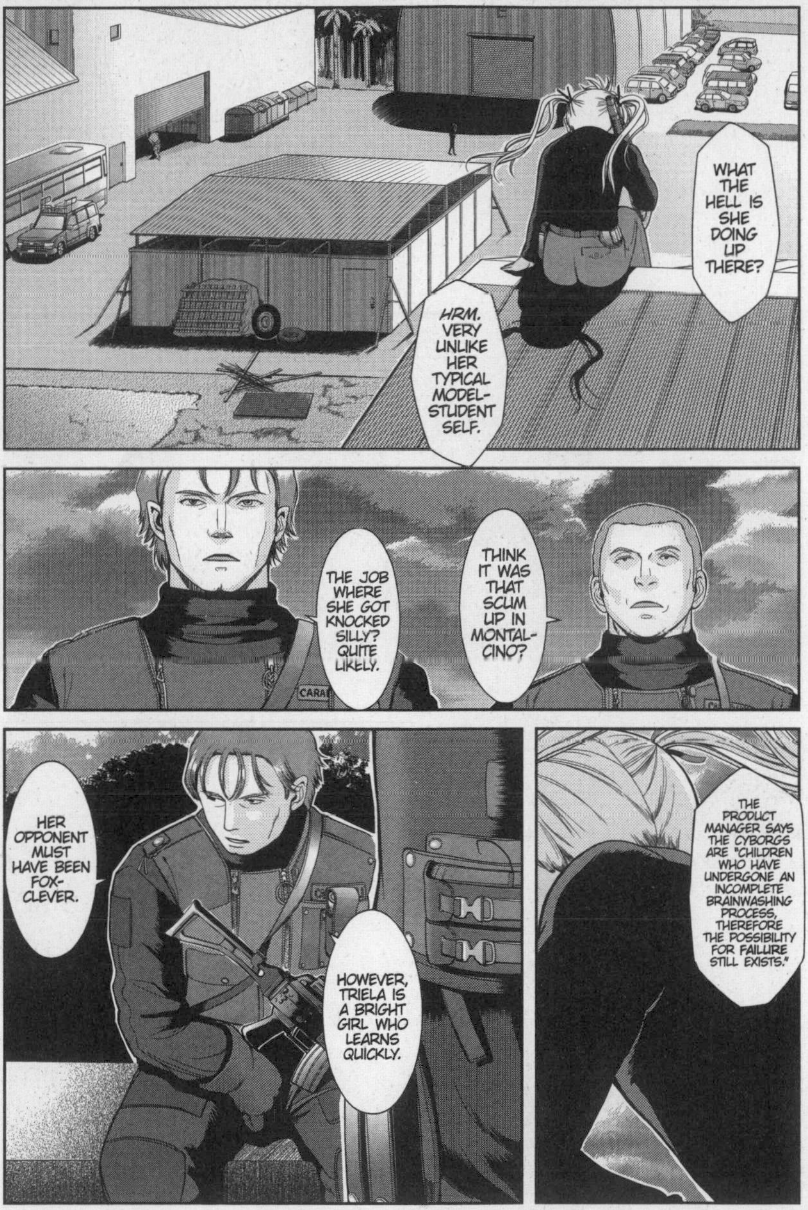
WHAT THE HELL IS SHE DOING UP THERE?
HRM. VERY UNLIKE HER TYPICAL MODEL-STUDENT SELF.
THINK IT WAS THAT SCUM UP IN MONTALCINO?
THE JOB WHERE SHE GOT KNOCKED SILLY? QUITE LIKELY.
THE PRODUCT MANAGER SAYS THE CYBORGS ARE "CHILDREN WHO HAVE UNDERGONE AN INCOMPLETE BRAINWASHING PROCESS, THEREFORE THE POSSIBILITY FOR FAILURE STILL EXISTS."
HER OPPONENT MUST HAVE BEEN FOX-CLEVER.
HOWEVER, TRIELA IS A BRIGHT GIRL WHO LEARNS QUICKLY.

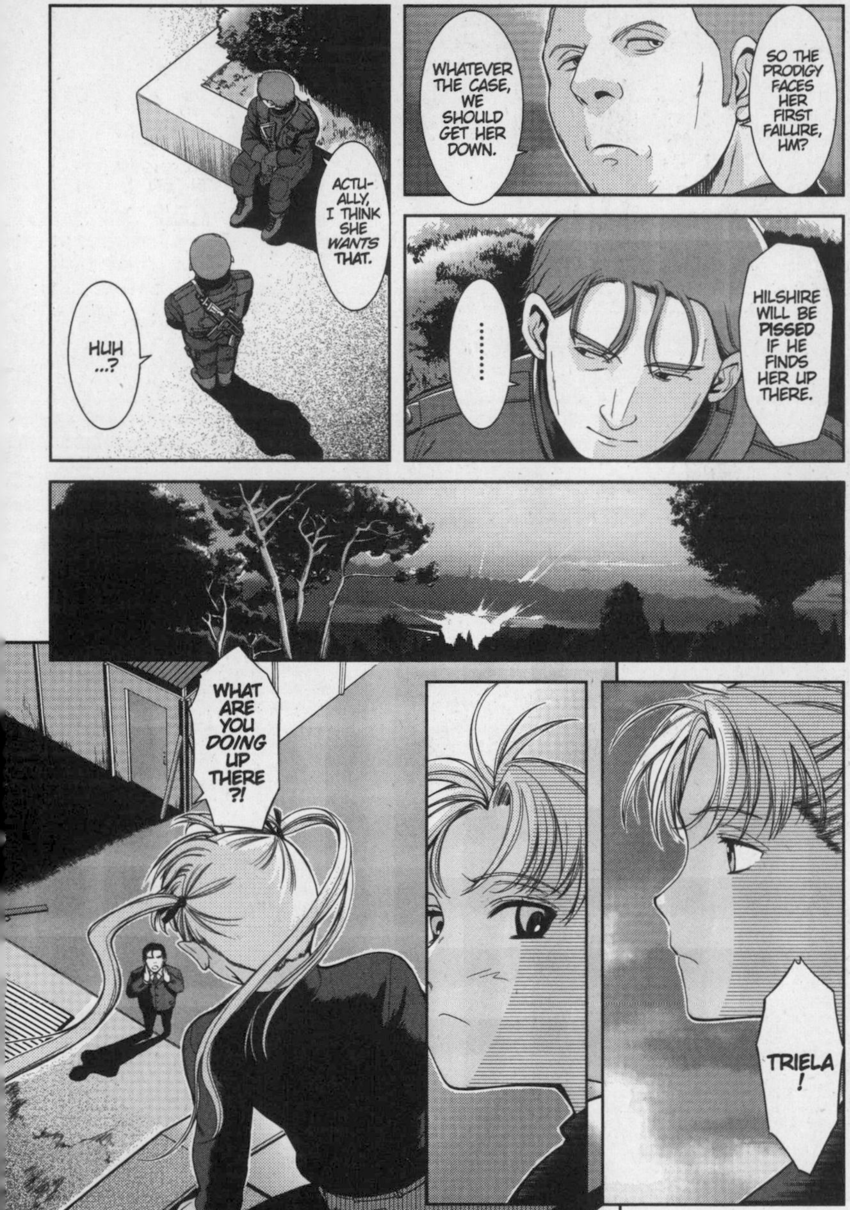
SO THE PRODIGY FACES HER FIRST FAILURE, HM?
WHATEVER THE CASE, WE SHOULD GET HER DOWN.
HILSHIRE WILL BE PISSED IF HE FINDS HER UP THERE.
....
ACTU-ALLY, I THINK SHE *WANTS* THAT.
HUH ...?
TRIELA!
WHAT ARE YOU *DOING* UP THERE?!

THIS IS THE ARMY'S TRAINING CENTER, NOT OURS!
COME DOWN AT ONCE !!
WHRL
るっ
....
ダッ
WHMP
....

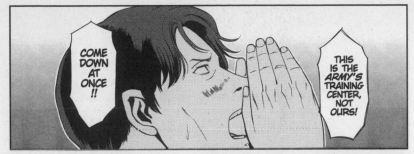

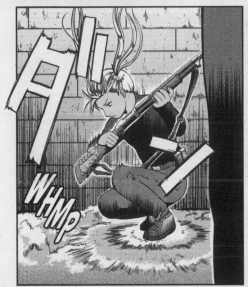

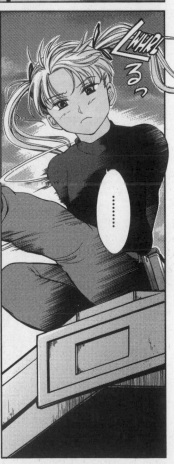

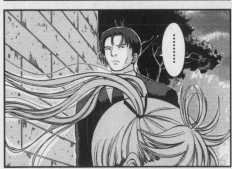

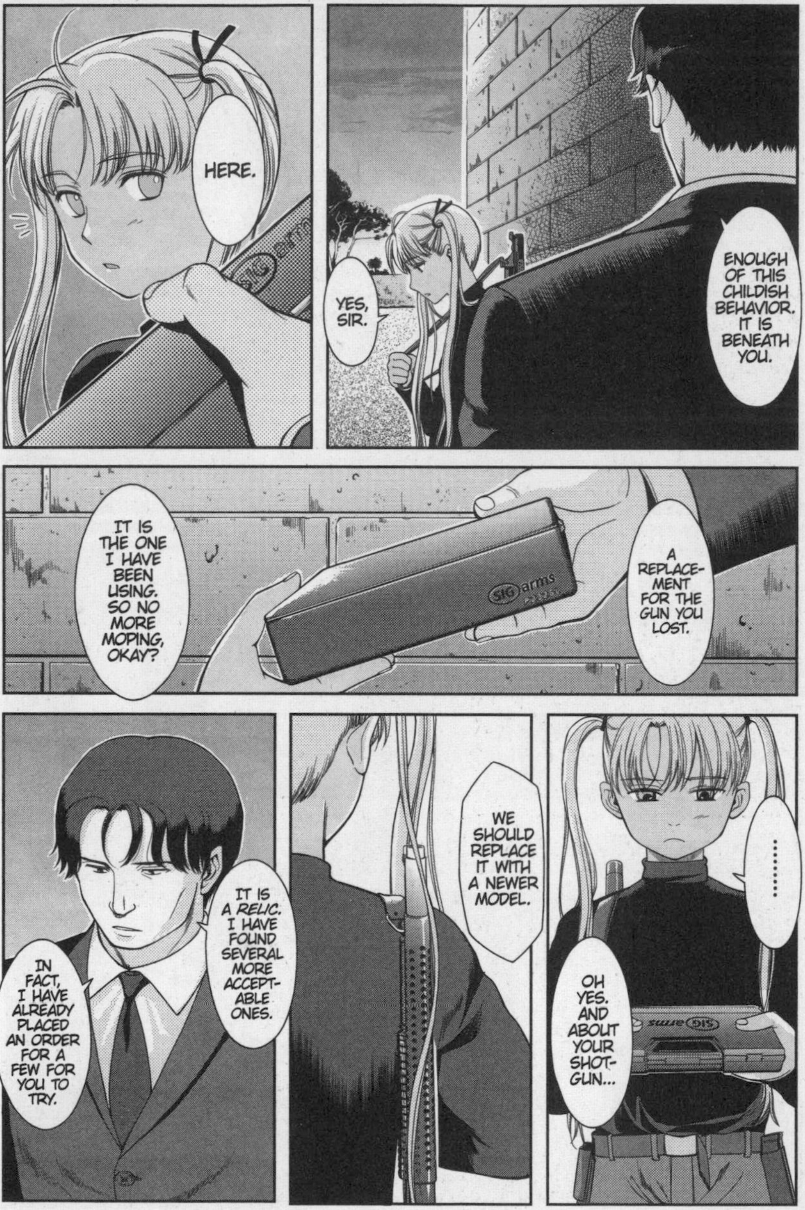
ENOUGH OF THIS CHILDISH BEHAVIOR. IT IS BENEATH YOU.
YES, SIR.
HERE.
A REPLACEMENT FOR THE GUN YOU LOST.
IT IS THE ONE I HAVE BEEN USING. SO NO MORE MOPING, OKAY?
......
OH YES. AND ABOUT YOUR SHOTGUN...
WE SHOULD REPLACE IT WITH A NEWER MODEL.
IT IS A *RELIC*. I HAVE FOUND SEVERAL MORE ACCEPTABLE ONES.
IN FACT, I HAVE ALREADY PLACED AN ORDER FOR A FEW FOR YOU TO TRY.

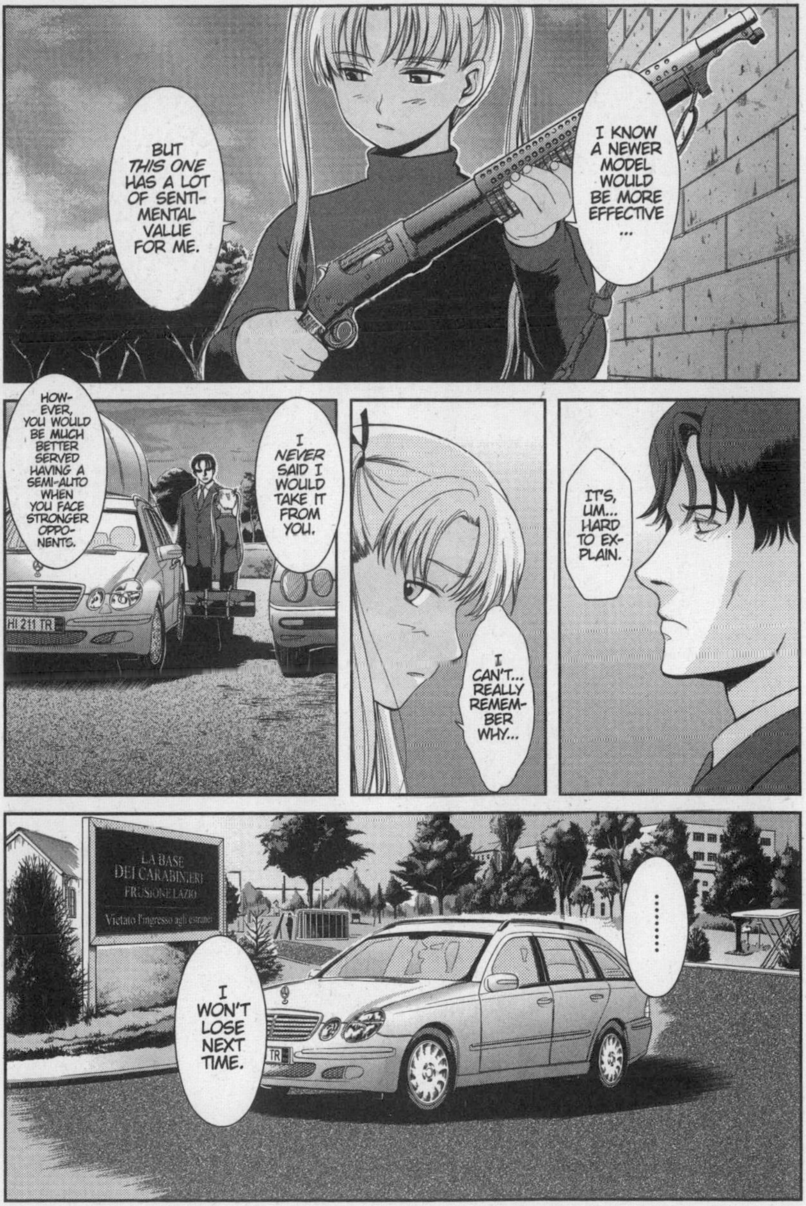
I KNOW A NEWER MODEL WOULD BE MORE EFFECTIVE ...
BUT *THIS ONE* HAS A LOT OF SENTI-MENTAL VALUE FOR ME.
IT'S, UM... HARD TO EX-PLAIN.
I CAN'T... REALLY REMEM-BER WHY...
I *NEVER* SAID I WOULD TAKE IT FROM YOU.
HOW-EVER, YOU WOULD BE MUCH BETTER SERVED HAVING A SEMI-AUTO WHEN YOU FACE STRONGER OPPO-NENTS.
HI 211 TR
....
LA BASE DEI CARABINIERI FRUSIONE LAZIO
Vietato l'ingresso agli estranei
I WON'T LOSE NEXT TIME.

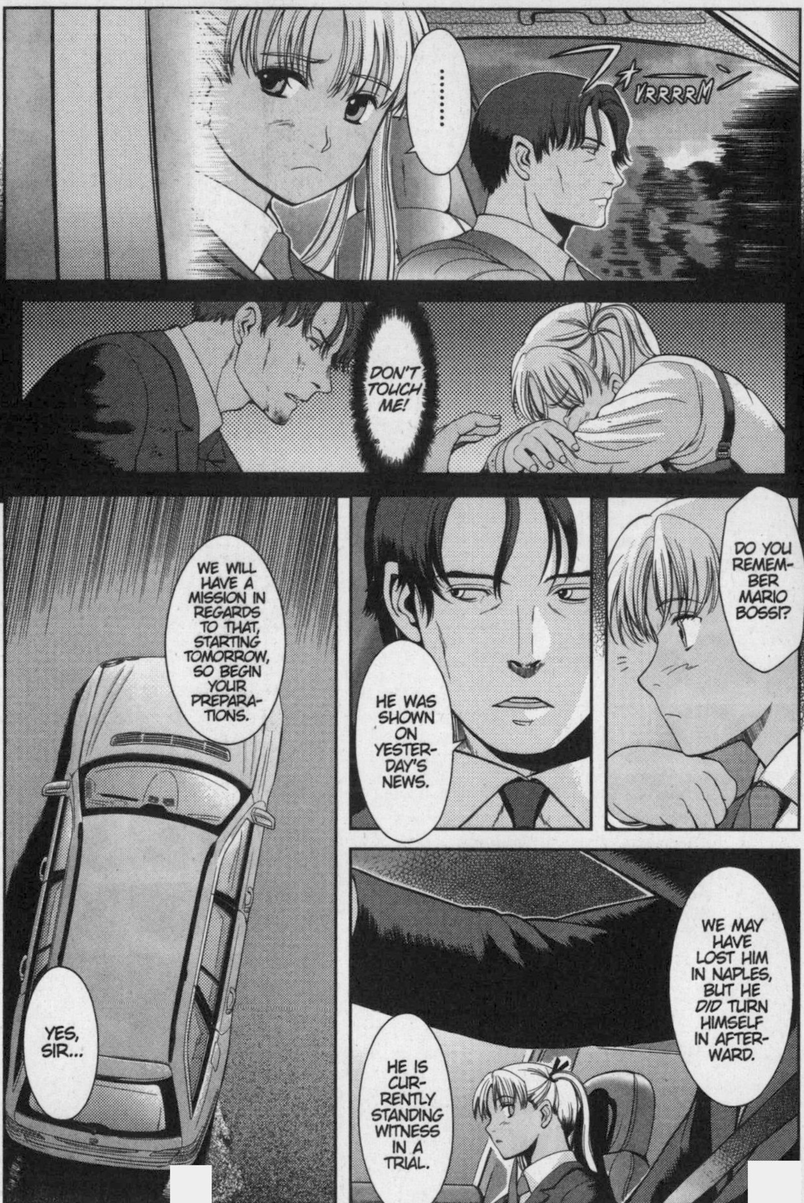
VRRRRM
......
DON'T TOUCH ME!
DO YOU REMEMBER MARIO BOSSI?
HE WAS SHOWN ON YESTERDAY'S NEWS.
WE MAY HAVE LOST HIM IN NAPLES, BUT HE *DID* TURN HIMSELF IN AFTERWARD.
HE IS CURRENTLY STANDING WITNESS IN A TRIAL.
WE WILL HAVE A MISSION IN REGARDS TO THAT, STARTING TOMORROW, SO BEGIN YOUR PREPARATIONS.
YES, SIR...

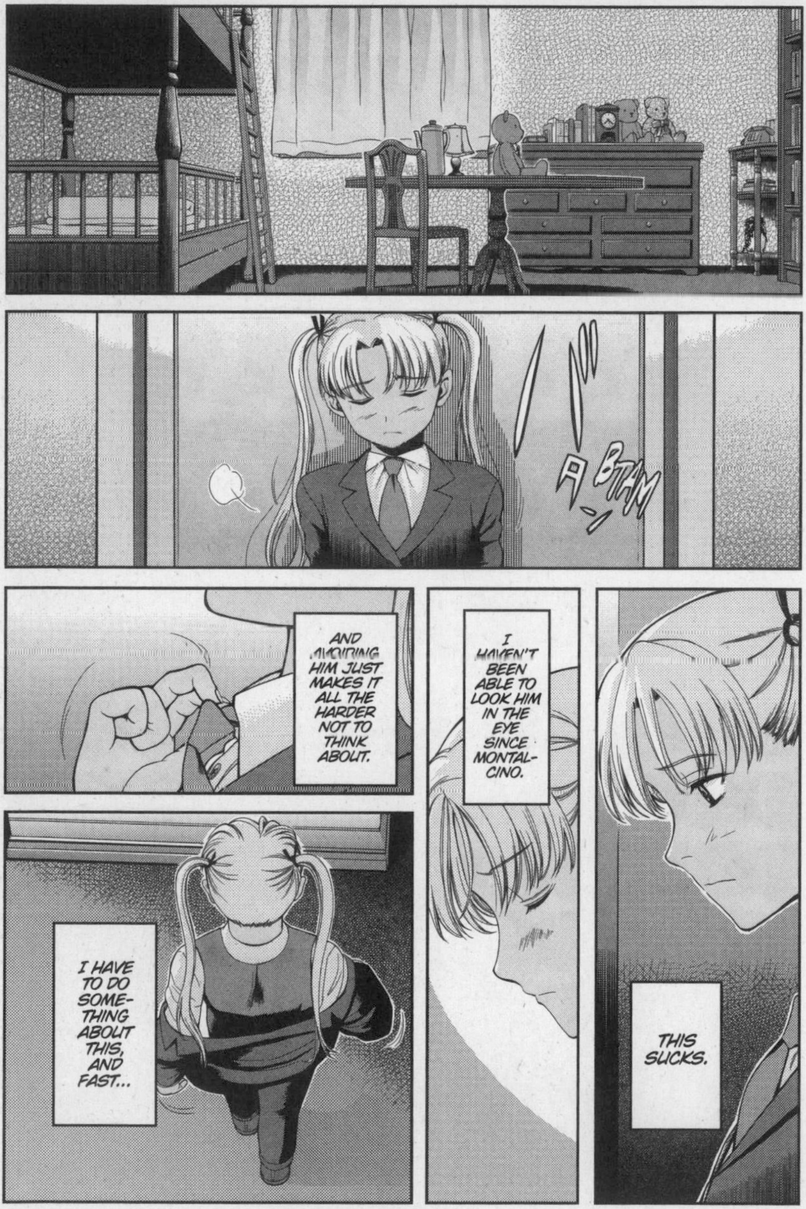
BTAM
THIS SUCKS.
I HAVEN'T BEEN ABLE TO LOOK HIM IN THE EYE SINCE MONTAL-CINO.
AND AVOIDING HIM JUST MAKES IT ALL THE HARDER NOT TO THINK ABOUT.
I HAVE TO DO SOME-THING ABOUT THIS, AND FAST...

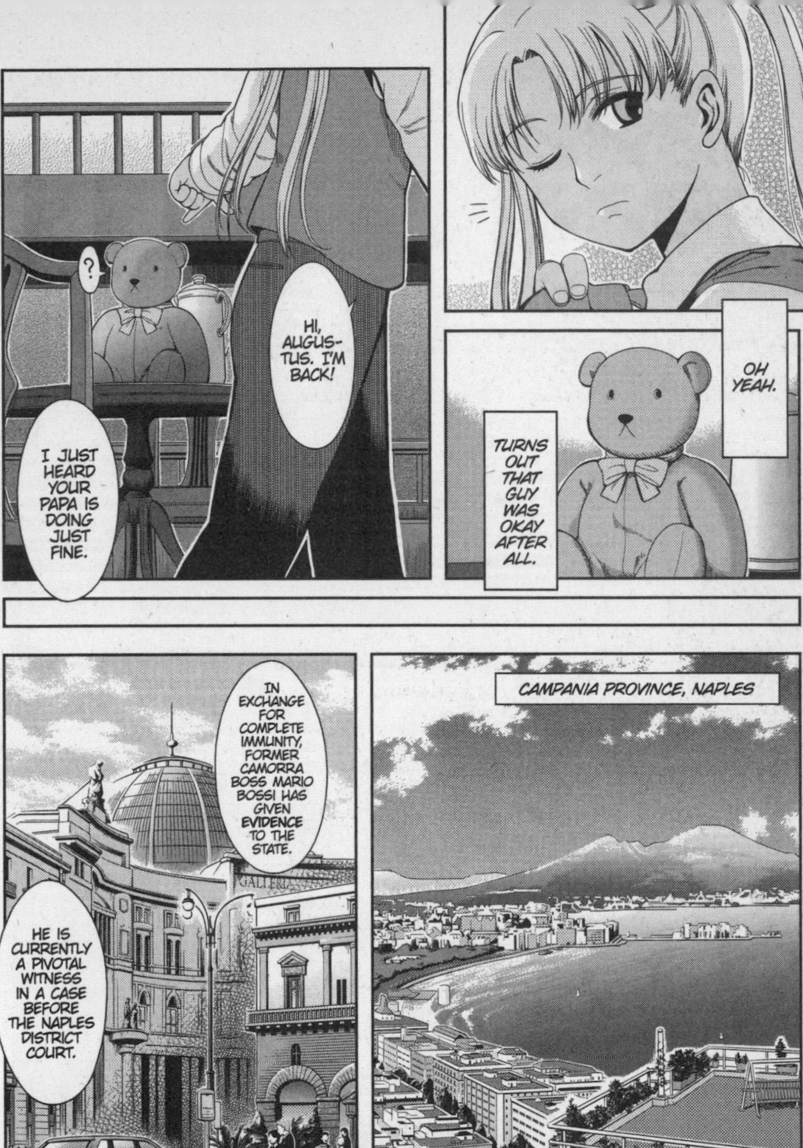
OH YEAH.
TURNS OUT THAT GUY WAS OKAY AFTER ALL.
?
HI, AUGUS-TUS. I'M BACK!
I JUST HEARD YOUR PAPA IS DOING JUST FINE.
CAMPANIA PROVINCE, NAPLES
IN EXCHANGE FOR COMPLETE IMMUNITY, FORMER CAMORRA BOSS MARIO BOSSI HAS GIVEN EVIDENCE TO THE STATE.
HE IS CURRENTLY A PIVOTAL WITNESS IN A CASE BEFORE THE NAPLES DISTRICT COURT.

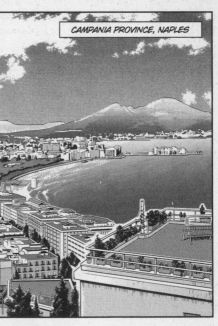

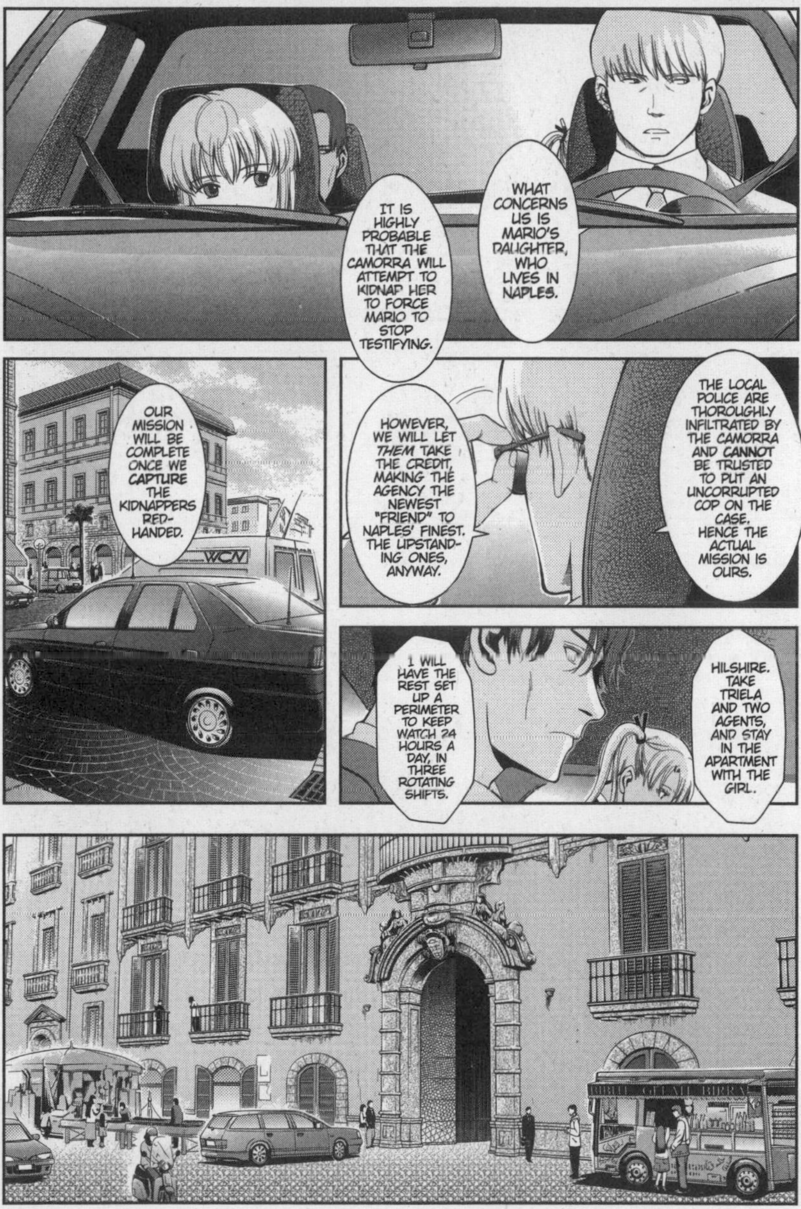
WHAT CONCERNS US IS MARIO'S DAUGHTER, WHO LIVES IN NAPLES.
IT IS HIGHLY PROBABLE THAT THE CAMORRA WILL ATTEMPT TO KIDNAP HER TO FORCE MARIO TO STOP TESTIFYING.
THE LOCAL POLICE ARE THOROUGHLY INFILTRATED BY THE CAMORRA AND CANNOT BE TRUSTED TO PUT AN UNCORRUPTED COP ON THE CASE. HENCE THE ACTUAL MISSION IS OURS.
HOWEVER, WE WILL LET *THEM* TAKE THE CREDIT, MAKING THE AGENCY THE NEWEST "FRIEND" TO NAPLES' FINEST. THE UPSTANDING ONES, ANYWAY.
HILSHIRE. TAKE TRIELA AND TWO AGENTS, AND STAY IN THE APARTMENT WITH THE GIRL.
I WILL HAVE THE REST SET UP A PERIMETER TO KEEP WATCH 24 HOURS A DAY, IN THREE ROTATING SHIFTS.
OUR MISSION WILL BE COMPLETE ONCE WE CAPTURE THE KIDNAPPERS RED-HANDED.
WCN

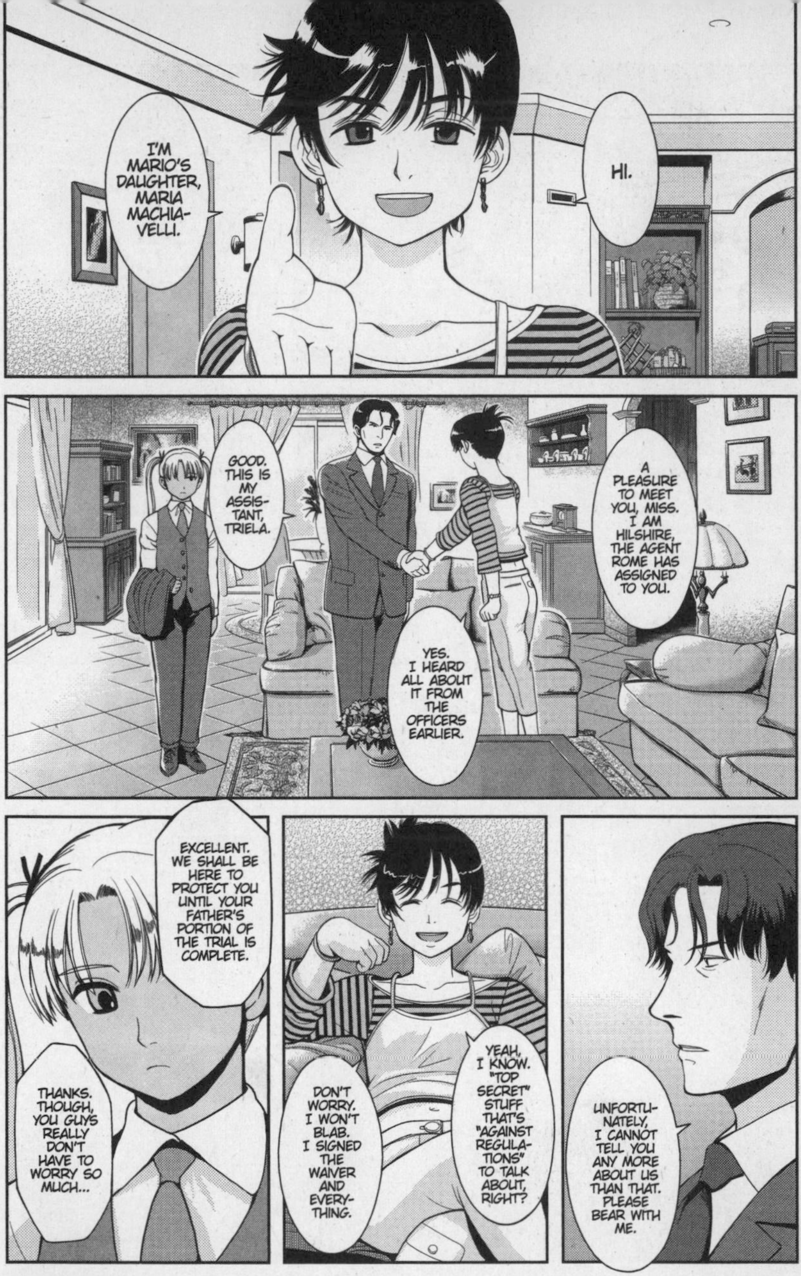
HI.
I'M MARIO'S DAUGHTER, MARIA MACHIAVELLI.
A PLEASURE TO MEET YOU, MISS. I AM HILSHIRE, THE AGENT ROME HAS ASSIGNED TO YOU.
YES. I HEARD ALL ABOUT IT FROM THE OFFICERS EARLIER.
GOOD. THIS IS MY ASSISTANT, TRIELA.
UNFORTUNATELY, I CANNOT TELL YOU ANY MORE ABOUT US THAN THAT. PLEASE BEAR WITH ME.
YEAH, I KNOW. "TOP SECRET" STUFF THAT'S "AGAINST REGULATIONS" TO TALK ABOUT, RIGHT?
DON'T WORRY. I WON'T BLAB. I SIGNED THE WAIVER AND EVERYTHING.
EXCELLENT. WE SHALL BE HERE TO PROTECT YOU UNTIL YOUR FATHER'S PORTION OF THE TRIAL IS COMPLETE.
THANKS. THOUGH, YOU GUYS REALLY DON'T HAVE TO WORRY SO MUCH...

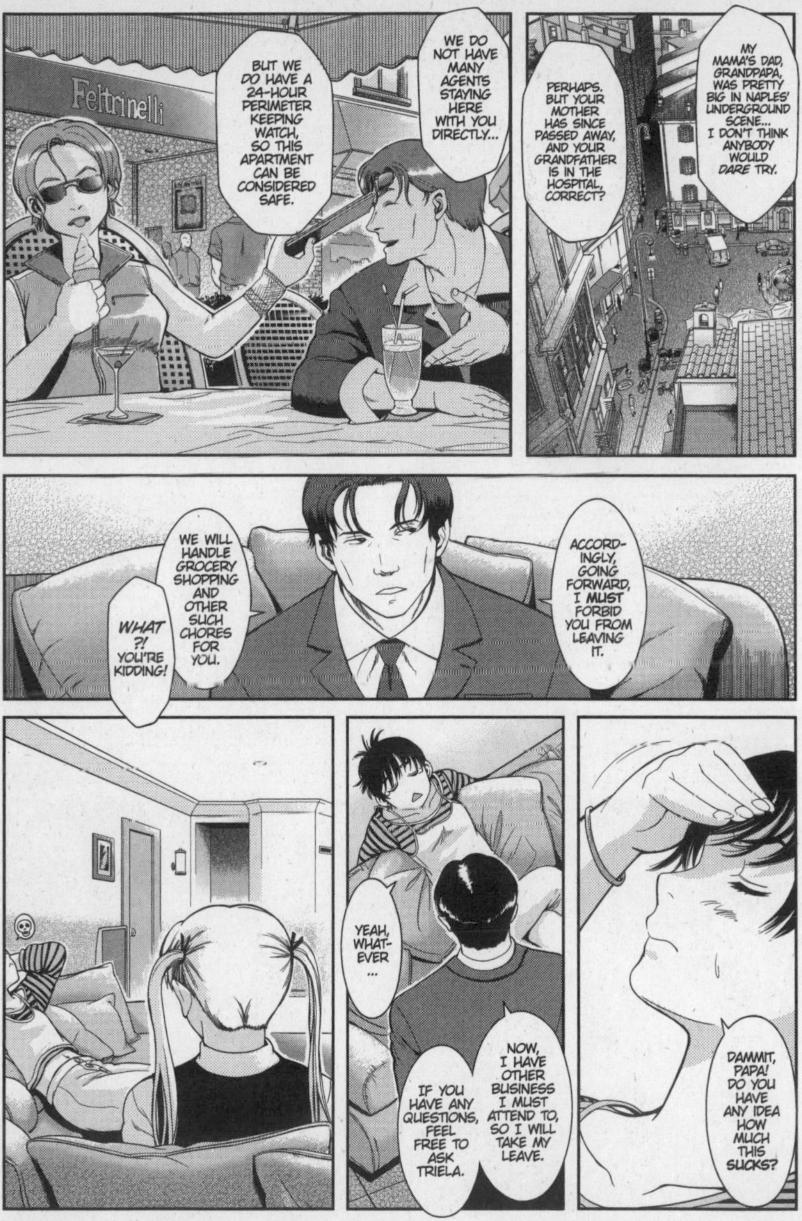
MY MAMA'S DAD, GRANDPAPA, WAS PRETTY BIG IN NAPLES' UNDERGROUND SCENE... I DON'T THINK ANYBODY WOULD *DARE* TRY.
PERHAPS. BUT YOUR MOTHER HAS SINCE PASSED AWAY, AND YOUR GRANDFATHER IS IN THE HOSPITAL, CORRECT?
Feltrinelli
WE DO NOT HAVE MANY AGENTS STAYING HERE WITH YOU DIRECTLY...
BUT WE *DO* HAVE A 24-HOUR PERIMETER KEEPING WATCH, SO THIS APARTMENT CAN BE CONSIDERED SAFE.
ACCORD-INGLY, GOING FORWARD, I **MUST** FORBID YOU FROM LEAVING IT.
WE WILL HANDLE GROCERY SHOPPING AND OTHER SUCH CHORES FOR YOU.
WHAT ?! YOU'RE KIDDING!
DAMMIT, PAPA! DO YOU HAVE ANY IDEA HOW MUCH THIS SUCKS?
NOW, I HAVE OTHER BUSINESS I MUST ATTEND TO, SO I WILL TAKE MY LEAVE.
IF YOU HAVE ANY QUESTIONS, FEEL FREE TO ASK TRIELA.
YEAH, WHAT-EVER ...

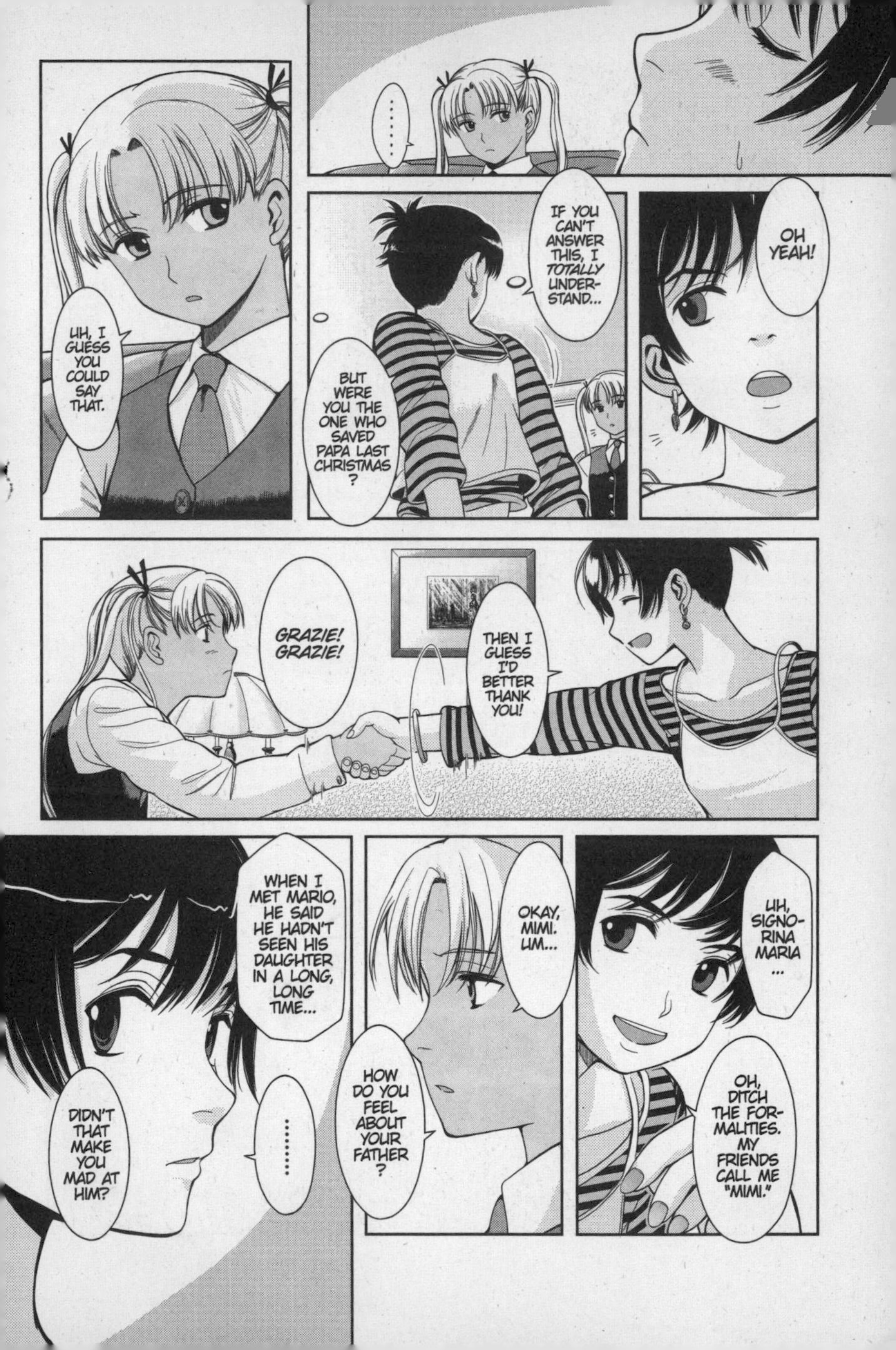
……
OH YEAH!
IF YOU CAN'T ANSWER THIS, I *TOTALLY* UNDER-STAND...
BUT WERE YOU THE ONE WHO SAVED PAPA LAST CHRISTMAS ?
UH, I GUESS YOU COULD SAY THAT.
THEN I GUESS I'D BETTER THANK YOU!
GRAZIE! GRAZIE!
UH, SIGNO-RINA MARIA ...
OH, DITCH THE FOR-MALITIES. MY FRIENDS CALL ME "MIMI."
OKAY, MIMI. UM...
HOW DO YOU FEEL ABOUT YOUR FATHER ?
WHEN I MET MARIO, HE SAID HE HADN'T SEEN HIS DAUGHTER IN A LONG, LONG TIME...
……
DIDN'T THAT MAKE YOU MAD AT HIM?

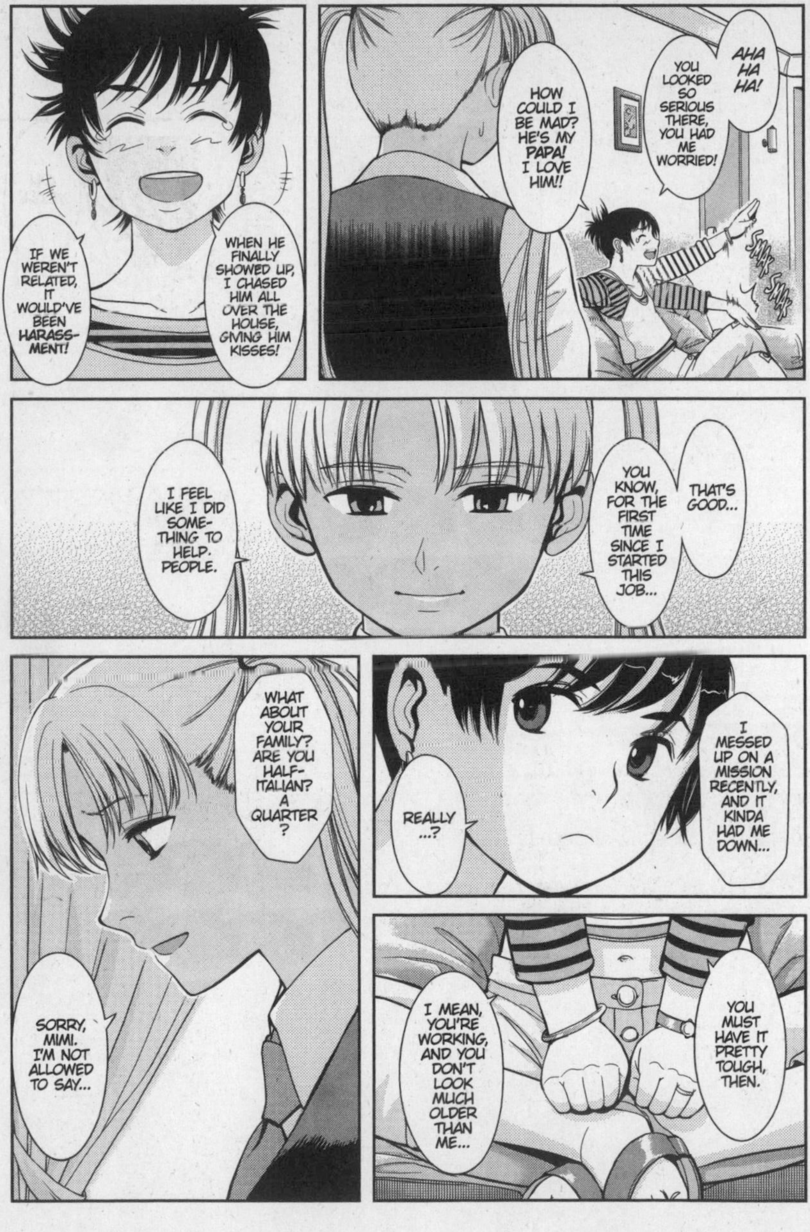
AHA HA HA!
YOU LOOKED SO SERIOUS THERE, YOU HAD ME WORRIED!
HOW COULD I BE MAD? HE'S MY PAPA! I LOVE HIM!!
SMAK SMAK
WHEN HE FINALLY SHOWED UP, I CHASED HIM ALL OVER THE HOUSE, GIVING HIM KISSES!
IF WE WEREN'T RELATED, IT WOULD'VE BEEN HARASS-MENT!
THAT'S GOOD...
YOU KNOW, FOR THE FIRST TIME SINCE I STARTED THIS JOB...
I FEEL LIKE I DID SOME-THING TO HELP. PEOPLE.
I MESSED UP ON A MISSION RECENTLY, AND IT KINDA HAD ME DOWN...
REALLY ...?
YOU MUST HAVE IT PRETTY TOUGH, THEN.
I MEAN, YOU'RE WORKING, AND YOU DON'T LOOK MUCH OLDER THAN ME...
WHAT ABOUT YOUR FAMILY? ARE YOU HALF-ITALIAN? A QUARTER ?
SORRY, MIMI. I'M NOT ALLOWED TO SAY...

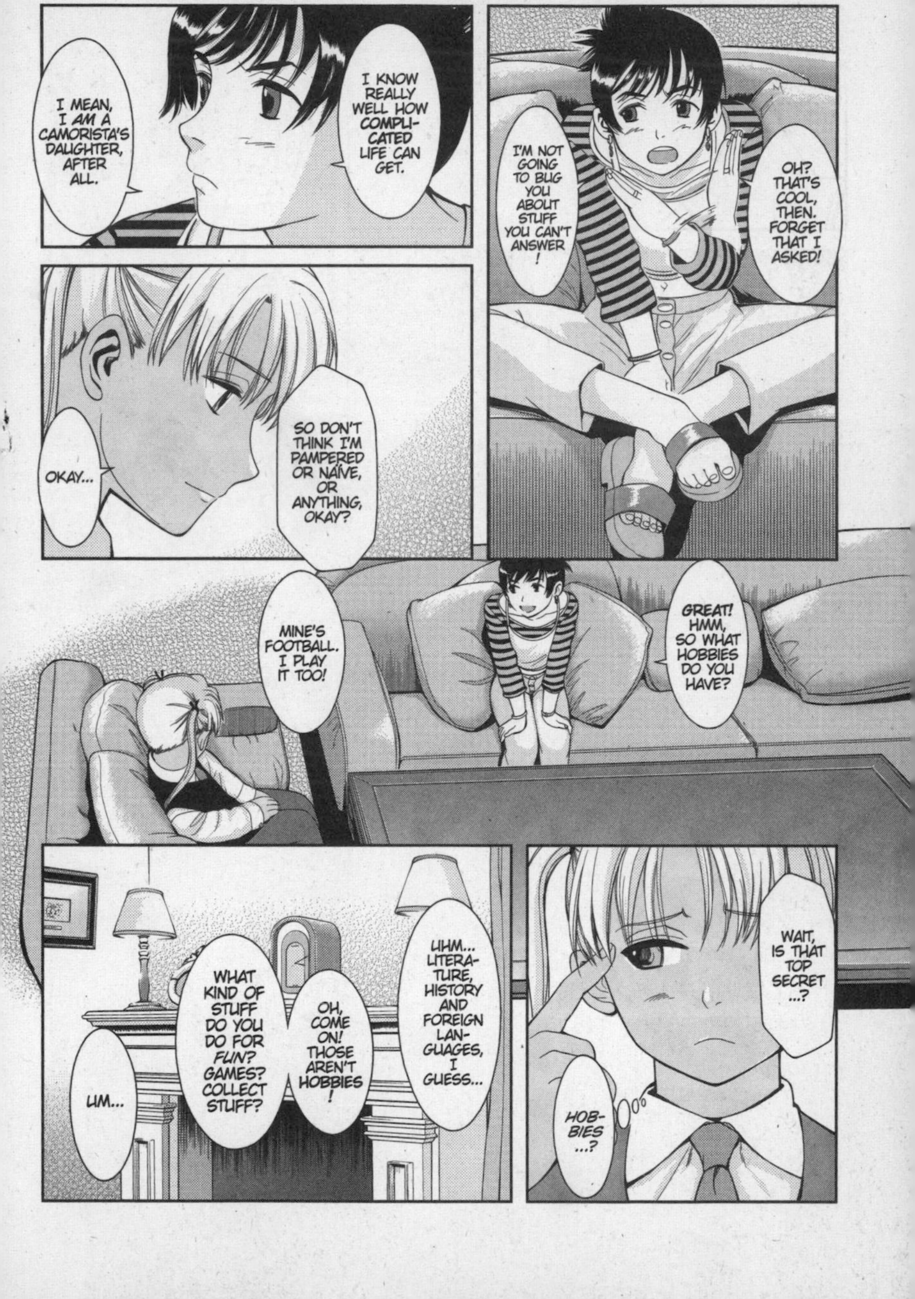
OH? THAT'S COOL, THEN. FORGET THAT I ASKED!
I'M NOT GOING TO BUG YOU ABOUT STUFF YOU CAN'T ANSWER!
I KNOW REALLY WELL HOW COMPLI-CATED LIFE CAN GET.
I MEAN, I AM A CAMORISTA'S DAUGHTER, AFTER ALL.
SO DON'T THINK I'M PAMPERED OR NAÏVE, OR ANYTHING, OKAY?
OKAY...
GREAT! HMM, SO WHAT HOBBIES DO YOU HAVE?
MINE'S FOOTBALL. I PLAY IT TOO!
WAIT, IS THAT TOP SECRET ...?
HOB-BIES ...?
UHM... LITERA-TURE, HISTORY AND FOREIGN LAN-GUAGES, I GUESS...
OH, COME ON! THOSE AREN'T HOBBIES!
WHAT KIND OF STUFF DO YOU DO FOR FUN? GAMES? COLLECT STUFF?
UM...

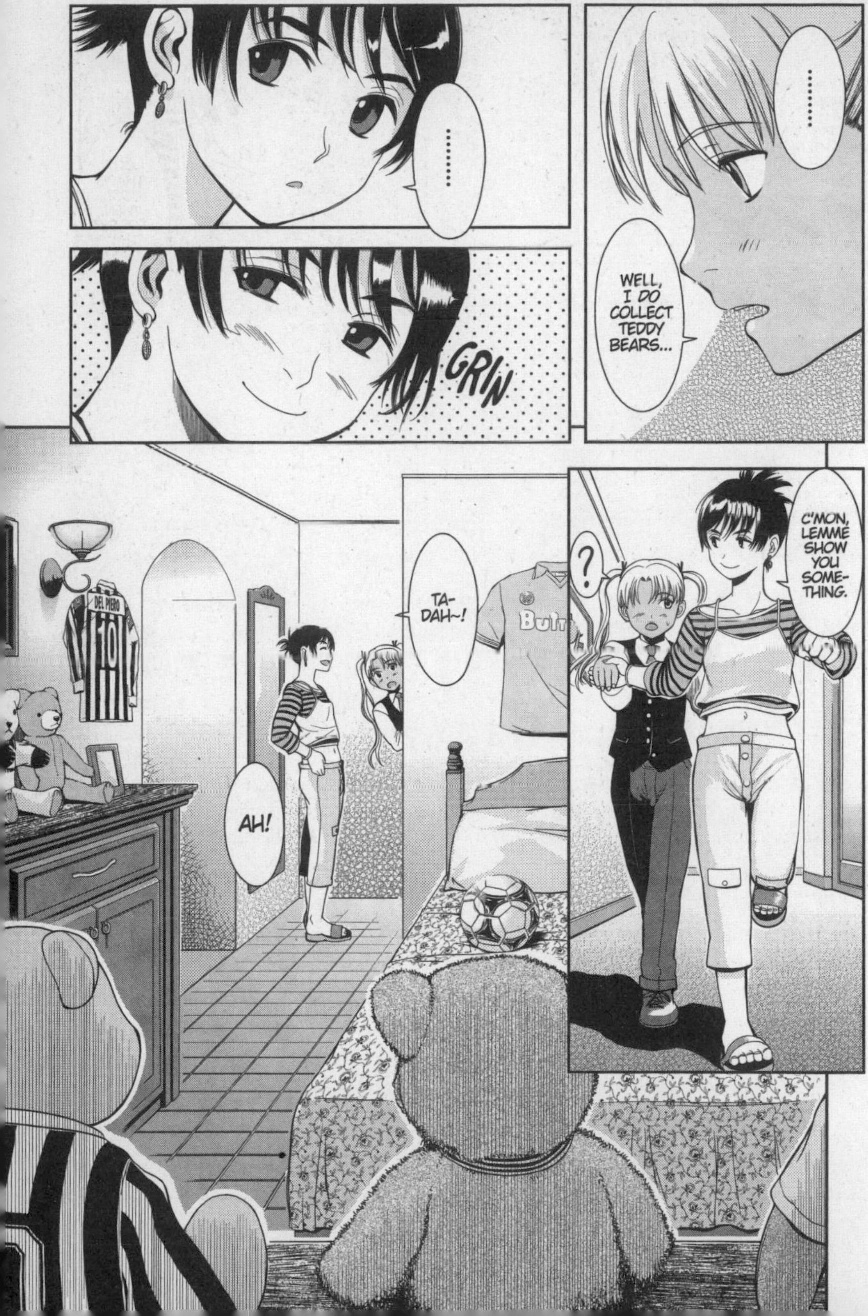

......
WELL, I DO COLLECT TEDDY BEARS...
......
GRIN
C'MON, LEMME SHOW YOU SOMETHING.
?
TA-DAH~!
AH!

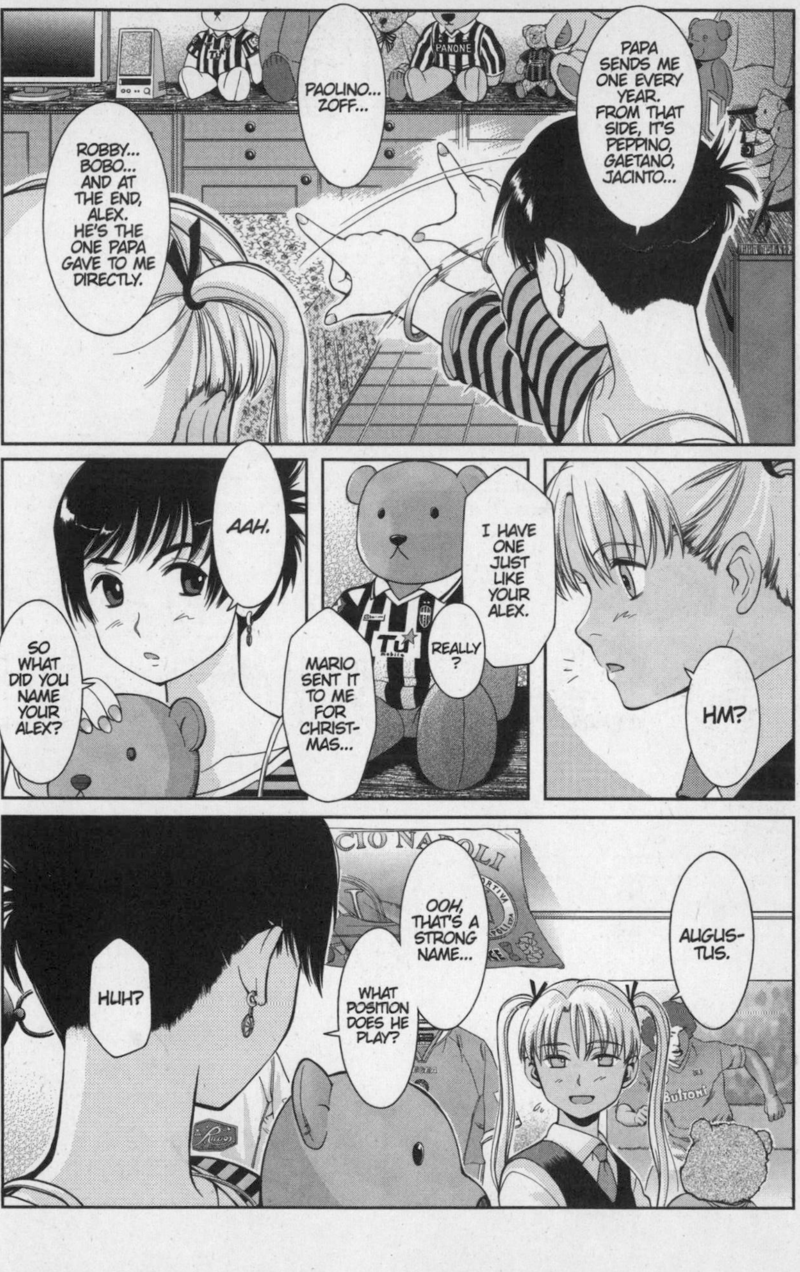
PAPA SENDS ME ONE EVERY YEAR. FROM THAT SIDE, IT'S PEPPINO, GAETANO, JACINTO...
PAOLINO... ZOFF...
ROBBY... BOBO... AND AT THE END, ALEX. HE'S THE ONE PAPA GAVE TO ME DIRECTLY.
HM?
I HAVE ONE JUST LIKE YOUR ALEX.
REALLY?
MARIO SENT IT TO ME FOR CHRIST-MAS...
AAH.
SO WHAT DID YOU NAME YOUR ALEX?
AUGUS-TUS.
OOH, THAT'S A STRONG NAME...
WHAT POSITION DOES HE PLAY?
HUH?

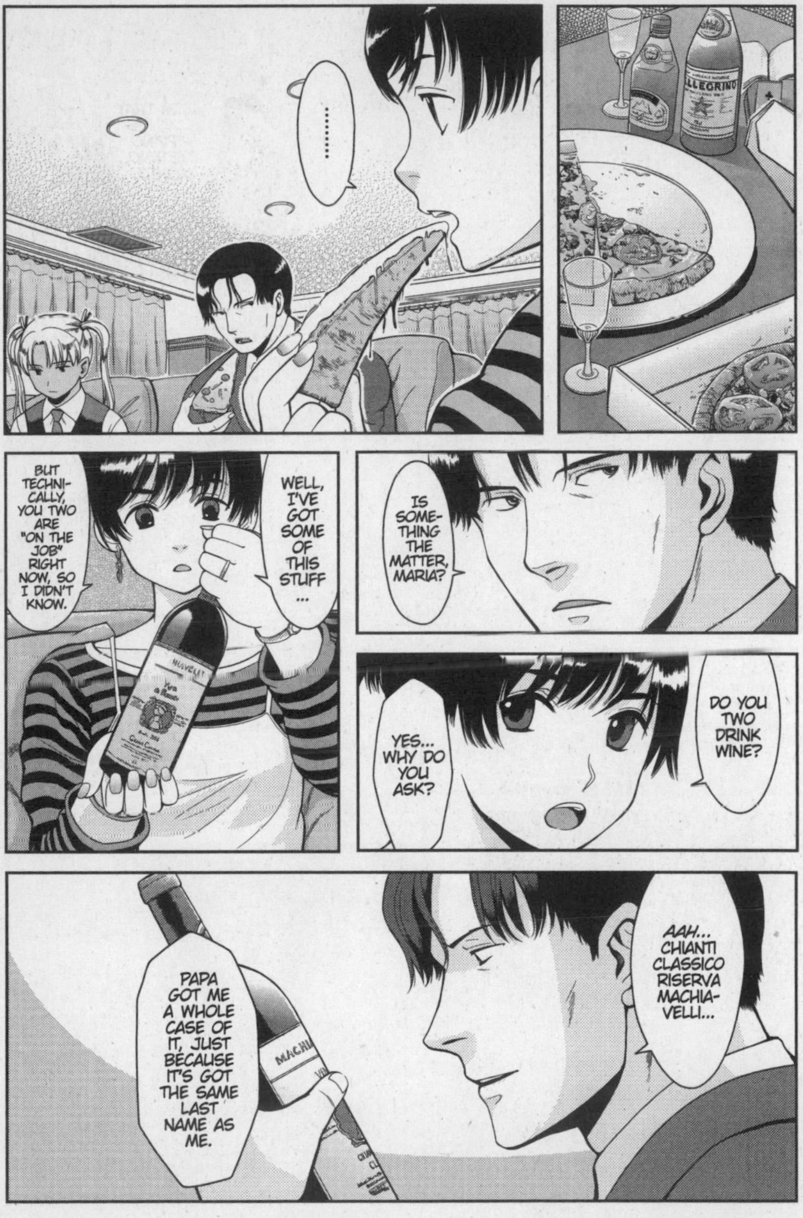
......
IS SOMETHING THE MATTER, MARIA?
DO YOU TWO DRINK WINE?
YES... WHY DO YOU ASK?
WELL, I'VE GOT SOME OF THIS STUFF ...
BUT TECHNICALLY, YOU TWO ARE "ON THE JOB" RIGHT NOW, SO I DIDN'T KNOW.
AAH... CHIANTI CLASSICO RISERVA MACHIAVELLI...
PAPA GOT ME A WHOLE CASE OF IT, JUST BECAUSE IT'S GOT THE SAME LAST NAME AS ME.

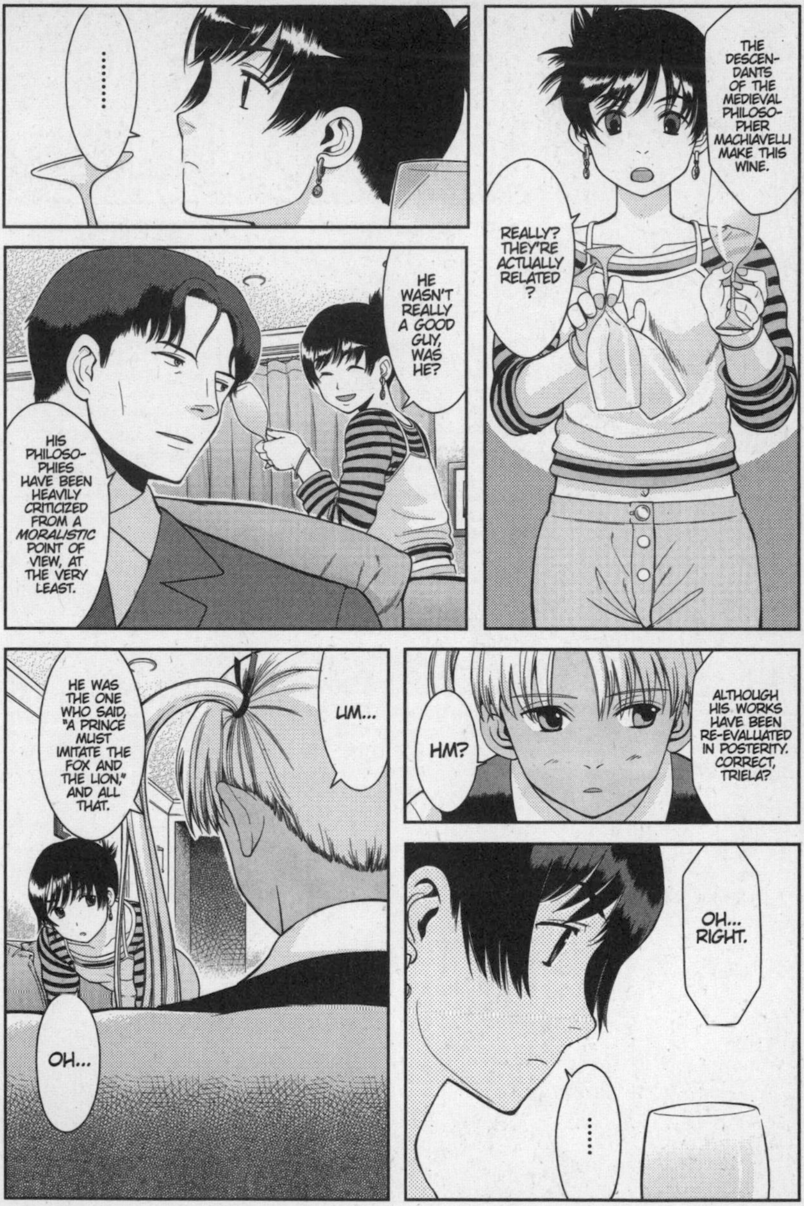
THE DESCENDANTS OF THE MEDIEVAL PHILOSOPHER MACHIAVELLI MAKE THIS WINE.
REALLY? THEY'RE ACTUALLY RELATED?
......
HE WASN'T REALLY A GOOD GUY, WAS HE?
HIS PHILOSOPHIES HAVE BEEN HEAVILY CRITICIZED FROM A *MORALISTIC* POINT OF VIEW, AT THE VERY LEAST.
ALTHOUGH HIS WORKS HAVE BEEN RE-EVALUATED IN POSTERITY. CORRECT, TRIELA?
HM?
OH... RIGHT.
......
UM...
HE WAS THE ONE WHO SAID, "A PRINCE MUST IMITATE THE FOX AND THE LION," AND ALL THAT.
OH...

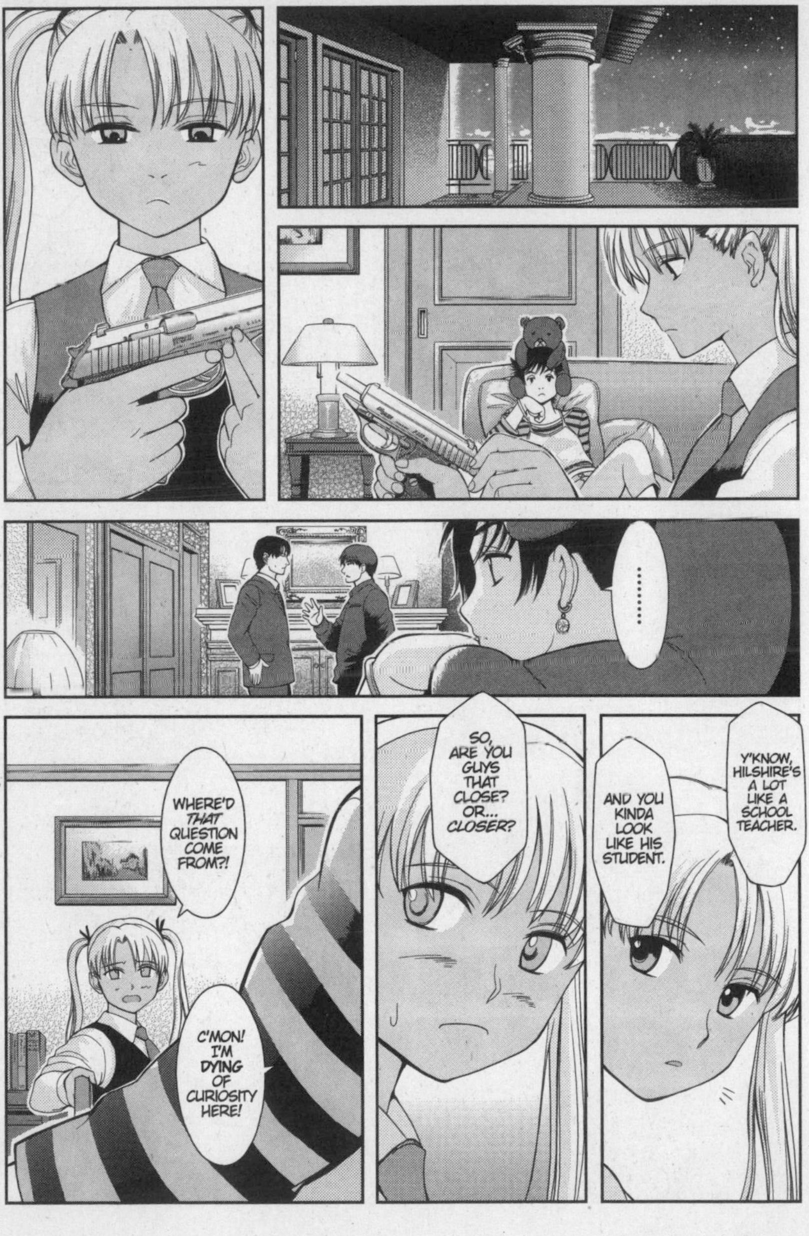
....
Y'KNOW, HILSHIRE'S A LOT LIKE A SCHOOL TEACHER.
AND YOU KINDA LOOK LIKE HIS STUDENT.
SO, ARE YOU GUYS THAT CLOSE? OR... CLOSER?
WHERE'D THAT QUESTION COME FROM?!
C'MON! I'M DYING OF CURIOSITY HERE!

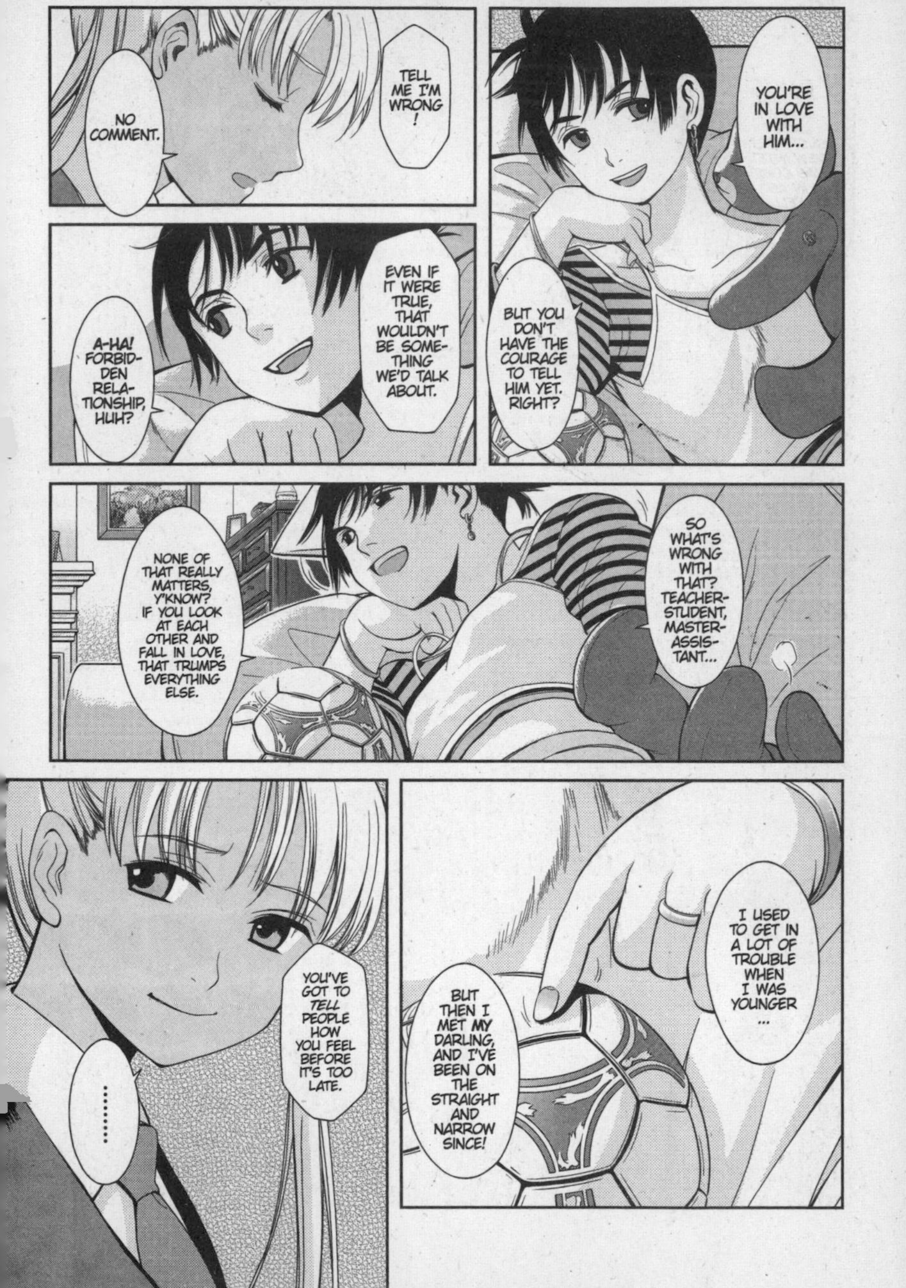
YOU'RE IN LOVE WITH HIM...
BUT YOU DON'T HAVE THE COURAGE TO TELL HIM YET. RIGHT?
TELL ME I'M WRONG!
NO COMMENT.
EVEN IF IT WERE TRUE, THAT WOULDN'T BE SOME-THING WE'D TALK ABOUT.
A-HA! FORBID-DEN RELA-TIONSHIP, HUH?
SO WHAT'S WRONG WITH THAT? TEACHER-STUDENT, MASTER-ASSIS-TANT...
NONE OF THAT REALLY MATTERS, Y'KNOW? IF YOU LOOK AT EACH OTHER AND FALL IN LOVE, THAT TRUMPS EVERYTHING ELSE.
I USED TO GET IN A LOT OF TROUBLE WHEN I WAS YOUNGER...
BUT THEN I MET MY DARLING, AND I'VE BEEN ON THE STRAIGHT AND NARROW SINCE!
YOU'VE GOT TO *TELL* PEOPLE HOW YOU FEEL BEFORE IT'S TOO LATE.
....

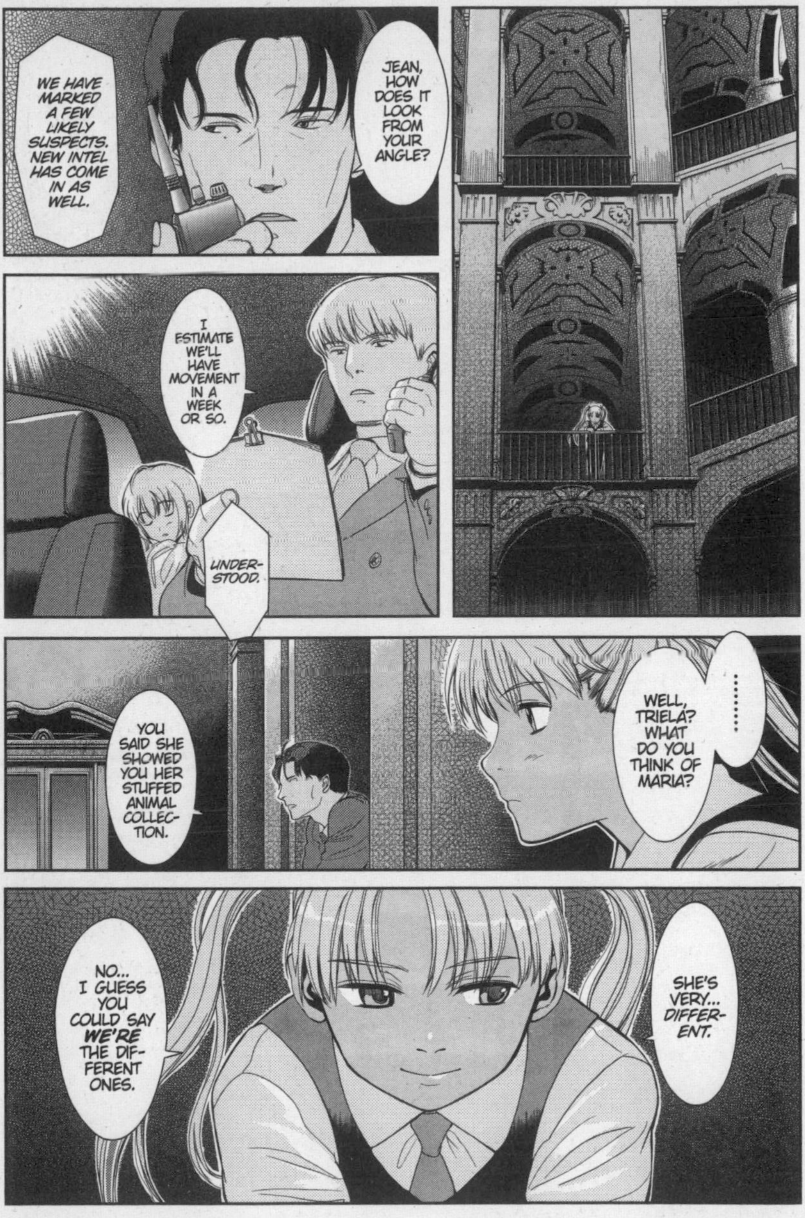
JEAN, HOW DOES IT LOOK FROM YOUR ANGLE?
WE HAVE MARKED A FEW LIKELY SUSPECTS. NEW INTEL HAS COME IN AS WELL.
I ESTIMATE WE'LL HAVE MOVEMENT IN A WEEK OR SO.
UNDERSTOOD.
......
WELL, TRIELA? WHAT DO YOU THINK OF MARIA?
YOU SAID SHE SHOWED YOU HER STUFFED ANIMAL COLLECTION.
SHE'S VERY... DIFFERENT.
NO... I GUESS YOU COULD SAY *WE'RE* THE DIFFERENT ONES.

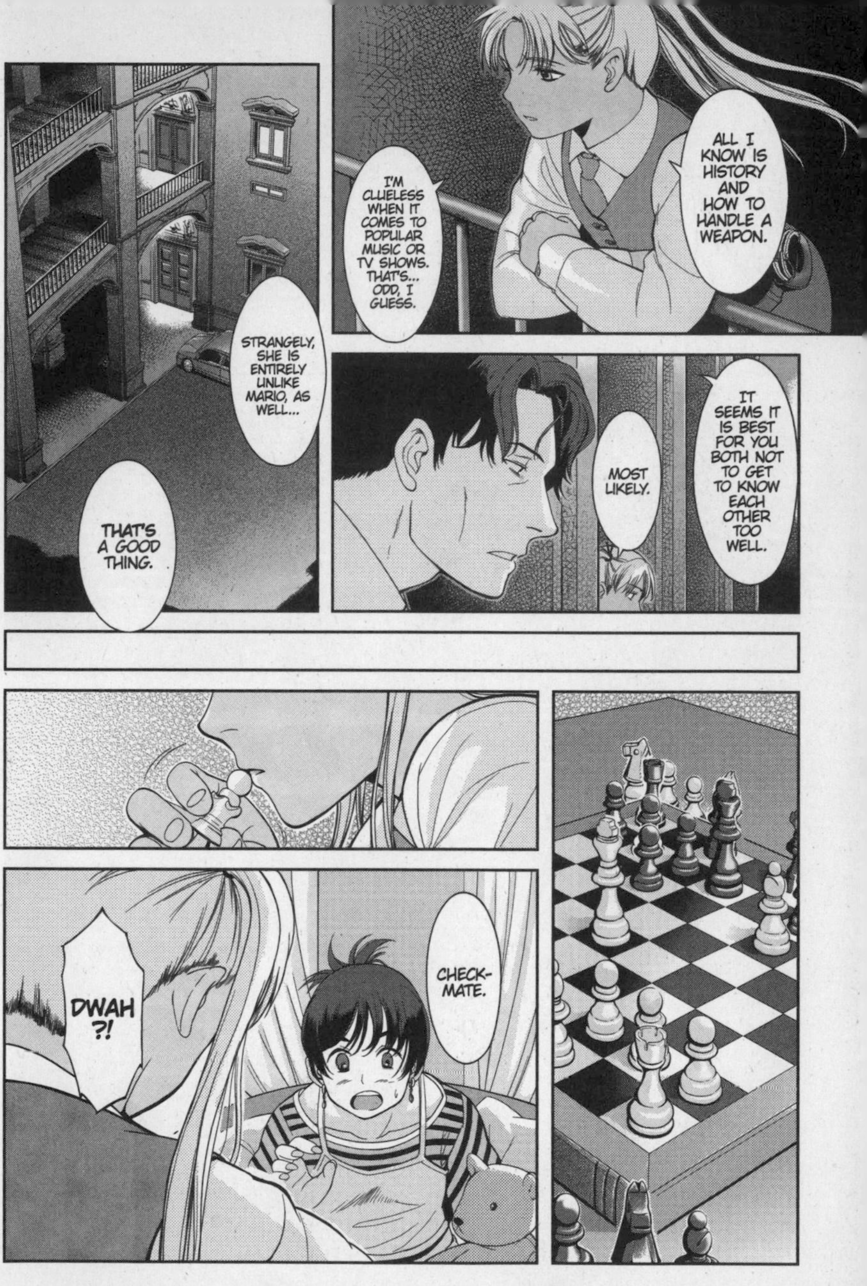
ALL I KNOW IS HISTORY AND HOW TO HANDLE A WEAPON.
I'M CLUELESS WHEN IT COMES TO POPULAR MUSIC OR TV SHOWS. THAT'S... ODD, I GUESS.
IT SEEMS IT IS BEST FOR YOU BOTH NOT TO GET TO KNOW EACH OTHER TOO WELL.
MOST LIKELY.
STRANGELY, SHE IS ENTIRELY UNLIKE MARIO, AS WELL...
THAT'S A GOOD THING.
CHECK-MATE.
DWAH ?!

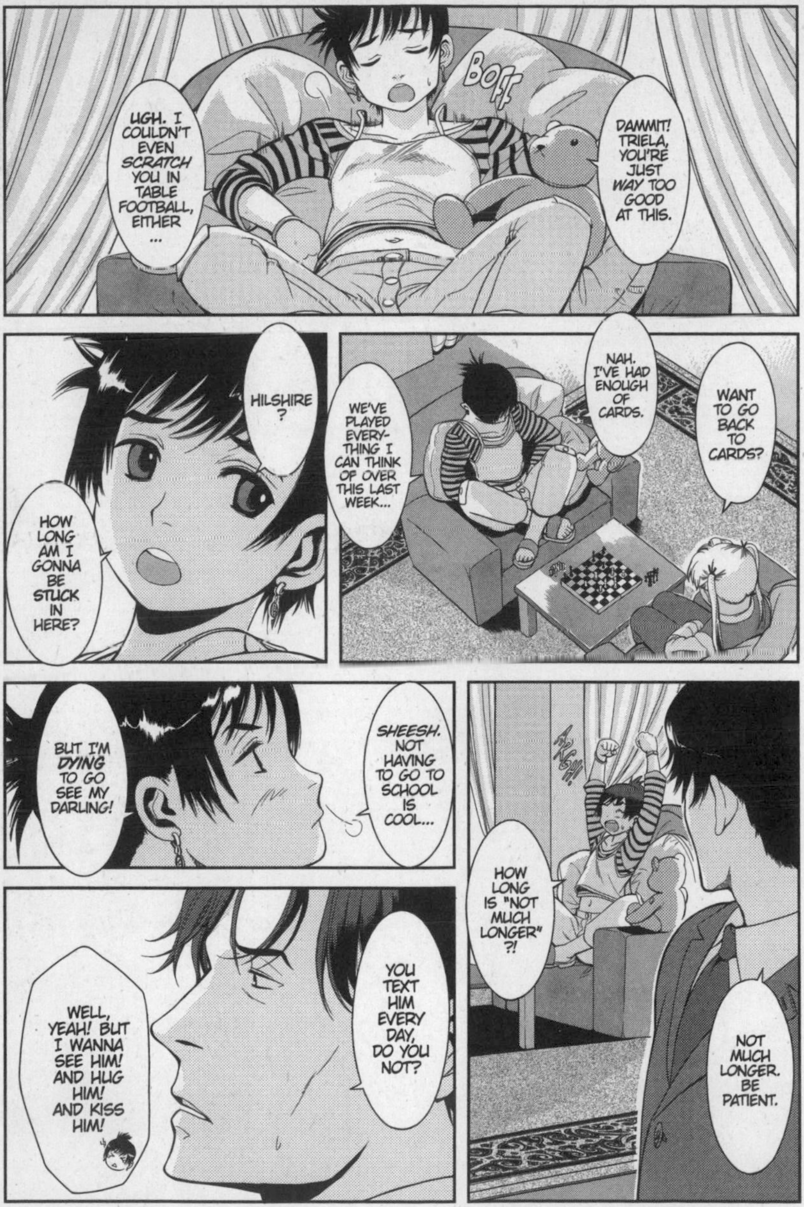
DAMMIT! TRIELA, YOU'RE JUST WAY TOO GOOD AT THIS.
BOFF
UGH. I COULDN'T EVEN SCRATCH YOU IN TABLE FOOTBALL, EITHER ...
WANT TO GO BACK TO CARDS?
NAH. I'VE HAD ENOUGH OF CARDS.
WE'VE PLAYED EVERY-THING I CAN THINK OF OVER THIS LAST WEEK...
HILSHIRE?
HOW LONG AM I GONNA BE STUCK IN HERE?
ARGH!
NOT MUCH LONGER. BE PATIENT.
HOW LONG IS "NOT MUCH LONGER"?!
SHEESH. NOT HAVING TO GO TO SCHOOL IS COOL...
BUT I'M DYING TO GO SEE MY DARLING!
YOU TEXT HIM EVERY DAY, DO YOU NOT?
WELL, YEAH! BUT I WANNA SEE HIM! AND HUG HIM! AND KISS HIM!

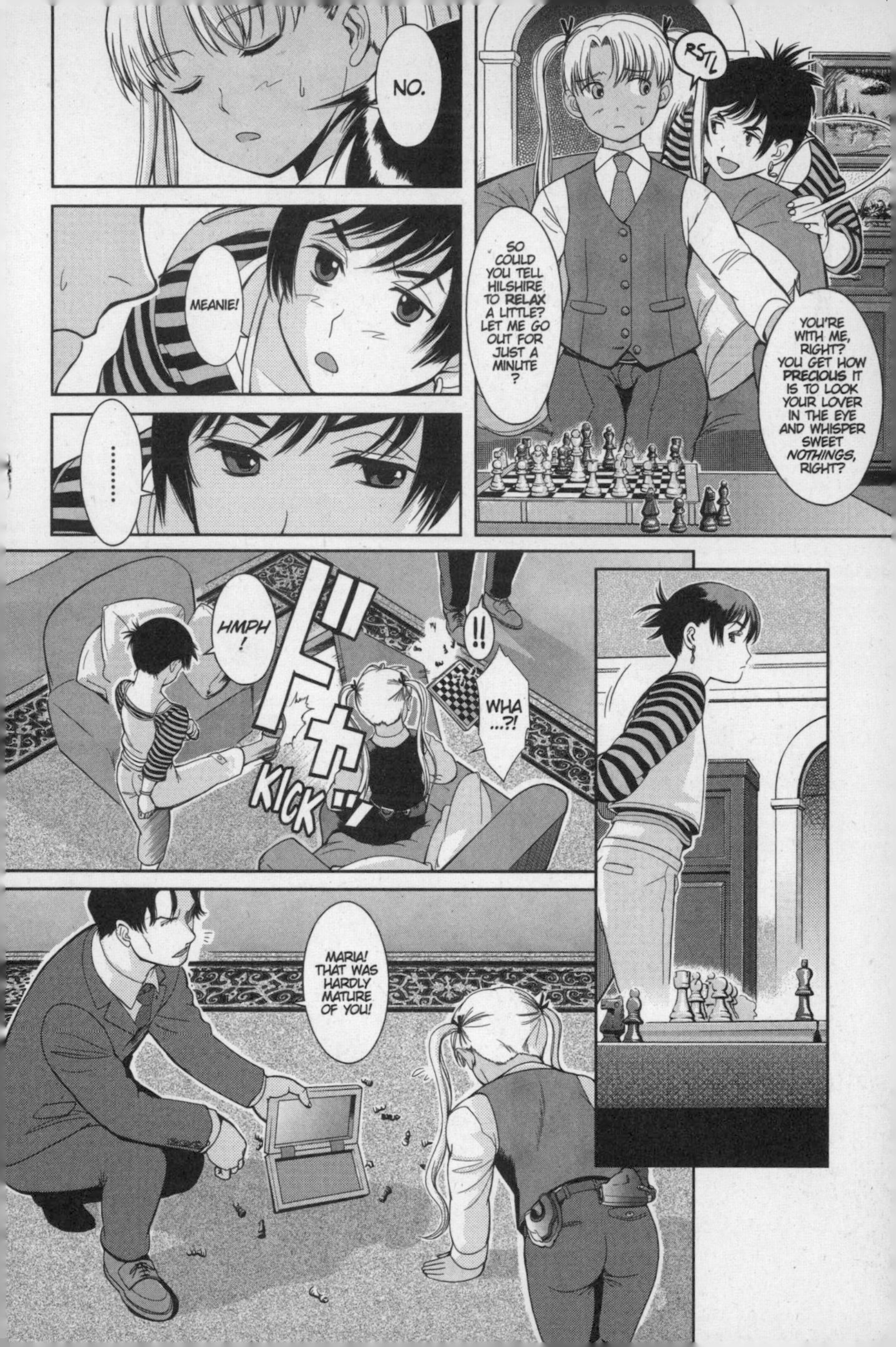
RSTL
SO COULD YOU TELL HILSHIRE TO RELAX A LITTLE? LET ME GO OUT FOR JUST A MINUTE?
YOU'RE WITH ME, RIGHT? YOU GET HOW PRECIOUS IT IS TO LOOK YOUR LOVER IN THE EYE AND WHISPER SWEET *NOTHINGS*, RIGHT?
NO.
MEANIE!
....
!!
WHA...?!
HMPH!
ドカッ
KICK
MARIA! THAT WAS HARDLY MATURE OF YOU!

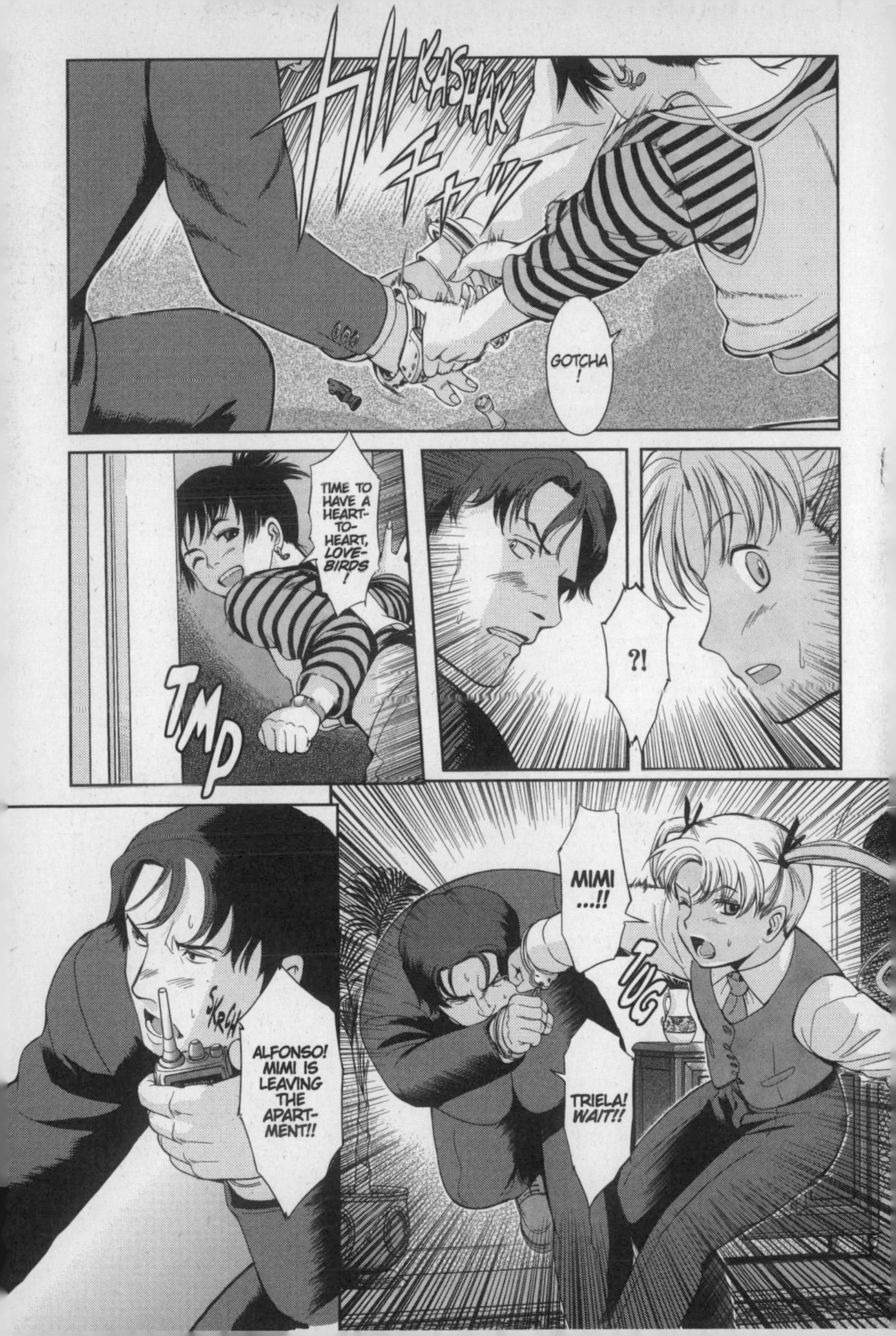
KASHAK
GOTCHA!
?!
TIME TO HAVE A HEART-TO-HEART, LOVEBIRDS!
TMP
MIMI...!!
TUG
TRIELA! WAIT!!
SKRCH
ALFONSO! MIMI IS LEAVING THE APARTMENT!!

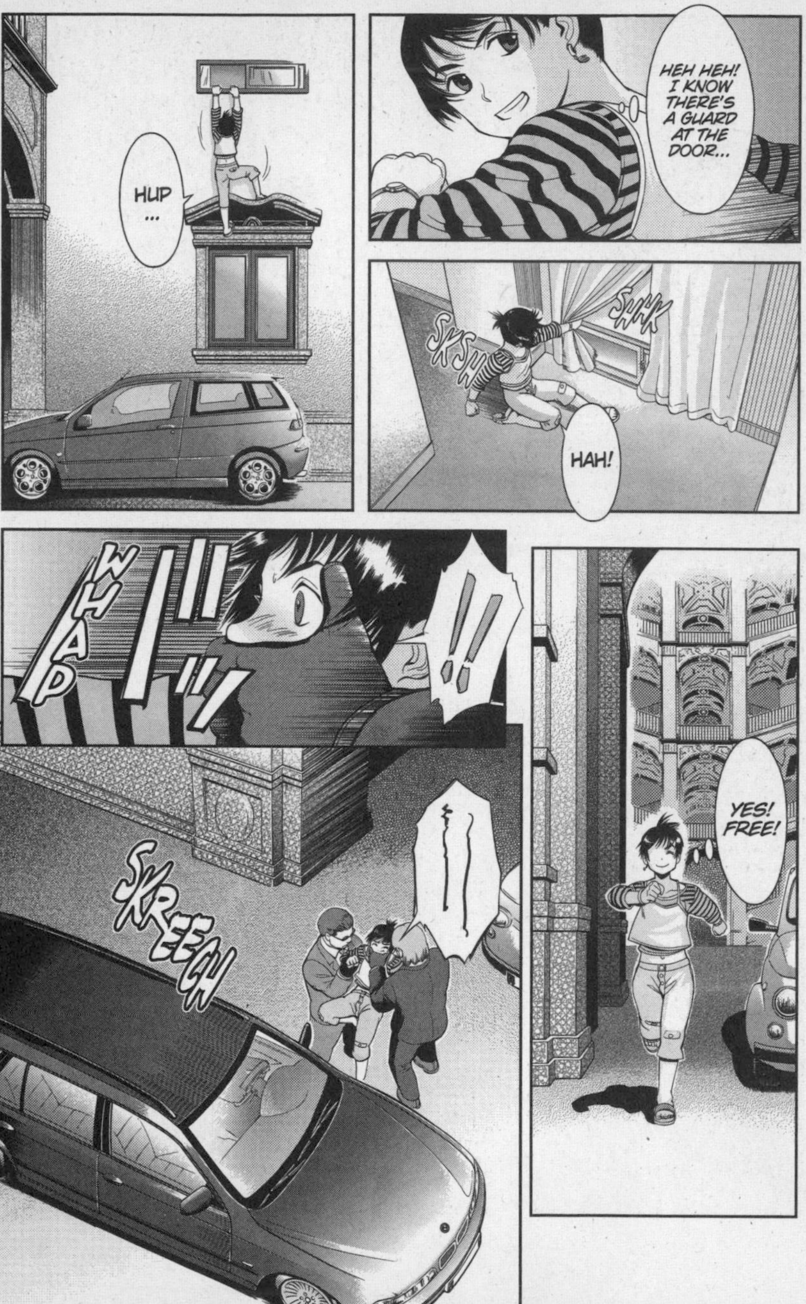
HEH HEH! I KNOW THERE'S A GUARD AT THE DOOR...
SKSH
SHHK
HAH!
HUP ...
YES! FREE!
WHAP
!!
SKREECH

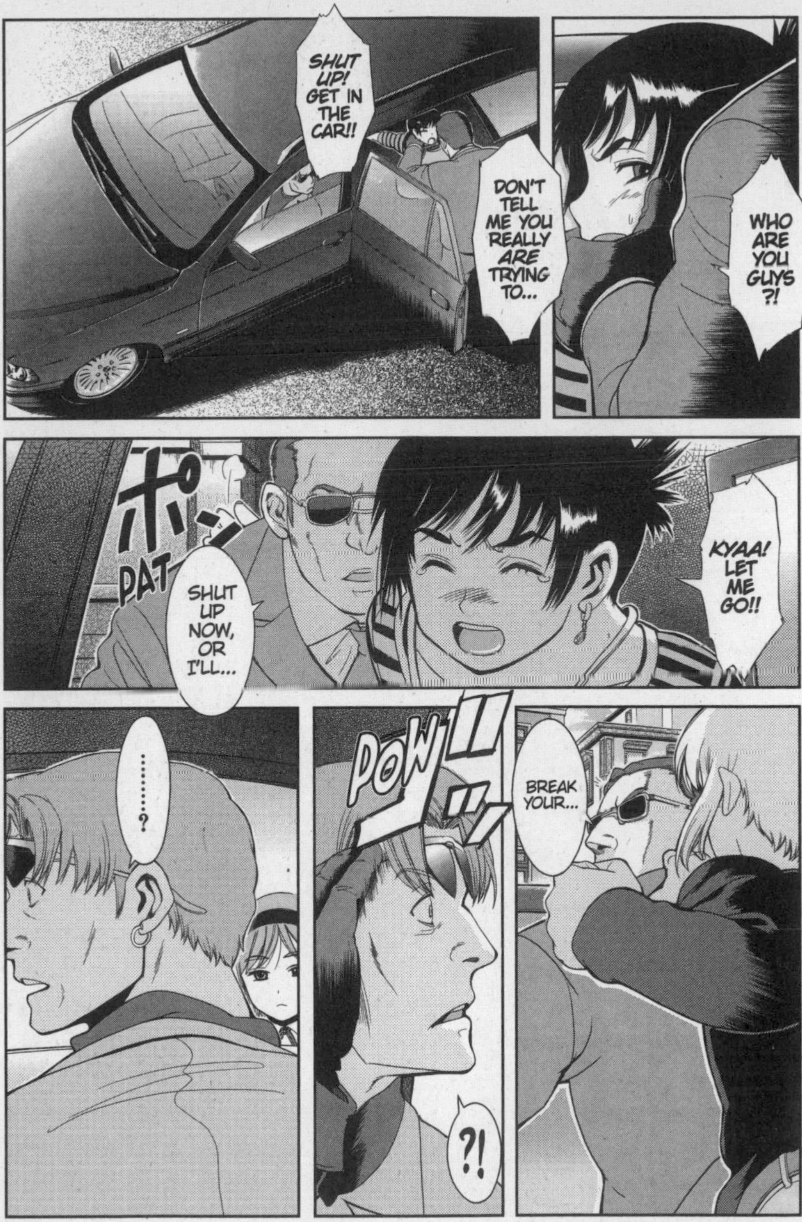

WHO ARE YOU GUYS ?!
DON'T TELL ME YOU REALLY ARE TRYING TO...
SHUT UP! GET IN THE CAR!!
KYAA! LET ME GO!!
ポン
PAT
SHUT UP NOW, OR I'LL...
BREAK YOUR...
POW!!
?!
......?

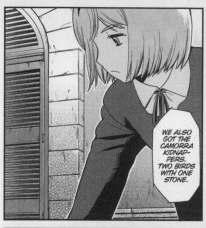

VREEE
HILSHIRE.
HERE.
WE HAVE MARIA. SHE IS SAFE.
WE ALSO GOT THE CAMORRA KIDNAP-PERS. TWO BIRDS WITH ONE STONE.
I'LL BRING MARIA UP PRES-ENTLY.
ROGER.
CHK CHK

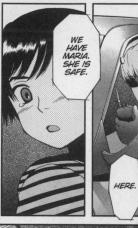

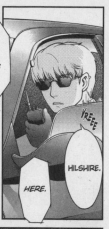

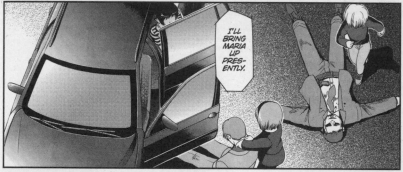

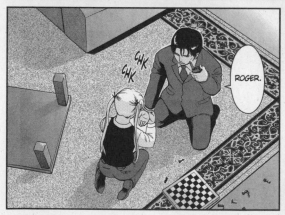

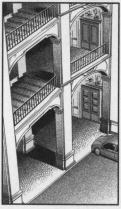

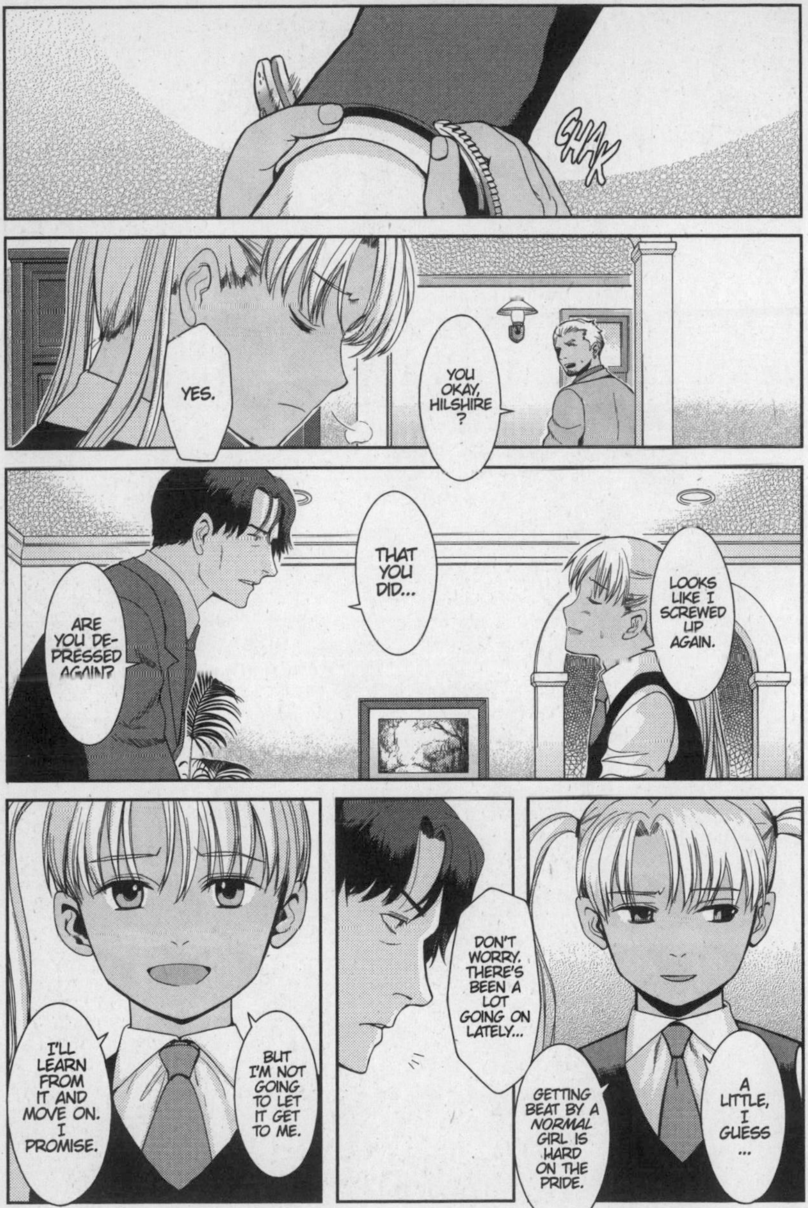
CHAK
YOU OKAY, HILSHIRE?
YES.
LOOKS LIKE I SCREWED UP AGAIN.
THAT YOU DID...
ARE YOU DE-PRESSED AGAIN?
A LITTLE, I GUESS...
GETTING BEAT BY A *NORMAL* GIRL IS HARD ON THE PRIDE.
DON'T WORRY. THERE'S BEEN A LOT GOING ON LATELY...
BUT I'M NOT GOING TO LET IT GET TO ME.
I'LL LEARN FROM IT AND MOVE ON. I PROMISE.

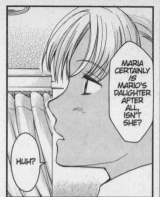

WHEW
......
......
MARIA CERTAINLY IS MARIO'S DAUGHTER AFTER ALL, ISN'T SHE?
HUH?
THEY MAY NOT LOOK ALIKE, BUT HER FINGERS ARE JUST AS NIMBLE AS HIS.
TRUE... AND SHE'LL DO ANYTHING TO GET WHAT SHE WANTS, TOO.
BY THE BY, DO YOU KNOW WHAT SHE MEANT BY THAT "HEART-TO-HEART" COMMENT?
WHO KNOWS? MAYBE SHE HAD THE WRONG IDEA ABOUT US.
I MEAN, THERE ISN'T ANY NEED FOR US TO HAVE "HEART-TO-HEART" TALKS.
WE'RE A FRATELLO.

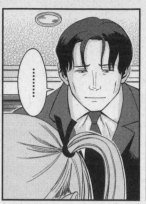

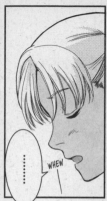

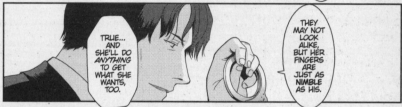

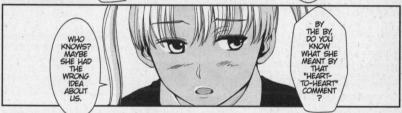

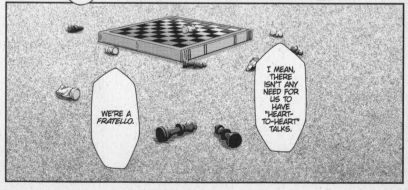

GUNSLINGERGIRL.

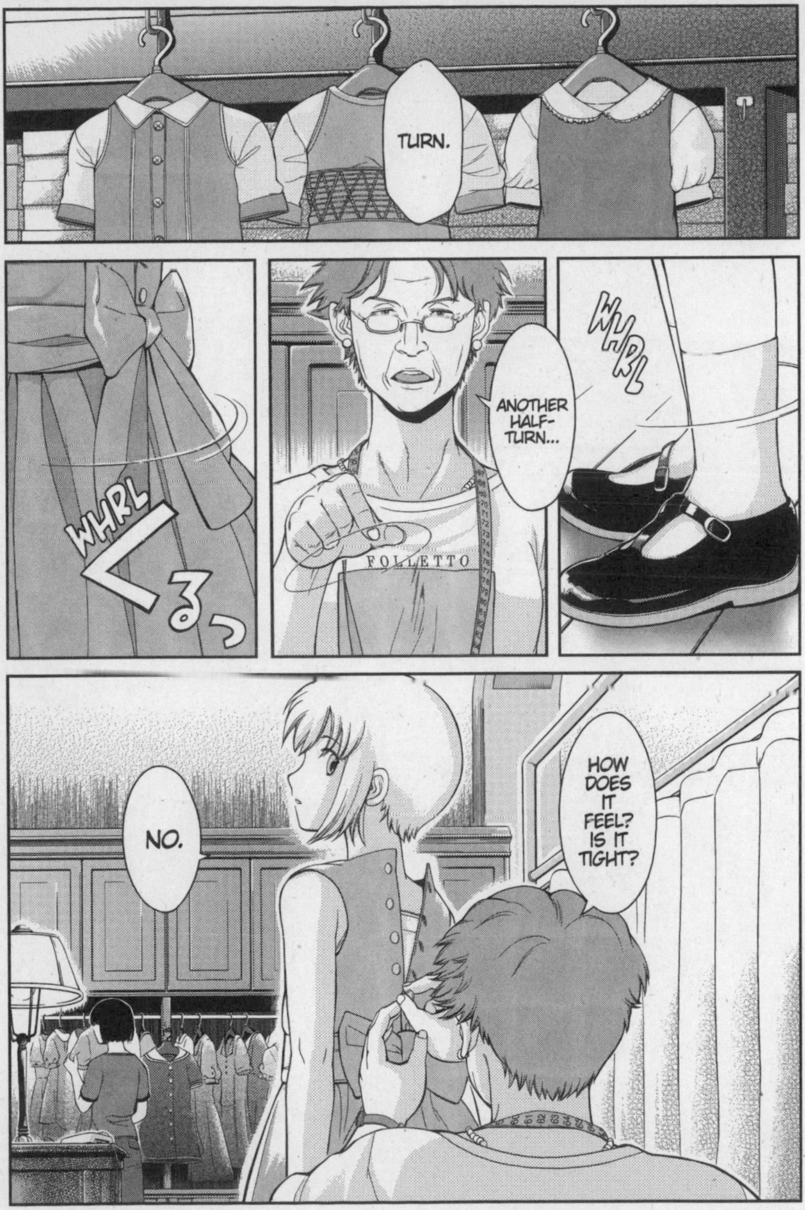
TURN.
WHRL
ANOTHER HALF-TURN...
WHRL
くるっ
HOW DOES IT FEEL? IS IT TIGHT?
NO.

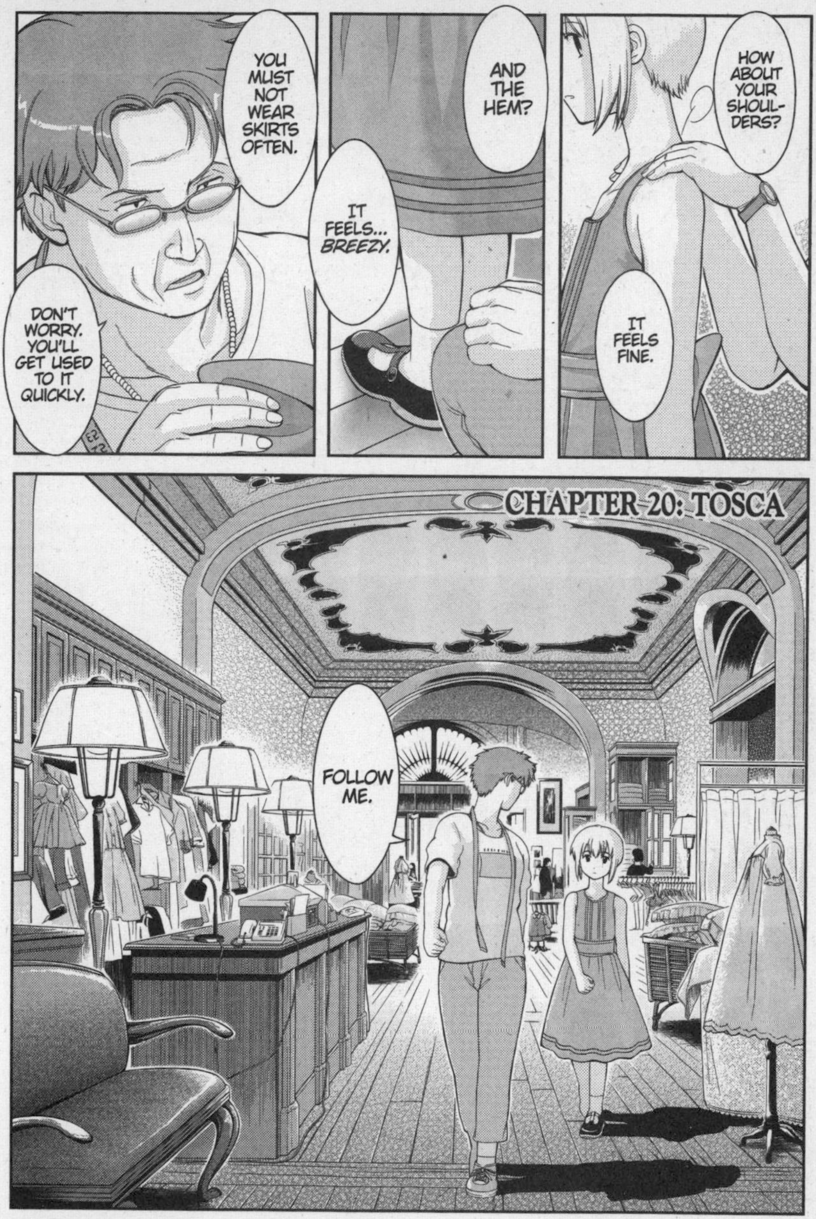
HOW ABOUT YOUR SHOULDERS?
IT FEELS FINE.
AND THE HEM?
IT FEELS... BREEZY.
YOU MUST NOT WEAR SKIRTS OFTEN.
DON'T WORRY. YOU'LL GET USED TO IT QUICKLY.
CHAPTER 20: TOSCA
FOLLOW ME.

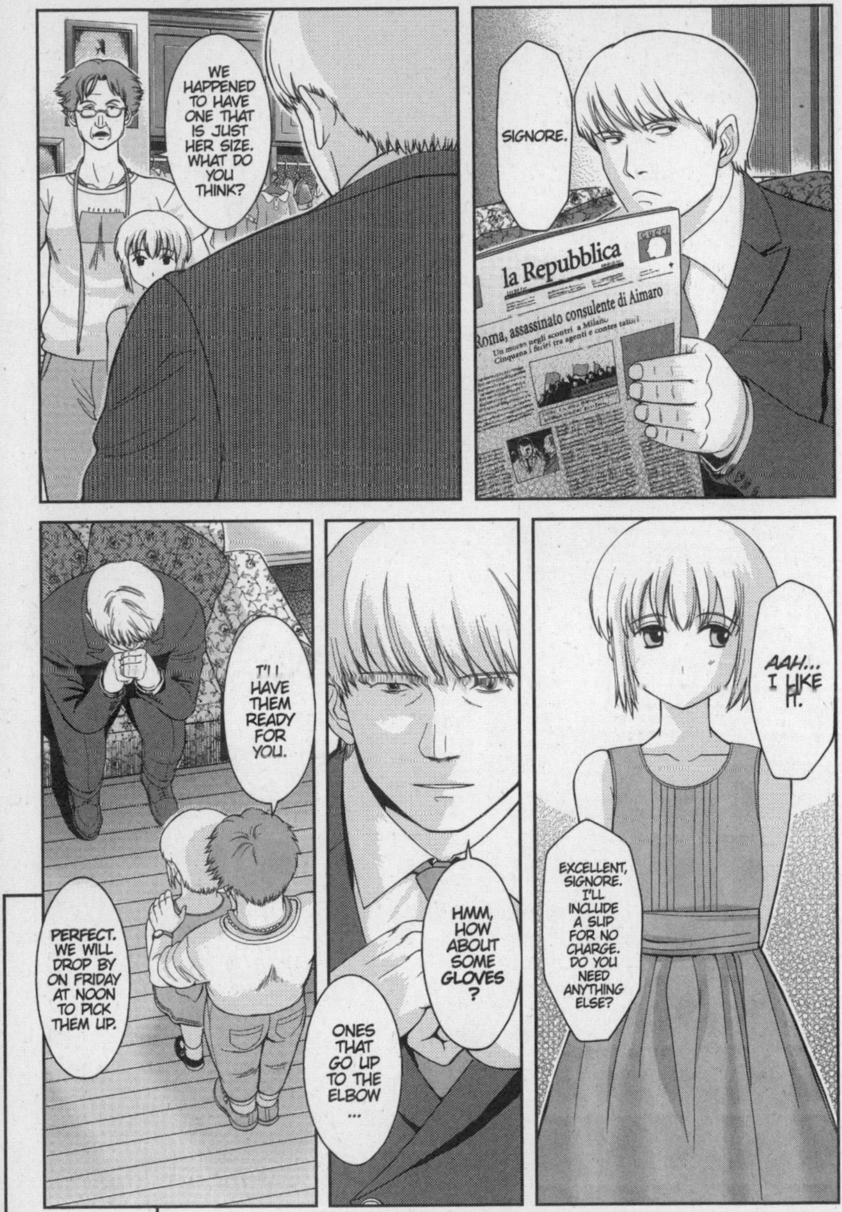
SIGNORE.
la Repubblica
Roma, assassinato consulente di Aimaro
WE HAPPENED TO HAVE ONE THAT IS JUST HER SIZE. WHAT DO YOU THINK?
AAH... I LIKE IT.
EXCELLENT, SIGNORE. I'LL INCLUDE A SLIP FOR NO CHARGE. DO YOU NEED ANYTHING ELSE?
HMM, HOW ABOUT SOME GLOVES?
ONES THAT GO UP TO THE ELBOW...
I'LL HAVE THEM READY FOR YOU.
PERFECT. WE WILL DROP BY ON FRIDAY AT NOON TO PICK THEM UP.

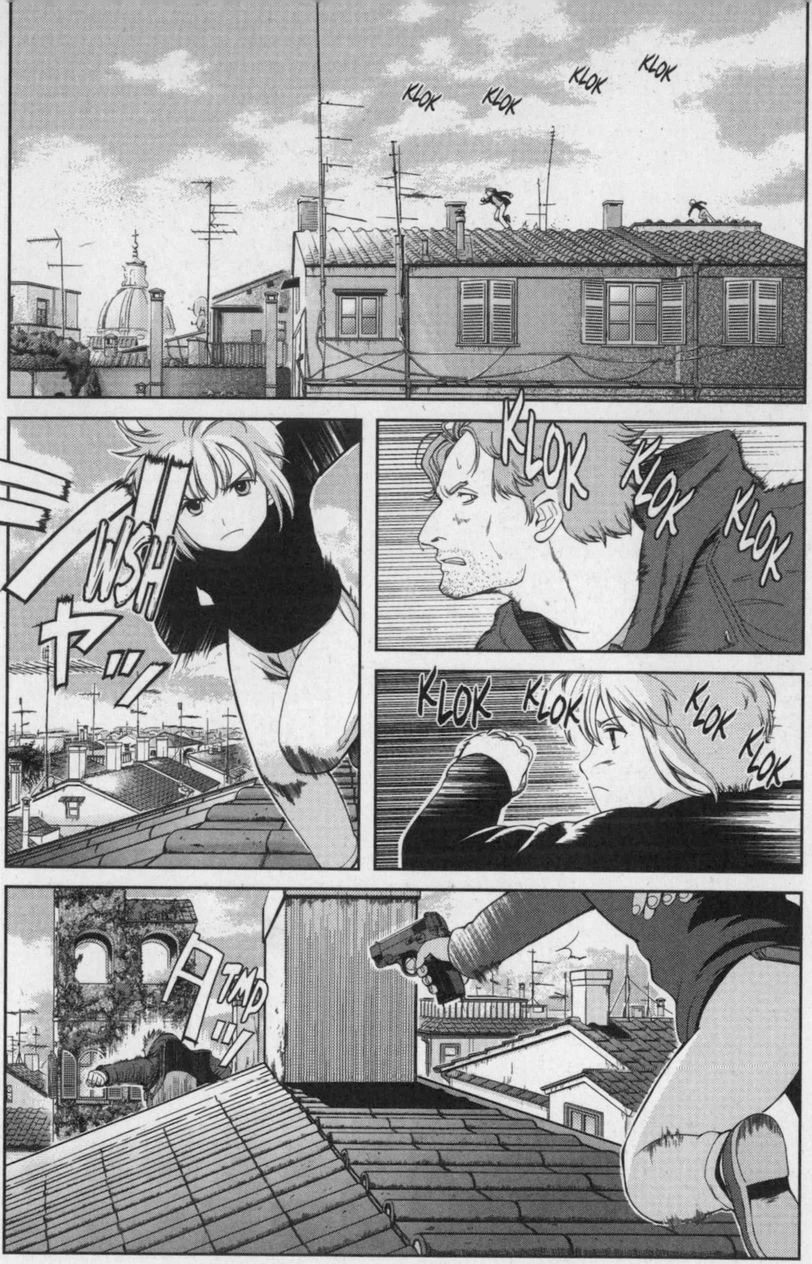
KLOK
KLOK
KLOK
KLOK
KLOK
KLOK
KLOK
KLOK
KLOK
KLOK
KLOK
WSH
TMP

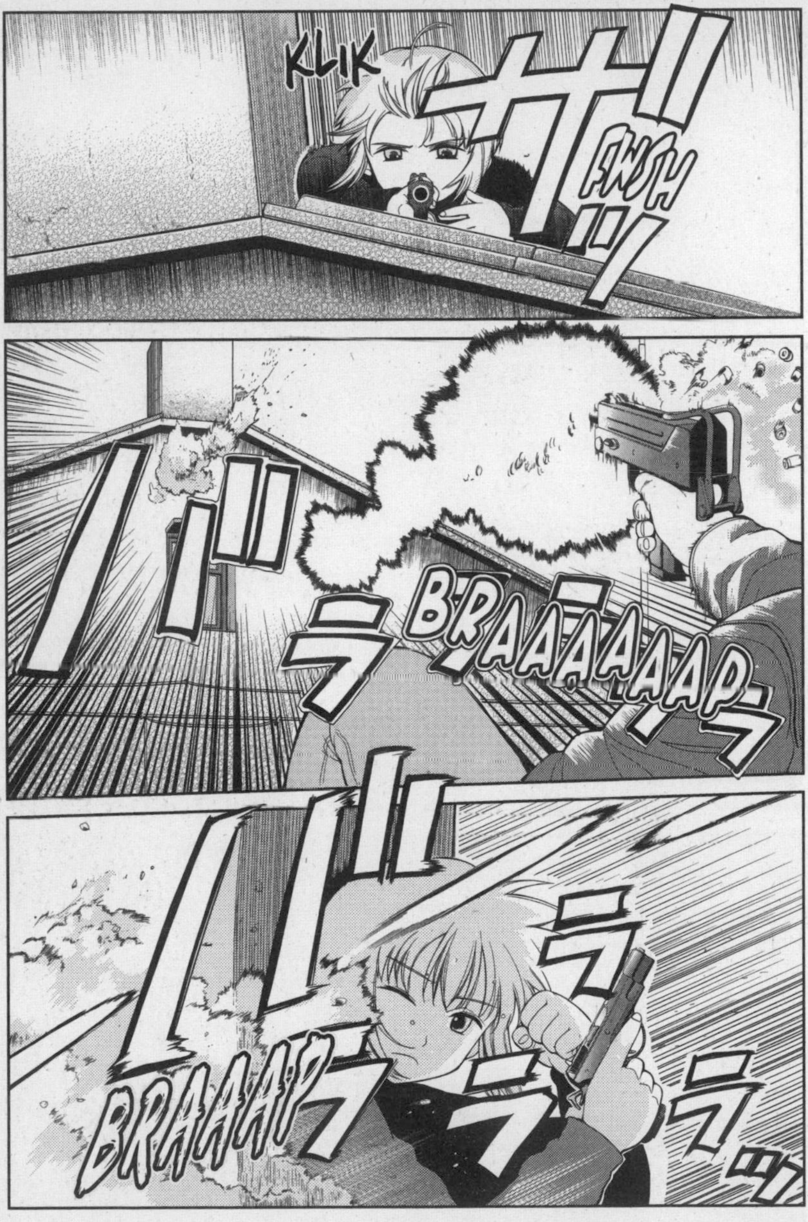
KLIK
FWSH
BRAAAAAAAP
BRAAAP

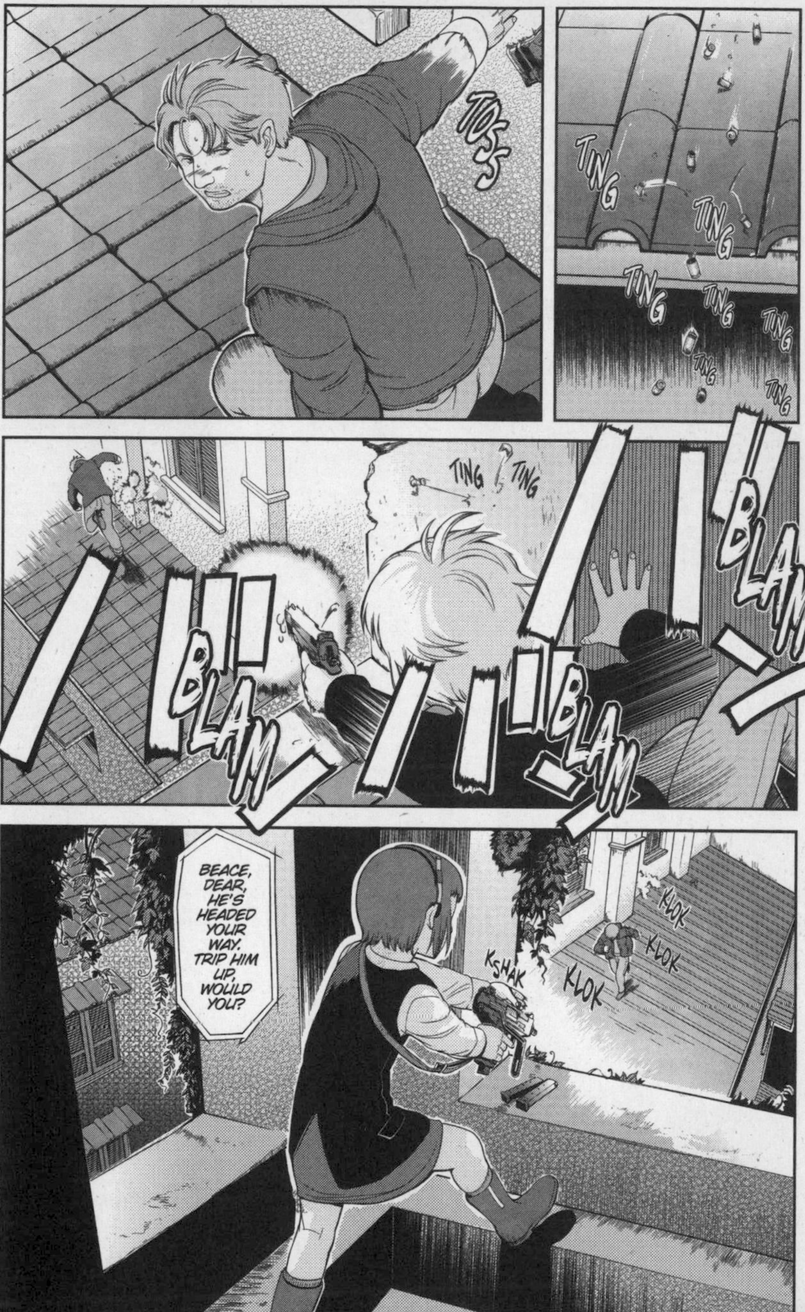
TING
TING
TING
TING
TING
TING
TING
TOSS
TING
TING
BLAM
BLAM
BLAM
KLOK
KLOK
KLOK
K'SHAK
BEACE, DEAR, HE'S HEADED YOUR WAY. TRIP HIM UP, WOULD YOU?

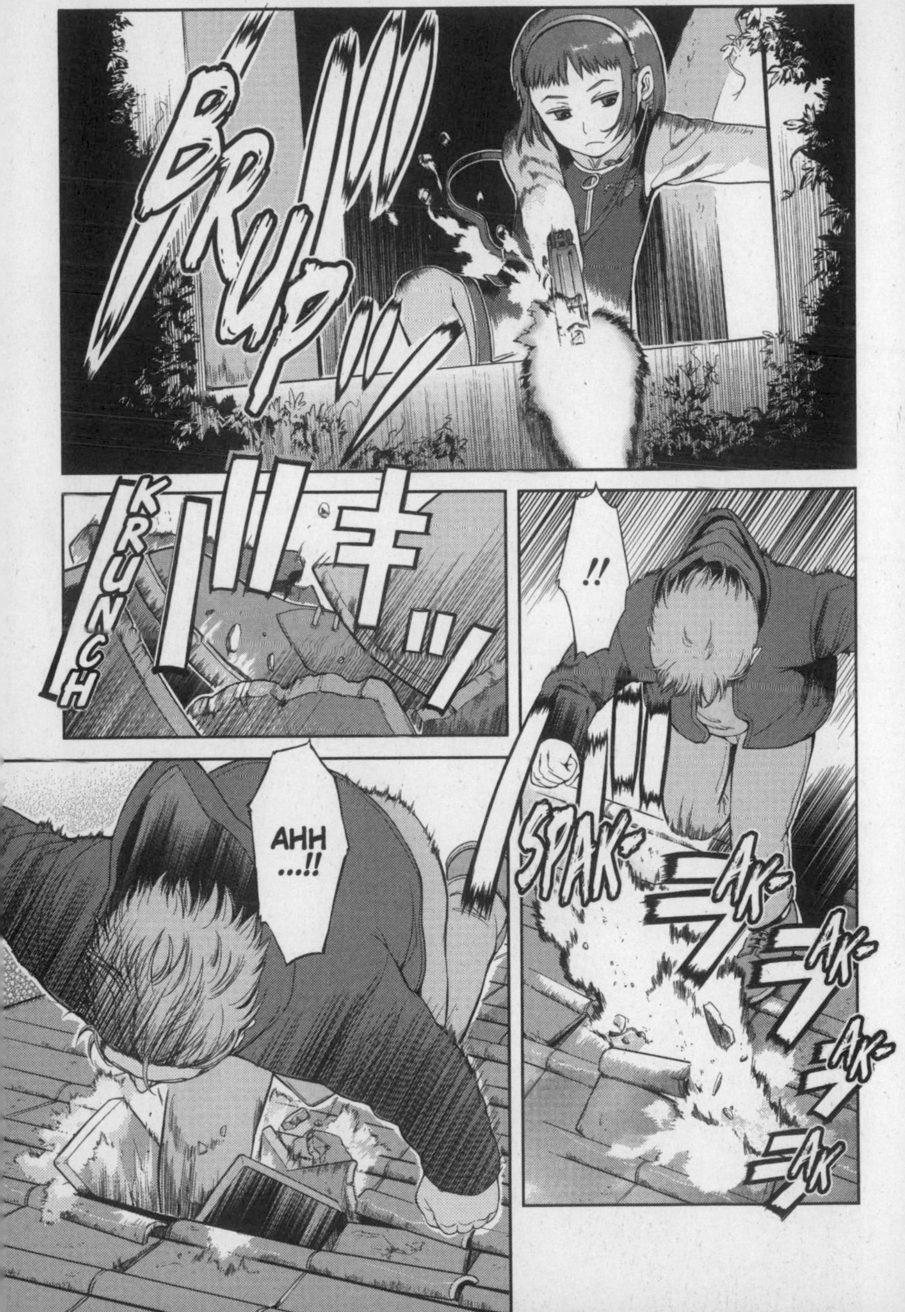
!!
SPAK-
AK-
AK-
AK-
AK
KRUNCH
AHH ...!!

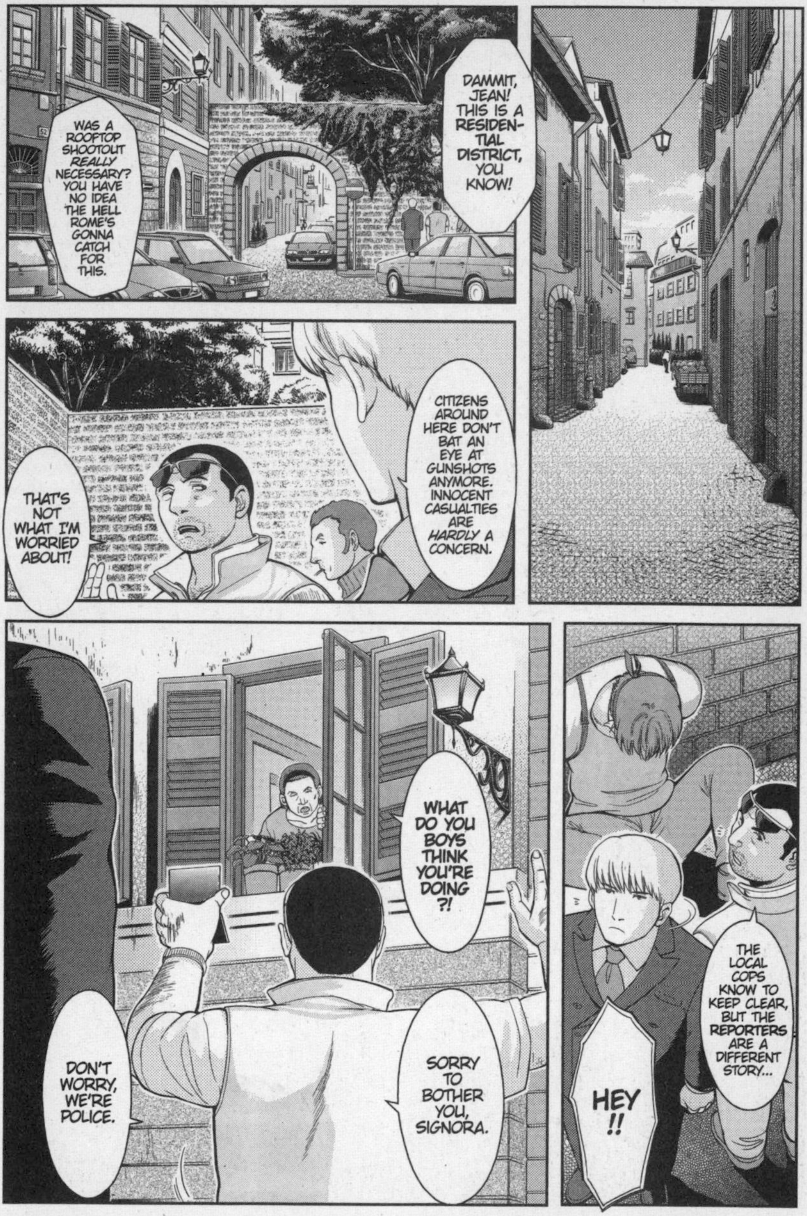
DAMMIT, JEAN! THIS IS A RESIDEN-TIAL DISTRICT, YOU KNOW!
WAS A ROOFTOP SHOOTOUT *REALLY* NECESSARY? YOU HAVE NO IDEA THE HELL ROME'S GONNA CATCH FOR THIS.
CITIZENS AROUND HERE DON'T BAT AN EYE AT GUNSHOTS ANYMORE. INNOCENT CASUALTIES ARE *HARDLY* A CONCERN.
THAT'S NOT WHAT I'M WORRIED ABOUT!
THE LOCAL COPS KNOW TO KEEP CLEAR, BUT THE REPORTERS ARE A DIFFERENT STORY...
HEY !!
WHAT DO YOU BOYS THINK YOU'RE DOING ?!
SORRY TO BOTHER YOU, SIGNORA.
DON'T WORRY, WE'RE POLICE.

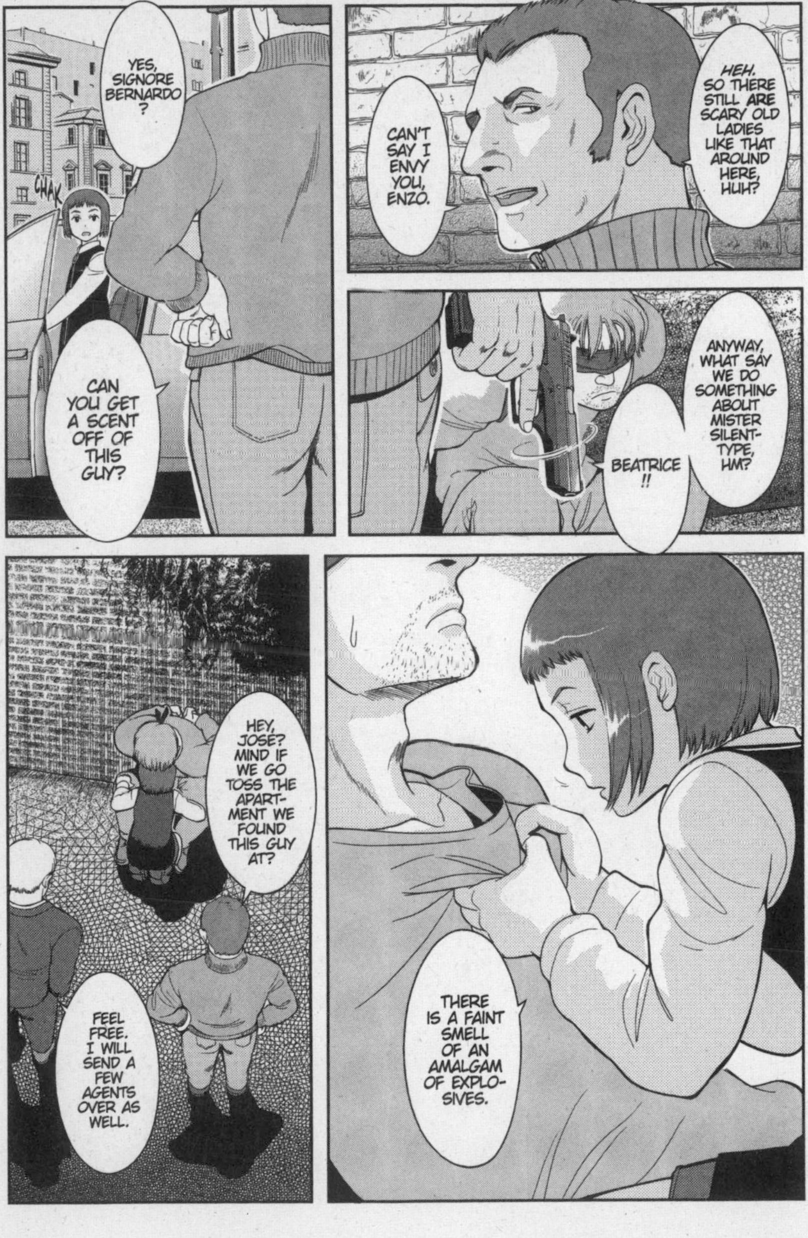
HEH. SO THERE STILL ARE SCARY OLD LADIES LIKE THAT AROUND HERE, HUH?
CAN'T SAY I ENVY YOU, ENZO.
ANYWAY, WHAT SAY WE DO SOMETHING ABOUT MISTER SILENT-TYPE, HM?
BEATRICE!!
YES, SIGNORE BERNARDO?
CHAK
CAN YOU GET A SCENT OFF OF THIS GUY?
THERE IS A FAINT SMELL OF AN AMALGAM OF EXPLOSIVES.
HEY, JOSÉ? MIND IF WE GO TOSS THE APARTMENT WE FOUND THIS GUY AT?
FEEL FREE. I WILL SEND A FEW AGENTS OVER AS WELL.

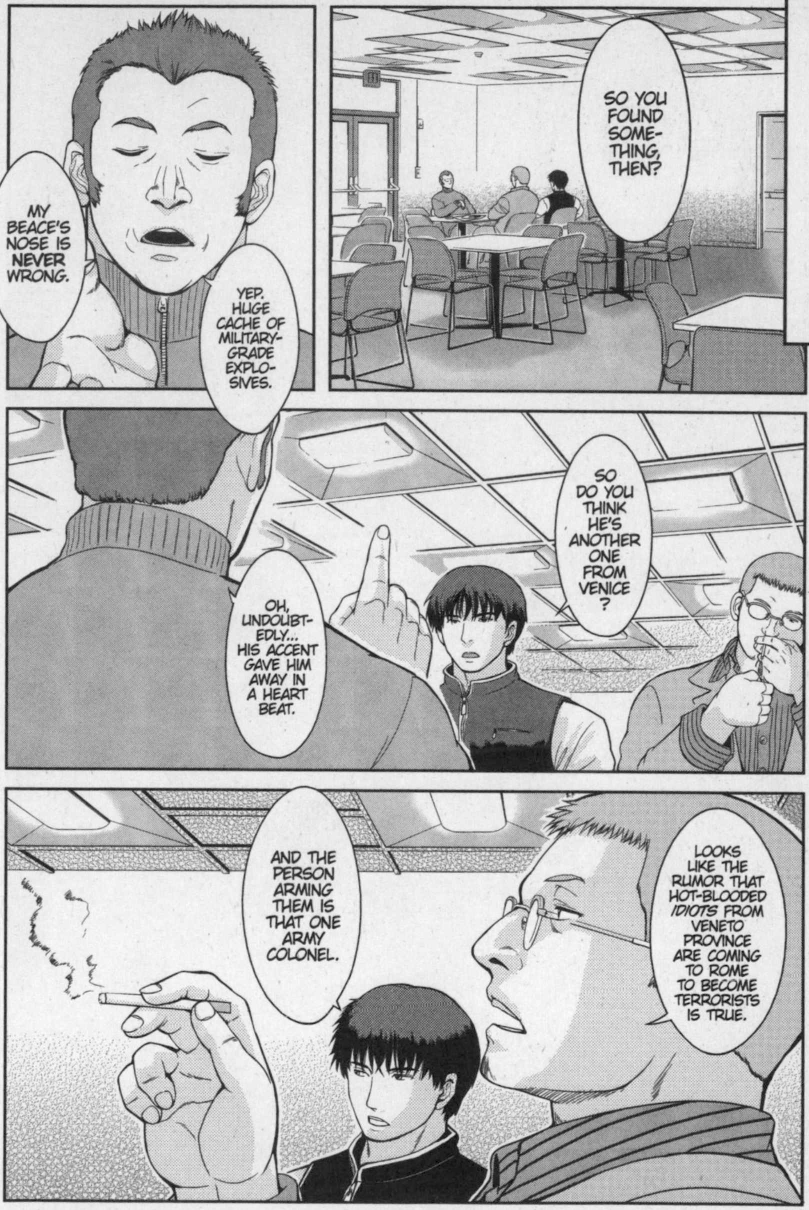
SO YOU FOUND SOME-THING, THEN?
YEP. HUGE CACHE OF MILITARY-GRADE EXPLO-SIVES.
MY BEACE'S NOSE IS NEVER WRONG.
SO DO YOU THINK HE'S ANOTHER ONE FROM VENICE ?
OH, UNDOUBT-EDLY... HIS ACCENT GAVE HIM AWAY IN A HEART BEAT.
LOOKS LIKE THE RUMOR THAT HOT-BLOODED *IDIOTS* FROM VENETO PROVINCE ARE COMING TO ROME TO BECOME TERRORISTS IS TRUE.
AND THE PERSON ARMING THEM IS THAT ONE ARMY COLONEL.

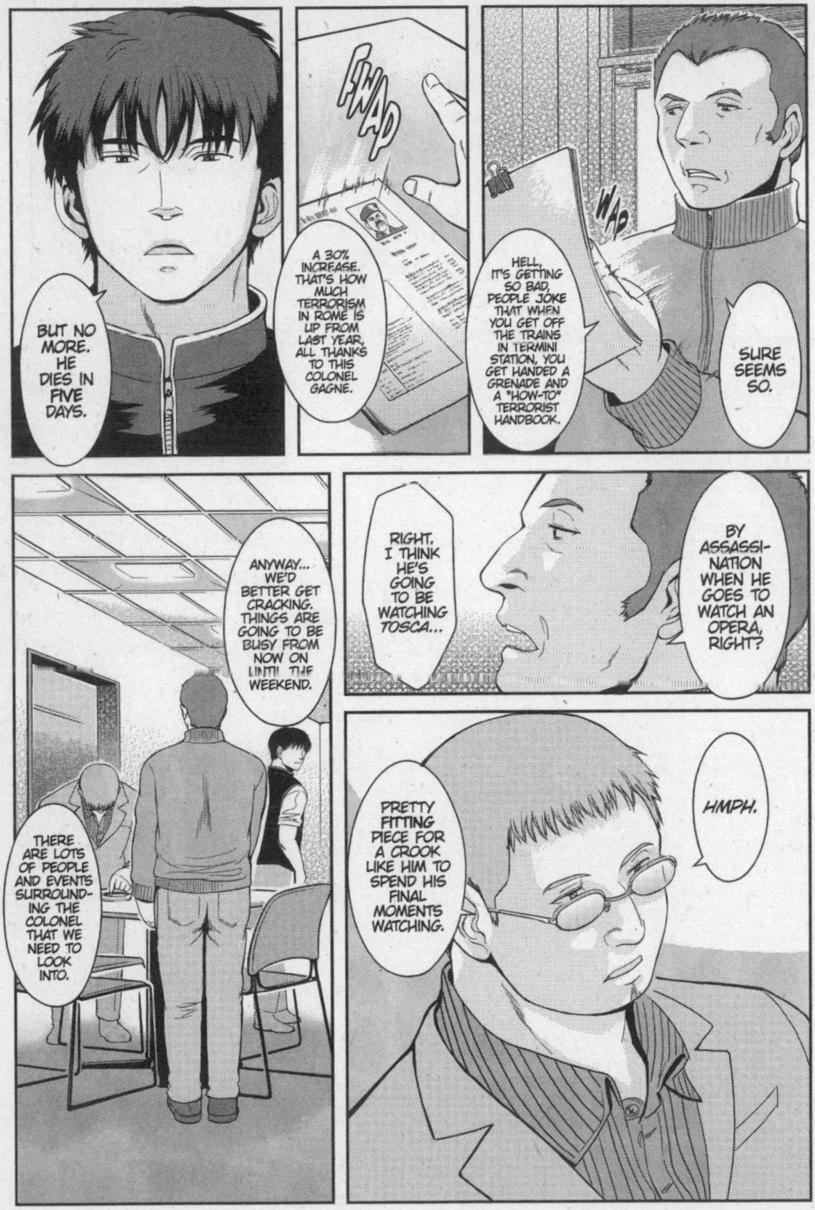
WAP
SURE SEEMS SO.
HELL, IT'S GETTING SO BAD, PEOPLE JOKE THAT WHEN YOU GET OFF THE TRAINS IN TERMINI STATION, YOU GET HANDED A GRENADE AND A "HOW-TO" TERRORIST HANDBOOK.
FWAP
A 30% INCREASE. THAT'S HOW MUCH TERRORISM IN ROME IS UP FROM LAST YEAR, ALL THANKS TO THIS COLONEL GAGNE.
BUT NO MORE. HE DIES IN FIVE DAYS.
BY ASSASSINATION WHEN HE GOES TO WATCH AN OPERA, RIGHT?
RIGHT. I THINK HE'S GOING TO BE WATCHING *TOSCA*...
HMPH.
PRETTY FITTING PIECE FOR A CROOK LIKE HIM TO SPEND HIS FINAL MOMENTS WATCHING.
ANYWAY... WE'D BETTER GET CRACKING. THINGS ARE GOING TO BE BUSY FROM NOW ON UNTIL THE WEEKEND.
THERE ARE LOTS OF PEOPLE AND EVENTS SURROUNDING THE COLONEL THAT WE NEED TO LOOK INTO.

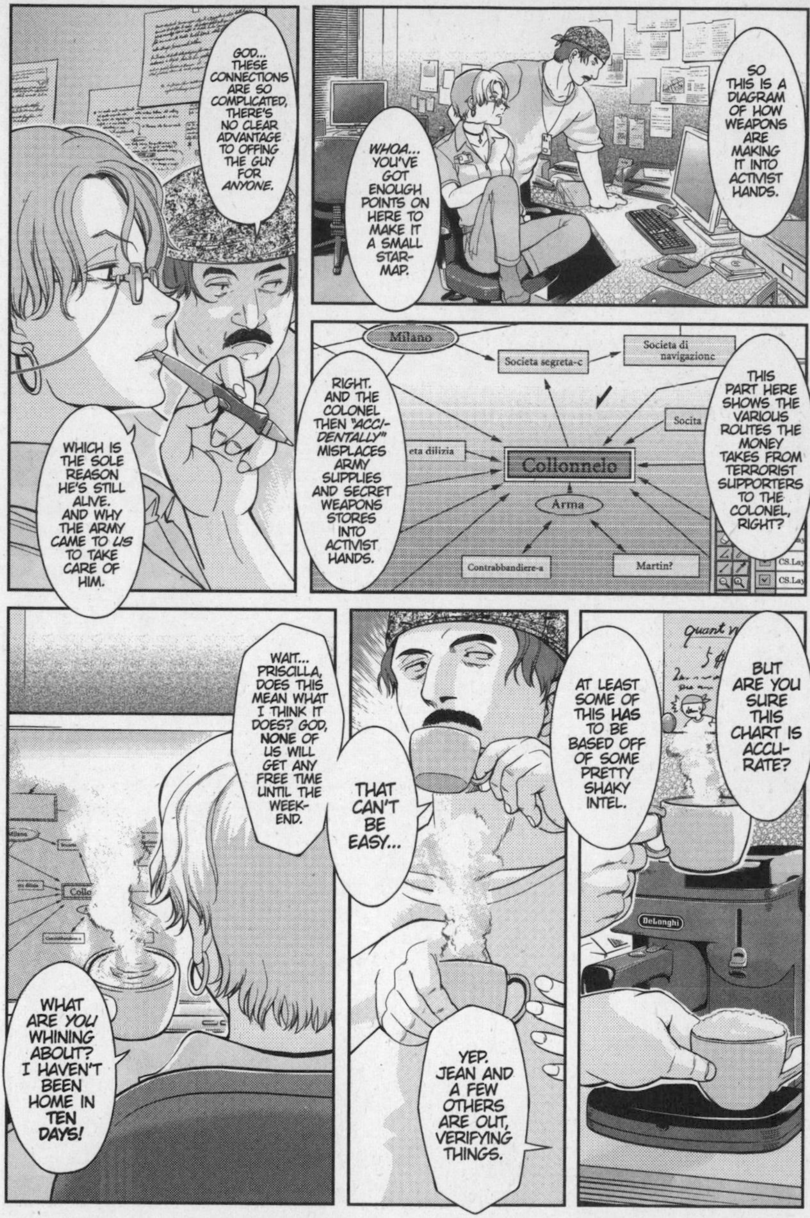
SO THIS IS A DIAGRAM OF HOW WEAPONS ARE MAKING IT INTO ACTIVIST HANDS.
WHOA... YOU'VE GOT ENOUGH POINTS ON HERE TO MAKE IT A SMALL STAR-MAP.
Milano
Societa segreta-c
Societa di navigazionc
Socita
eta dilizia
Collonnelo
Arma
Contrabbandiere-a
Martin?
THIS PART HERE SHOWS THE VARIOUS ROUTES THE MONEY TAKES FROM TERRORIST SUPPORTERS TO THE COLONEL, RIGHT?
RIGHT. AND THE COLONEL THEN "*ACCI-DENTALLY*" MISPLACES ARMY SUPPLIES AND SECRET WEAPONS STORES INTO ACTIVIST HANDS.
GOD... THESE CONNECTIONS ARE SO COMPLICATED, THERE'S NO CLEAR ADVANTAGE TO OFFING THE GUY FOR *ANYONE*.
WHICH IS THE SOLE REASON HE'S STILL ALIVE. AND WHY THE ARMY CAME TO *US* TO TAKE CARE OF HIM.
BUT ARE YOU SURE THIS CHART IS ACCU-RATE?
AT LEAST SOME OF THIS HAS TO BE BASED OFF OF SOME PRETTY SHAKY INTEL.
DeLonghi
THAT CAN'T BE EASY...
YEP. JEAN AND A FEW OTHERS ARE OUT, VERIFYING THINGS.
WAIT... PRISCILLA, DOES THIS MEAN WHAT I THINK IT DOES? GOD, NONE OF US WILL GET ANY FREE TIME UNTIL THE WEEK-END.
WHAT ARE *YOU* WHINING ABOUT? I HAVEN'T BEEN HOME IN TEN DAYS!

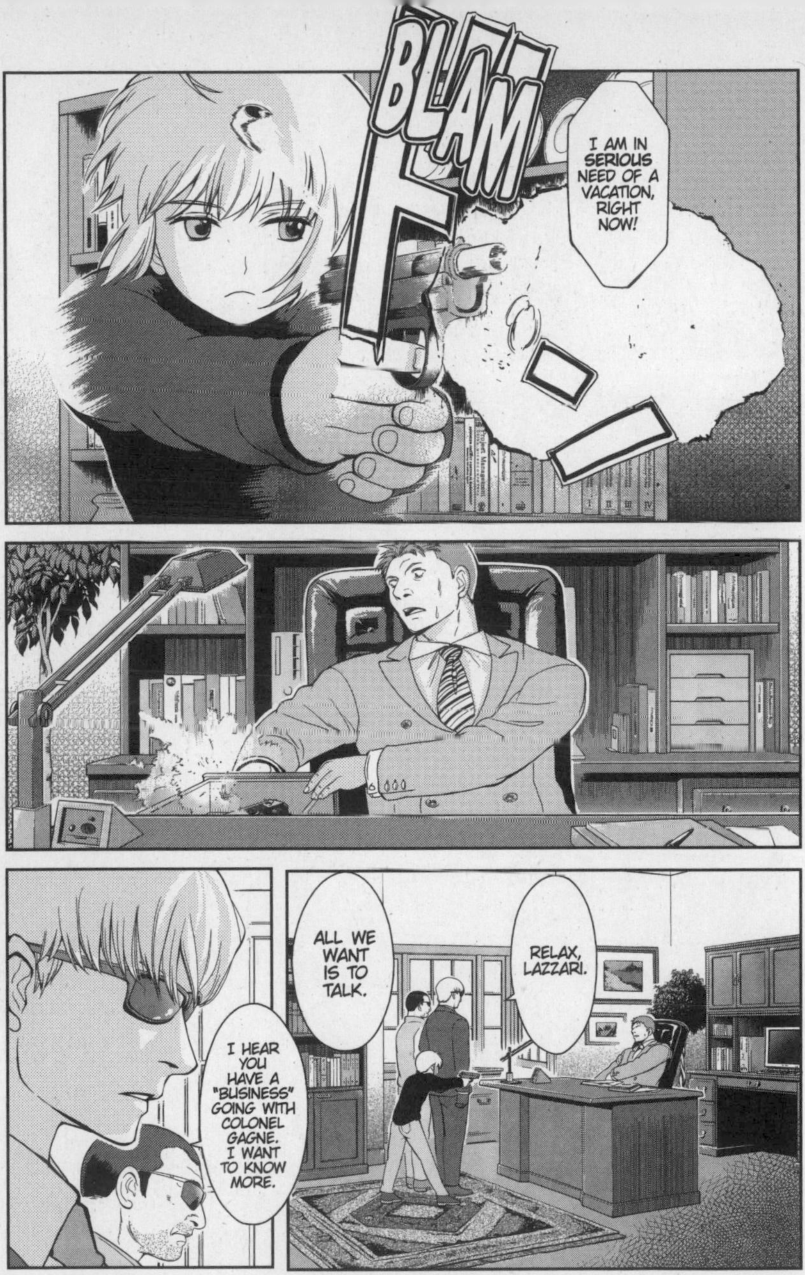
BLAM
I AM IN SERIOUS NEED OF A VACATION, RIGHT NOW!
RELAX, LAZZARI.
ALL WE WANT IS TO TALK.
I HEAR YOU HAVE A "BUSINESS" GOING WITH COLONEL GAGNE. I WANT TO KNOW MORE.

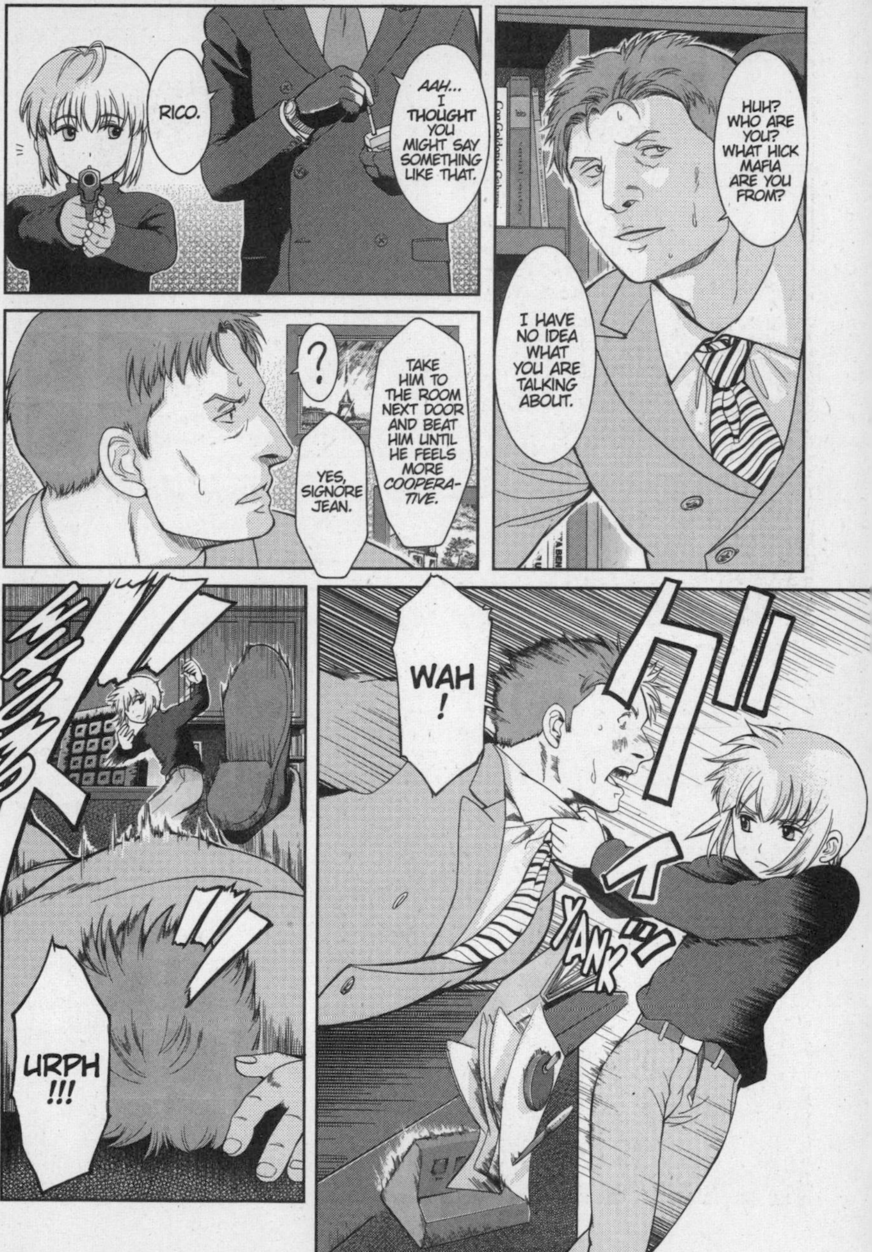
HUH? WHO ARE YOU? WHAT HICK MAFIA ARE YOU FROM?
I HAVE NO IDEA WHAT YOU ARE TALKING ABOUT.
AAH... I THOUGHT YOU MIGHT SAY SOMETHING LIKE THAT.
RICO.
TAKE HIM TO THE ROOM NEXT DOOR AND BEAT HIM UNTIL HE FEELS MORE COOPERA-TIVE.
?
YES, SIGNORE JEAN.
WAH!
YANK
WHOMP
URPH!!!

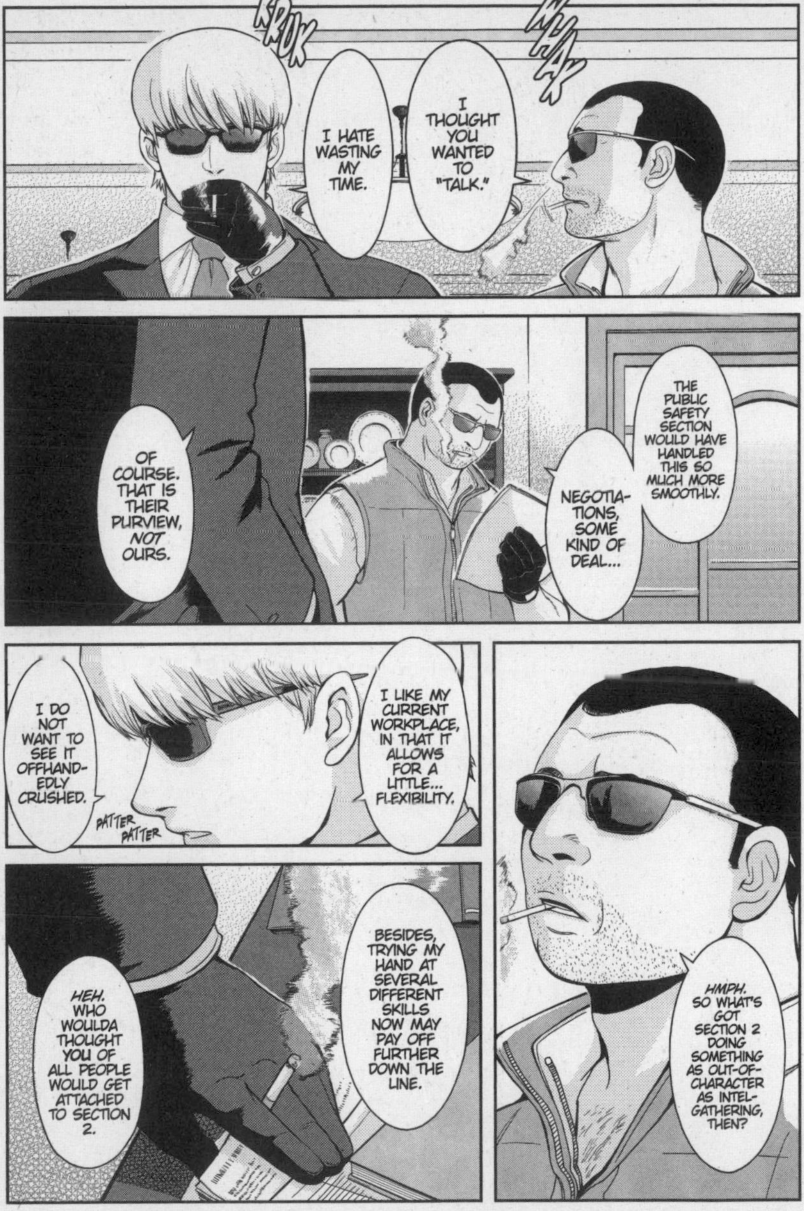
WHAK
I THOUGHT YOU WANTED TO "TALK."
KRUK
I HATE WASTING MY TIME.
THE PUBLIC SAFETY SECTION WOULD HAVE HANDLED THIS SO MUCH MORE SMOOTHLY.
NEGOTIATIONS, SOME KIND OF DEAL...
OF COURSE. THAT IS THEIR PURVIEW, *NOT* OURS.
HMPH. SO WHAT'S GOT SECTION 2 DOING SOMETHING AS OUT-OF-CHARACTER AS INTEL-GATHERING, THEN?
I LIKE MY CURRENT WORKPLACE, IN THAT IT ALLOWS FOR A LITTLE... FLEXIBILITY.
I DO NOT WANT TO SEE IT OFFHANDEDLY CRUSHED.
PATTER PATTER
BESIDES, TRYING MY HAND AT SEVERAL DIFFERENT SKILLS NOW MAY PAY OFF FURTHER DOWN THE LINE.
HEH. WHO WOULDA THOUGHT YOU OF ALL PEOPLE WOULD GET ATTACHED TO SECTION 2.

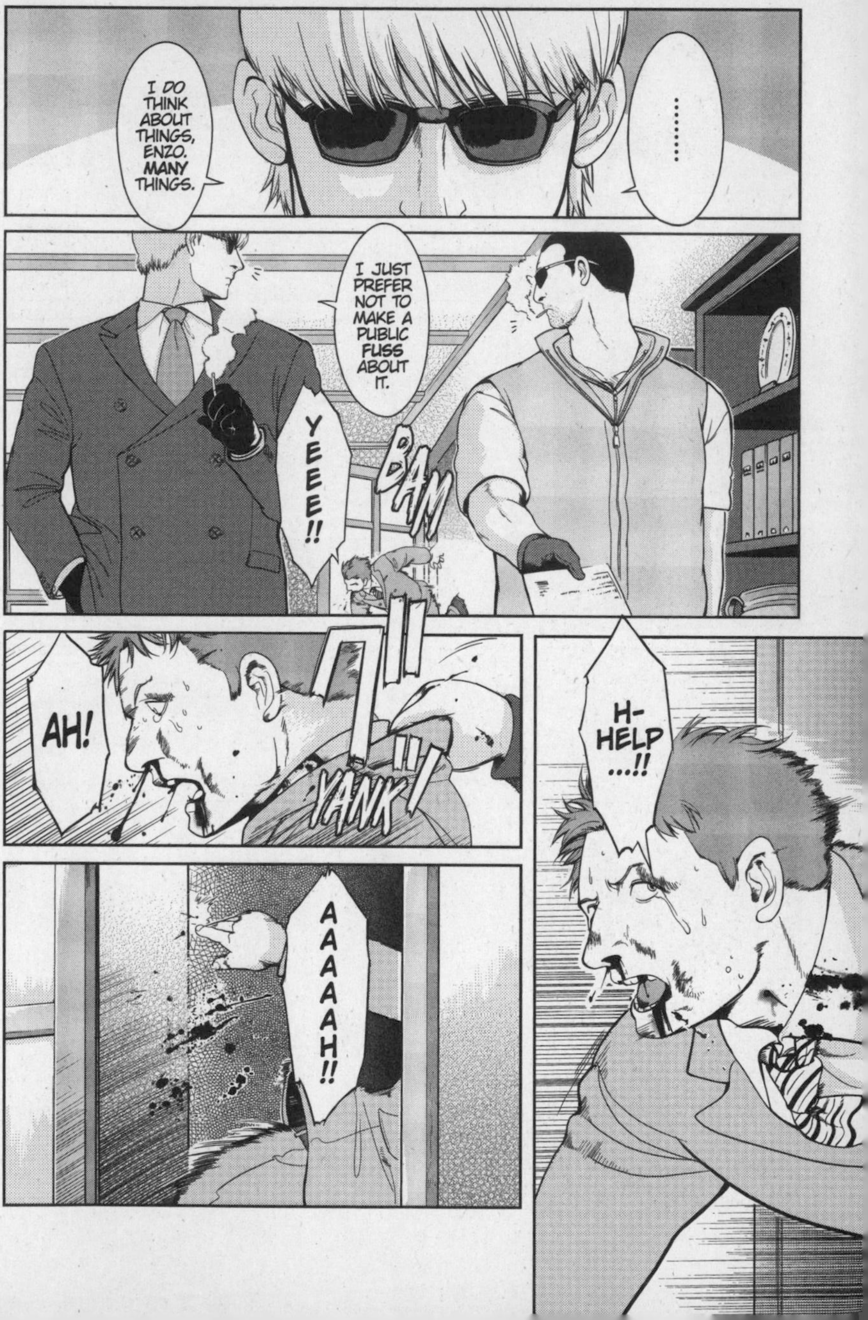
……
I DO THINK ABOUT THINGS, ENZO. MANY THINGS.
I JUST PREFER NOT TO MAKE A PUBLIC FUSS ABOUT IT.
BAM
YEEEE!!
H-HELP...!!
AH!
YANK
AAAAAAH!!

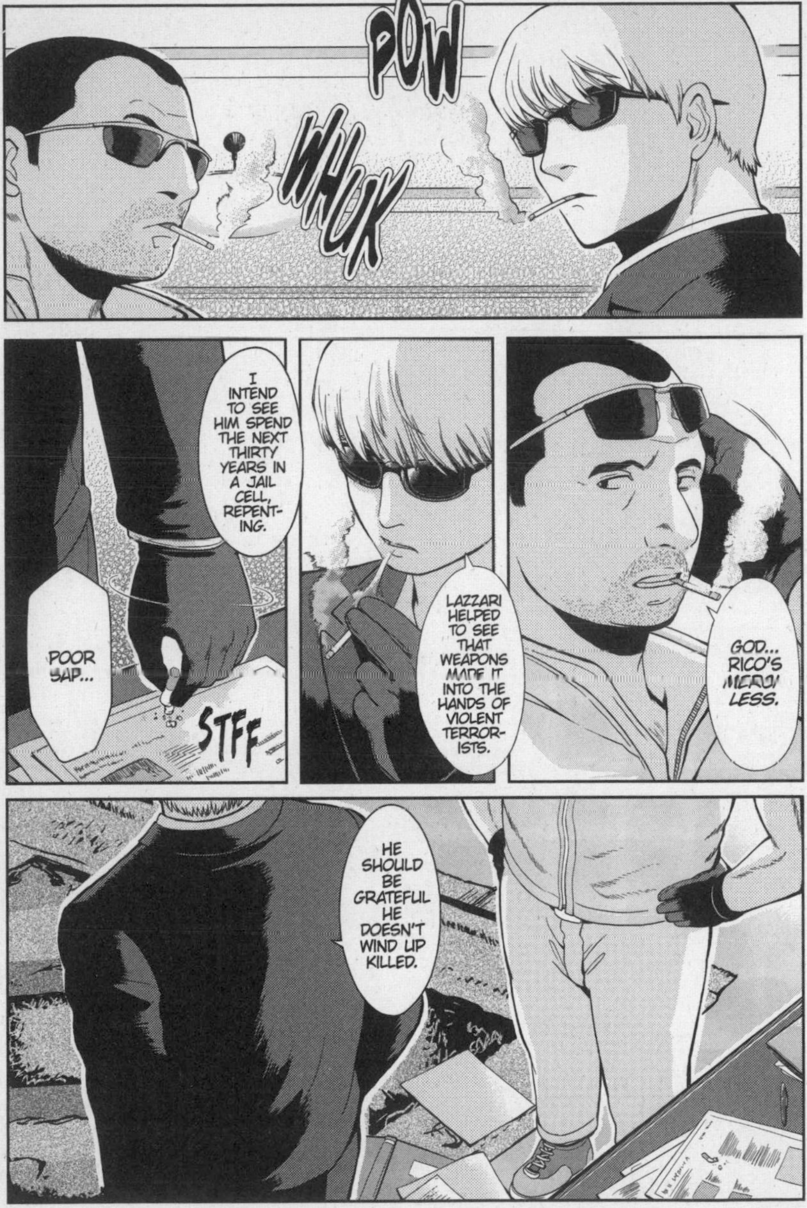
POW
WHUK
GOD... RICO'S MERCILESS.
LAZZARI HELPED TO SEE THAT WEAPONS MADE IT INTO THE HANDS OF VIOLENT TERRORISTS.
I INTEND TO SEE HIM SPEND THE NEXT THIRTY YEARS IN A JAIL CELL, REPENTING.
POOR SAP...
STFF
HE SHOULD BE GRATEFUL HE DOESN'T WIND UP KILLED.

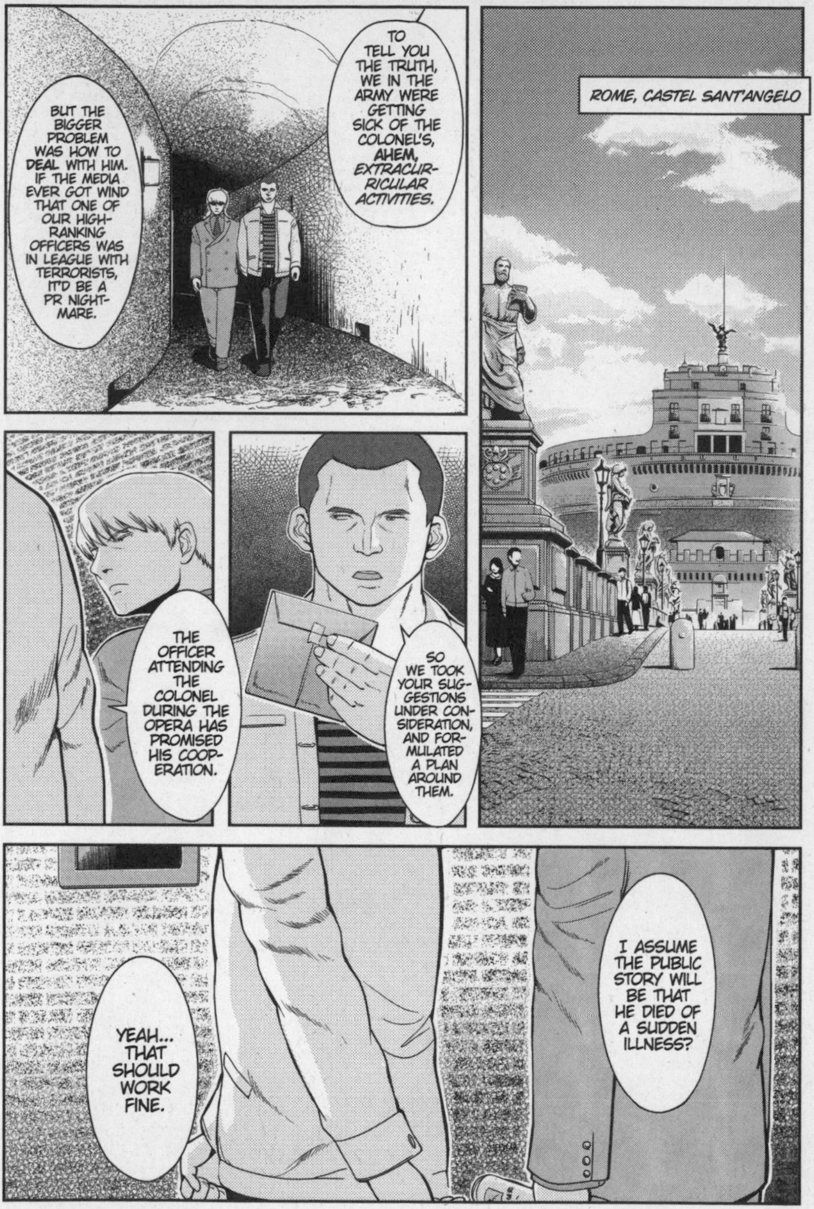
ROME, CASTEL SANT'ANGELO
TO TELL YOU THE TRUTH, WE IN THE ARMY WERE GETTING SICK OF THE COLONEL'S, AHEM, EXTRACURRICULAR ACTIVITIES.
BUT THE BIGGER PROBLEM WAS HOW TO DEAL WITH HIM. IF THE MEDIA EVER GOT WIND THAT ONE OF OUR HIGH-RANKING OFFICERS WAS IN LEAGUE WITH TERRORISTS, IT'D BE A PR NIGHTMARE.
SO WE TOOK YOUR SUGGESTIONS UNDER CONSIDERATION, AND FORMULATED A PLAN AROUND THEM.
THE OFFICER ATTENDING THE COLONEL DURING THE OPERA HAS PROMISED HIS COOPERATION.
I ASSUME THE PUBLIC STORY WILL BE THAT HE DIED OF A SUDDEN ILLNESS?
YEAH... THAT SHOULD WORK FINE.

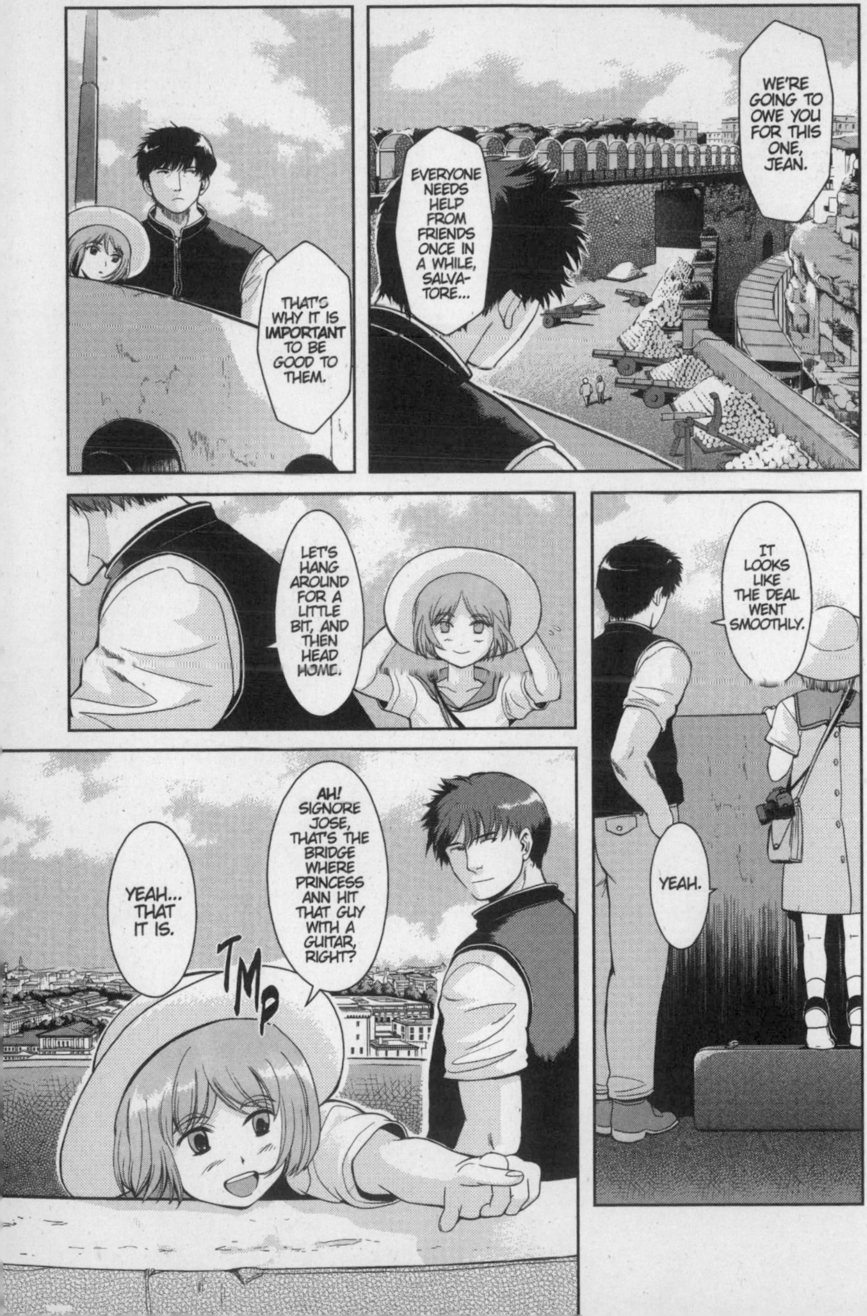
WE'RE GOING TO OWE YOU FOR THIS ONE, JEAN.
EVERYONE NEEDS HELP FROM FRIENDS ONCE IN A WHILE, SALVATORE...
THAT'S WHY IT IS IMPORTANT TO BE GOOD TO THEM.
IT LOOKS LIKE THE DEAL WENT SMOOTHLY.
YEAH.
LET'S HANG AROUND FOR A LITTLE BIT, AND THEN HEAD HOME.
AH! SIGNORE JOSE, THAT'S THE BRIDGE WHERE PRINCESS ANN HIT THAT GUY WITH A GUITAR, RIGHT?
TMP
YEAH... THAT IT IS.

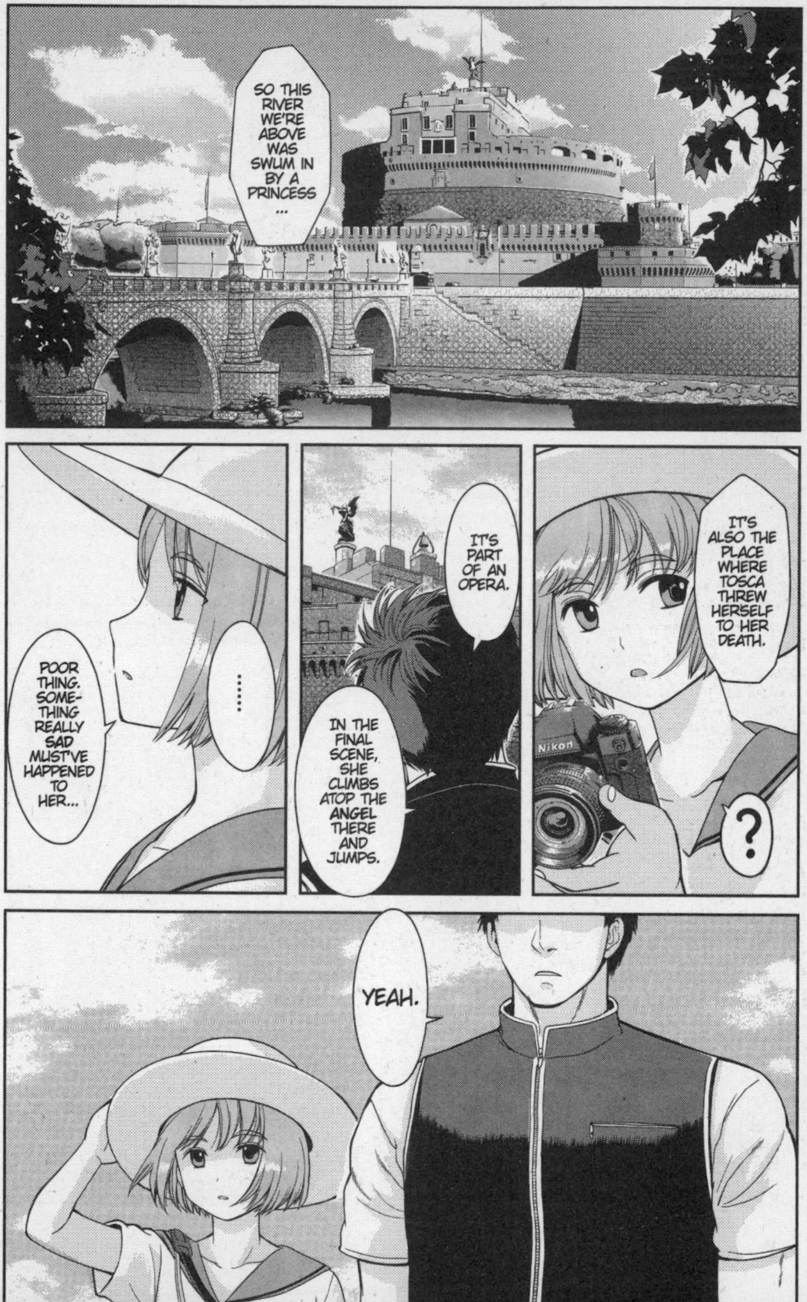
SO THIS RIVER WE'RE ABOVE WAS SWUM IN BY A PRINCESS ...
IT'S ALSO THE PLACE WHERE TOSCA THREW HERSELF TO HER DEATH.
?
IT'S PART OF AN OPERA.
IN THE FINAL SCENE, SHE CLIMBS ATOP THE ANGEL THERE AND JUMPS.
......
POOR THING. SOME-THING REALLY SAD MUST'VE HAPPENED TO HER...
YEAH.

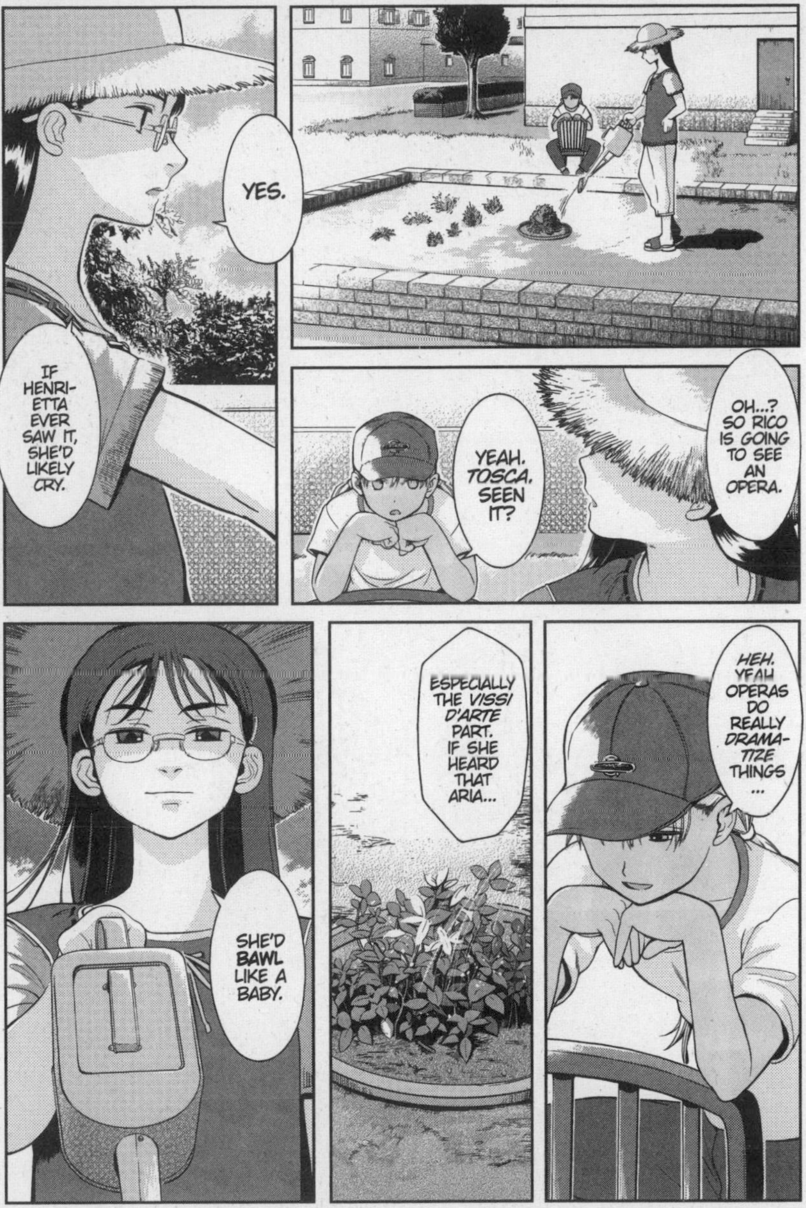
OH...? SO RICO IS GOING TO SEE AN OPERA.
YEAH. *TOSCA.* SEEN IT?
YES.
IF HENRIETTA EVER SAW IT, SHE'D LIKELY CRY.
HEH. YEAH OPERAS DO REALLY *DRAMATIZE* THINGS...
ESPECIALLY THE *VISSI D'ARTE* PART. IF SHE HEARD THAT ARIA...
SHE'D **BAWL** LIKE A BABY.

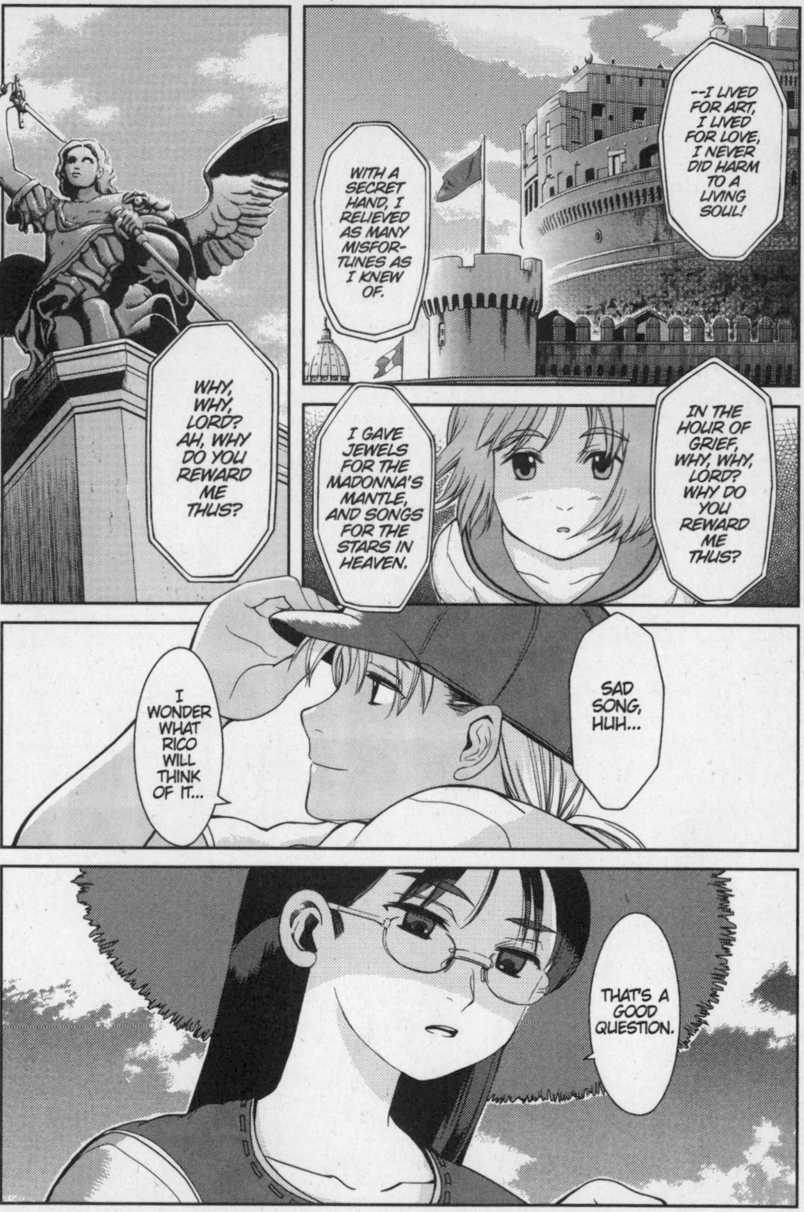
--I LIVED FOR ART, I LIVED FOR LOVE, I NEVER DID HARM TO A LIVING SOUL!
WITH A SECRET HAND, I RELIEVED AS MANY MISFORTUNES AS I KNEW OF.
IN THE HOUR OF GRIEF, WHY, WHY, LORD? WHY DO YOU REWARD ME THUS?
I GAVE JEWELS FOR THE MADONNA'S MANTLE, AND SONGS FOR THE STARS IN HEAVEN.
WHY, WHY, LORD? AH, WHY DO YOU REWARD ME THUS?
SAD SONG, HUH...
I WONDER WHAT RICO WILL THINK OF IT...
THAT'S A GOOD QUESTION.

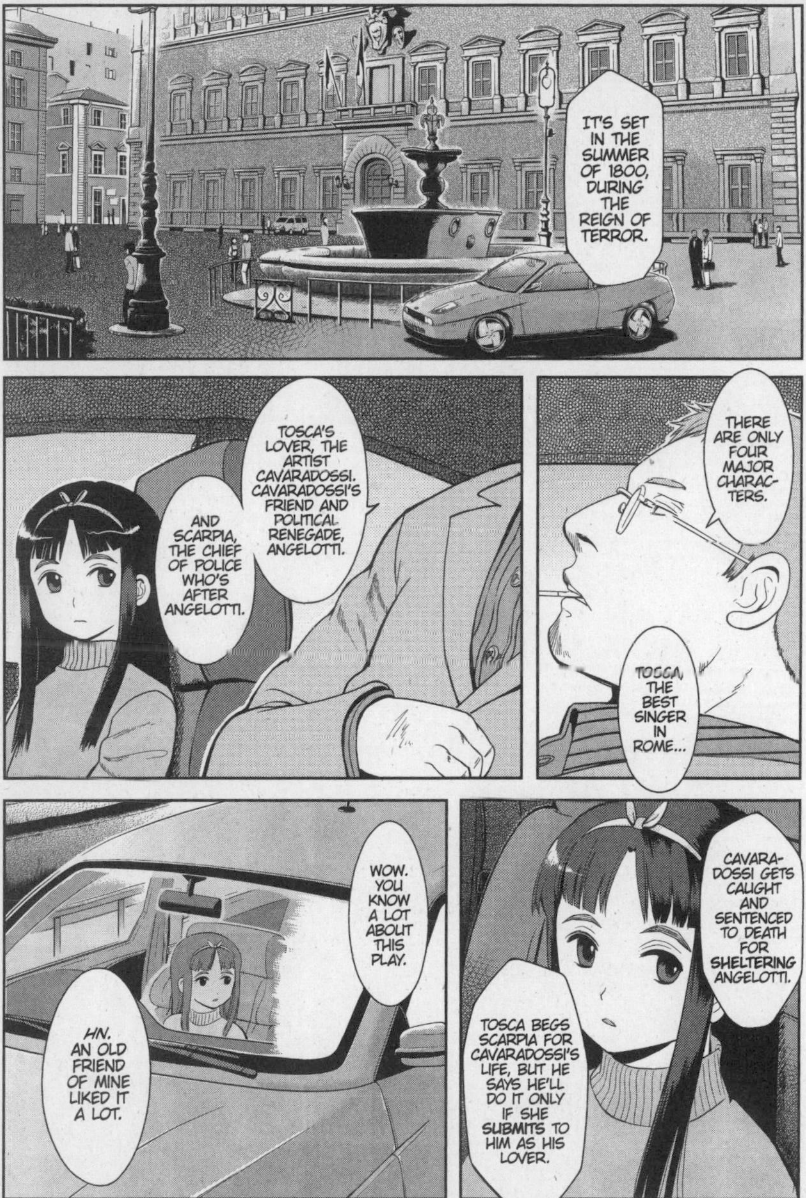
IT'S SET IN THE SUMMER OF 1800, DURING THE REIGN OF TERROR.
THERE ARE ONLY FOUR MAJOR CHARAC-TERS.
TOSCA, THE BEST SINGER IN ROME...
TOSCA'S LOVER, THE ARTIST CAVARADOSSI. CAVARADOSSI'S FRIEND AND POLITICAL RENEGADE, ANGELOTTI.
AND SCARPIA, THE CHIEF OF POLICE WHO'S AFTER ANGELOTTI.
CAVARA-DOSSI GETS CAUGHT AND SENTENCED TO DEATH FOR SHELTERING ANGELOTTI.
TOSCA BEGS SCARPIA FOR CAVARADOSSI'S LIFE, BUT HE SAYS HE'LL DO IT ONLY IF SHE SUBMITS TO HIM AS HIS LOVER.
WOW. YOU KNOW A LOT ABOUT THIS PLAY.
HN. AN OLD FRIEND OF MINE LIKED IT A LOT.

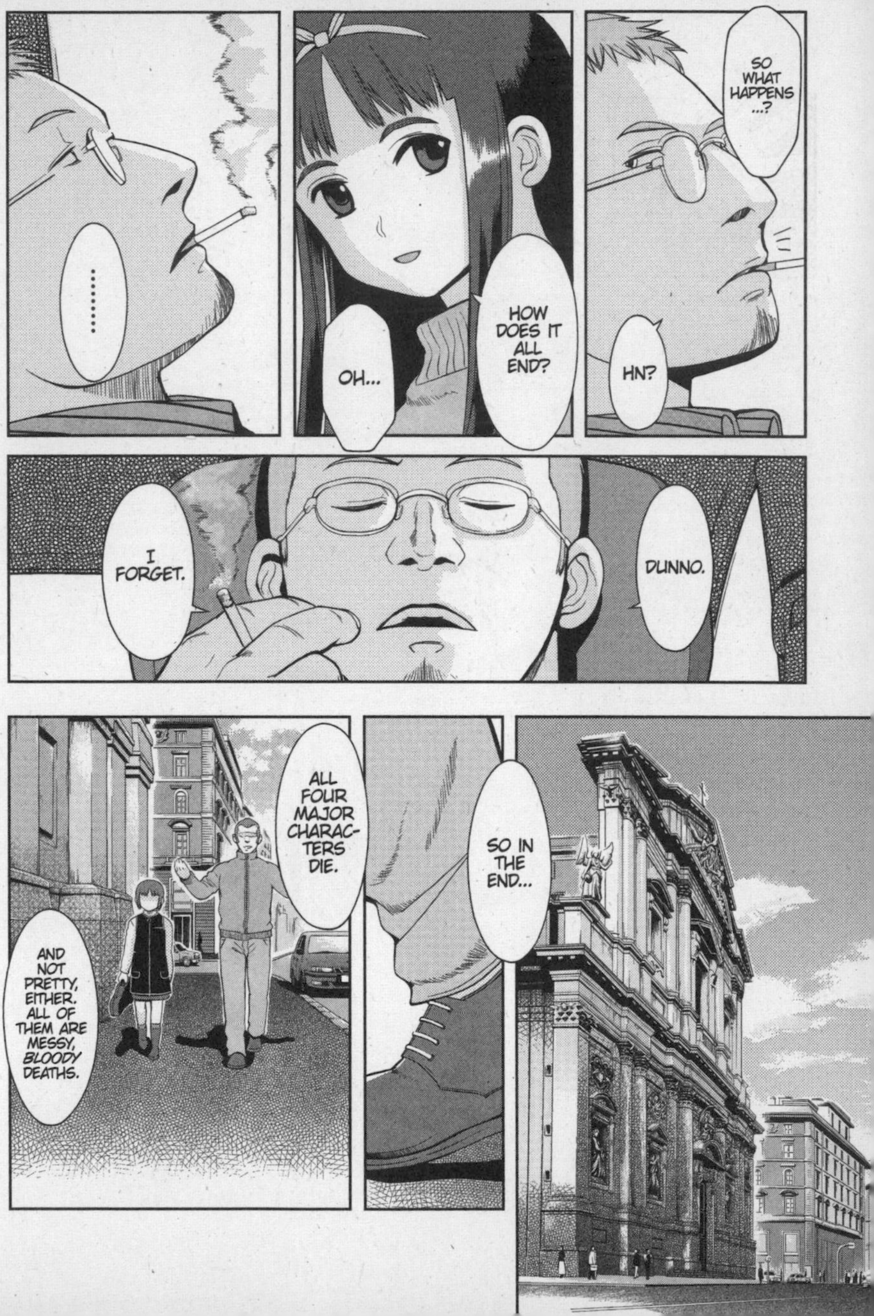
SO WHAT HAPPENS ...?
HN?
HOW DOES IT ALL END?
OH...
......
DUNNO.
I FORGET.
SO IN THE END...
ALL FOUR MAJOR CHARACTERS DIE.
AND NOT PRETTY, EITHER. ALL OF THEM ARE MESSY, BLOODY DEATHS.

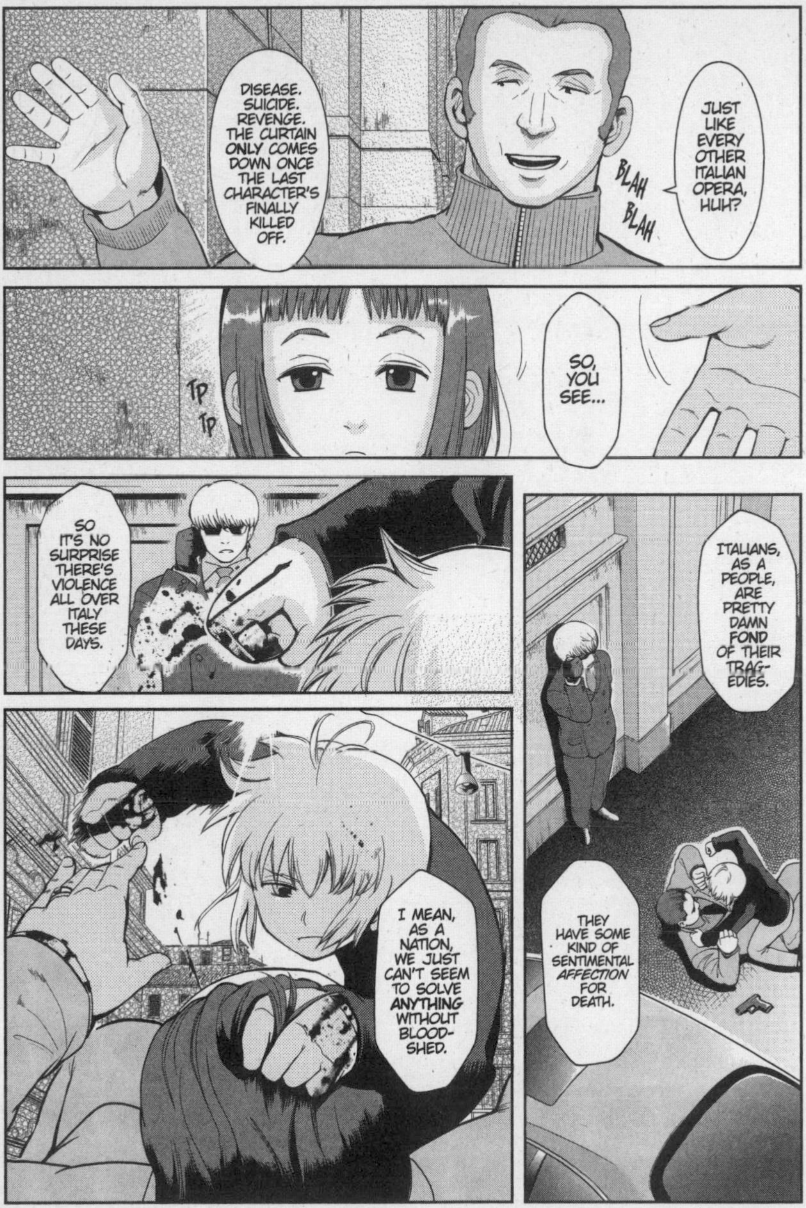
JUST LIKE EVERY OTHER ITALIAN OPERA, HUH?
BLAH BLAH
DISEASE. SUICIDE. REVENGE. THE CURTAIN ONLY COMES DOWN ONCE THE LAST CHARACTER'S FINALLY KILLED OFF.
SO, YOU SEE...
Tp Tp
ITALIANS, AS A PEOPLE, ARE PRETTY DAMN FOND OF THEIR TRAG-EDIES.
THEY HAVE SOME KIND OF SENTIMENTAL *AFFECTION* FOR DEATH.
SO IT'S NO SURPRISE THERE'S VIOLENCE ALL OVER ITALY THESE DAYS.
I MEAN, AS A NATION, WE JUST CAN'T SEEM TO SOLVE **ANYTHING** WITHOUT BLOOD-SHED.

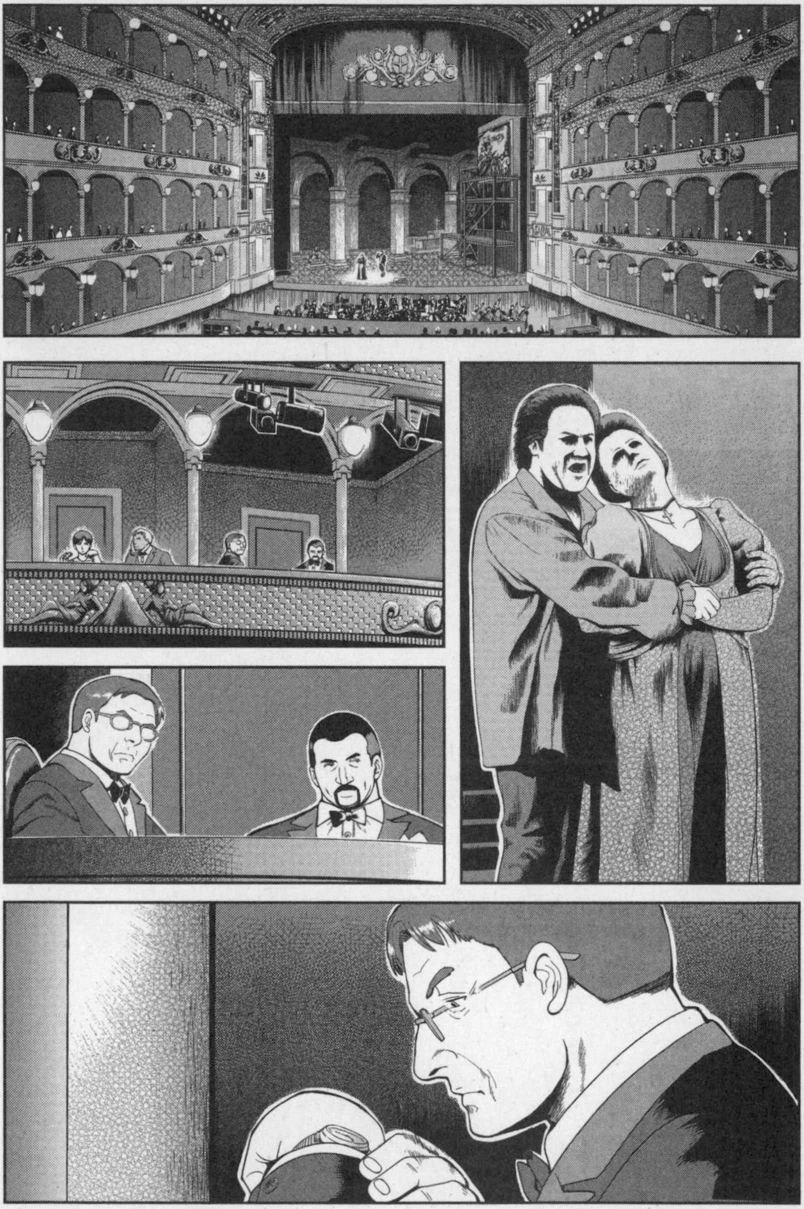

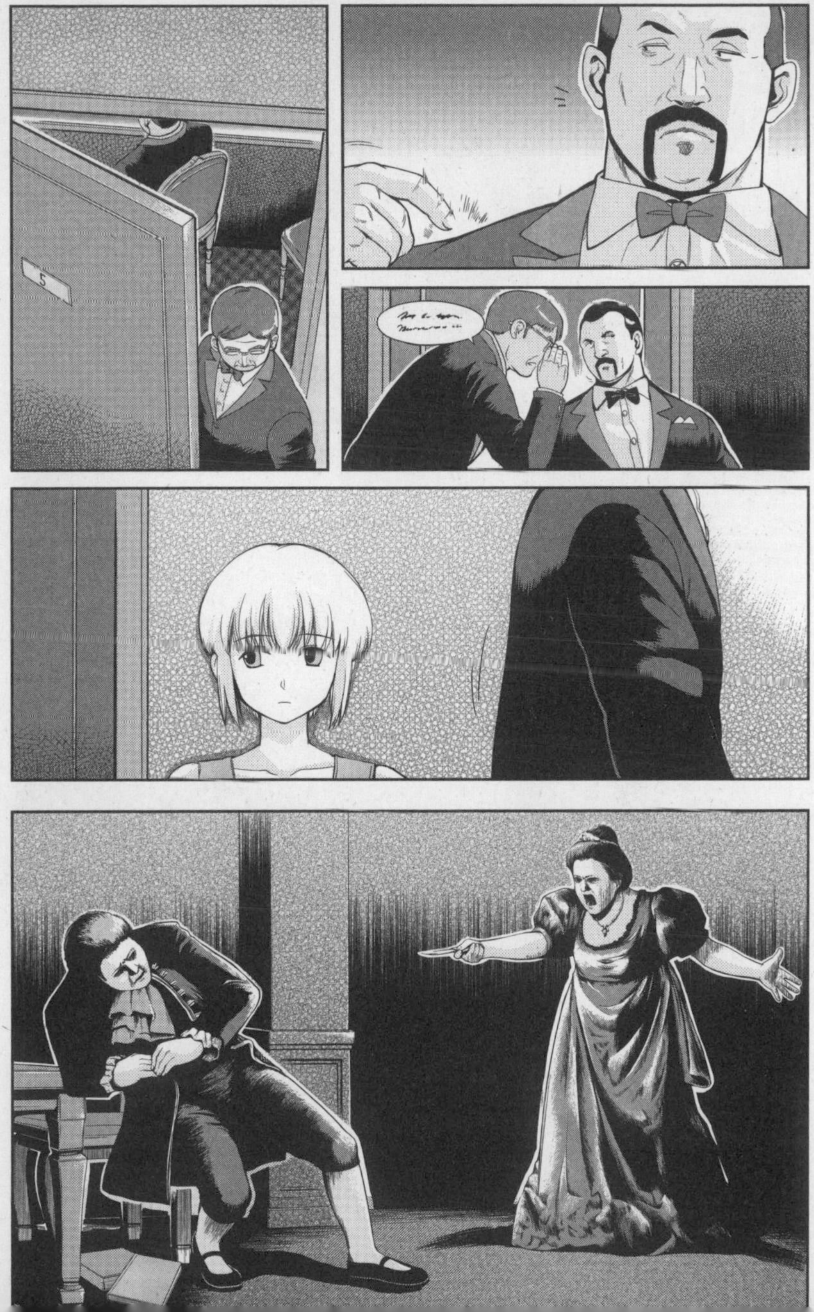

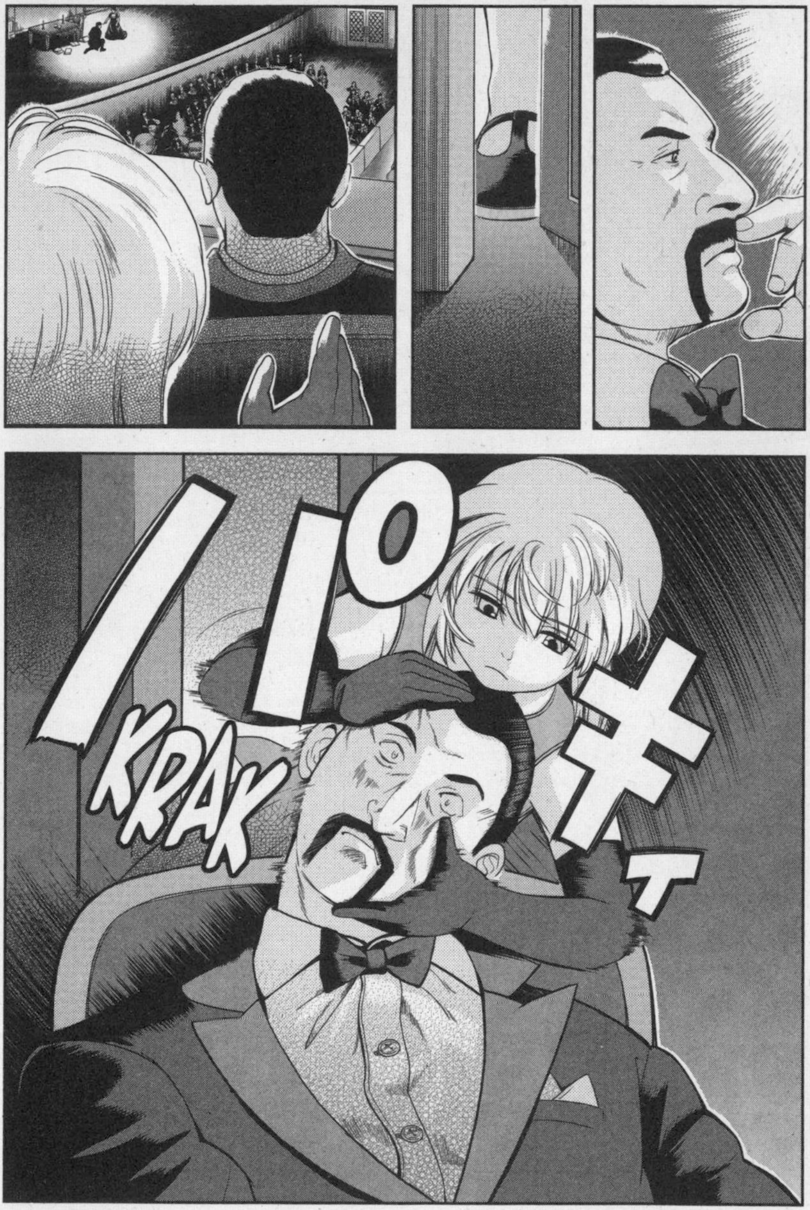
パキッ
KRAK

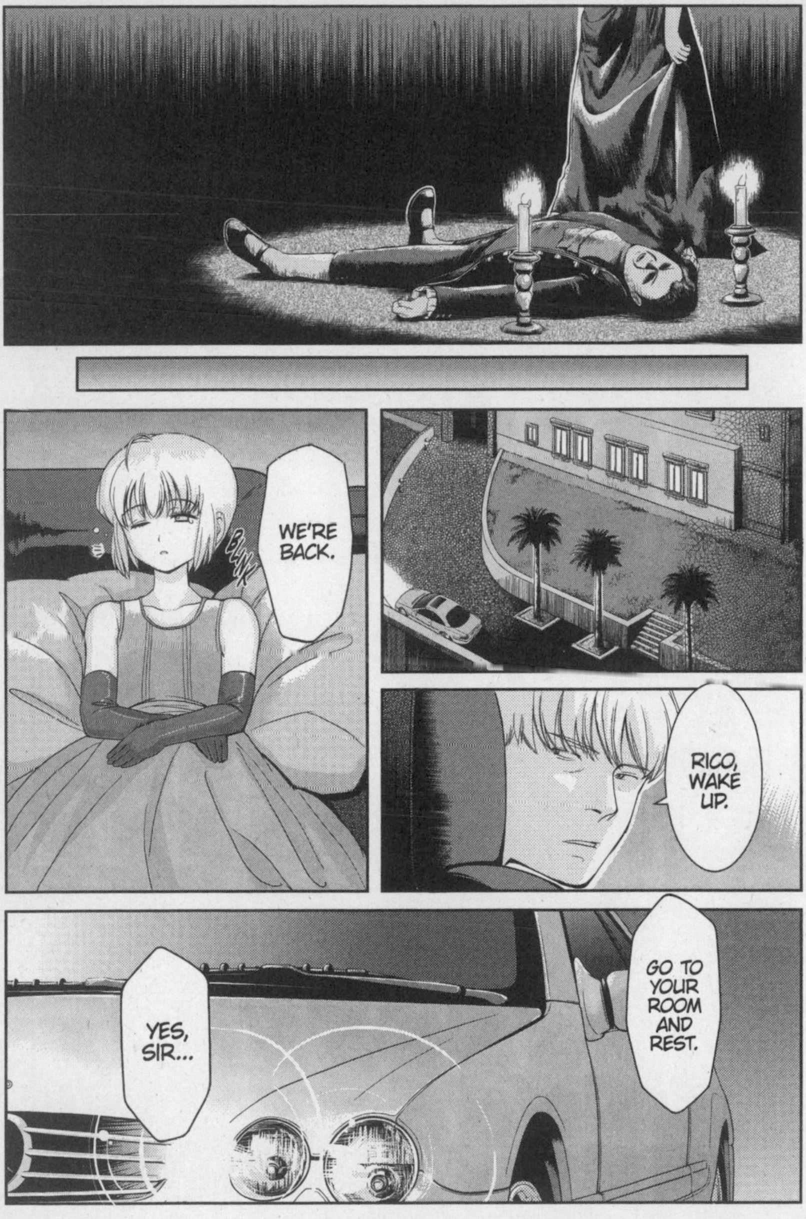
RICO, WAKE UP.
WE'RE BACK.
BLINK
GO TO YOUR ROOM AND REST.
YES, SIR...

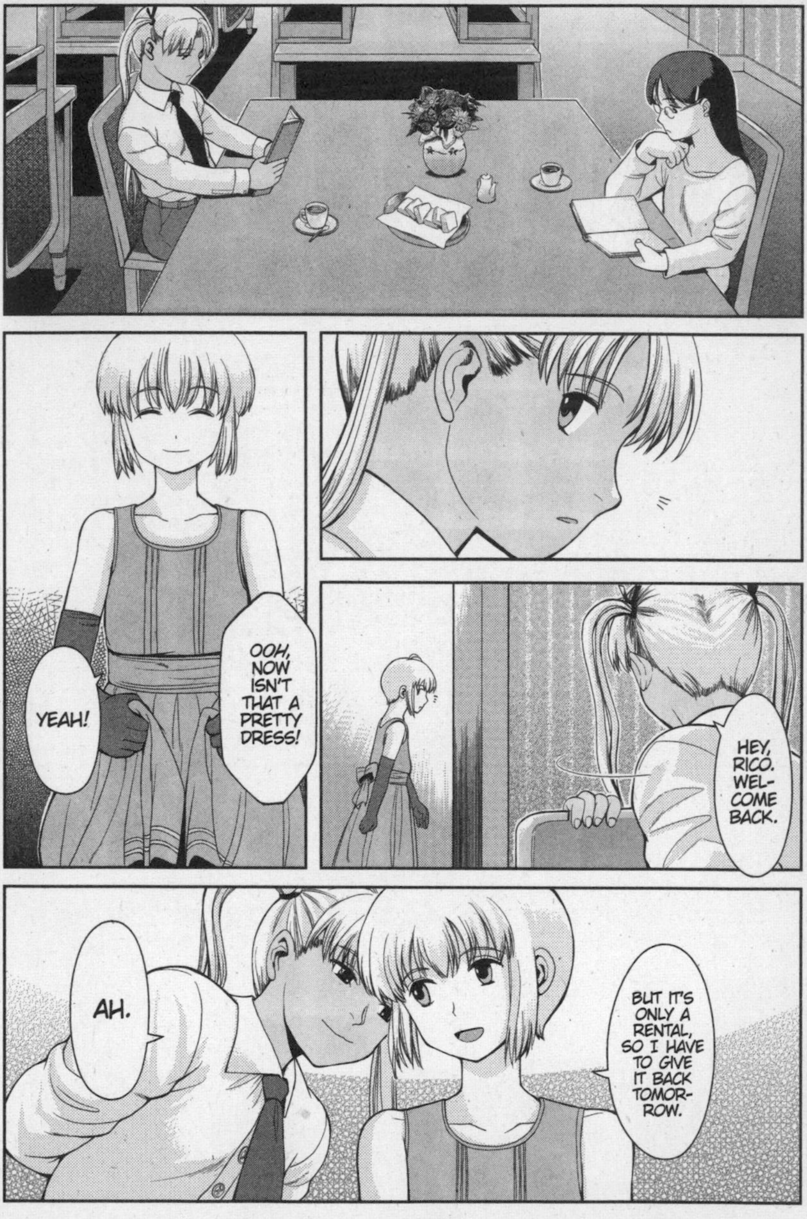
HEY, RICO. WEL-COME BACK.
OOH, NOW ISN'T THAT A PRETTY DRESS!
YEAH!
BUT IT'S ONLY A RENTAL, SO I HAVE TO GIVE IT BACK TOMOR-ROW.
AH.

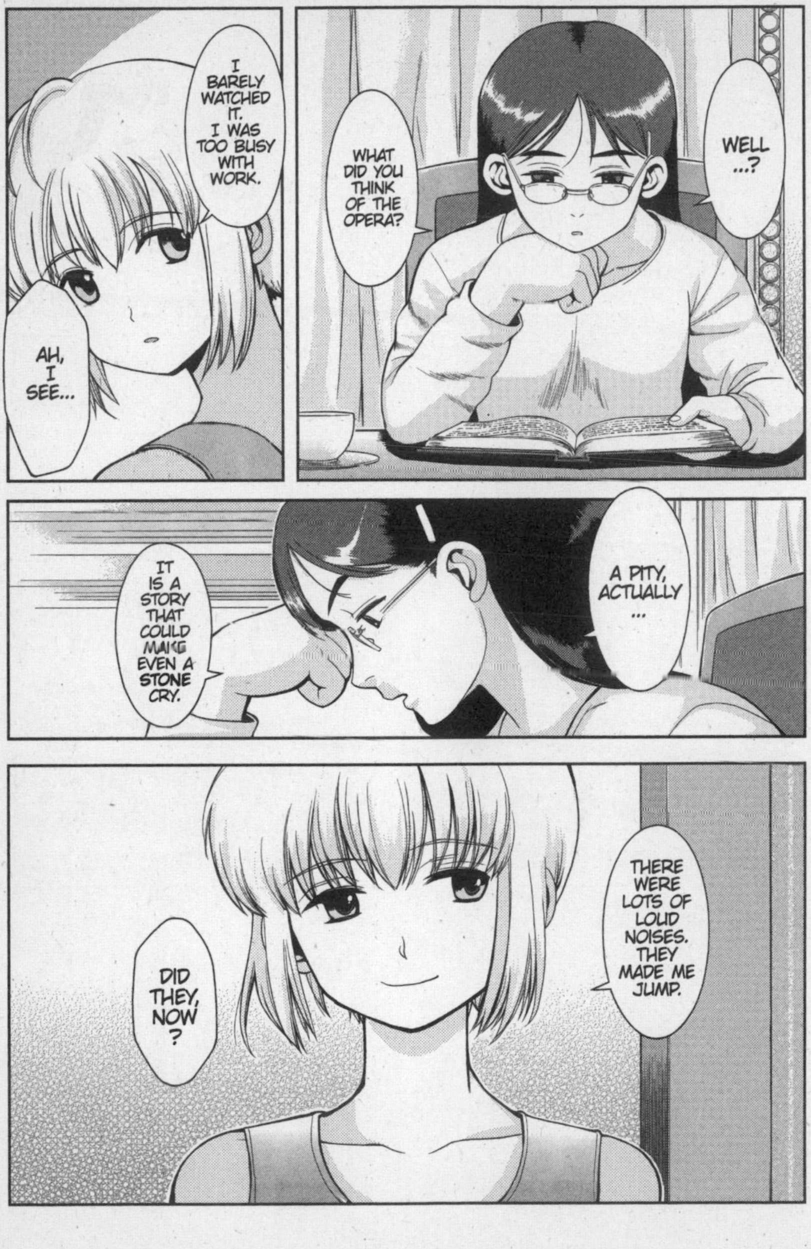
WELL ...?
WHAT DID YOU THINK OF THE OPERA?
I BARELY WATCHED IT. I WAS TOO BUSY WITH WORK.
AH, I SEE...
A PITY, ACTUALLY ...
IT IS A STORY THAT COULD MAKE EVEN A STONE CRY.
THERE WERE LOTS OF LOUD NOISES. THEY MADE ME JUMP.
DID THEY, NOW ?

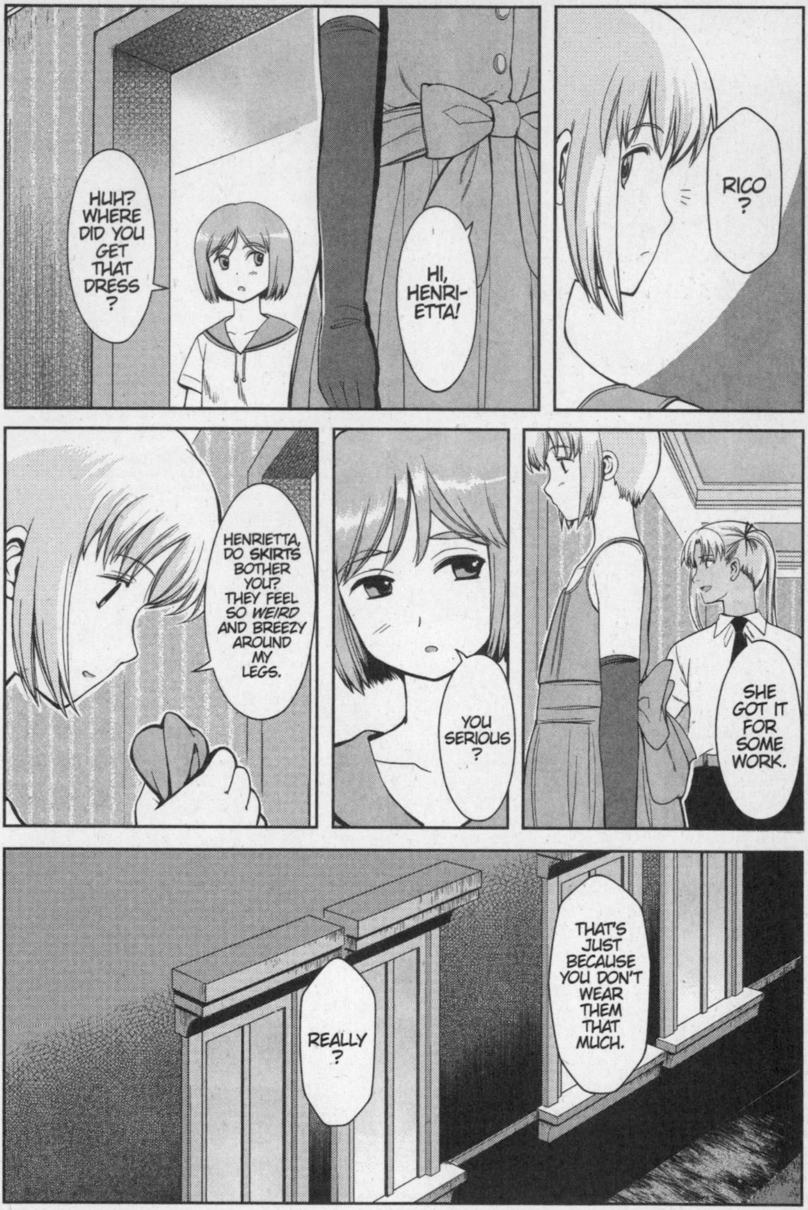
RICO?
HI, HENRIETTA!
HUH? WHERE DID YOU GET THAT DRESS?
SHE GOT IT FOR SOME WORK.
YOU SERIOUS?
HENRIETTA, DO SKIRTS BOTHER YOU? THEY FEEL SO *WEIRD* AND BREEZY AROUND MY LEGS.
THAT'S JUST BECAUSE YOU DON'T WEAR THEM THAT MUCH.
REALLY?

GUNSLINGERGIRL.

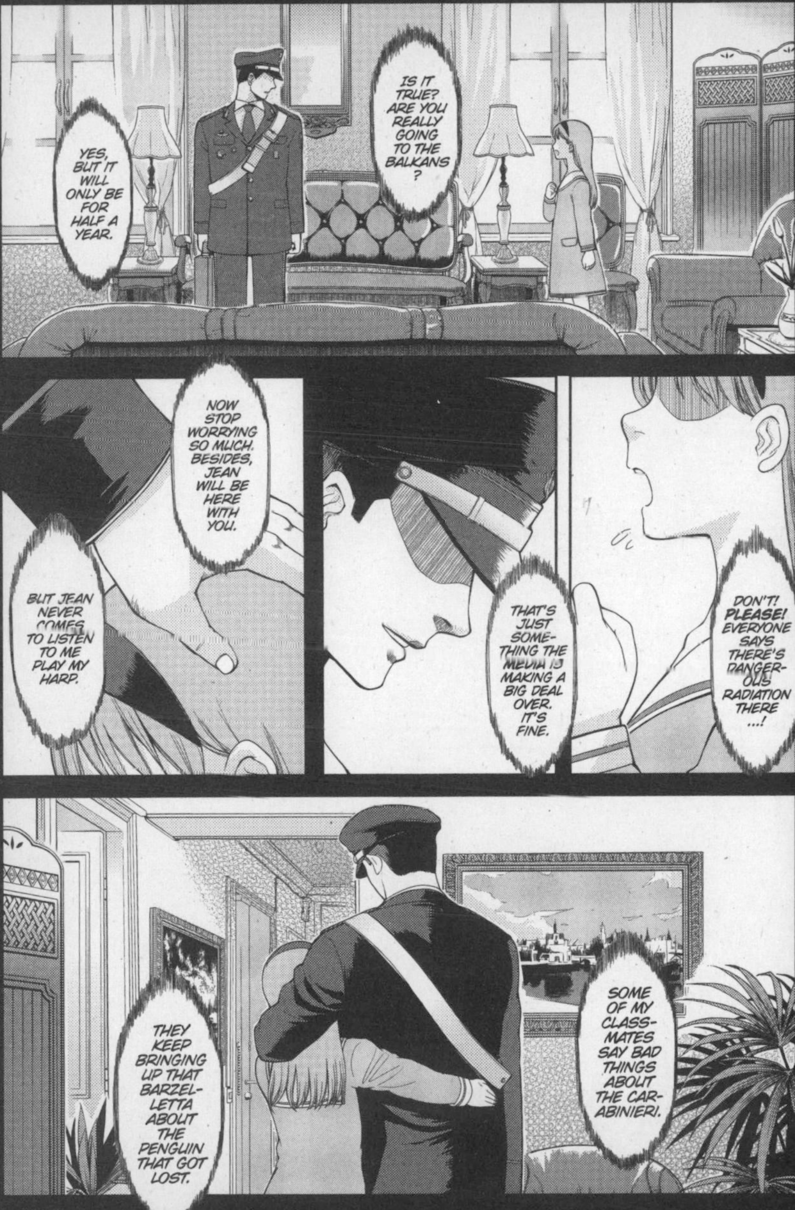
IS IT TRUE? ARE YOU REALLY GOING TO THE BALKANS?
YES, BUT IT WILL ONLY BE FOR HALF A YEAR.
DON'T! PLEASE! EVERYONE SAYS THERE'S DANGEROUS RADIATION THERE...!
THAT'S JUST SOMETHING THE MEDIA IS MAKING A BIG DEAL OVER. IT'S FINE.
NOW STOP WORRYING SO MUCH. BESIDES, JEAN WILL BE HERE WITH YOU.
BUT JEAN NEVER COMES TO LISTEN TO ME PLAY MY HARP.
SOME OF MY CLASSMATES SAY BAD THINGS ABOUT THE CARABINIERI.
THEY KEEP BRINGING UP THAT BARZELLETTA ABOUT THE PENGUIN THAT GOT LOST.

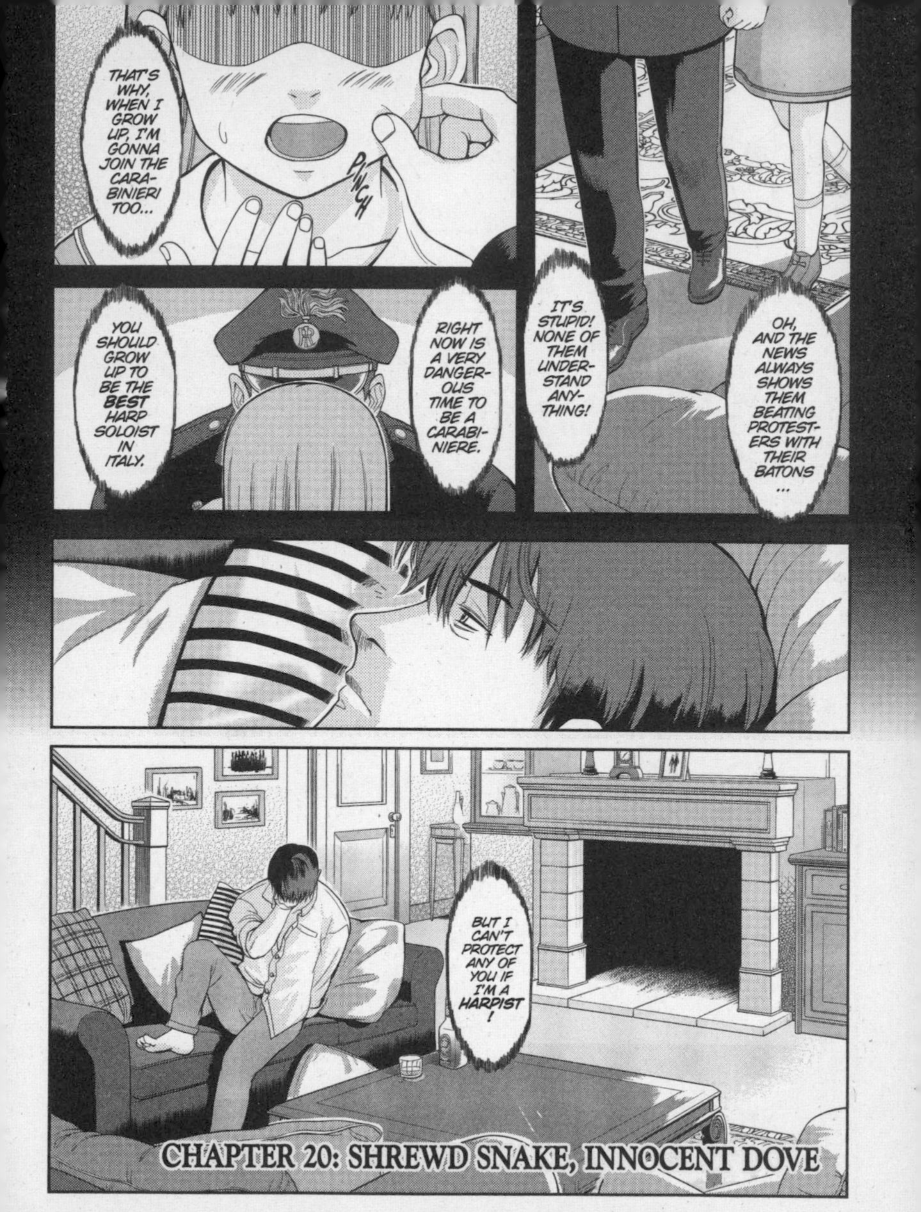
OH, AND THE NEWS ALWAYS SHOWS THEM BEATING PROTESTERS WITH THEIR BATONS ...
IT'S STUPID! NONE OF THEM UNDERSTAND ANYTHING!
THAT'S WHY, WHEN I GROW UP, I'M GONNA JOIN THE CARABINIERI TOO...
PINCH
RIGHT NOW IS A VERY DANGEROUS TIME TO BE A CARABINIERE.
YOU SHOULD GROW UP TO BE THE BEST HARP SOLOIST IN ITALY.
BUT I CAN'T PROTECT ANY OF YOU IF I'M A HARPIST!
CHAPTER 20: SHREWD SNAKE, INNOCENT DOVE

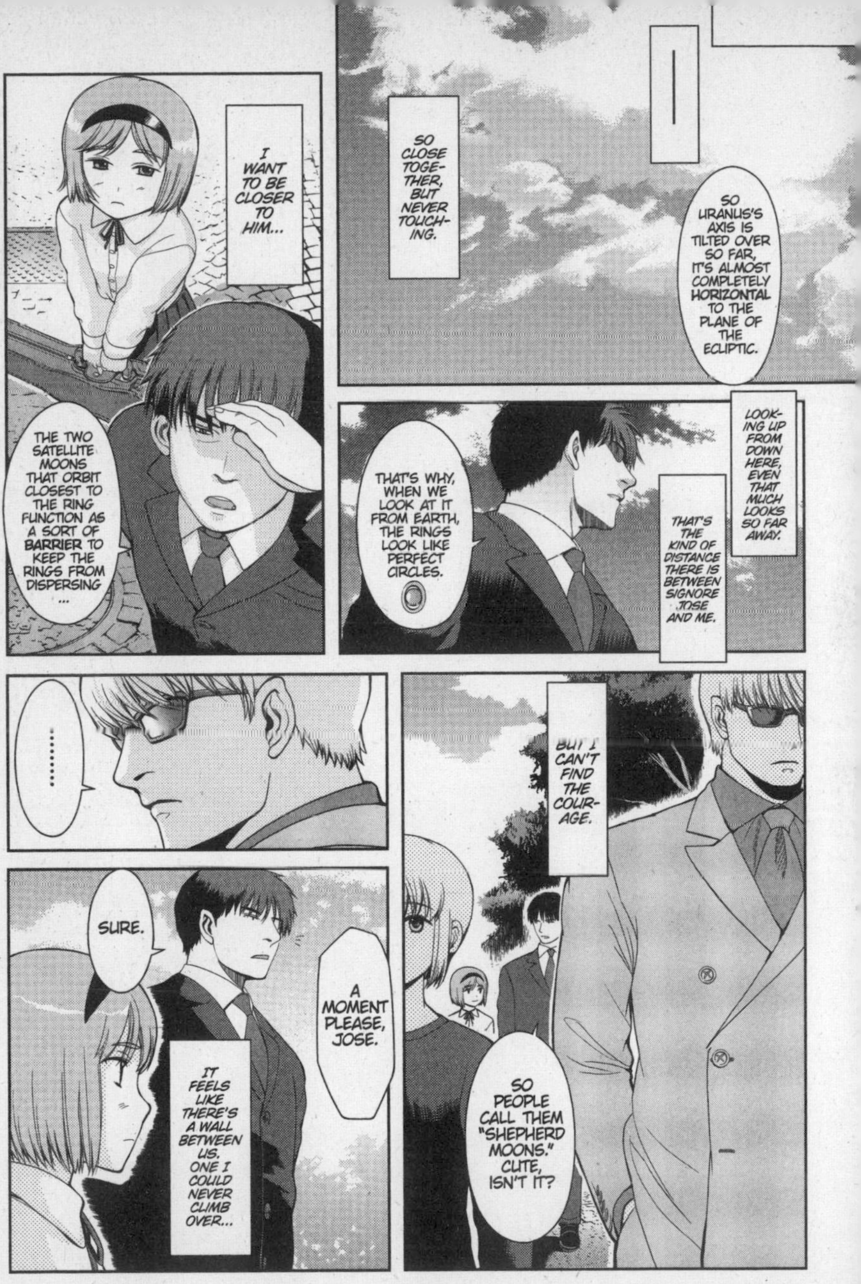

SO URANUS'S AXIS IS TILTED OVER SO FAR, IT'S ALMOST COMPLETELY HORIZONTAL TO THE PLANE OF THE ECLIPTIC.
SO CLOSE TOGETHER, BUT NEVER TOUCHING.
LOOKING UP FROM DOWN HERE, EVEN THAT MUCH LOOKS SO FAR AWAY.
THAT'S THE KIND OF DISTANCE THERE IS BETWEEN SIGNORE JOSE AND ME.
THAT'S WHY, WHEN WE LOOK AT IT FROM EARTH, THE RINGS LOOK LIKE PERFECT CIRCLES.
I WANT TO BE CLOSER TO HIM...
THE TWO SATELLITE MOONS THAT ORBIT CLOSEST TO THE RING FUNCTION AS A SORT OF BARRIER TO KEEP THE RINGS FROM DISPERSING...
BUT I CAN'T FIND THE COURAGE.
SO PEOPLE CALL THEM "SHEPHERD MOONS." CUTE, ISN'T IT?
......
A MOMENT PLEASE, JOSE.
IT FEELS LIKE THERE'S A WALL BETWEEN US. ONE I COULD NEVER CLIMB OVER...
SURE.

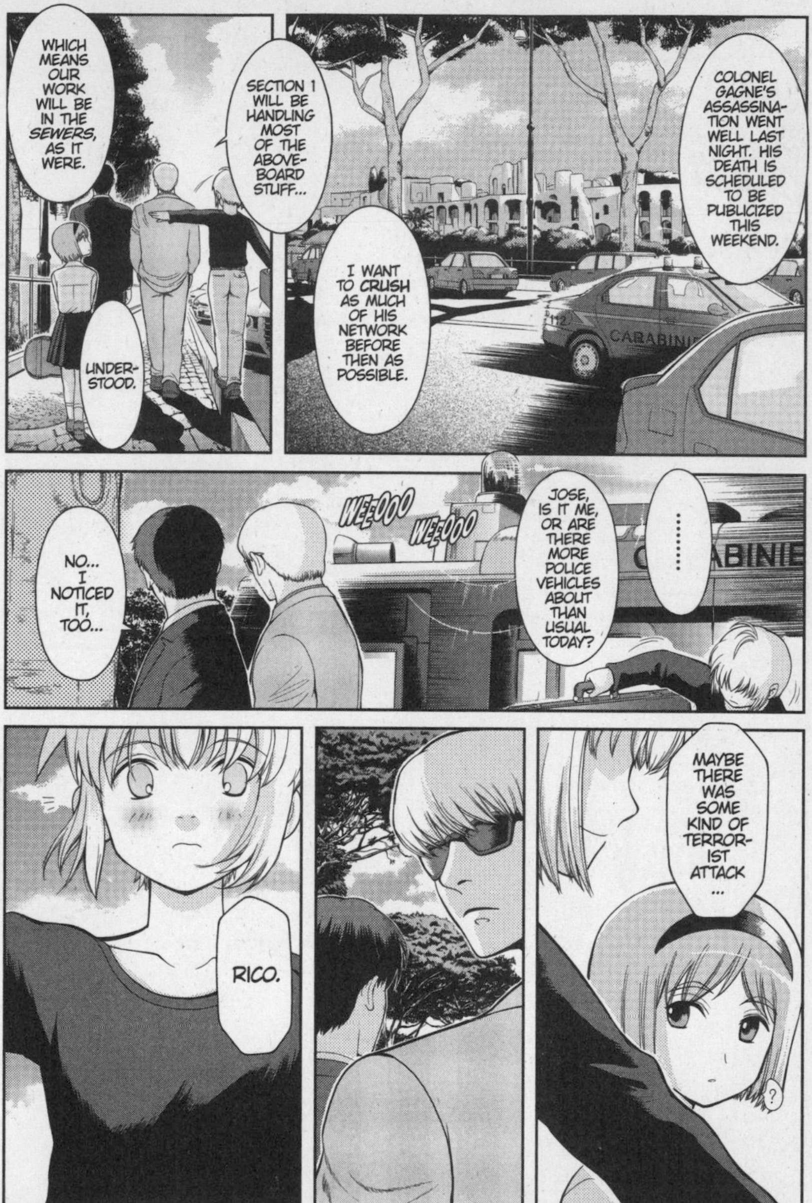
COLONEL GAGNE'S ASSASSINATION WENT WELL LAST NIGHT. HIS DEATH IS SCHEDULED TO BE PUBLICIZED THIS WEEKEND.
I WANT TO CRUSH AS MUCH OF HIS NETWORK BEFORE THEN AS POSSIBLE.
SECTION 1 WILL BE HANDLING MOST OF THE ABOVE-BOARD STUFF...
WHICH MEANS OUR WORK WILL BE IN THE SEWERS, AS IT WERE.
UNDERSTOOD.
CARABINIE
......
JOSE, IS IT ME, OR ARE THERE MORE POLICE VEHICLES ABOUT THAN USUAL TODAY?
WEEEOOO
WEEEOOO
NO... I NOTICED IT, TOO...
MAYBE THERE WAS SOME KIND OF TERRORIST ATTACK...
?
RICO.

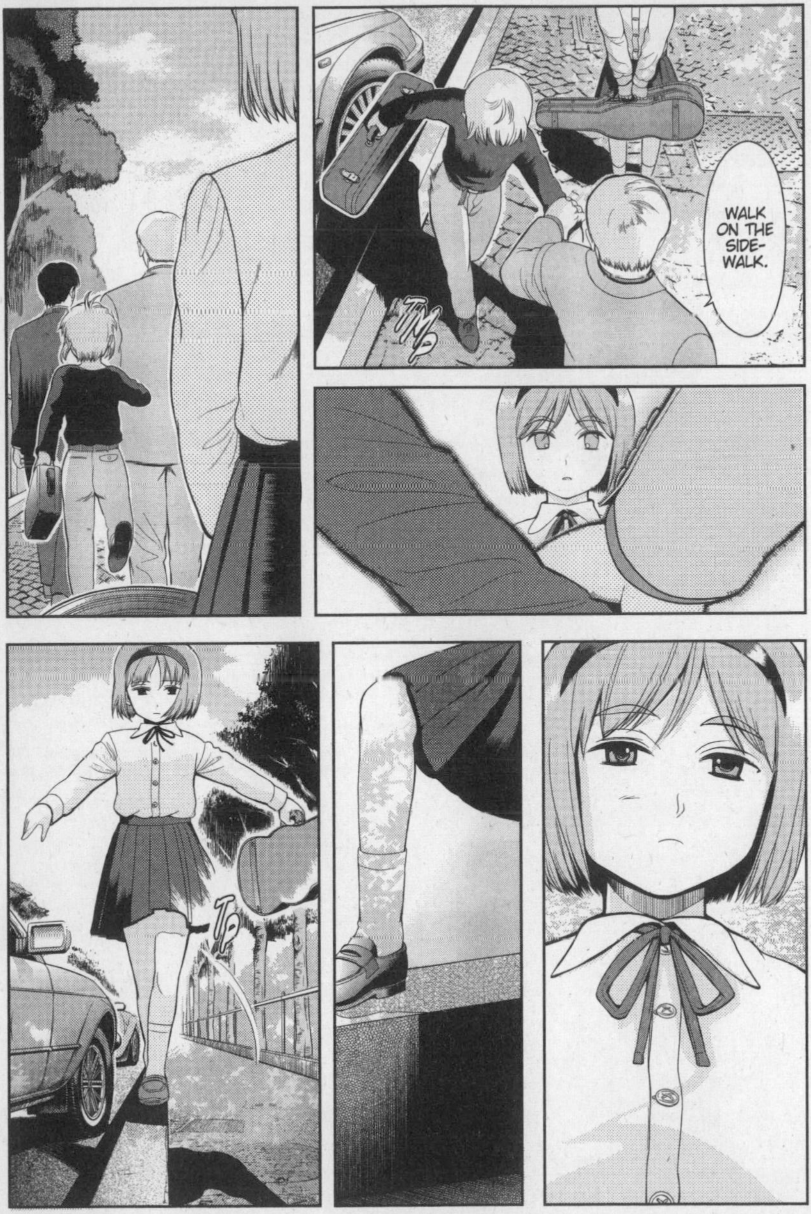
WALK ON THE SIDE-WALK.
TMP
TP

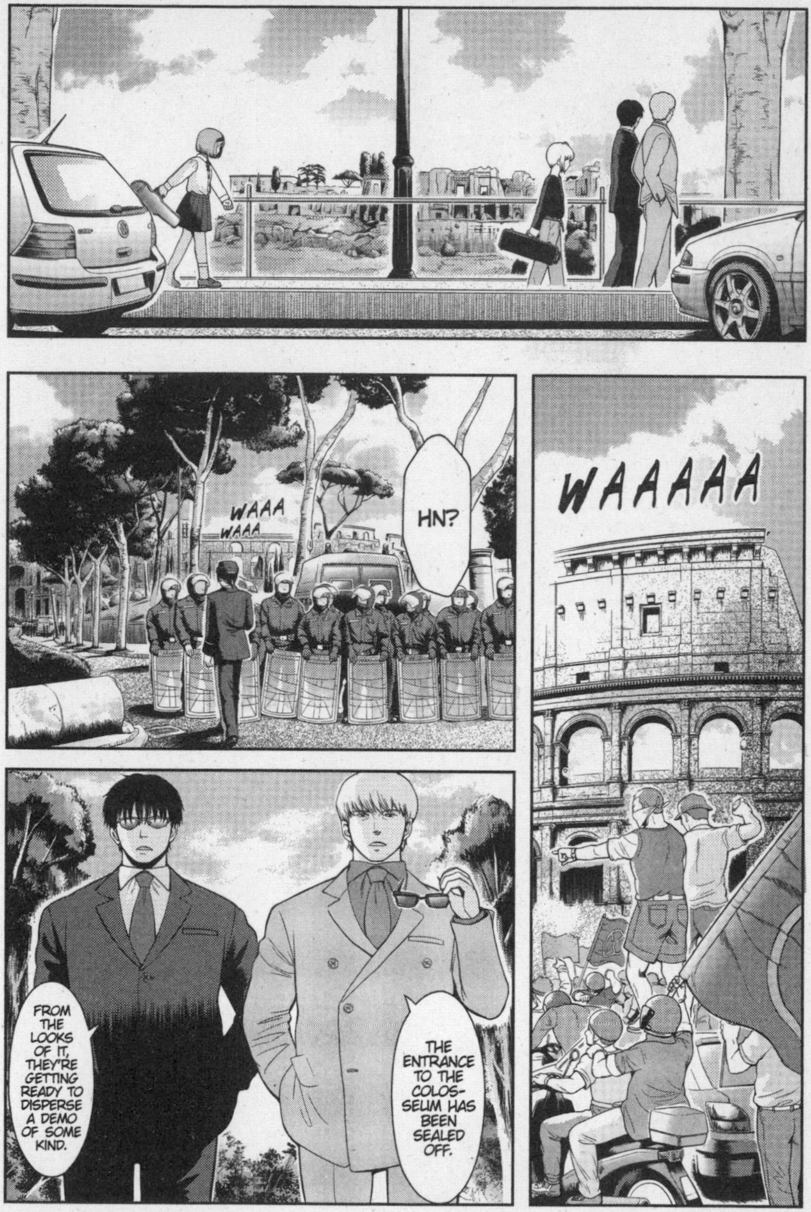
WAAAAA
HN?
WAAA
WAAA
THE ENTRANCE TO THE COLOS-SEUM HAS BEEN SEALED OFF.
FROM THE LOOKS OF IT, THEY'RE GETTING READY TO DISPERSE A DEMO OF SOME KIND.

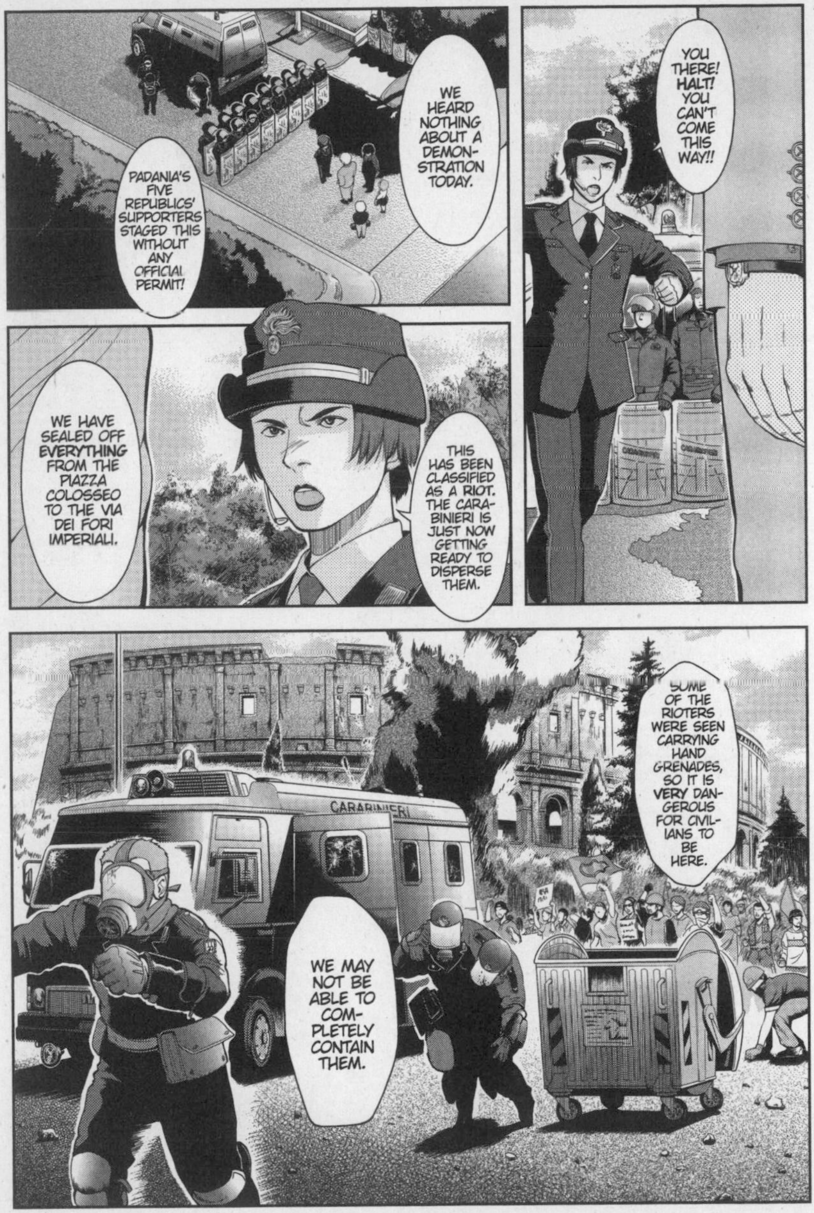
YOU THERE! HALT! YOU CAN'T COME THIS WAY!!
WE HEARD NOTHING ABOUT A DEMON-STRATION TODAY.
PADANIA'S FIVE REPUBLICS' SUPPORTERS STAGED THIS WITHOUT ANY OFFICIAL PERMIT!
THIS HAS BEEN CLASSIFIED AS A RIOT. THE CARA-BINIERI IS JUST NOW GETTING READY TO DISPERSE THEM.
WE HAVE SEALED OFF EVERYTHING FROM THE PIAZZA COLOSSEO TO THE VIA DEI FORI IMPERIALI.
SOME OF THE RIOTERS WERE SEEN CARRYING HAND GRENADES, SO IT IS VERY DAN-GEROUS FOR CIVIL-IANS TO BE HERE.
CARABINIERI
WE MAY NOT BE ABLE TO COM-PLETELY CONTAIN THEM.

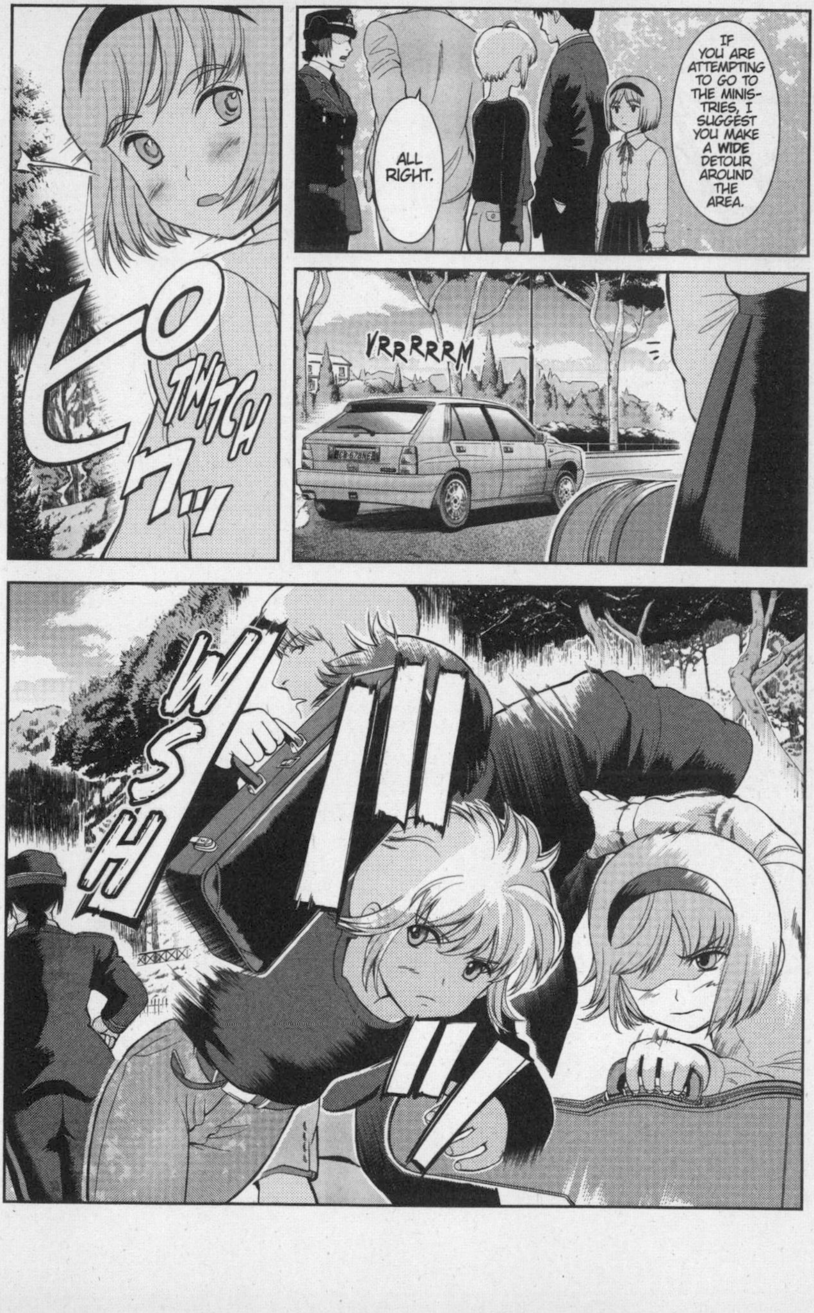
IF YOU ARE ATTEMPTING TO GO TO THE MINISTRIES, I SUGGEST YOU MAKE A WIDE DETOUR AROUND THE AREA.
ALL RIGHT.
VRRRRRM
ピクッ
TWITCH
WSSH

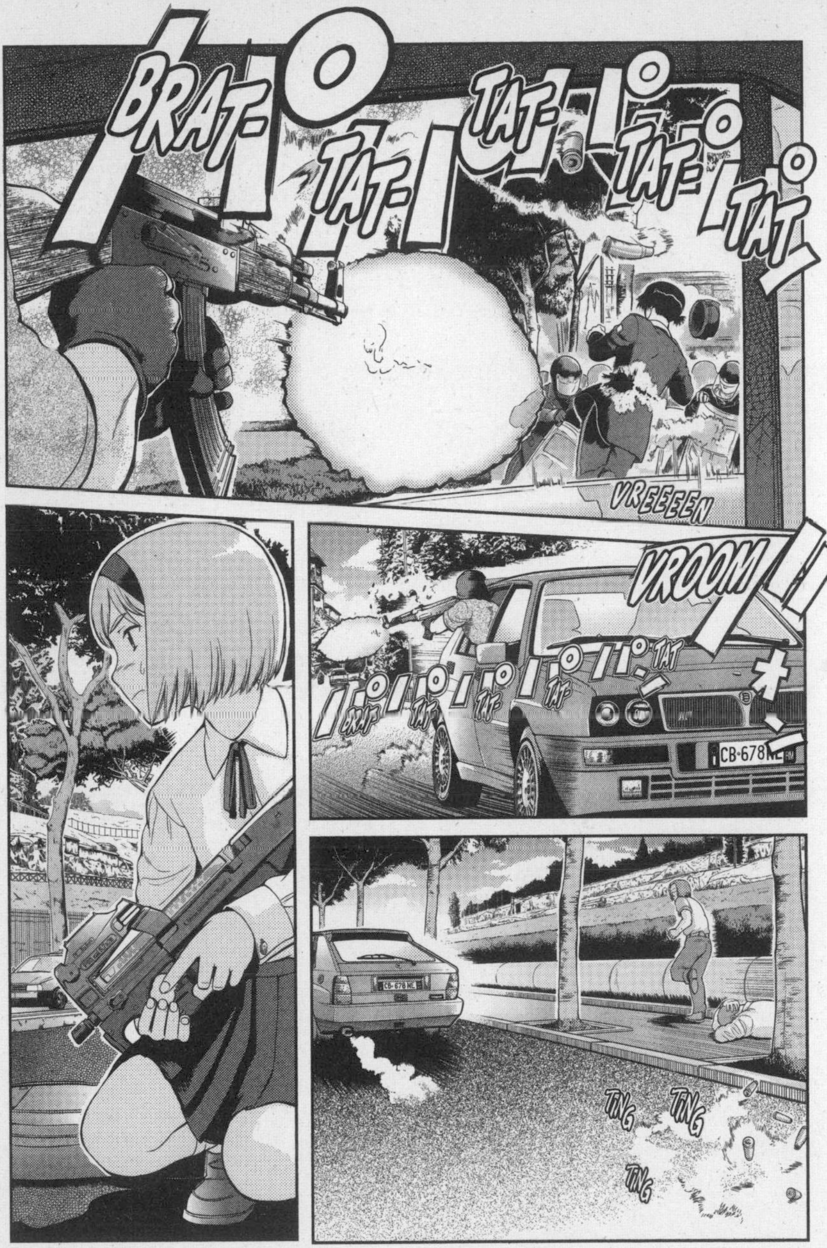
BRAT-TAT-TAT-TAT-TAT
VREEEEN
VROOM
BRAT TAT TAT TAT TAT TAT
TING TING TING

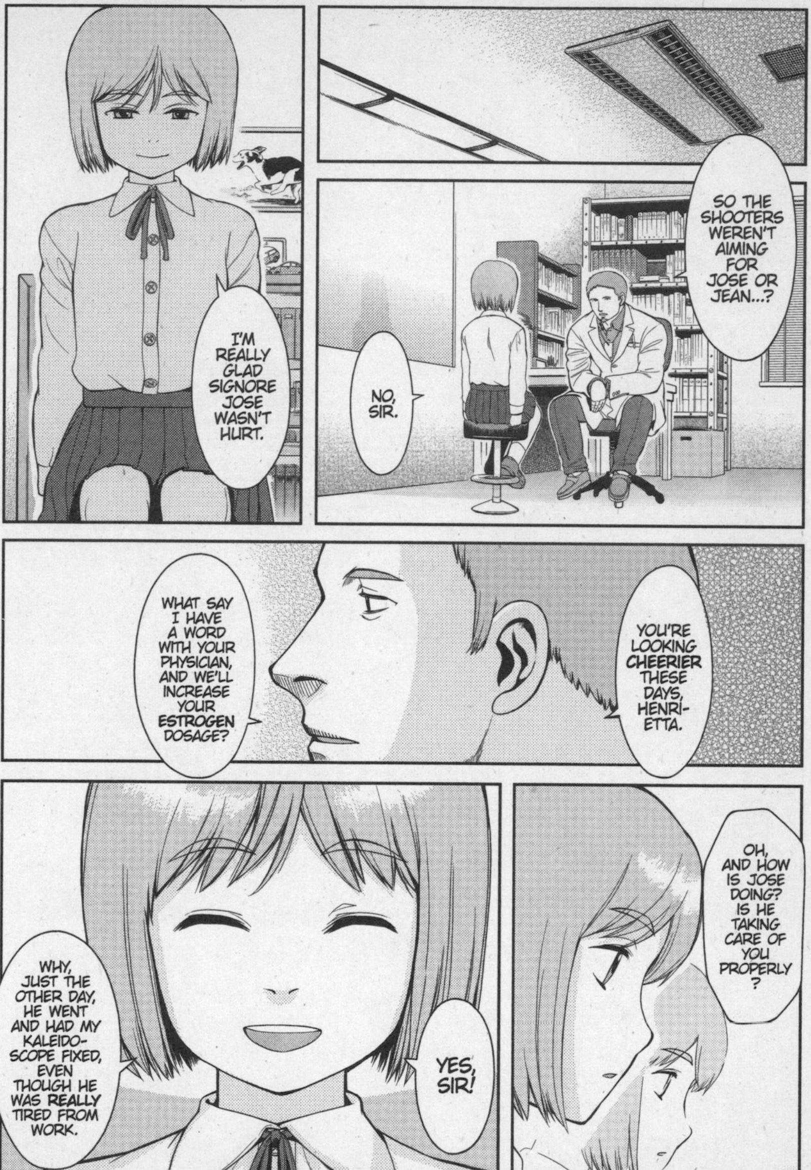
SO THE SHOOTERS WEREN'T AIMING FOR JOSE OR JEAN...?
NO, SIR.
I'M REALLY GLAD SIGNORE JOSE WASN'T HURT.
YOU'RE LOOKING CHEERIER THESE DAYS, HENRI-ETTA.
WHAT SAY I HAVE A WORD WITH YOUR PHYSICIAN, AND WE'LL INCREASE YOUR ESTROGEN DOSAGE?
OH, AND HOW IS JOSE DOING? IS HE TAKING CARE OF YOU PROPERLY?
YES, SIR!
WHY, JUST THE OTHER DAY, HE WENT AND HAD MY KALEIDO-SCOPE FIXED, EVEN THOUGH HE WAS REALLY TIRED FROM WORK.

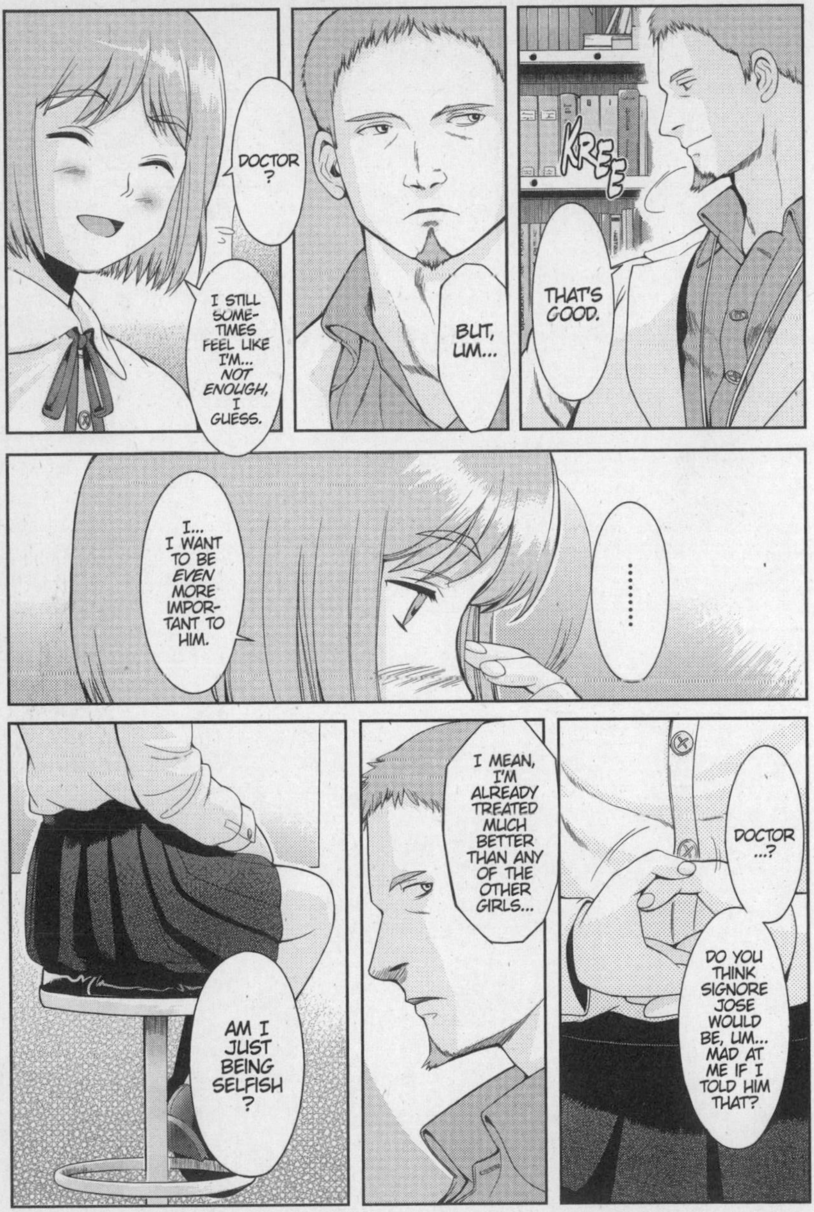
KREE
THAT'S GOOD.
BUT, UM...
DOCTOR?
I STILL SOMETIMES FEEL LIKE I'M... NOT ENOUGH, I GUESS.
......
I... I WANT TO BE EVEN MORE IMPORTANT TO HIM.
DOCTOR...?
DO YOU THINK SIGNORE JOSE WOULD BE, UM... MAD AT ME IF I TOLD HIM THAT?
I MEAN, I'M ALREADY TREATED MUCH BETTER THAN ANY OF THE OTHER GIRLS...
AM I JUST BEING SELFISH?

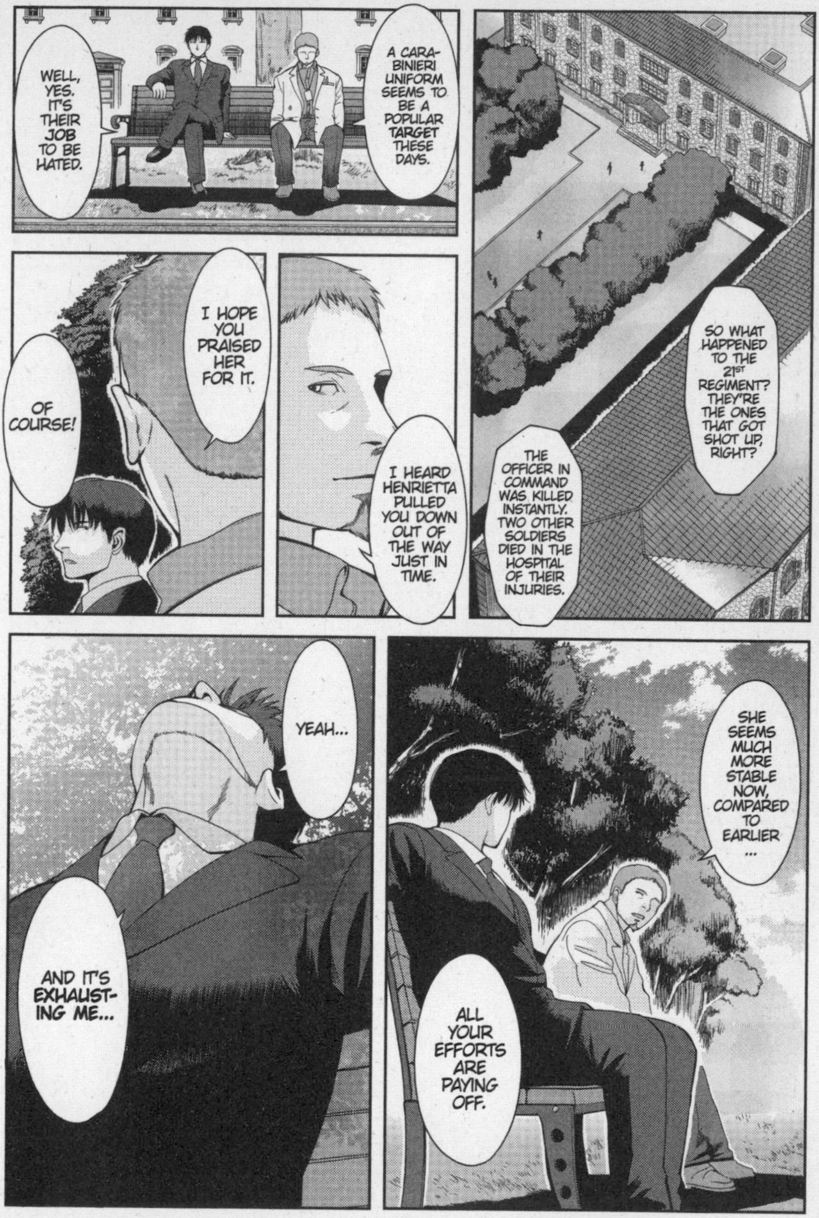
SO WHAT HAPPENED TO THE 21ST REGIMENT? THEY'RE THE ONES THAT GOT SHOT UP, RIGHT?
THE OFFICER IN COMMAND WAS KILLED INSTANTLY. TWO OTHER SOLDIERS DIED IN THE HOSPITAL OF THEIR INJURIES.
A CARABINIERI UNIFORM SEEMS TO BE A POPULAR TARGET THESE DAYS.
WELL, YES. IT'S THEIR JOB TO BE HATED.
I HEARD HENRIETTA PULLED YOU DOWN OUT OF THE WAY JUST IN TIME.
I HOPE YOU PRAISED HER FOR IT.
OF COURSE!
SHE SEEMS MUCH MORE STABLE NOW, COMPARED TO EARLIER ...
ALL YOUR EFFORTS ARE PAYING OFF.
YEAH...
AND IT'S EXHAUSTING ME...

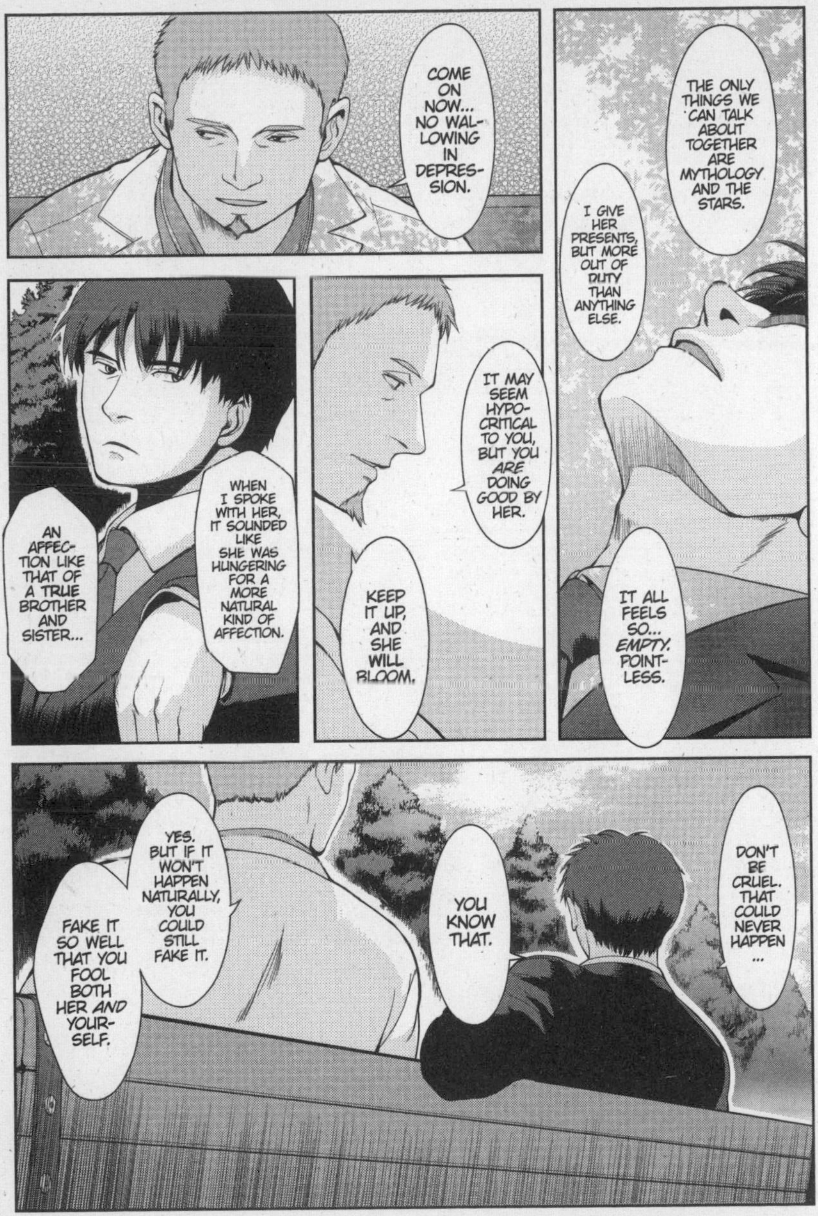
THE ONLY THINGS WE CAN TALK ABOUT TOGETHER ARE MYTHOLOGY AND THE STARS.
I GIVE HER PRESENTS, BUT MORE OUT OF DUTY THAN ANYTHING ELSE.
IT ALL FEELS SO... *EMPTY.* POINTLESS.
COME ON NOW... NO WAL-LOWING IN DEPRES-SION.
IT MAY SEEM HYPO-CRITICAL TO YOU, BUT YOU *ARE* DOING GOOD BY HER.
KEEP IT UP, AND SHE WILL BLOOM.
WHEN I SPOKE WITH HER, IT SOUNDED LIKE SHE WAS HUNGERING FOR A MORE NATURAL KIND OF AFFECTION.
AN AFFEC-TION LIKE THAT OF A TRUE BROTHER AND SISTER...
DON'T BE CRUEL. THAT COULD NEVER HAPPEN ...
YOU KNOW THAT.
YES. BUT IF IT WON'T HAPPEN NATURALLY, YOU COULD STILL FAKE IT.
FAKE IT SO WELL THAT YOU FOOL BOTH HER *AND* YOUR-SELF.

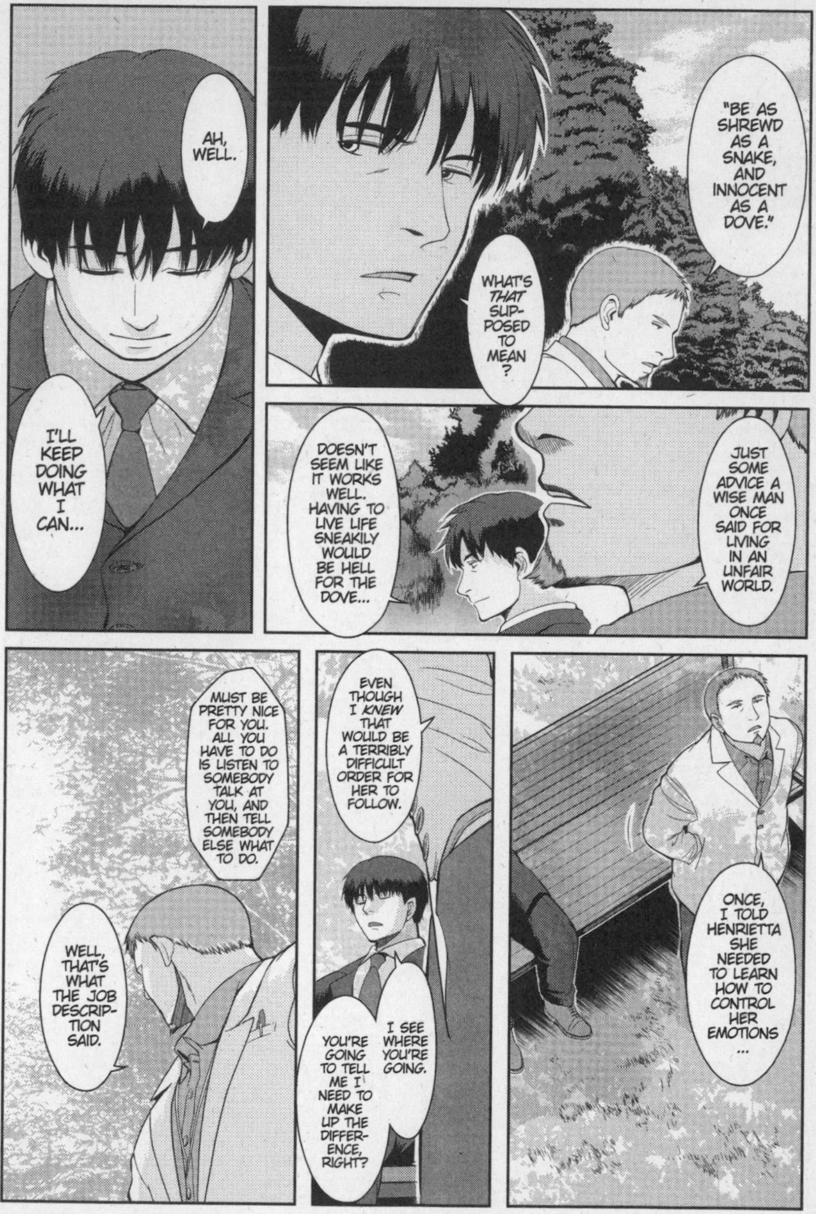
"BE AS SHREWD AS A SNAKE, AND INNOCENT AS A DOVE."
WHAT'S *THAT* SUP-POSED TO MEAN?
JUST SOME ADVICE A WISE MAN ONCE SAID FOR LIVING IN AN UNFAIR WORLD.
DOESN'T SEEM LIKE IT WORKS WELL. HAVING TO LIVE LIFE SNEAKILY WOULD BE HELL FOR THE DOVE...
AH, WELL.
I'LL KEEP DOING WHAT I CAN...
ONCE, I TOLD HENRIETTA SHE NEEDED TO LEARN HOW TO CONTROL HER EMOTIONS...
EVEN THOUGH I *KNEW* THAT WOULD BE A TERRIBLY DIFFICULT ORDER FOR HER TO FOLLOW.
I SEE WHERE YOU'RE GOING.
YOU'RE GOING TO TELL ME I NEED TO MAKE UP THE DIFFER-ENCE, RIGHT?
MUST BE PRETTY NICE FOR YOU. ALL YOU HAVE TO DO IS LISTEN TO SOMEBODY TALK AT YOU, AND THEN TELL SOMEBODY ELSE WHAT TO DO.
WELL, THAT'S WHAT THE JOB DESCRIP-TION SAID.

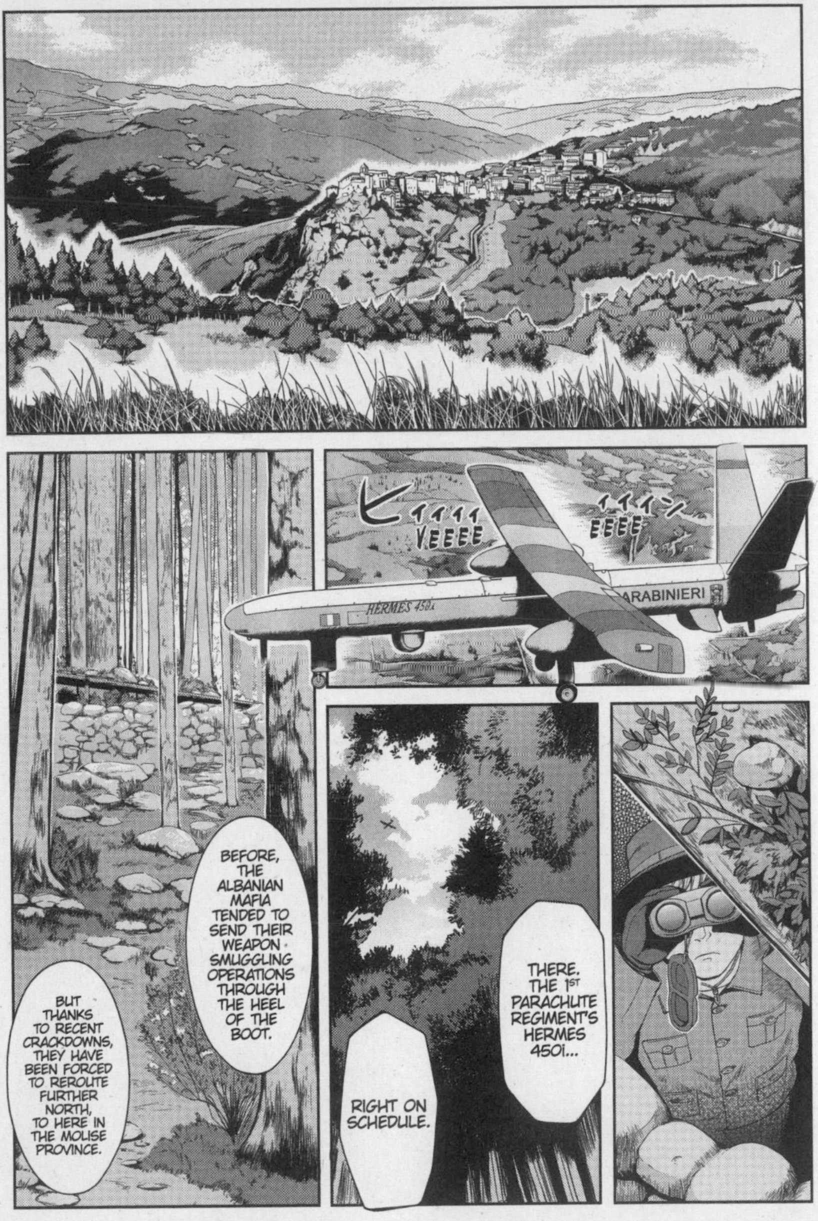
ヒイイイイ
VEEEE
イイイン
EEEE
HERMES 450i
ARABINIERI
THERE. THE 1ST PARACHUTE REGIMENT'S HERMES 450i...
RIGHT ON SCHEDULE.
BEFORE, THE ALBANIAN MAFIA TENDED TO SEND THEIR WEAPON SMUGGLING OPERATIONS THROUGH THE HEEL OF THE BOOT.
BUT THANKS TO RECENT CRACKDOWNS, THEY HAVE BEEN FORCED TO REROUTE FURTHER NORTH, TO HERE IN THE MOLISE PROVINCE.

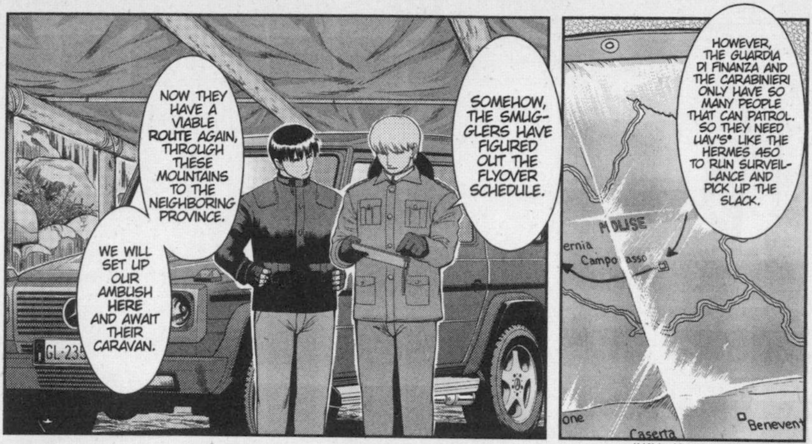
HOWEVER, THE GUARDIA DI FINANZA AND THE CARABINIERI ONLY HAVE SO MANY PEOPLE THAT CAN PATROL. SO THEY NEED UAV'S* LIKE THE HERMES 450 TO RUN SURVEILLANCE AND PICK UP THE SLACK.
MOLISE
Caserta
SOMEHOW, THE SMUGGLERS HAVE FIGURED OUT THE FLYOVER SCHEDULE.
NOW THEY HAVE A VIABLE ROUTE AGAIN, THROUGH THESE MOUNTAINS TO THE NEIGHBORING PROVINCE.
WE WILL SET UP OUR AMBUSH HERE AND AWAIT THEIR CARAVAN.

*UAV = Unmanned Aerial Vehicle

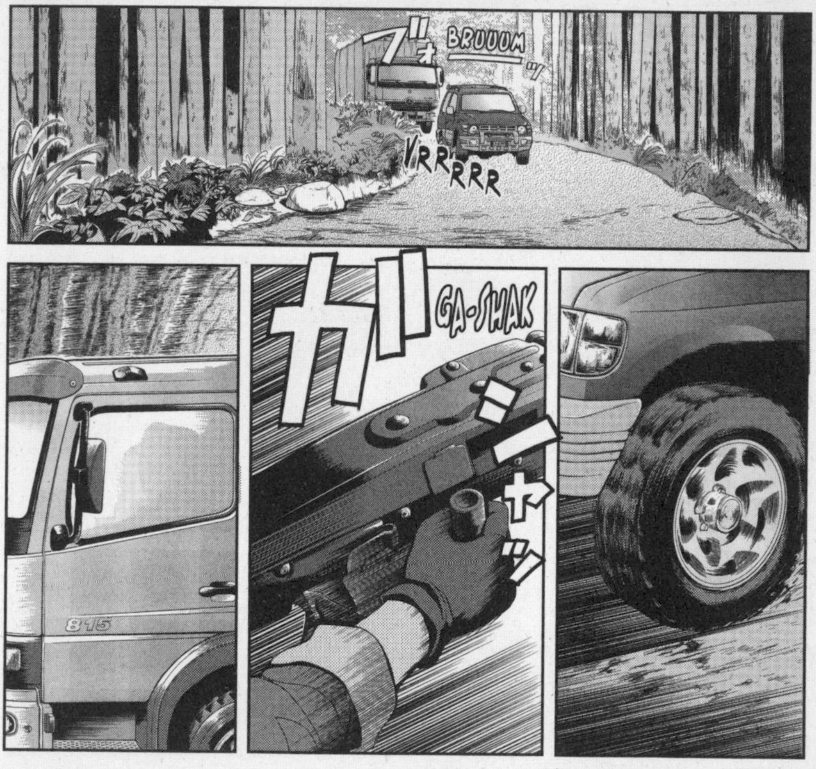
ブォ
BRUUUM
VRRRRRR
ガシャッ
GA-SHAK

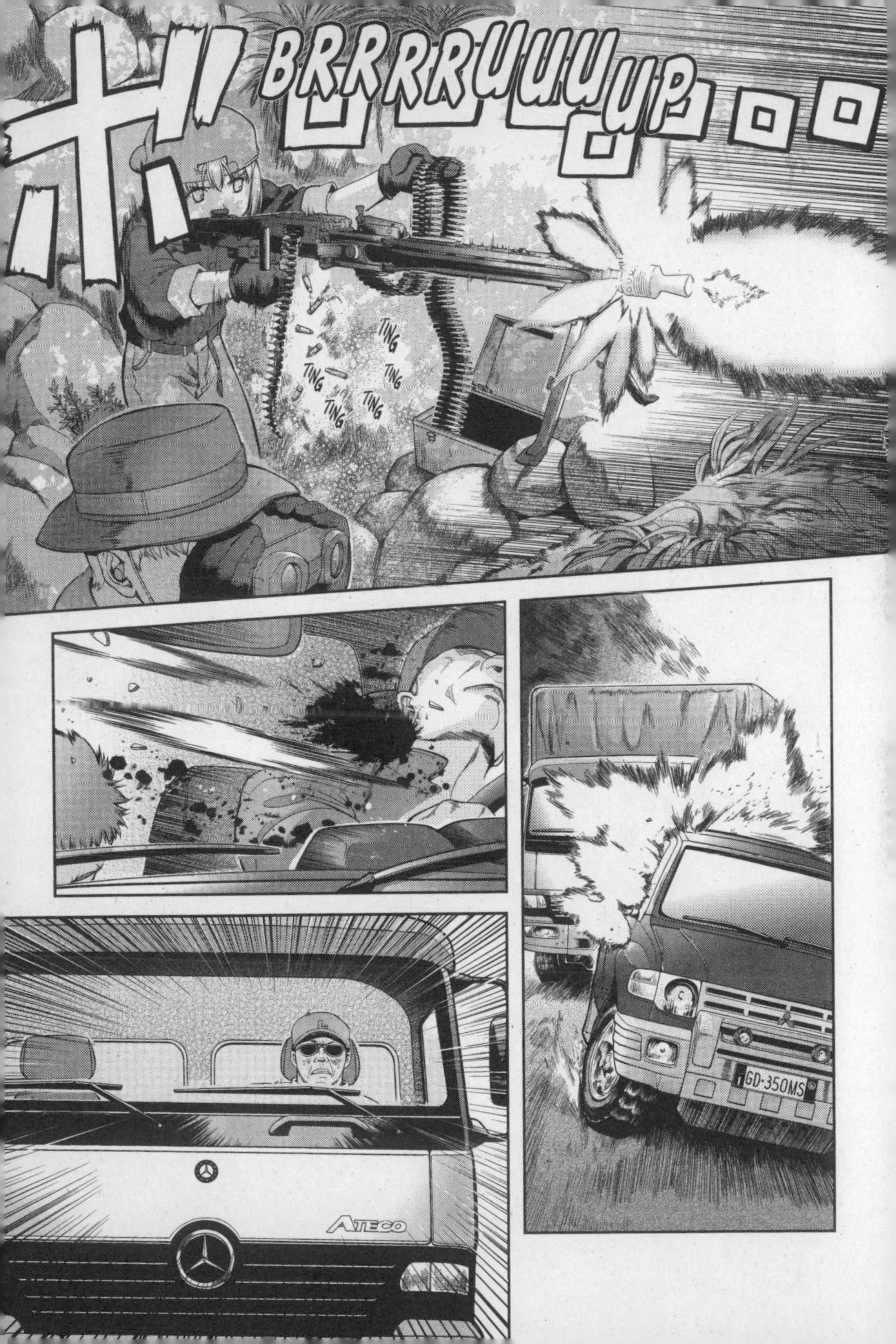
BRRRRRUUUUUP
TING
TING
TING
TING
TING
GD-350MS
ATECO

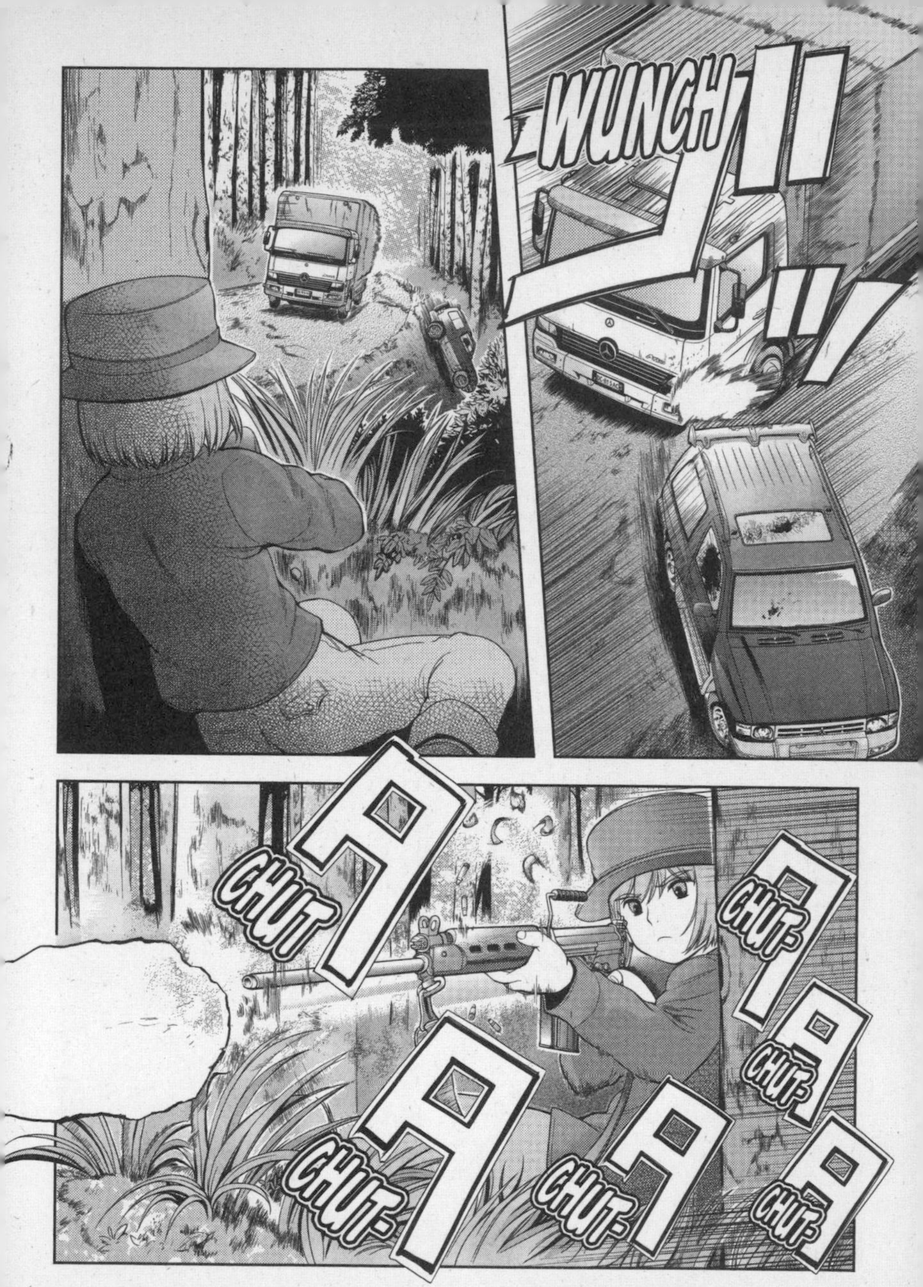
WUNCH!!
CHUT-A
CHUT-A
CHUT-A
CHUTA
CHUT-A
CHUT-A

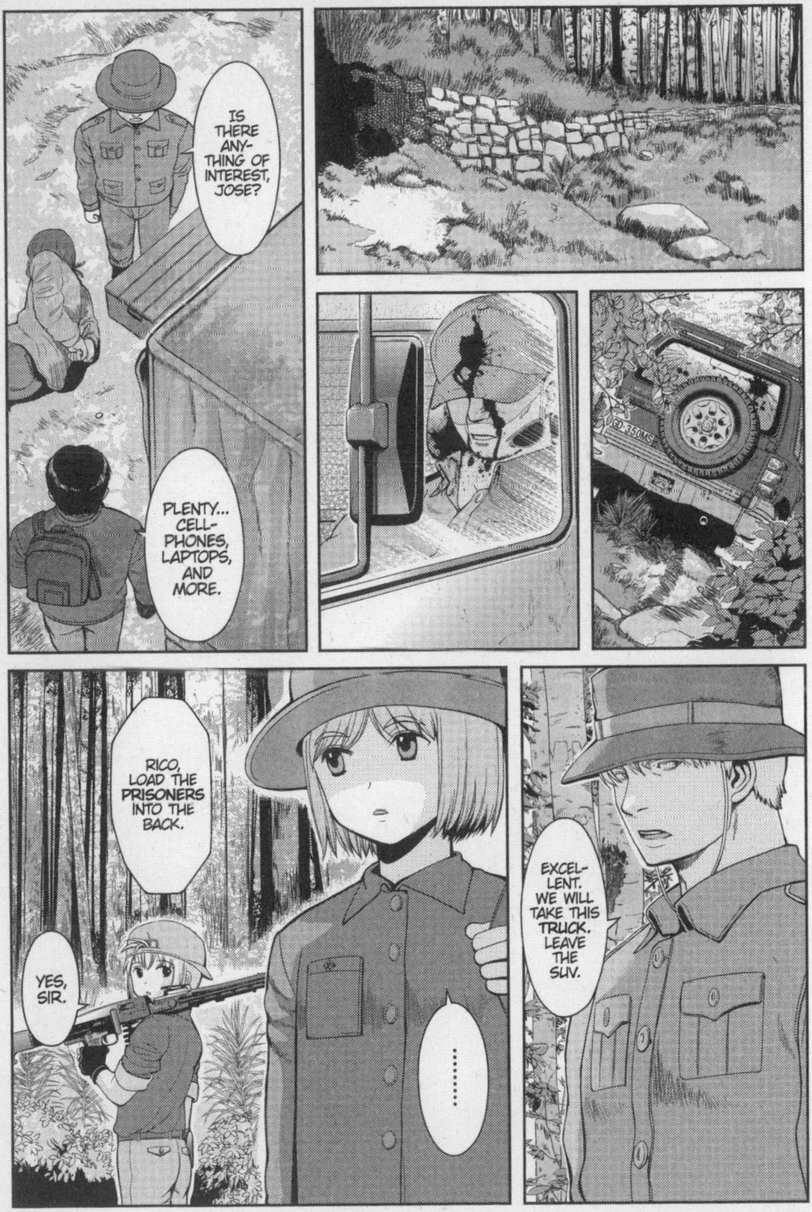
GD-350MS
IS THERE ANY-THING OF INTEREST, JOSE?
PLENTY... CELL-PHONES, LAPTOPS, AND MORE.
EXCEL-LENT. WE WILL TAKE THIS TRUCK. LEAVE THE SUV.
RICO, LOAD THE PRISONERS INTO THE BACK.
......
YES, SIR.

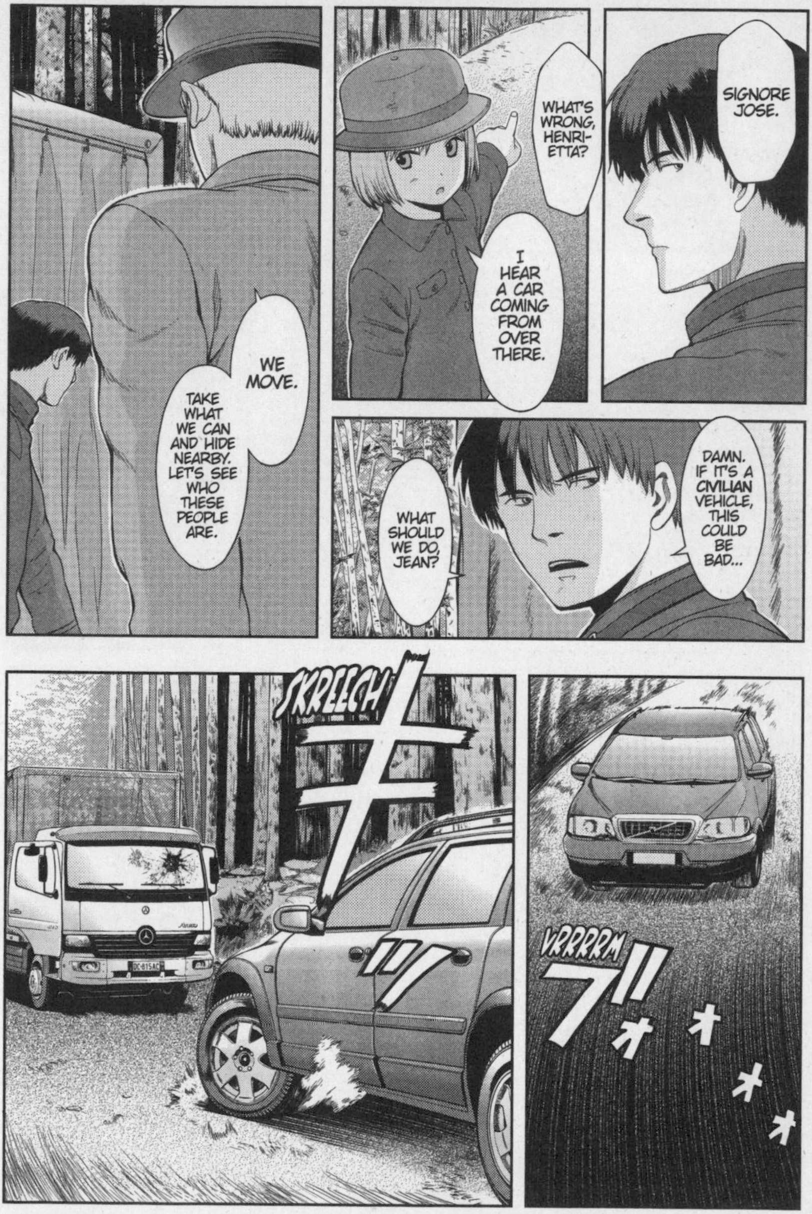

SIGNORE JOSE.
WHAT'S WRONG, HENRI-ETTA?
I HEAR A CAR COMING FROM OVER THERE.
DAMN. IF IT'S A CIVILIAN VEHICLE, THIS COULD BE BAD...
WHAT SHOULD WE DO, JEAN?
WE MOVE.
TAKE WHAT WE CAN AND HIDE NEARBY. LET'S SEE WHO THESE PEOPLE ARE.
VRRRRM
SKREECH

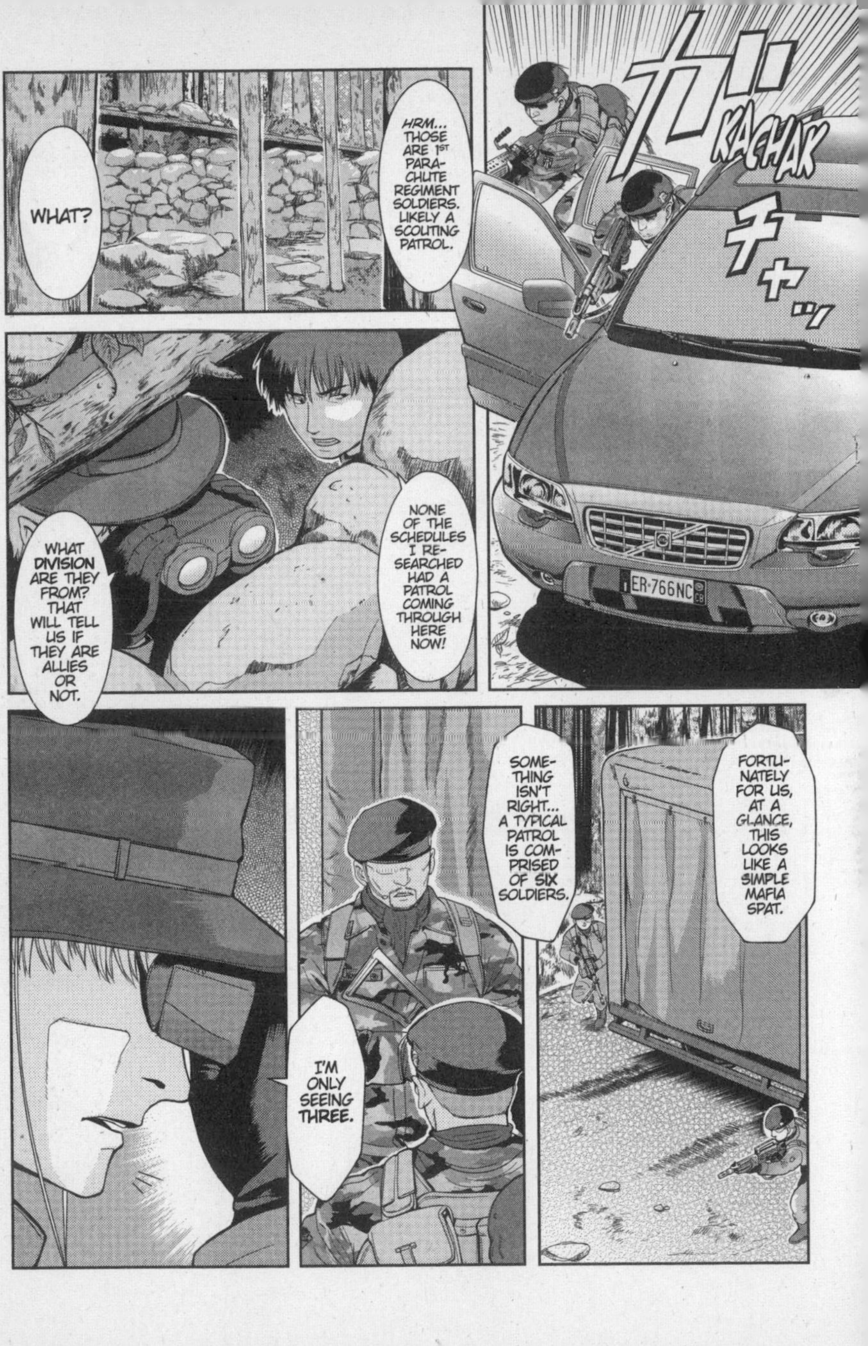
ガチャッ
KACHAK
HRM... THOSE ARE 1ST PARACHUTE REGIMENT SOLDIERS. LIKELY A SCOUTING PATROL.
WHAT?
NONE OF THE SCHEDULES I RESEARCHED HAD A PATROL COMING THROUGH HERE NOW!
WHAT DIVISION ARE THEY FROM? THAT WILL TELL US IF THEY ARE ALLIES OR NOT.
FORTUNATELY FOR US, AT A GLANCE, THIS LOOKS LIKE A SIMPLE MAFIA SPAT.
SOMETHING ISN'T RIGHT... A TYPICAL PATROL IS COMPRISED OF SIX SOLDIERS.
I'M ONLY SEEING THREE.
ER·766NC

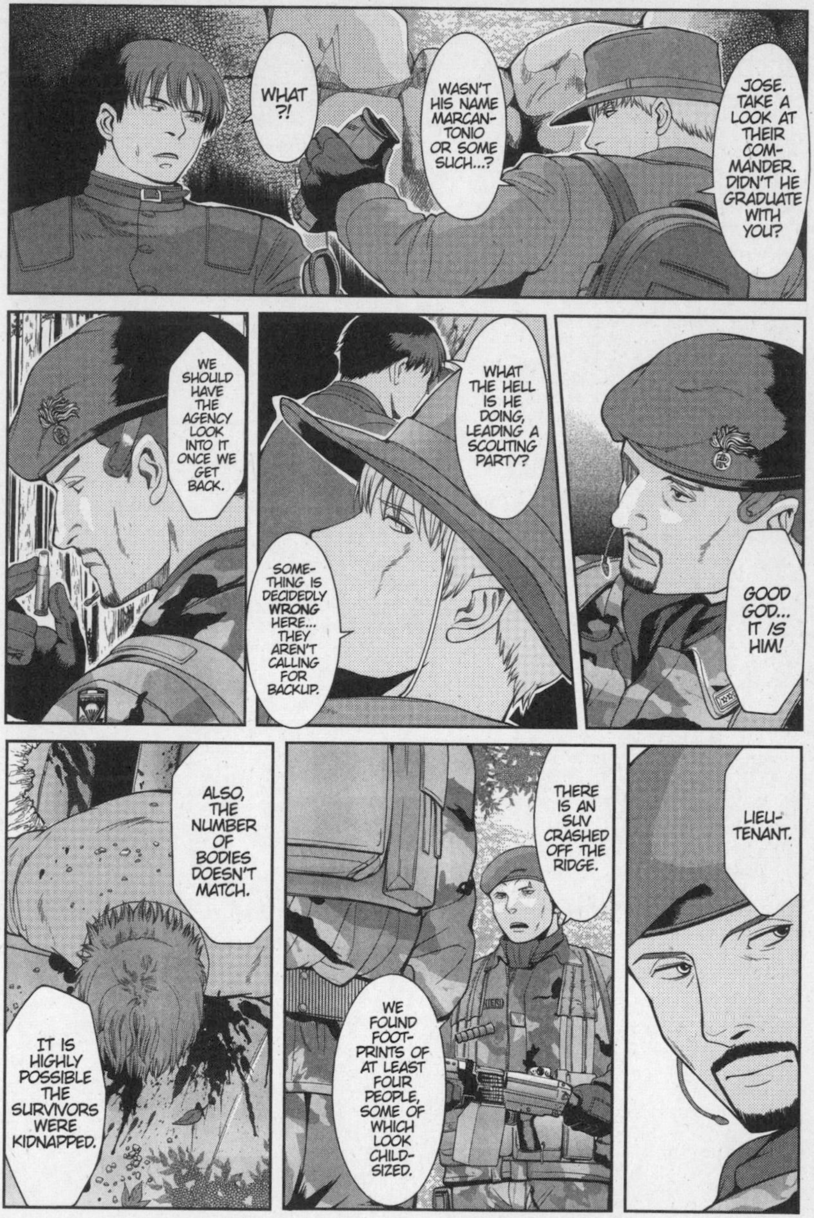

JOSE. TAKE A LOOK AT THEIR COMMANDER. DIDN'T HE GRADUATE WITH YOU?
WASN'T HIS NAME MARCANTONIO OR SOME SUCH...?
WHAT ?!
GOOD GOD... IT IS HIM!
WHAT THE HELL IS HE DOING, LEADING A SCOUTING PARTY?
SOMETHING IS DECIDEDLY WRONG HERE... THEY AREN'T CALLING FOR BACKUP.
WE SHOULD HAVE THE AGENCY LOOK INTO IT ONCE WE GET BACK.
LIEUTENANT.
THERE IS AN SUV CRASHED OFF THE RIDGE.
WE FOUND FOOTPRINTS OF AT LEAST FOUR PEOPLE, SOME OF WHICH LOOK CHILD-SIZED.
ALSO, THE NUMBER OF BODIES DOESN'T MATCH.
IT IS HIGHLY POSSIBLE THE SURVIVORS WERE KIDNAPPED.

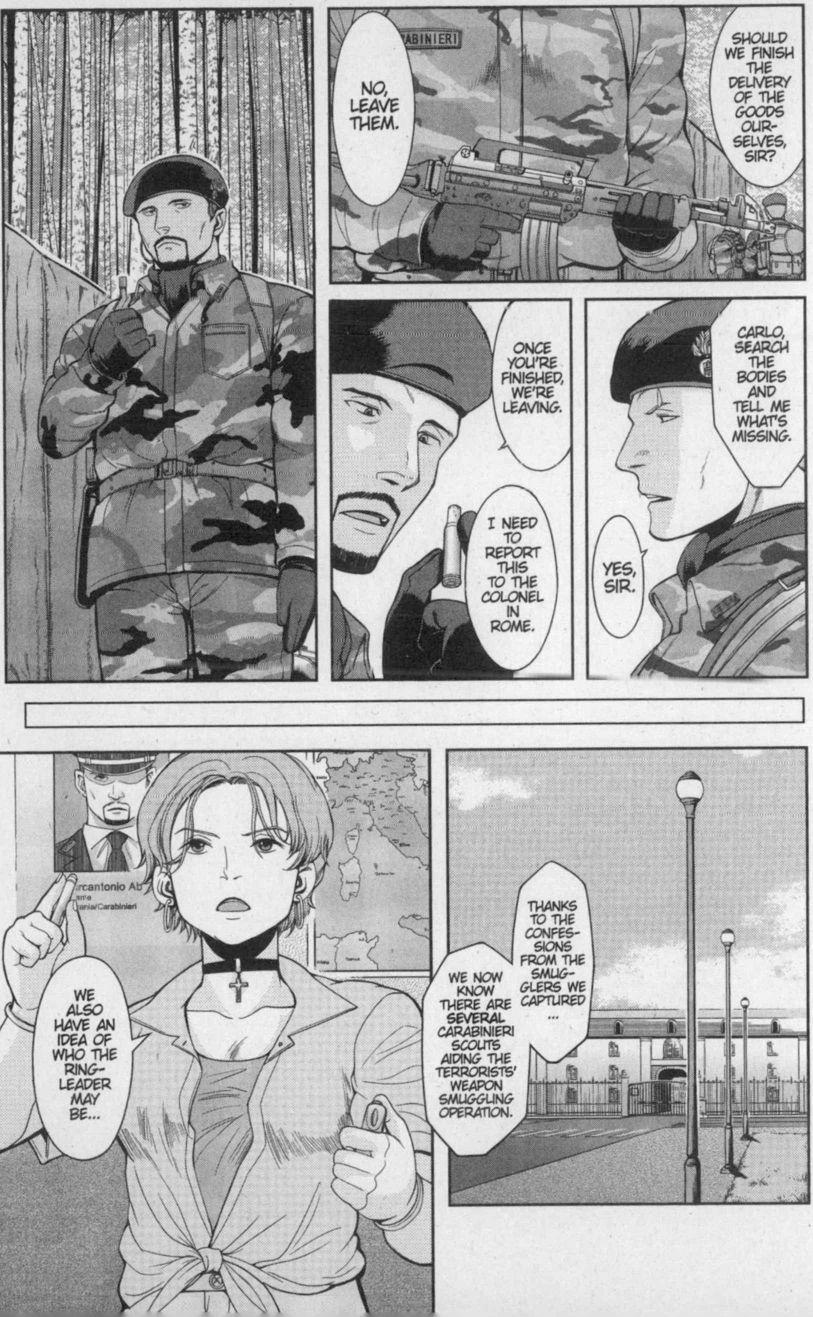
SHOULD WE FINISH THE DELIVERY OF THE GOODS OUR-SELVES, SIR?
NO, LEAVE THEM.
CARLO, SEARCH THE BODIES AND TELL ME WHAT'S MISSING.
YES, SIR.
ONCE YOU'RE FINISHED, WE'RE LEAVING.
I NEED TO REPORT THIS TO THE COLONEL IN ROME.
THANKS TO THE CONFES-SIONS FROM THE SMUG-GLERS WE CAPTURED ...
WE NOW KNOW THERE ARE **SEVERAL** CARABINIERI SCOUTS AIDING THE TERRORISTS' WEAPON SMUGGLING OPERATION.
WE ALSO HAVE AN IDEA OF WHO THE RING-LEADER MAY BE...

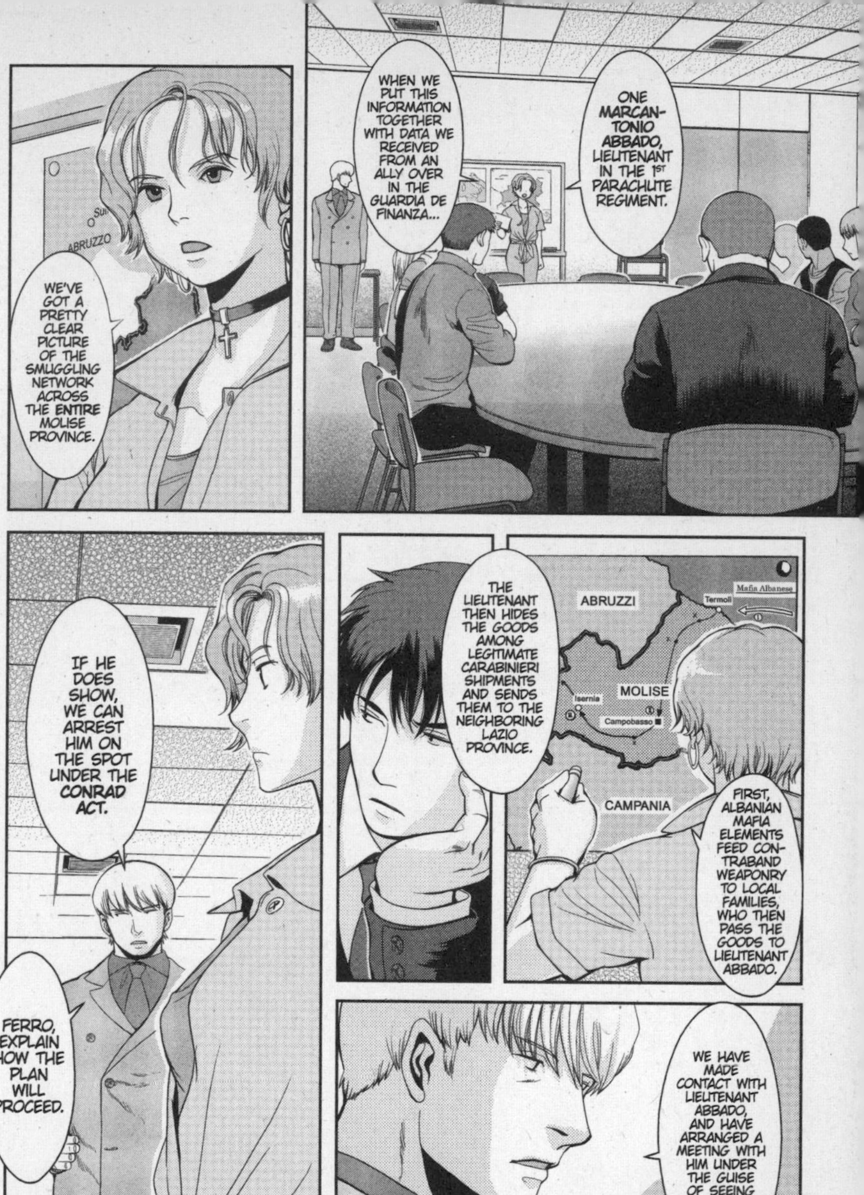
ONE MARCANTONIO ABBADO, LIEUTENANT IN THE 1ST PARACHUTE REGIMENT.
WHEN WE PUT THIS INFORMATION TOGETHER WITH DATA WE RECEIVED FROM AN ALLY OVER IN THE GUARDIA DE FINANZA...
ABRUZZO
WE'VE GOT A PRETTY CLEAR PICTURE OF THE SMUGGLING NETWORK ACROSS THE ENTIRE MOLISE PROVINCE.
Mafia Albanese
ABRUZZI
Termoli
MOLISE
Isernia
Campobasso
CAMPANIA
FIRST, ALBANIAN MAFIA ELEMENTS FEED CONTRABAND WEAPONRY TO LOCAL FAMILIES, WHO THEN PASS THE GOODS TO LIEUTENANT ABBADO.
THE LIEUTENANT THEN HIDES THE GOODS AMONG LEGITIMATE CARABINIERI SHIPMENTS AND SENDS THEM TO THE NEIGHBORING LAZIO PROVINCE.
WE HAVE MADE CONTACT WITH LIEUTENANT ABBADO, AND HAVE ARRANGED A MEETING WITH HIM UNDER THE GUISE OF SEEING AN OLD FRIEND.
IF HE DOES SHOW, WE CAN ARREST HIM ON THE SPOT UNDER THE CONRAD ACT.
FERRO, EXPLAIN HOW THE PLAN WILL PROCEED.

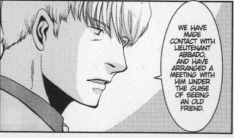

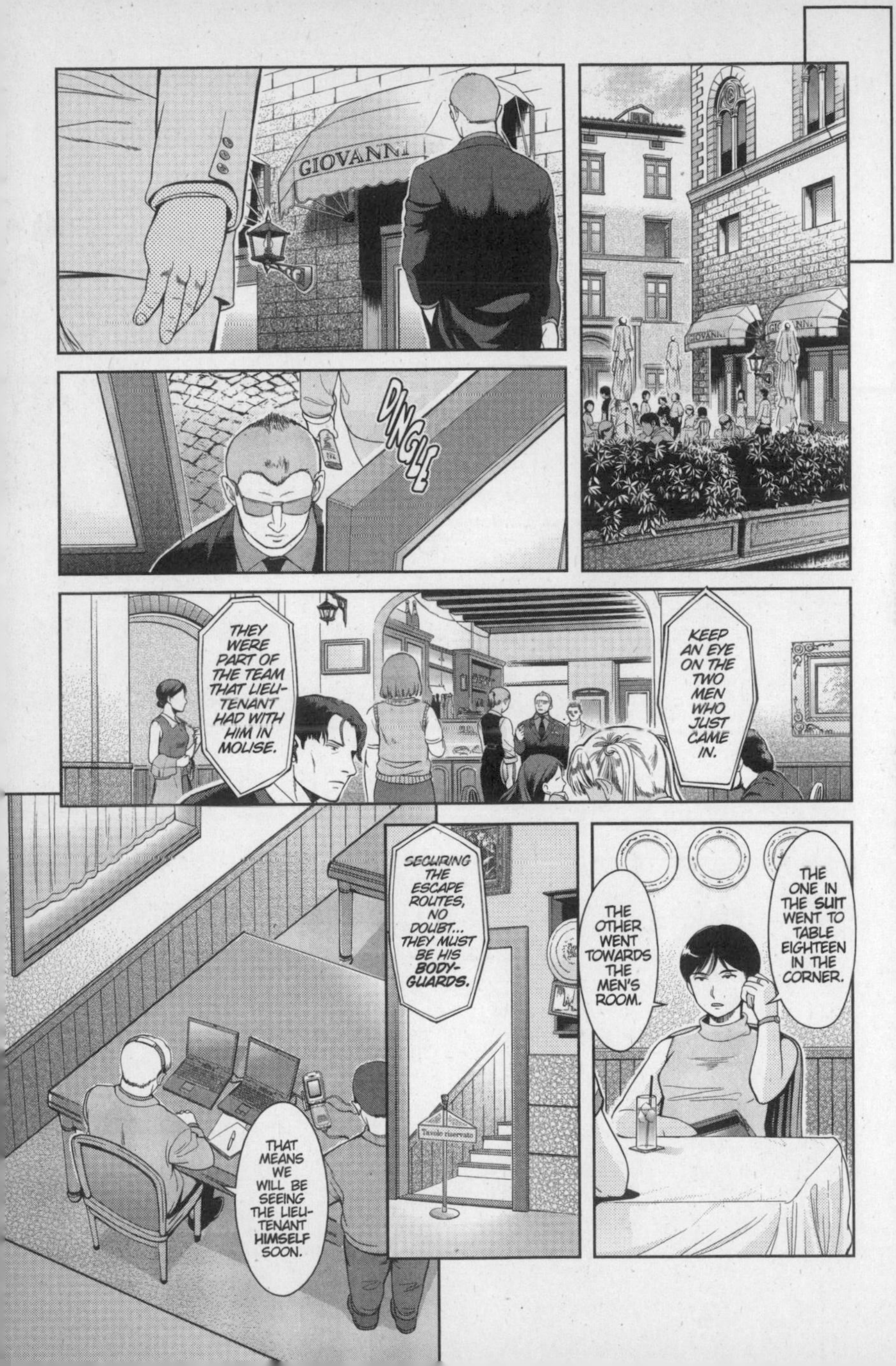
GIOVANNI
GIOVANNI
GIOVANNI
DINGLE
KEEP AN EYE ON THE TWO MEN WHO JUST CAME IN.
THEY WERE PART OF THE TEAM THAT LIEUTENANT HAD WITH HIM IN MOLISE.
THE ONE IN THE SUIT WENT TO TABLE EIGHTEEN IN THE CORNER.
THE OTHER WENT TOWARDS THE MEN'S ROOM.
SECURING THE ESCAPE ROUTES, NO DOUBT... THEY MUST BE HIS BODYGUARDS.
Tavolo riservato
THAT MEANS WE WILL BE SEEING THE LIEUTENANT HIMSELF SOON.

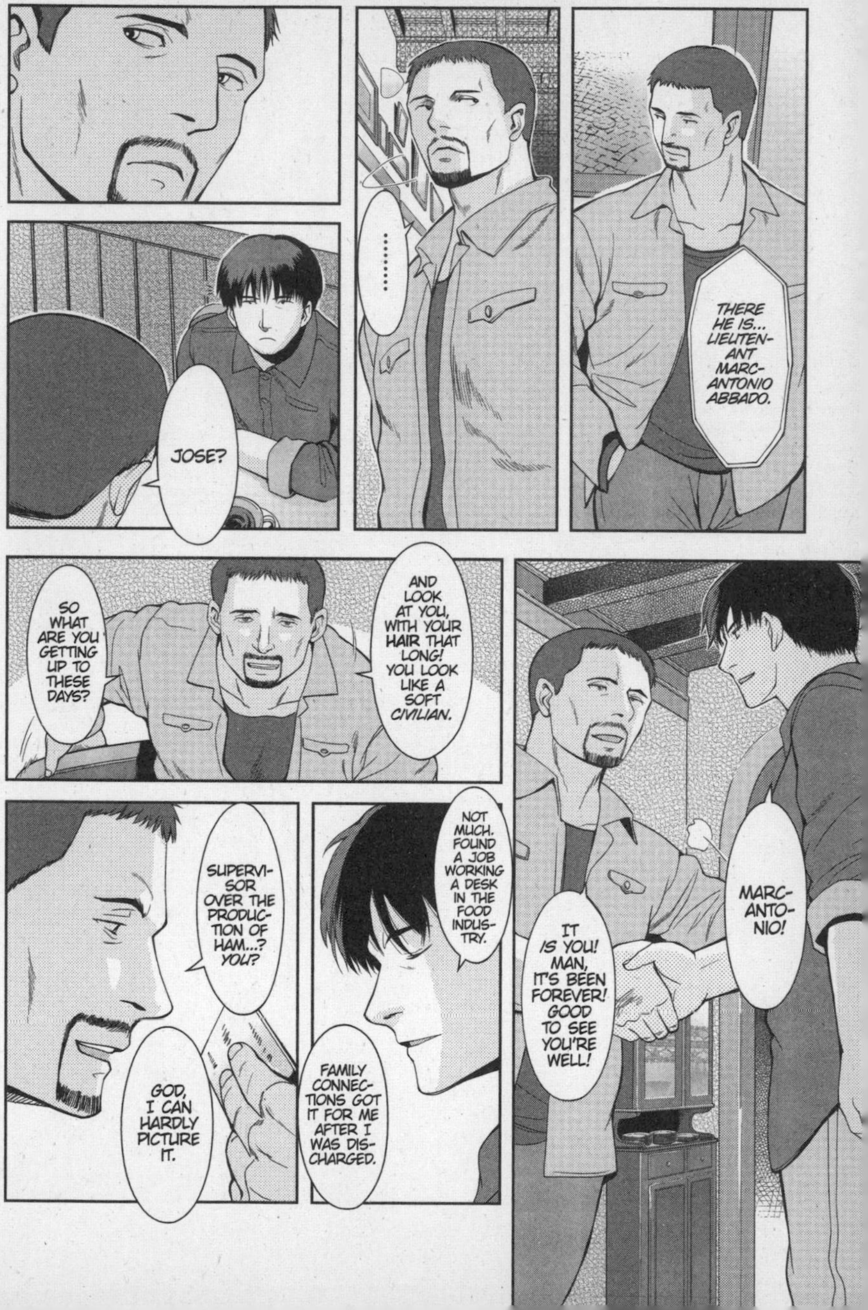
THERE HE IS... LIEUTEN-ANT MARC-ANTONIO ABBADO.
......
JOSE?
MARC-ANTO-NIO!
IT IS YOU! MAN, IT'S BEEN FOREVER! GOOD TO SEE YOU'RE WELL!
AND LOOK AT YOU, WITH YOUR HAIR THAT LONG! YOU LOOK LIKE A SOFT CIVILIAN.
SO WHAT ARE YOU GETTING UP TO THESE DAYS?
NOT MUCH. FOUND A JOB WORKING A DESK IN THE FOOD INDUS-TRY.
FAMILY CONNEC-TIONS GOT IT FOR ME AFTER I WAS DIS-CHARGED.
SUPERVI-SOR OVER THE PRODUC-TION OF HAM...? YOU?
GOD, I CAN HARDLY PICTURE IT.

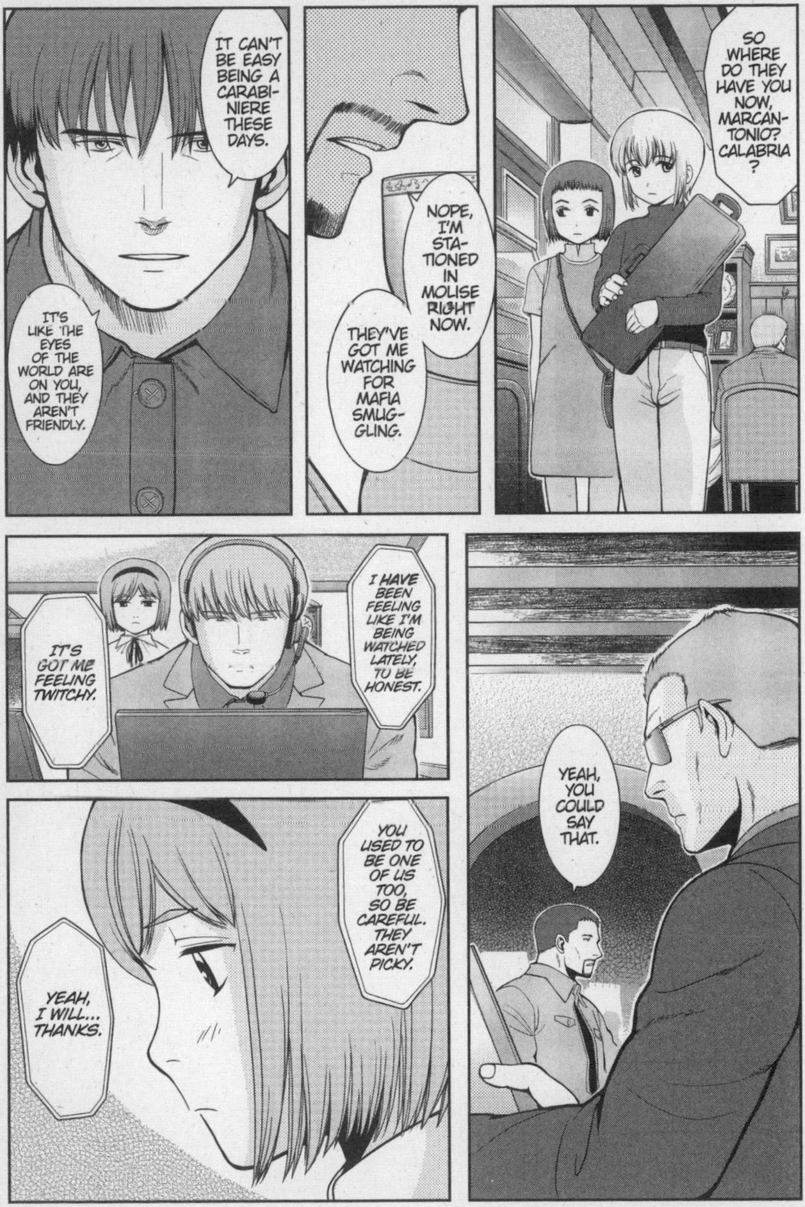
SO WHERE DO THEY HAVE YOU NOW, MARCANTONIO? CALABRIA?
NOPE, I'M STATIONED IN MOLISE RIGHT NOW.
THEY'VE GOT ME WATCHING FOR MAFIA SMUGGLING.
IT CAN'T BE EASY BEING A CARABINIERE THESE DAYS.
IT'S LIKE THE EYES OF THE WORLD ARE ON YOU, AND THEY AREN'T FRIENDLY.
YEAH, YOU COULD SAY THAT.
I HAVE BEEN FEELING LIKE I'M BEING WATCHED LATELY, TO BE HONEST.
IT'S GOT ME FEELING TWITCHY.
YOU USED TO BE ONE OF US TOO, SO BE CAREFUL. THEY AREN'T PICKY.
YEAH, I WILL... THANKS.

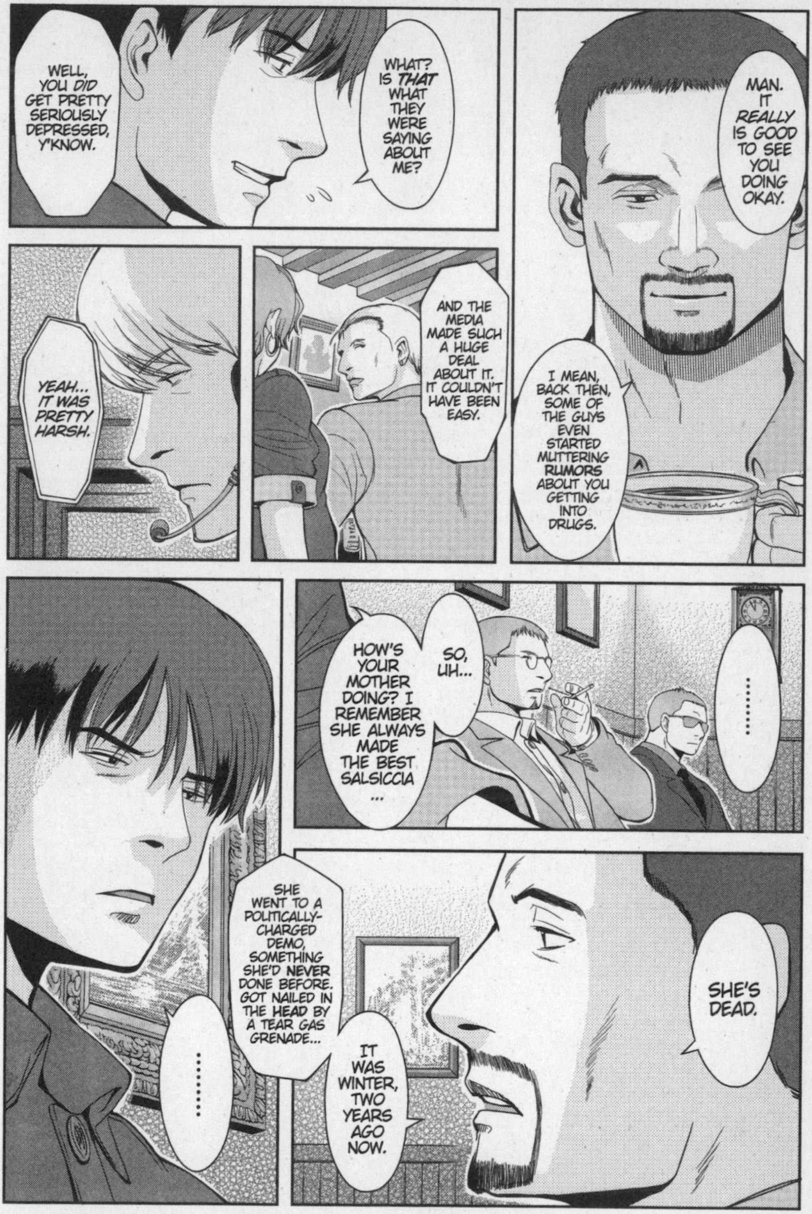
MAN. IT *REALLY* IS GOOD TO SEE YOU DOING OKAY.
I MEAN, BACK THEN, SOME OF THE GUYS EVEN STARTED MUTTERING RUMORS ABOUT YOU GETTING INTO DRUGS.
WHAT? IS *THAT* WHAT THEY WERE SAYING ABOUT ME?
WELL, YOU *DID* GET PRETTY SERIOUSLY DEPRESSED, Y'KNOW.
AND THE MEDIA MADE SUCH A HUGE DEAL ABOUT IT. IT COULDN'T HAVE BEEN EASY.
YEAH... IT WAS PRETTY HARSH.
....
SO, UH...
HOW'S YOUR MOTHER DOING? I REMEMBER SHE ALWAYS MADE THE BEST SALSICCIA ...
SHE'S DEAD.
SHE WENT TO A POLITICALLY-CHARGED DEMO, SOMETHING SHE'D NEVER DONE BEFORE. GOT NAILED IN THE HEAD BY A TEAR GAS GRENADE...
IT WAS WINTER, TWO YEARS AGO NOW.
....

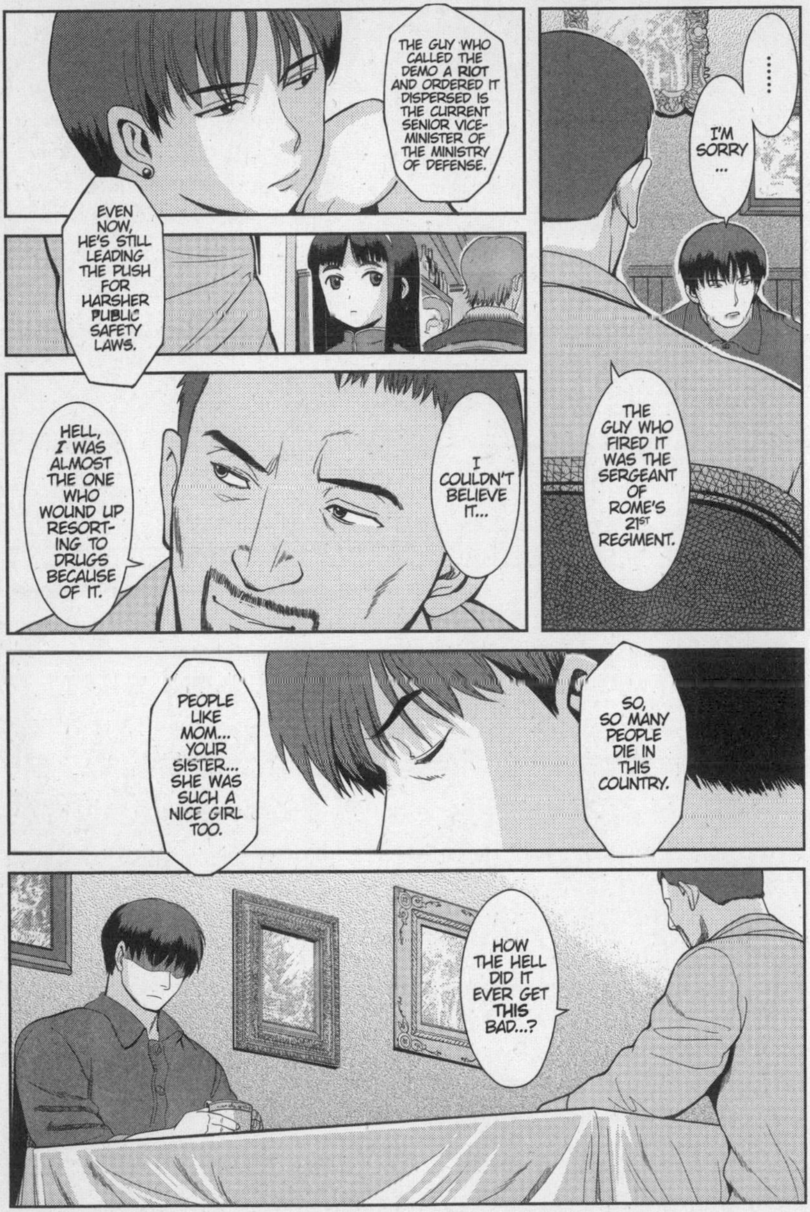
......
I'M SORRY...
THE GUY WHO FIRED IT WAS THE SERGEANT OF ROME'S 21ST REGIMENT.
THE GUY WHO CALLED THE DEMO A RIOT AND ORDERED IT DISPERSED IS THE CURRENT SENIOR VICE-MINISTER OF THE MINISTRY OF DEFENSE.
EVEN NOW, HE'S STILL LEADING THE PUSH FOR HARSHER PUBLIC SAFETY LAWS.
I COULDN'T BELIEVE IT...
HELL, I WAS ALMOST THE ONE WHO WOUND UP RESORTING TO DRUGS BECAUSE OF IT.
SO, SO MANY PEOPLE DIE IN THIS COUNTRY.
PEOPLE LIKE MOM... YOUR SISTER... SHE WAS SUCH A NICE GIRL TOO.
HOW THE HELL DID IT EVER GET THIS BAD...?

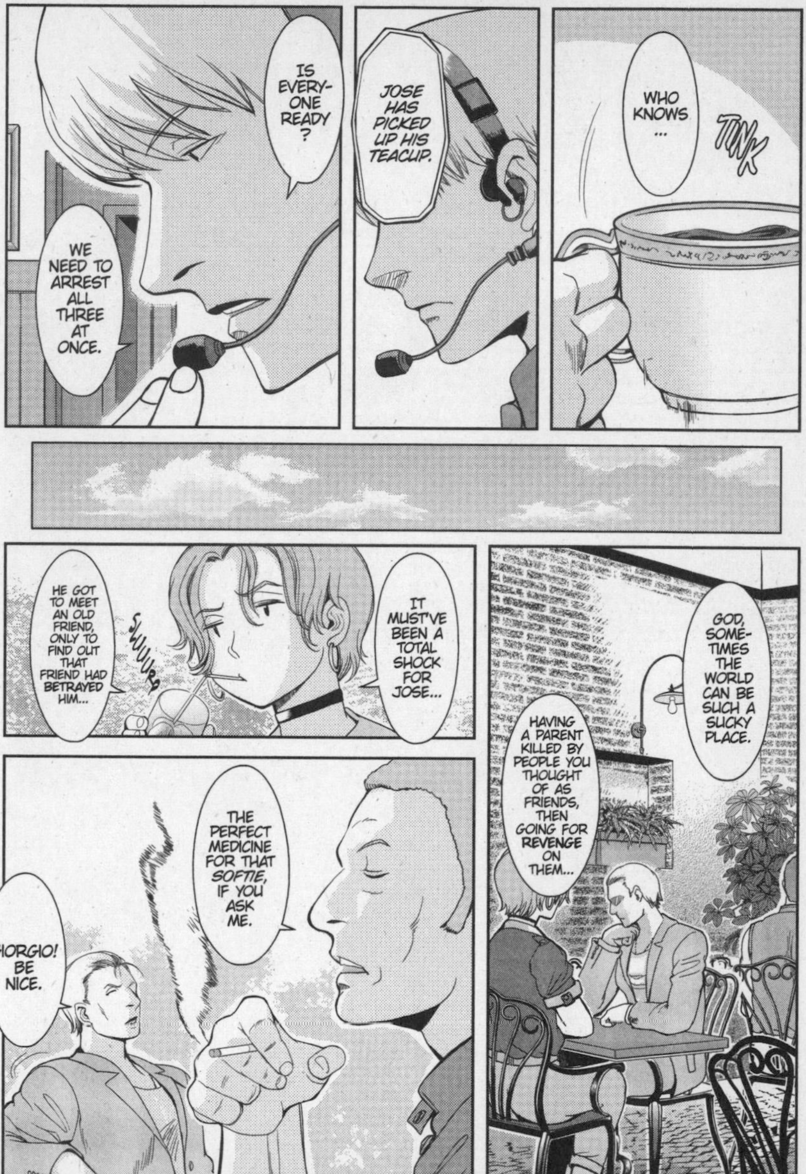
WHO KNOWS ...
TINK
JOSE HAS PICKED UP HIS TEACUP.
IS EVERY-ONE READY?
WE NEED TO ARREST ALL THREE AT ONCE.
GOD, SOME-TIMES THE WORLD CAN BE SUCH A SUCKY PLACE.
HAVING A PARENT KILLED BY PEOPLE YOU THOUGHT OF AS FRIENDS, THEN GOING FOR REVENGE ON THEM...
IT MUST'VE BEEN A TOTAL SHOCK FOR JOSE...
HE GOT TO MEET AN OLD FRIEND, ONLY TO FIND OUT THAT FRIEND HAD BETRAYED HIM...
THE PERFECT MEDICINE FOR THAT *SOFTIE*, IF YOU ASK ME.
GIORGIO! BE NICE.

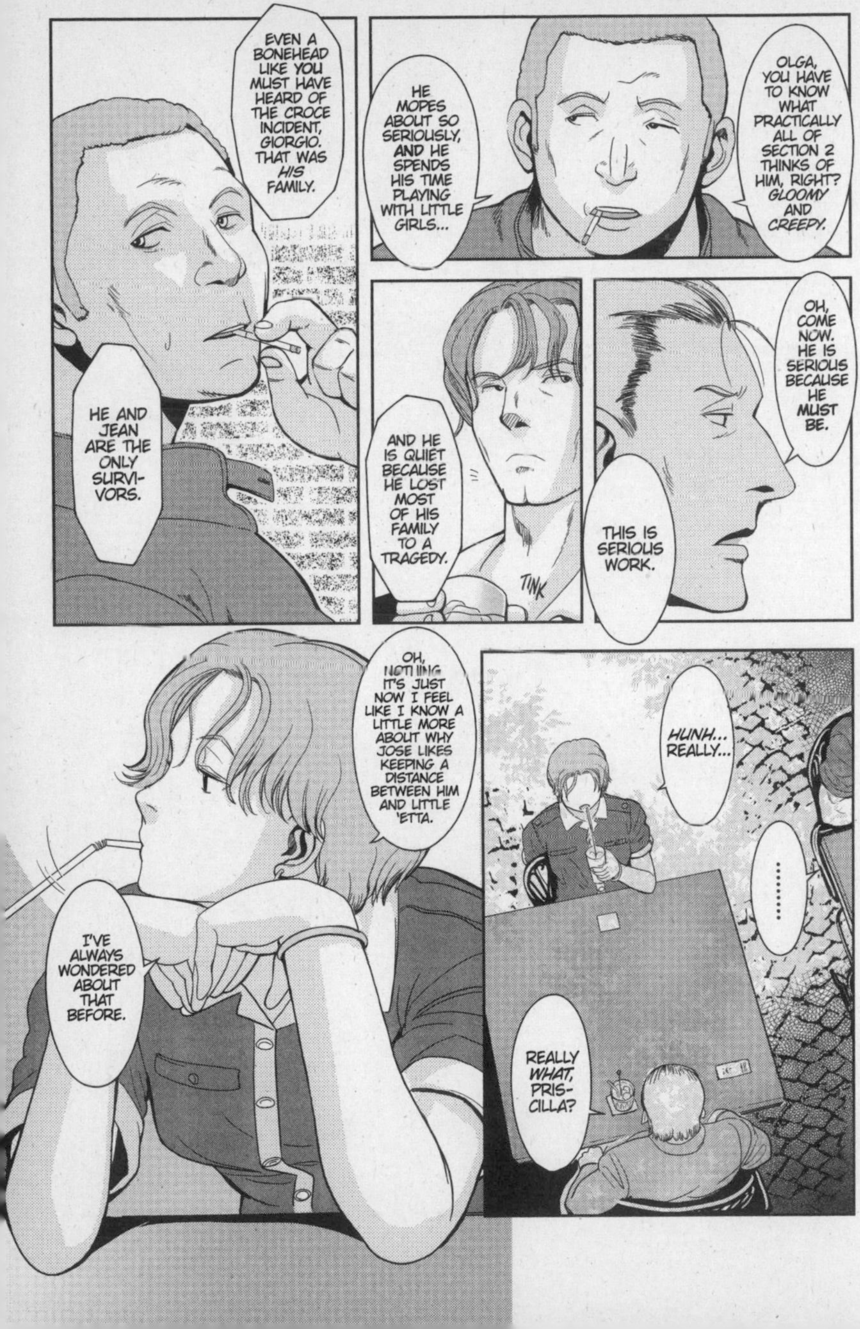

OLGA, YOU HAVE TO KNOW WHAT PRACTICALLY ALL OF SECTION 2 THINKS OF HIM, RIGHT? *GLOOMY* AND *CREEPY.*
HE MOPES ABOUT SO SERIOUSLY, AND HE SPENDS HIS TIME PLAYING WITH LITTLE GIRLS...
OH, COME NOW. HE IS SERIOUS BECAUSE HE MUST BE.
THIS IS SERIOUS WORK.
AND HE IS QUIET BECAUSE HE LOST MOST OF HIS FAMILY TO A TRAGEDY.
TINK
EVEN A BONEHEAD LIKE YOU MUST HAVE HEARD OF THE CROCE INCIDENT, GIORGIO. THAT WAS *HIS* FAMILY.
HE AND JEAN ARE THE ONLY SURVIVORS.
HUNH... REALLY...
......
REALLY *WHAT,* PRISCILLA?
OH, NOTHING. IT'S JUST NOW I FEEL LIKE I KNOW A LITTLE MORE ABOUT WHY JOSE LIKES KEEPING A DISTANCE BETWEEN HIM AND LITTLE 'ETTA.
I'VE ALWAYS WONDERED ABOUT THAT BEFORE.

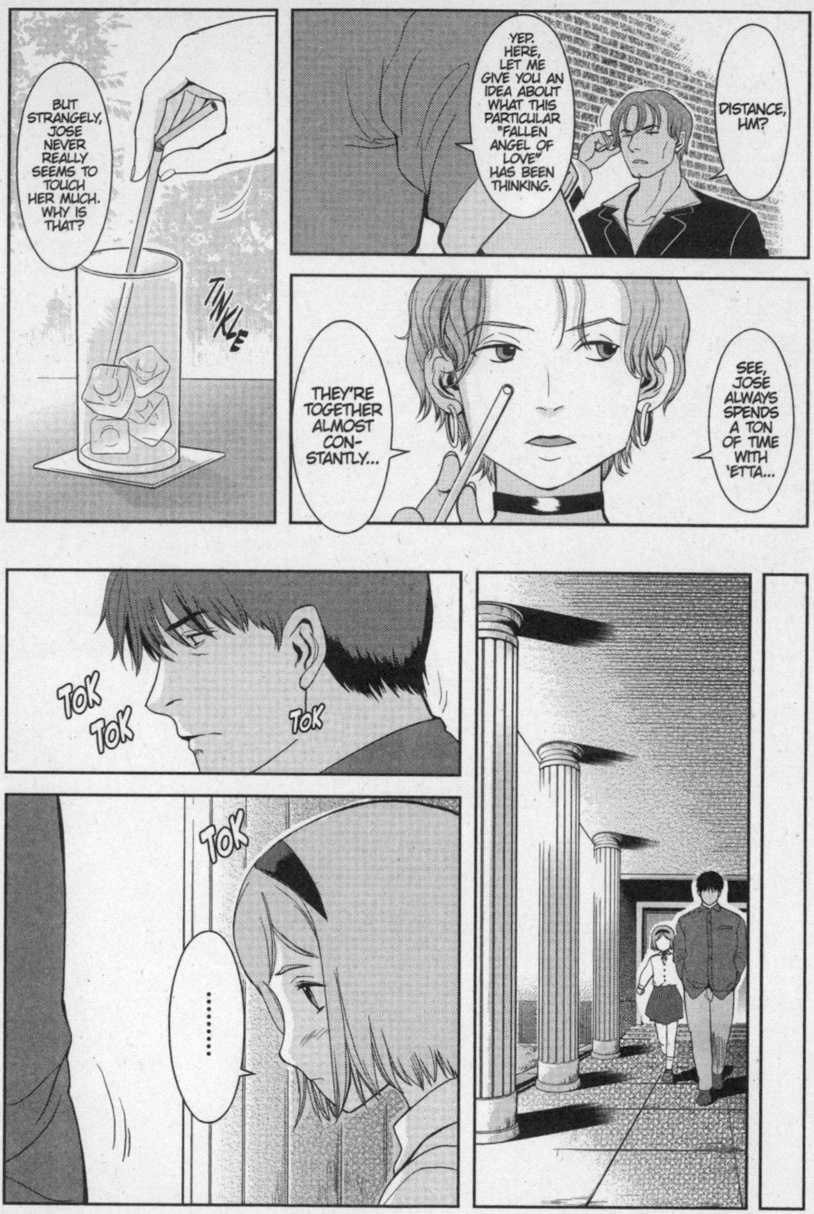
DISTANCE, HM?
YEP. HERE, LET ME GIVE YOU AN IDEA ABOUT WHAT THIS PARTICULAR "FALLEN ANGEL OF LOVE" HAS BEEN THINKING.
SEE, JOSE ALWAYS SPENDS A TON OF TIME WITH 'ETTA...
THEY'RE TOGETHER ALMOST CON-STANTLY...
BUT STRANGELY, JOSE NEVER REALLY SEEMS TO TOUCH HER MUCH. WHY IS THAT?
TINKLE
TOK
TOK
TOK
TOK
....

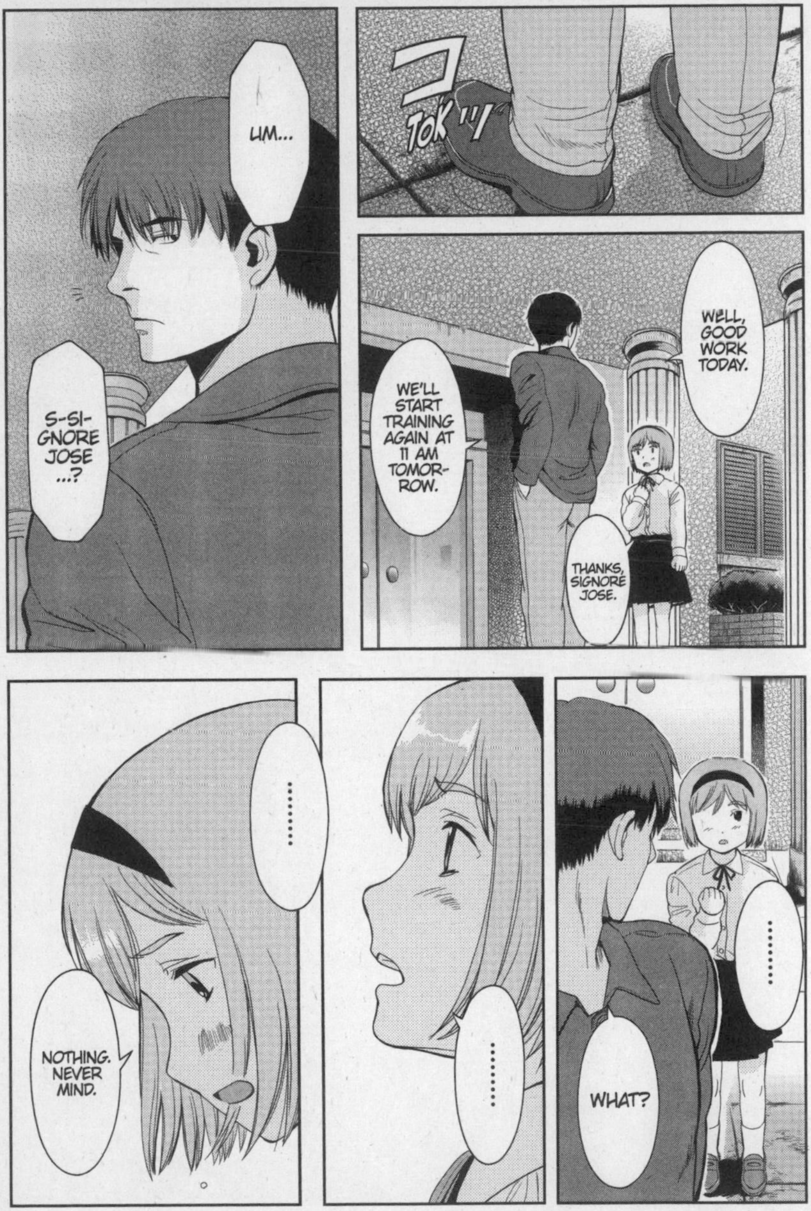
TOK
WELL, GOOD WORK TODAY.
WE'LL START TRAINING AGAIN AT 11 AM TOMORROW.
THANKS, SIGNORE JOSE.
UM...
S-SI-GNORE JOSE ...?
....
WHAT?
....
....
NOTHING. NEVER MIND.

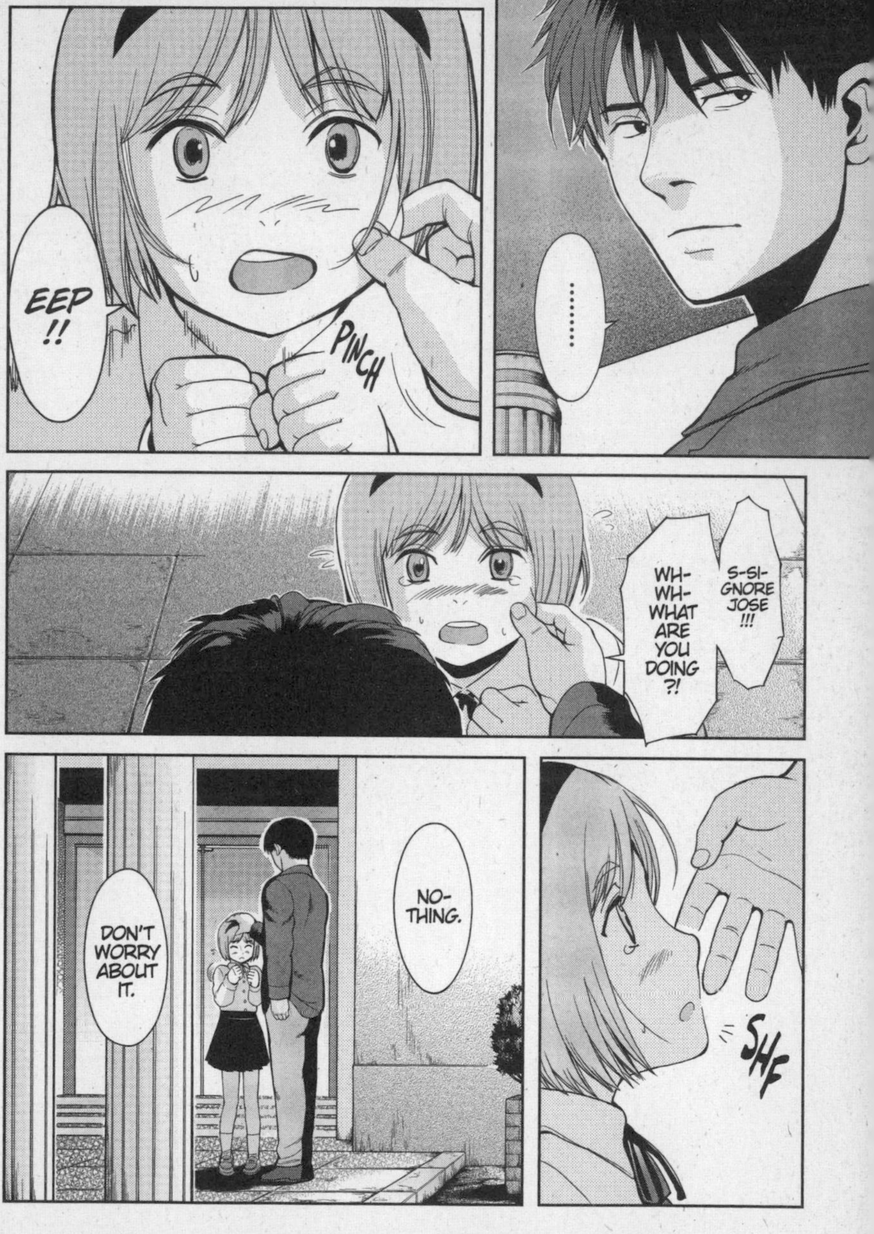
......
EEP!!
PINCH
S-SIGNORE JOSE!!!
WH-WH-WHAT ARE YOU DOING?!
SHF
NO-THING.
DON'T WORRY ABOUT IT.

GUNSLINGERGIRL.

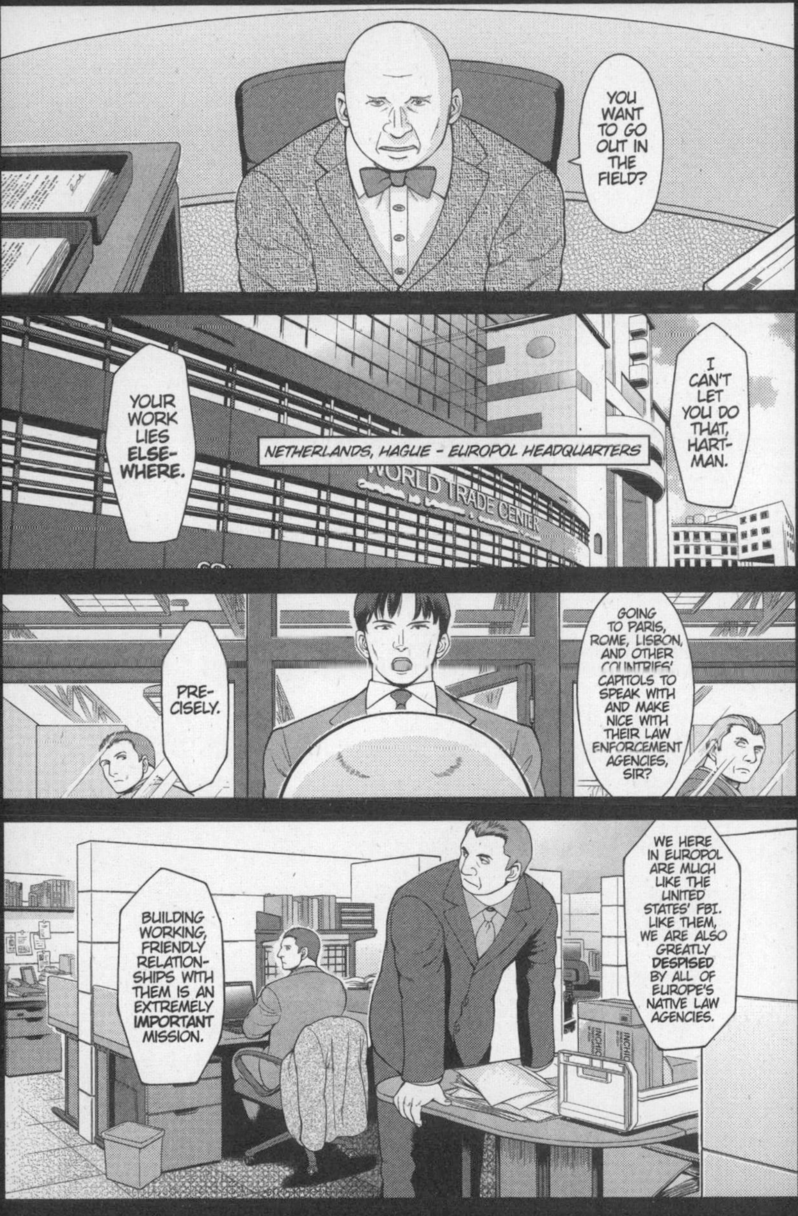
YOU WANT TO GO OUT IN THE FIELD?
I CAN'T LET YOU DO THAT, HART-MAN.
NETHERLANDS, HAGUE - EUROPOL HEADQUARTERS
WORLD TRADE CENTER
YOUR WORK LIES ELSE-WHERE.
GOING TO PARIS, ROME, LISBON, AND OTHER COUNTRIES' CAPITOLS TO SPEAK WITH AND MAKE NICE WITH THEIR LAW ENFORCEMENT AGENCIES, SIR?
PRE-CISELY.
WE HERE IN EUROPOL ARE MUCH LIKE THE UNITED STATES' FBI. LIKE THEM, WE ARE ALSO GREATLY DESPISED BY ALL OF EUROPE'S NATIVE LAW AGENCIES.
BUILDING WORKING, FRIENDLY RELATION-SHIPS WITH THEM IS AN EXTREMELY IMPORTANT MISSION.

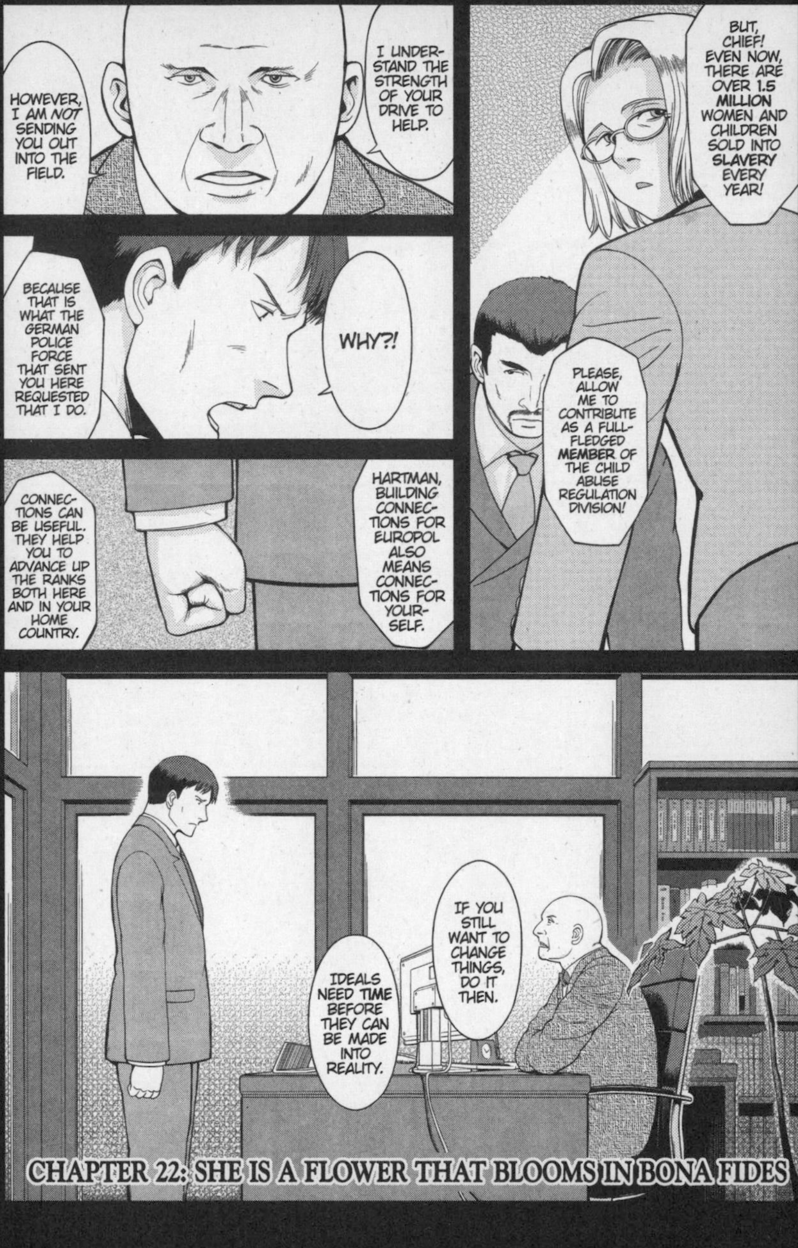
BUT, CHIEF! EVEN NOW, THERE ARE OVER 1.5 MILLION WOMEN AND CHILDREN SOLD INTO SLAVERY EVERY YEAR!
PLEASE, ALLOW ME TO CONTRIBUTE AS A FULL-FLEDGED MEMBER OF THE CHILD ABUSE REGULATION DIVISION!
I UNDERSTAND THE STRENGTH OF YOUR DRIVE TO HELP.
HOWEVER, I AM *NOT* SENDING YOU OUT INTO THE FIELD.
WHY?!
BECAUSE THAT IS WHAT THE GERMAN POLICE FORCE THAT SENT YOU HERE REQUESTED THAT I DO.
HARTMAN, BUILDING CONNECTIONS FOR EUROPOL ALSO MEANS CONNECTIONS FOR YOURSELF.
CONNECTIONS CAN BE USEFUL. THEY HELP YOU TO ADVANCE UP THE RANKS BOTH HERE AND IN YOUR HOME COUNTRY.
IF YOU STILL WANT TO CHANGE THINGS, DO IT THEN.
IDEALS NEED TIME BEFORE THEY CAN BE MADE INTO REALITY.

CHAPTER 22: SHE IS A FLOWER THAT BLOOMS IN BONA FIDES

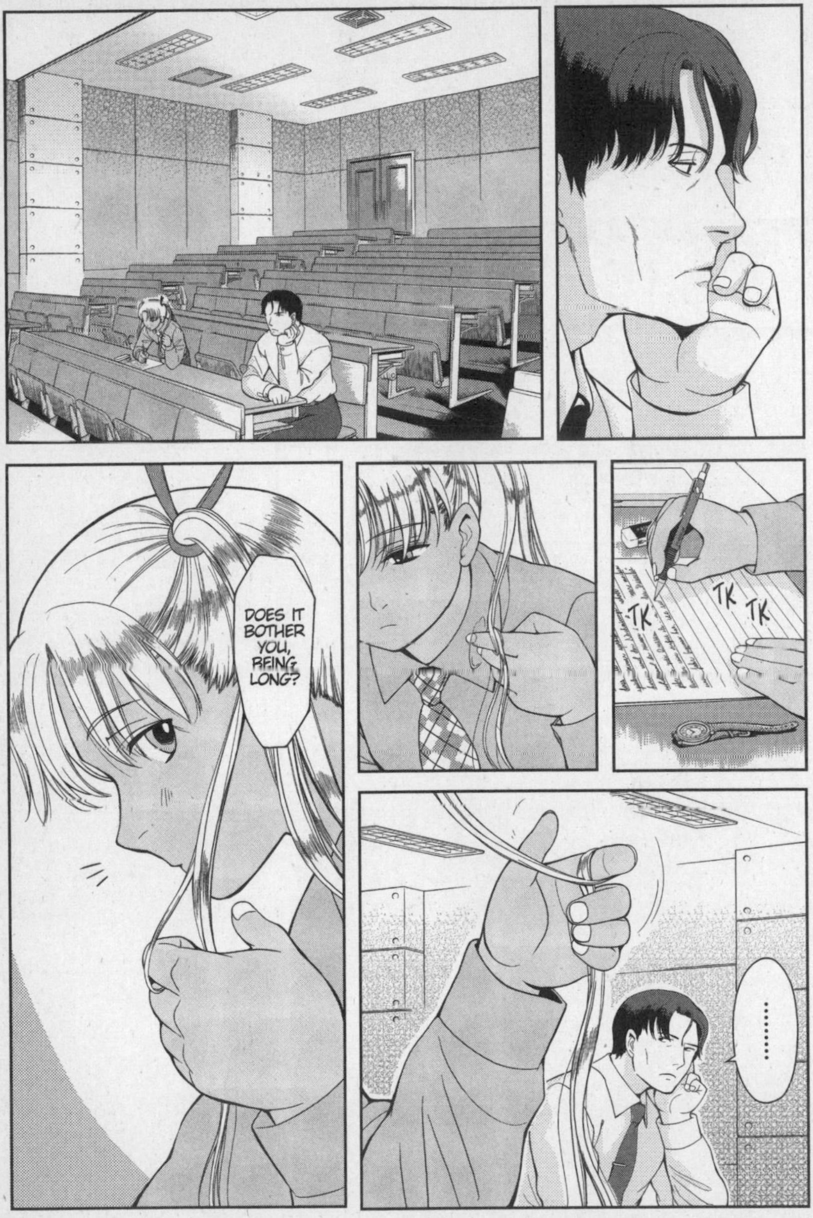
DOES IT BOTHER YOU, BEING LONG?
TK TK TK
......

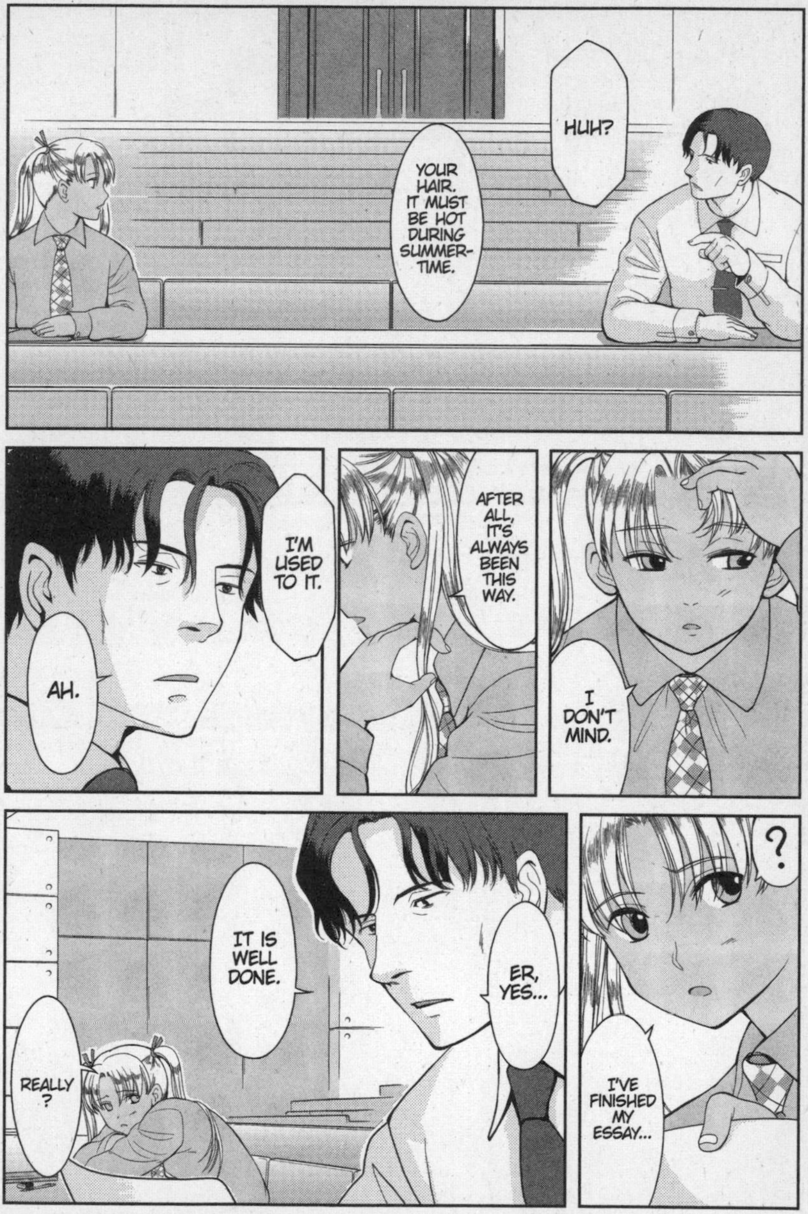
HUH?
YOUR HAIR. IT MUST BE HOT DURING SUMMER-TIME.
I DON'T MIND.
AFTER ALL, IT'S ALWAYS BEEN THIS WAY.
I'M USED TO IT.
AH.
?
I'VE FINISHED MY ESSAY...
ER, YES...
IT IS WELL DONE.
REALLY?

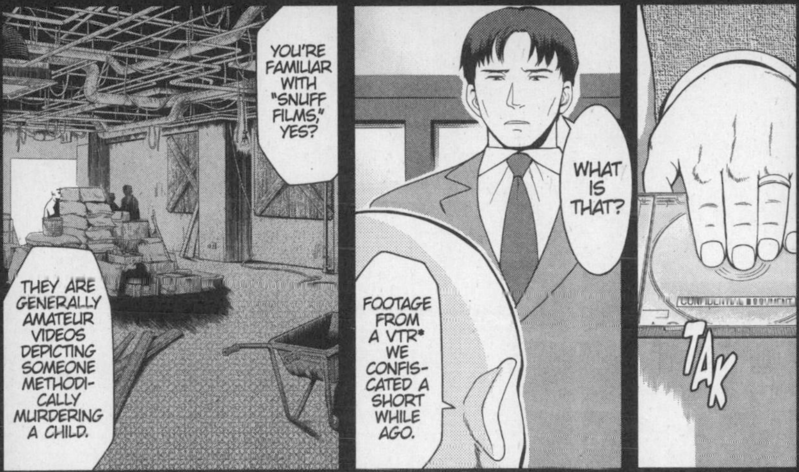
TAK
WHAT IS THAT?
FOOTAGE FROM A VTR* WE CONFISCATED A SHORT WHILE AGO.
CONFIDENTIAL DOCUMENT
YOU'RE FAMILIAR WITH "SNUFF FILMS," YES?
THEY ARE GENERALLY AMATEUR VIDEOS DEPICTING SOMEONE METHODICALLY MURDERING A CHILD.

*VTR = Video Tape Recorder

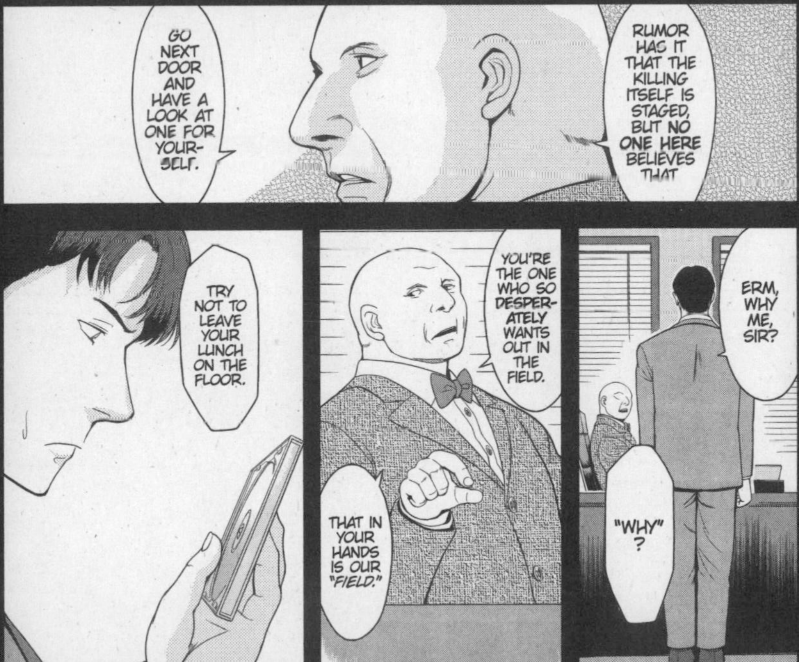
RUMOR HAS IT THAT THE KILLING ITSELF IS STAGED, BUT NO ONE HERE BELIEVES THAT
GO NEXT DOOR AND HAVE A LOOK AT ONE FOR YOURSELF.
ERM, WHY ME, SIR?
"WHY"?
YOU'RE THE ONE WHO SO DESPERATELY WANTS OUT IN THE FIELD.
THAT IN YOUR HANDS IS OUR "FIELD."
TRY NOT TO LEAVE YOUR LUNCH ON THE FLOOR.

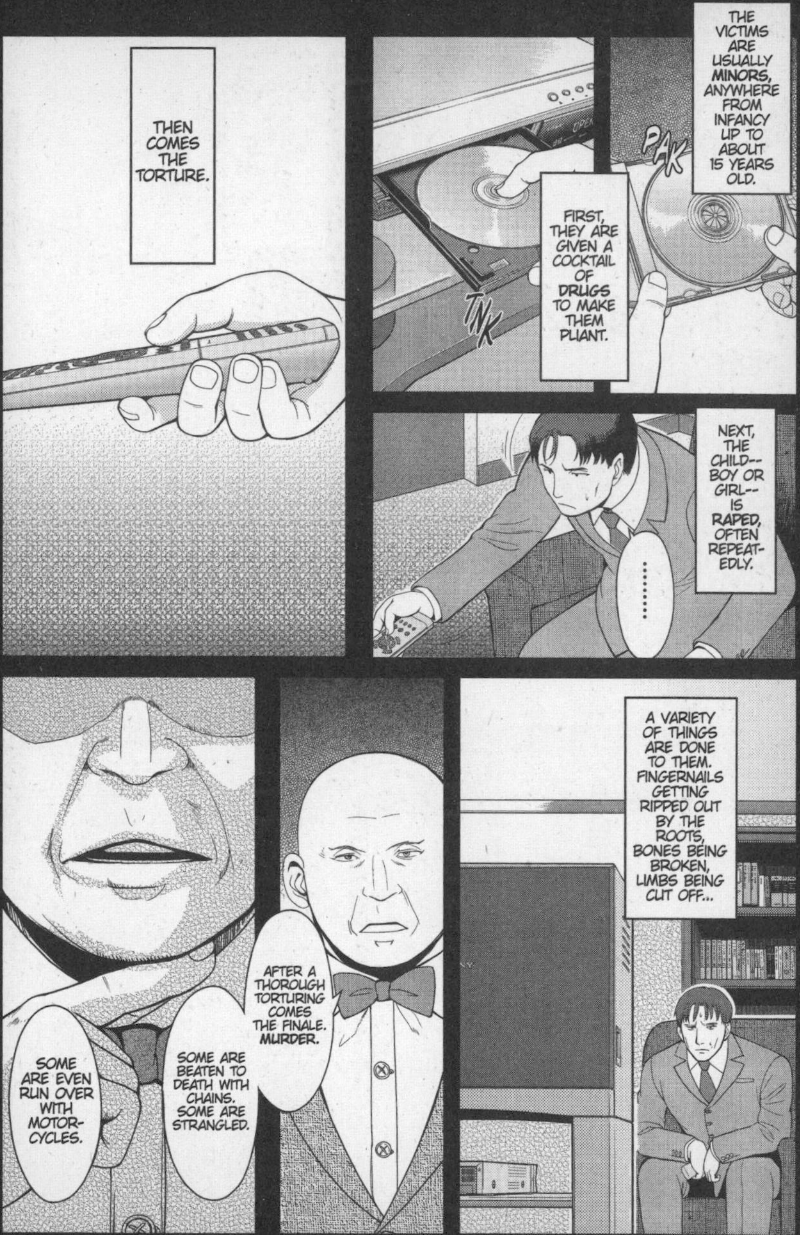
THE VICTIMS ARE USUALLY MINORS, ANYWHERE FROM INFANCY UP TO ABOUT 15 YEARS OLD.
PAK
FIRST, THEY ARE GIVEN A COCKTAIL OF DRUGS TO MAKE THEM PLIANT.
TNK
NEXT, THE CHILD--BOY OR GIRL--IS RAPED, OFTEN REPEATEDLY.
......
THEN COMES THE TORTURE.
A VARIETY OF THINGS ARE DONE TO THEM. FINGERNAILS GETTING RIPPED OUT BY THE ROOTS, BONES BEING BROKEN, LIMBS BEING CUT OFF...
AFTER A THOROUGH TORTURING COMES THE FINALE. MURDER.
SOME ARE BEATEN TO DEATH WITH CHAINS. SOME ARE STRANGLED.
SOME ARE EVEN RUN OVER WITH MOTORCYCLES.

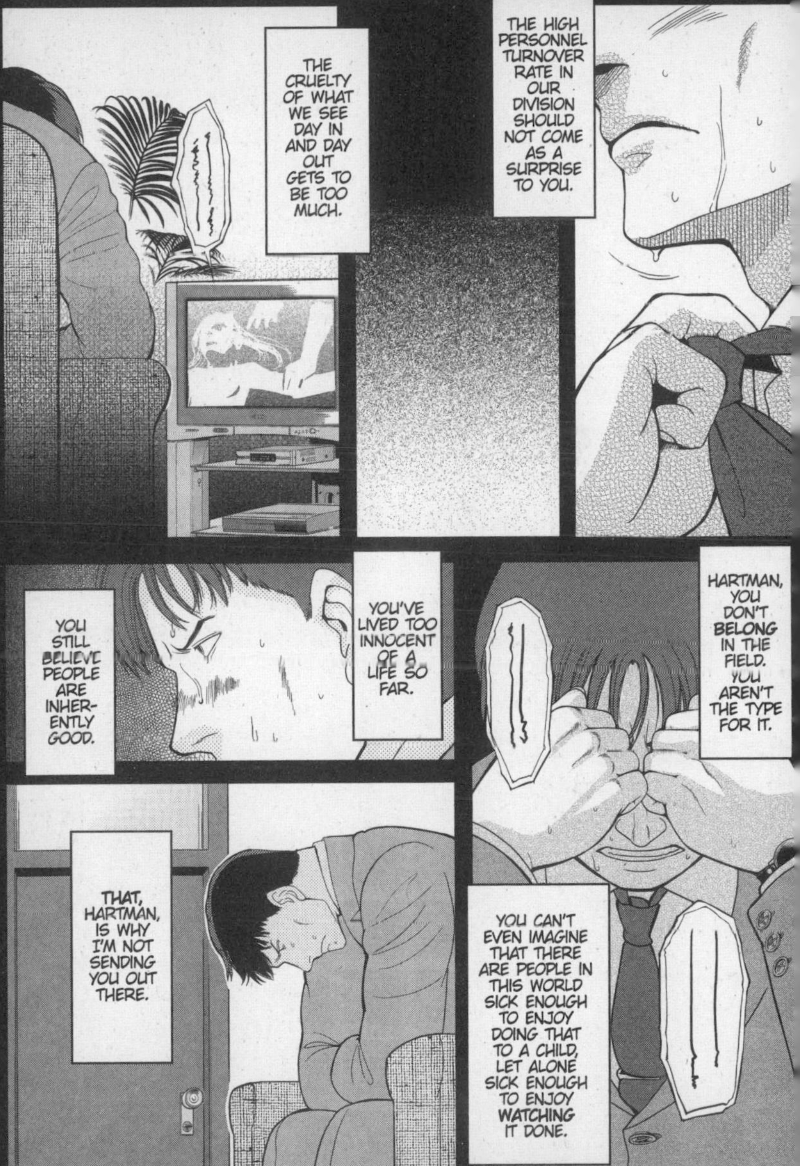
THE HIGH PERSONNEL TURNOVER RATE IN OUR DIVISION SHOULD NOT COME AS A SURPRISE TO YOU.
THE CRUELTY OF WHAT WE SEE DAY IN AND DAY OUT GETS TO BE TOO MUCH.
HARTMAN, YOU DON'T BELONG IN THE FIELD. YOU AREN'T THE TYPE FOR IT.
YOU CAN'T EVEN IMAGINE THAT THERE ARE PEOPLE IN THIS WORLD SICK ENOUGH TO ENJOY DOING THAT TO A CHILD, LET ALONE SICK ENOUGH TO ENJOY WATCHING IT DONE.
YOU'VE LIVED TOO INNOCENT OF A LIFE SO FAR.
YOU STILL BELIEVE PEOPLE ARE INHERENTLY GOOD.
THAT, HARTMAN, IS WHY I'M NOT SENDING YOU OUT THERE.

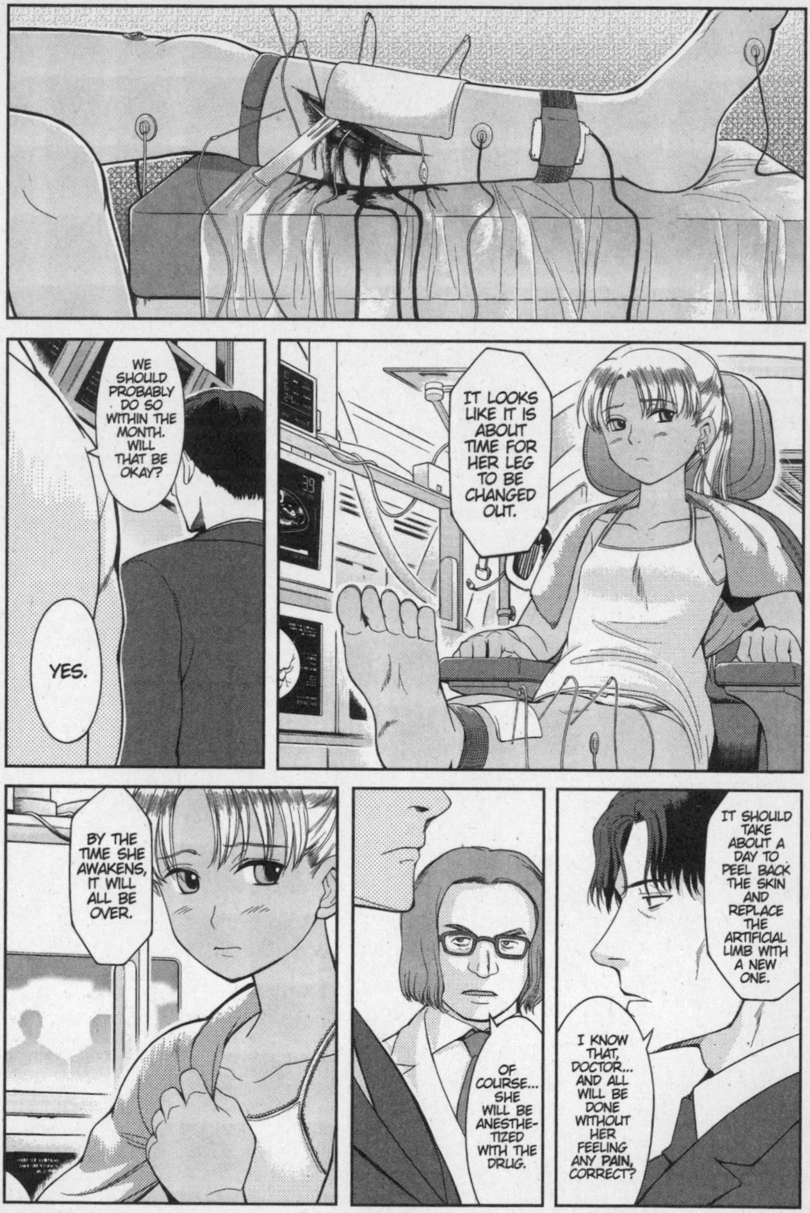
IT LOOKS LIKE IT IS ABOUT TIME FOR HER LEG TO BE CHANGED OUT.
WE SHOULD PROBABLY DO SO WITHIN THE MONTH. WILL THAT BE OKAY?
YES.
IT SHOULD TAKE ABOUT A DAY TO PEEL BACK THE SKIN AND REPLACE THE ARTIFICIAL LIMB WITH A NEW ONE.
I KNOW THAT, DOCTOR... AND ALL WILL BE DONE WITHOUT HER FEELING ANY PAIN, CORRECT?
OF COURSE... SHE WILL BE ANESTHE-TIZED WITH THE DRUG.
BY THE TIME SHE AWAKENS, IT WILL ALL BE OVER.

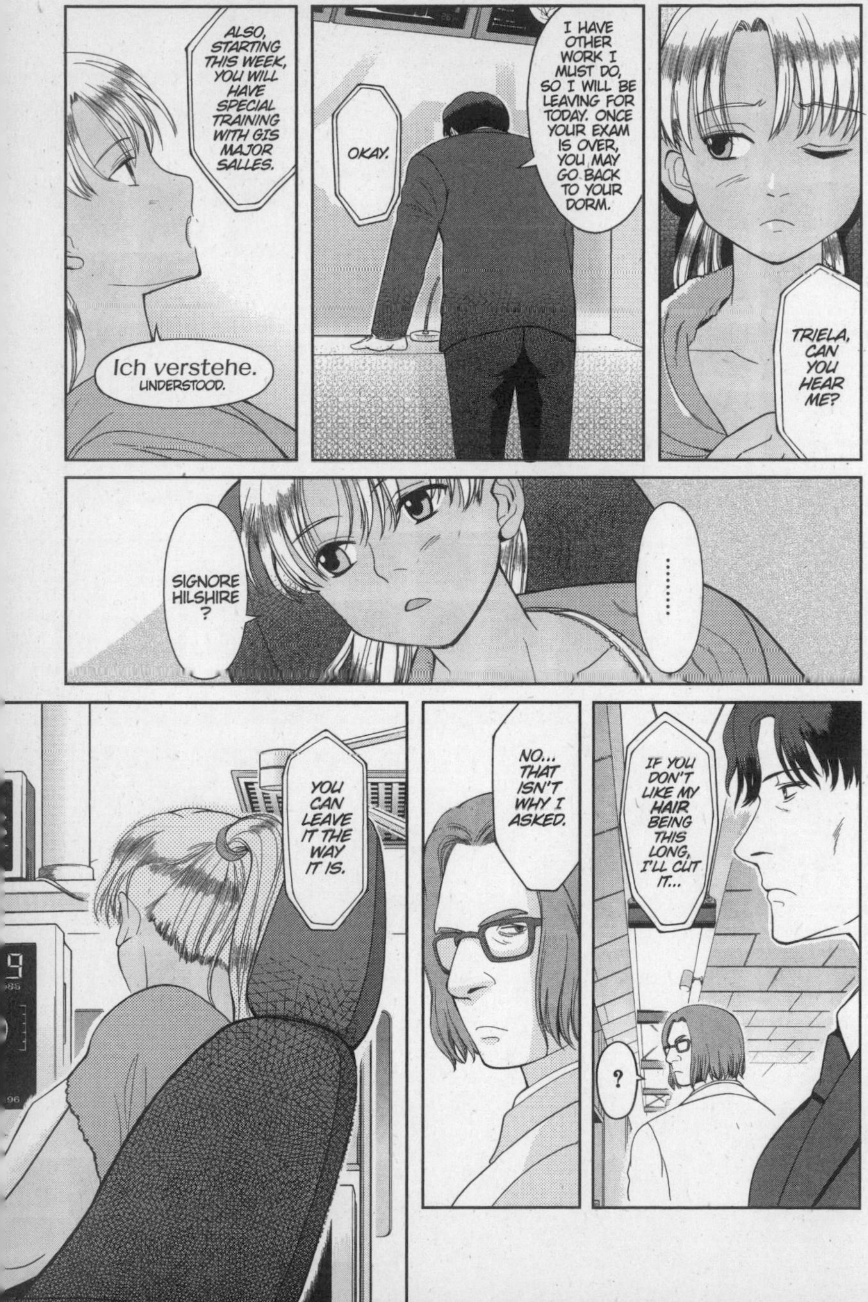
TRIELA, CAN YOU HEAR ME?
I HAVE OTHER WORK I MUST DO, SO I WILL BE LEAVING FOR TODAY. ONCE YOUR EXAM IS OVER, YOU MAY GO BACK TO YOUR DORM.
OKAY.
ALSO, STARTING THIS WEEK, YOU WILL HAVE SPECIAL TRAINING WITH GIS MAJOR SALLES.
Ich verstehe.
UNDERSTOOD.
......
SIGNORE HILSHIRE?
IF YOU DON'T LIKE MY HAIR BEING THIS LONG, I'LL CUT IT...
?
NO... THAT ISN'T WHY I ASKED.
YOU CAN LEAVE IT THE WAY IT IS.

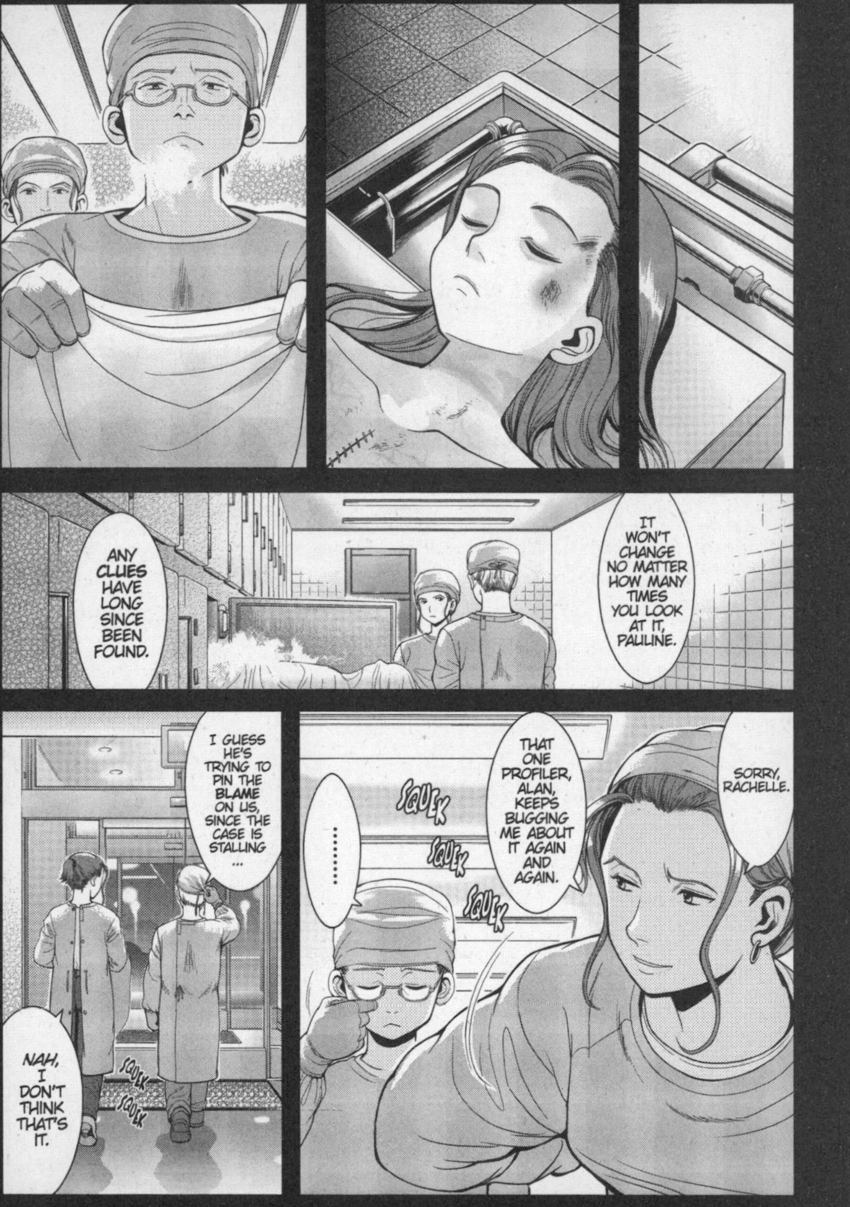
IT WON'T CHANGE NO MATTER HOW MANY TIMES YOU LOOK AT IT, PAULINE.
ANY CLUES HAVE LONG SINCE BEEN FOUND.
SORRY, RACHELLE.
THAT ONE PROFILER, ALAN, KEEPS BUGGING ME ABOUT IT AGAIN AND AGAIN.
SQUEK
SQUEK
SQUEK
......
I GUESS HE'S TRYING TO PIN THE BLAME ON US, SINCE THE CASE IS STALLING ...
NAH, I DON'T THINK THAT'S IT.
SQUEK
SQUEK

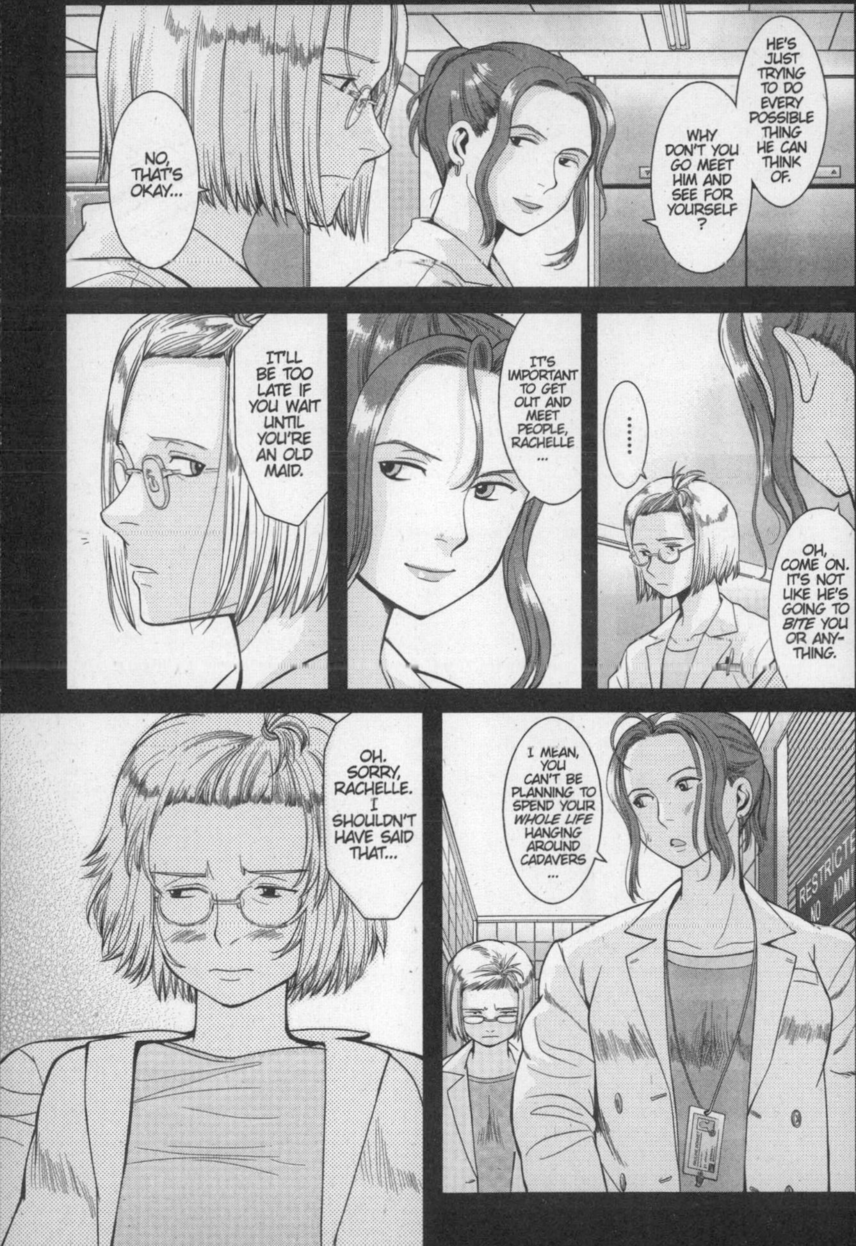
HE'S JUST TRYING TO DO EVERY POSSIBLE THING HE CAN THINK OF.
WHY DON'T YOU GO MEET HIM AND SEE FOR YOURSELF?
NO, THAT'S OKAY...
OH, COME ON. IT'S NOT LIKE HE'S GOING TO *BITE* YOU OR ANY-THING.
......
IT'S IMPORTANT TO GET OUT AND MEET PEOPLE, RACHELLE...
IT'LL BE TOO LATE IF YOU WAIT UNTIL YOU'RE AN OLD MAID.
I MEAN, YOU CAN'T BE PLANNING TO SPEND YOUR *WHOLE LIFE* HANGING AROUND CADAVERS...
OH. SORRY, RACHELLE. I SHOULDN'T HAVE SAID THAT...

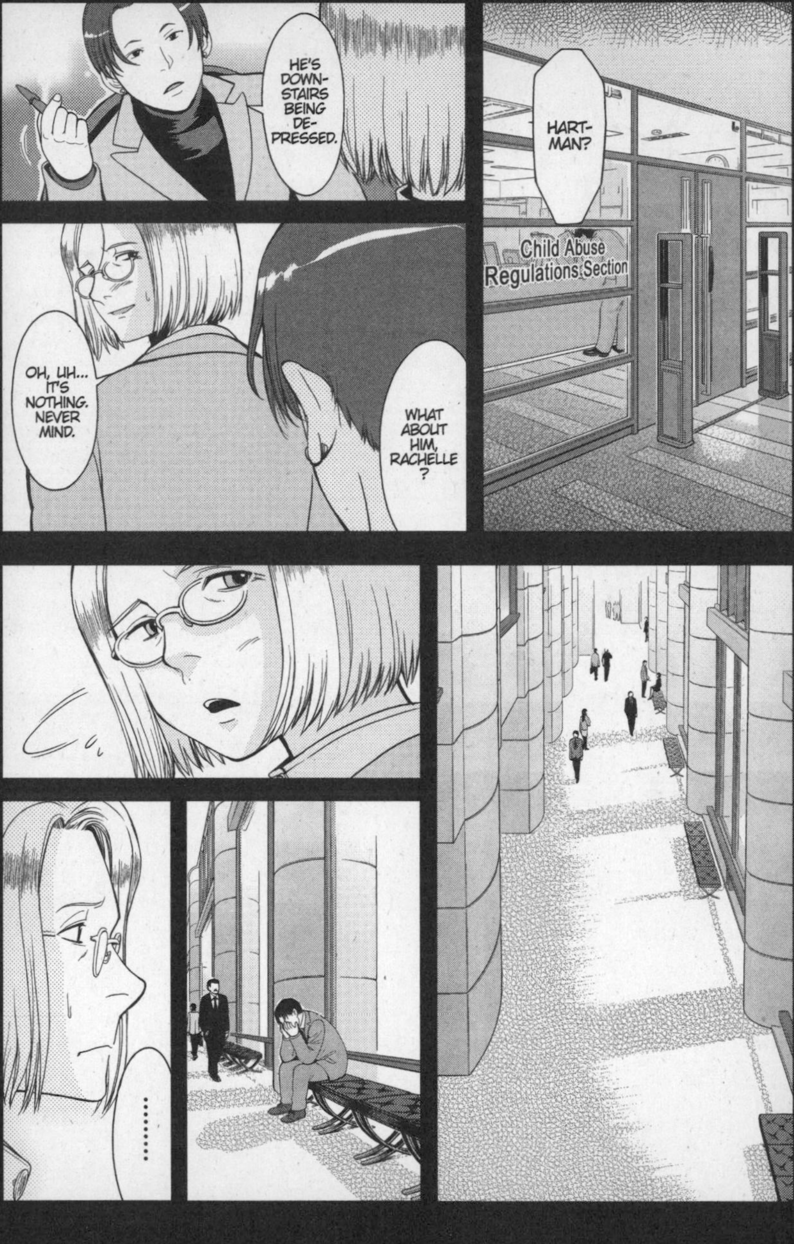
HART-MAN?
Child Abuse Regulations Section
HE'S DOWN-STAIRS BEING DE-PRESSED.
WHAT ABOUT HIM, RACHELLE?
OH, UH... IT'S NOTHING. NEVER MIND.
....

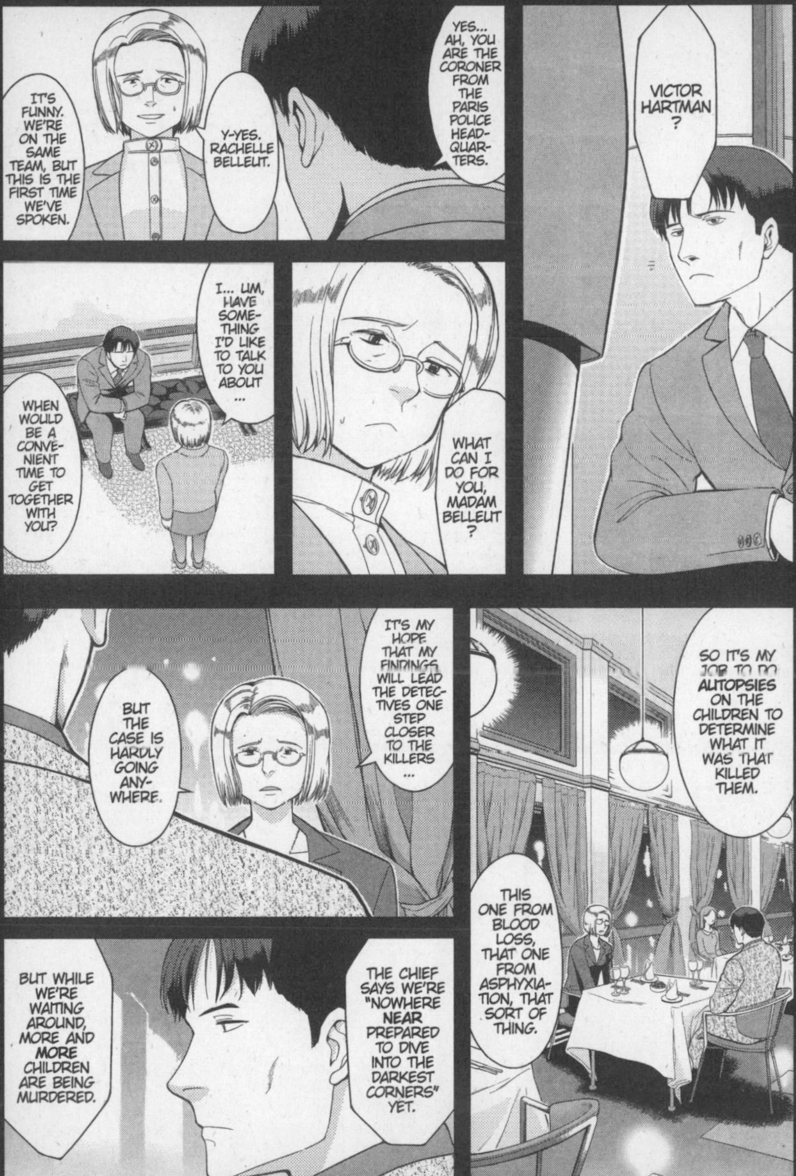
VICTOR HARTMAN?
YES... AH, YOU ARE THE CORONER FROM THE PARIS POLICE HEADQUARTERS.
Y-YES. RACHELLE BELLEUT.
IT'S FUNNY. WE'RE ON THE SAME TEAM, BUT THIS IS THE FIRST TIME WE'VE SPOKEN.
WHAT CAN I DO FOR YOU, MADAM BELLEUT?
I... UM, HAVE SOMETHING I'D LIKE TO TALK TO YOU ABOUT...
WHEN WOULD BE A CONVENIENT TIME TO GET TOGETHER WITH YOU?
SO IT'S MY JOB TO DO AUTOPSIES ON THE CHILDREN TO DETERMINE WHAT IT WAS THAT KILLED THEM.
THIS ONE FROM BLOOD LOSS, THAT ONE FROM ASPHYXIATION, THAT SORT OF THING.
IT'S MY HOPE THAT MY FINDINGS WILL LEAD THE DETECTIVES ONE STEP CLOSER TO THE KILLERS...
BUT THE CASE IS HARDLY GOING ANYWHERE.
THE CHIEF SAYS WE'RE "NOWHERE NEAR PREPARED TO DIVE INTO THE DARKEST CORNERS" YET.
BUT WHILE WE'RE WAITING AROUND, MORE AND MORE CHILDREN ARE BEING MURDERED.

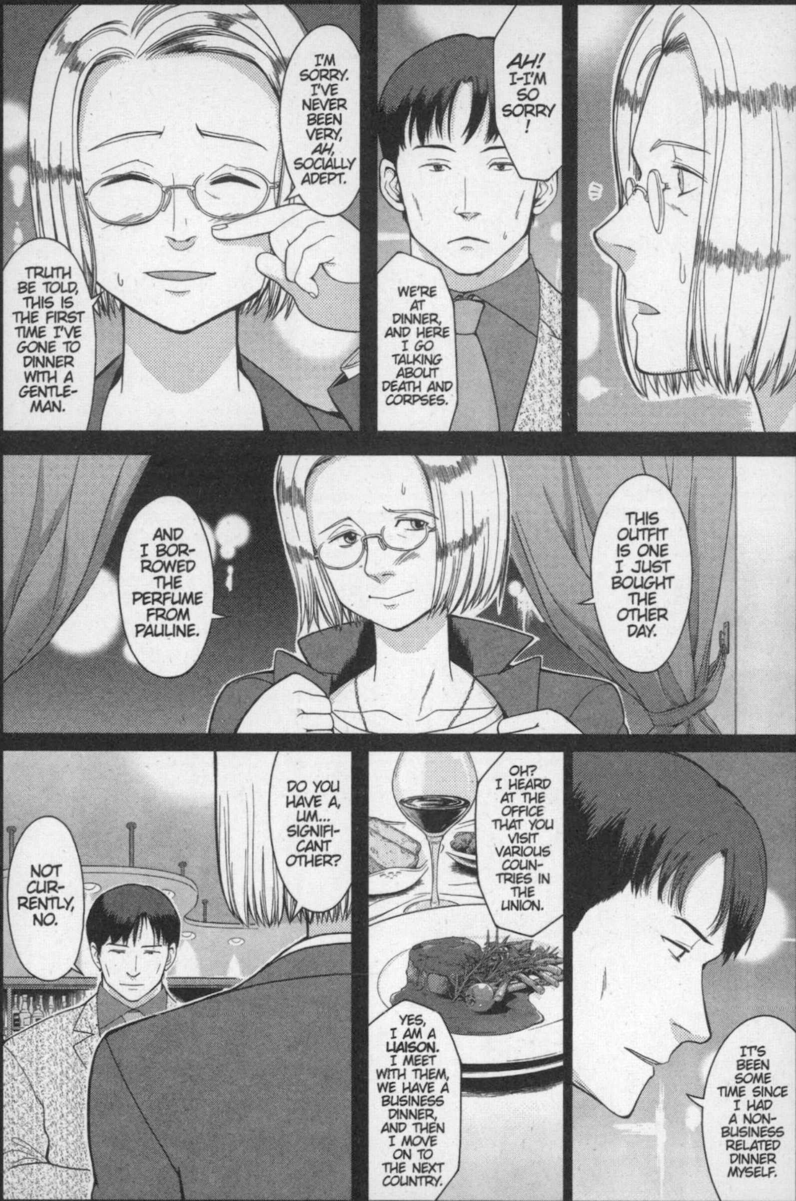
AH! I-I'M SO SORRY!
WE'RE AT DINNER, AND HERE I GO TALKING ABOUT DEATH AND CORPSES.
I'M SORRY. I'VE NEVER BEEN VERY, AH, SOCIALLY ADEPT.
TRUTH BE TOLD, THIS IS THE FIRST TIME I'VE GONE TO DINNER WITH A GENTLEMAN.
THIS OUTFIT IS ONE I JUST BOUGHT THE OTHER DAY.
AND I BORROWED THE PERFUME FROM PAULINE.
IT'S BEEN SOME TIME SINCE I HAD A NON-BUSINESS RELATED DINNER MYSELF.
OH? I HEARD AT THE OFFICE THAT YOU VISIT VARIOUS COUNTRIES IN THE UNION.
YES, I AM A LIAISON. I MEET WITH THEM, WE HAVE A BUSINESS DINNER, AND THEN I MOVE ON TO THE NEXT COUNTRY.
DO YOU HAVE A, UM... SIGNIFICANT OTHER?
NOT CURRENTLY, NO.

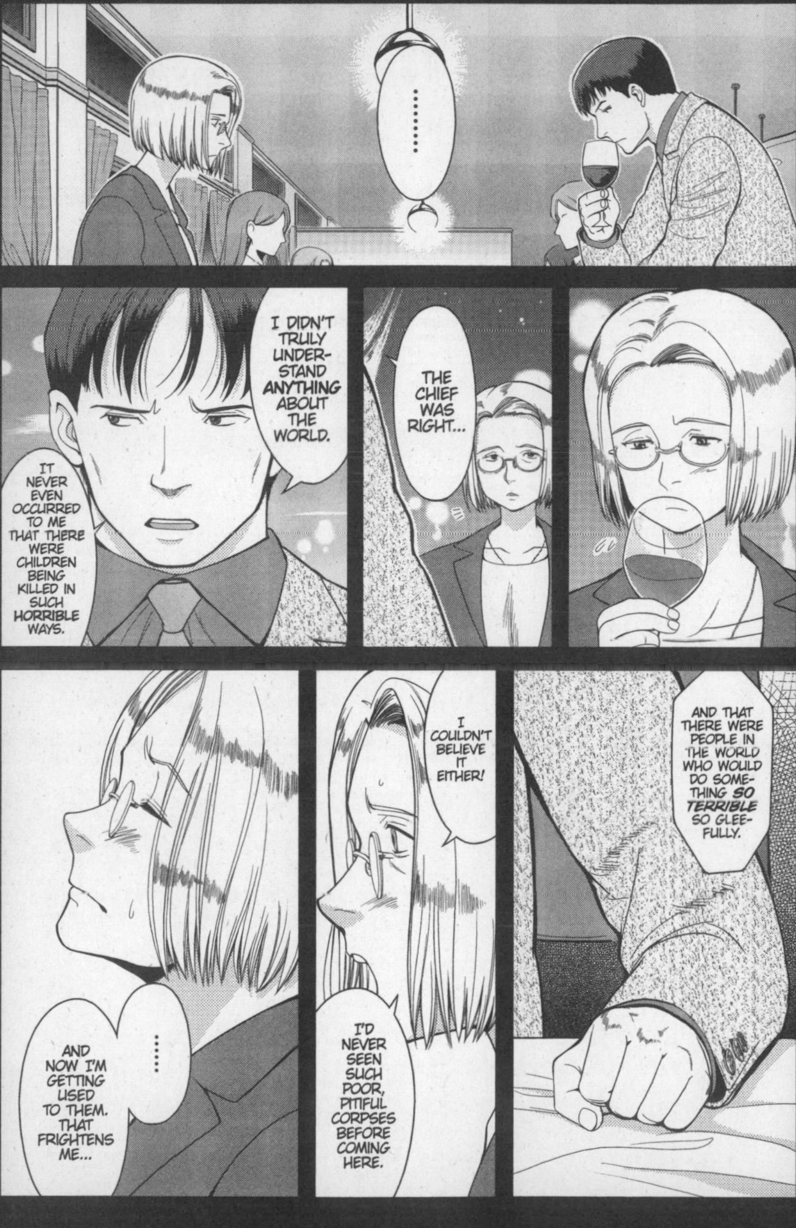
......
THE CHIEF WAS RIGHT...
I DIDN'T TRULY UNDERSTAND ANYTHING ABOUT THE WORLD.
IT NEVER EVEN OCCURRED TO ME THAT THERE WERE CHILDREN BEING KILLED IN SUCH HORRIBLE WAYS.
AND THAT THERE WERE PEOPLE IN THE WORLD WHO WOULD DO SOMETHING SO TERRIBLE SO GLEEFULLY.
I COULDN'T BELIEVE IT EITHER!
I'D NEVER SEEN SUCH POOR, PITIFUL CORPSES BEFORE COMING HERE.
......
AND NOW I'M GETTING USED TO THEM. THAT FRIGHTENS ME...

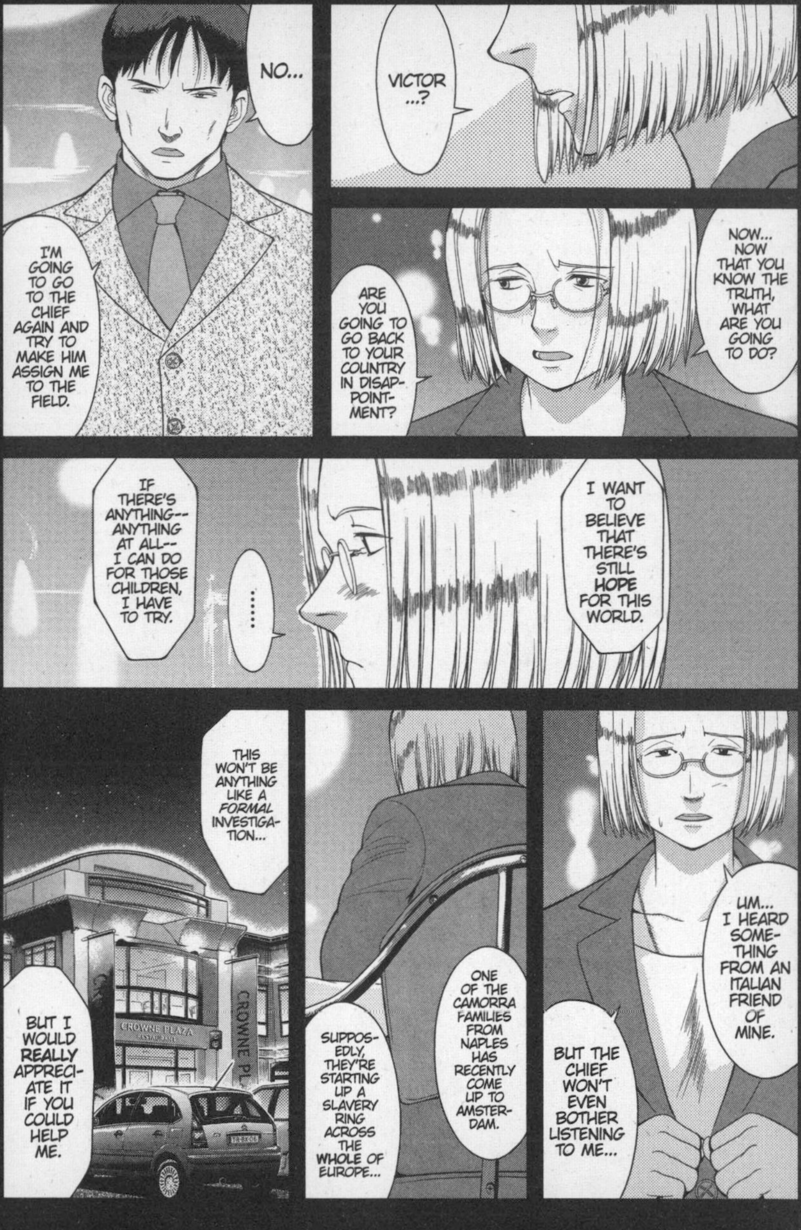
VICTOR ...?
NOW... NOW THAT YOU KNOW THE TRUTH, WHAT ARE YOU GOING TO DO?
ARE YOU GOING TO GO BACK TO YOUR COUNTRY IN DISAPPOINTMENT?
NO...
I'M GOING TO GO TO THE CHIEF AGAIN AND TRY TO MAKE HIM ASSIGN ME TO THE FIELD.
I WANT TO BELIEVE THAT THERE'S STILL HOPE FOR THIS WORLD.
......
IF THERE'S ANYTHING-- ANYTHING AT ALL-- I CAN DO FOR THOSE CHILDREN, I HAVE TO TRY.
UM... I HEARD SOMETHING FROM AN ITALIAN FRIEND OF MINE.
BUT THE CHIEF WON'T EVEN BOTHER LISTENING TO ME...
ONE OF THE CAMORRA FAMILIES FROM NAPLES HAS RECENTLY COME UP TO AMSTERDAM.
SUPPOSEDLY, THEY'RE STARTING UP A SLAVERY RING ACROSS THE WHOLE OF EUROPE...
THIS WON'T BE ANYTHING LIKE A *FORMAL* INVESTIGATION...
CROWNE PLAZA
RESTAURANT
CROWNE PL
BUT I WOULD **REALLY** APPRECIATE IT IF YOU COULD HELP ME.

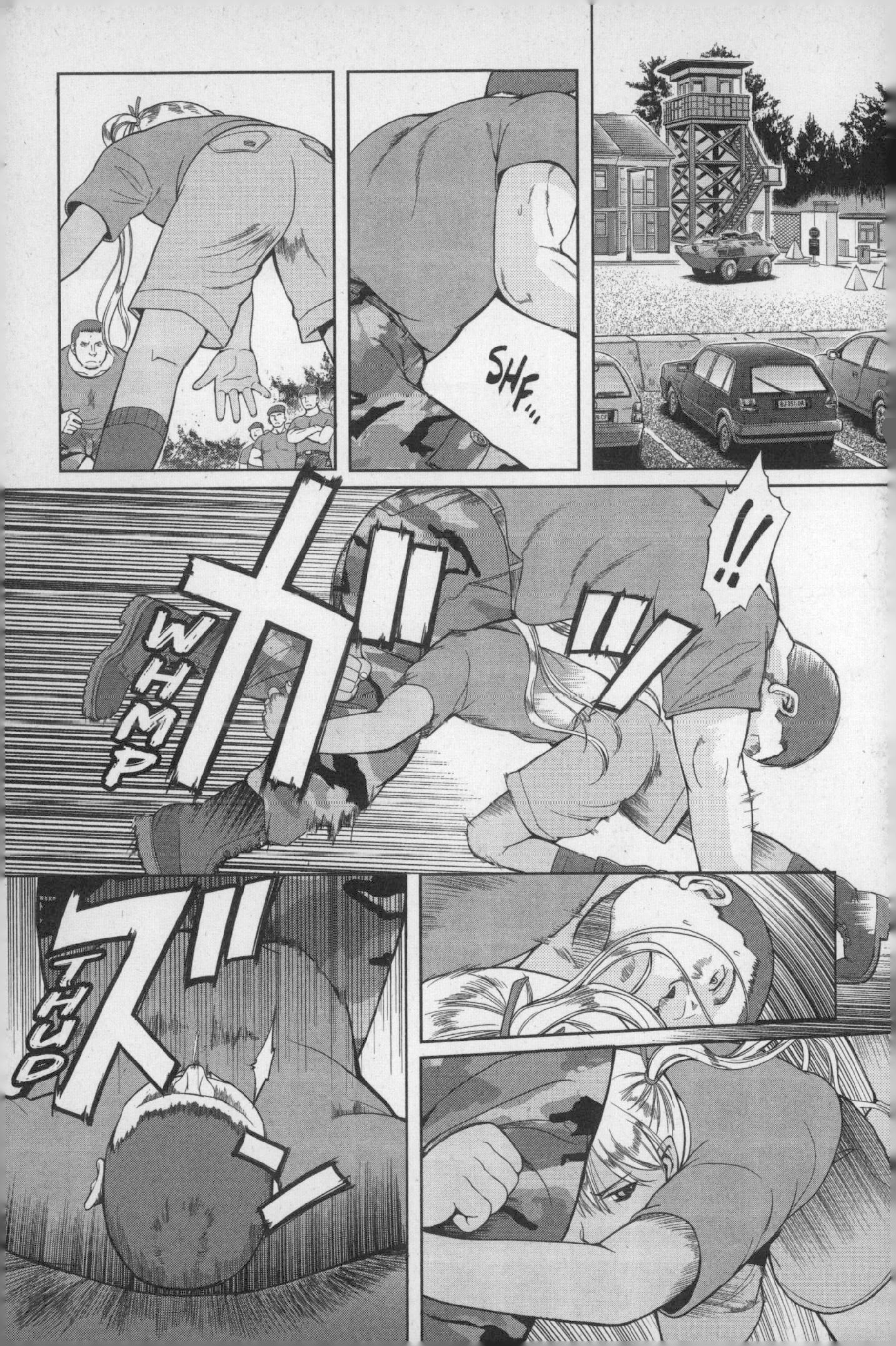
SHF...
!!
WHMP
THUD

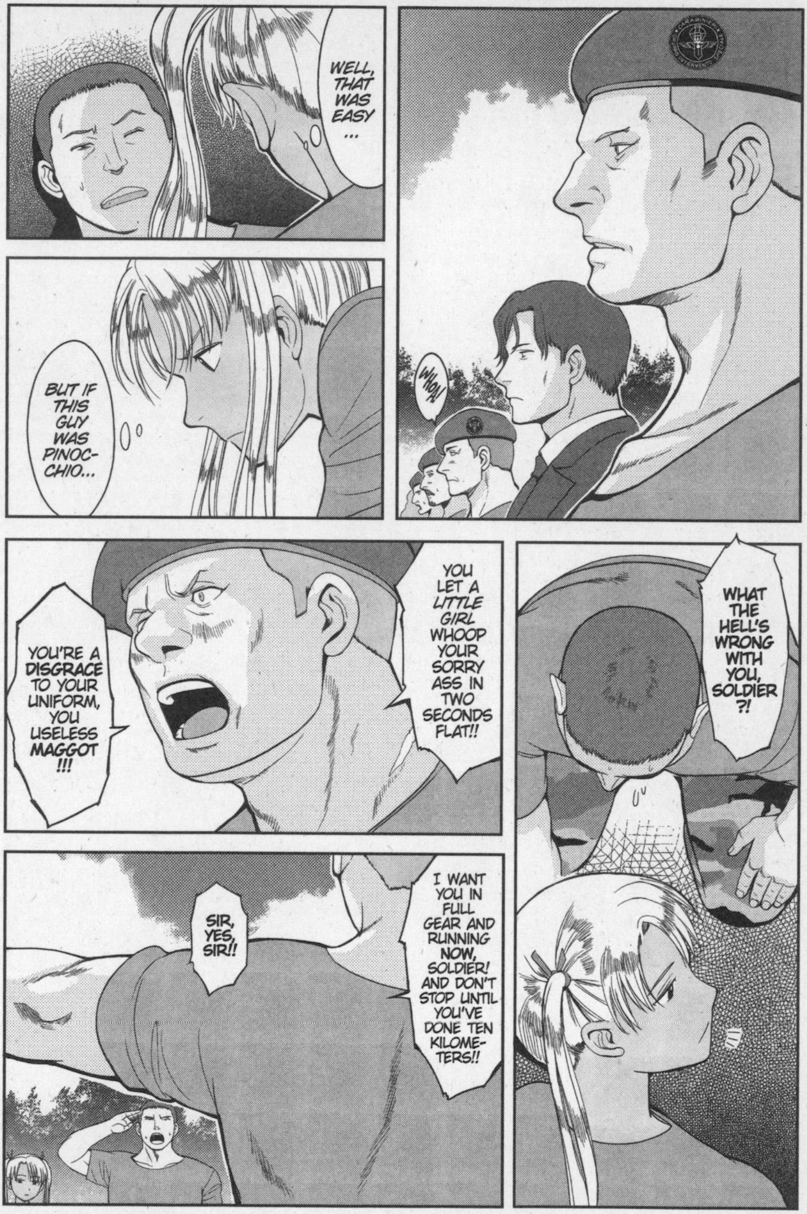
WHOA!
WELL, THAT WAS EASY...
BUT IF THIS GUY WAS PINOCCHIO...
WHAT THE HELL'S WRONG WITH YOU, SOLDIER?!
YOU LET A LITTLE GIRL WHOOP YOUR SORRY ASS IN TWO SECONDS FLAT!!
YOU'RE A DISGRACE TO YOUR UNIFORM, YOU USELESS MAGGOT!!!
I WANT YOU IN FULL GEAR AND RUNNING NOW, SOLDIER! AND DON'T STOP UNTIL YOU'VE DONE TEN KILOMETERS!!
SIR, YES, SIR!!

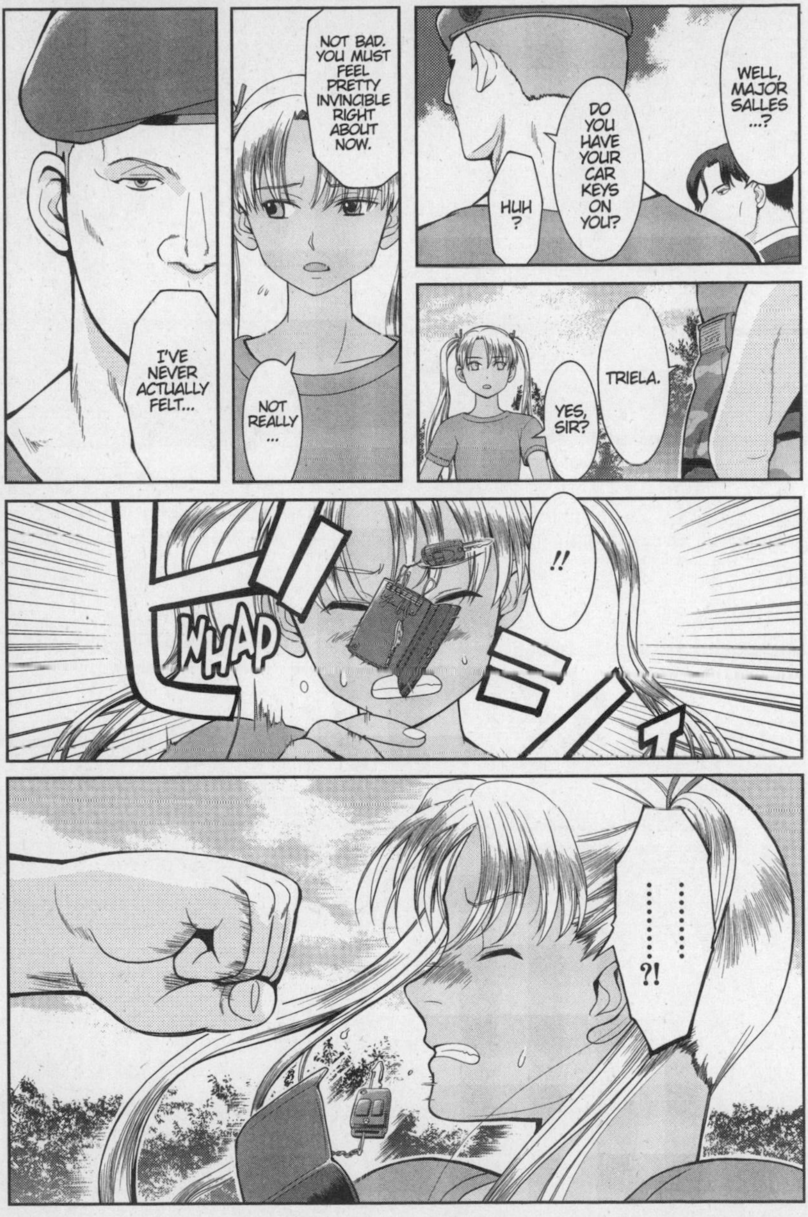
WELL, MAJOR SALLES ...?
DO YOU HAVE YOUR CAR KEYS ON YOU?
HUH ?
TRIELA.
YES, SIR?
NOT BAD. YOU MUST FEEL PRETTY INVINCIBLE RIGHT ABOUT NOW.
NOT REALLY ...
I'VE NEVER ACTUALLY FELT...
!!
WHAP
......
......?!

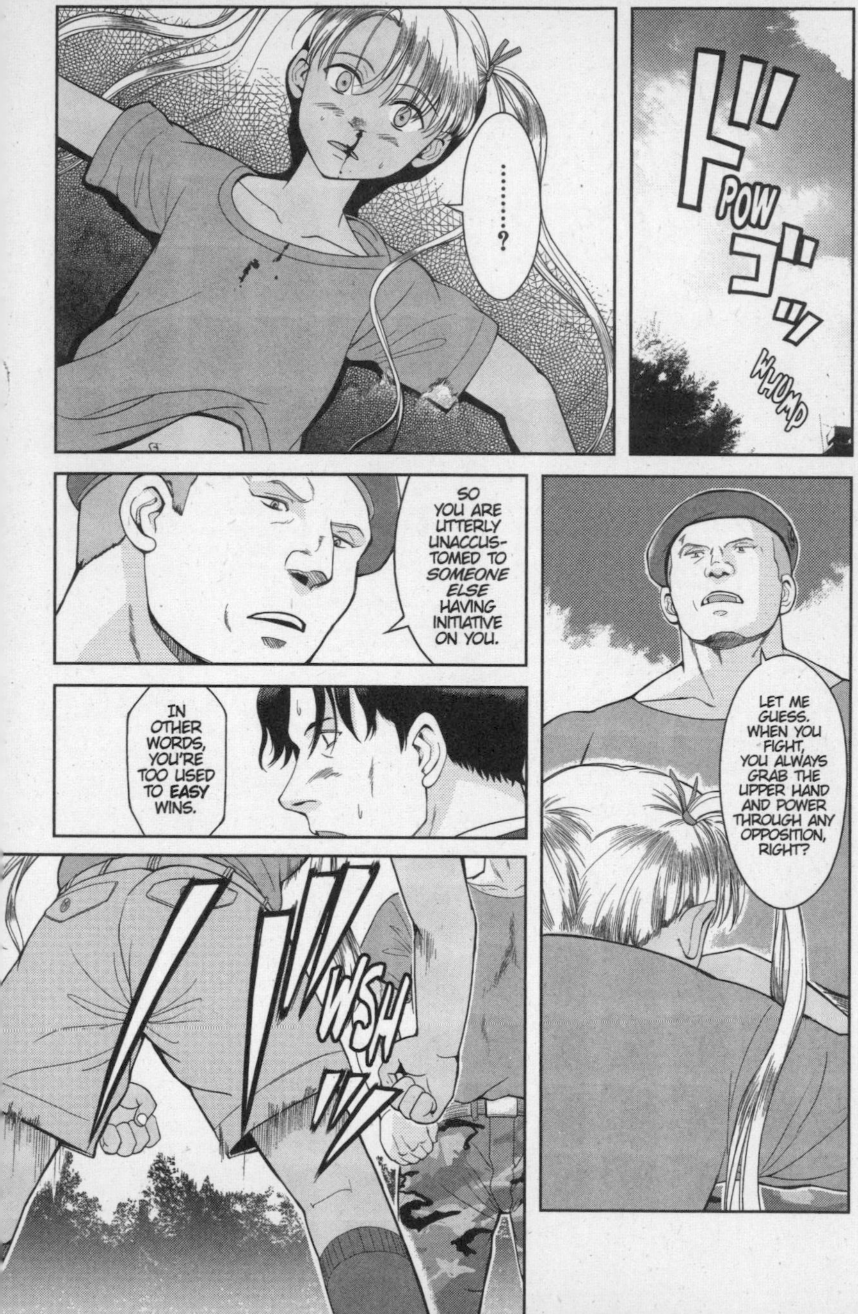
ド
POW
ゴッ
WHUMP
......?
LET ME GUESS. WHEN YOU FIGHT, YOU ALWAYS GRAB THE UPPER HAND AND POWER THROUGH ANY OPPOSITION, RIGHT?
SO YOU ARE UTTERLY UNACCUSTOMED TO *SOMEONE ELSE* HAVING INITIATIVE ON YOU.
IN OTHER WORDS, YOU'RE TOO USED TO **EASY** WINS.
WSH

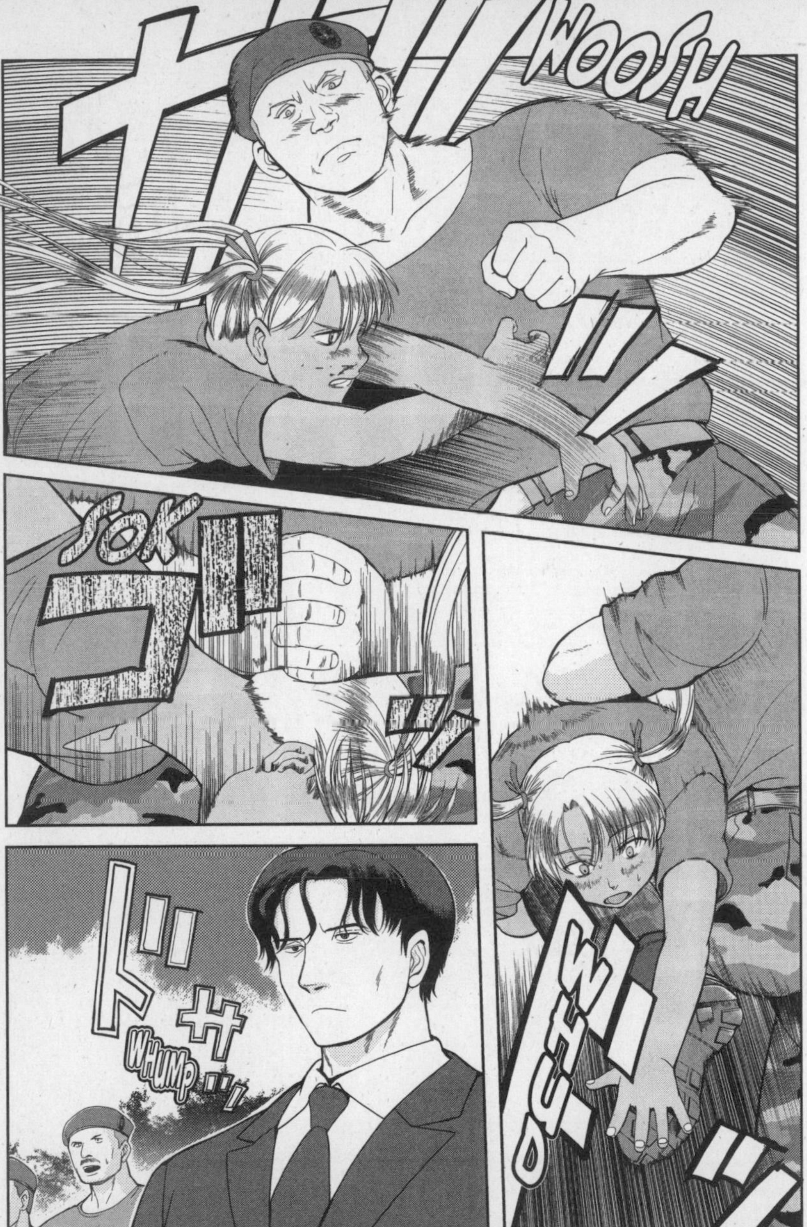
WOOSH
WHUD
SOK
WHUMP

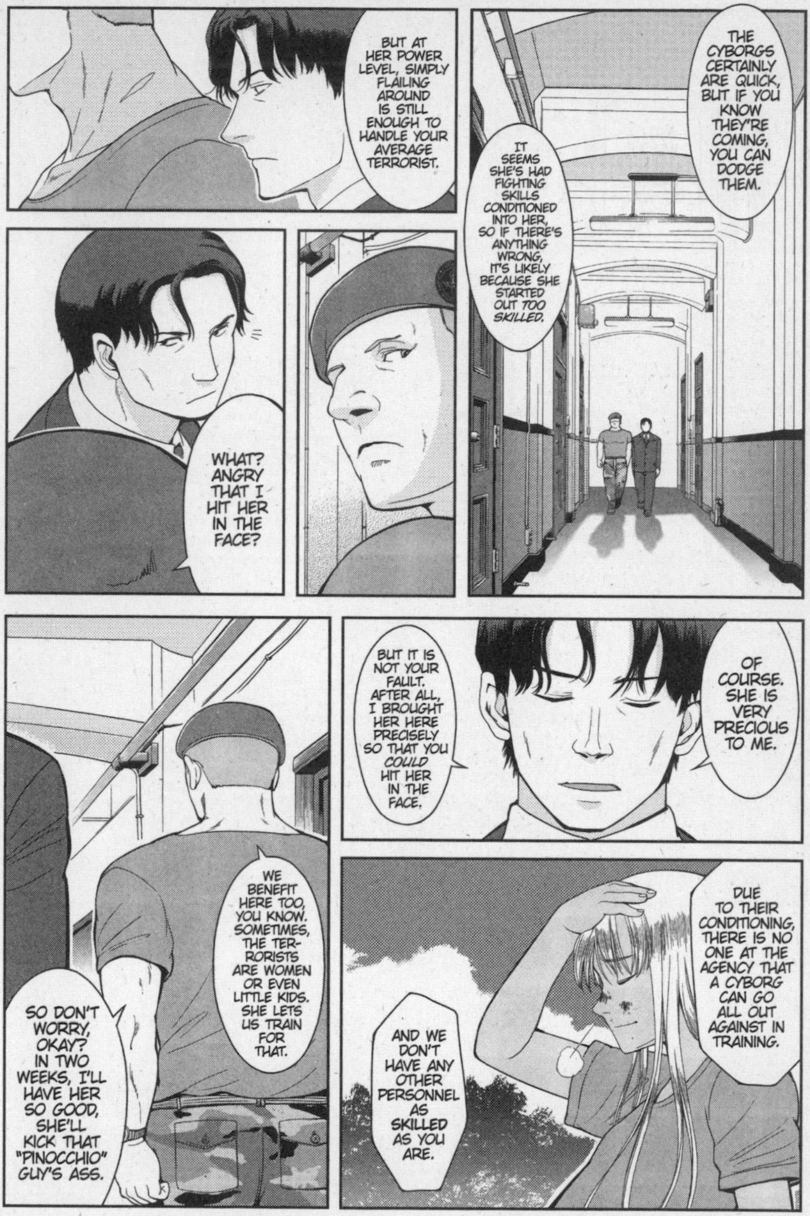
THE CYBORGS CERTAINLY ARE QUICK, BUT IF YOU KNOW THEY'RE COMING, YOU CAN DODGE THEM.
IT SEEMS SHE'S HAD FIGHTING SKILLS CONDITIONED INTO HER, SO IF THERE'S ANYTHING WRONG, IT'S LIKELY BECAUSE SHE STARTED OUT *TOO* SKILLED.
BUT AT HER POWER LEVEL, SIMPLY FLAILING AROUND IS STILL ENOUGH TO HANDLE YOUR AVERAGE TERRORIST.
WHAT? ANGRY THAT I HIT HER IN THE FACE?
OF COURSE. SHE IS VERY PRECIOUS TO ME.
BUT IT IS NOT YOUR FAULT. AFTER ALL, I BROUGHT HER HERE PRECISELY SO THAT YOU *COULD* HIT HER IN THE FACE.
DUE TO THEIR CONDITIONING, THERE IS NO ONE AT THE AGENCY THAT A CYBORG CAN GO ALL OUT AGAINST IN TRAINING.
AND WE DON'T HAVE ANY OTHER PERSONNEL AS SKILLED AS YOU ARE.
WE BENEFIT HERE TOO, YOU KNOW. SOMETIMES, THE TER-RORISTS ARE WOMEN OR EVEN LITTLE KIDS. SHE LETS US TRAIN FOR THAT.
SO DON'T WORRY, OKAY? IN TWO WEEKS, I'LL HAVE HER SO GOOD, SHE'LL KICK THAT "PINOCCHIO" GUY'S ASS.

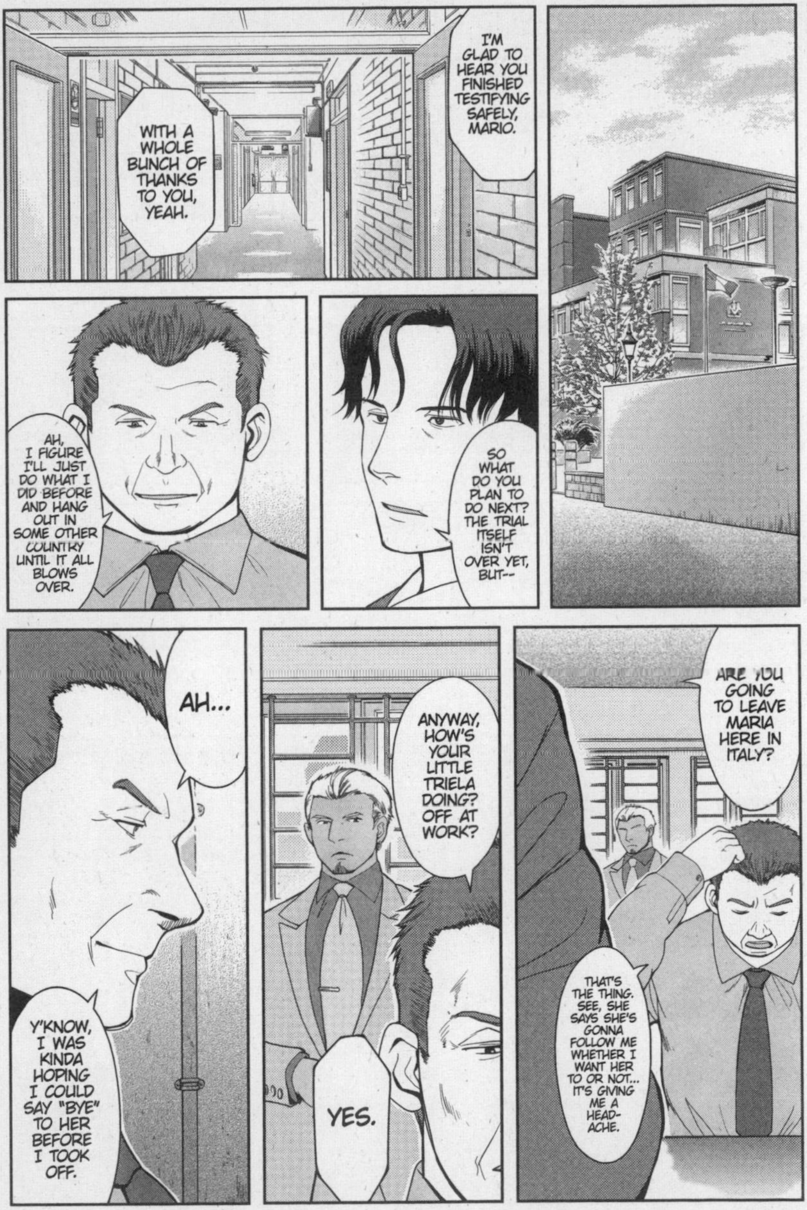
I'M GLAD TO HEAR YOU FINISHED TESTIFYING SAFELY, MARIO.
WITH A WHOLE BUNCH OF THANKS TO YOU, YEAH.
SO WHAT DO YOU PLAN TO DO NEXT? THE TRIAL ITSELF ISN'T OVER YET, BUT--
AH, I FIGURE I'LL JUST DO WHAT I DID BEFORE AND HANG OUT IN SOME OTHER COUNTRY UNTIL IT ALL BLOWS OVER.
ARE YOU GOING TO LEAVE MARIA HERE IN ITALY?
THAT'S THE THING. SEE, SHE SAYS SHE'S GONNA FOLLOW ME WHETHER I WANT HER TO OR NOT... IT'S GIVING ME A HEAD-ACHE.
ANYWAY, HOW'S YOUR LITTLE TRIELA DOING? OFF AT WORK?
YES.
AH...
Y'KNOW, I WAS KINDA HOPING I COULD SAY "BYE" TO HER BEFORE I TOOK OFF.

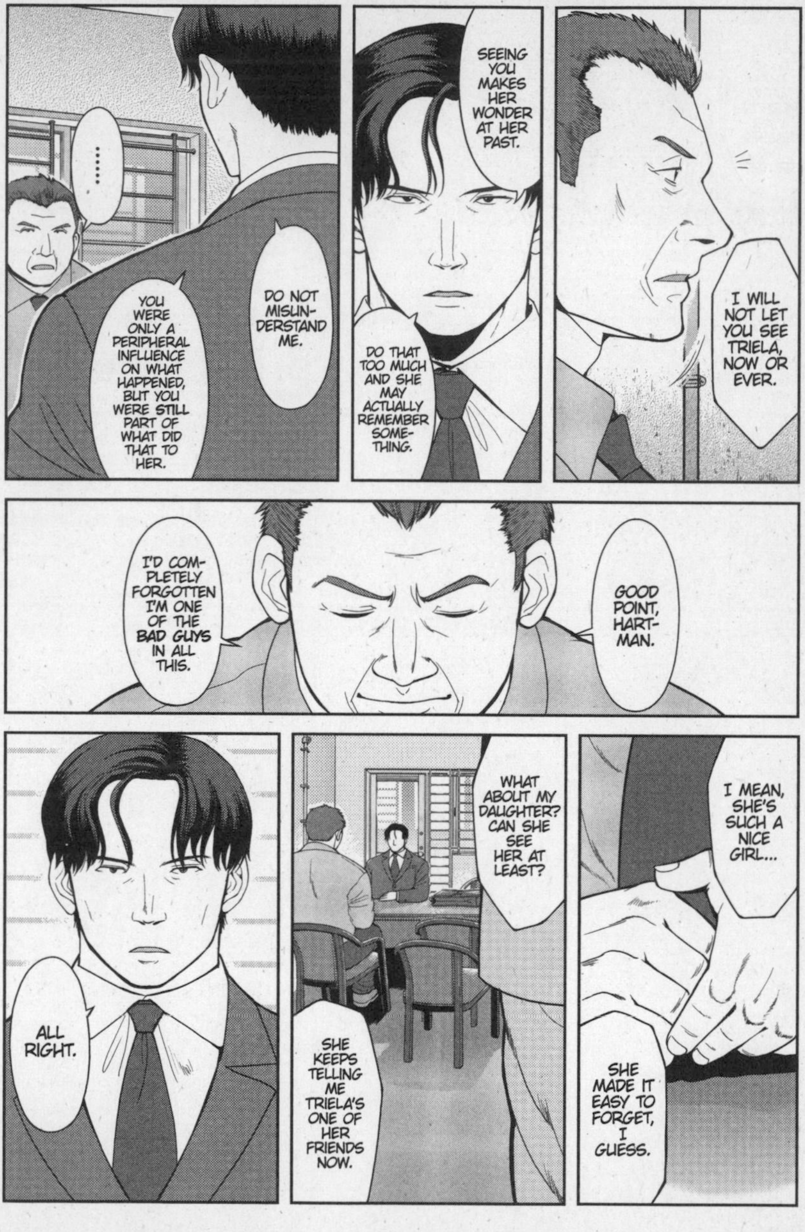
I WILL NOT LET YOU SEE TRIELA, NOW OR EVER.
SEEING YOU MAKES HER WONDER AT HER PAST.
DO THAT TOO MUCH AND SHE MAY ACTUALLY REMEMBER SOMETHING.
......
DO NOT MISUNDERSTAND ME.
YOU WERE ONLY A PERIPHERAL INFLUENCE ON WHAT HAPPENED, BUT YOU WERE STILL PART OF WHAT DID THAT TO HER.
GOOD POINT, HARTMAN.
I'D COMPLETELY FORGOTTEN I'M ONE OF THE BAD GUYS IN ALL THIS.
I MEAN, SHE'S SUCH A NICE GIRL...
SHE MADE IT EASY TO FORGET, I GUESS.
WHAT ABOUT MY DAUGHTER? CAN SHE SEE HER AT LEAST?
SHE KEEPS TELLING ME TRIELA'S ONE OF HER FRIENDS NOW.
ALL RIGHT.

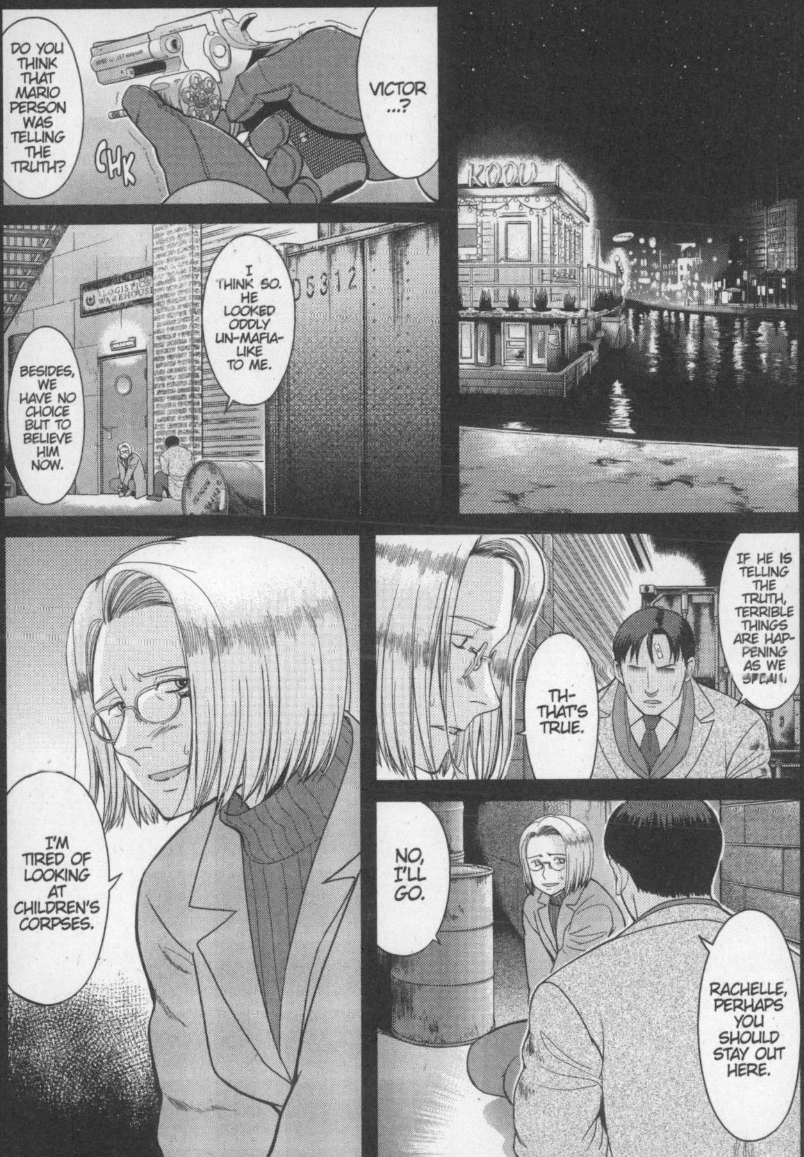
VICTOR ...?
DO YOU THINK THAT MARIO PERSON WAS TELLING THE TRUTH?
CHK
I THINK SO. HE LOOKED ODDLY UN-MAFIA-LIKE TO ME.
BESIDES, WE HAVE NO CHOICE BUT TO BELIEVE HIM NOW.
IF HE IS TELLING THE TRUTH, TERRIBLE THINGS ARE HAPPENING AS WE SPEAK.
TH-THAT'S TRUE.
RACHELLE, PERHAPS YOU SHOULD STAY OUT HERE.
NO, I'LL GO.
I'M TIRED OF LOOKING AT CHILDREN'S CORPSES.

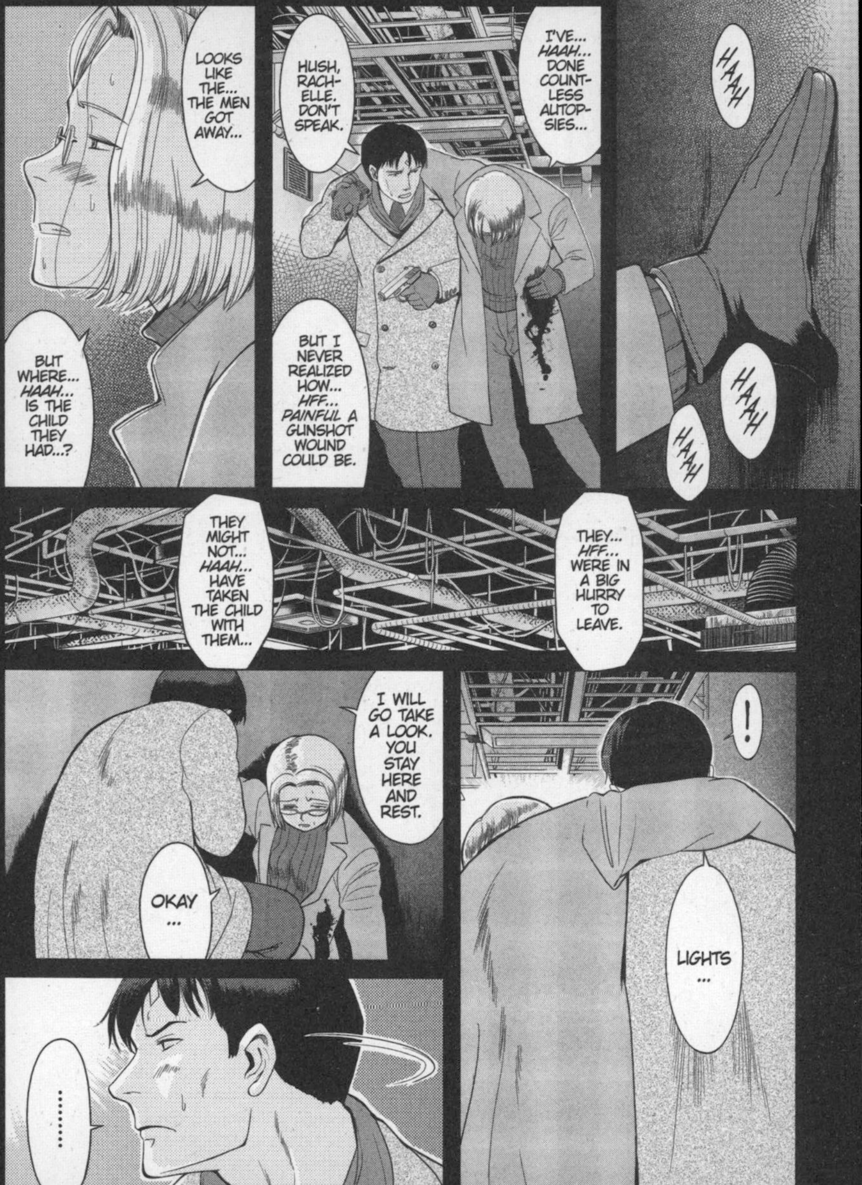
HAAH
HAAH
HAAH
I'VE... HAAH... DONE COUNTLESS AUTOPSIES...
HUSH, RACHELLE. DON'T SPEAK.
BUT I NEVER REALIZED HOW... HFF... PAINFUL A GUNSHOT WOUND COULD BE.
LOOKS LIKE THE... THE MEN GOT AWAY...
BUT WHERE... HAAH... IS THE CHILD THEY HAD...?
THEY... HFF... WERE IN A BIG HURRY TO LEAVE.
THEY MIGHT NOT... HAAH... HAVE TAKEN THE CHILD WITH THEM...
!
LIGHTS...
I WILL GO TAKE A LOOK. YOU STAY HERE AND REST.
OKAY...
....

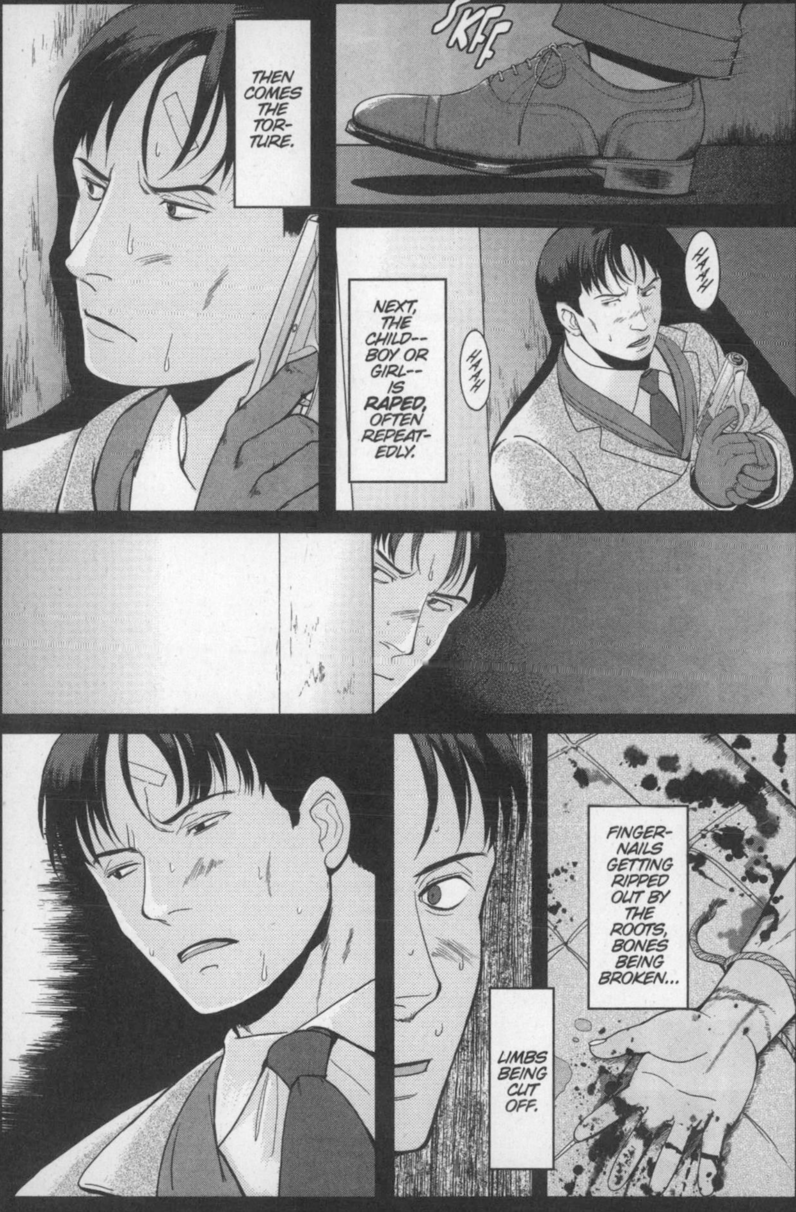
SKFF
HAAH
NEXT, THE CHILD--BOY OR GIRL--IS **RAPED**, OFTEN REPEATEDLY.
HAAH
THEN COMES THE TORTURE.
FINGERNAILS GETTING RIPPED OUT BY THE ROOTS, BONES BEING BROKEN...
LIMBS BEING CUT OFF.

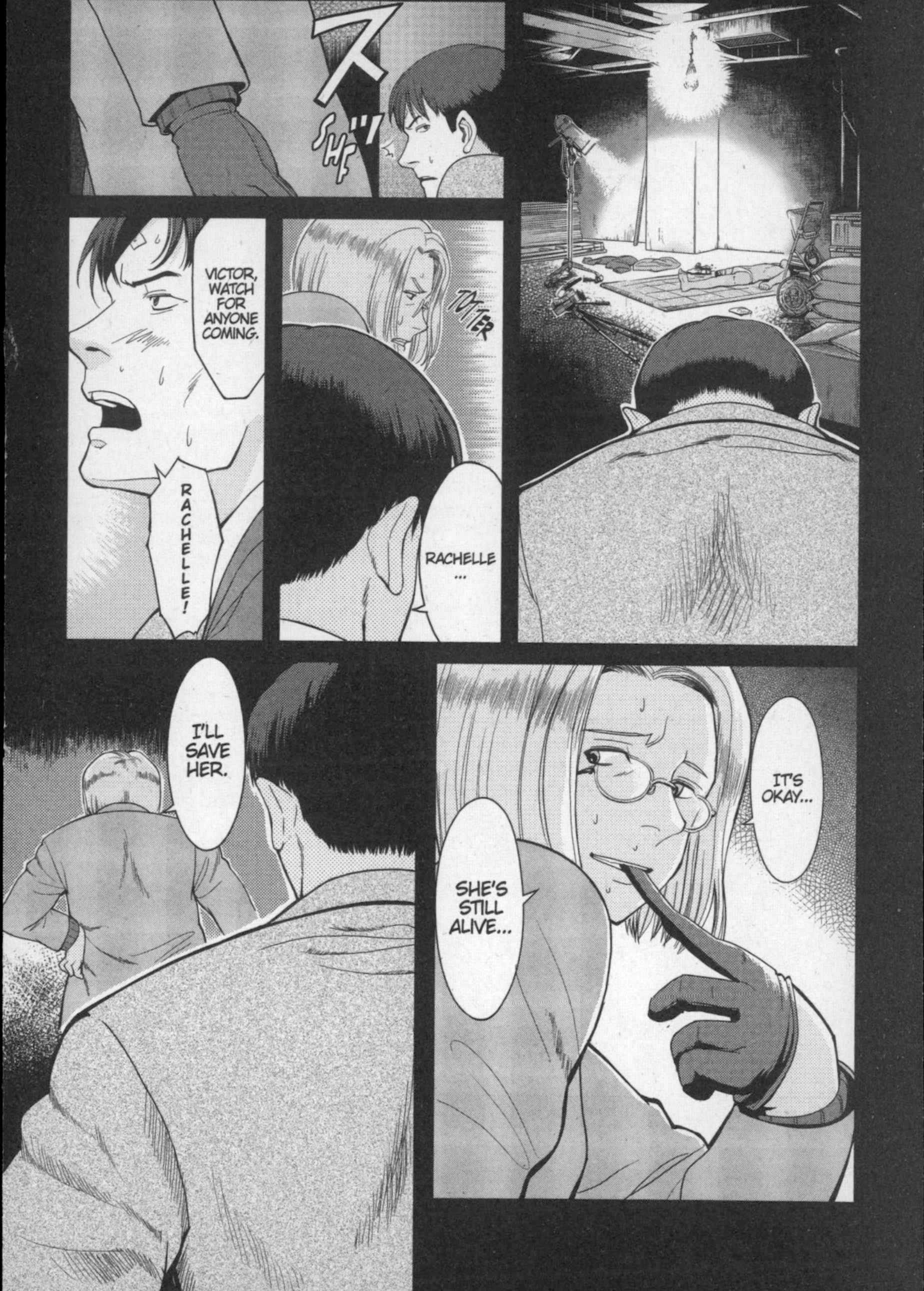

ス
SHF
TWITTER
RACHELLE...
VICTOR, WATCH FOR ANYONE COMING.
RACHELLE!
IT'S OKAY...
SHE'S STILL ALIVE...
I'LL SAVE HER.

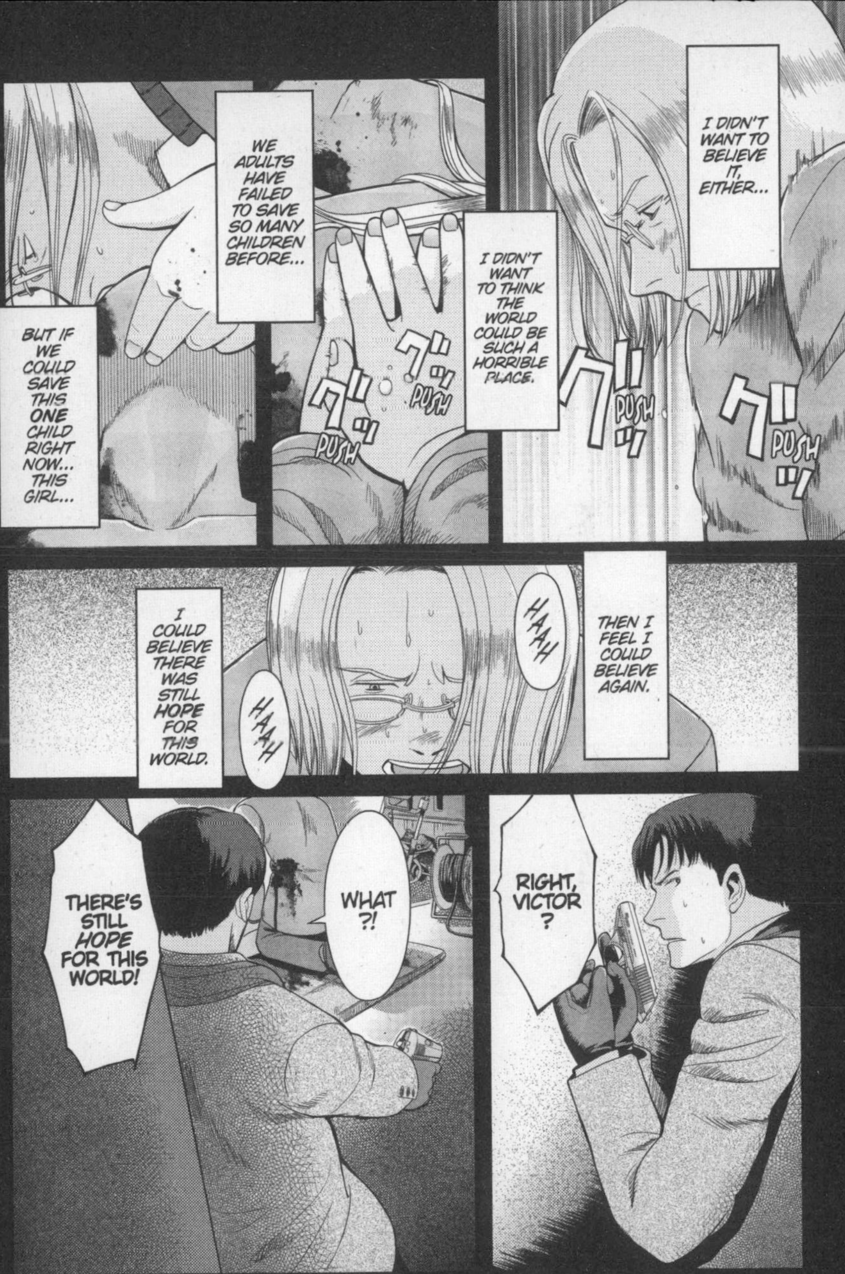
I DIDN'T WANT TO BELIEVE IT, EITHER...
グッ
PUSH
グッ
PUSH
I DIDN'T WANT TO THINK THE WORLD COULD BE SUCH A HORRIBLE PLACE.
WE ADULTS HAVE FAILED TO SAVE SO MANY CHILDREN BEFORE...
グッ
PUSH
グッ
PUSH
BUT IF WE COULD SAVE THIS ONE CHILD RIGHT NOW... THIS GIRL...
THEN I FEEL I COULD BELIEVE AGAIN.
HAAAH
HAAAH
I COULD BELIEVE THERE WAS STILL HOPE FOR THIS WORLD.
RIGHT, VICTOR?
WHAT?!
THERE'S STILL HOPE FOR THIS WORLD!

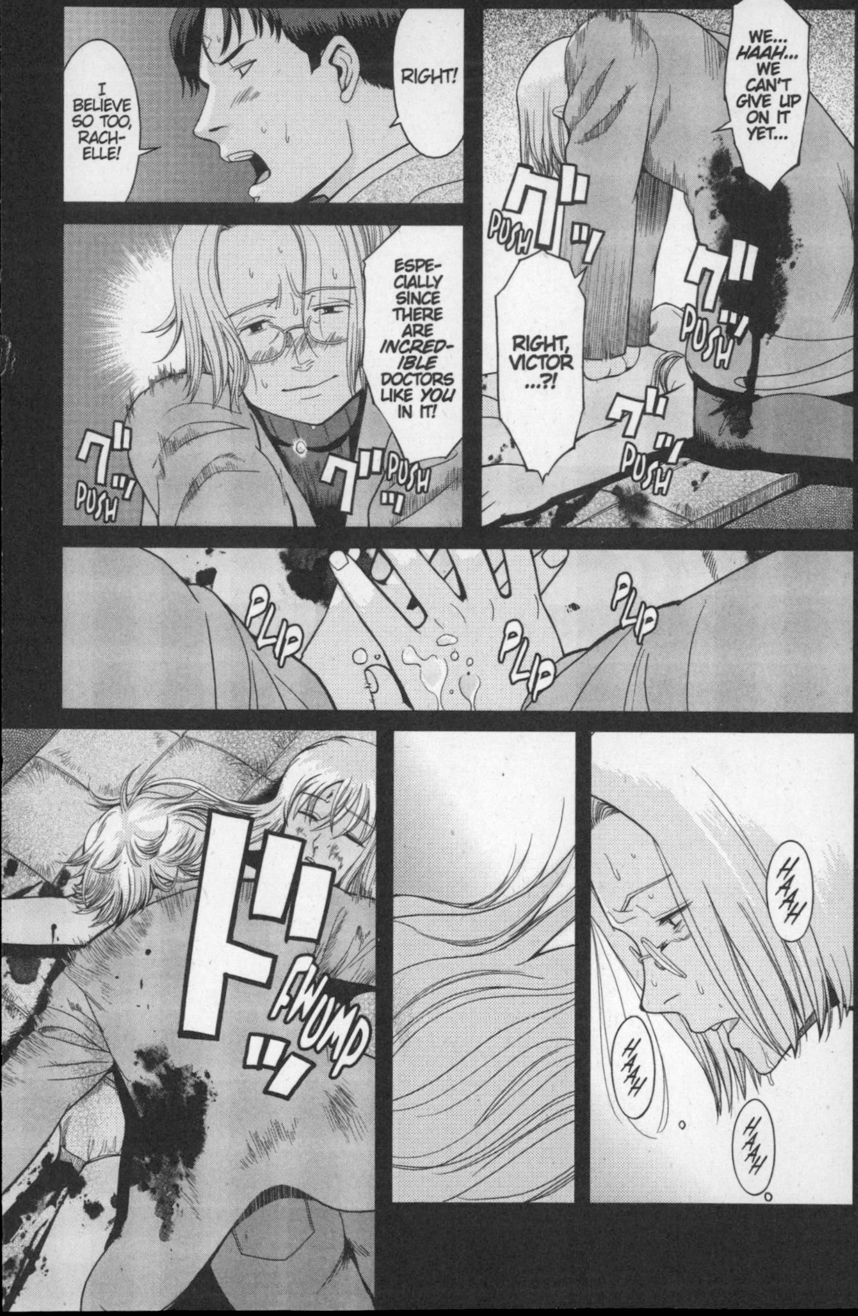

WE... HAAH... WE CAN'T GIVE UP ON IT YET...
グッ
PUSH
グッ
PUSH
RIGHT, VICTOR ...?!
グッ
PUSH
RIGHT!
I BELIEVE SO TOO, RACHELLE!
ESPECIALLY SINCE THERE ARE INCREDIBLE DOCTORS LIKE YOU IN IT!
グッ
PUSH
グッ
PUSH
PLIP
PLIP
PLIP
HAAH
HAAH
HAAH
ドッ
FWUMP

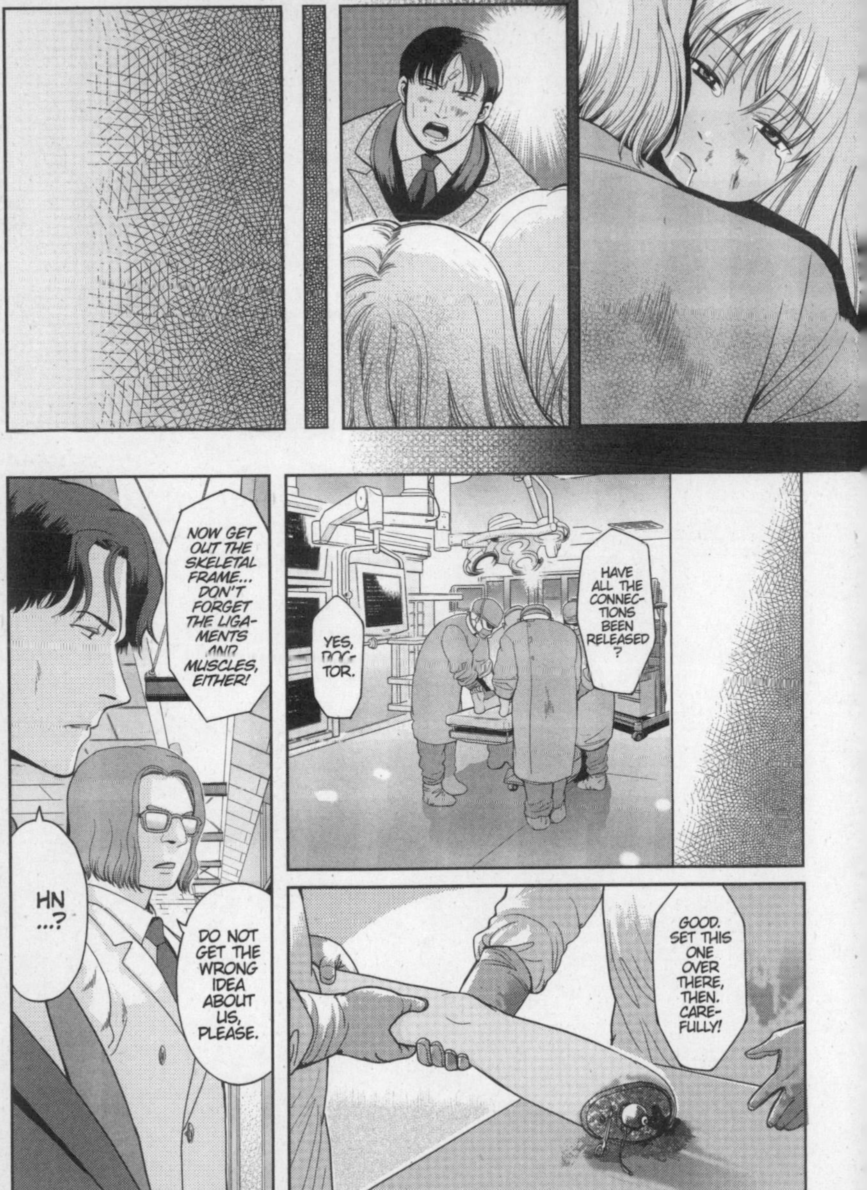
HAVE ALL THE CONNECTIONS BEEN RELEASED?
YES, DOCTOR.
GOOD. SET THIS ONE OVER THERE, THEN. CAREFULLY!
NOW GET OUT THE SKELETAL FRAME... DON'T FORGET THE LIGAMENTS AND MUSCLES, EITHER!
HN ...?
DO NOT GET THE WRONG IDEA ABOUT US, PLEASE.

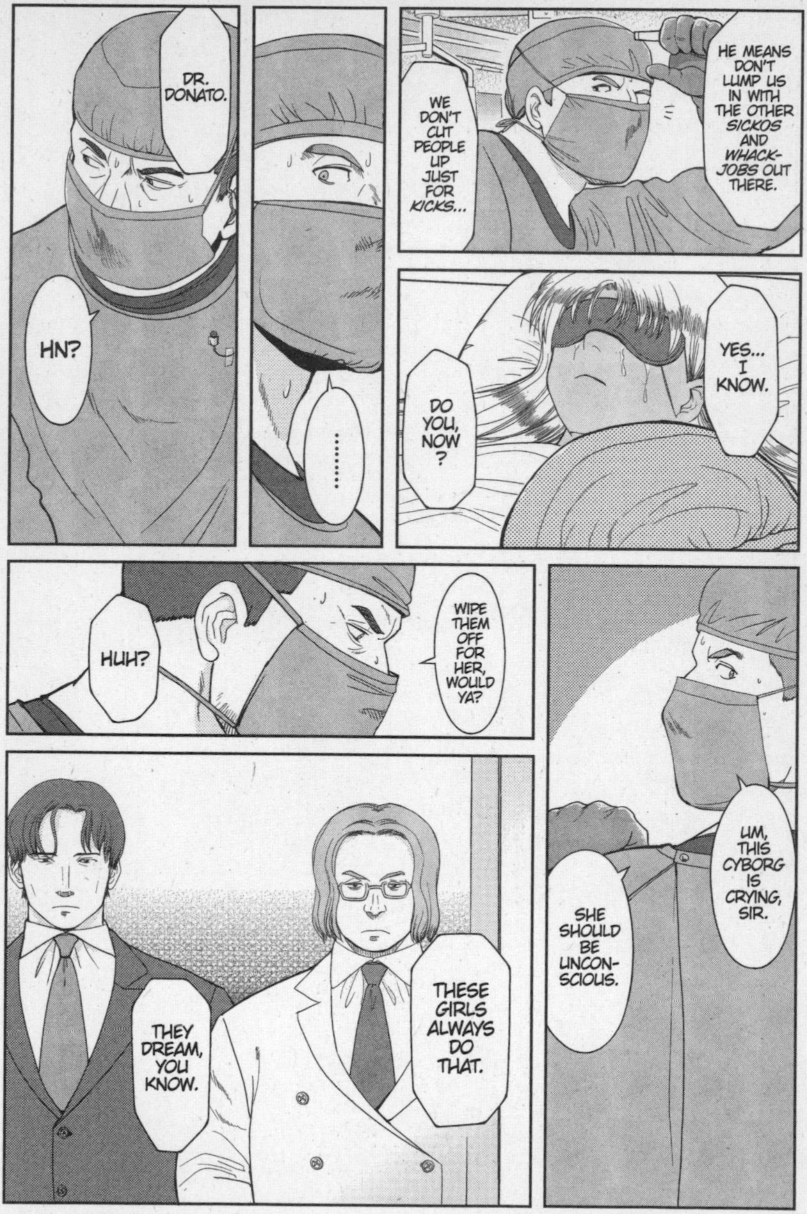
HE MEANS DON'T LUMP US IN WITH THE OTHER *SICKOS* AND *WHACK-JOBS* OUT THERE.
WE DON'T CUT PEOPLE UP JUST FOR *KICKS*...
YES... I KNOW.
DO YOU, NOW?
....
DR. DONATO.
HN?
UM, THIS CYBORG IS CRYING, SIR.
SHE SHOULD BE UNCON-SCIOUS.
WIPE THEM OFF FOR HER, WOULD YA?
HUH?
THESE GIRLS ALWAYS DO THAT.
THEY DREAM, YOU KNOW.

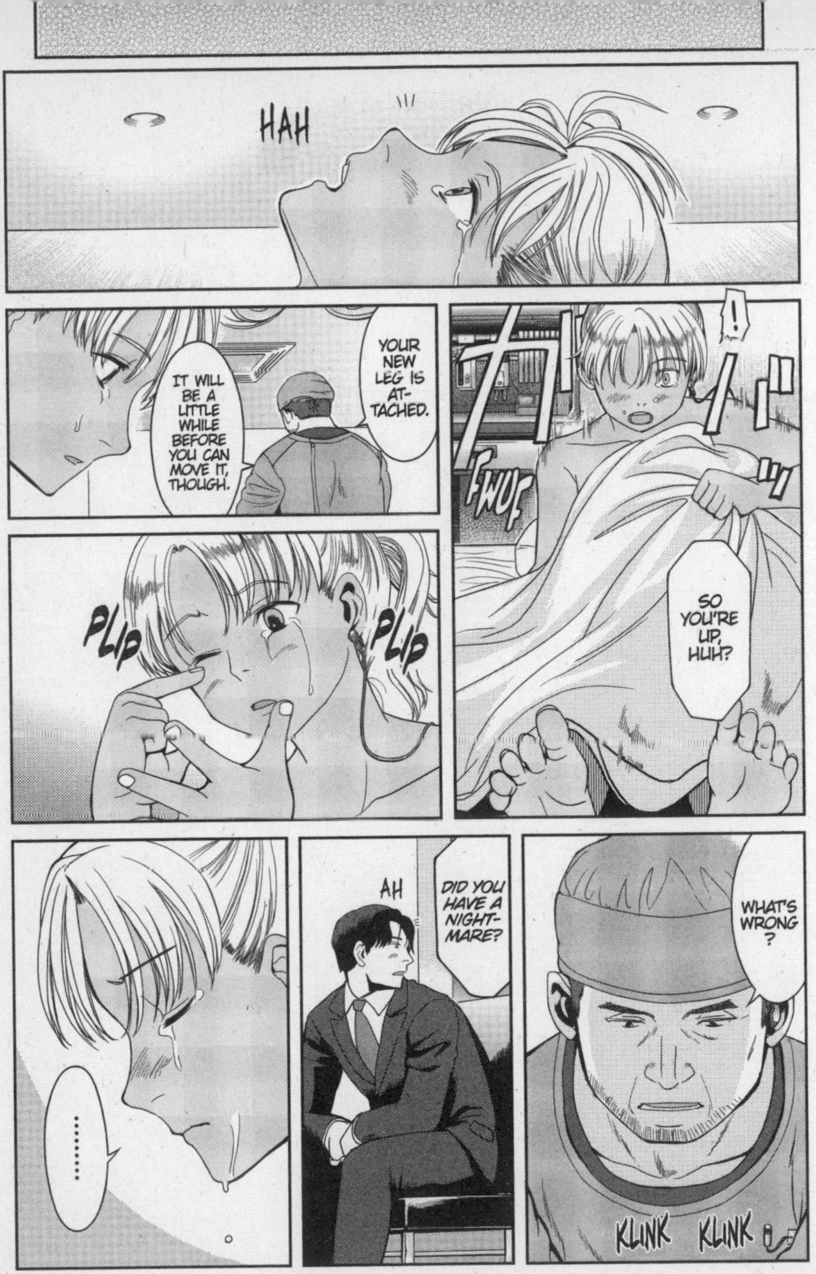
HAH
!
FWUF
SO YOU'RE UP, HUH?
YOUR NEW LEG IS AT-TACHED.
IT WILL BE A LITTLE WHILE BEFORE YOU CAN MOVE IT, THOUGH.
PLIP
PLIP
WHAT'S WRONG?
KLINK KLINK
AH
DID YOU HAVE A NIGHT-MARE?
....

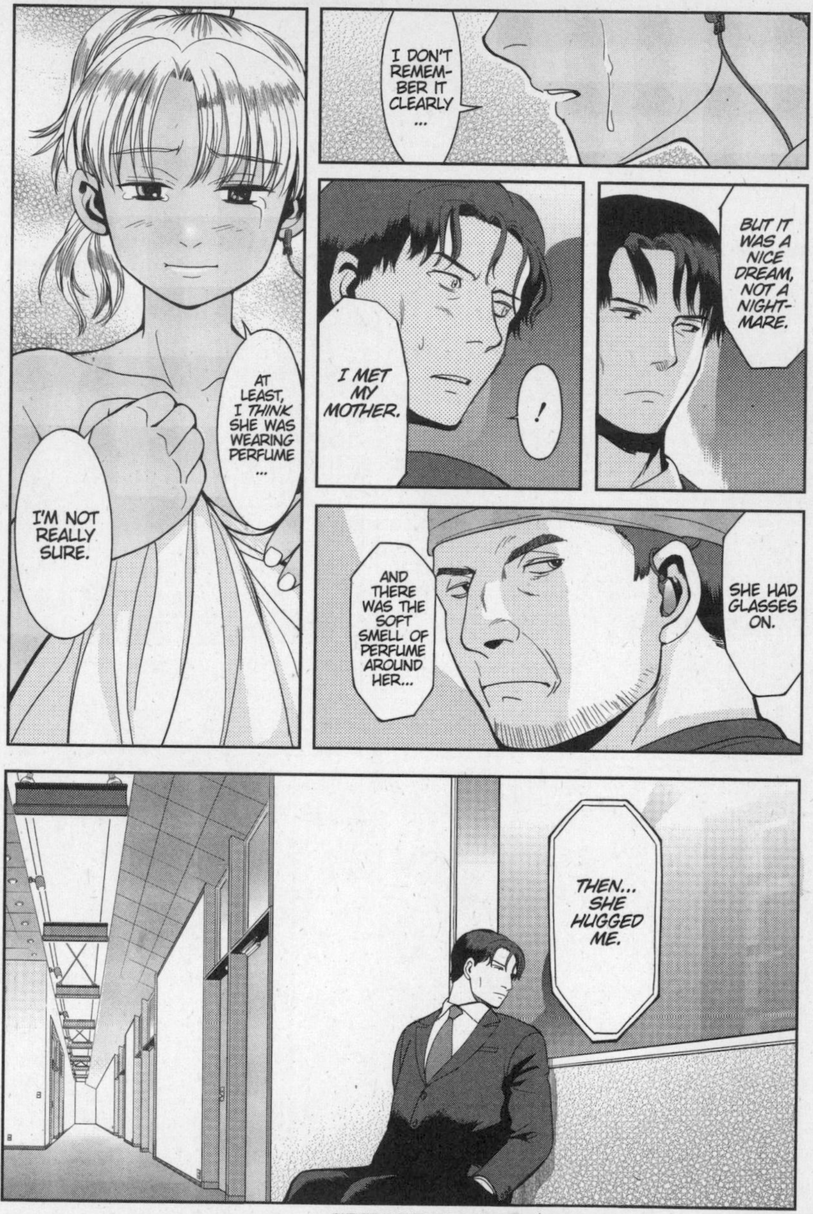
I DON'T REMEMBER IT CLEARLY ...
BUT IT WAS A NICE DREAM, NOT A NIGHTMARE.
!
I MET MY MOTHER.
SHE HAD GLASSES ON.
AND THERE WAS THE SOFT SMELL OF PERFUME AROUND HER...
AT LEAST, I *THINK* SHE WAS WEARING PERFUME ...
I'M NOT REALLY SURE.
THEN... SHE HUGGED ME.

GUNSLINGER GIRL Vol.4 END

GUNSLINGER GIRL vol.4

EDITOR
CHIAKI SUGIHARA

ASSISTANT
TAKAHIRO ENDO
JUNICHIRO YAGI

SPECIAL THANKS
And everyone who so helpfully offered advice and research materials.

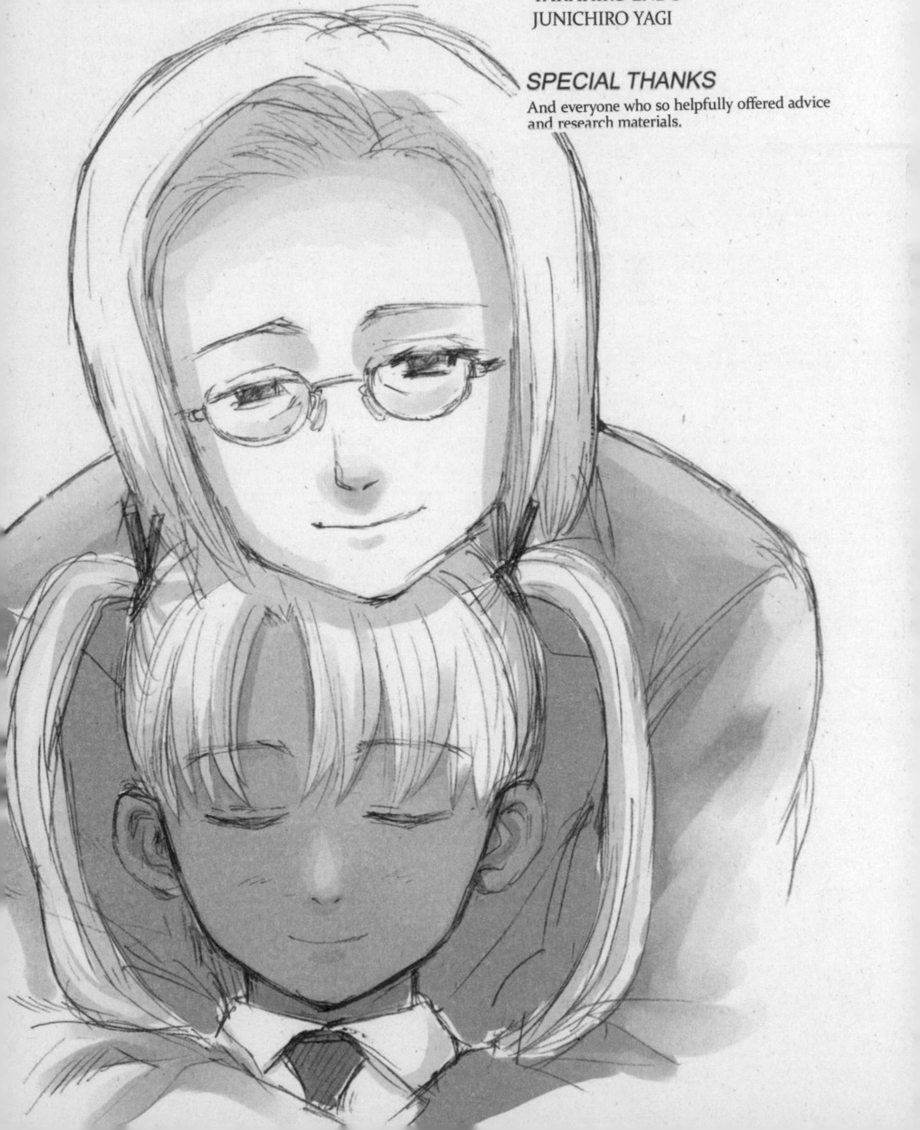

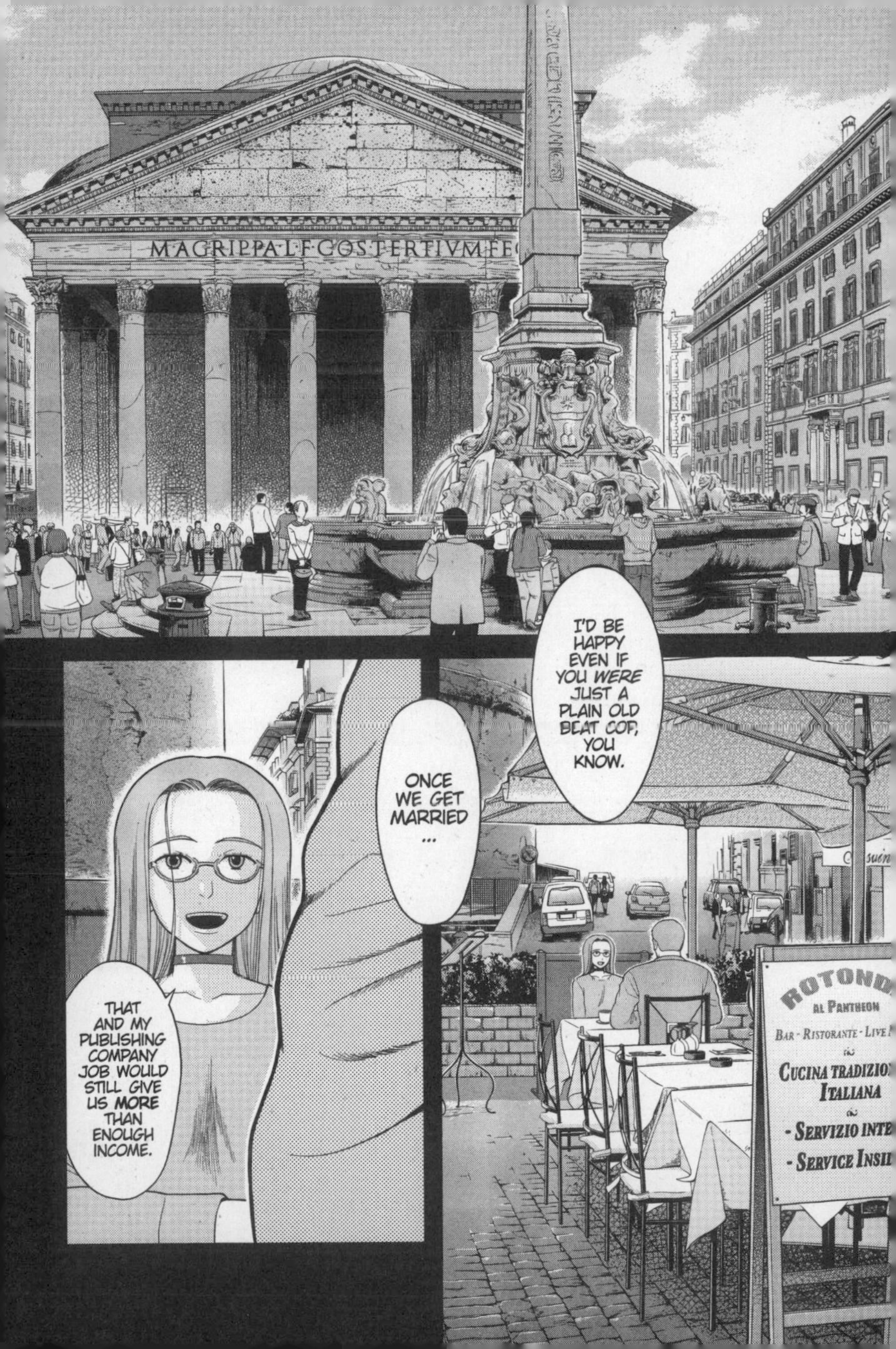
M·AGRIPPA·L·F·COS·TERTIVM·FE
I'D BE HAPPY EVEN IF YOU WERE JUST A PLAIN OLD BEAT COP, YOU KNOW.
ONCE WE GET MARRIED ...
ROTOND
AL PANTHEON
BAR - RISTORANTE - LIVE
CUCINA TRADIZIO
ITALIANA
- SERVIZIO INTE
- SERVICE INSI
THAT AND MY PUBLISHING COMPANY JOB WOULD STILL GIVE US MORE THAN ENOUGH INCOME.

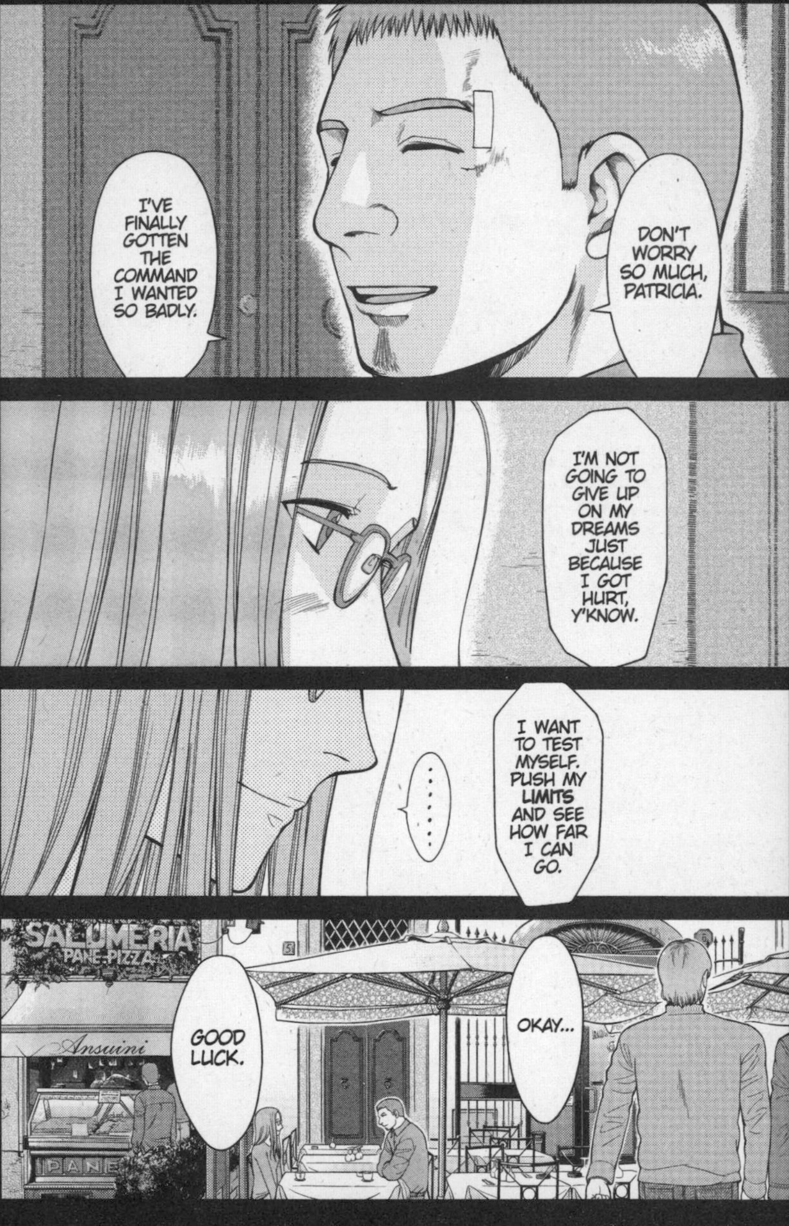
DON'T WORRY SO MUCH, PATRICIA.
I'VE FINALLY GOTTEN THE COMMAND I WANTED SO BADLY.
I'M NOT GOING TO GIVE UP ON MY DREAMS JUST BECAUSE I GOT HURT, Y'KNOW.
I WANT TO TEST MYSELF. PUSH MY LIMITS AND SEE HOW FAR I CAN GO.
......
OKAY...
GOOD LUCK.
SALUMERIA
PANE-PIZZA
5
Ansuini
PANE

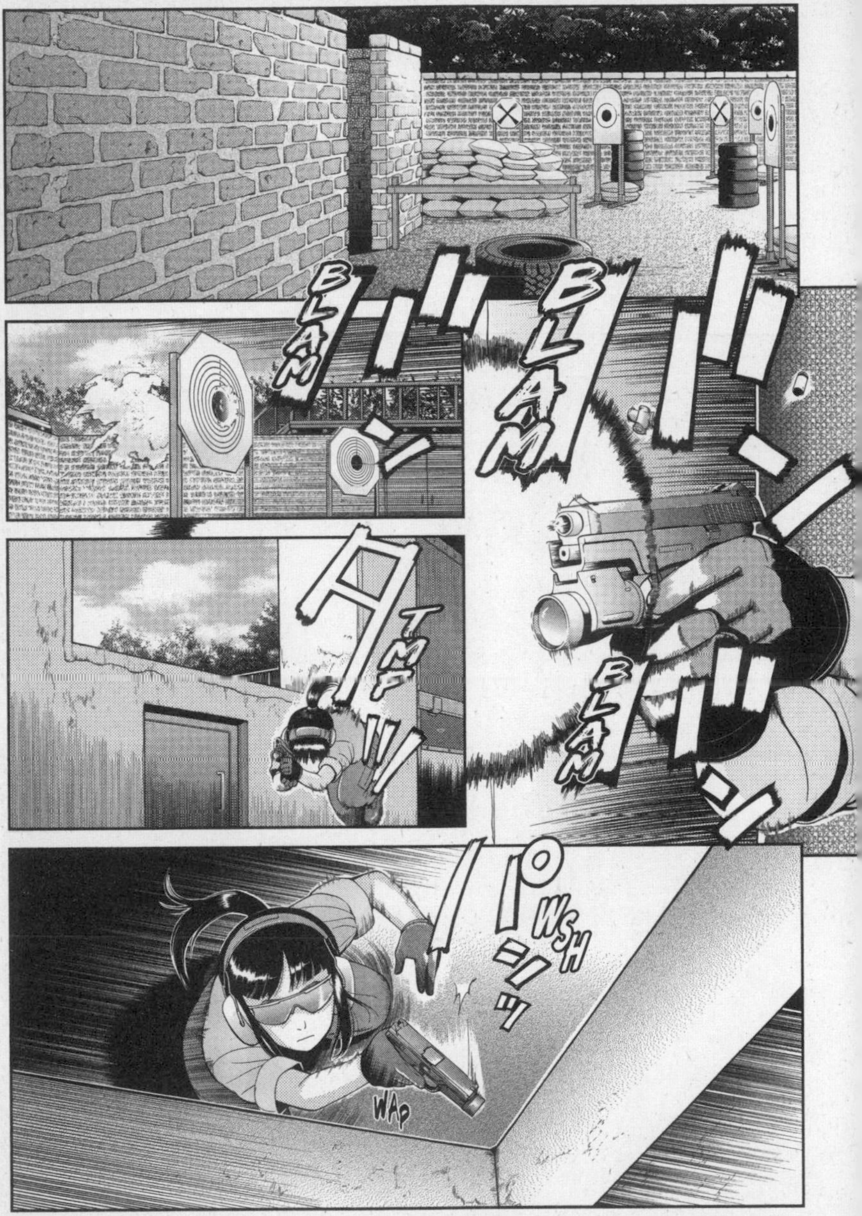
BLAM
BLAM
BLAM
TMP
WSH
WAP

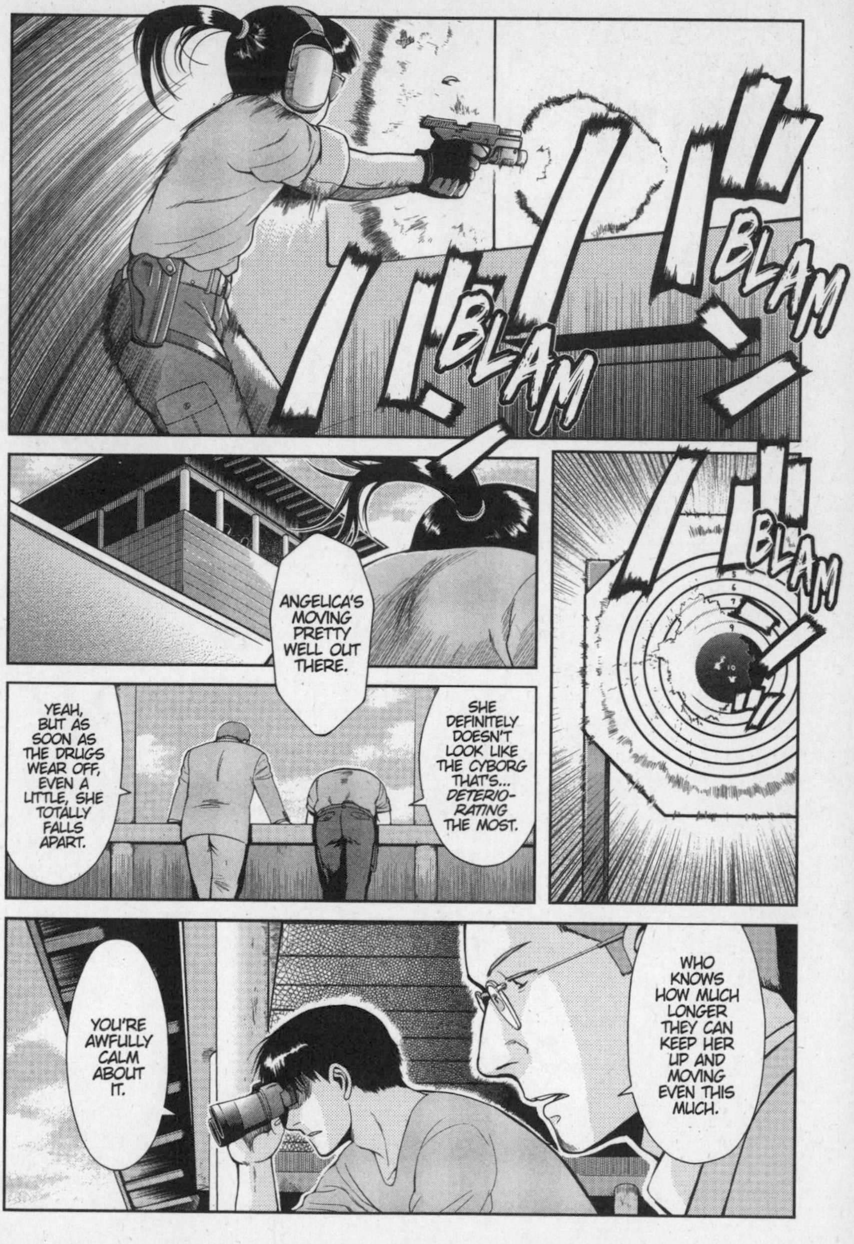
BLAM
BLAM
BLAM
ANGELICA'S MOVING PRETTY WELL OUT THERE.
SHE DEFINITELY DOESN'T LOOK LIKE THE CYBORG THAT'S... *DETERIORATING* THE MOST.
YEAH, BUT AS SOON AS THE DRUGS WEAR OFF, EVEN A LITTLE, SHE TOTALLY FALLS APART.
WHO KNOWS HOW MUCH LONGER THEY CAN KEEP HER UP AND MOVING EVEN THIS MUCH.
YOU'RE AWFULLY CALM ABOUT IT.

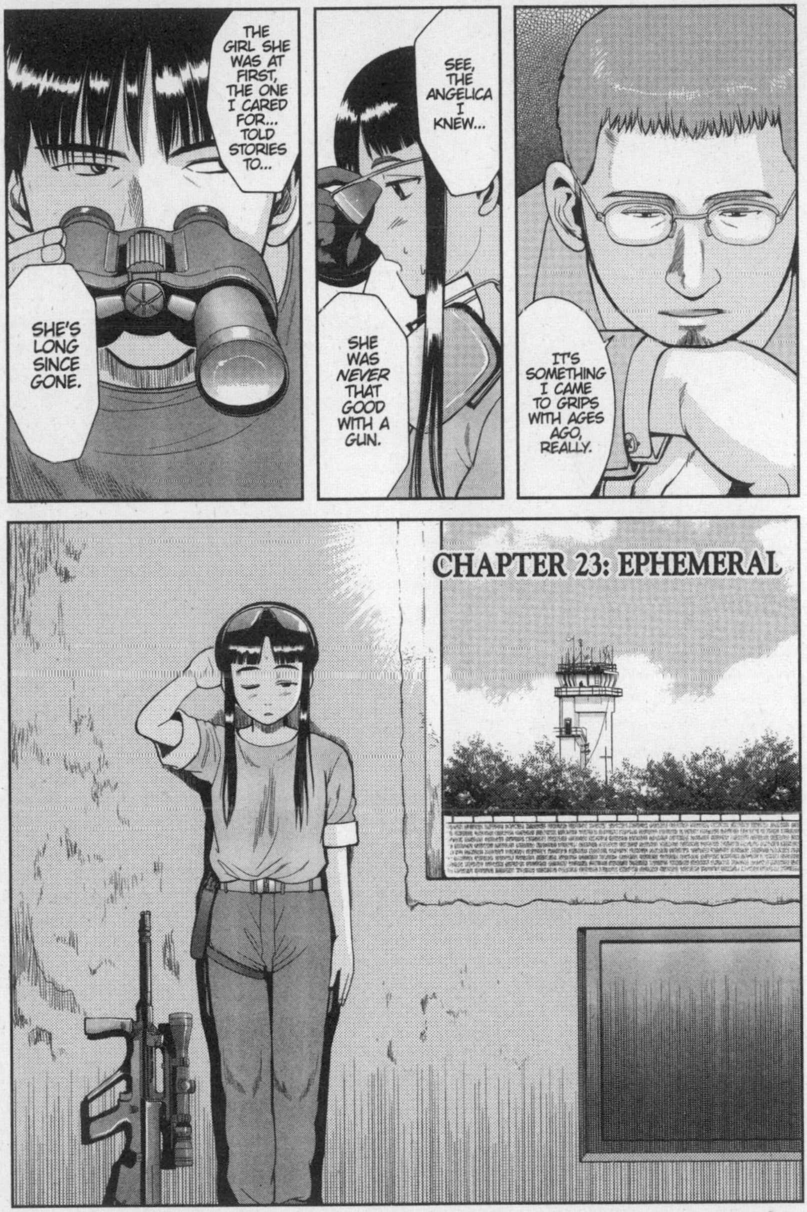
IT'S SOMETHING I CAME TO GRIPS WITH AGES AGO, REALLY.
SEE, THE ANGELICA I KNEW...
SHE WAS *NEVER* THAT GOOD WITH A GUN.
THE GIRL SHE WAS AT FIRST, THE ONE I CARED FOR... TOLD STORIES TO...
SHE'S LONG SINCE GONE.
CHAPTER 23: EPHEMERAL

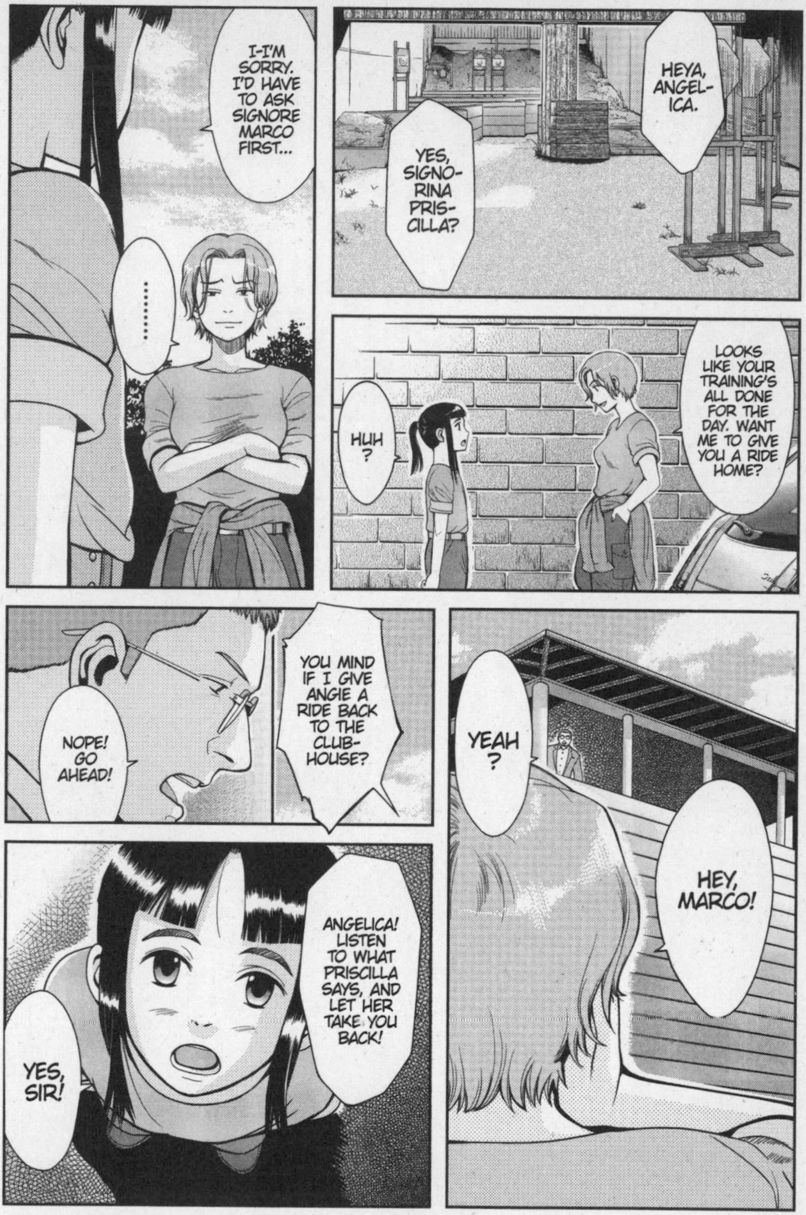
HEYA, ANGEL-ICA.
YES, SIGNO-RINA PRIS-CILLA?
LOOKS LIKE YOUR TRAINING'S ALL DONE FOR THE DAY. WANT ME TO GIVE YOU A RIDE HOME?
HUH?
I-I'M SORRY. I'D HAVE TO ASK SIGNORE MARCO FIRST...
....
HEY, MARCO!
YEAH?
YOU MIND IF I GIVE ANGIE A RIDE BACK TO THE CLUB-HOUSE?
NOPE! GO AHEAD!
ANGELICA! LISTEN TO WHAT PRISCILLA SAYS, AND LET HER TAKE YOU BACK!
YES, SIR!

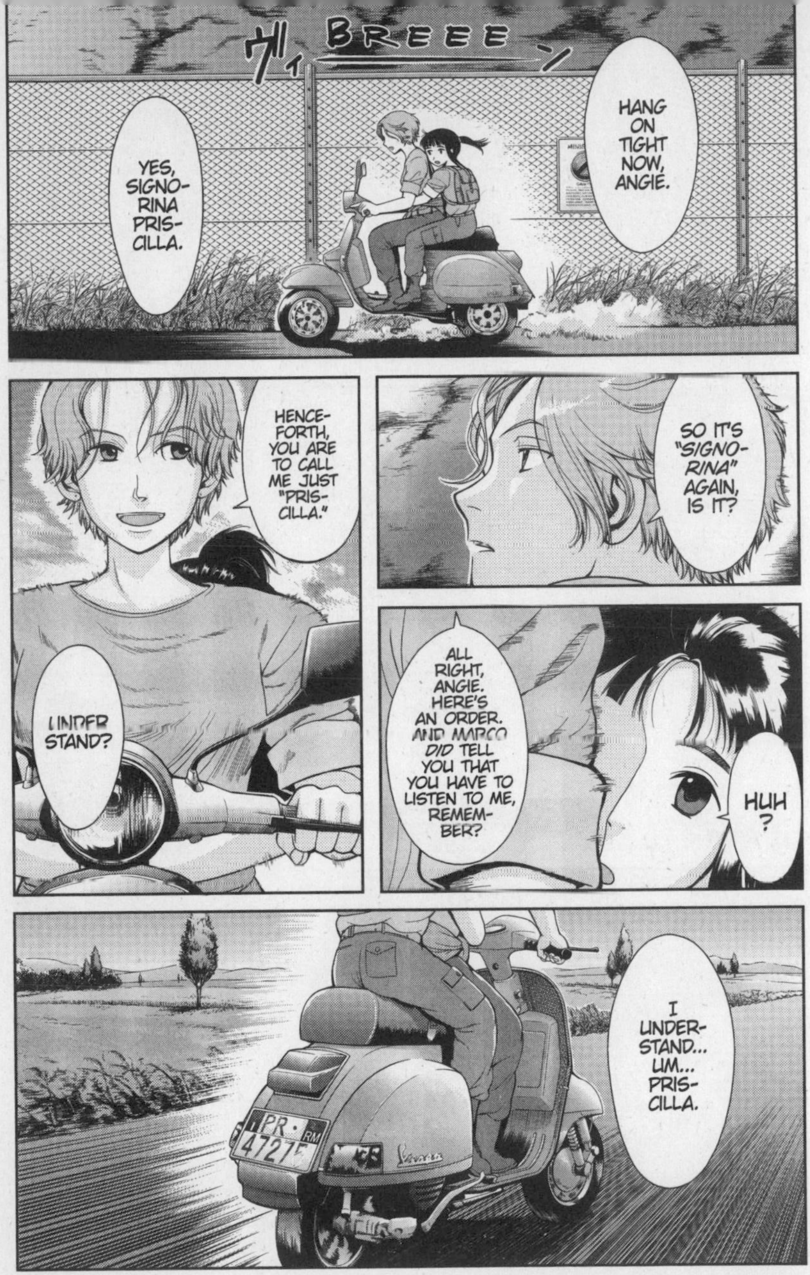
ヴィ BREEEE ン
HANG ON TIGHT NOW, ANGIE.
YES, SIGNORINA PRISCILLA.
SO IT'S "SIGNORINA" AGAIN, IS IT?
HUH?
ALL RIGHT, ANGIE. HERE'S AN ORDER. AND MARCO DID TELL YOU THAT YOU HAVE TO LISTEN TO ME, REMEMBER?
HENCEFORTH, YOU ARE TO CALL ME JUST "PRISCILLA."
UNDERSTAND?
I UNDERSTAND... UM... PRISCILLA.

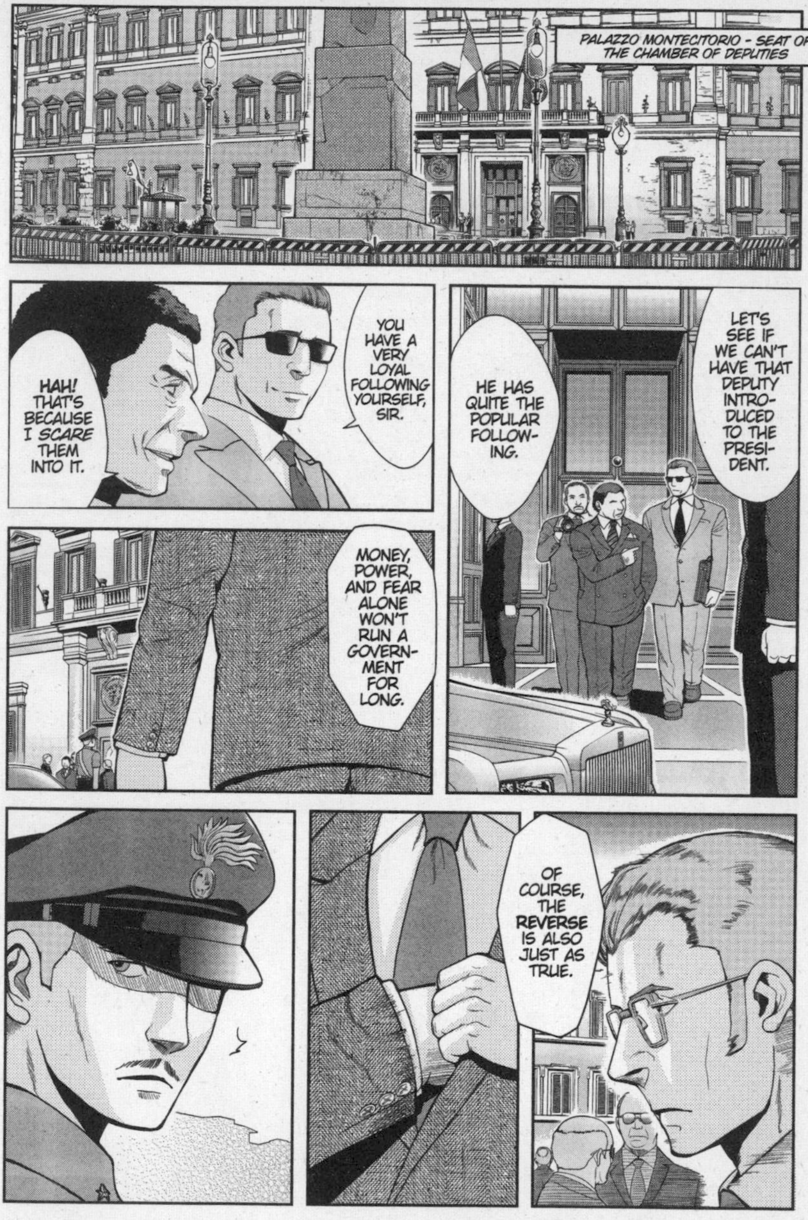
PALAZZO MONTECITORIO - SEAT OF THE CHAMBER OF DEPUTIES
LET'S SEE IF WE CAN'T HAVE THAT DEPUTY INTRODUCED TO THE PRESIDENT.
HE HAS QUITE THE POPULAR FOLLOWING.
YOU HAVE A VERY LOYAL FOLLOWING YOURSELF, SIR.
HAH! THAT'S BECAUSE I SCARE THEM INTO IT.
MONEY, POWER, AND FEAR ALONE WON'T RUN A GOVERNMENT FOR LONG.
OF COURSE, THE REVERSE IS ALSO JUST AS TRUE.

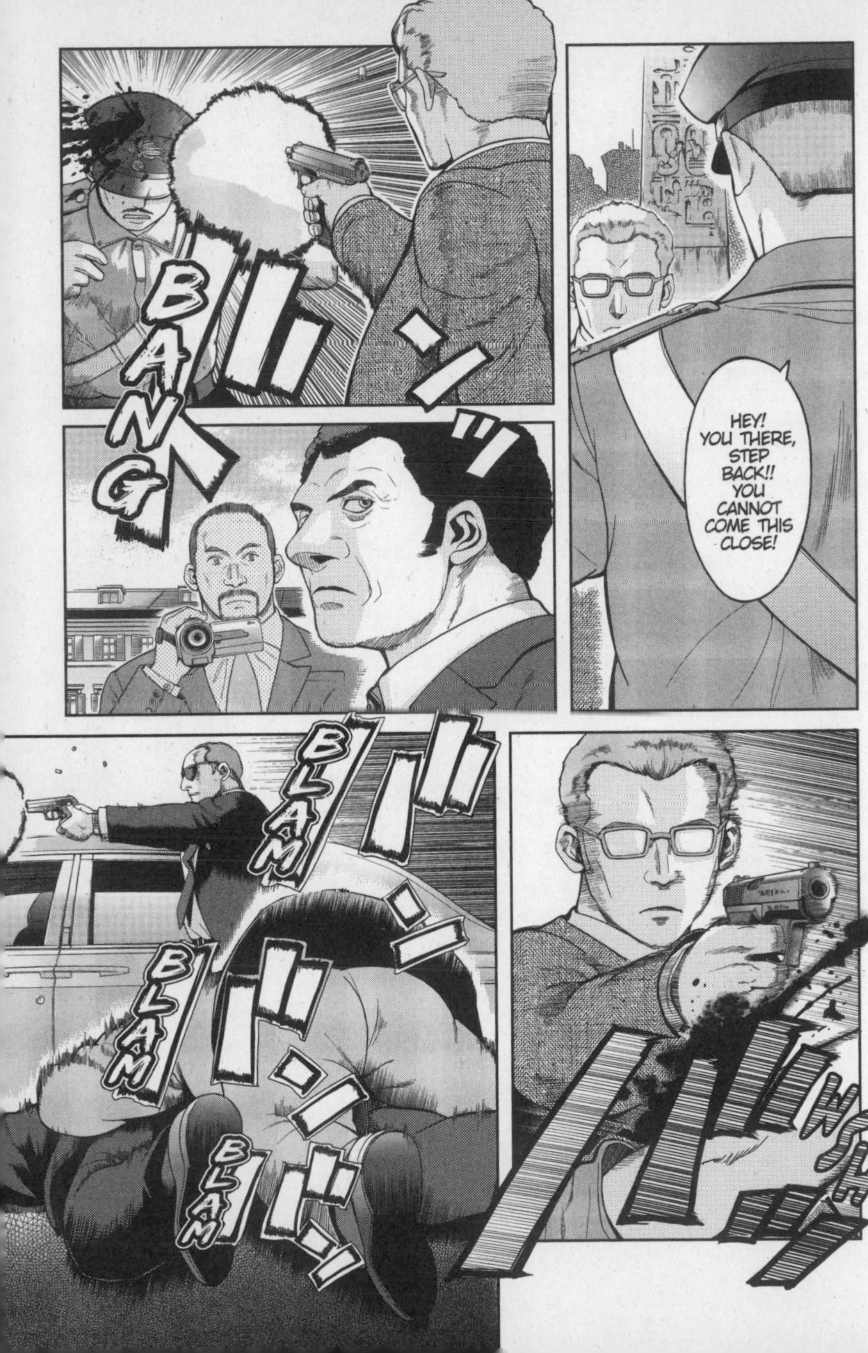
HEY! YOU THERE, STEP BACK!! YOU CANNOT COME THIS CLOSE!
BANG
WSH
BLAM
BLAM
BLAM

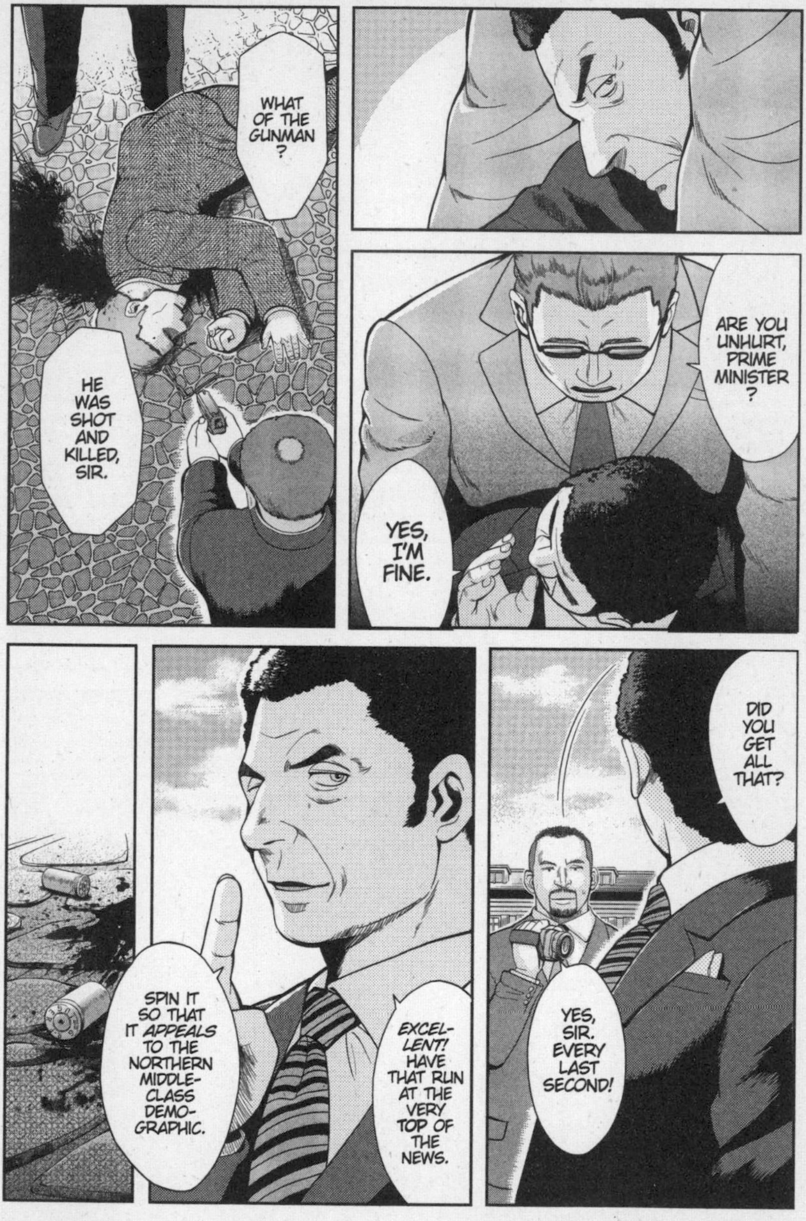
ARE YOU UNHURT, PRIME MINISTER?
YES, I'M FINE.
WHAT OF THE GUNMAN?
HE WAS SHOT AND KILLED, SIR.
DID YOU GET ALL THAT?
YES, SIR. EVERY LAST SECOND!
EXCELLENT! HAVE THAT RUN AT THE VERY TOP OF THE NEWS.
SPIN IT SO THAT IT *APPEALS* TO THE NORTHERN MIDDLE-CLASS DEMOGRAPHIC.

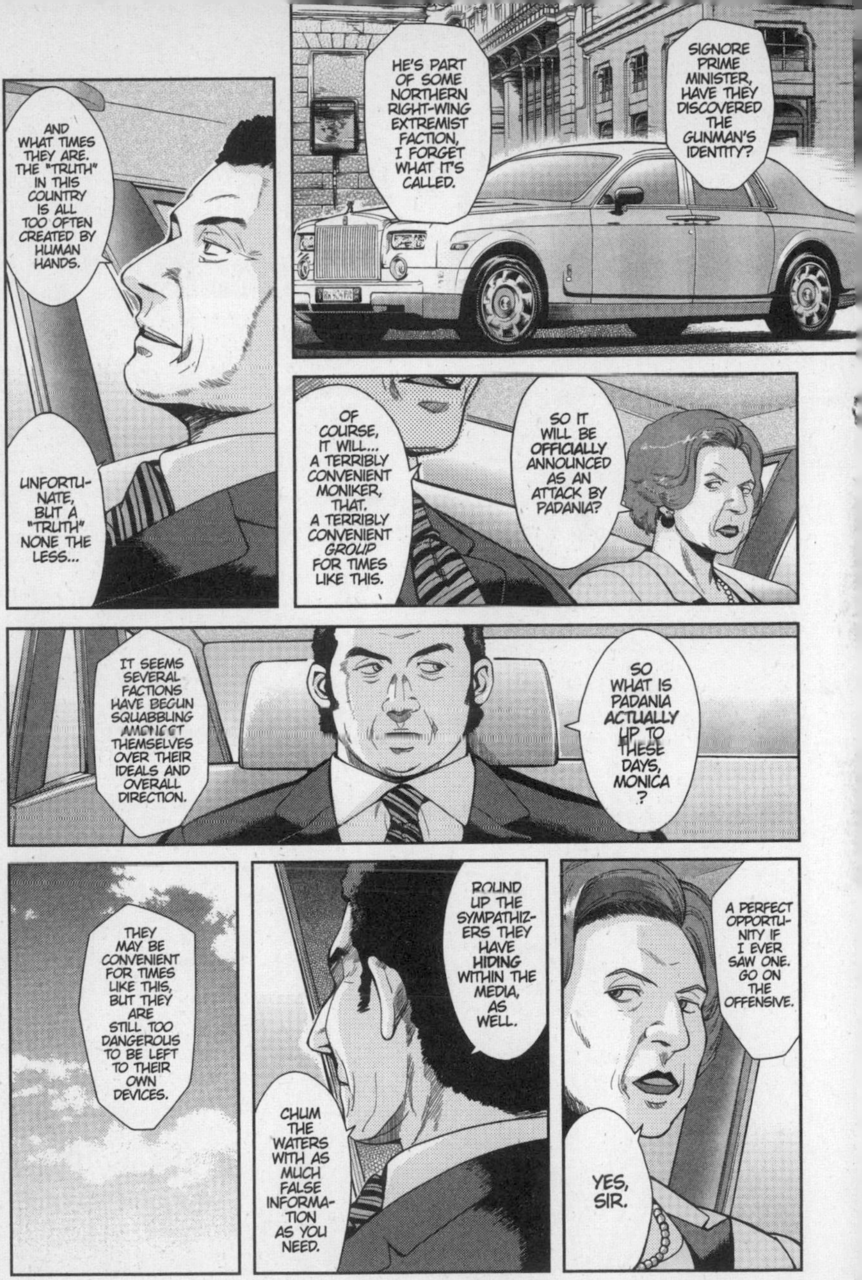
SIGNORE PRIME MINISTER, HAVE THEY DISCOVERED THE GUNMAN'S IDENTITY?
HE'S PART OF SOME NORTHERN RIGHT-WING EXTREMIST FACTION, I FORGET WHAT IT'S CALLED.
SO IT WILL BE OFFICIALLY ANNOUNCED AS AN ATTACK BY PADANIA?
OF COURSE, IT WILL... A TERRIBLY CONVENIENT MONIKER, THAT. A TERRIBLY CONVENIENT GROUP FOR TIMES LIKE THIS.
AND WHAT TIMES THEY ARE. THE "TRUTH" IN THIS COUNTRY IS ALL TOO OFTEN CREATED BY HUMAN HANDS.
UNFORTUNATE, BUT A "TRUTH" NONE THE LESS...
SO WHAT IS PADANIA ACTUALLY UP TO THESE DAYS, MONICA?
IT SEEMS SEVERAL FACTIONS HAVE BEGUN SQUABBLING AMONGST THEMSELVES OVER THEIR IDEALS AND OVERALL DIRECTION.
A PERFECT OPPORTUNITY IF I EVER SAW ONE. GO ON THE OFFENSIVE.
YES, SIR.
ROUND UP THE SYMPATHIZERS THEY HAVE HIDING WITHIN THE MEDIA, AS WELL.
CHUM THE WATERS WITH AS MUCH FALSE INFORMATION AS YOU NEED.
THEY MAY BE CONVENIENT FOR TIMES LIKE THIS, BUT THEY ARE STILL TOO DANGEROUS TO BE LEFT TO THEIR OWN DEVICES.

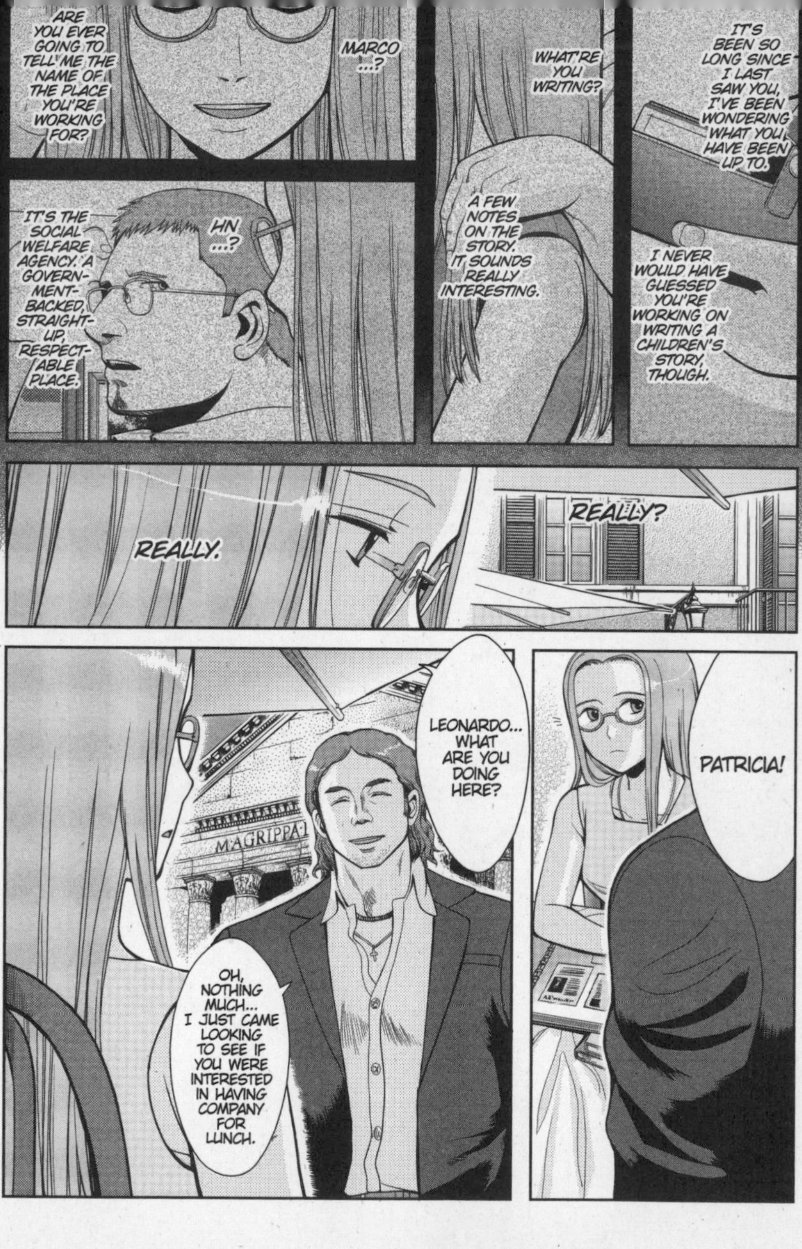
IT'S BEEN SO LONG SINCE I LAST SAW YOU, I'VE BEEN WONDERING WHAT YOU HAVE BEEN UP TO.
I NEVER WOULD HAVE GUESSED YOU'RE WORKING ON WRITING A CHILDREN'S STORY, THOUGH.
WHAT'RE YOU WRITING?
A FEW NOTES ON THE STORY. IT SOUNDS REALLY INTERESTING.
MARCO ...?
ARE YOU EVER GOING TO TELL ME THE NAME OF THE PLACE YOU'RE WORKING FOR?
HN ...?
IT'S THE SOCIAL WELFARE AGENCY. A GOVERNMENT-BACKED, STRAIGHT-UP, RESPECTABLE PLACE.
REALLY?
REALLY.
PATRICIA!
LEONARDO... WHAT ARE YOU DOING HERE?
OH, NOTHING MUCH... I JUST CAME LOOKING TO SEE IF YOU WERE INTERESTED IN HAVING COMPANY FOR LUNCH.

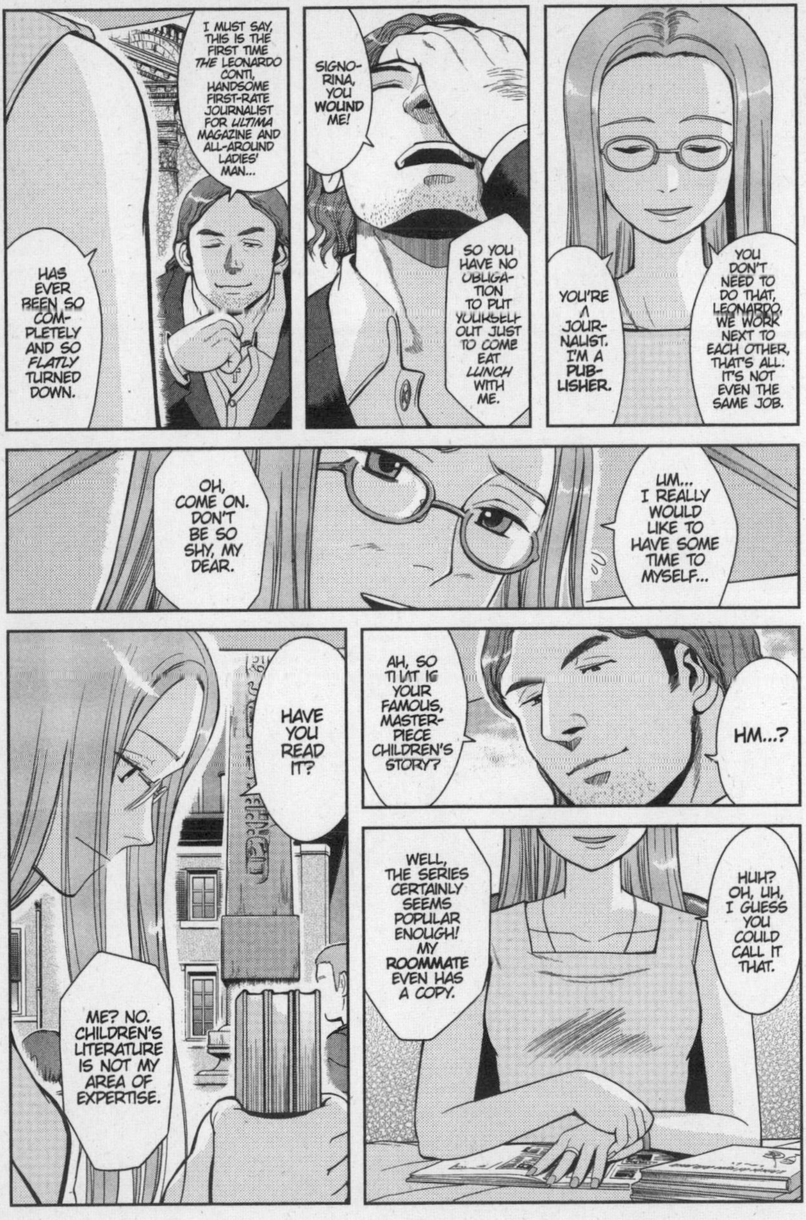
YOU DON'T NEED TO DO THAT, LEONARDO. WE WORK NEXT TO EACH OTHER, THAT'S ALL. IT'S NOT EVEN THE SAME JOB.
YOU'RE A JOURNALIST. I'M A PUBLISHER.
SIGNORINA, YOU WOUND ME!
SO YOU HAVE NO OBLIGATION TO PUT YOURSELF OUT JUST TO COME EAT *LUNCH* WITH ME.
I MUST SAY, THIS IS THE FIRST TIME *THE* LEONARDO CONTI, HANDSOME FIRST-RATE JOURNALIST FOR *ULTIMA* MAGAZINE AND ALL-AROUND LADIES' MAN...
HAS EVER BEEN SO COMPLETELY AND SO *FLATLY* TURNED DOWN.
UM... I REALLY WOULD LIKE TO HAVE SOME TIME TO MYSELF...
OH, COME ON. DON'T BE SO SHY, MY DEAR.
HM...?
AH, SO THAT IS YOUR FAMOUS, MASTERPIECE CHILDREN'S STORY?
HUH? OH, UH, I GUESS YOU COULD CALL IT THAT.
WELL, THE SERIES CERTAINLY SEEMS POPULAR ENOUGH! MY ROOMMATE EVEN HAS A COPY.
HAVE YOU READ IT?
ME? NO. CHILDREN'S LITERATURE IS NOT MY AREA OF EXPERTISE.

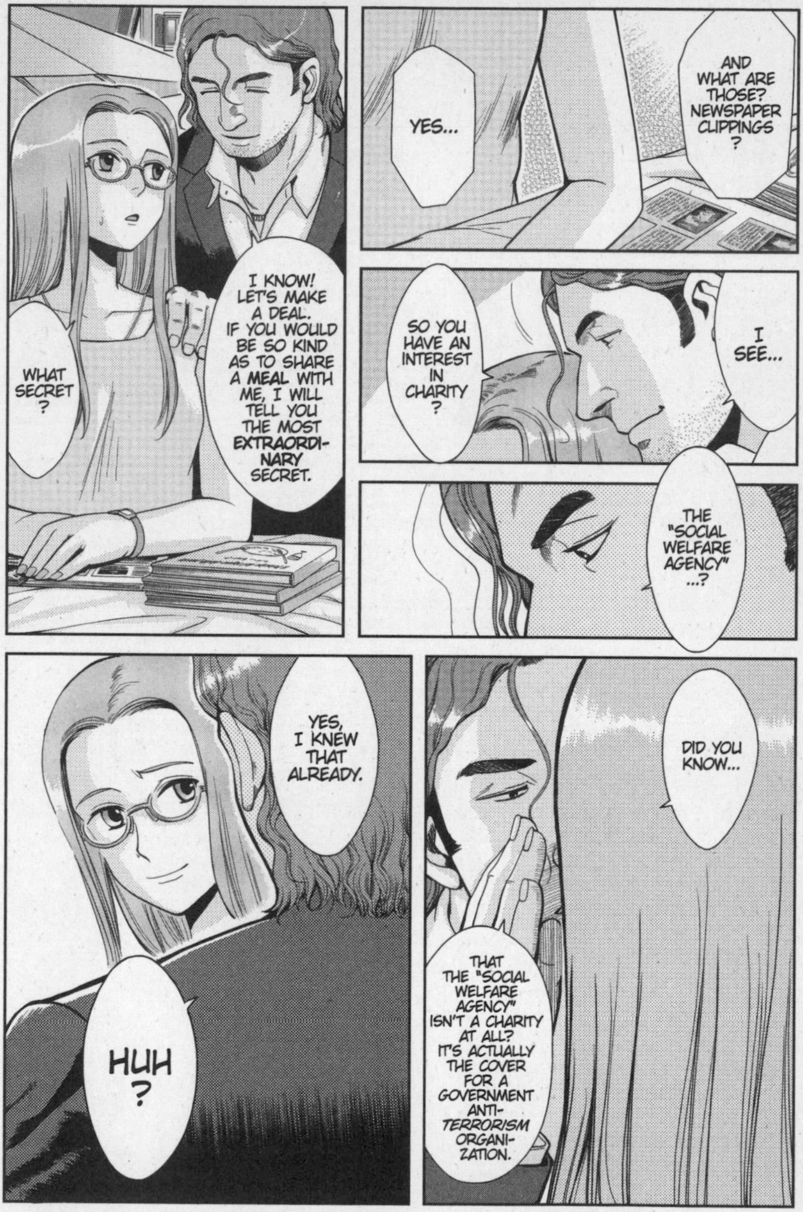
AND WHAT ARE THOSE? NEWSPAPER CLIPPINGS?
YES...
I SEE...
SO YOU HAVE AN INTEREST IN CHARITY?
THE "SOCIAL WELFARE AGENCY" ...?
I KNOW! LET'S MAKE A DEAL. IF YOU WOULD BE SO KIND AS TO SHARE A **MEAL** WITH ME, I WILL TELL YOU THE MOST **EXTRAORDINARY** SECRET.
WHAT SECRET?
DID YOU KNOW...
THAT THE "SOCIAL WELFARE AGENCY" ISN'T A CHARITY AT ALL? IT'S ACTUALLY THE COVER FOR A GOVERNMENT ANTI-TERRORISM ORGANIZATION.
YES, I KNEW THAT ALREADY.
HUH?

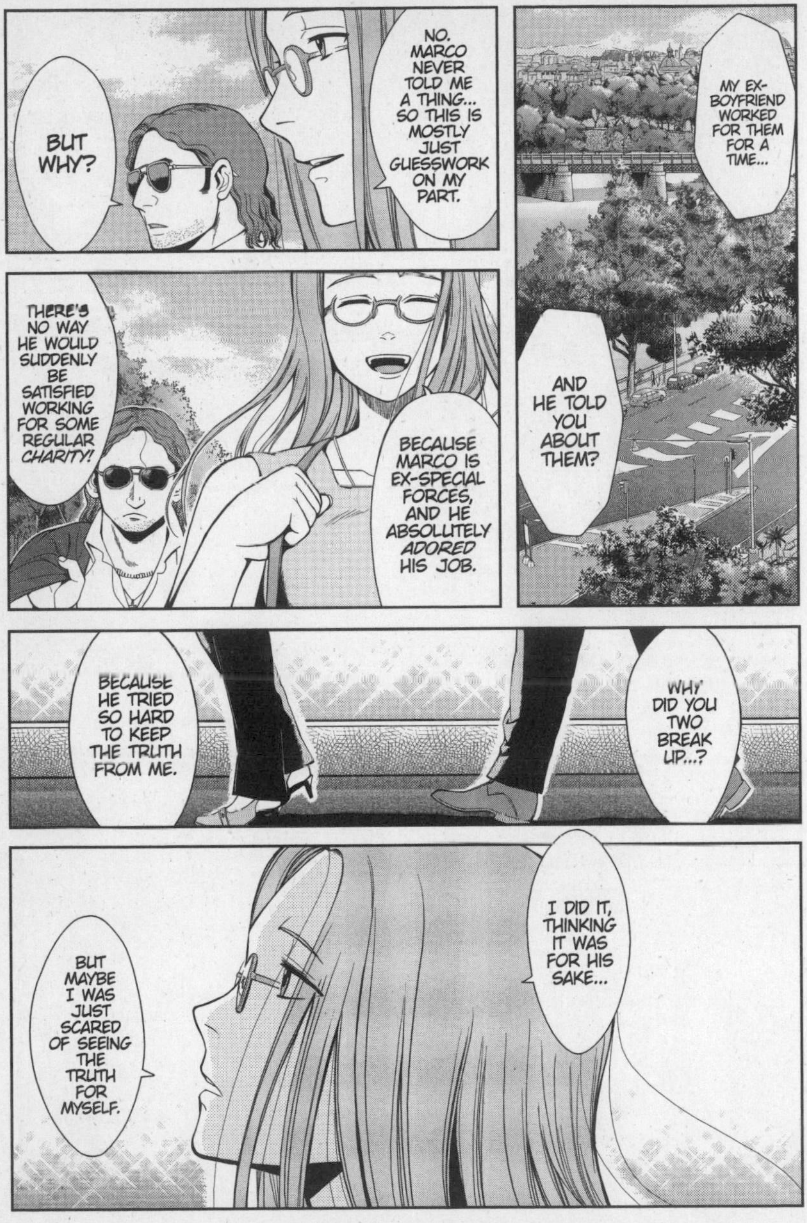
MY EX-BOYFRIEND WORKED FOR THEM FOR A TIME...
AND HE TOLD YOU ABOUT THEM?
NO. MARCO NEVER TOLD ME A THING... SO THIS IS MOSTLY JUST GUESSWORK ON MY PART.
BUT WHY?
BECAUSE MARCO IS EX-SPECIAL FORCES, AND HE ABSOLUTELY *ADORED* HIS JOB.
THERE'S NO WAY HE WOULD SUDDENLY BE SATISFIED WORKING FOR SOME REGULAR *CHARITY!*
WHY DID YOU TWO BREAK UP...?
BECAUSE HE TRIED SO HARD TO KEEP THE TRUTH FROM ME.
I DID IT, THINKING IT WAS FOR HIS SAKE...
BUT MAYBE I WAS JUST SCARED OF SEEING THE TRUTH FOR MYSELF.

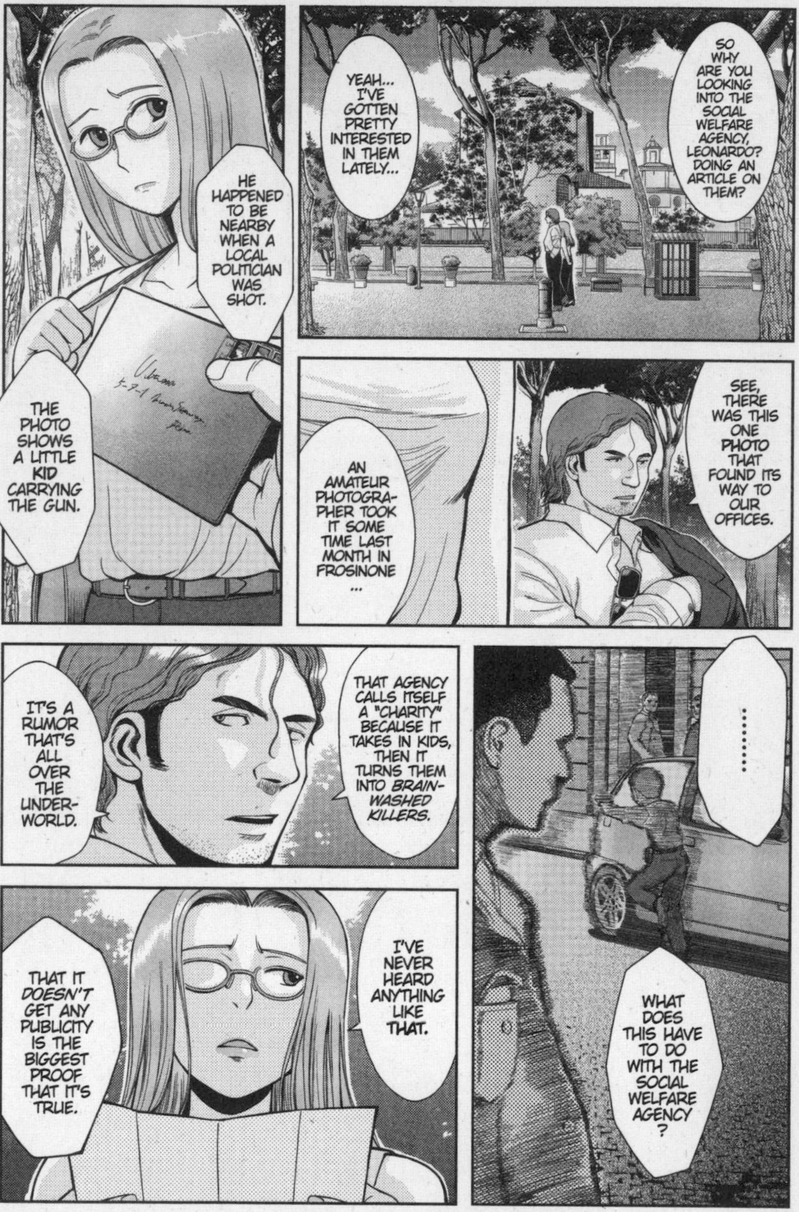
SO WHY ARE YOU LOOKING INTO THE SOCIAL WELFARE AGENCY, LEONARDO? DOING AN ARTICLE ON THEM?
YEAH... I'VE GOTTEN PRETTY INTERESTED IN THEM LATELY...
SEE, THERE WAS THIS ONE PHOTO THAT FOUND ITS WAY TO OUR OFFICES.
AN AMATEUR PHOTOGRAPHER TOOK IT SOME TIME LAST MONTH IN FROSINONE ...
HE HAPPENED TO BE NEARBY WHEN A LOCAL POLITICIAN WAS SHOT.
THE PHOTO SHOWS A LITTLE KID CARRYING THE GUN.
......
WHAT DOES THIS HAVE TO DO WITH THE SOCIAL WELFARE AGENCY?
THAT AGENCY CALLS ITSELF A "CHARITY" BECAUSE IT TAKES IN KIDS, THEN IT TURNS THEM INTO *BRAIN-WASHED KILLERS.*
IT'S A RUMOR THAT'S ALL OVER THE UNDER-WORLD.
I'VE NEVER HEARD ANYTHING LIKE **THAT.**
THAT IT DOESN'T GET ANY PUBLICITY IS THE BIGGEST PROOF THAT IT'S TRUE.

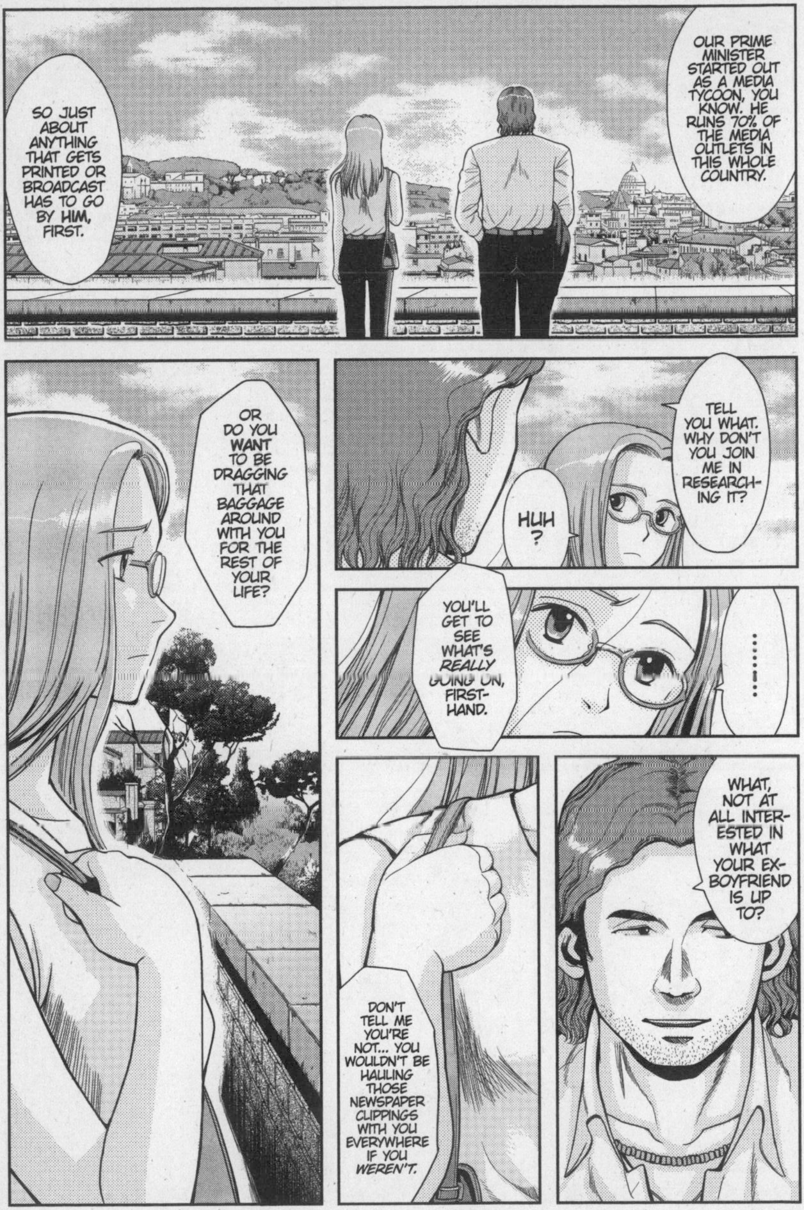
OUR PRIME MINISTER STARTED OUT AS A MEDIA TYCOON, YOU KNOW. HE RUNS 70% OF THE MEDIA OUTLETS IN THIS WHOLE COUNTRY.
SO JUST ABOUT ANYTHING THAT GETS PRINTED OR BROADCAST HAS TO GO BY **HIM**, FIRST.
TELL YOU WHAT. WHY DON'T YOU JOIN ME IN RESEARCHING IT?
HUH?
......
YOU'LL GET TO SEE WHAT'S *REALLY* GOING ON, FIRST-HAND.
WHAT, NOT AT ALL INTERESTED IN WHAT YOUR EX-BOYFRIEND IS UP TO?
DON'T TELL ME YOU'RE NOT... YOU WOULDN'T BE HAULING THOSE NEWSPAPER CLIPPINGS WITH YOU EVERYWHERE IF YOU *WEREN'T*.
OR DO YOU WANT TO BE DRAGGING THAT BAGGAGE AROUND WITH YOU FOR THE REST OF YOUR LIFE?

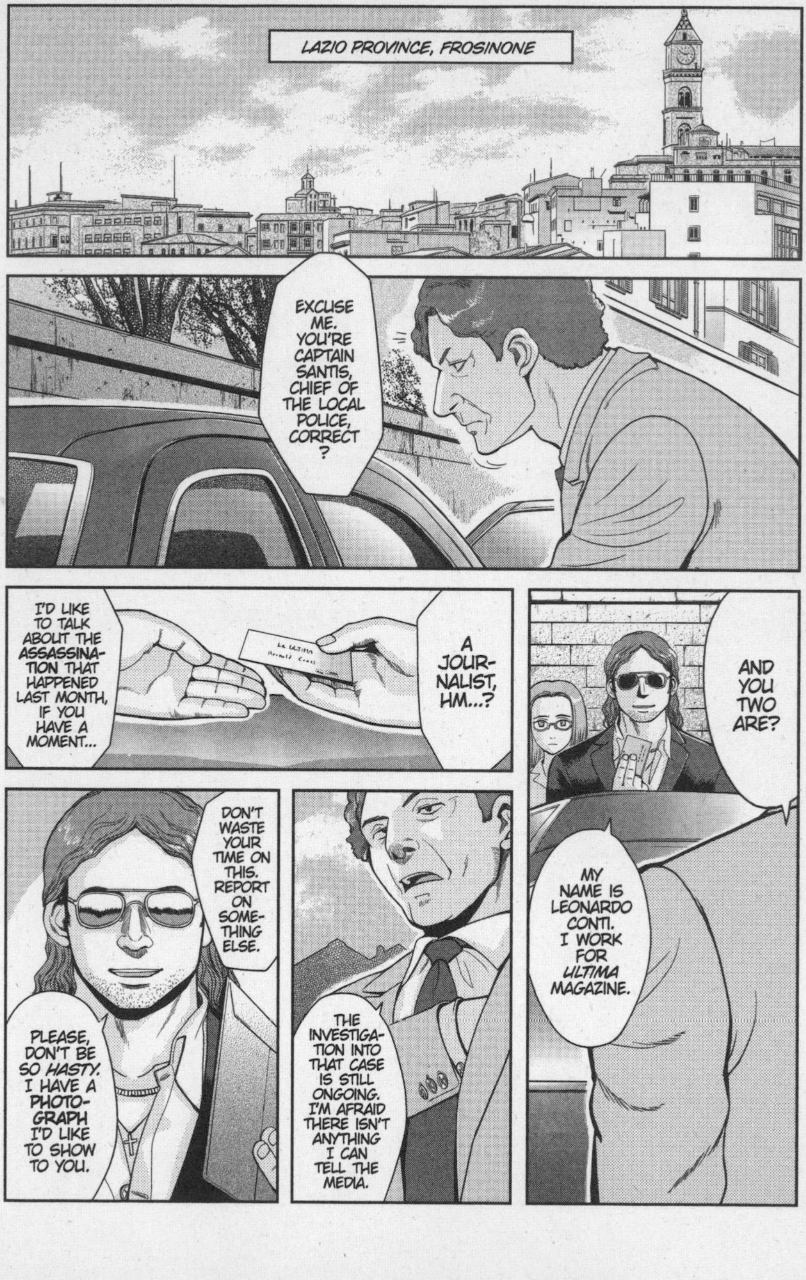
LAZIO PROVINCE, FROSINONE
EXCUSE ME. YOU'RE CAPTAIN SANTIS, CHIEF OF THE LOCAL POLICE, CORRECT?
AND YOU TWO ARE?
MY NAME IS LEONARDO CONTI. I WORK FOR *ULTIMA* MAGAZINE.
A JOURNALIST, HM...?
I'D LIKE TO TALK ABOUT THE ASSASSINATION THAT HAPPENED LAST MONTH, IF YOU HAVE A MOMENT...
THE INVESTIGATION INTO THAT CASE IS STILL ONGOING. I'M AFRAID THERE ISN'T ANYTHING I CAN TELL THE MEDIA.
DON'T WASTE YOUR TIME ON THIS. REPORT ON SOMETHING ELSE.
PLEASE, DON'T BE SO *HASTY*. I HAVE A PHOTOGRAPH I'D LIKE TO SHOW TO YOU.

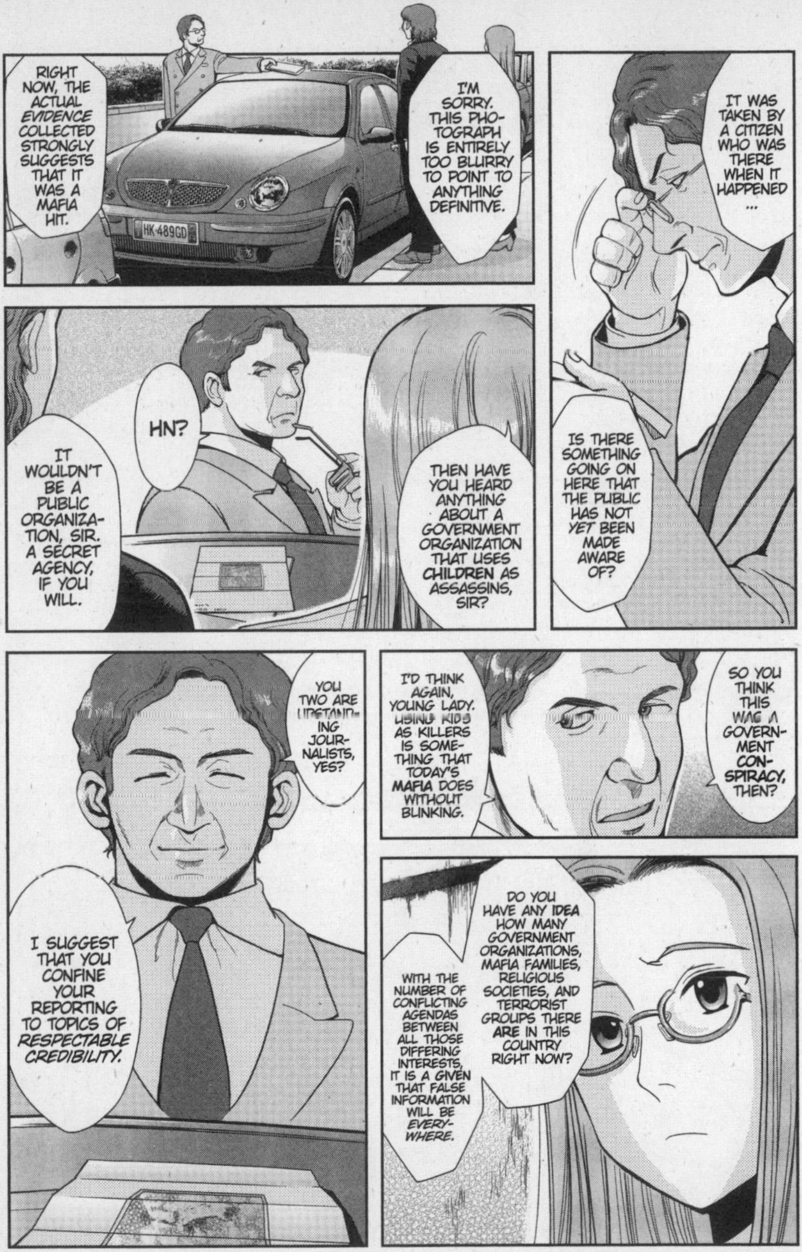
IT WAS TAKEN BY A CITIZEN WHO WAS THERE WHEN IT HAPPENED ...
I'M SORRY. THIS PHOTOGRAPH IS ENTIRELY TOO BLURRY TO POINT TO ANYTHING DEFINITIVE.
RIGHT NOW, THE ACTUAL *EVIDENCE* COLLECTED STRONGLY SUGGESTS THAT IT WAS A MAFIA HIT.
HK 489GD
IS THERE SOMETHING GOING ON HERE THAT THE PUBLIC HAS NOT *YET* BEEN MADE AWARE OF?
THEN HAVE YOU HEARD ANYTHING ABOUT A GOVERNMENT ORGANIZATION THAT USES **CHILDREN** AS ASSASSINS, SIR?
HN?
IT WOULDN'T BE A PUBLIC ORGANIZATION, SIR. A SECRET AGENCY, IF YOU WILL.
SO YOU THINK THIS WAS A GOVERNMENT **CONSPIRACY**, THEN?
I'D THINK AGAIN, YOUNG LADY. USING KIDS AS KILLERS IS SOMETHING THAT TODAY'S **MAFIA** DOES WITHOUT BLINKING.
DO YOU HAVE ANY **IDEA** HOW MANY GOVERNMENT ORGANIZATIONS, MAFIA FAMILIES, RELIGIOUS SOCIETIES, AND TERRORIST GROUPS THERE **ARE** IN THIS COUNTRY RIGHT NOW?
WITH THE NUMBER OF CONFLICTING AGENDAS BETWEEN ALL THOSE DIFFERING INTERESTS, IT IS A GIVEN THAT FALSE INFORMATION WILL BE *EVERYWHERE.*
YOU TWO ARE UPSTANDING JOURNALISTS, YES?
I SUGGEST THAT YOU CONFINE YOUR REPORTING TO TOPICS OF *RESPECTABLE CREDIBILITY.*

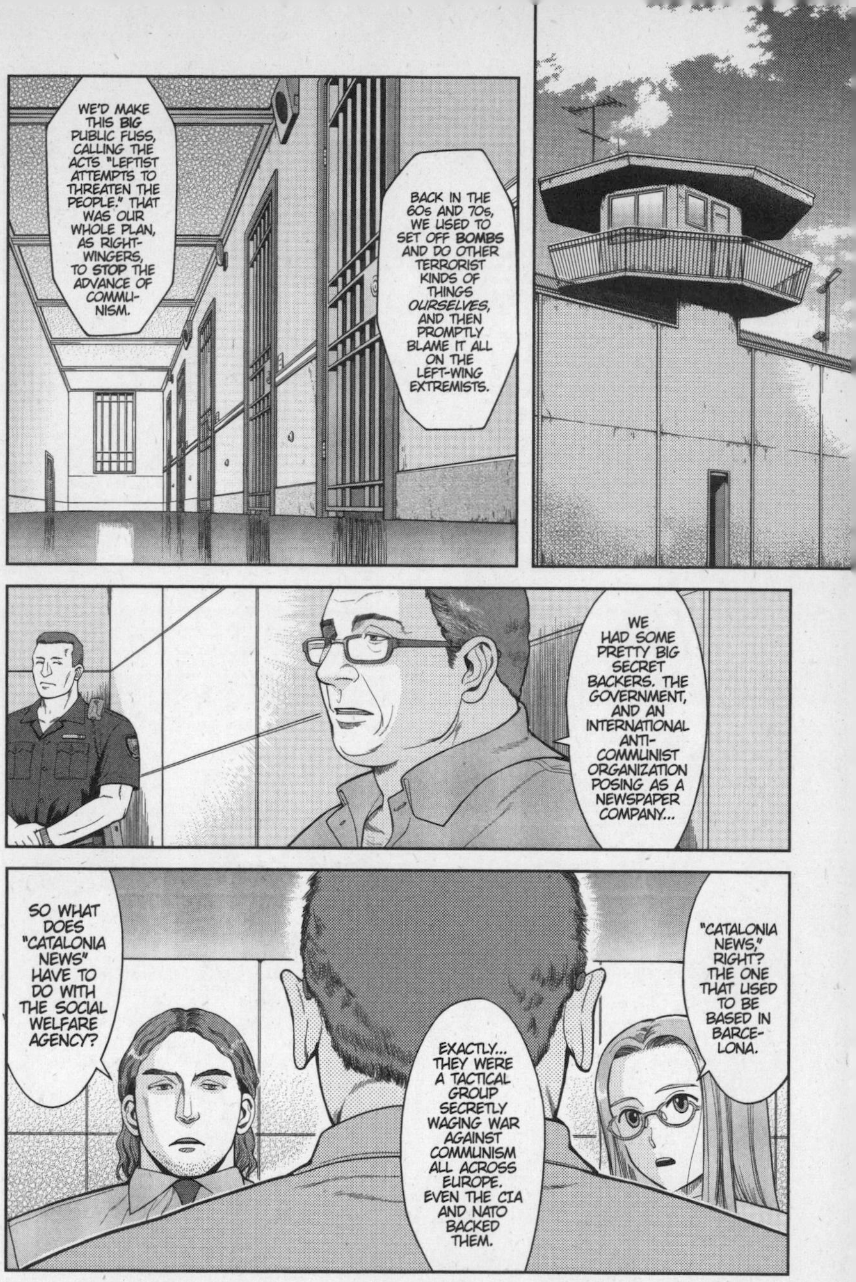
BACK IN THE 60s AND 70s, WE USED TO SET OFF BOMBS AND DO OTHER TERRORIST KINDS OF THINGS *OURSELVES,* AND THEN PROMPTLY BLAME IT ALL ON THE LEFT-WING EXTREMISTS.
WE'D MAKE THIS BIG PUBLIC FUSS, CALLING THE ACTS "LEFTIST ATTEMPTS TO THREATEN THE PEOPLE." THAT WAS OUR WHOLE PLAN, AS RIGHT-WINGERS, TO STOP THE ADVANCE OF COMMUNISM.
WE HAD SOME PRETTY BIG SECRET BACKERS. THE GOVERNMENT, AND AN INTERNATIONAL ANTI-COMMUNIST ORGANIZATION POSING AS A NEWSPAPER COMPANY...
"CATALONIA NEWS," RIGHT? THE ONE THAT USED TO BE BASED IN BARCELONA.
EXACTLY... THEY WERE A TACTICAL GROUP SECRETLY WAGING WAR AGAINST COMMUNISM ALL ACROSS EUROPE. EVEN THE CIA AND NATO BACKED THEM.
SO WHAT DOES "CATALONIA NEWS" HAVE TO DO WITH THE SOCIAL WELFARE AGENCY?

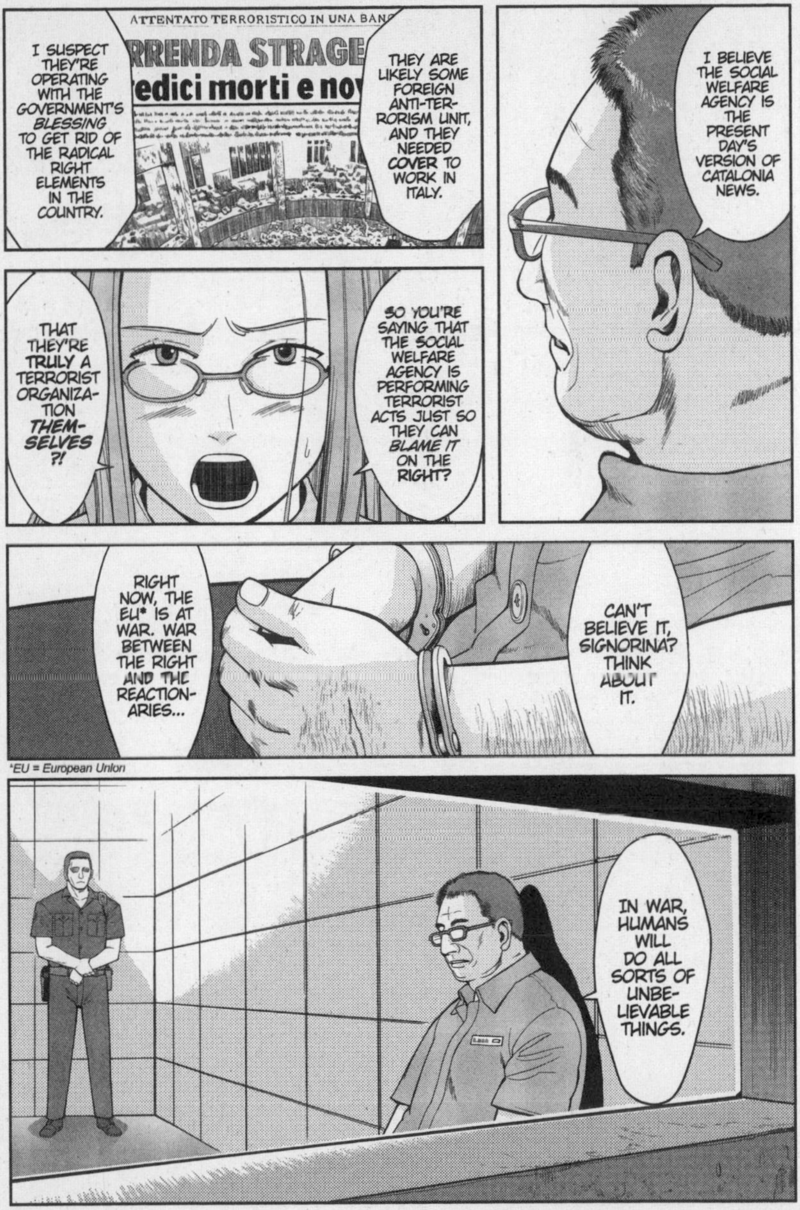
I BELIEVE THE SOCIAL WELFARE AGENCY IS THE PRESENT DAY'S VERSION OF CATALONIA NEWS.
ATTENTATO TERRORISTICO IN UNA BANC
RRENDA STRAGE
redici morti e nov
THEY ARE LIKELY SOME FOREIGN ANTI-TERRORISM UNIT, AND THEY NEEDED COVER TO WORK IN ITALY.
I SUSPECT THEY'RE OPERATING WITH THE GOVERNMENT'S *BLESSING* TO GET RID OF THE RADICAL RIGHT ELEMENTS IN THE COUNTRY.
SO YOU'RE SAYING THAT THE SOCIAL WELFARE AGENCY IS PERFORMING TERRORIST ACTS JUST SO THEY CAN *BLAME IT* ON THE RIGHT?
THAT THEY'RE TRULY A TERRORIST ORGANIZATION *THEMSELVES*?!
CAN'T BELIEVE IT, SIGNORINA? THINK ABOUT IT.
RIGHT NOW, THE EU* IS AT WAR. WAR BETWEEN THE RIGHT AND THE REACTIONARIES...
IN WAR, HUMANS WILL DO ALL SORTS OF UNBELIEVABLE THINGS.

*EU = European Union

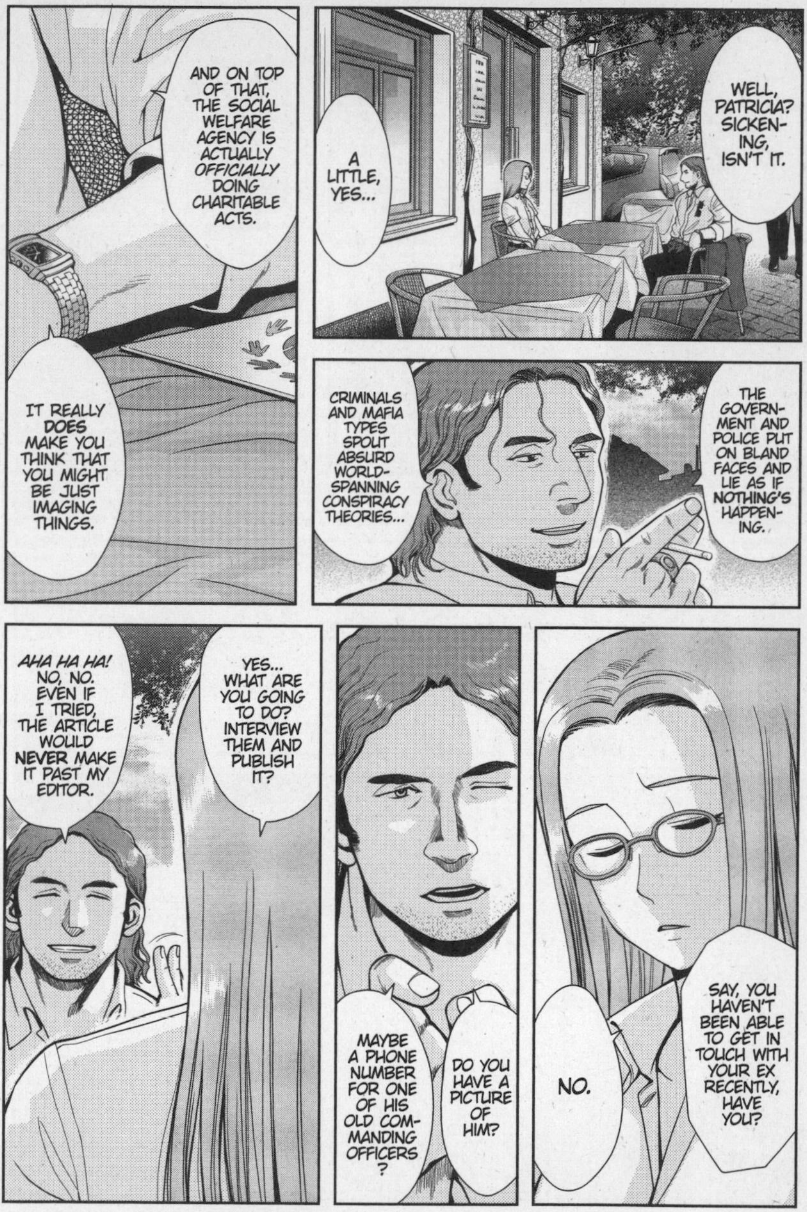
WELL, PATRICIA? SICKENING, ISN'T IT.
A LITTLE, YES...
THE GOVERNMENT AND POLICE PUT ON BLAND FACES AND LIE AS IF NOTHING'S HAPPENING.
CRIMINALS AND MAFIA TYPES SPOUT ABSURD WORLD-SPANNING CONSPIRACY THEORIES...
AND ON TOP OF THAT, THE SOCIAL WELFARE AGENCY IS ACTUALLY *OFFICIALLY* DOING CHARITABLE ACTS.
IT REALLY **DOES** MAKE YOU THINK THAT YOU MIGHT BE JUST IMAGING THINGS.
SAY, YOU HAVEN'T BEEN ABLE TO GET IN TOUCH WITH YOUR EX RECENTLY, HAVE YOU?
NO.
DO YOU HAVE A PICTURE OF HIM?
MAYBE A PHONE NUMBER FOR ONE OF HIS OLD COMMANDING OFFICERS?
YES... WHAT ARE YOU GOING TO DO? INTERVIEW THEM AND PUBLISH IT?
AHA HA HA! NO, NO. EVEN IF I TRIED, THE ARTICLE WOULD **NEVER** MAKE IT PAST MY EDITOR.

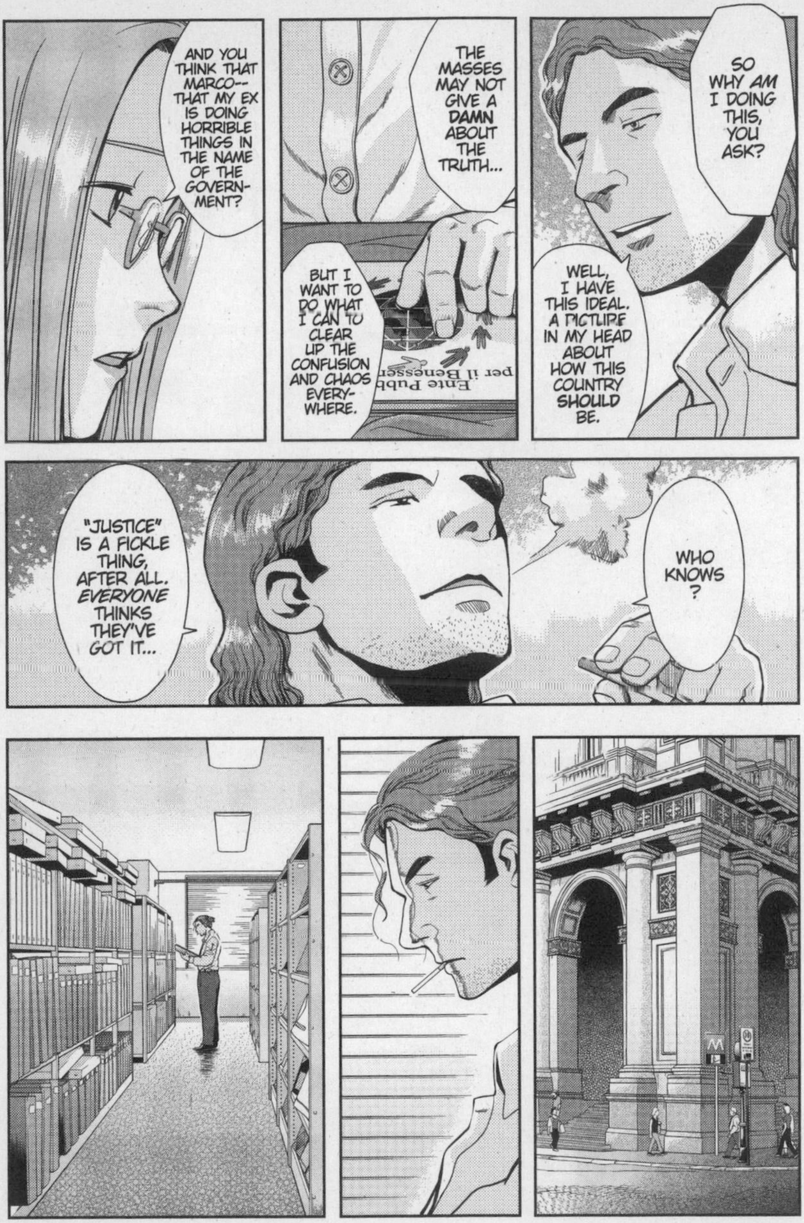
SO WHY AM I DOING THIS, YOU ASK?
WELL, I HAVE THIS IDEAL. A PICTURE IN MY HEAD ABOUT HOW THIS COUNTRY SHOULD BE.
THE MASSES MAY NOT GIVE A DAMN ABOUT THE TRUTH...
BUT I WANT TO DO WHAT I CAN TO CLEAR UP THE CONFUSION AND CHAOS EVERY-WHERE.
AND YOU THINK THAT MARCO-- THAT MY EX IS DOING HORRIBLE THINGS IN THE NAME OF THE GOVERN-MENT?
WHO KNOWS?
"JUSTICE" IS A FICKLE THING, AFTER ALL. EVERYONE THINKS THEY'VE GOT IT...

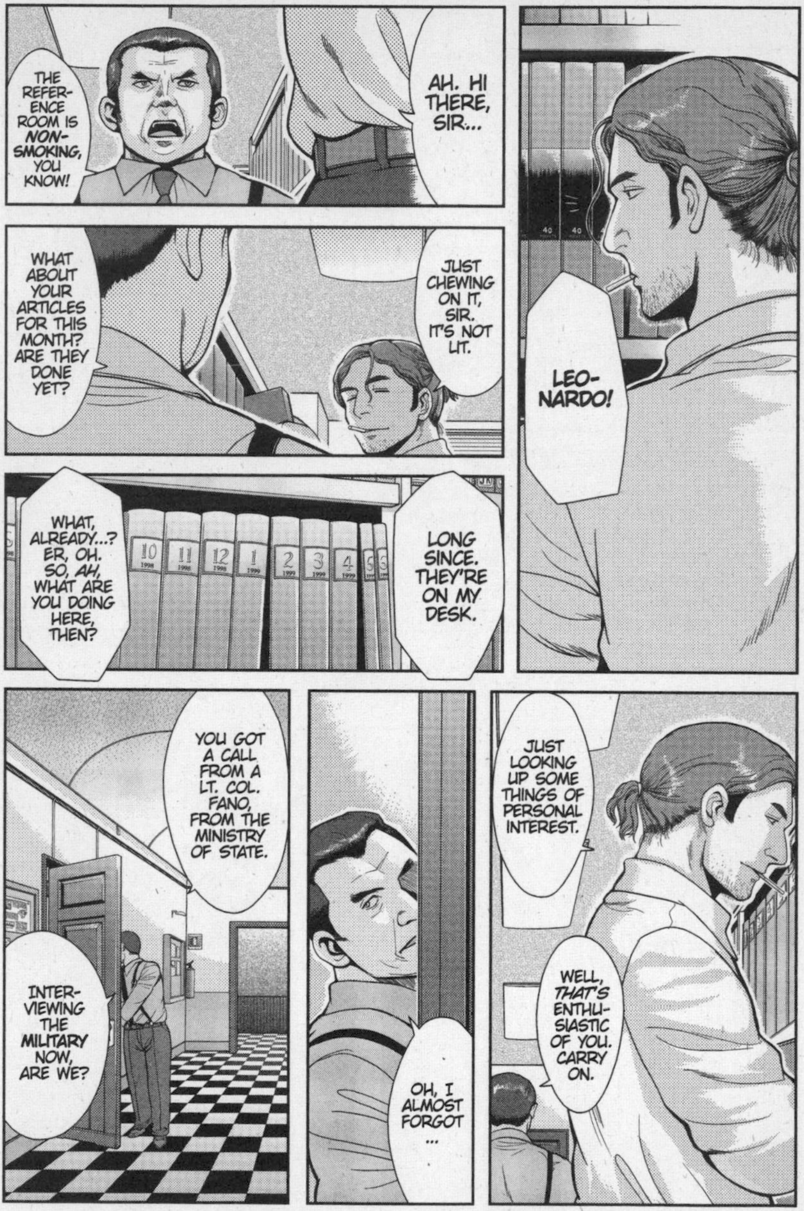
LEO-NARDO!
AH. HI THERE, SIR...
THE REFER-ENCE ROOM IS NON-SMOKING, YOU KNOW!
JUST CHEWING ON IT, SIR. IT'S NOT LIT.
WHAT ABOUT YOUR ARTICLES FOR THIS MONTH? ARE THEY DONE YET?
LONG SINCE. THEY'RE ON MY DESK.
WHAT, ALREADY...? ER, OH. SO, AH, WHAT ARE YOU DOING HERE, THEN?
JUST LOOKING UP SOME THINGS OF PERSONAL INTEREST.
WELL, THAT'S ENTHU-SIASTIC OF YOU. CARRY ON.
OH, I ALMOST FORGOT ...
YOU GOT A CALL FROM A LT. COL. FANO, FROM THE MINISTRY OF STATE.
INTER-VIEWING THE MILITARY NOW, ARE WE?

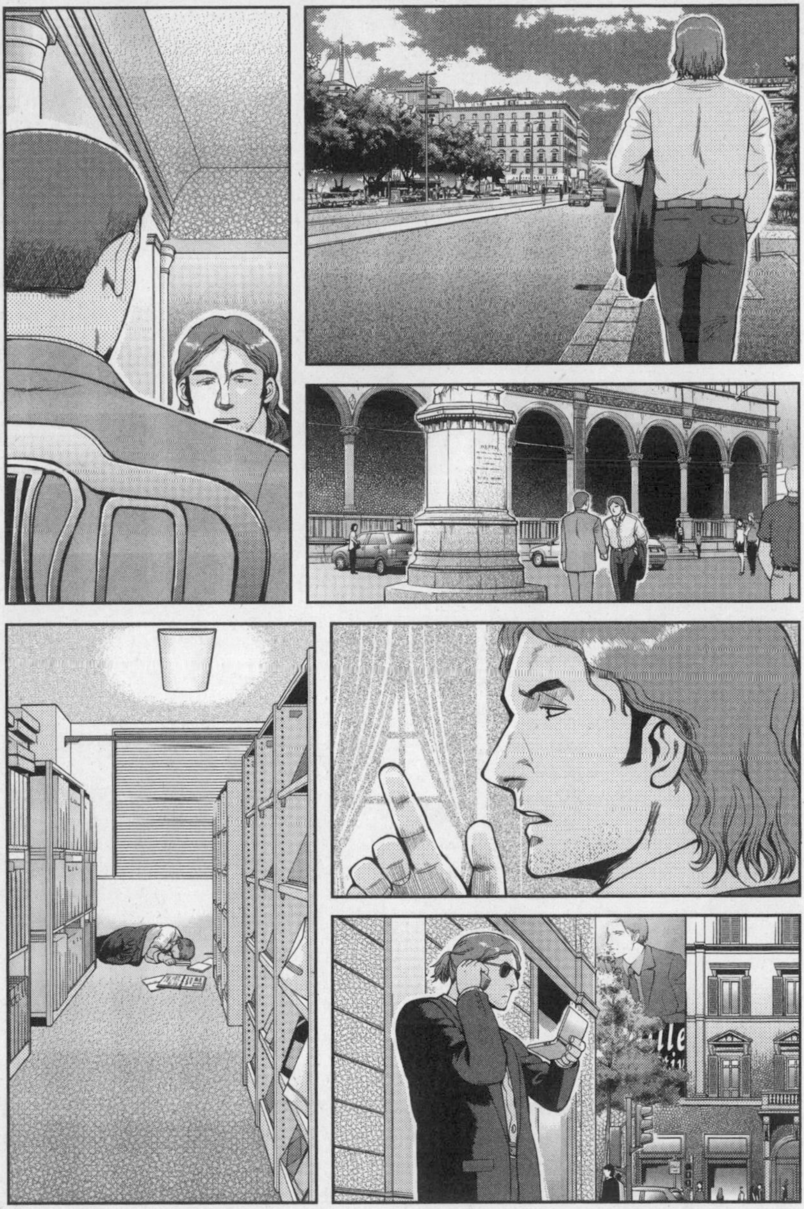

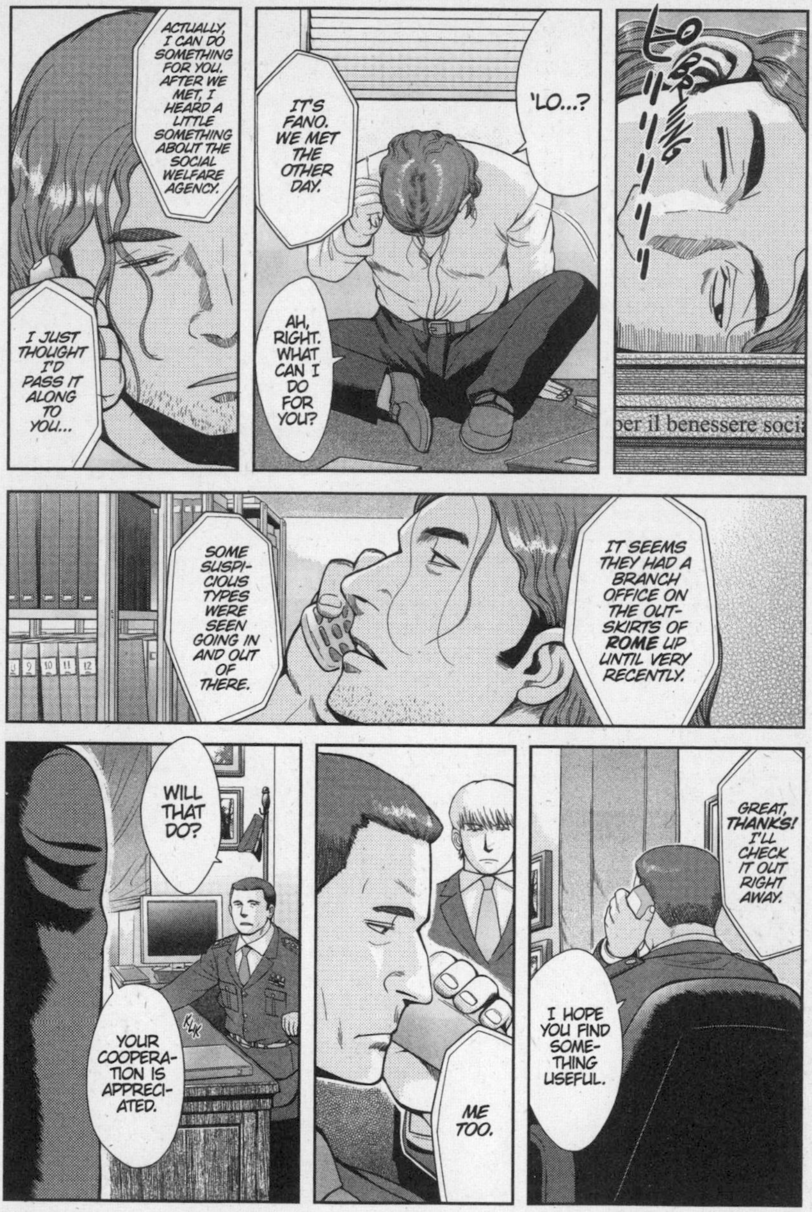
BRRING
per il benessere soci
'LO...?
IT'S FANO. WE MET THE OTHER DAY.
AH, RIGHT. WHAT CAN I DO FOR YOU?
ACTUALLY, I CAN DO SOMETHING FOR YOU. AFTER WE MET, I HEARD A LITTLE SOMETHING ABOUT THE SOCIAL WELFARE AGENCY.
I JUST THOUGHT I'D PASS IT ALONG TO YOU...
IT SEEMS THEY HAD A BRANCH OFFICE ON THE OUTSKIRTS OF ROME UP UNTIL VERY RECENTLY.
SOME SUSPICIOUS TYPES WERE SEEN GOING IN AND OUT OF THERE.
GREAT, THANKS! I'LL CHECK IT OUT RIGHT AWAY.
I HOPE YOU FIND SOMETHING USEFUL.
ME TOO.
WILL THAT DO?
KLIK
YOUR COOPERATION IS APPRECIATED.

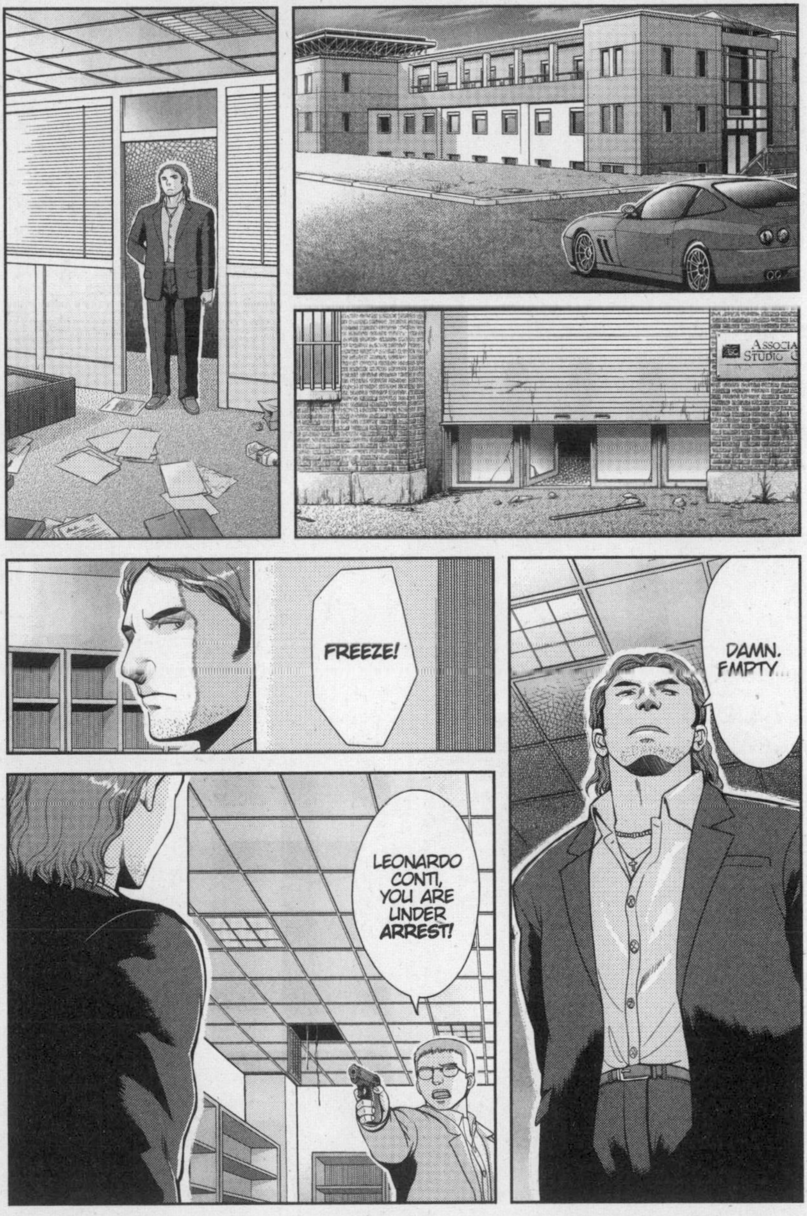
DAMN. EMPTY...
FREEZE!
LEONARDO CONTI, YOU ARE UNDER ARREST!

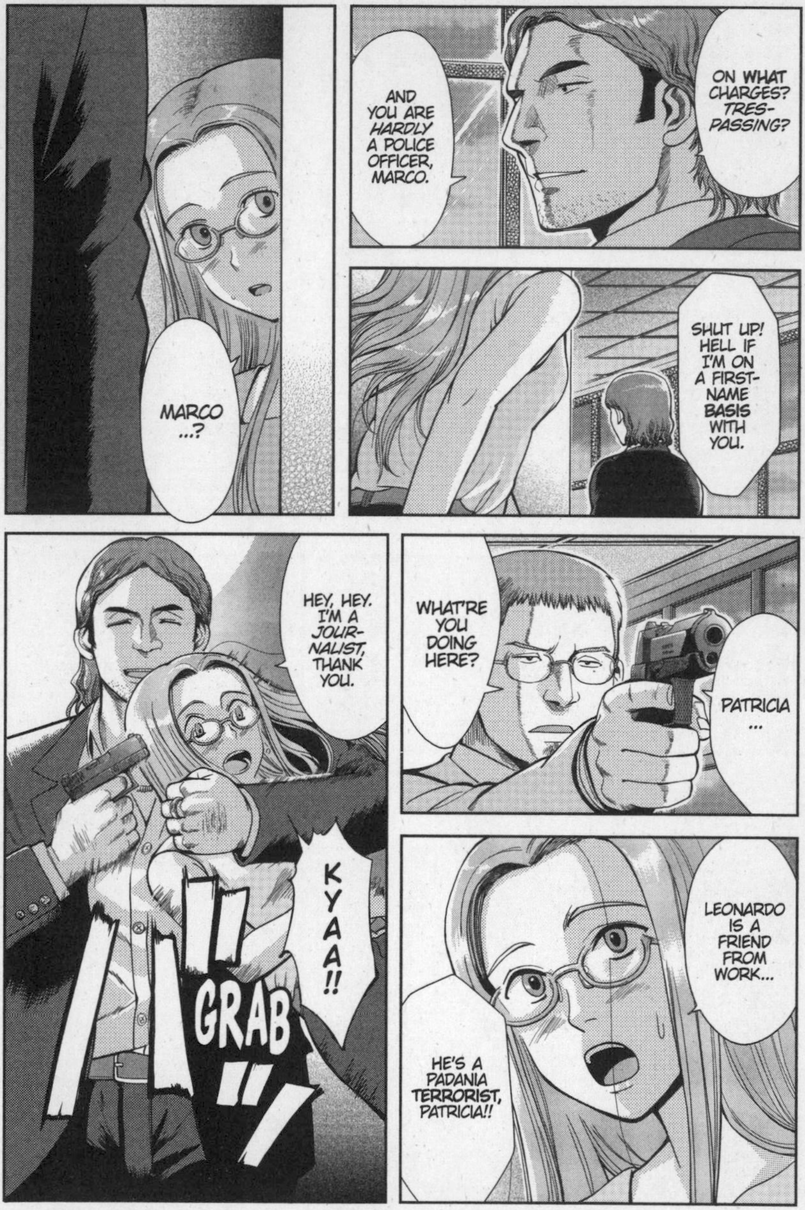
ON WHAT CHARGES? TRES-PASSING?
AND YOU ARE HARDLY A POLICE OFFICER, MARCO.
SHUT UP! HELL IF I'M ON A FIRST-NAME BASIS WITH YOU.
MARCO ...?
PATRICIA ...
WHAT'RE YOU DOING HERE?
LEONARDO IS A FRIEND FROM WORK...
HE'S A PADANIA TERRORIST, PATRICIA!!
HEY, HEY. I'M A JOURNALIST, THANK YOU.
KYAA!!
GRAB

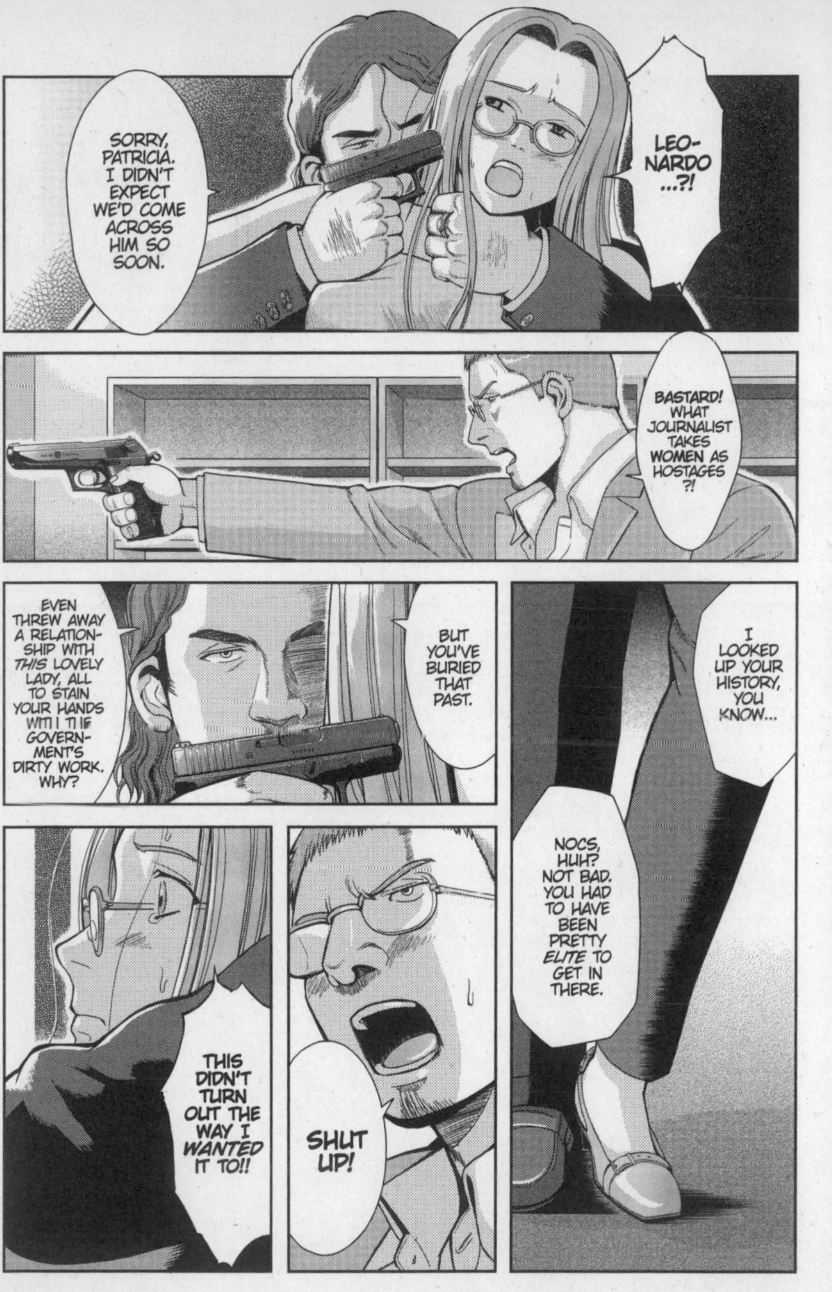
LEO-NARDO ...?!
SORRY, PATRICIA. I DIDN'T EXPECT WE'D COME ACROSS HIM SO SOON.
BASTARD! WHAT JOURNALIST TAKES WOMEN AS HOSTAGES ?!
I LOOKED UP YOUR HISTORY, YOU KNOW...
NOCS, HUH? NOT BAD. YOU HAD TO HAVE BEEN PRETTY *ELITE* TO GET IN THERE.
BUT YOU'VE BURIED THAT PAST.
EVEN THREW AWAY A RELATION-SHIP WITH *THIS* LOVELY LADY, ALL TO STAIN YOUR HANDS WITH THE GOVERN-MENT'S DIRTY WORK. WHY?
SHUT UP!
THIS DIDN'T TURN OUT THE WAY I *WANTED* IT TO!!

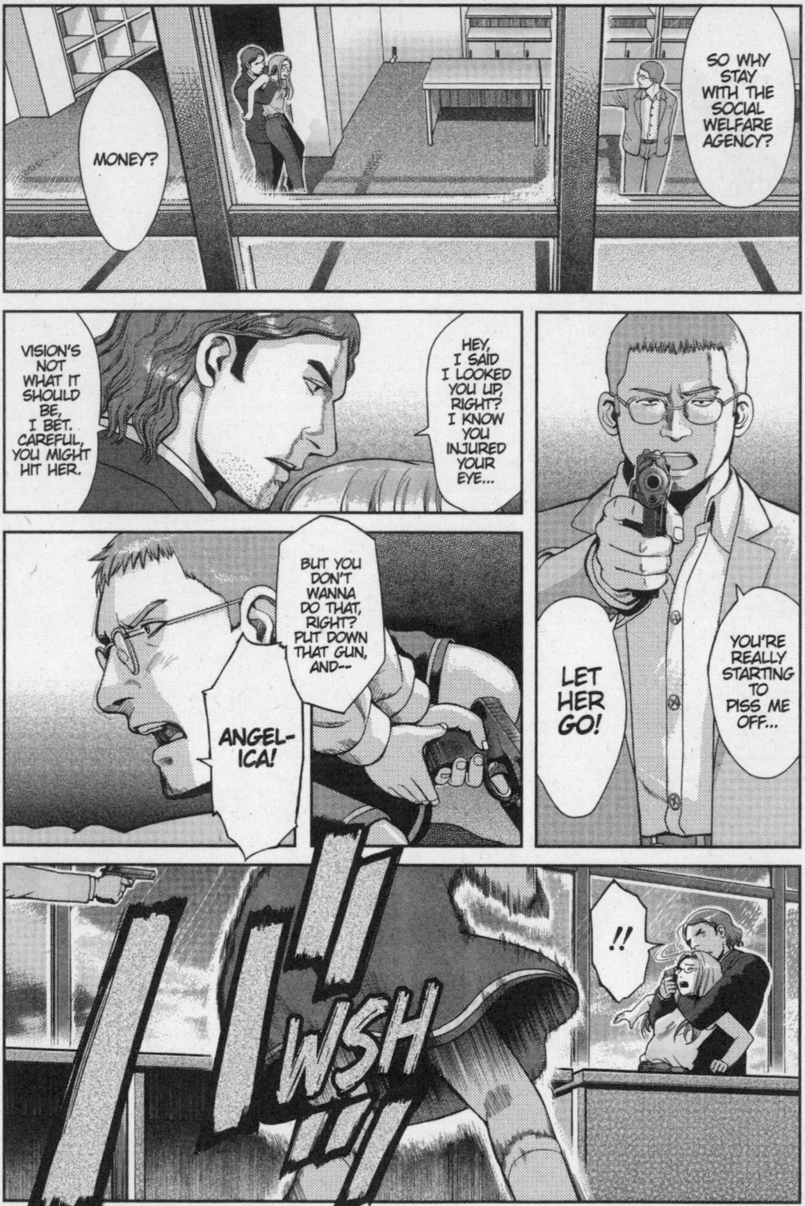
SO WHY STAY WITH THE SOCIAL WELFARE AGENCY?
MONEY?
YOU'RE REALLY STARTING TO PISS ME OFF...
LET HER GO!
HEY, I SAID I LOOKED YOU UP, RIGHT? I KNOW YOU INJURED YOUR EYE...
VISION'S NOT WHAT IT SHOULD BE, I BET. CAREFUL, YOU MIGHT HIT HER.
BUT YOU DON'T WANNA DO THAT, RIGHT? PUT DOWN THAT GUN, AND--
ANGEL-ICA!
!!
WSH

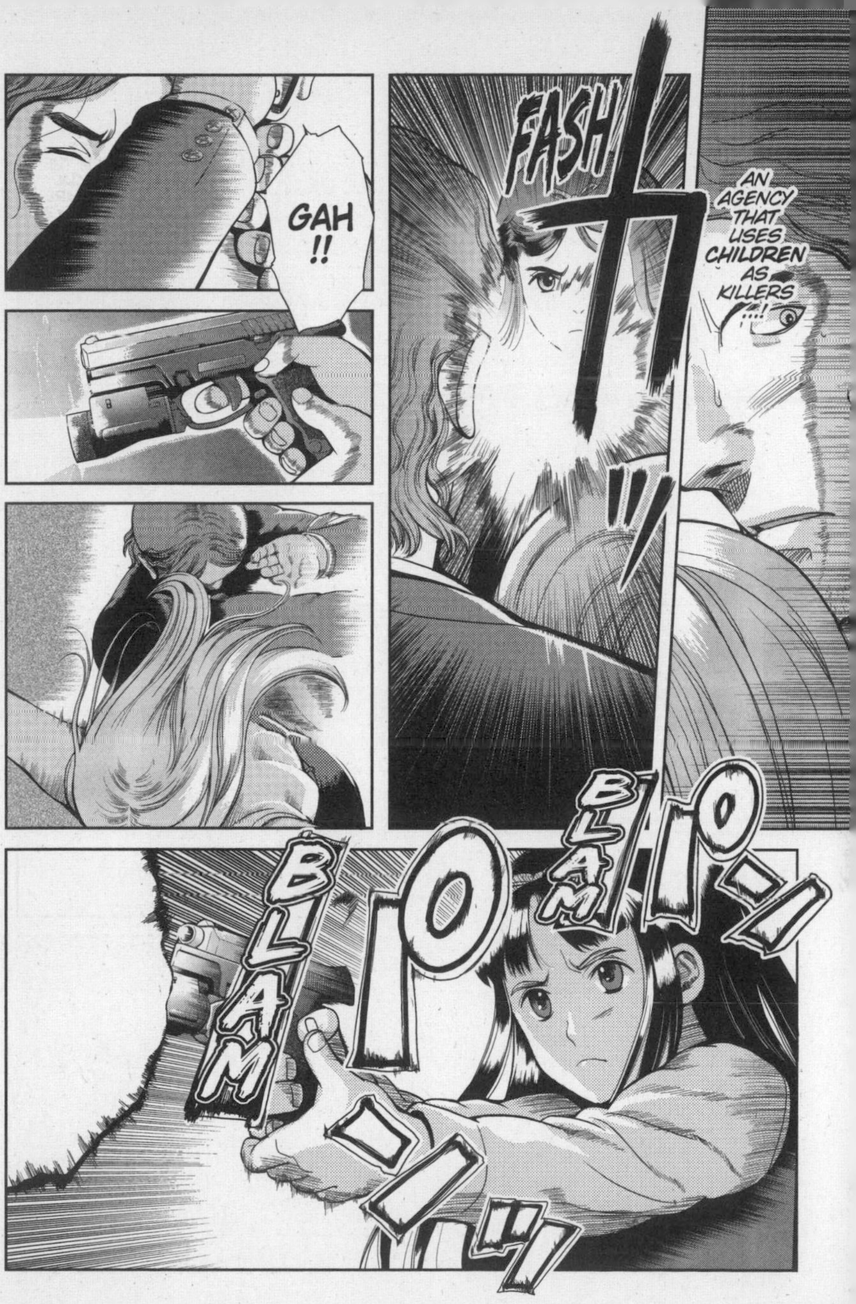
FASH
AN AGENCY THAT USES CHILDREN AS KILLERS...!
GAH!!
BLAM
BLAM

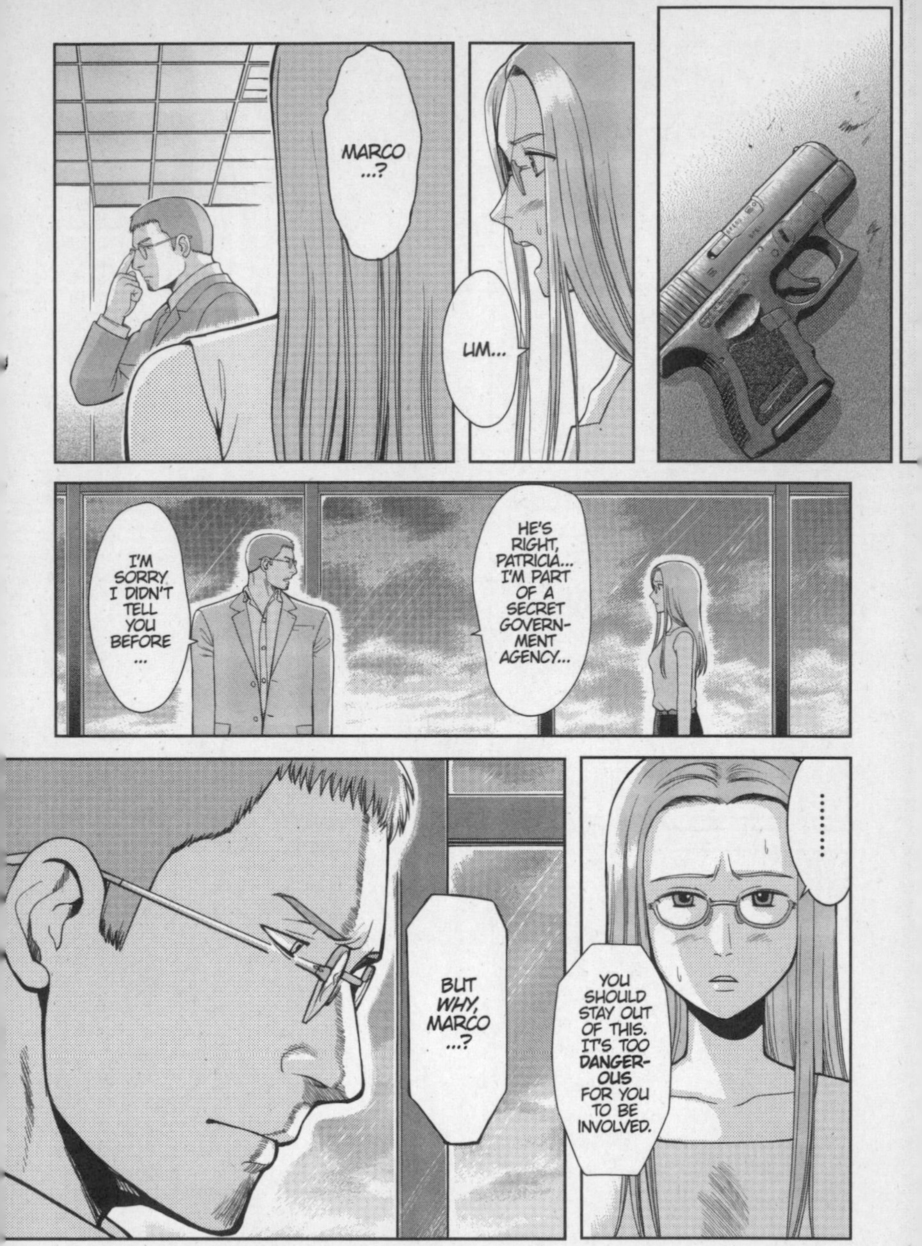
UM...
MARCO ...?
HE'S RIGHT, PATRICIA... I'M PART OF A SECRET GOVERNMENT AGENCY...
I'M SORRY I DIDN'T TELL YOU BEFORE ...
......
YOU SHOULD STAY OUT OF THIS. IT'S TOO DANGEROUS FOR YOU TO BE INVOLVED.
BUT WHY, MARCO ...?

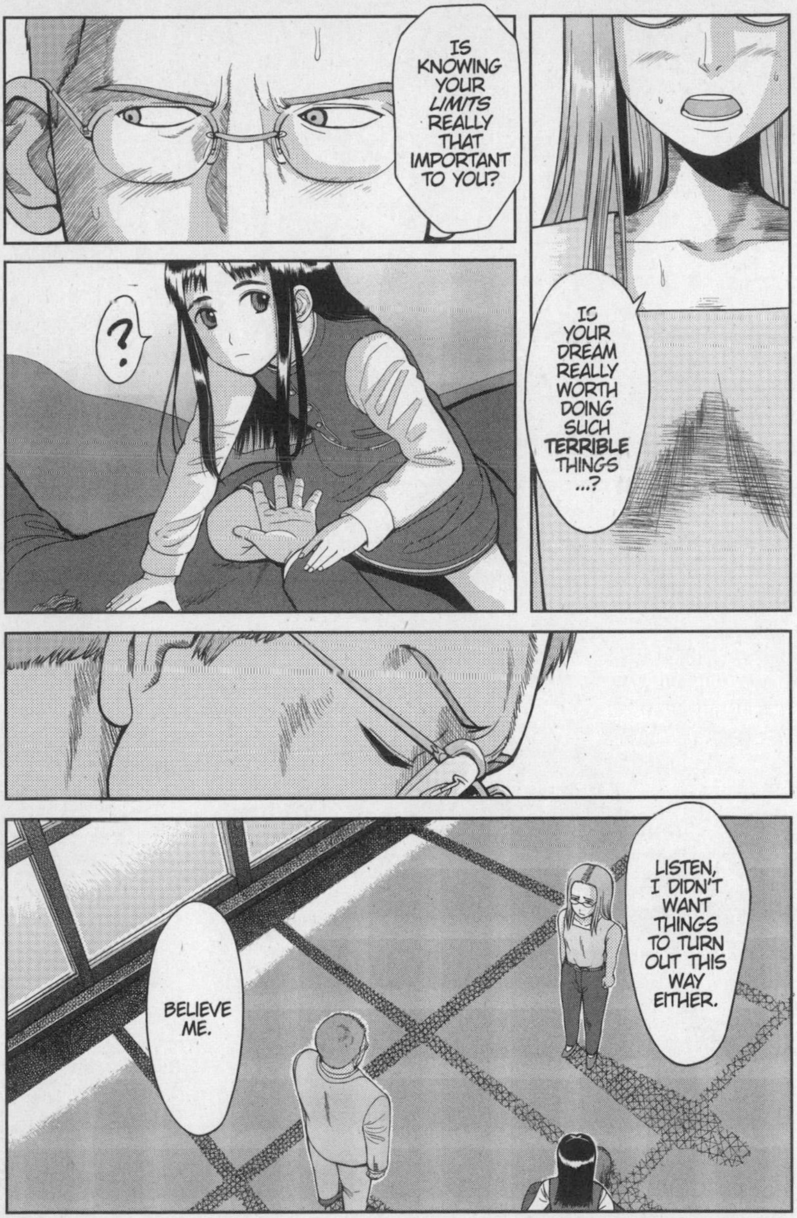
IS YOUR DREAM REALLY WORTH DOING SUCH TERRIBLE THINGS ...?
IS KNOWING YOUR *LIMITS* REALLY THAT IMPORTANT TO YOU?
?
LISTEN, I DIDN'T WANT THINGS TO TURN OUT THIS WAY EITHER.
BELIEVE ME.

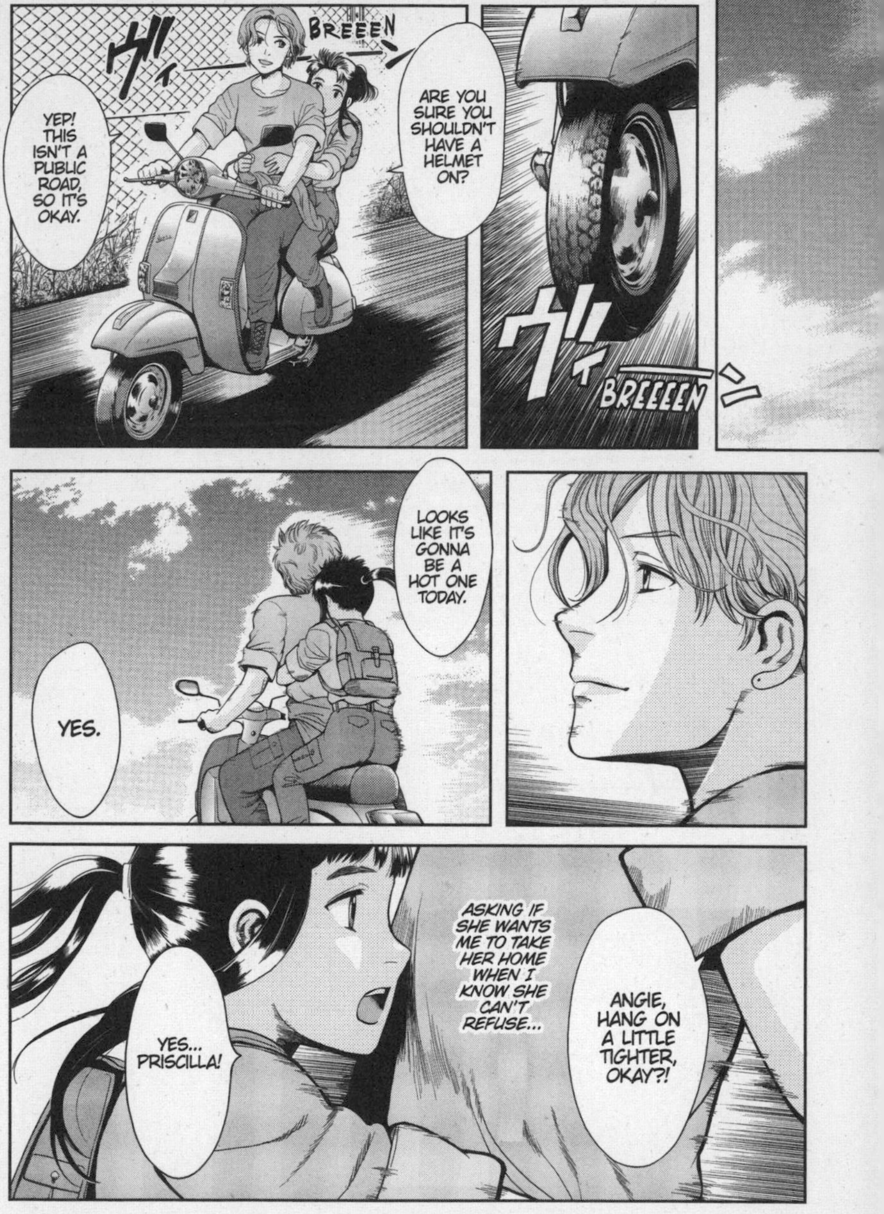
BREEEEEN
BREEEN
ARE YOU SURE YOU SHOULDN'T HAVE A HELMET ON?
YEP! THIS ISN'T A PUBLIC ROAD, SO IT'S OKAY.
LOOKS LIKE IT'S GONNA BE A HOT ONE TODAY.
YES.
ANGIE, HANG ON A LITTLE TIGHTER, OKAY?!
ASKING IF SHE WANTS ME TO TAKE HER HOME WHEN I KNOW SHE CAN'T REFUSE...
YES... PRISCILLA!

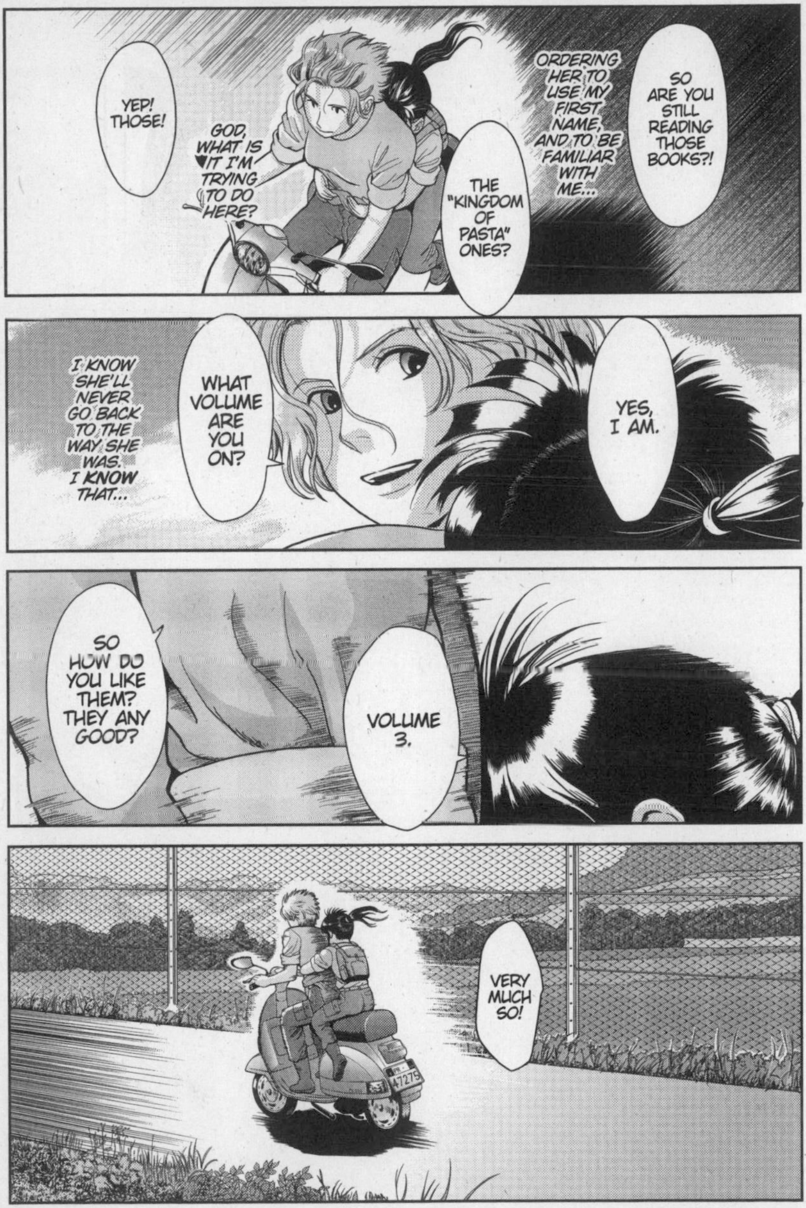
SO ARE YOU STILL READING THOSE BOOKS?!
ORDERING HER TO USE MY FIRST NAME, AND TO BE FAMILIAR WITH ME...
THE "KINGDOM OF PASTA" ONES?
GOD, WHAT IS IT I'M TRYING TO DO HERE?
YEP! THOSE!
YES, I AM.
WHAT VOLUME ARE YOU ON?
I KNOW SHE'LL NEVER GO BACK TO THE WAY SHE WAS. I KNOW THAT...
VOLUME 3.
SO HOW DO YOU LIKE THEM? THEY ANY GOOD?
VERY MUCH SO!

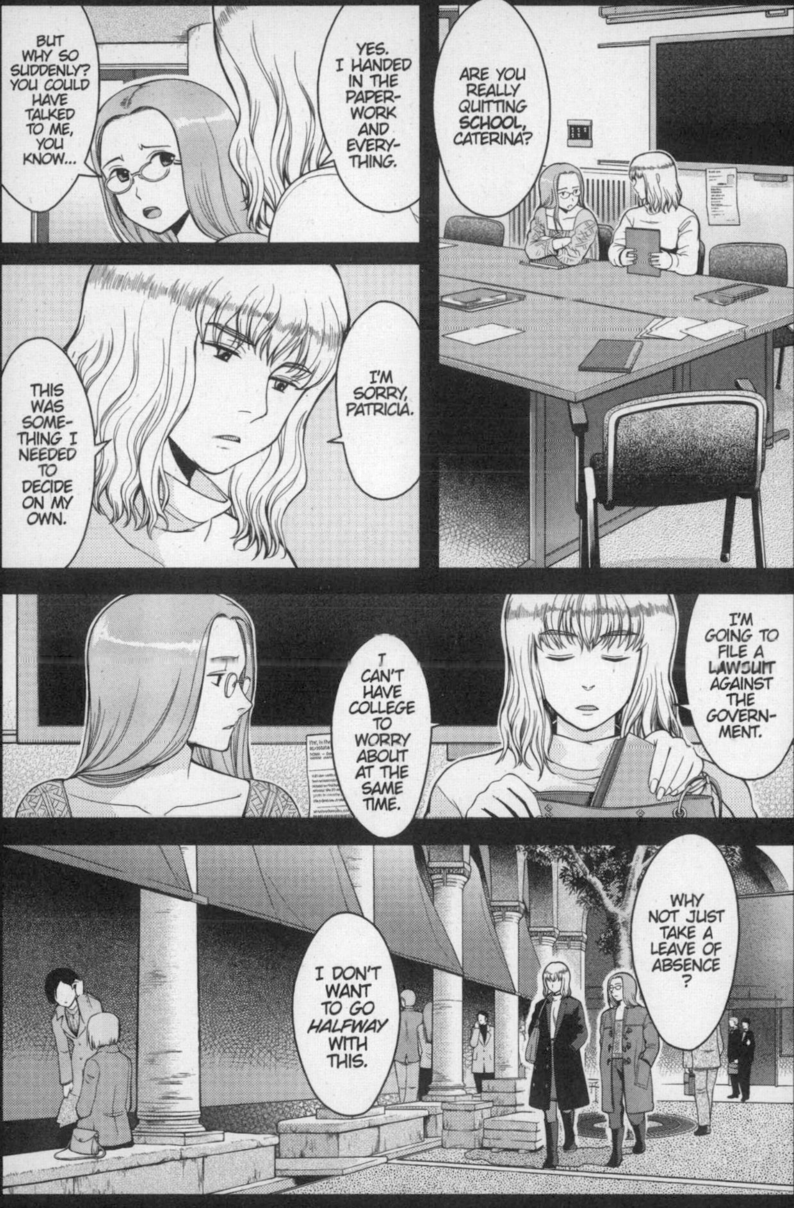
ARE YOU REALLY QUITTING SCHOOL, CATERINA?
YES. I HANDED IN THE PAPER-WORK AND EVERY-THING.
BUT WHY SO SUDDENLY? YOU COULD HAVE TALKED TO ME, YOU KNOW...
I'M SORRY, PATRICIA.
THIS WAS SOME-THING I NEEDED TO DECIDE ON MY OWN.
I'M GOING TO FILE A LAWSUIT AGAINST THE GOVERN-MENT.
I CAN'T HAVE COLLEGE TO WORRY ABOUT AT THE SAME TIME.
WHY NOT JUST TAKE A LEAVE OF ABSENCE?
I DON'T WANT TO GO *HALFWAY* WITH THIS.

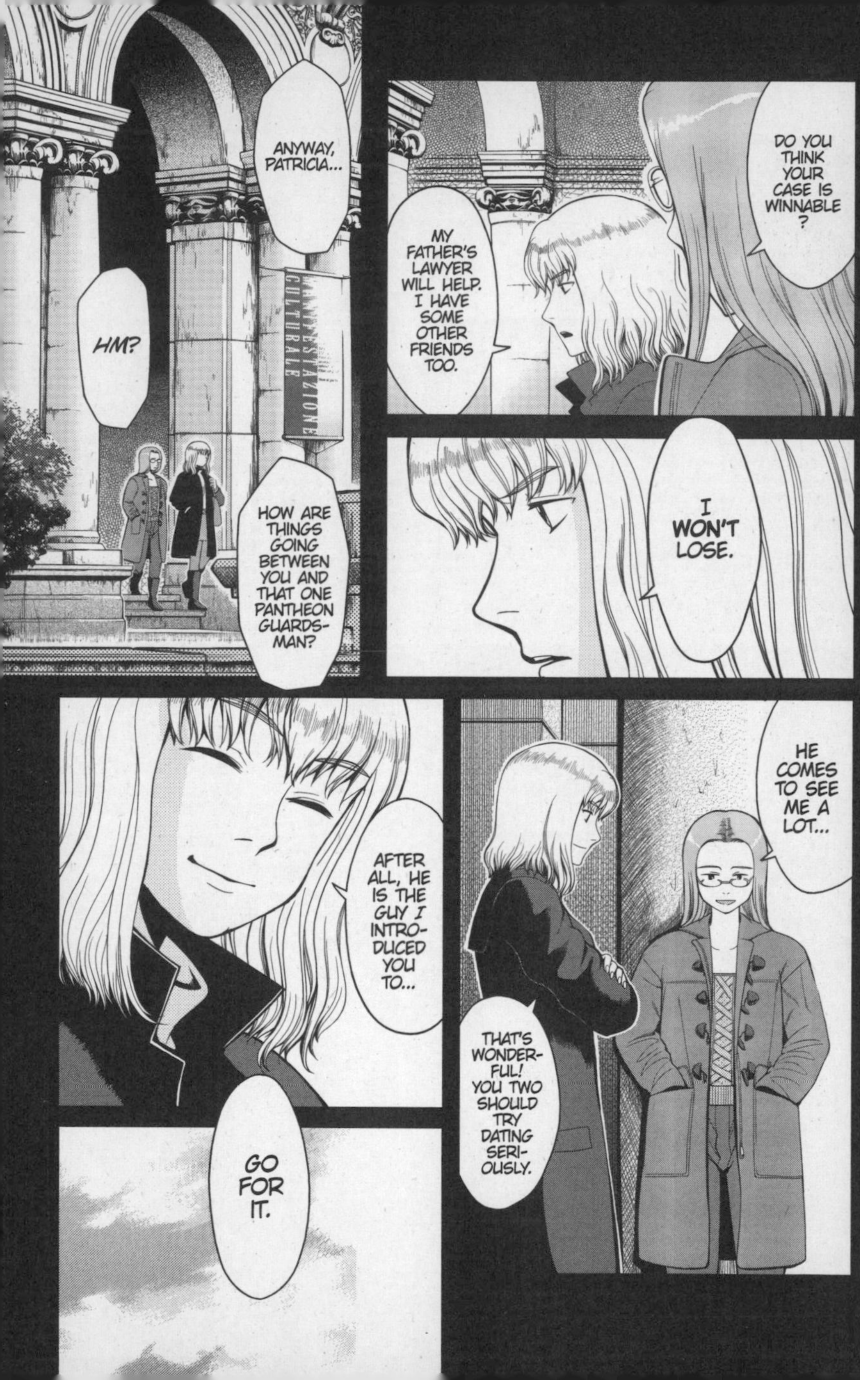
DO YOU THINK YOUR CASE IS WINNABLE?
MY FATHER'S LAWYER WILL HELP. I HAVE SOME OTHER FRIENDS TOO.
I WON'T LOSE.
ANYWAY, PATRICIA...
HM?
HOW ARE THINGS GOING BETWEEN YOU AND THAT ONE PANTHEON GUARDSMAN?
HE COMES TO SEE ME A LOT...
THAT'S WONDERFUL! YOU TWO SHOULD TRY DATING SERIOUSLY.
AFTER ALL, HE IS THE GUY *I* INTRODUCED YOU TO...
GO FOR IT.

CHAPTER 24: CATERINA

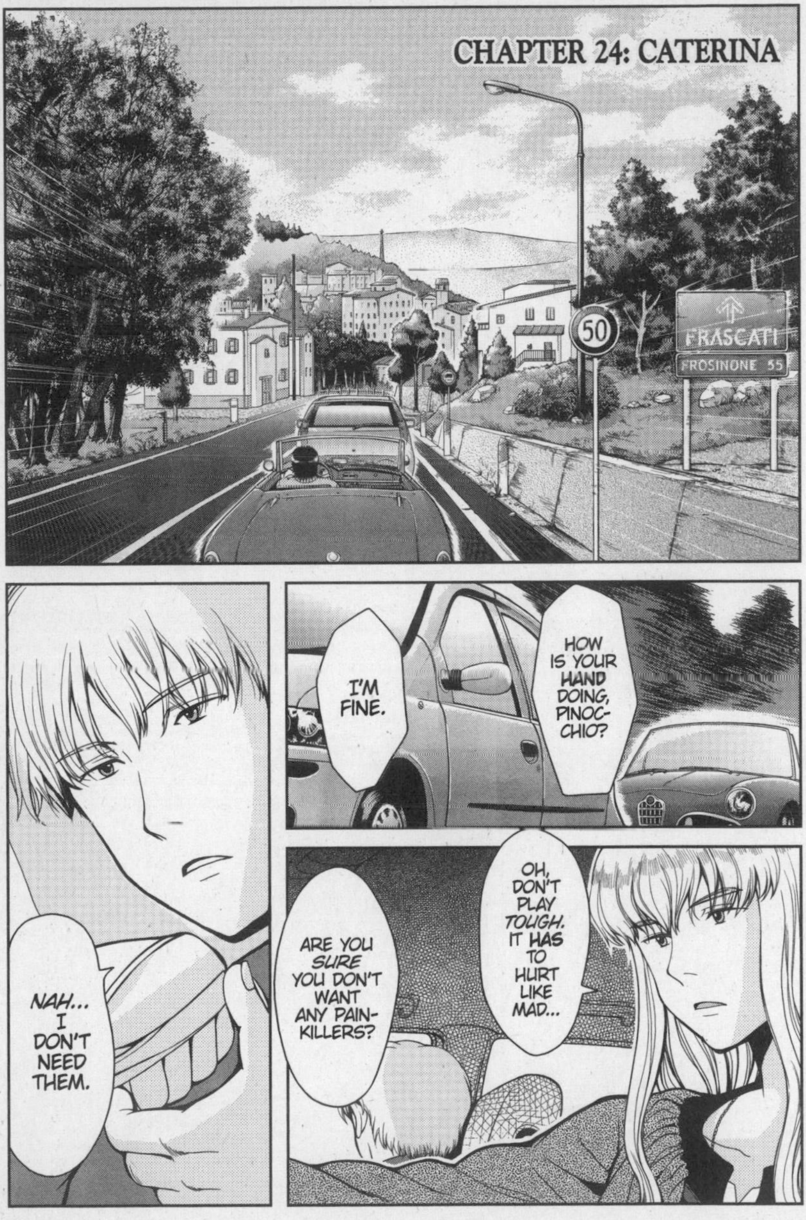
50
FRASCATI
FROSINONE 55
HOW IS YOUR HAND DOING, PINOCCHIO?
I'M FINE.
OH, DON'T PLAY *TOUGH.* IT HAS TO HURT LIKE MAD...
ARE YOU *SURE* YOU DON'T WANT ANY PAIN-KILLERS?
NAH... I DON'T NEED THEM.

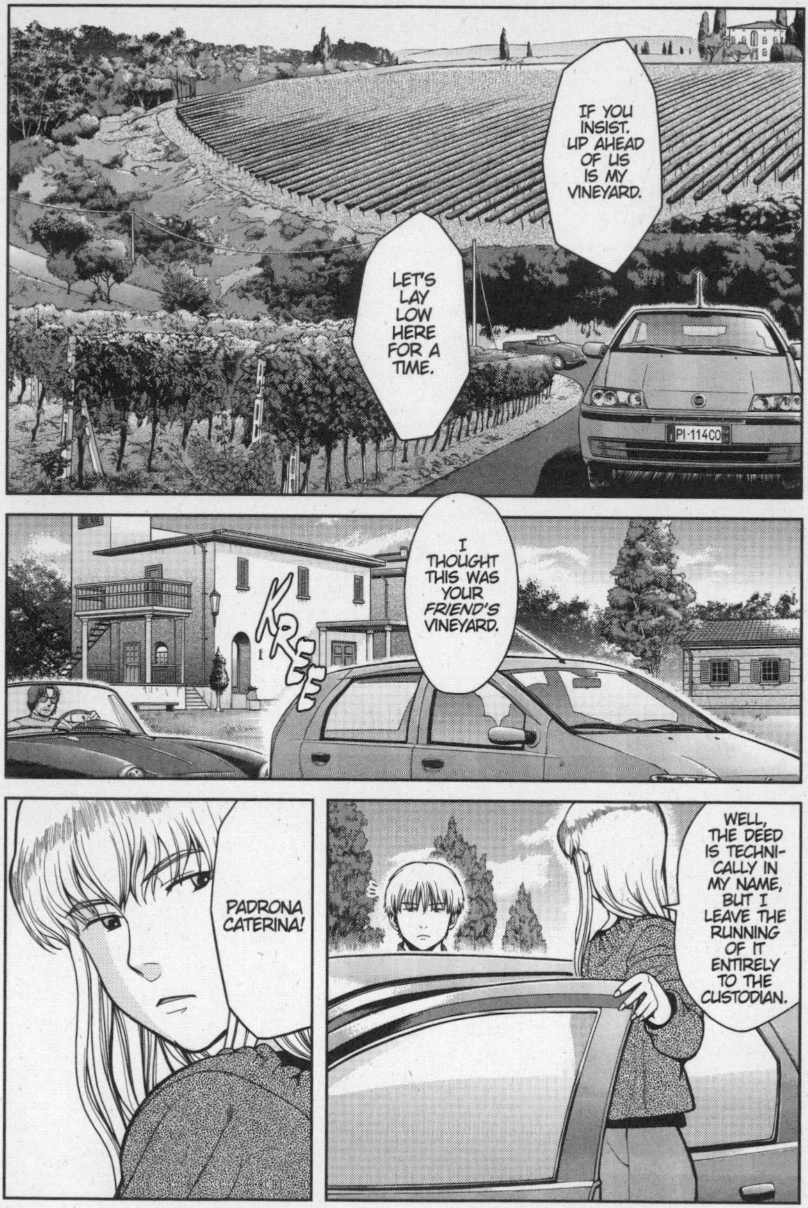
IF YOU INSIST. UP AHEAD OF US IS MY VINEYARD.
LET'S LAY LOW HERE FOR A TIME.
I THOUGHT THIS WAS YOUR *FRIEND'S* VINEYARD.
KREE
WELL, THE DEED IS TECHNICALLY IN MY NAME, BUT I LEAVE THE RUNNING OF IT ENTIRELY TO THE CUSTODIAN.
PADRONA CATERINA!

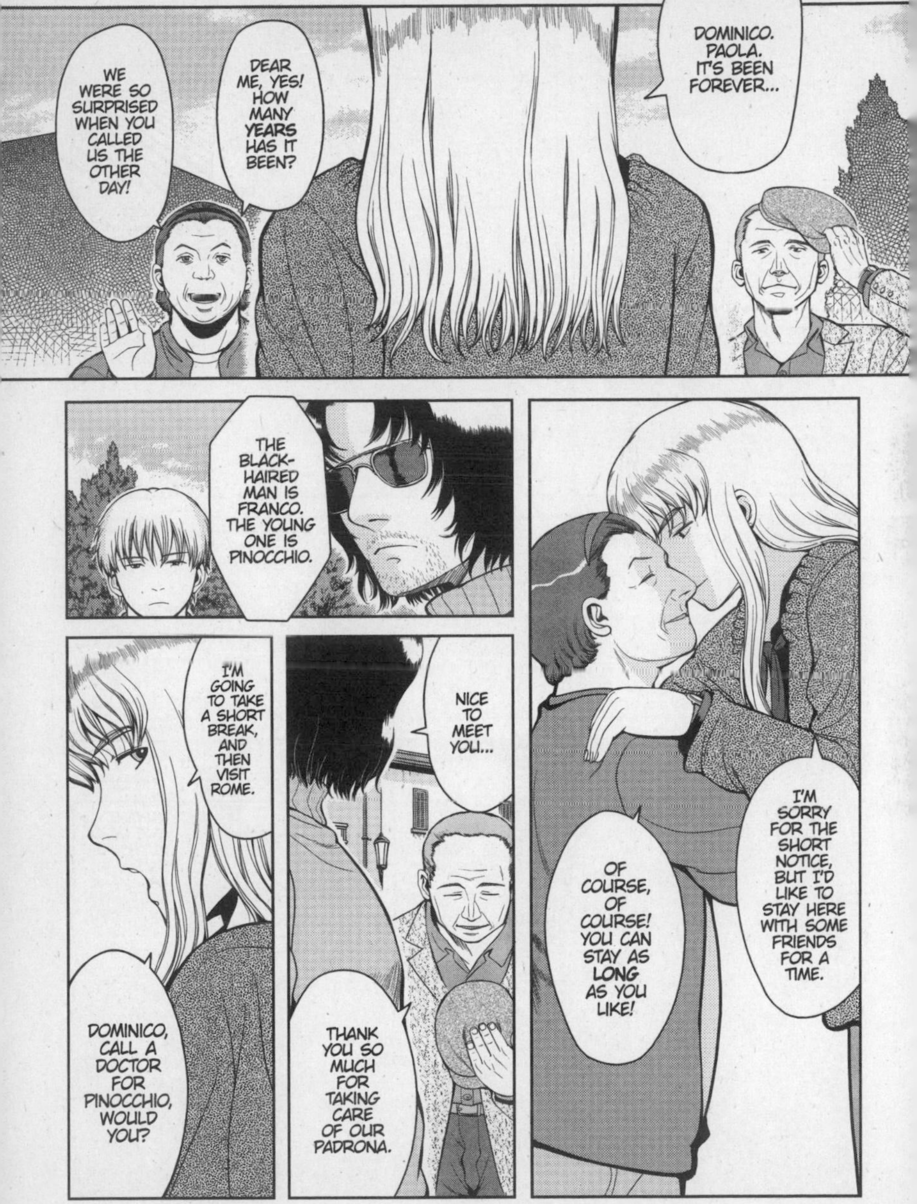
DOMINICO. PAOLA. IT'S BEEN FOREVER...
DEAR ME, YES! HOW MANY YEARS HAS IT BEEN?
WE WERE SO SURPRISED WHEN YOU CALLED US THE OTHER DAY!
I'M SORRY FOR THE SHORT NOTICE, BUT I'D LIKE TO STAY HERE WITH SOME FRIENDS FOR A TIME.
OF COURSE, OF COURSE! YOU CAN STAY AS LONG AS YOU LIKE!
THE BLACK-HAIRED MAN IS FRANCO. THE YOUNG ONE IS PINOCCHIO.
NICE TO MEET YOU...
THANK YOU SO MUCH FOR TAKING CARE OF OUR PADRONA.
I'M GOING TO TAKE A SHORT BREAK, AND THEN VISIT ROME.
DOMINICO, CALL A DOCTOR FOR PINOCCHIO, WOULD YOU?

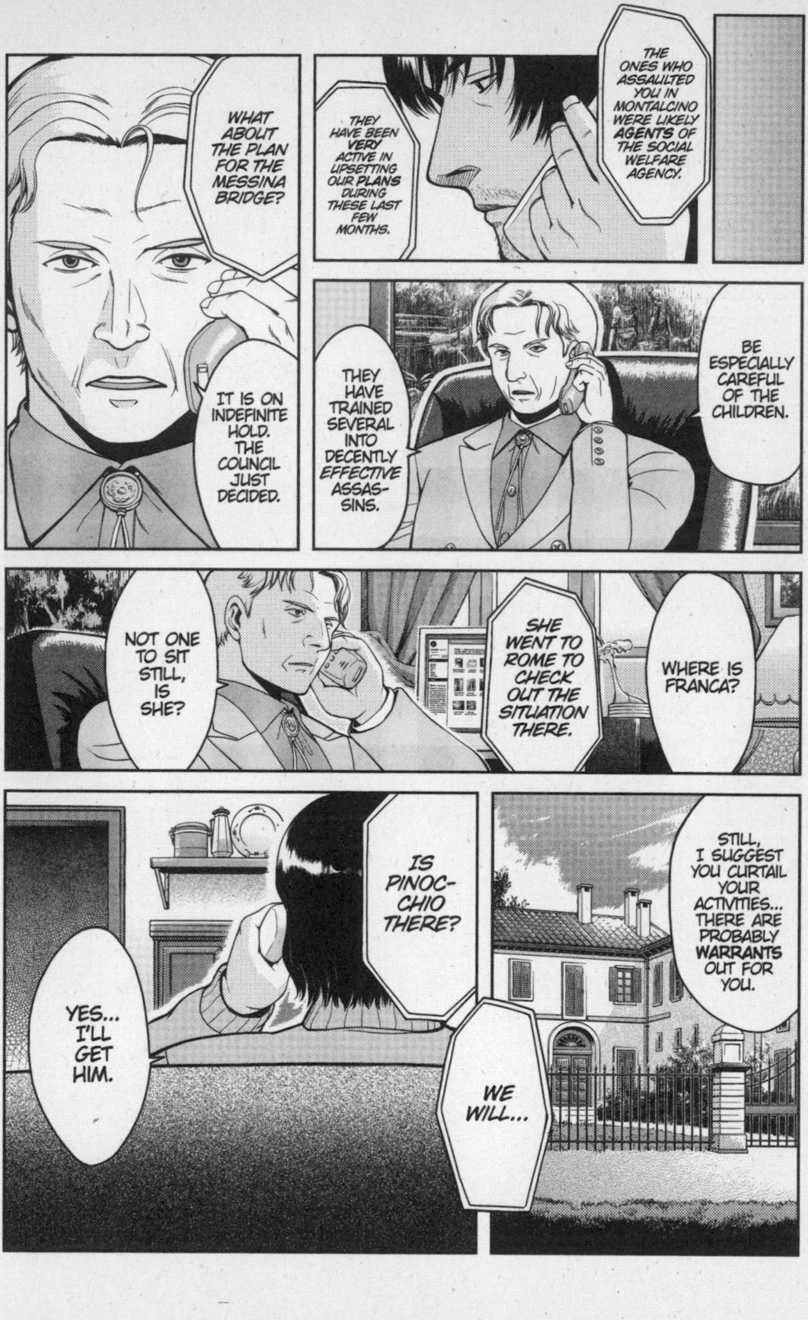
THE ONES WHO ASSAULTED YOU IN MONTALCINO WERE LIKELY AGENTS OF THE SOCIAL WELFARE AGENCY.
THEY HAVE BEEN VERY ACTIVE IN UPSETTING OUR PLANS DURING THESE LAST FEW MONTHS.
BE ESPECIALLY CAREFUL OF THE CHILDREN.
THEY HAVE TRAINED SEVERAL INTO DECENTLY EFFECTIVE ASSAS-SINS.
WHAT ABOUT THE PLAN FOR THE MESSINA BRIDGE?
IT IS ON INDEFINITE HOLD. THE COUNCIL JUST DECIDED.
WHERE IS FRANCA?
SHE WENT TO ROME TO CHECK OUT THE SITUATION THERE.
NOT ONE TO SIT STILL, IS SHE?
STILL, I SUGGEST YOU CURTAIL YOUR ACTIVITIES... THERE ARE PROBABLY WARRANTS OUT FOR YOU.
WE WILL...
IS PINOC-CHIO THERE?
YES... I'LL GET HIM.

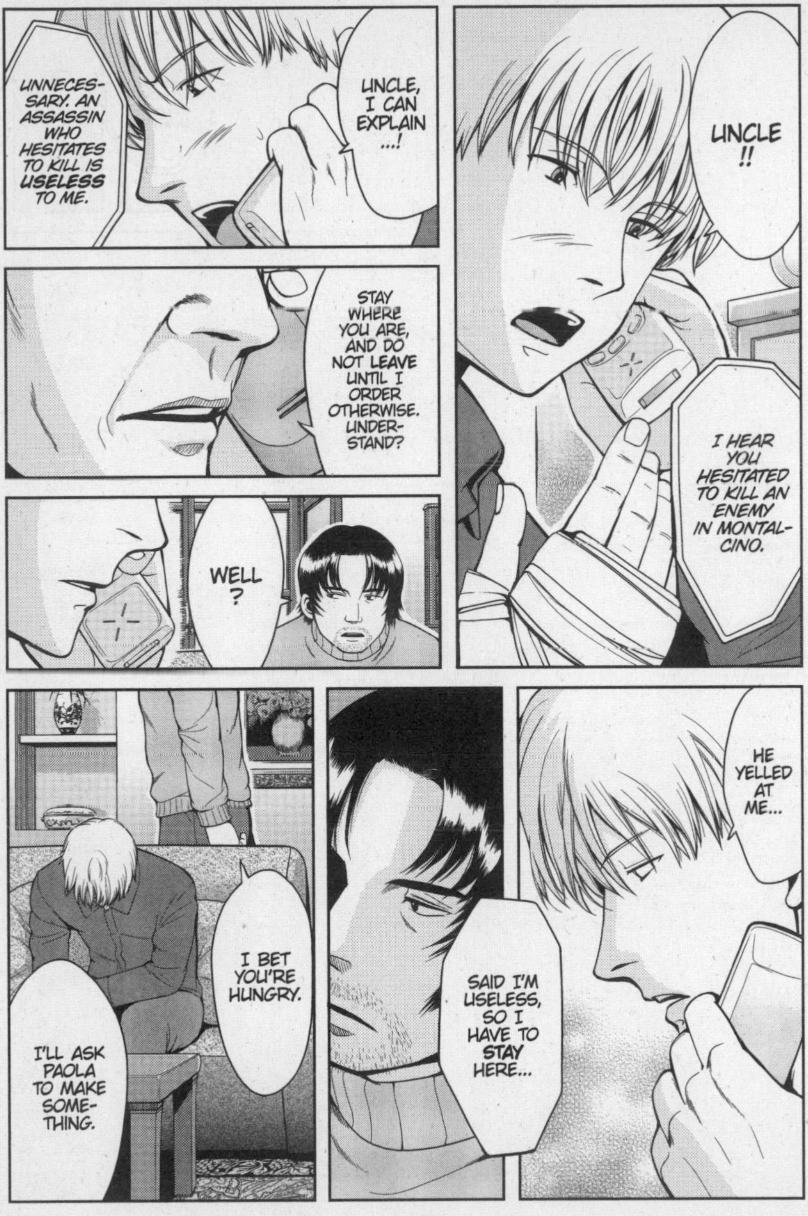
UNCLE !!
I HEAR YOU HESITATED TO KILL AN ENEMY IN MONTALCINO.
UNCLE, I CAN EXPLAIN ...!
UNNECESSARY. AN ASSASSIN WHO HESITATES TO KILL IS USELESS TO ME.
STAY WHERE YOU ARE, AND DO NOT LEAVE UNTIL I ORDER OTHERWISE. UNDERSTAND?
WELL ?
HE YELLED AT ME...
SAID I'M USELESS, SO I HAVE TO STAY HERE...
I BET YOU'RE HUNGRY.
I'LL ASK PAOLA TO MAKE SOMETHING.

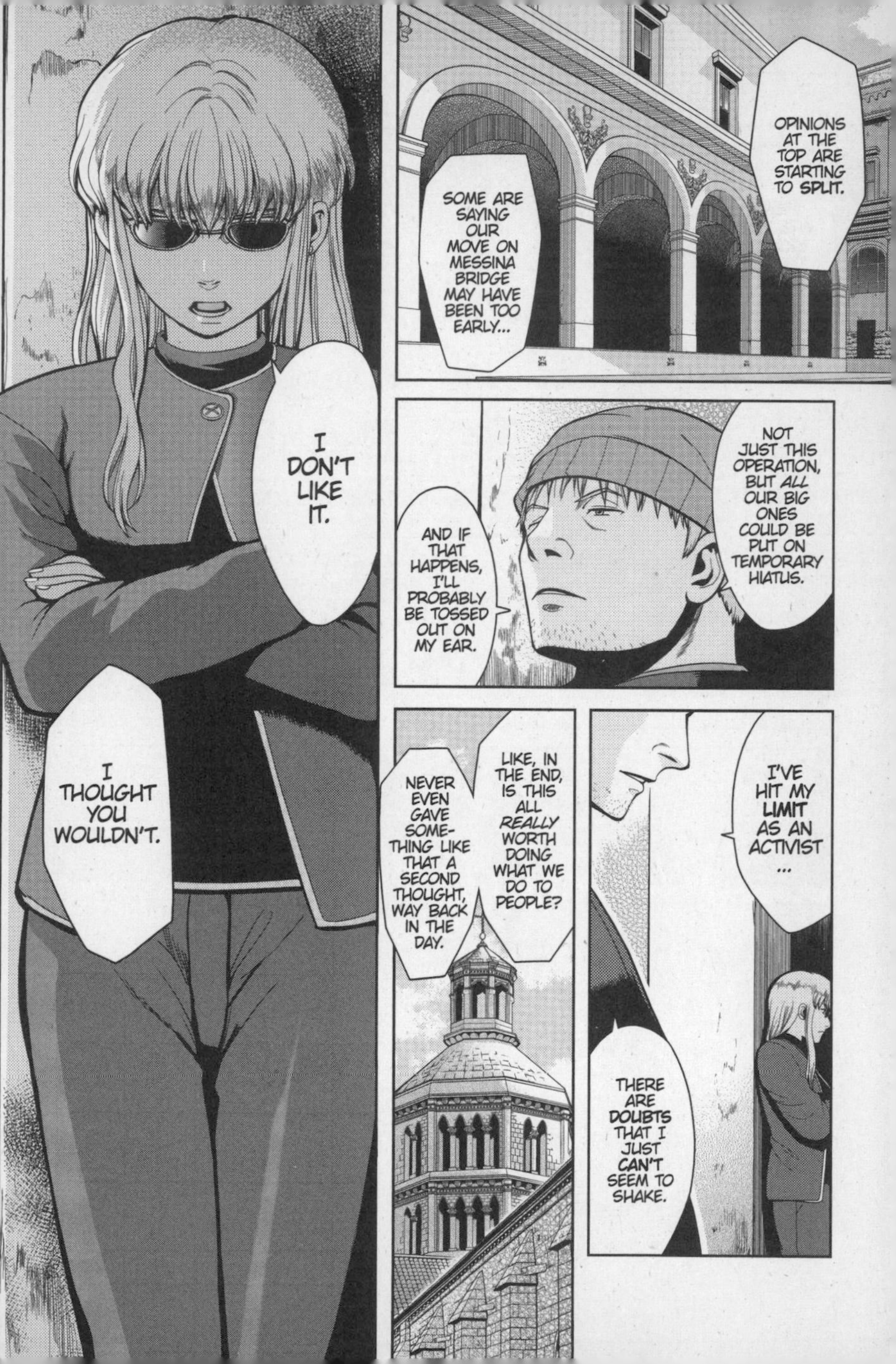
OPINIONS AT THE TOP ARE STARTING TO SPLIT.
SOME ARE SAYING OUR MOVE ON MESSINA BRIDGE MAY HAVE BEEN TOO EARLY...
NOT JUST THIS OPERATION, BUT *ALL* OUR BIG ONES COULD BE PUT ON TEMPORARY HIATUS.
AND IF THAT HAPPENS, I'LL PROBABLY BE TOSSED OUT ON MY EAR.
I'VE HIT MY **LIMIT** AS AN ACTIVIST...
THERE ARE **DOUBTS** THAT I JUST **CAN'T** SEEM TO SHAKE.
LIKE, IN THE END, IS THIS ALL *REALLY* WORTH DOING WHAT WE DO TO PEOPLE?
NEVER EVEN GAVE SOME-THING LIKE THAT A SECOND THOUGHT, WAY BACK IN THE DAY.
I DON'T LIKE IT.
I THOUGHT YOU WOULDN'T.

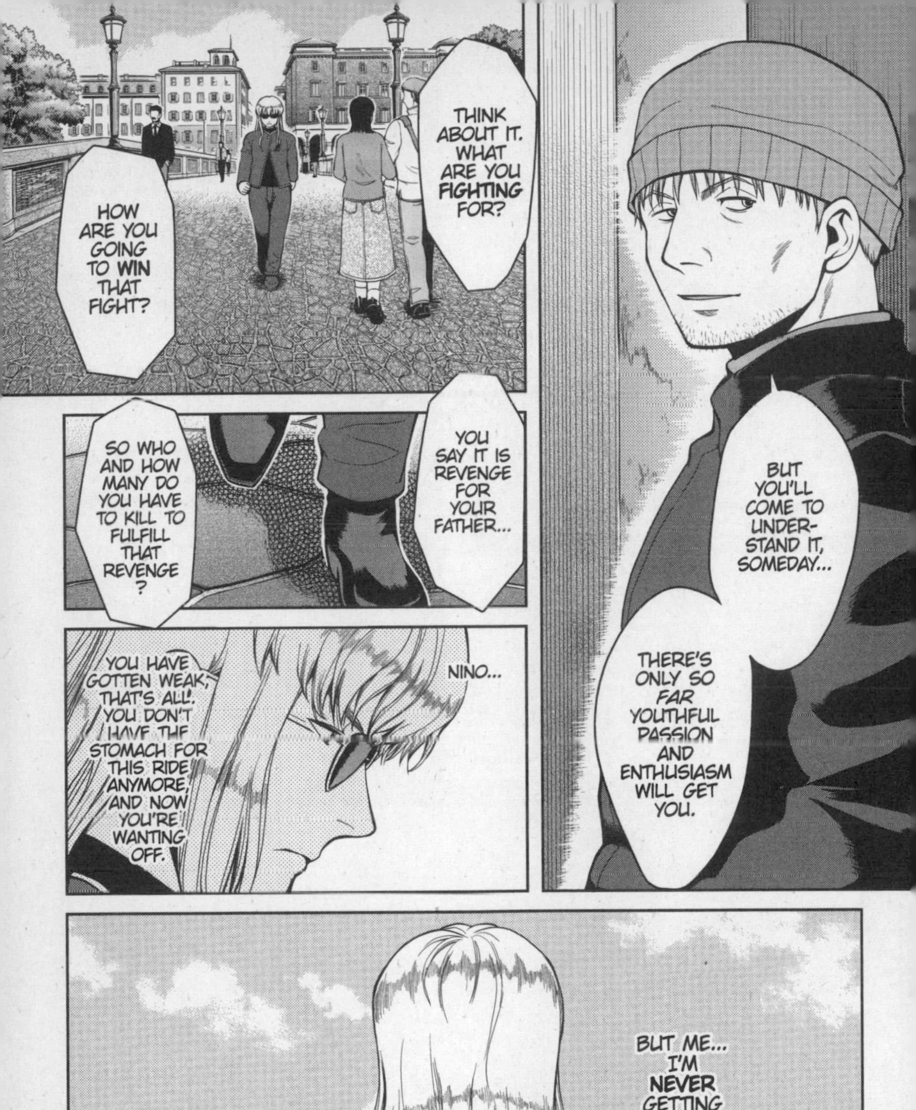
BUT YOU'LL COME TO UNDER-STAND IT, SOMEDAY...
THERE'S ONLY SO *FAR* YOUTHFUL PASSION AND ENTHUSIASM WILL GET YOU.
THINK ABOUT IT. WHAT ARE YOU **FIGHTING** FOR?
HOW ARE YOU GOING TO **WIN** THAT FIGHT?
YOU SAY IT IS REVENGE FOR YOUR FATHER...
SO WHO AND HOW MANY DO YOU HAVE TO KILL TO FULFILL THAT REVENGE ?
NINO...
YOU HAVE GOTTEN WEAK, THAT'S ALL. YOU DON'T HAVE THE STOMACH FOR THIS RIDE ANYMORE, AND NOW YOU'RE WANTING OFF.
BUT ME... I'M **NEVER** GETTING OFF.

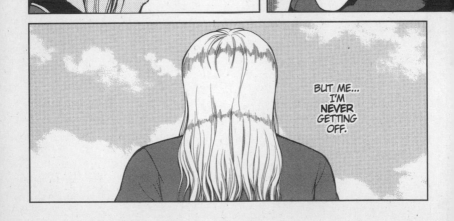

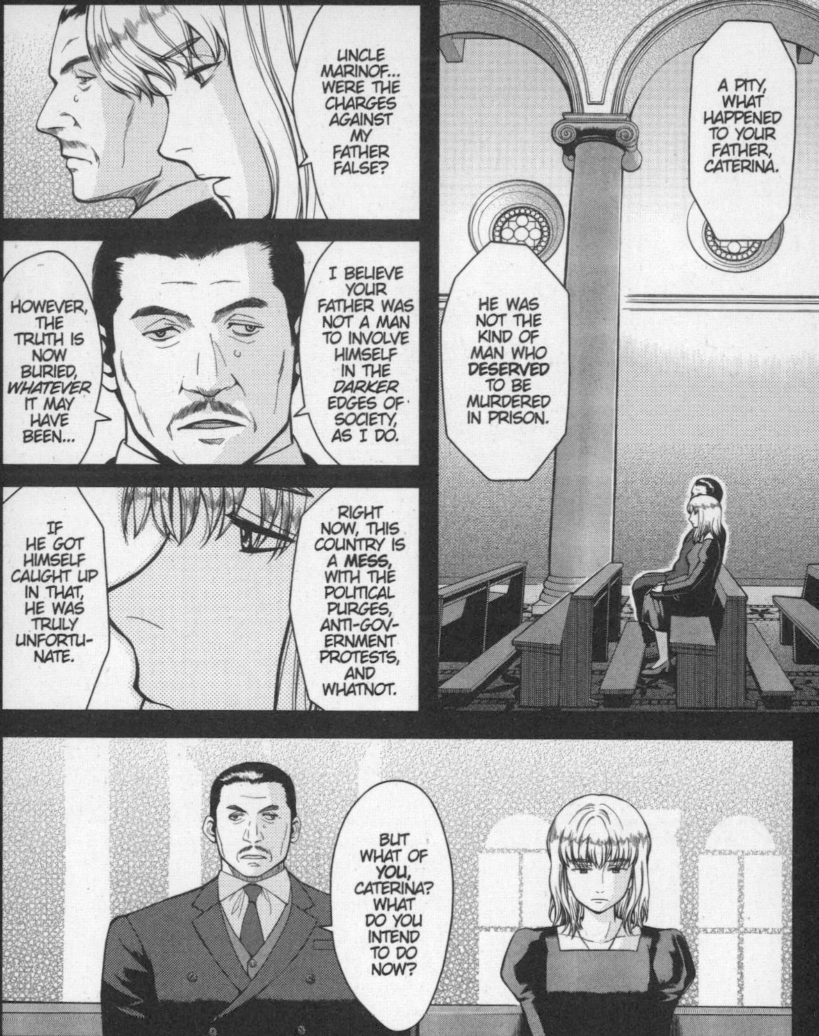
A PITY, WHAT HAPPENED TO YOUR FATHER, CATERINA.
HE WAS NOT THE KIND OF MAN WHO DESERVED TO BE MURDERED IN PRISON.
UNCLE MARINOF... WERE THE CHARGES AGAINST MY FATHER FALSE?
I BELIEVE YOUR FATHER WAS NOT A MAN TO INVOLVE HIMSELF IN THE DARKER EDGES OF SOCIETY, AS I DO.
HOWEVER, THE TRUTH IS NOW BURIED, WHATEVER IT MAY HAVE BEEN...
RIGHT NOW, THIS COUNTRY IS A MESS, WITH THE POLITICAL PURGES, ANTI-GOVERNMENT PROTESTS, AND WHATNOT.
IF HE GOT HIMSELF CAUGHT UP IN THAT, HE WAS TRULY UNFORTUNATE.
BUT WHAT OF YOU, CATERINA? WHAT DO YOU INTEND TO DO NOW?

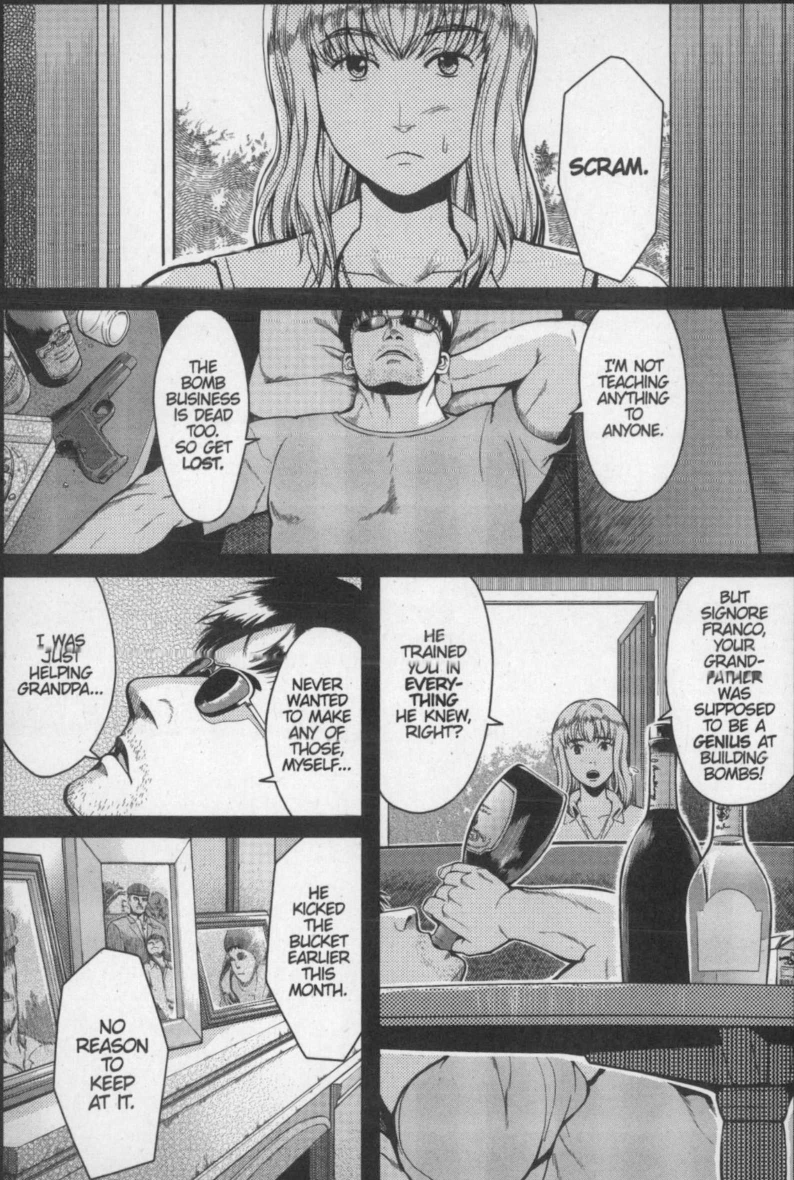
SCRAM.
I'M NOT TEACHING ANYTHING TO ANYONE.
THE BOMB BUSINESS IS DEAD TOO. SO GET LOST.
BUT SIGNORE FRANCO, YOUR GRAND-FATHER WAS SUPPOSED TO BE A GENIUS AT BUILDING BOMBS!
HE TRAINED YOU IN EVERY-THING HE KNEW, RIGHT?
NEVER WANTED TO MAKE ANY OF THOSE, MYSELF...
I WAS JUST HELPING GRANDPA...
HE KICKED THE BUCKET EARLIER THIS MONTH.
NO REASON TO KEEP AT IT.

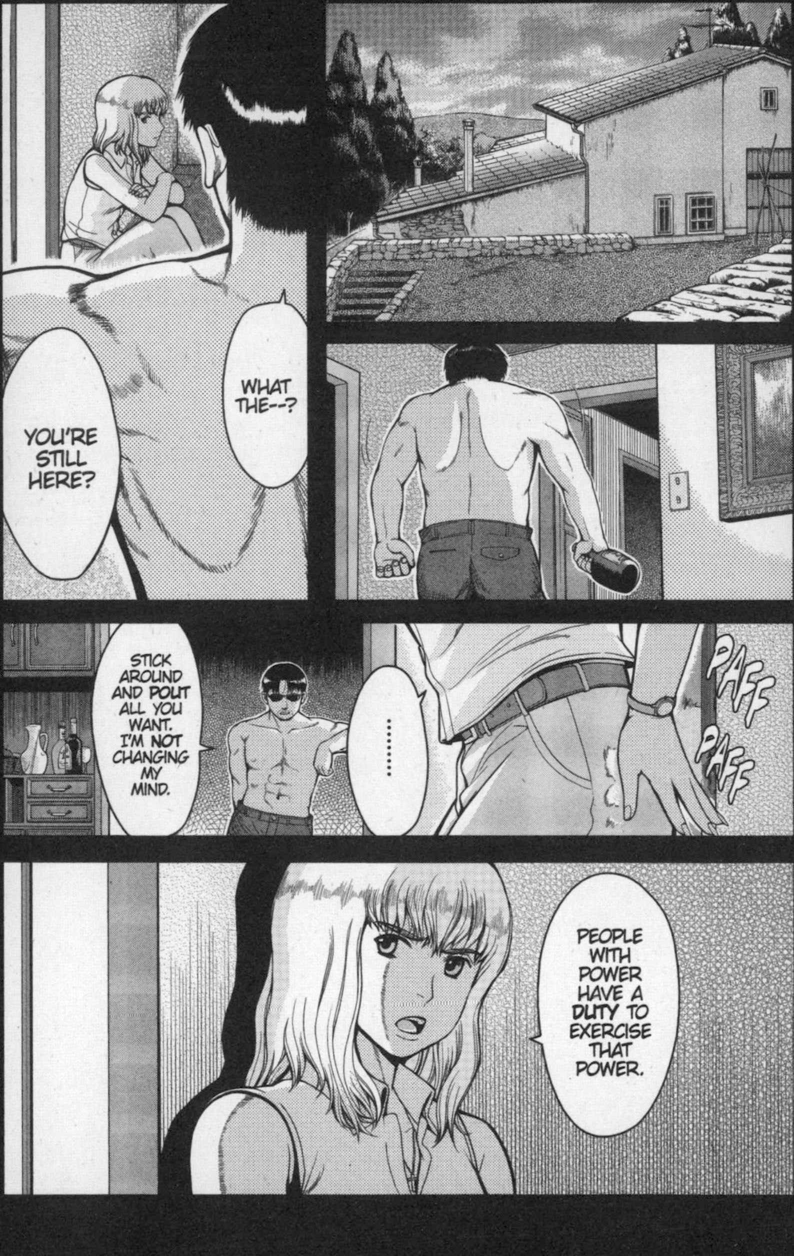
WHAT THE--?
YOU'RE STILL HERE?
PAFF
PAFF
......
STICK AROUND AND POUT ALL YOU WANT. I'M NOT CHANGING MY MIND.
PEOPLE WITH POWER HAVE A DUTY TO EXERCISE THAT POWER.

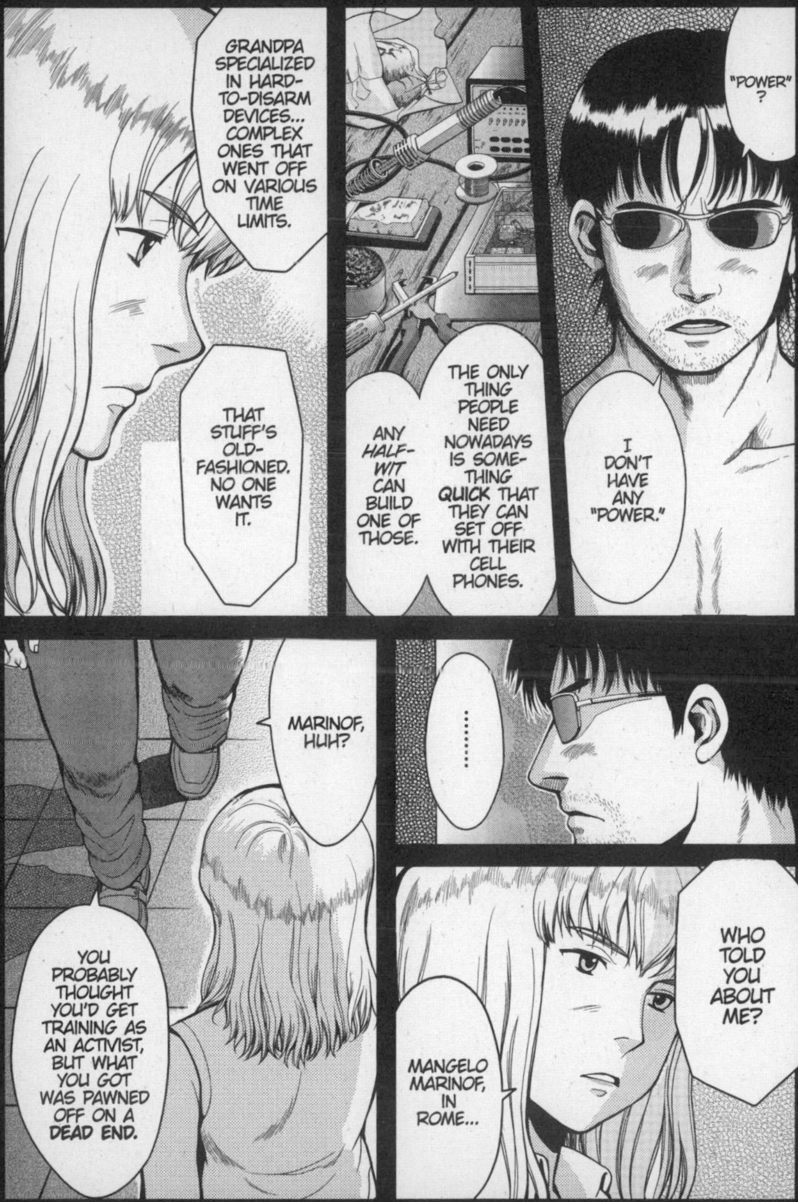
"POWER"?
I DON'T HAVE ANY "POWER."
THE ONLY THING PEOPLE NEED NOWADAYS IS SOMETHING QUICK THAT THEY CAN SET OFF WITH THEIR CELL PHONES.
ANY HALF-WIT CAN BUILD ONE OF THOSE.
GRANDPA SPECIALIZED IN HARD-TO-DISARM DEVICES... COMPLEX ONES THAT WENT OFF ON VARIOUS TIME LIMITS.
THAT STUFF'S OLD-FASHIONED. NO ONE WANTS IT.
....
WHO TOLD YOU ABOUT ME?
MANGELO MARINOF, IN ROME...
MARINOF, HUH?
YOU PROBABLY THOUGHT YOU'D GET TRAINING AS AN ACTIVIST, BUT WHAT YOU GOT WAS PAWNED OFF ON A DEAD END.

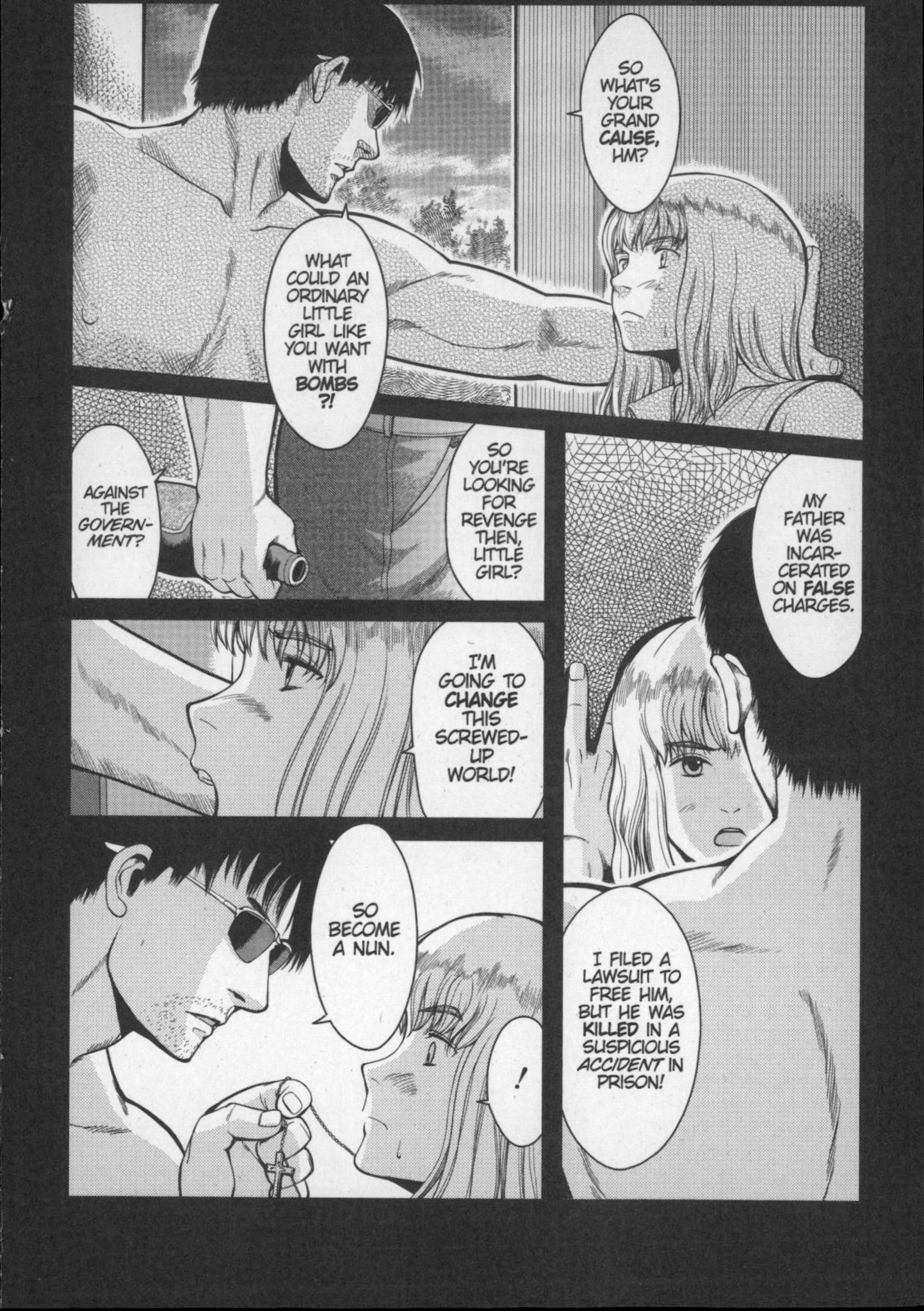
SO WHAT'S YOUR GRAND CAUSE, HM?
WHAT COULD AN ORDINARY LITTLE GIRL LIKE YOU WANT WITH BOMBS ?!
MY FATHER WAS INCARCERATED ON FALSE CHARGES.
I FILED A LAWSUIT TO FREE HIM, BUT HE WAS KILLED IN A SUSPICIOUS ACCIDENT IN PRISON!
SO YOU'RE LOOKING FOR REVENGE THEN, LITTLE GIRL?
AGAINST THE GOVERNMENT?
I'M GOING TO CHANGE THIS SCREWED-UP WORLD!
!
SO BECOME A NUN.

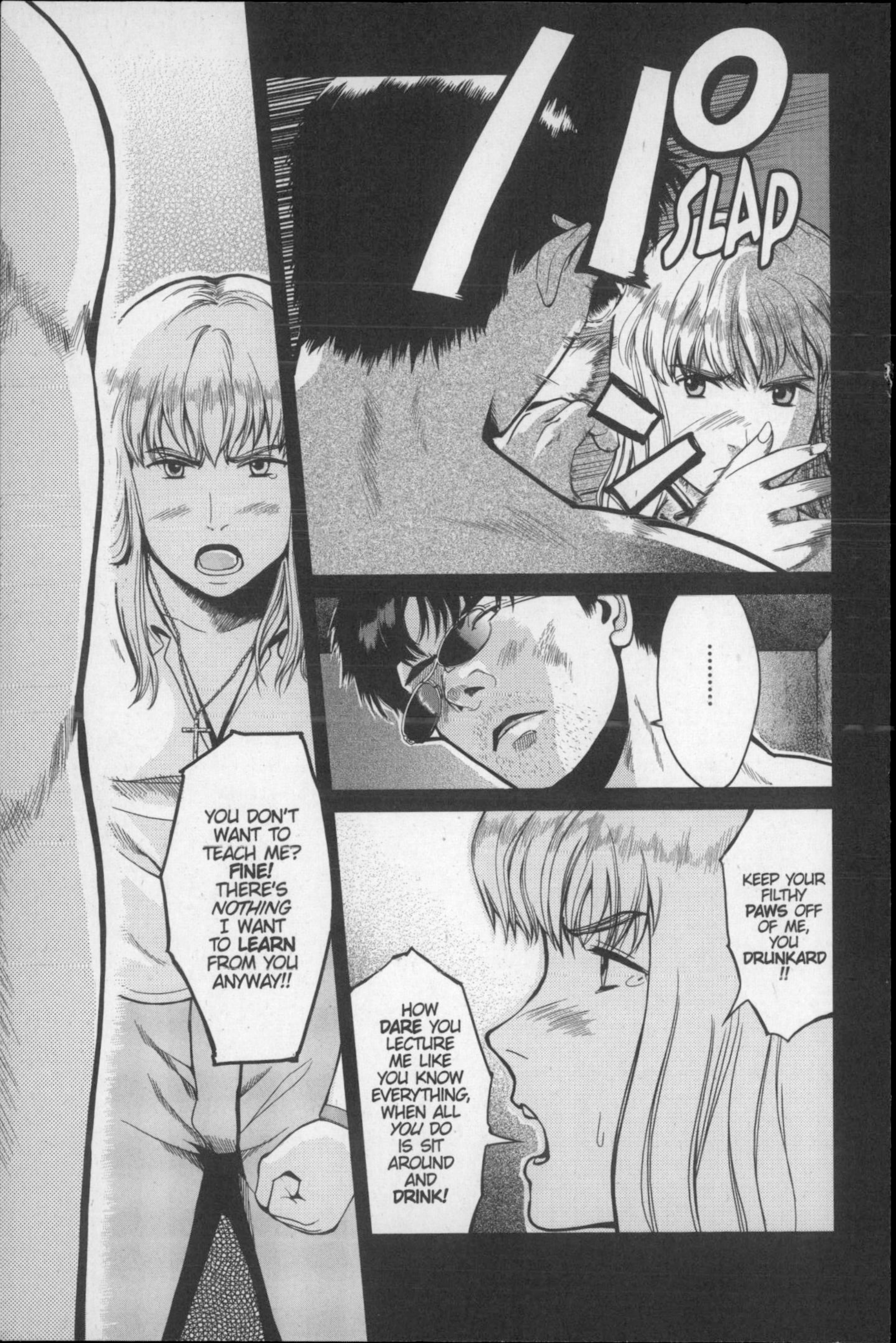

SLAP
......
KEEP YOUR FILTHY PAWS OFF OF ME, YOU DRUNKARD!!
HOW DARE YOU LECTURE ME LIKE YOU KNOW EVERYTHING, WHEN ALL YOU DO IS SIT AROUND AND DRINK!
YOU DON'T WANT TO TEACH ME? FINE! THERE'S NOTHING I WANT TO LEARN FROM YOU ANYWAY!!

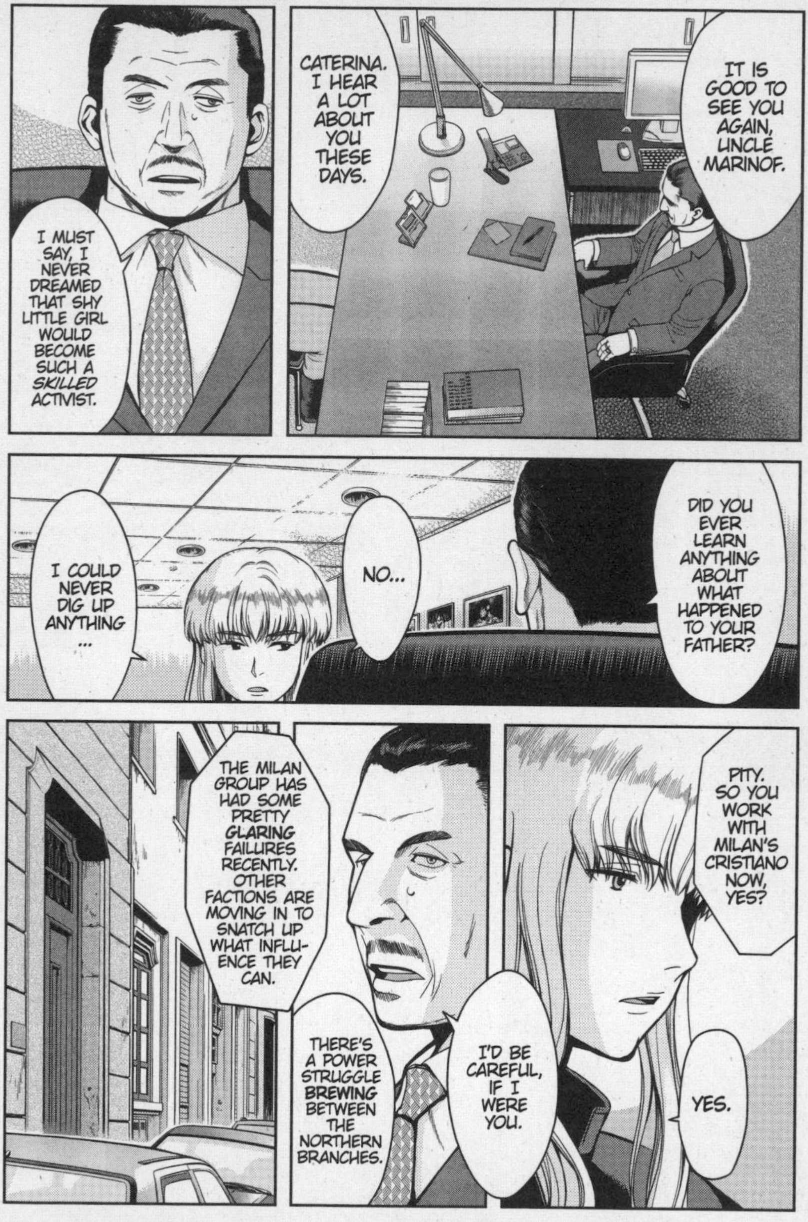
IT IS GOOD TO SEE YOU AGAIN, UNCLE MARINOF.
CATERINA. I HEAR A LOT ABOUT YOU THESE DAYS.
I MUST SAY, I NEVER DREAMED THAT SHY LITTLE GIRL WOULD BECOME SUCH A *SKILLED* ACTIVIST.
DID YOU EVER LEARN ANYTHING ABOUT WHAT HAPPENED TO YOUR FATHER?
NO...
I COULD NEVER DIG UP ANYTHING ...
PITY. SO YOU WORK WITH MILAN'S CRISTIANO NOW, YES?
YES.
THE MILAN GROUP HAS HAD SOME PRETTY **GLARING** FAILURES RECENTLY. OTHER FACTIONS ARE MOVING IN TO SNATCH UP WHAT INFLUENCE THEY CAN.
THERE'S A POWER STRUGGLE **BREWING** BETWEEN THE NORTHERN BRANCHES.
I'D BE CAREFUL, IF I WERE YOU.

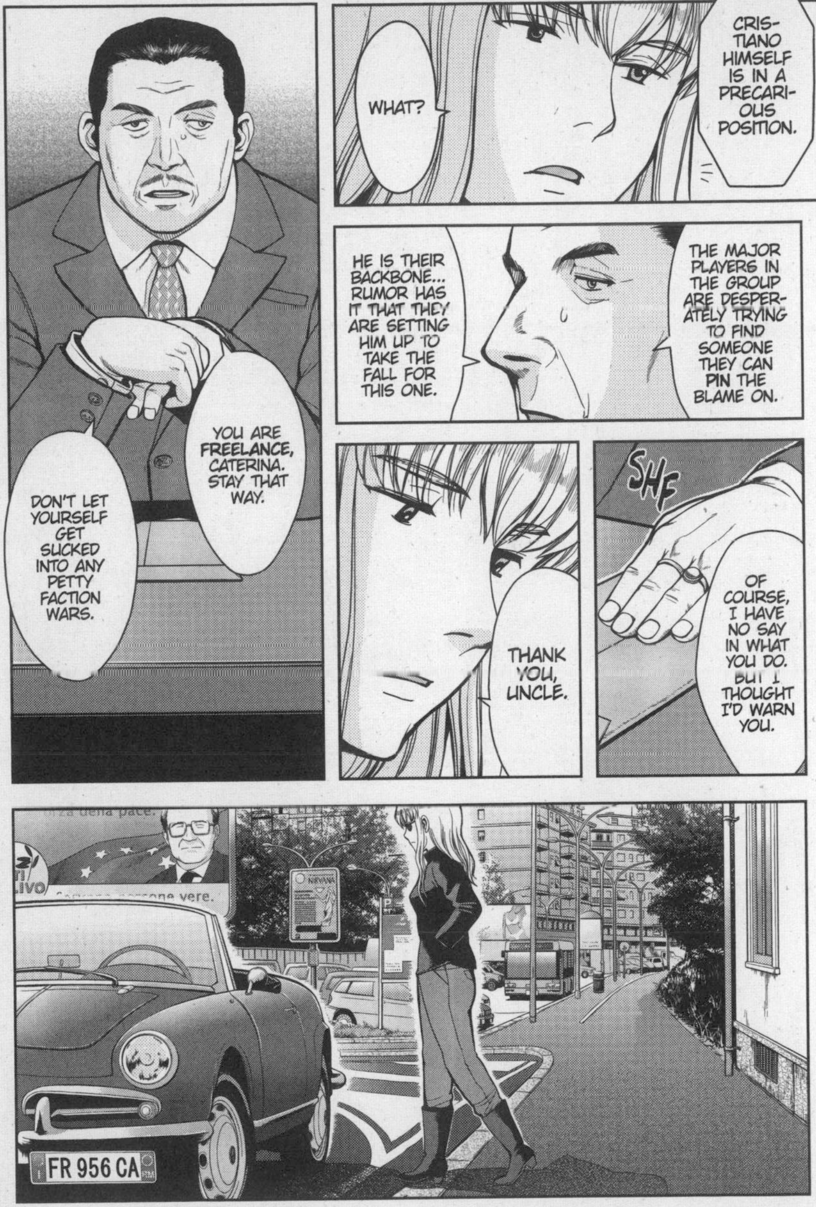
CRISTIANO HIMSELF IS IN A PRECARIOUS POSITION.
WHAT?
THE MAJOR PLAYERS IN THE GROUP ARE DESPERATELY TRYING TO FIND SOMEONE THEY CAN PIN THE BLAME ON.
HE IS THEIR BACKBONE... RUMOR HAS IT THAT THEY ARE SETTING HIM UP TO TAKE THE FALL FOR THIS ONE.
OF COURSE, I HAVE NO SAY IN WHAT YOU DO. BUT I THOUGHT I'D WARN YOU.
SHF
THANK YOU, UNCLE.
YOU ARE FREELANCE, CATERINA. STAY THAT WAY.
DON'T LET YOURSELF GET SUCKED INTO ANY PETTY FACTION WARS.
FR 956 CA

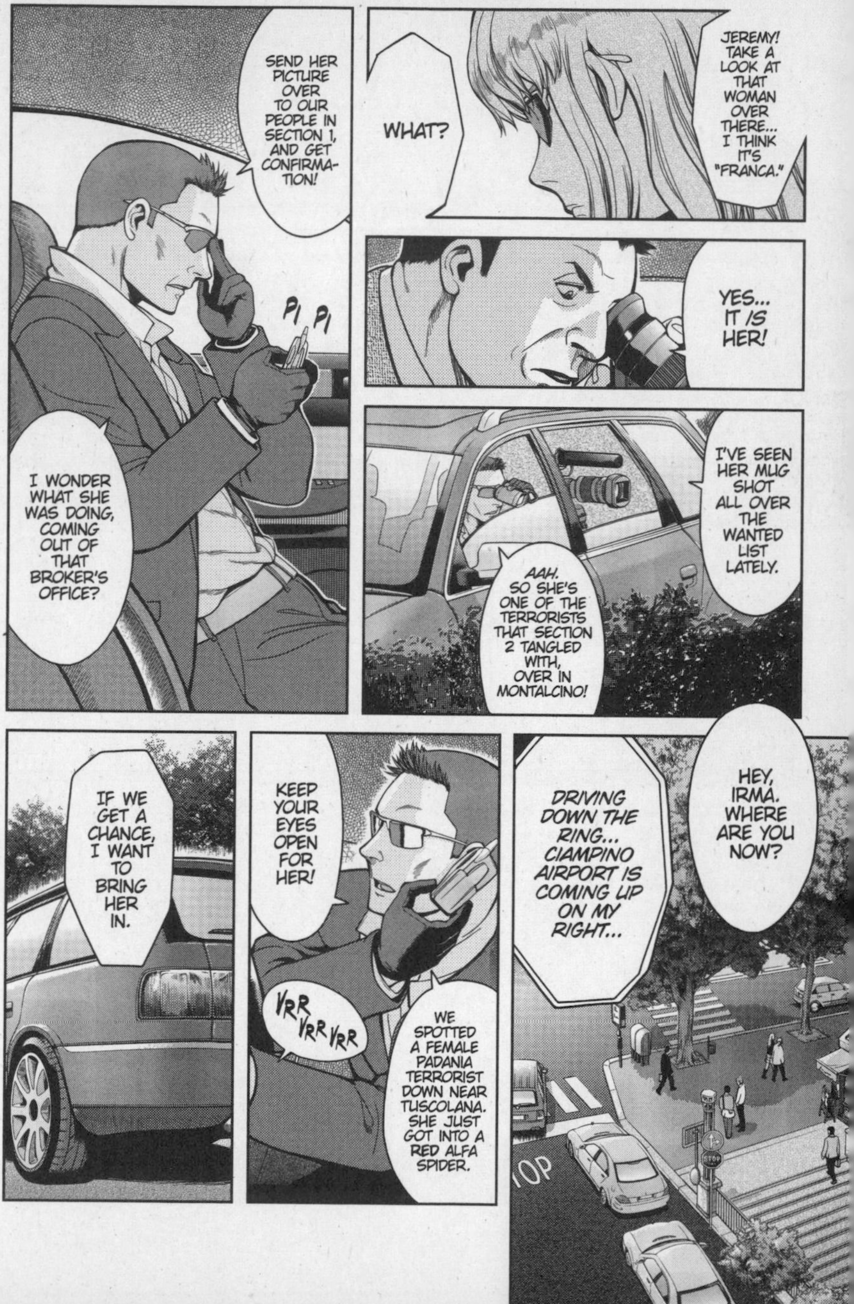
JEREMY! TAKE A LOOK AT THAT WOMAN OVER THERE... I THINK IT'S "FRANCA."
WHAT?
YES... IT IS HER!
I'VE SEEN HER MUG SHOT ALL OVER THE WANTED LIST LATELY.
AAH. SO SHE'S ONE OF THE TERRORISTS THAT SECTION 2 TANGLED WITH, OVER IN MONTALCINO!
SEND HER PICTURE OVER TO OUR PEOPLE IN SECTION 1, AND GET CONFIRMATION!
PI PI
I WONDER WHAT SHE WAS DOING, COMING OUT OF THAT BROKER'S OFFICE?
HEY, IRMA. WHERE ARE YOU NOW?
DRIVING DOWN THE RING... CIAMPINO AIRPORT IS COMING UP ON MY RIGHT...
VRR VRR VRR
WE SPOTTED A FEMALE PADANIA TERRORIST DOWN NEAR TUSCOLANA. SHE JUST GOT INTO A RED ALFA SPIDER.
KEEP YOUR EYES OPEN FOR HER!
IF WE GET A CHANCE, I WANT TO BRING HER IN.

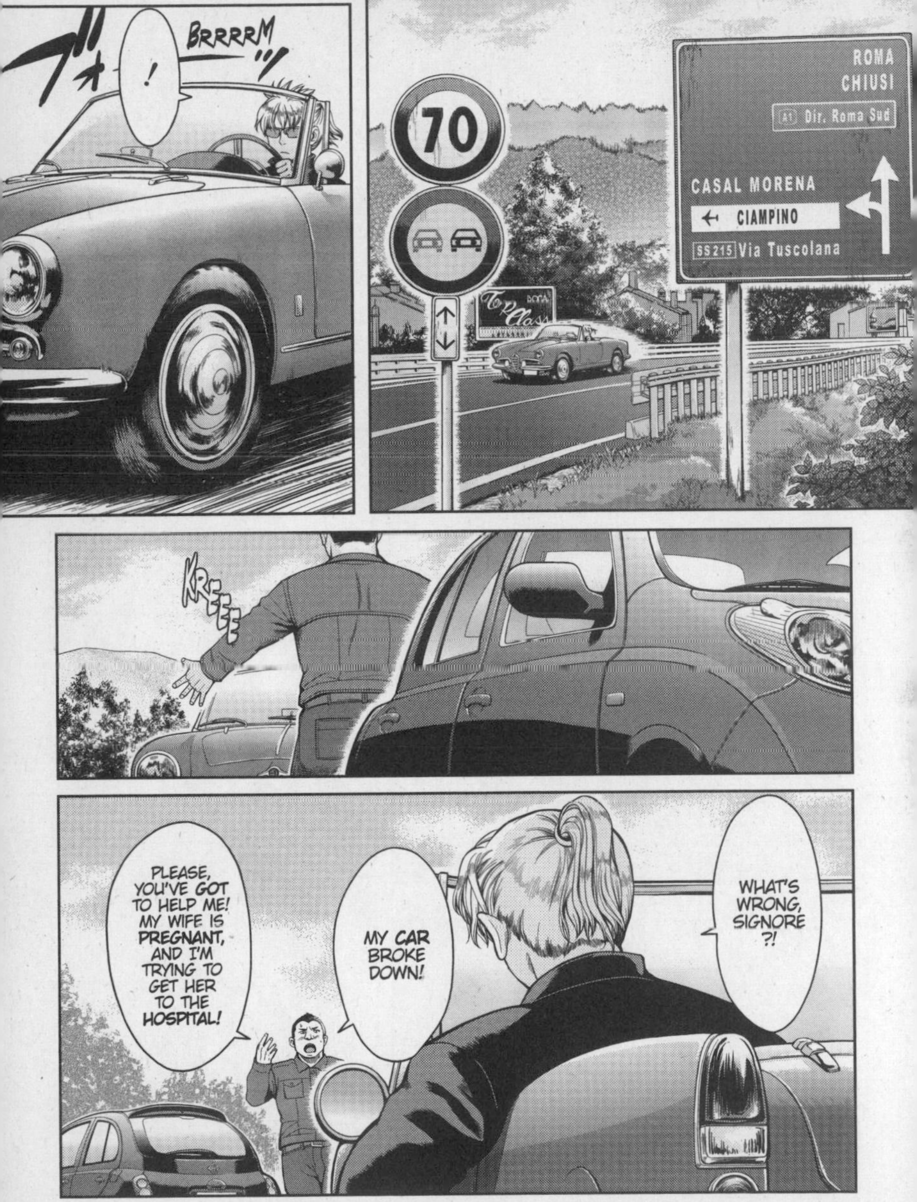
ROMA
CHIUSI
A1 Dir. Roma Sud
CASAL MORENA
CIAMPINO
SS215 Via Tuscolana
70
BRRRRM
!
KREEE
WHAT'S WRONG, SIGNORE?!
MY CAR BROKE DOWN!
PLEASE, YOU'VE GOT TO HELP ME! MY WIFE IS PREGNANT, AND I'M TRYING TO GET HER TO THE HOSPITAL!

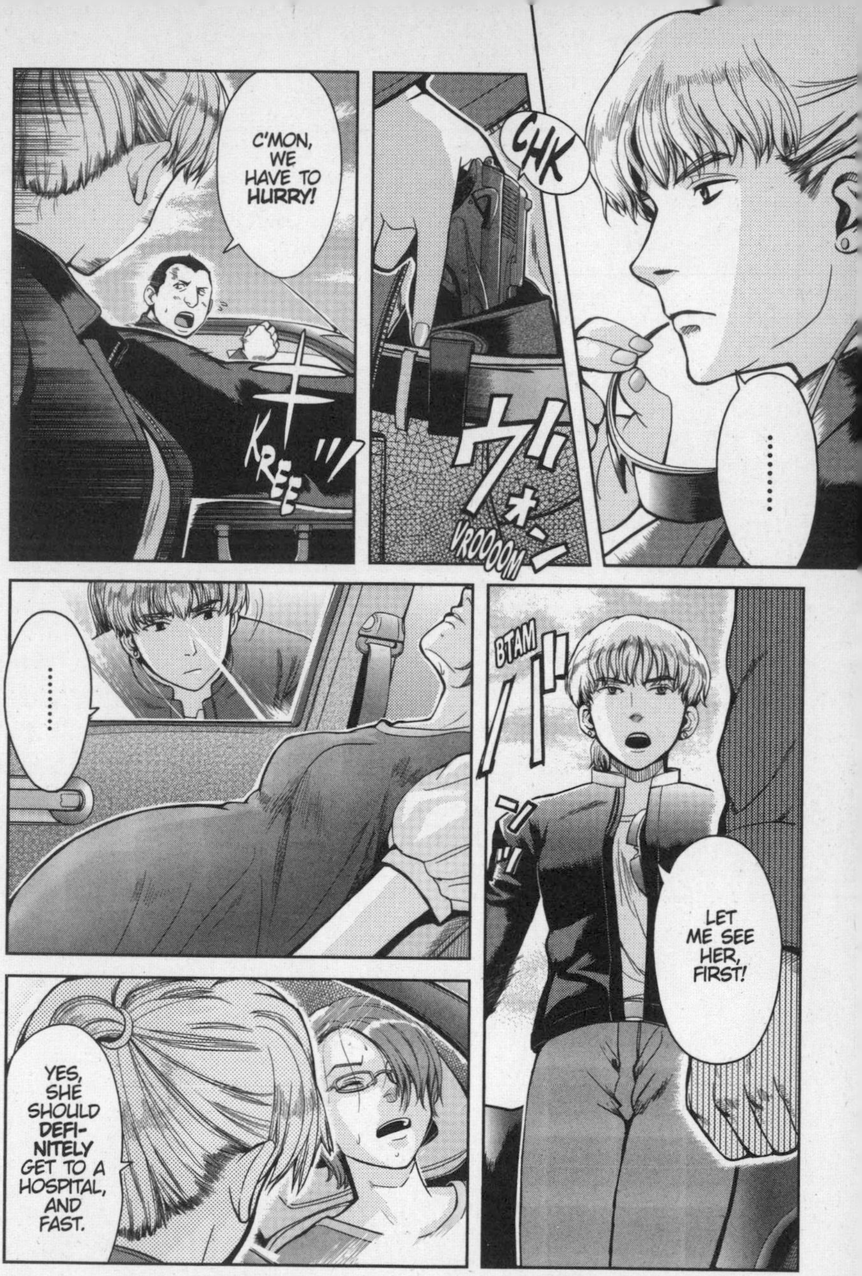
......
CHK
VROOOOM
C'MON, WE HAVE TO HURRY!
KREE
BTAM
LET ME SEE HER, FIRST!
......
YES, SHE SHOULD DEFI-NITELY GET TO A HOSPITAL, AND FAST.

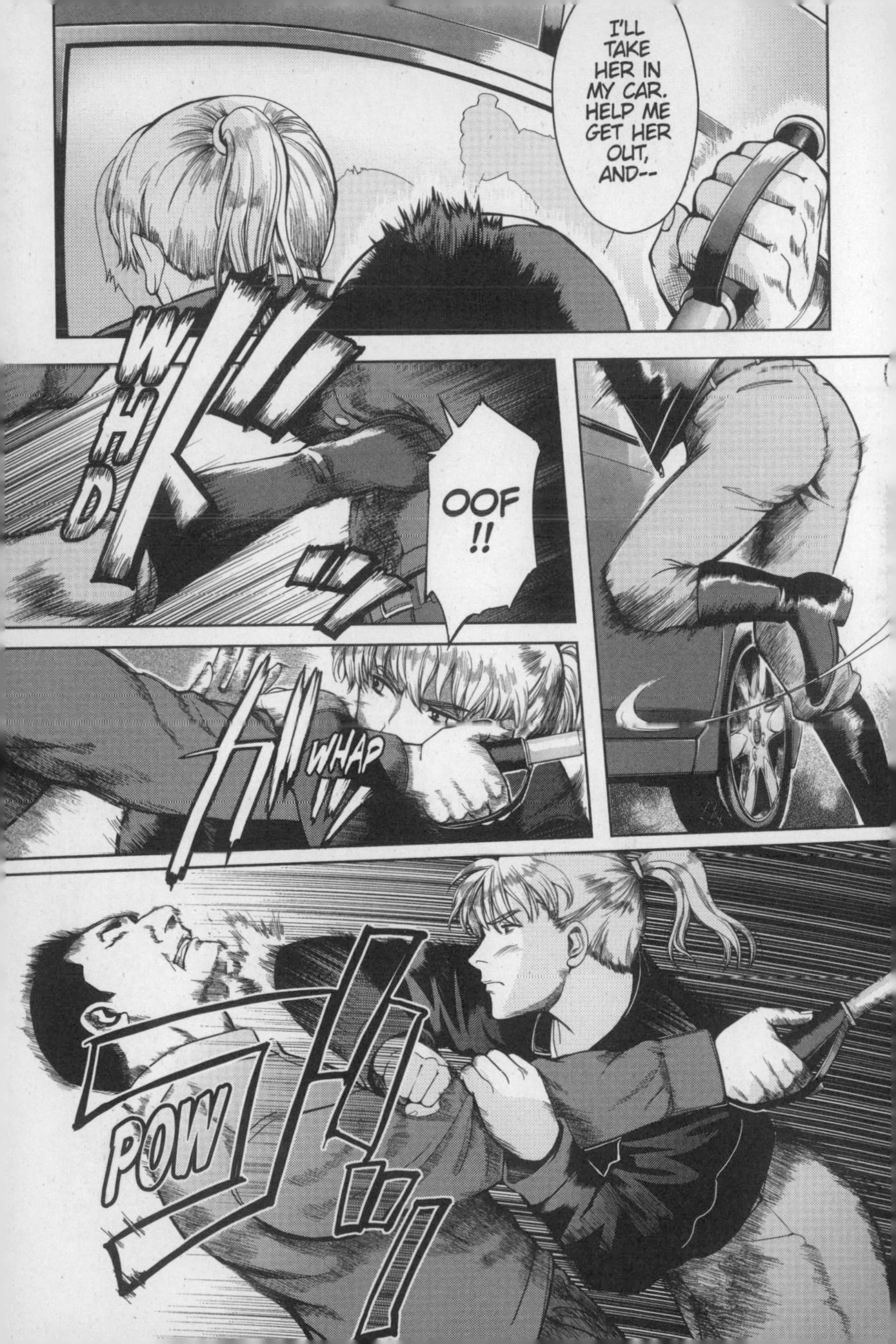
I'LL TAKE HER IN MY CAR. HELP ME GET HER OUT, AND--
WHD
OOF !!
WHAP
POW

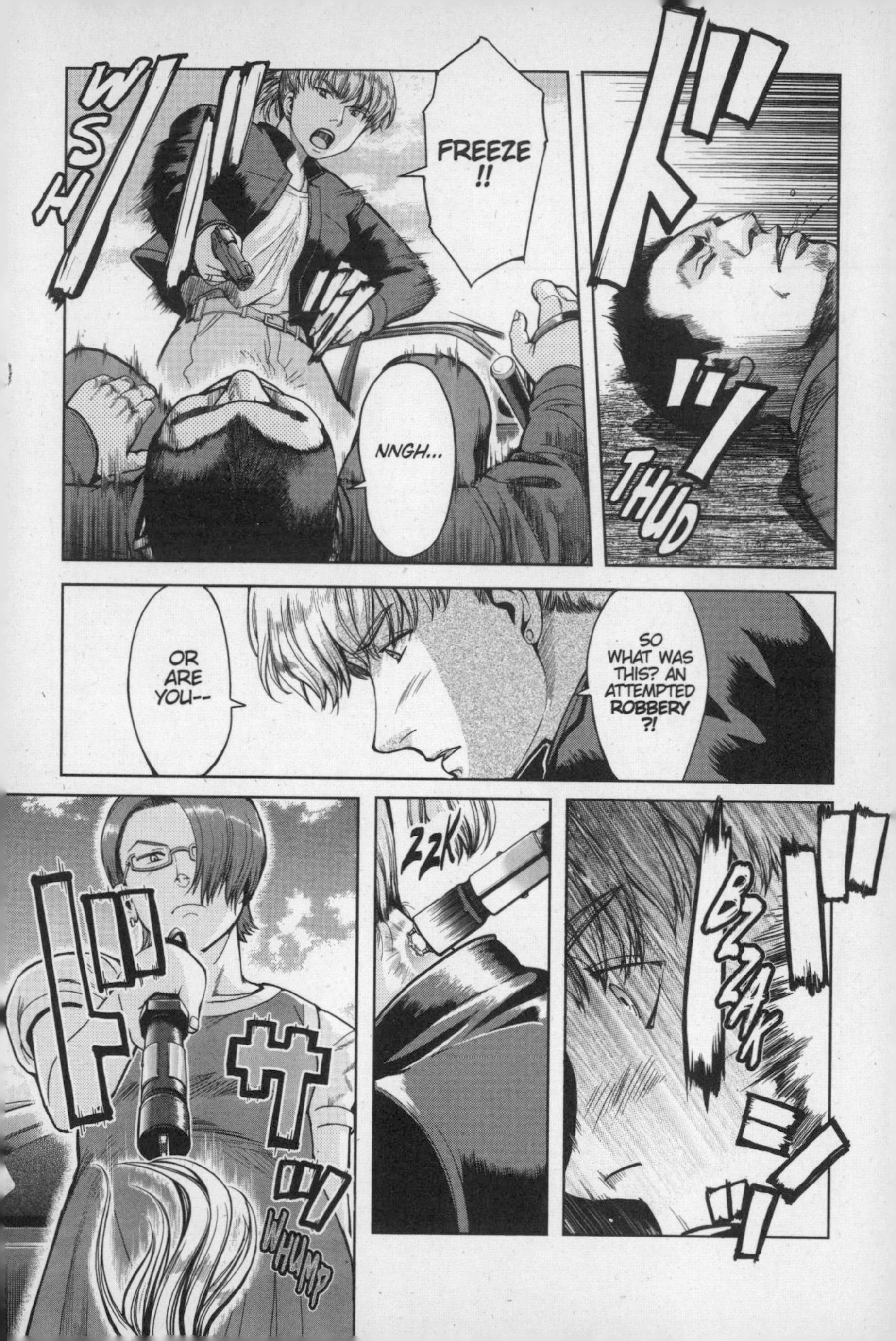
THUD
FREEZE !!
WSH
NNGH...
SO WHAT WAS THIS? AN ATTEMPTED ROBBERY ?!
OR ARE YOU--
BZZAK
ZZK
WHUMP

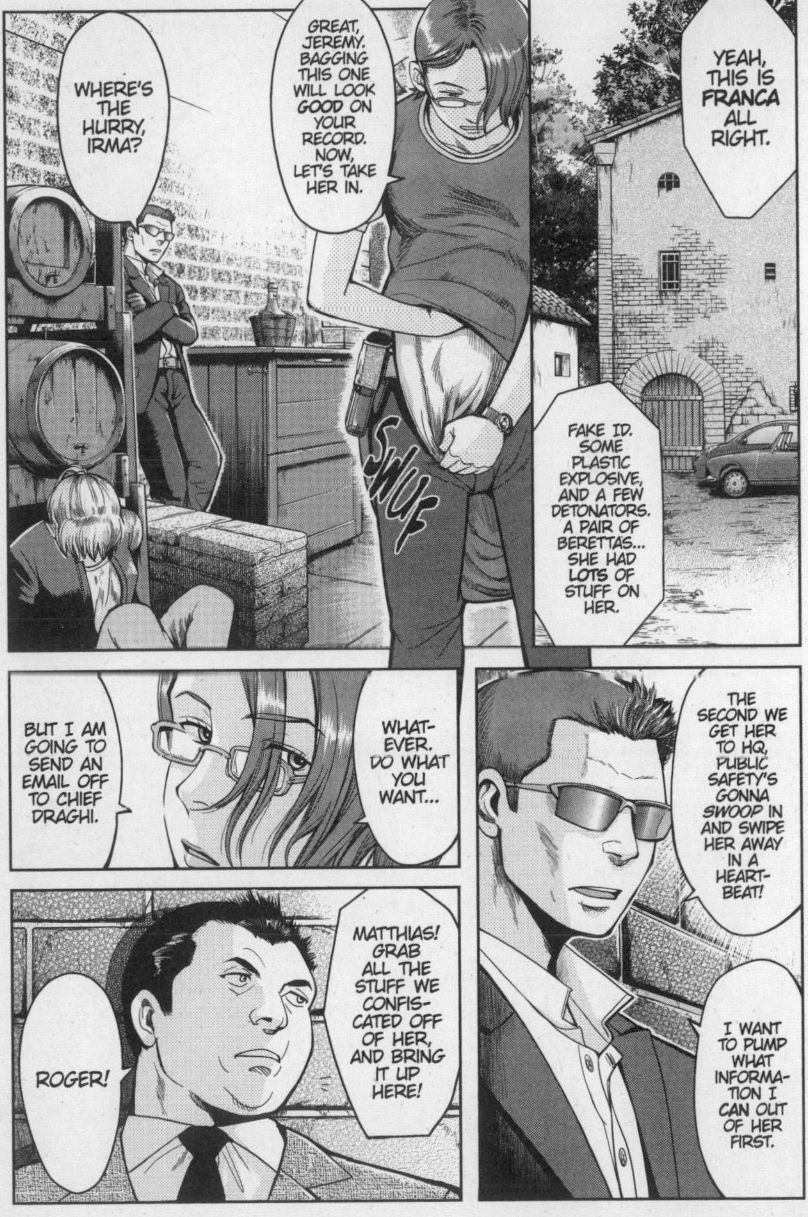
YEAH, THIS IS FRANCA ALL RIGHT.
FAKE ID. SOME PLASTIC EXPLOSIVE, AND A FEW DETONATORS. A PAIR OF BERETTAS... SHE HAD LOTS OF STUFF ON HER.
GREAT, JEREMY. BAGGING THIS ONE WILL LOOK GOOD ON YOUR RECORD. NOW, LET'S TAKE HER IN.
WHERE'S THE HURRY, IRMA?
SWUF
THE SECOND WE GET HER TO HQ, PUBLIC SAFETY'S GONNA SWOOP IN AND SWIPE HER AWAY IN A HEART-BEAT!
I WANT TO PUMP WHAT INFORMA-TION I CAN OUT OF HER FIRST.
WHAT-EVER. DO WHAT YOU WANT...
BUT I AM GOING TO SEND AN EMAIL OFF TO CHIEF DRAGHI.
MATTHIAS! GRAB ALL THE STUFF WE CONFIS-CATED OFF OF HER, AND BRING IT UP HERE!
ROGER!

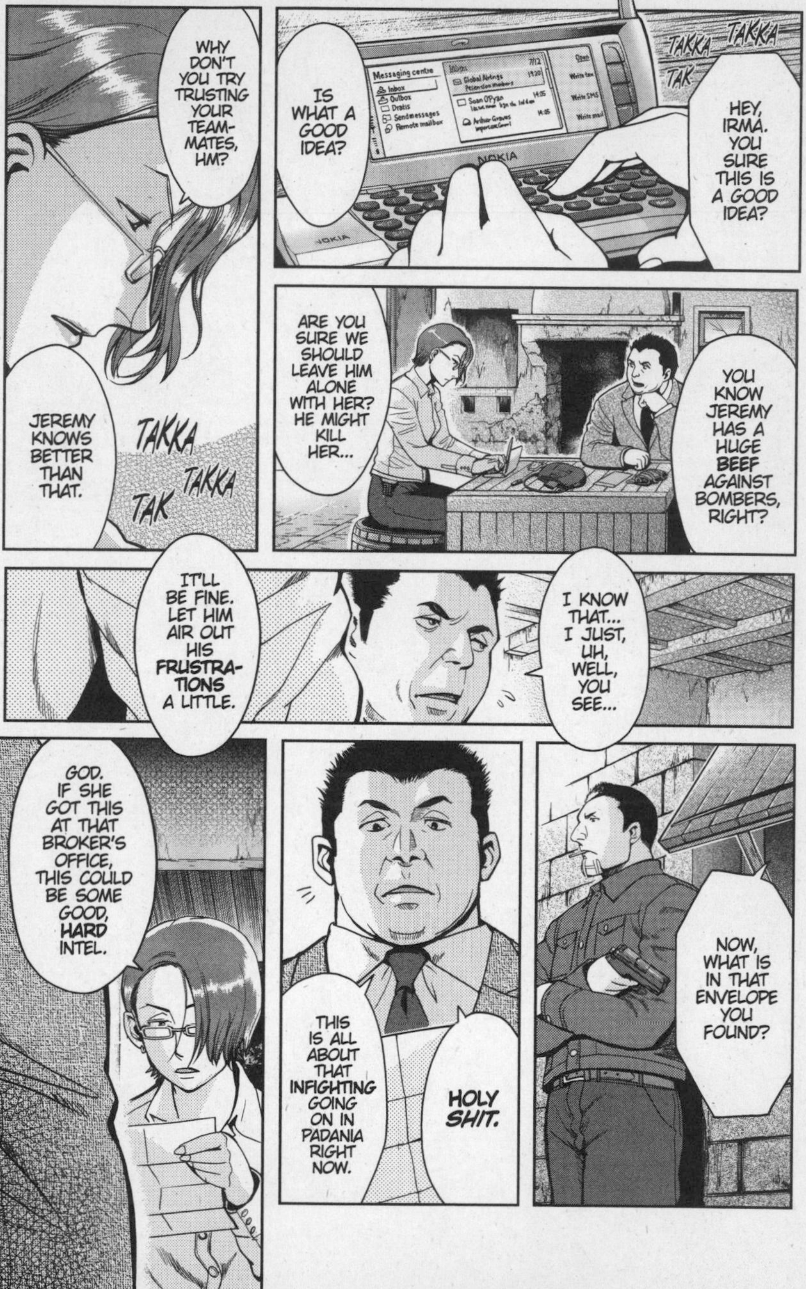
TAKKA TAKKA TAK
HEY, IRMA. YOU SURE THIS IS A GOOD IDEA?
IS WHAT A GOOD IDEA?
YOU KNOW JEREMY HAS A HUGE **BEEF** AGAINST BOMBERS, RIGHT?
ARE YOU SURE WE SHOULD LEAVE HIM ALONE WITH HER? HE MIGHT KILL HER...
WHY DON'T YOU TRY TRUSTING YOUR TEAM-MATES, HM?
TAKKA TAKKA TAK
JEREMY KNOWS BETTER THAN THAT.
I KNOW THAT... I JUST, UH, WELL, YOU SEE...
IT'LL BE FINE. LET HIM AIR OUT HIS **FRUSTRATIONS** A LITTLE.
NOW, WHAT IS IN THAT ENVELOPE YOU FOUND?
HOLY SHIT.
THIS IS ALL ABOUT THAT **INFIGHTING** GOING ON IN PADANIA RIGHT NOW.
GOD. IF SHE GOT THIS AT THAT BROKER'S OFFICE, THIS COULD BE SOME GOOD, **HARD** INTEL.

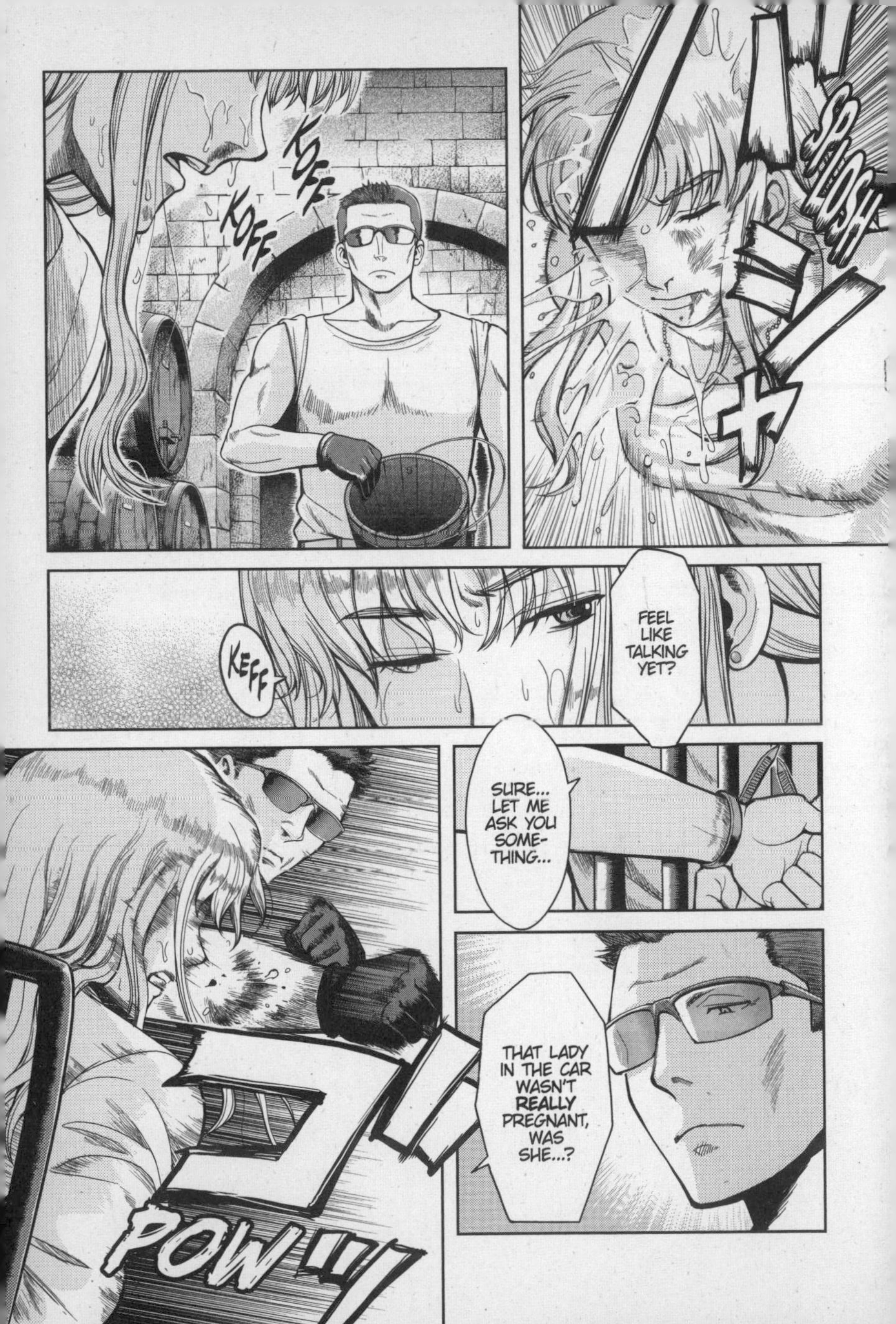
SPLOSH
KOFF
KOFF
FEEL LIKE TALKING YET?
KEFF
SURE... LET ME ASK YOU SOME-THING...
THAT LADY IN THE CAR WASN'T **REALLY** PREGNANT, WAS SHE...?
POW!!!

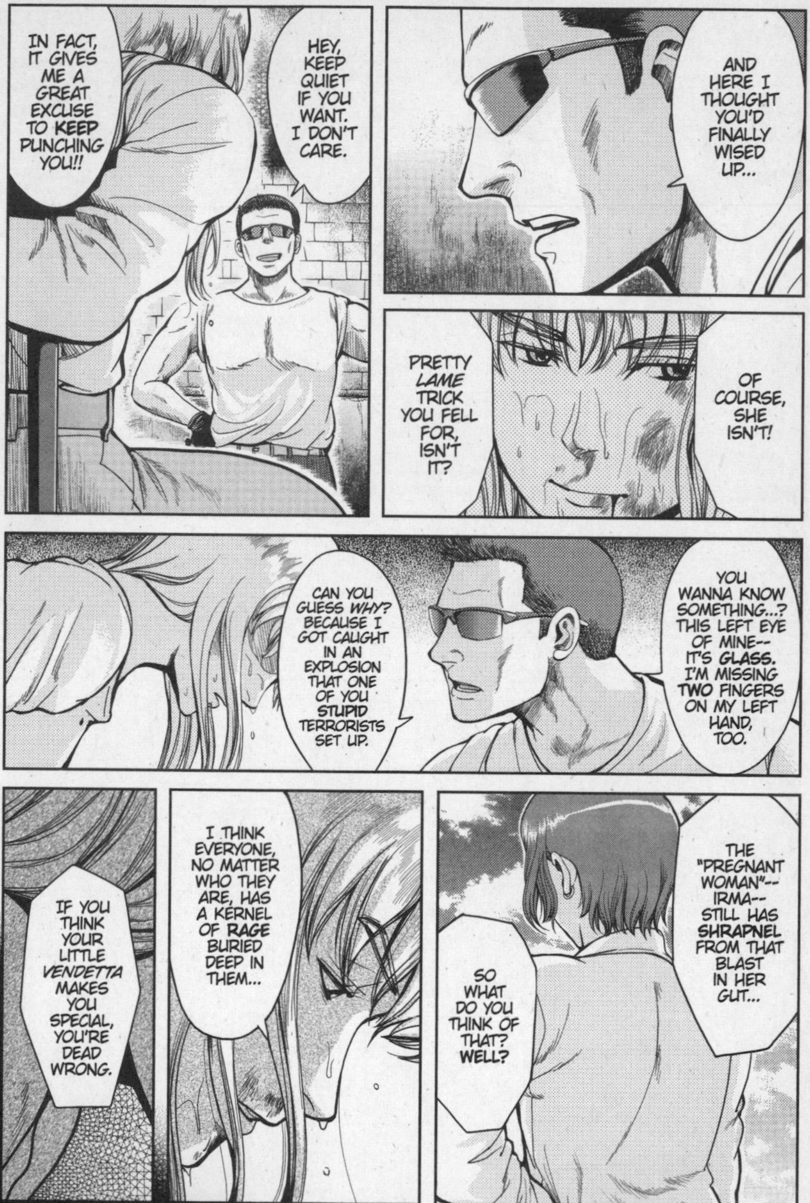
AND HERE I THOUGHT YOU'D FINALLY WISED UP...
OF COURSE, SHE ISN'T!
PRETTY LAME TRICK YOU FELL FOR, ISN'T IT?
HEY, KEEP QUIET IF YOU WANT. I DON'T CARE.
IN FACT, IT GIVES ME A GREAT EXCUSE TO KEEP PUNCHING YOU!!
YOU WANNA KNOW SOMETHING...? THIS LEFT EYE OF MINE-- IT'S GLASS. I'M MISSING TWO FINGERS ON MY LEFT HAND, TOO.
CAN YOU GUESS WHY? BECAUSE I GOT CAUGHT IN AN EXPLOSION THAT ONE OF YOU STUPID TERRORISTS SET UP.
THE "PREGNANT WOMAN"-- IRMA-- STILL HAS SHRAPNEL FROM THAT BLAST IN HER GUT...
SO WHAT DO YOU THINK OF THAT? WELL?
I THINK EVERYONE, NO MATTER WHO THEY ARE, HAS A KERNEL OF RAGE BURIED DEEP IN THEM...
IF YOU THINK YOUR LITTLE VENDETTA MAKES YOU SPECIAL, YOU'RE DEAD WRONG.

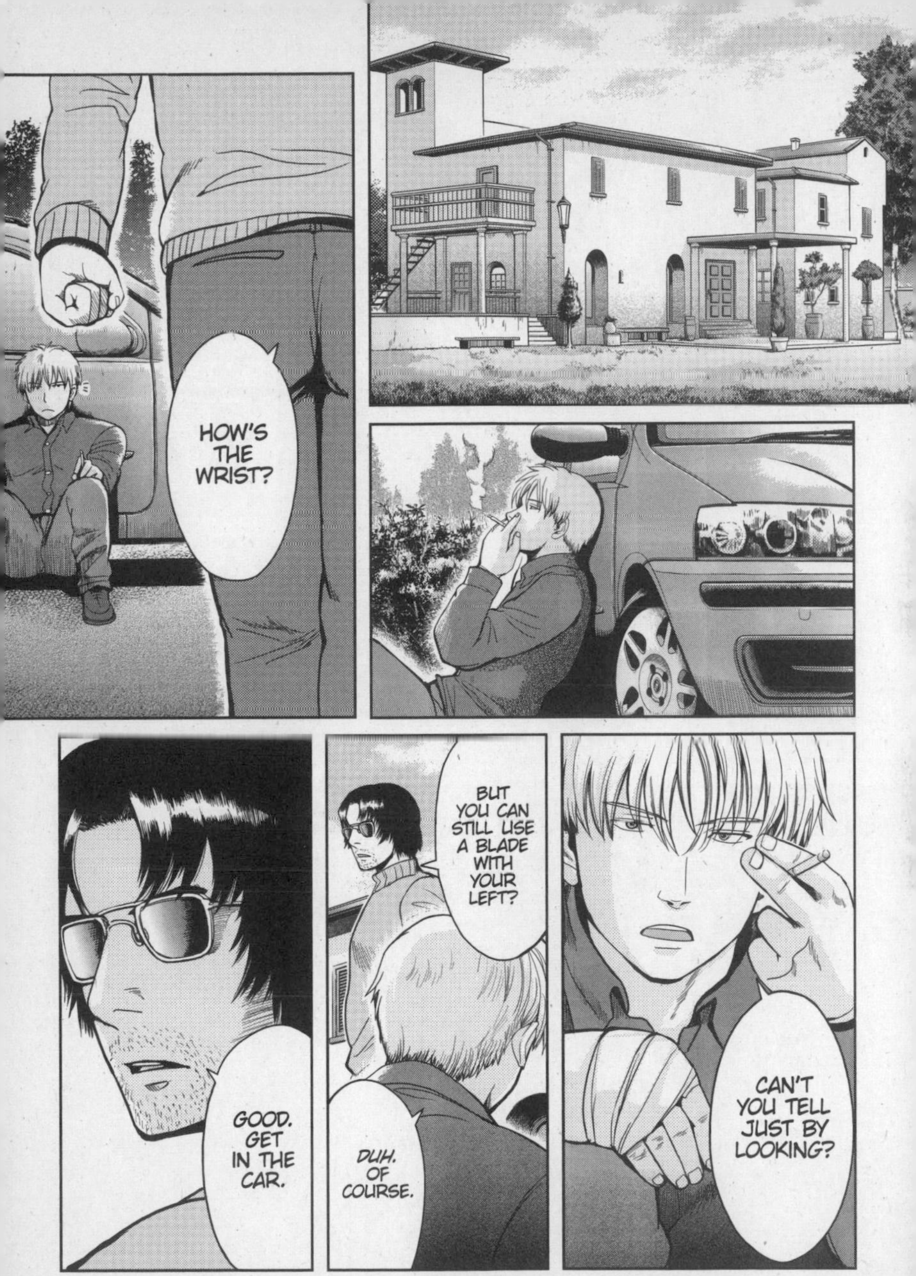
HOW'S THE WRIST?
CAN'T YOU TELL JUST BY LOOKING?
BUT YOU CAN STILL USE A BLADE WITH YOUR LEFT?
DUH. OF COURSE.
GOOD. GET IN THE CAR.

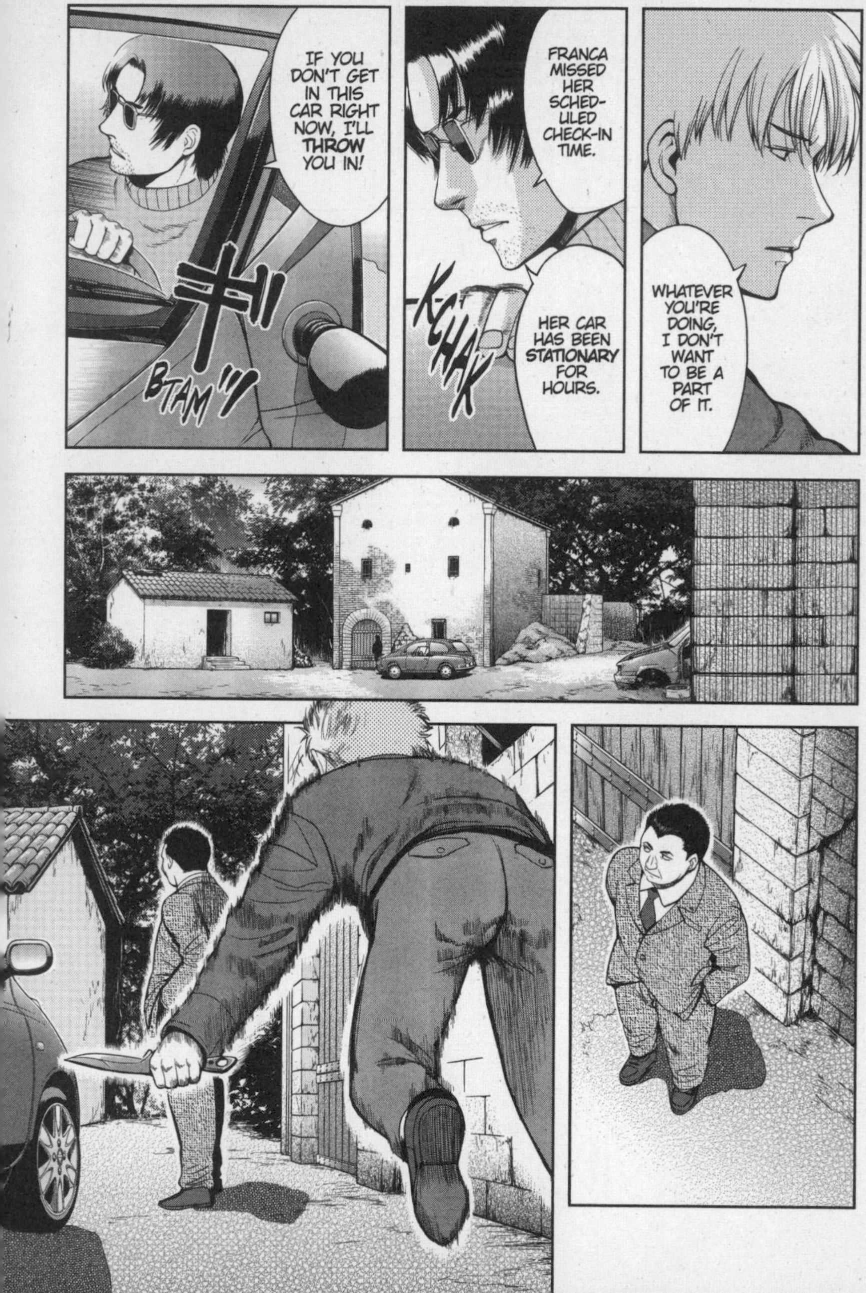
WHATEVER YOU'RE DOING, I DON'T WANT TO BE A PART OF IT.
FRANCA MISSED HER SCHED-ULED CHECK-IN TIME.
HER CAR HAS BEEN **STATIONARY** FOR HOURS.
K-CHAK
IF YOU DON'T GET IN THIS CAR RIGHT NOW, I'LL **THROW** YOU IN!
BTAM

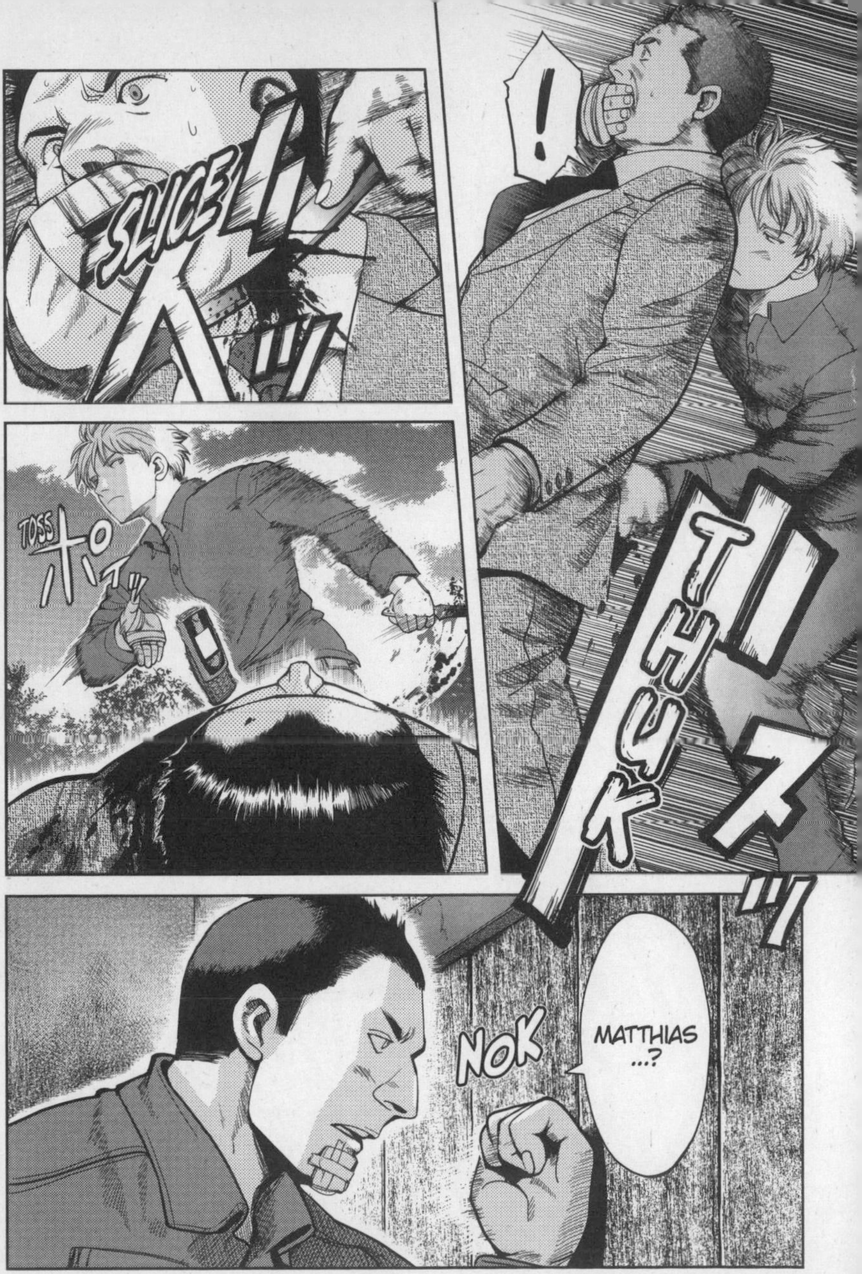
!
THUK
SLICE
TOSS
NOK
MATTHIAS ...?

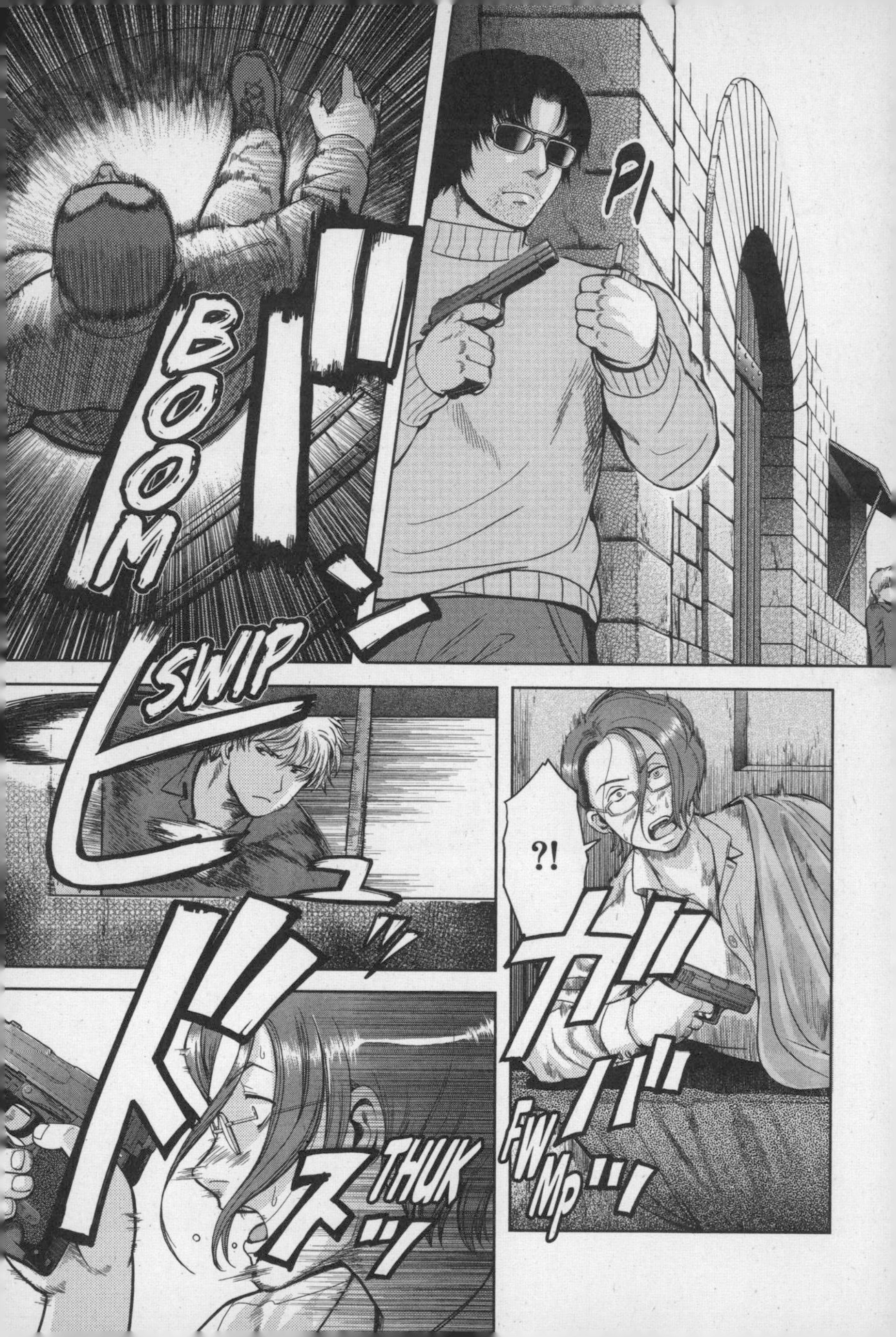
PI
BOOM
?!
FWMp
SWIP
THUK

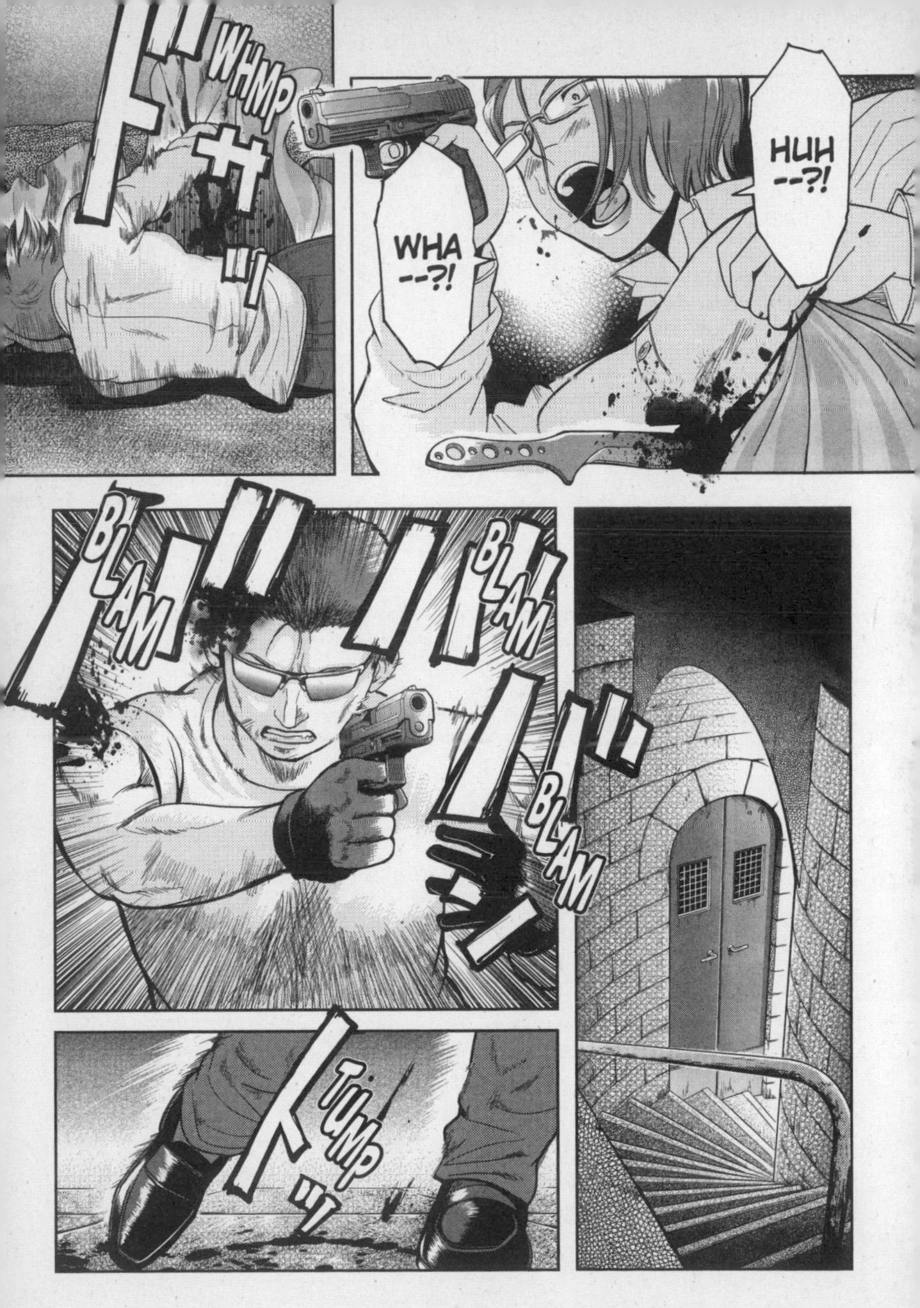

HUH --?!
WHA --?!
WHMP
BLAM
BLAM
BLAM
TUMP

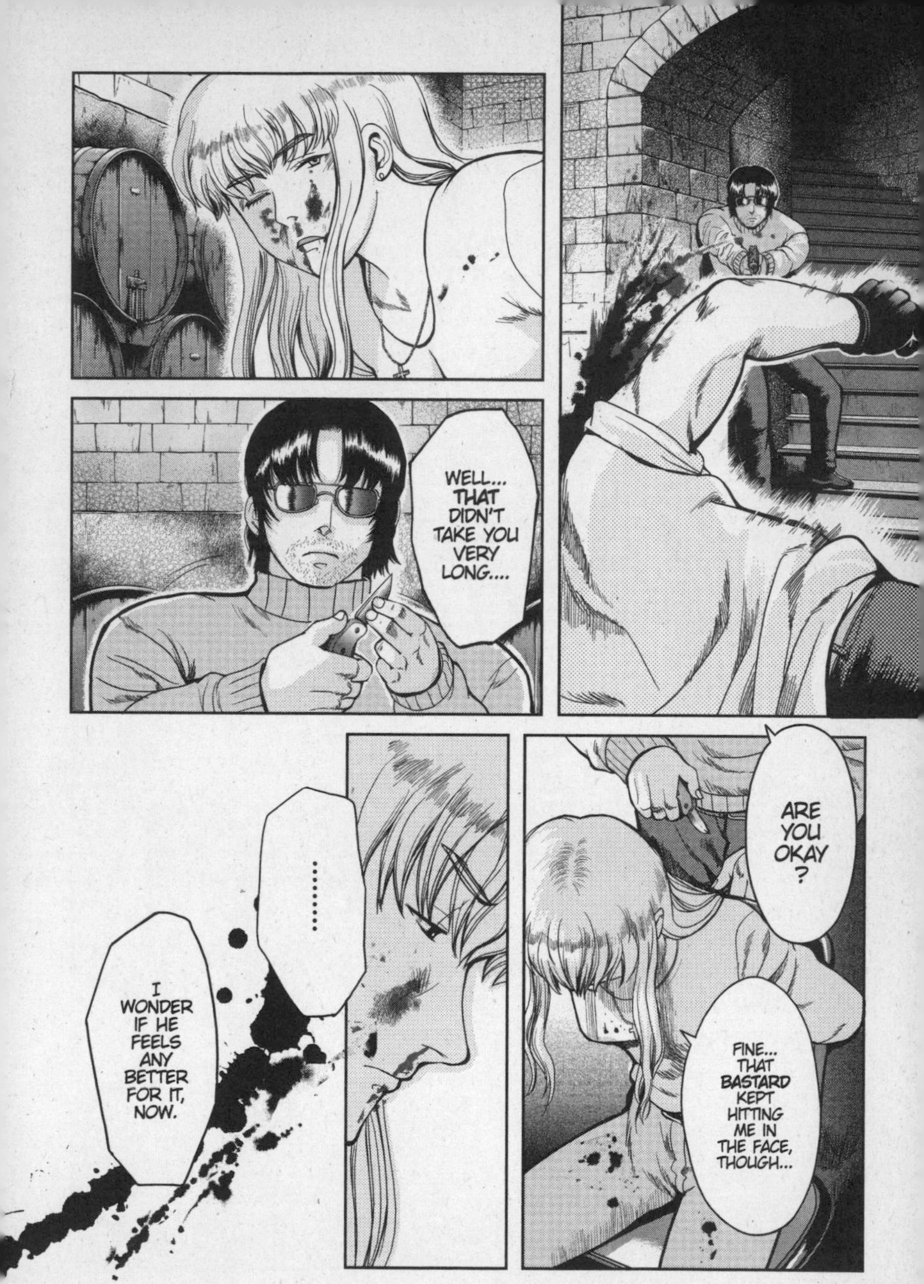
WELL... THAT DIDN'T TAKE YOU VERY LONG....
ARE YOU OKAY?
FINE... THAT BASTARD KEPT HITTING ME IN THE FACE, THOUGH...
......
I WONDER IF HE FEELS ANY BETTER FOR IT, NOW.

GUNSLINGERGIRL.

CHAPTER 25: PINOCCHIO (4)

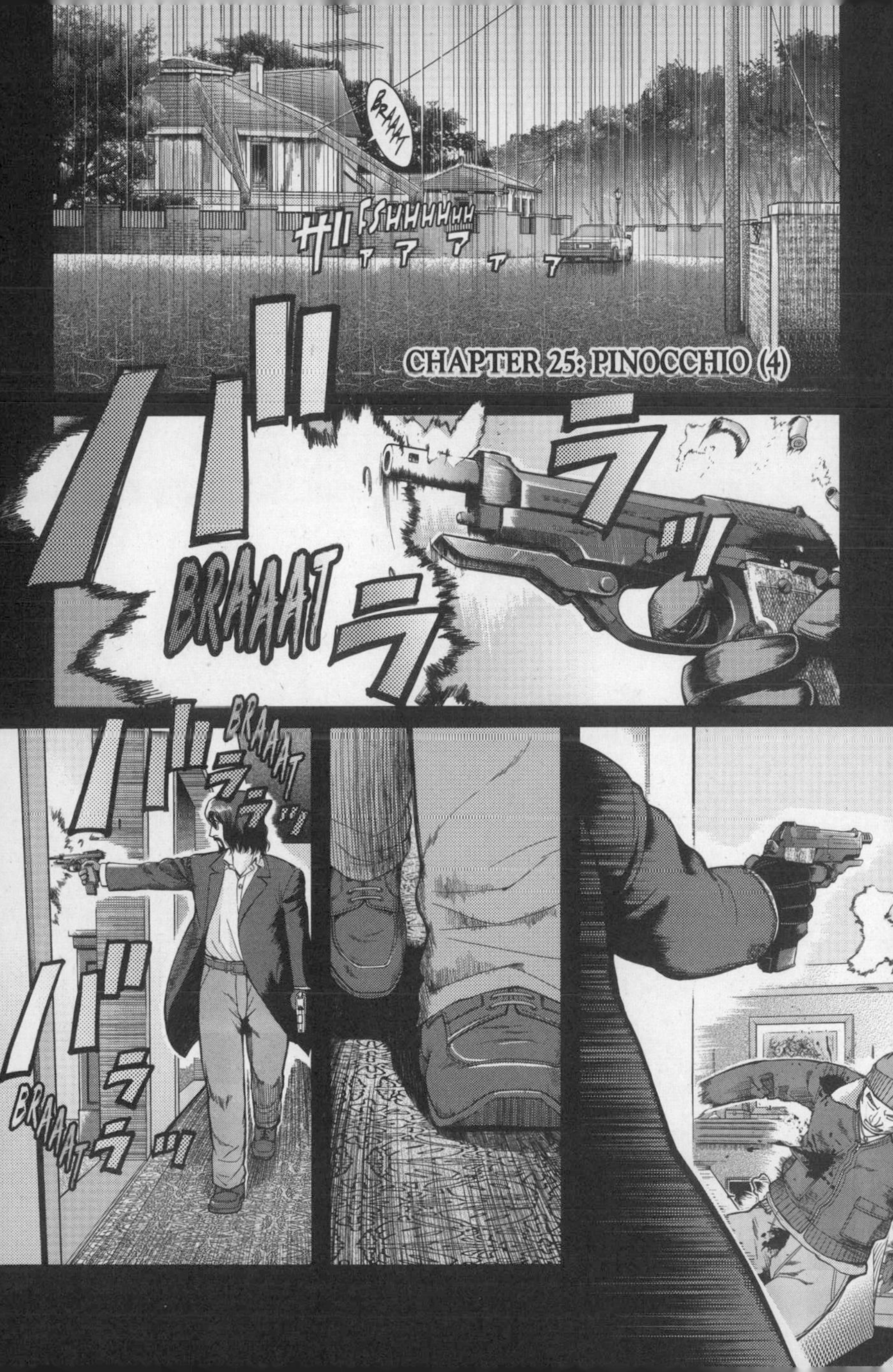

BRAAM
FSHHHHHH
BRAAAT
BRAAAT
BRAAAT

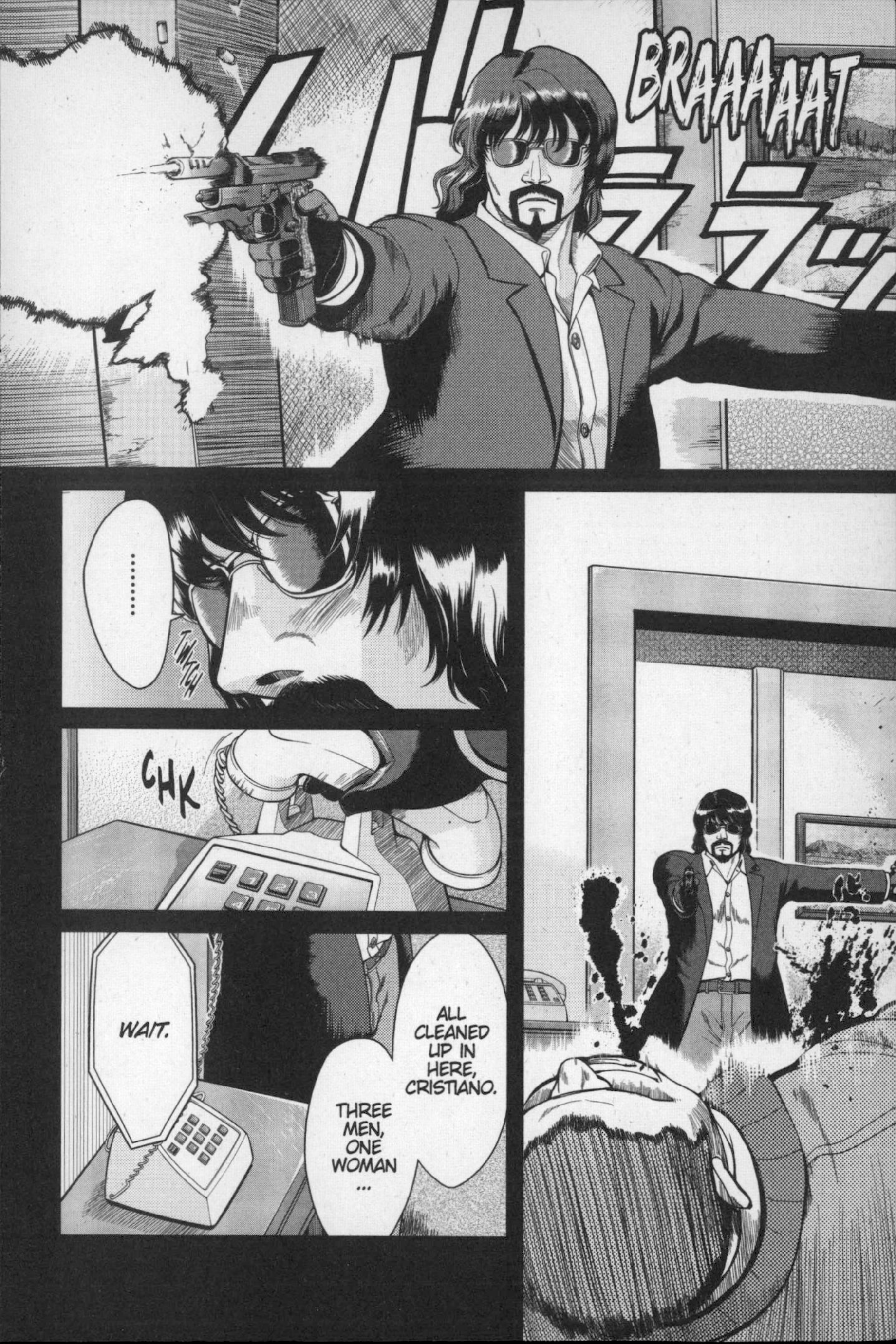
BRAAAAAT
......
TWITCH
CHK
ALL CLEANED UP IN HERE, CRISTIANO.
THREE MEN, ONE WOMAN ...
WAIT.

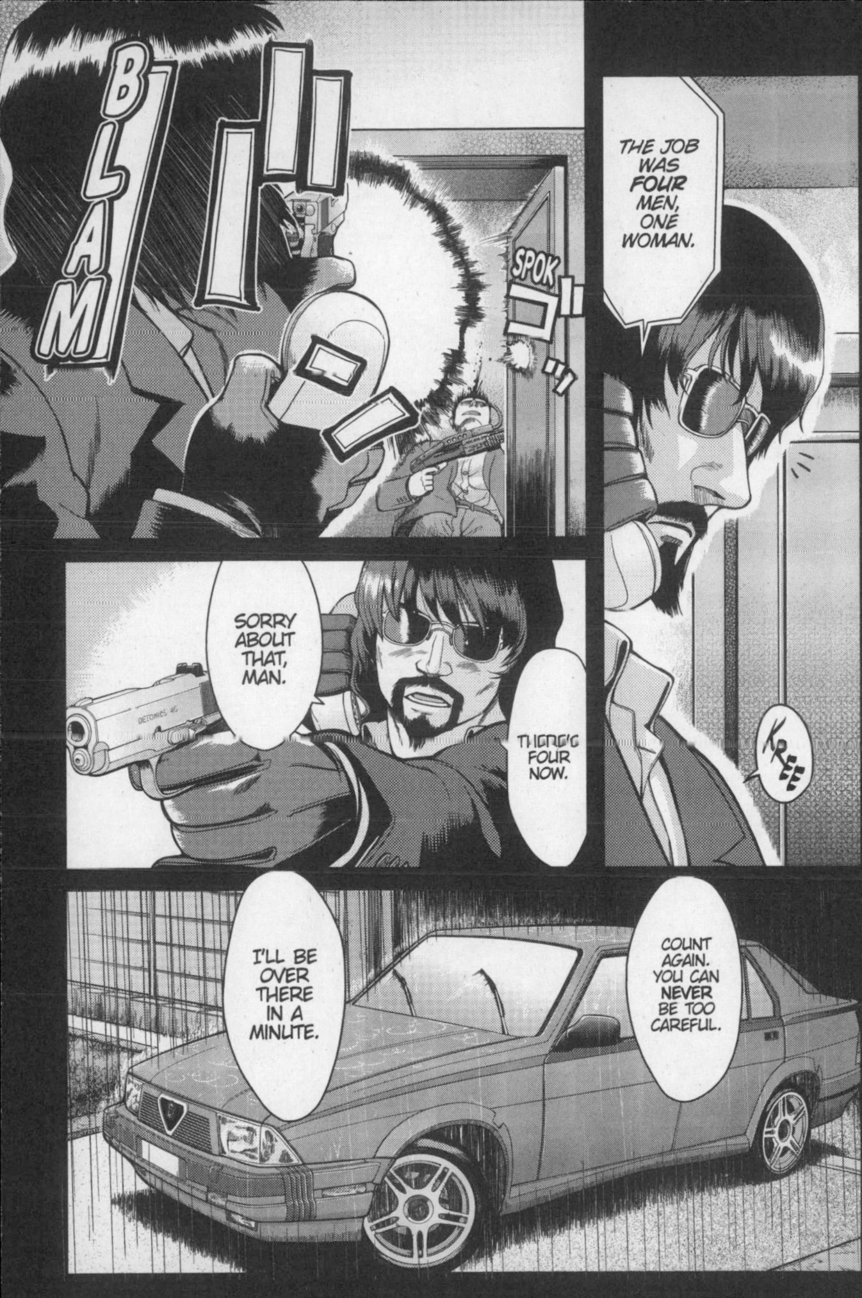
THE JOB WAS FOUR MEN, ONE WOMAN.
KREE
BLAM
SPOK
SORRY ABOUT THAT, MAN.
THERE'S FOUR NOW.
COUNT AGAIN. YOU CAN NEVER BE TOO CAREFUL.
I'LL BE OVER THERE IN A MINUTE.

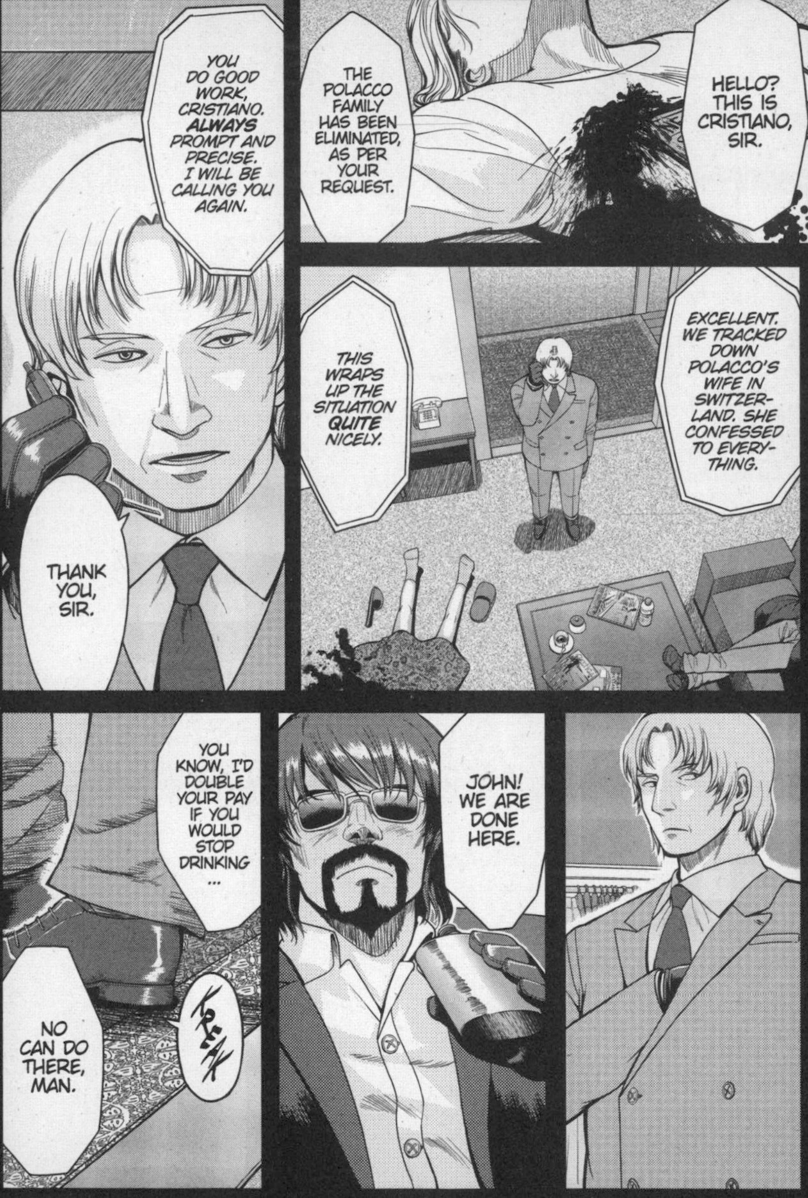
HELLO? THIS IS CRISTIANO, SIR.
THE POLACCO FAMILY HAS BEEN ELIMINATED, AS PER YOUR REQUEST.
EXCELLENT. WE TRACKED DOWN POLACCO'S WIFE IN SWITZER-LAND. SHE CONFESSED TO EVERY-THING.
THIS WRAPS UP THE SITUATION QUITE NICELY.
YOU DO GOOD WORK, CRISTIANO. ALWAYS PROMPT AND PRECISE. I WILL BE CALLING YOU AGAIN.
THANK YOU, SIR.
JOHN! WE ARE DONE HERE.
YOU KNOW, I'D DOUBLE YOUR PAY IF YOU WOULD STOP DRINKING ...
KREAK
NO CAN DO THERE, MAN.

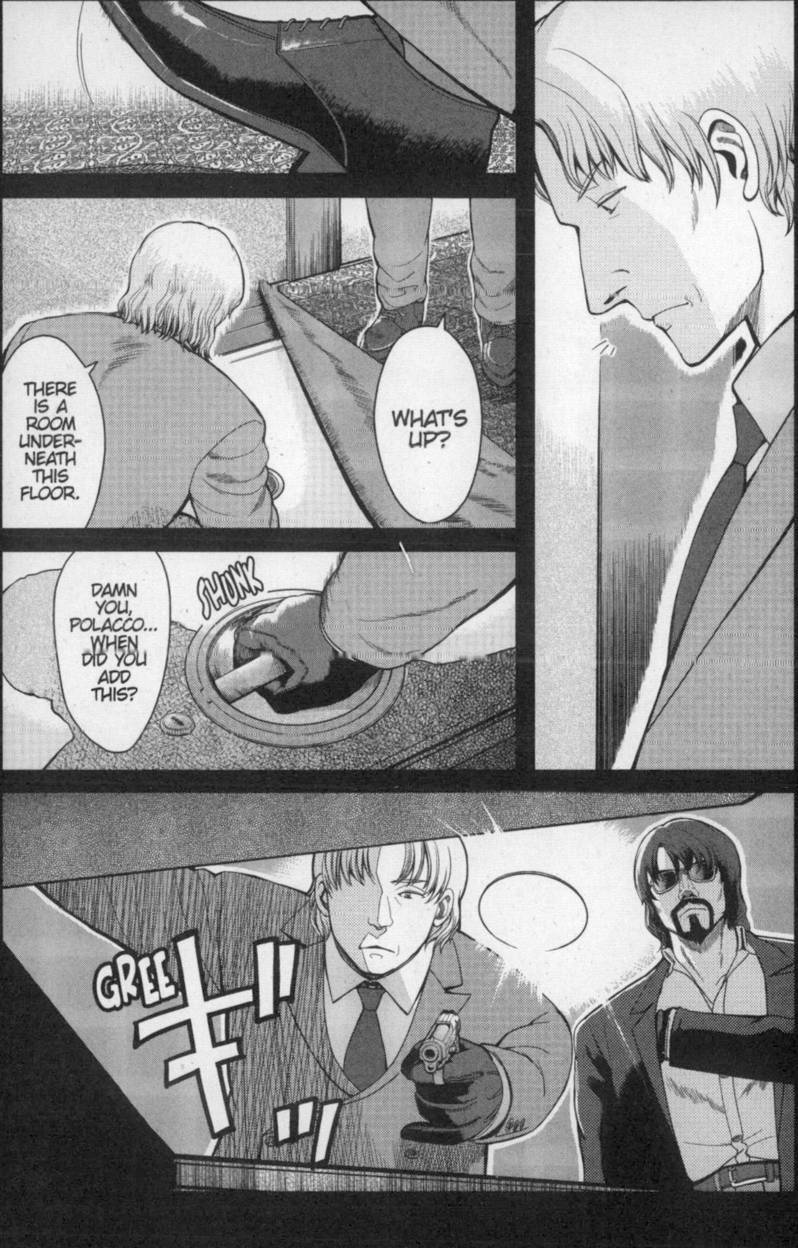
WHAT'S UP?
THERE IS A ROOM UNDER-NEATH THIS FLOOR.
SHUNK
DAMN YOU, POLACCO... WHEN DID YOU ADD THIS?
GREE

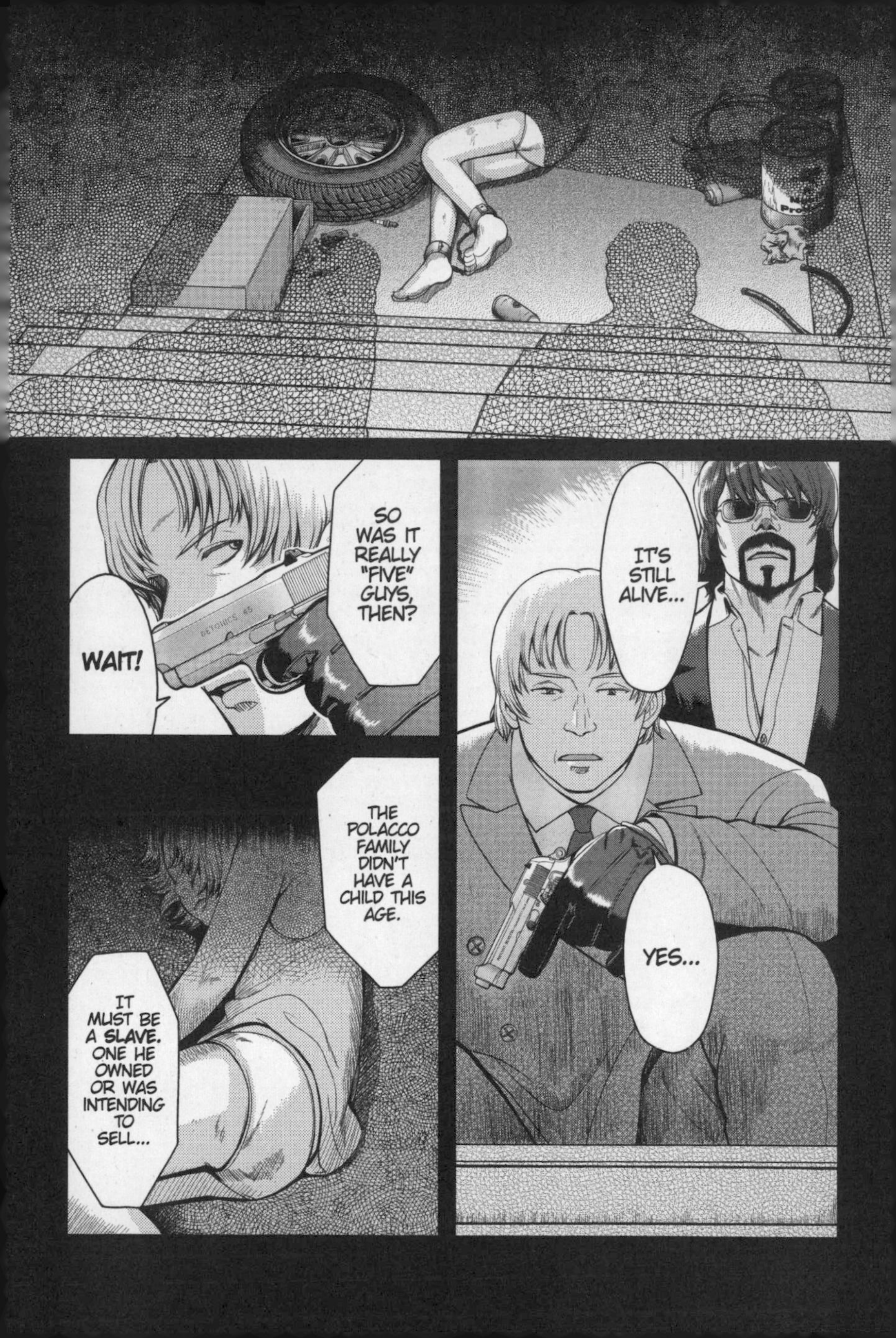
IT'S STILL ALIVE...
YES...
SO WAS IT REALLY "FIVE" GUYS, THEN?
WAIT!
THE POLACCO FAMILY DIDN'T HAVE A CHILD THIS AGE.
IT MUST BE A SLAVE. ONE HE OWNED OR WAS INTENDING TO SELL...

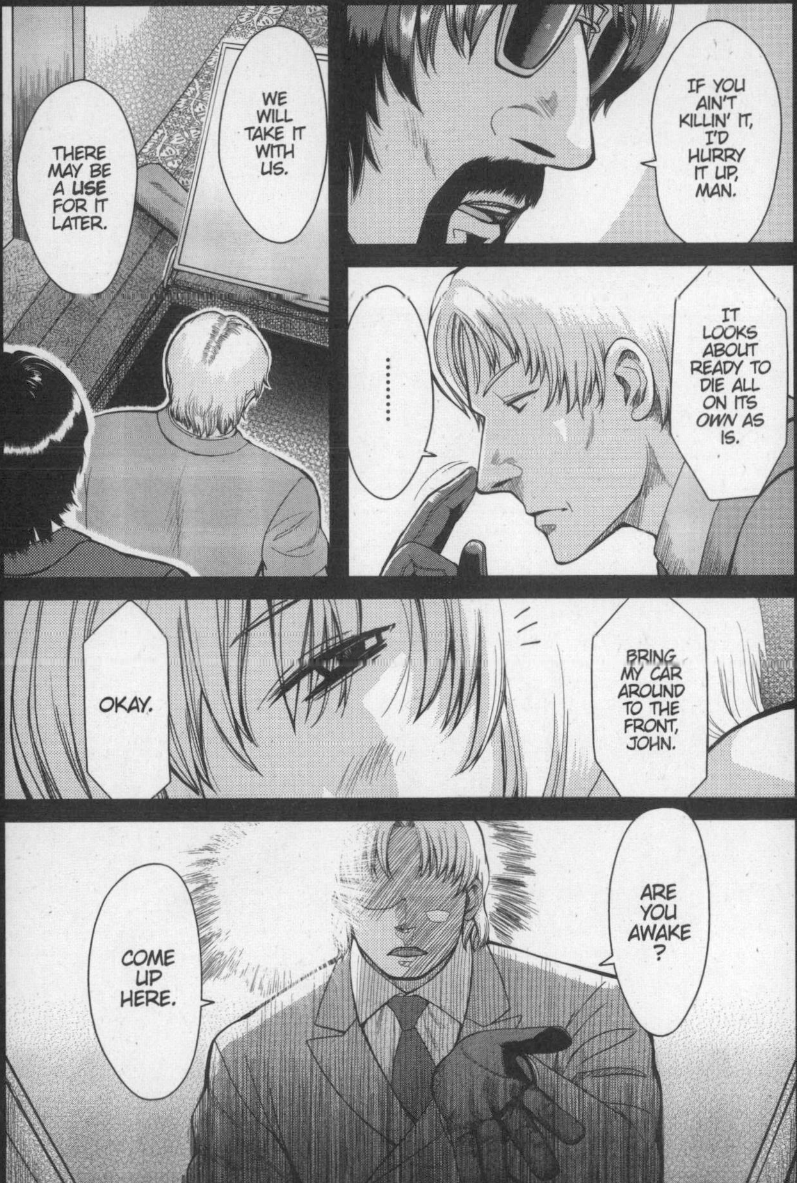
IF YOU AIN'T KILLIN' IT, I'D HURRY IT UP, MAN.
IT LOOKS ABOUT READY TO DIE ALL ON ITS *OWN* AS IS.
....
WE WILL TAKE IT WITH US.
THERE MAY BE A USE FOR IT LATER.
BRING MY CAR AROUND TO THE FRONT, JOHN.
OKAY.
ARE YOU AWAKE?
COME UP HERE.

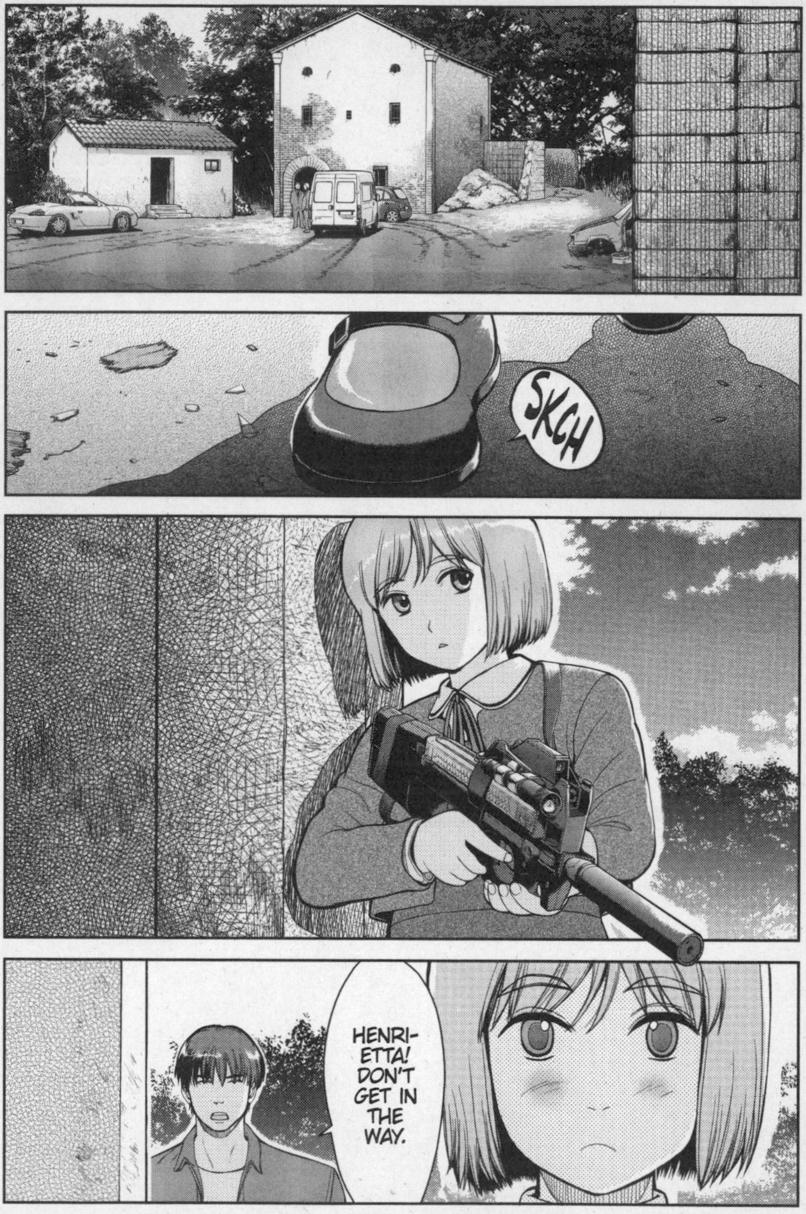
SKCH
HENRIETTA! DON'T GET IN THE WAY.

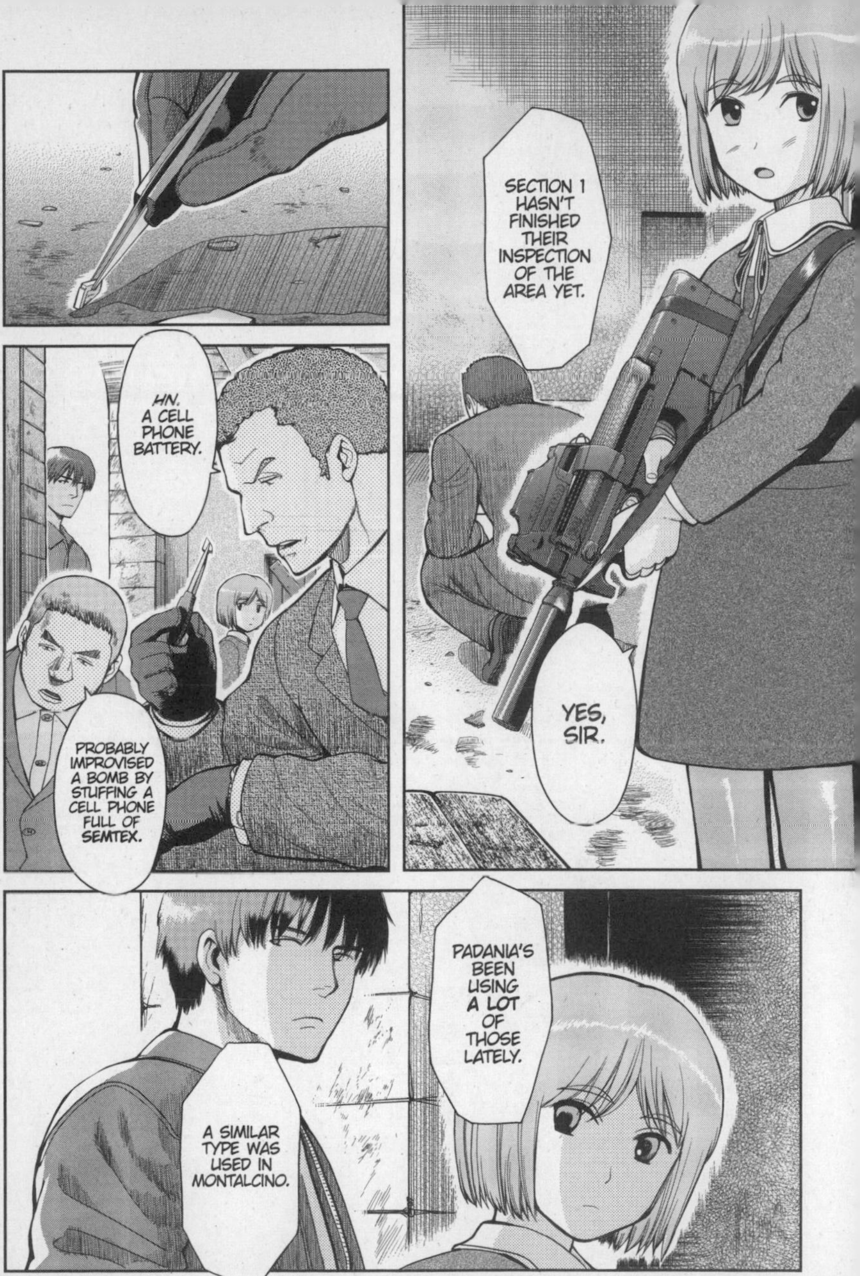
SECTION 1 HASN'T FINISHED THEIR INSPECTION OF THE AREA YET.
YES, SIR.
HN. A CELL PHONE BATTERY.
PROBABLY IMPROVISED A BOMB BY STUFFING A CELL PHONE FULL OF SEMTEX.
PADANIA'S BEEN USING A LOT OF THOSE LATELY.
A SIMILAR TYPE WAS USED IN MONTALCINO.

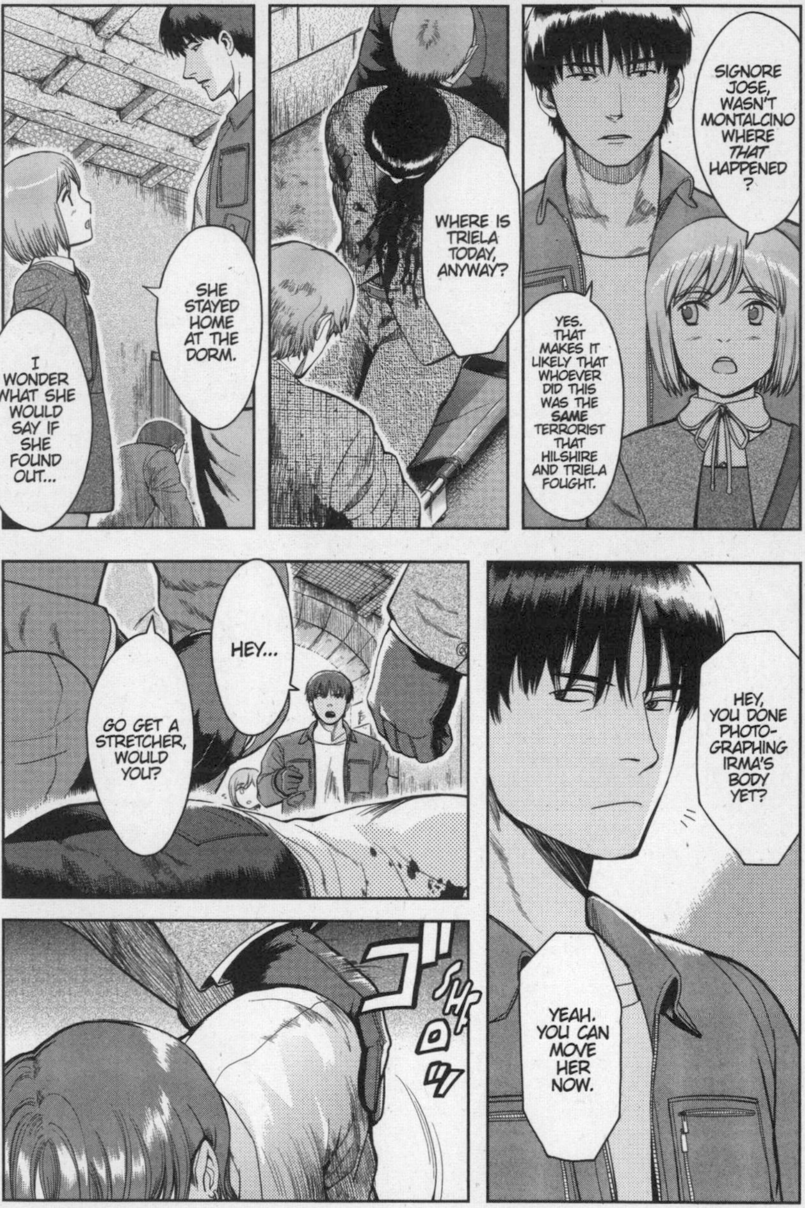
SIGNORE JOSE, WASN'T MONTALCINO WHERE THAT HAPPENED?
YES. THAT MAKES IT LIKELY THAT WHOEVER DID THIS WAS THE SAME TERRORIST THAT HILSHIRE AND TRIELA FOUGHT.
WHERE IS TRIELA TODAY, ANYWAY?
SHE STAYED HOME AT THE DORM.
I WONDER WHAT SHE WOULD SAY IF SHE FOUND OUT...
HEY, YOU DONE PHOTOGRAPHING IRMA'S BODY YET?
YEAH. YOU CAN MOVE HER NOW.
HEY...
GO GET A STRETCHER, WOULD YOU?
SHF

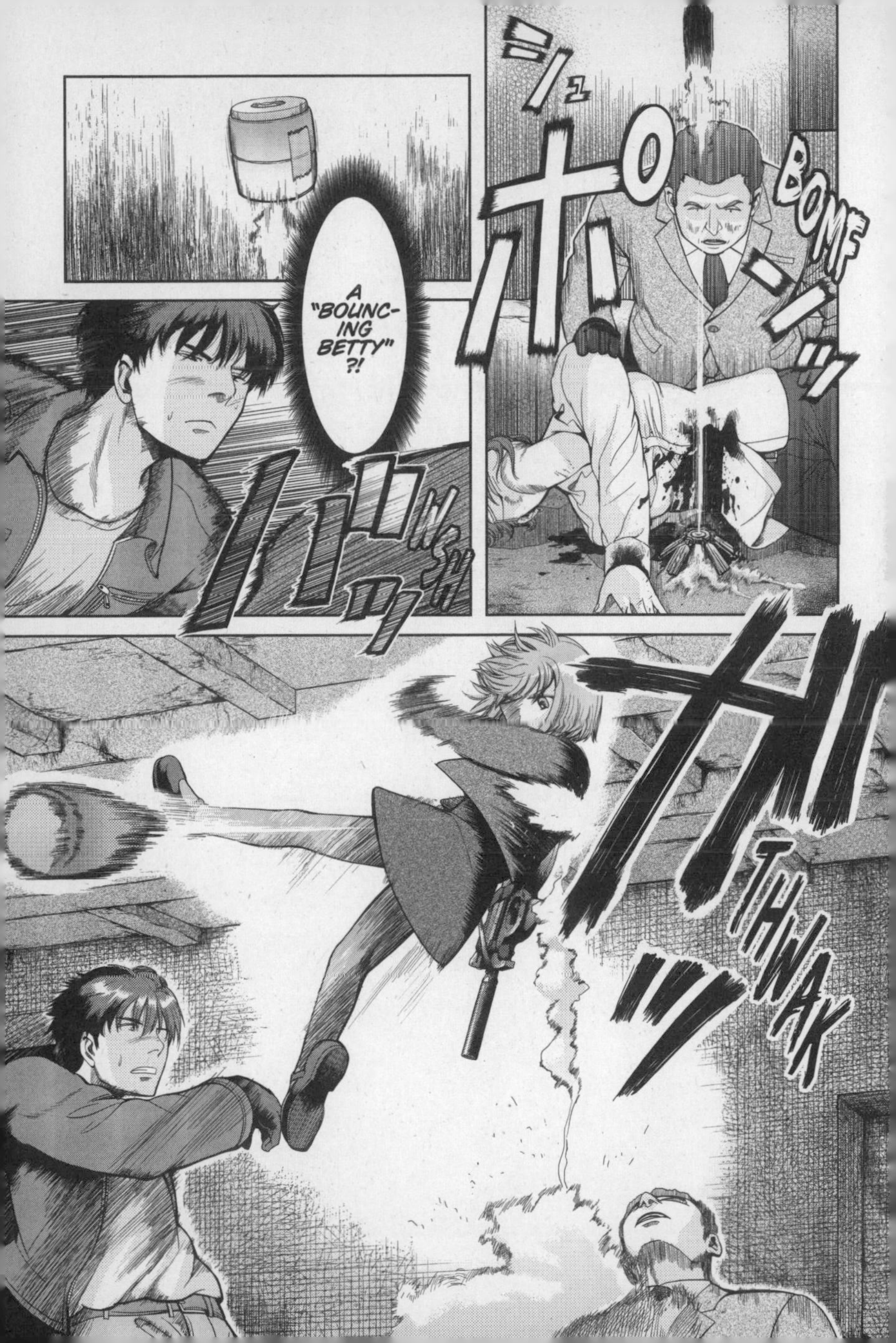
BOMF
A "BOUNCING BETTY"?!
WHSH
THWAK

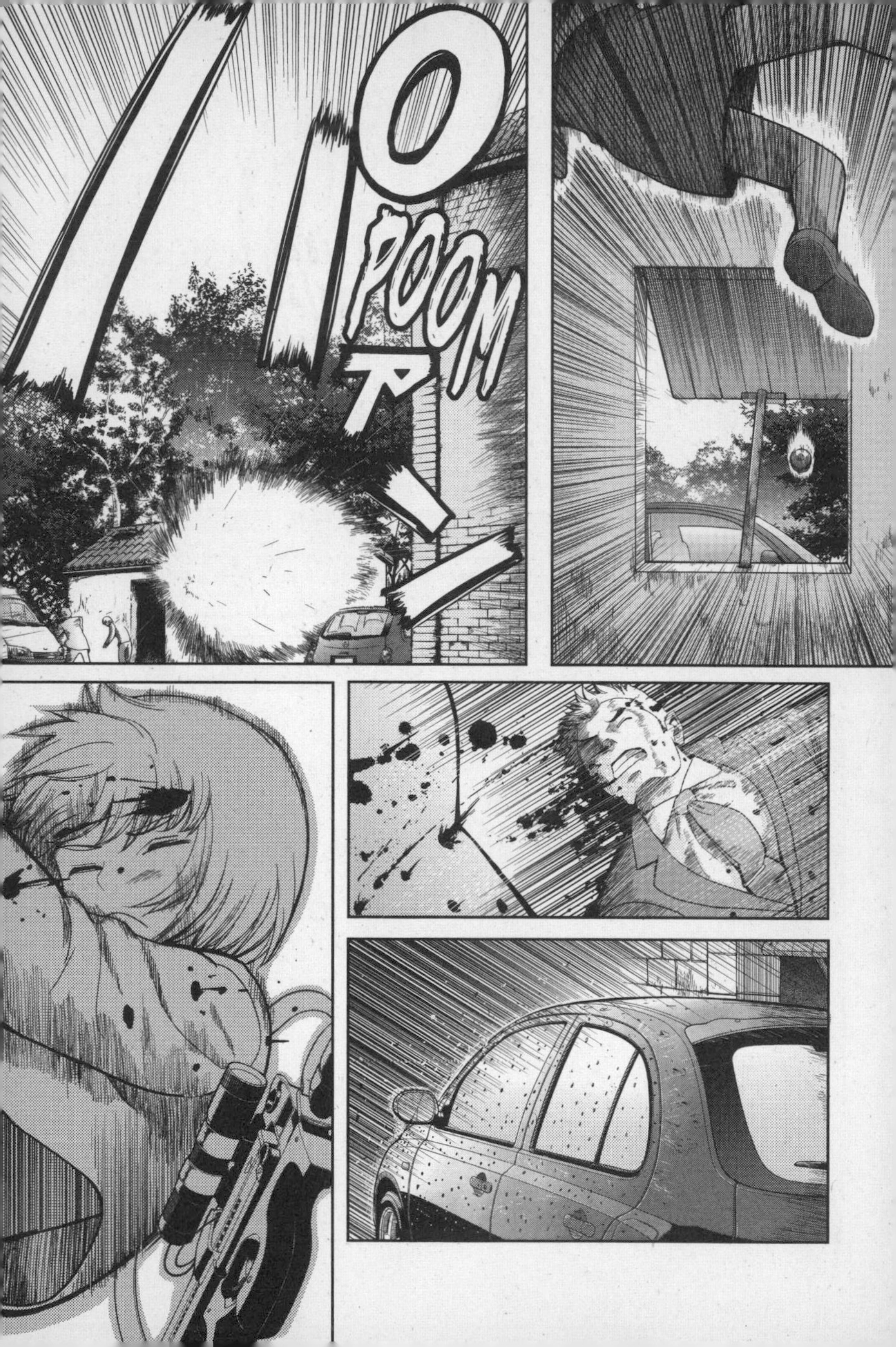
POOM

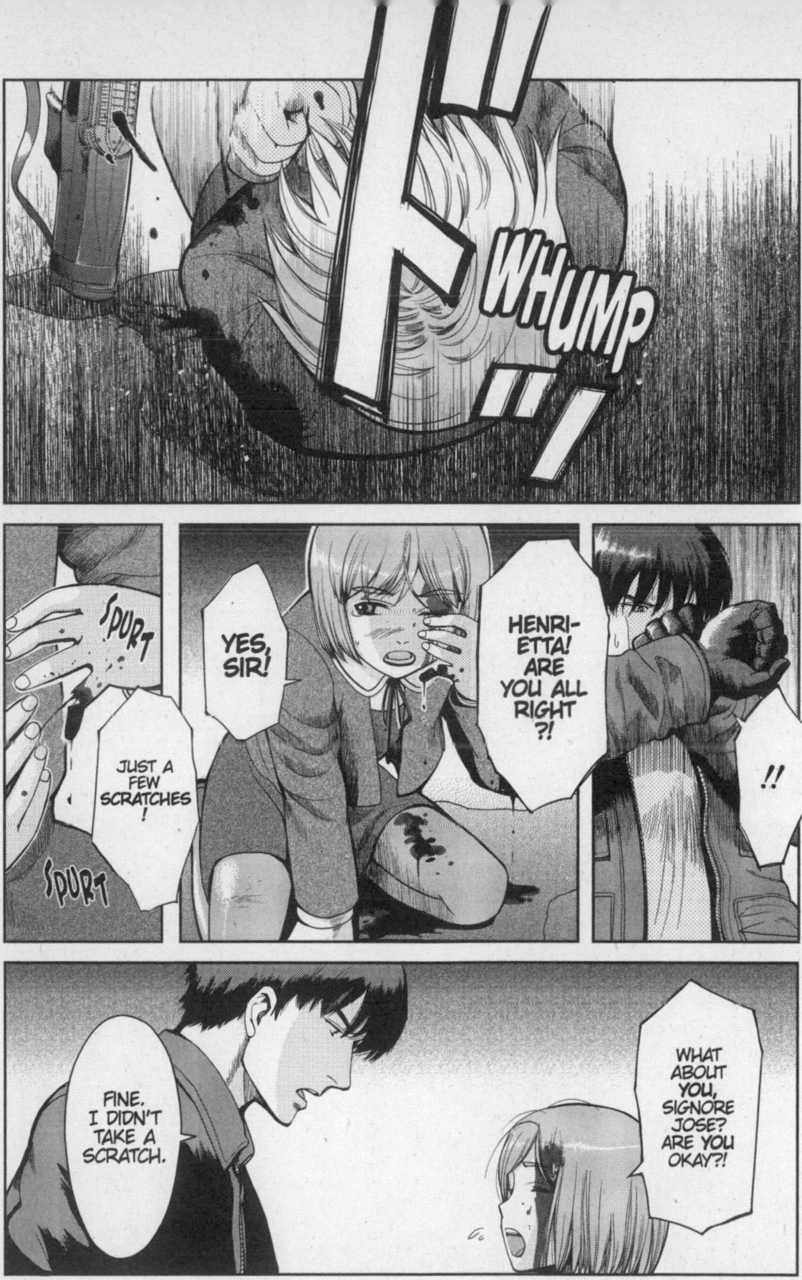
WHUMP
!!
HENRI-ETTA! ARE YOU ALL RIGHT?!
YES, SIR!
SPURT
JUST A FEW SCRATCHES!
SPURT
WHAT ABOUT YOU, SIGNORE JOSE? ARE YOU OKAY?!
FINE. I DIDN'T TAKE A SCRATCH.

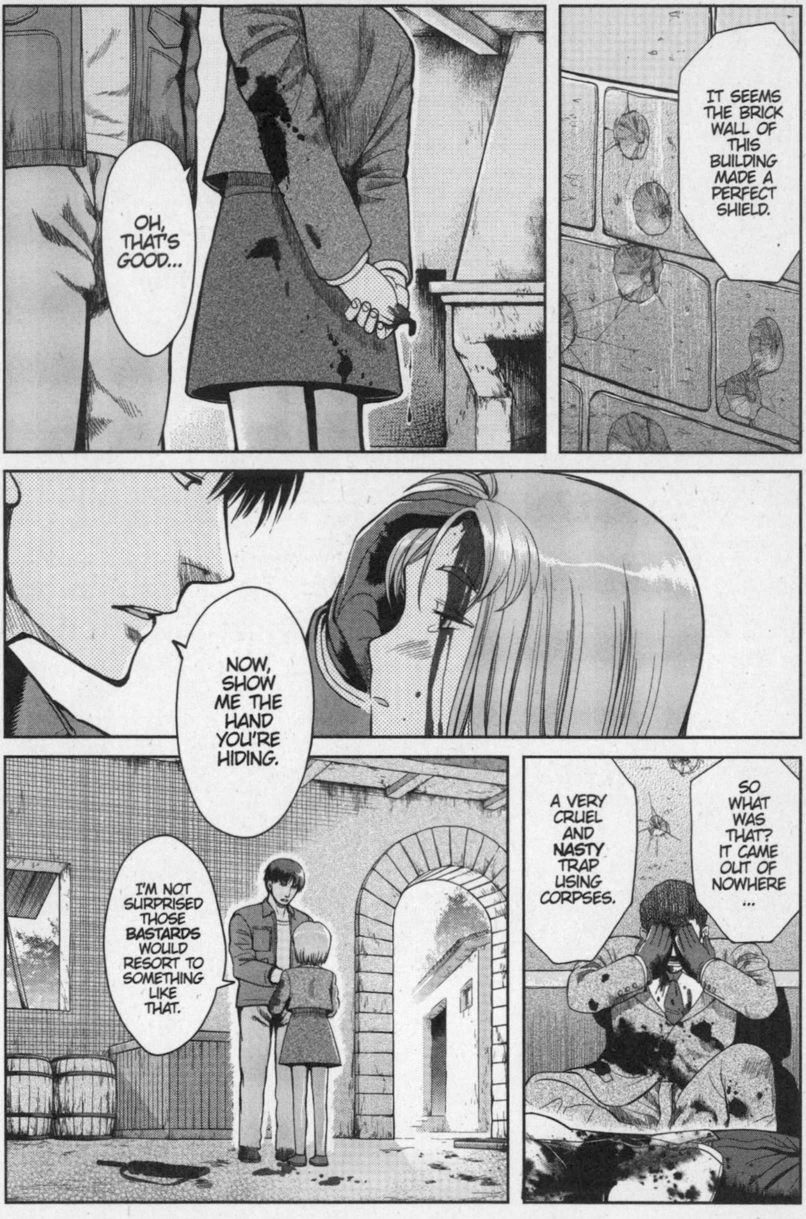
IT SEEMS THE BRICK WALL OF THIS BUILDING MADE A PERFECT SHIELD.
OH, THAT'S GOOD...
NOW, SHOW ME THE HAND YOU'RE HIDING.
SO WHAT WAS THAT? IT CAME OUT OF NOWHERE ...
A VERY CRUEL AND NASTY TRAP USING CORPSES.
I'M NOT SURPRISED THOSE BASTARDS WOULD RESORT TO SOMETHING LIKE THAT.

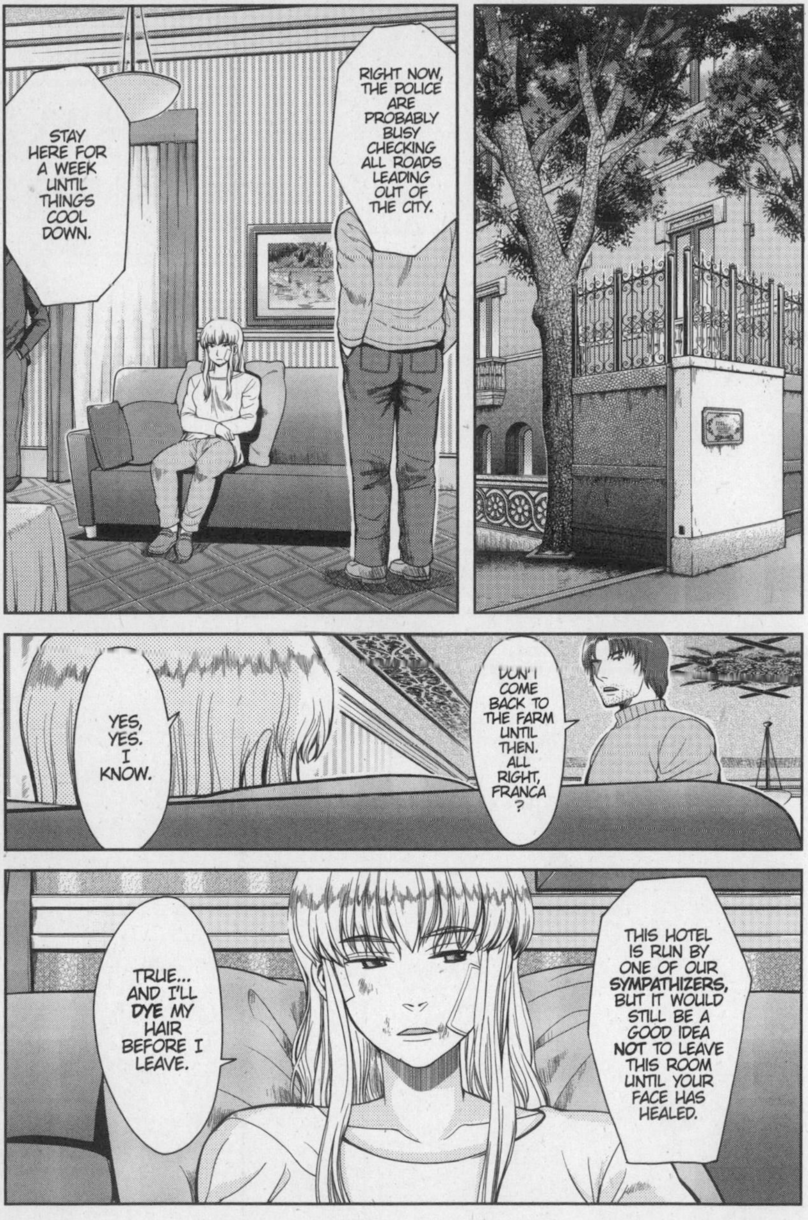

RIGHT NOW, THE POLICE ARE PROBABLY BUSY CHECKING ALL ROADS LEADING OUT OF THE CITY.
STAY HERE FOR A WEEK UNTIL THINGS COOL DOWN.
DON'T COME BACK TO THE FARM UNTIL THEN. ALL RIGHT, FRANCA?
YES, YES. I KNOW.
THIS HOTEL IS RUN BY ONE OF OUR **SYMPATHIZERS**, BUT IT WOULD STILL BE A GOOD IDEA **NOT** TO LEAVE THIS ROOM UNTIL YOUR FACE HAS HEALED.
TRUE... AND I'LL **DYE** MY HAIR BEFORE I LEAVE.

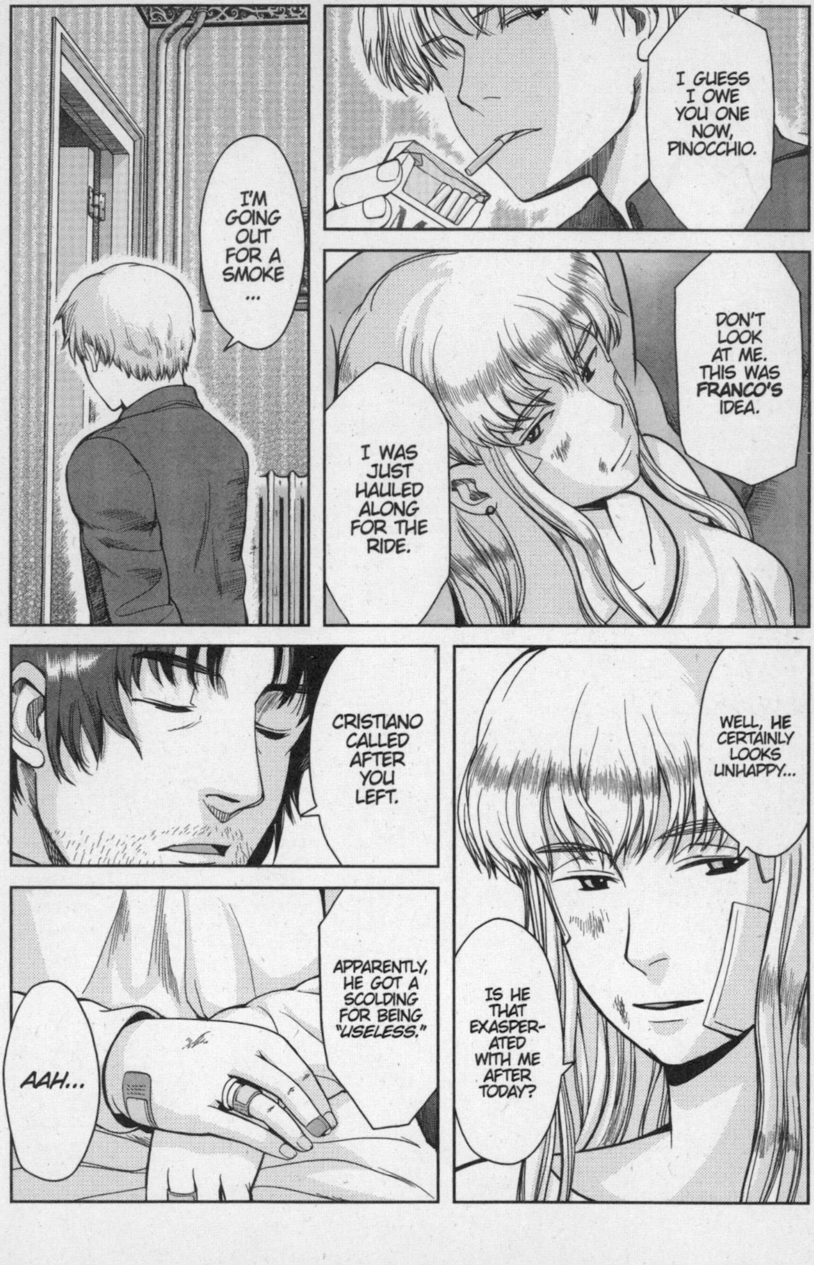
I GUESS I OWE YOU ONE NOW, PINOCCHIO.
DON'T LOOK AT ME. THIS WAS FRANCO'S IDEA.
I WAS JUST HAULED ALONG FOR THE RIDE.
I'M GOING OUT FOR A SMOKE ...
WELL, HE CERTAINLY LOOKS UNHAPPY...
IS HE THAT EXASPER-ATED WITH ME AFTER TODAY?
CRISTIANO CALLED AFTER YOU LEFT.
APPARENTLY, HE GOT A SCOLDING FOR BEING "USELESS."
AAH...

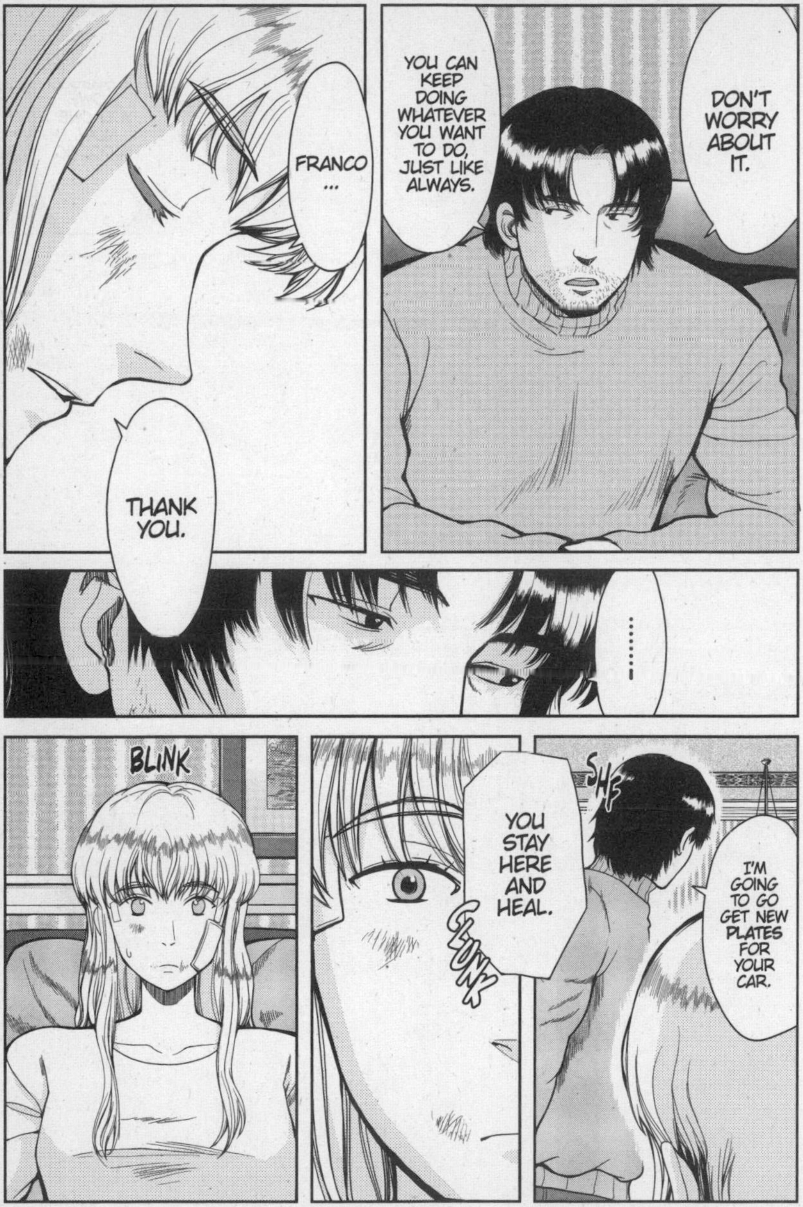
DON'T WORRY ABOUT IT.
YOU CAN KEEP DOING WHATEVER YOU WANT TO DO, JUST LIKE ALWAYS.
FRANCO ...
THANK YOU.
......
SHF
I'M GOING TO GO GET NEW PLATES FOR YOUR CAR.
YOU STAY HERE AND HEAL.
CLUNK
BLINK

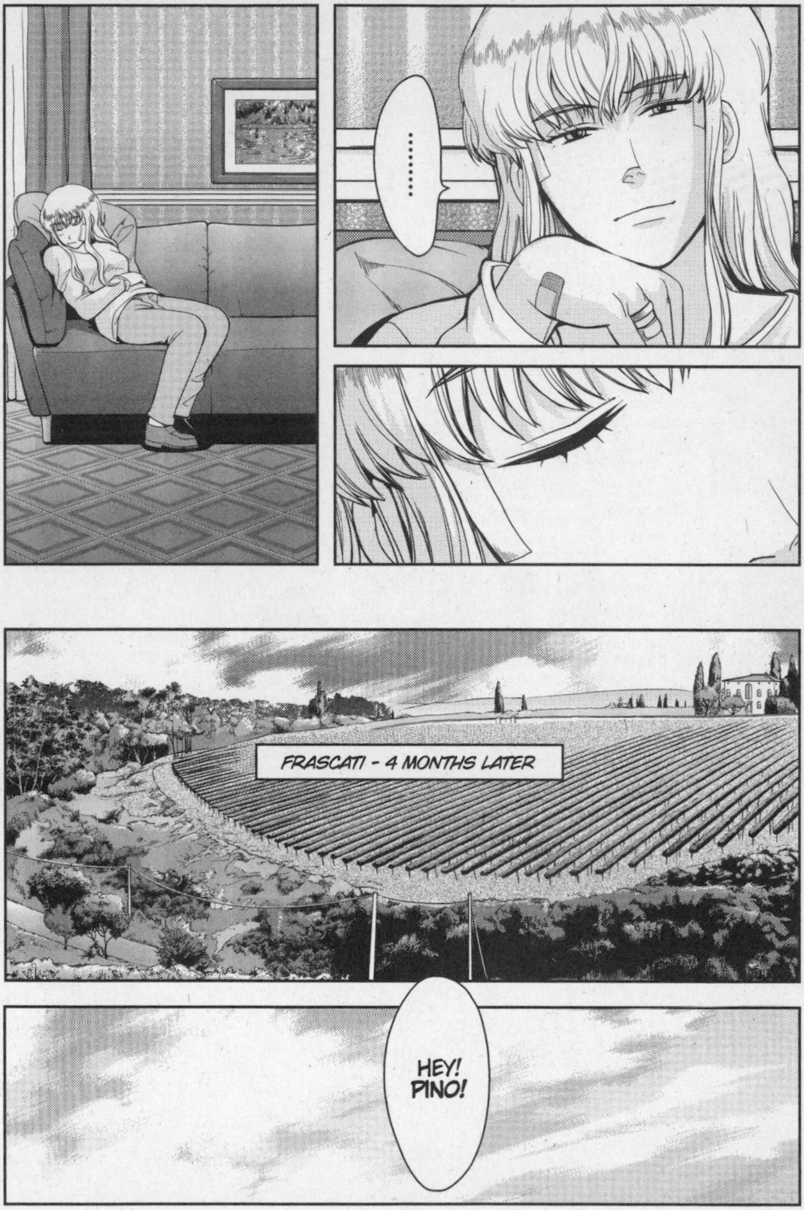
....
FRASCATI - 4 MONTHS LATER
HEY! PINO!

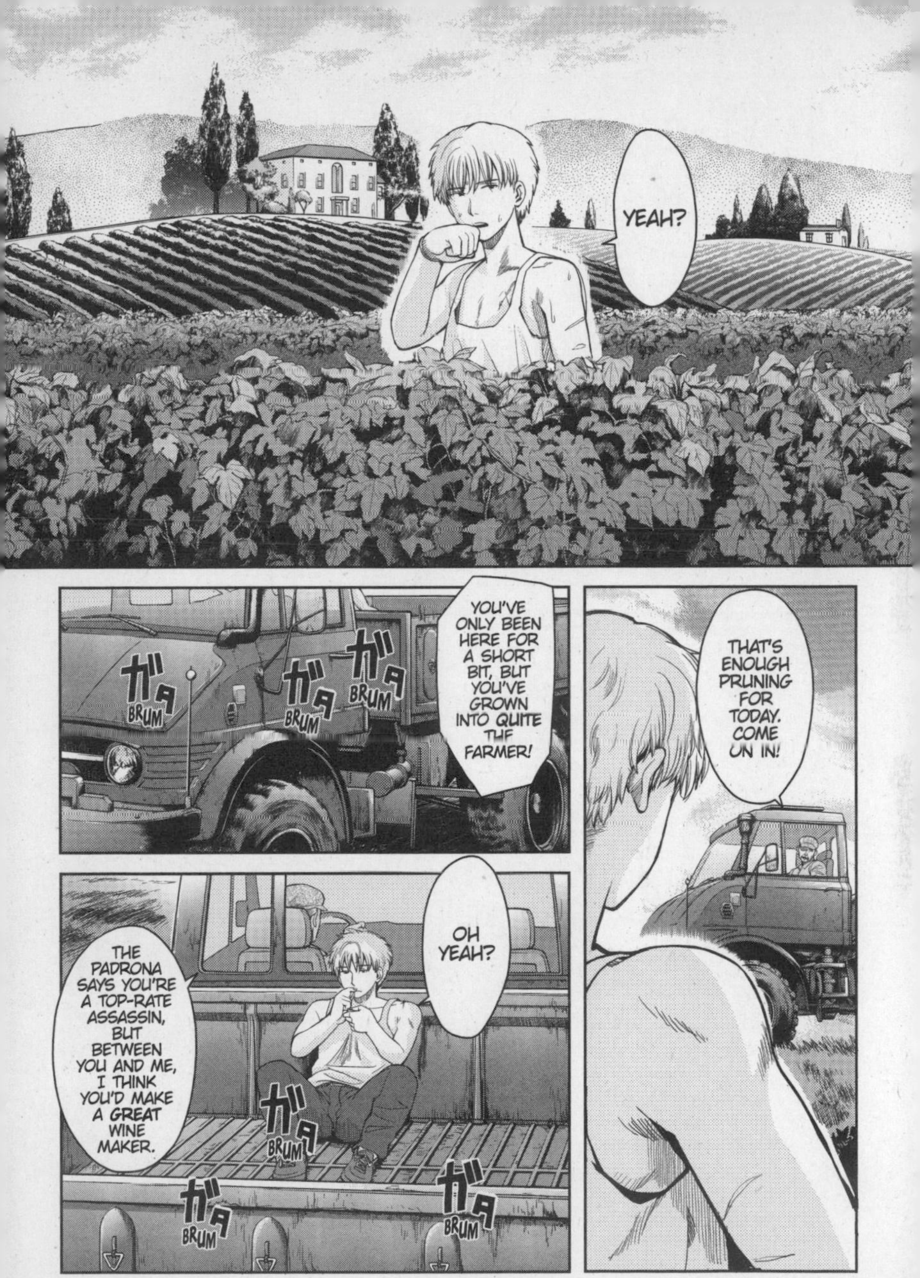
YEAH?
THAT'S ENOUGH PRUNING FOR TODAY. COME ON IN!
ガタ BRUM
ガタ BRUM
ガタ BRUM
YOU'VE ONLY BEEN HERE FOR A SHORT BIT, BUT YOU'VE GROWN INTO QUITE THE FARMER!
OH YEAH?
THE PADRONA SAYS YOU'RE A TOP-RATE ASSASSIN, BUT BETWEEN YOU AND ME, I THINK YOU'D MAKE A GREAT WINE MAKER.
ガタ BRUM
ガタ BRUM
ガタ BRUM

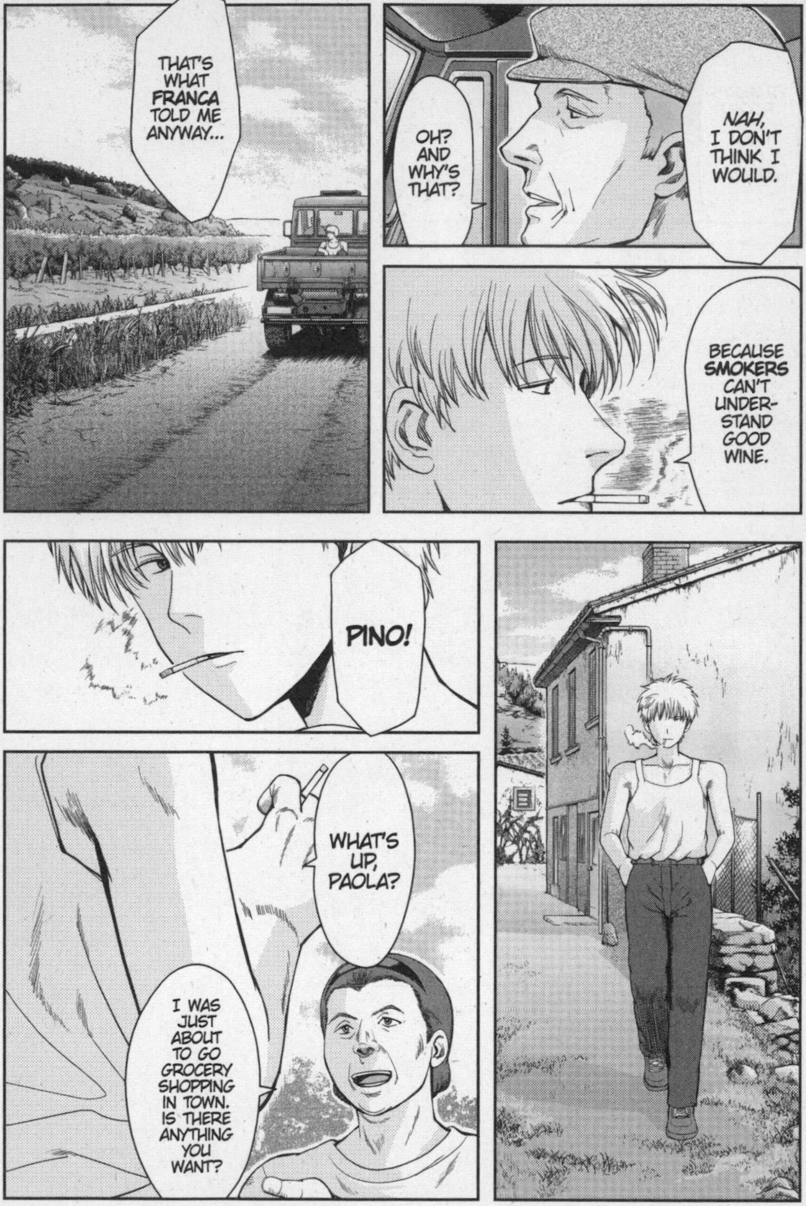
NAH, I DON'T THINK I WOULD.
OH? AND WHY'S THAT?
BECAUSE SMOKERS CAN'T UNDER-STAND GOOD WINE.
THAT'S WHAT FRANCA TOLD ME ANYWAY...
PINO!
WHAT'S UP, PAOLA?
I WAS JUST ABOUT TO GO GROCERY SHOPPING IN TOWN. IS THERE ANYTHING YOU WANT?

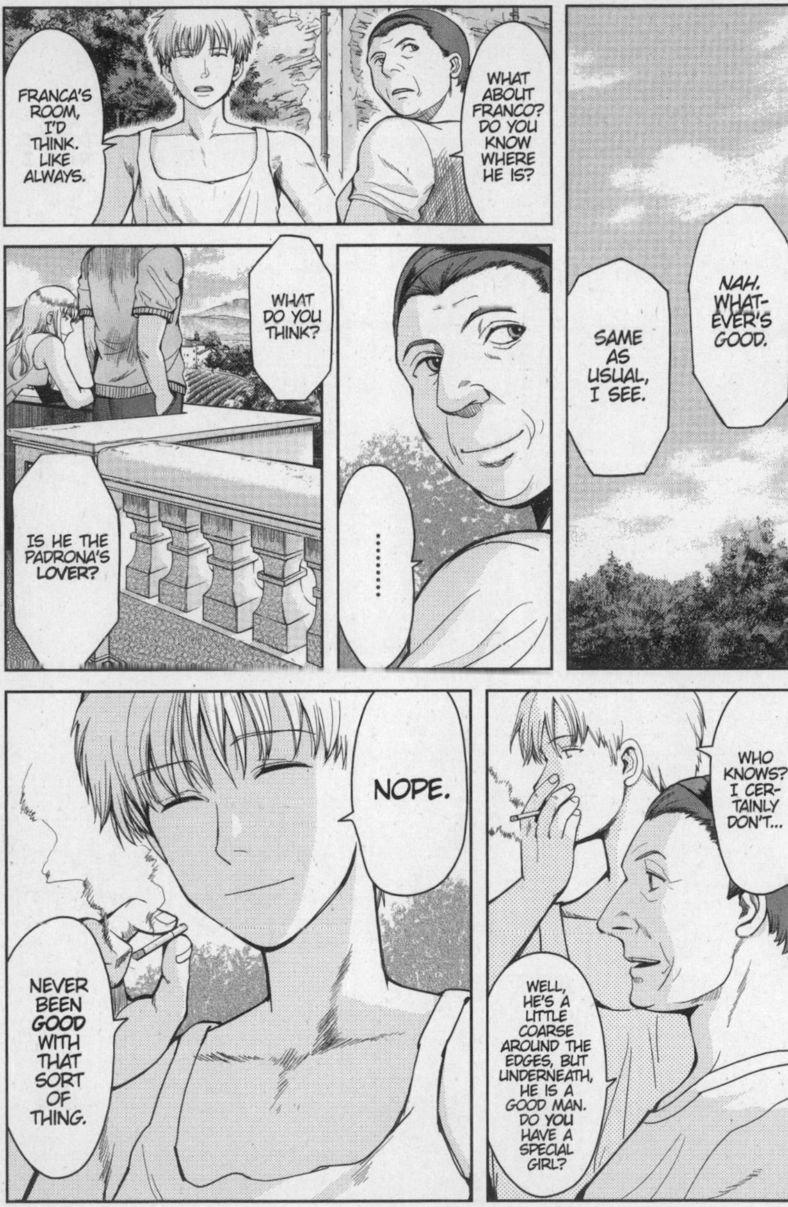
NAH. WHATEVER'S GOOD.
SAME AS USUAL, I SEE.
WHAT ABOUT FRANCO? DO YOU KNOW WHERE HE IS?
FRANCA'S ROOM, I'D THINK. LIKE ALWAYS.
......
WHAT DO YOU THINK?
IS HE THE PADRONA'S LOVER?
WHO KNOWS? I CERTAINLY DON'T...
WELL, HE'S A LITTLE COARSE AROUND THE EDGES, BUT UNDERNEATH, HE IS A GOOD MAN. DO YOU HAVE A SPECIAL GIRL?
NOPE.
NEVER BEEN GOOD WITH THAT SORT OF THING.

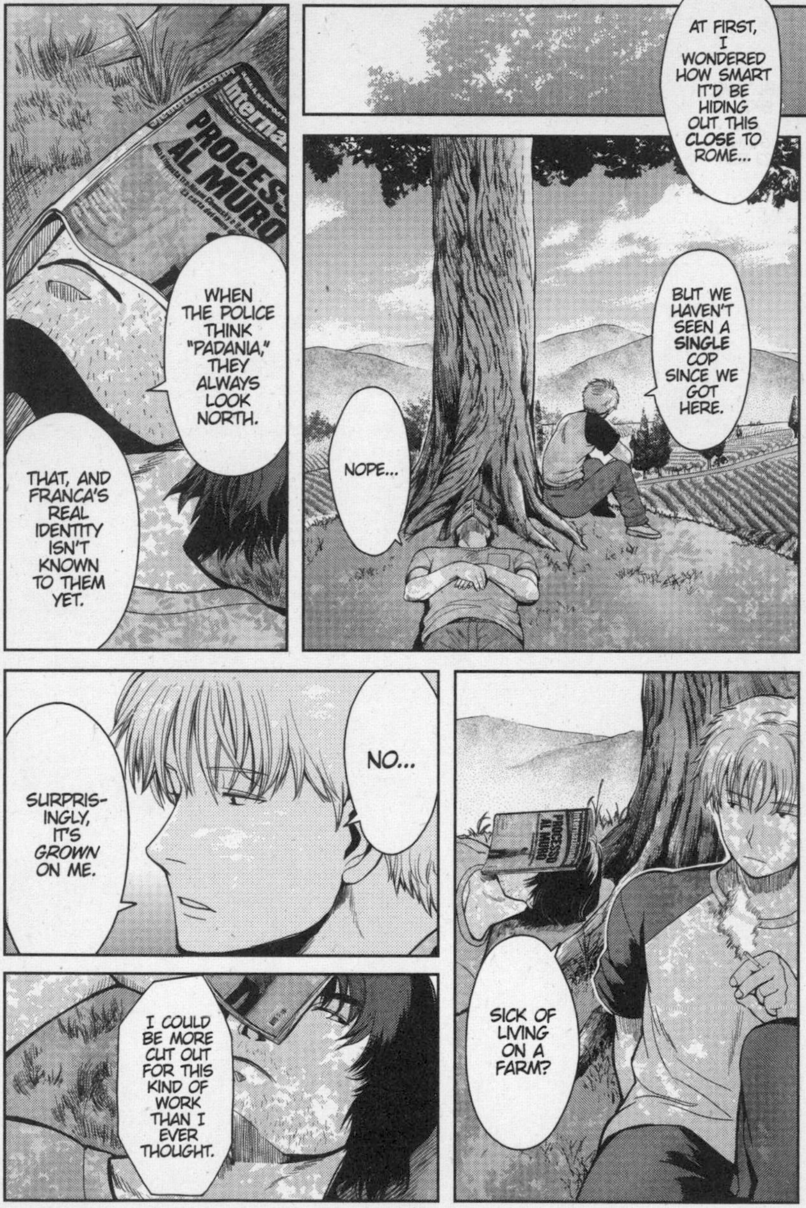
AT FIRST, I WONDERED HOW SMART IT'D BE HIDING OUT THIS CLOSE TO ROME...
BUT WE HAVEN'T SEEN A SINGLE COP SINCE WE GOT HERE.
NOPE...
PROCESSO AL MURO
WHEN THE POLICE THINK "PADANIA," THEY ALWAYS LOOK NORTH.
THAT, AND FRANCA'S REAL IDENTITY ISN'T KNOWN TO THEM YET.
SICK OF LIVING ON A FARM?
NO...
SURPRISINGLY, IT'S *GROWN* ON ME.
I COULD BE MORE CUT OUT FOR THIS KIND OF WORK THAN I EVER THOUGHT.

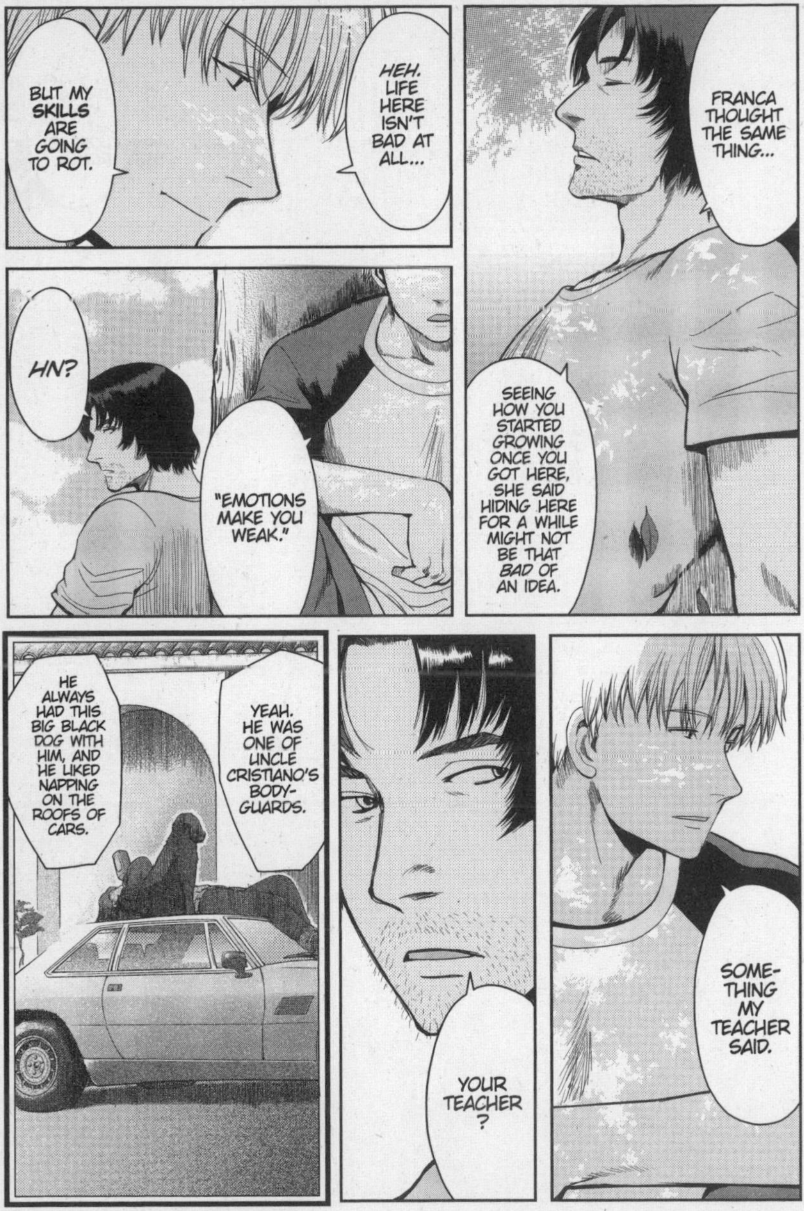
FRANCA THOUGHT THE SAME THING...
SEEING HOW YOU STARTED GROWING ONCE YOU GOT HERE, SHE SAID HIDING HERE FOR A WHILE MIGHT NOT BE THAT *BAD* OF AN IDEA.
HEH. LIFE HERE ISN'T BAD AT ALL...
BUT MY **SKILLS** ARE GOING TO ROT.
"EMOTIONS MAKE YOU WEAK."
HN?
SOME-THING MY TEACHER SAID.
YOUR TEACHER?
YEAH. HE WAS ONE OF UNCLE CRISTIANO'S BODY-GUARDS.
HE ALWAYS HAD THIS BIG BLACK DOG WITH HIM, AND HE LIKED NAPPING ON THE ROOFS OF CARS.

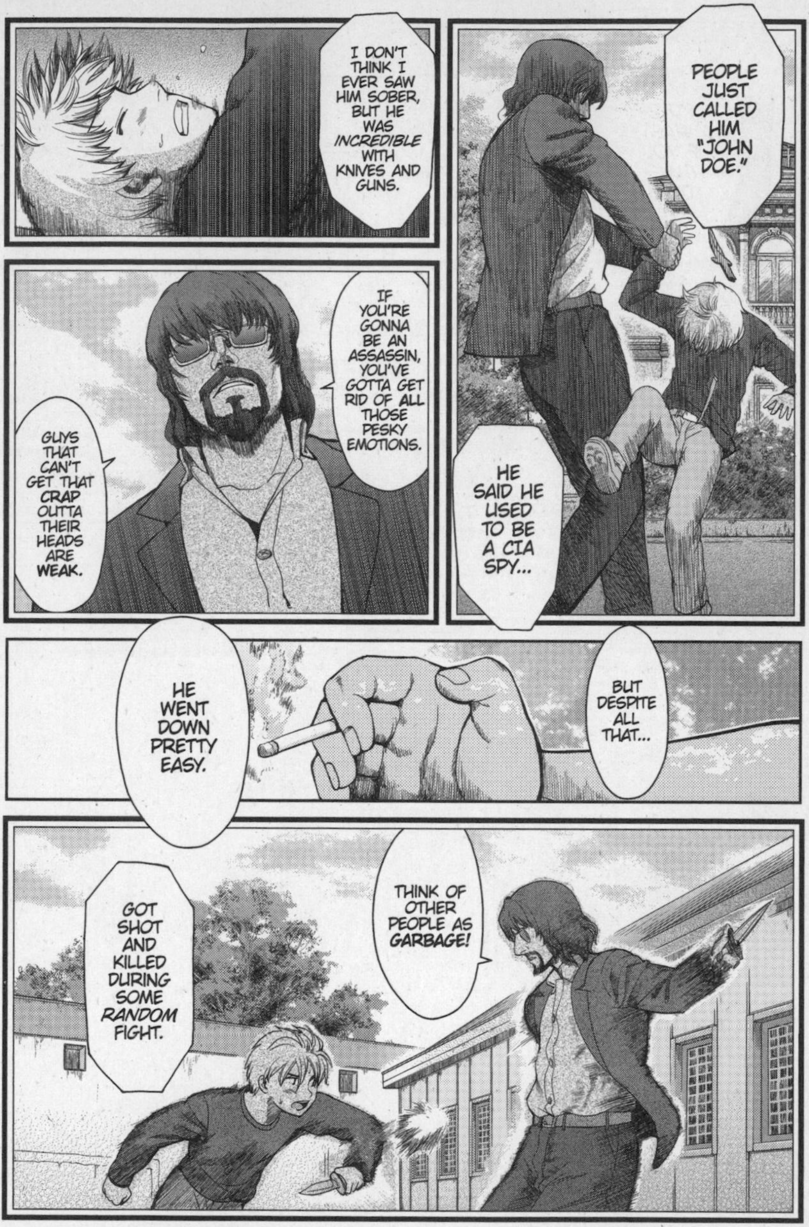
PEOPLE JUST CALLED HIM "JOHN DOE."
HE SAID HE USED TO BE A CIA SPY...
I DON'T THINK I EVER SAW HIM SOBER, BUT HE WAS *INCREDIBLE* WITH KNIVES AND GUNS.
IF YOU'RE GONNA BE AN ASSASSIN, YOU'VE GOTTA GET RID OF ALL THOSE PESKY EMOTIONS.
GUYS THAT CAN'T GET THAT CRAP OUTTA THEIR HEADS ARE WEAK.
BUT DESPITE ALL THAT...
HE WENT DOWN PRETTY EASY.
THINK OF OTHER PEOPLE AS GARBAGE!
GOT SHOT AND KILLED DURING SOME *RANDOM* FIGHT.

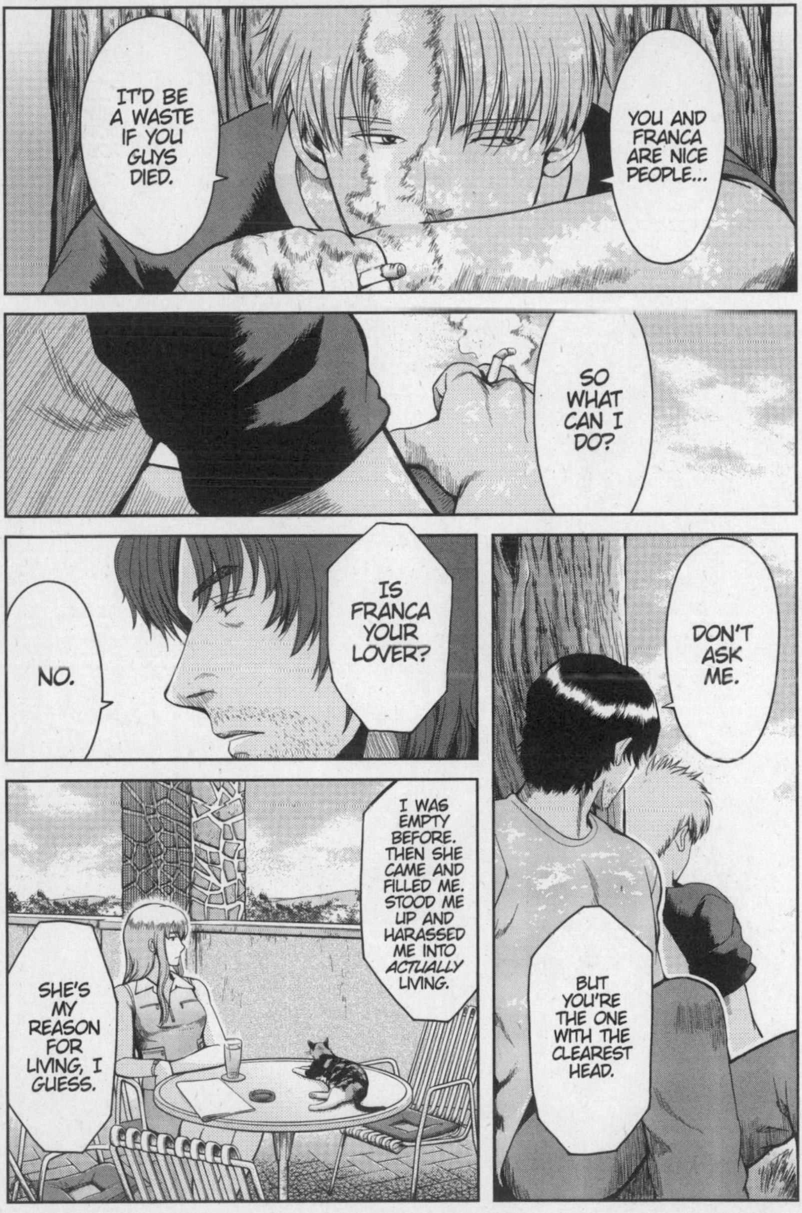
YOU AND FRANCA ARE NICE PEOPLE...
IT'D BE A WASTE IF YOU GUYS DIED.
SO WHAT CAN I DO?
DON'T ASK ME.
BUT YOU'RE THE ONE WITH THE CLEAREST HEAD.
IS FRANCA YOUR LOVER?
NO.
I WAS EMPTY BEFORE. THEN SHE CAME AND FILLED ME. STOOD ME UP AND HARASSED ME INTO *ACTUALLY* LIVING.
SHE'S MY REASON FOR LIVING, I GUESS.

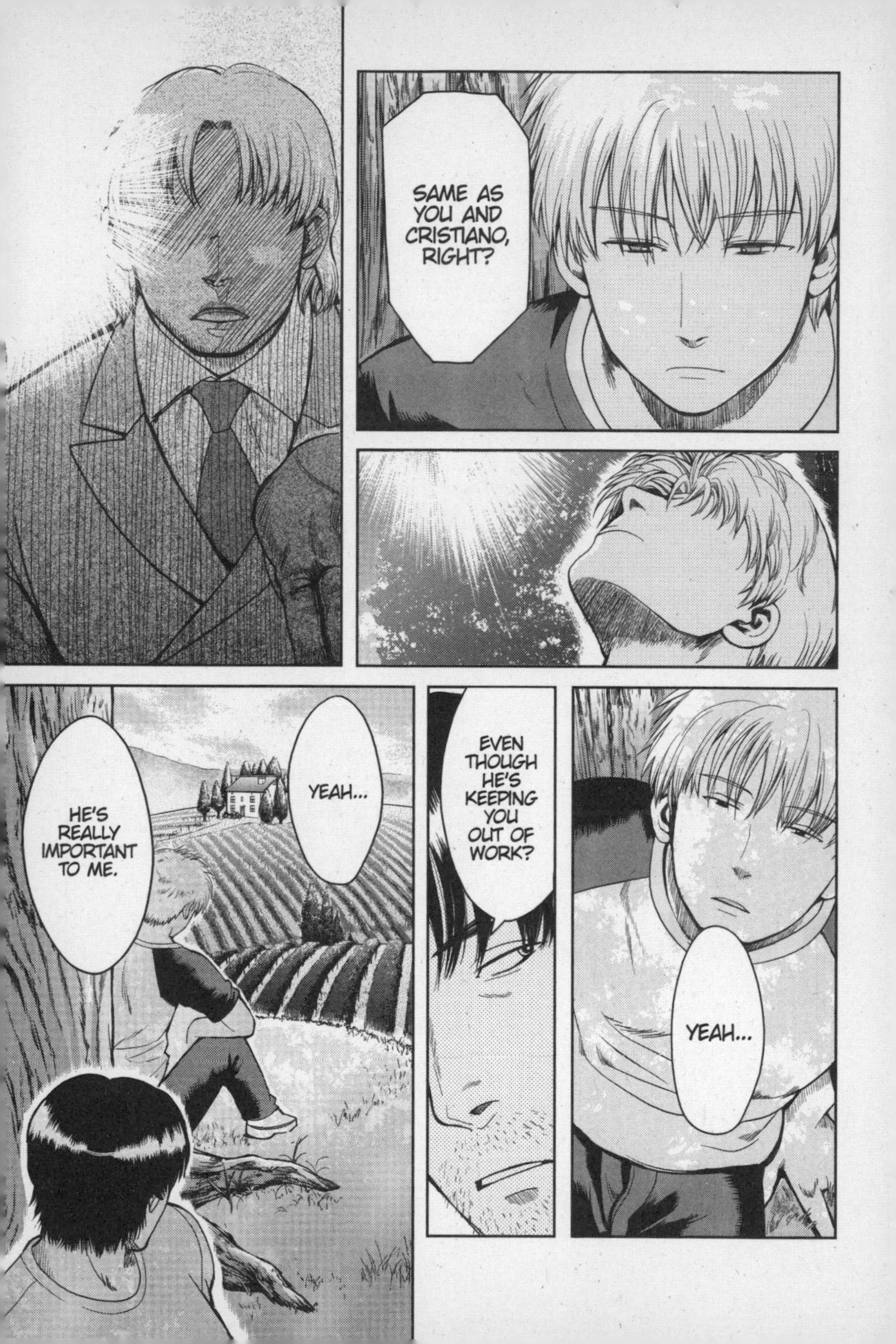
SAME AS YOU AND CRISTIANO, RIGHT?
YEAH...
EVEN THOUGH HE'S KEEPING YOU OUT OF WORK?
YEAH...
HE'S REALLY IMPORTANT TO ME.

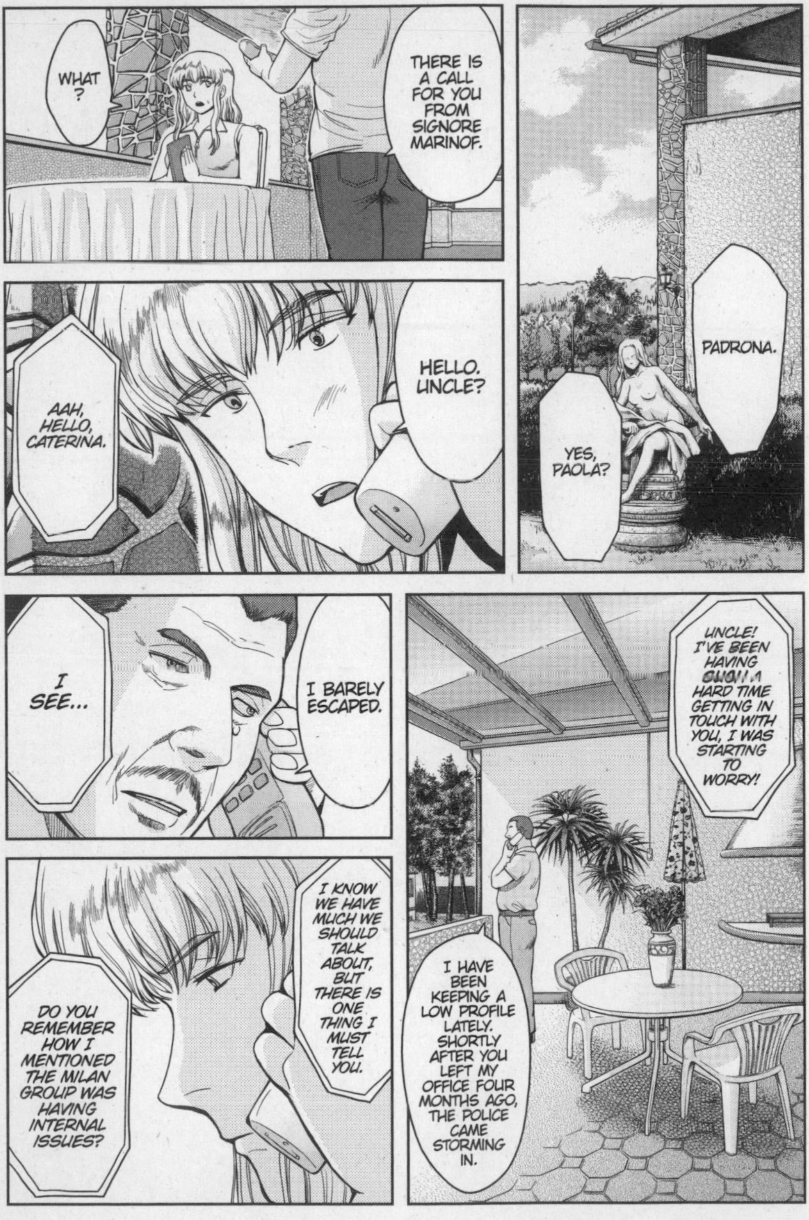
PADRONA.
YES, PAOLA?
THERE IS A CALL FOR YOU FROM SIGNORE MARINOF.
WHAT?
HELLO. UNCLE?
AAH, HELLO, CATERINA.
UNCLE! I'VE BEEN HAVING SUCH A HARD TIME GETTING IN TOUCH WITH YOU, I WAS STARTING TO WORRY!
I HAVE BEEN KEEPING A LOW PROFILE LATELY. SHORTLY AFTER YOU LEFT MY OFFICE FOUR MONTHS AGO, THE POLICE CAME STORMING IN.
I BARELY ESCAPED.
I SEE...
I KNOW WE HAVE MUCH WE SHOULD TALK ABOUT, BUT THERE IS ONE THING I MUST TELL YOU.
DO YOU REMEMBER HOW I MENTIONED THE MILAN GROUP WAS HAVING INTERNAL ISSUES?

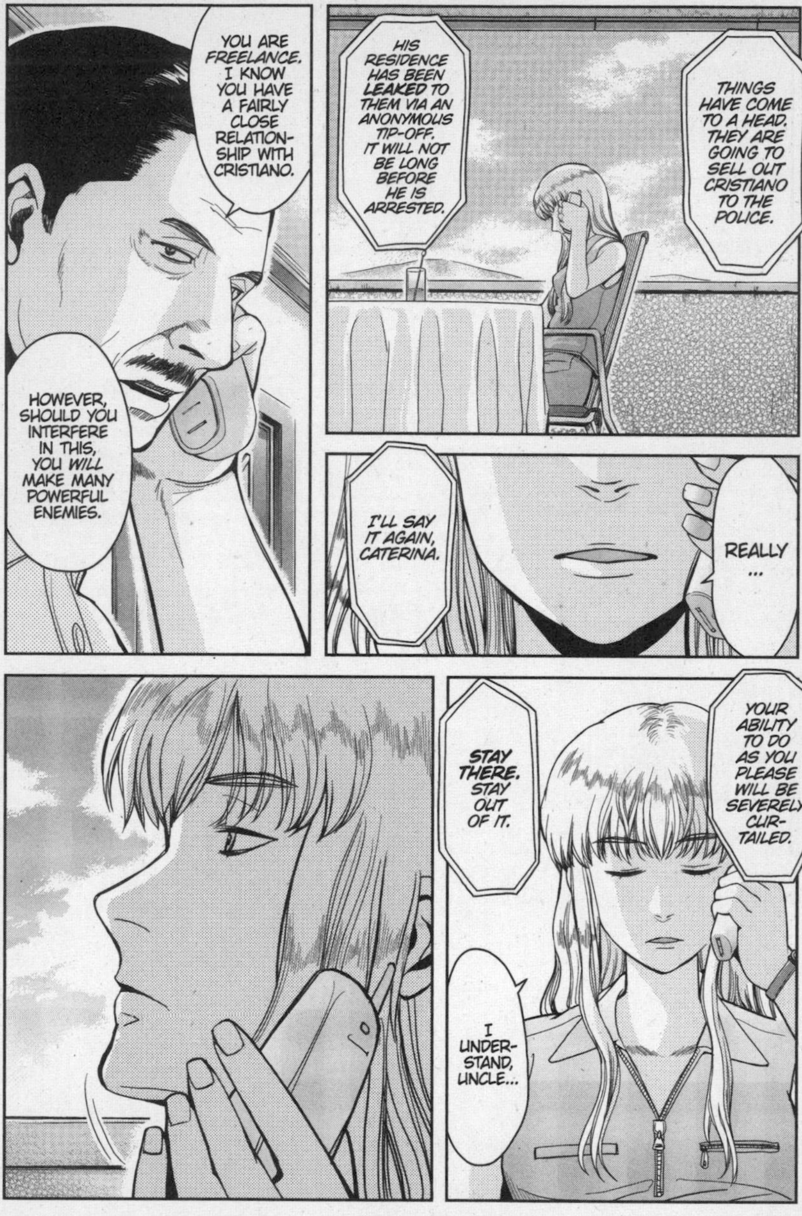
THINGS HAVE COME TO A HEAD. THEY ARE GOING TO SELL OUT CRISTIANO TO THE POLICE.
HIS RESIDENCE HAS BEEN **LEAKED** TO THEM VIA AN ANONYMOUS TIP-OFF. IT WILL NOT BE LONG BEFORE HE IS ARRESTED.
REALLY ...
I'LL SAY IT AGAIN, CATERINA.
YOU ARE FREELANCE. I KNOW YOU HAVE A FAIRLY CLOSE RELATION-SHIP WITH CRISTIANO.
HOWEVER, SHOULD YOU INTERFERE IN THIS, YOU *WILL* MAKE MANY POWERFUL ENEMIES.
YOUR ABILITY TO DO AS YOU PLEASE WILL BE SEVERELY CUR-TAILED.
STAY THERE. STAY OUT OF IT.
I UNDER-STAND, UNCLE...

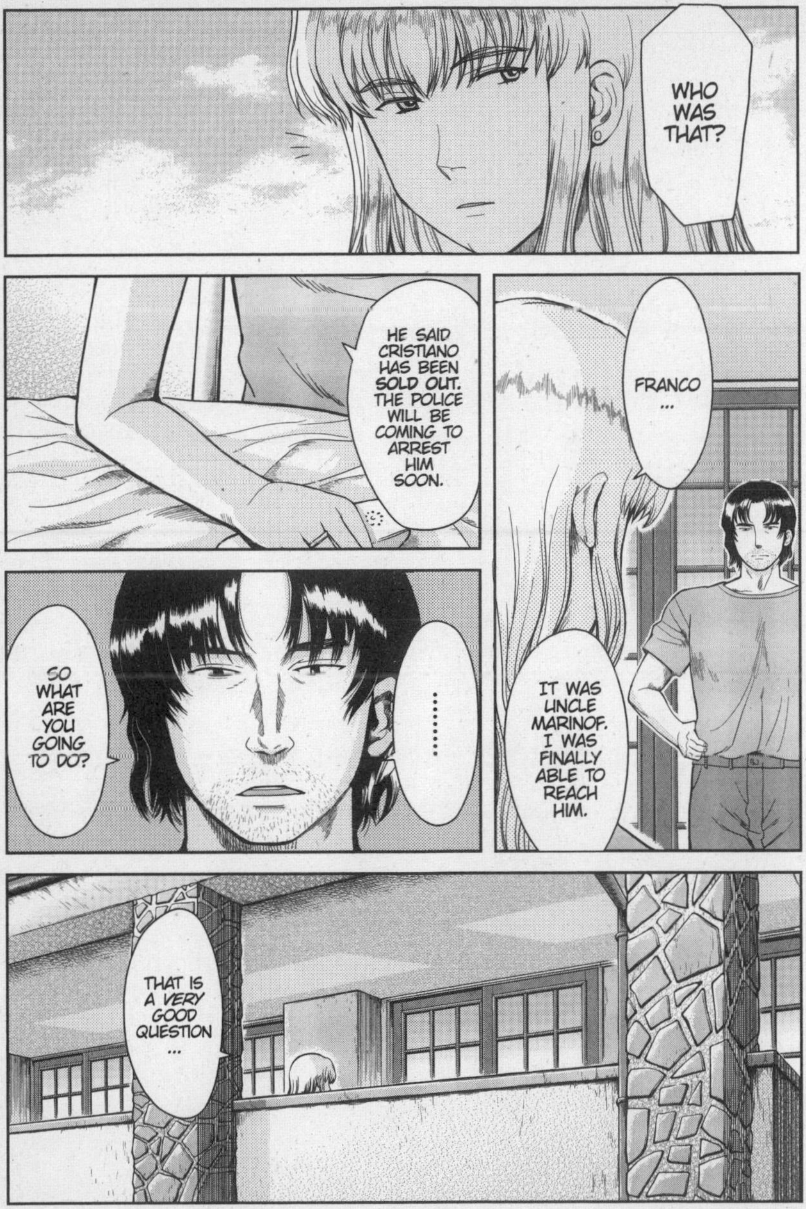
WHO WAS THAT?
FRANCO ...
IT WAS UNCLE MARINOF. I WAS FINALLY ABLE TO REACH HIM.
HE SAID CRISTIANO HAS BEEN SOLD OUT. THE POLICE WILL BE COMING TO ARREST HIM SOON.
....
SO WHAT ARE YOU GOING TO DO?
THAT IS A *VERY* GOOD QUESTION ...

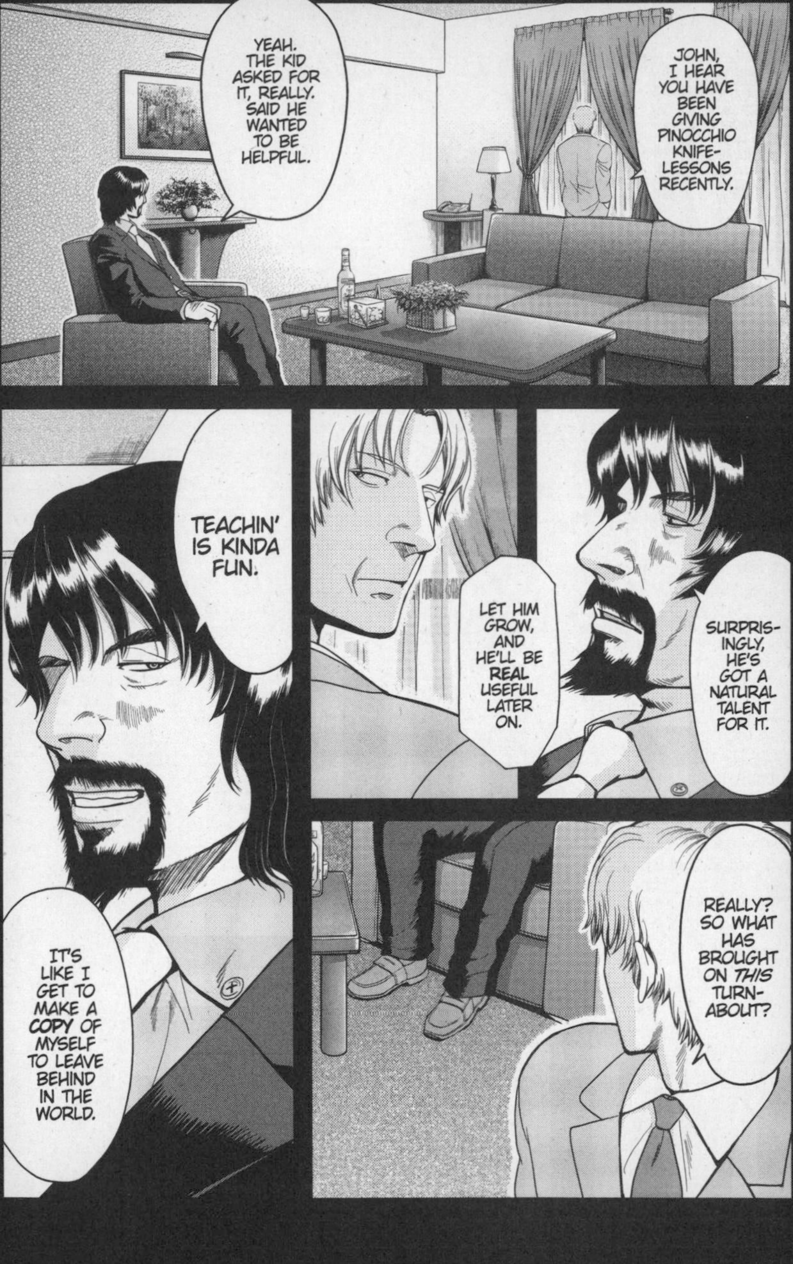
JOHN, I HEAR YOU HAVE BEEN GIVING PINOCCHIO KNIFE-LESSONS RECENTLY.
YEAH. THE KID ASKED FOR IT, REALLY. SAID HE WANTED TO BE HELPFUL.
SURPRIS-INGLY, HE'S GOT A NATURAL TALENT FOR IT.
LET HIM GROW, AND HE'LL BE **REAL** USEFUL LATER ON.
REALLY? SO WHAT HAS BROUGHT ON *THIS* TURN-ABOUT?
TEACHIN' IS KINDA FUN.
IT'S LIKE I GET TO MAKE A **COPY** OF MYSELF TO LEAVE BEHIND IN THE WORLD.

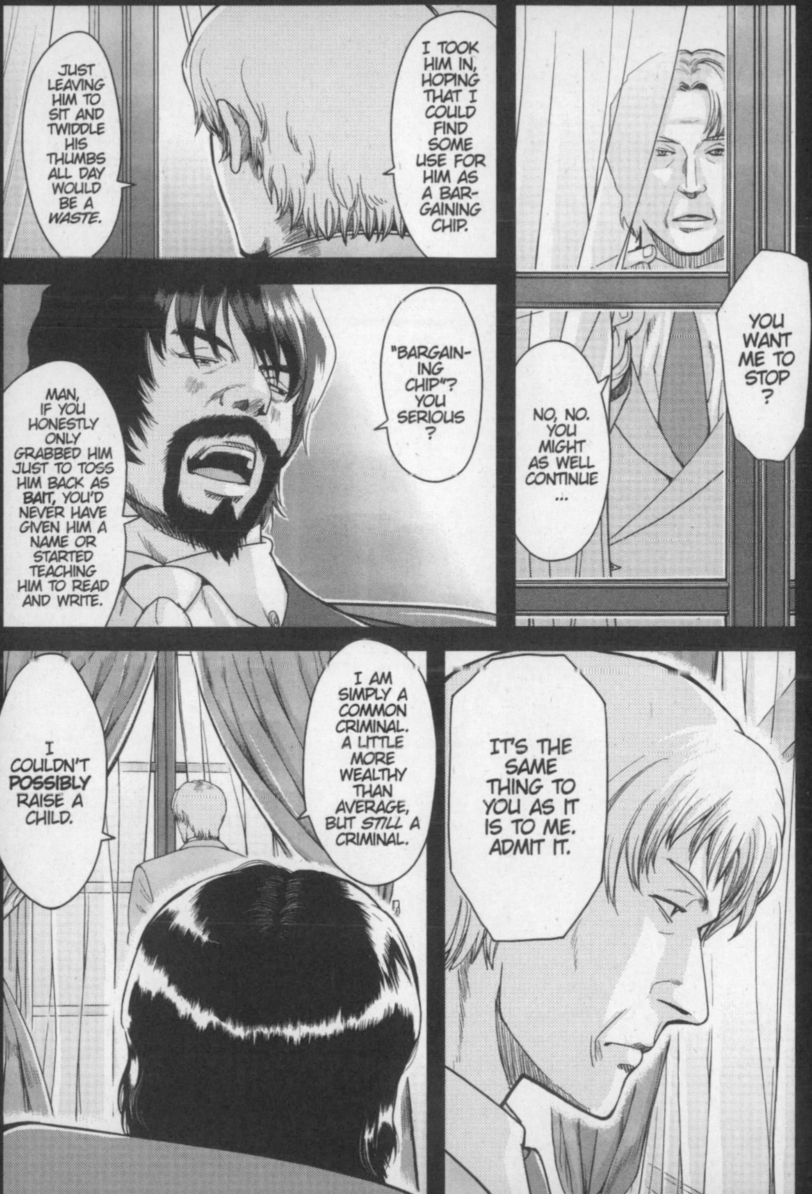
I TOOK HIM IN, HOPING THAT I COULD FIND SOME USE FOR HIM AS A BAR-GAINING CHIP.
JUST LEAVING HIM TO SIT AND TWIDDLE HIS THUMBS ALL DAY WOULD BE A *WASTE*.
YOU WANT ME TO STOP?
NO, NO. YOU MIGHT AS WELL CONTINUE...
"BARGAIN-ING CHIP"? YOU SERIOUS?
MAN, IF YOU HONESTLY ONLY GRABBED HIM JUST TO TOSS HIM BACK AS BAIT, YOU'D NEVER HAVE GIVEN HIM A NAME OR STARTED TEACHING HIM TO READ AND WRITE.
IT'S THE SAME THING TO YOU AS IT IS TO ME. ADMIT IT.
I AM SIMPLY A COMMON CRIMINAL. A LITTLE MORE WEALTHY THAN AVERAGE, BUT *STILL* A CRIMINAL.
I COULDN'T **POSSIBLY** RAISE A CHILD.

THERE ARE MORE WAYS OF EXPRESSING AFFECTION OUT THERE THAN JUST THAT OF A DAD FOR HIS KID.

A BOSS FOR HIS LACKEYS. A MAN FOR HIS TOOLS.

EVEN A GUY TEACHIN' A KID HOW TO KILL.

"EMOTIONS MAKE YOU WEAK." IS THAT NOT WHAT YOU ALWAYS SAY?

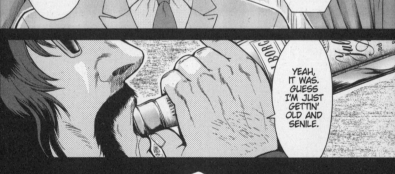

YEAH, IT WAS. GUESS I'M JUST GETTIN' OLD AND SENILE.

PERHAPS. STILL, IT COULD BE AMUSING TO TRY.

GUNSLINGERGIRL.

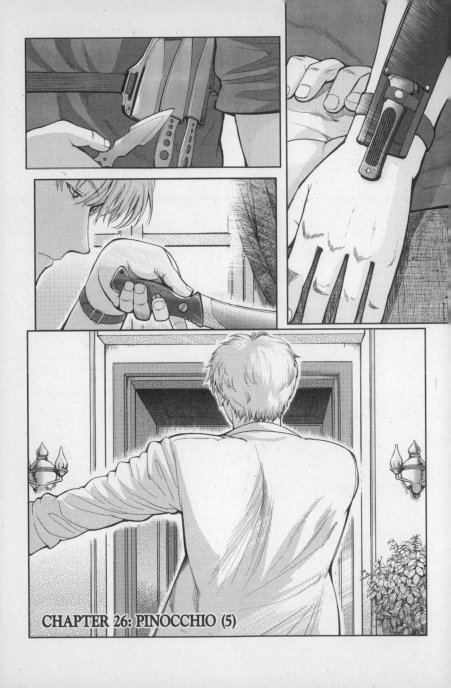

CHAPTER 26: PINOCCHIO (5)

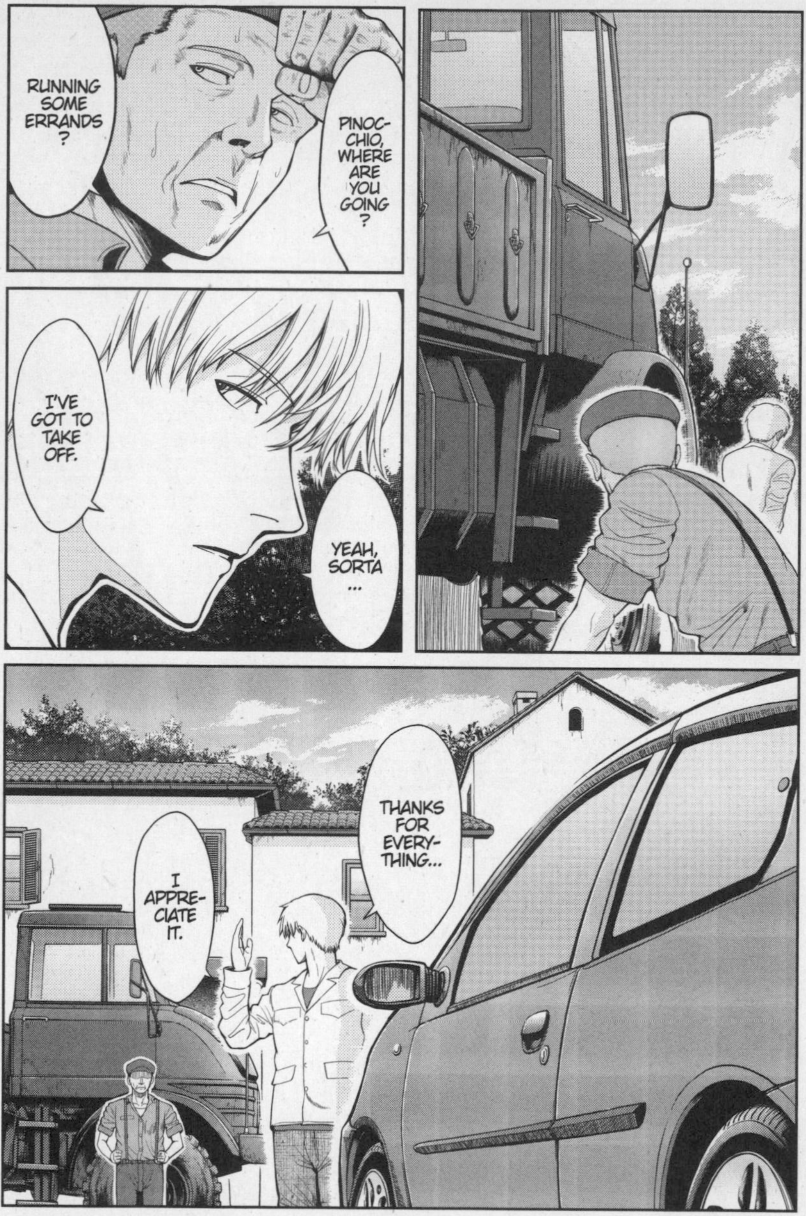
PINOC-CHIO, WHERE ARE YOU GOING?
RUNNING SOME ERRANDS?
YEAH, SORTA...
I'VE GOT TO TAKE OFF.
THANKS FOR EVERY-THING...
I APPRECI-ATE IT.

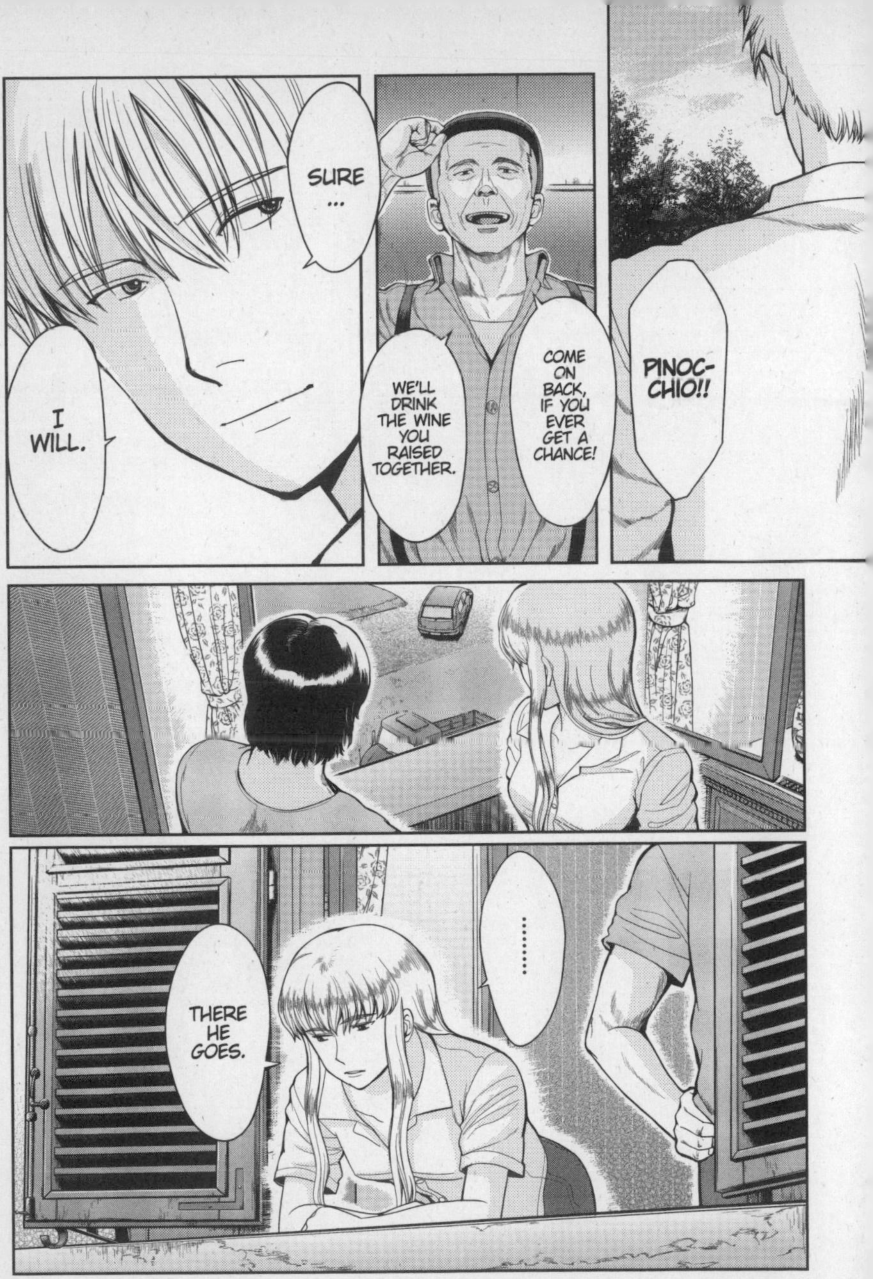
PINOC-CHIO!!
COME ON BACK, IF YOU EVER GET A CHANCE!
WE'LL DRINK THE WINE YOU RAISED TOGETHER.
SURE ...
I WILL.
......
THERE HE GOES.

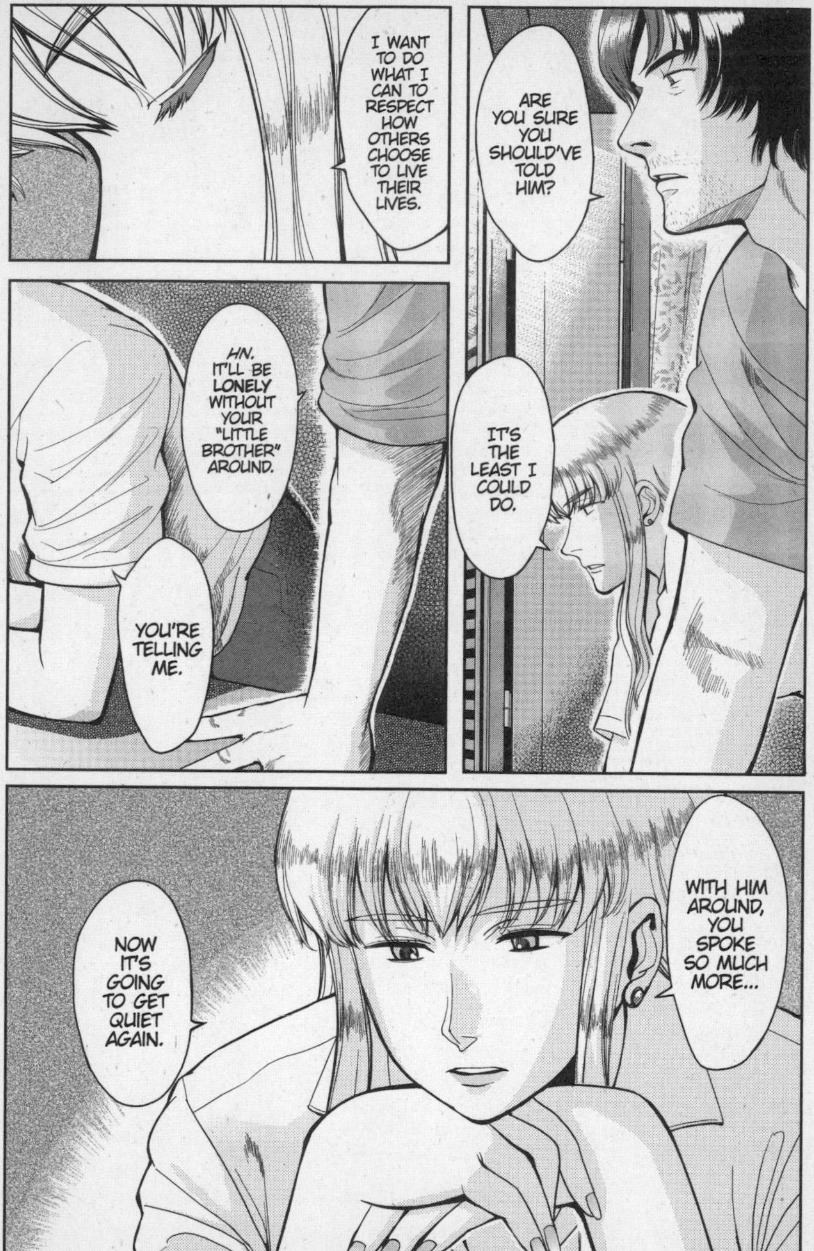
ARE YOU SURE YOU SHOULD'VE TOLD HIM?
IT'S THE LEAST I COULD DO.
I WANT TO DO WHAT I CAN TO RESPECT HOW OTHERS CHOOSE TO LIVE THEIR LIVES.
HN. IT'LL BE LONELY WITHOUT YOUR "LITTLE BROTHER" AROUND.
YOU'RE TELLING ME.
WITH HIM AROUND, YOU SPOKE SO MUCH MORE...
NOW IT'S GOING TO GET QUIET AGAIN.

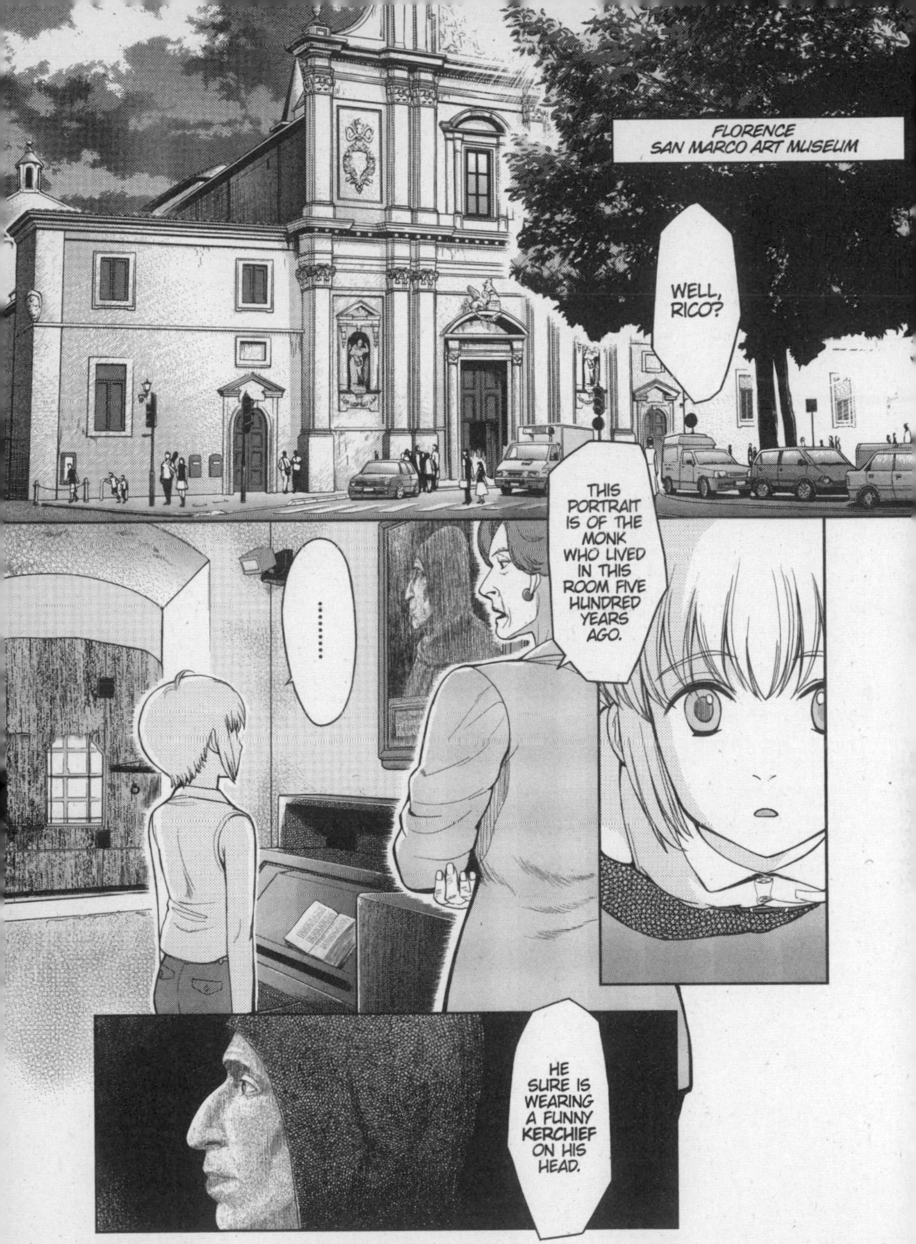
FLORENCE SAN MARCO ART MUSEUM
WELL, RICO?
THIS PORTRAIT IS OF THE MONK WHO LIVED IN THIS ROOM FIVE HUNDRED YEARS AGO.
....
HE SURE IS WEARING A FUNNY KERCHIEF ON HIS HEAD.

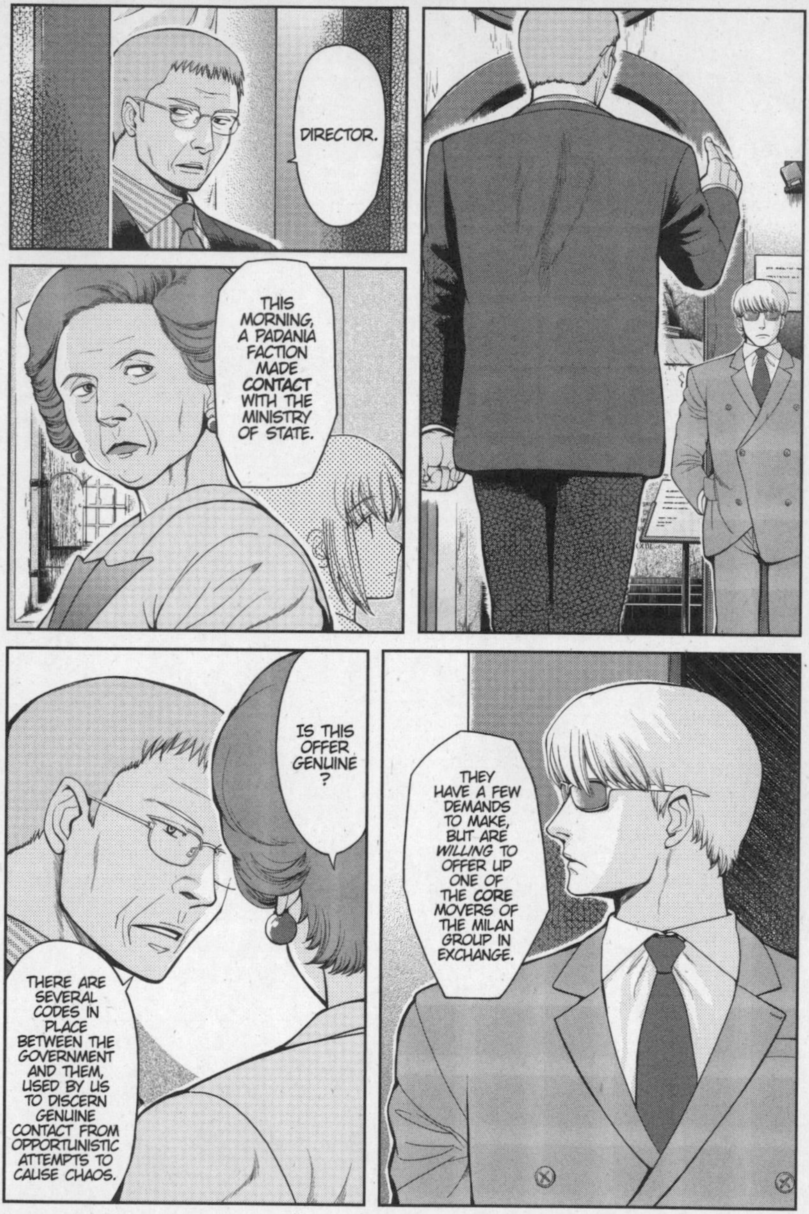
DIRECTOR.
THIS MORNING, A PADANIA FACTION MADE CONTACT WITH THE MINISTRY OF STATE.
THEY HAVE A FEW DEMANDS TO MAKE, BUT ARE *WILLING* TO OFFER UP ONE OF THE CORE MOVERS OF THE MILAN GROUP IN EXCHANGE.
IS THIS OFFER GENUINE?
THERE ARE SEVERAL CODES IN PLACE BETWEEN THE GOVERNMENT AND THEM, USED BY US TO DISCERN GENUINE CONTACT FROM OPPORTUNISTIC ATTEMPTS TO CAUSE CHAOS.

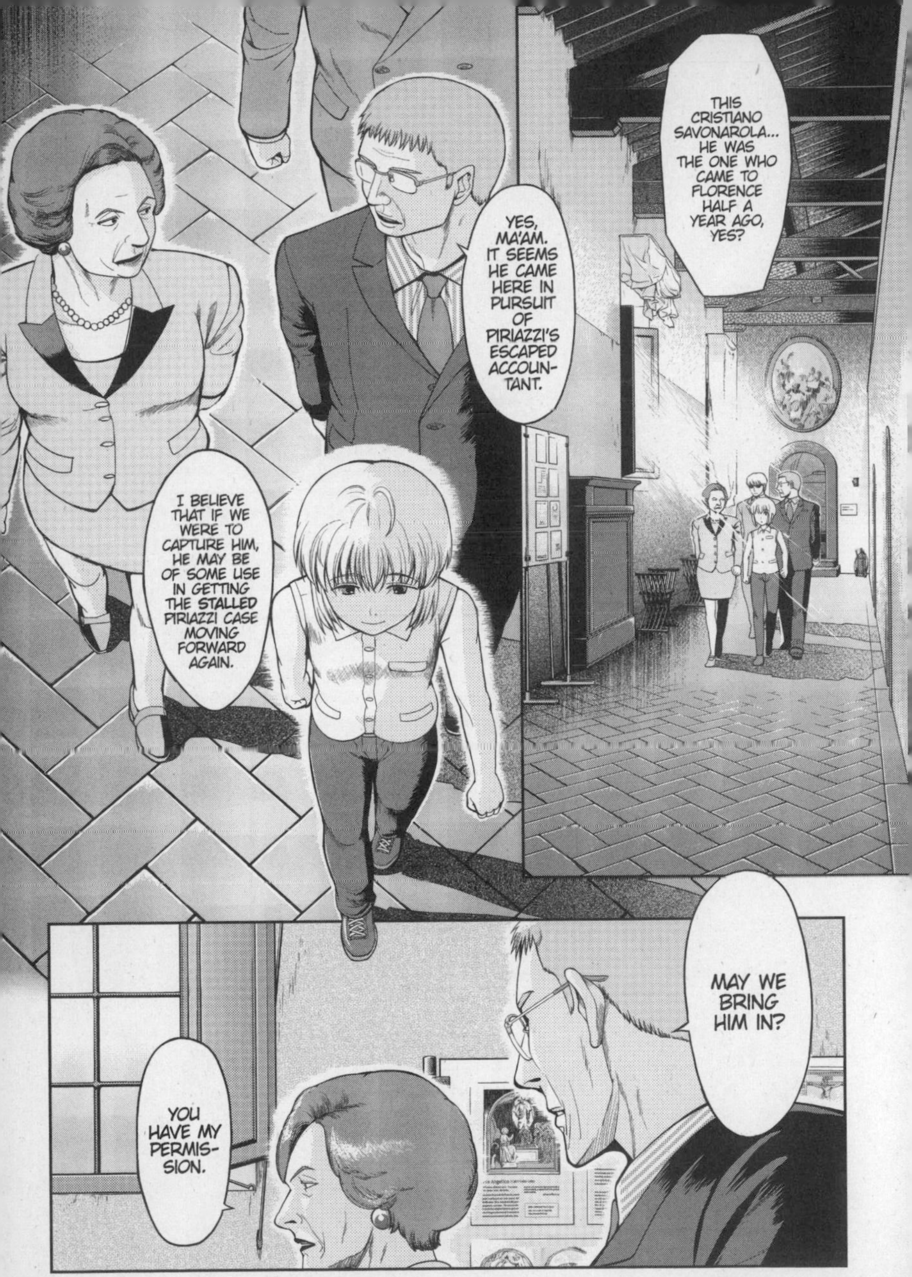
THIS CRISTIANO SAVONAROLA... HE WAS THE ONE WHO CAME TO FLORENCE HALF A YEAR AGO, YES?
YES, MA'AM. IT SEEMS HE CAME HERE IN PURSUIT OF PIRIAZZI'S ESCAPED ACCOUN-TANT.
I BELIEVE THAT IF WE WERE TO CAPTURE HIM, HE MAY BE OF SOME USE IN GETTING THE STALLED PIRIAZZI CASE MOVING FORWARD AGAIN.
MAY WE BRING HIM IN?
YOU HAVE MY PERMIS-SION.

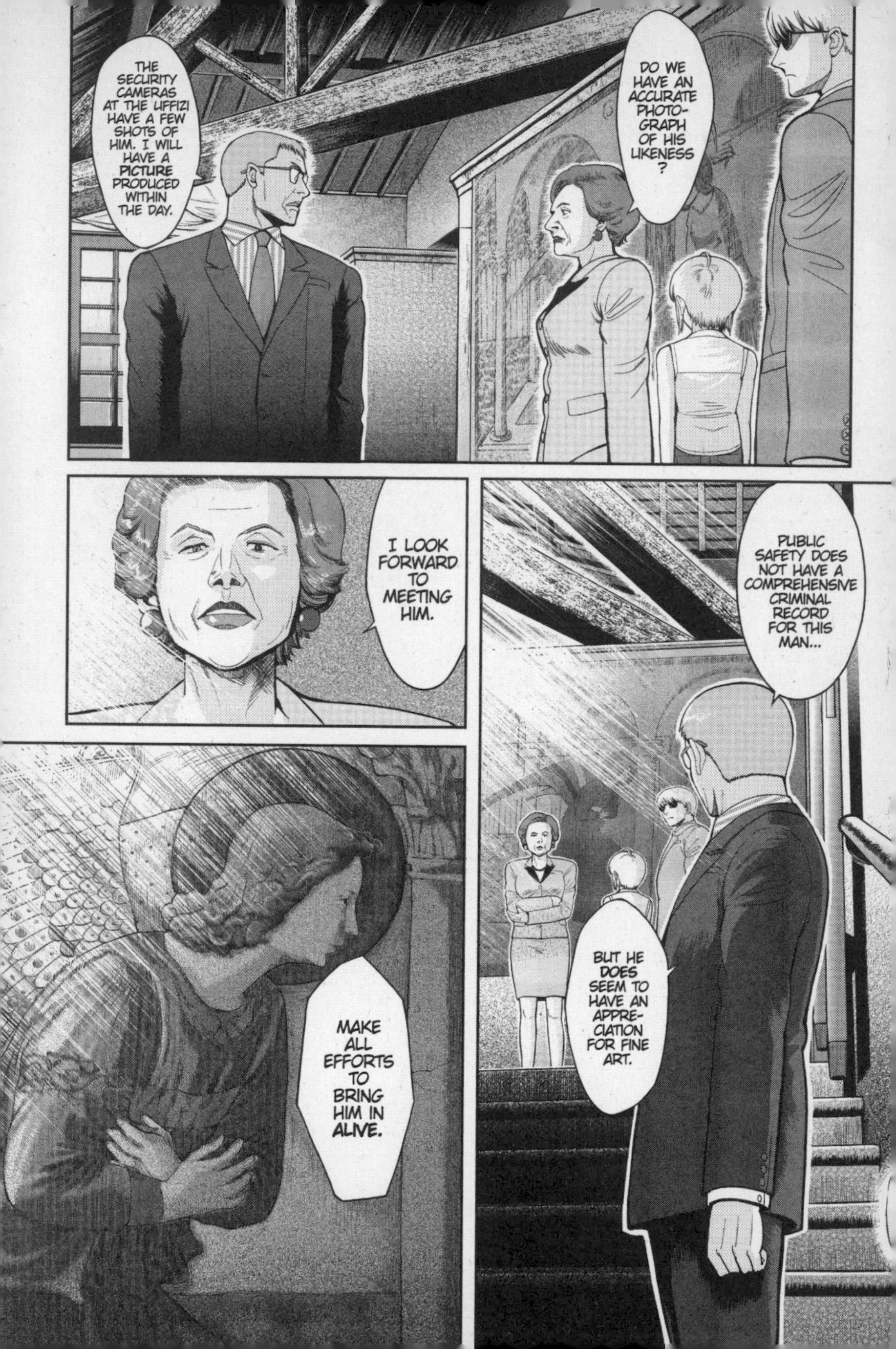
DO WE HAVE AN ACCURATE PHOTOGRAPH OF HIS LIKENESS?
THE SECURITY CAMERAS AT THE UFFIZI HAVE A FEW SHOTS OF HIM. I WILL HAVE A PICTURE PRODUCED WITHIN THE DAY.
PUBLIC SAFETY DOES NOT HAVE A COMPREHENSIVE CRIMINAL RECORD FOR THIS MAN...
BUT HE DOES SEEM TO HAVE AN APPRECIATION FOR FINE ART.
I LOOK FORWARD TO MEETING HIM.
MAKE ALL EFFORTS TO BRING HIM IN ALIVE.

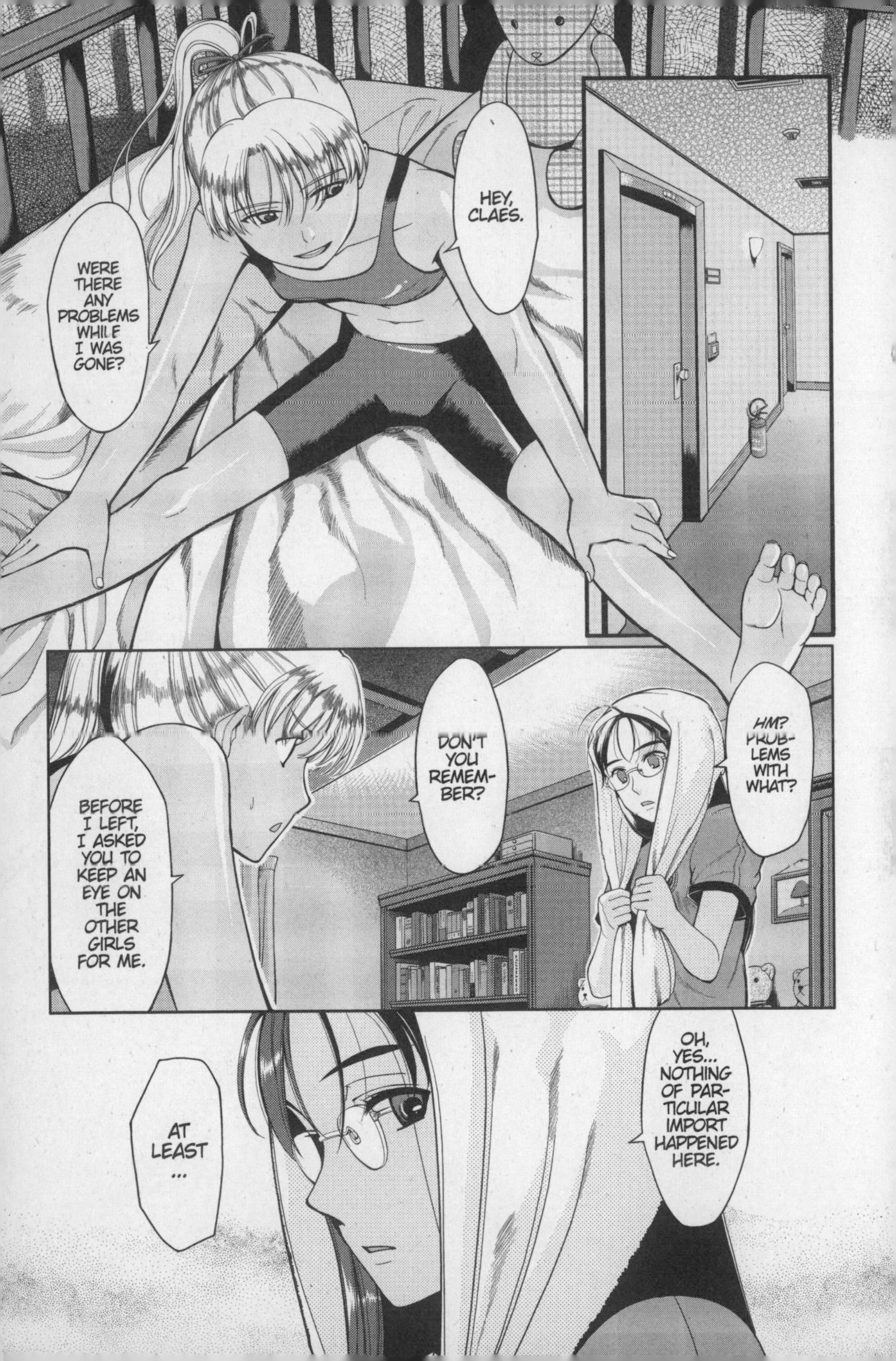
HEY, CLAES.
WERE THERE ANY PROBLEMS WHILE I WAS GONE?
HM? PROB-LEMS WITH WHAT?
DON'T YOU REMEM-BER?
BEFORE I LEFT, I ASKED YOU TO KEEP AN EYE ON THE OTHER GIRLS FOR ME.
OH, YES... NOTHING OF PAR-TICULAR IMPORT HAPPENED HERE.
AT LEAST ...

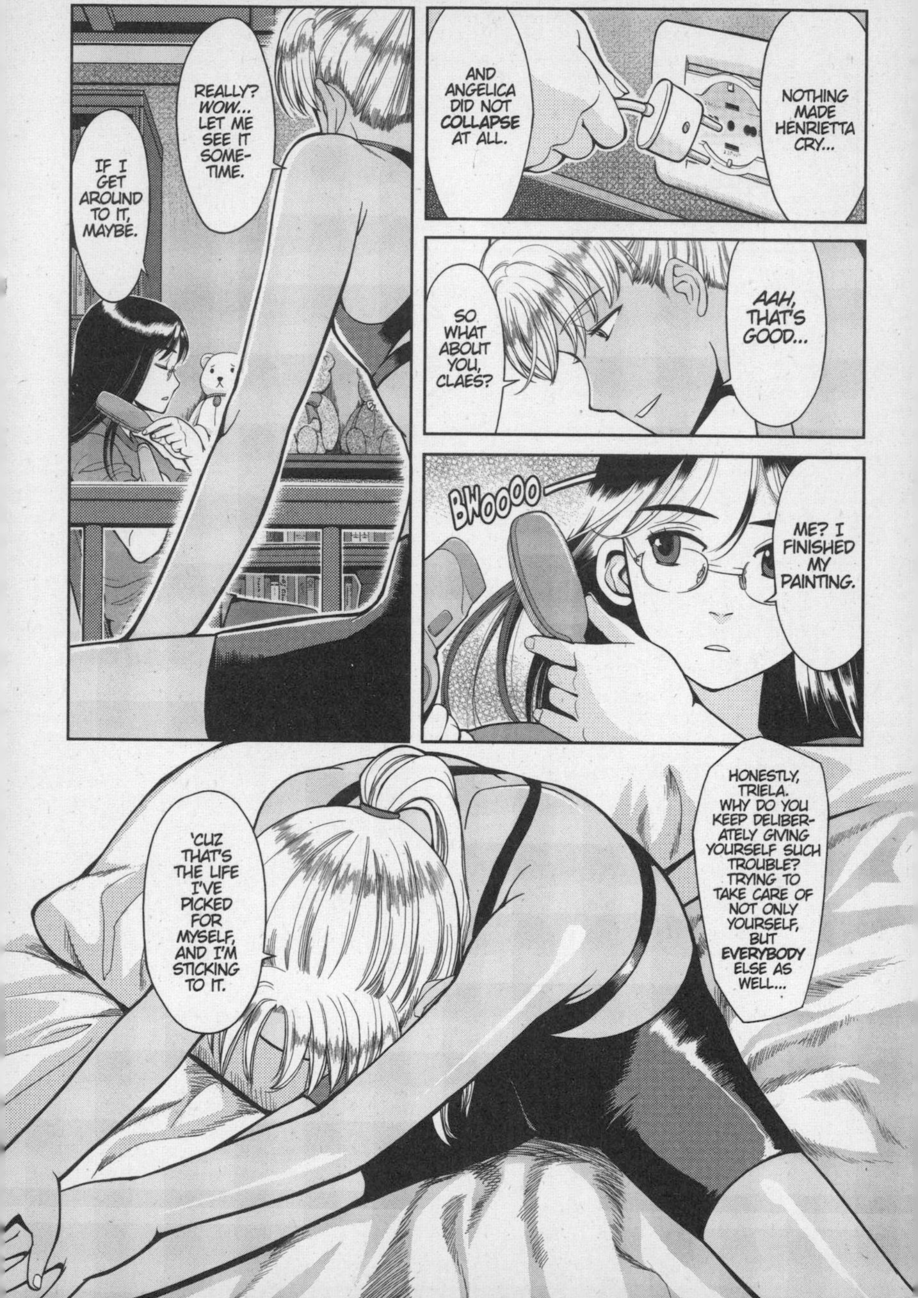
NOTHING MADE HENRIETTA CRY...
AND ANGELICA DID NOT COLLAPSE AT ALL.
AAH, THAT'S GOOD...
SO WHAT ABOUT YOU, CLAES?
BWOOOO
ME? I FINISHED MY PAINTING.
REALLY? WOW... LET ME SEE IT SOMETIME.
IF I GET AROUND TO IT, MAYBE.
HONESTLY, TRIELA. WHY DO YOU KEEP DELIBERATELY GIVING YOURSELF SUCH TROUBLE? TRYING TO TAKE CARE OF NOT ONLY YOURSELF, BUT EVERYBODY ELSE AS WELL...
'CUZ THAT'S THE LIFE I'VE PICKED FOR MYSELF, AND I'M STICKING TO IT.

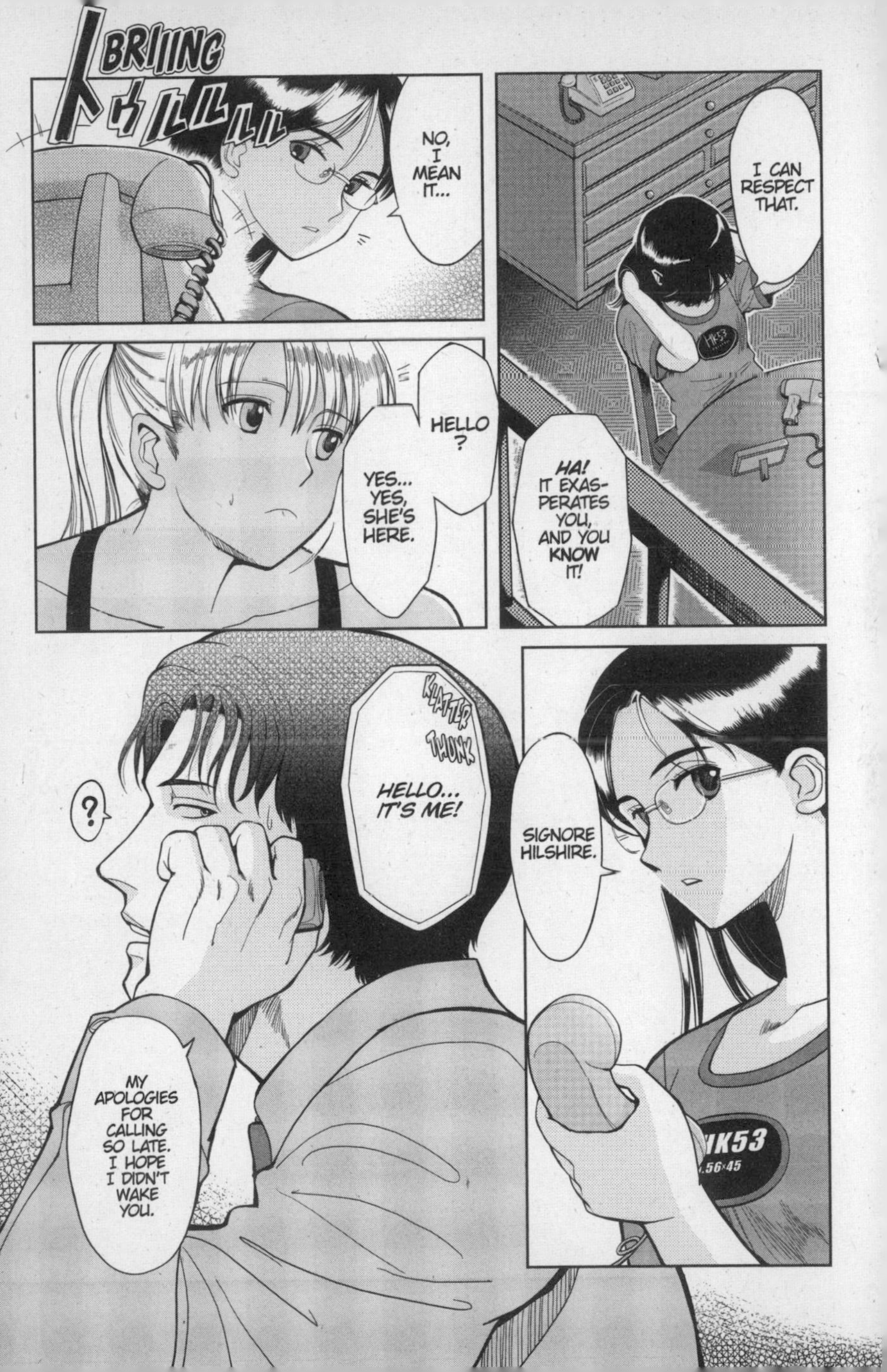
I CAN RESPECT THAT.
HA! IT EXASPERATES YOU, AND YOU KNOW IT!
BRIIING
NO, I MEAN IT...
HELLO?
YES... YES, SHE'S HERE.
SIGNORE HILSHIRE.
KLATTER
THUNK
HELLO... IT'S ME!
?
MY APOLOGIES FOR CALLING SO LATE. I HOPE I DIDN'T WAKE YOU.

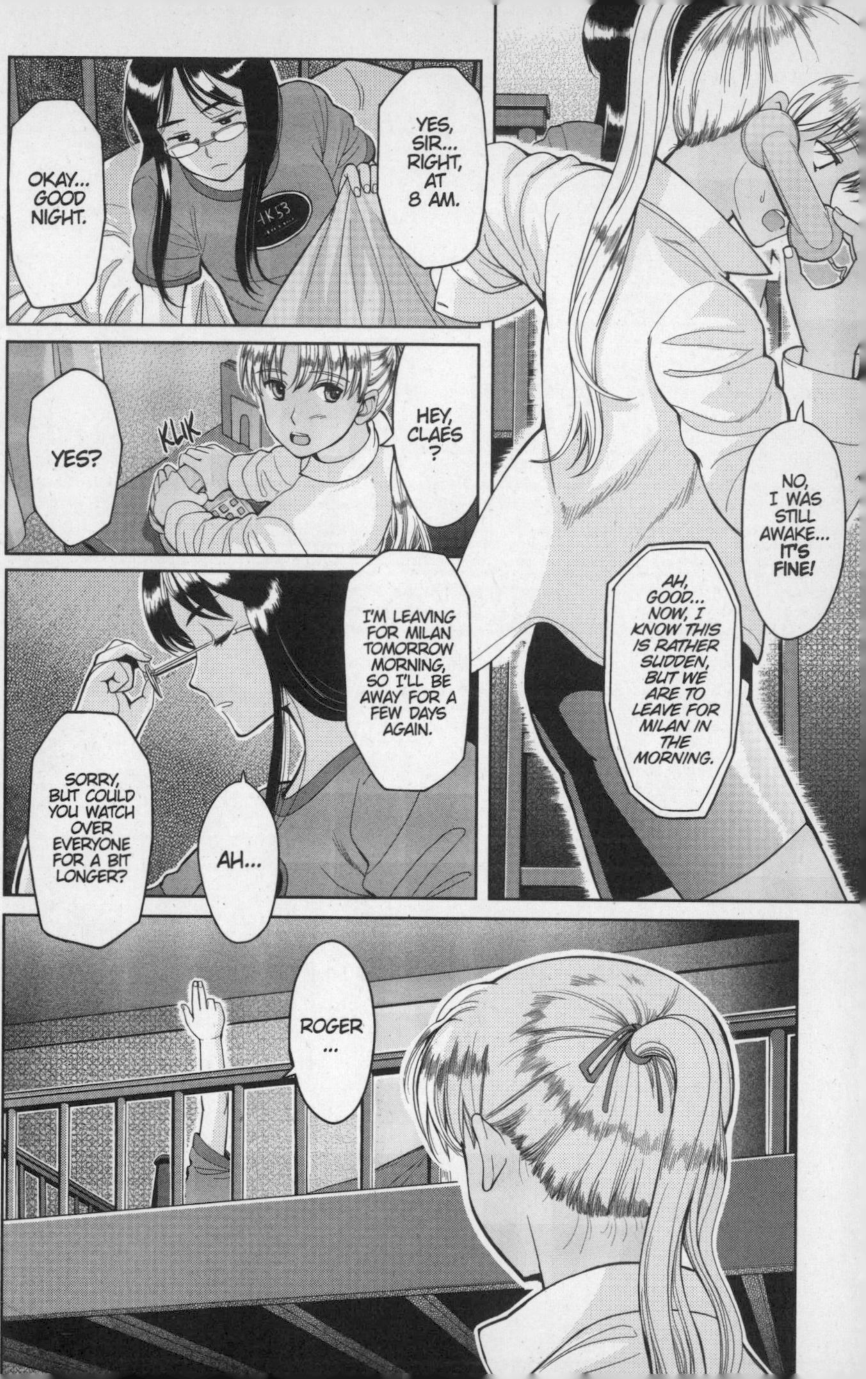
NO, I WAS STILL AWAKE... IT'S FINE!
AH, GOOD... NOW, I KNOW THIS IS RATHER SUDDEN, BUT WE ARE TO LEAVE FOR MILAN IN THE MORNING.
YES, SIR... RIGHT, AT 8 AM.
OKAY... GOOD NIGHT.
HEY, CLAES?
KLIK
YES?
I'M LEAVING FOR MILAN TOMORROW MORNING, SO I'LL BE AWAY FOR A FEW DAYS AGAIN.
AH...
SORRY, BUT COULD YOU WATCH OVER EVERYONE FOR A BIT LONGER?
ROGER ...

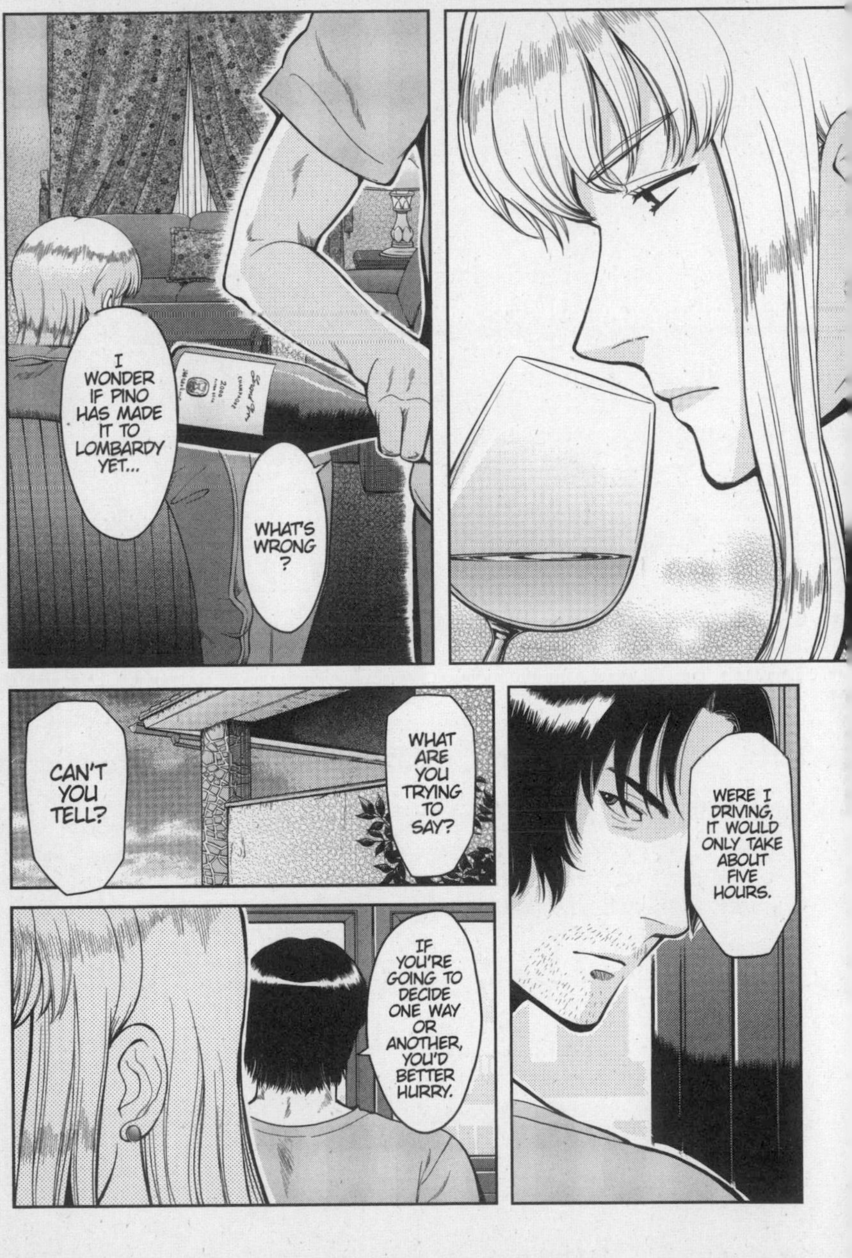
I WONDER IF PINO HAS MADE IT TO LOMBARDY YET...
WHAT'S WRONG?
WERE I DRIVING, IT WOULD ONLY TAKE ABOUT FIVE HOURS.
WHAT ARE YOU TRYING TO SAY?
CAN'T YOU TELL?
IF YOU'RE GOING TO DECIDE ONE WAY OR ANOTHER, YOU'D BETTER HURRY.

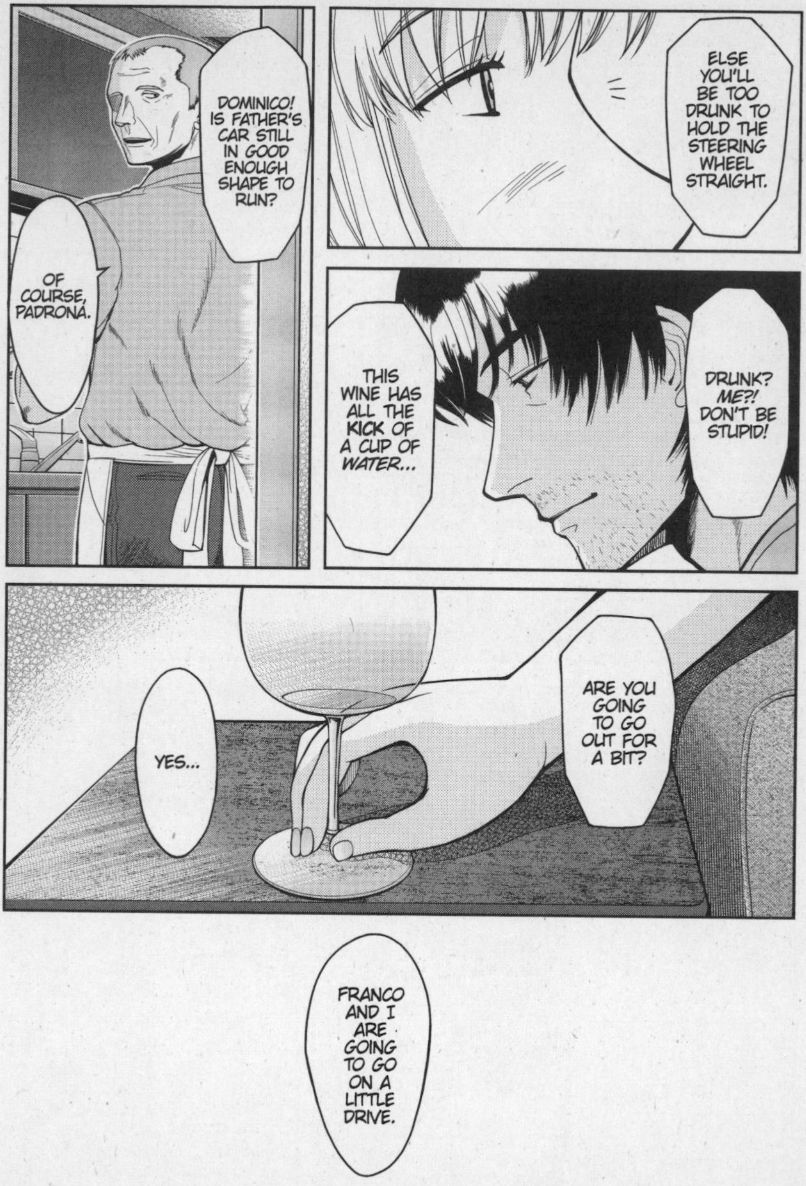
ELSE YOU'LL BE TOO DRUNK TO HOLD THE STEERING WHEEL STRAIGHT.
DRUNK? *ME?!* DON'T BE STUPID!
THIS WINE HAS ALL THE KICK OF A CUP OF *WATER*...
DOMINICO! IS FATHER'S CAR STILL IN GOOD ENOUGH SHAPE TO RUN?
OF COURSE, PADRONA.
ARE YOU GOING TO GO OUT FOR A BIT?
YES...
FRANCO AND I ARE GOING TO GO ON A LITTLE DRIVE.

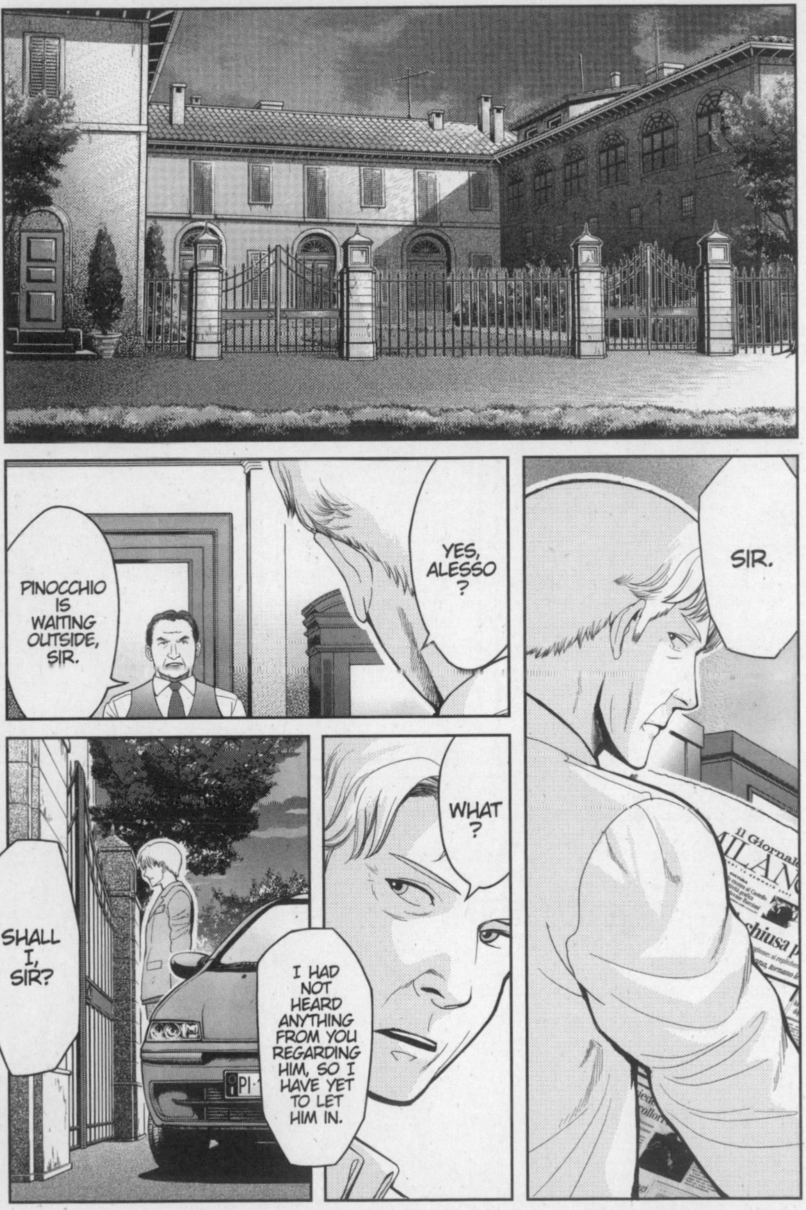
SIR.
YES, ALESSO?
PINOCCHIO IS WAITING OUTSIDE, SIR.
WHAT?
I HAD NOT HEARD ANYTHING FROM YOU REGARDING HIM, SO I HAVE YET TO LET HIM IN.
SHALL I, SIR?

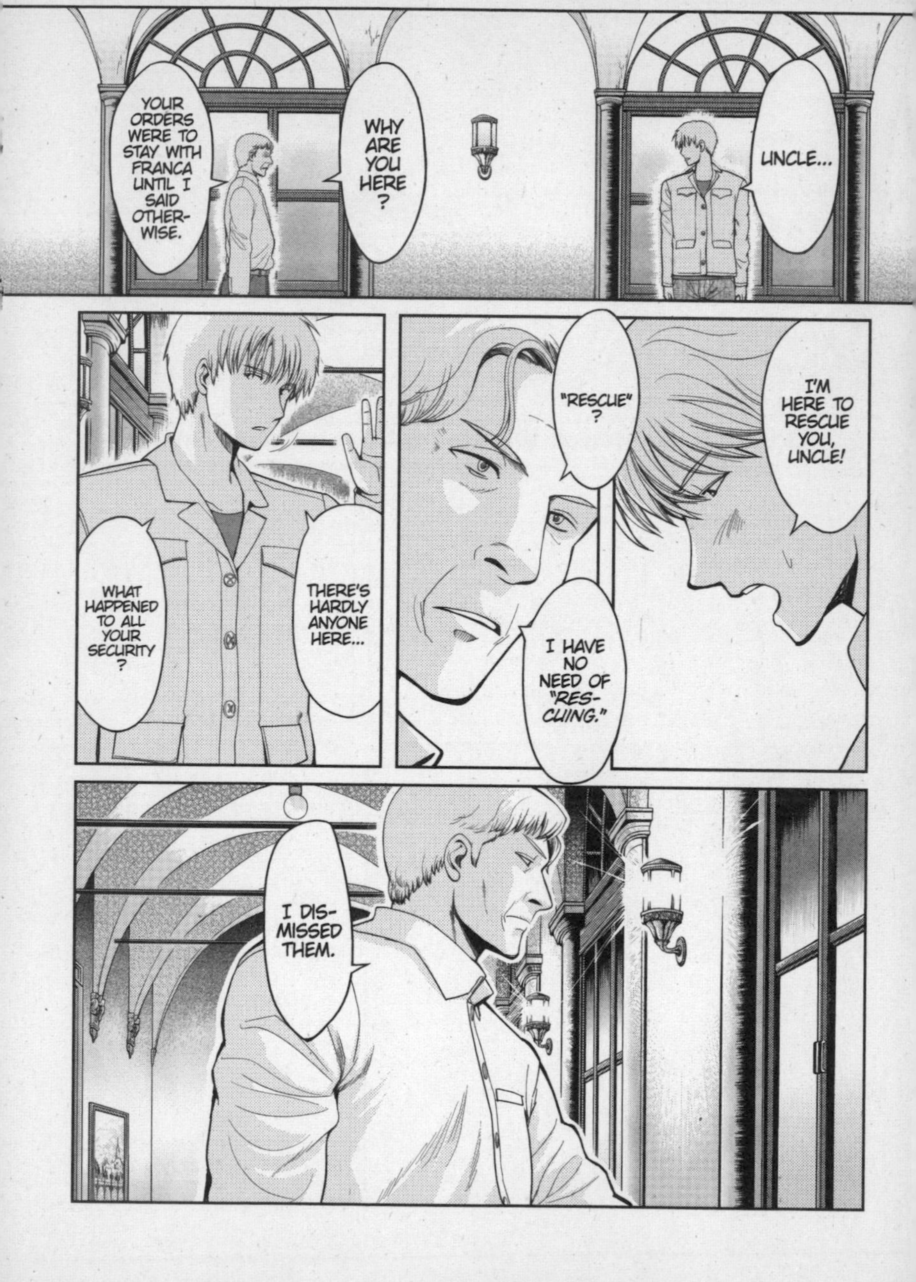
UNCLE...
WHY ARE YOU HERE?
YOUR ORDERS WERE TO STAY WITH FRANCA UNTIL I SAID OTHERWISE.
I'M HERE TO RESCUE YOU, UNCLE!
"RESCUE"?
I HAVE NO NEED OF "RESCUING."
THERE'S HARDLY ANYONE HERE...
WHAT HAPPENED TO ALL YOUR SECURITY?
I DISMISSED THEM.

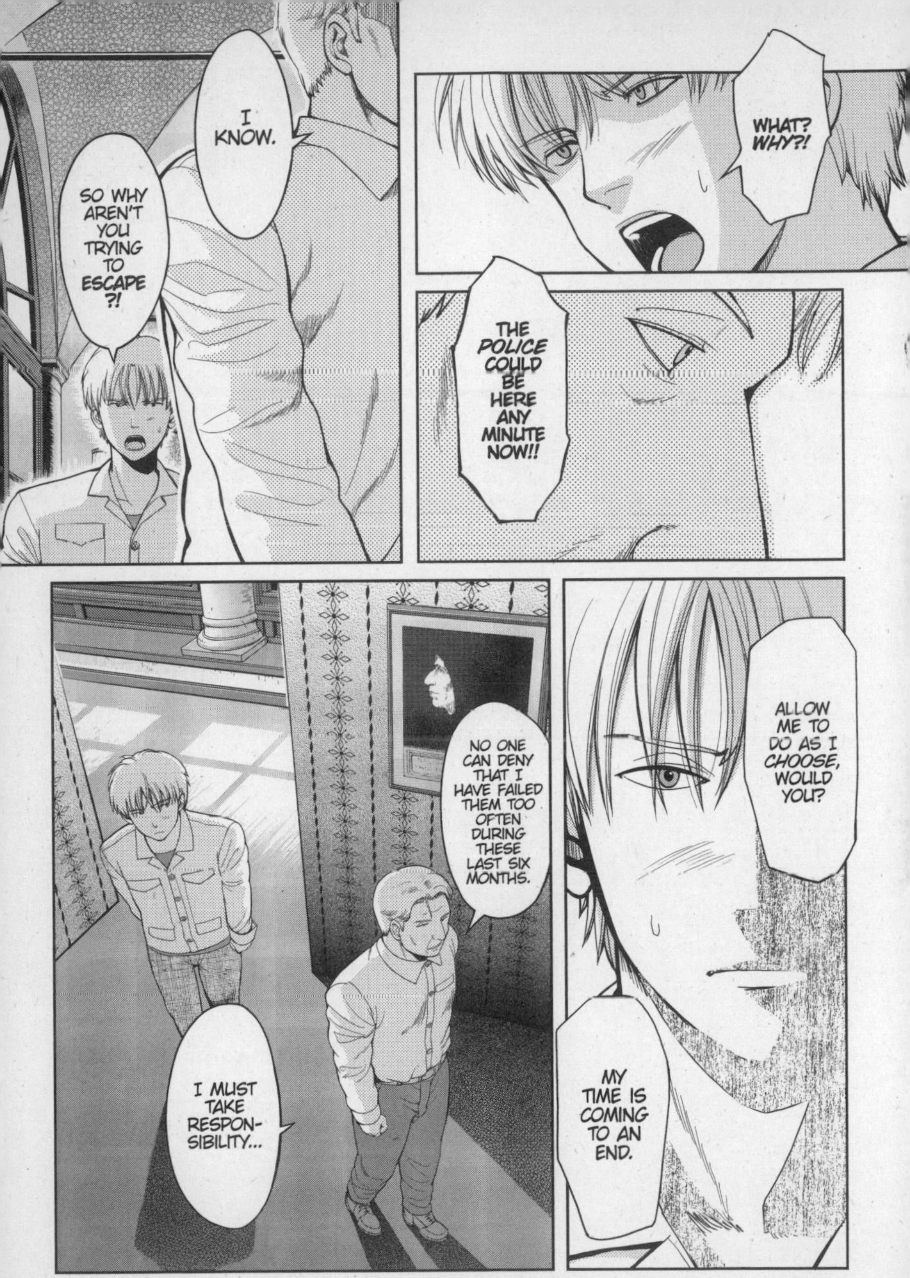
WHAT? *WHY?!*
THE *POLICE* COULD BE HERE ANY MINUTE NOW!!
I KNOW.
SO WHY AREN'T YOU TRYING TO ESCAPE?!
ALLOW ME TO DO AS I *CHOOSE,* WOULD YOU?
MY TIME IS COMING TO AN END.
NO ONE CAN DENY THAT I HAVE FAILED THEM TOO OFTEN DURING THESE LAST SIX MONTHS.
I MUST TAKE RESPON-SIBILITY...

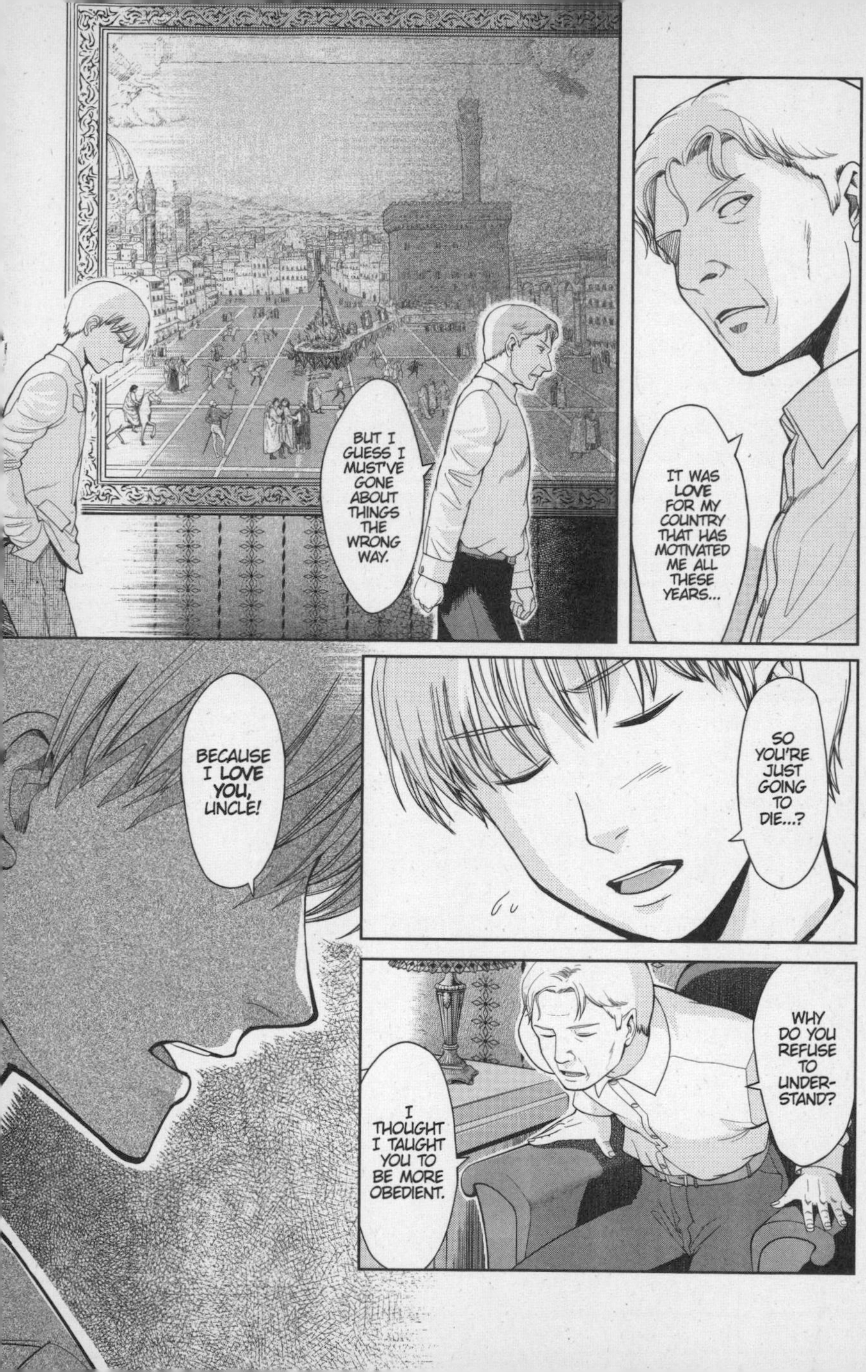
IT WAS LOVE FOR MY COUNTRY THAT HAS MOTIVATED ME ALL THESE YEARS...
BUT I GUESS I MUST'VE GONE ABOUT THINGS THE WRONG WAY.
SO YOU'RE JUST GOING TO DIE...?
WHY DO YOU REFUSE TO UNDERSTAND?
I THOUGHT I TAUGHT YOU TO BE MORE OBEDIENT.
BECAUSE I LOVE YOU, UNCLE!

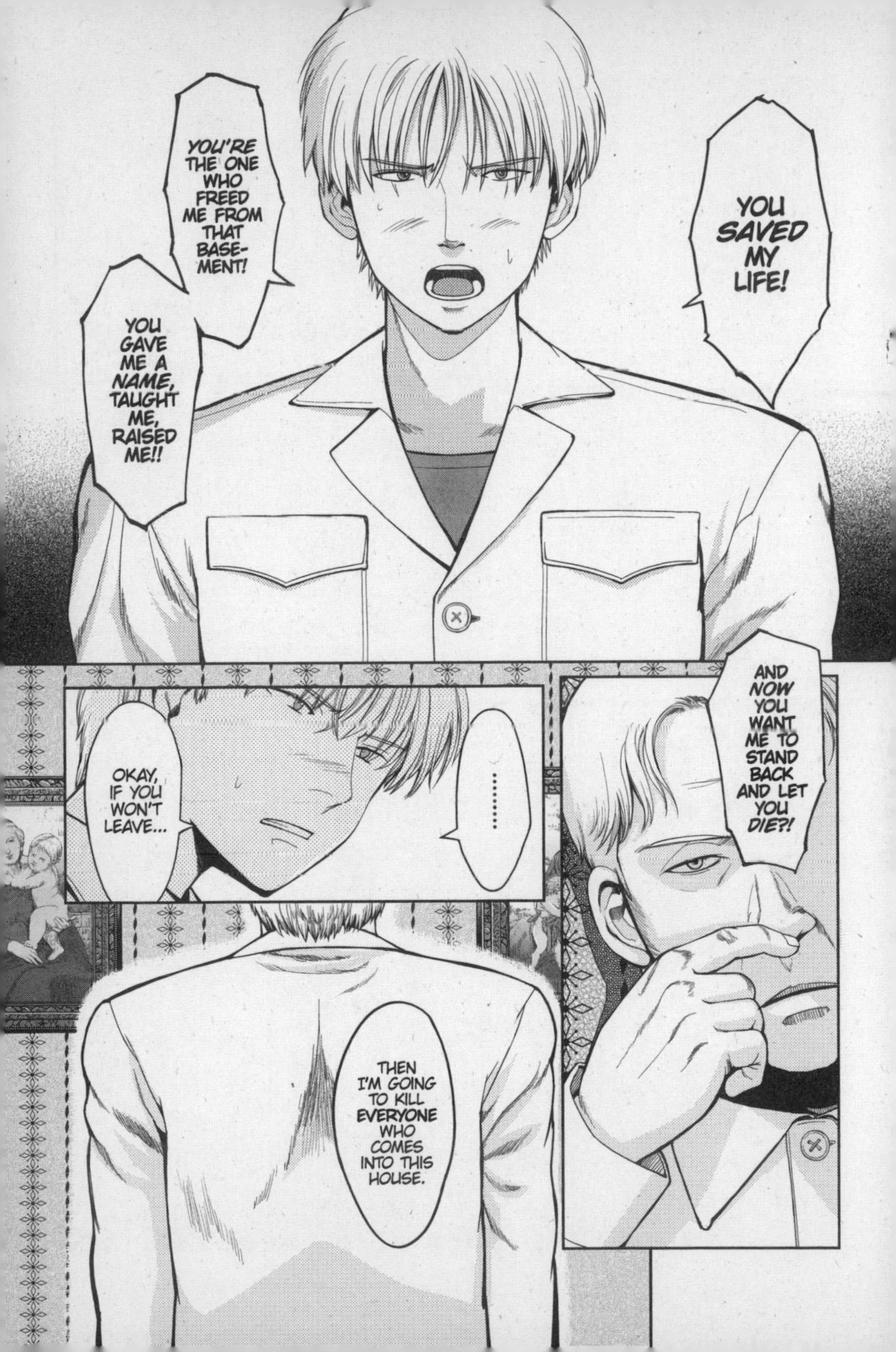
YOU SAVED MY LIFE!
YOU'RE THE ONE WHO FREED ME FROM THAT BASE-MENT!
YOU GAVE ME A NAME, TAUGHT ME, RAISED ME!!
AND NOW YOU WANT ME TO STAND BACK AND LET YOU DIE?!
......
OKAY, IF YOU WON'T LEAVE...
THEN I'M GOING TO KILL EVERYONE WHO COMES INTO THIS HOUSE.

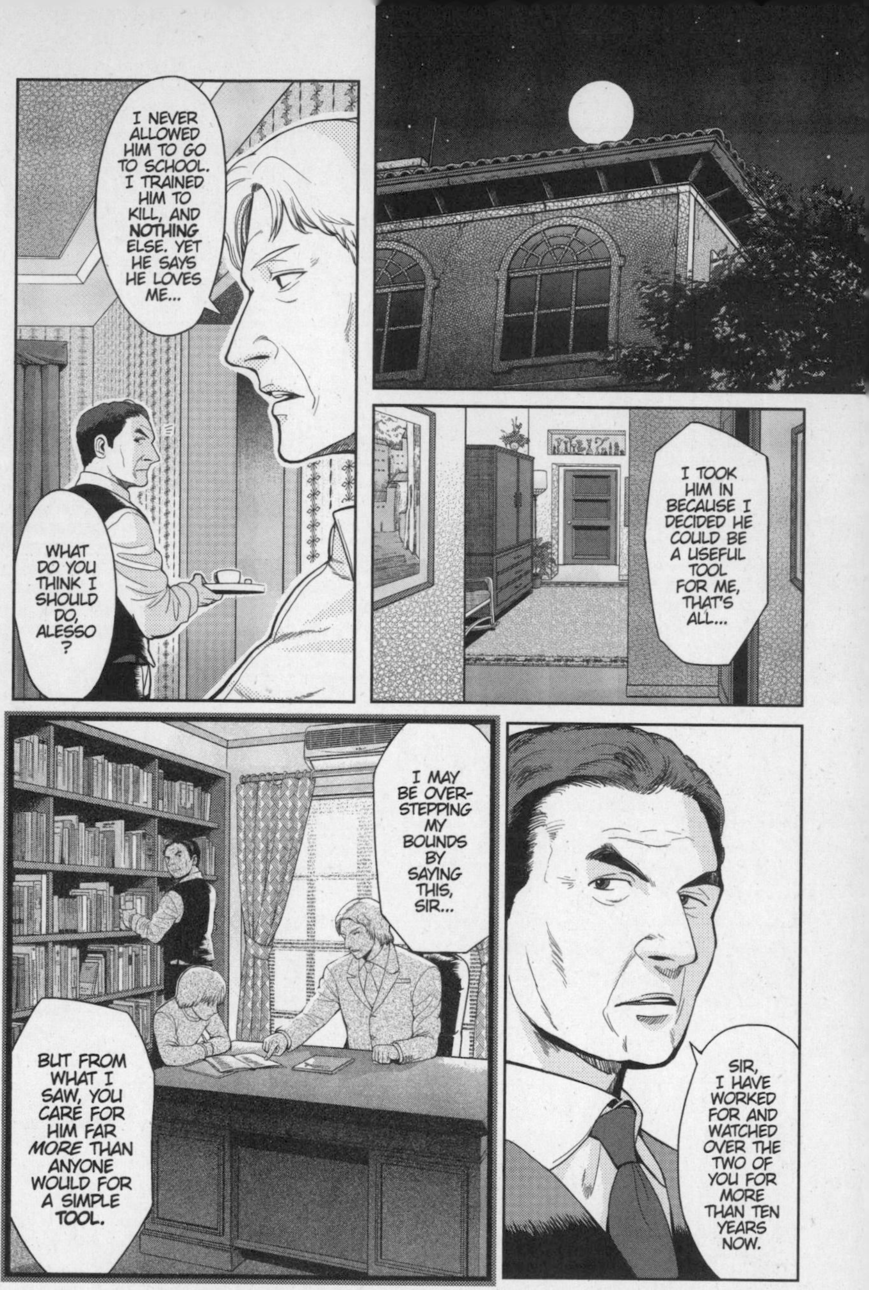
I TOOK HIM IN BECAUSE I DECIDED HE COULD BE A USEFUL TOOL FOR ME, THAT'S ALL...
I NEVER ALLOWED HIM TO GO TO SCHOOL. I TRAINED HIM TO KILL, AND NOTHING ELSE. YET HE SAYS HE LOVES ME...
WHAT DO YOU THINK I SHOULD DO, ALESSO?
SIR, I HAVE WORKED FOR AND WATCHED OVER THE TWO OF YOU FOR MORE THAN TEN YEARS NOW.
I MAY BE OVER-STEPPING MY BOUNDS BY SAYING THIS, SIR...
BUT FROM WHAT I SAW, YOU CARE FOR HIM FAR MORE THAN ANYONE WOULD FOR A SIMPLE TOOL.

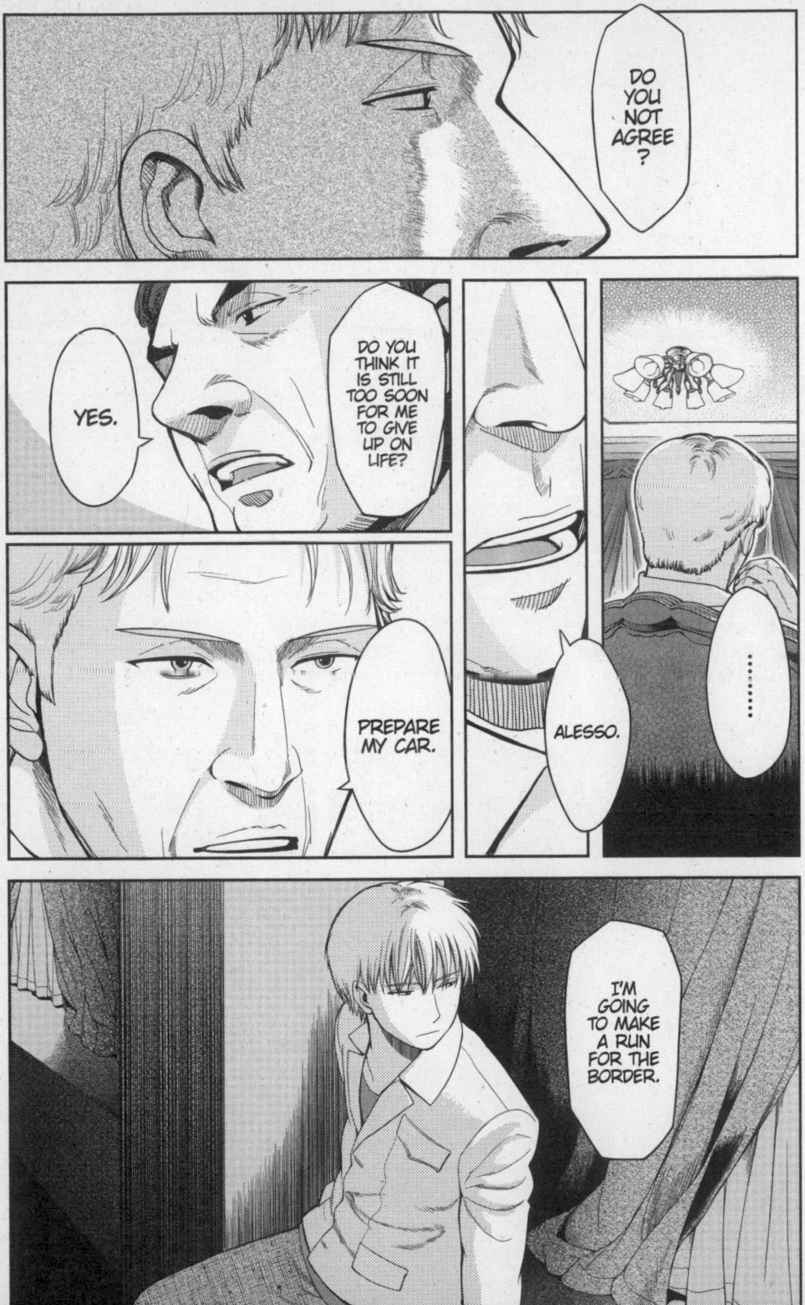
DO YOU NOT AGREE ?
……
ALESSO.
DO YOU THINK IT IS STILL TOO SOON FOR ME TO GIVE UP ON LIFE?
YES.
PREPARE MY CAR.
I'M GOING TO MAKE A RUN FOR THE BORDER.

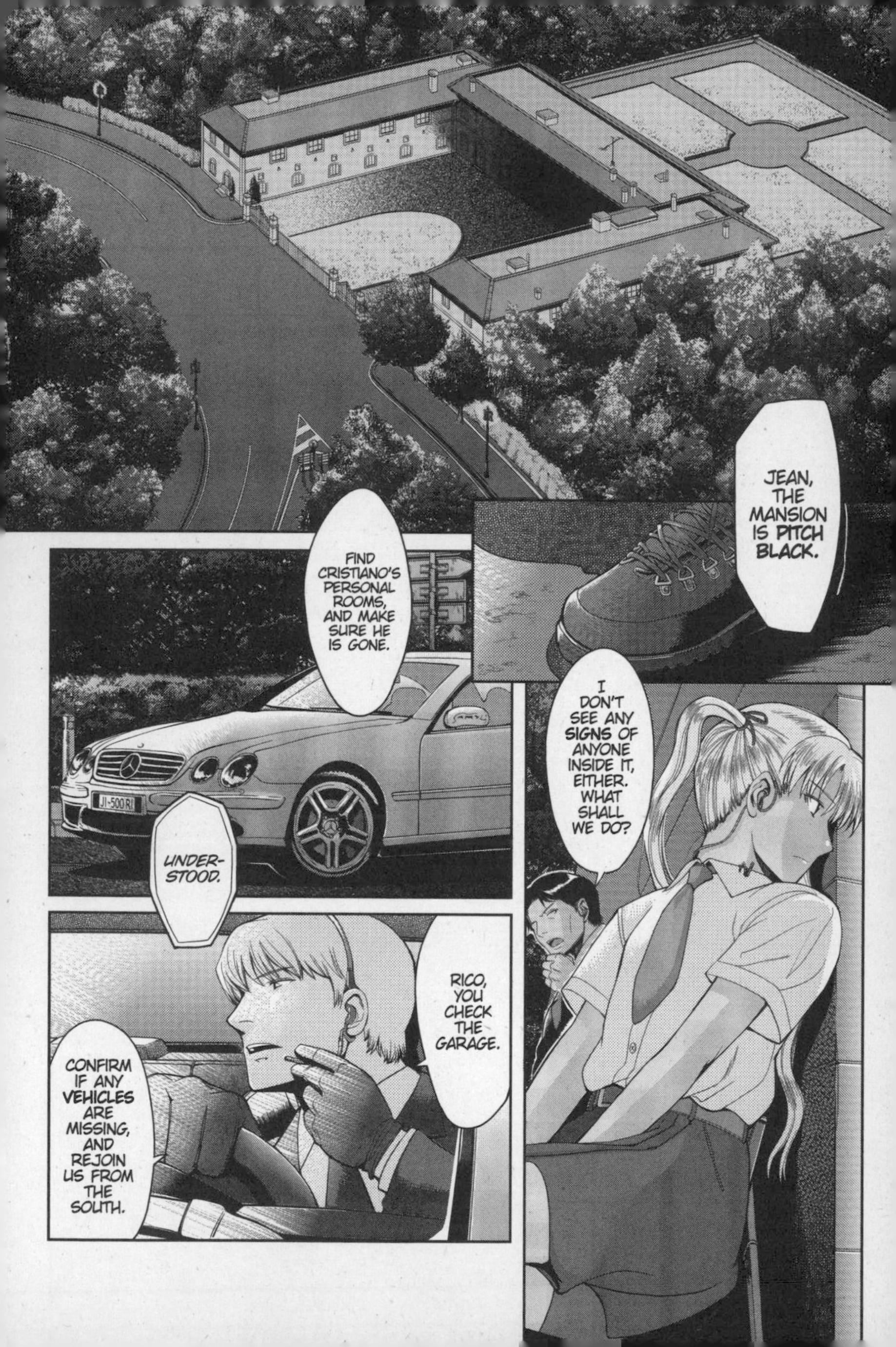
JEAN, THE MANSION IS PITCH BLACK.
I DON'T SEE ANY SIGNS OF ANYONE INSIDE IT, EITHER. WHAT SHALL WE DO?
FIND CRISTIANO'S PERSONAL ROOMS, AND MAKE SURE HE IS GONE.
UNDER-STOOD.
RICO, YOU CHECK THE GARAGE.
CONFIRM IF ANY VEHICLES ARE MISSING, AND REJOIN US FROM THE SOUTH.
JI-500RI

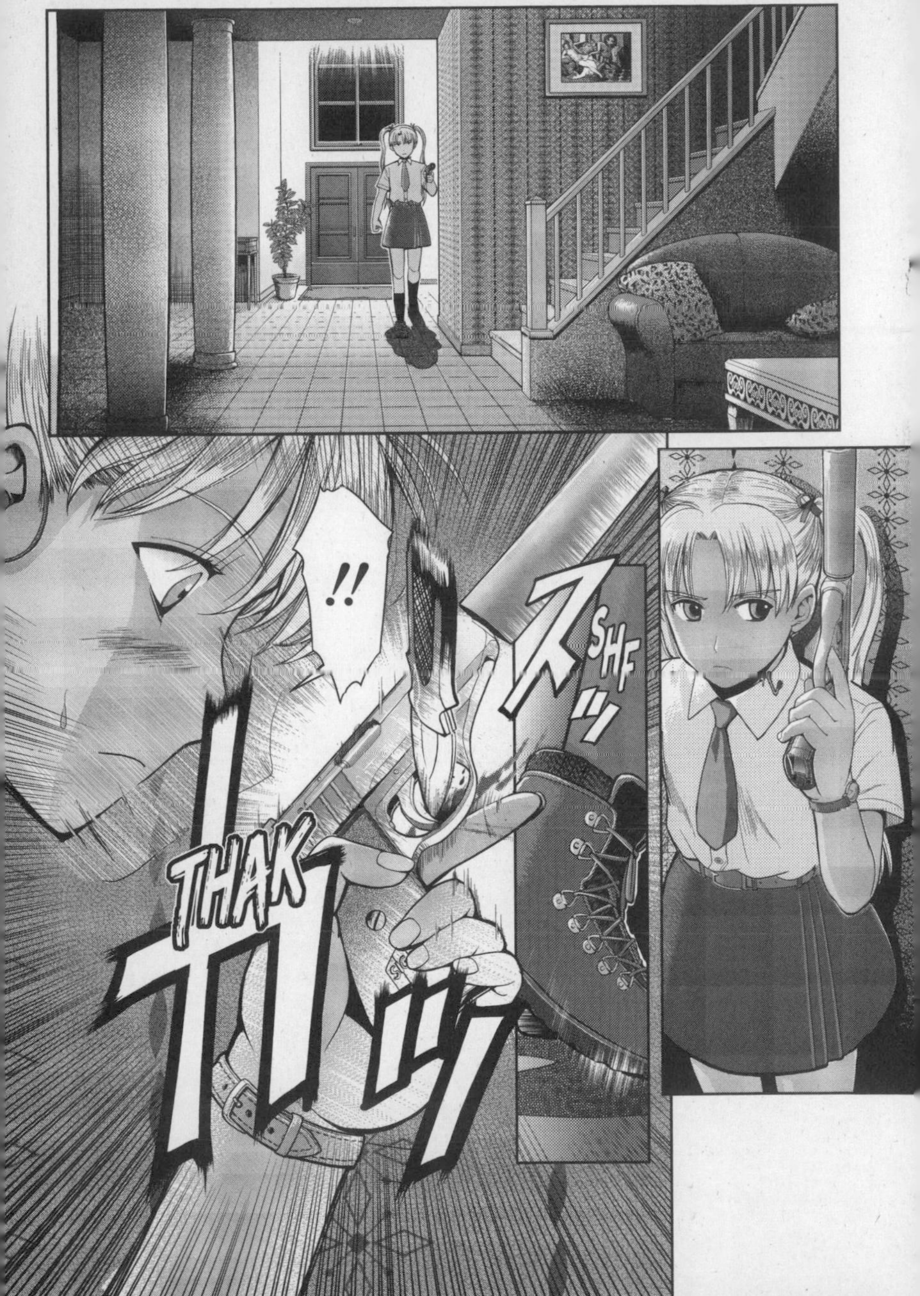

スッ
SHF
!!
カッ
THAK

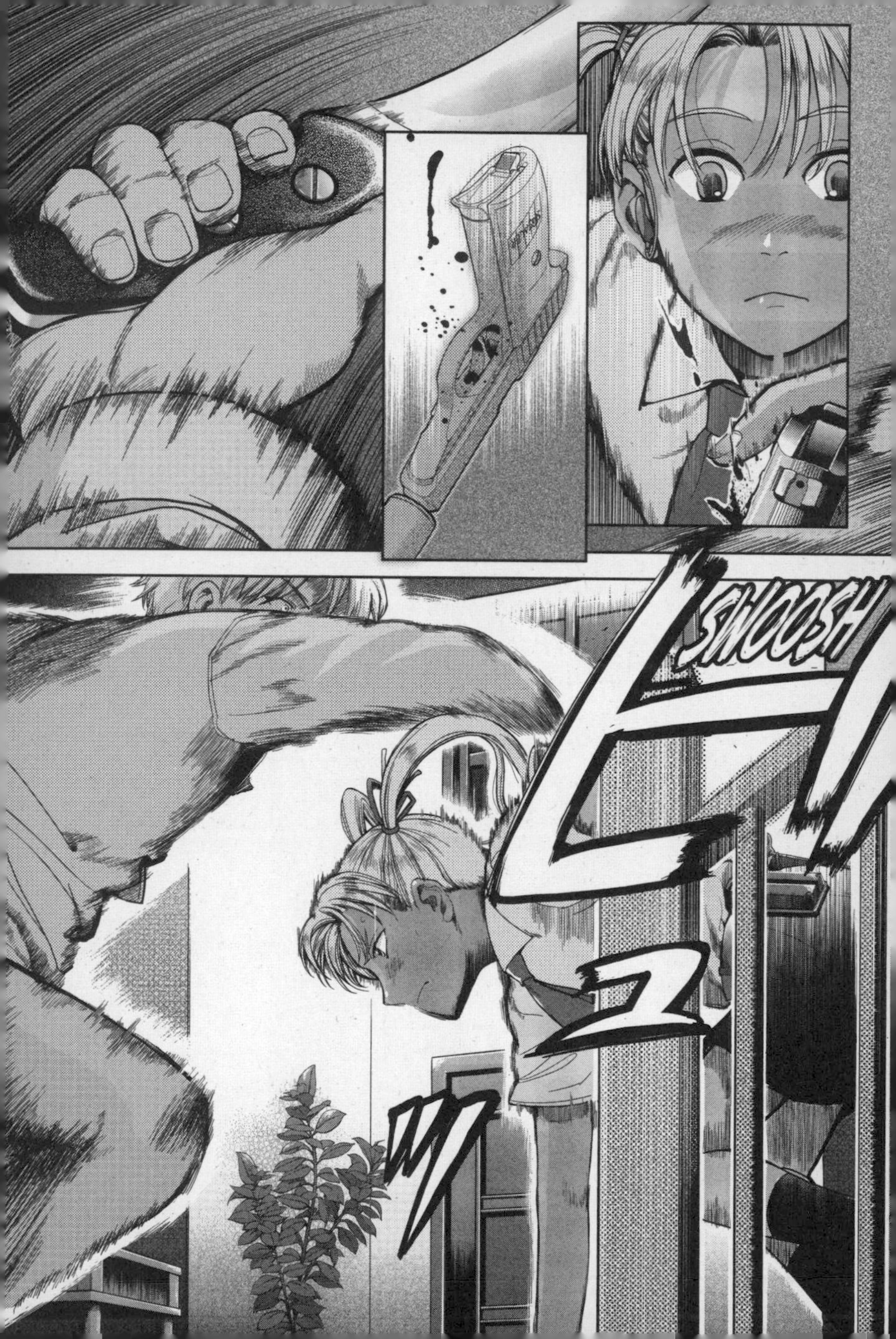
SWOOSH

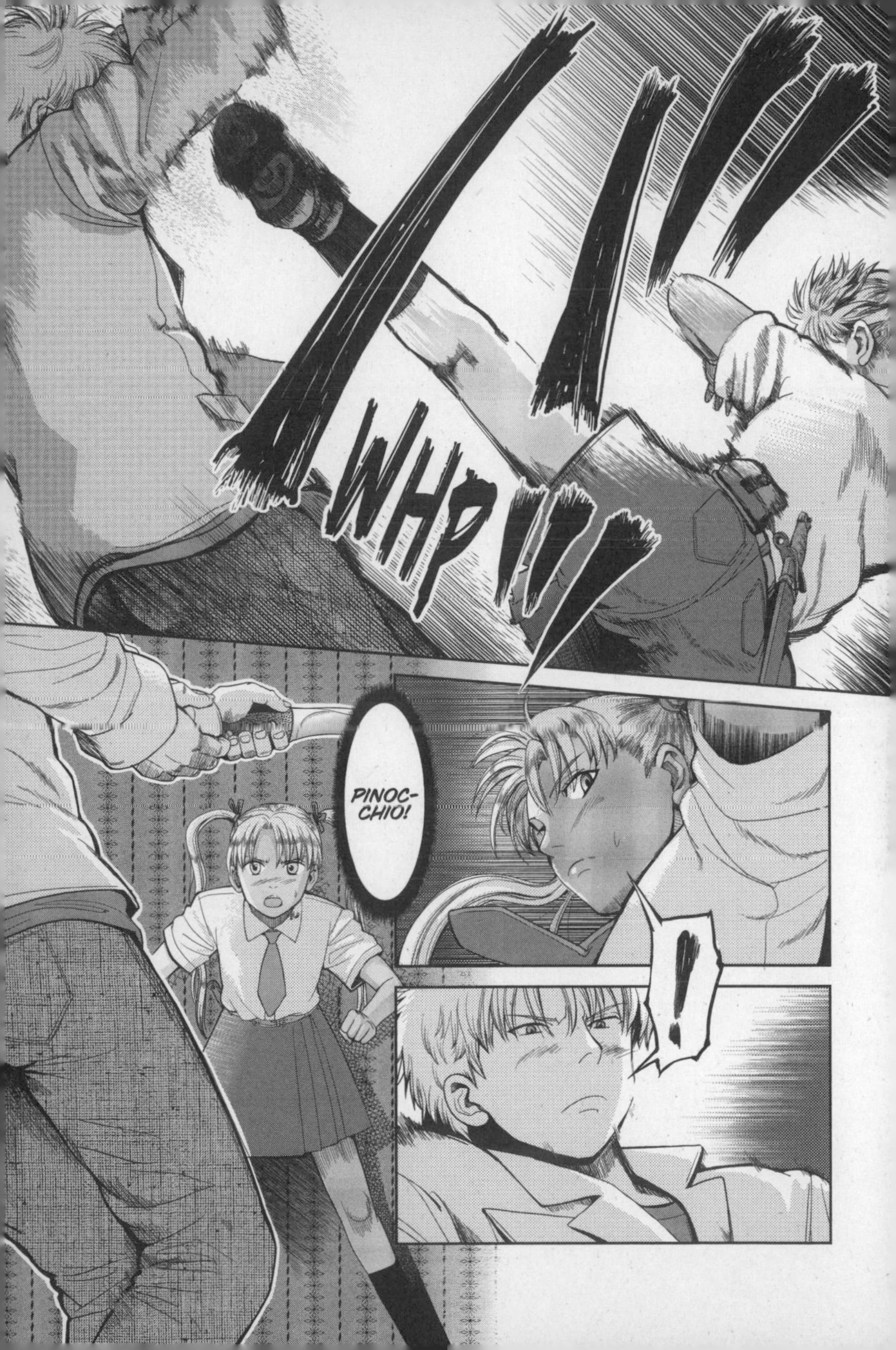
WHP!!
PINOC-
CHIO!
!

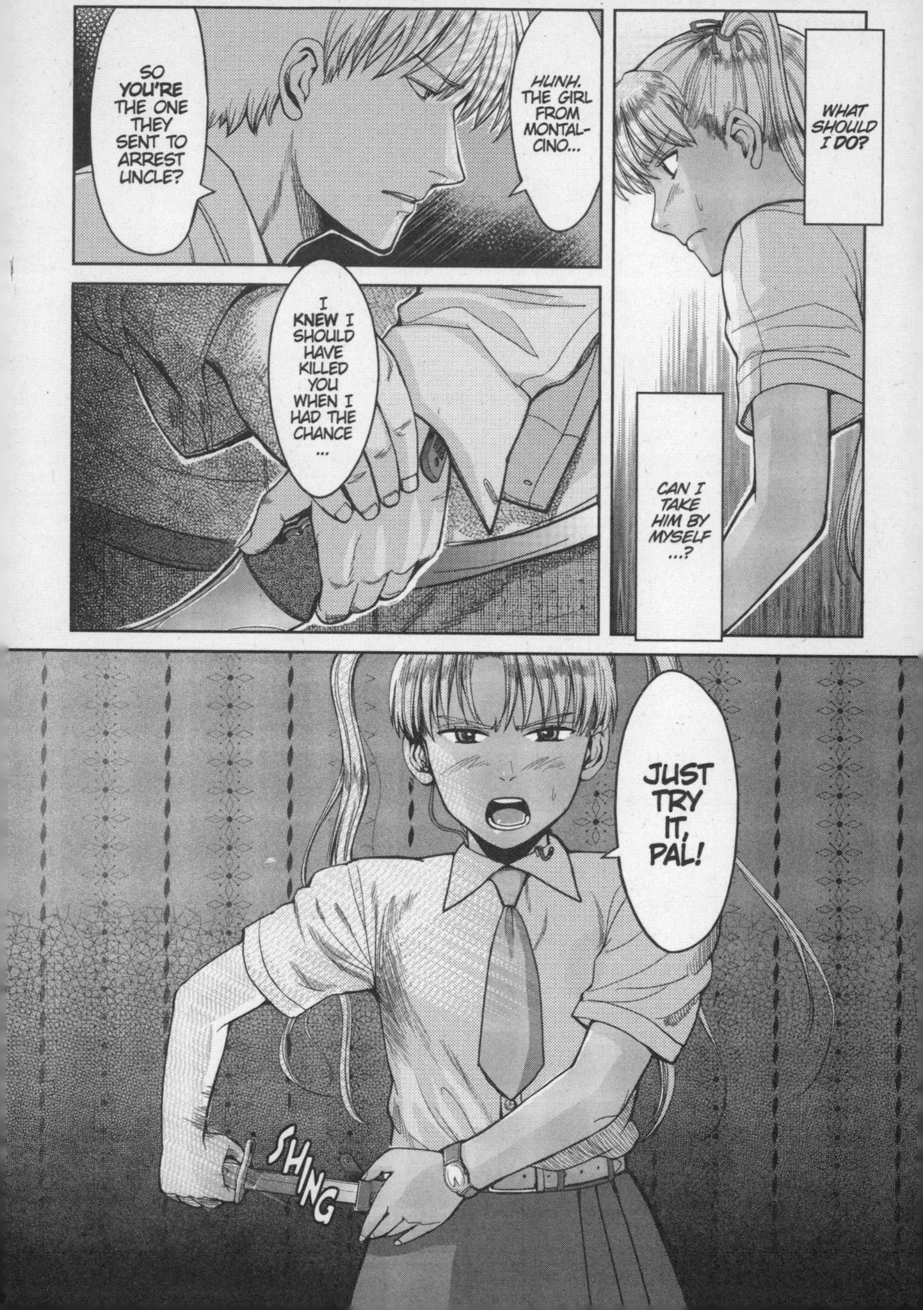
WHAT SHOULD I DO?
CAN I TAKE HIM BY MYSELF ...?
HUNH. THE GIRL FROM MONTAL-CINO...
SO YOU'RE THE ONE THEY SENT TO ARREST UNCLE?
I KNEW I SHOULD HAVE KILLED YOU WHEN I HAD THE CHANCE ...
JUST TRY IT, PAL!
SHING

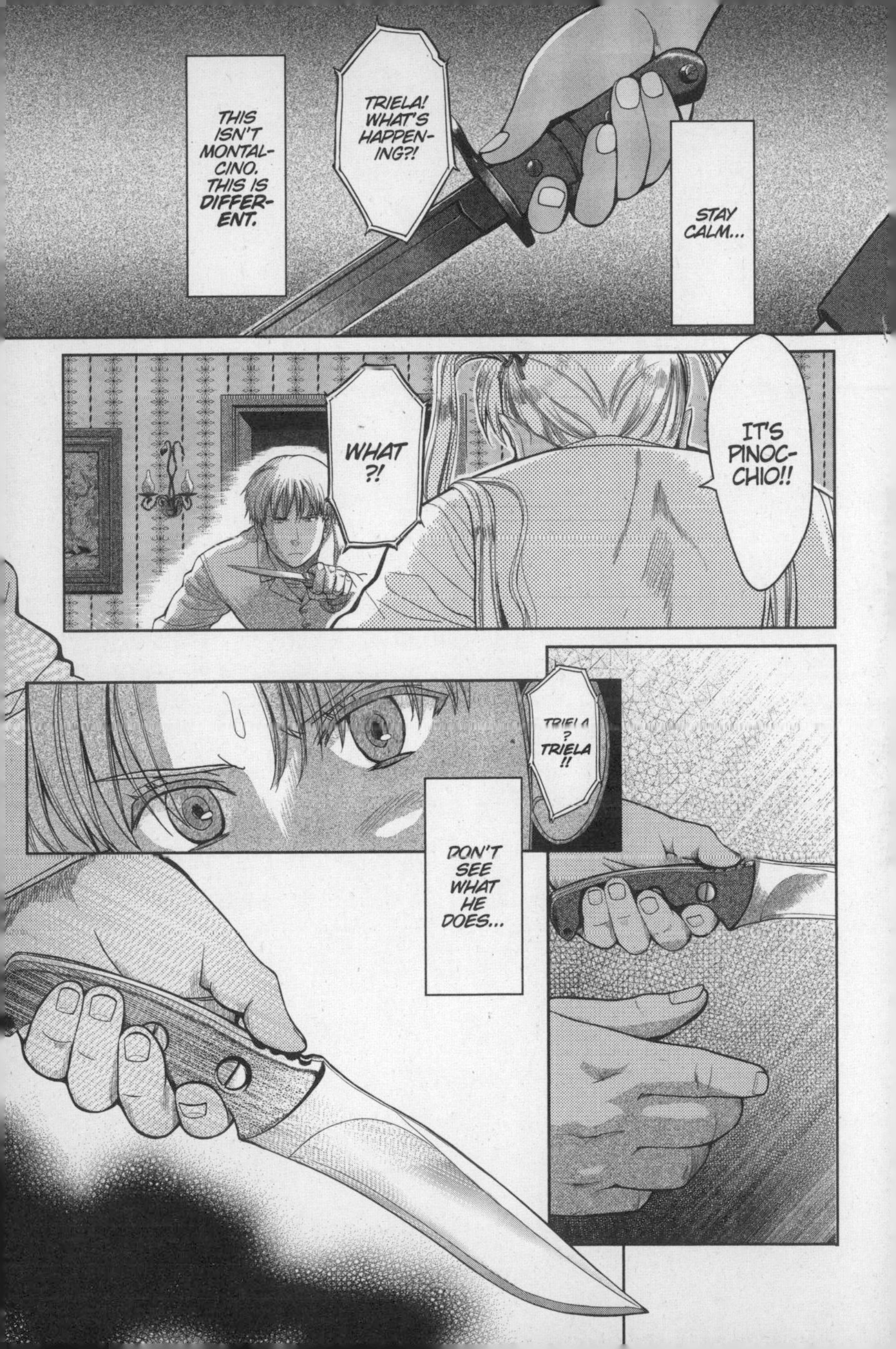
STAY CALM...
TRIELA! WHAT'S HAPPEN-ING?!
THIS ISN'T MONTAL-CINO. THIS IS DIFFER-ENT.
IT'S PINOC-CHIO!!
WHAT?!
TRIELA? TRIELA!!
DON'T SEE WHAT HE DOES...

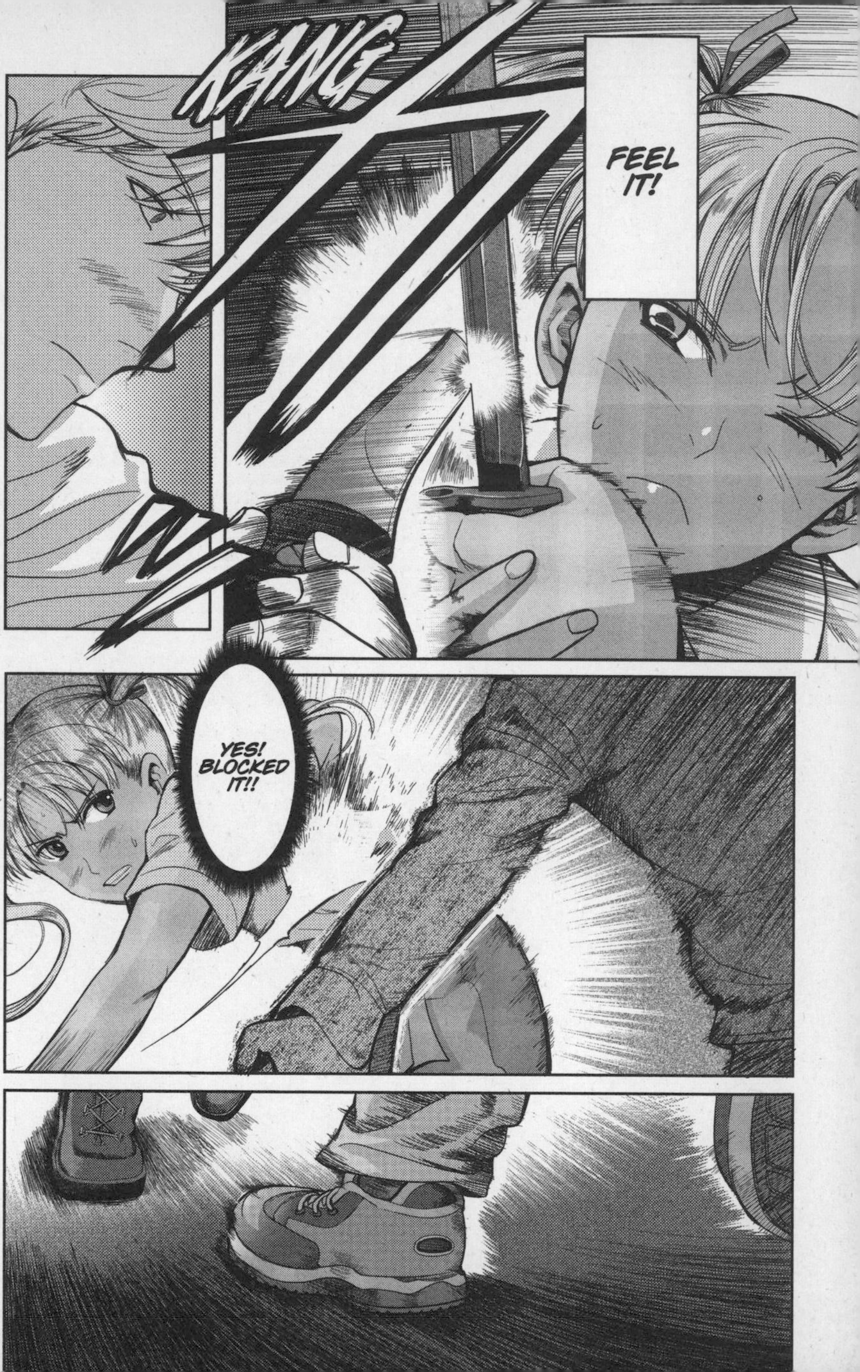
FEEL IT!
KANG
YES! BLOCKED IT!!

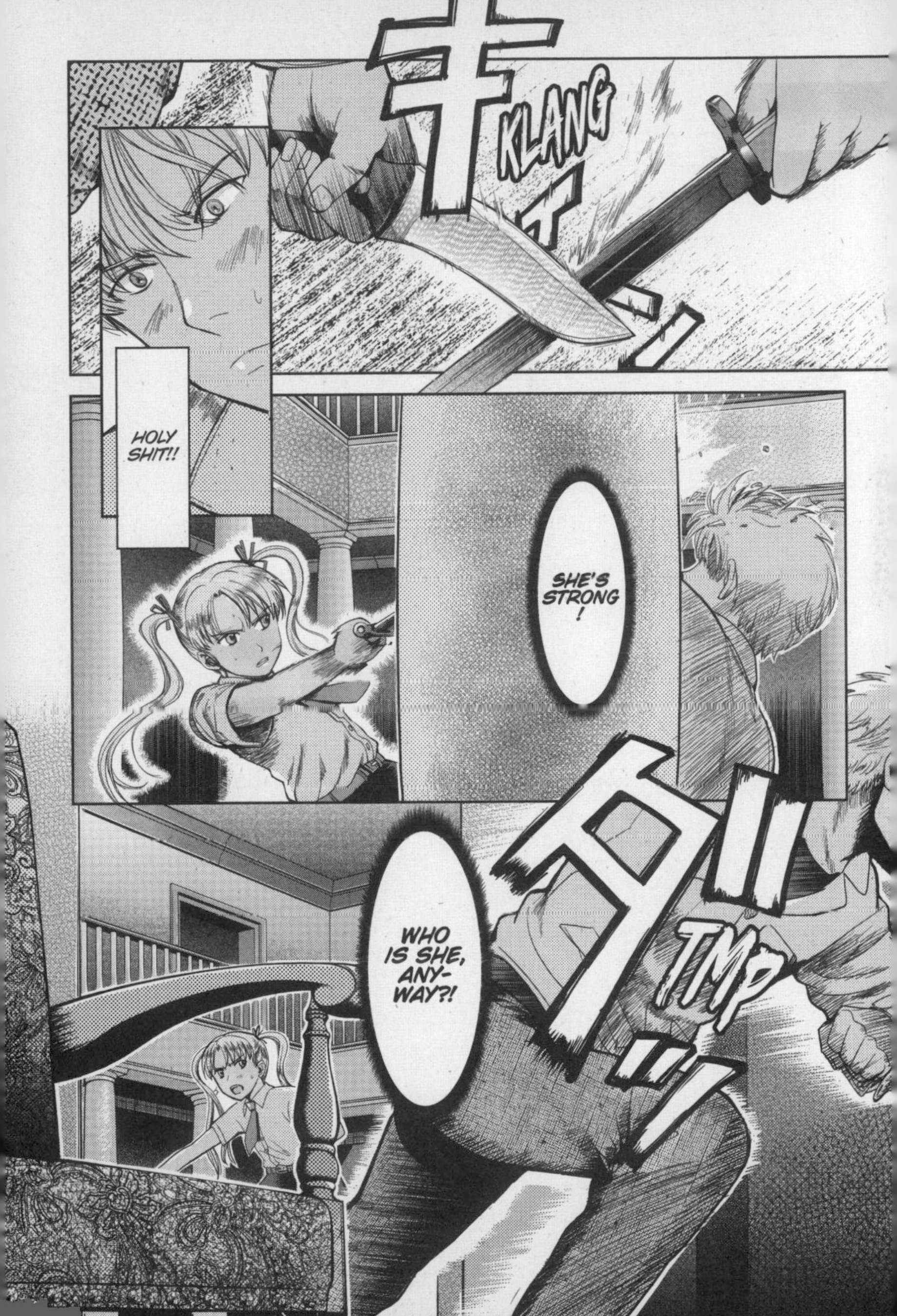
KLANG
HOLY SHIT!!
SHE'S STRONG!
TMP
WHO IS SHE, ANYWAY?!

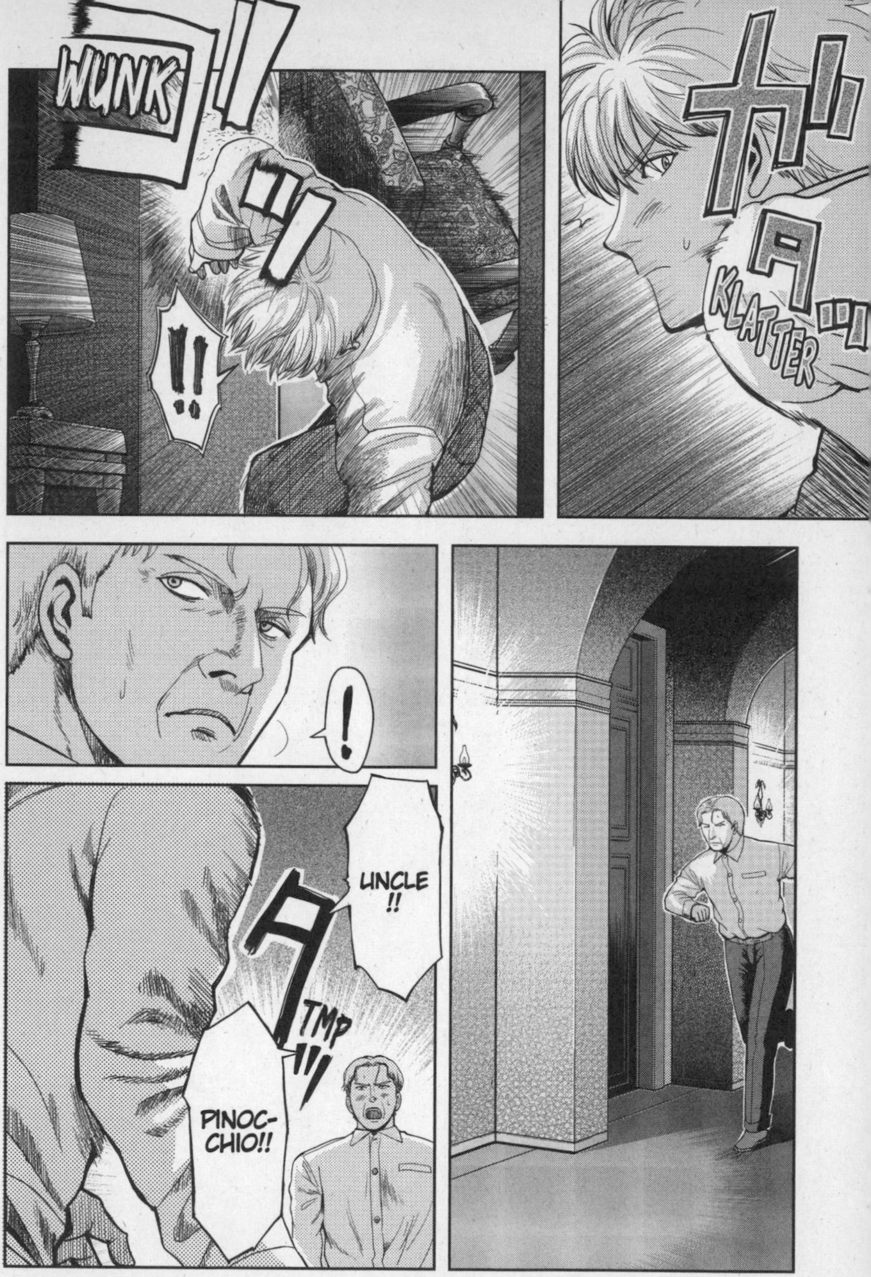
KLATTER
WUNK
!!
!
UNCLE !!
TMP
PINOC-CHIO!!

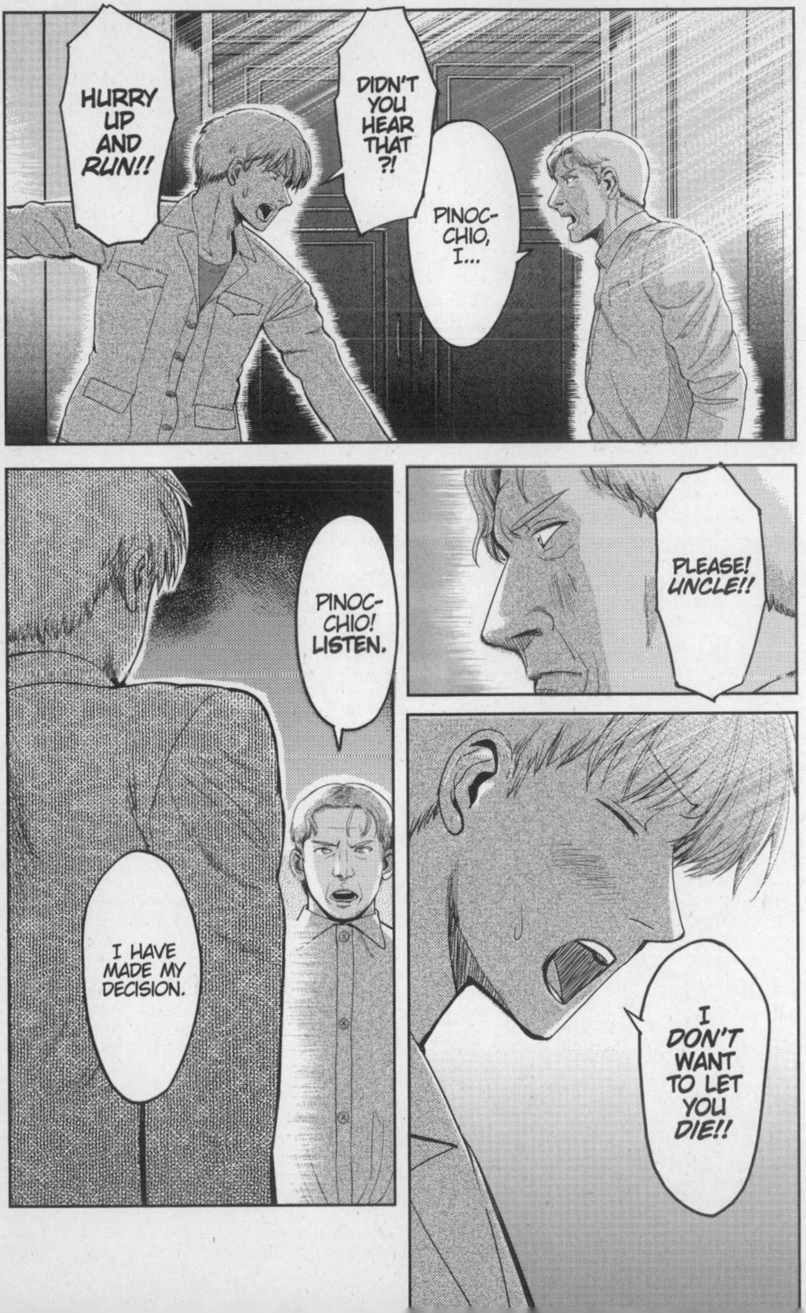
PINOCCHIO, I...
DIDN'T YOU HEAR THAT?!
HURRY UP AND RUN!!
PLEASE! UNCLE!!
I DON'T WANT TO LET YOU DIE!!
PINOCCHIO! LISTEN.
I HAVE MADE MY DECISION.

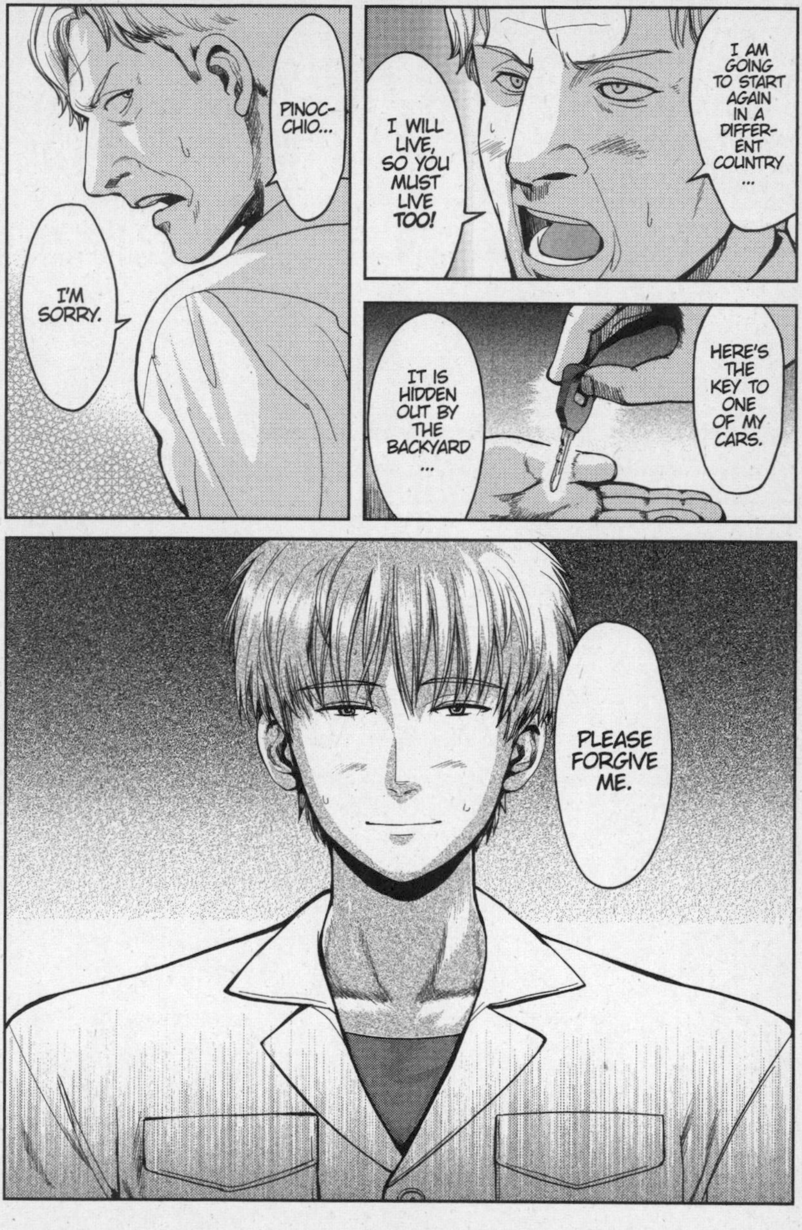
I AM GOING TO START AGAIN IN A DIFFERENT COUNTRY ...
I WILL LIVE, SO YOU MUST LIVE TOO!
HERE'S THE KEY TO ONE OF MY CARS.
IT IS HIDDEN OUT BY THE BACKYARD ...
PINOCCHIO...
I'M SORRY.
PLEASE FORGIVE ME.

GUNSLINGERGIRL.

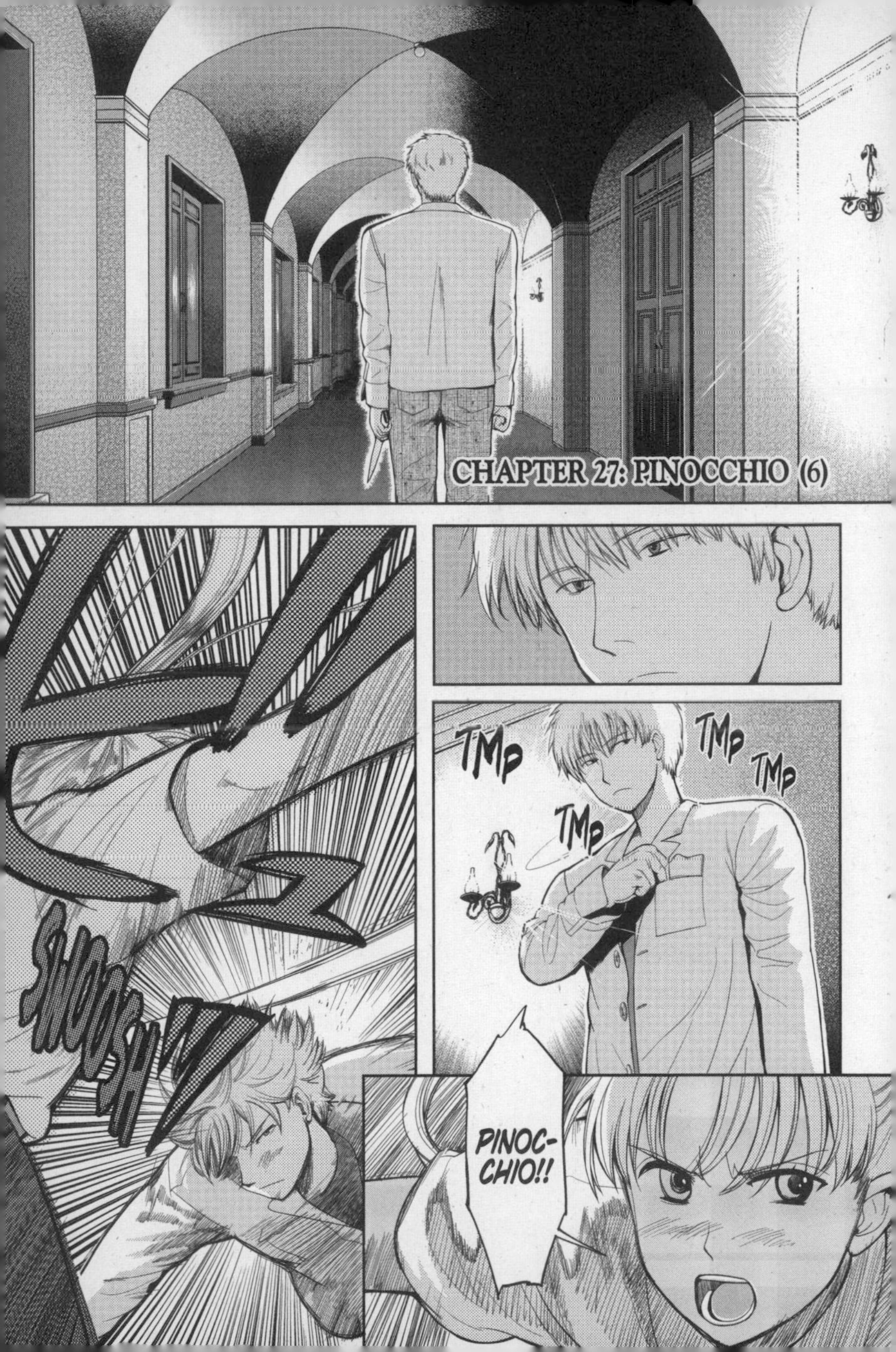
CHAPTER 27: PINOCCHIO (6)
TMP
TMP
TMP
TMP
PINOC-
CHIO!!
SHOOSH

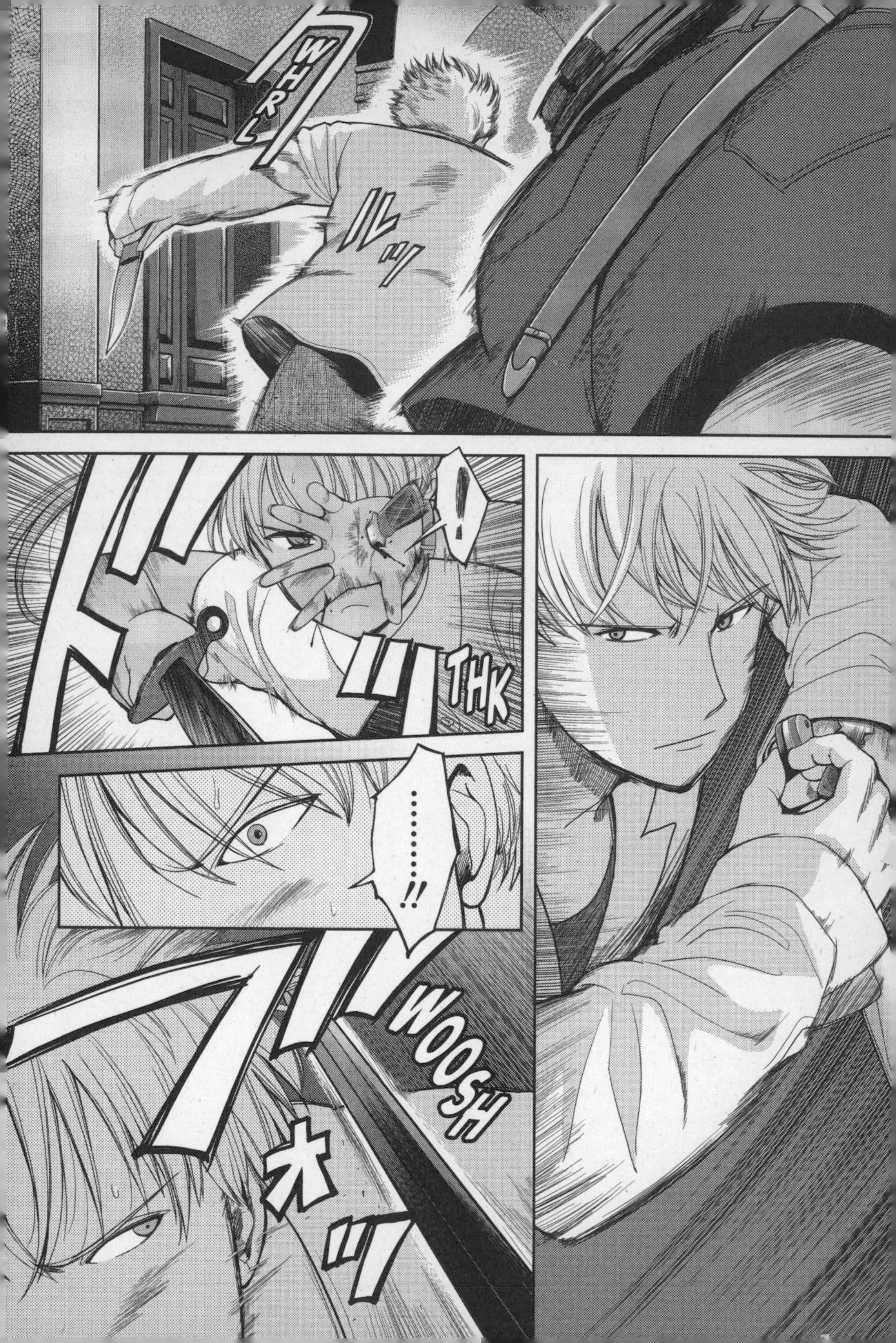
WHRL
ルッ
!
THK
......!!
WOOSH
オッ

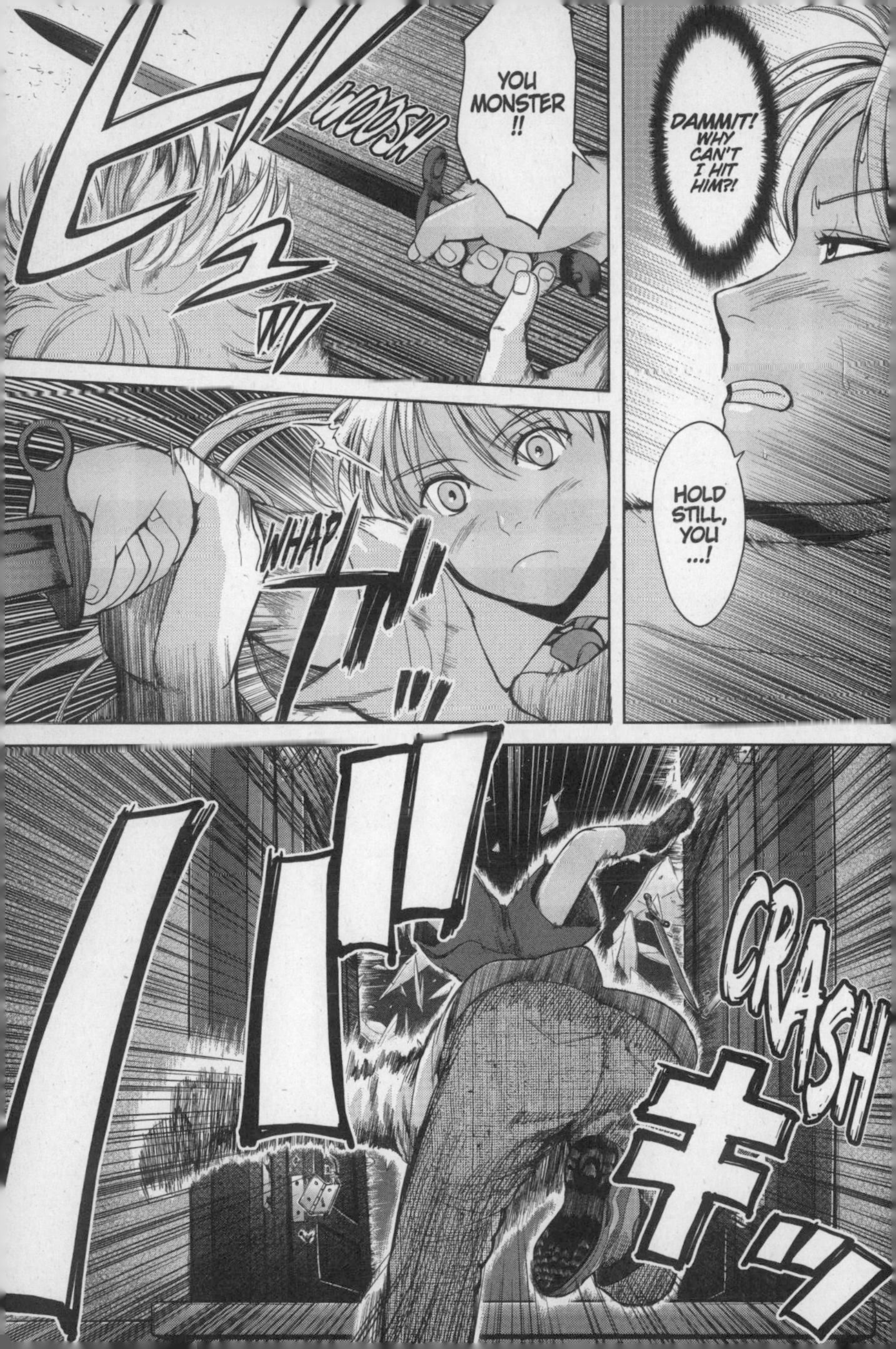
DAMMIT! WHY CAN'T I HIT HIM?!
HOLD STILL, YOU ...!
YOU MONSTER !!
WHOOSH
WHAP
CRASH

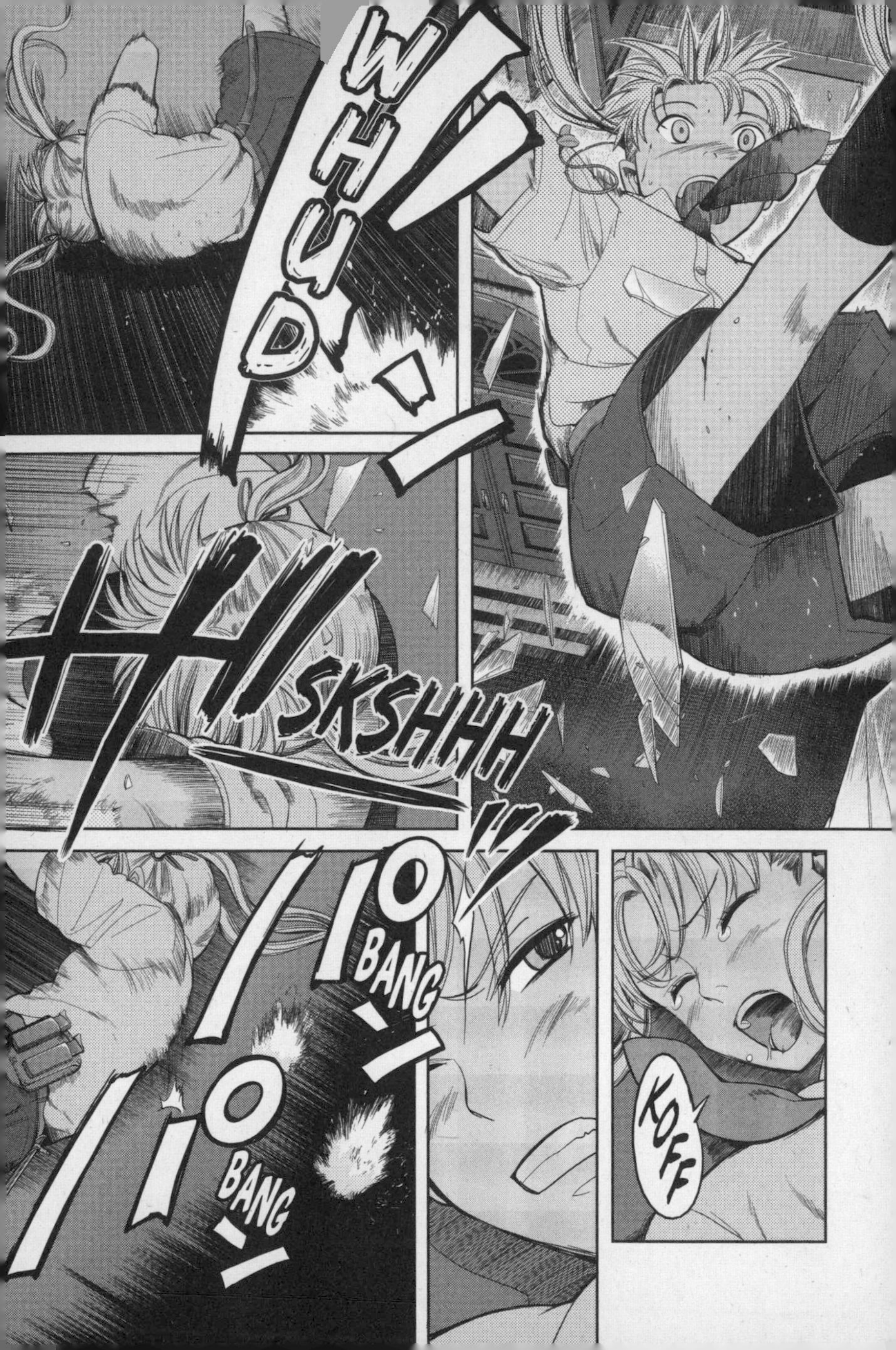
WHUD!!
SKSHHH!!
KOFF
BANG!
BANG!

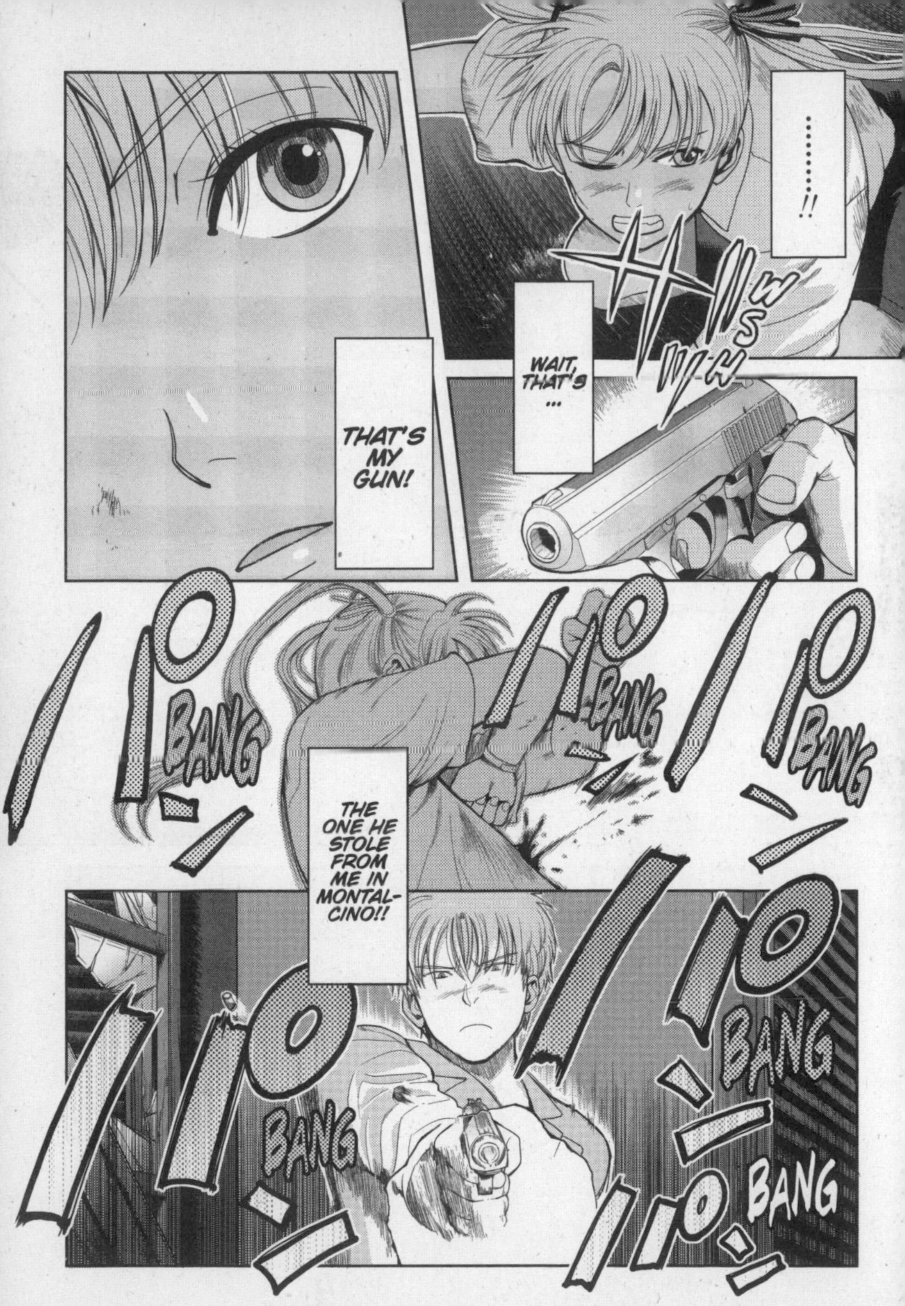

......!!
WSH
WAIT, THAT'S ...
THAT'S MY GUN!
BANG
BANG
BANG
THE ONE HE STOLE FROM ME IN MONTAL-CINO!!
BANG
BANG
BANG

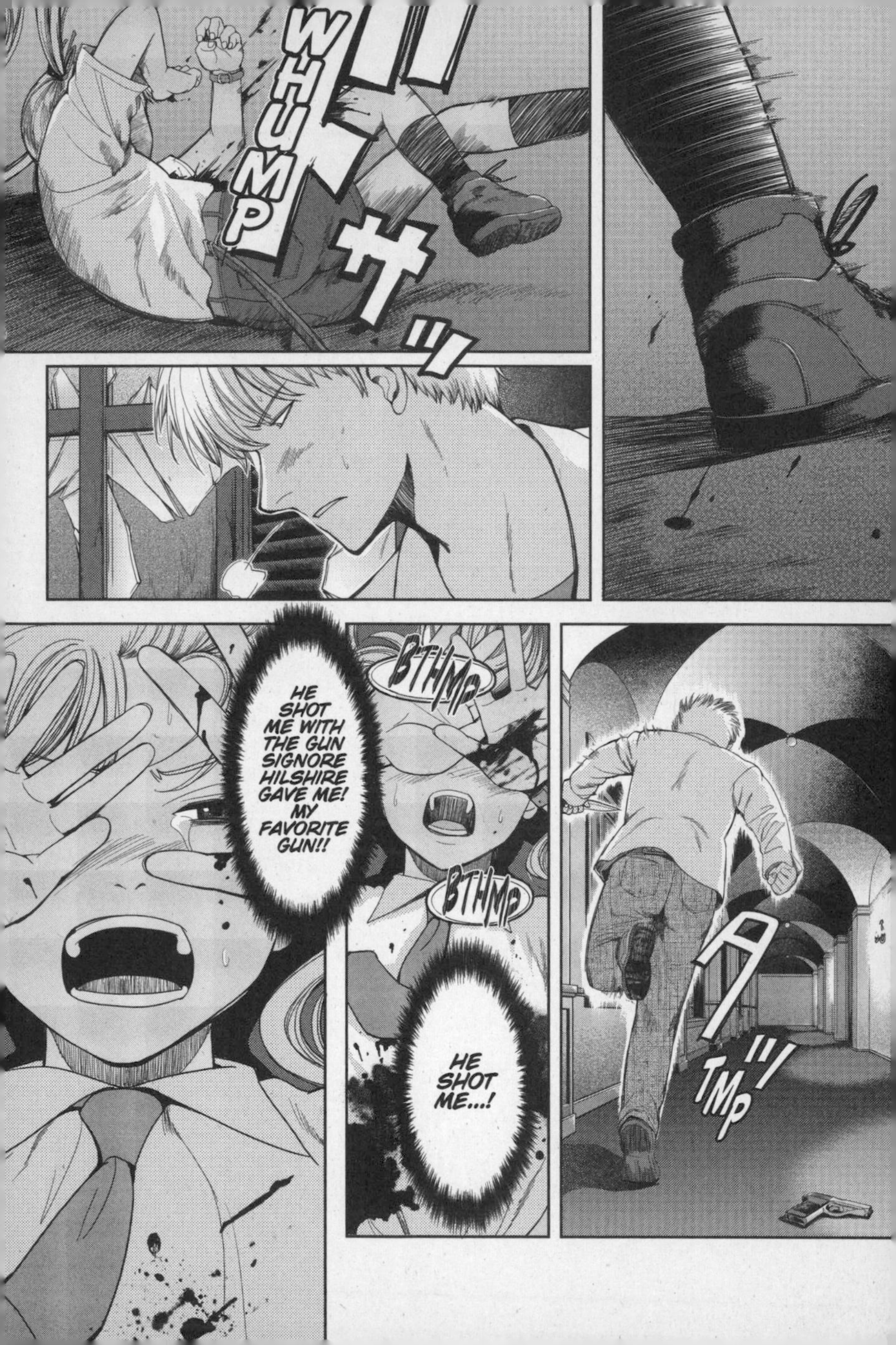
WHUMP
サッ
A
TMP
BTHMP
BTHMP
HE SHOT ME...!
HE SHOT ME WITH THE GUN SIGNORE HILSHIRE GAVE ME! MY FAVORITE GUN!!

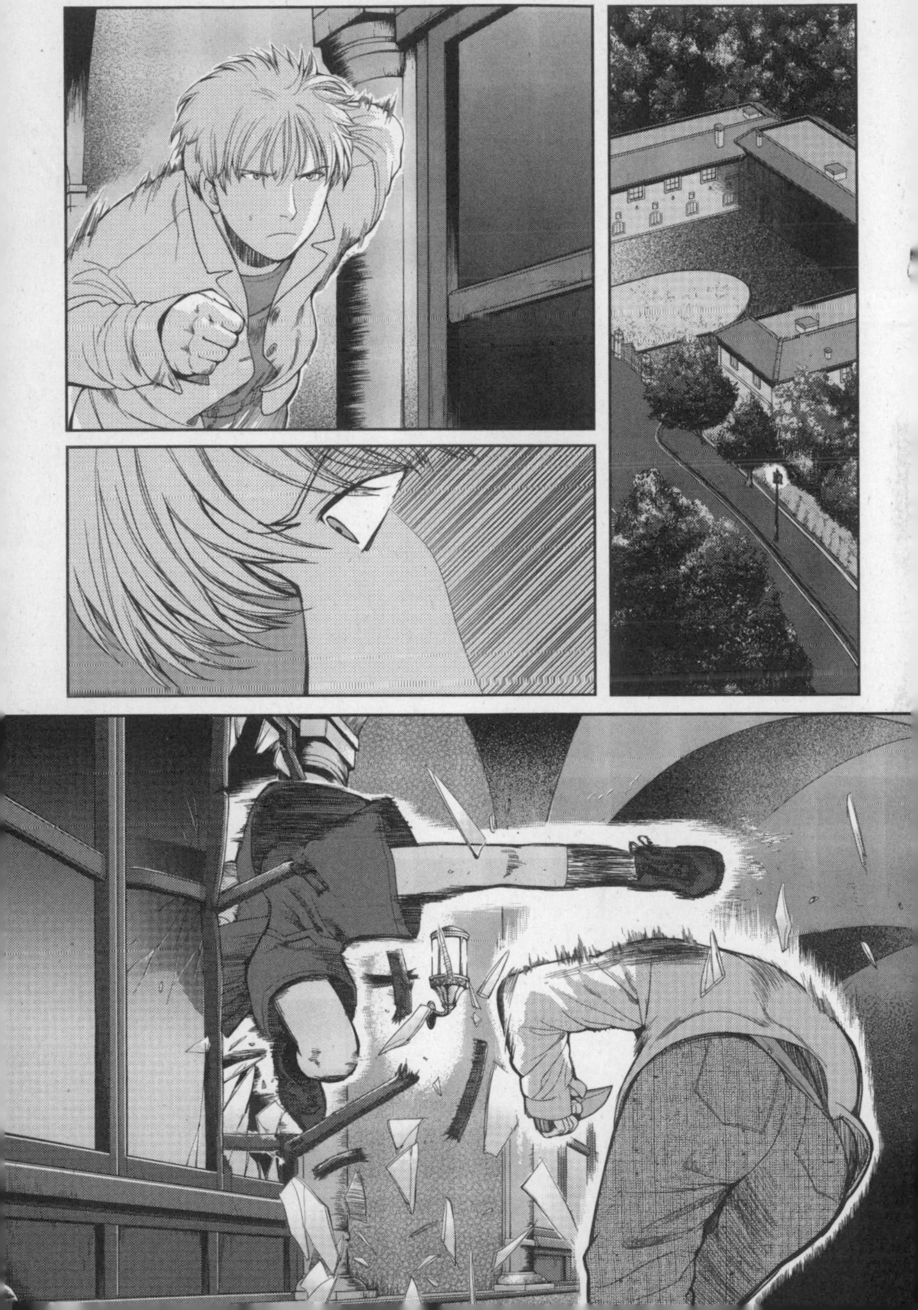

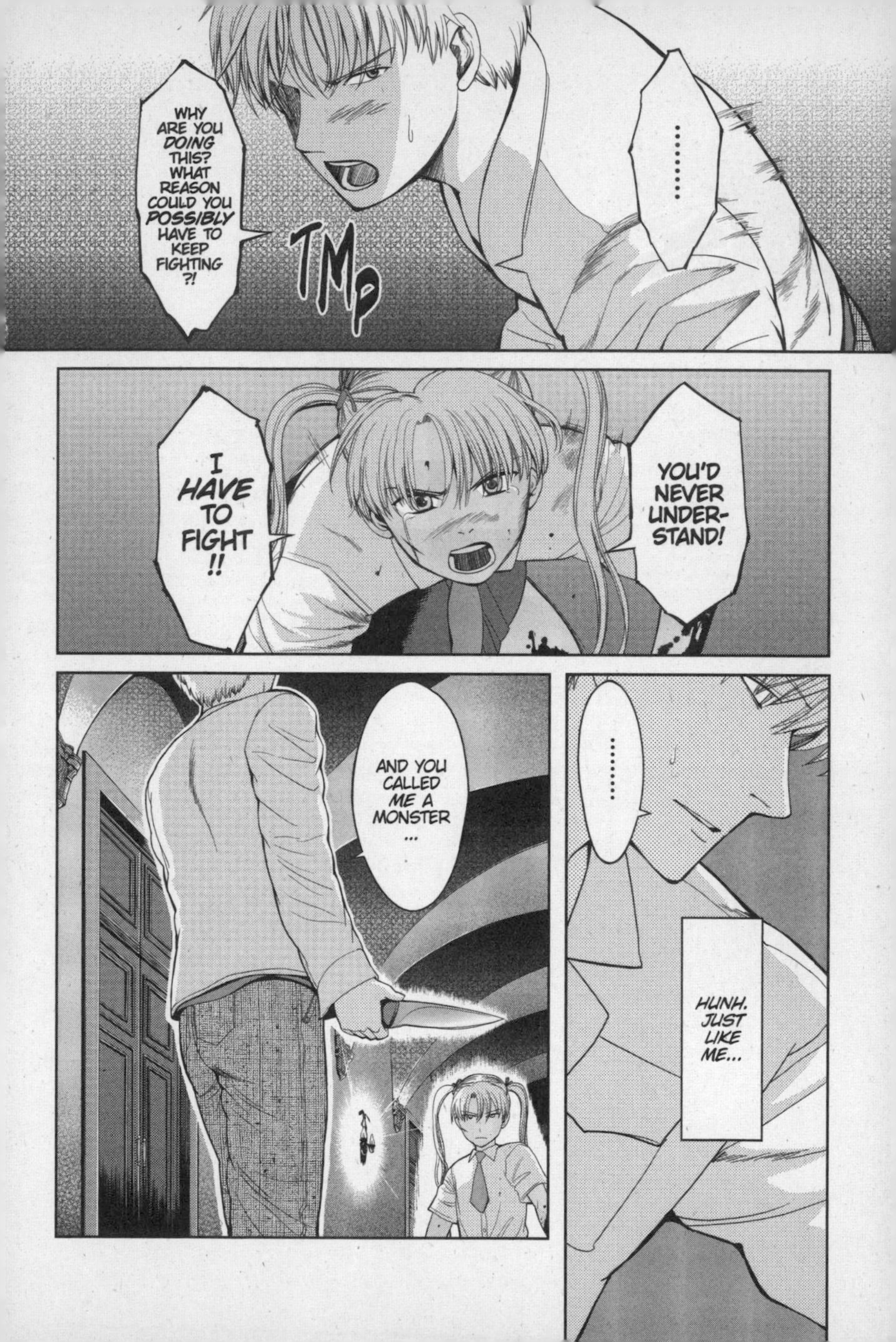
......
WHY ARE YOU DOING THIS? WHAT REASON COULD YOU POSSIBLY HAVE TO KEEP FIGHTING ?!
TMP
YOU'D NEVER UNDER-STAND!
I HAVE TO FIGHT !!
......
HUNH. JUST LIKE ME...
AND YOU CALLED ME A MONSTER ...

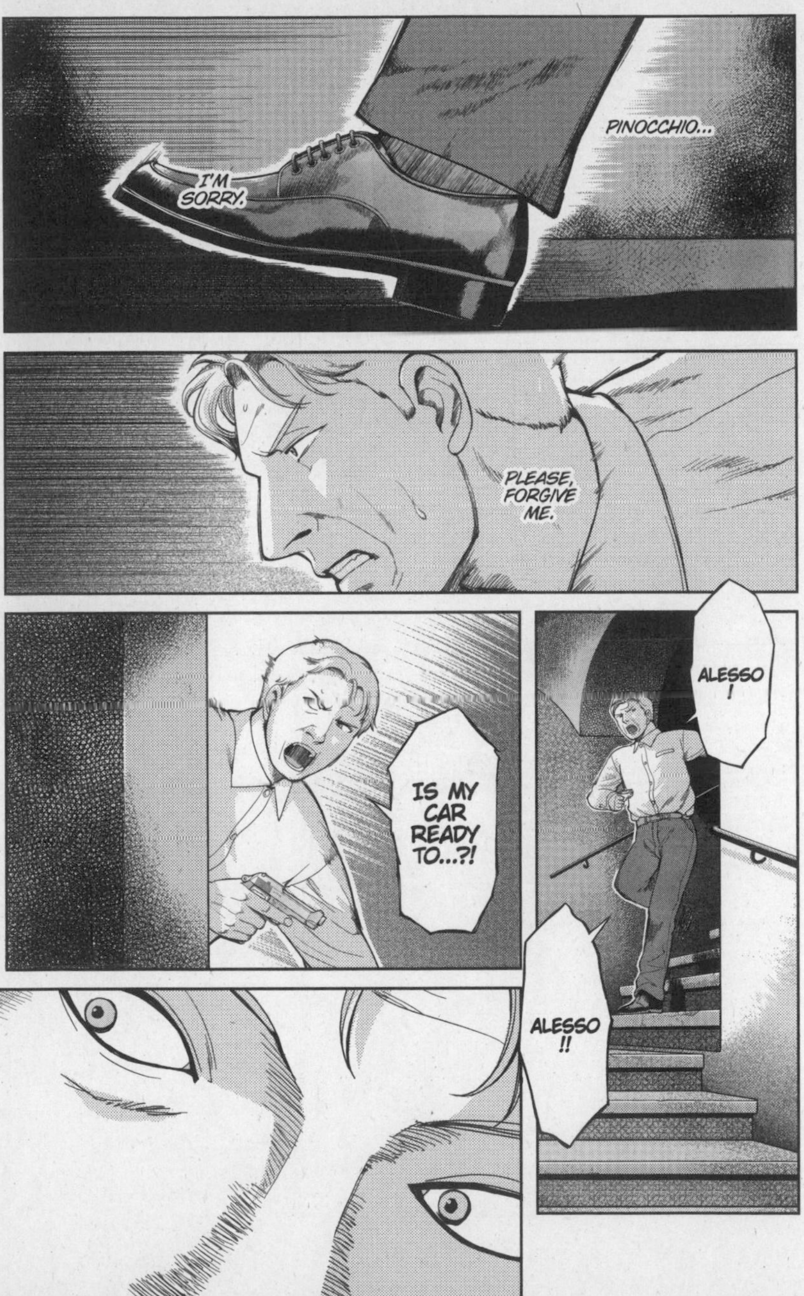
PINOCCHIO...
I'M SORRY.
PLEASE, FORGIVE ME.
ALESSO!
ALESSO!!
IS MY CAR READY TO...?!

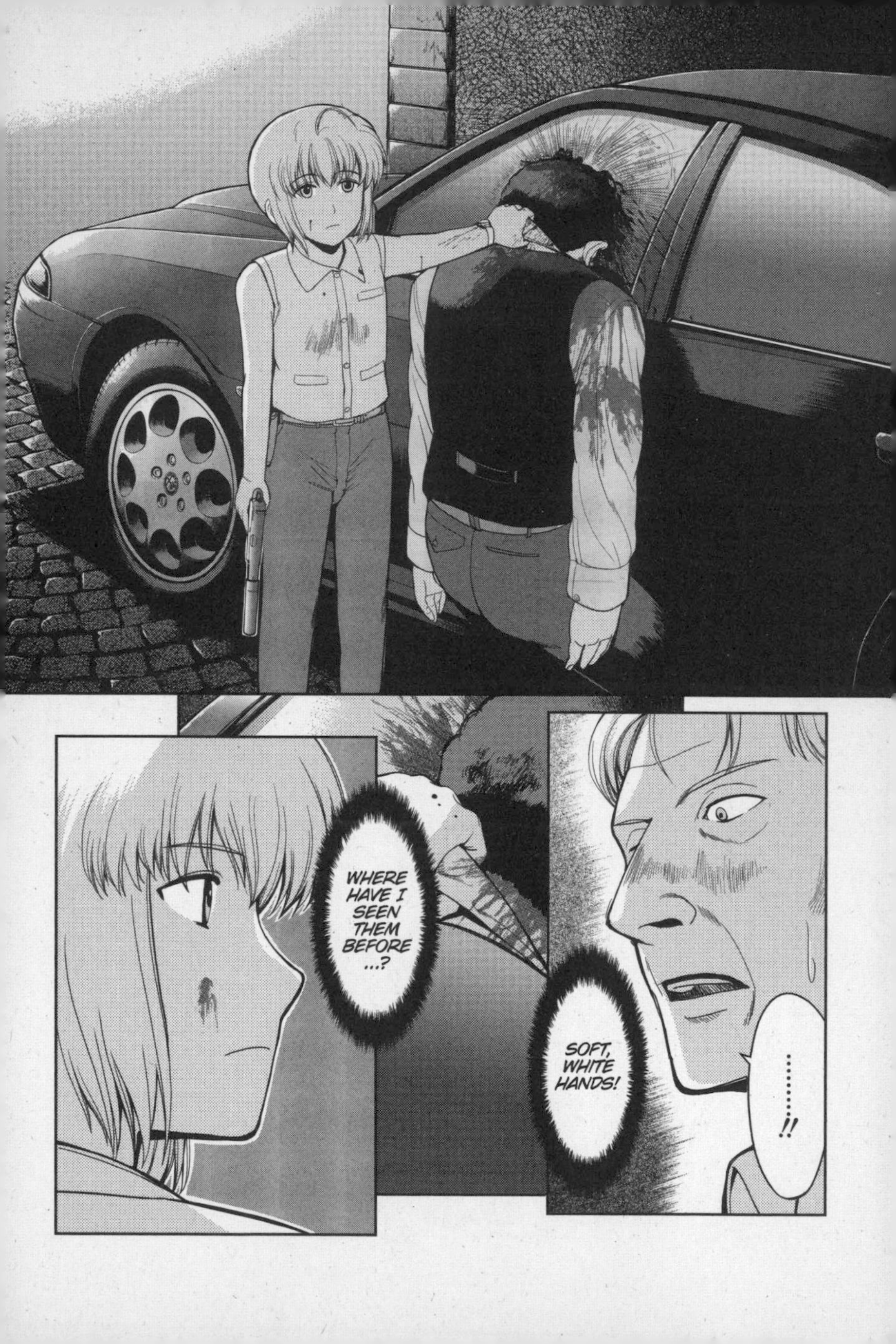
......!!
SOFT, WHITE HANDS!
WHERE HAVE I SEEN THEM BEFORE ...?

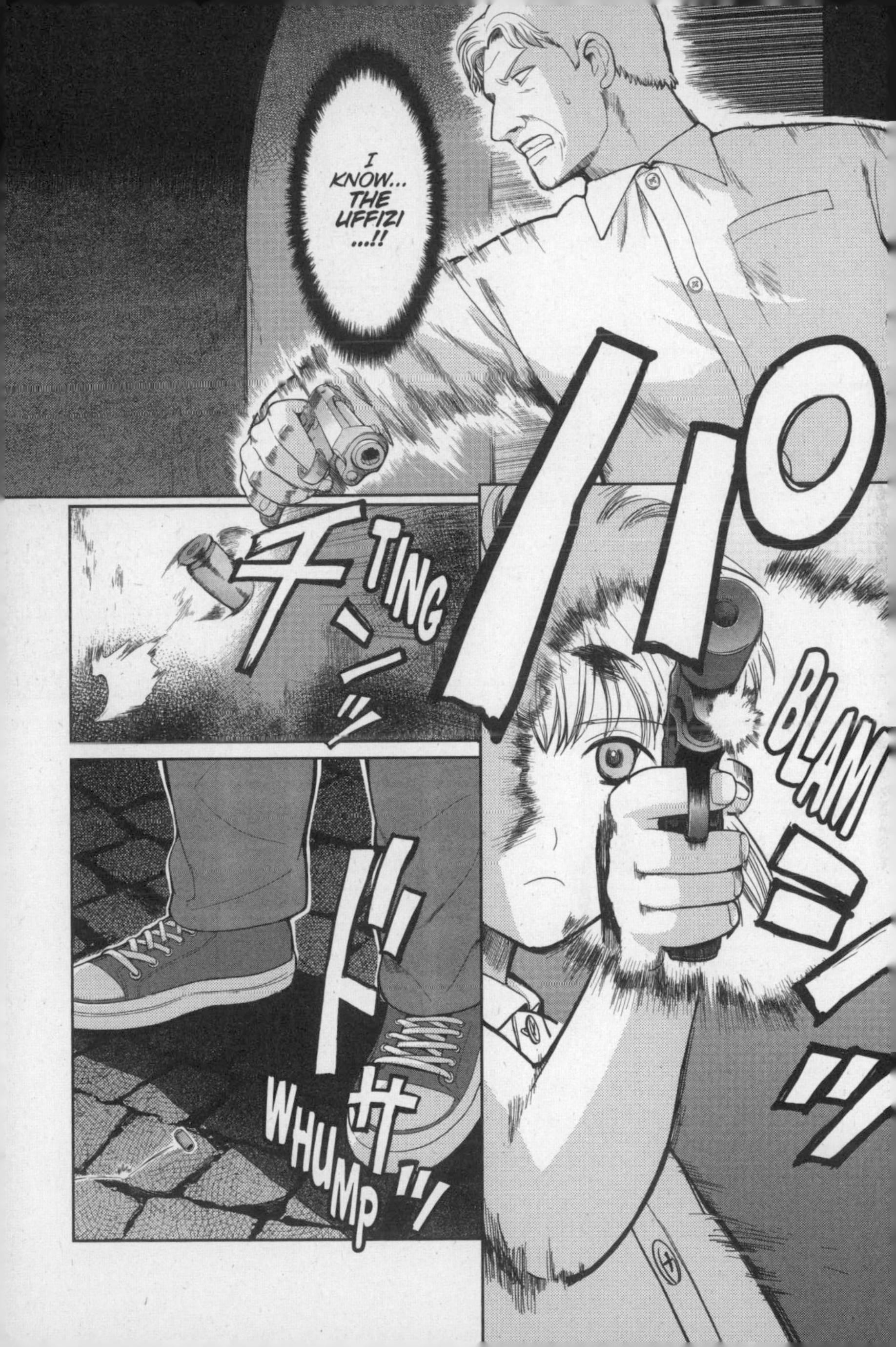
I KNOW... THE UFFIZI ...!!
BLAM
TING
WHUMP

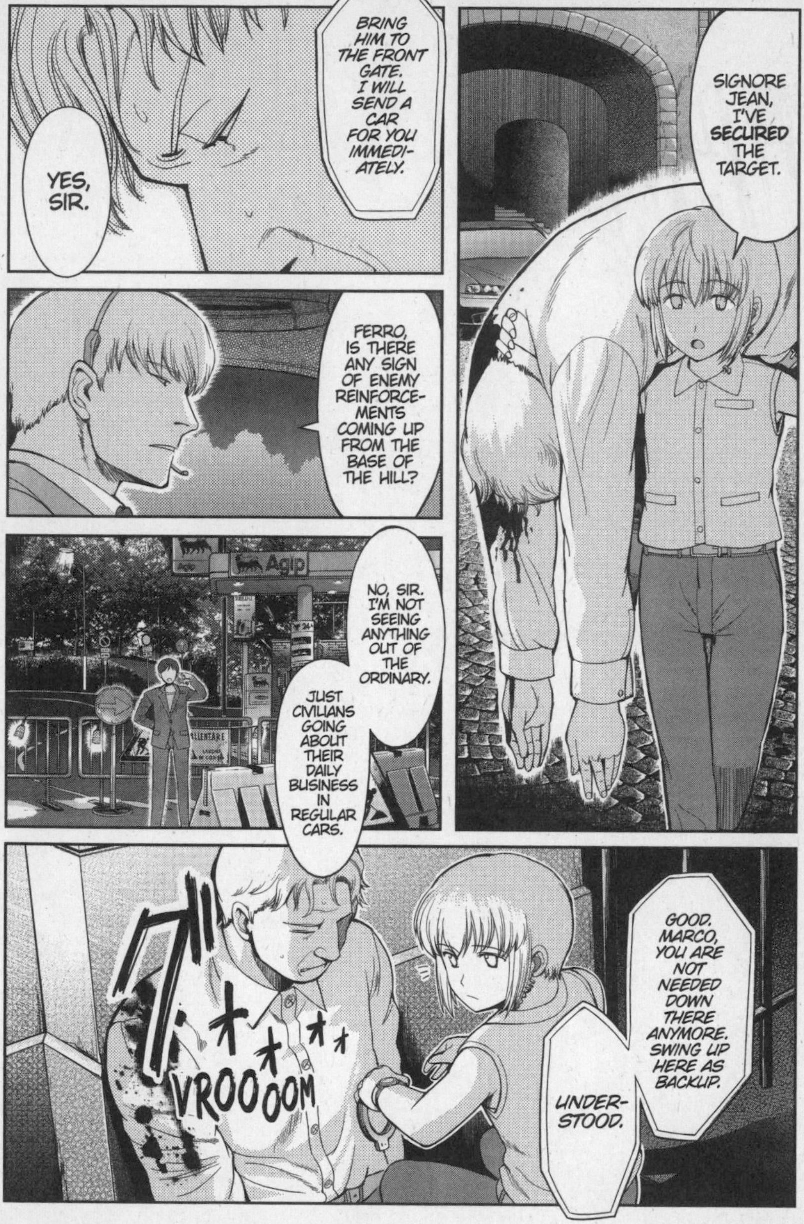
SIGNORE JEAN, I'VE SECURED THE TARGET.
BRING HIM TO THE FRONT GATE. I WILL SEND A CAR FOR YOU IMMEDIATELY.
YES, SIR.
FERRO, IS THERE ANY SIGN OF ENEMY REINFORCEMENTS COMING UP FROM THE BASE OF THE HILL?
Agip
NO, SIR. I'M NOT SEEING ANYTHING OUT OF THE ORDINARY.
JUST CIVILIANS GOING ABOUT THEIR DAILY BUSINESS IN REGULAR CARS.
VROOOOM
GOOD. MARCO, YOU ARE NOT NEEDED DOWN THERE ANYMORE. SWING UP HERE AS BACKUP.
UNDERSTOOD.

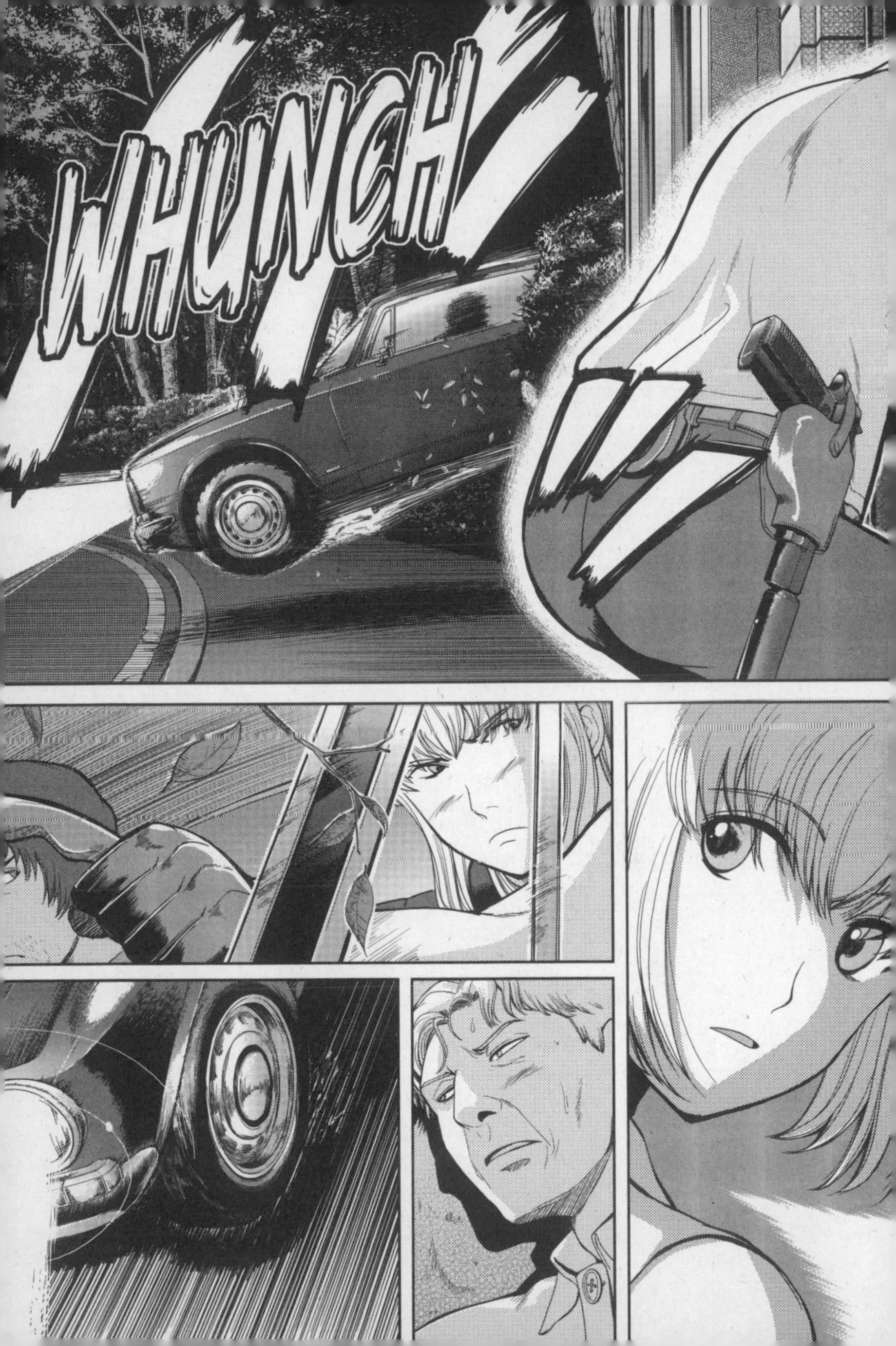
WHUNCH

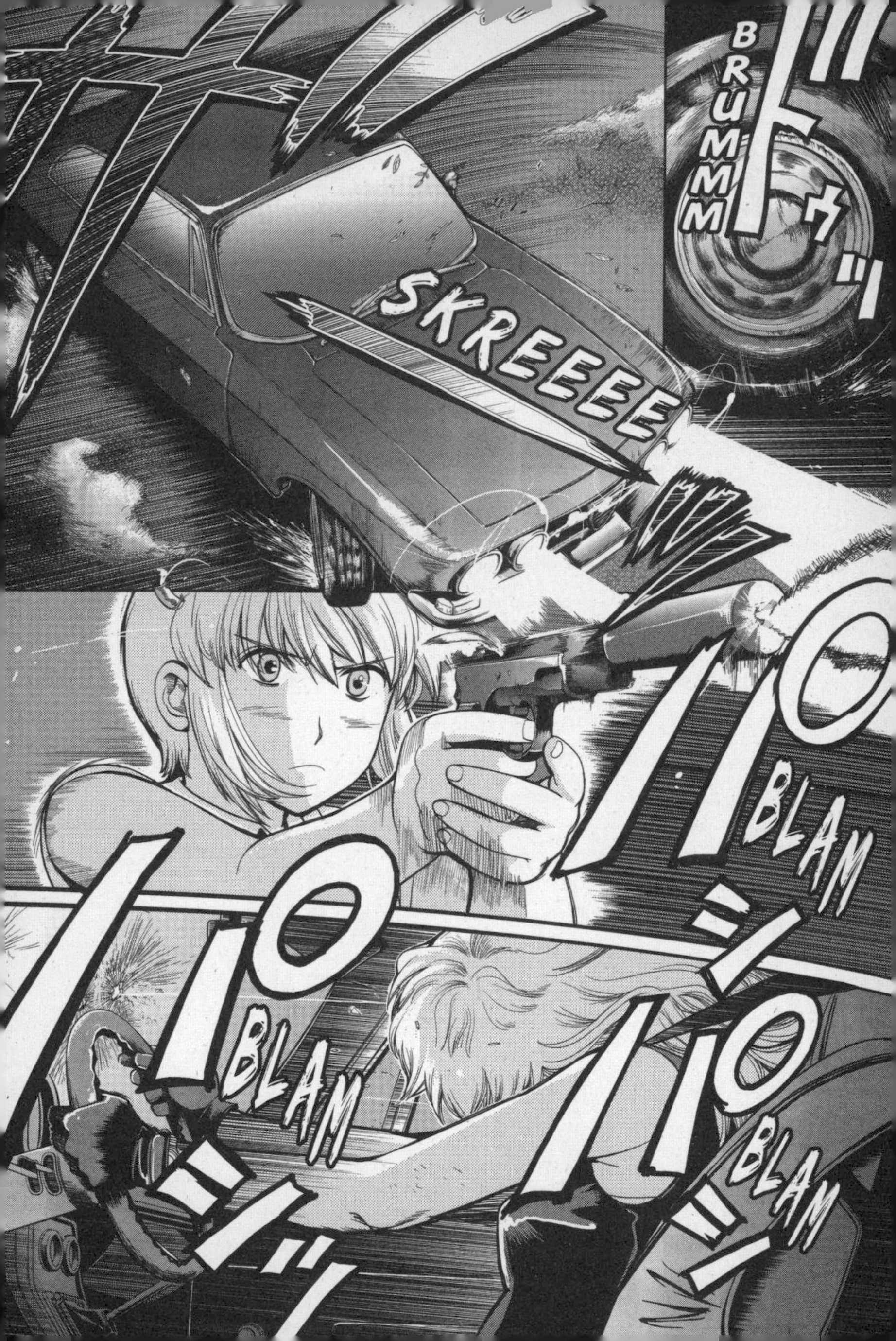
BRUMMM
SKREEEEE
BLAM
BLAM
BLAM

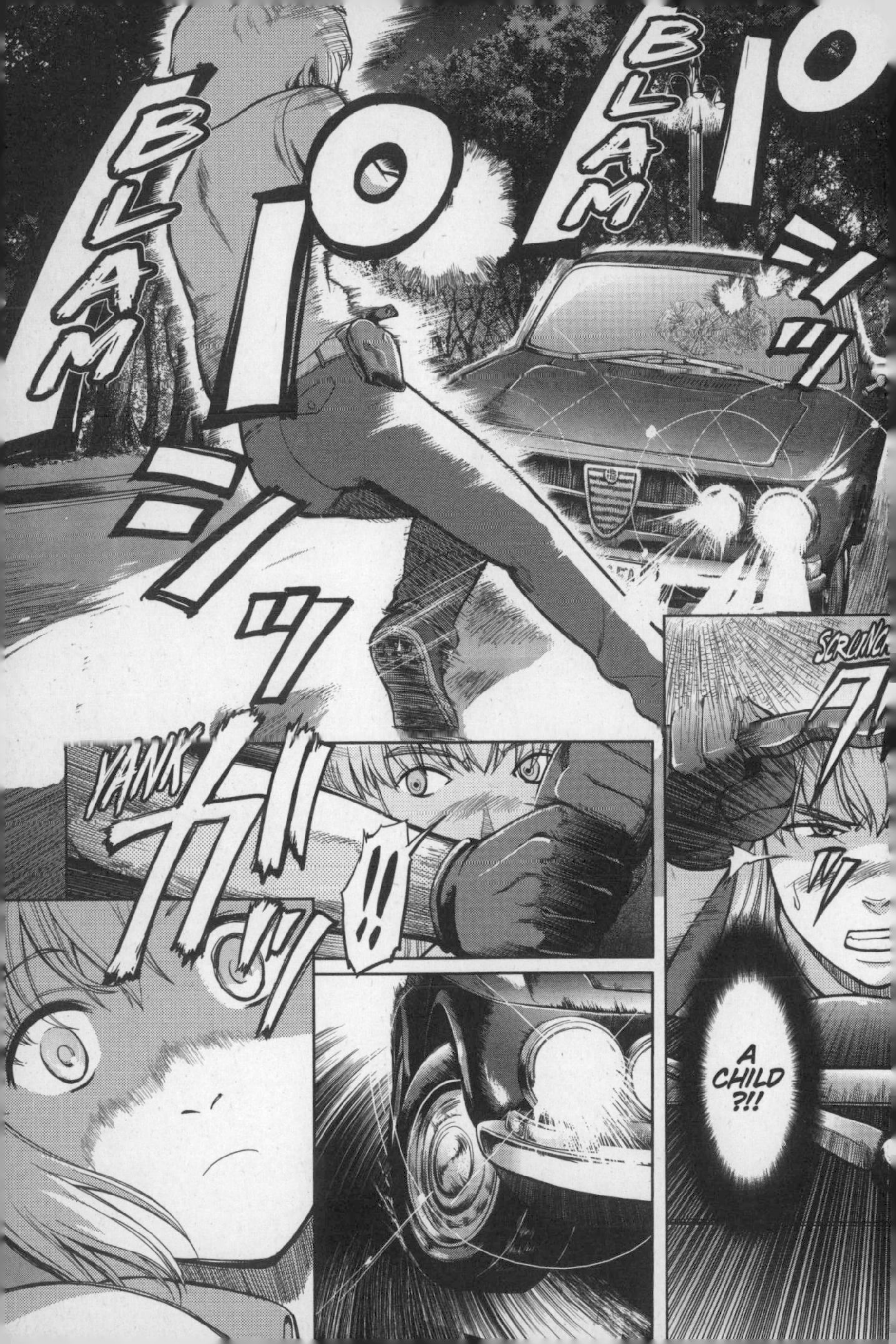
BLAM
BLAM
SCRUNC
A CHILD ?!!
YANK
!!

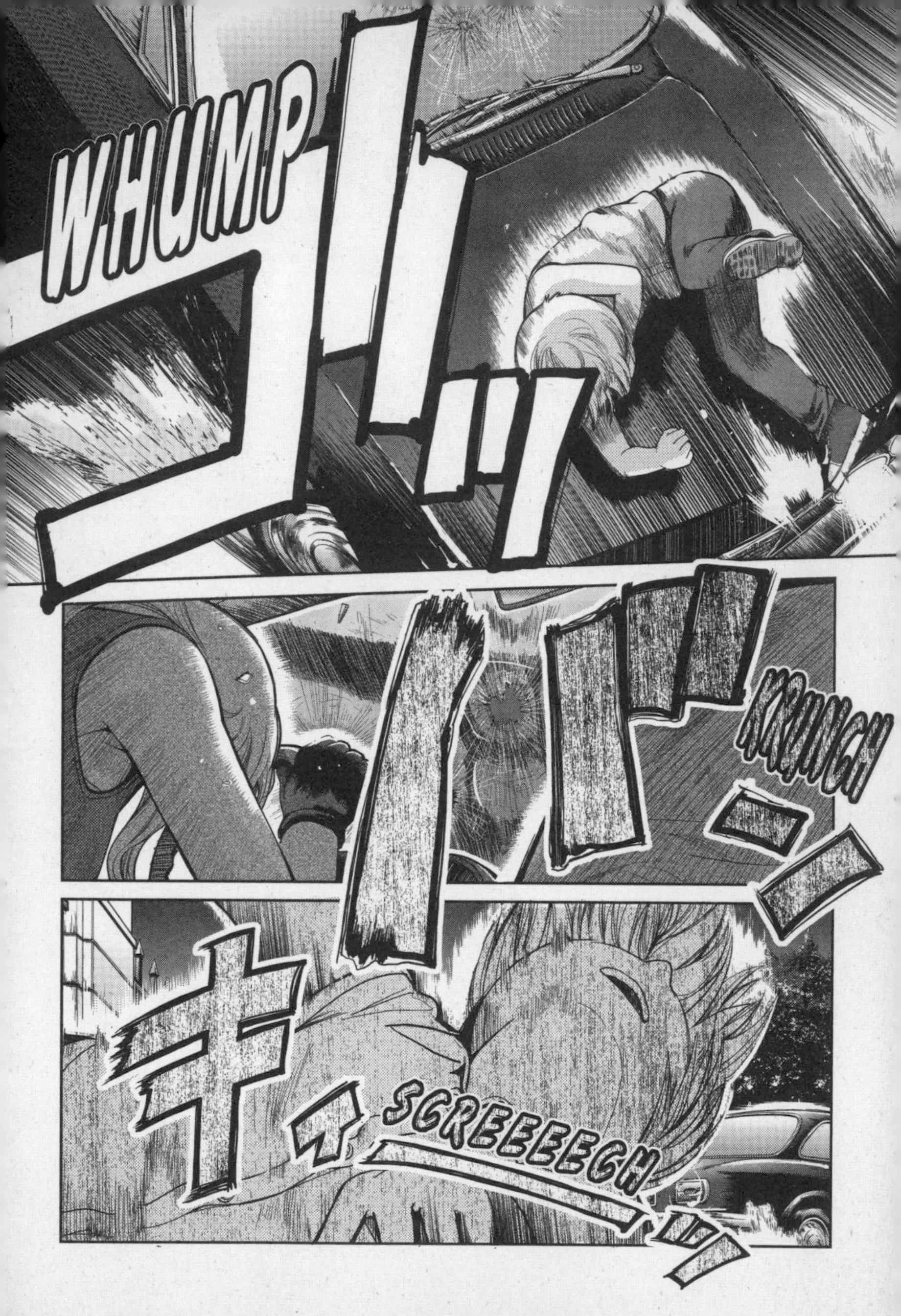
WHUMP
KRUNCH
SCREEEEEGH

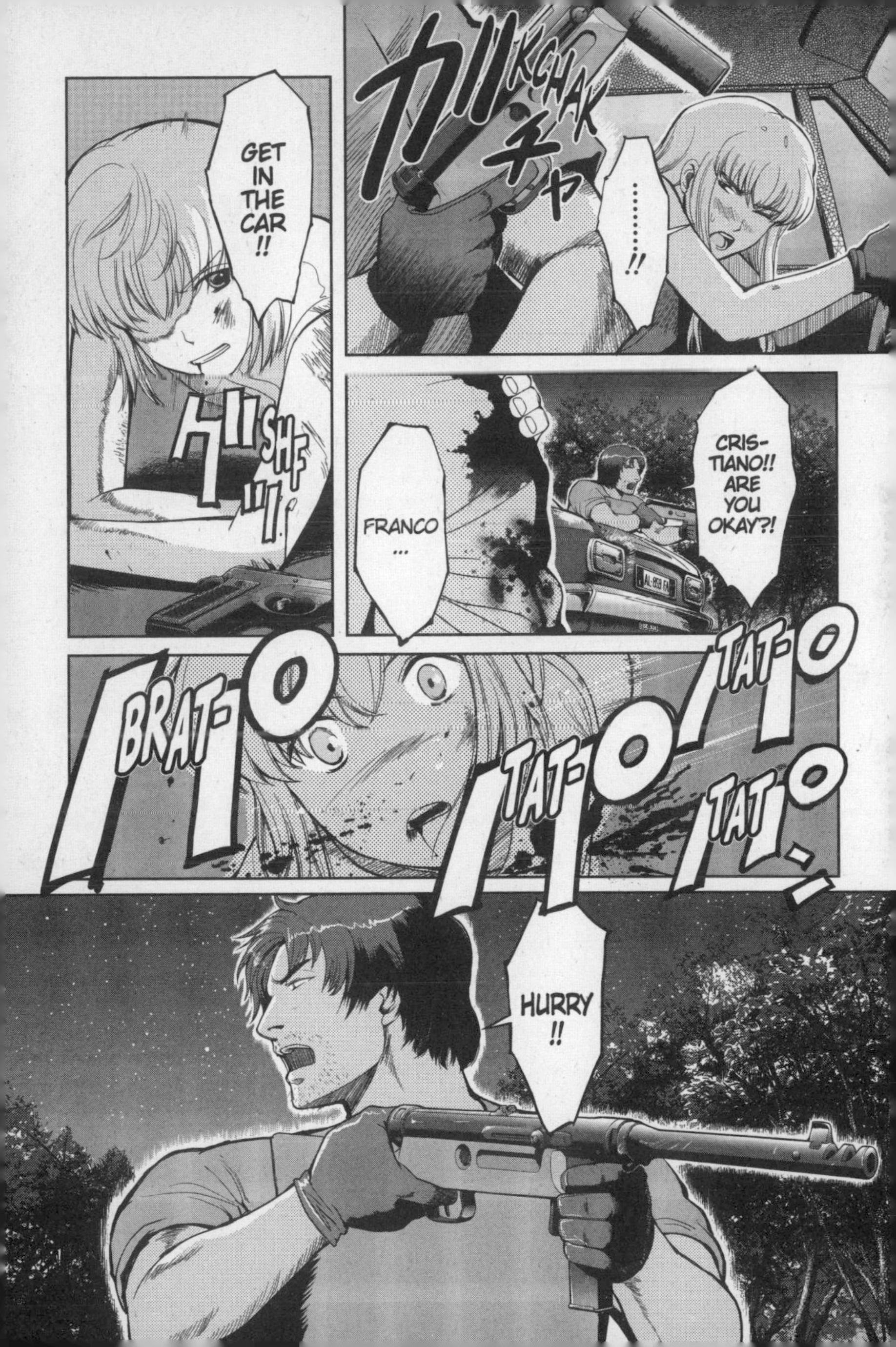
KCHAK
......!!
CRIS-TIANO!! ARE YOU OKAY?!
FRANCO ...
GET IN THE CAR!!
SHF
BRAT-TAT-TAT-TAT
HURRY!!

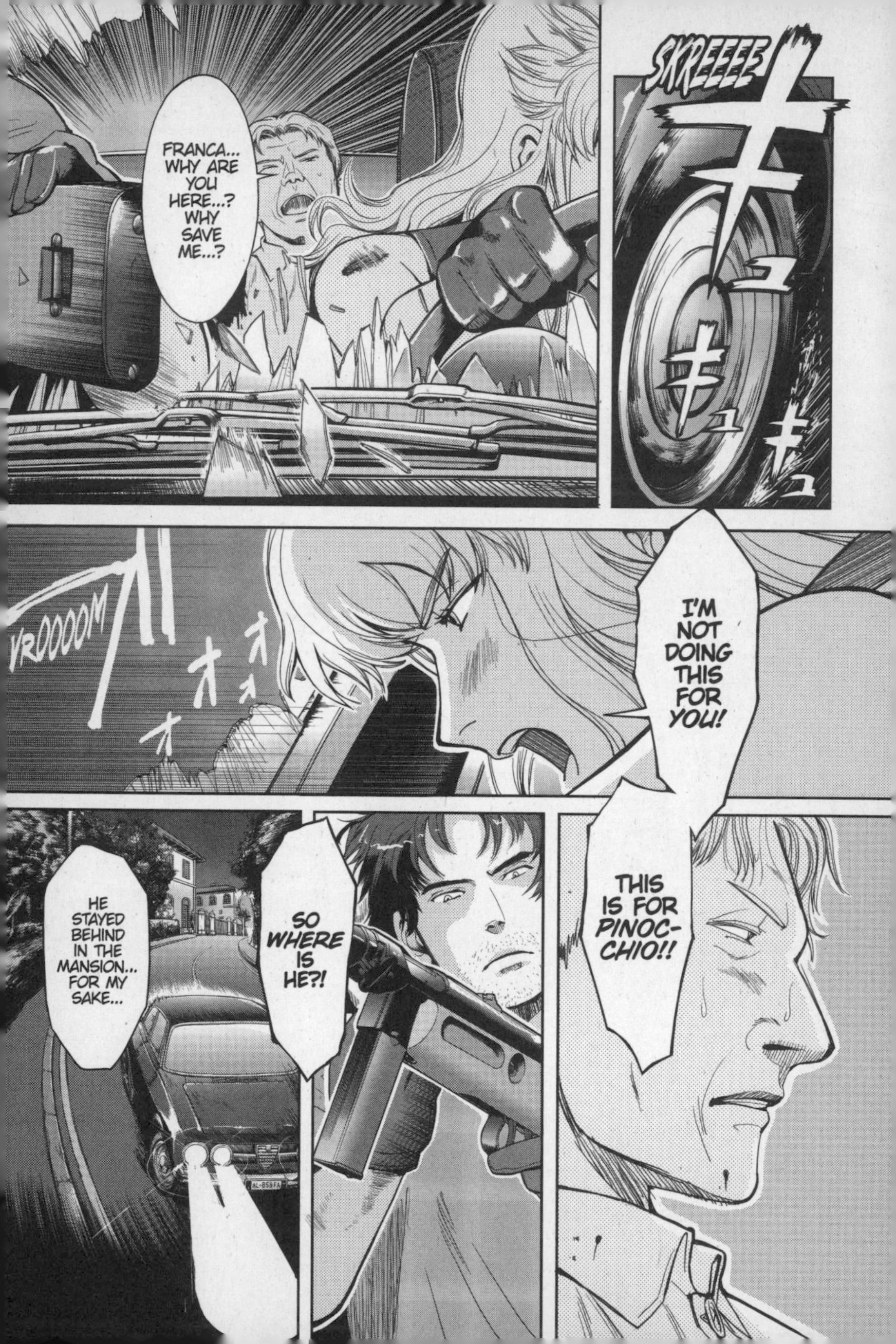
SKREEEE
FRANCA... WHY ARE YOU HERE...? WHY SAVE ME...?
I'M NOT DOING THIS FOR YOU!
VROOOOM
THIS IS FOR PINOC-CHIO!!
SO WHERE IS HE?!
HE STAYED BEHIND IN THE MANSION... FOR MY SAKE...

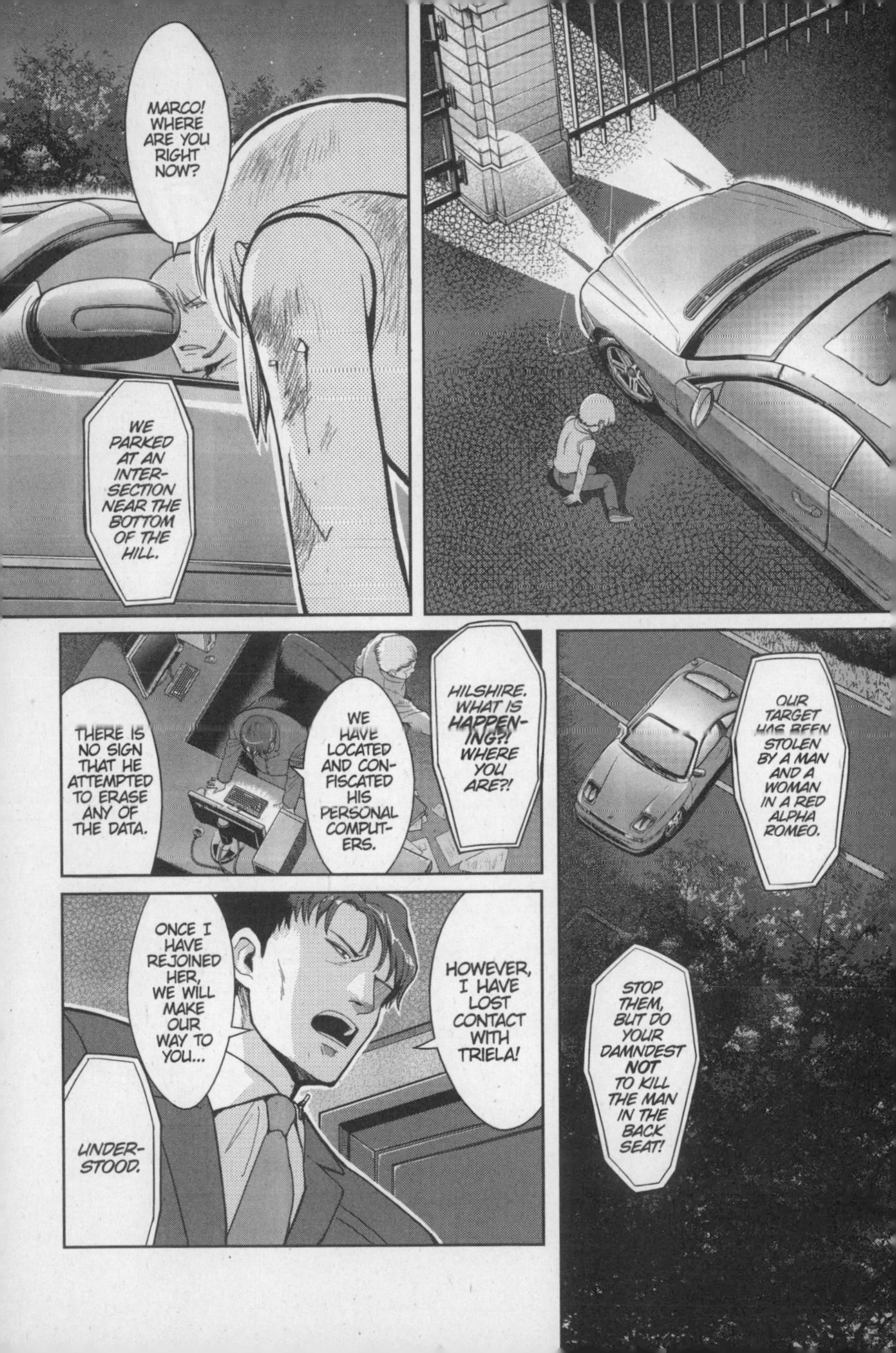
MARCO! WHERE ARE YOU RIGHT NOW?
WE PARKED AT AN INTERSECTION NEAR THE BOTTOM OF THE HILL.
OUR TARGET HAS BEEN STOLEN BY A MAN AND A WOMAN IN A RED ALPHA ROMEO.
STOP THEM, BUT DO YOUR DAMNDEST NOT TO KILL THE MAN IN THE BACK SEAT!
HILSHIRE. WHAT IS HAPPENING?! WHERE YOU ARE?!
WE HAVE LOCATED AND CONFISCATED HIS PERSONAL COMPUTERS.
THERE IS NO SIGN THAT HE ATTEMPTED TO ERASE ANY OF THE DATA.
HOWEVER, I HAVE LOST CONTACT WITH TRIELA!
ONCE I HAVE REJOINED HER, WE WILL MAKE OUR WAY TO YOU...
UNDERSTOOD.

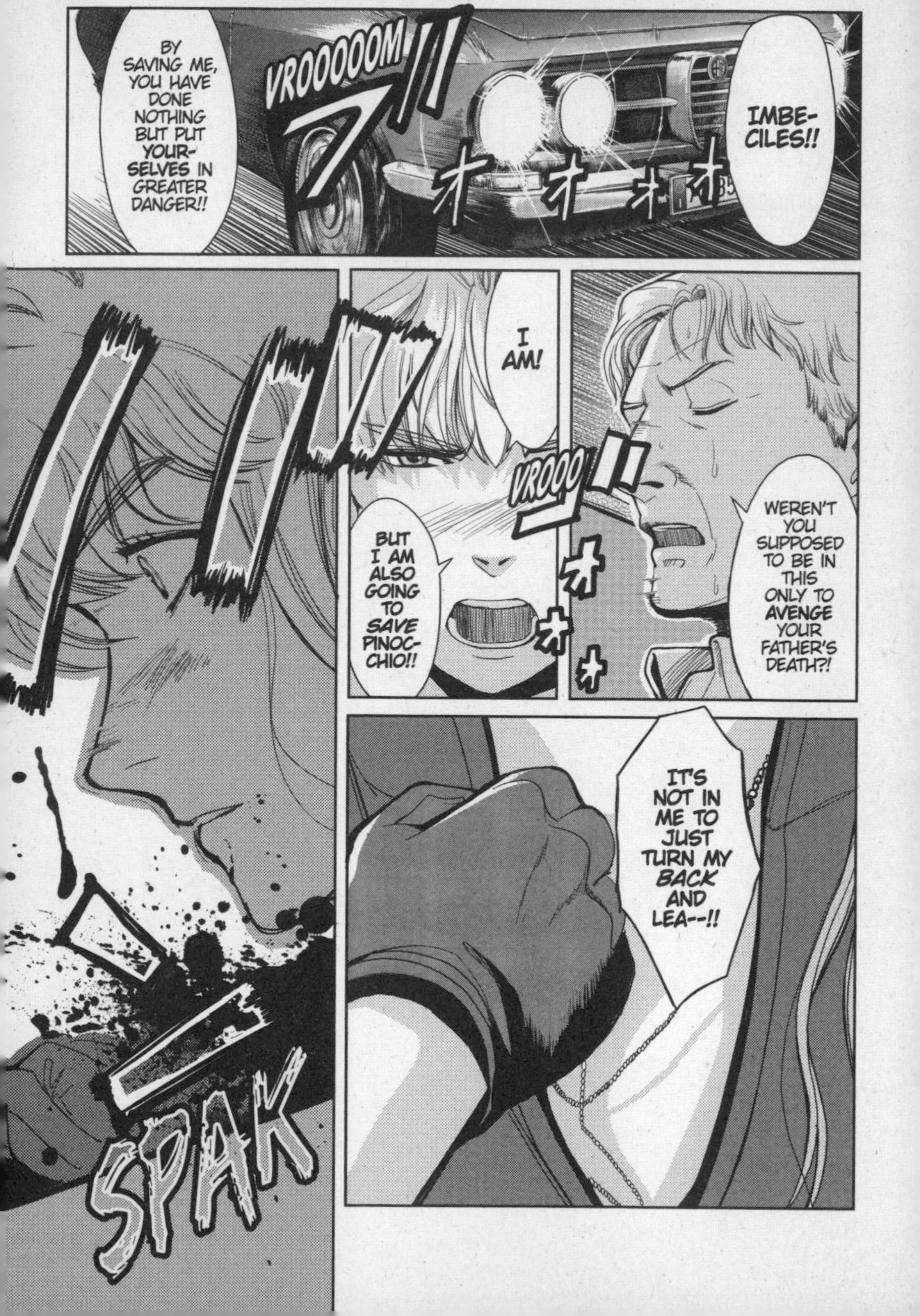
IMBE-CILES!!
VROOOOOM!!
オ オ オ オ
BY SAVING ME, YOU HAVE DONE NOTHING BUT PUT YOUR-SELVES IN GREATER DANGER!!
WEREN'T YOU SUPPOSED TO BE IN THIS ONLY TO AVENGE YOUR FATHER'S DEATH?!
I AM!
VROOO!!
オ オ オ
BUT I AM ALSO GOING TO SAVE PINOC-CHIO!!
IT'S NOT IN ME TO JUST TURN MY BACK AND LEA--!!
SPAK

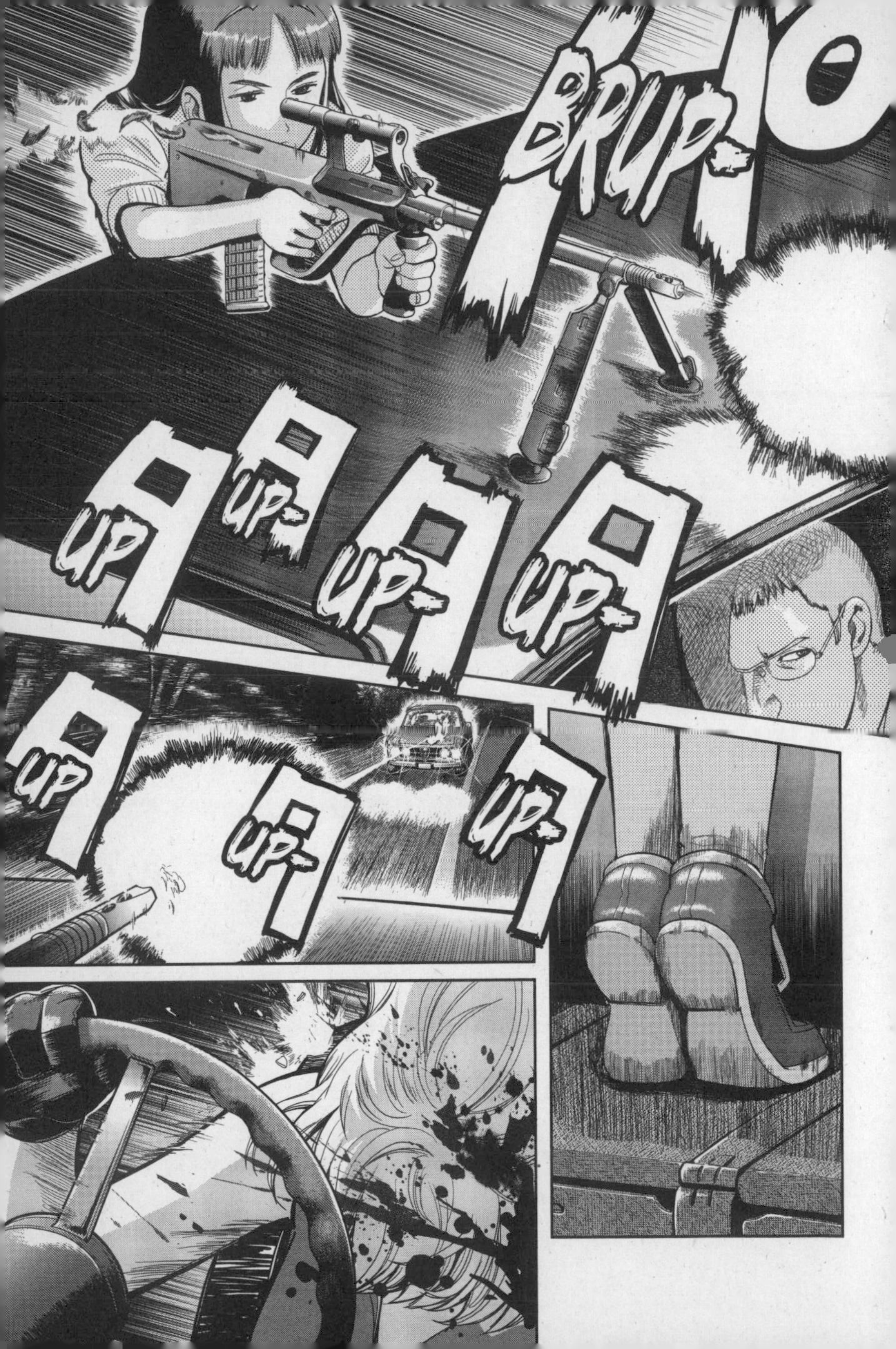
BRUP-
UP-
UP-
UP-
UP
UP-
UP-
UP

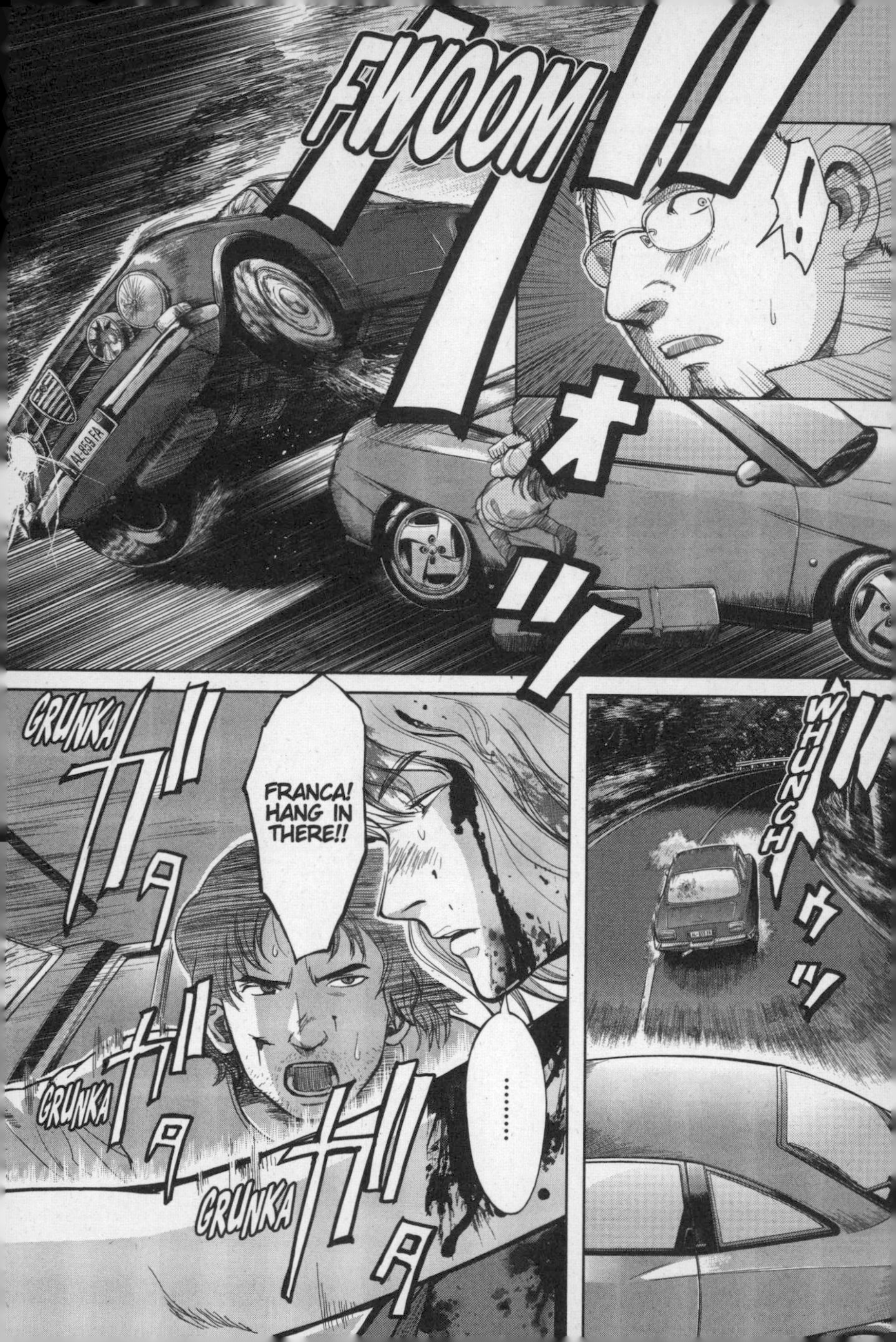
FWOOM
!
WHUNCH
GRUNKA
FRANCA! HANG IN THERE!!
GRUNKA
GRUNKA
......

FRANCA!!

I'M SORRY...

FRANCO...

THERE'S NO WAY WE'LL MAKE THIS TURN IF YOU DON'T SLOW DOWN!!

KEEP YOUR EYES OPEN! WATCH THE ROAD!!

YOU HAVE TO HIT THE BRAKES!!

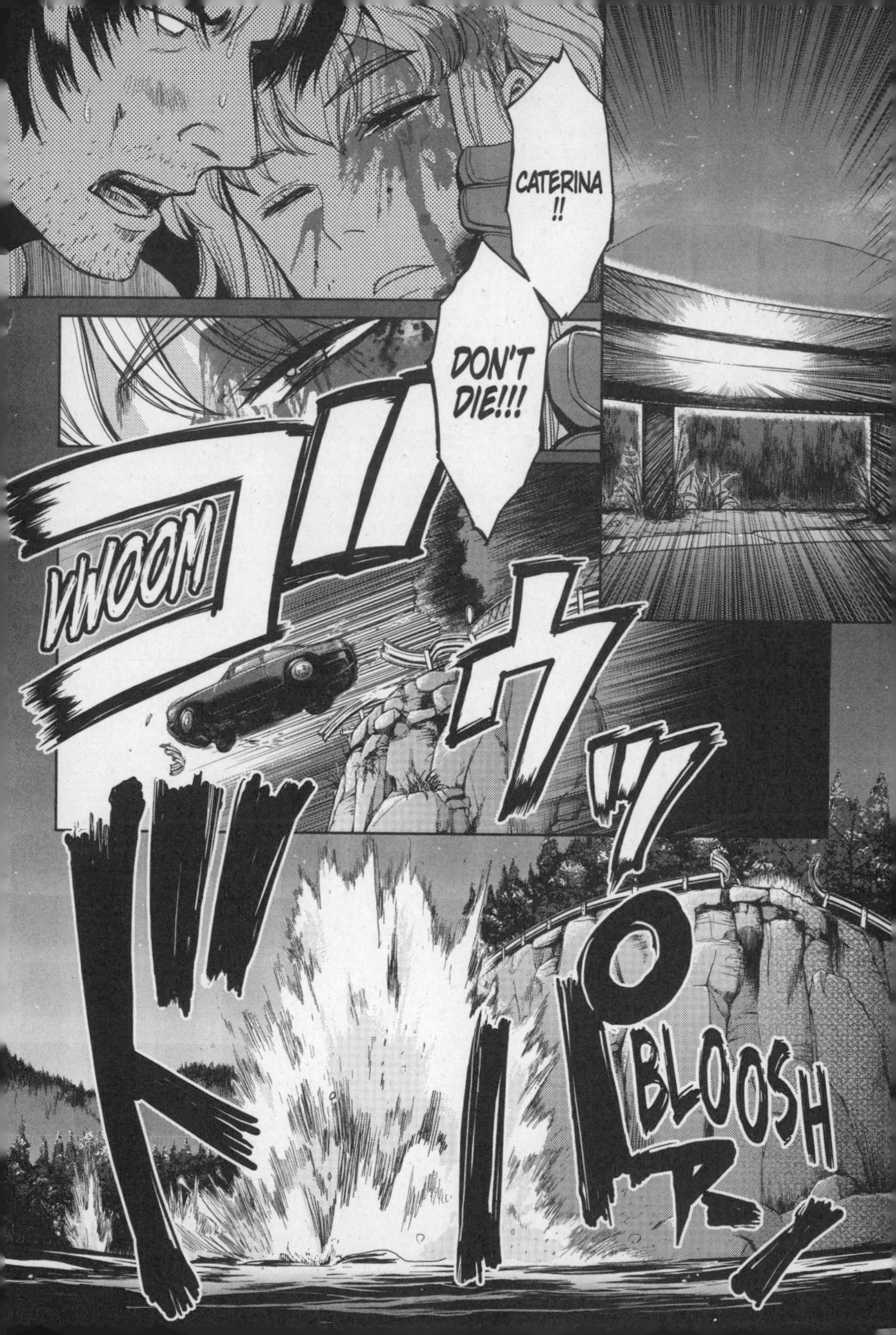
CATERINA!!
DON'T DIE!!!
VWOOM
BLOOSH

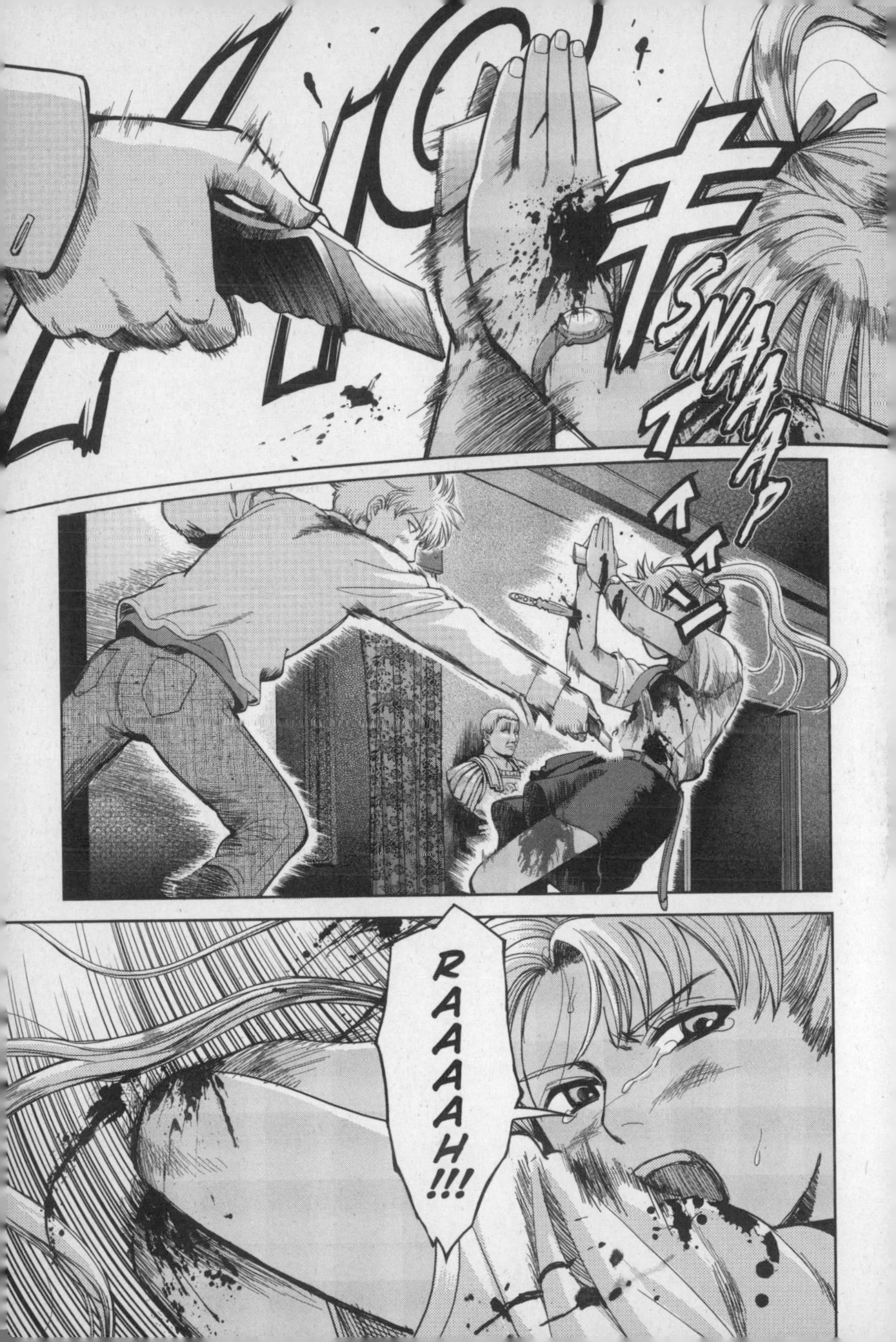
SNAAAP
RAAAAAH!!!

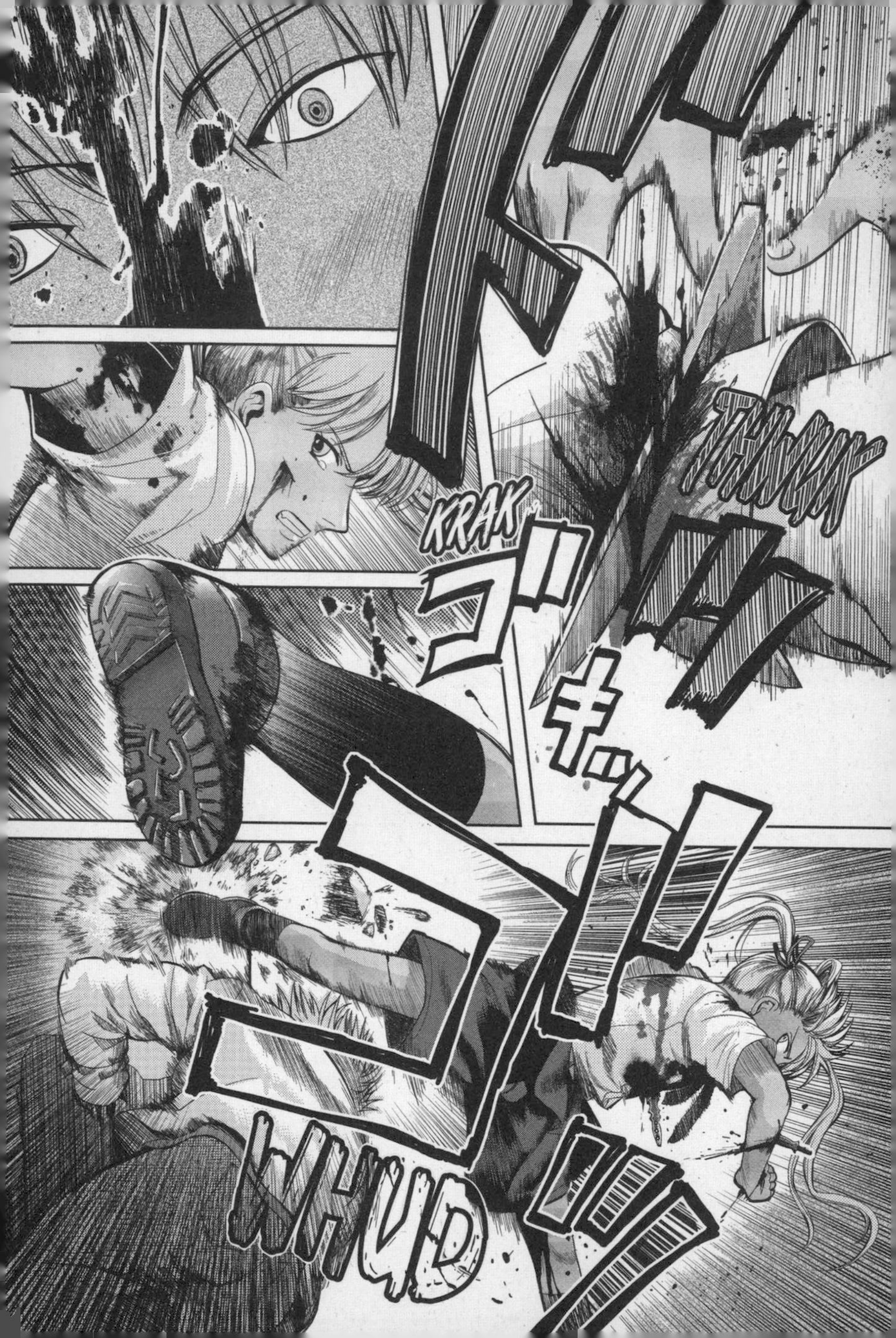
THWACK
KRAK
WHUD

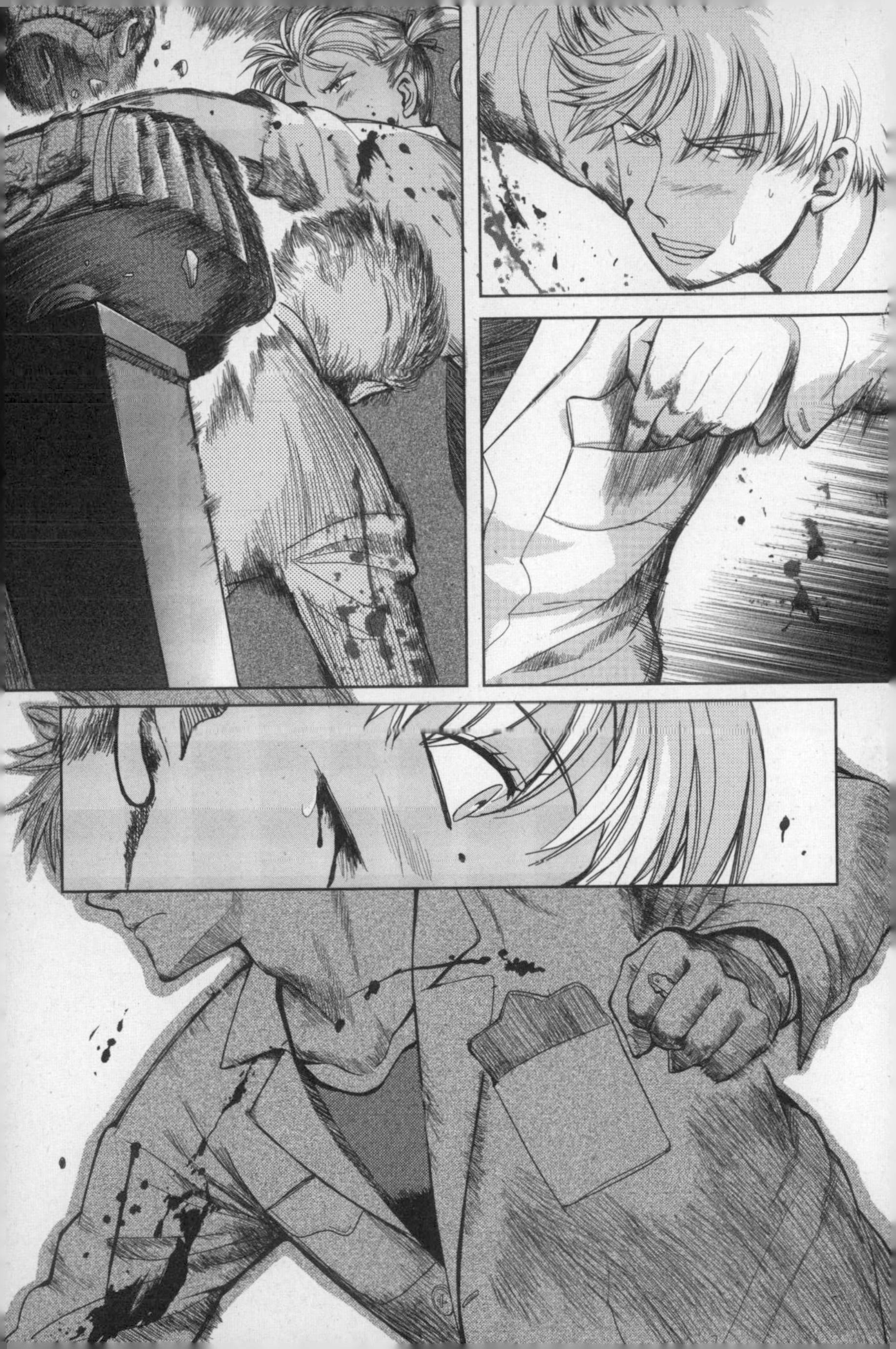

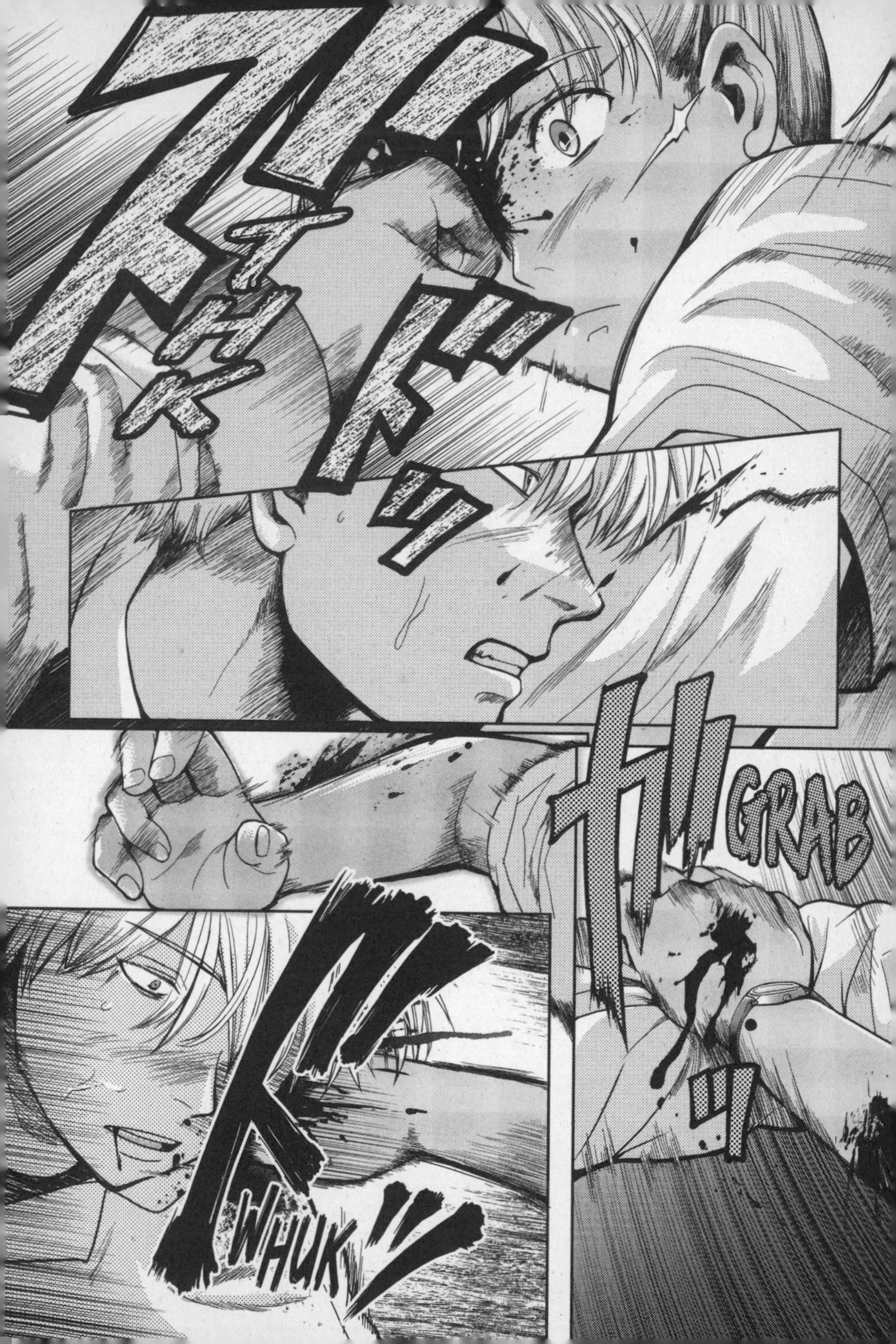
GRAB
WHUK

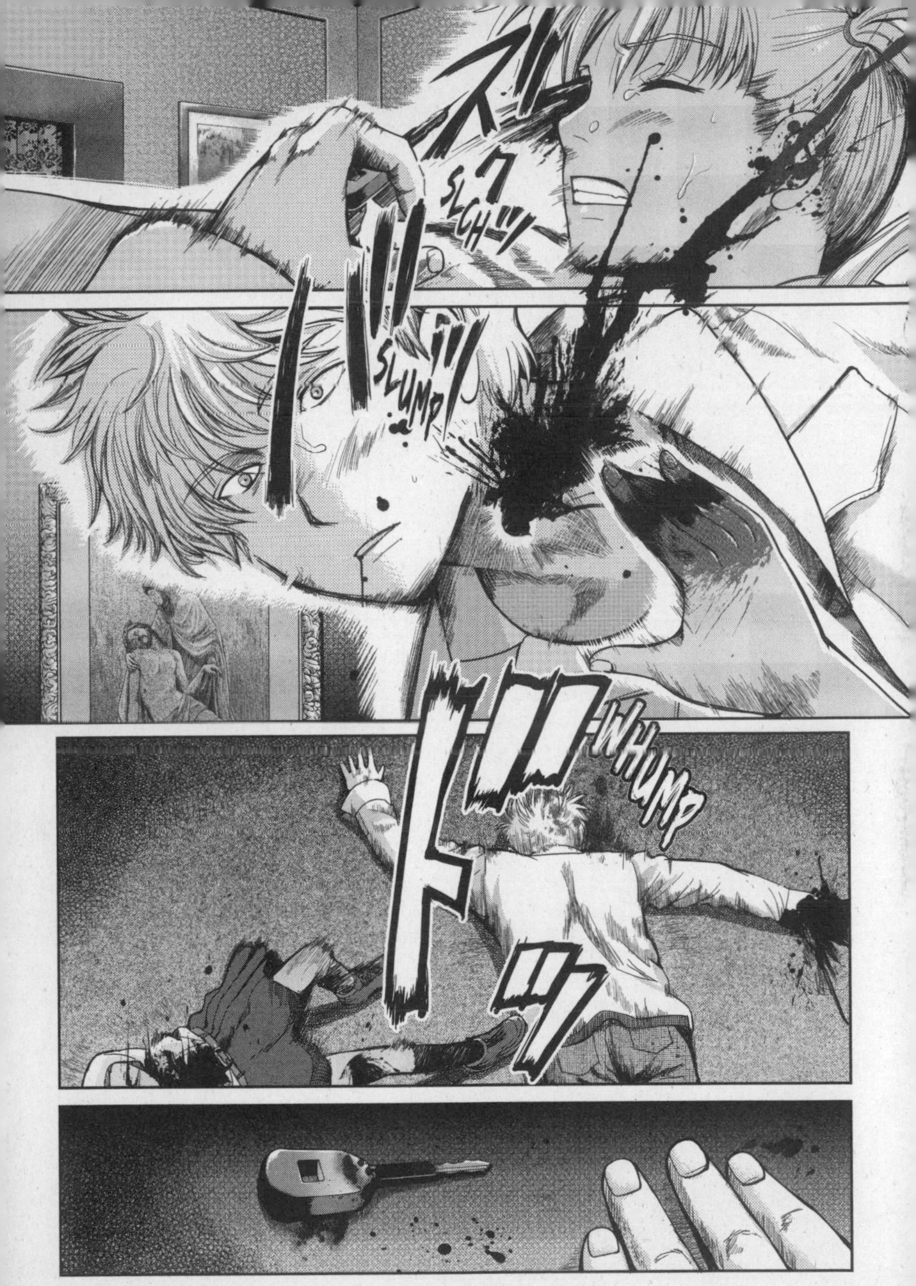
SLCH
SLUMP
WHUMP

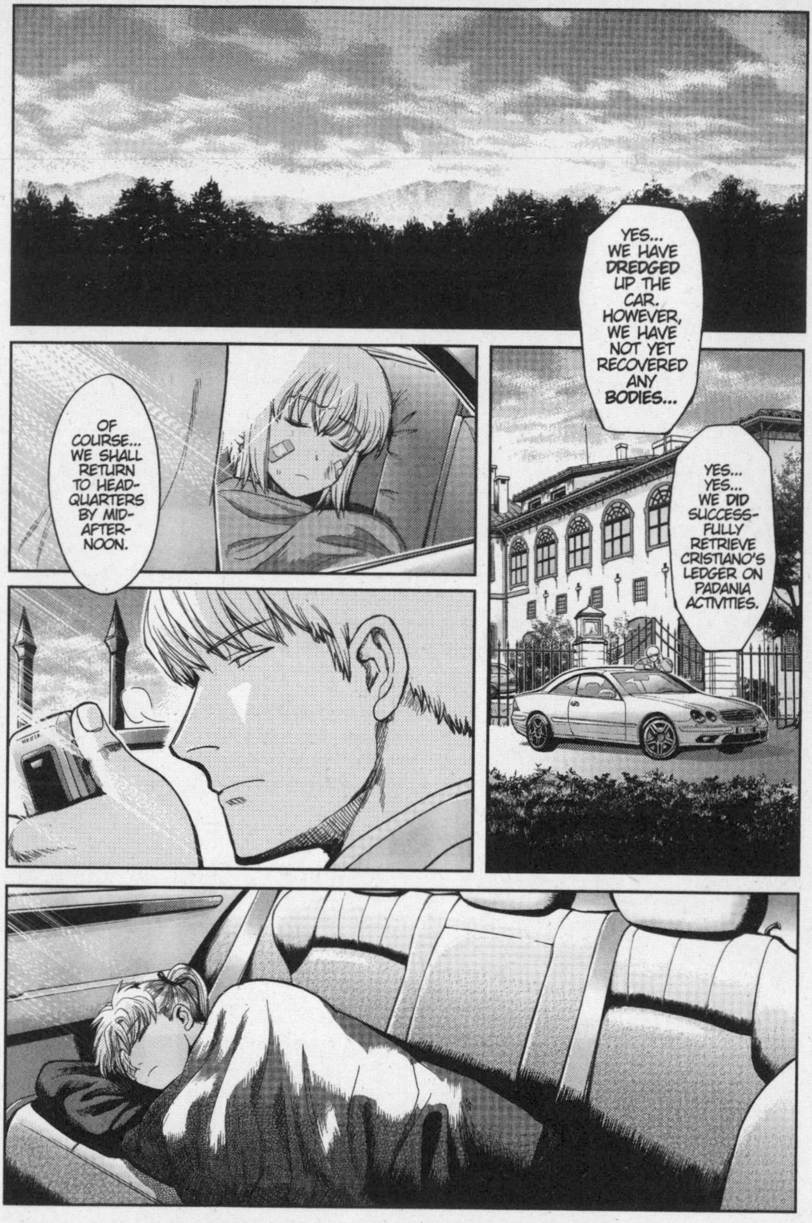
YES... WE HAVE DREDGED UP THE CAR. HOWEVER, WE HAVE NOT YET RECOVERED ANY BODIES...
YES... YES... WE DID SUCCESSFULLY RETRIEVE CRISTIANO'S LEDGER ON PADANIA ACTIVITIES.
OF COURSE... WE SHALL RETURN TO HEAD-QUARTERS BY MID-AFTER-NOON.

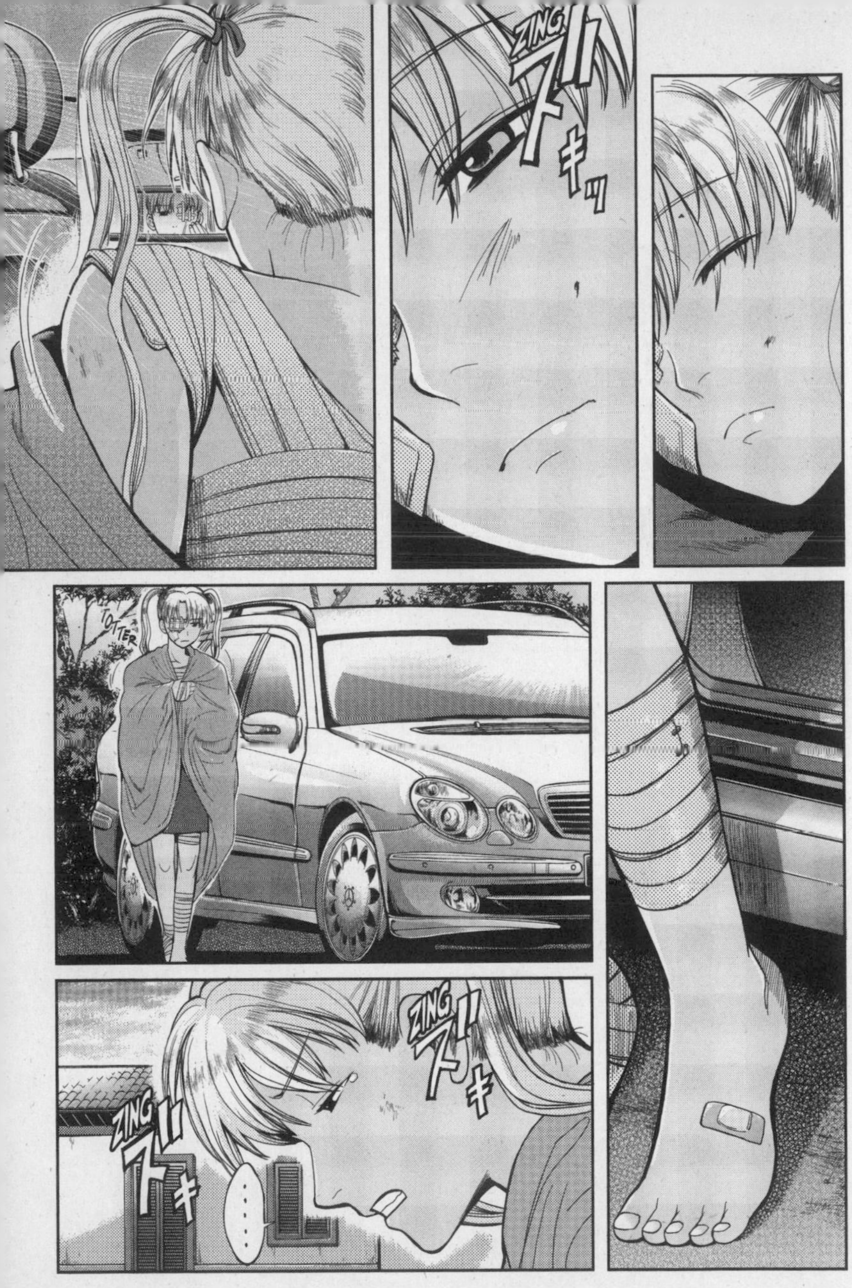
ZING
ズキッ
TOTTER
ZING
ズキ
ZING
ズキ
......

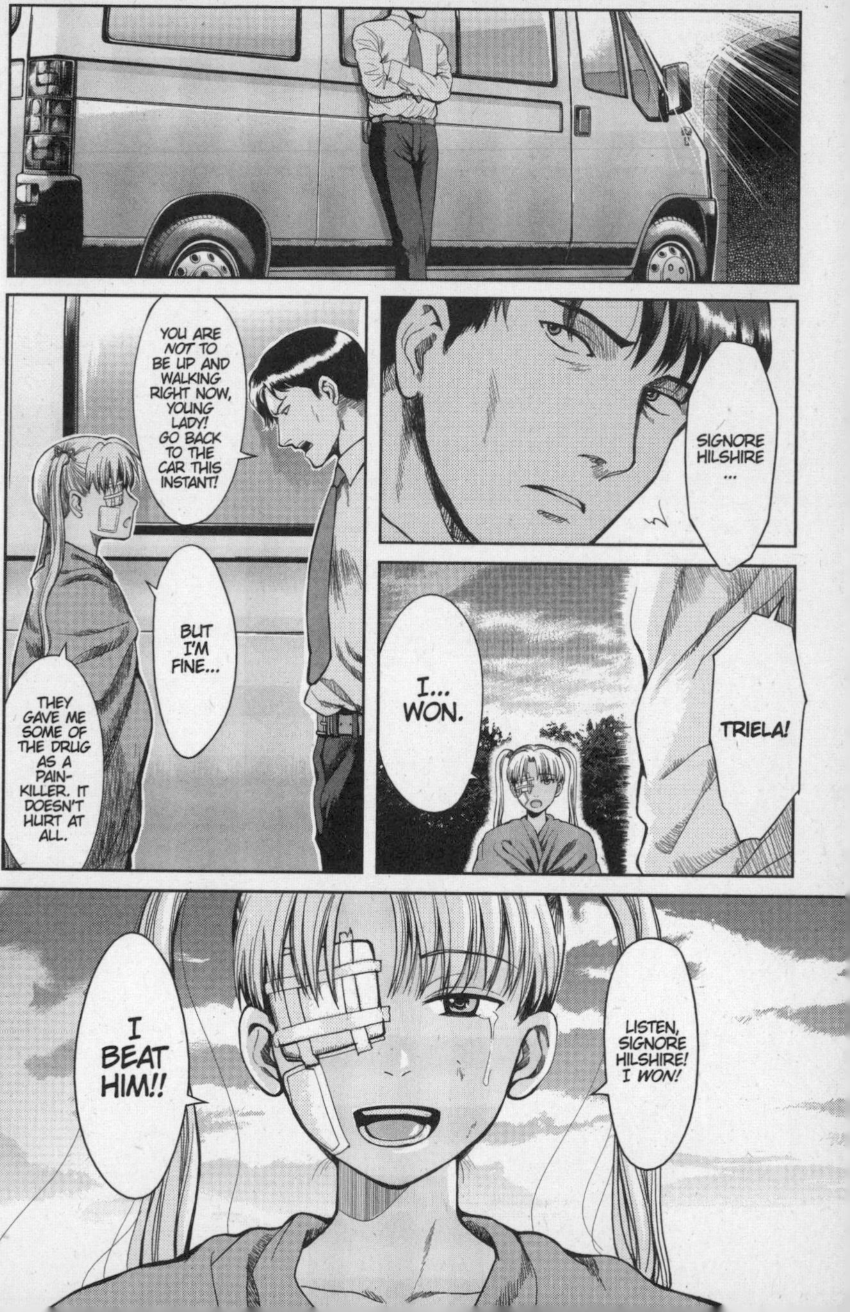
SIGNORE HILSHIRE ...
TRIELA!
I... WON.
YOU ARE *NOT* TO BE UP AND WALKING RIGHT NOW, YOUNG LADY! GO BACK TO THE CAR THIS INSTANT!
BUT I'M FINE...
THEY GAVE ME SOME OF THE DRUG AS A PAIN-KILLER. IT DOESN'T HURT AT ALL.
LISTEN, SIGNORE HILSHIRE! I *WON*!
I BEAT HIM!!

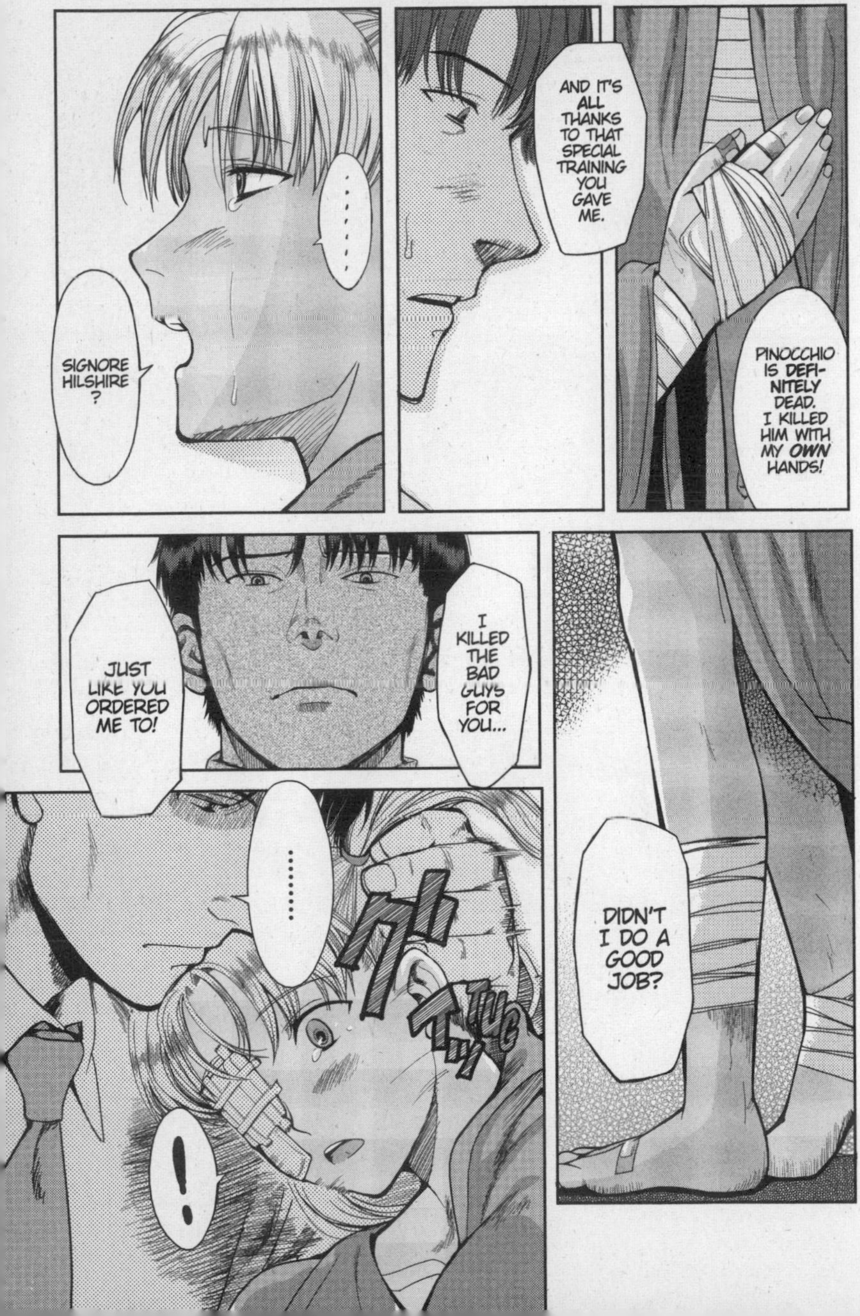
PINOCCHIO IS DEFINITELY DEAD. I KILLED HIM WITH MY OWN HANDS!
AND IT'S ALL THANKS TO THAT SPECIAL TRAINING YOU GAVE ME.
......
SIGNORE HILSHIRE?
DIDN'T I DO A GOOD JOB?
I KILLED THE BAD GUYS FOR YOU...
JUST LIKE YOU ORDERED ME TO!
......
TUG
!

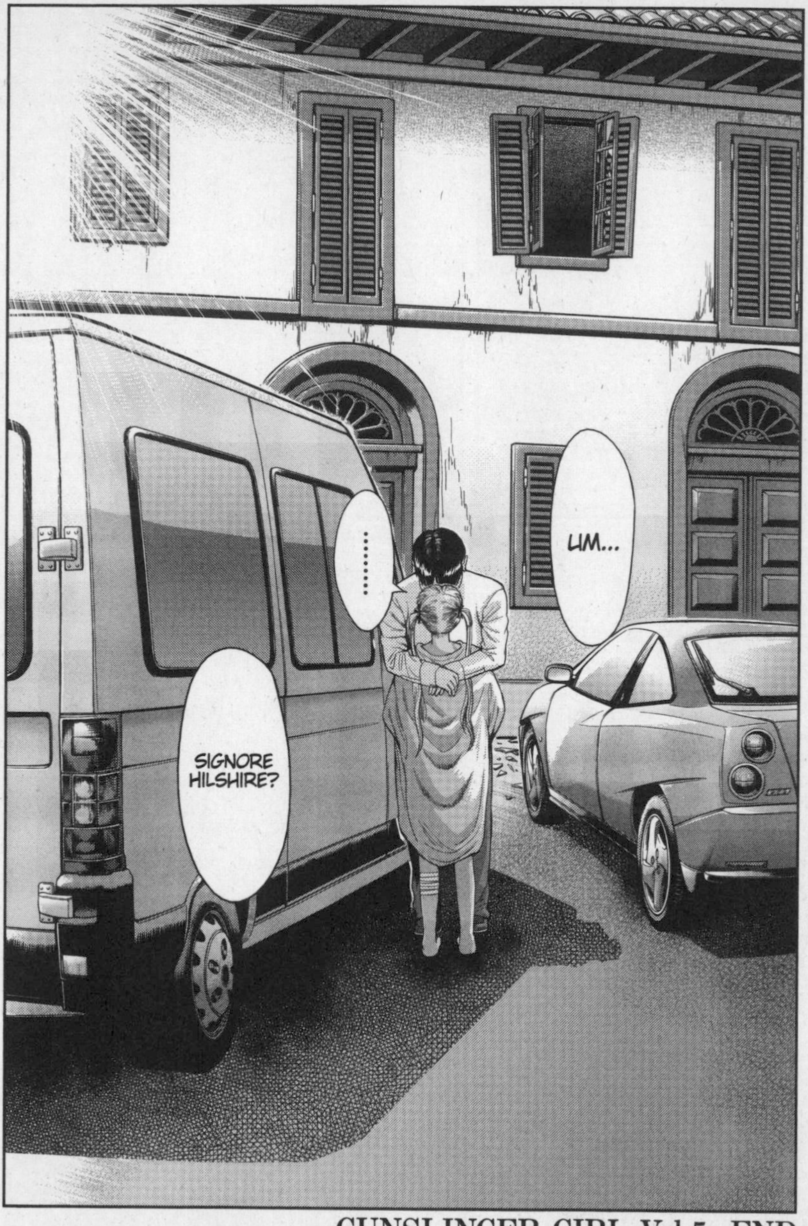
UM...
......
SIGNORE HILSHIRE?

GUNSLINGER GIRL Vol.5 END

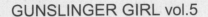

GUNSLINGER GIRL vol.5

EDITOR

CHIAKI SUGIHARA

ASSISTANT

TAKAHIRO ENDO
JUNICHIRO YAGI

SPECIAL THANKS

Everyone who so helpfully offered advice and research materials.

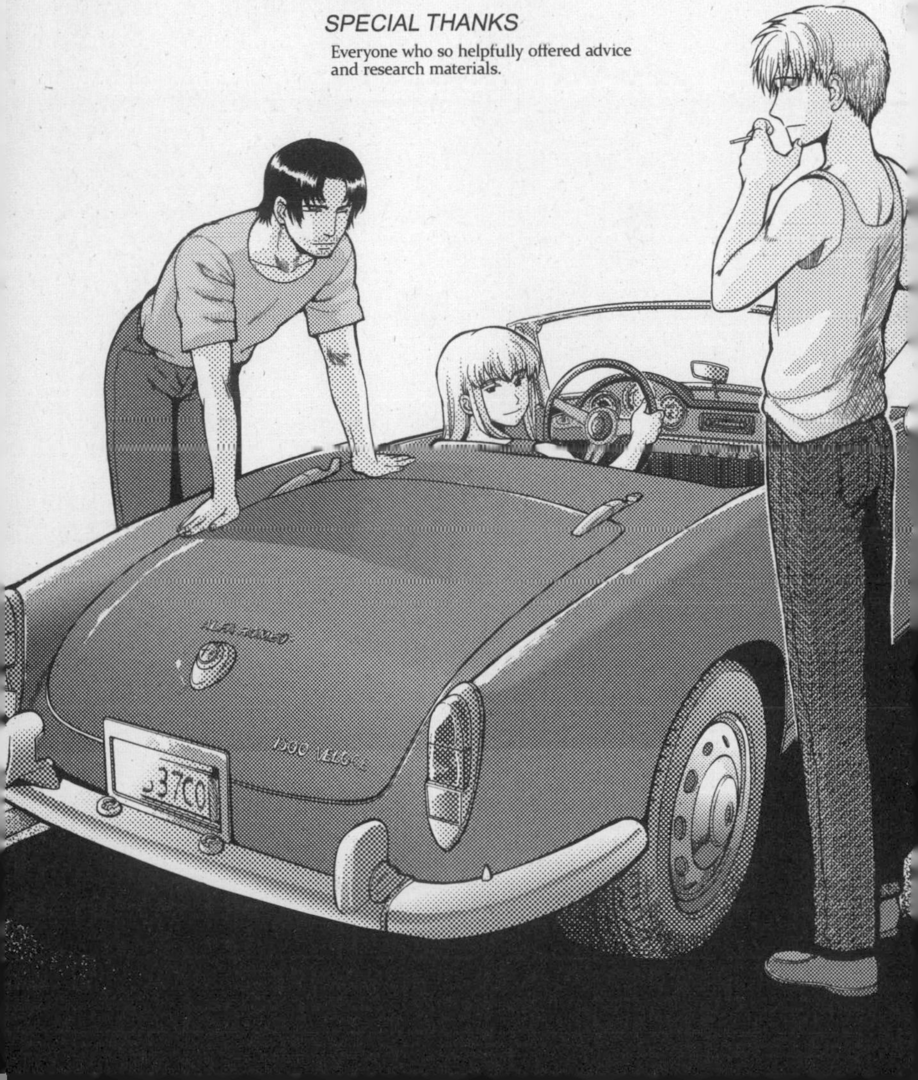

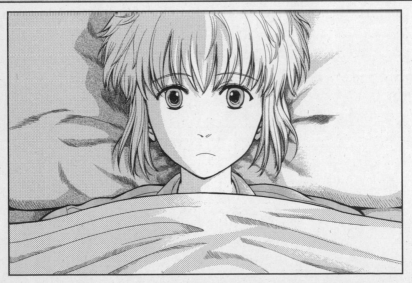

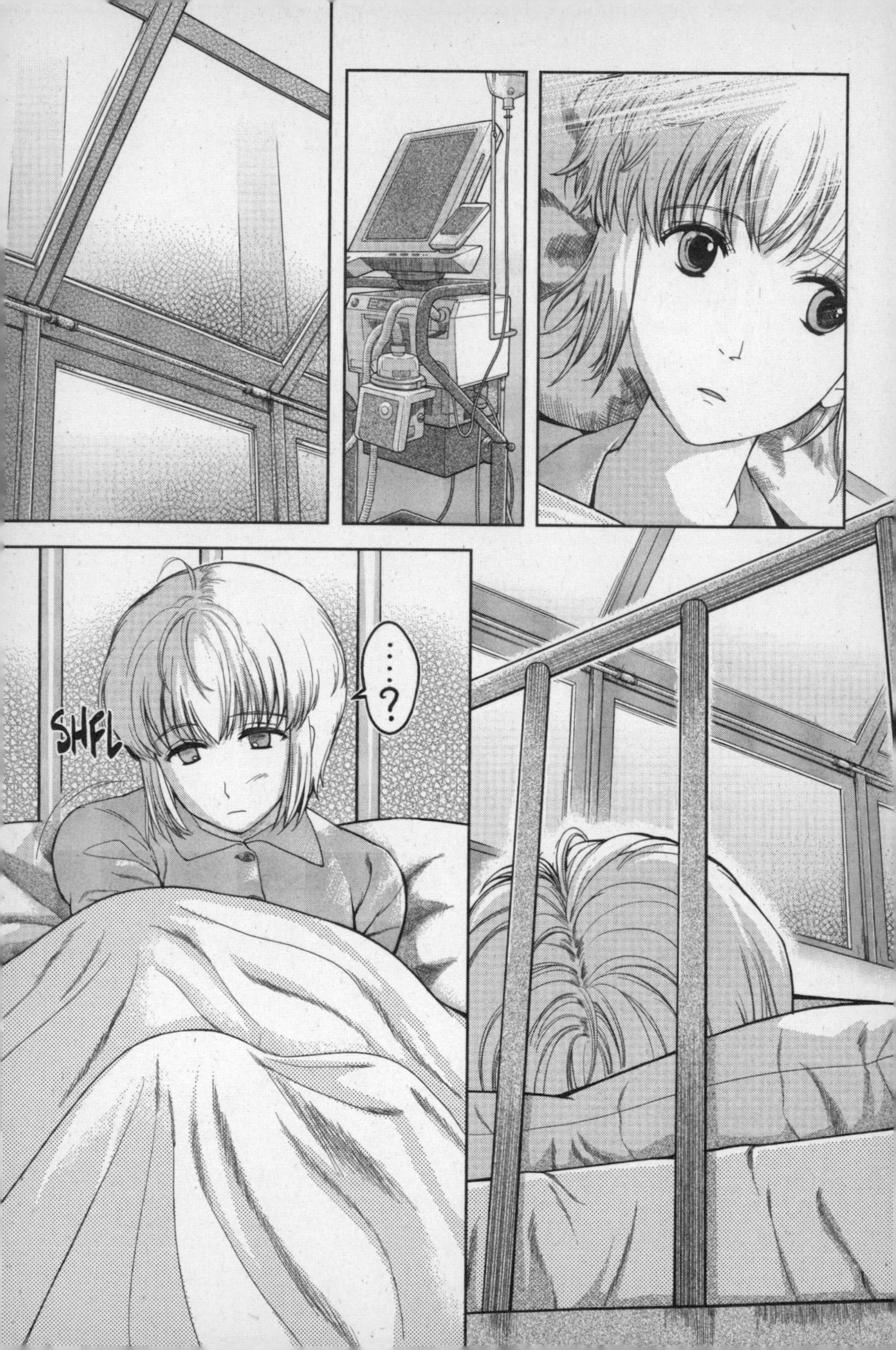
....?
SHFL

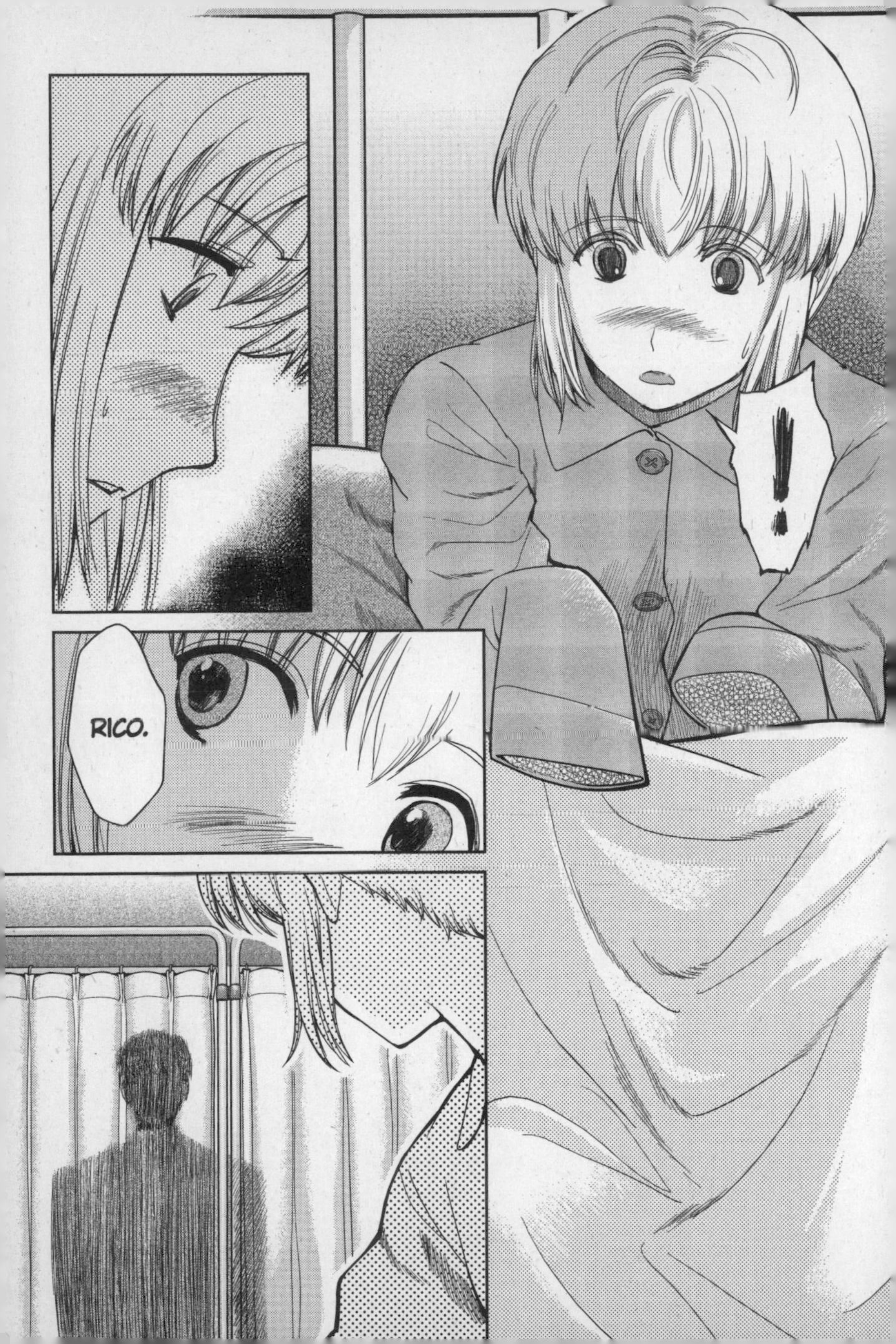
!!
RICO.

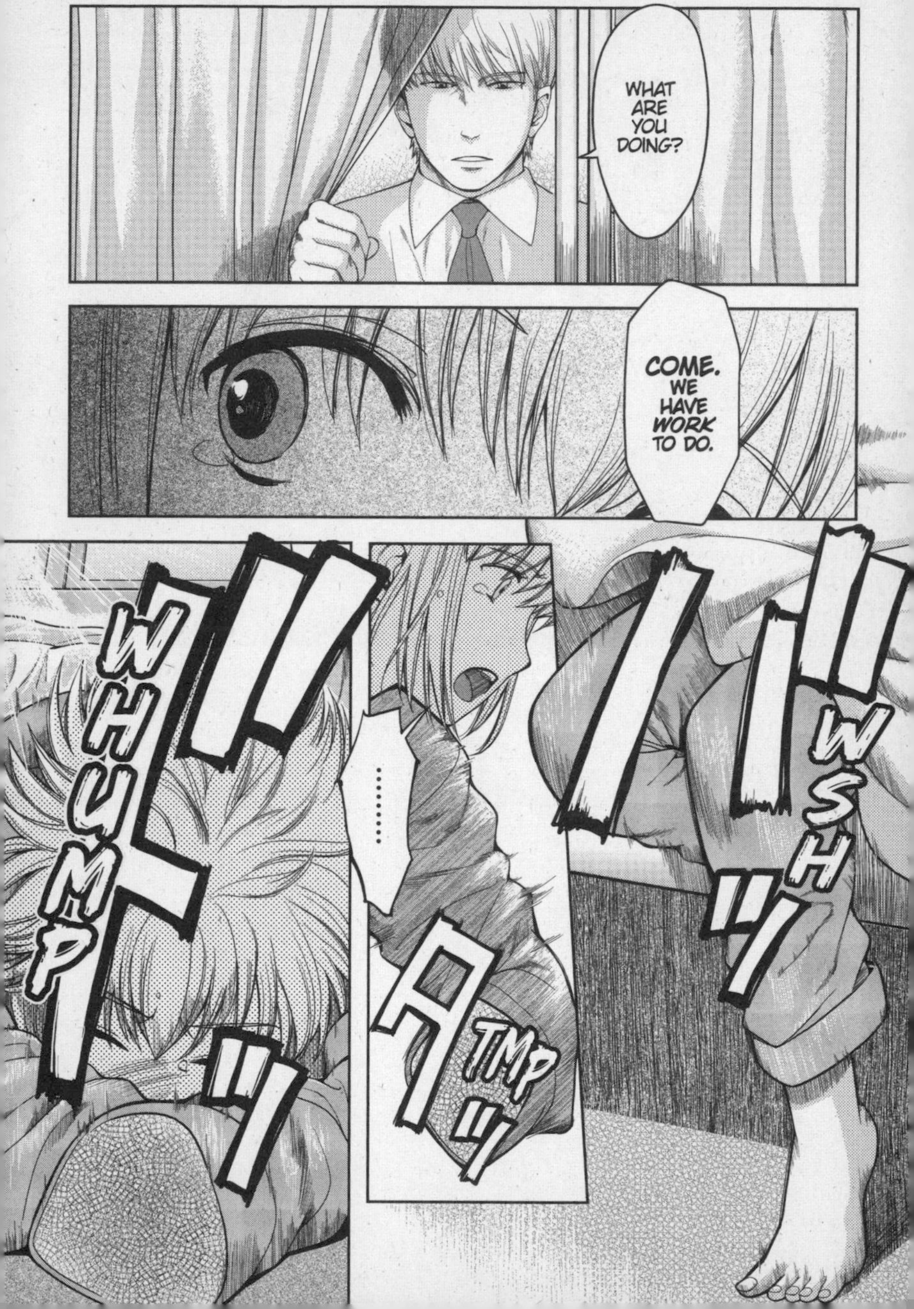
WHAT ARE YOU DOING?
COME. WE HAVE WORK TO DO.
WSHH
......
TMP
WHUMP

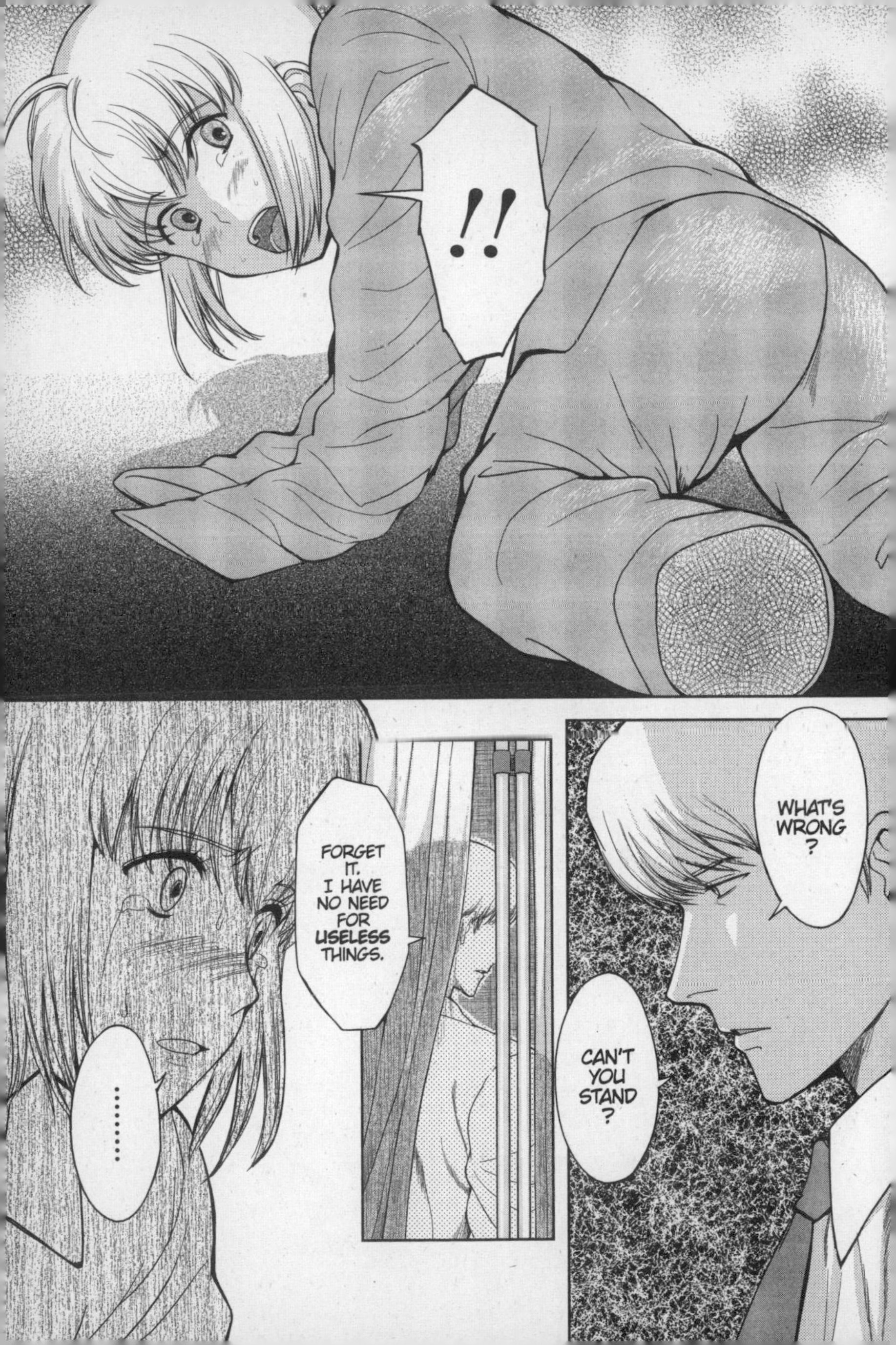
!!
WHAT'S WRONG?
CAN'T YOU STAND?
FORGET IT. I HAVE NO NEED FOR USELESS THINGS.
......

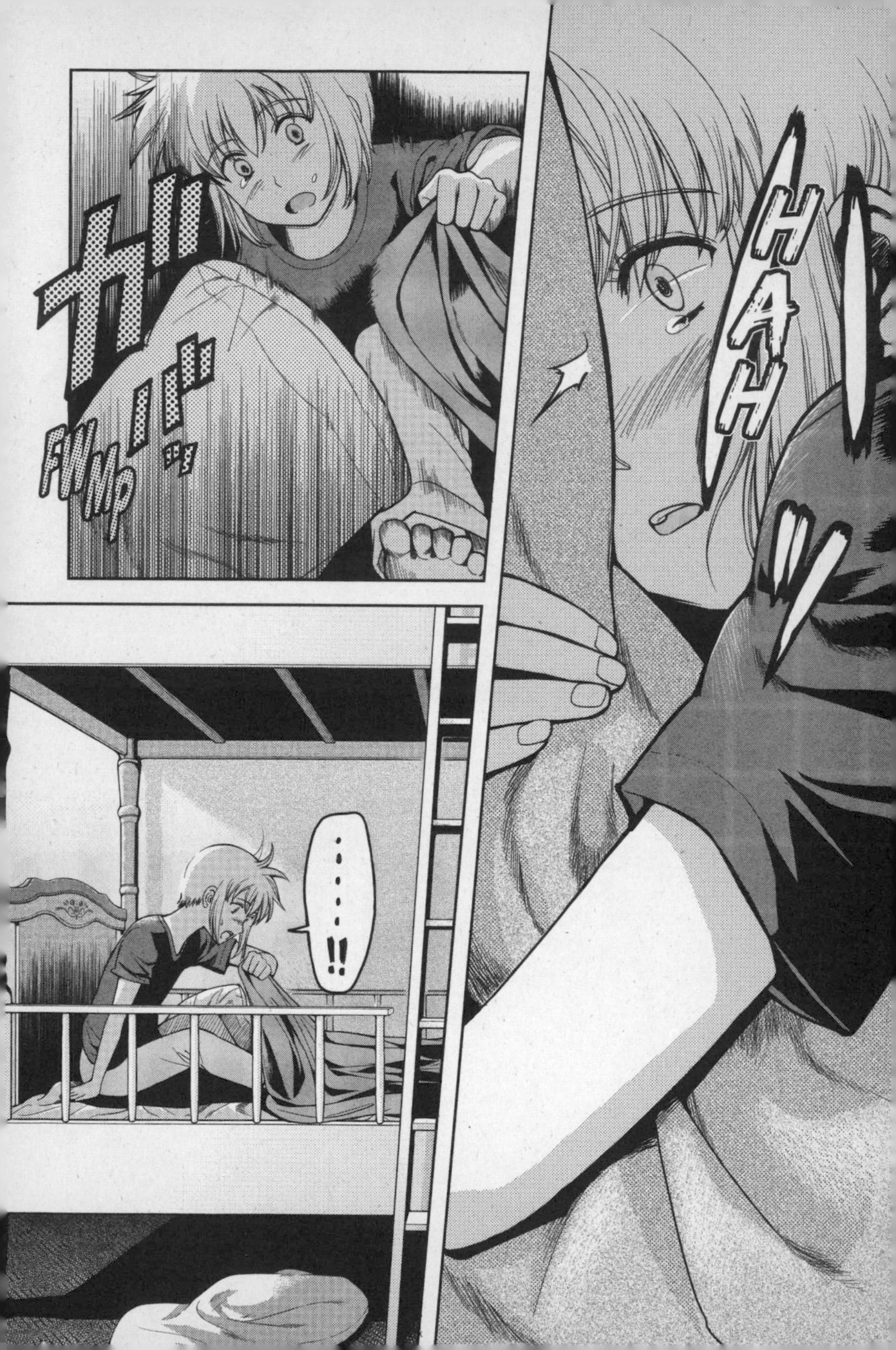
HAHH
ガバッ
FWMP
......!!

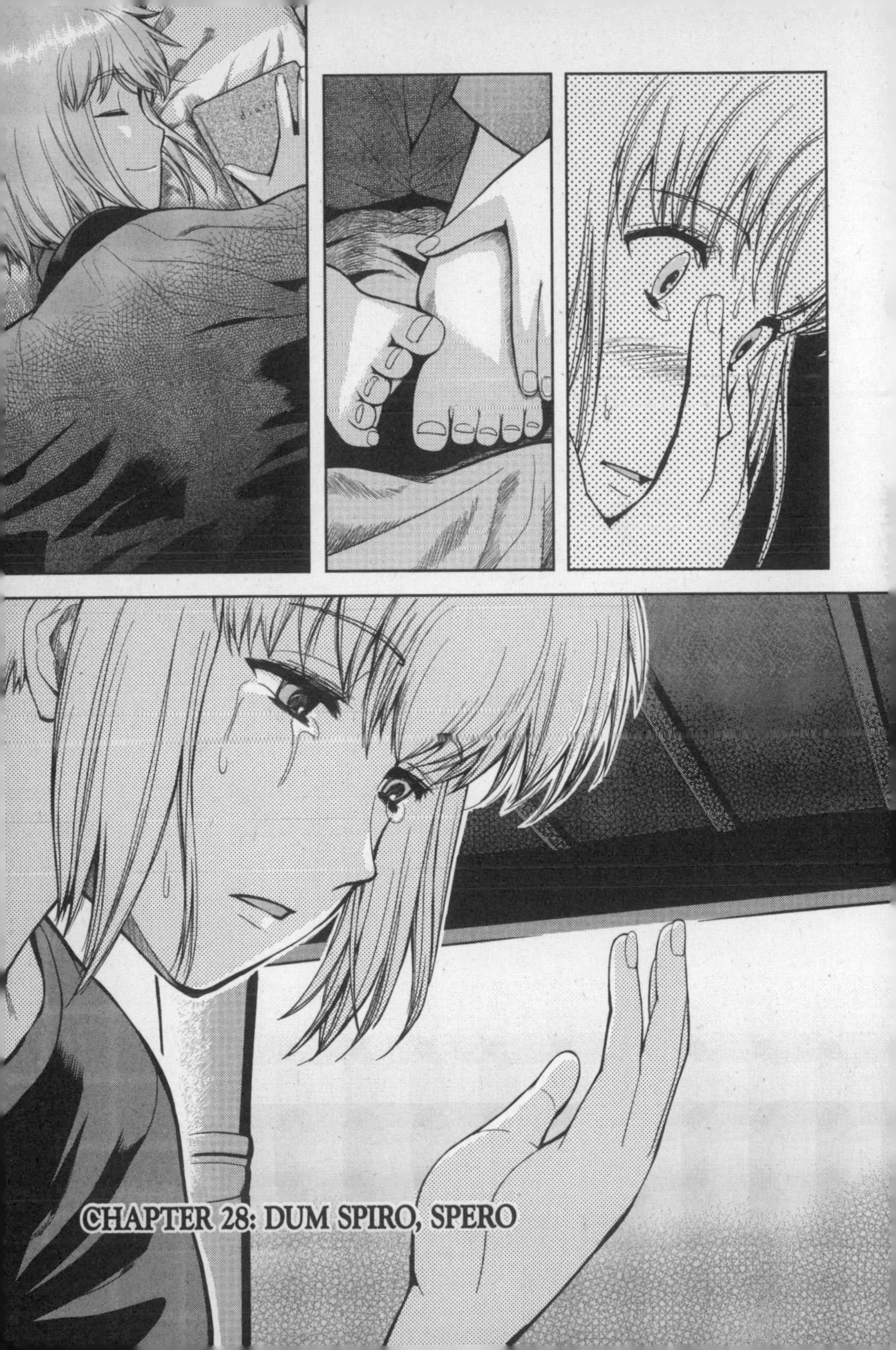
CHAPTER 28: DUM SPIRO, SPERO

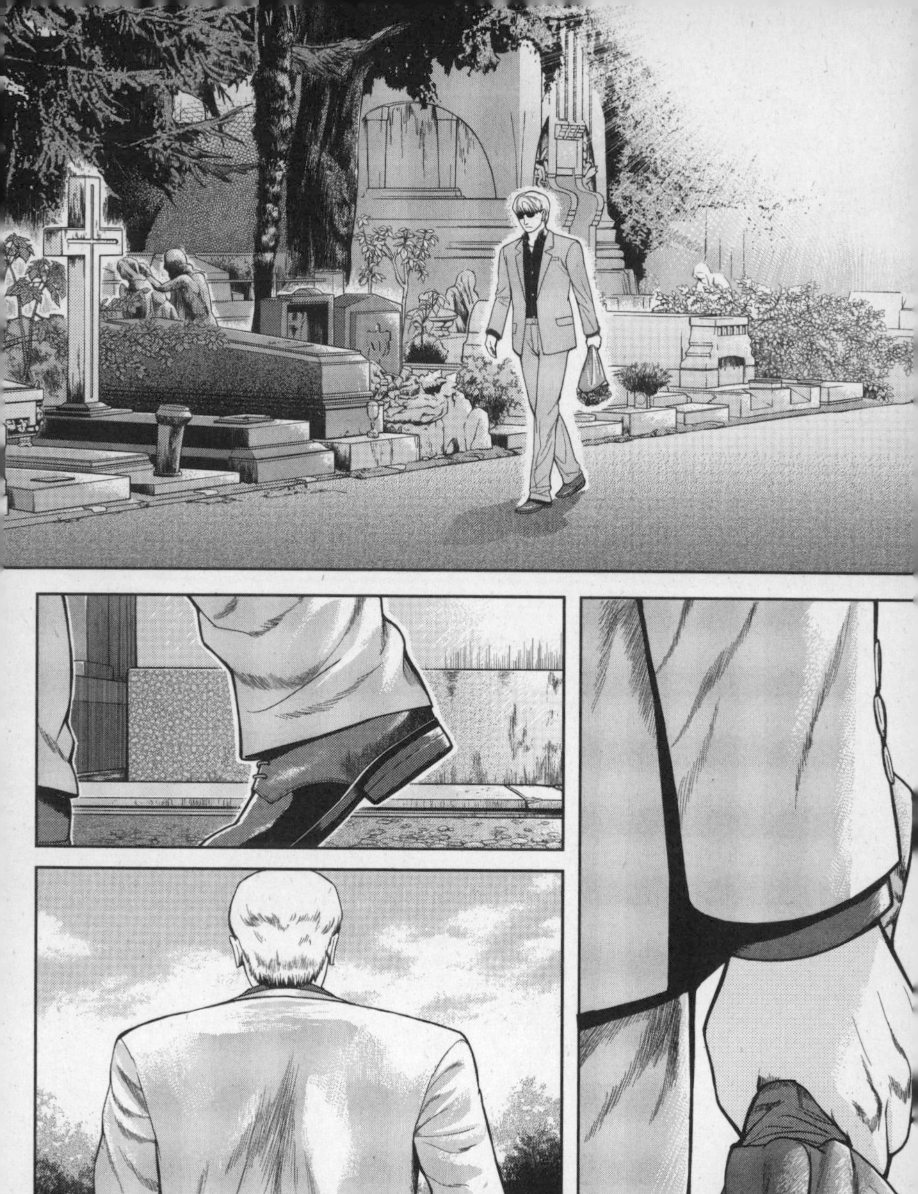

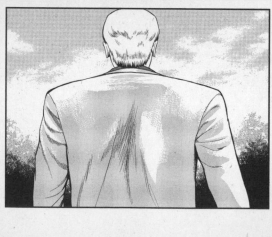

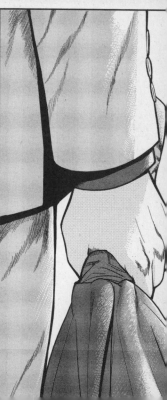

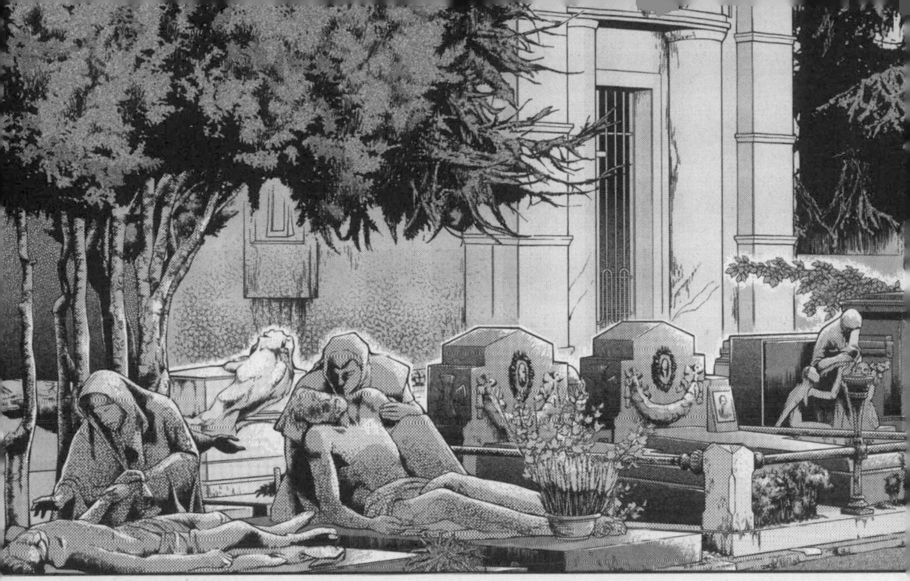
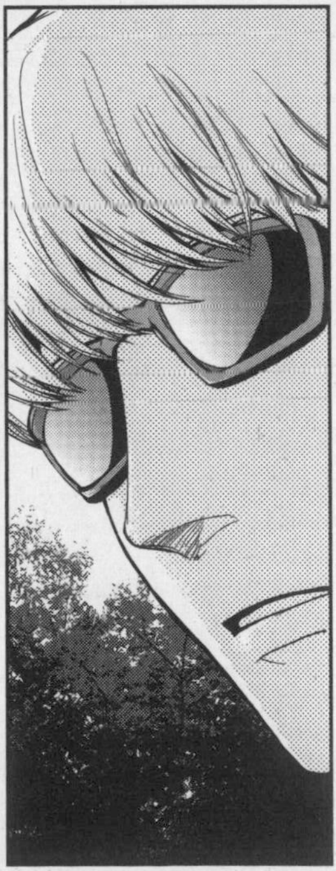
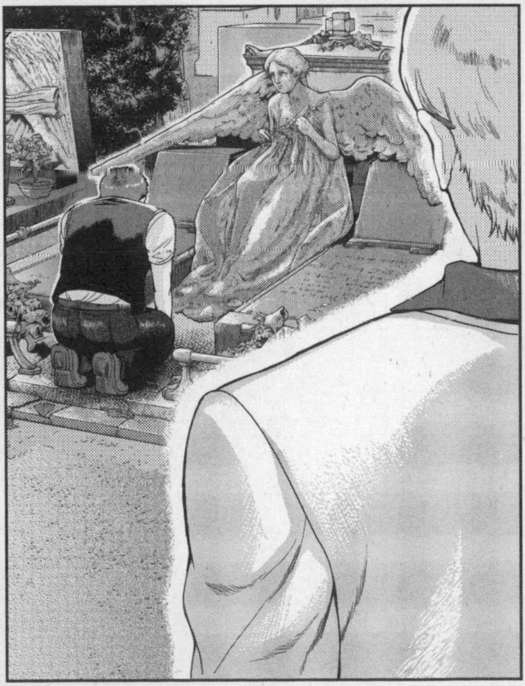

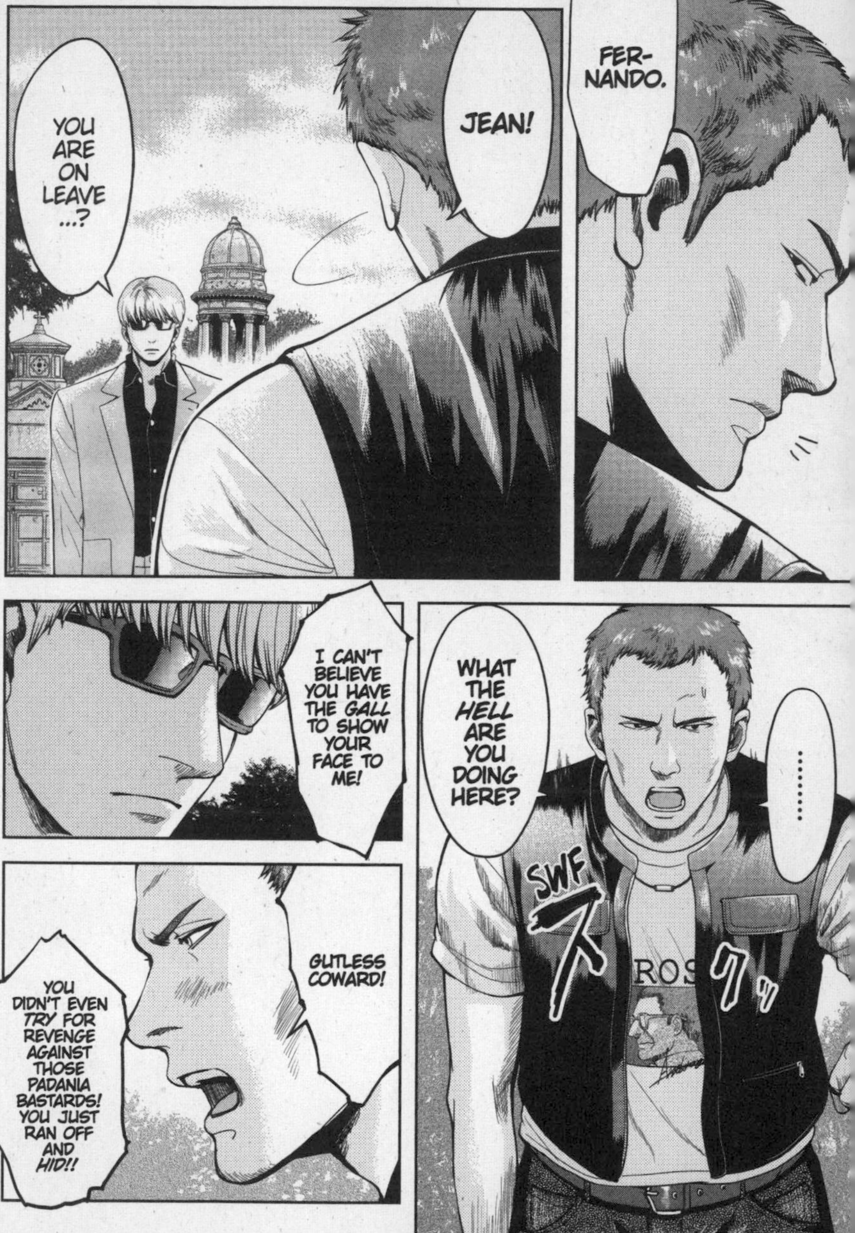
FER-NANDO.
JEAN!
YOU ARE ON LEAVE ...?
......
WHAT THE *HELL* ARE YOU DOING HERE?
SWF
スッ
I CAN'T BELIEVE YOU HAVE THE *GALL* TO SHOW YOUR FACE TO ME!
GUTLESS COWARD!
YOU DIDN'T EVEN *TRY* FOR REVENGE AGAINST THOSE PADANIA BASTARDS! YOU JUST RAN OFF AND *HID!!*

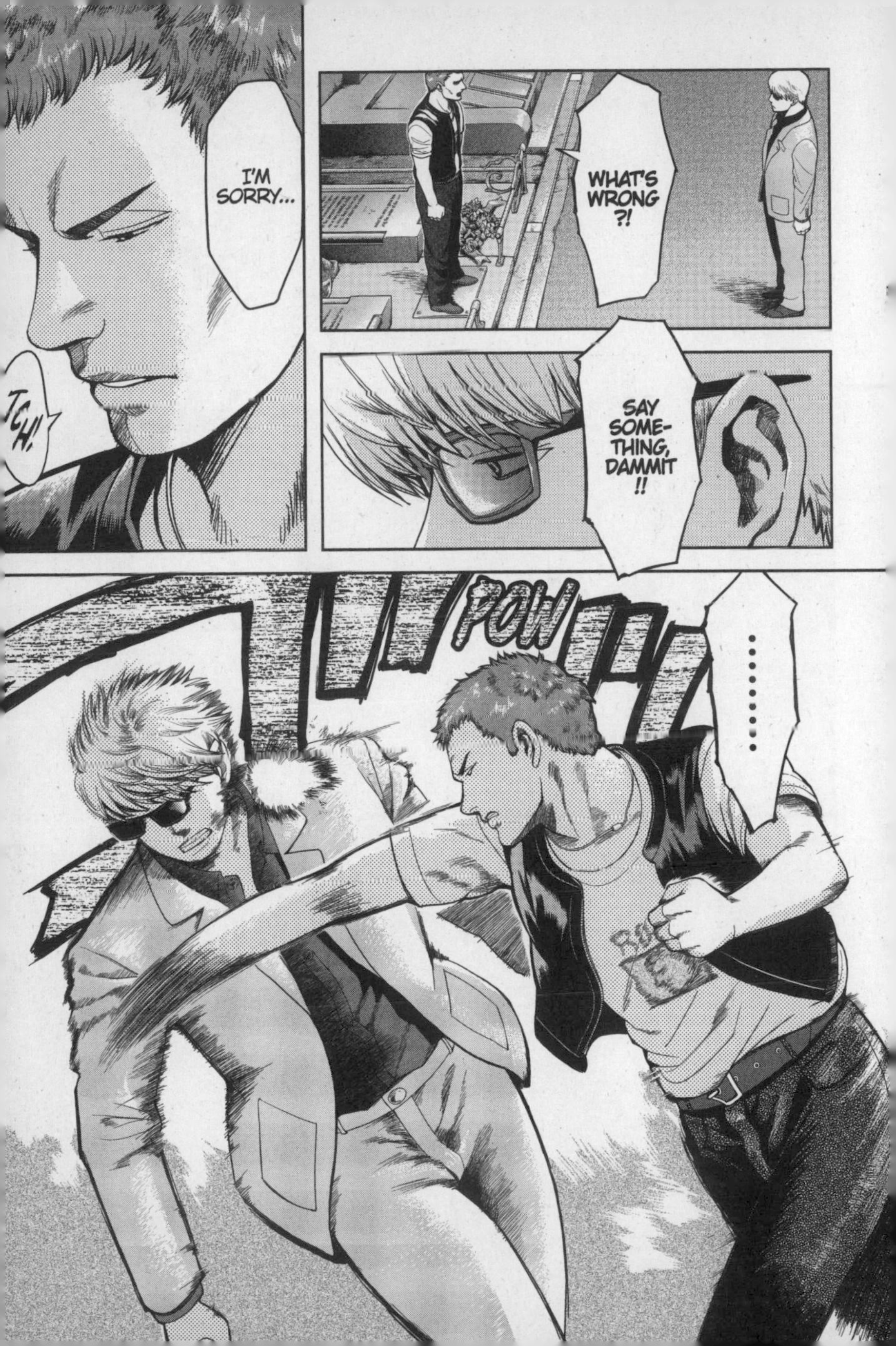
WHAT'S WRONG ?!
SAY SOME-THING, DAMMIT !!
I'M SORRY...
TCH!
....
POW

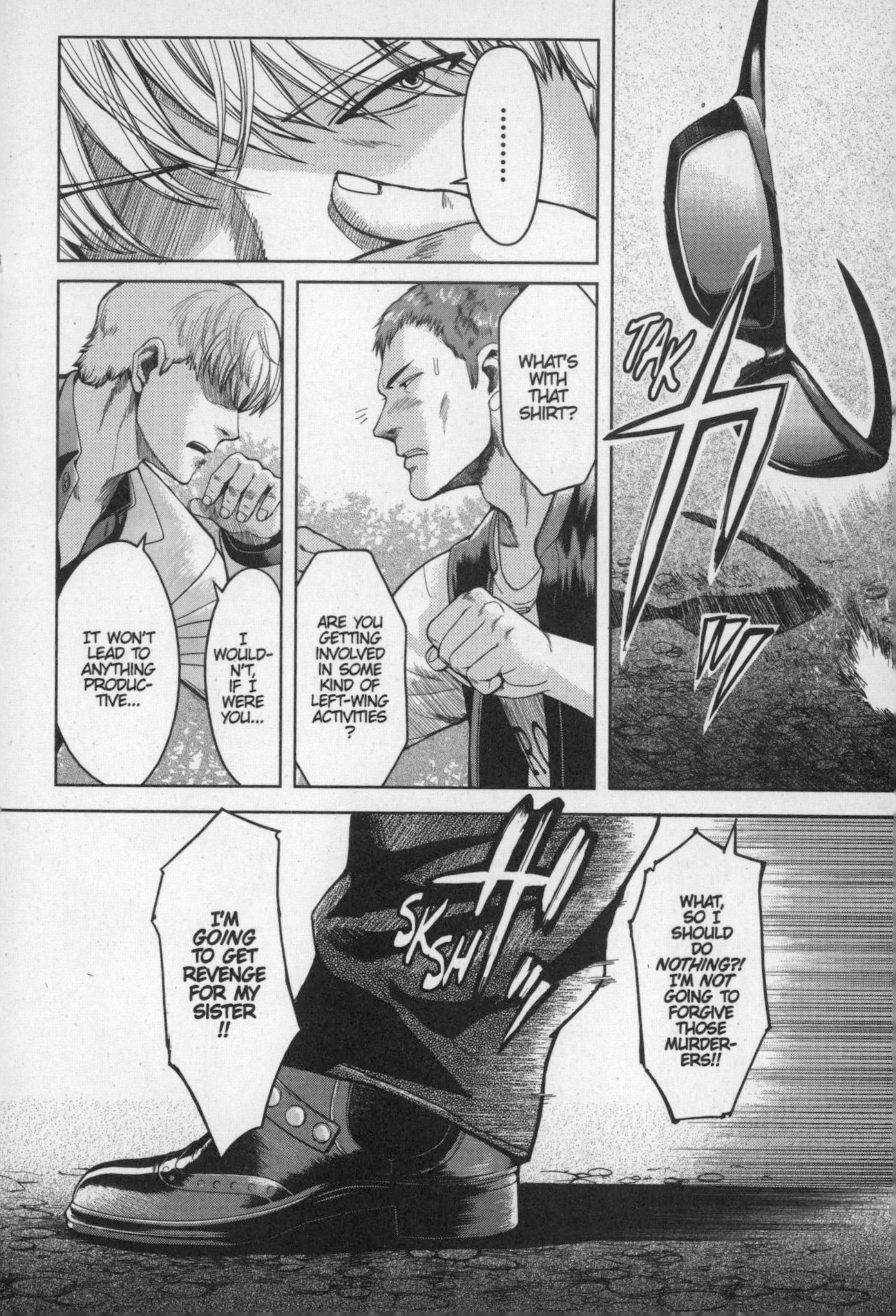
TAK
......
WHAT'S WITH THAT SHIRT?
ARE YOU GETTING INVOLVED IN SOME KIND OF LEFT-WING ACTIVITIES?
I WOULDN'T, IF I WERE YOU...
IT WON'T LEAD TO ANYTHING PRODUCTIVE...
WHAT, SO I SHOULD DO *NOTHING*?! I'M *NOT* GOING TO FORGIVE THOSE MURDERERS!!
SKSH
I'M *GOING* TO GET REVENGE FOR MY SISTER!!

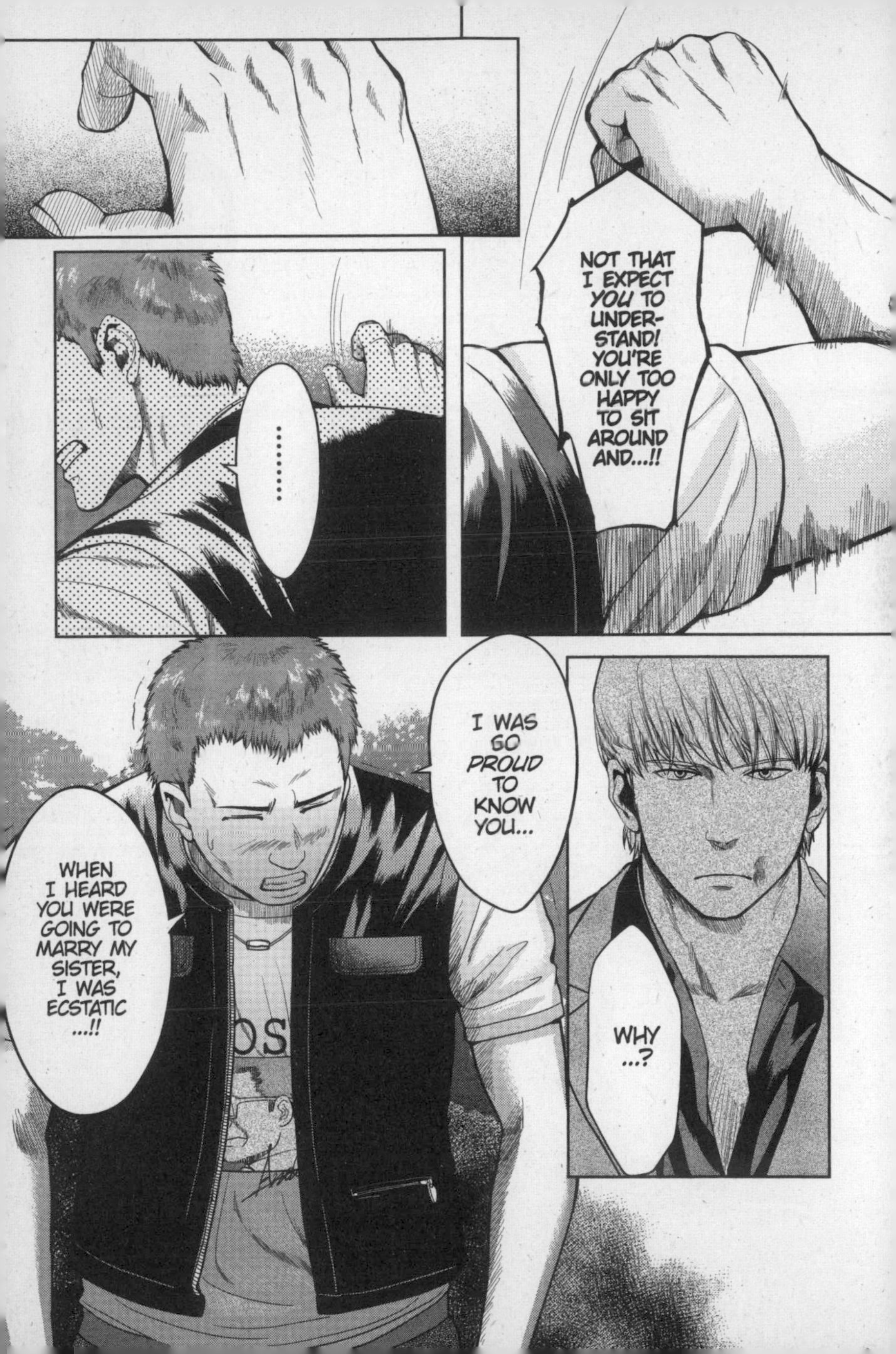
NOT THAT I EXPECT *YOU* TO UNDER-STAND! YOU'RE ONLY TOO *HAPPY* TO SIT AROUND AND...!!
......
WHY ...?
I WAS SO *PROUD* TO KNOW YOU...
WHEN I HEARD YOU WERE GOING TO MARRY MY SISTER, I WAS ECSTATIC ...!!

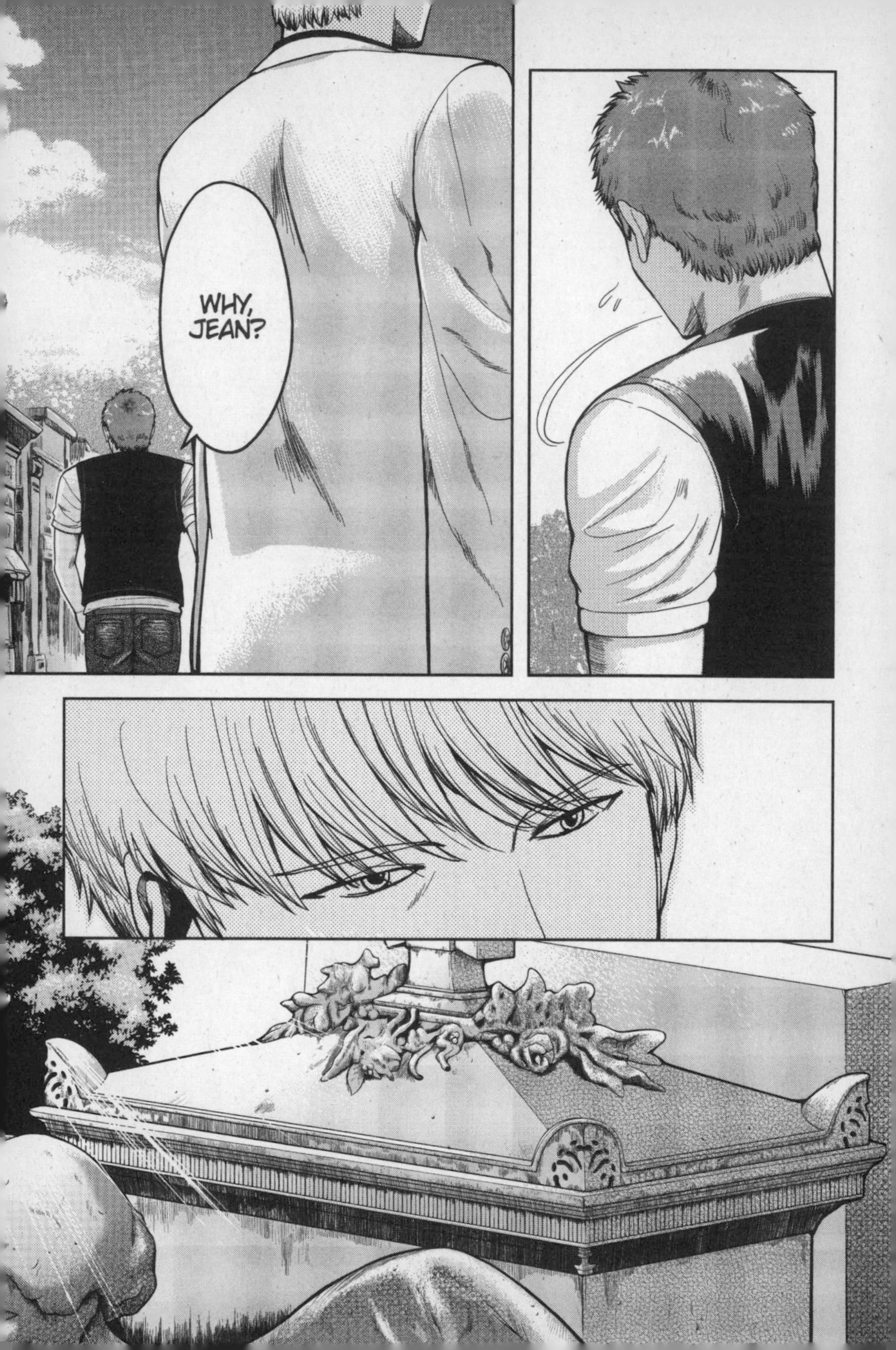
WHY, JEAN?

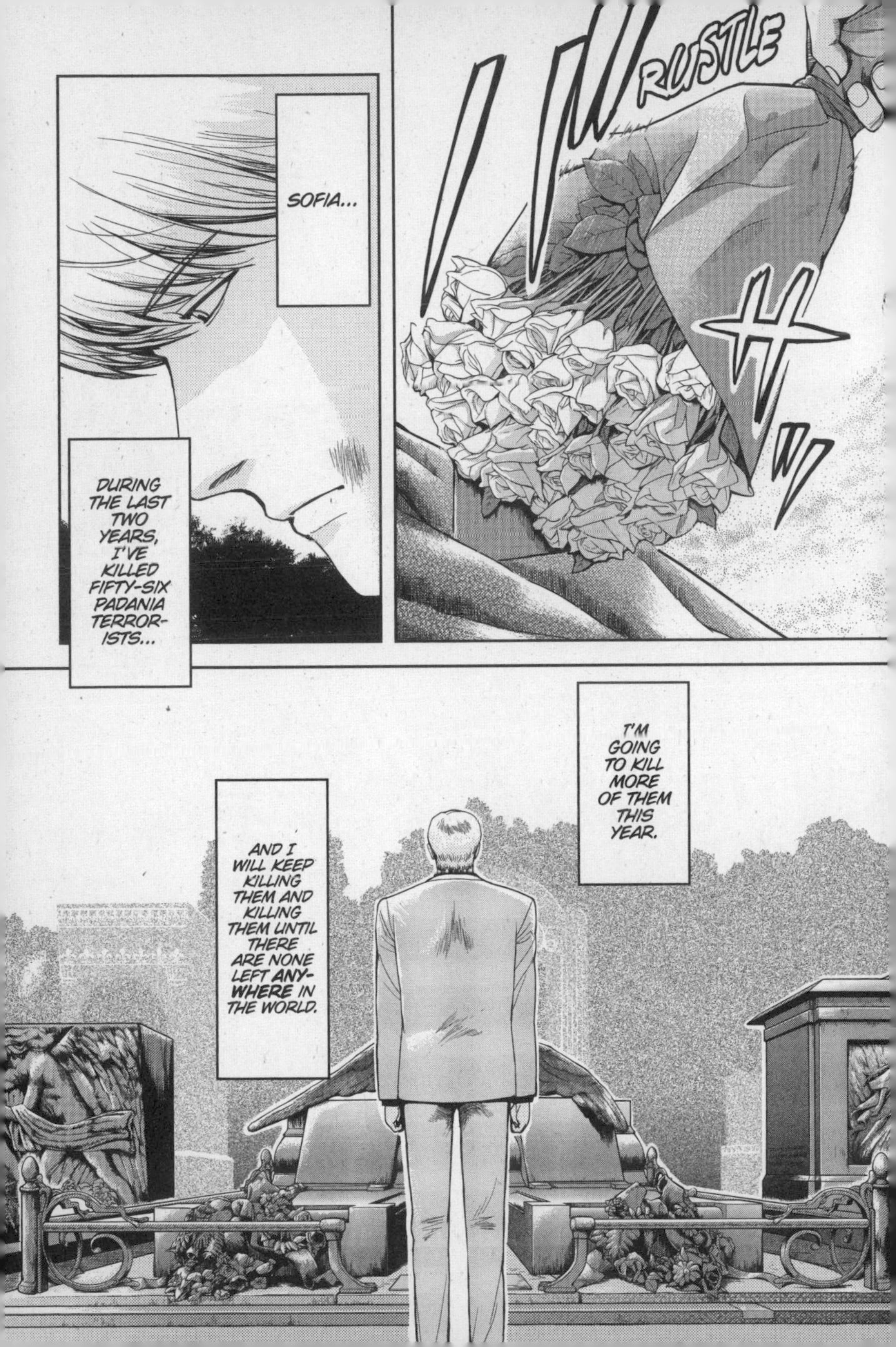
RUSTLE
SOFIA...
DURING THE LAST TWO YEARS, I'VE KILLED FIFTY-SIX PADANIA TERROR-ISTS...
I'M GOING TO KILL MORE OF THEM THIS YEAR.
AND I WILL KEEP KILLING THEM AND KILLING THEM UNTIL THERE ARE NONE LEFT ANY-WHERE IN THE WORLD.

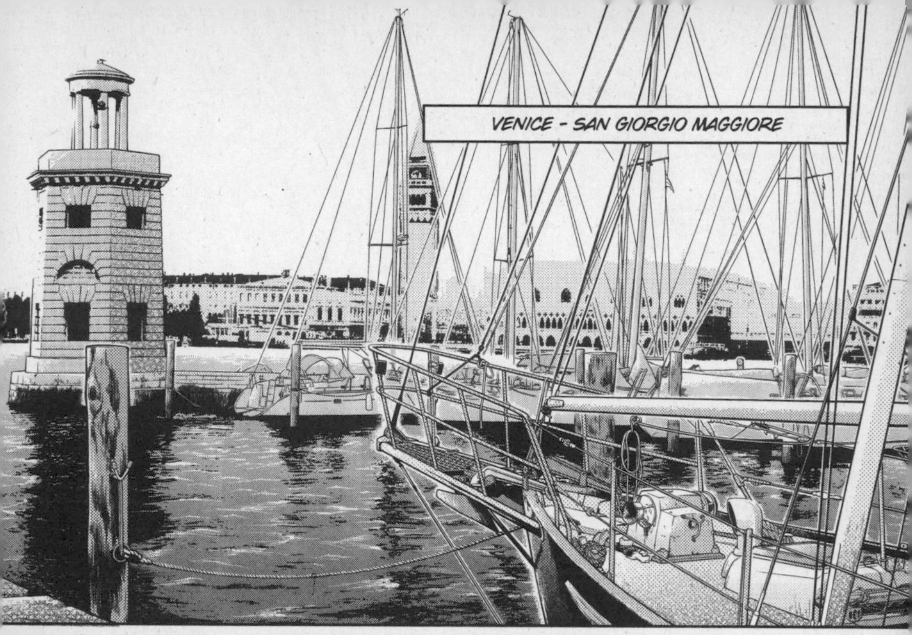
VENICE - SAN GIORGIO MAGGIORE

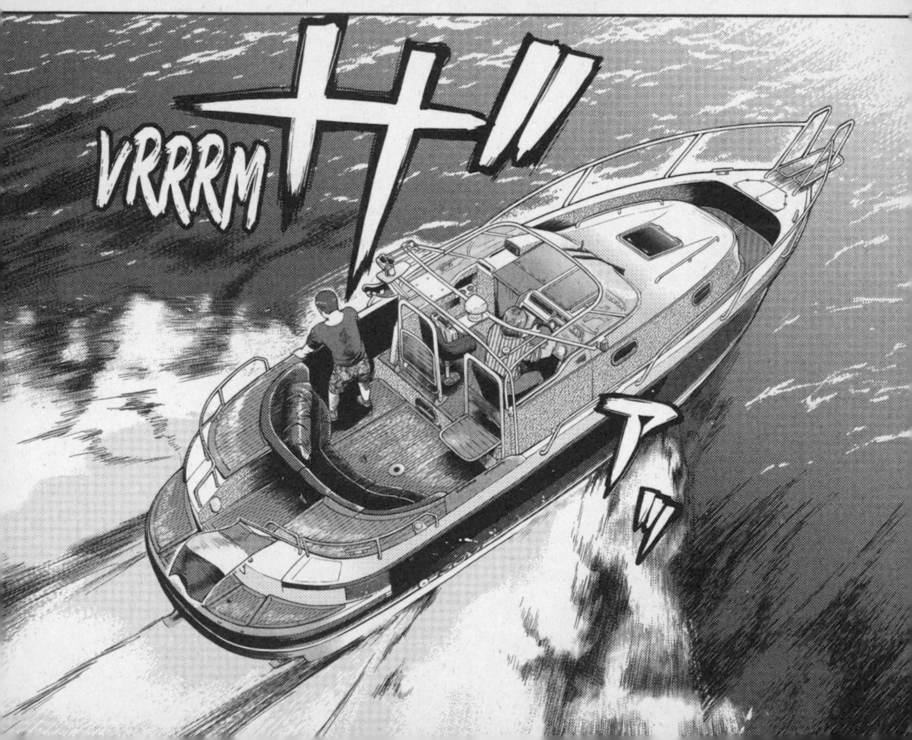
VRRRM

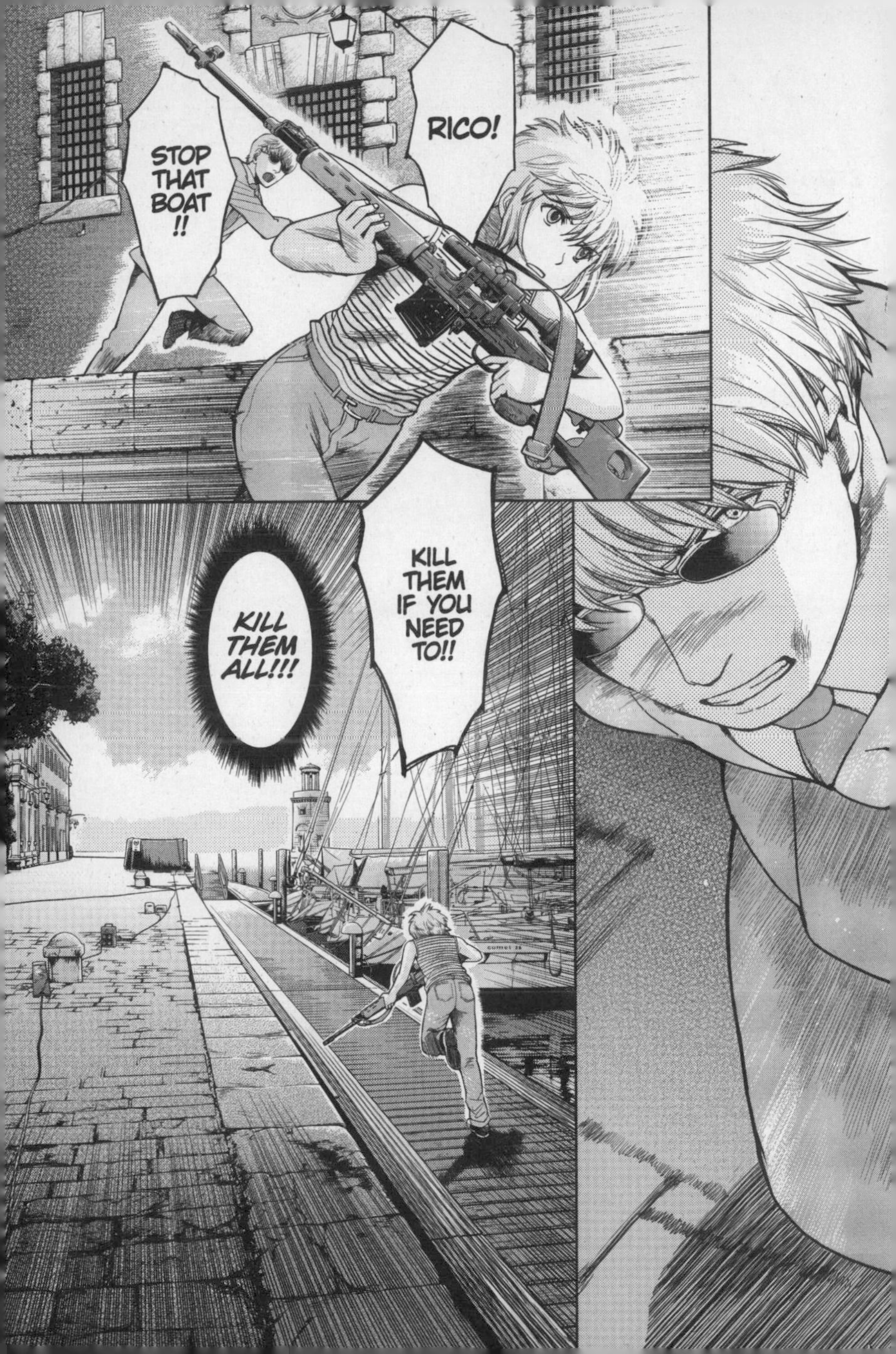
RICO!
STOP THAT BOAT !!
KILL THEM IF YOU NEED TO!!
KILL THEM ALL!!!

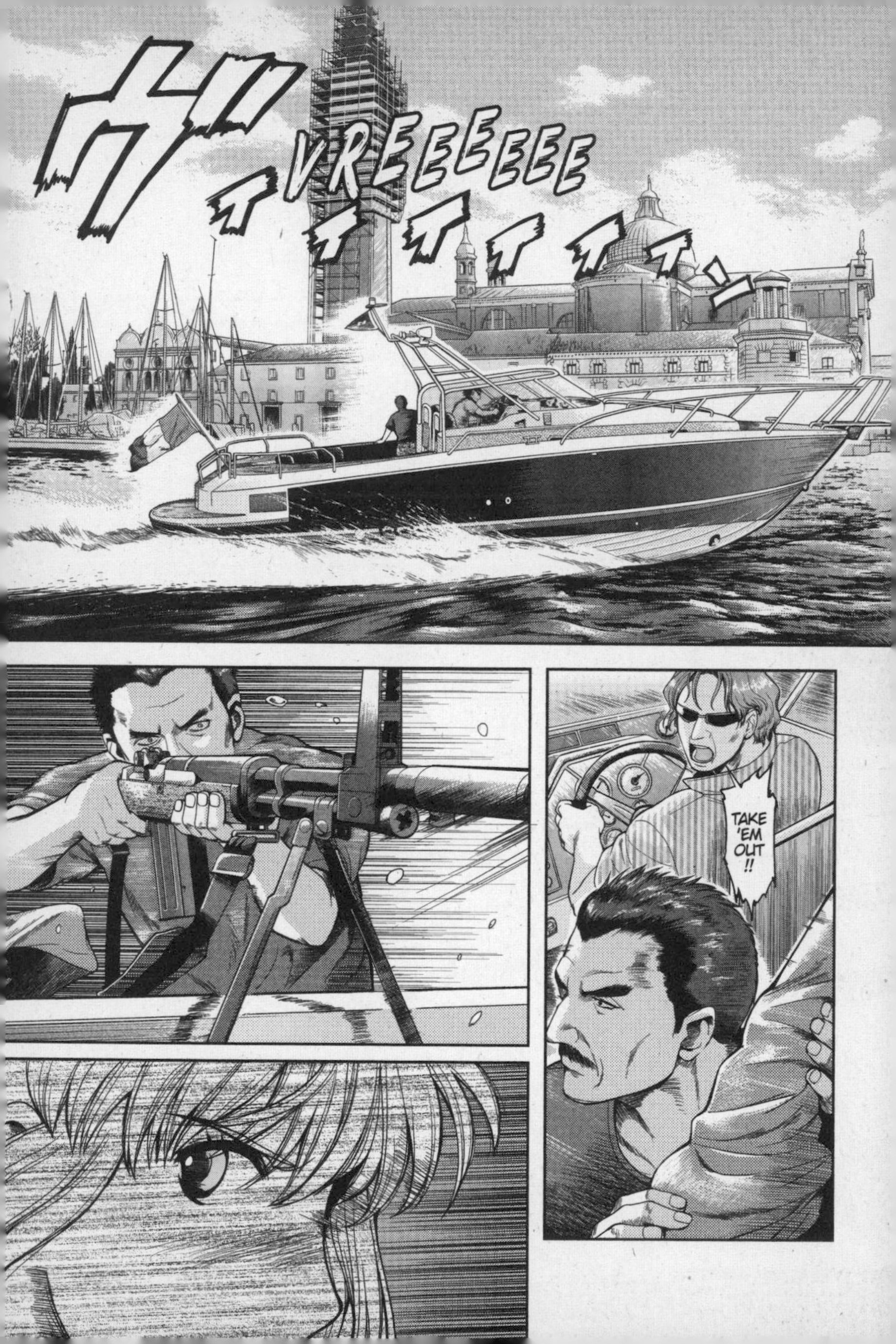
VREEEEEEE
TAKE 'EM OUT !!

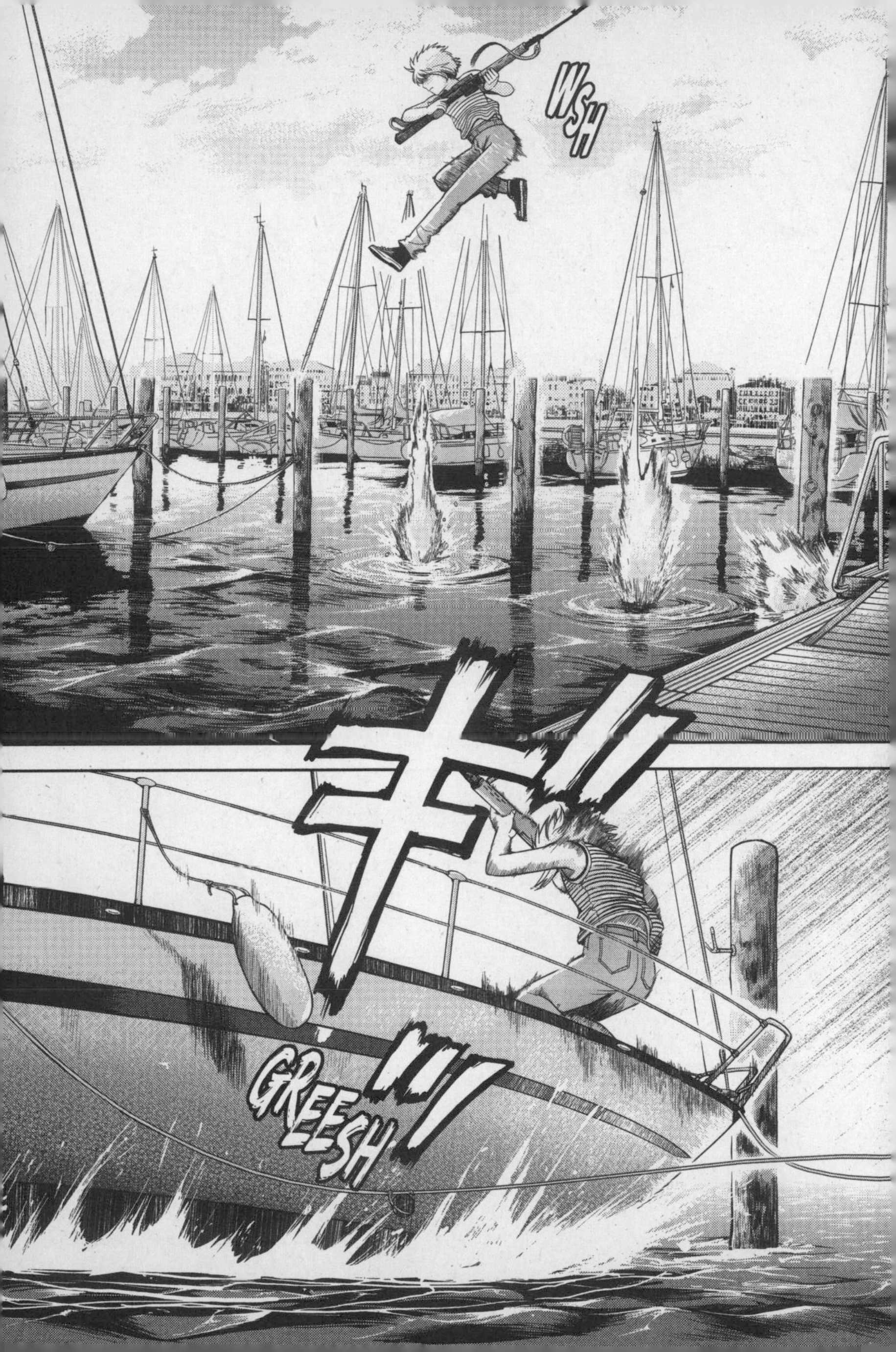
WSH
キ!!
GREESH

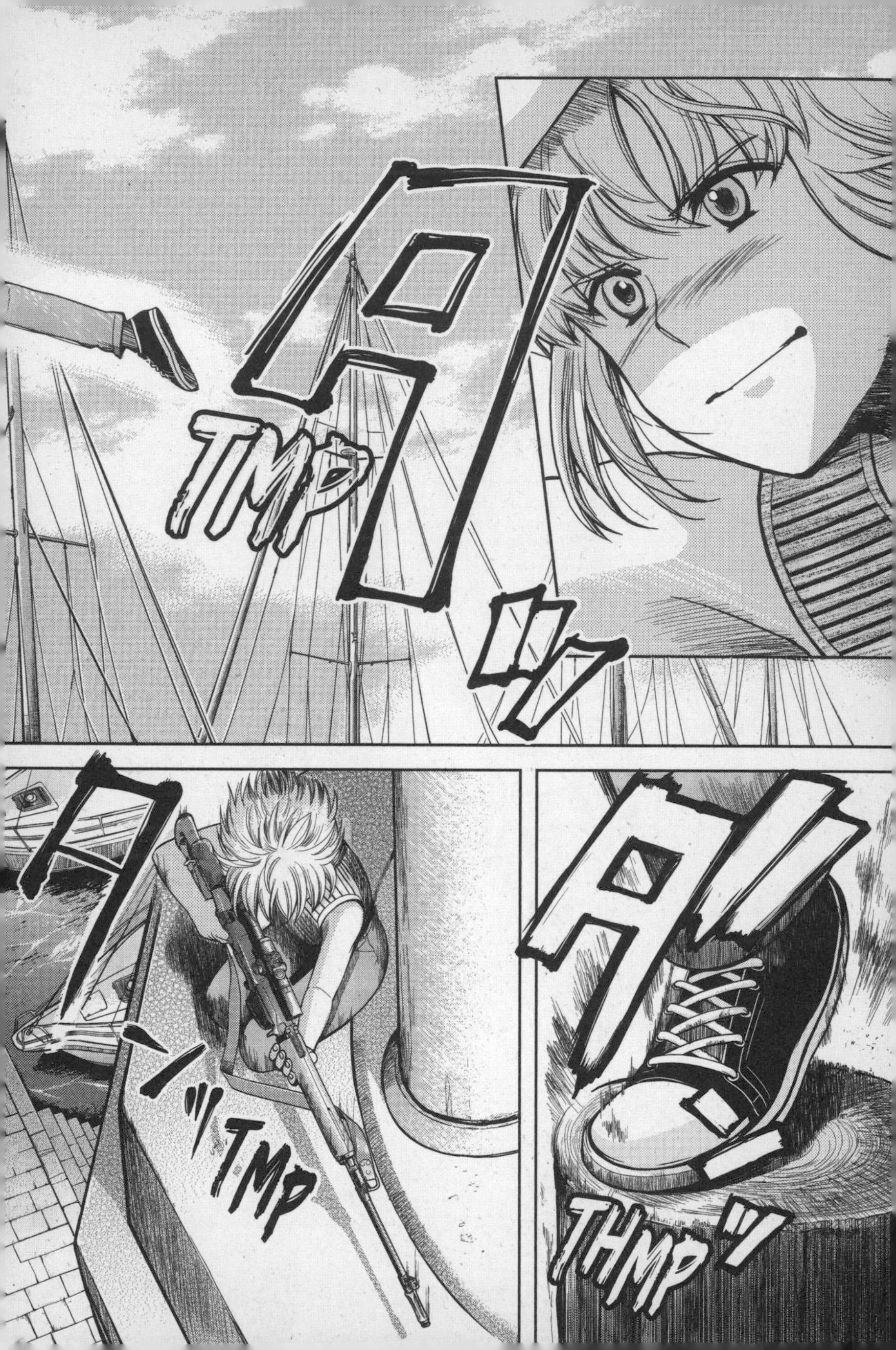
TMP
THMP
TMP

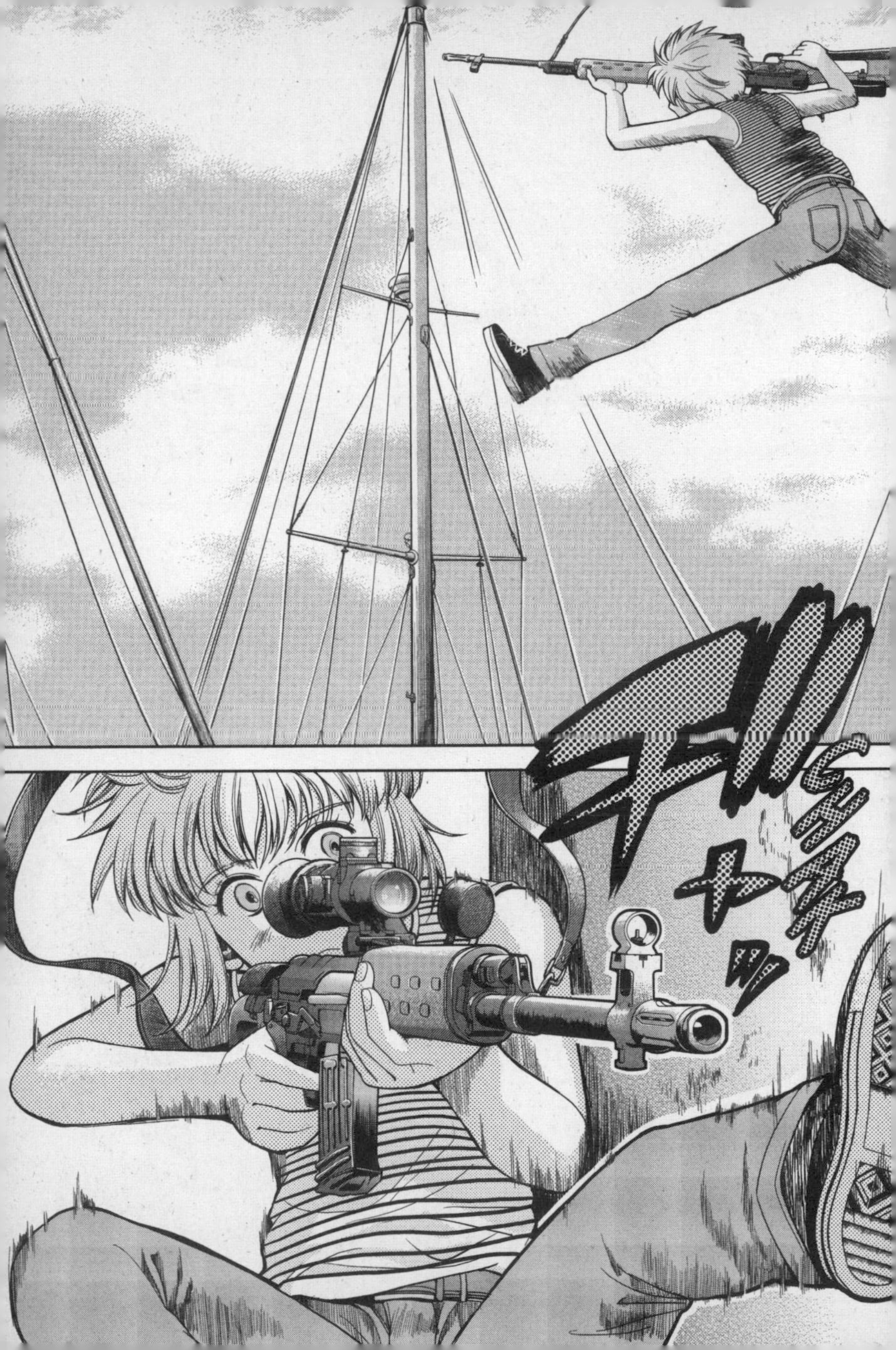
ズチャッ
SHAK

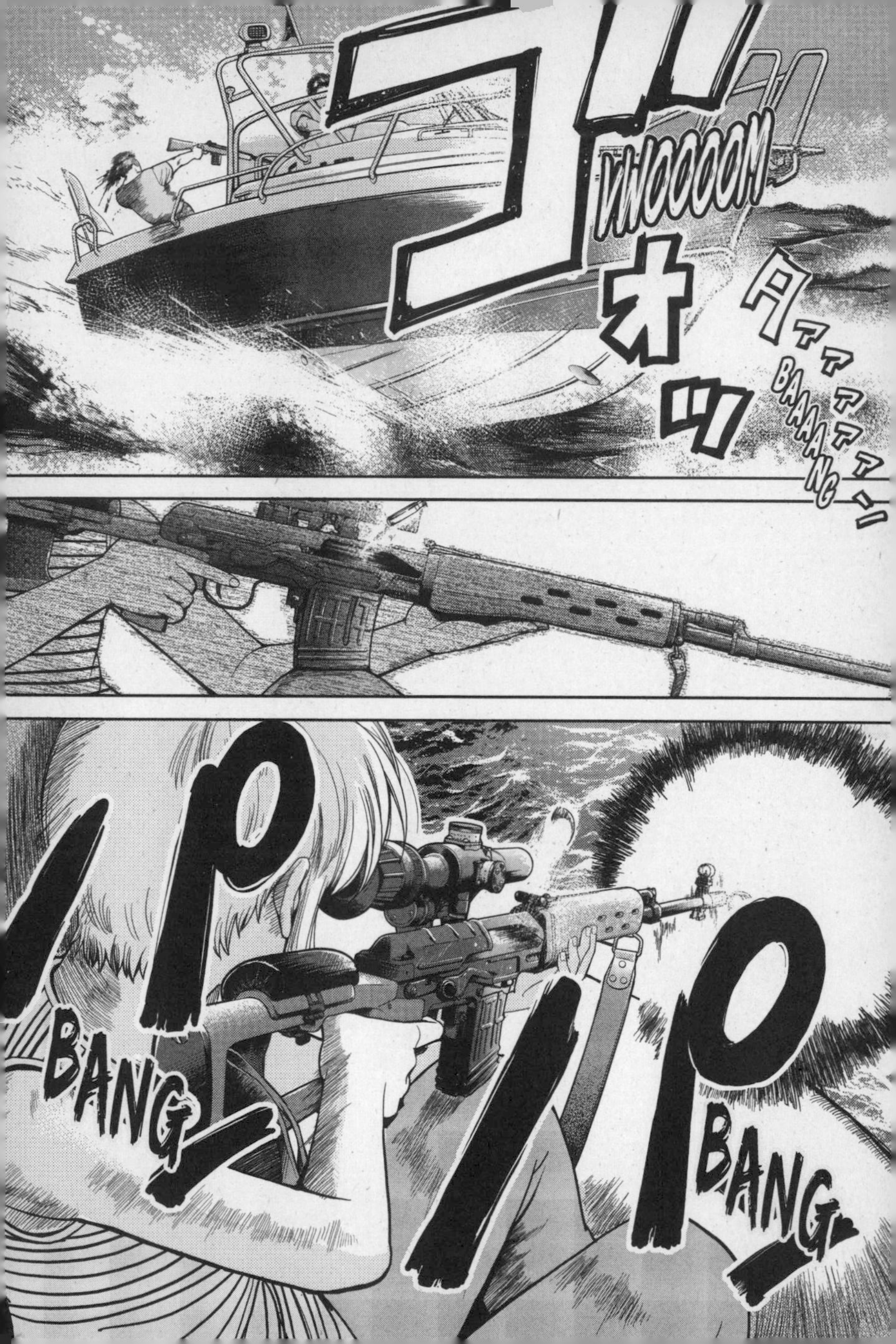

ゴオッ
VWOOOOM
ダァァァァーン
BAAAANG
パン
BANG
パン
BANG

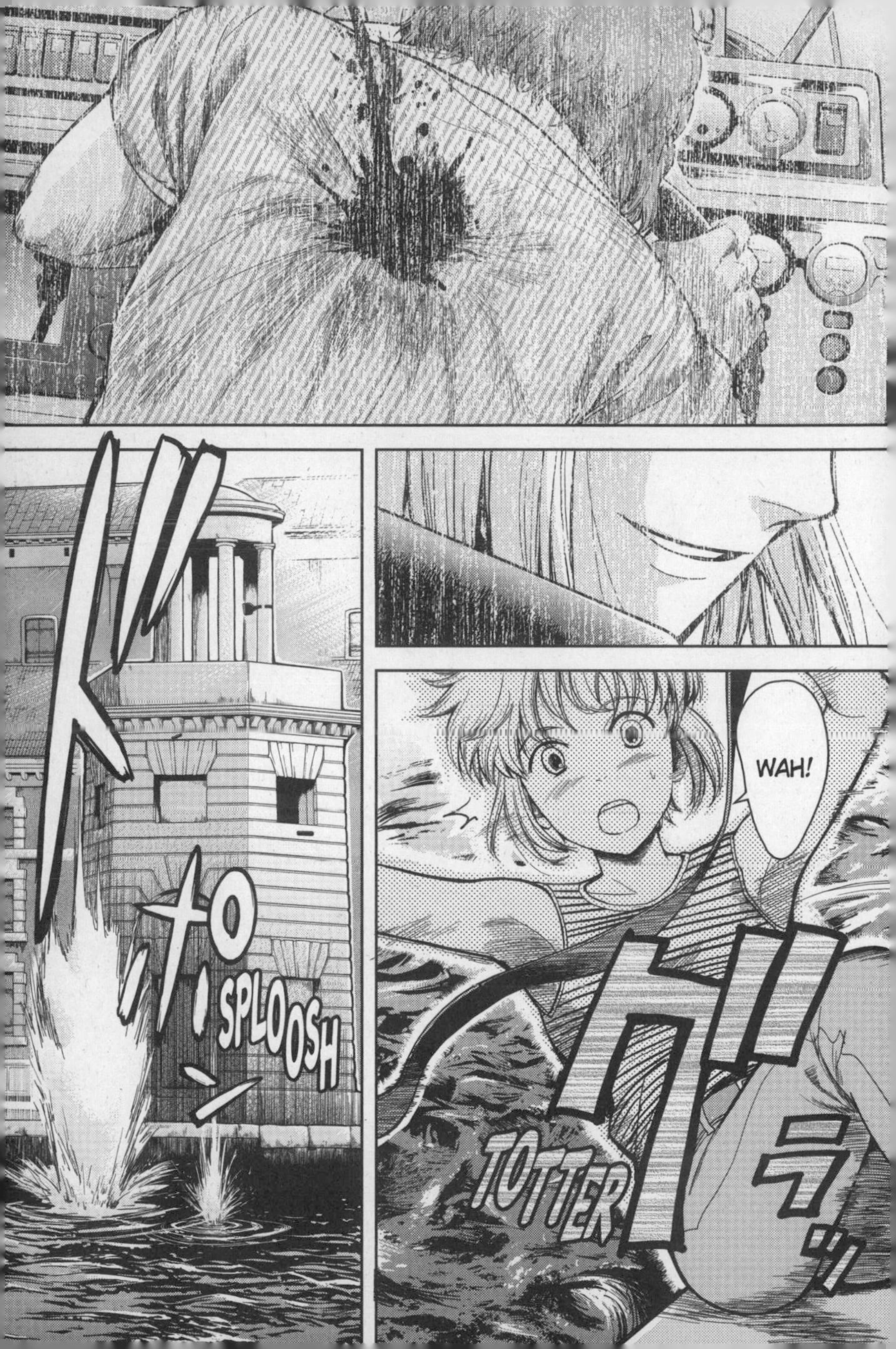
WAH!
TOTTER
SPLOOSH

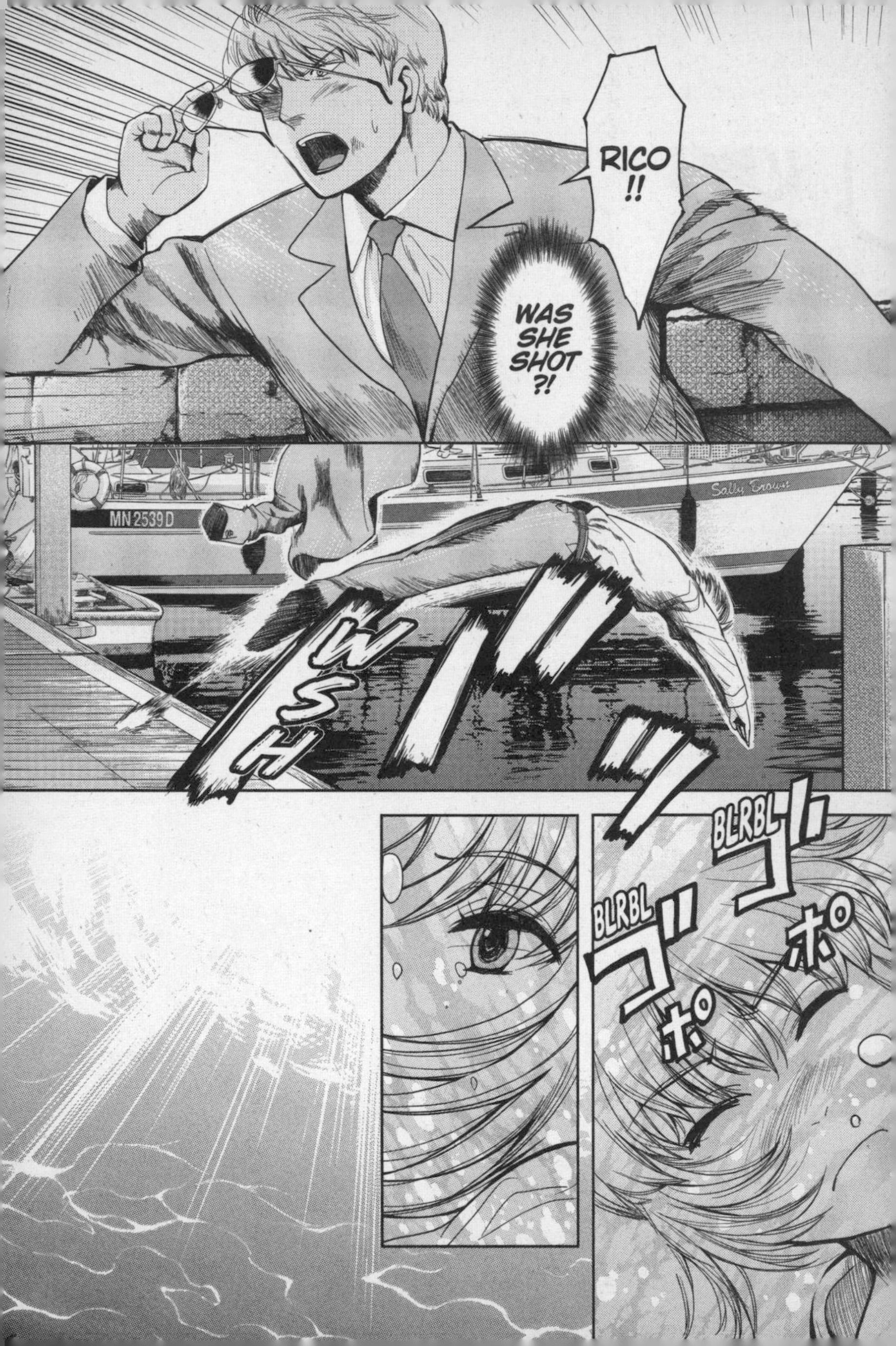
RICO !!
WAS SHE SHOT ?!
WSH
BLRBL
ゴポ
BLRBL
ゴポ

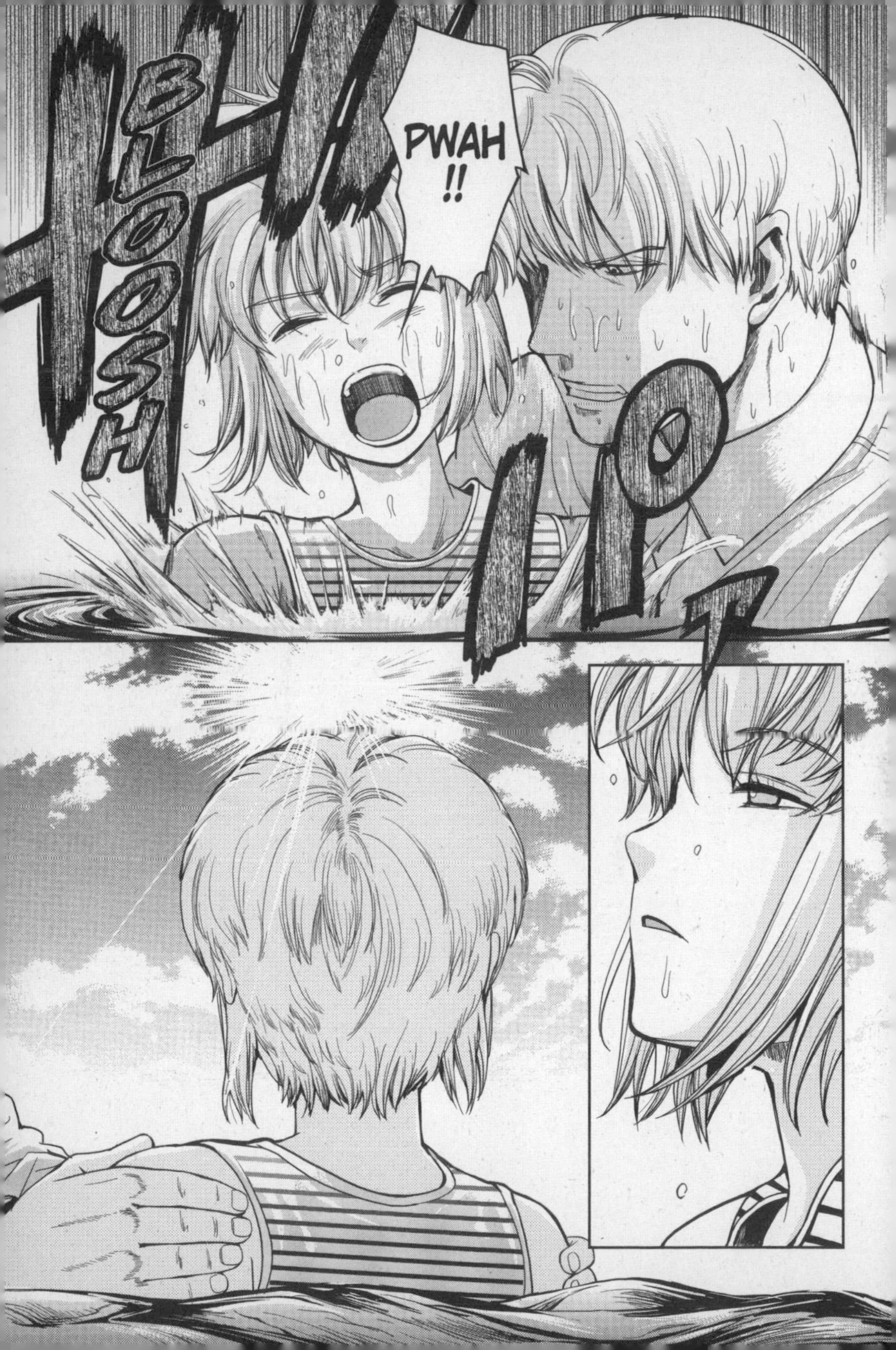
PWAH
!!
BLOOSH

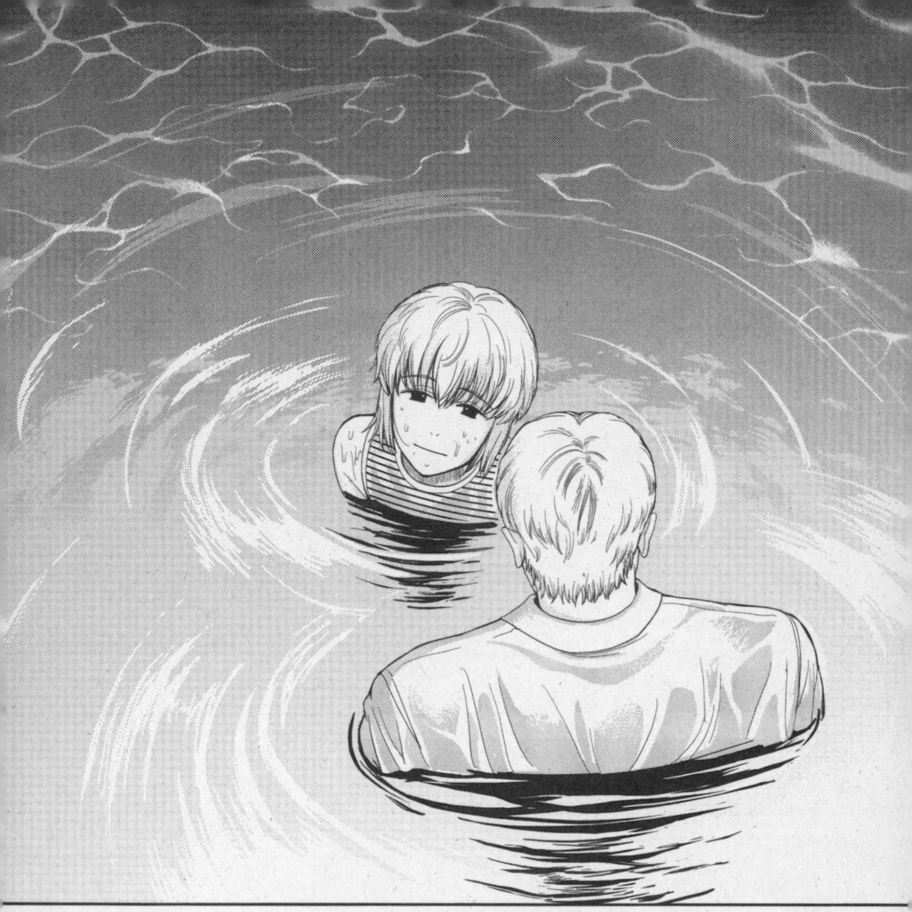
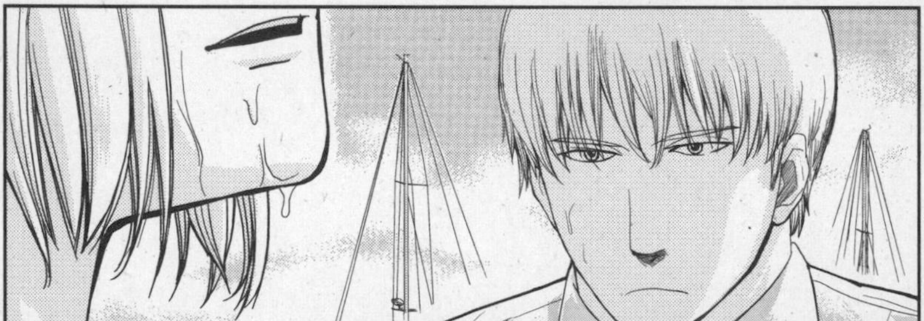

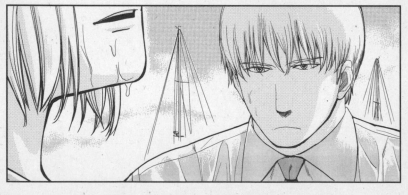

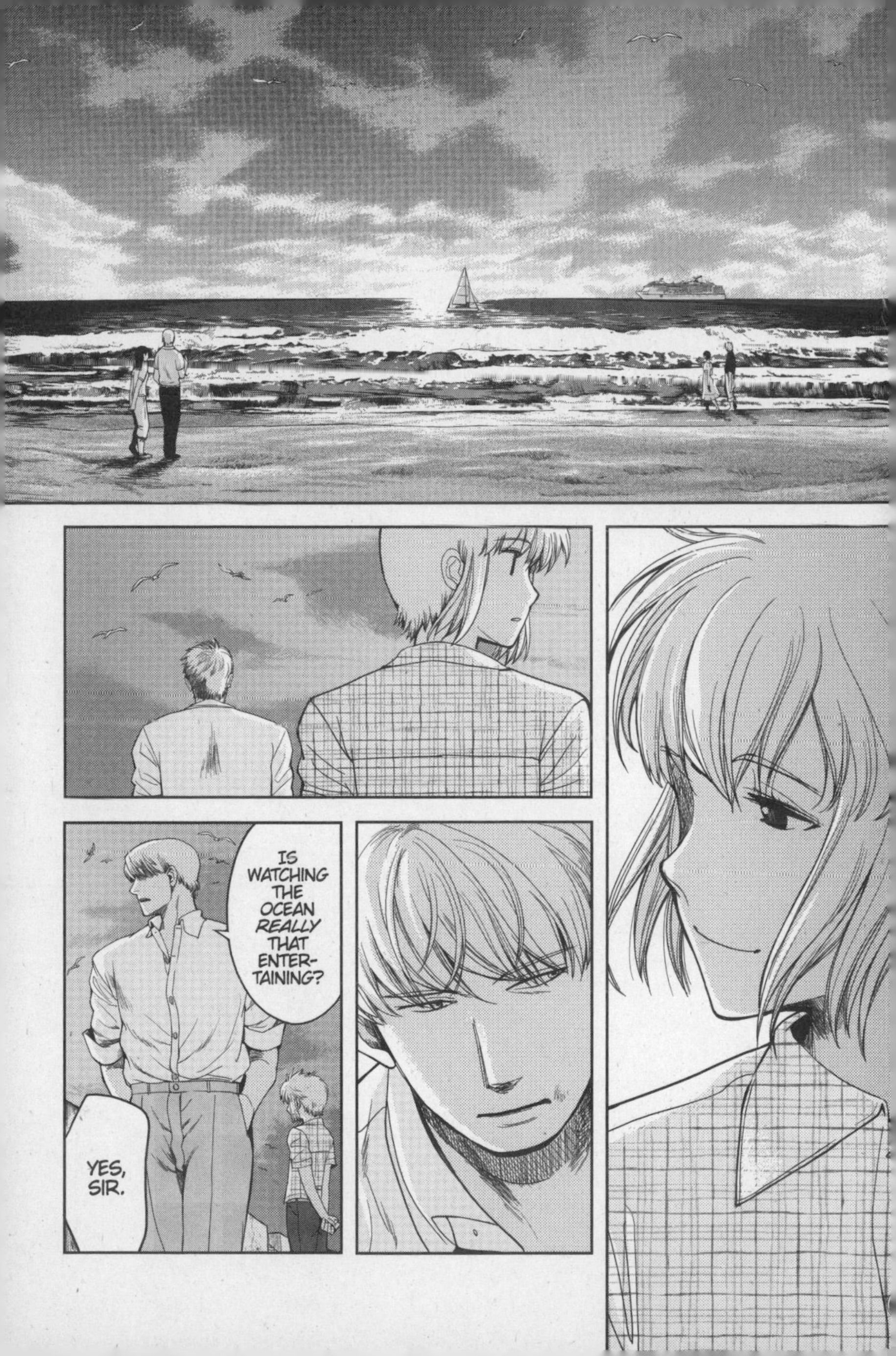
IS WATCHING THE OCEAN *REALLY* THAT ENTERTAINING?
YES, SIR.

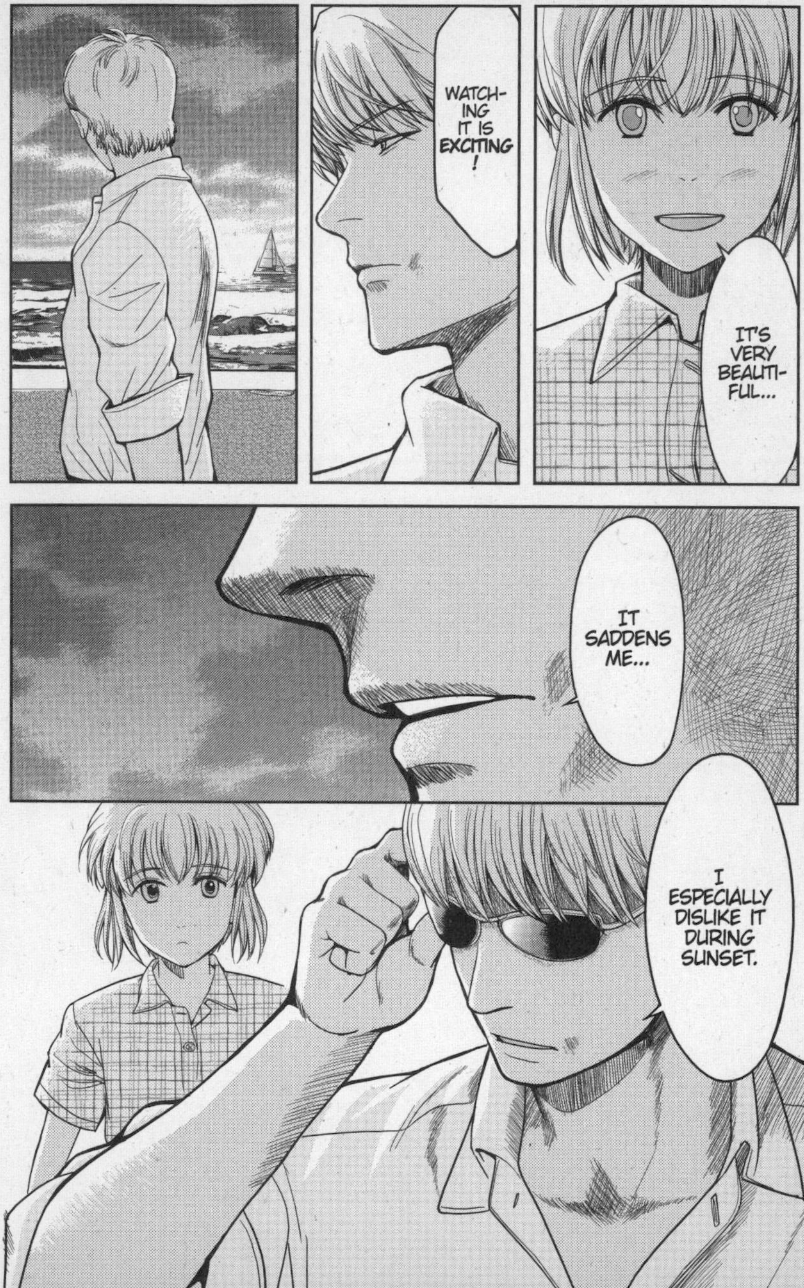
IT'S VERY BEAUTIFUL...
WATCHING IT IS EXCITING!
IT SADDENS ME...
I ESPECIALLY DISLIKE IT DURING SUNSET.

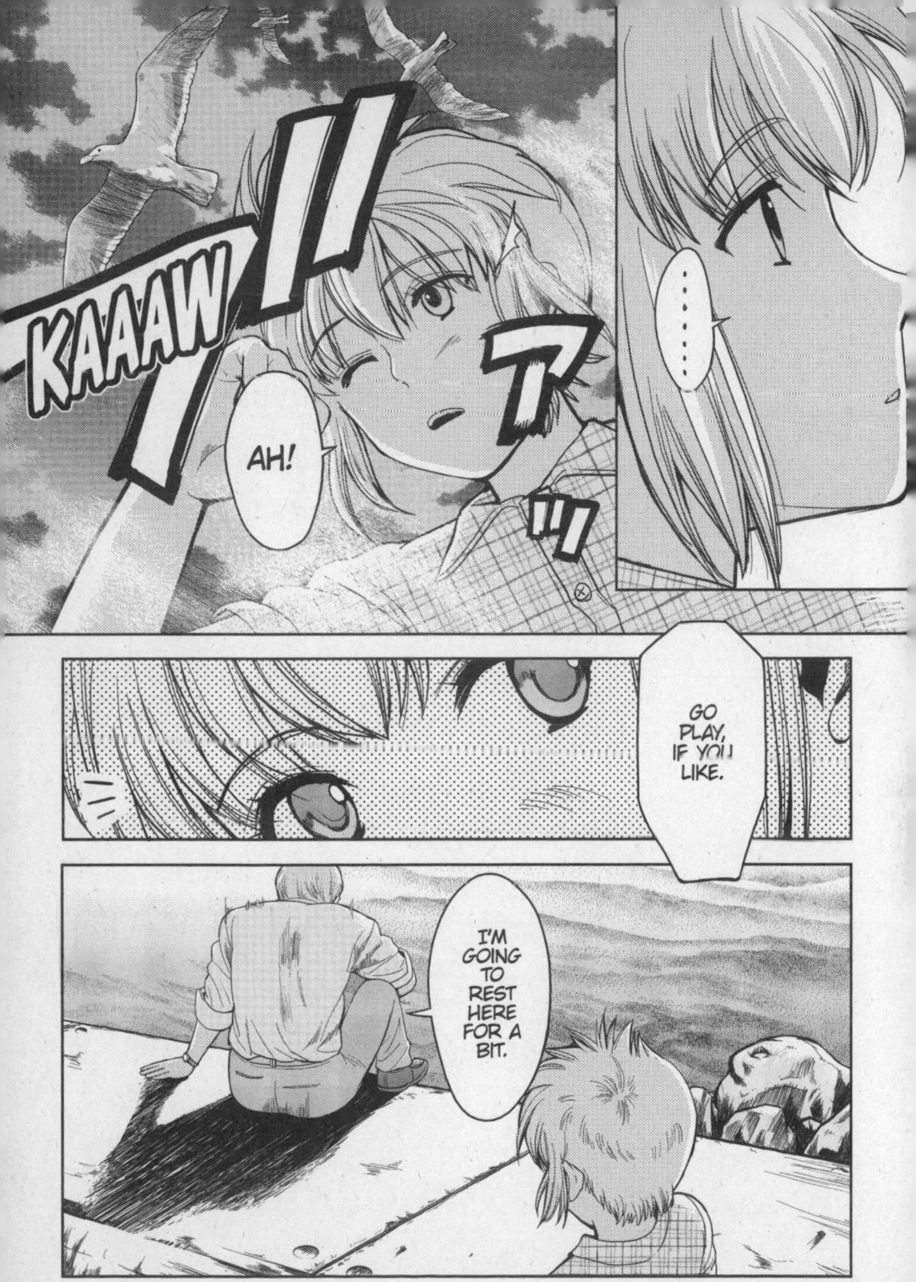
......
KAAAW
AH!
GO PLAY, IF YOU LIKE.
I'M GOING TO REST HERE FOR A BIT.

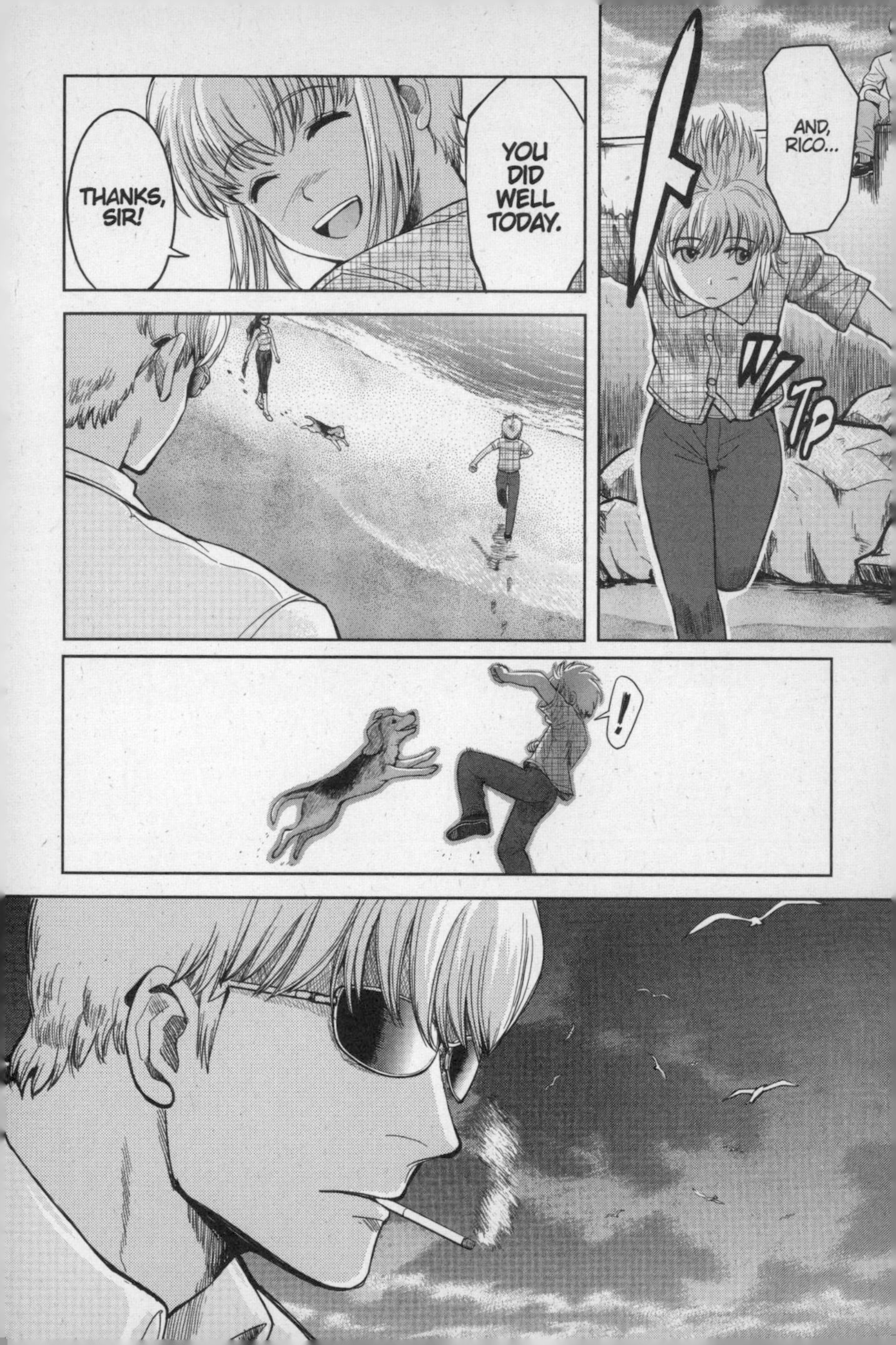
AND, RICO...
TP
YOU DID WELL TODAY.
THANKS, SIR!
!

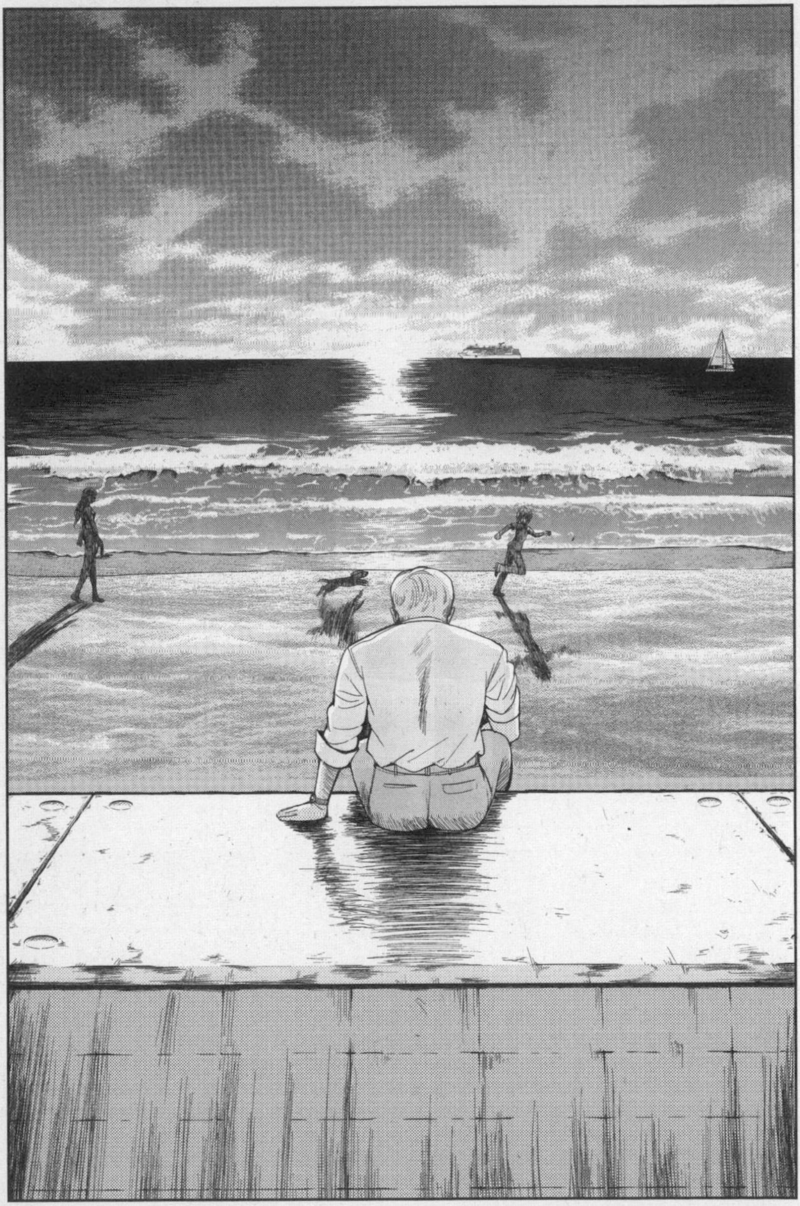

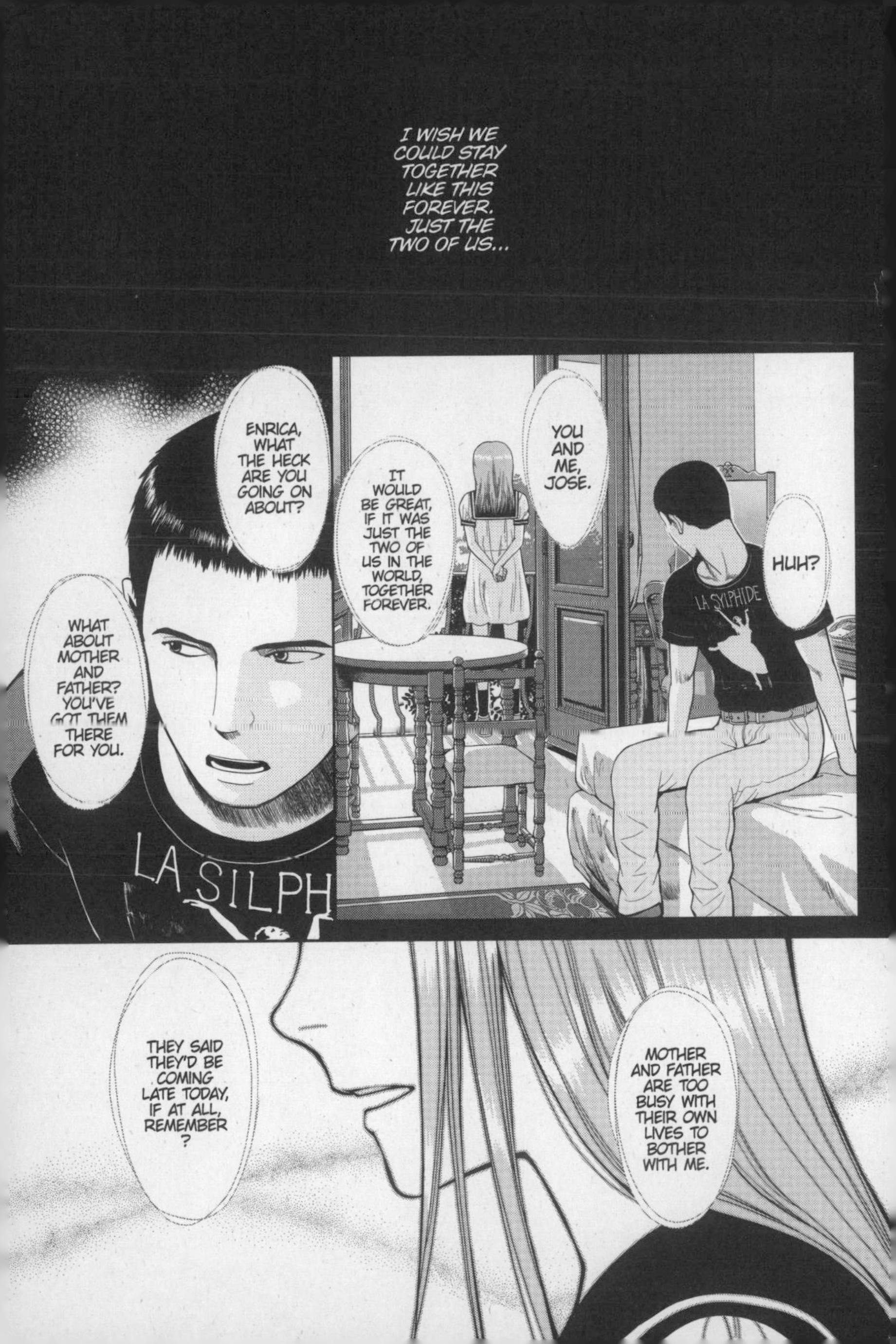
I WISH WE COULD STAY TOGETHER LIKE THIS FOREVER. JUST THE TWO OF US...
IT WOULD BE GREAT, IF IT WAS JUST THE TWO OF US IN THE WORLD, TOGETHER FOREVER.
YOU AND ME, JOSE.
HUH?
LA SYLPHIDE
ENRICA, WHAT THE HECK ARE YOU GOING ON ABOUT?
WHAT ABOUT MOTHER AND FATHER? YOU'VE GOT THEM THERE FOR YOU.
LA SILPH
MOTHER AND FATHER ARE TOO BUSY WITH THEIR OWN LIVES TO BOTHER WITH ME.
THEY SAID THEY'D BE COMING LATE TODAY, IF AT ALL, REMEMBER?

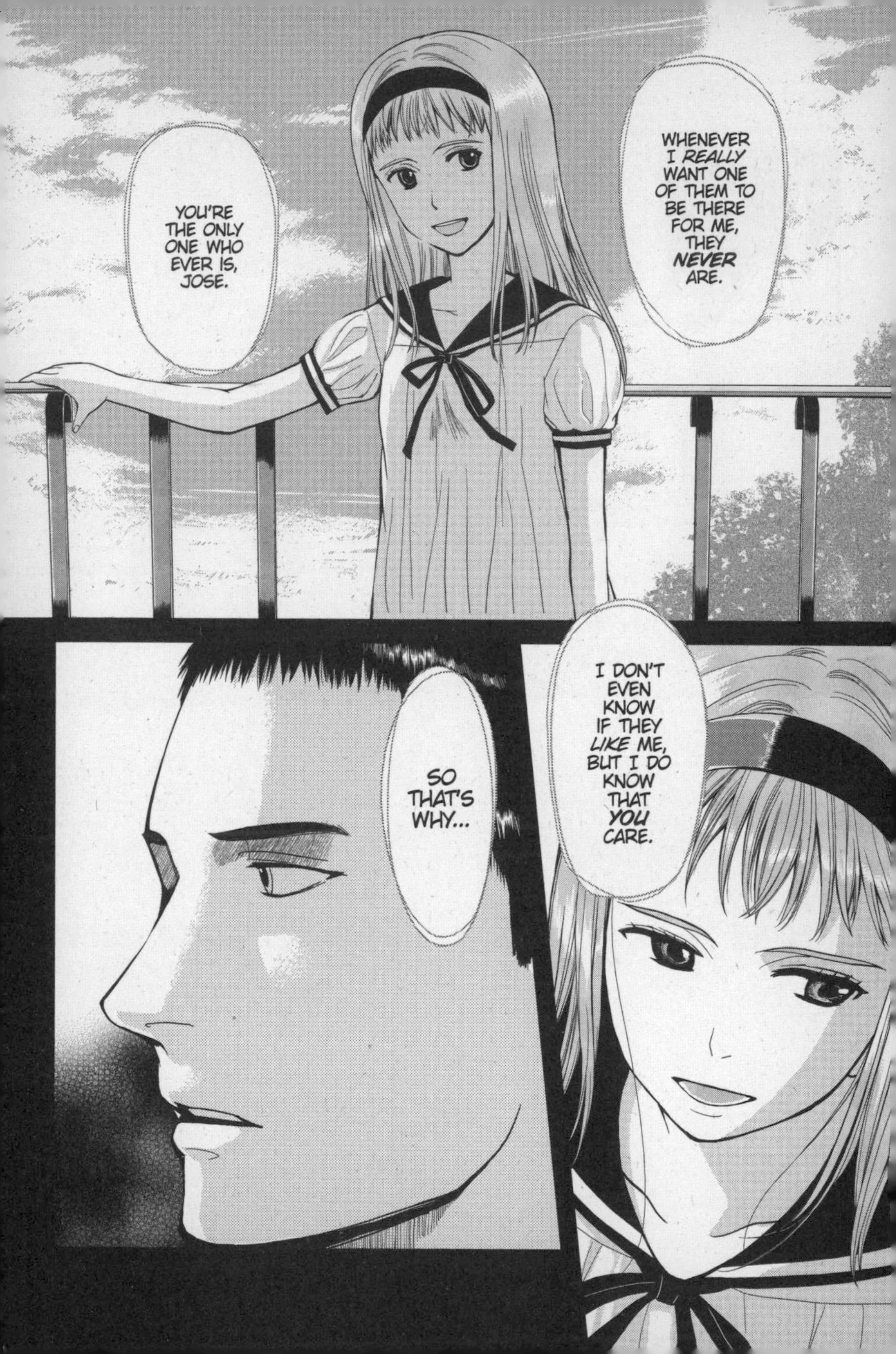
WHENEVER I *REALLY* WANT ONE OF THEM TO BE THERE FOR ME, THEY ***NEVER*** ARE.
YOU'RE THE ONLY ONE WHO EVER IS, JOSE.
I DON'T EVEN KNOW IF THEY *LIKE* ME, BUT I DO KNOW THAT ***YOU*** CARE.
SO THAT'S WHY...

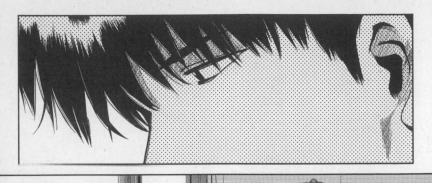

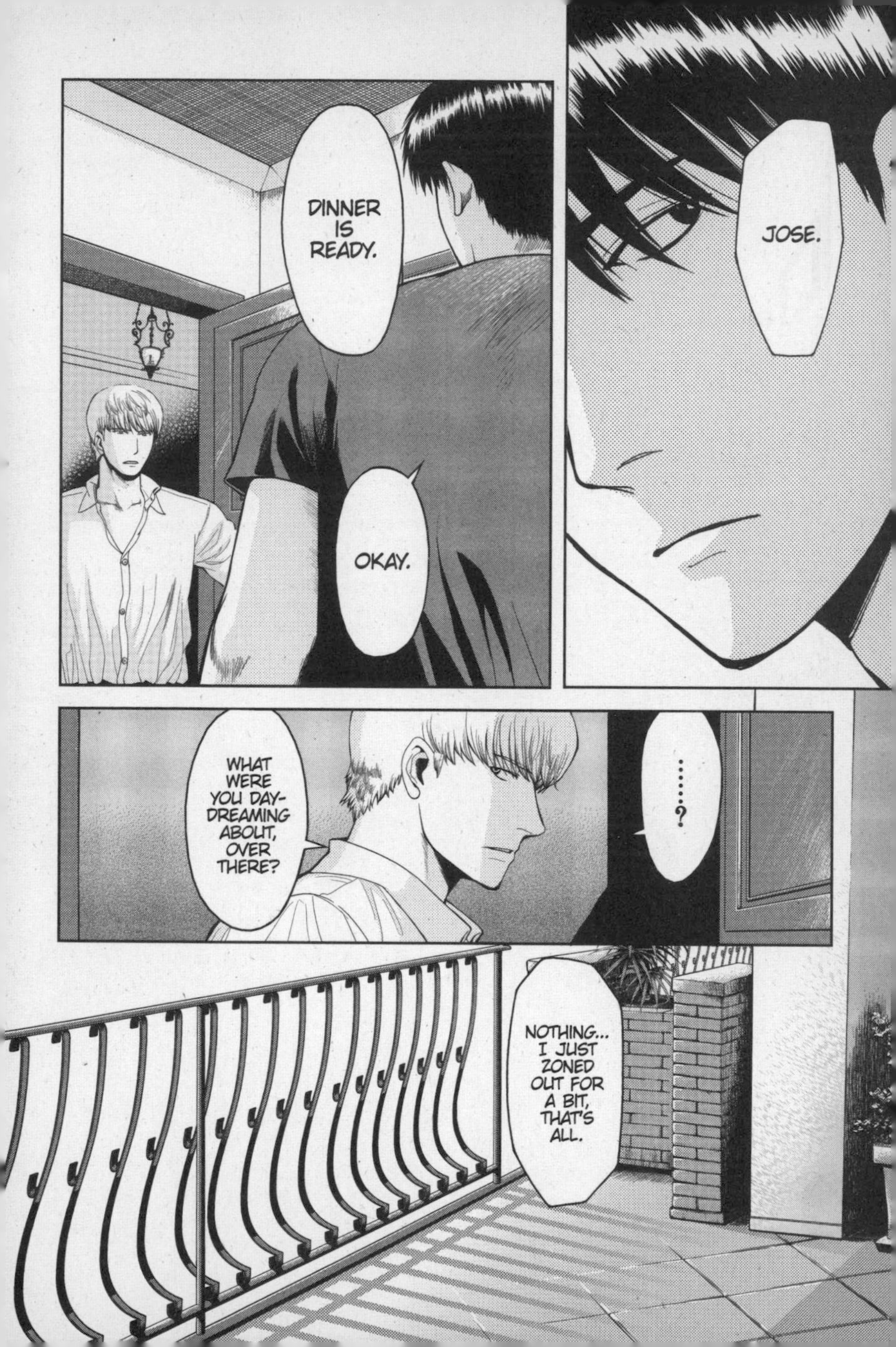
JOSE.
DINNER IS READY.
OKAY.
......?
WHAT WERE YOU DAY-DREAMING ABOUT, OVER THERE?
NOTHING... I JUST ZONED OUT FOR A BIT, THAT'S ALL.

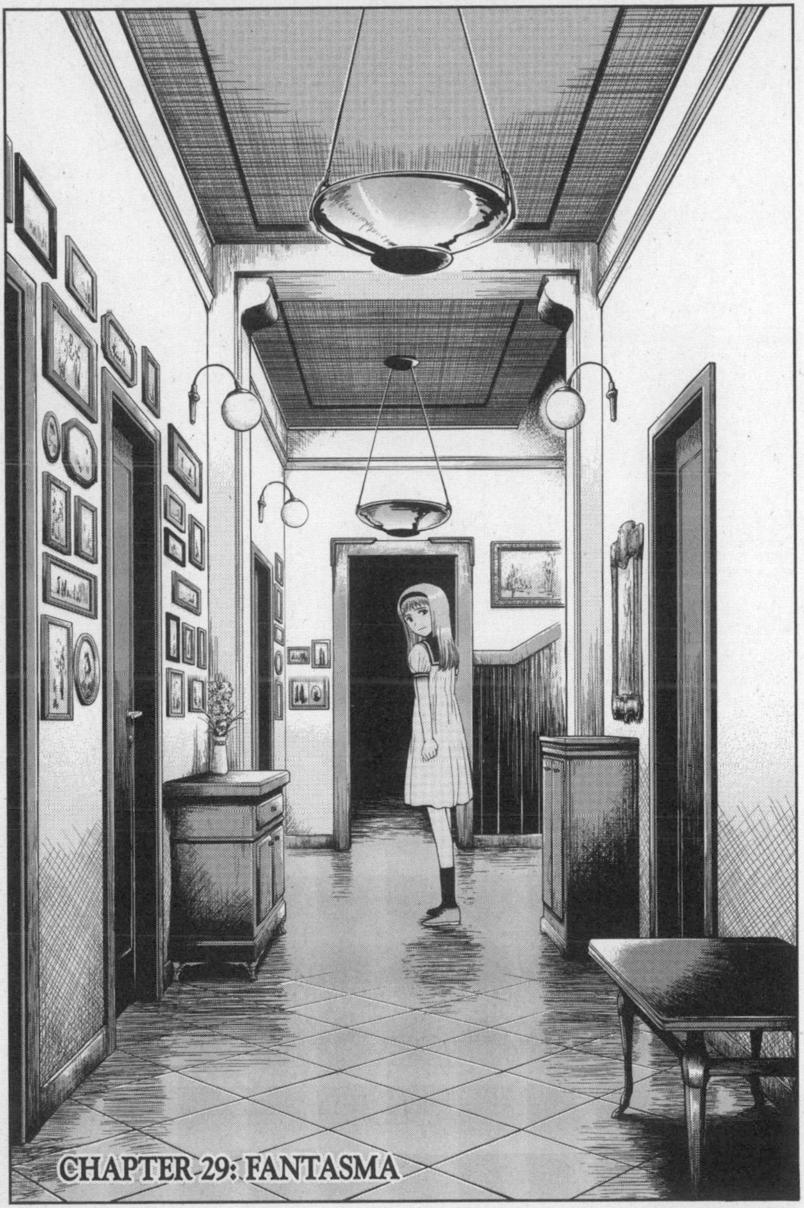
CHAPTER 29: FANTASMA

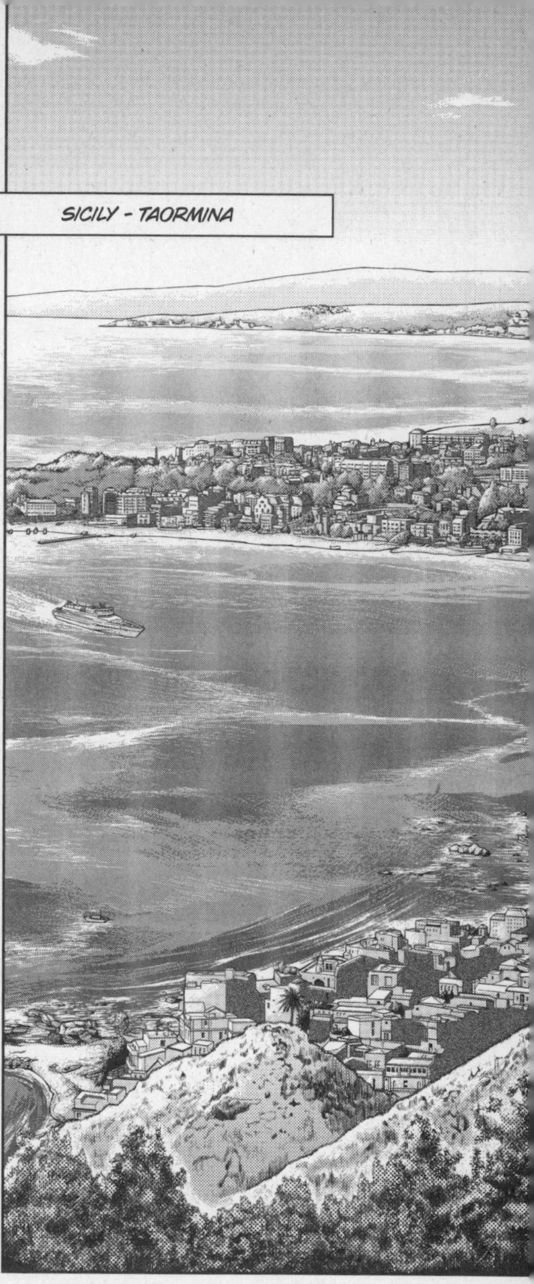
SICILY - TAORMINA

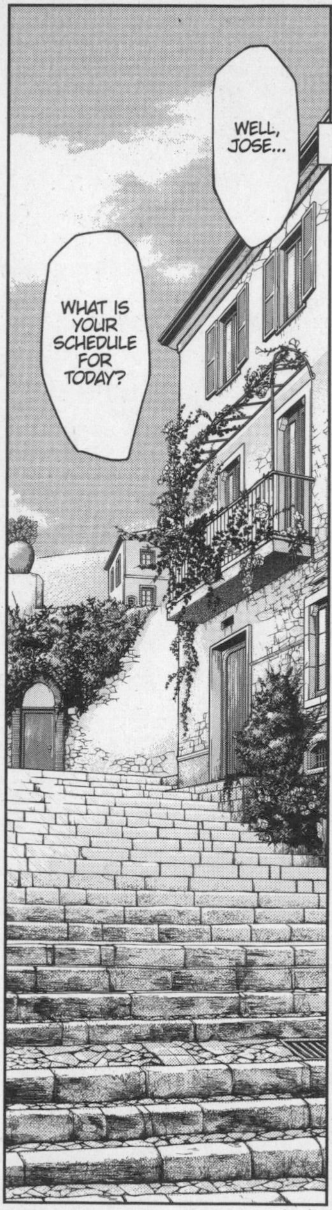
WELL, JOSE...
WHAT IS YOUR SCHEDULE FOR TODAY?

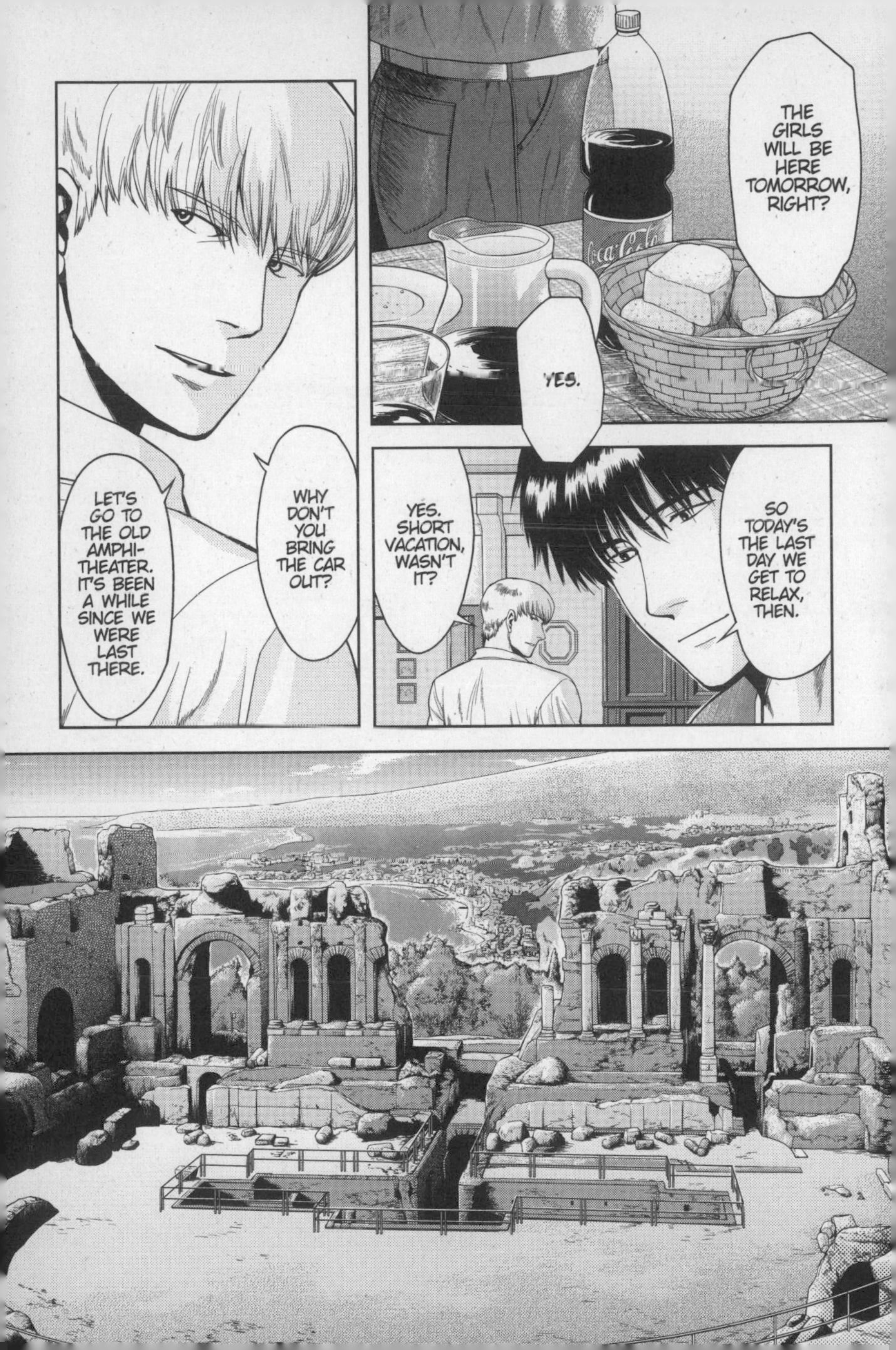

THE GIRLS WILL BE HERE TOMORROW, RIGHT?
YES.
SO TODAY'S THE LAST DAY WE GET TO RELAX, THEN.
YES. SHORT VACATION, WASN'T IT?
WHY DON'T YOU BRING THE CAR OUT?
LET'S GO TO THE OLD AMPHI-THEATER. IT'S BEEN A WHILE SINCE WE WERE LAST THERE.

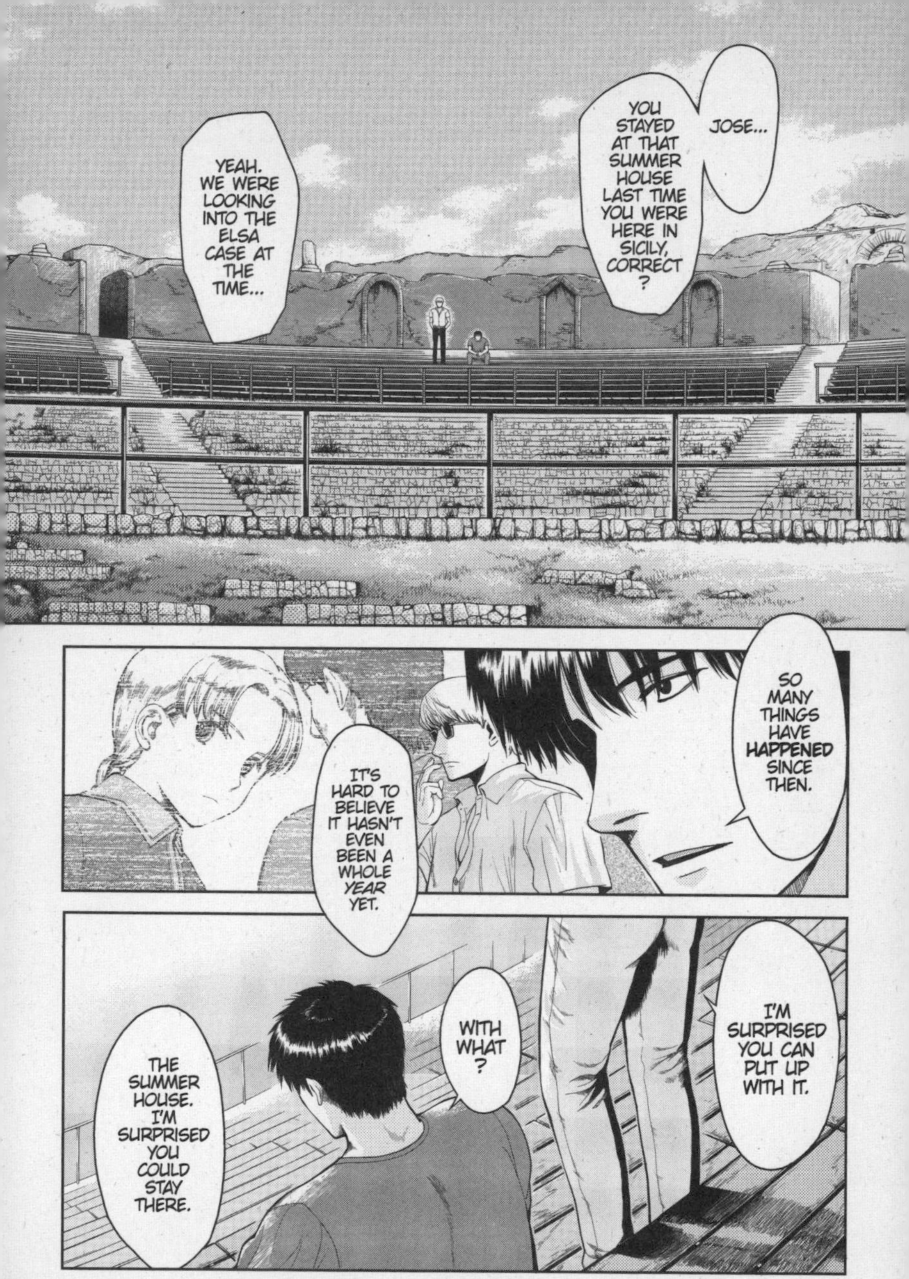
JOSE...
YOU STAYED AT THAT SUMMER HOUSE LAST TIME YOU WERE HERE IN SICILY, CORRECT?
YEAH. WE WERE LOOKING INTO THE ELSA CASE AT THE TIME...
SO MANY THINGS HAVE HAPPENED SINCE THEN.
IT'S HARD TO BELIEVE IT HASN'T EVEN BEEN A WHOLE YEAR YET.
I'M SURPRISED YOU CAN PUT UP WITH IT.
WITH WHAT?
THE SUMMER HOUSE. I'M SURPRISED YOU COULD STAY THERE.

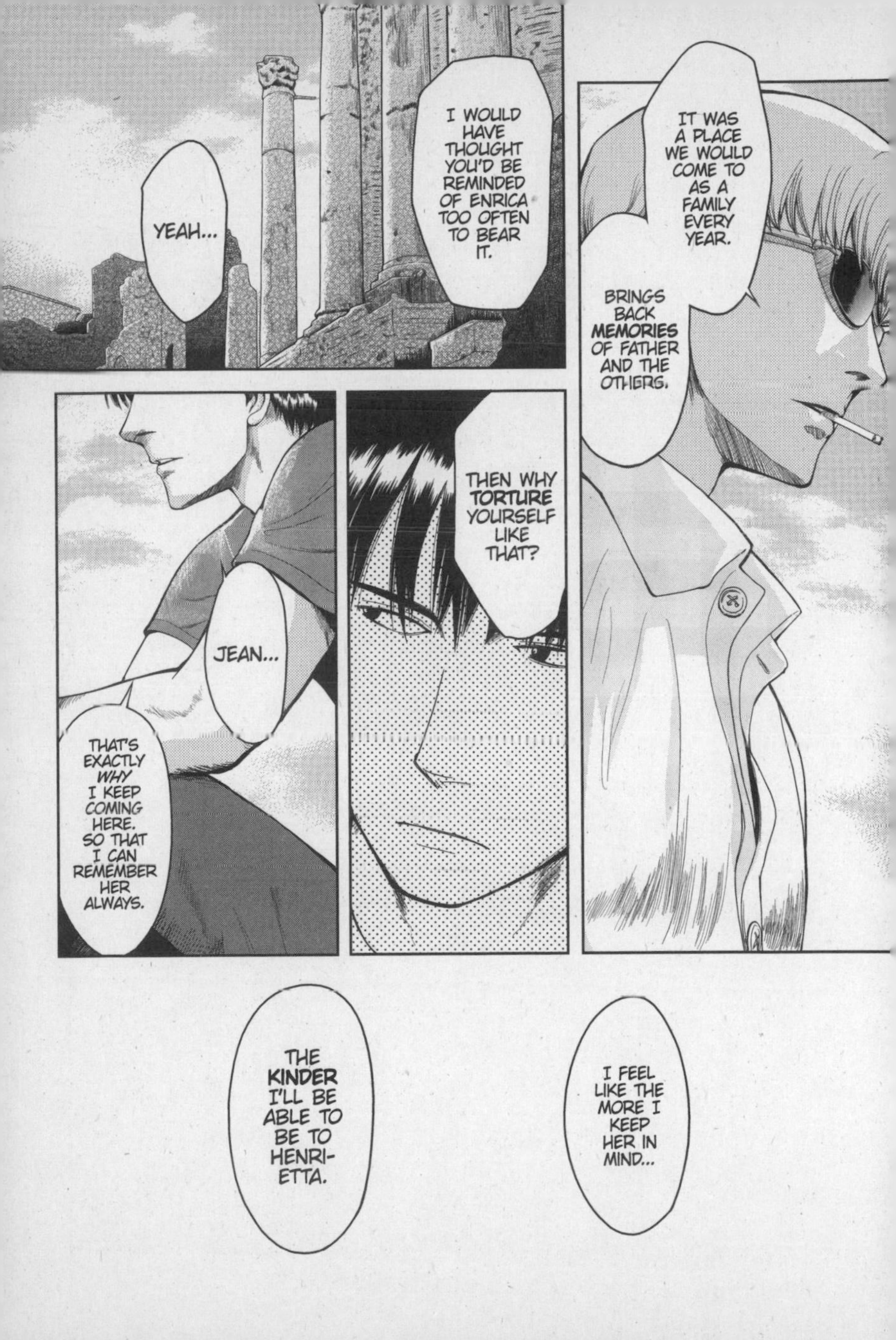
IT WAS A PLACE WE WOULD COME TO AS A FAMILY EVERY YEAR.
BRINGS BACK MEMORIES OF FATHER AND THE OTHERS.
I WOULD HAVE THOUGHT YOU'D BE REMINDED OF ENRICA TOO OFTEN TO BEAR IT.
YEAH...
THEN WHY TORTURE YOURSELF LIKE THAT?
JEAN...
THAT'S EXACTLY WHY I KEEP COMING HERE. SO THAT I CAN REMEMBER HER ALWAYS.
I FEEL LIKE THE MORE I KEEP HER IN MIND...
THE KINDER I'LL BE ABLE TO BE TO HENRIETTA.

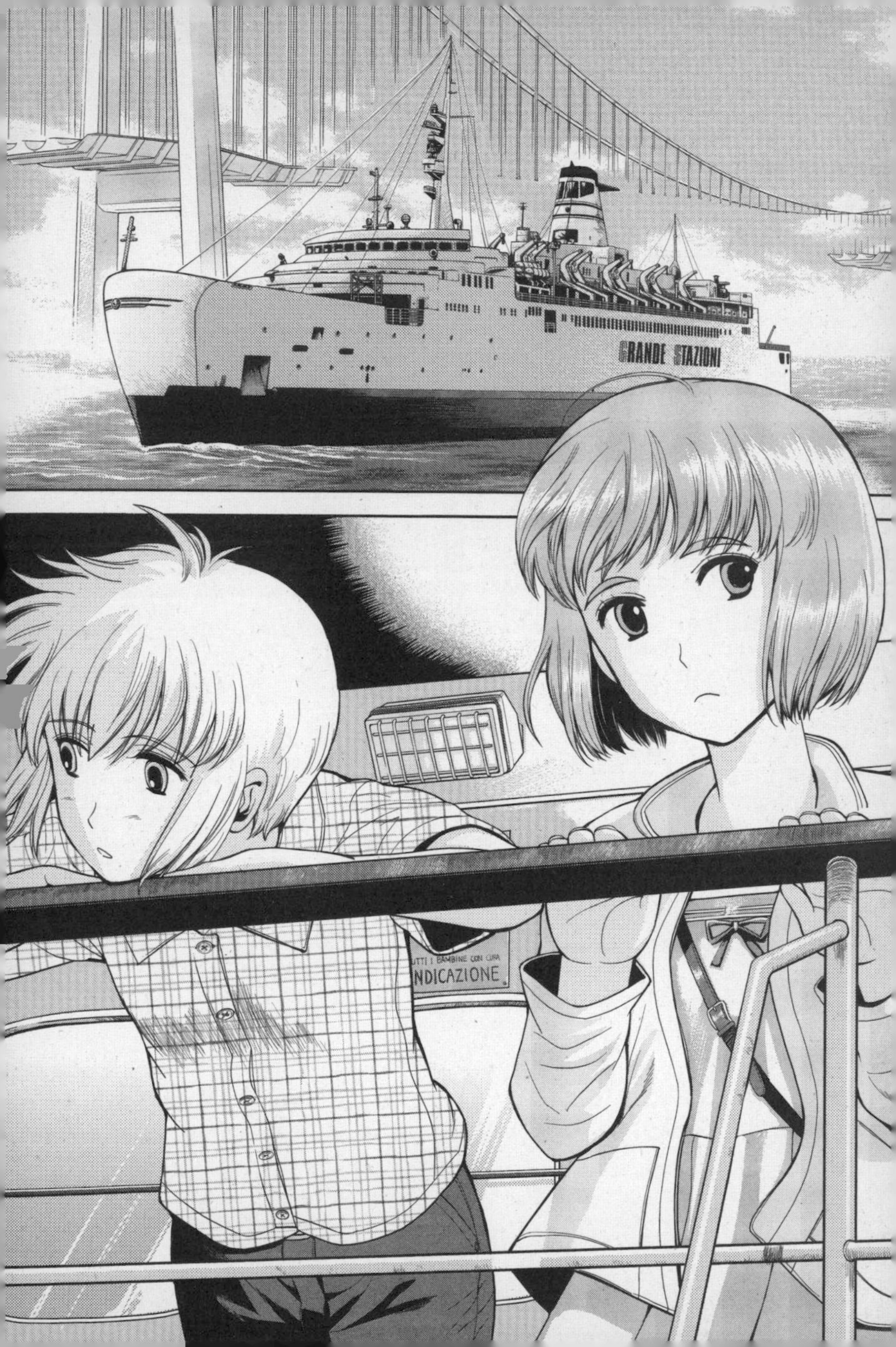
GRANDE STAZIONI
NDICAZIONE

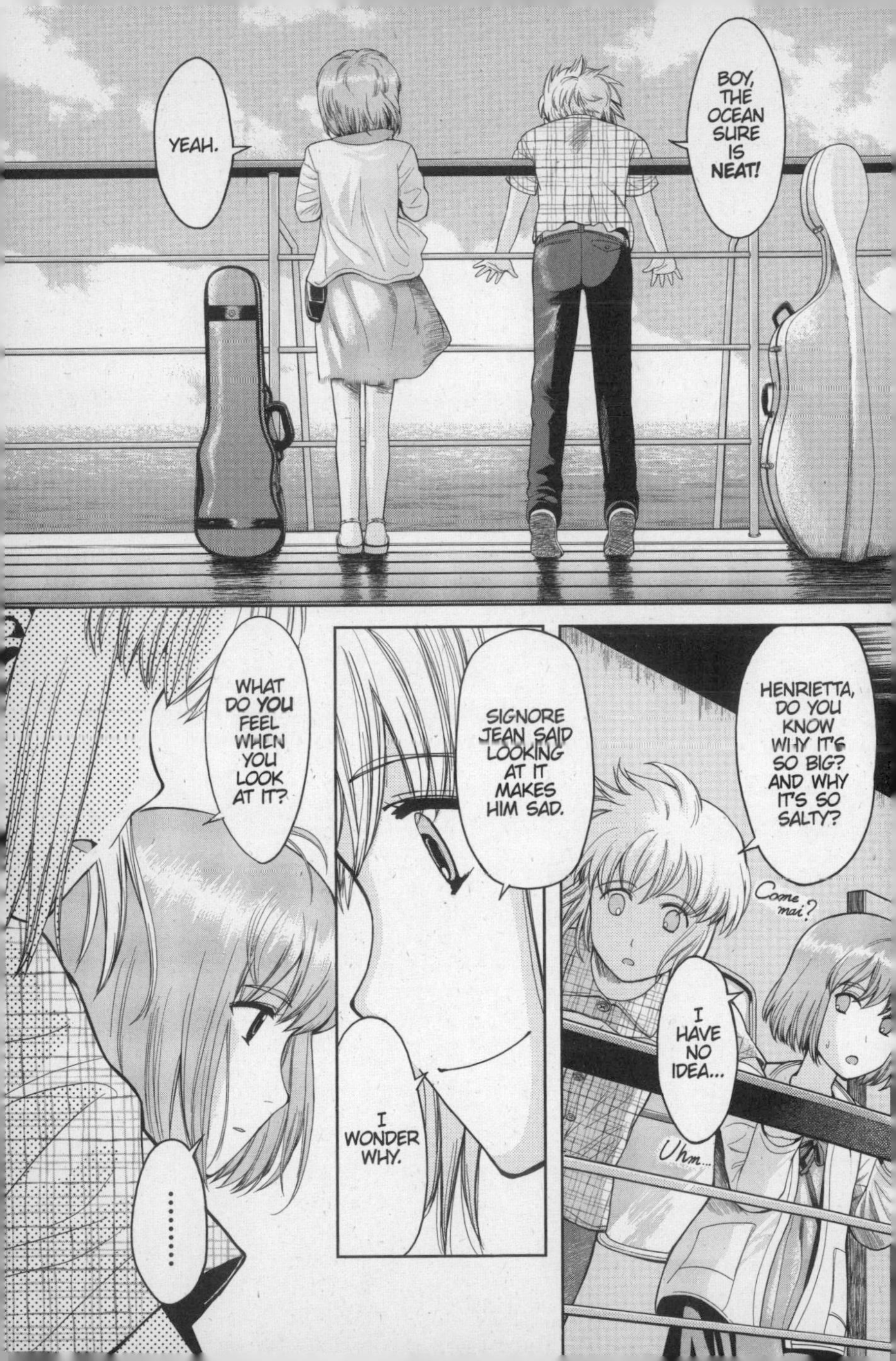
BOY, THE OCEAN SURE IS NEAT!
YEAH.
HENRIETTA, DO YOU KNOW WHY IT'S SO BIG? AND WHY IT'S SO SALTY?
Come mai?
I HAVE NO IDEA...
Uhm...
SIGNORE JEAN SAID LOOKING AT IT MAKES HIM SAD.
I WONDER WHY.
WHAT DO YOU FEEL WHEN YOU LOOK AT IT?
......

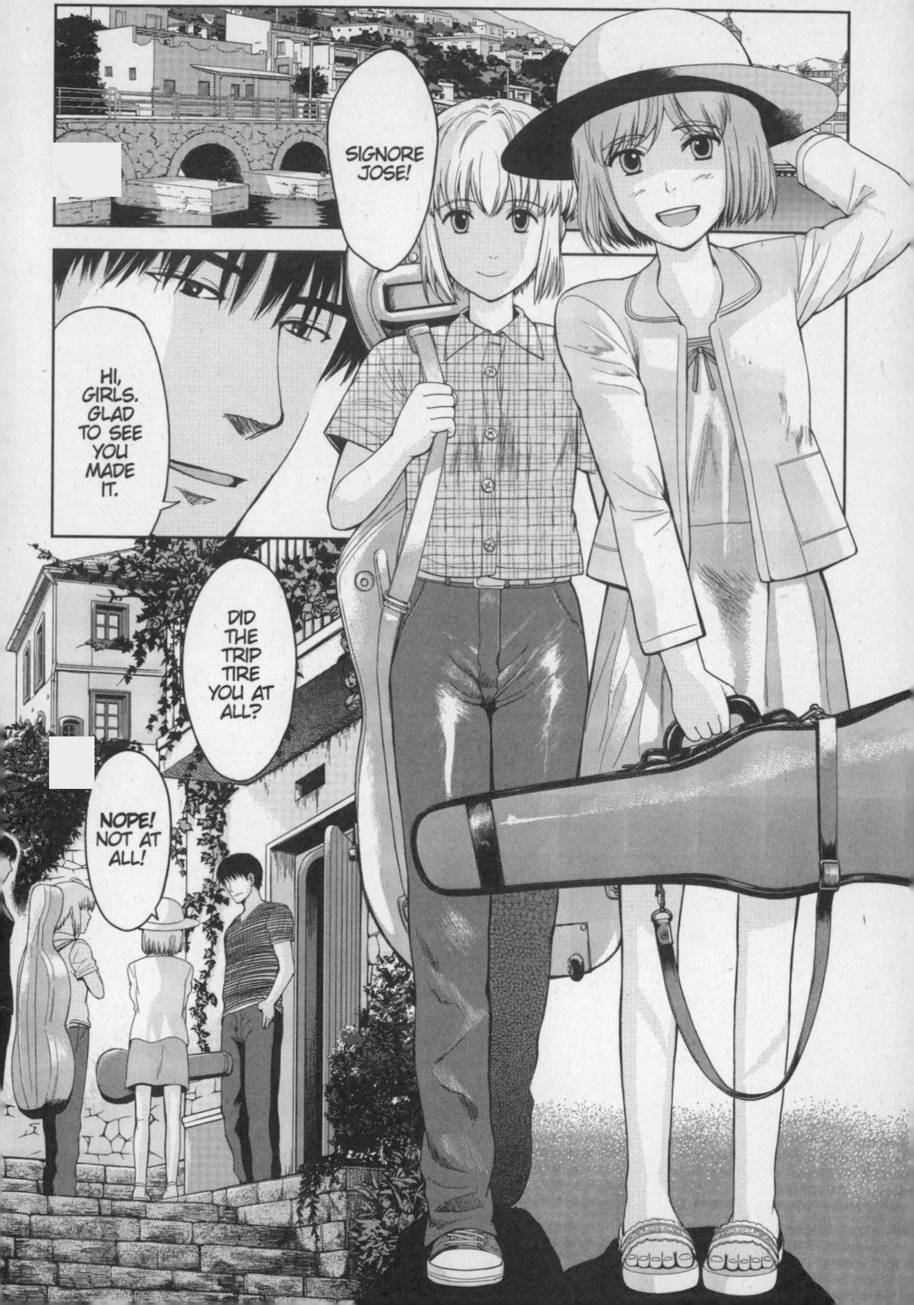
SIGNORE JOSE!
HI, GIRLS. GLAD TO SEE YOU MADE IT.
DID THE TRIP TIRE YOU AT ALL?
NOPE! NOT AT ALL!

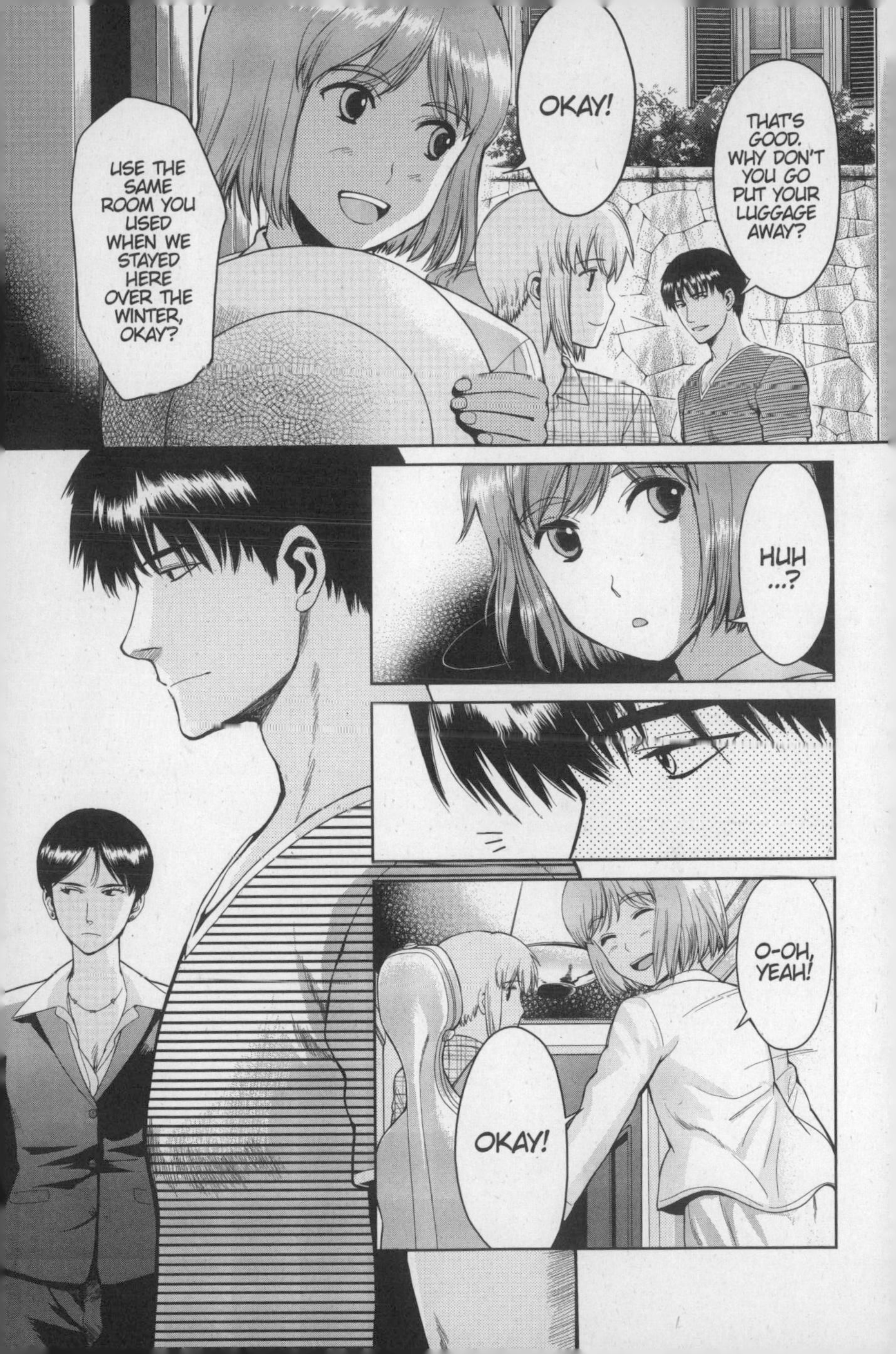
THAT'S GOOD. WHY DON'T YOU GO PUT YOUR LUGGAGE AWAY?
OKAY!
USE THE SAME ROOM YOU USED WHEN WE STAYED HERE OVER THE WINTER, OKAY?
HUH ...?
O-OH, YEAH!
OKAY!

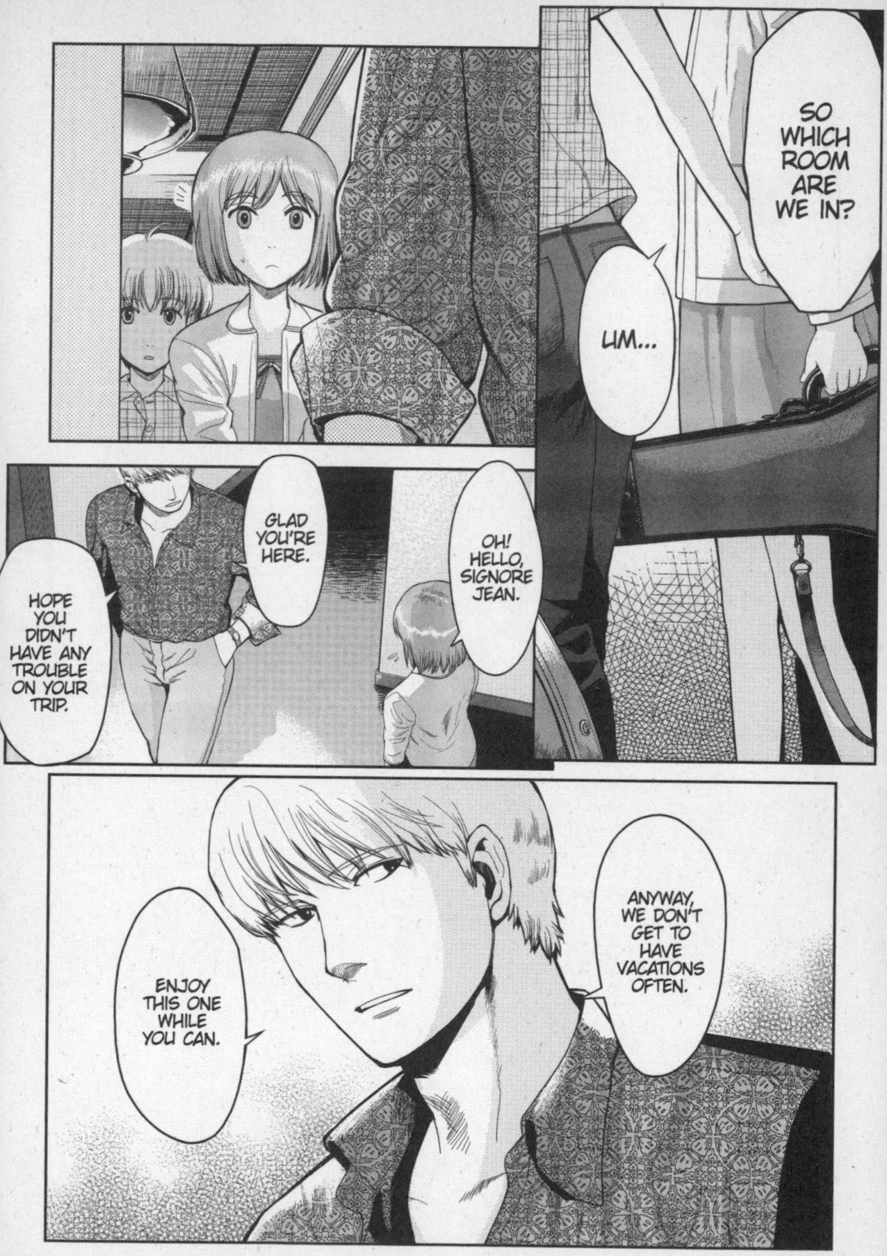
SO WHICH ROOM ARE WE IN?
UM...
OH! HELLO, SIGNORE JEAN.
GLAD YOU'RE HERE.
HOPE YOU DIDN'T HAVE ANY TROUBLE ON YOUR TRIP.
ANYWAY, WE DON'T GET TO HAVE VACATIONS OFTEN.
ENJOY THIS ONE WHILE YOU CAN.

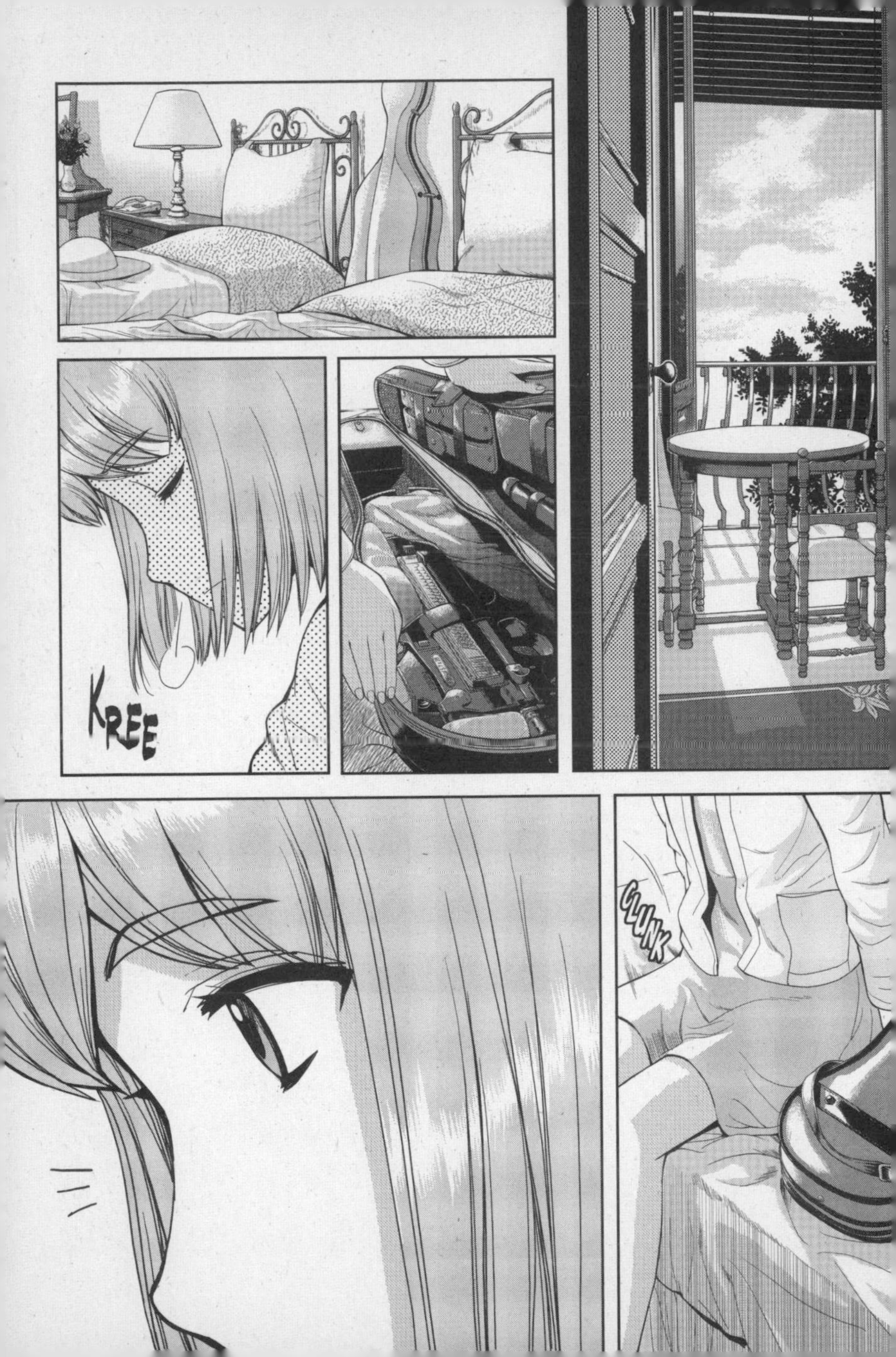
KREE
CLUNK

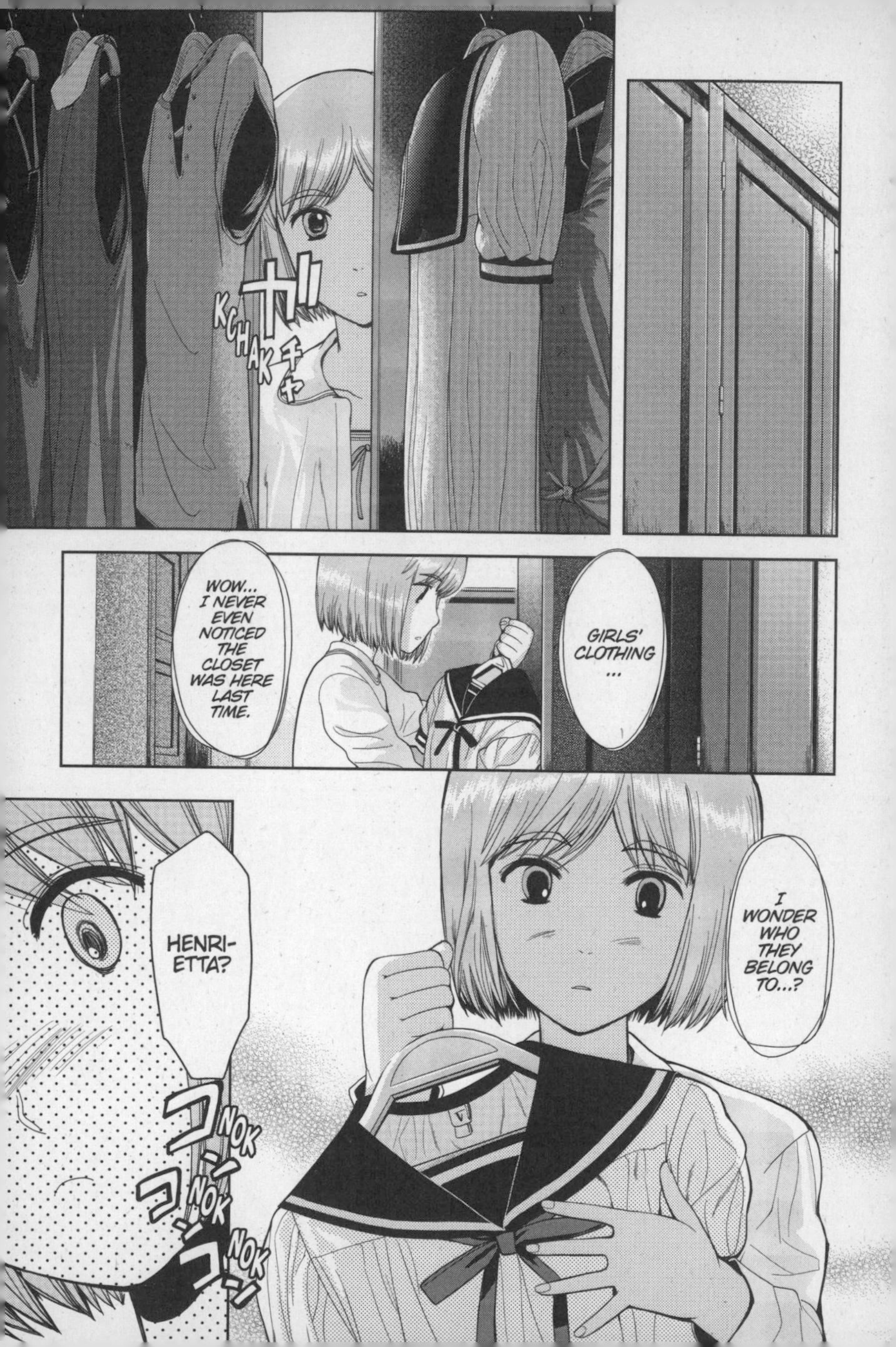
KCHAK
GIRLS' CLOTHING ...
WOW... I NEVER EVEN NOTICED THE CLOSET WAS HERE LAST TIME.
I WONDER WHO THEY BELONG TO...?
HENRI-ETTA?
NOK
NOK
NOK

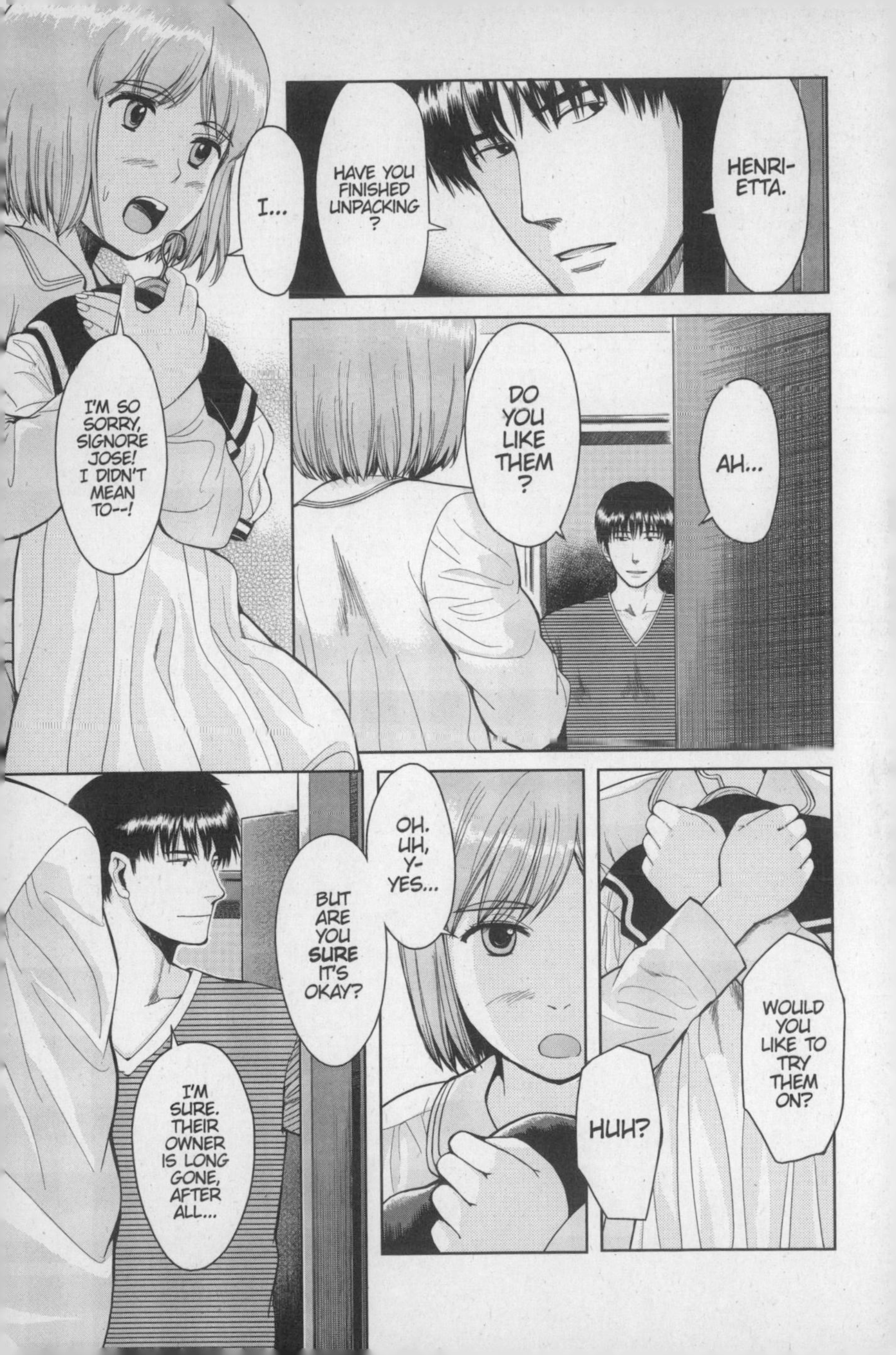
HENRI-ETTA.
HAVE YOU FINISHED UNPACKING?
AH...
DO YOU LIKE THEM?
I...
I'M SO SORRY, SIGNORE JOSE! I DIDN'T MEAN TO--!
WOULD YOU LIKE TO TRY THEM ON?
HUH?
OH. UH, Y-YES...
BUT ARE YOU SURE IT'S OKAY?
I'M SURE. THEIR OWNER IS LONG GONE, AFTER ALL...

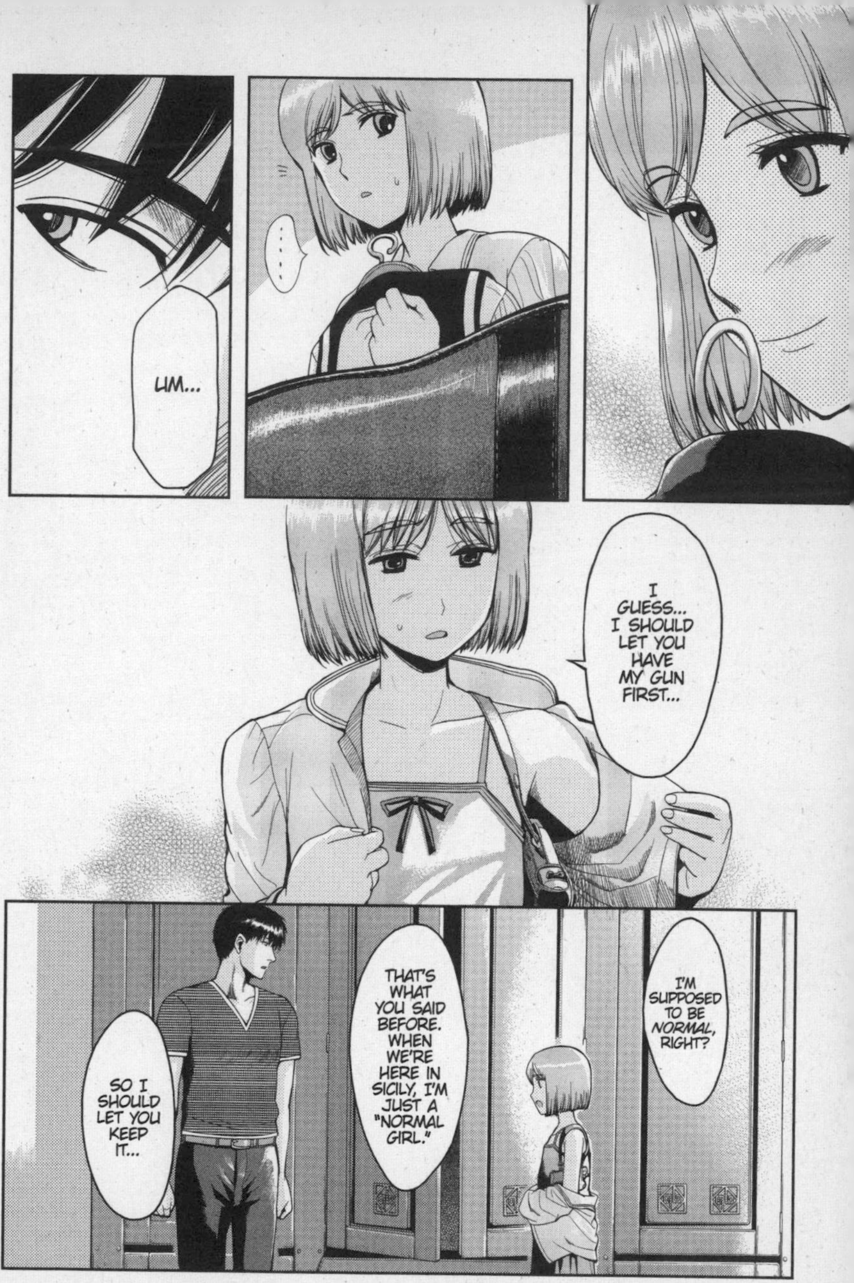
...
UM...
I GUESS... I SHOULD LET YOU HAVE MY GUN FIRST...
I'M SUPPOSED TO BE *NORMAL*, RIGHT?
THAT'S WHAT YOU SAID BEFORE. WHEN WE'RE HERE IN SICILY, I'M JUST A "NORMAL GIRL."
SO I SHOULD LET YOU KEEP IT...

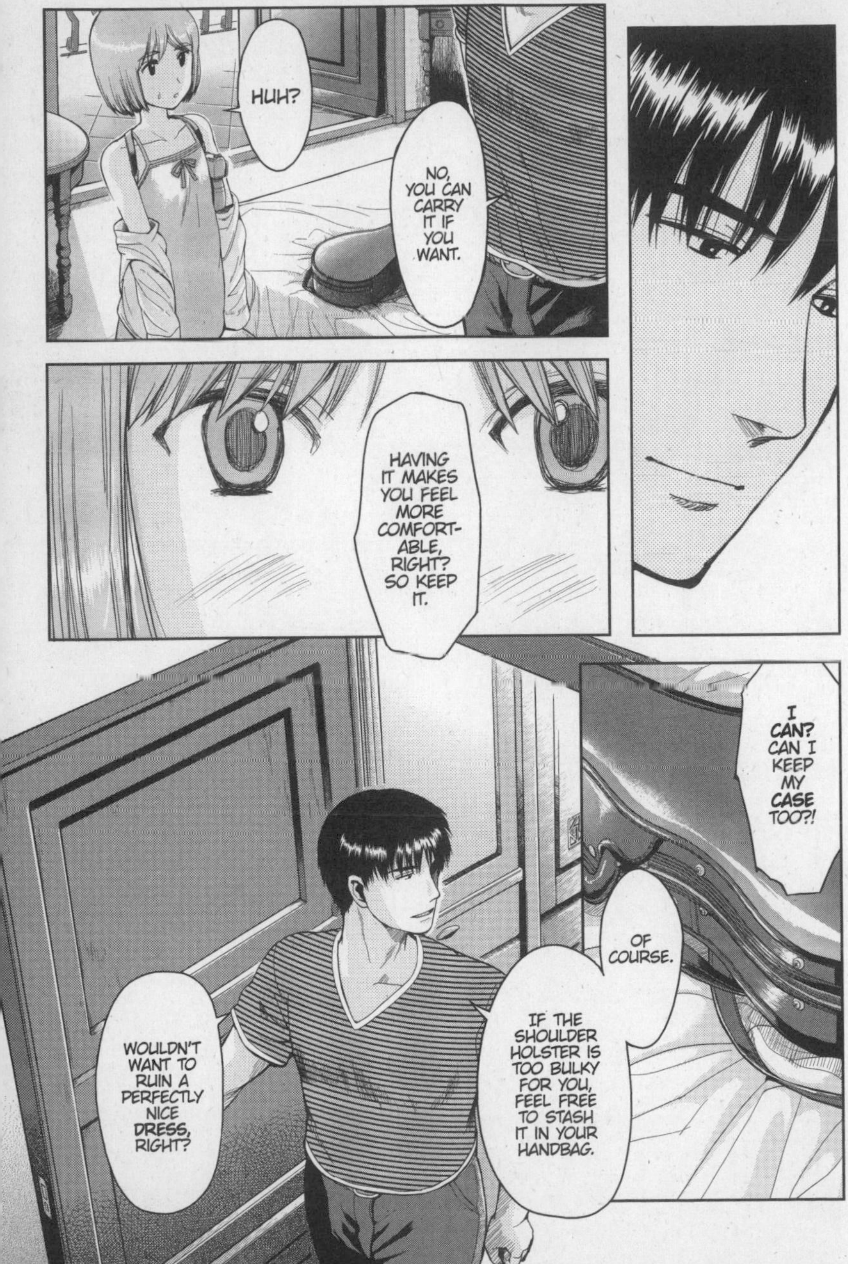
HUH?
NO, YOU CAN CARRY IT IF YOU WANT.
HAVING IT MAKES YOU FEEL MORE COMFORT-ABLE, RIGHT? SO KEEP IT.
I CAN? CAN I KEEP MY CASE TOO?!
OF COURSE.
IF THE SHOULDER HOLSTER IS TOO BULKY FOR YOU, FEEL FREE TO STASH IT IN YOUR HANDBAG.
WOULDN'T WANT TO RUIN A PERFECTLY NICE DRESS, RIGHT?

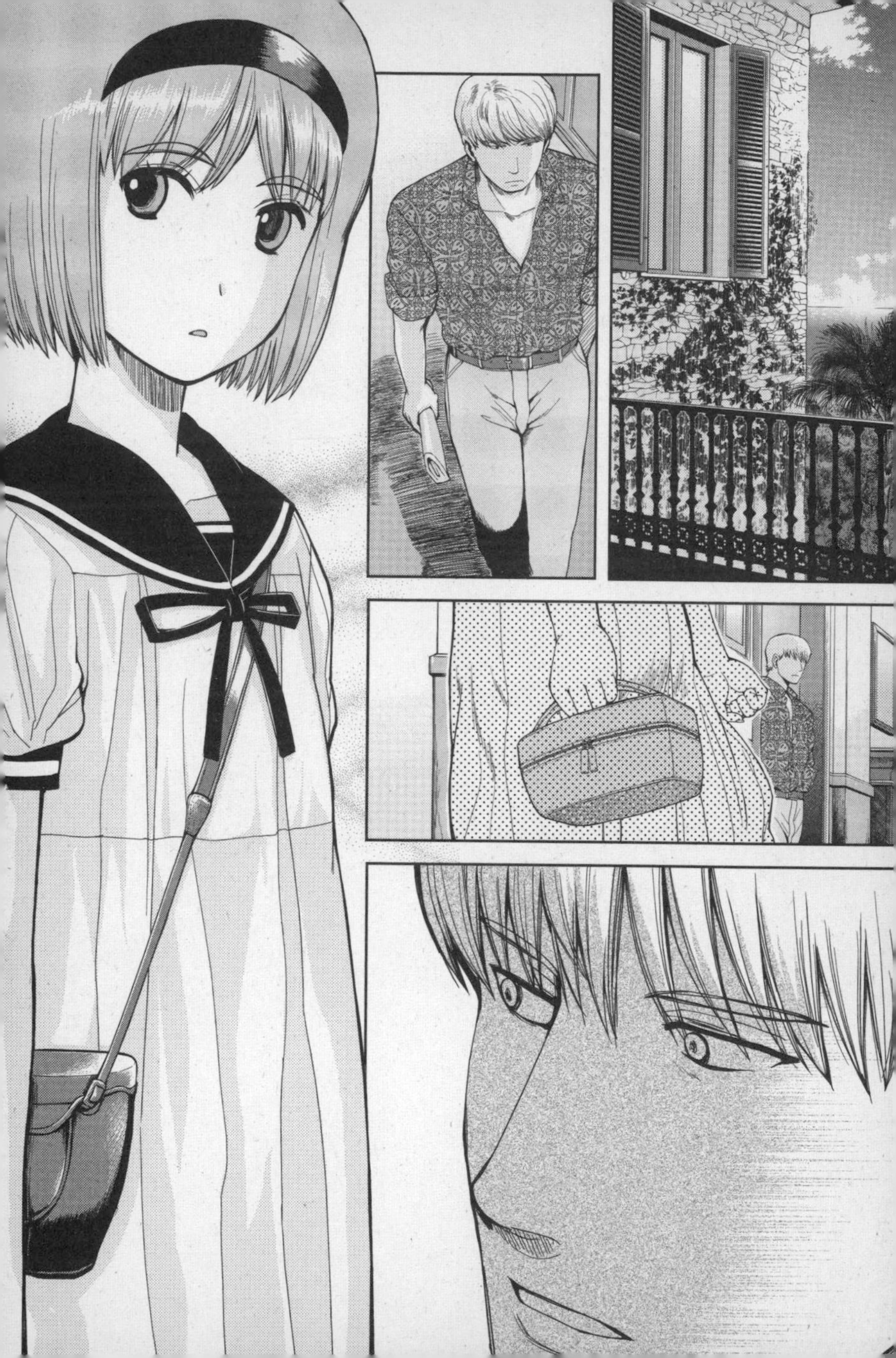

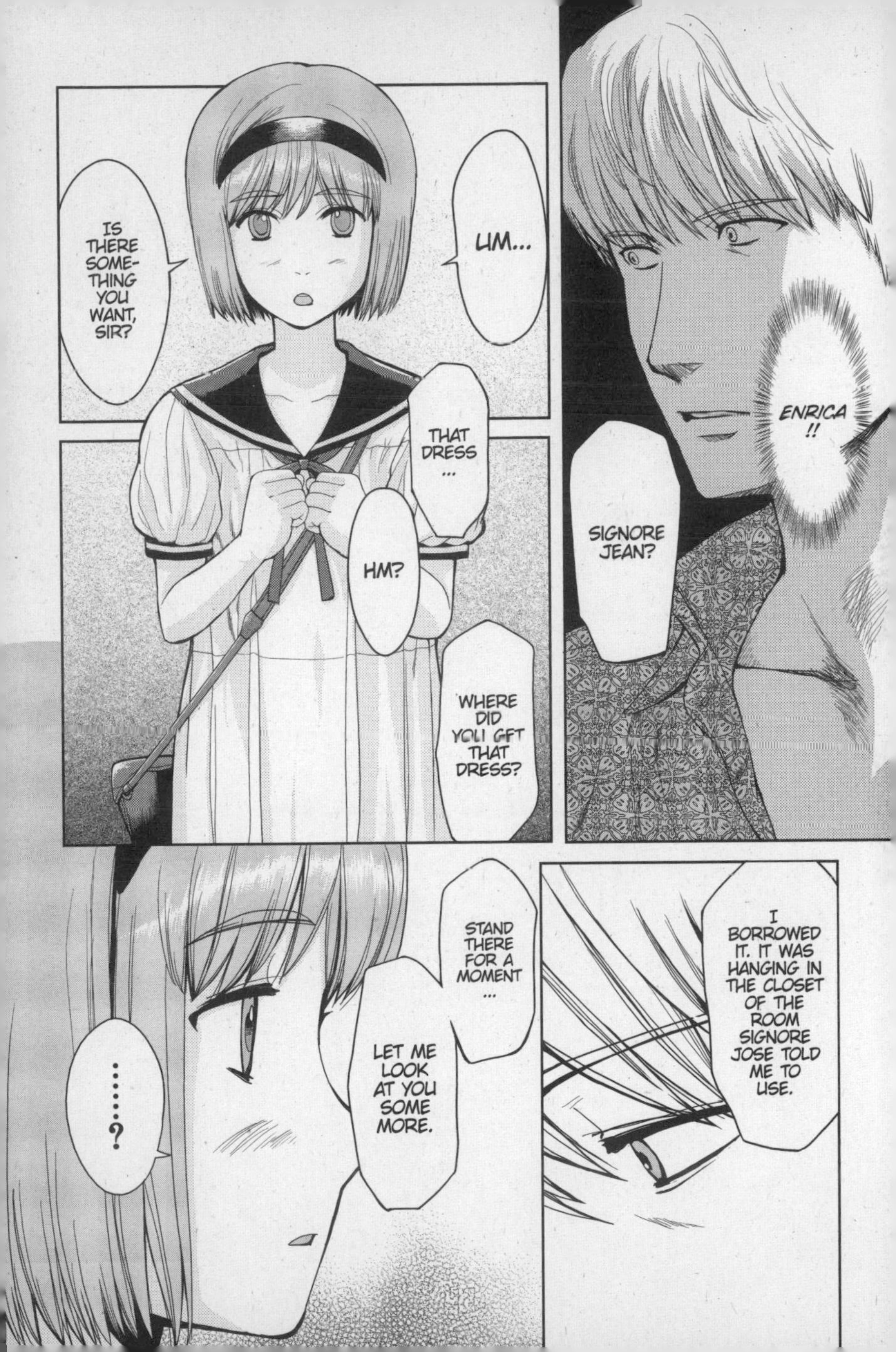
ENRICA !!
SIGNORE JEAN?
UM...
IS THERE SOME-THING YOU WANT, SIR?
THAT DRESS ...
HM?
WHERE DID YOU GET THAT DRESS?
I BORROWED IT. IT WAS HANGING IN THE CLOSET OF THE ROOM SIGNORE JOSE TOLD ME TO USE.
STAND THERE FOR A MOMENT ...
LET ME LOOK AT YOU SOME MORE.
......?

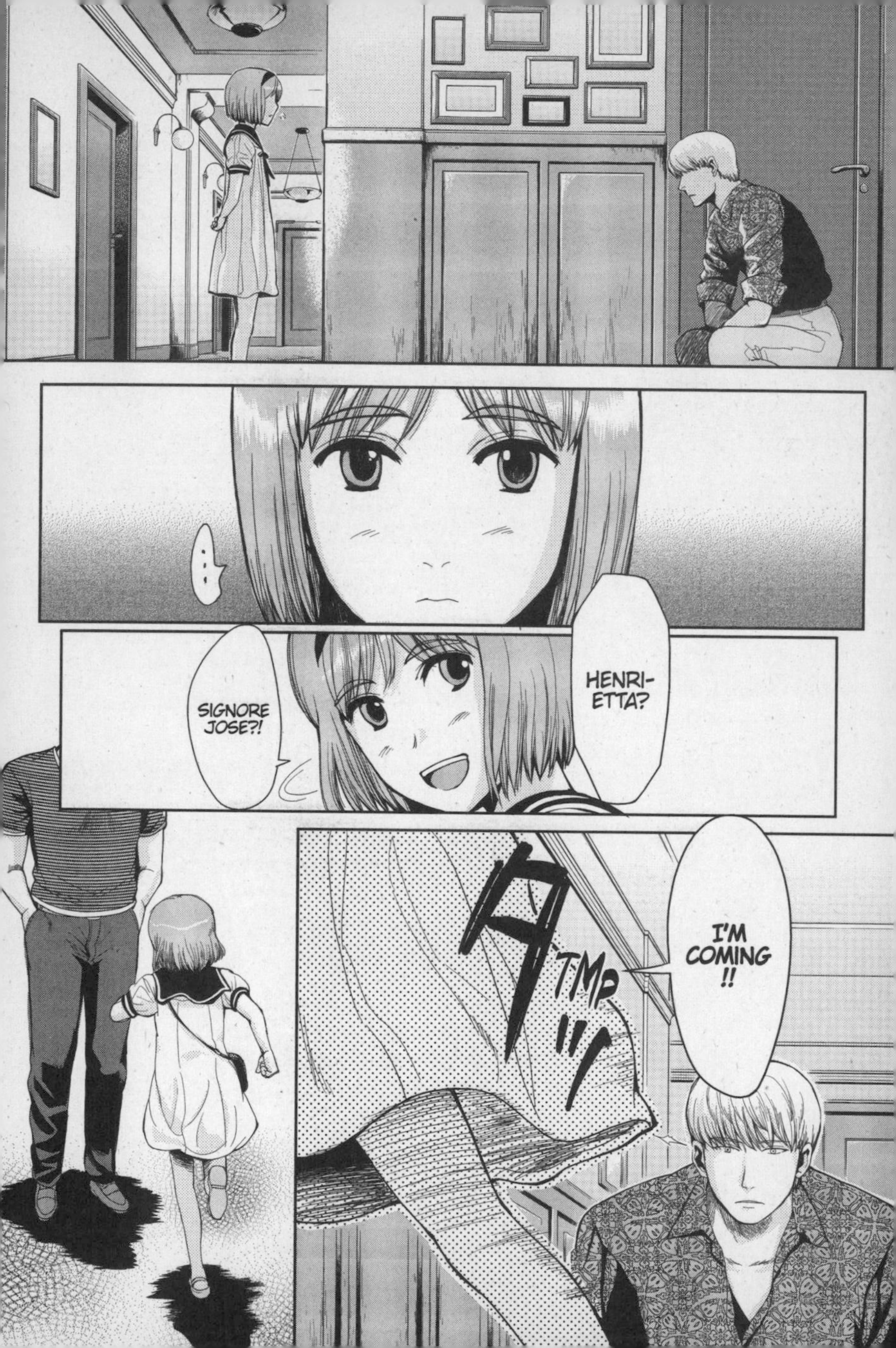
...
HENRI-ETTA?
SIGNORE JOSE?!
I'M COMING !!
TMP

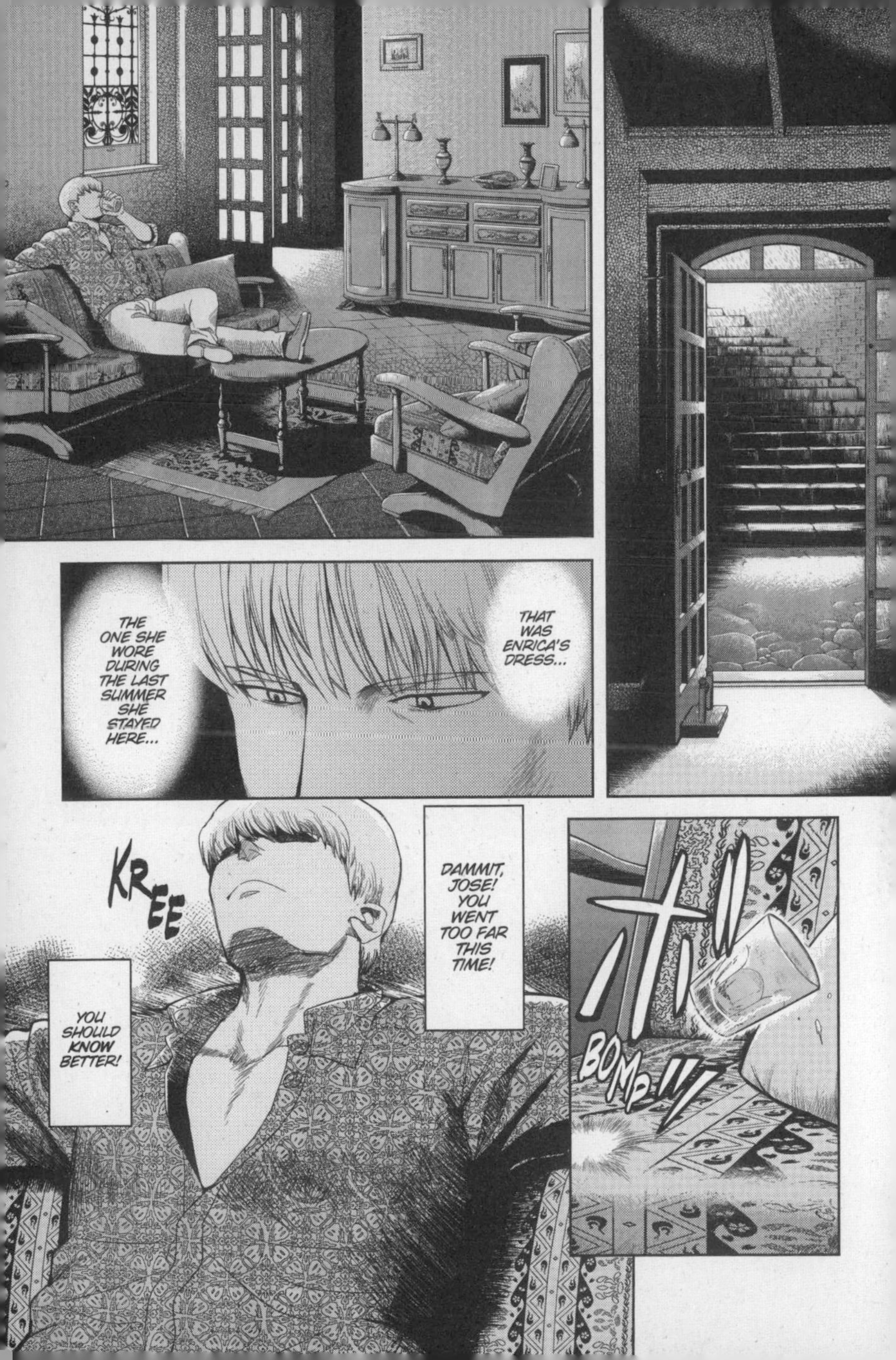
THAT WAS ENRICA'S DRESS...
THE ONE SHE WORE DURING THE LAST SUMMER SHE STAYED HERE...
BOMP!!!
DAMMIT, JOSE! YOU WENT TOO FAR THIS TIME!
KREE
YOU SHOULD KNOW BETTER!

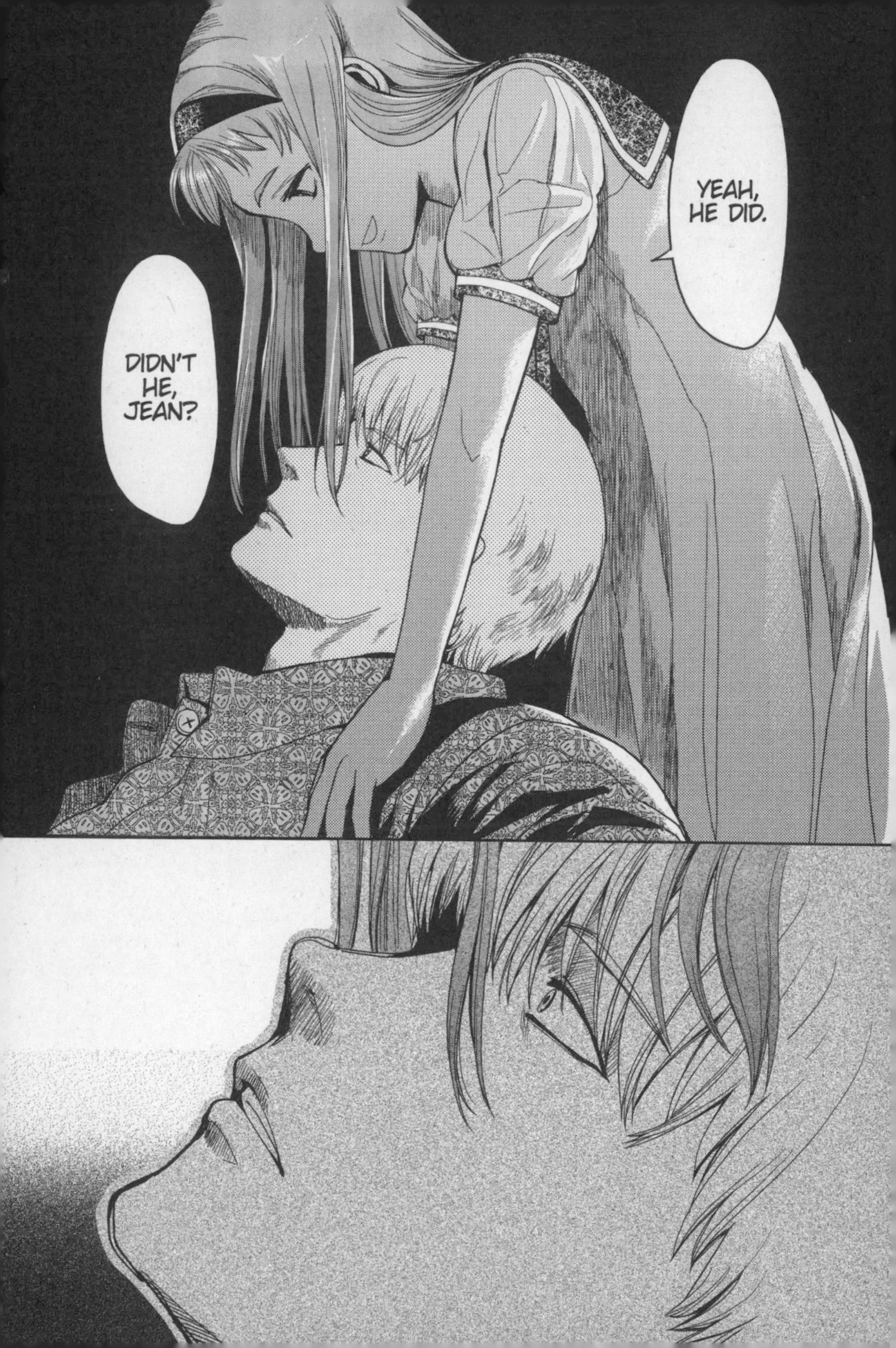
YEAH, HE DID.
DIDN'T HE, JEAN?

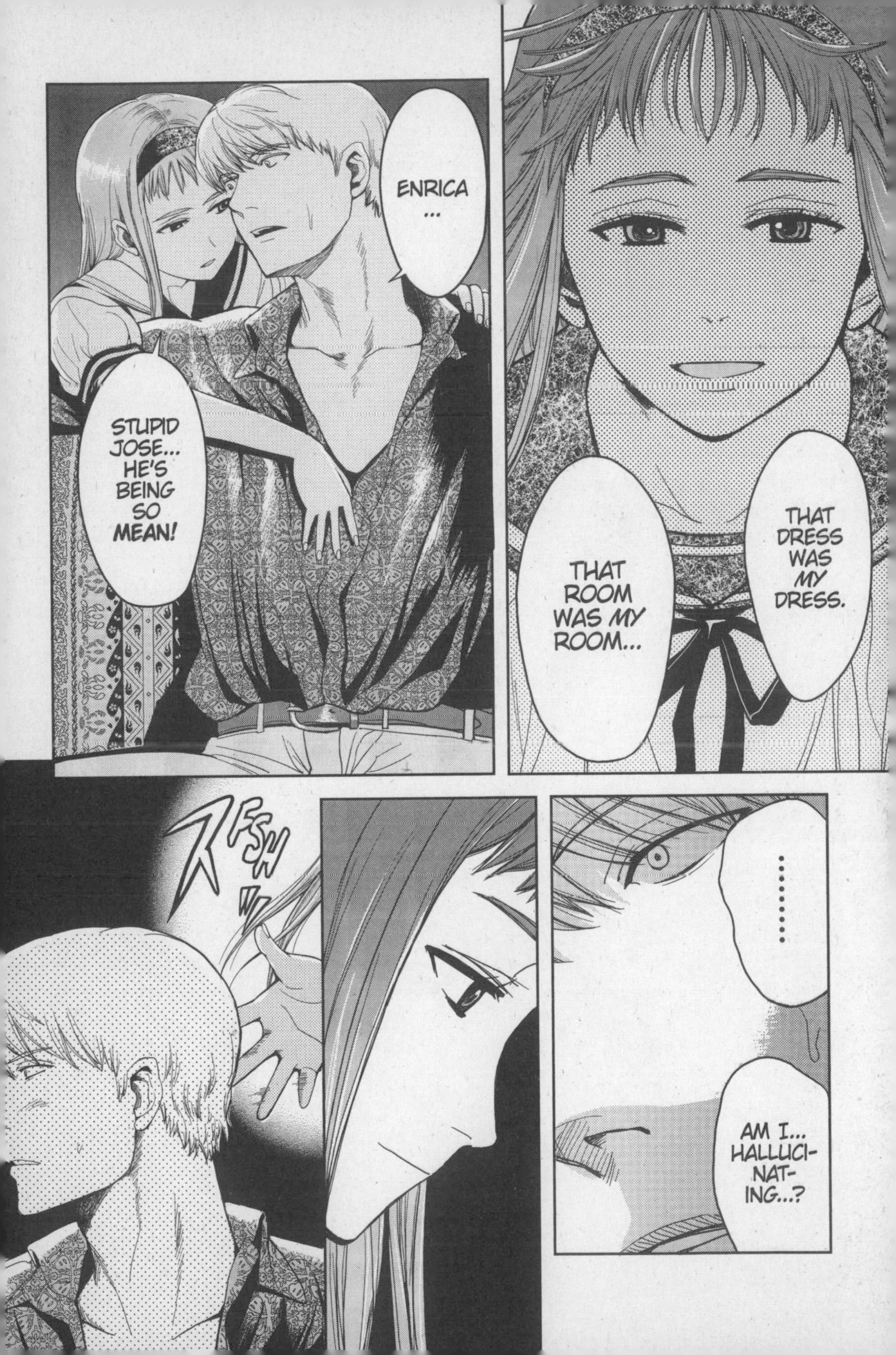
THAT DRESS WAS MY DRESS.
THAT ROOM WAS MY ROOM...
ENRICA ...
STUPID JOSE... HE'S BEING SO MEAN!
......
AM I... HALLUCI-NAT-ING...?
FSH

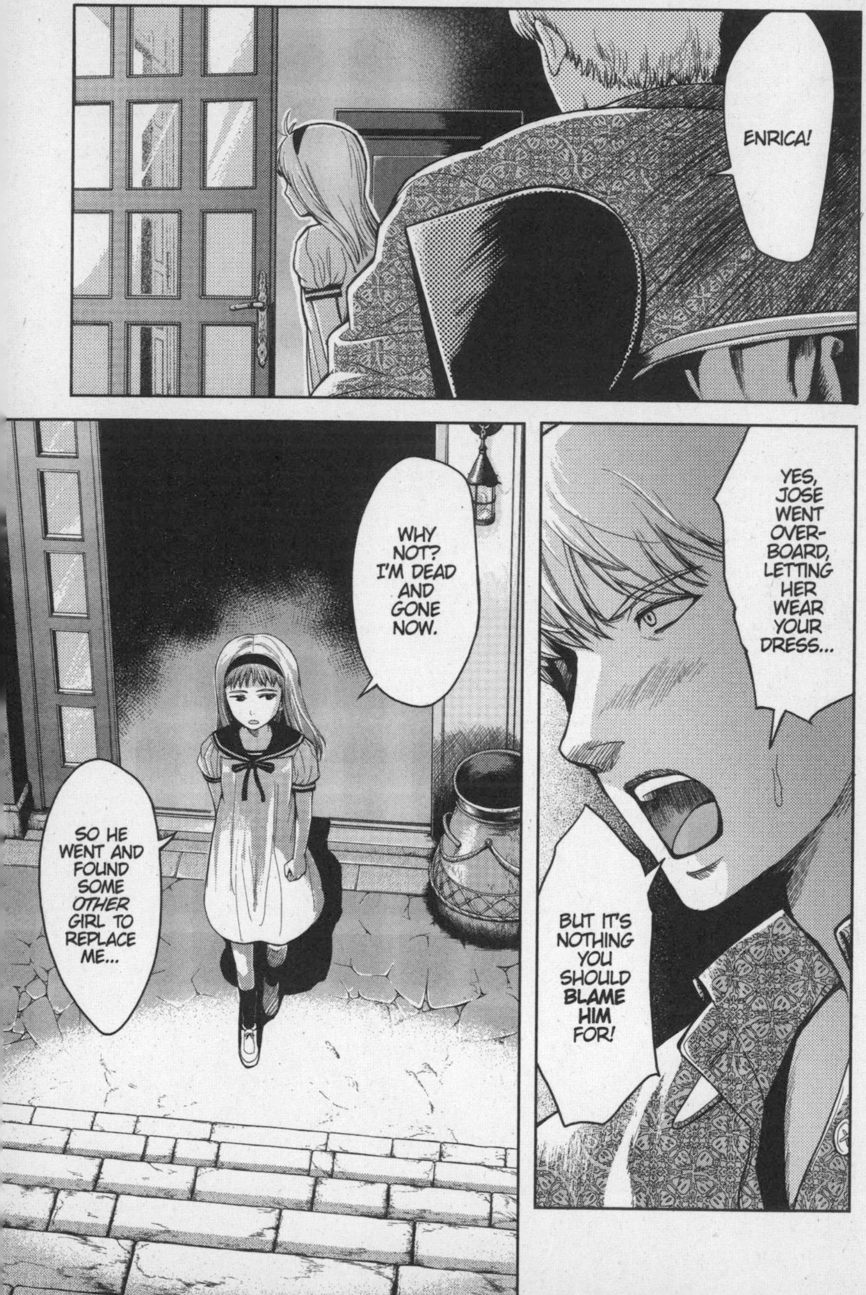
ENRICA!
YES, JOSE WENT OVER-BOARD, LETTING HER WEAR YOUR DRESS...
BUT IT'S NOTHING YOU SHOULD BLAME HIM FOR!
WHY NOT? I'M DEAD AND GONE NOW.
SO HE WENT AND FOUND SOME OTHER GIRL TO REPLACE ME...

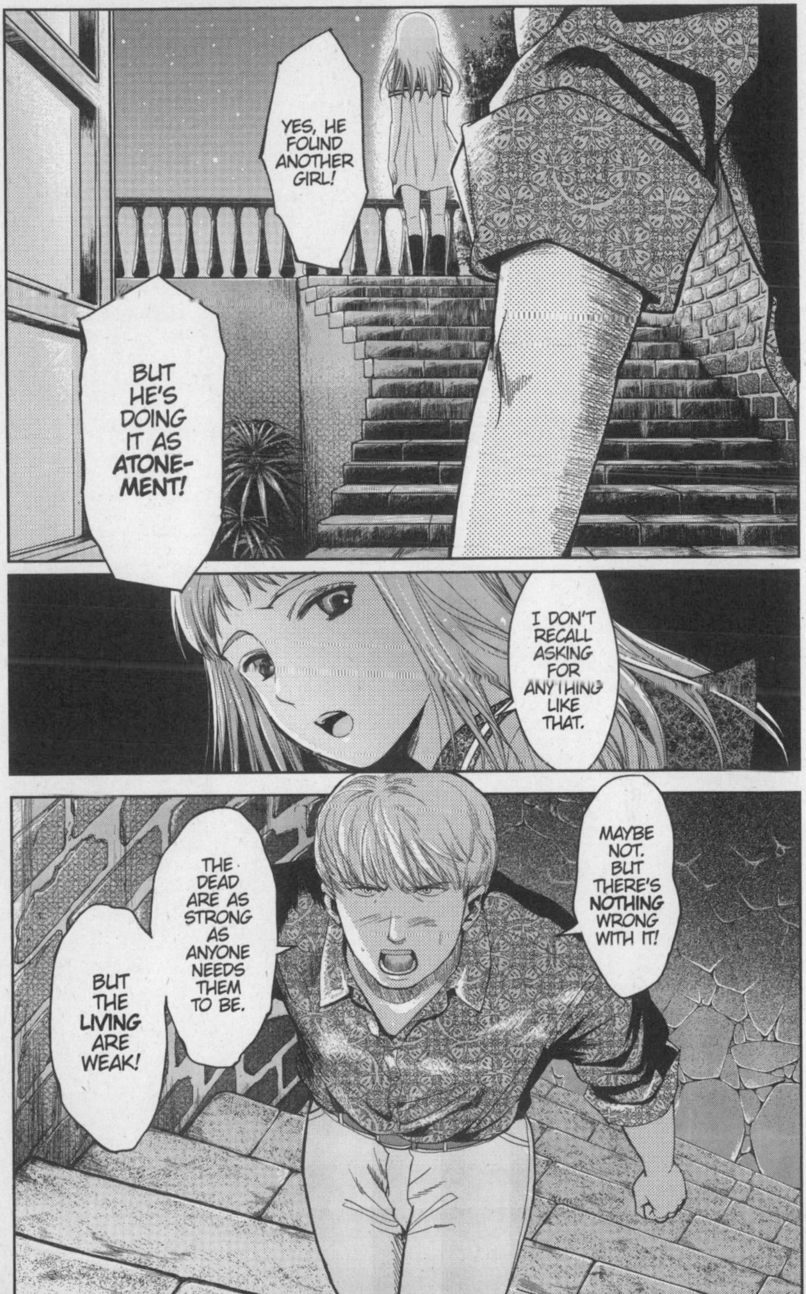
YES, HE FOUND ANOTHER GIRL!
BUT HE'S DOING IT AS ATONEMENT!
I DON'T RECALL ASKING FOR ANYTHING LIKE THAT.
MAYBE NOT. BUT THERE'S NOTHING WRONG WITH IT!
THE DEAD ARE AS STRONG AS ANYONE NEEDS THEM TO BE.
BUT THE LIVING ARE WEAK!

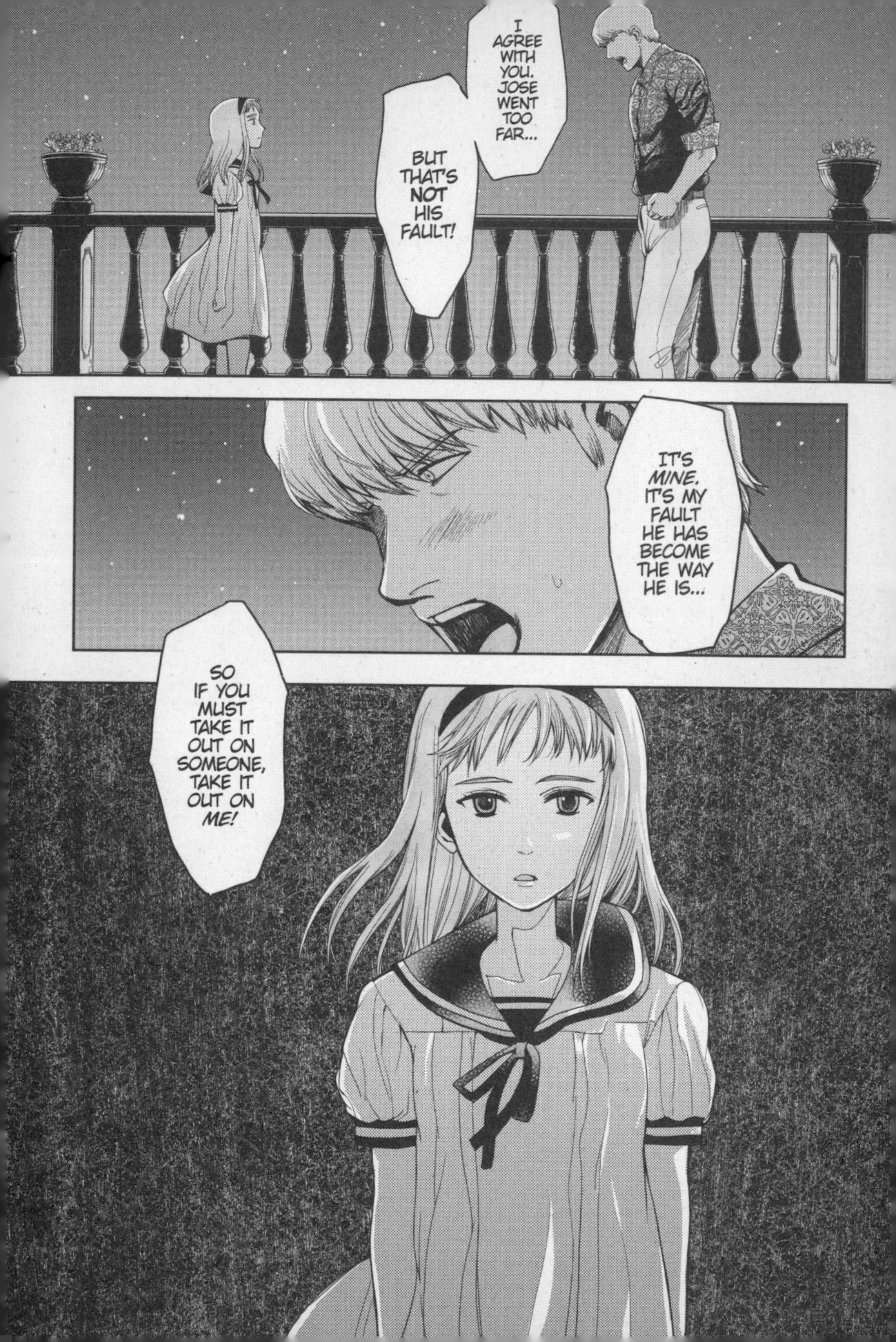
I AGREE WITH YOU. JOSE WENT TOO FAR...
BUT THAT'S NOT HIS FAULT!
IT'S *MINE.* IT'S MY FAULT HE HAS BECOME THE WAY HE IS...
SO IF YOU MUST TAKE IT OUT ON SOMEONE, TAKE IT OUT ON *ME!*

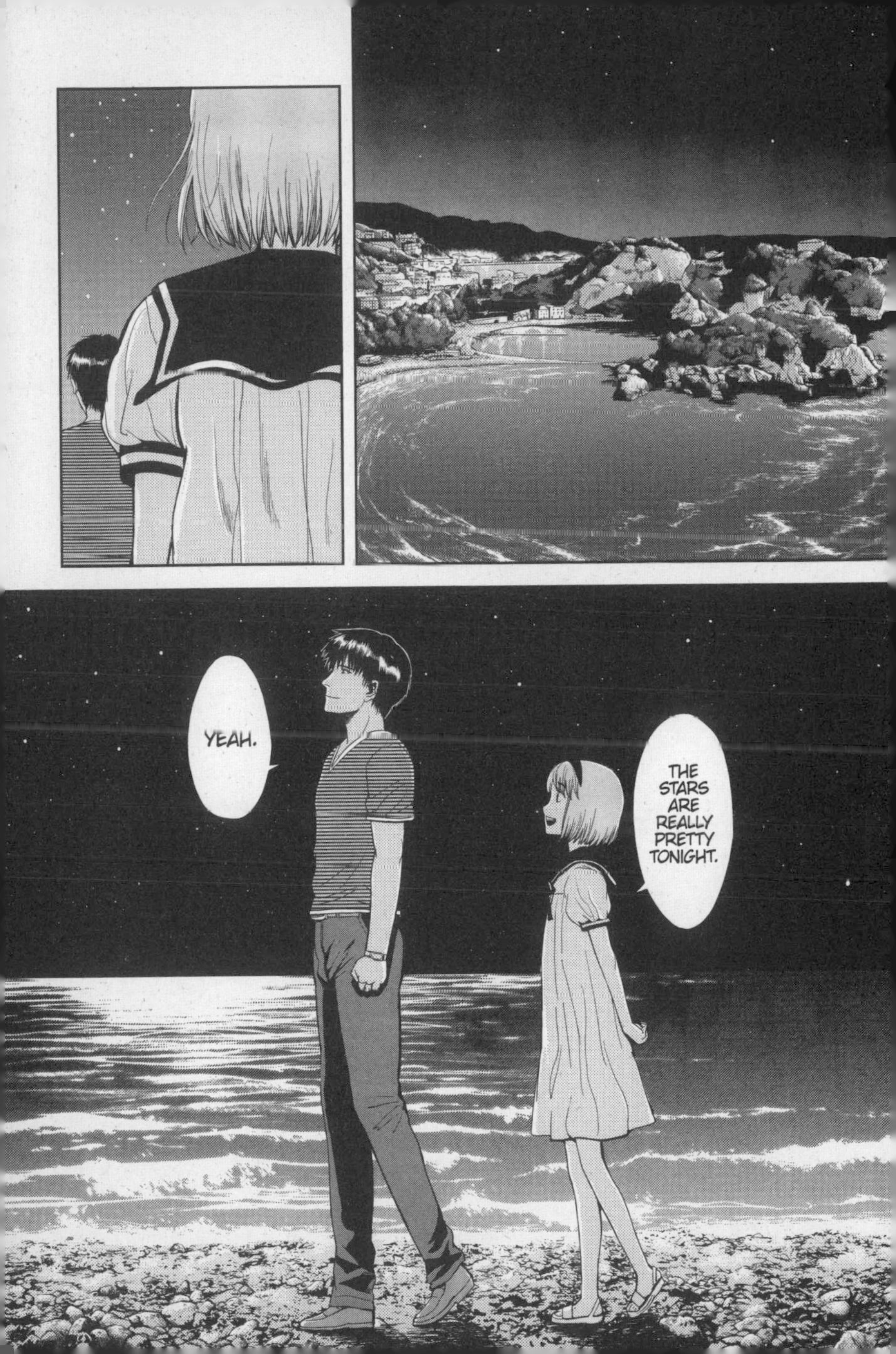
THE STARS ARE REALLY PRETTY TONIGHT.
YEAH.

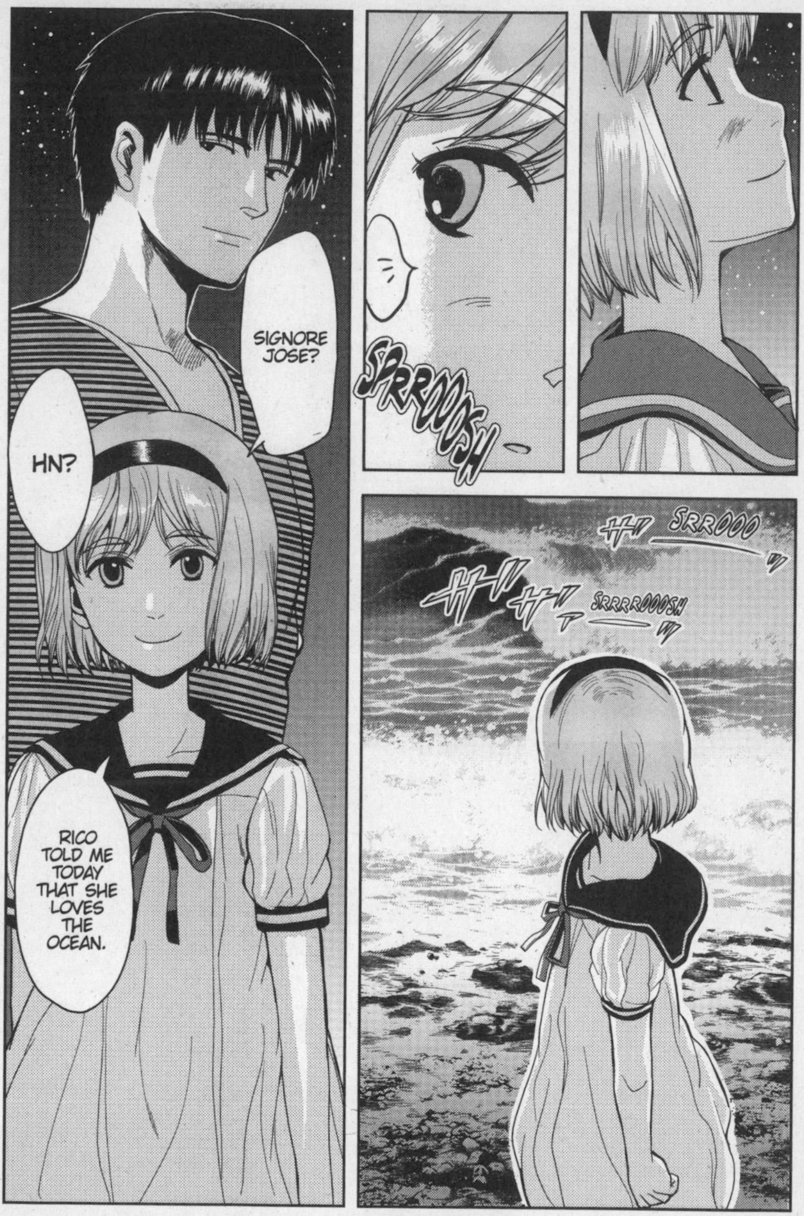

SPRROOOSH
SRROOO
SRRRROOOSH
SIGNORE JOSE?
HN?
RICO TOLD ME TODAY THAT SHE LOVES THE OCEAN.

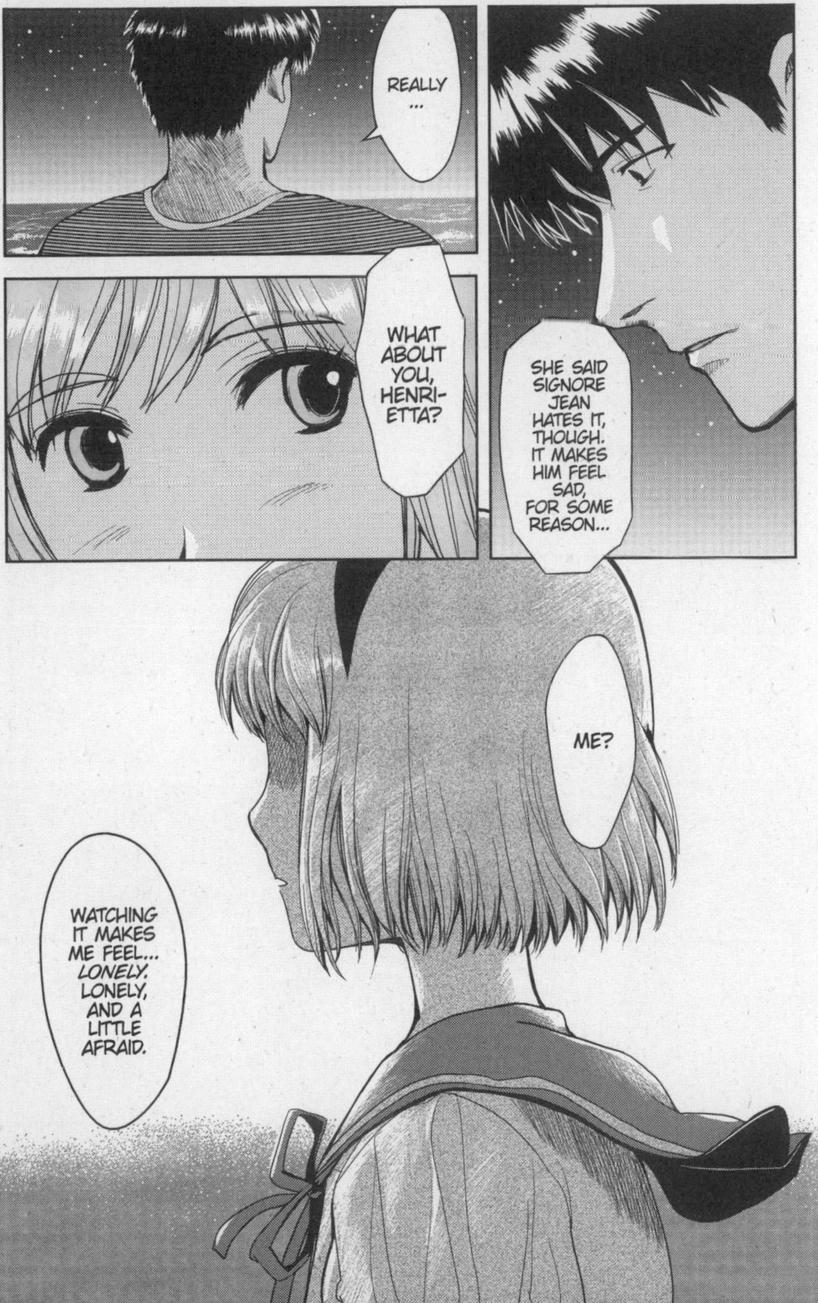
SHE SAID SIGNORE JEAN HATES IT, THOUGH. IT MAKES HIM FEEL SAD, FOR SOME REASON...
REALLY ...
WHAT ABOUT YOU, HENRI-ETTA?
ME?
WATCHING IT MAKES ME FEEL... *LONELY.* LONELY, AND A LITTLE AFRAID.

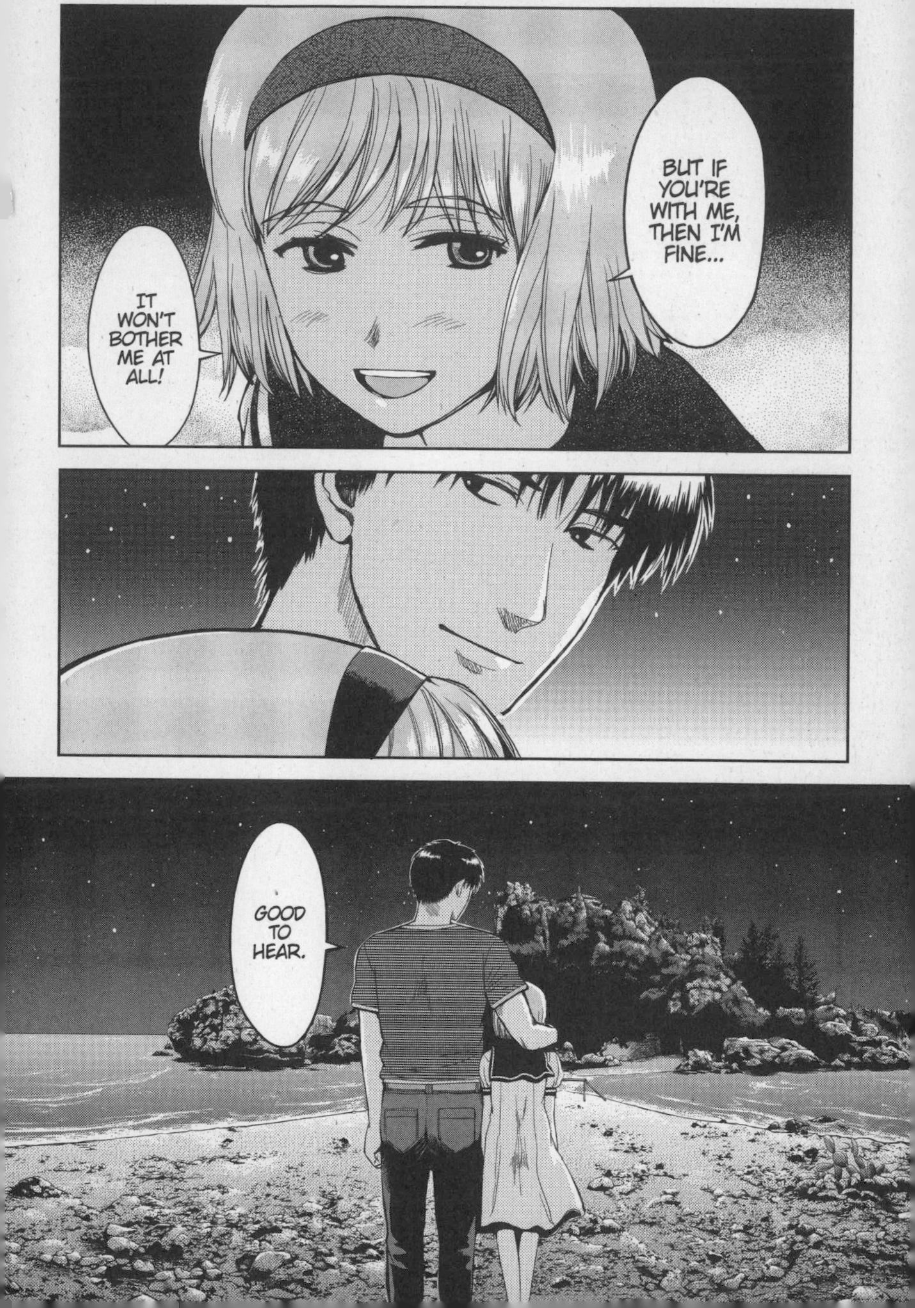
BUT IF YOU'RE WITH ME, THEN I'M FINE...
IT WON'T BOTHER ME AT ALL!
GOOD TO HEAR.

GUNSLINGERGIRL.

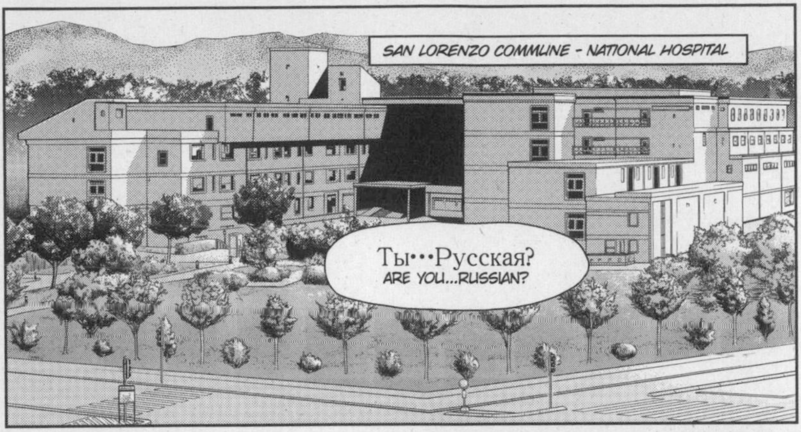
SAN LORENZO COMMUNE - NATIONAL HOSPITAL
Ты•••Русская?
ARE YOU...RUSSIAN?
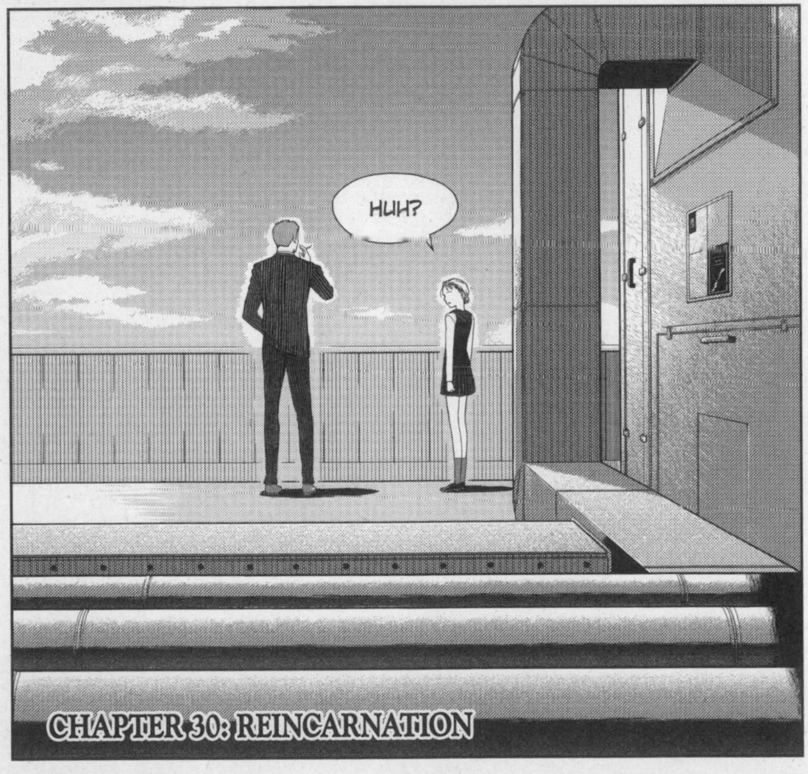
HUH?
CHAPTER 30: REINCARNATION

WAS I WRONG?

IN THAT CASE, I AM SORRY.

NO, YOU'RE RIGHT...

HOW DID YOU KNOW?

WATCHING PEOPLE IS MY JOB.

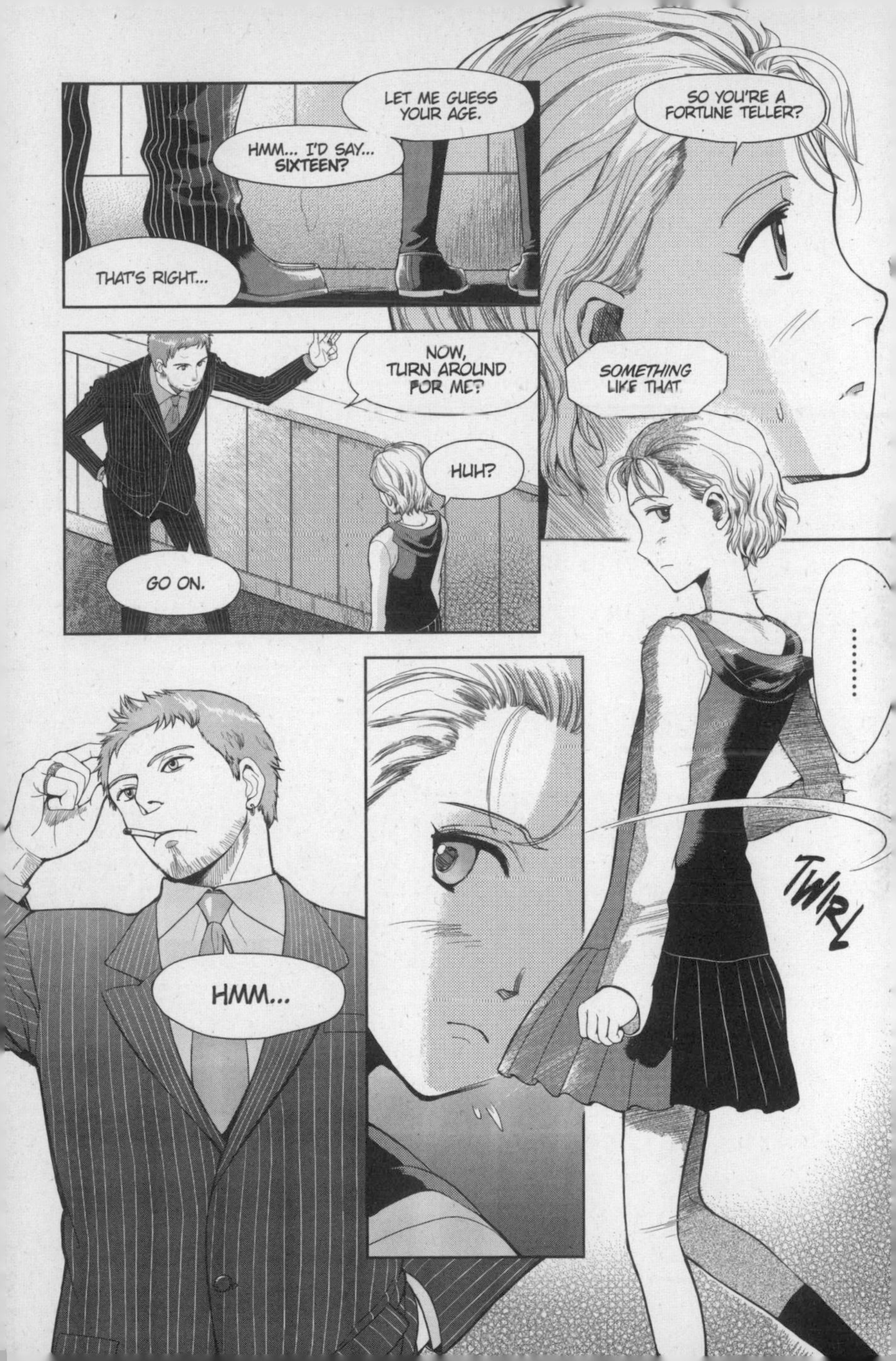
SO YOU'RE A FORTUNE TELLER?
SOMETHING LIKE THAT
LET ME GUESS YOUR AGE.
HMM... I'D SAY... SIXTEEN?
THAT'S RIGHT...
NOW, TURN AROUND FOR ME?
HUH?
GO ON.
......
TWIRL
HMM...

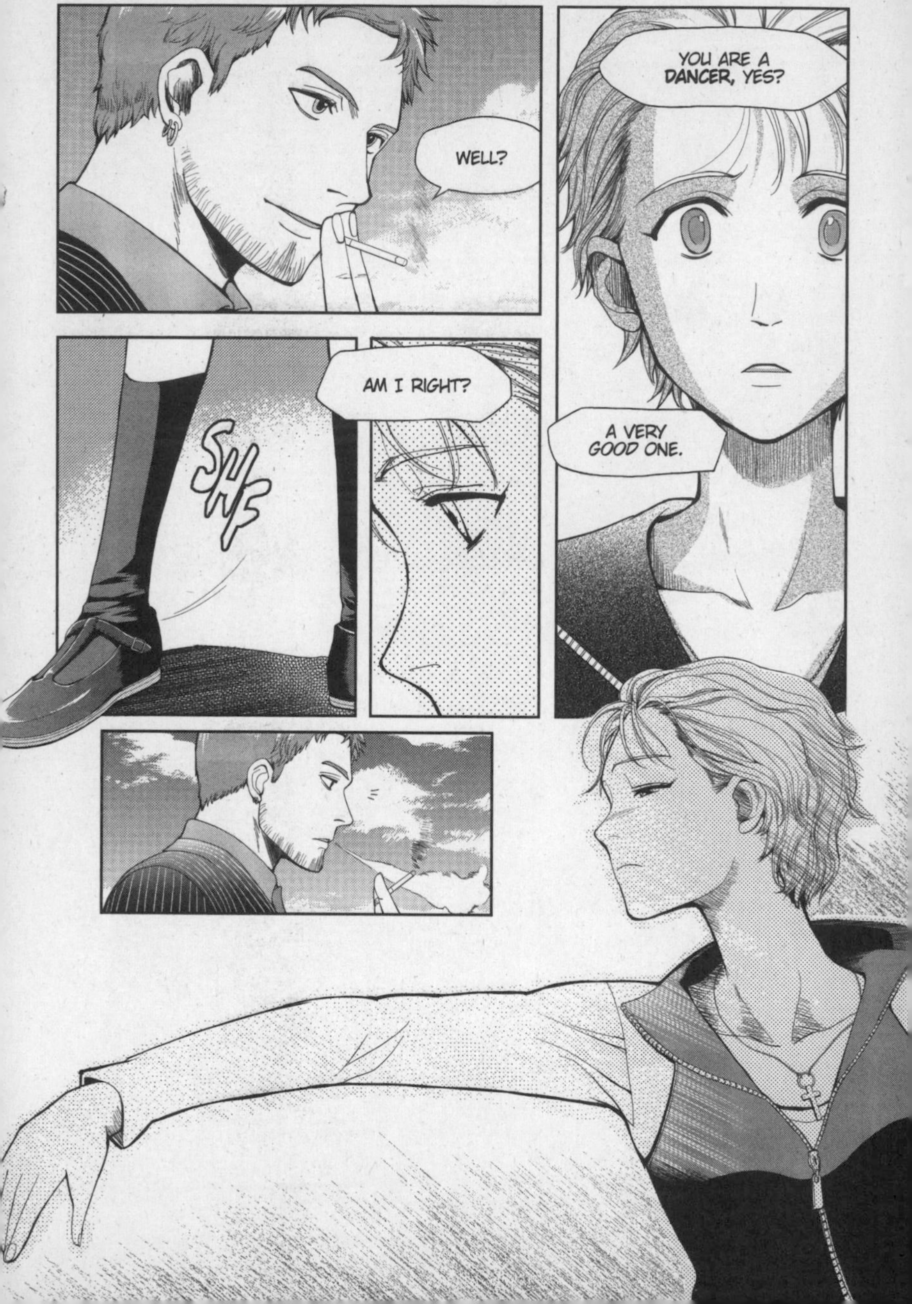
YOU ARE A DANCER, YES?
A VERY GOOD ONE.
WELL?
AM I RIGHT?
SHF

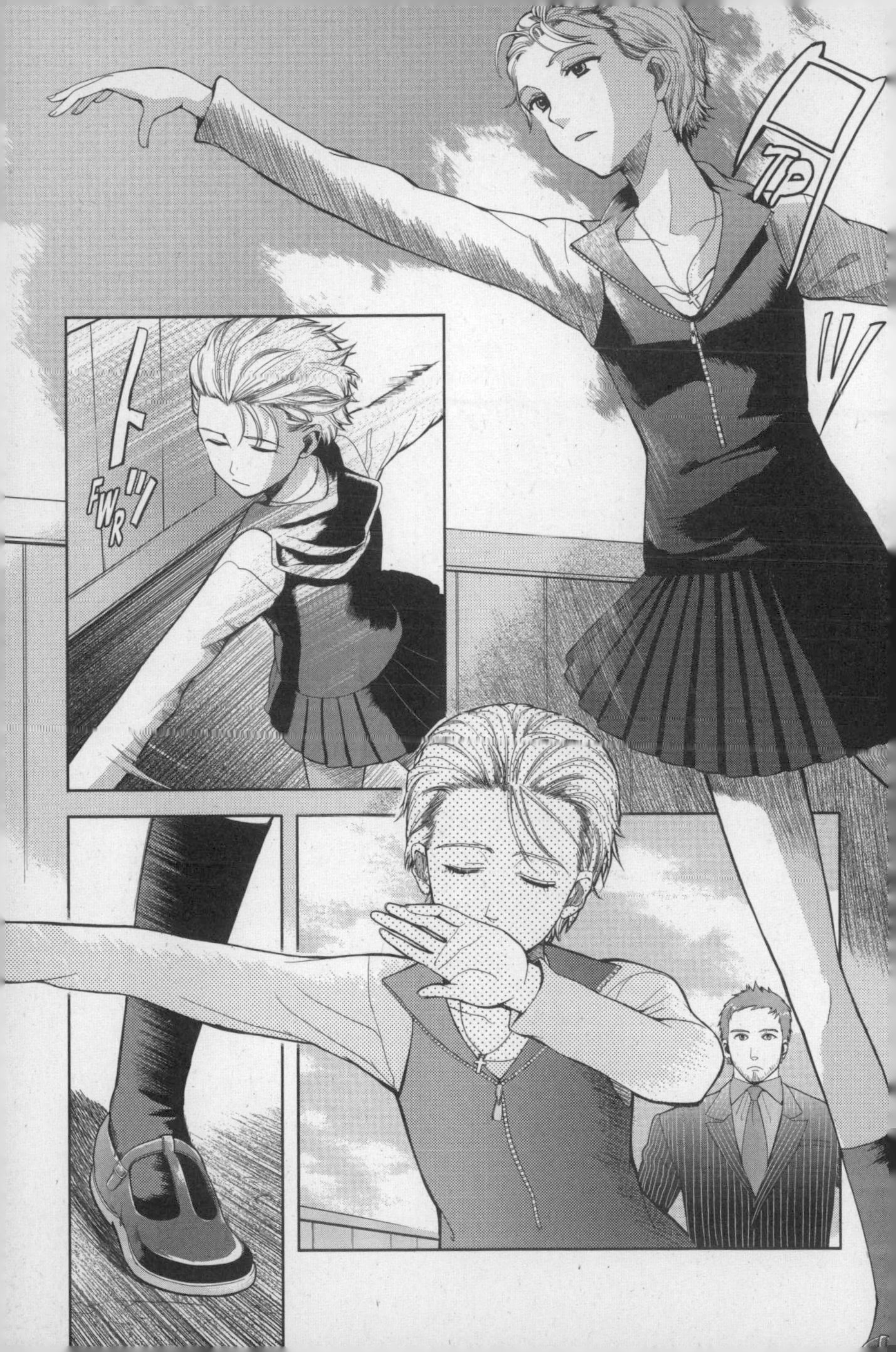
TP
FWR

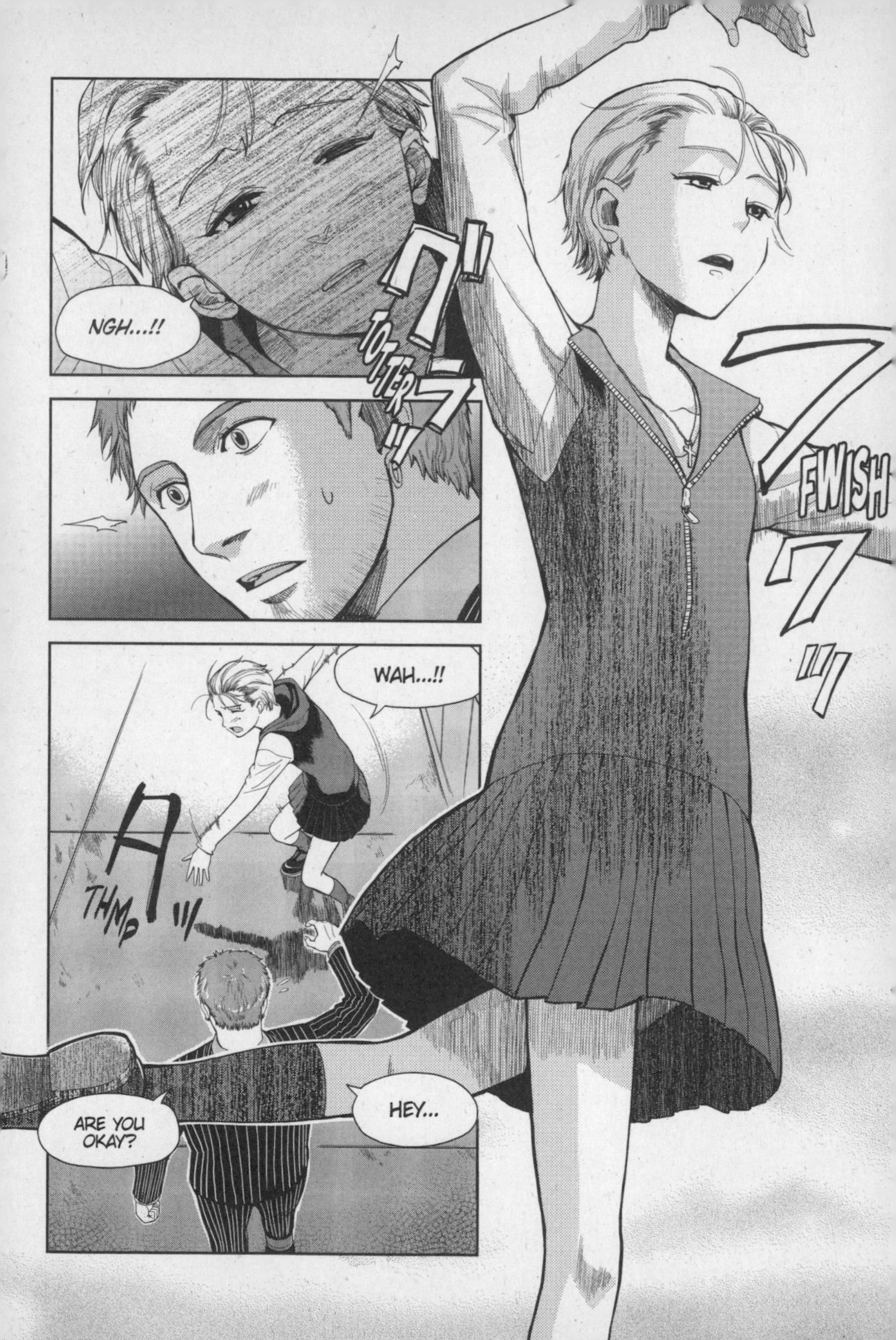
FWISH
NGH...!!
TOTTER
WAH...!!
THMP
HEY...
ARE YOU OKAY?

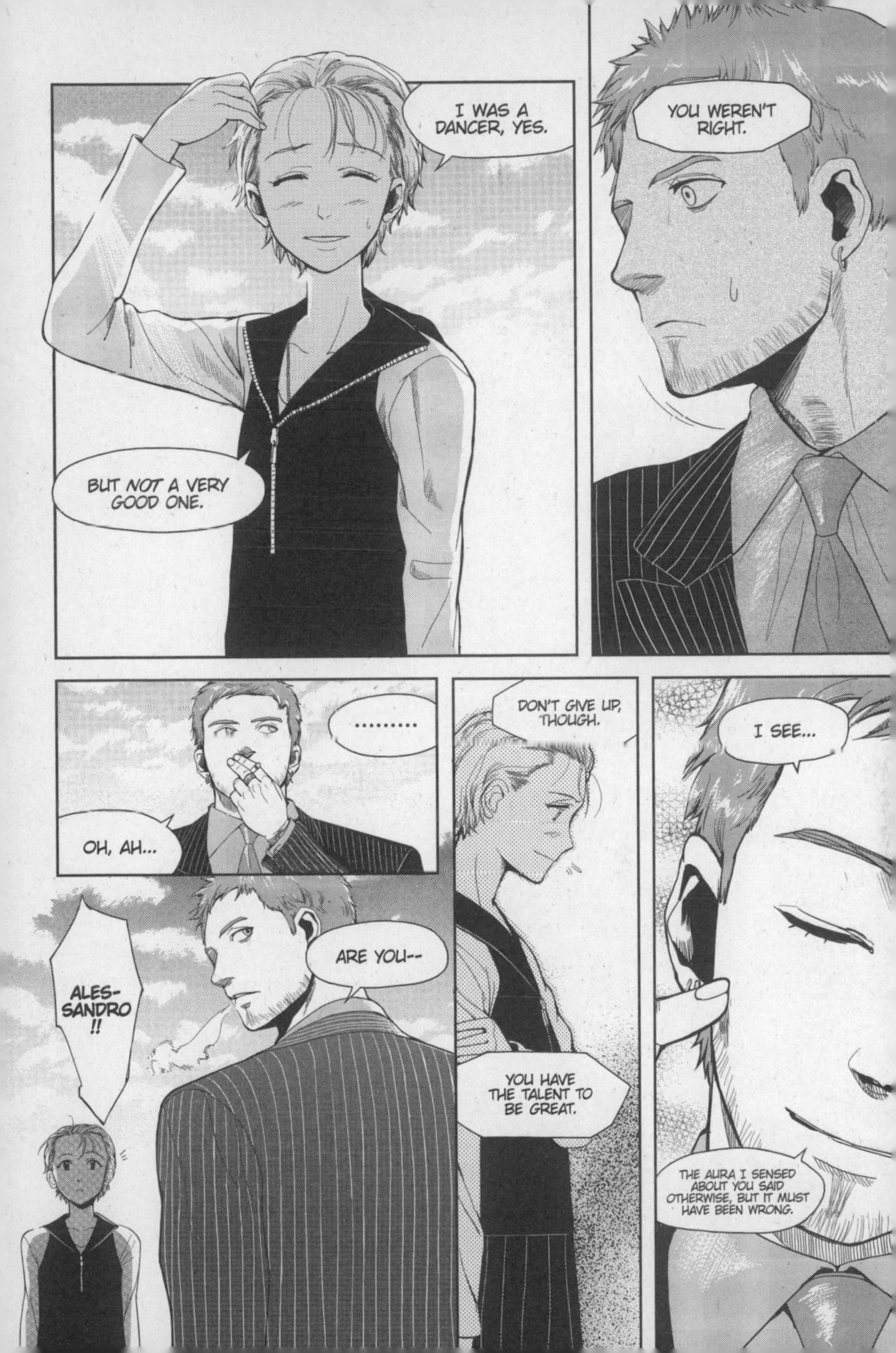
YOU WEREN'T RIGHT.
I WAS A DANCER, YES.
BUT *NOT* A VERY GOOD ONE.
I SEE...
THE AURA I SENSED ABOUT YOU SAID OTHERWISE, BUT IT MUST HAVE BEEN WRONG.
DON'T GIVE UP, THOUGH.
YOU HAVE THE TALENT TO BE GREAT.
....
OH, AH...
ARE YOU--
ALES-SANDRO !!

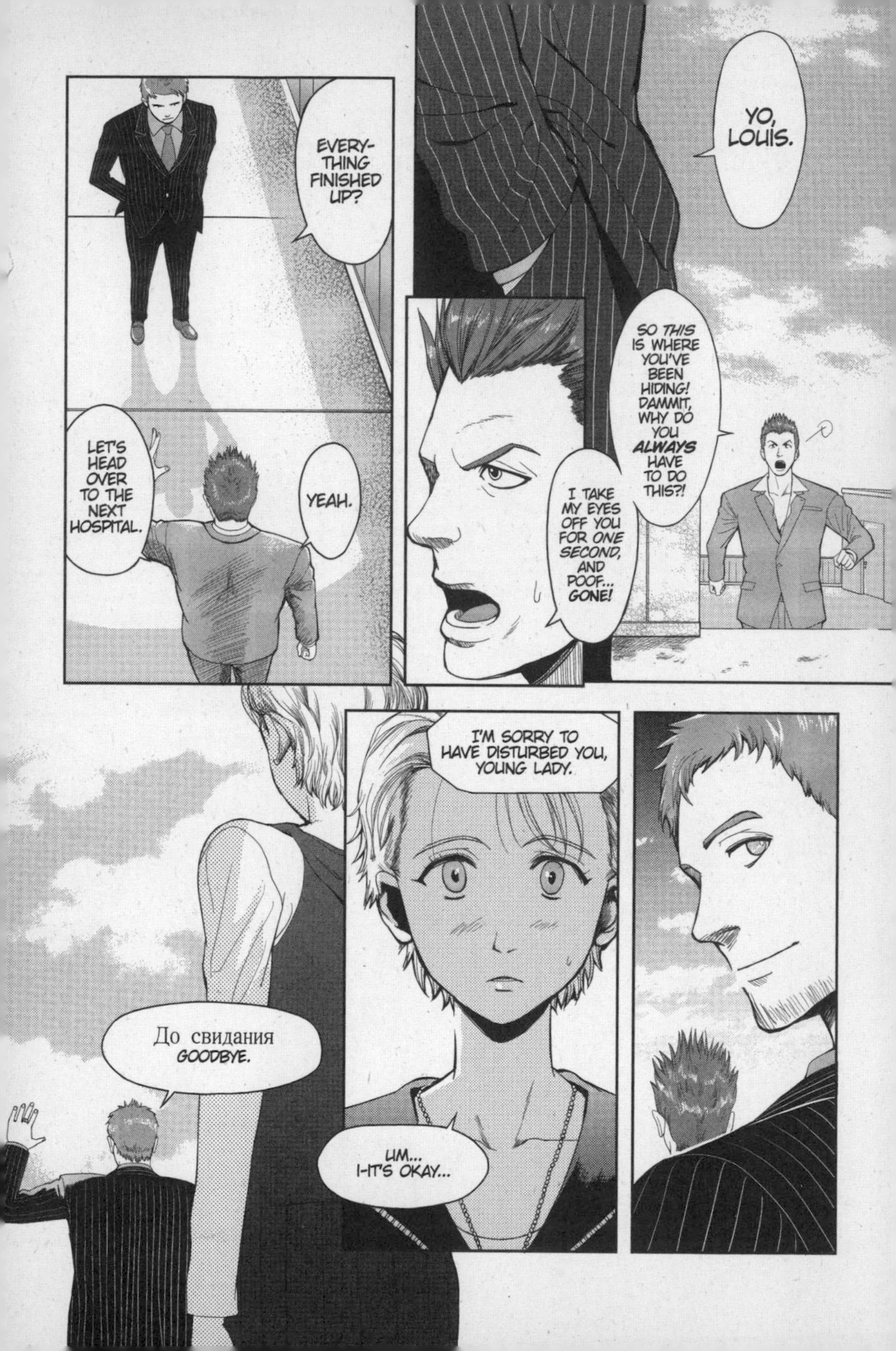
YO, LOUIS.
SO THIS IS WHERE YOU'VE BEEN HIDING! DAMMIT, WHY DO YOU **ALWAYS** HAVE TO DO THIS?!
I TAKE MY EYES OFF YOU FOR *ONE SECOND*, AND POOF... GONE!
EVERY-THING FINISHED UP?
YEAH.
LET'S HEAD OVER TO THE NEXT HOSPITAL.
I'M SORRY TO HAVE DISTURBED YOU, YOUNG LADY.
UM... I-IT'S OKAY...
До свидания
GOODBYE.

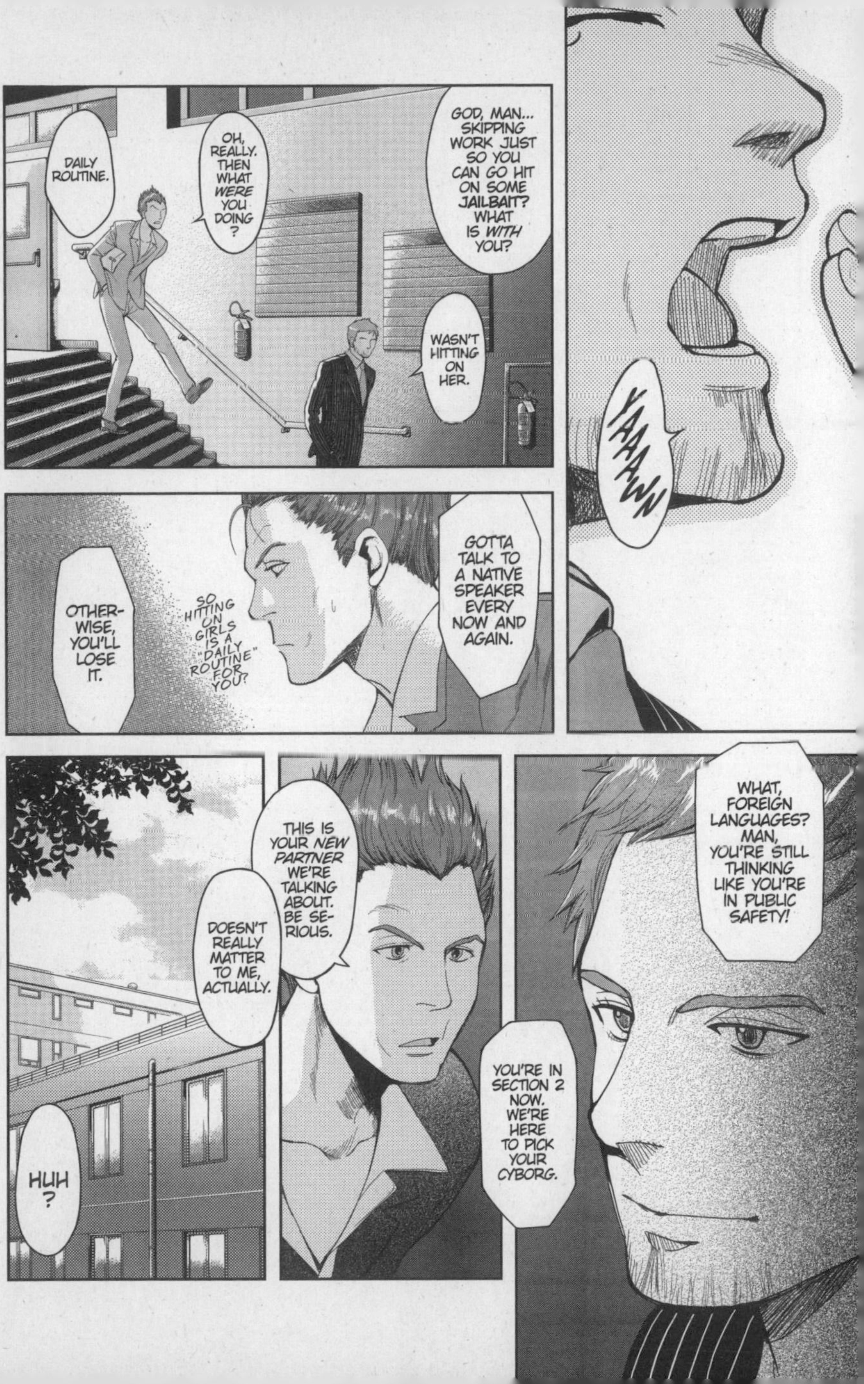
YAAAAWN
GOD, MAN... SKIPPING WORK JUST SO YOU CAN GO HIT ON SOME JAILBAIT? WHAT IS *WITH* YOU?
WASN'T HITTING ON HER.
OH, REALLY. THEN WHAT *WERE* YOU DOING?
DAILY ROUTINE.
GOTTA TALK TO A NATIVE SPEAKER EVERY NOW AND AGAIN.
OTHER-WISE, YOU'LL LOSE IT.
SO HITTING ON GIRLS IS A "DAILY ROUTINE" FOR YOU?
WHAT, FOREIGN LANGUAGES? MAN, YOU'RE STILL THINKING LIKE YOU'RE IN PUBLIC SAFETY!
YOU'RE IN SECTION 2 NOW. WE'RE HERE TO PICK YOUR CYBORG.
THIS IS YOUR *NEW PARTNER* WE'RE TALKING ABOUT. BE SE-RIOUS.
DOESN'T REALLY MATTER TO ME, ACTUALLY.
HUH?

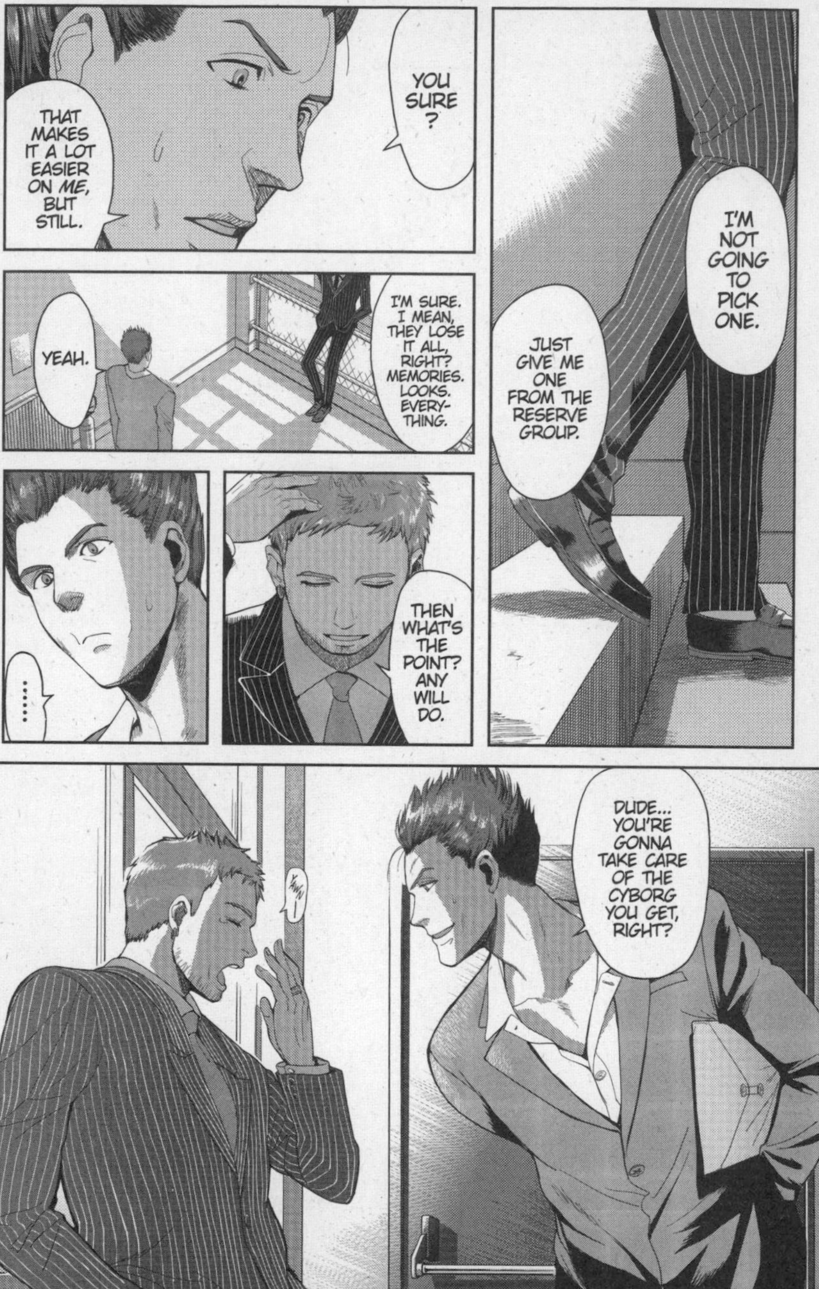
I'M NOT GOING TO PICK ONE.
JUST GIVE ME ONE FROM THE RESERVE GROUP.
YOU SURE?
THAT MAKES IT A LOT EASIER ON ME, BUT STILL.
I'M SURE. I MEAN, THEY LOSE IT ALL, RIGHT? MEMORIES. LOOKS. EVERYTHING.
YEAH.
THEN WHAT'S THE POINT? ANY WILL DO.
......
DUDE... YOU'RE GONNA TAKE CARE OF THE CYBORG YOU GET, RIGHT?
YAWN

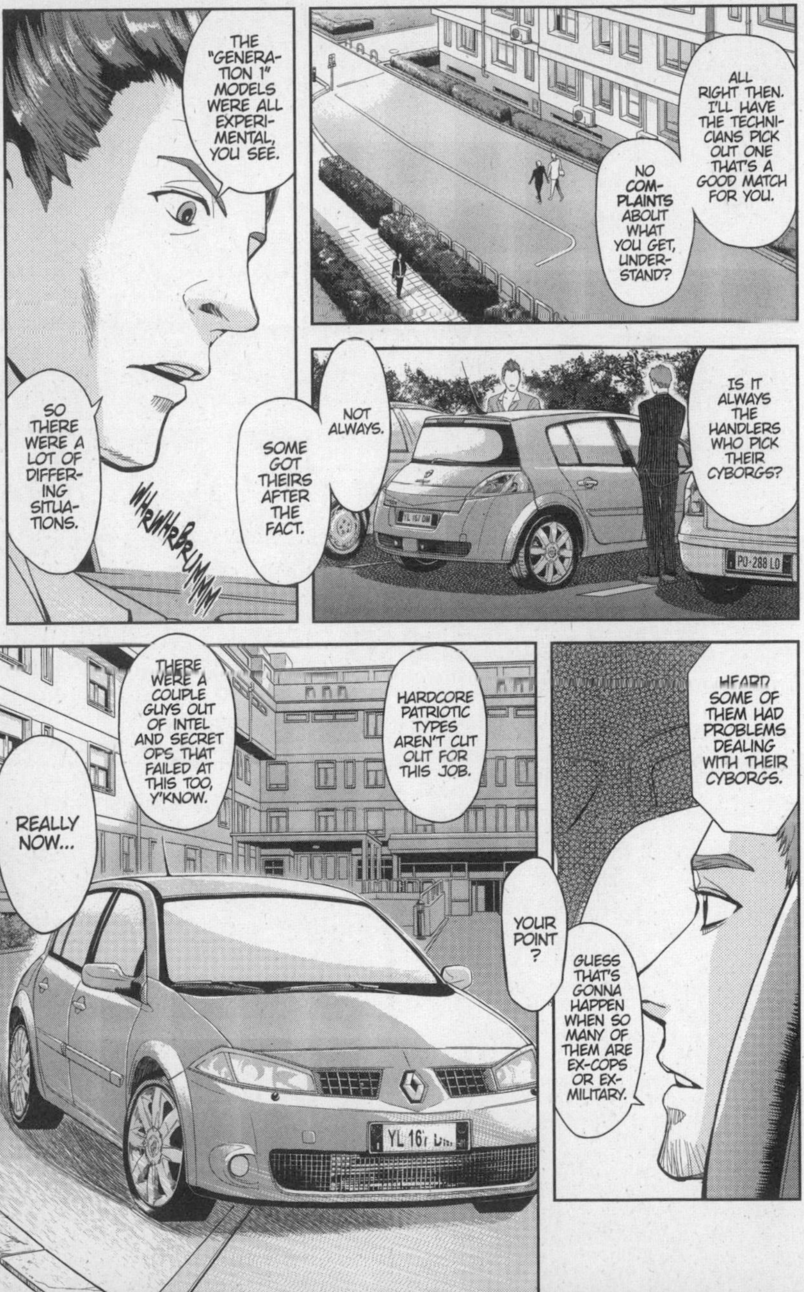
ALL RIGHT THEN. I'LL HAVE THE TECHNICIANS PICK OUT ONE THAT'S A GOOD MATCH FOR YOU.
NO COMPLAINTS ABOUT WHAT YOU GET, UNDERSTAND?
IS IT ALWAYS THE HANDLERS WHO PICK THEIR CYBORGS?
NOT ALWAYS.
SOME GOT THEIRS AFTER THE FACT.
THE "GENERATION 1" MODELS WERE ALL EXPERIMENTAL, YOU SEE.
SO THERE WERE A LOT OF DIFFERING SITUATIONS.
WHRWHRBRUMMM
HEARD SOME OF THEM HAD PROBLEMS DEALING WITH THEIR CYBORGS.
YOUR POINT?
GUESS THAT'S GONNA HAPPEN WHEN SO MANY OF THEM ARE EX-COPS OR EX-MILITARY.
HARDCORE PATRIOTIC TYPES AREN'T CUT OUT FOR THIS JOB.
THERE WERE A COUPLE GUYS OUT OF INTEL AND SECRET OPS THAT FAILED AT THIS TOO, Y'KNOW.
REALLY NOW...

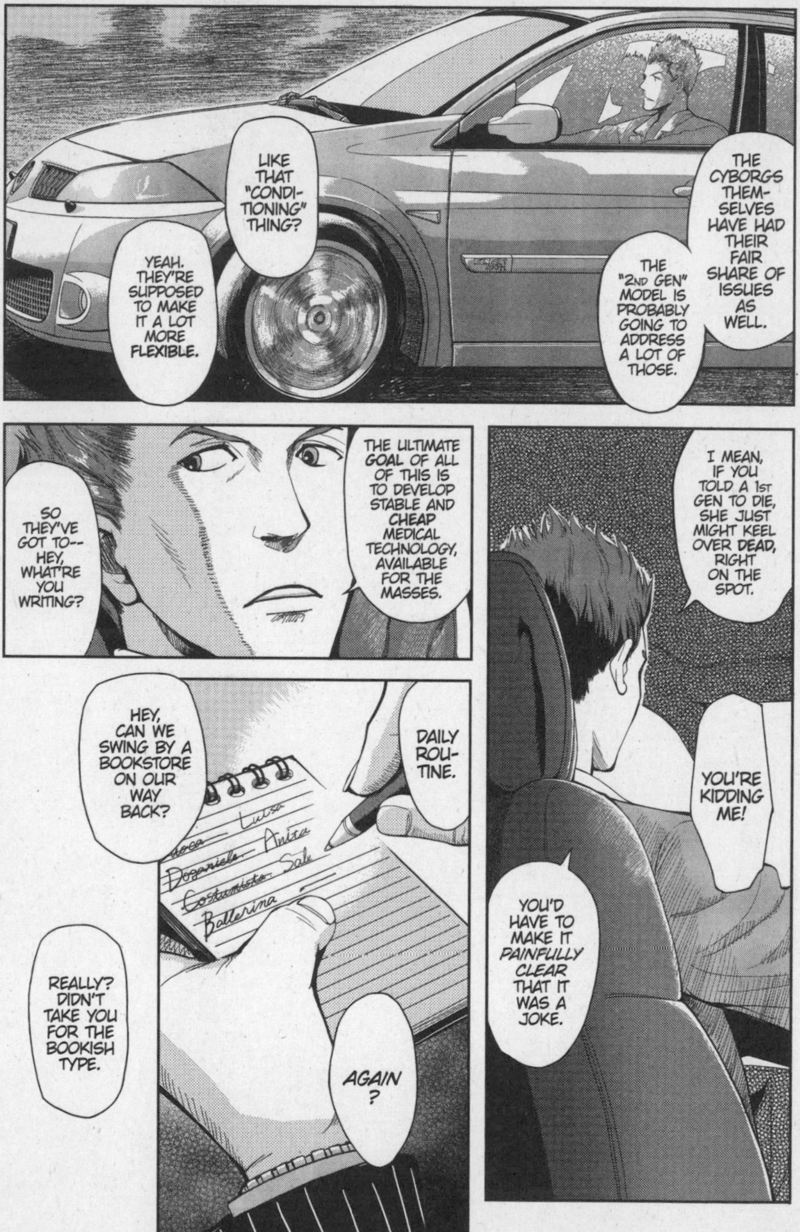
THE CYBORGS THEMSELVES HAVE HAD THEIR FAIR SHARE OF ISSUES AS WELL.
THE "2ND GEN" MODEL IS PROBABLY GOING TO ADDRESS A LOT OF THOSE.
LIKE THAT "CONDITIONING" THING?
YEAH. THEY'RE SUPPOSED TO MAKE IT A LOT MORE FLEXIBLE.
I MEAN, IF YOU TOLD A 1ST GEN TO DIE, SHE JUST MIGHT KEEL OVER DEAD, RIGHT ON THE SPOT.
YOU'RE KIDDING ME!
YOU'D HAVE TO MAKE IT *PAINFULLY CLEAR* THAT IT WAS A JOKE.
THE ULTIMATE GOAL OF ALL OF THIS IS TO DEVELOP STABLE AND CHEAP MEDICAL TECHNOLOGY, AVAILABLE FOR THE MASSES.
SO THEY'VE GOT TO-- HEY, WHAT'RE YOU WRITING?
DAILY ROUTINE.
HEY, CAN WE SWING BY A BOOKSTORE ON OUR WAY BACK?
REALLY? DIDN'T TAKE YOU FOR THE BOOKISH TYPE.
AGAIN?

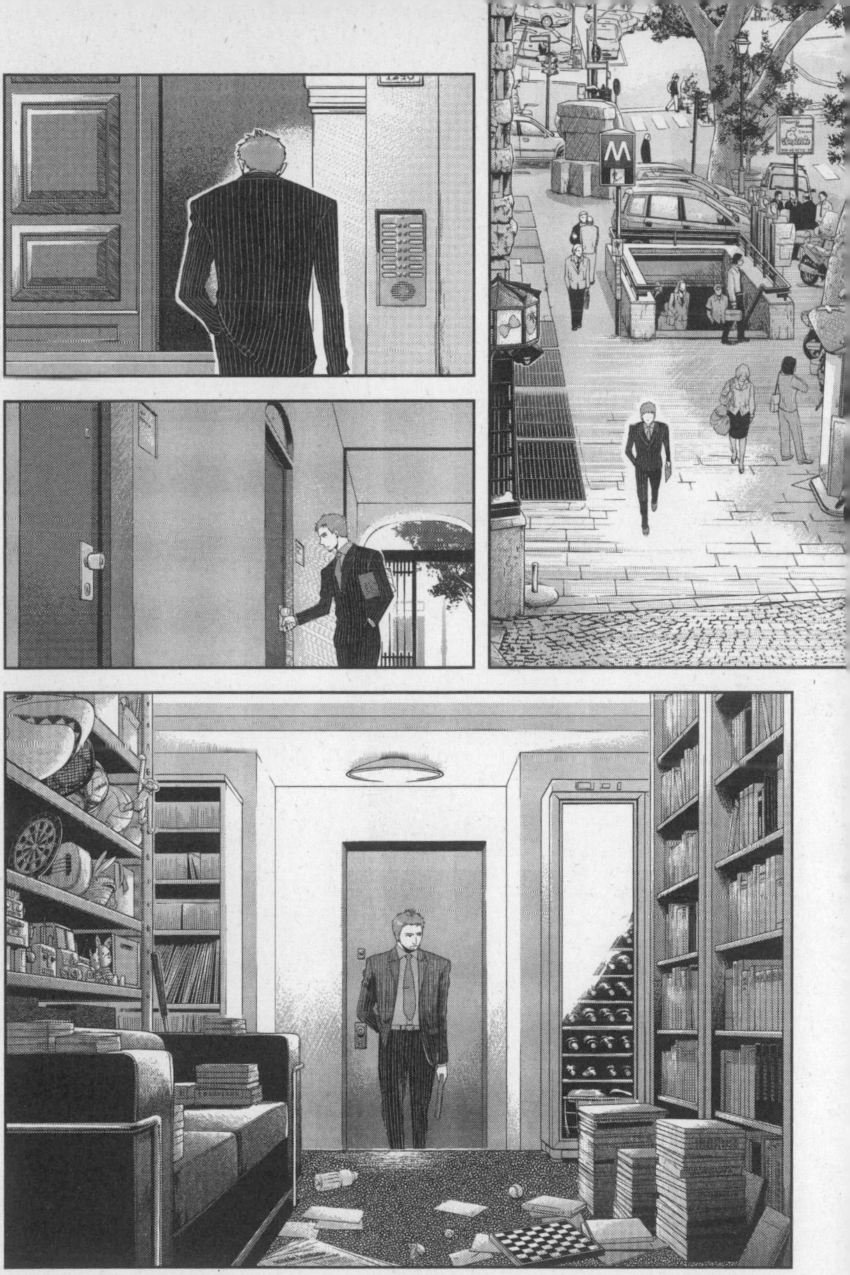
M

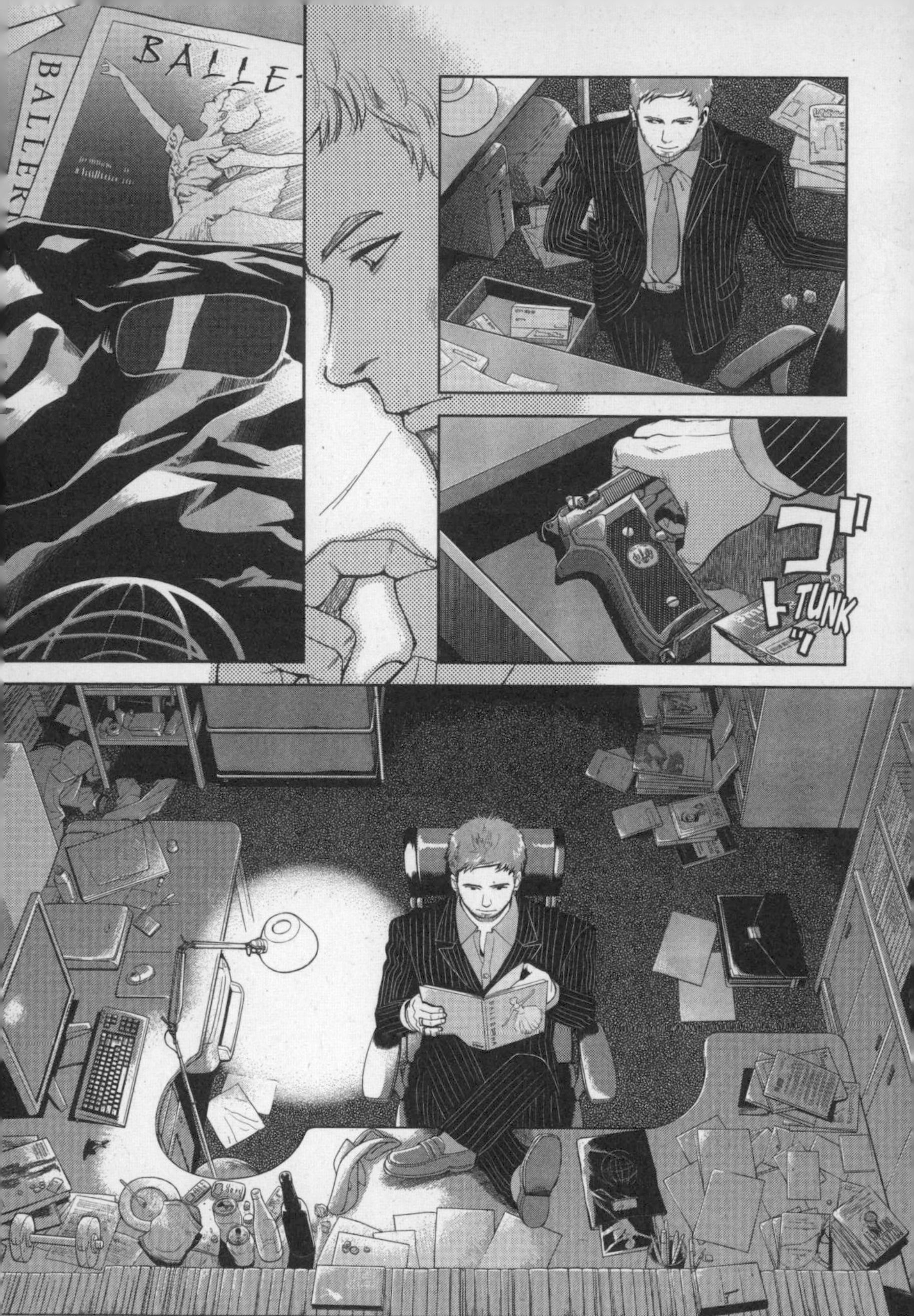
ゴトッ
TUNK
BALLE
BALLER

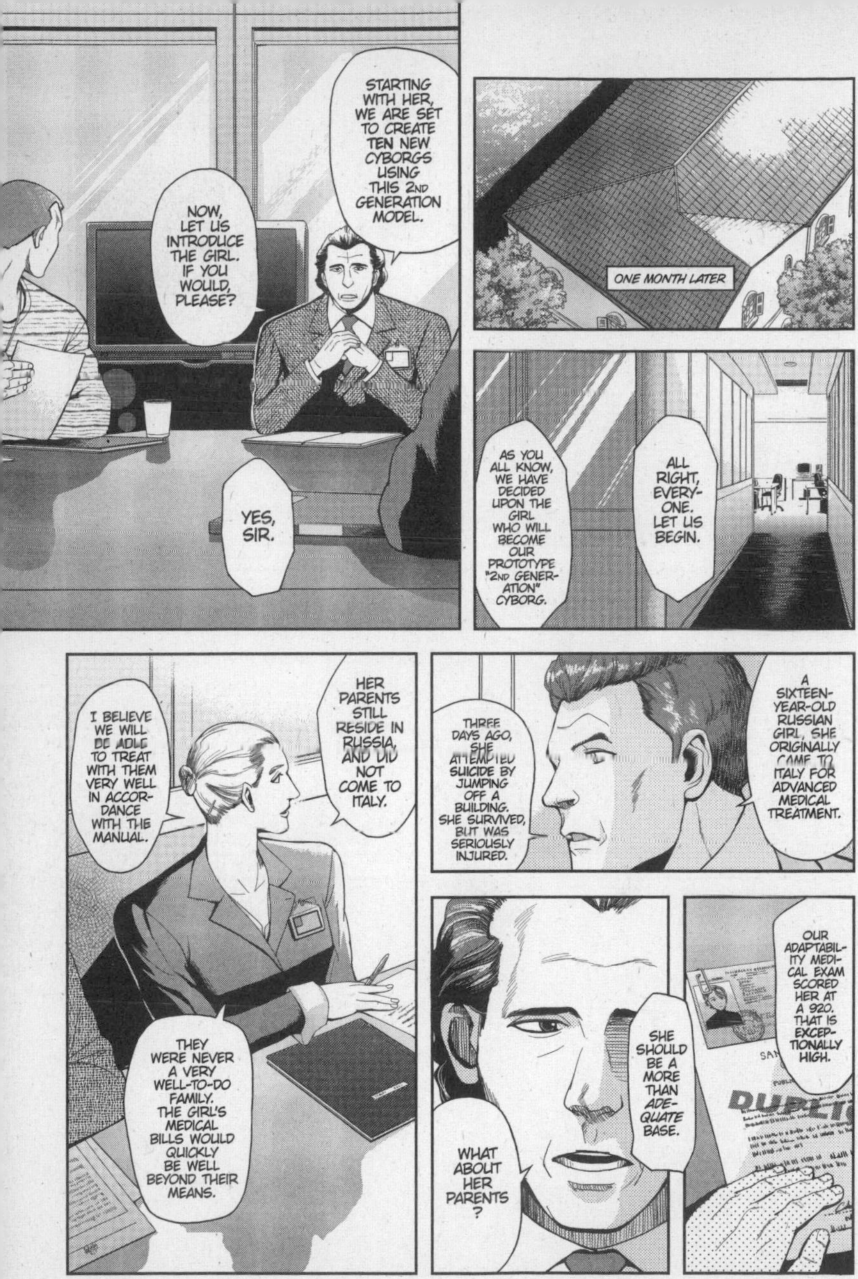
ONE MONTH LATER
ALL RIGHT, EVERY-ONE. LET US BEGIN.
AS YOU ALL KNOW, WE HAVE DECIDED UPON THE GIRL WHO WILL BECOME OUR PROTOTYPE "2ND GENERATION" CYBORG.
STARTING WITH HER, WE ARE SET TO CREATE TEN NEW CYBORGS USING THIS 2ND GENERATION MODEL.
NOW, LET US INTRODUCE THE GIRL. IF YOU WOULD, PLEASE?
YES, SIR.
A SIXTEEN-YEAR-OLD RUSSIAN GIRL, SHE ORIGINALLY CAME TO ITALY FOR ADVANCED MEDICAL TREATMENT.
THREE DAYS AGO, SHE ATTEMPTED SUICIDE BY JUMPING OFF A BUILDING. SHE SURVIVED, BUT WAS SERIOUSLY INJURED.
OUR ADAPTABILITY MEDICAL EXAM SCORED HER AT A 920. THAT IS EXCEPTIONALLY HIGH.
SHE SHOULD BE A MORE THAN ADEQUATE BASE.
WHAT ABOUT HER PARENTS?
HER PARENTS STILL RESIDE IN RUSSIA, AND DID NOT COME TO ITALY.
I BELIEVE WE WILL BE ABLE TO TREAT WITH THEM VERY WELL IN ACCORDANCE WITH THE MANUAL.
THEY WERE NEVER A VERY WELL-TO-DO FAMILY. THE GIRL'S MEDICAL BILLS WOULD QUICKLY BE WELL BEYOND THEIR MEANS.

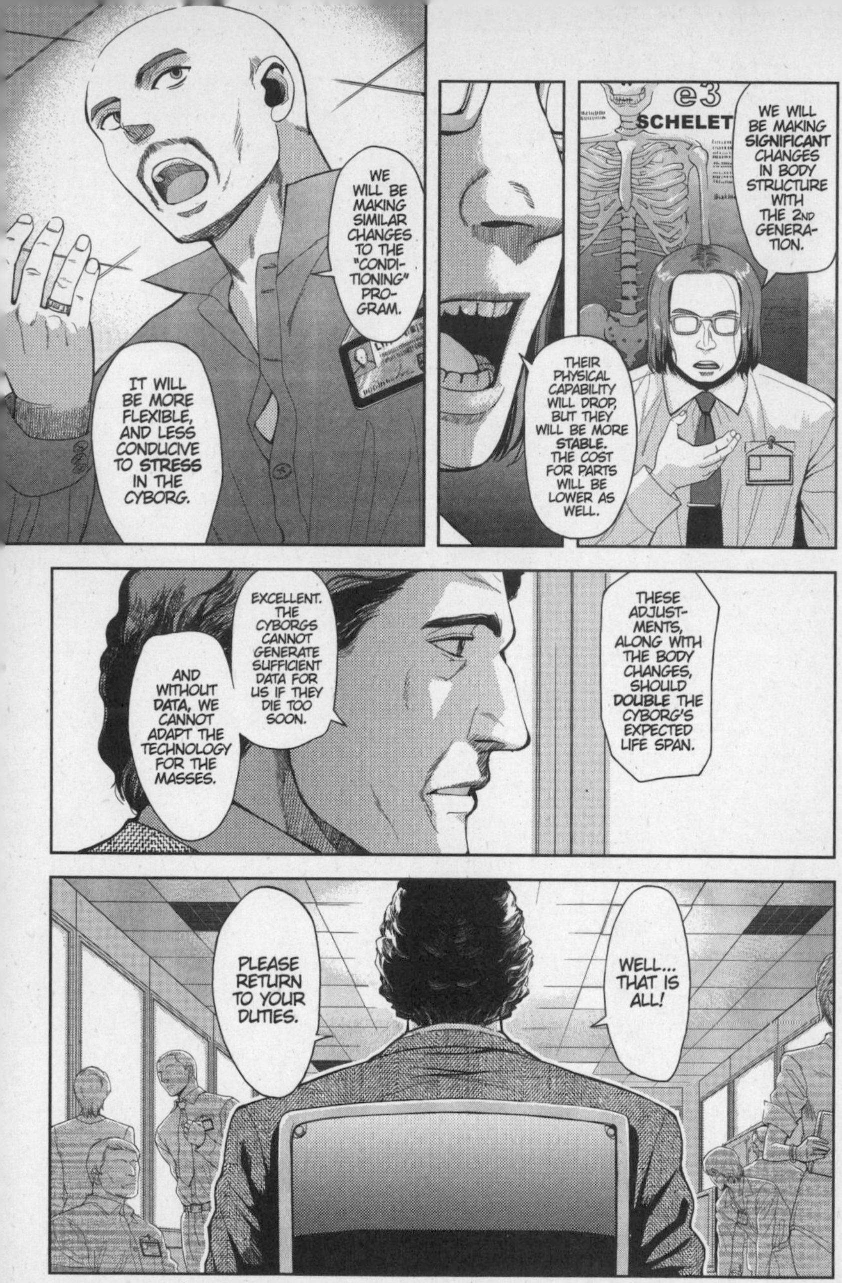
e3
SCHELET
WE WILL BE MAKING SIGNIFICANT CHANGES IN BODY STRUCTURE WITH THE 2ND GENERATION.
THEIR PHYSICAL CAPABILITY WILL DROP, BUT THEY WILL BE MORE STABLE. THE COST FOR PARTS WILL BE LOWER AS WELL.
WE WILL BE MAKING SIMILAR CHANGES TO THE "CONDITIONING" PROGRAM.
IT WILL BE MORE FLEXIBLE, AND LESS CONDUCIVE TO STRESS IN THE CYBORG.
THESE ADJUSTMENTS, ALONG WITH THE BODY CHANGES, SHOULD DOUBLE THE CYBORG'S EXPECTED LIFE SPAN.
EXCELLENT. THE CYBORGS CANNOT GENERATE SUFFICIENT DATA FOR US IF THEY DIE TOO SOON.
AND WITHOUT DATA, WE CANNOT ADAPT THE TECHNOLOGY FOR THE MASSES.
WELL... THAT IS ALL!
PLEASE RETURN TO YOUR DUTIES.

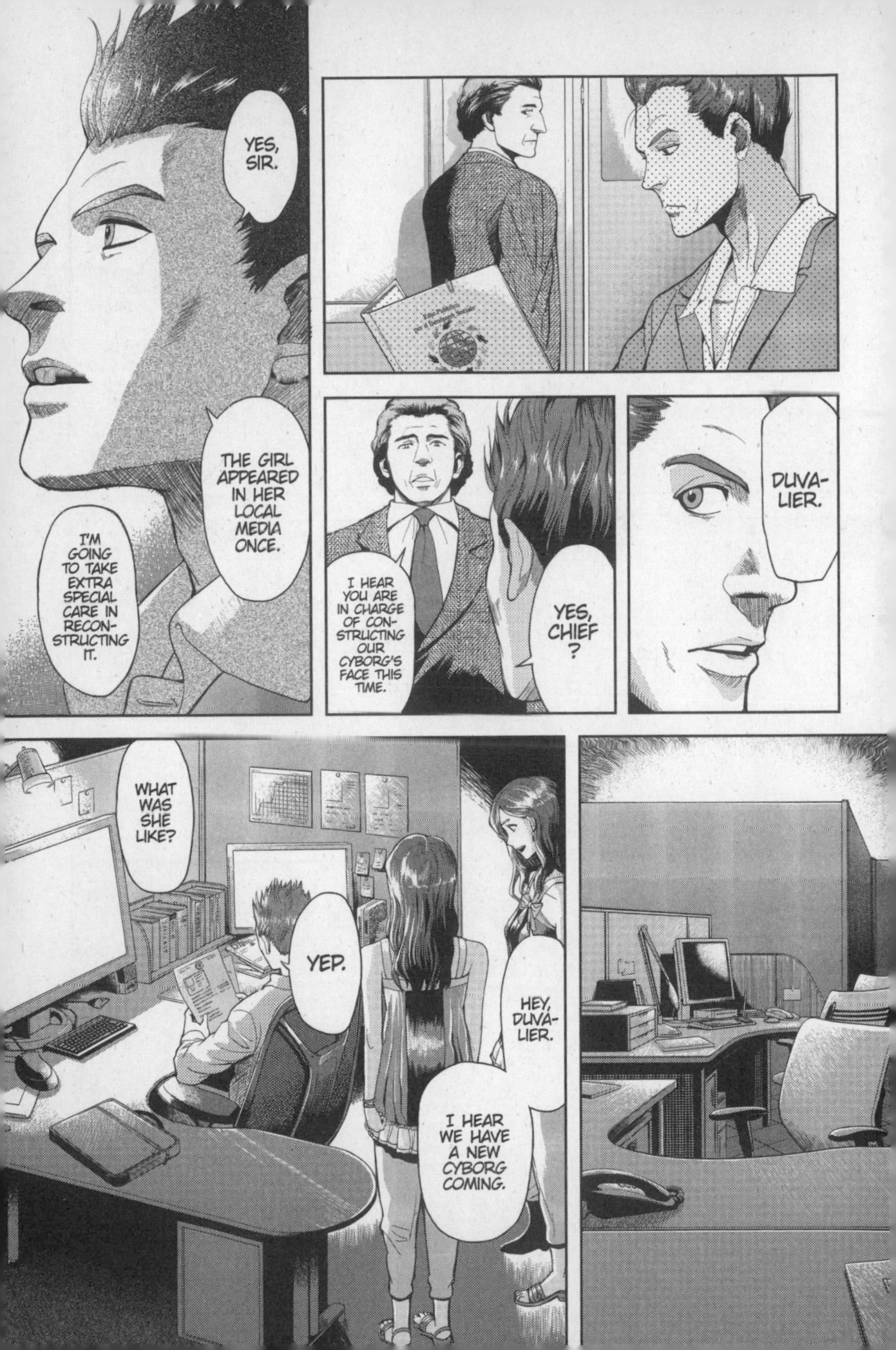
DUVA-
LIER.
YES, CHIEF?
I HEAR YOU ARE IN CHARGE OF CON-STRUCTING OUR CYBORG'S FACE THIS TIME.
YES, SIR.
THE GIRL APPEARED IN HER LOCAL MEDIA ONCE.
I'M GOING TO TAKE EXTRA SPECIAL CARE IN RECON-STRUCTING IT.
HEY, DUVA-LIER.
I HEAR WE HAVE A NEW CYBORG COMING.
YEP.
WHAT WAS SHE LIKE?

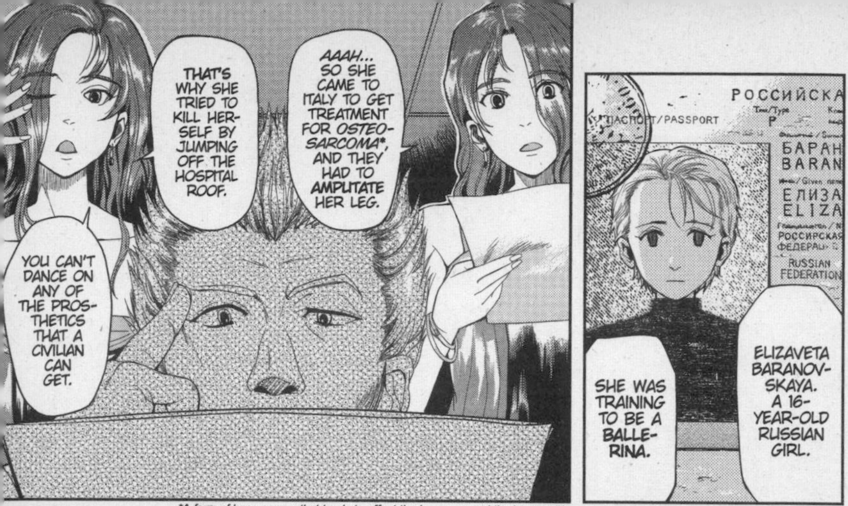
РОССИЙСКА
ПАСПОРТ/PASSPORT
БАРАН
BARAN
ЕЛИЗА
ELIZA
РОССИРСКАЯ ФЕДЕРАЦ
RUSSIAN FEDERATION
ELIZAVETA BARANOV-SKAYA. A 16-YEAR-OLD RUSSIAN GIRL.
SHE WAS TRAINING TO BE A BALLERINA.
AAAH... SO SHE CAME TO ITALY TO GET TREATMENT FOR *OSTEO-SARCOMA**, AND THEY HAD TO **AMPUTATE** HER LEG.
THAT'S WHY SHE TRIED TO KILL HER-SELF BY JUMPING OFF THE HOSPITAL ROOF.
YOU CAN'T DANCE ON ANY OF THE PROS-THETICS THAT A CIVILIAN CAN GET.

A form of bone cancer that tends to affect the bones around the knee or hip.

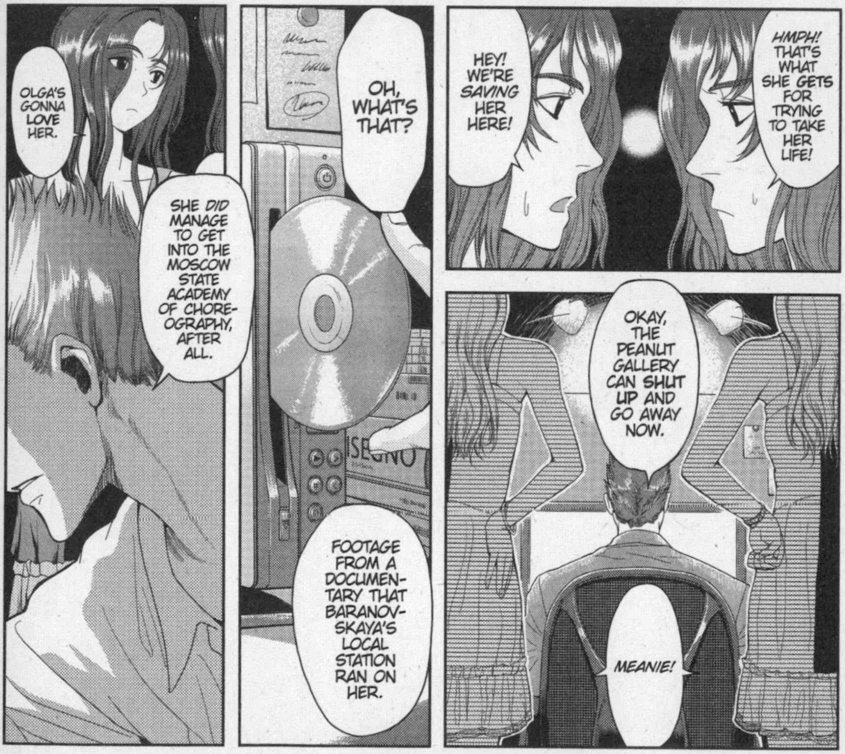
HMPH! THAT'S WHAT SHE **GETS** FOR TRYING TO TAKE HER LIFE!
HEY! WE'RE *SAVING* HER HERE!
OKAY, THE PEANUT GALLERY CAN **SHUT UP** AND GO AWAY NOW.
MEANIE!
OH, WHAT'S THAT?
ISEGNO
FOOTAGE FROM A DOCUMEN-TARY THAT BARANOV-SKAYA'S LOCAL STATION RAN ON HER.
OLGA'S GONNA LOVE HER.
SHE *DID* MANAGE TO GET INTO THE MOSCOW STATE ACADEMY OF CHOREO-OGRAPHY, AFTER ALL.

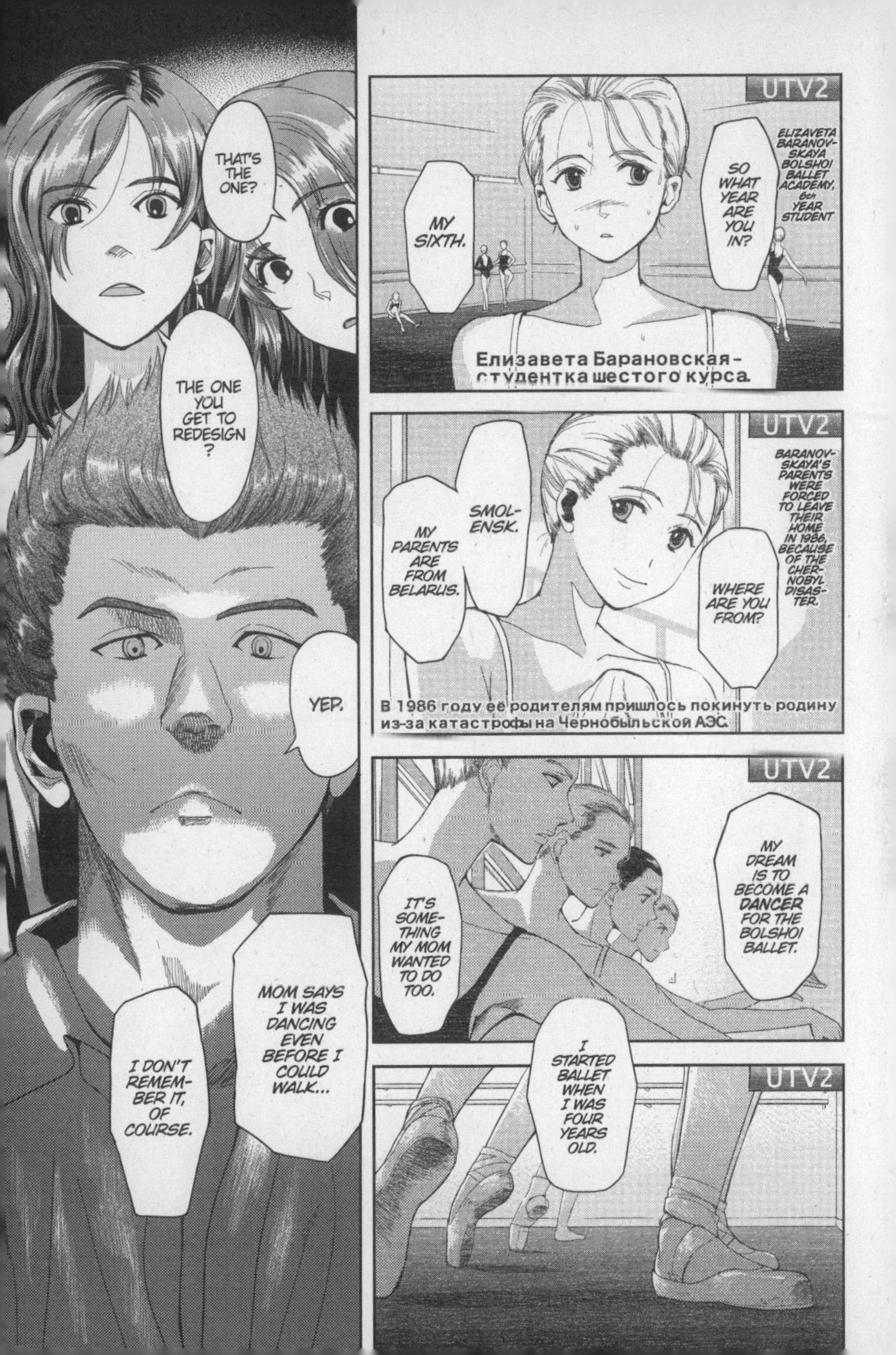
UTV2
ELIZAVETA BARANOVSKAYA BOLSHOI BALLET ACADEMY, 6th YEAR STUDENT
SO WHAT YEAR ARE YOU IN?
MY SIXTH.
Елизавета Барановская - студентка шестого курса.
UTV2
BARANOVSKAYA'S PARENTS WERE FORCED TO LEAVE THEIR HOME IN 1986, BECAUSE OF THE CHERNOBYL DISASTER.
WHERE ARE YOU FROM?
SMOLENSK.
MY PARENTS ARE FROM BELARUS.
В 1986 году её родителям пришлось покинуть родину из-за катастрофы на Чернобыльской АЭС.
UTV2
MY DREAM IS TO BECOME A DANCER FOR THE BOLSHOI BALLET.
IT'S SOMETHING MY MOM WANTED TO DO TOO.
UTV2
I STARTED BALLET WHEN I WAS FOUR YEARS OLD.
THAT'S THE ONE?
THE ONE YOU GET TO REDESIGN?
YEP.
MOM SAYS I WAS DANCING EVEN BEFORE I COULD WALK...
I DON'T REMEMBER IT, OF COURSE.

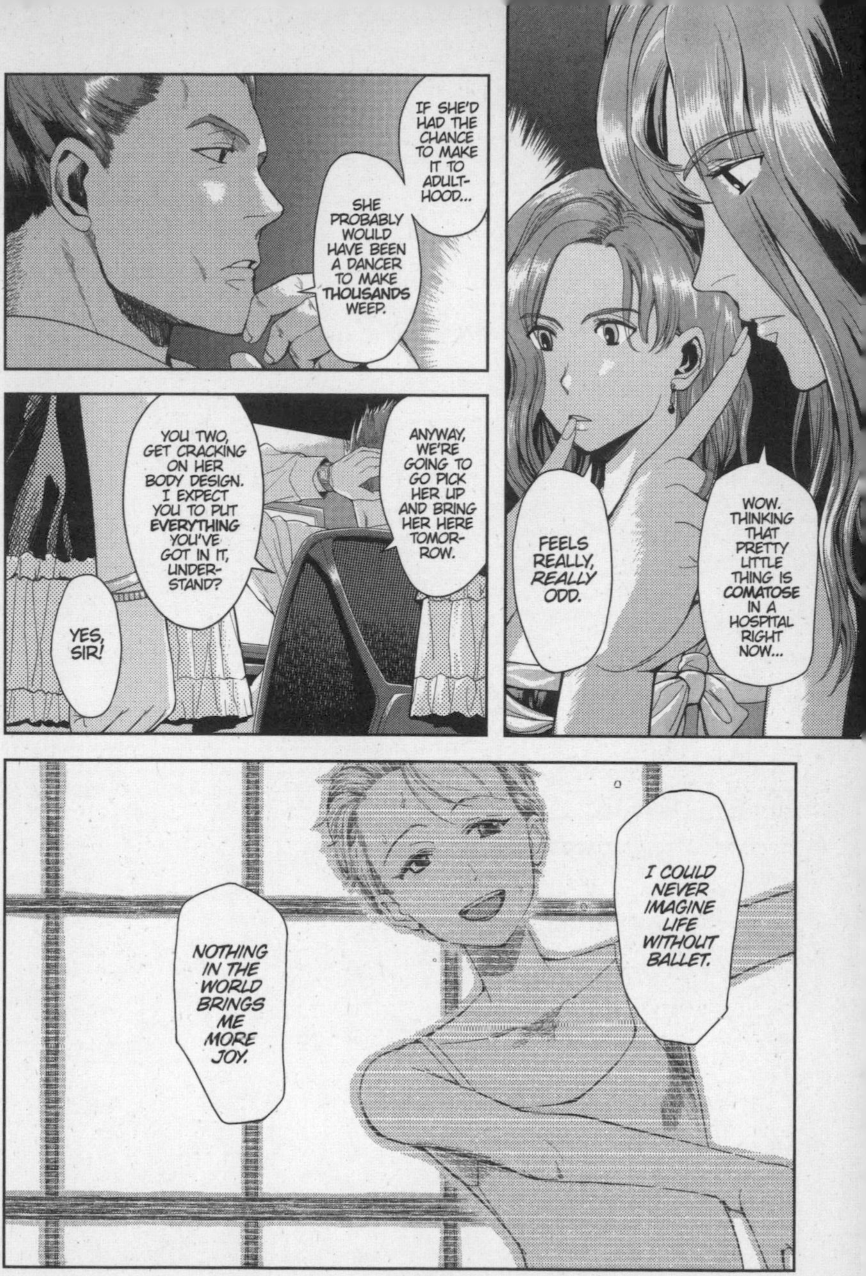
WOW. THINKING THAT PRETTY LITTLE THING IS **COMATOSE** IN A HOSPITAL RIGHT NOW...
FEELS REALLY, *REALLY* ODD.
IF SHE'D HAD THE CHANCE TO MAKE IT TO ADULTHOOD...
SHE PROBABLY WOULD HAVE BEEN A DANCER TO MAKE **THOUSANDS** WEEP.
ANYWAY, WE'RE GOING TO GO PICK HER UP AND BRING HER HERE TOMORROW.
YOU TWO, GET CRACKING ON HER BODY DESIGN. I EXPECT YOU TO PUT **EVERYTHING** YOU'VE GOT IN IT, UNDERSTAND?
YES, SIR!
I COULD NEVER IMAGINE LIFE WITHOUT BALLET.
NOTHING IN THE WORLD BRINGS ME MORE JOY.

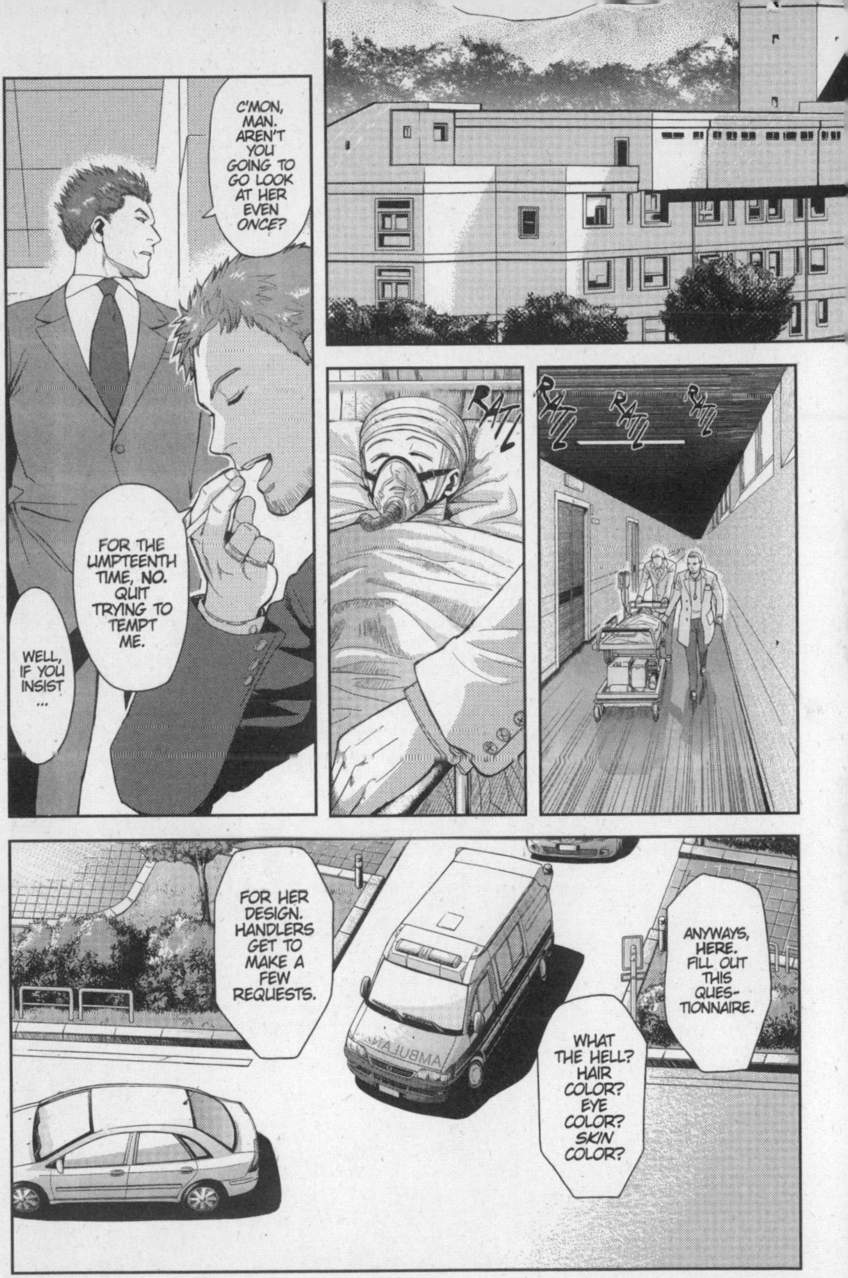
RATTL
RATTL
RATTL
RATTL
C'MON, MAN. AREN'T YOU GOING TO GO LOOK AT HER EVEN ONCE?
FOR THE UMPTEENTH TIME, NO. QUIT TRYING TO TEMPT ME.
WELL, IF YOU INSIST ...
ANYWAYS, HERE. FILL OUT THIS QUES-TIONNAIRE.
WHAT THE HELL? HAIR COLOR? EYE COLOR? SKIN COLOR?
FOR HER DESIGN. HANDLERS GET TO MAKE A FEW REQUESTS.

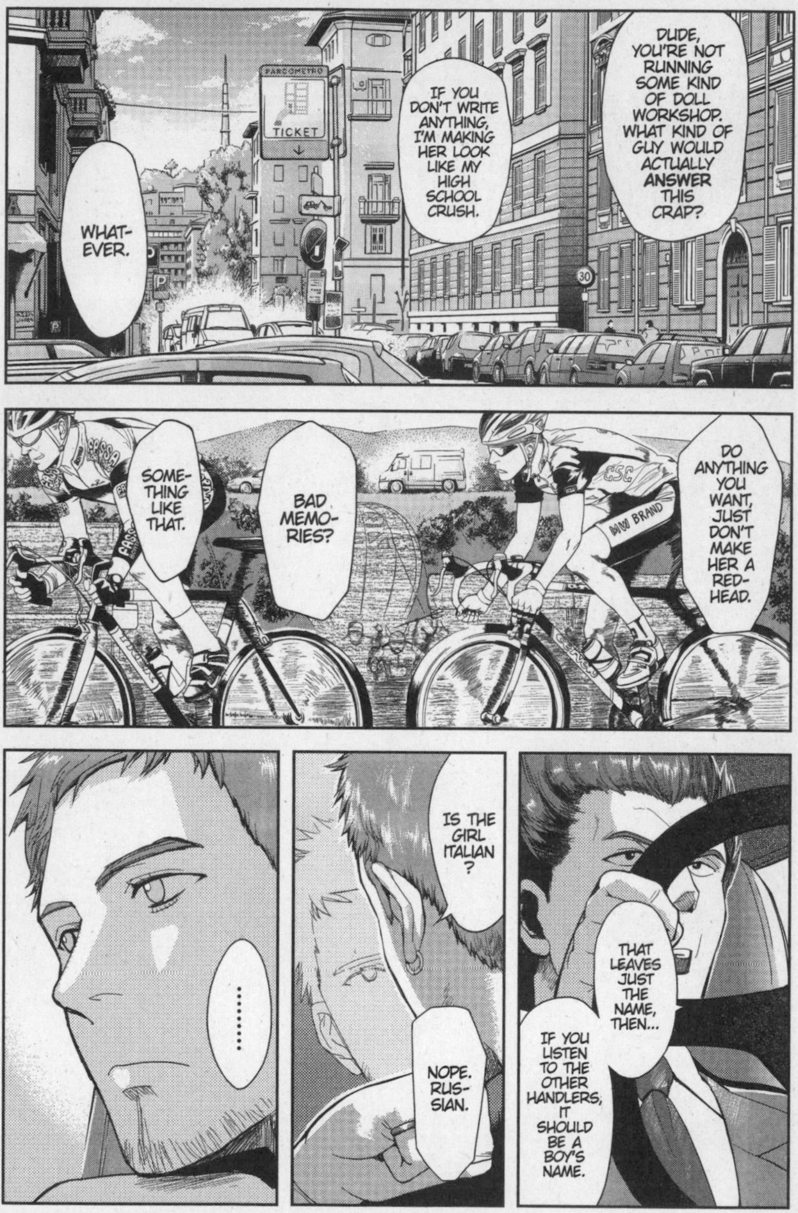
DUDE, YOU'RE NOT RUNNING SOME KIND OF DOLL WORKSHOP. WHAT KIND OF GUY WOULD ACTUALLY **ANSWER** THIS CRAP?
IF YOU DON'T WRITE ANYTHING, I'M MAKING HER LOOK LIKE MY HIGH SCHOOL CRUSH.
PARCOMETRO
TICKET
WHAT-EVER.
DO ANYTHING YOU WANT, JUST DON'T MAKE HER A RED-HEAD.
BAD MEMO-RIES?
SOME-THING LIKE THAT.
THAT LEAVES JUST THE NAME, THEN...
IF YOU LISTEN TO THE OTHER HANDLERS, IT SHOULD BE A BOY'S NAME.
IS THE GIRL ITALIAN?
NOPE. RUS-SIAN.
......

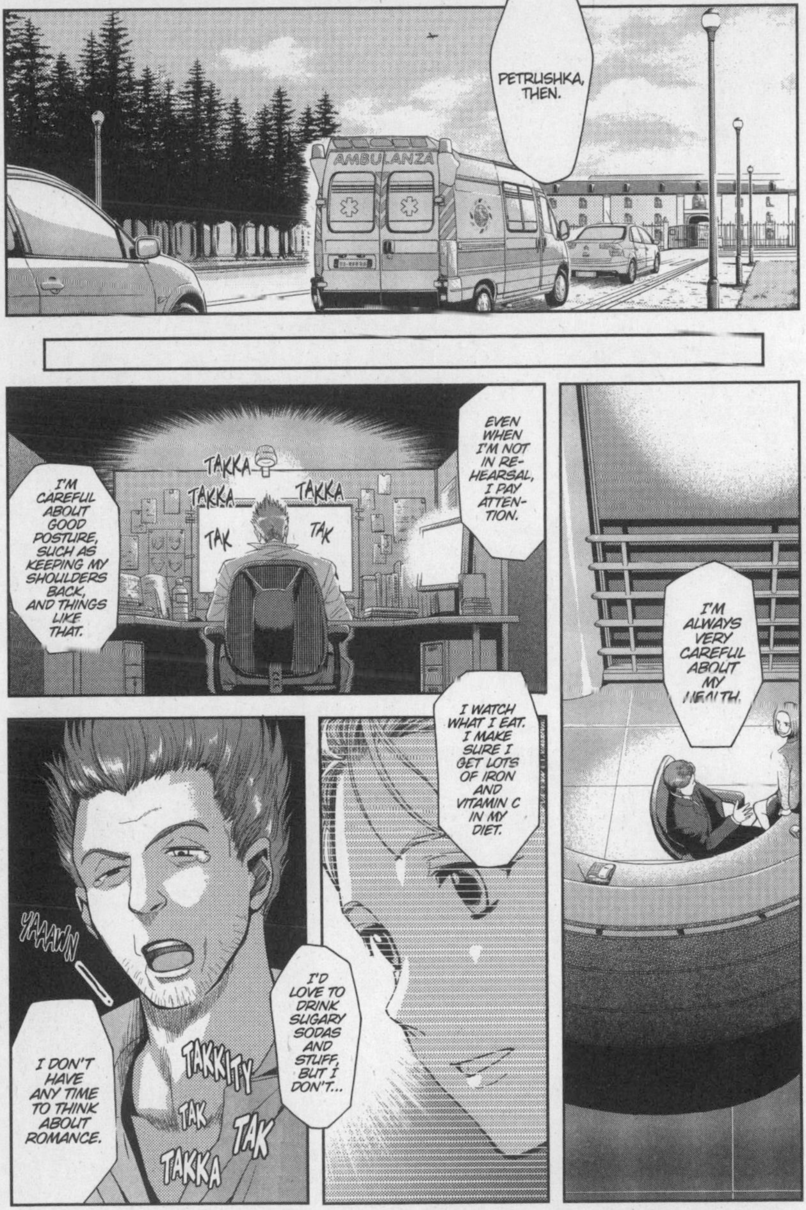
PETRUSHKA, THEN.
I'M ALWAYS VERY CAREFUL ABOUT MY HEALTH.
EVEN WHEN I'M NOT IN RE-HEARSAL, I PAY ATTEN-TION.
I'M CAREFUL ABOUT GOOD POSTURE, SUCH AS KEEPING MY SHOULDERS BACK, AND THINGS LIKE THAT.
TAKKA
TAKKA
TAKKA
TAK
TAK
I WATCH WHAT I EAT. I MAKE SURE I GET LOTS OF IRON AND VITAMIN C IN MY DIET.
I'D LOVE TO DRINK SUGARY SODAS AND STUFF, BUT I DON'T...
YAAAWN
TAKKITY
TAK
TAK
TAKKA
I DON'T HAVE ANY TIME TO THINK ABOUT ROMANCE.

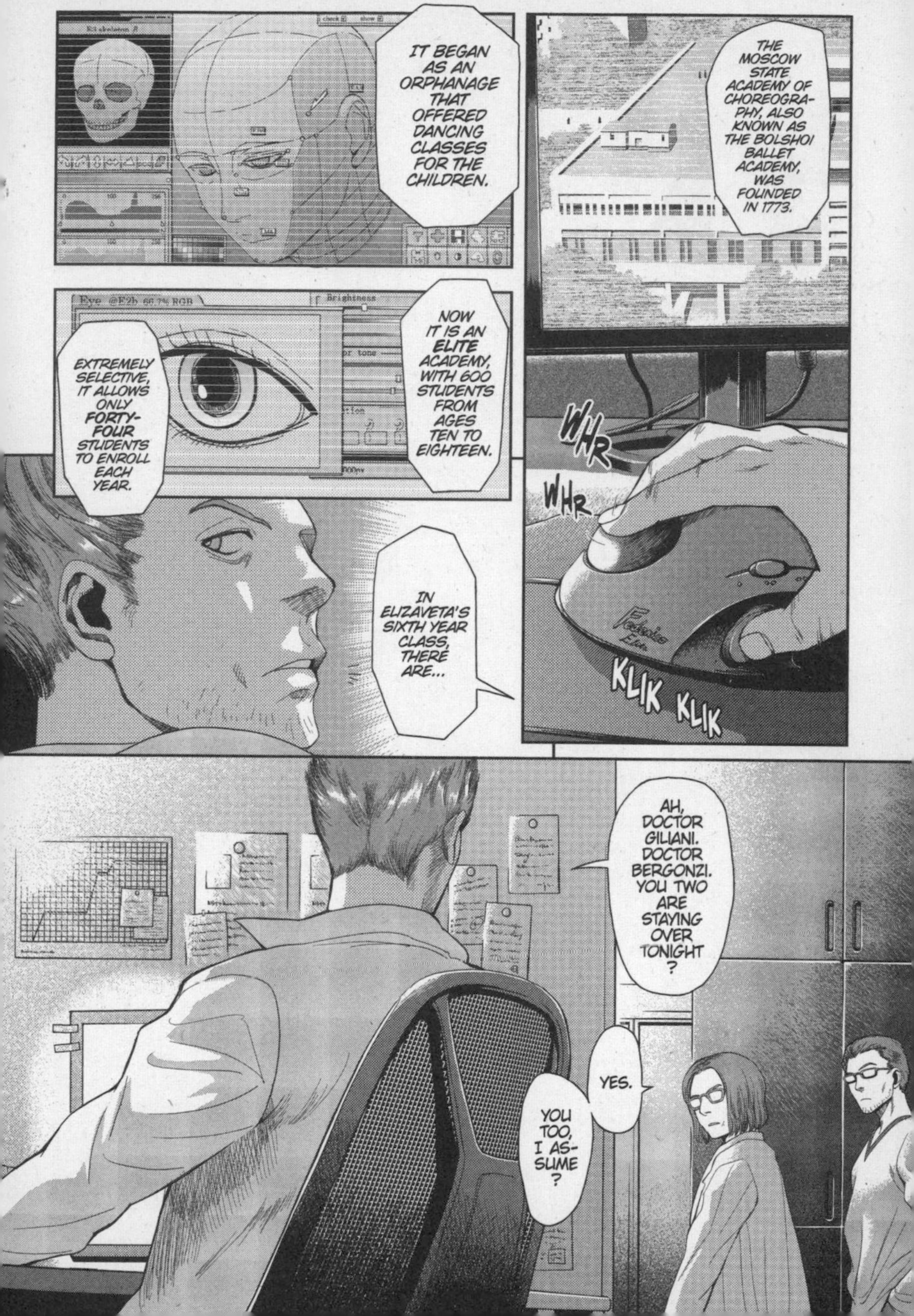
THE MOSCOW STATE ACADEMY OF CHOREOGRAPHY, ALSO KNOWN AS THE BOLSHOI BALLET ACADEMY, WAS FOUNDED IN 1773.
IT BEGAN AS AN ORPHANAGE THAT OFFERED DANCING CLASSES FOR THE CHILDREN.
NOW IT IS AN ELITE ACADEMY, WITH 600 STUDENTS FROM AGES TEN TO EIGHTEEN.
EXTREMELY SELECTIVE, IT ALLOWS ONLY FORTY-FOUR STUDENTS TO ENROLL EACH YEAR.
IN ELIZAVETA'S SIXTH YEAR CLASS, THERE ARE...
WHR
WHR
KLIK KLIK
AH, DOCTOR GILIANI. DOCTOR BERGONZI. YOU TWO ARE STAYING OVER TONIGHT?
YES.
YOU TOO, I ASSUME?

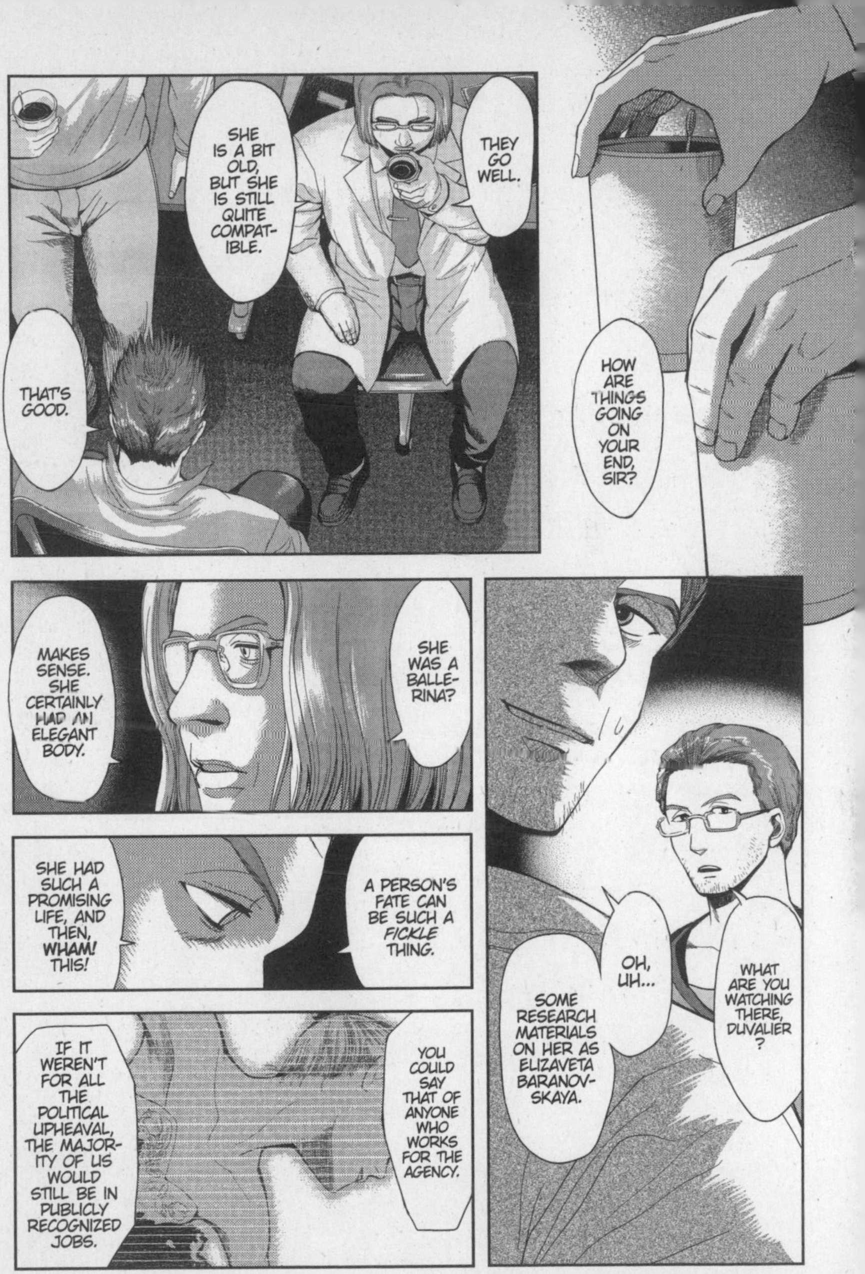
HOW ARE THINGS GOING ON YOUR END, SIR?
THEY GO WELL.
SHE IS A BIT OLD, BUT SHE IS STILL QUITE COMPATIBLE.
THAT'S GOOD.
WHAT ARE YOU WATCHING THERE, DUVALIER?
OH, UH...
SOME RESEARCH MATERIALS ON HER AS ELIZAVETA BARANOVSKAYA.
SHE WAS A BALLERINA?
MAKES SENSE. SHE CERTAINLY HAD AN ELEGANT BODY.
A PERSON'S FATE CAN BE SUCH A *FICKLE* THING.
SHE HAD SUCH A PROMISING LIFE, AND THEN, **WHAM!** THIS!
YOU COULD SAY THAT OF ANYONE WHO WORKS FOR THE AGENCY.
IF IT WEREN'T FOR ALL THE POLITICAL UPHEAVAL, THE MAJORITY OF US WOULD STILL BE IN PUBLICLY RECOGNIZED JOBS.

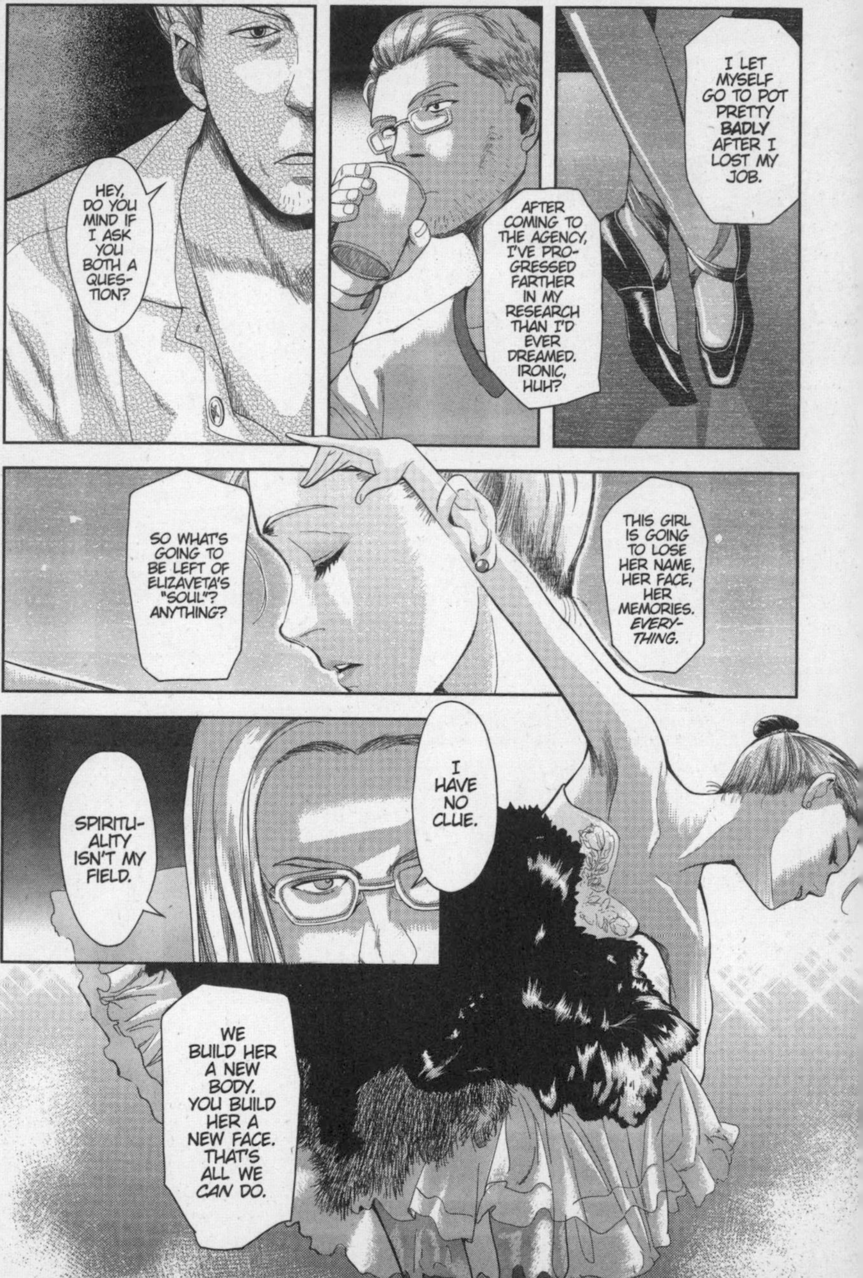
I LET MYSELF GO TO POT PRETTY **BADLY** AFTER I LOST MY JOB.
AFTER COMING TO THE AGENCY, I'VE PROGRESSED FARTHER IN MY RESEARCH THAN I'D EVER DREAMED. IRONIC, HUH?
HEY, DO YOU MIND IF I ASK YOU BOTH A QUES-TION?
THIS GIRL IS GOING TO LOSE HER NAME, HER FACE, HER MEMORIES. *EVERY-THING.*
SO WHAT'S GOING TO BE LEFT OF ELIZAVETA'S "SOUL"? ANYTHING?
I HAVE NO CLUE.
SPIRITU-ALITY ISN'T MY FIELD.
WE BUILD HER A NEW BODY. YOU BUILD HER A NEW FACE. THAT'S ALL WE CAN DO.

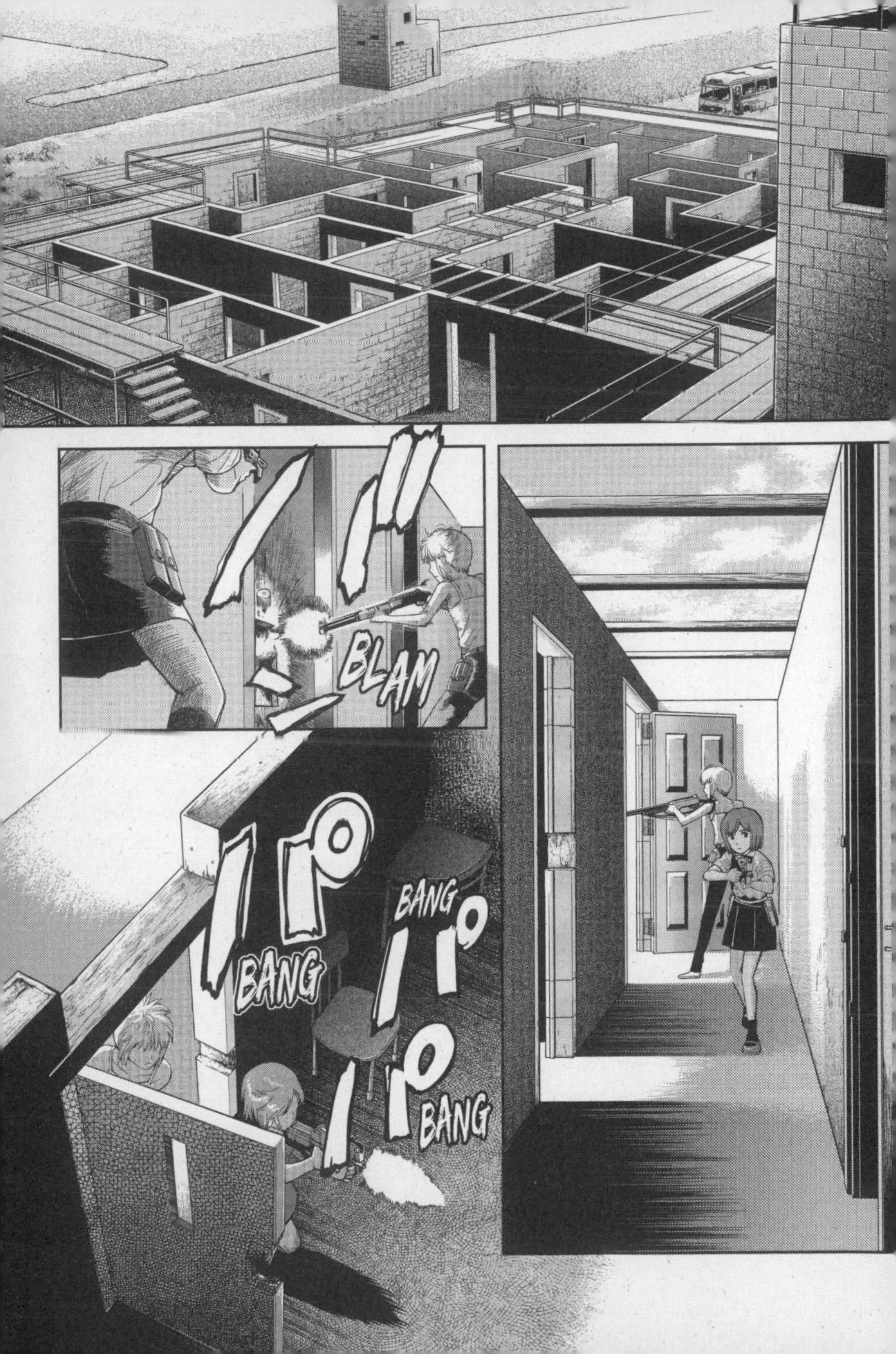
BLAM
BANG
BANG
BANG

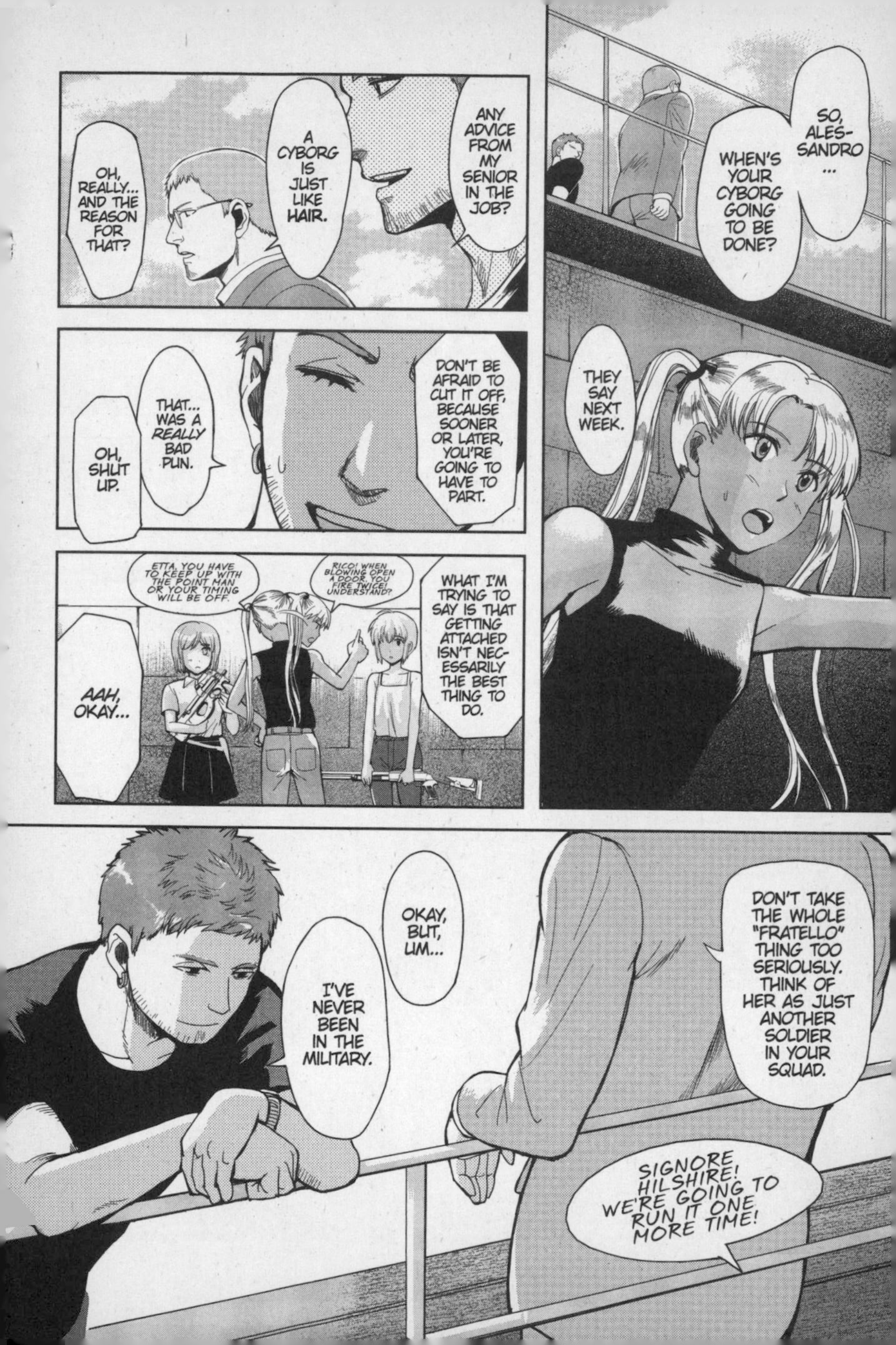
SO, ALESSANDRO...
WHEN'S YOUR CYBORG GOING TO BE DONE?
THEY SAY NEXT WEEK.
ANY ADVICE FROM MY SENIOR IN THE JOB?
A CYBORG IS JUST LIKE HAIR.
OH, REALLY... AND THE REASON FOR THAT?
DON'T BE AFRAID TO CUT IT OFF, BECAUSE SOONER OR LATER, YOU'RE GOING TO HAVE TO PART.
THAT... WAS A REALLY BAD PUN.
OH, SHUT UP.
WHAT I'M TRYING TO SAY IS THAT GETTING ATTACHED ISN'T NECESSARILY THE BEST THING TO DO.
RICO! WHEN BLOWING OPEN A DOOR, YOU FIRE TWICE! UNDERSTAND?
ETTA, YOU HAVE TO KEEP UP WITH THE POINT MAN OR YOUR TIMING WILL BE OFF.
AAH, OKAY...
DON'T TAKE THE WHOLE "FRATELLO" THING TOO SERIOUSLY. THINK OF HER AS JUST ANOTHER SOLDIER IN YOUR SQUAD.
OKAY, BUT, UM...
I'VE NEVER BEEN IN THE MILITARY.
SIGNORE HILSHIRE! WE'RE GOING TO RUN IT ONE MORE TIME!

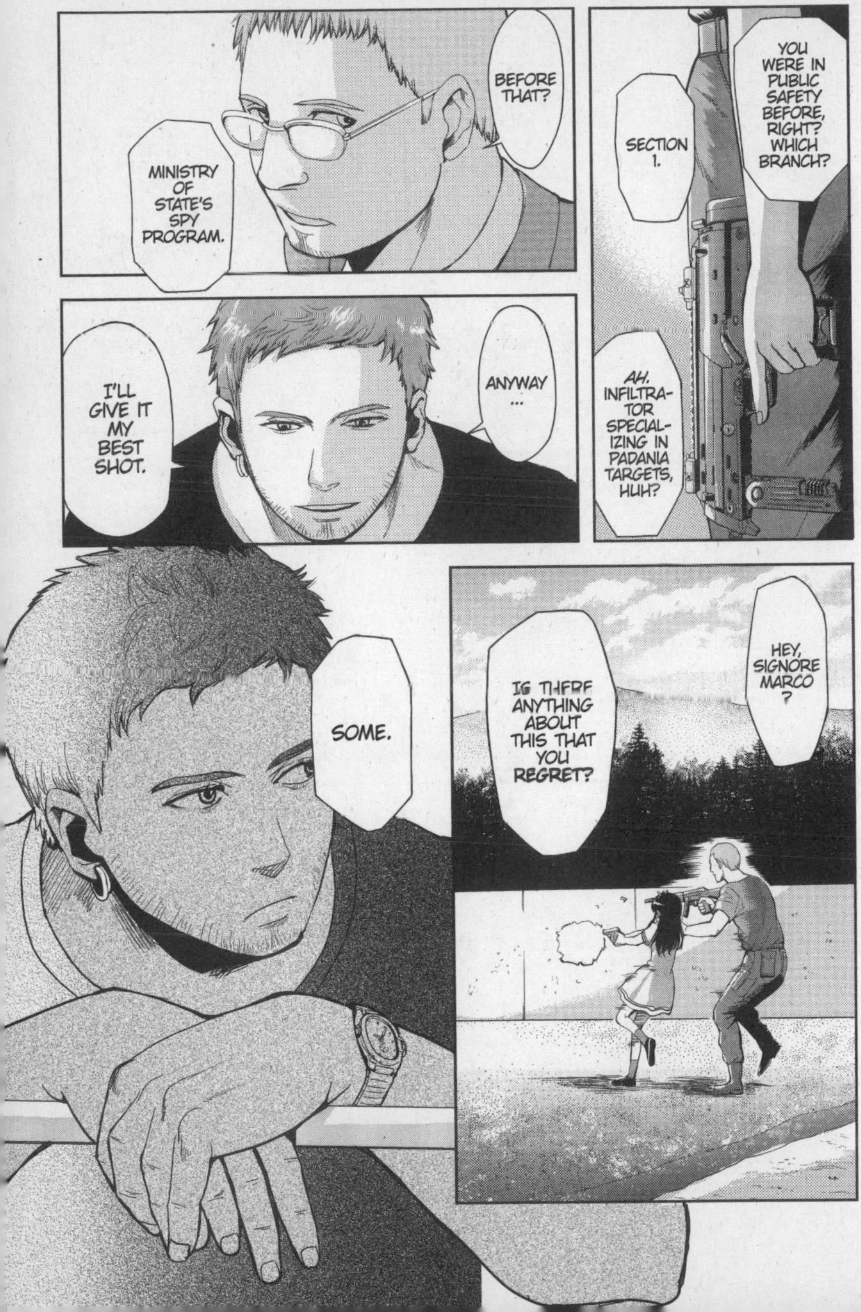
YOU WERE IN PUBLIC SAFETY BEFORE, RIGHT? WHICH BRANCH?
SECTION 1.
AH. INFILTRATOR SPECIALIZING IN PADANIA TARGETS, HUH?
BEFORE THAT?
MINISTRY OF STATE'S SPY PROGRAM.
ANYWAY ...
I'LL GIVE IT MY BEST SHOT.
HEY, SIGNORE MARCO?
IS THERE ANYTHING ABOUT THIS THAT YOU REGRET?
SOME.

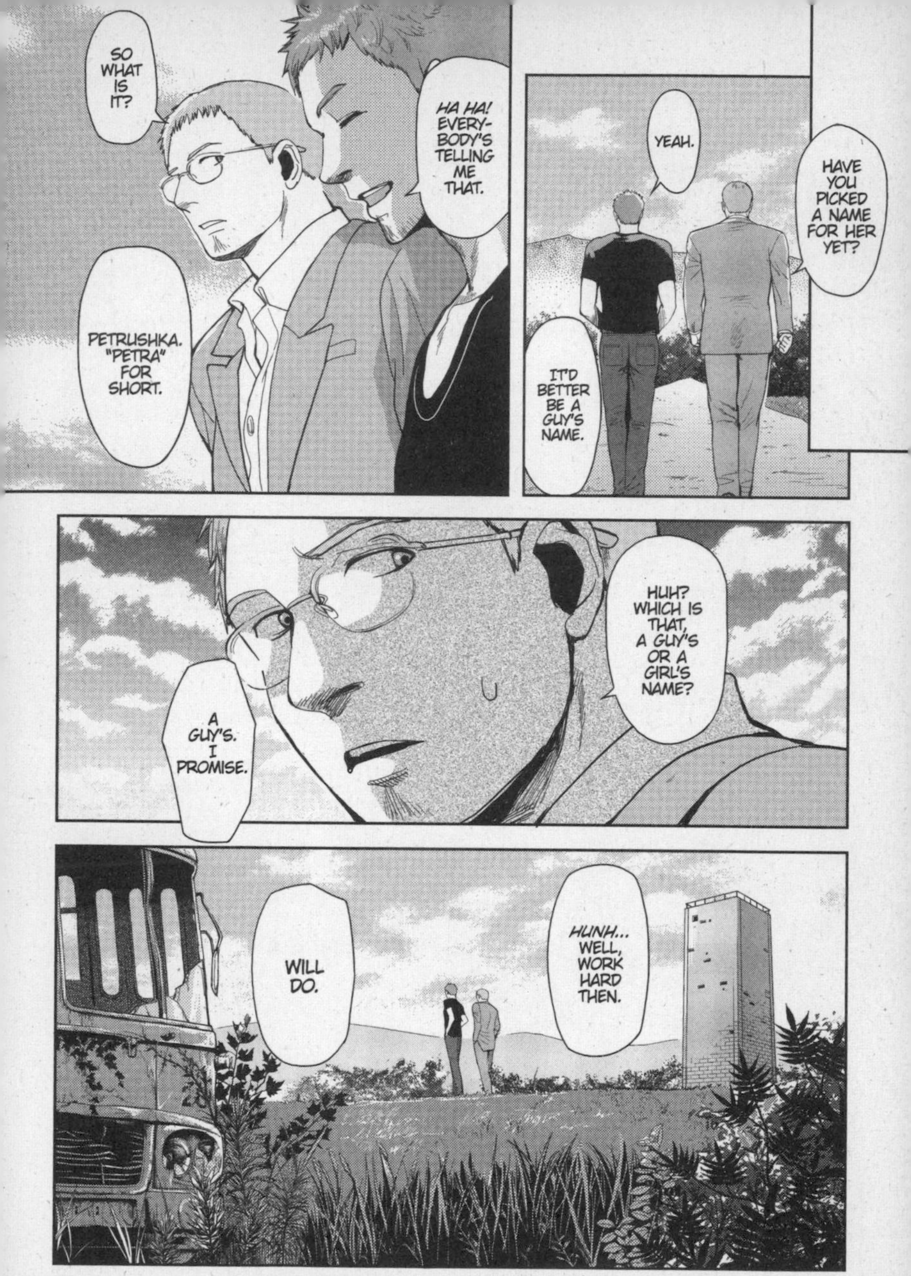
HAVE YOU PICKED A NAME FOR HER YET?
YEAH.
IT'D BETTER BE A GUY'S NAME.
HA HA! EVERY-BODY'S TELLING ME THAT.
SO WHAT IS IT?
PETRUSHKA. "PETRA" FOR SHORT.
HUH? WHICH IS THAT, A GUY'S OR A GIRL'S NAME?
A GUY'S. I PROMISE.
HUNH... WELL, WORK HARD THEN.
WILL DO.

GUNSLINGERGIRL.

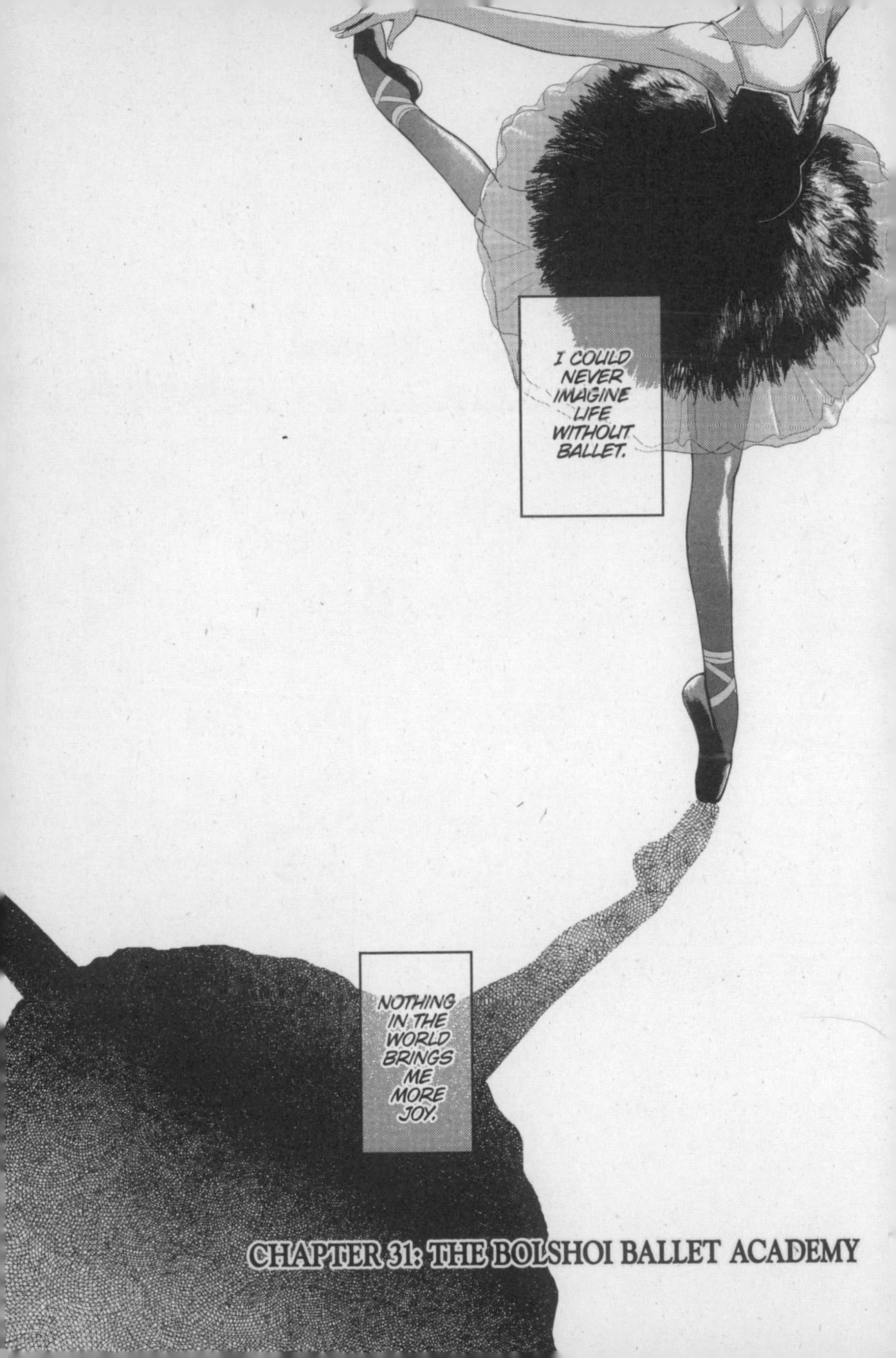
I COULD NEVER IMAGINE LIFE WITHOUT BALLET.
NOTHING IN THE WORLD BRINGS ME MORE JOY.
CHAPTER 31: THE BOLSHOI BALLET ACADEMY

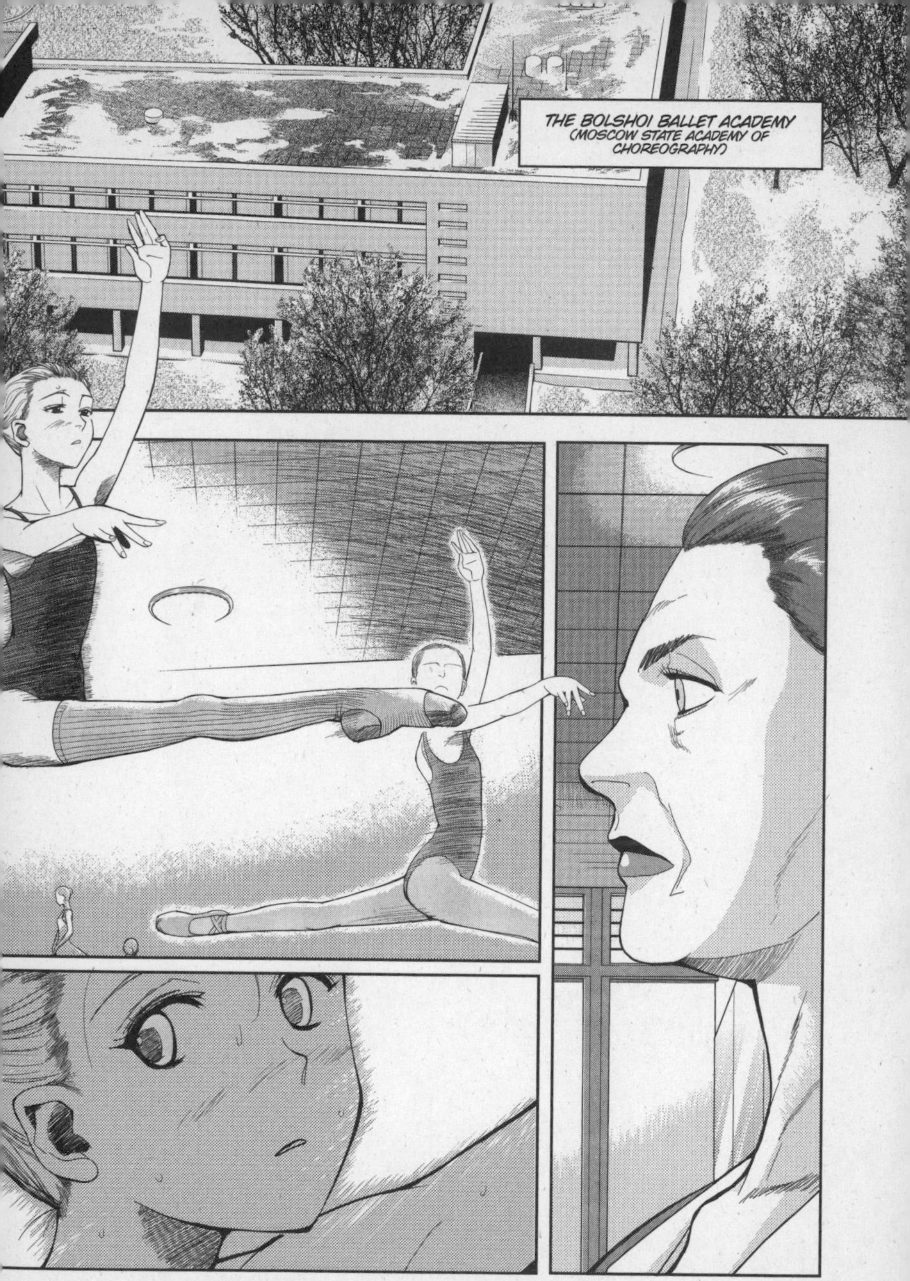
THE BOLSHOI BALLET ACADEMY (MOSCOW STATE ACADEMY OF CHOREOGRAPHY)

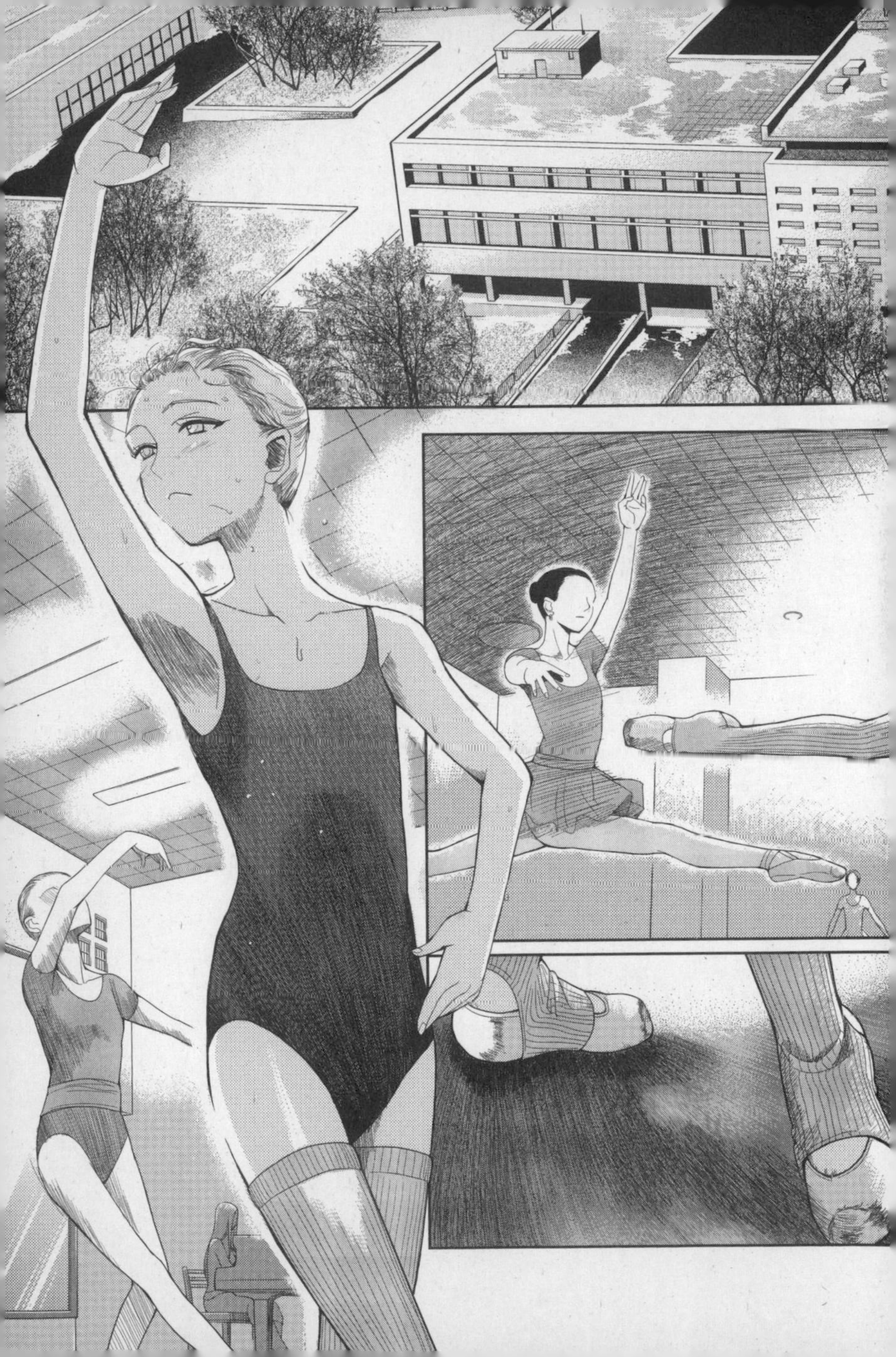

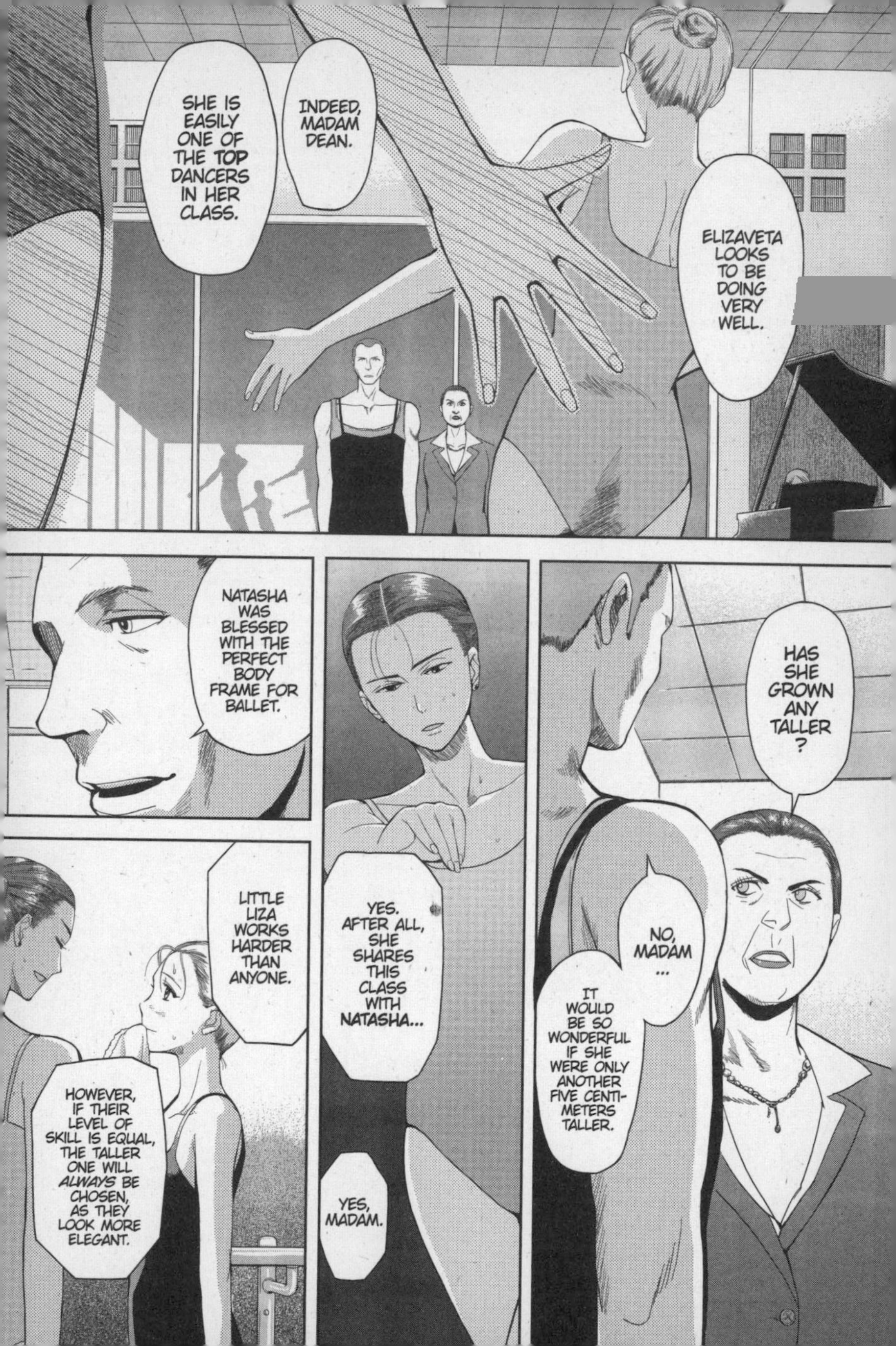
ELIZAVETA LOOKS TO BE DOING VERY WELL.
INDEED, MADAM DEAN.
SHE IS EASILY ONE OF THE TOP DANCERS IN HER CLASS.
HAS SHE GROWN ANY TALLER?
NO, MADAM...
IT WOULD BE SO WONDERFUL IF SHE WERE ONLY ANOTHER FIVE CENTIMETERS TALLER.
YES. AFTER ALL, SHE SHARES THIS CLASS WITH NATASHA...
YES, MADAM.
NATASHA WAS BLESSED WITH THE PERFECT BODY FRAME FOR BALLET.
LITTLE LIZA WORKS HARDER THAN ANYONE.
HOWEVER, IF THEIR LEVEL OF SKILL IS EQUAL, THE TALLER ONE WILL *ALWAYS* BE CHOSEN, AS THEY LOOK MORE ELEGANT.

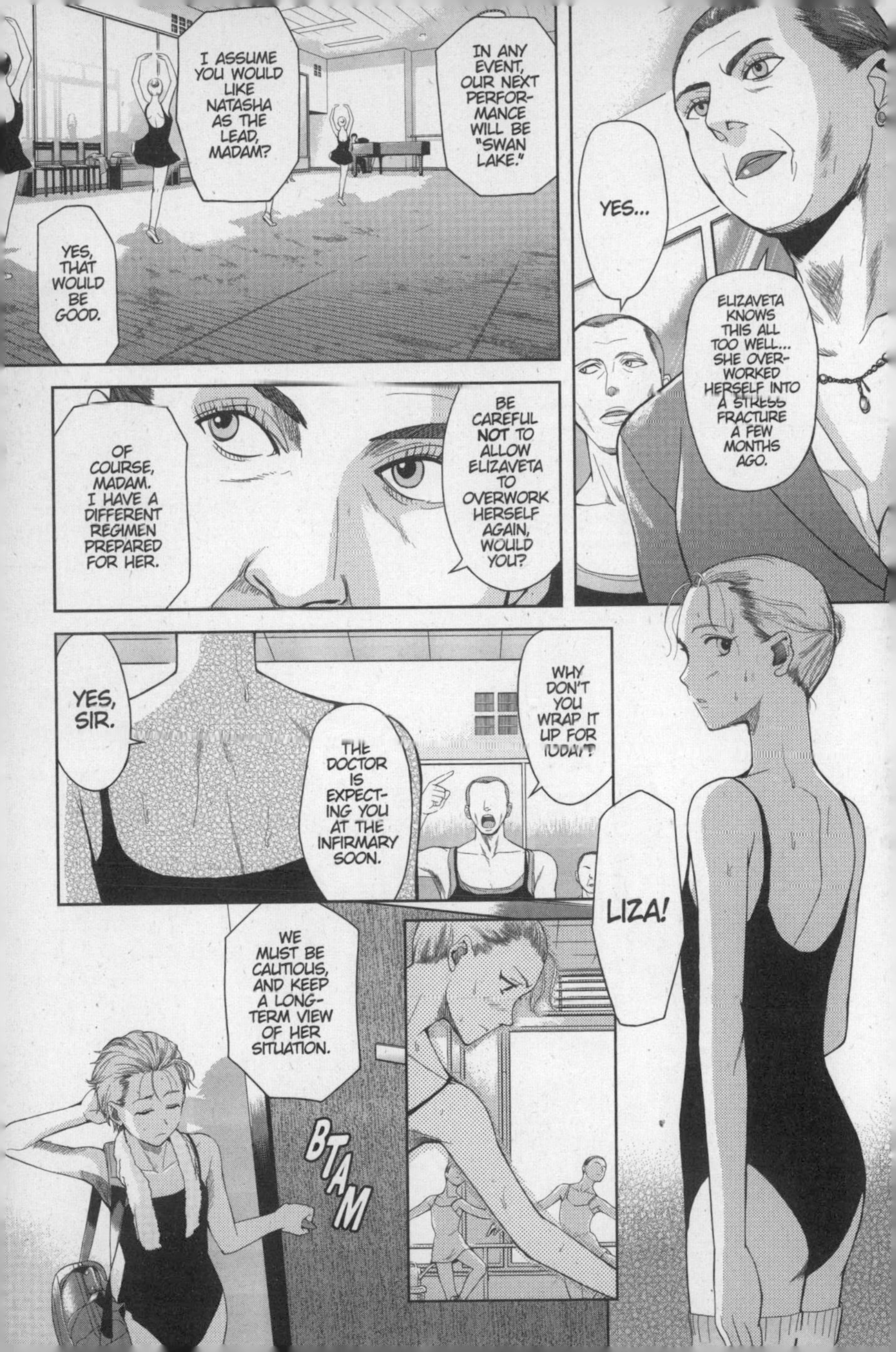
YES...
ELIZAVETA KNOWS THIS ALL TOO WELL... SHE OVER-WORKED HERSELF INTO A STRESS FRACTURE A FEW MONTHS AGO.
IN ANY EVENT, OUR NEXT PERFORM-ANCE WILL BE "SWAN LAKE."
I ASSUME YOU WOULD LIKE NATASHA AS THE LEAD, MADAM?
YES, THAT WOULD BE GOOD.
BE CAREFUL NOT TO ALLOW ELIZAVETA TO OVERWORK HERSELF AGAIN, WOULD YOU?
OF COURSE, MADAM. I HAVE A DIFFERENT REGIMEN PREPARED FOR HER.
LIZA!
WHY DON'T YOU WRAP IT UP FOR TODAY?
THE DOCTOR IS EXPECT-ING YOU AT THE INFIRMARY SOON.
YES, SIR.
WE MUST BE CAUTIOUS, AND KEEP A LONG-TERM VIEW OF HER SITUATION.
BTAM

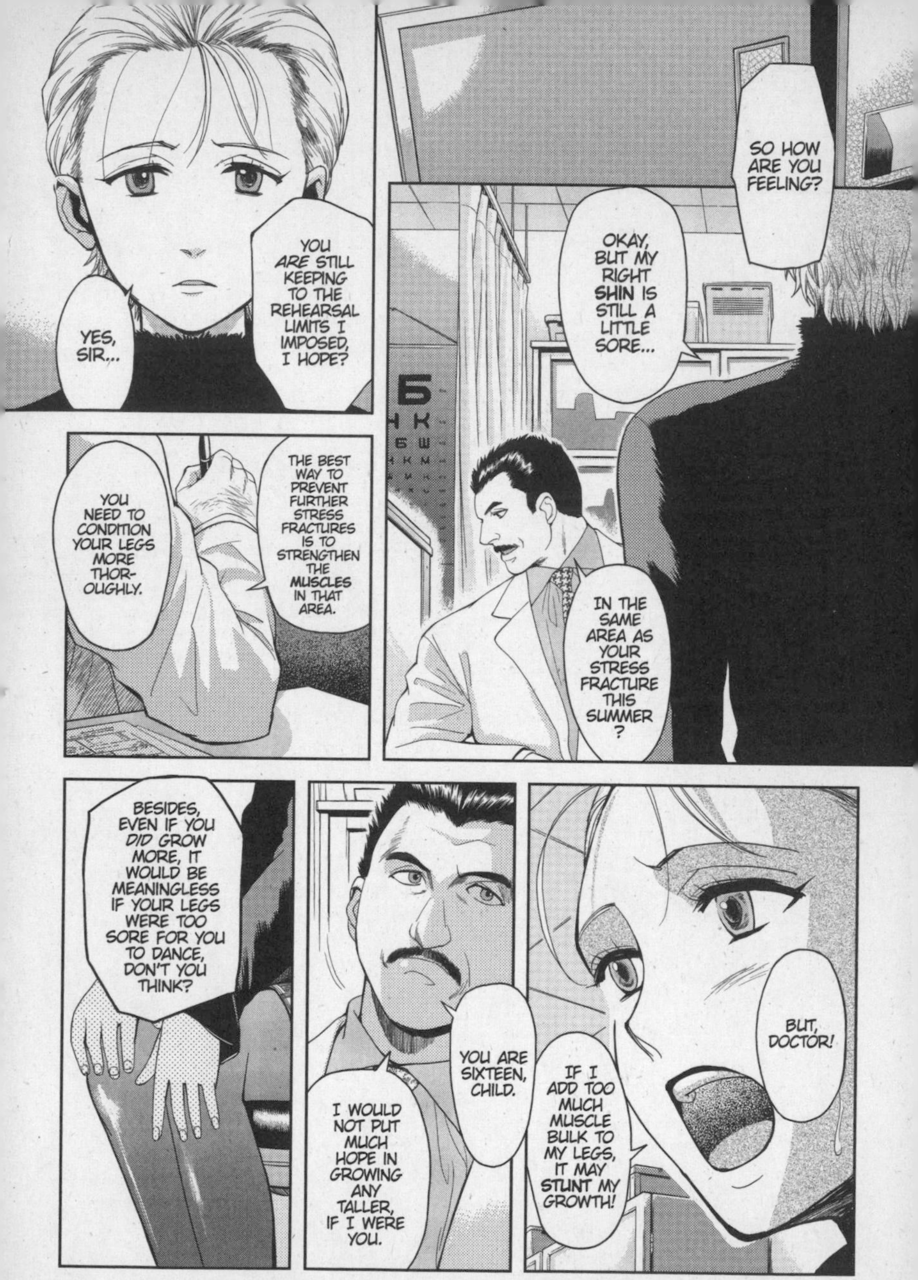
SO HOW ARE YOU FEELING?
OKAY, BUT MY RIGHT SHIN IS STILL A LITTLE SORE...
IN THE SAME AREA AS YOUR STRESS FRACTURE THIS SUMMER?
YOU *ARE* STILL KEEPING TO THE REHEARSAL LIMITS I IMPOSED, I HOPE?
YES, SIR...
THE BEST WAY TO PREVENT FURTHER STRESS FRACTURES IS TO STRENGTHEN THE MUSCLES IN THAT AREA.
YOU NEED TO CONDITION YOUR LEGS MORE THOROUGHLY.
BUT, DOCTOR!
IF I ADD TOO MUCH MUSCLE BULK TO MY LEGS, IT MAY STUNT MY GROWTH!
YOU ARE SIXTEEN, CHILD.
I WOULD NOT PUT MUCH HOPE IN GROWING ANY TALLER, IF I WERE YOU.
BESIDES, EVEN IF YOU *DID* GROW MORE, IT WOULD BE MEANINGLESS IF YOUR LEGS WERE TOO SORE FOR YOU TO DANCE, DON'T YOU THINK?

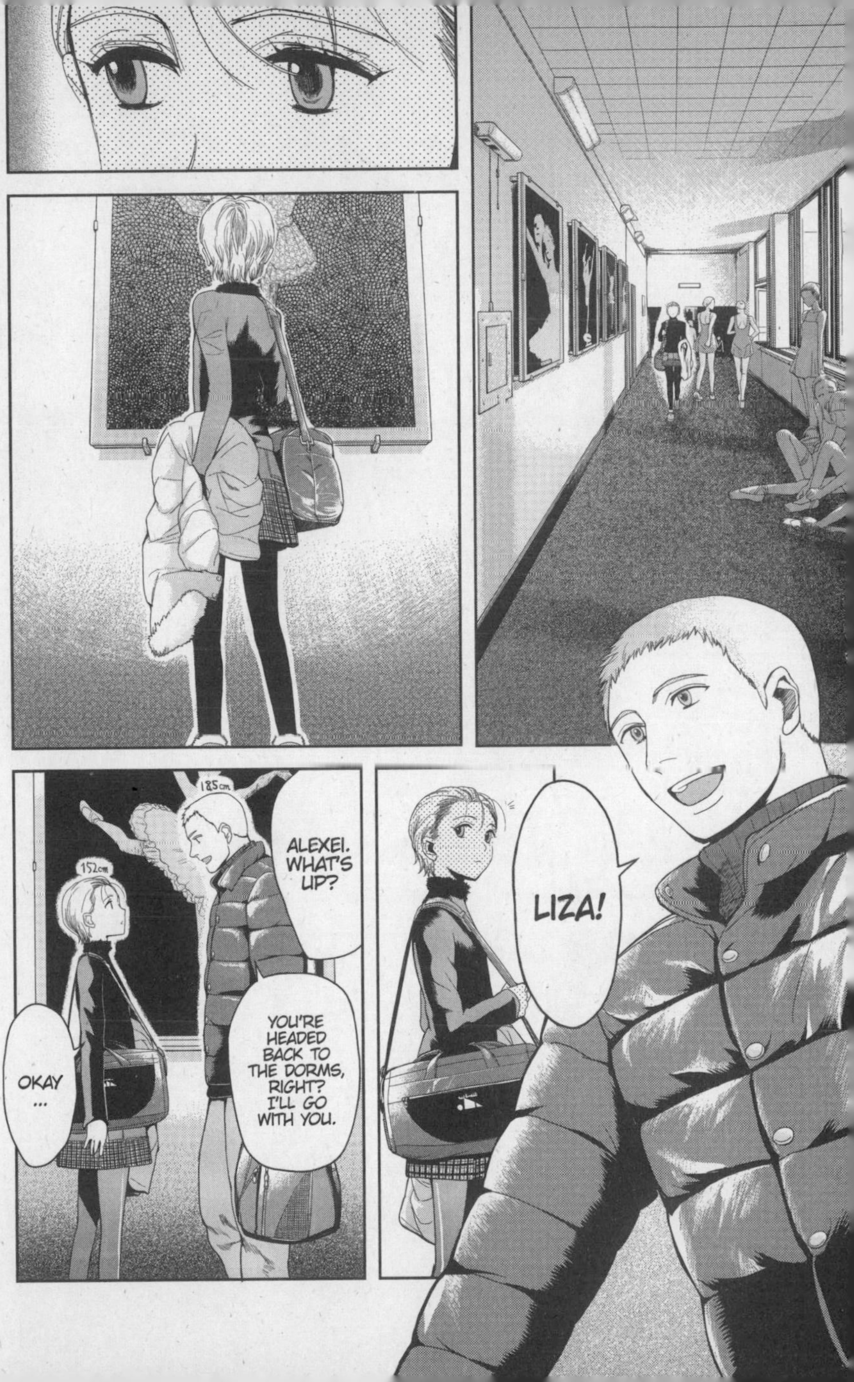
LIZA!
ALEXEI. WHAT'S UP?
185cm
152cm
YOU'RE HEADED BACK TO THE DORMS, RIGHT? I'LL GO WITH YOU.
OKAY ...

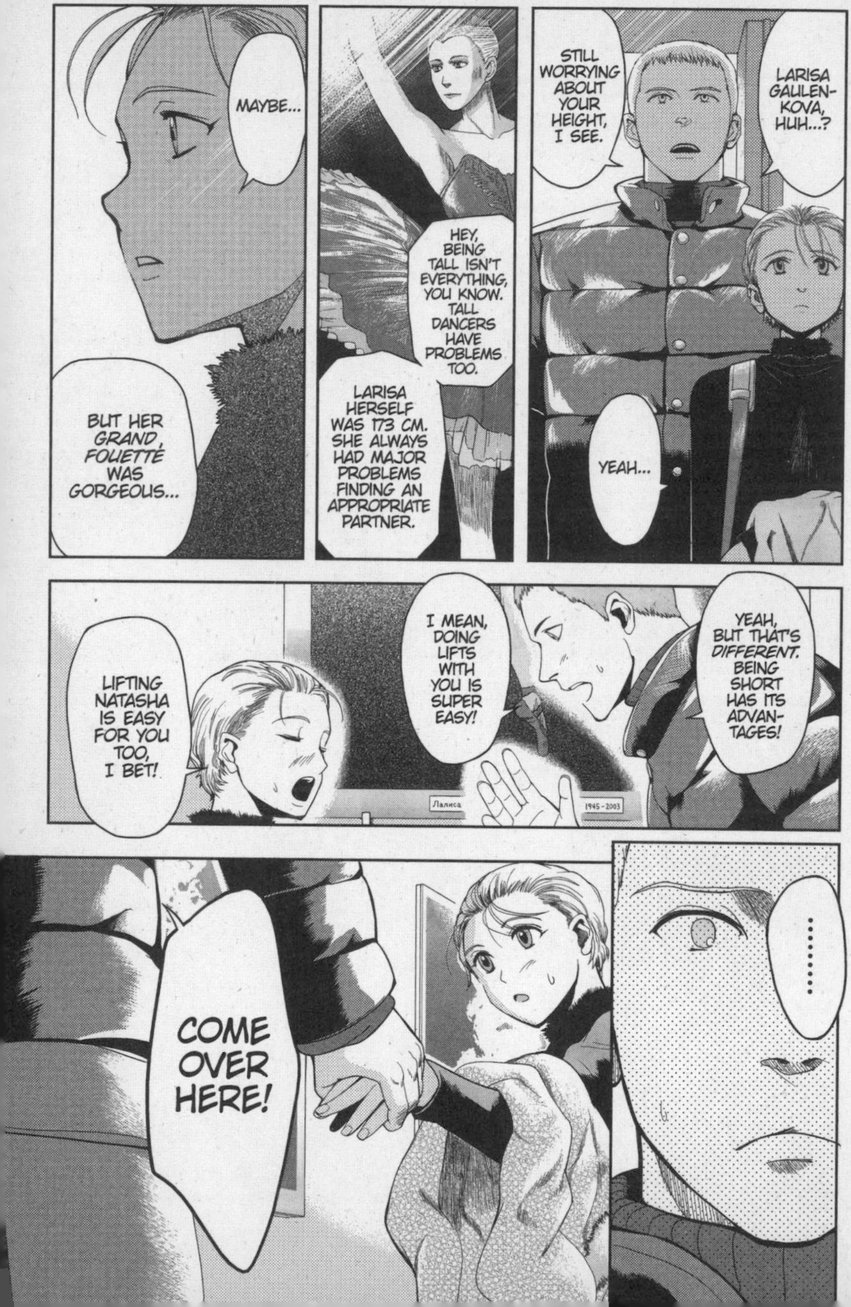
LARISA GAULEN-KOVA, HUH...?
STILL WORRYING ABOUT YOUR HEIGHT, I SEE.
YEAH...
HEY, BEING TALL ISN'T EVERYTHING, YOU KNOW. TALL DANCERS HAVE PROBLEMS TOO.
LARISA HERSELF WAS 173 CM. SHE ALWAYS HAD MAJOR PROBLEMS FINDING AN APPROPRIATE PARTNER.
MAYBE...
BUT HER *GRAND FOUETTÉ* WAS GORGEOUS...
YEAH, BUT THAT'S *DIFFERENT*. BEING SHORT HAS ITS ADVAN-TAGES!
I MEAN, DOING LIFTS WITH YOU IS SUPER EASY!
Лалиса
1945-2003
LIFTING NATASHA IS EASY FOR YOU TOO, I BET!
......
COME OVER HERE!

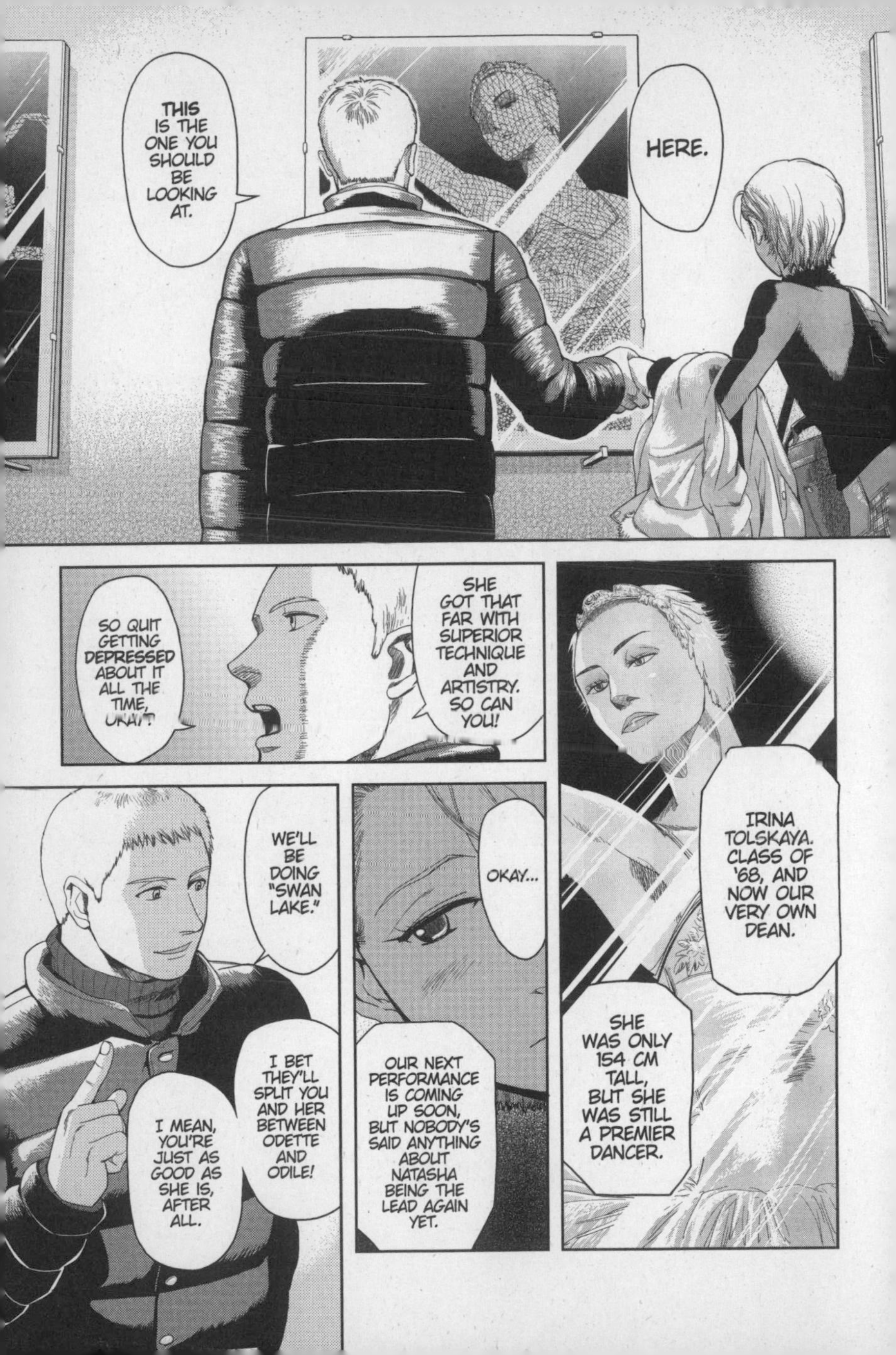
HERE.
THIS IS THE ONE YOU SHOULD BE LOOKING AT.
IRINA TOLSKAYA. CLASS OF '68, AND NOW OUR VERY OWN DEAN.
SHE WAS ONLY 154 CM TALL, BUT SHE WAS STILL A PREMIER DANCER.
SHE GOT THAT FAR WITH SUPERIOR TECHNIQUE AND ARTISTRY. SO CAN YOU!
SO QUIT GETTING DEPRESSED ABOUT IT ALL THE TIME, OKAY?
OKAY...
OUR NEXT PERFORMANCE IS COMING UP SOON, BUT NOBODY'S SAID ANYTHING ABOUT NATASHA BEING THE LEAD AGAIN YET.
WE'LL BE DOING "SWAN LAKE."
I BET THEY'LL SPLIT YOU AND HER BETWEEN ODETTE AND ODILE!
I MEAN, YOU'RE JUST AS GOOD AS SHE IS, AFTER ALL.

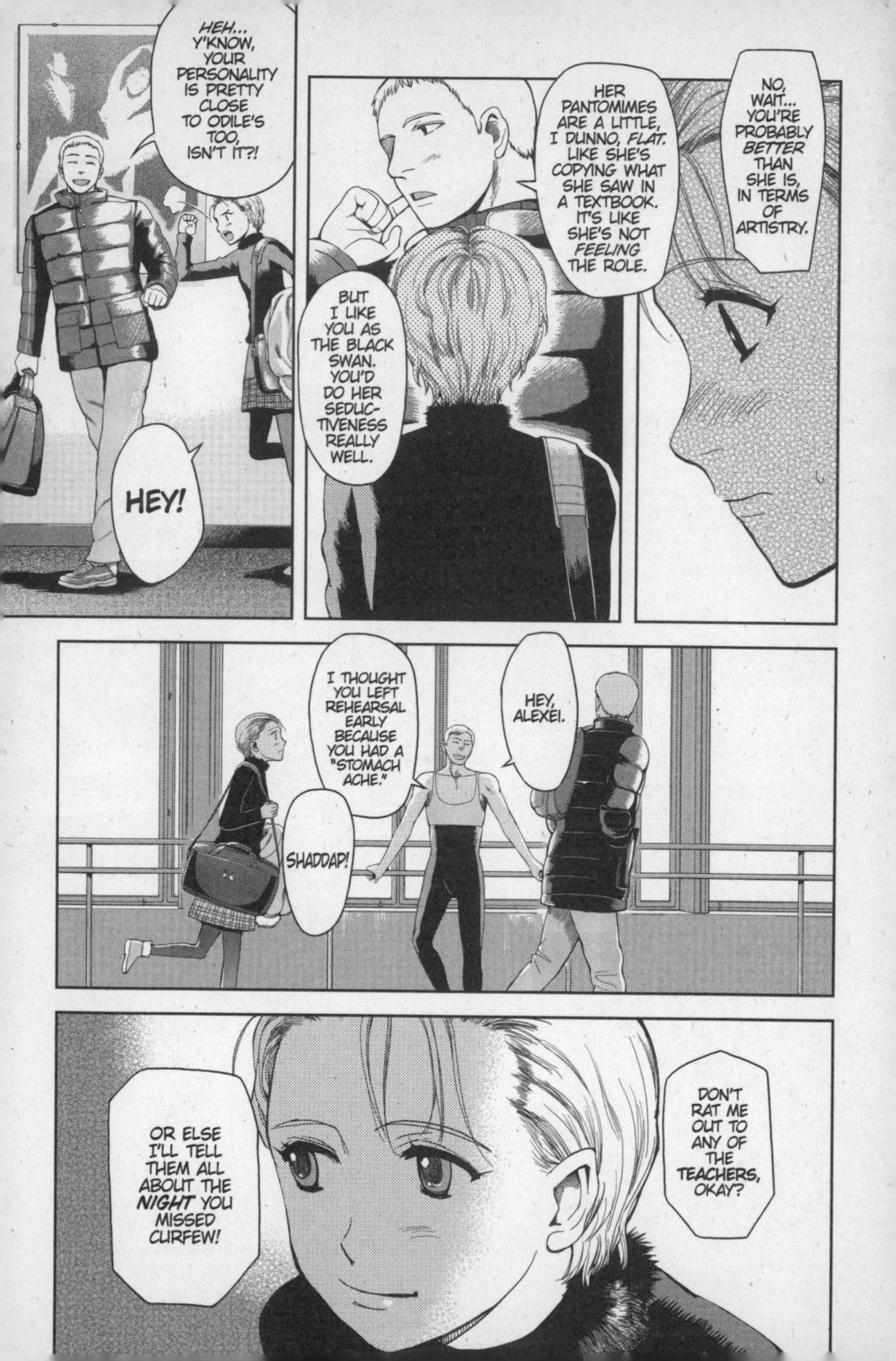
NO, WAIT... YOU'RE PROBABLY *BETTER* THAN SHE IS, IN TERMS OF ARTISTRY.
HER PANTOMIMES ARE A LITTLE, I DUNNO, *FLAT.* LIKE SHE'S COPYING WHAT SHE SAW IN A TEXTBOOK. IT'S LIKE SHE'S NOT *FEELING* THE ROLE.
BUT I LIKE YOU AS THE BLACK SWAN. YOU'D DO HER SEDUC-TIVENESS REALLY WELL.
HEH... Y'KNOW, YOUR PERSONALITY IS PRETTY CLOSE TO ODILE'S TOO, ISN'T IT?!
HEY!
HEY, ALEXEI.
I THOUGHT YOU LEFT REHEARSAL EARLY BECAUSE YOU HAD A "STOMACH ACHE."
SHADDAP!
DON'T RAT ME OUT TO ANY OF THE TEACHERS, OKAY?
OR ELSE I'LL TELL THEM ALL ABOUT THE ***NIGHT*** YOU MISSED CURFEW!

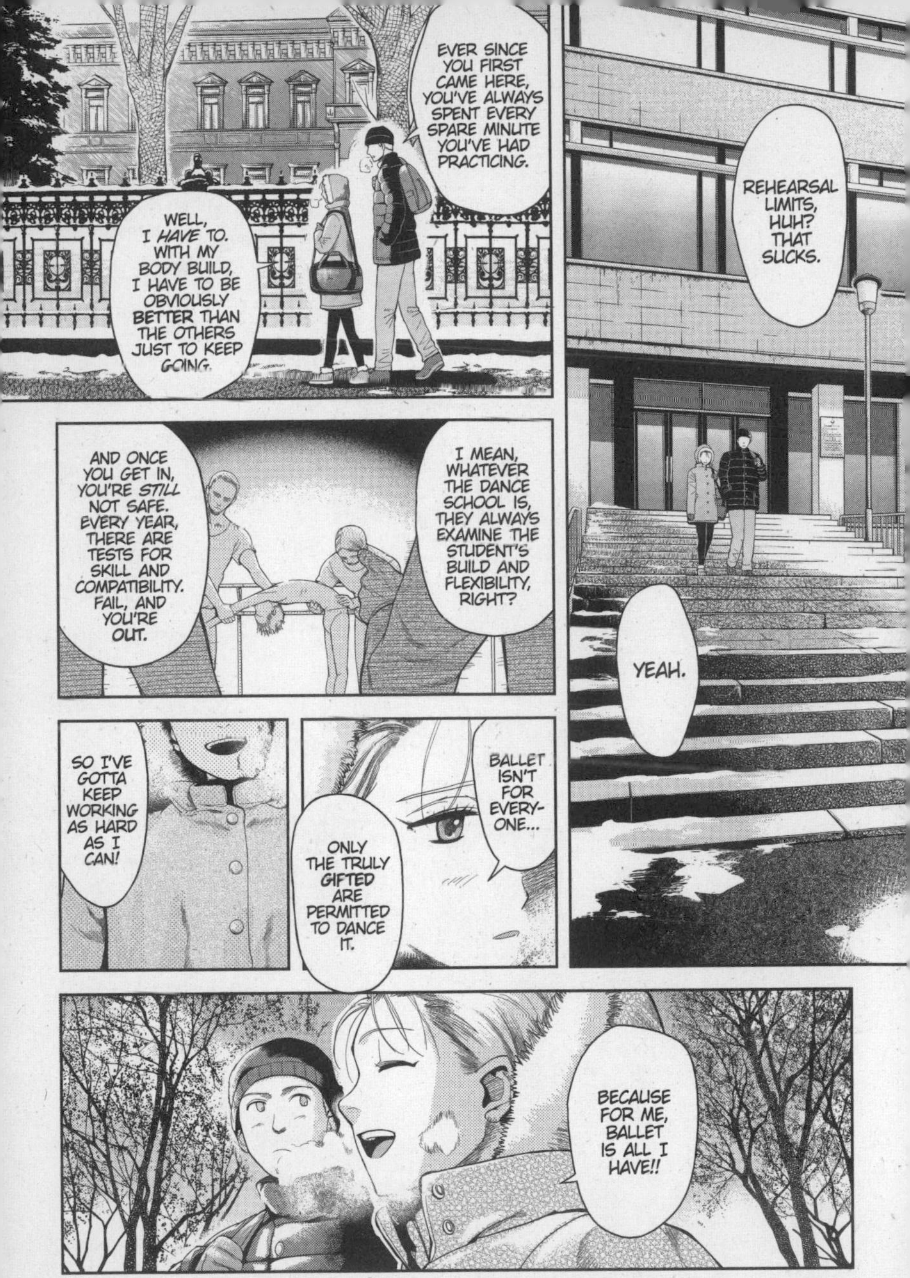
REHEARSAL LIMITS, HUH? THAT SUCKS.
YEAH.
EVER SINCE YOU FIRST CAME HERE, YOU'VE ALWAYS SPENT EVERY SPARE MINUTE YOU'VE HAD PRACTICING.
WELL, I *HAVE* TO. WITH MY BODY BUILD, I HAVE TO BE OBVIOUSLY BETTER THAN THE OTHERS JUST TO KEEP GOING.
I MEAN, WHATEVER THE DANCE SCHOOL IS, THEY ALWAYS EXAMINE THE STUDENT'S BUILD AND FLEXIBILITY, RIGHT?
AND ONCE YOU GET IN, YOU'RE *STILL* NOT SAFE. EVERY YEAR, THERE ARE TESTS FOR SKILL AND COMPATIBILITY. FAIL, AND YOU'RE OUT.
BALLET ISN'T FOR EVERY-ONE...
ONLY THE TRULY GIFTED ARE PERMITTED TO DANCE IT.
SO I'VE GOTTA KEEP WORKING AS HARD AS I CAN!
BECAUSE FOR ME, BALLET IS ALL I HAVE!!

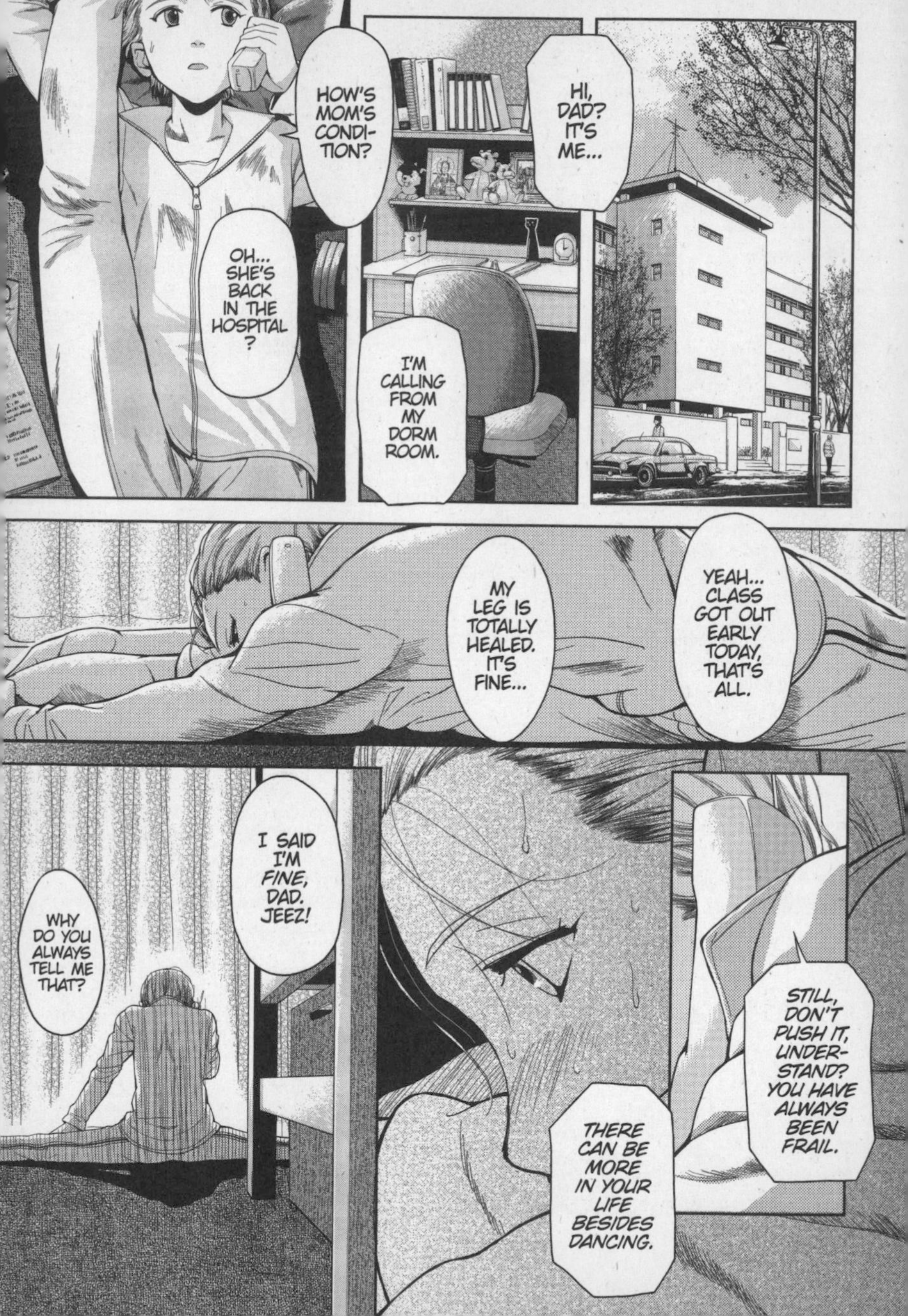
HI, DAD? IT'S ME...
HOW'S MOM'S CONDITION?
I'M CALLING FROM MY DORM ROOM.
OH... SHE'S BACK IN THE HOSPITAL?
YEAH... CLASS GOT OUT EARLY TODAY, THAT'S ALL.
MY LEG IS TOTALLY HEALED. IT'S FINE...
STILL, DON'T PUSH IT, UNDERSTAND? YOU HAVE ALWAYS BEEN FRAIL.
THERE CAN BE MORE IN YOUR LIFE BESIDES DANCING.
I SAID I'M *FINE*, DAD. JEEZ!
WHY DO YOU ALWAYS TELL ME THAT?

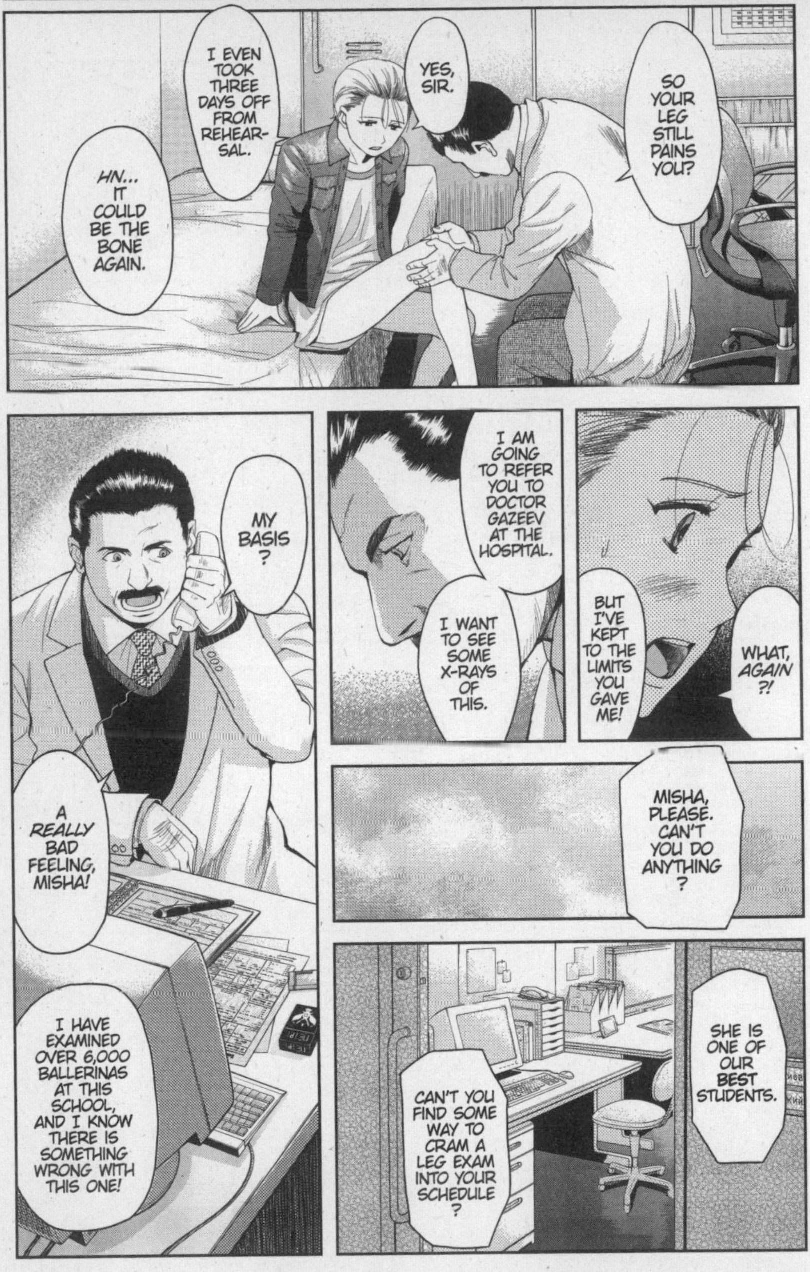
SO YOUR LEG STILL PAINS YOU?
YES, SIR.
I EVEN TOOK THREE DAYS OFF FROM REHEAR-SAL.
HN... IT COULD BE THE BONE AGAIN.
WHAT, AGAIN?!
BUT I'VE KEPT TO THE LIMITS YOU GAVE ME!
I AM GOING TO REFER YOU TO DOCTOR GAZEEV AT THE HOSPITAL.
I WANT TO SEE SOME X-RAYS OF THIS.
MISHA, PLEASE. CAN'T YOU DO ANYTHING?
SHE IS ONE OF OUR BEST STUDENTS.
CAN'T YOU FIND SOME WAY TO CRAM A LEG EXAM INTO YOUR SCHEDULE?
MY BASIS?
A REALLY BAD FEELING, MISHA!
I HAVE EXAMINED OVER 6,000 BALLERINAS AT THIS SCHOOL, AND I KNOW THERE IS SOMETHING WRONG WITH THIS ONE!

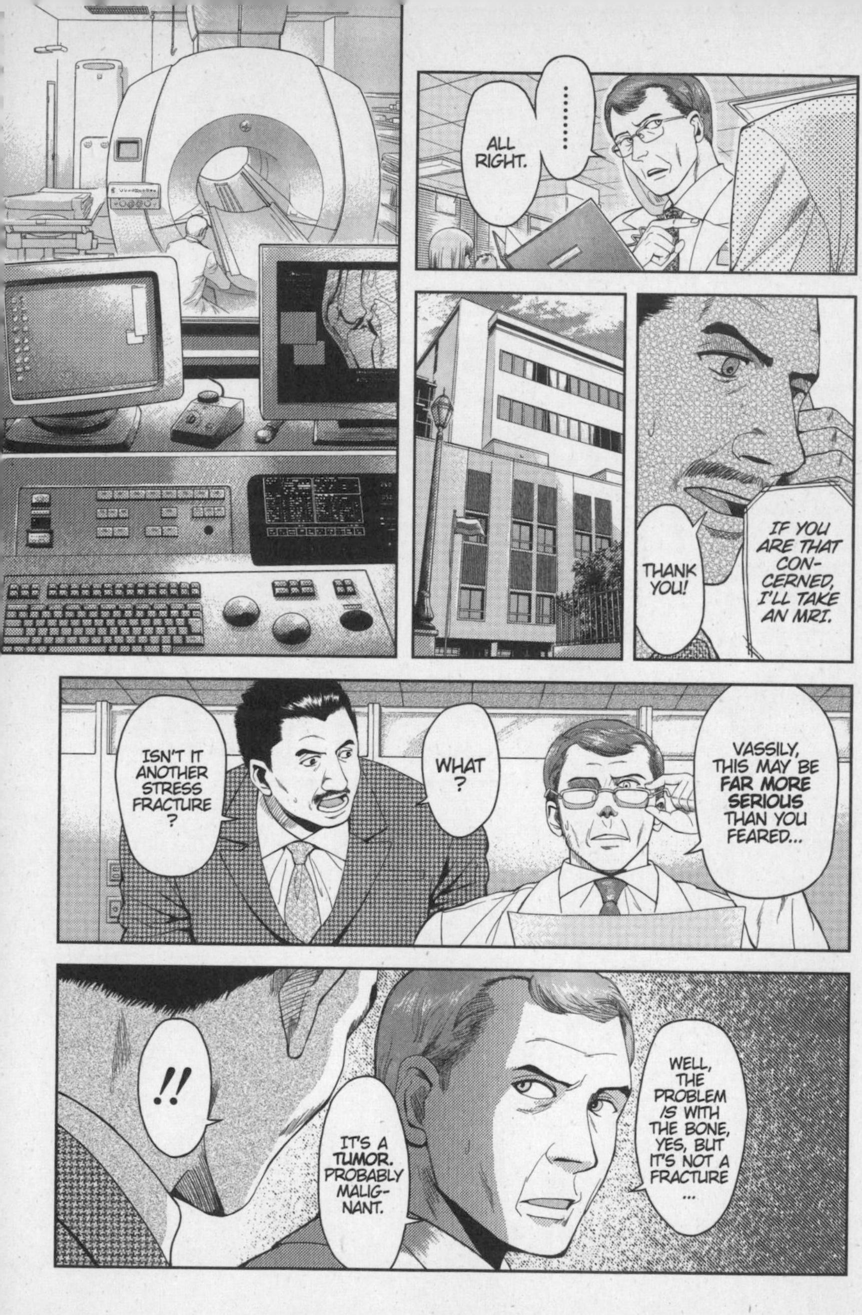
......
ALL RIGHT.
IF YOU ARE THAT CONCERNED, I'LL TAKE AN MRI.
THANK YOU!
VASSILY, THIS MAY BE **FAR MORE SERIOUS** THAN YOU FEARED...
WHAT?
ISN'T IT ANOTHER STRESS FRACTURE?
WELL, THE PROBLEM IS WITH THE BONE, YES, BUT IT'S NOT A FRACTURE...
IT'S A **TUMOR.** PROBABLY MALIGNANT.
!!

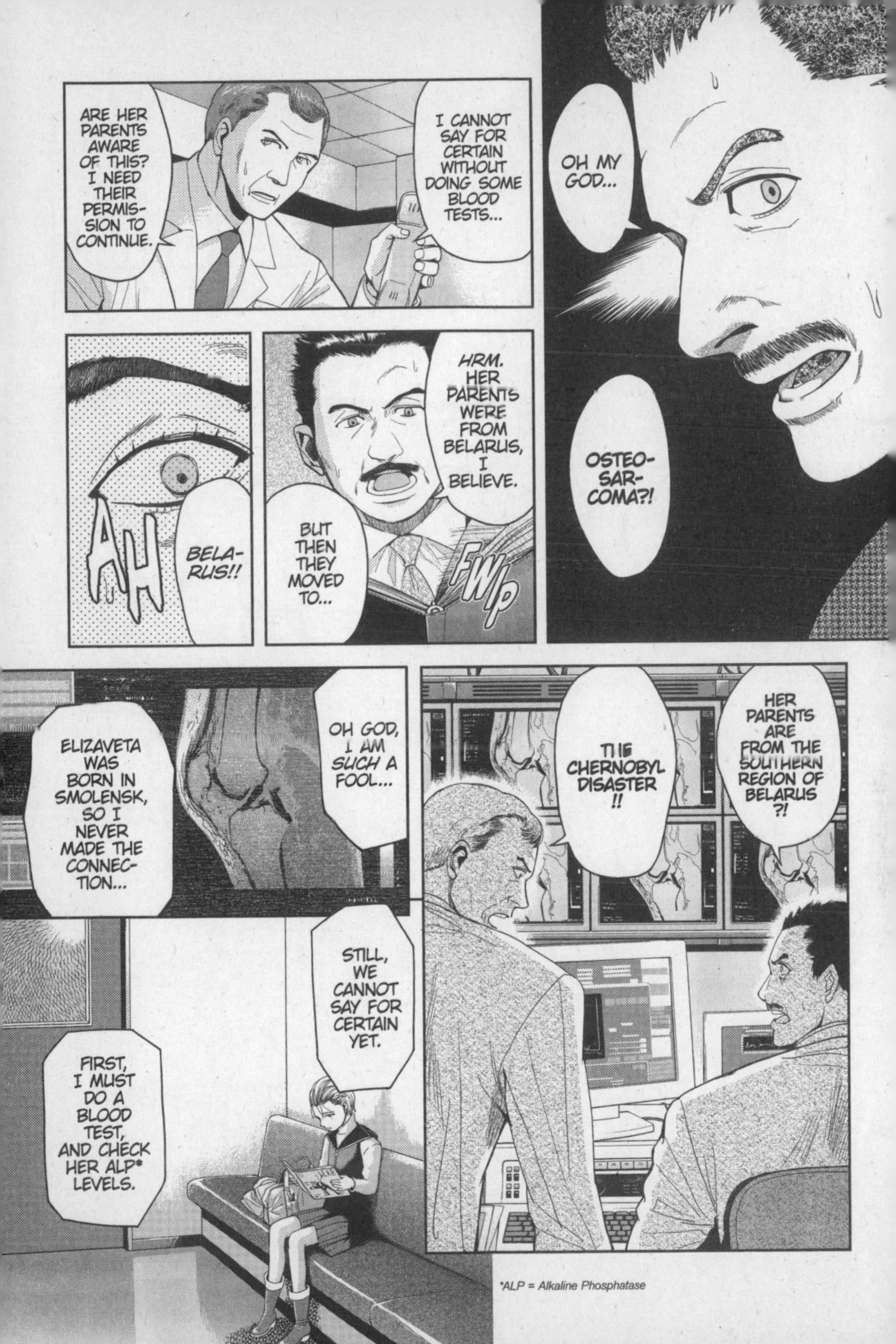
OH MY GOD...
OSTEO-SAR-COMA?!
I CANNOT SAY FOR CERTAIN WITHOUT DOING SOME BLOOD TESTS...
ARE HER PARENTS AWARE OF THIS? I NEED THEIR PERMIS-SION TO CONTINUE.
HRM. HER PARENTS WERE FROM BELARUS, I BELIEVE.
FWIP
BUT THEN THEY MOVED TO...
BELA-RUS!!
AH
HER PARENTS ARE FROM THE SOUTHERN REGION OF BELARUS?!
THE CHERNOBYL DISASTER!!
OH GOD, I AM SUCH A FOOL...
ELIZAVETA WAS BORN IN SMOLENSK, SO I NEVER MADE THE CONNEC-TION...
STILL, WE CANNOT SAY FOR CERTAIN YET.
FIRST, I MUST DO A BLOOD TEST, AND CHECK HER ALP* LEVELS.

*ALP = Alkaline Phosphatase

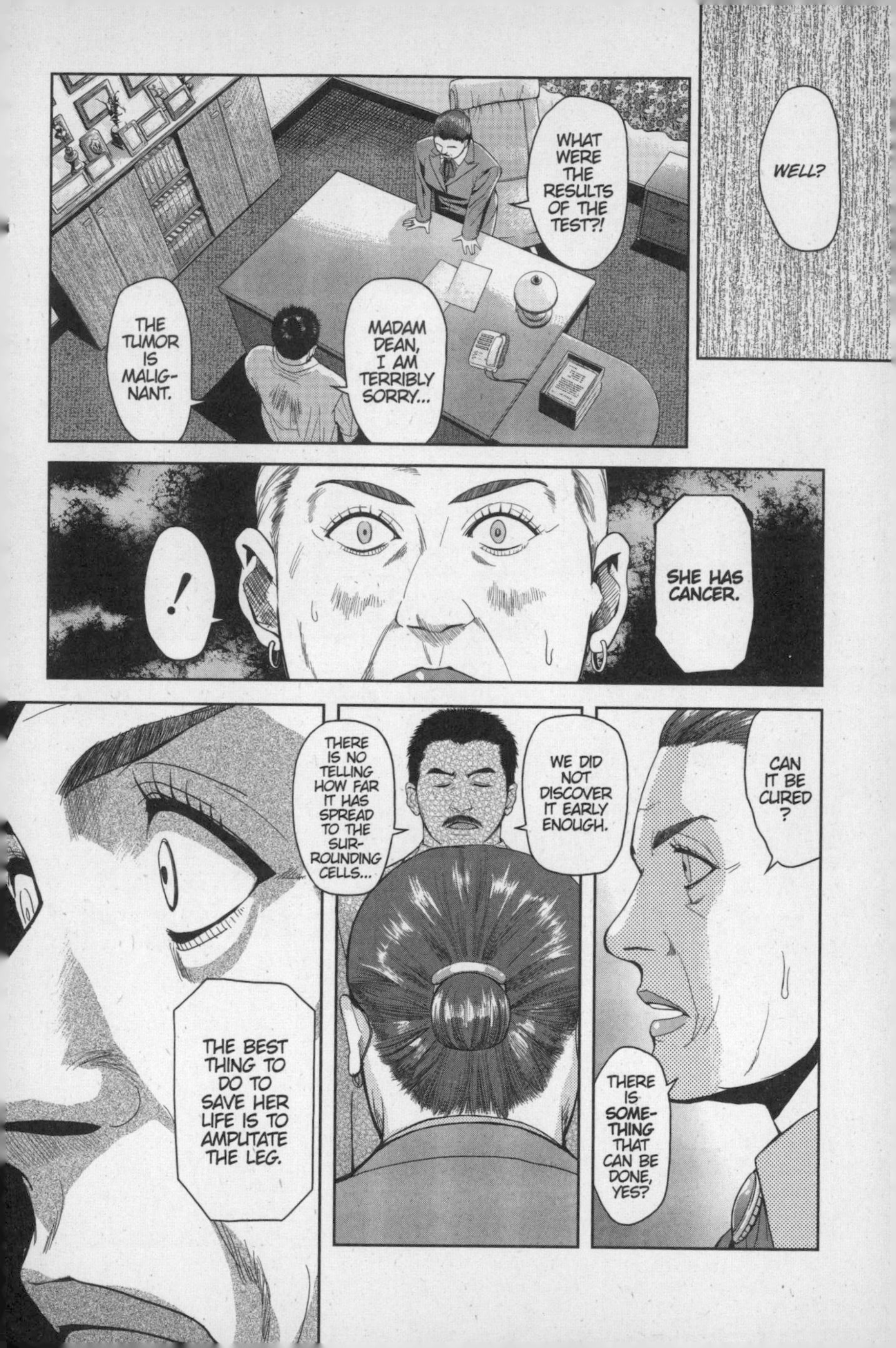
WELL?
WHAT WERE THE RESULTS OF THE TEST?!
MADAM DEAN, I AM TERRIBLY SORRY...
THE TUMOR IS MALIGNANT.
SHE HAS CANCER.
!
CAN IT BE CURED?
THERE IS SOMETHING THAT CAN BE DONE, YES?
WE DID NOT DISCOVER IT EARLY ENOUGH.
THERE IS NO TELLING HOW FAR IT HAS SPREAD TO THE SURROUNDING CELLS...
THE BEST THING TO DO TO SAVE HER LIFE IS TO AMPUTATE THE LEG.

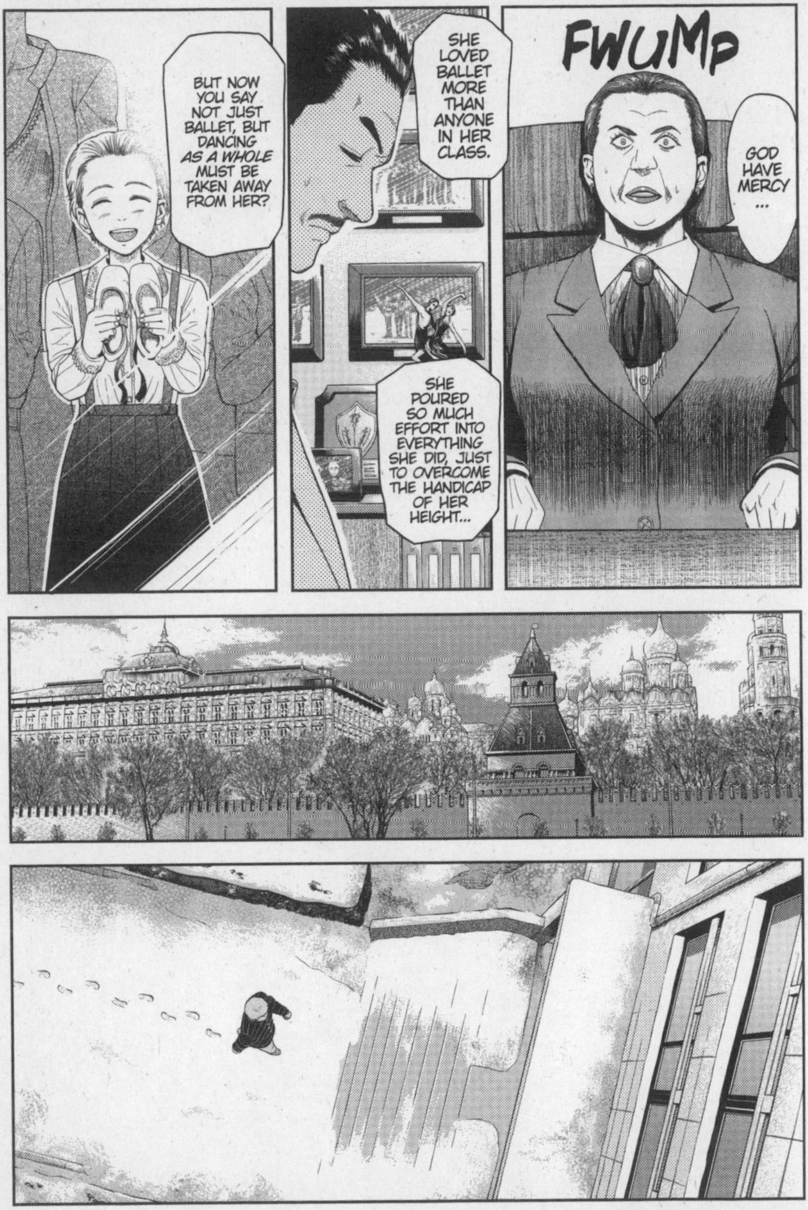
FWUMP
GOD HAVE MERCY...
SHE LOVED BALLET MORE THAN ANYONE IN HER CLASS.
SHE POURED SO MUCH EFFORT INTO EVERYTHING SHE DID, JUST TO OVERCOME THE HANDICAP OF HER HEIGHT...
BUT NOW YOU SAY NOT JUST BALLET, BUT DANCING *AS A WHOLE* MUST BE TAKEN AWAY FROM HER?

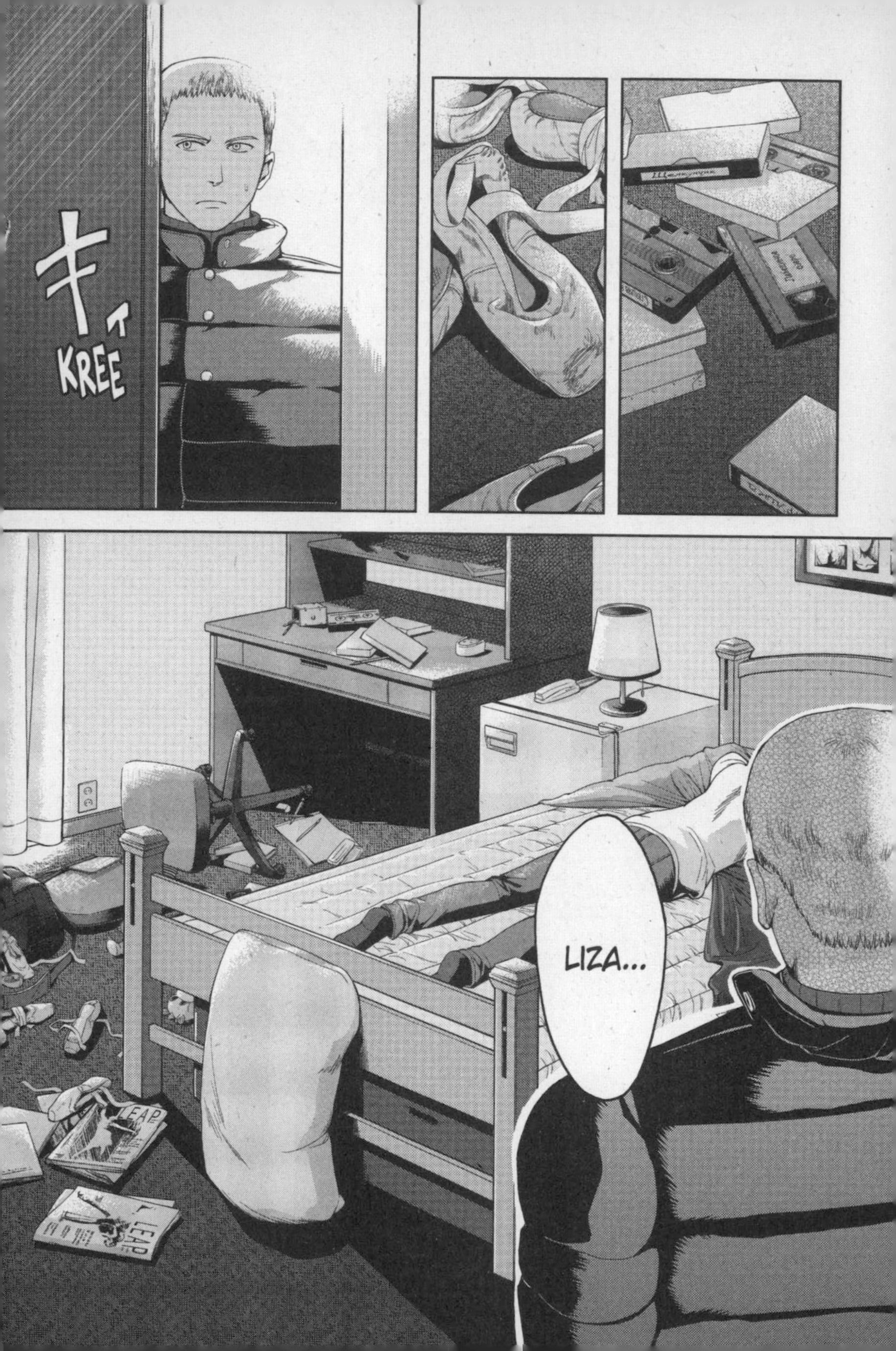
キィ
KREE
LEAP
LEAP
LIZA...

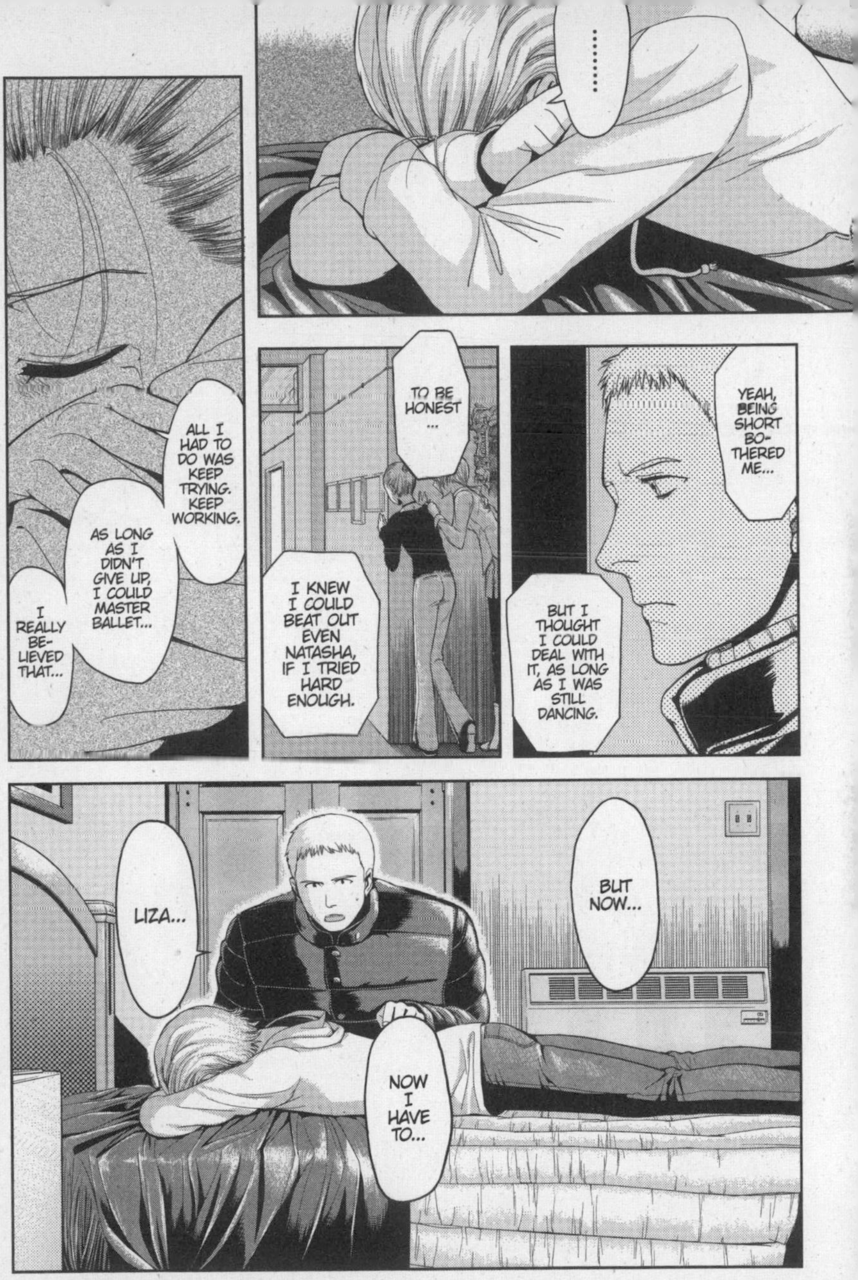
....
YEAH, BEING SHORT BOTHERED ME...
BUT I THOUGHT I COULD DEAL WITH IT, AS LONG AS I WAS STILL DANCING.
TO BE HONEST...
I KNEW I COULD BEAT OUT EVEN NATASHA, IF I TRIED HARD ENOUGH.
ALL I HAD TO DO WAS KEEP TRYING. KEEP WORKING.
AS LONG AS I DIDN'T GIVE UP, I COULD MASTER BALLET...
I REALLY BELIEVED THAT...
BUT NOW...
LIZA...
NOW I HAVE TO...

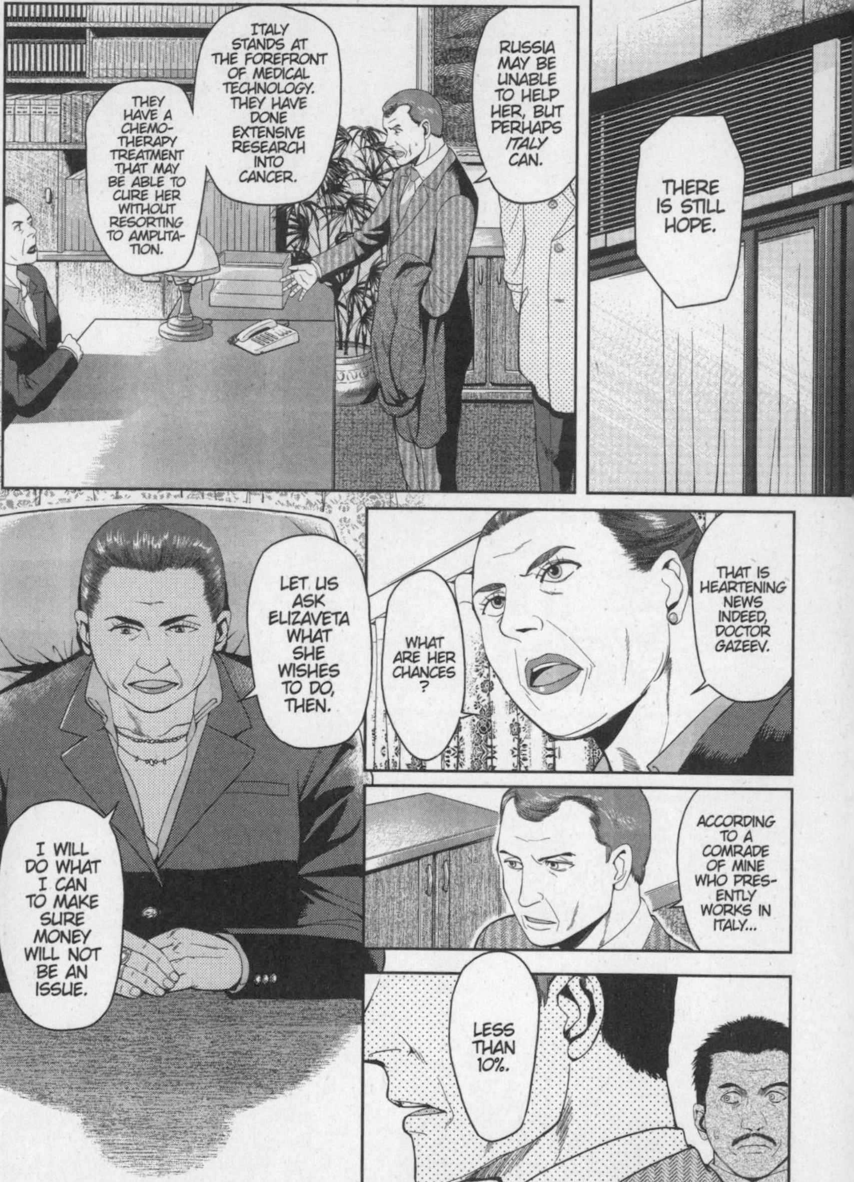
THERE IS STILL HOPE.
RUSSIA MAY BE UNABLE TO HELP HER, BUT PERHAPS *ITALY* CAN.
ITALY STANDS AT THE FOREFRONT OF MEDICAL TECHNOLOGY. THEY HAVE DONE EXTENSIVE RESEARCH INTO CANCER.
THEY HAVE A CHEMO-THERAPY TREATMENT THAT MAY BE ABLE TO CURE HER WITHOUT RESORTING TO AMPUTA-TION.
THAT IS HEARTENING NEWS INDEED, DOCTOR GAZEEV.
WHAT ARE HER CHANCES ?
ACCORDING TO A COMRADE OF MINE WHO PRES-ENTLY WORKS IN ITALY...
LESS THAN 10%.
LET US ASK ELIZAVETA WHAT SHE WISHES TO DO, THEN.
I WILL DO WHAT I CAN TO MAKE SURE MONEY WILL NOT BE AN ISSUE.

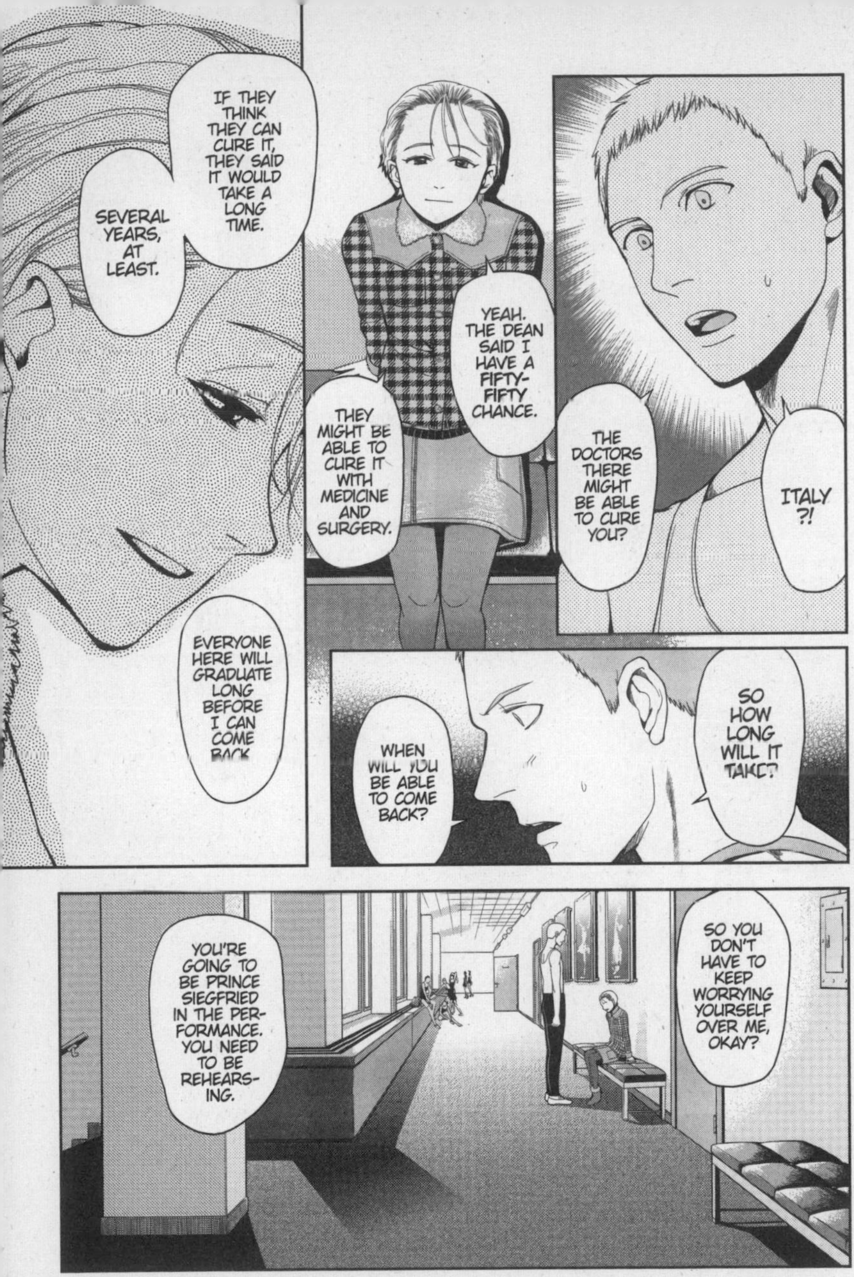
ITALY ?!
THE DOCTORS THERE MIGHT BE ABLE TO CURE YOU?
YEAH. THE DEAN SAID I HAVE A FIFTY-FIFTY CHANCE.
THEY MIGHT BE ABLE TO CURE IT WITH MEDICINE AND SURGERY.
SO HOW LONG WILL IT TAKE?
WHEN WILL YOU BE ABLE TO COME BACK?
IF THEY THINK THEY CAN CURE IT, THEY SAID IT WOULD TAKE A LONG TIME.
SEVERAL YEARS, AT LEAST.
EVERYONE HERE WILL GRADUATE LONG BEFORE I CAN COME BACK
SO YOU DON'T HAVE TO KEEP WORRYING YOURSELF OVER ME, OKAY?
YOU'RE GOING TO BE PRINCE SIEGFRIED IN THE PERFORMANCE. YOU NEED TO BE REHEARSING.

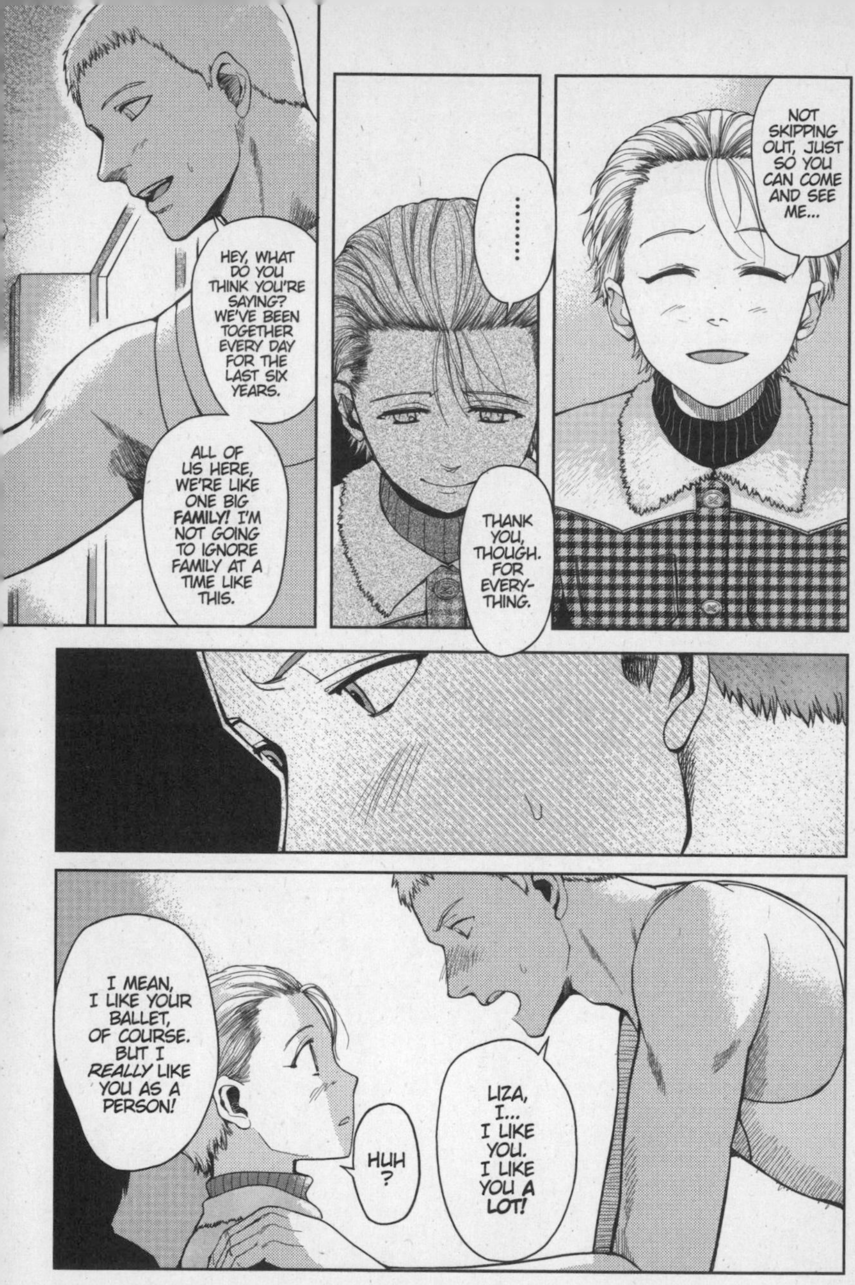
NOT SKIPPING OUT, JUST SO YOU CAN COME AND SEE ME...
......
THANK YOU, THOUGH. FOR EVERYTHING.
HEY, WHAT DO YOU THINK YOU'RE SAYING? WE'VE BEEN TOGETHER EVERY DAY FOR THE LAST SIX YEARS.
ALL OF US HERE, WE'RE LIKE ONE BIG **FAMILY!** I'M NOT GOING TO IGNORE FAMILY AT A TIME LIKE THIS.
LIZA, I... I LIKE YOU. I LIKE YOU A **LOT!**
HUH?
I MEAN, I LIKE YOUR BALLET, OF COURSE. BUT I *REALLY* LIKE YOU AS A PERSON!

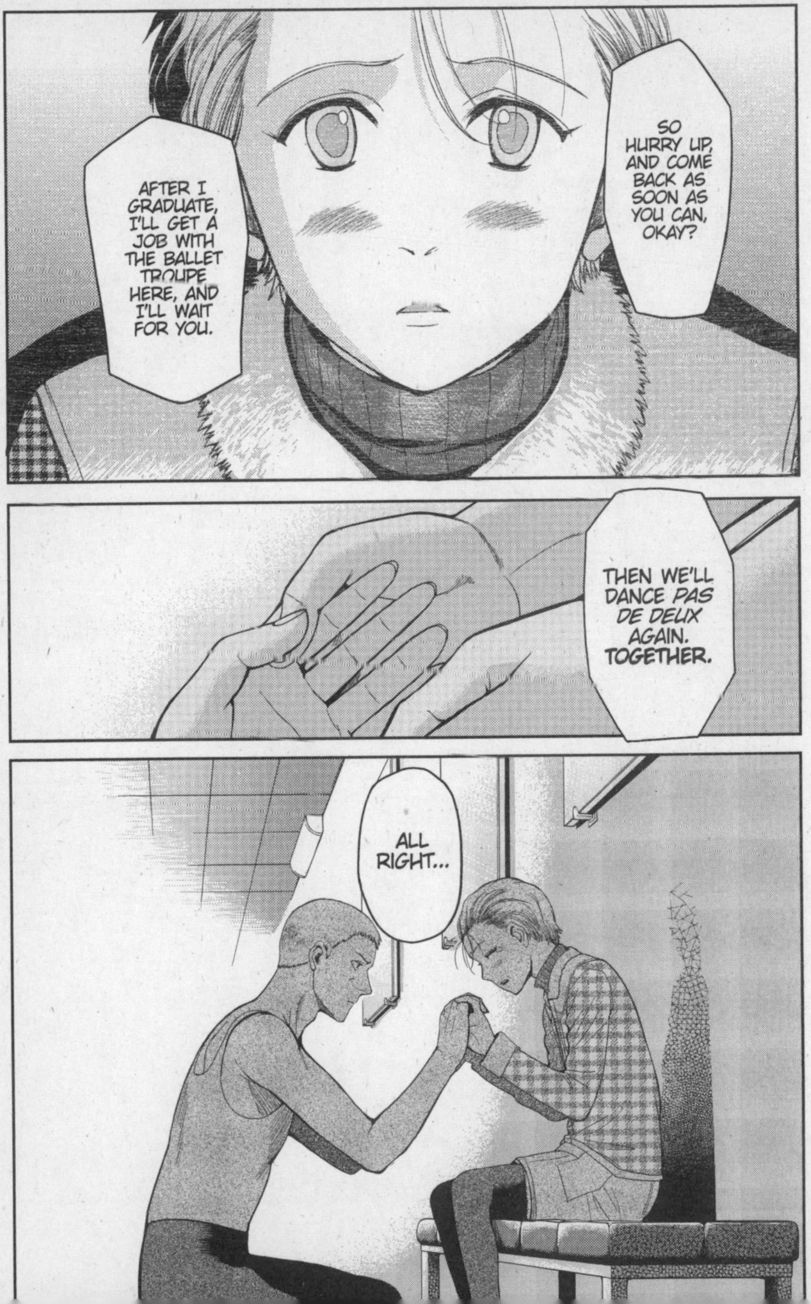
SO HURRY UP, AND COME BACK AS SOON AS YOU CAN, OKAY?
AFTER I GRADUATE, I'LL GET A JOB WITH THE BALLET TROUPE HERE, AND I'LL WAIT FOR YOU.
THEN WE'LL DANCE *PAS DE DEUX* AGAIN. TOGETHER.
ALL RIGHT...

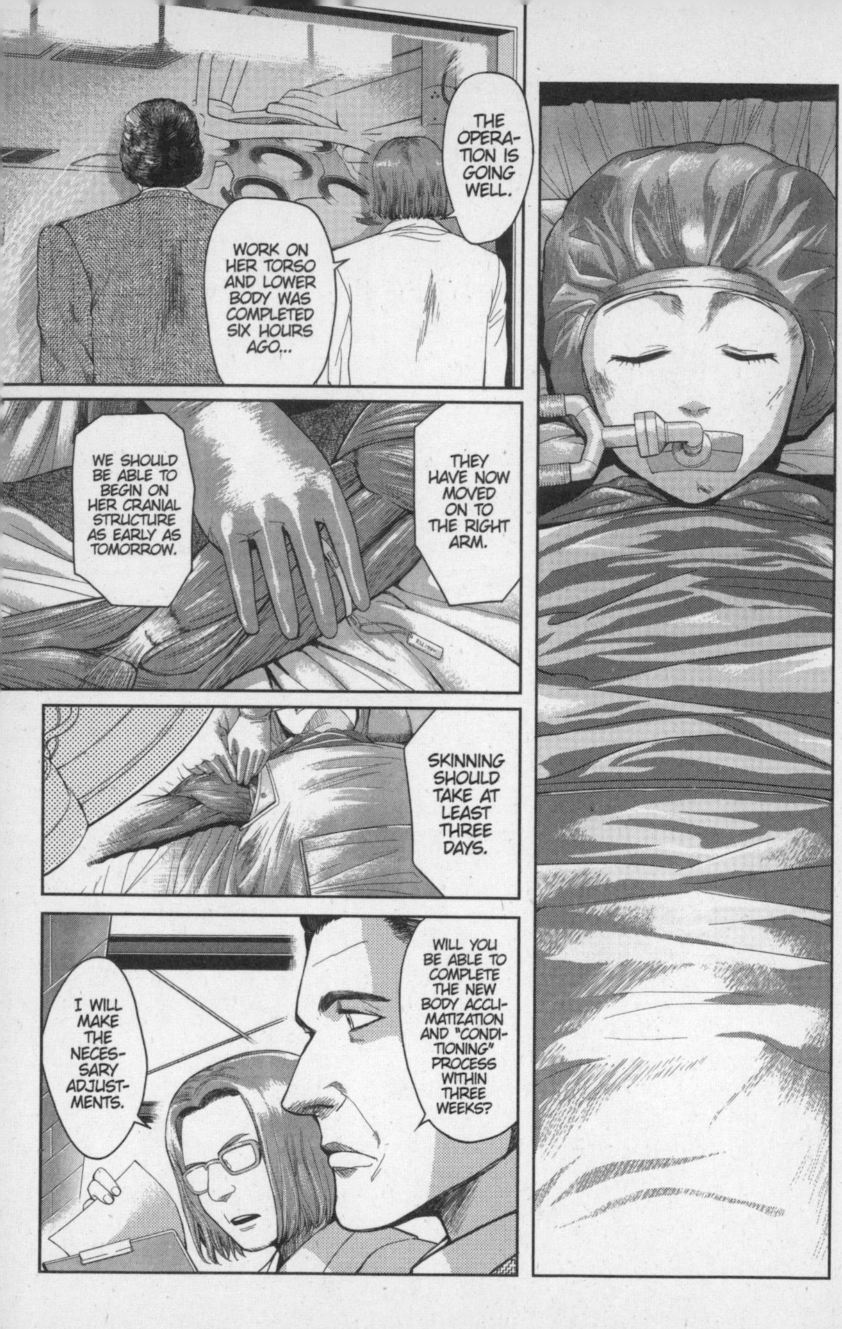
THE OPERATION IS GOING WELL.
WORK ON HER TORSO AND LOWER BODY WAS COMPLETED SIX HOURS AGO...
THEY HAVE NOW MOVED ON TO THE RIGHT ARM.
WE SHOULD BE ABLE TO BEGIN ON HER CRANIAL STRUCTURE AS EARLY AS TOMORROW.
SKINNING SHOULD TAKE AT LEAST THREE DAYS.
WILL YOU BE ABLE TO COMPLETE THE NEW BODY ACCLIMATIZATION AND "CONDITIONING" PROCESS WITHIN THREE WEEKS?
I WILL MAKE THE NECESSARY ADJUSTMENTS.

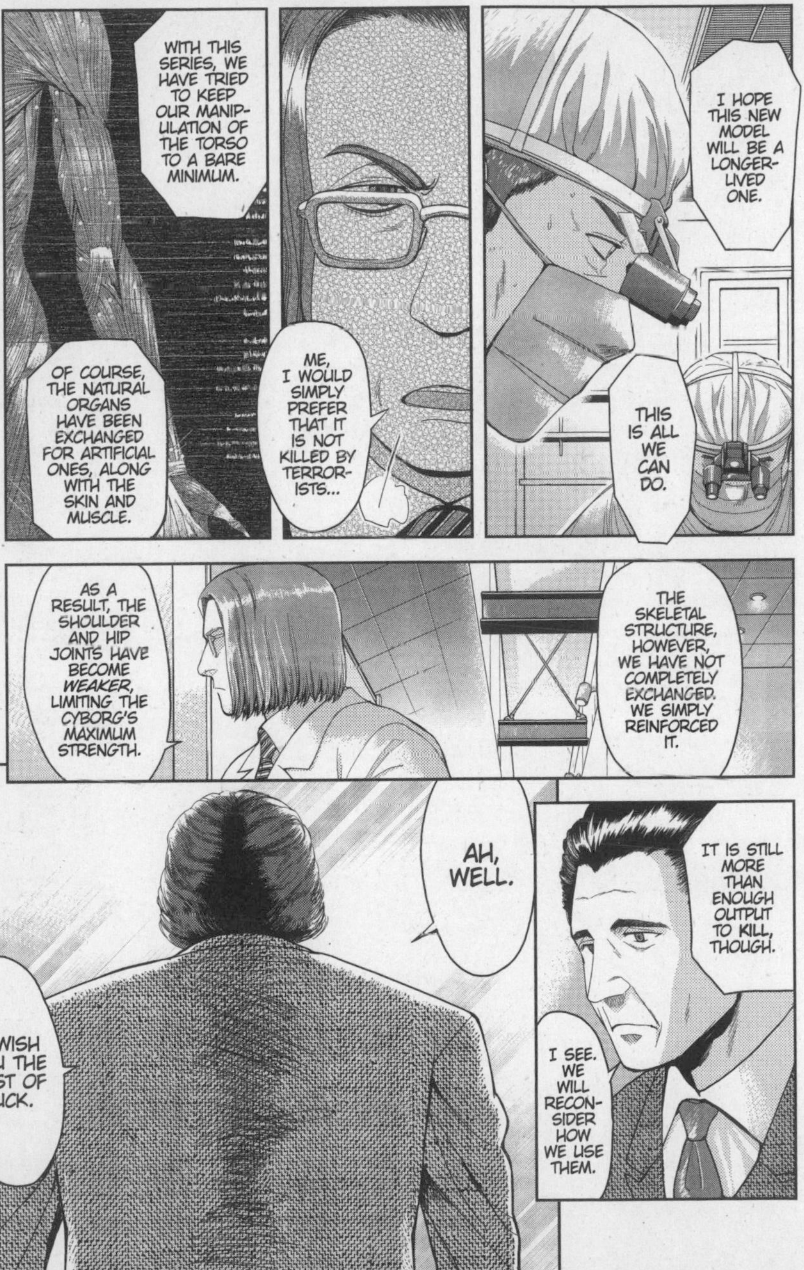
I HOPE THIS NEW MODEL WILL BE A LONGER-LIVED ONE.
THIS IS ALL WE CAN DO.
ME, I WOULD SIMPLY PREFER THAT IT IS NOT KILLED BY TERRORISTS...
WITH THIS SERIES, WE HAVE TRIED TO KEEP OUR MANIPULATION OF THE TORSO TO A BARE MINIMUM.
OF COURSE, THE NATURAL ORGANS HAVE BEEN EXCHANGED FOR ARTIFICIAL ONES, ALONG WITH THE SKIN AND MUSCLE.
THE SKELETAL STRUCTURE, HOWEVER, WE HAVE NOT COMPLETELY EXCHANGED. WE SIMPLY REINFORCED IT.
AS A RESULT, THE SHOULDER AND HIP JOINTS HAVE BECOME *WEAKER*, LIMITING THE CYBORG'S MAXIMUM STRENGTH.
IT IS STILL MORE THAN ENOUGH OUTPUT TO KILL, THOUGH.
I SEE. WE WILL RECONSIDER HOW WE USE THEM.
AH, WELL.
I WISH YOU THE BEST OF LUCK.

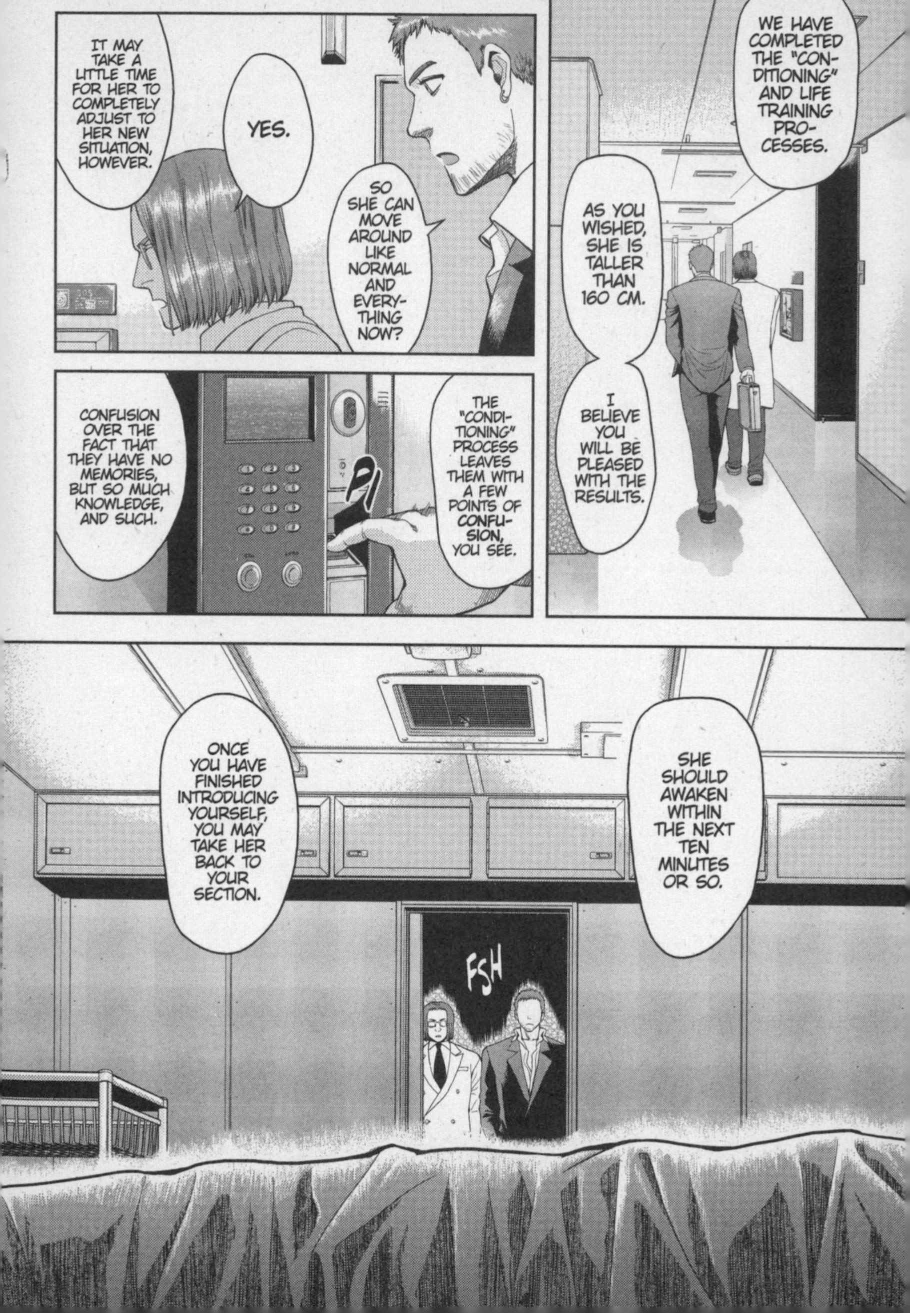
WE HAVE COMPLETED THE "CONDITIONING" AND LIFE TRAINING PROCESSES.
AS YOU WISHED, SHE IS TALLER THAN 160 CM.
I BELIEVE YOU WILL BE PLEASED WITH THE RESULTS.
SO SHE CAN MOVE AROUND LIKE NORMAL AND EVERYTHING NOW?
YES.
IT MAY TAKE A LITTLE TIME FOR HER TO COMPLETELY ADJUST TO HER NEW SITUATION, HOWEVER.
THE "CONDITIONING" PROCESS LEAVES THEM WITH A FEW POINTS OF CONFUSION, YOU SEE.
CONFUSION OVER THE FACT THAT THEY HAVE NO MEMORIES, BUT SO MUCH KNOWLEDGE, AND SUCH.
SHE SHOULD AWAKEN WITHIN THE NEXT TEN MINUTES OR SO.
ONCE YOU HAVE FINISHED INTRODUCING YOURSELF, YOU MAY TAKE HER BACK TO YOUR SECTION.
FSH

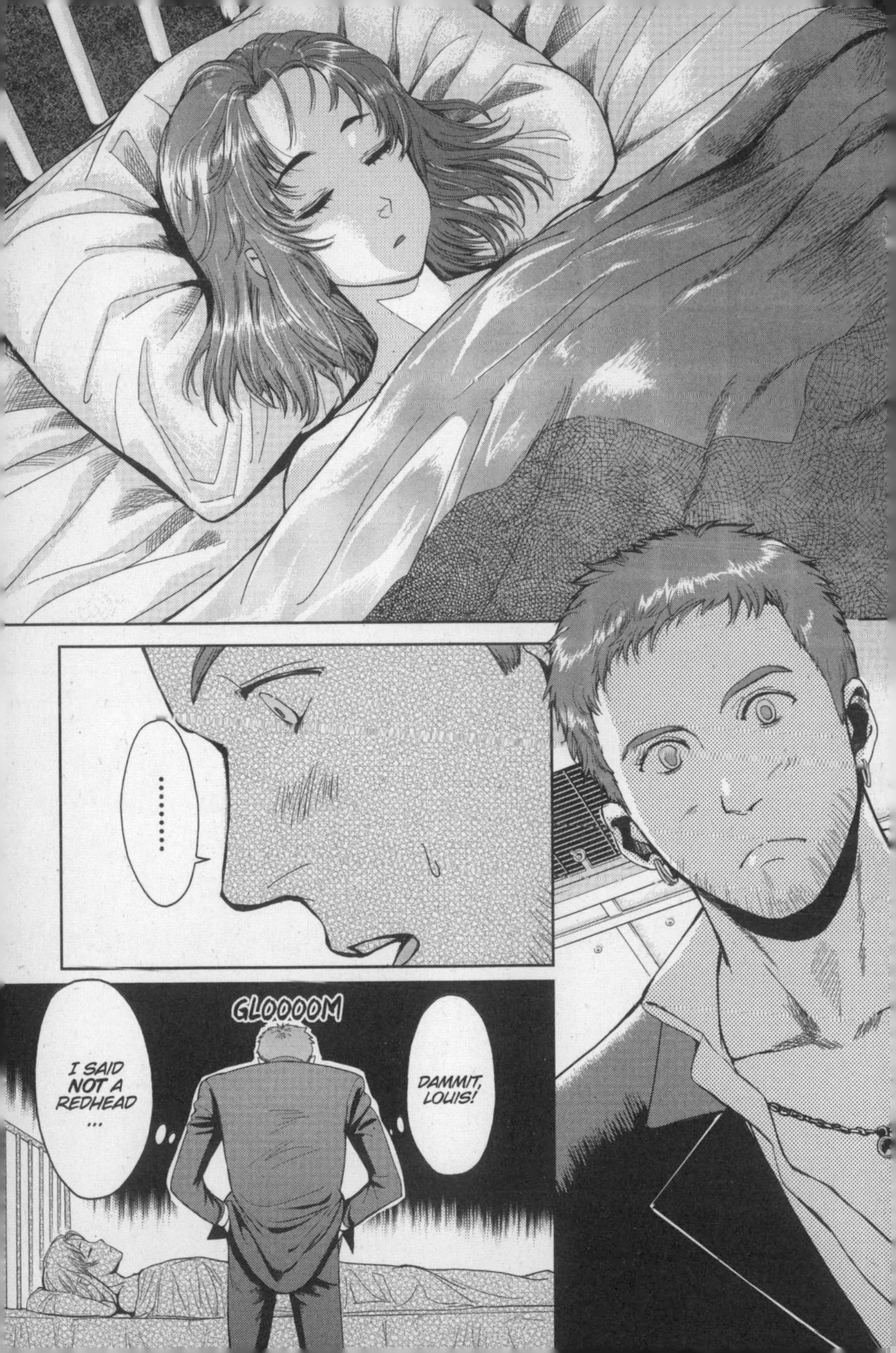
......
GLOOOOM
DAMMIT, LOUIS!
I SAID NOT A REDHEAD ...

ANYWAY...

HUNH. SHE LOOKS JUST LIKE ANY OTHER NORMAL GIRL...

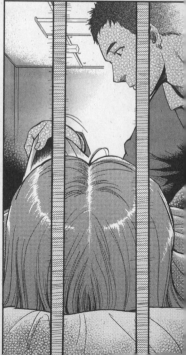

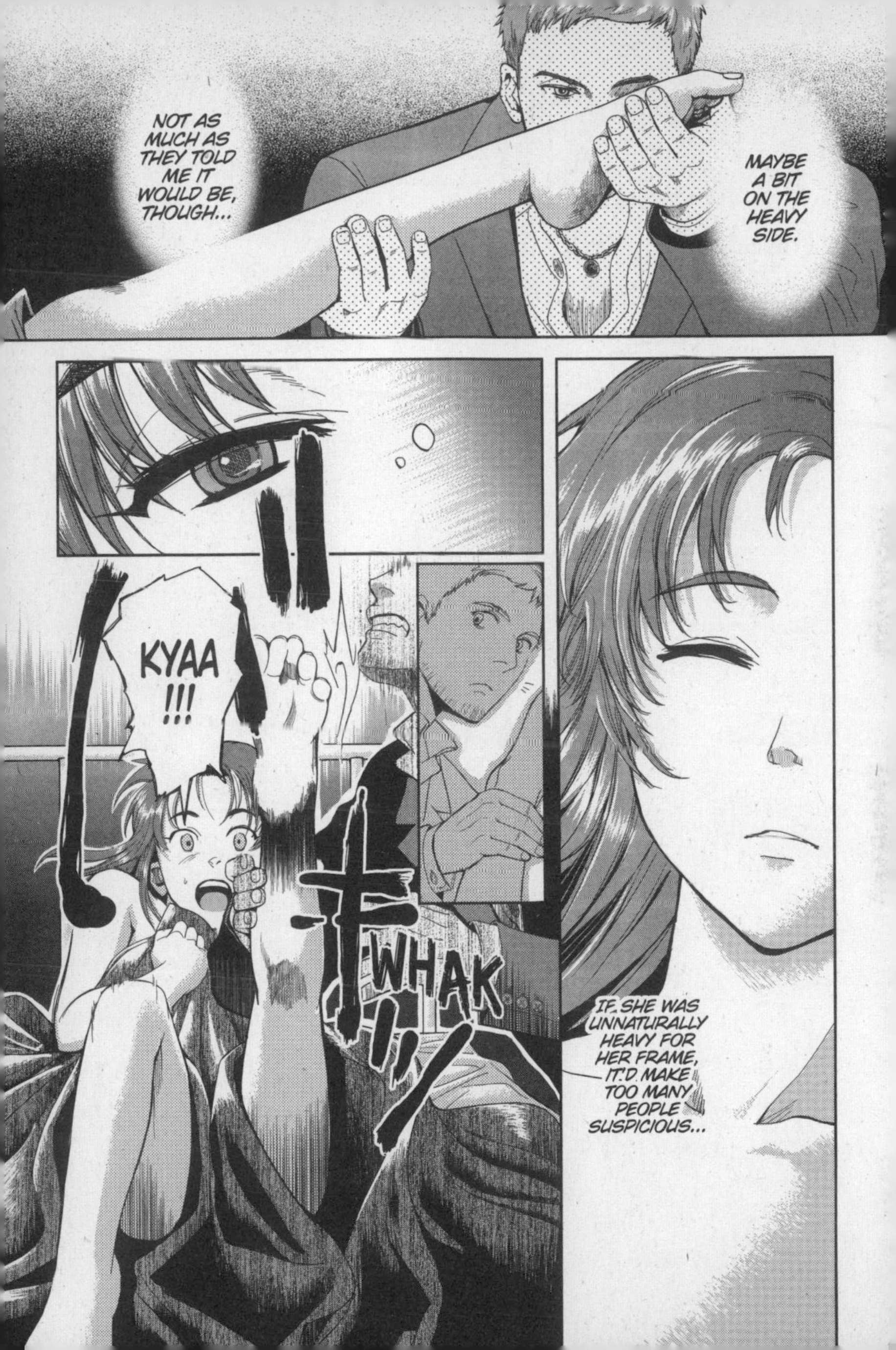
MAYBE A BIT ON THE HEAVY SIDE.
NOT AS MUCH AS THEY TOLD ME IT WOULD BE, THOUGH...
IF SHE WAS UNNATURALLY HEAVY FOR HER FRAME, IT'D MAKE TOO MANY PEOPLE SUSPICIOUS...
KYAA !!!
WHAK

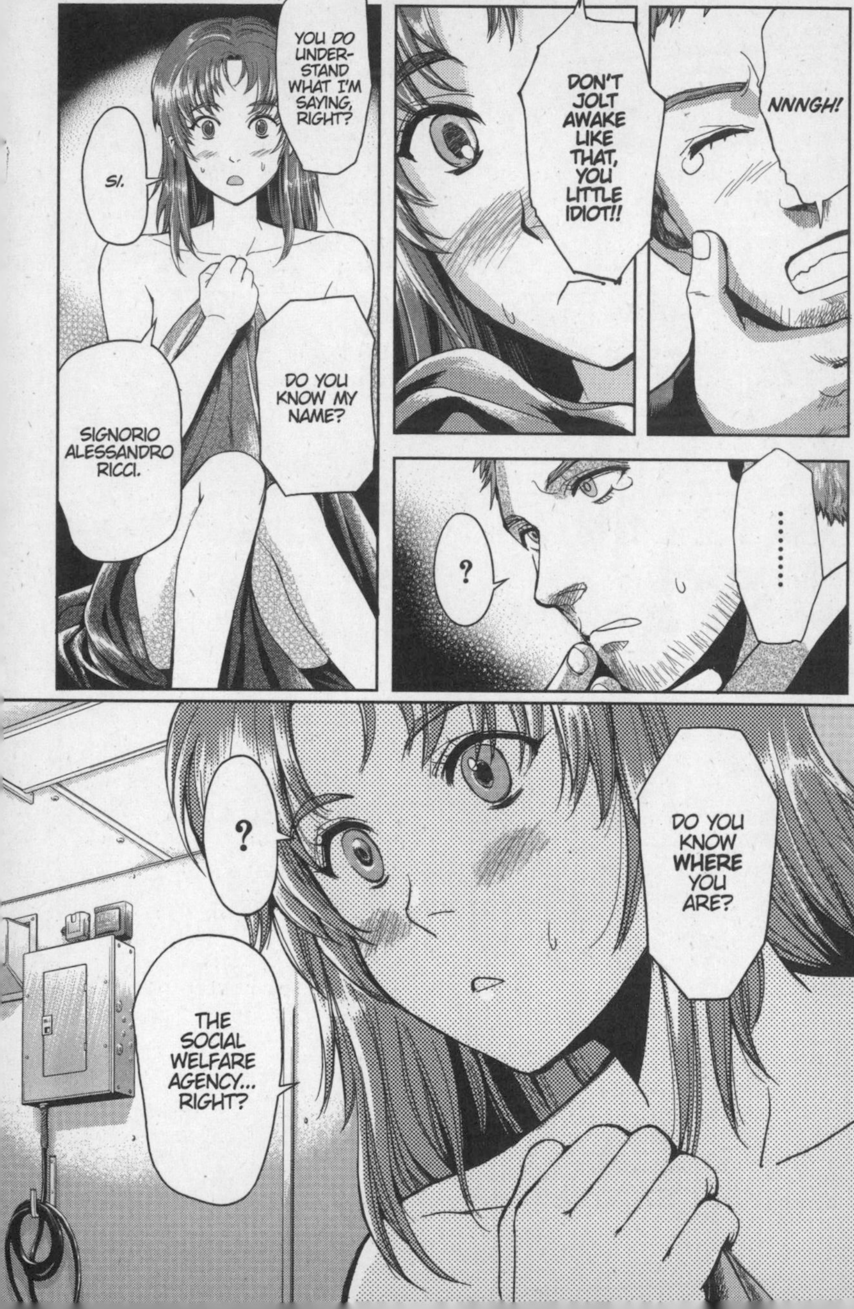
NNNGH!
DON'T JOLT AWAKE LIKE THAT, YOU LITTLE IDIOT!!
......
?
YOU DO UNDER-STAND WHAT I'M SAYING, RIGHT?
SÌ.
DO YOU KNOW MY NAME?
SIGNORIO ALESSANDRO RICCI.
DO YOU KNOW WHERE YOU ARE?
?
THE SOCIAL WELFARE AGENCY... RIGHT?

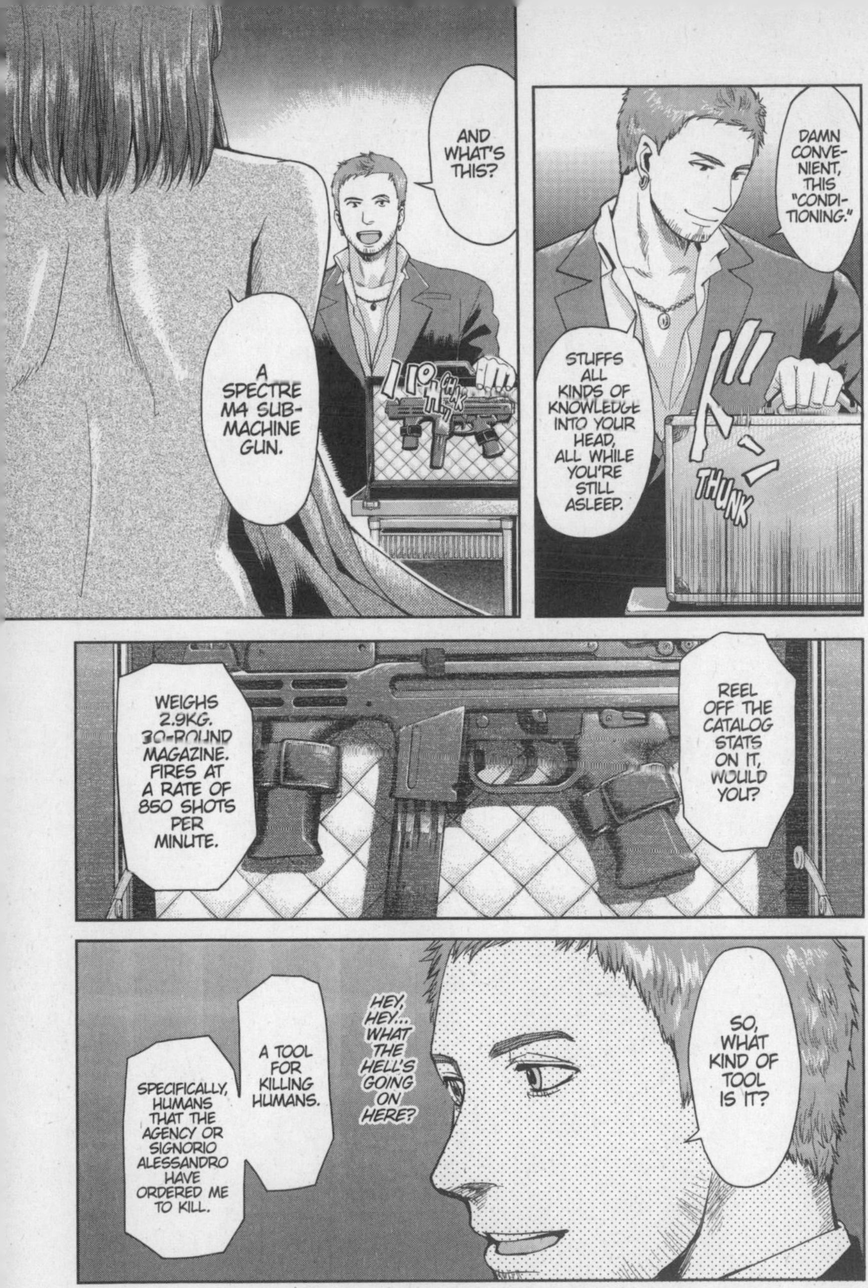
DAMN CONVENIENT, THIS "CONDITIONING."
STUFFS ALL KINDS OF KNOWLEDGE INTO YOUR HEAD, ALL WHILE YOU'RE STILL ASLEEP.
THUNK
AND WHAT'S THIS?
A SPECTRE M4 SUBMACHINE GUN.
CHAK
REEL OFF THE CATALOG STATS ON IT, WOULD YOU?
WEIGHS 2.9KG. 30-ROUND MAGAZINE. FIRES AT A RATE OF 850 SHOTS PER MINUTE.
SO, WHAT KIND OF TOOL IS IT?
HEY, HEY... WHAT THE HELL'S GOING ON HERE?
A TOOL FOR KILLING HUMANS.
SPECIFICALLY, HUMANS THAT THE AGENCY OR SIGNORIO ALESSANDRO HAVE ORDERED ME TO KILL.

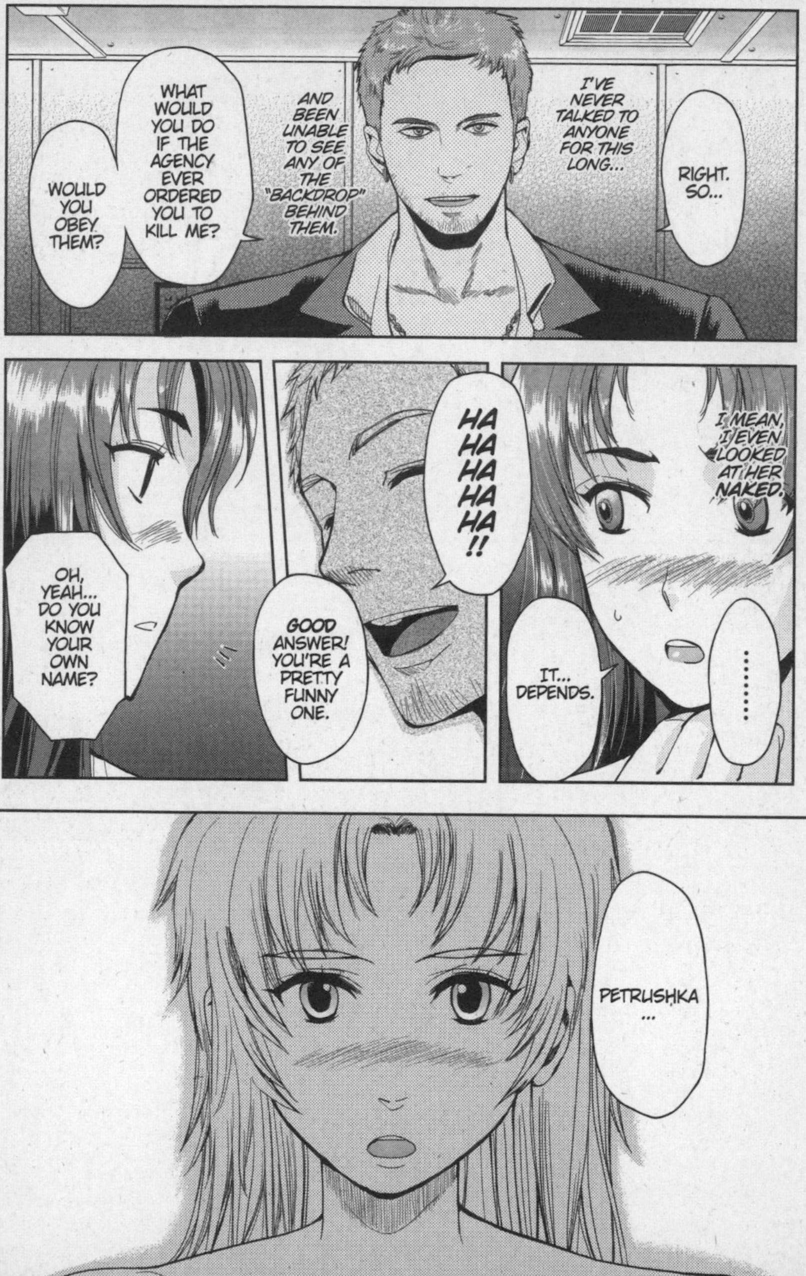
RIGHT. SO...
I'VE NEVER TALKED TO ANYONE FOR THIS LONG...
AND BEEN UNABLE TO SEE ANY OF THE "BACKDROP" BEHIND THEM.
WHAT WOULD YOU DO IF THE AGENCY EVER ORDERED YOU TO KILL ME?
WOULD YOU OBEY THEM?
I MEAN, I EVEN LOOKED AT HER NAKED.
......
IT... DEPENDS.
HA HA HA HA HA!!
GOOD ANSWER! YOU'RE A PRETTY FUNNY ONE.
OH, YEAH... DO YOU KNOW YOUR OWN NAME?
PETRUSHKA...

GUNSLINGERGIRL.

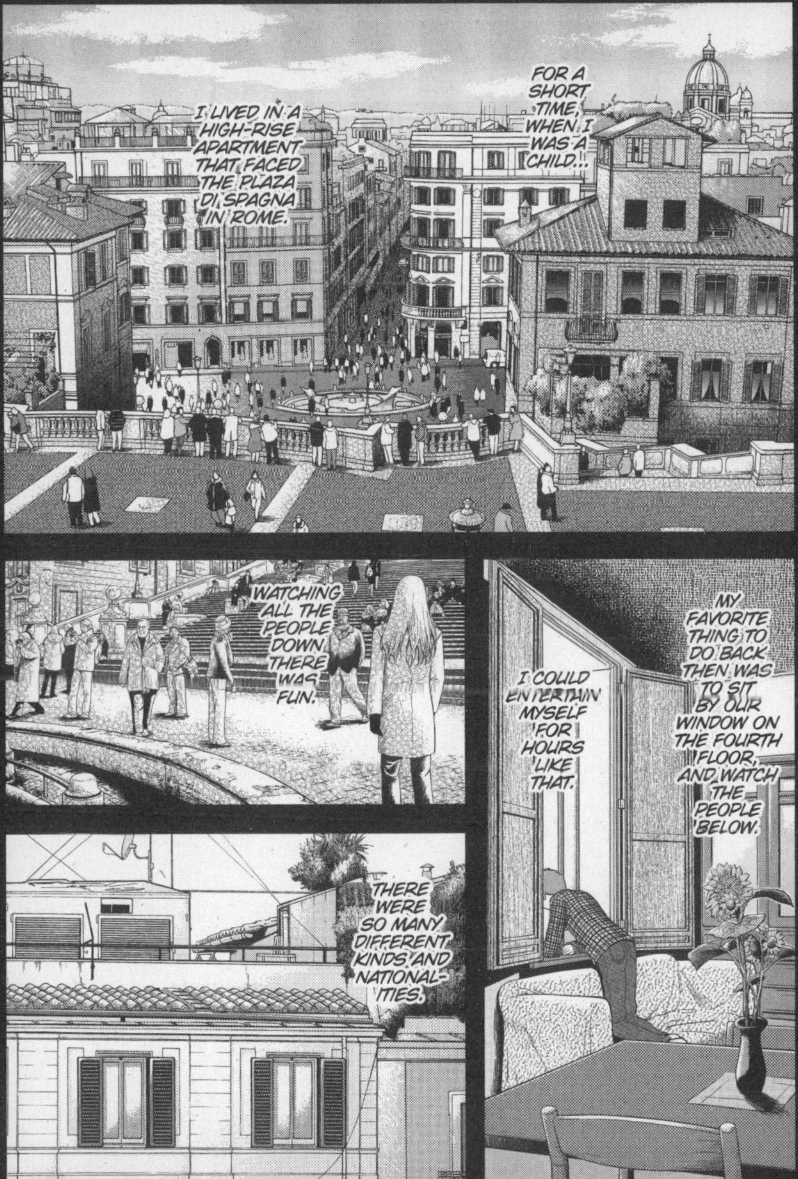
FOR A SHORT TIME, WHEN I WAS A CHILD...
I LIVED IN A HIGH-RISE APARTMENT THAT FACED THE PLAZA DI SPAGNA IN ROME.
MY FAVORITE THING TO DO BACK THEN WAS TO SIT BY OUR WINDOW ON THE FOURTH FLOOR, AND WATCH THE PEOPLE BELOW.
I COULD ENTERTAIN MYSELF FOR HOURS LIKE THAT.
WATCHING ALL THE PEOPLE DOWN THERE WAS FUN.
THERE WERE SO MANY DIFFERENT KINDS AND NATIONAL-ITIES.

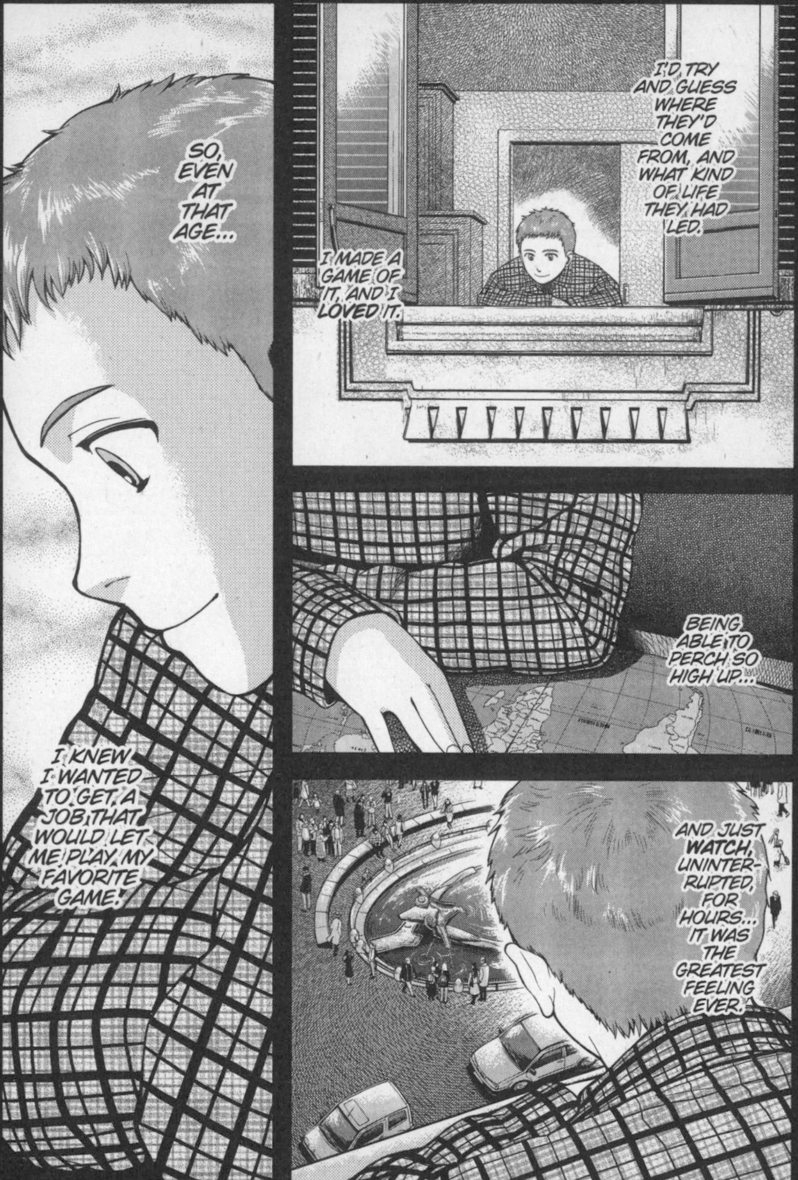
I'D TRY AND GUESS WHERE THEY'D COME FROM, AND WHAT KIND OF LIFE THEY HAD LED.
I MADE A GAME OF IT, AND I LOVED IT.
BEING ABLE TO PERCH SO HIGH UP...
AND JUST **WATCH**, UNINTERRUPTED, FOR HOURS... IT WAS THE GREATEST FEELING EVER.
SO, EVEN AT THAT AGE...
I KNEW I WANTED TO GET A JOB THAT WOULD LET ME PLAY MY FAVORITE GAME!

CHAPTER 32: GLANCES

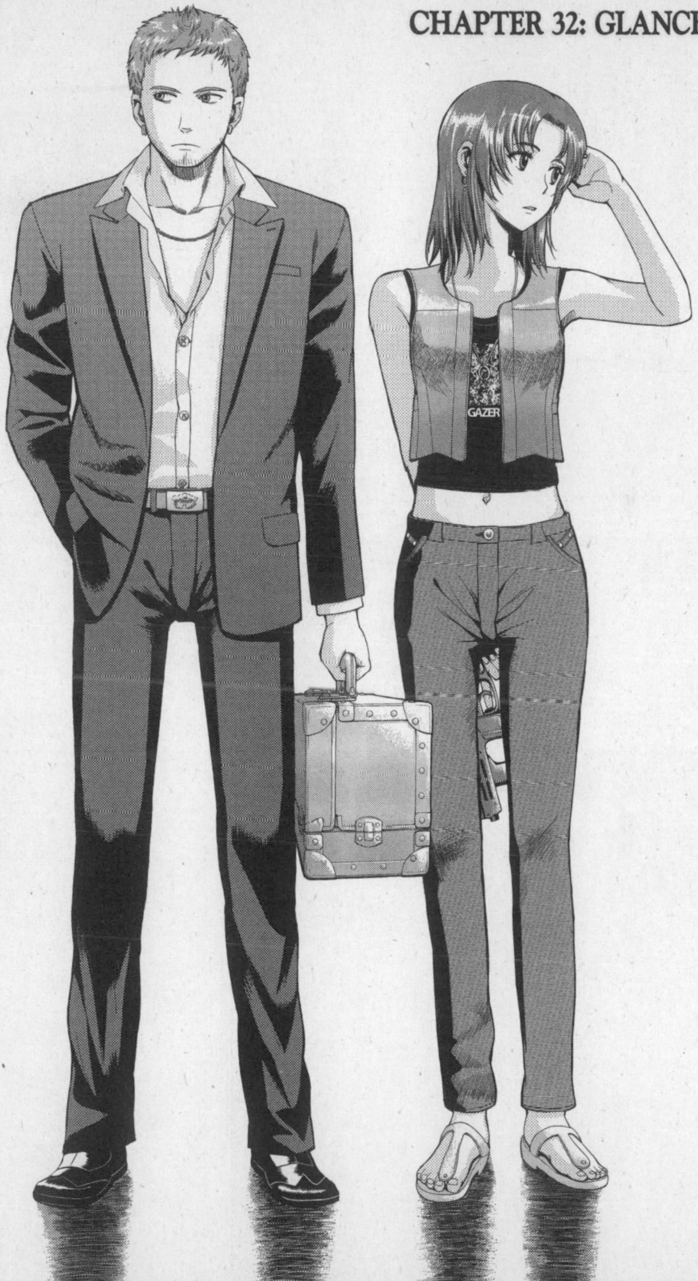
GAZER

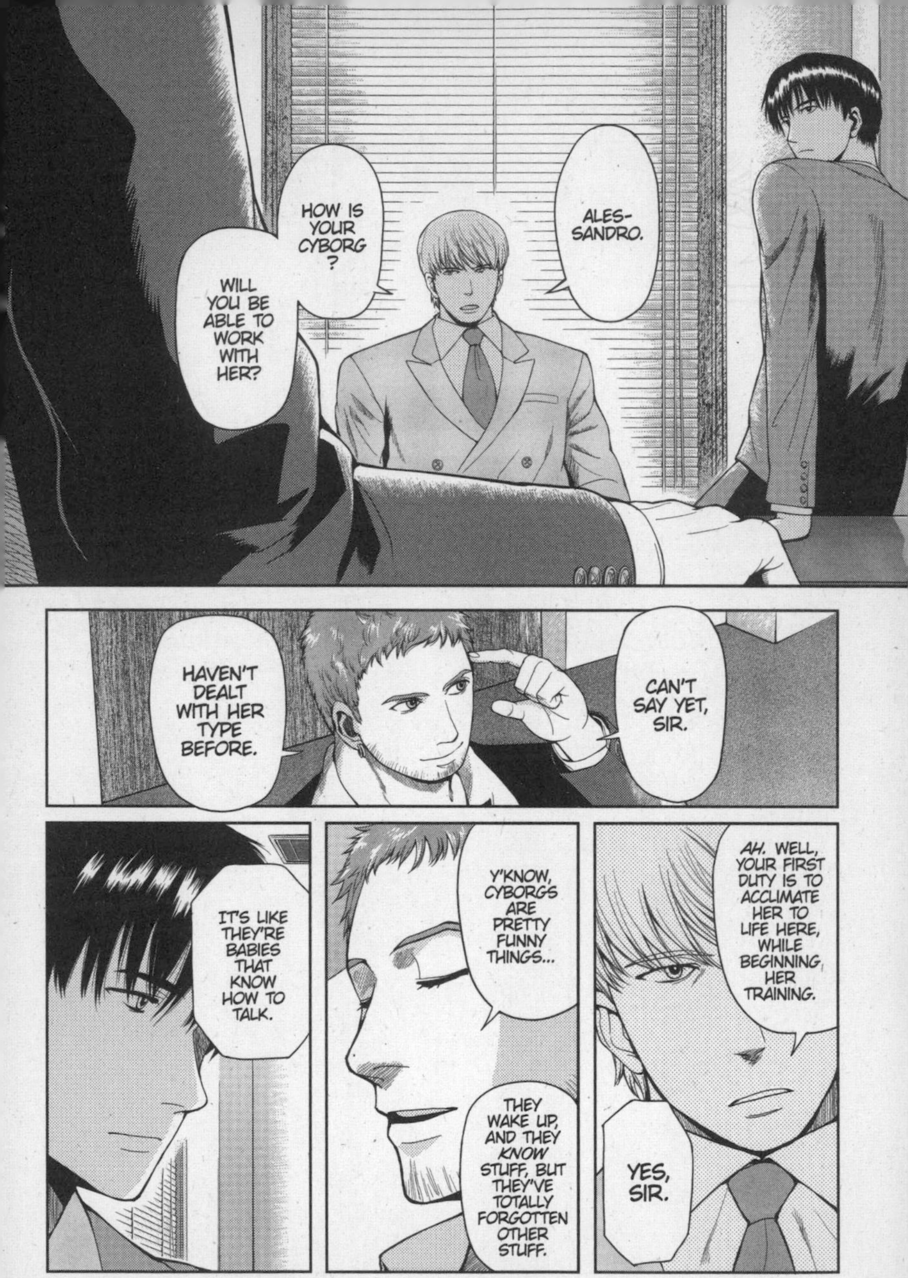
ALES-SANDRO.
HOW IS YOUR CYBORG?
WILL YOU BE ABLE TO WORK WITH HER?
CAN'T SAY YET, SIR.
HAVEN'T DEALT WITH HER TYPE BEFORE.
AH. WELL, YOUR FIRST DUTY IS TO ACCLIMATE HER TO LIFE HERE, WHILE BEGINNING HER TRAINING.
YES, SIR.
Y'KNOW, CYBORGS ARE PRETTY FUNNY THINGS...
THEY WAKE UP, AND THEY *KNOW* STUFF, BUT THEY'VE TOTALLY FORGOTTEN OTHER STUFF.
IT'S LIKE THEY'RE BABIES THAT KNOW HOW TO TALK.

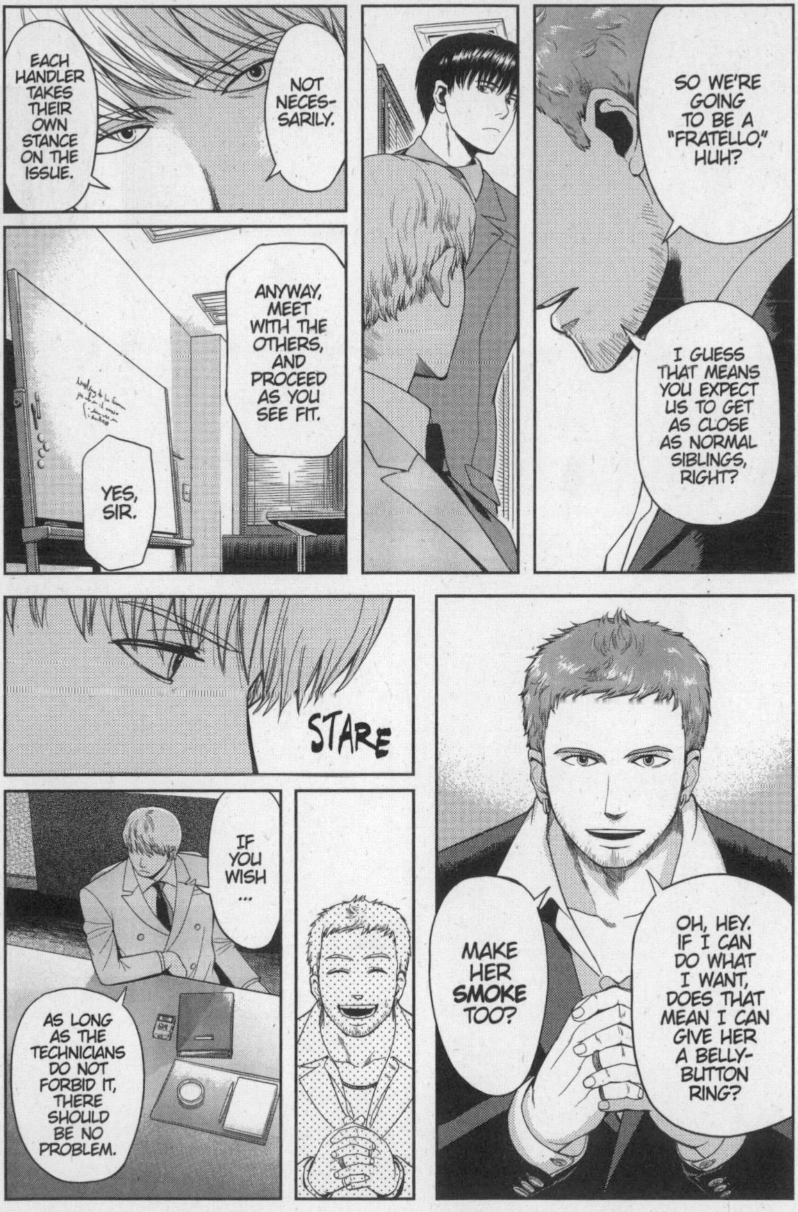

SO WE'RE GOING TO BE A "FRATELLO," HUH?
I GUESS THAT MEANS YOU EXPECT US TO GET AS CLOSE AS NORMAL SIBLINGS, RIGHT?
NOT NECES-SARILY.
EACH HANDLER TAKES THEIR OWN STANCE ON THE ISSUE.
ANYWAY, MEET WITH THE OTHERS, AND PROCEED AS YOU SEE FIT.
YES, SIR.
OH, HEY. IF I CAN DO WHAT I WANT, DOES THAT MEAN I CAN GIVE HER A BELLY-BUTTON RING?
MAKE HER SMOKE TOO?
STARE
IF YOU WISH ...
AS LONG AS THE TECHNICIANS DO NOT FORBID IT, THERE SHOULD BE NO PROBLEM.

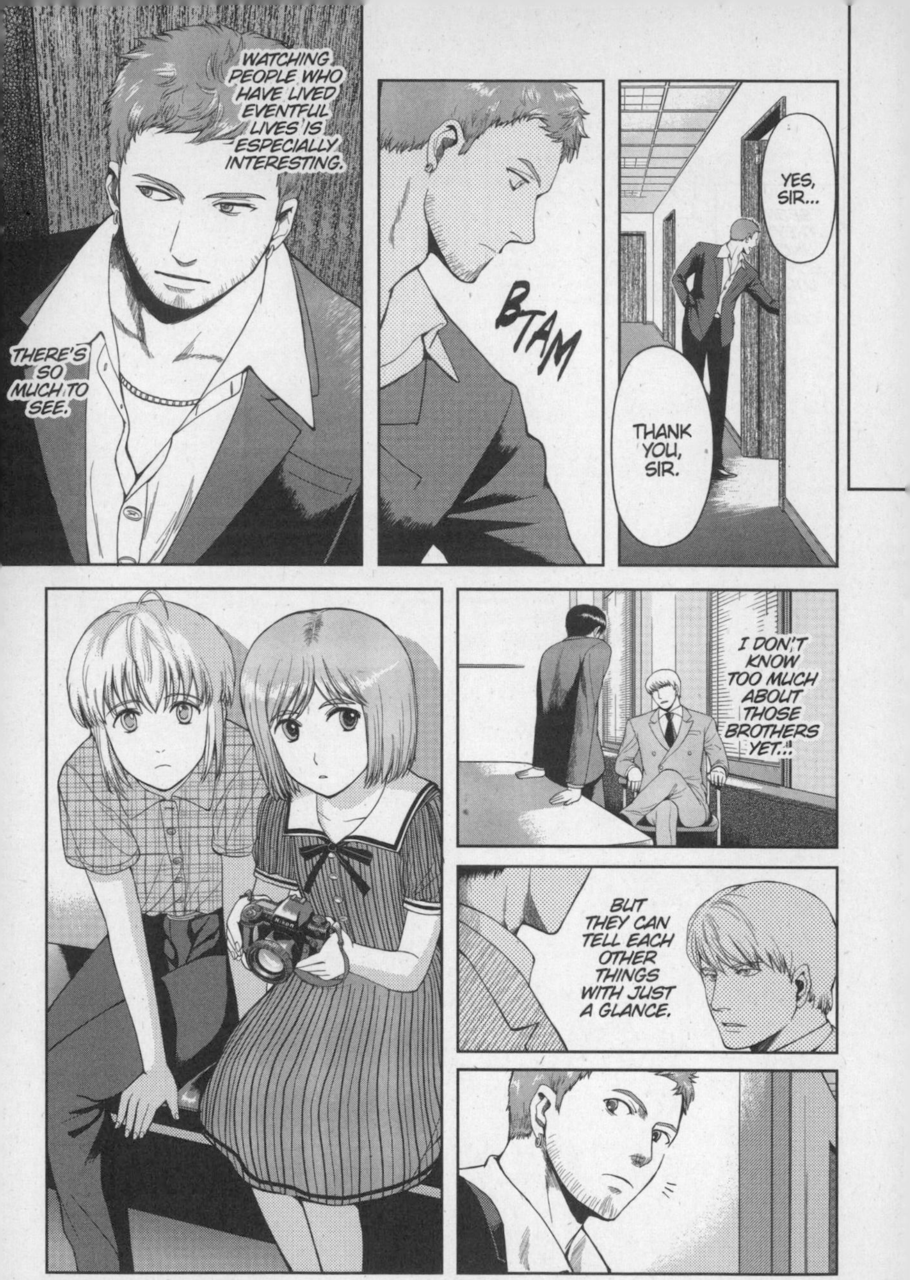
YES, SIR...
THANK YOU, SIR.
BTAM
WATCHING PEOPLE WHO HAVE LIVED EVENTFUL LIVES IS ESPECIALLY INTERESTING.
THERE'S SO MUCH TO SEE.
I DON'T KNOW TOO MUCH ABOUT THOSE BROTHERS YET...
BUT THEY CAN TELL EACH OTHER THINGS WITH JUST A GLANCE.

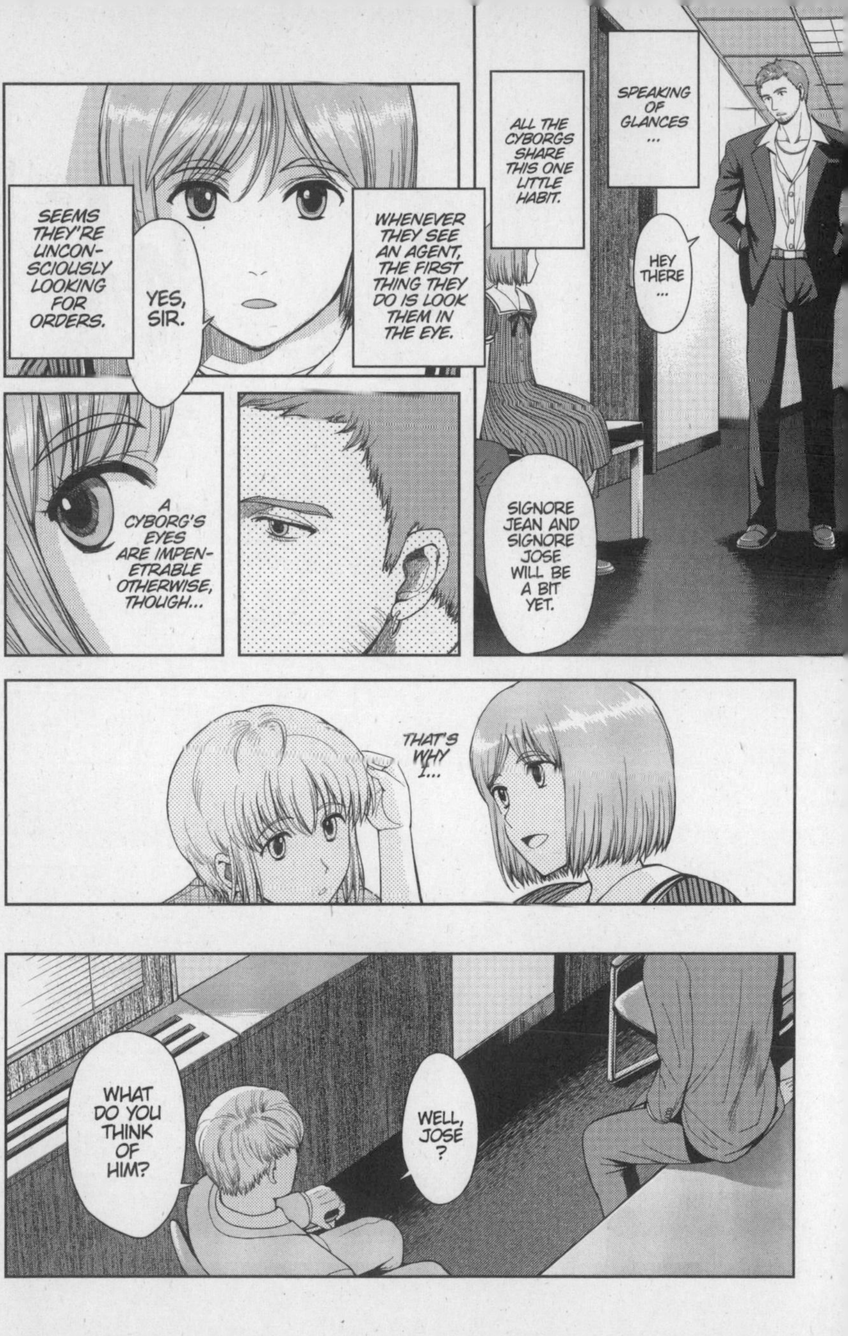
SPEAKING OF GLANCES ...
ALL THE CYBORGS SHARE THIS ONE LITTLE HABIT.
HEY THERE ...
SIGNORE JEAN AND SIGNORE JOSE WILL BE A BIT YET.
WHENEVER THEY SEE AN AGENT, THE FIRST THING THEY DO IS LOOK THEM IN THE EYE.
YES, SIR.
SEEMS THEY'RE UNCON-SCIOUSLY LOOKING FOR ORDERS.
A CYBORG'S EYES ARE IMPEN-ETRABLE OTHERWISE, THOUGH...
THAT'S WHY I...
WELL, JOSE ?
WHAT DO YOU THINK OF HIM?

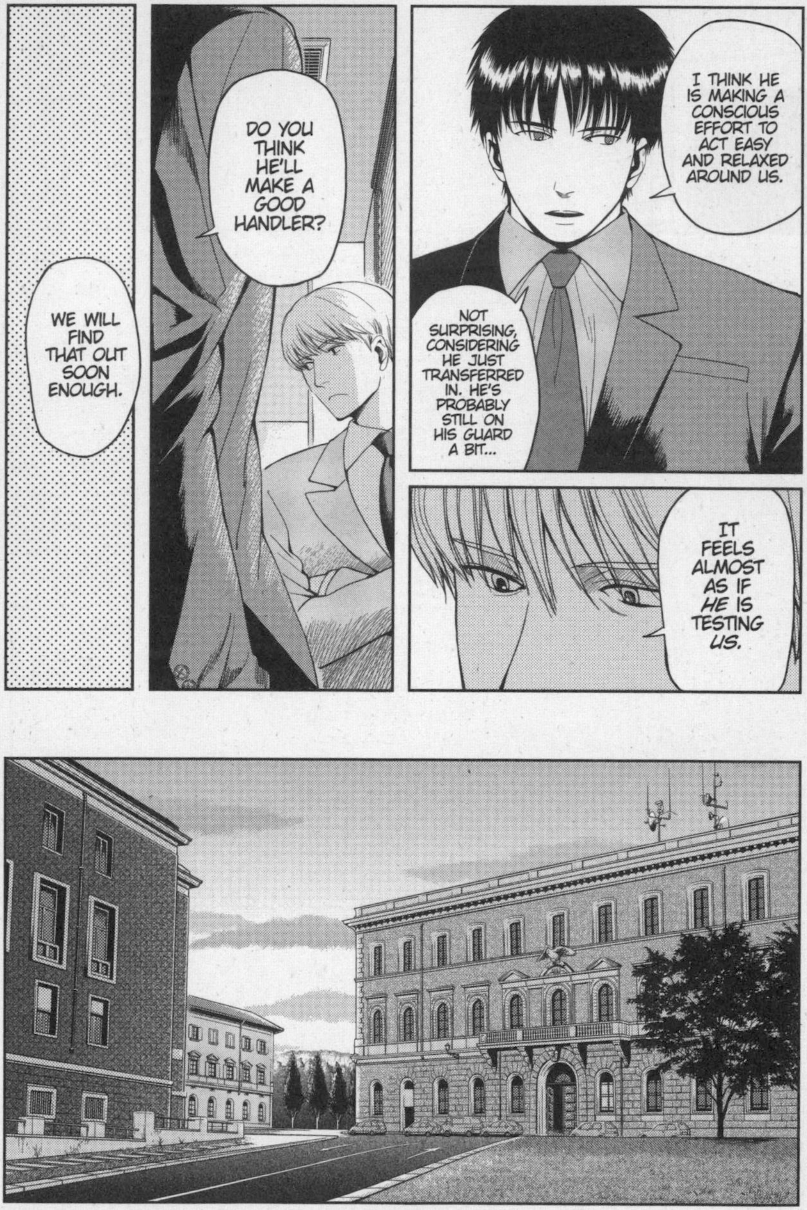
I THINK HE IS MAKING A CONSCIOUS EFFORT TO ACT EASY AND RELAXED AROUND US.
NOT SURPRISING, CONSIDERING HE JUST TRANSFERRED IN. HE'S PROBABLY STILL ON HIS GUARD A BIT...
IT FEELS ALMOST AS IF *HE* IS TESTING *US*.
DO YOU THINK HE'LL MAKE A GOOD HANDLER?
WE WILL FIND THAT OUT SOON ENOUGH.

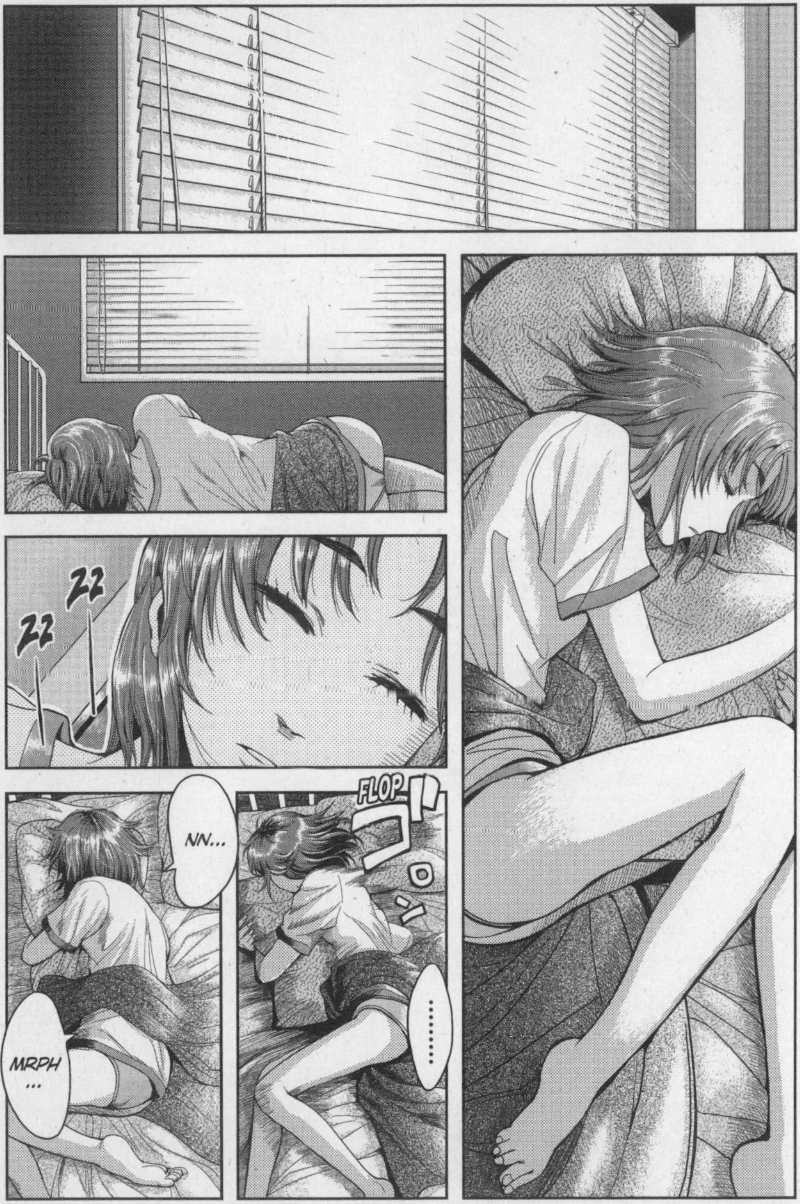
ZZ
ZZ
FLOP
....
NN...
MRPH ...

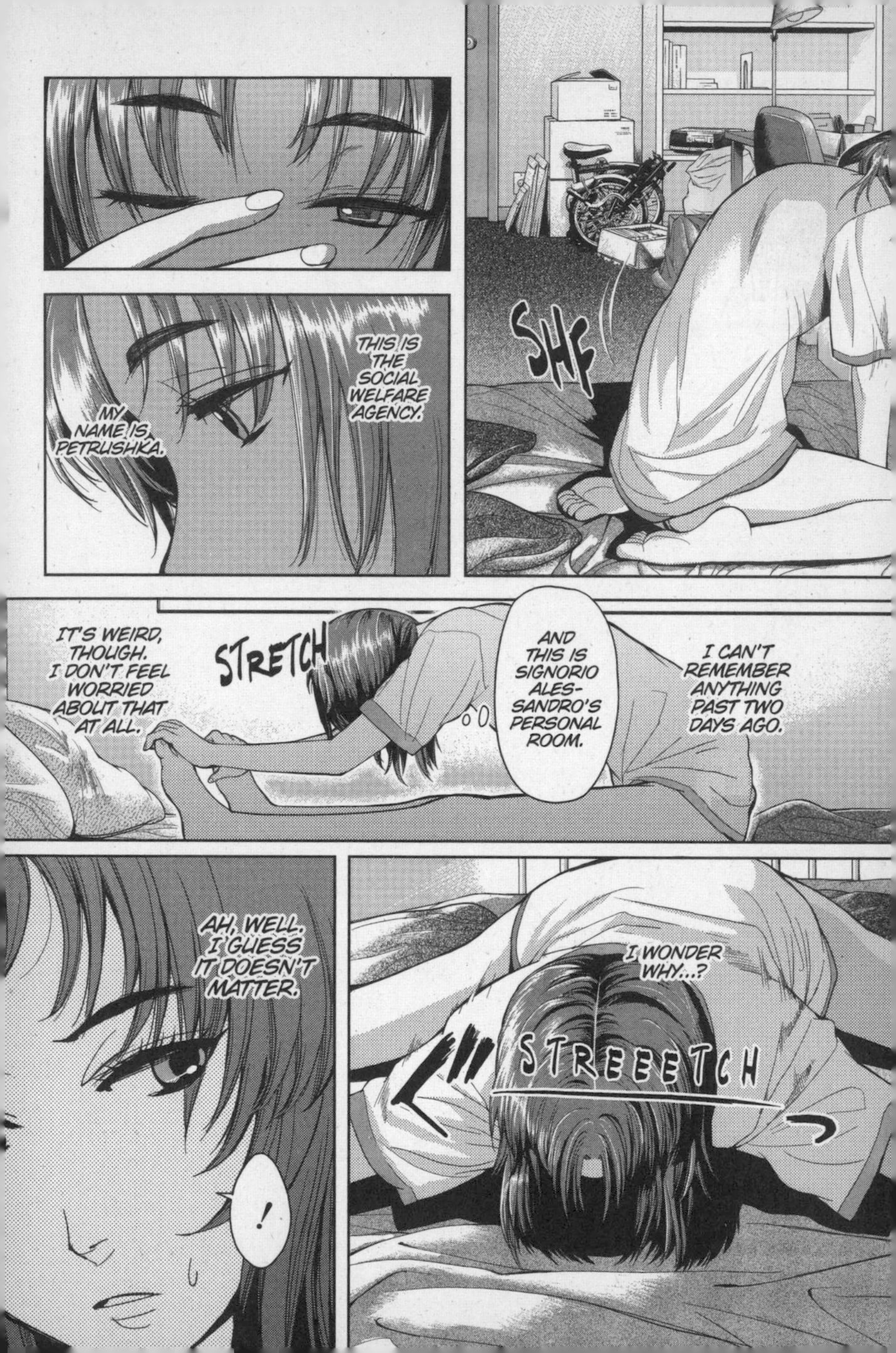
SHF
THIS IS THE SOCIAL WELFARE AGENCY.
MY NAME IS, PETRUSHKA.
I CAN'T REMEMBER ANYTHING PAST TWO DAYS AGO.
AND THIS IS SIGNORIO ALES-SANDRO'S PERSONAL ROOM.
STRETCH
IT'S WEIRD, THOUGH. I DON'T FEEL WORRIED ABOUT THAT AT ALL.
I WONDER WHY...?
STREEETCH
AH, WELL. I GUESS IT DOESN'T MATTER.
!

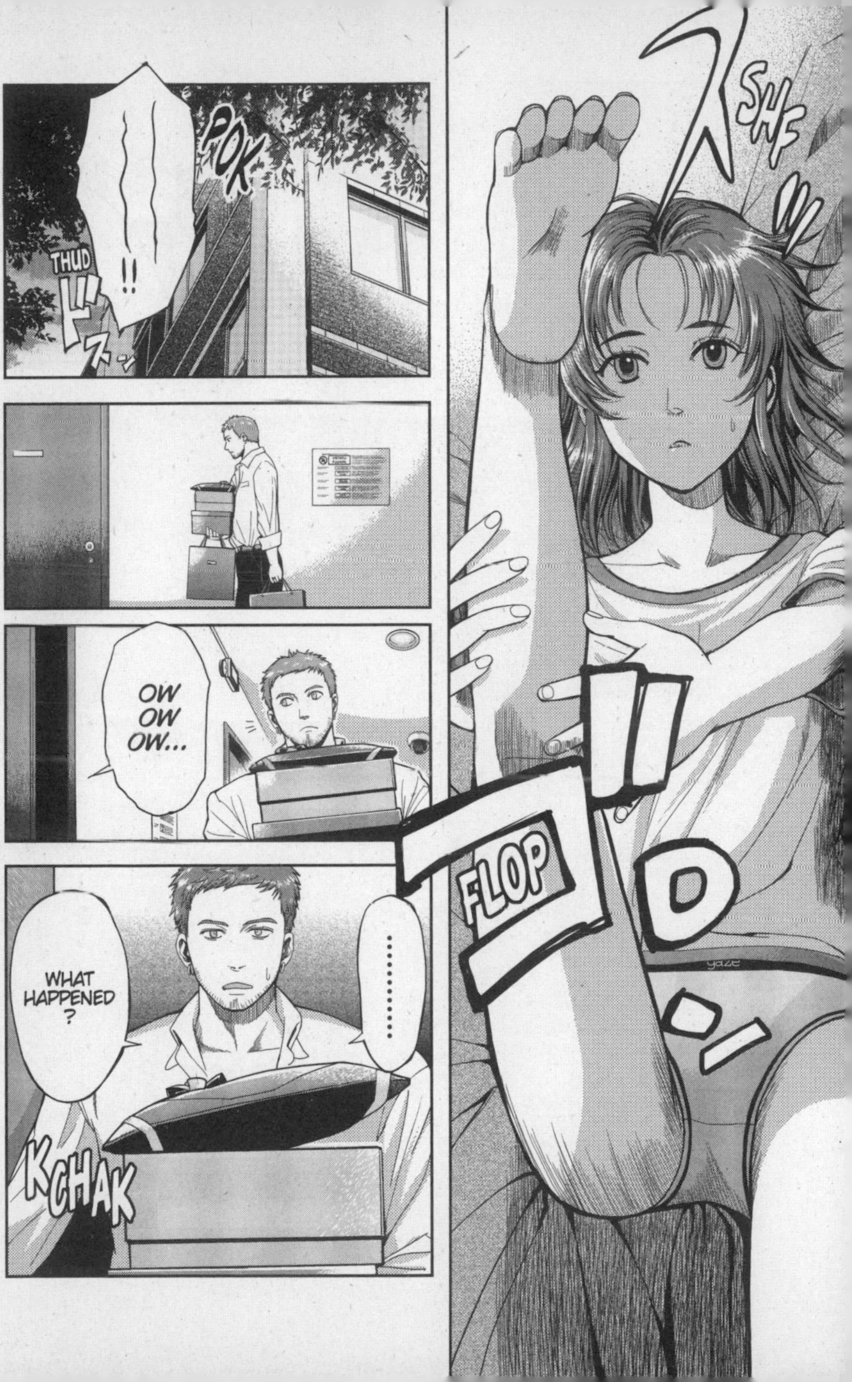
SHF
FLOP
POK
!!
THUD
ドス
OW OW OW...
......
WHAT HAPPENED ?
KCHAK

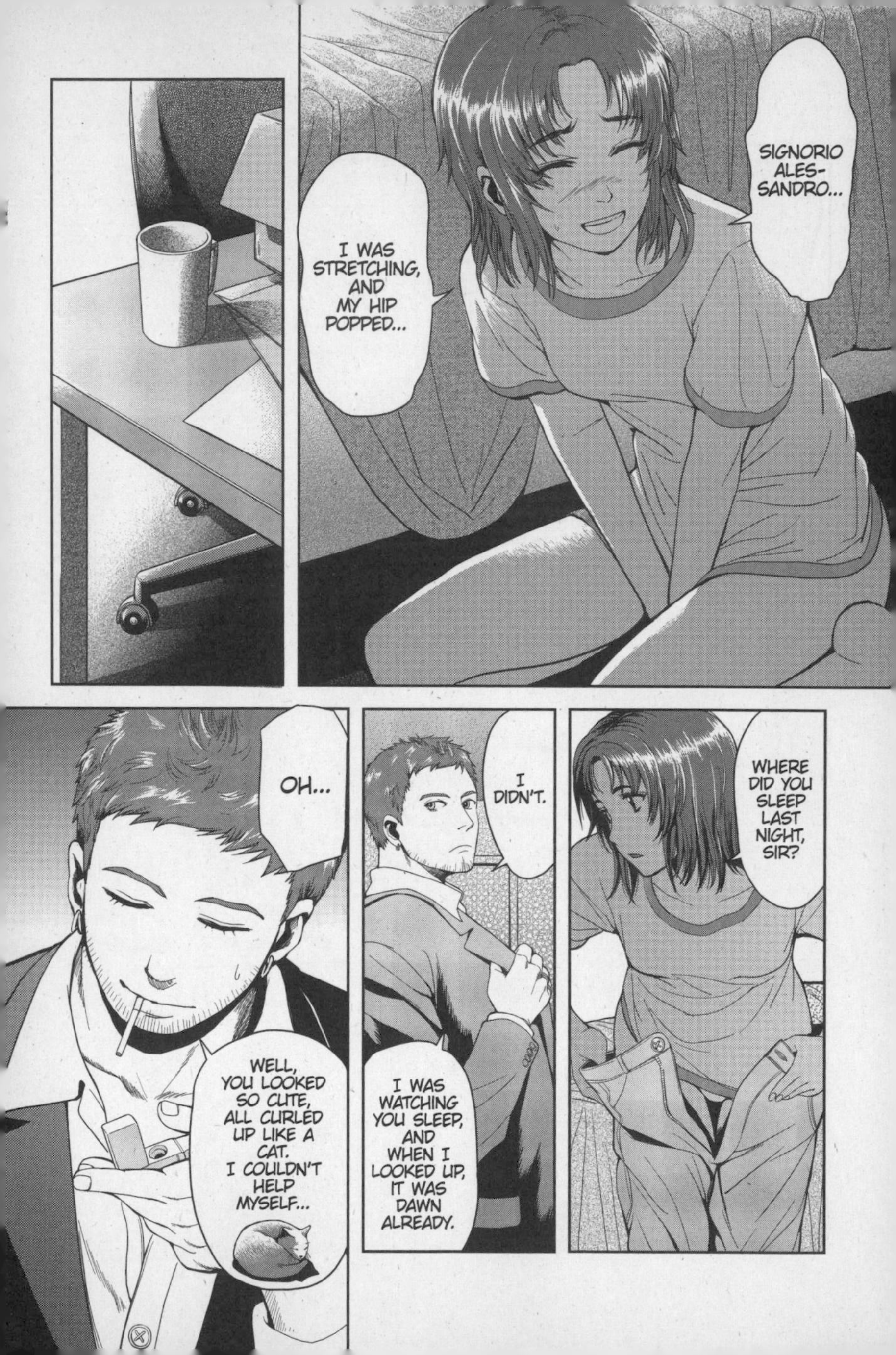
SIGNORIO ALES-SANDRO...
I WAS STRETCHING, AND MY HIP POPPED...
WHERE DID YOU SLEEP LAST NIGHT, SIR?
I DIDN'T.
I WAS WATCHING YOU SLEEP, AND WHEN I LOOKED UP, IT WAS DAWN ALREADY.
OH...
WELL, YOU LOOKED SO CUTE, ALL CURLED UP LIKE A CAT. I COULDN'T HELP MYSELF...

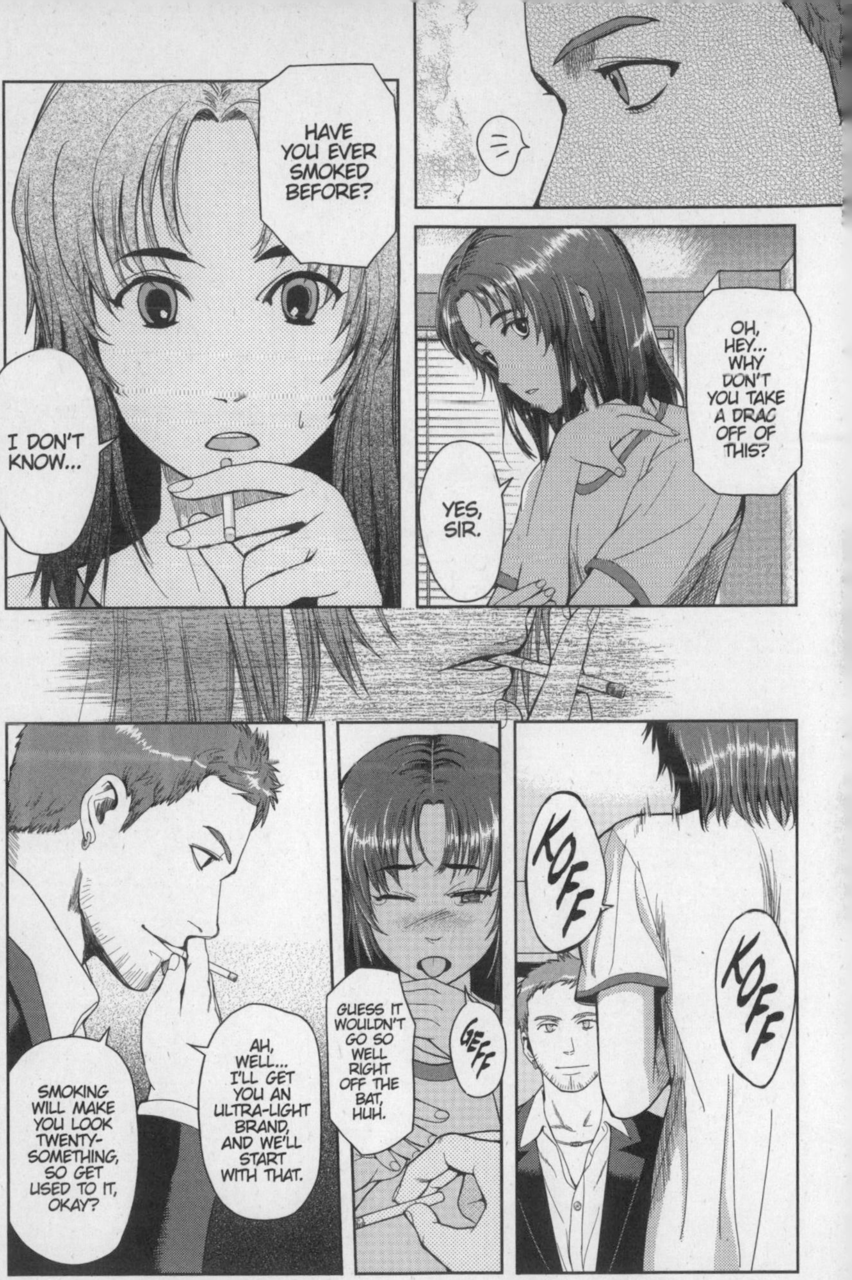
OH, HEY... WHY DON'T YOU TAKE A DRAG OFF OF THIS?
YES, SIR.
HAVE YOU EVER SMOKED BEFORE?
I DON'T KNOW...
KOFF
KOFF
GEFF
GUESS IT WOULDN'T GO SO WELL RIGHT OFF THE BAT, HUH.
AH, WELL... I'LL GET YOU AN ULTRA-LIGHT BRAND, AND WE'LL START WITH THAT.
SMOKING WILL MAKE YOU LOOK TWENTY-SOMETHING, SO GET USED TO IT, OKAY?

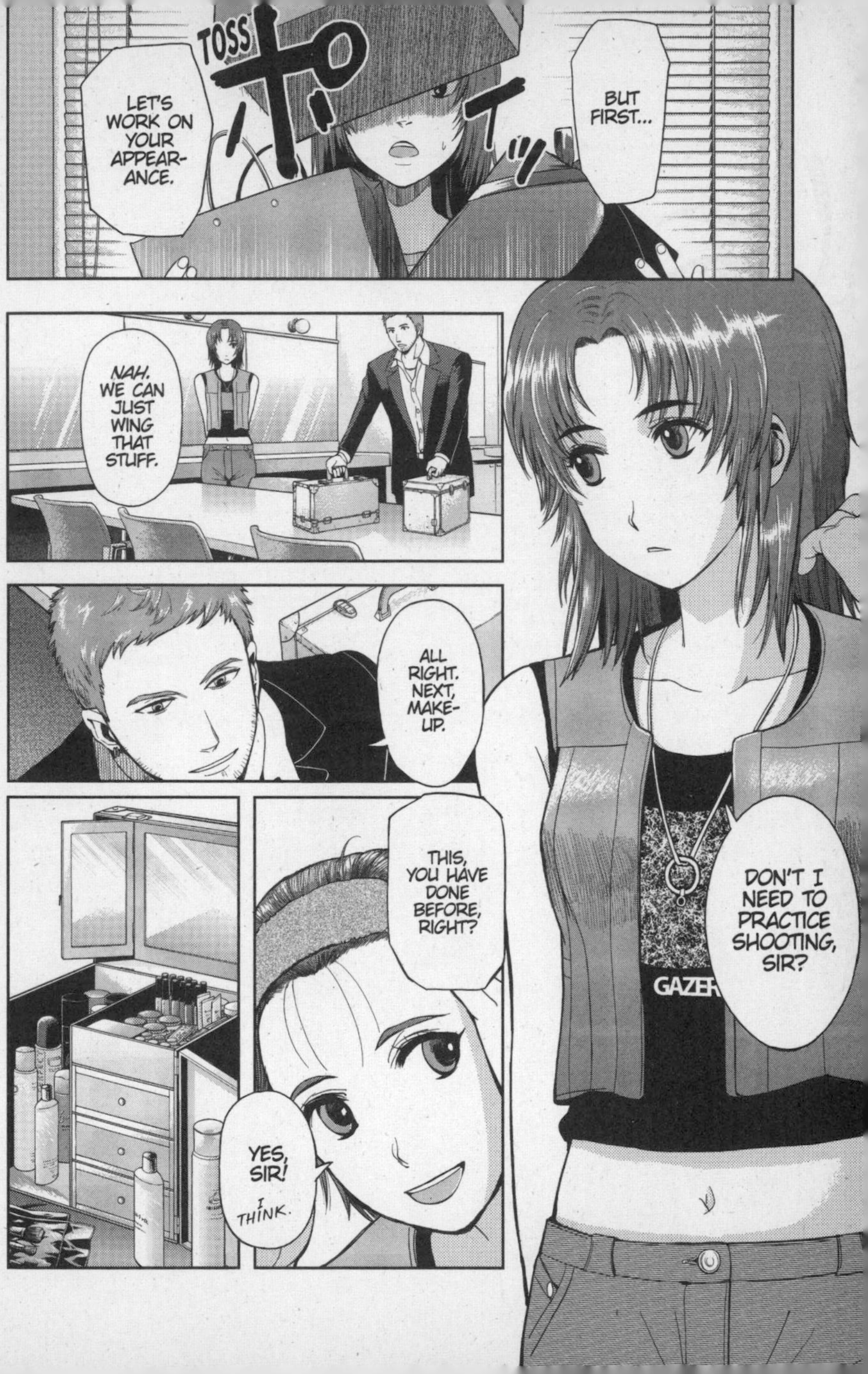
BUT FIRST...
TOSS
LET'S WORK ON YOUR APPEARANCE.
DON'T I NEED TO PRACTICE SHOOTING, SIR?
GAZER
NAH. WE CAN JUST WING THAT STUFF.
ALL RIGHT. NEXT, MAKE-UP.
THIS, YOU HAVE DONE BEFORE, RIGHT?
YES, SIR!
I THINK.

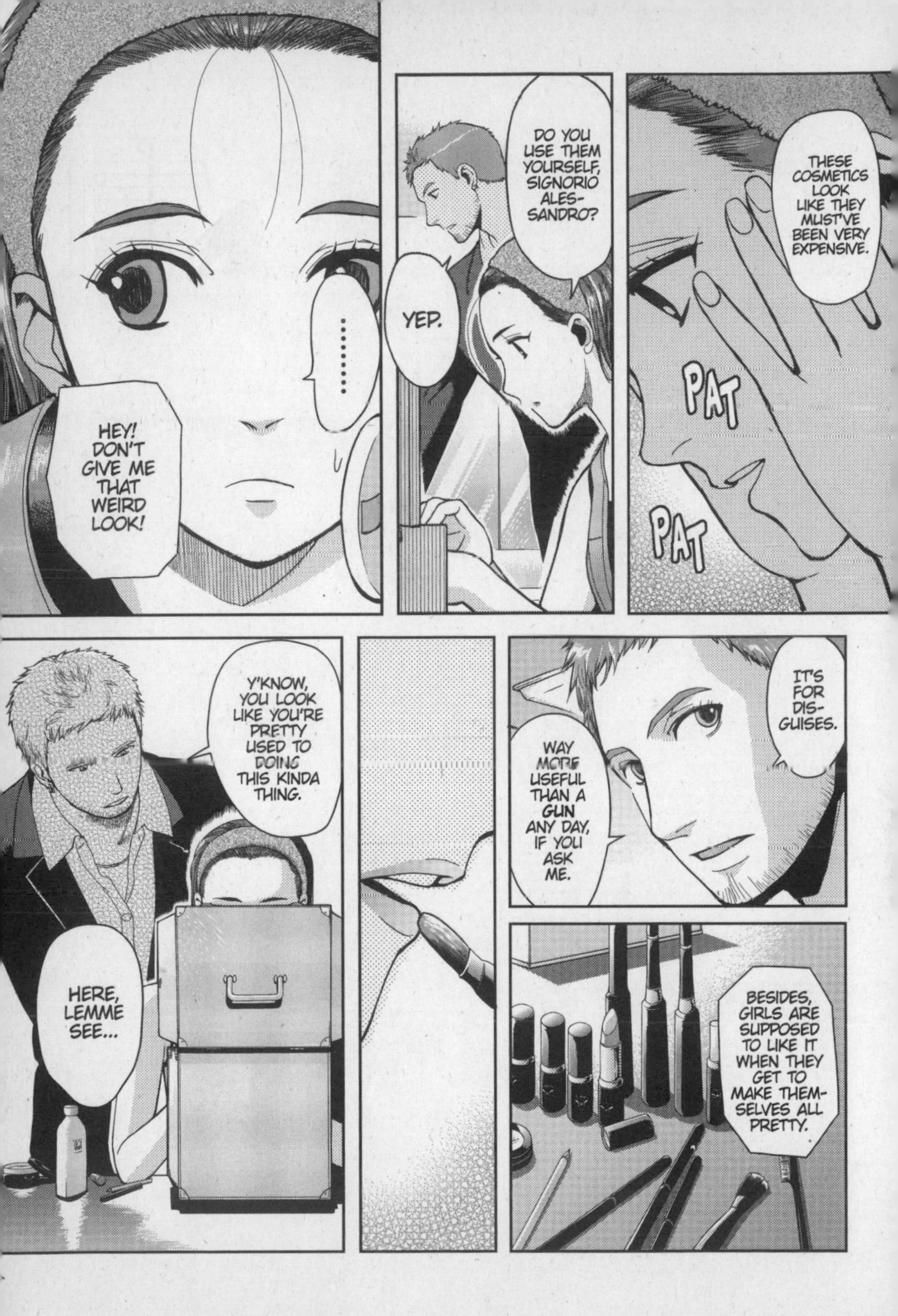
THESE COSMETICS LOOK LIKE THEY MUST'VE BEEN VERY EXPENSIVE.
PAT
PAT
DO YOU USE THEM YOURSELF, SIGNORIO ALESSANDRO?
YEP.
......
HEY! DON'T GIVE ME THAT WEIRD LOOK!
IT'S FOR DISGUISES.
WAY MORE USEFUL THAN A GUN ANY DAY, IF YOU ASK ME.
BESIDES, GIRLS ARE SUPPOSED TO LIKE IT WHEN THEY GET TO MAKE THEMSELVES ALL PRETTY.
Y'KNOW, YOU LOOK LIKE YOU'RE PRETTY USED TO DOING THIS KINDA THING.
HERE, LEMME SEE...

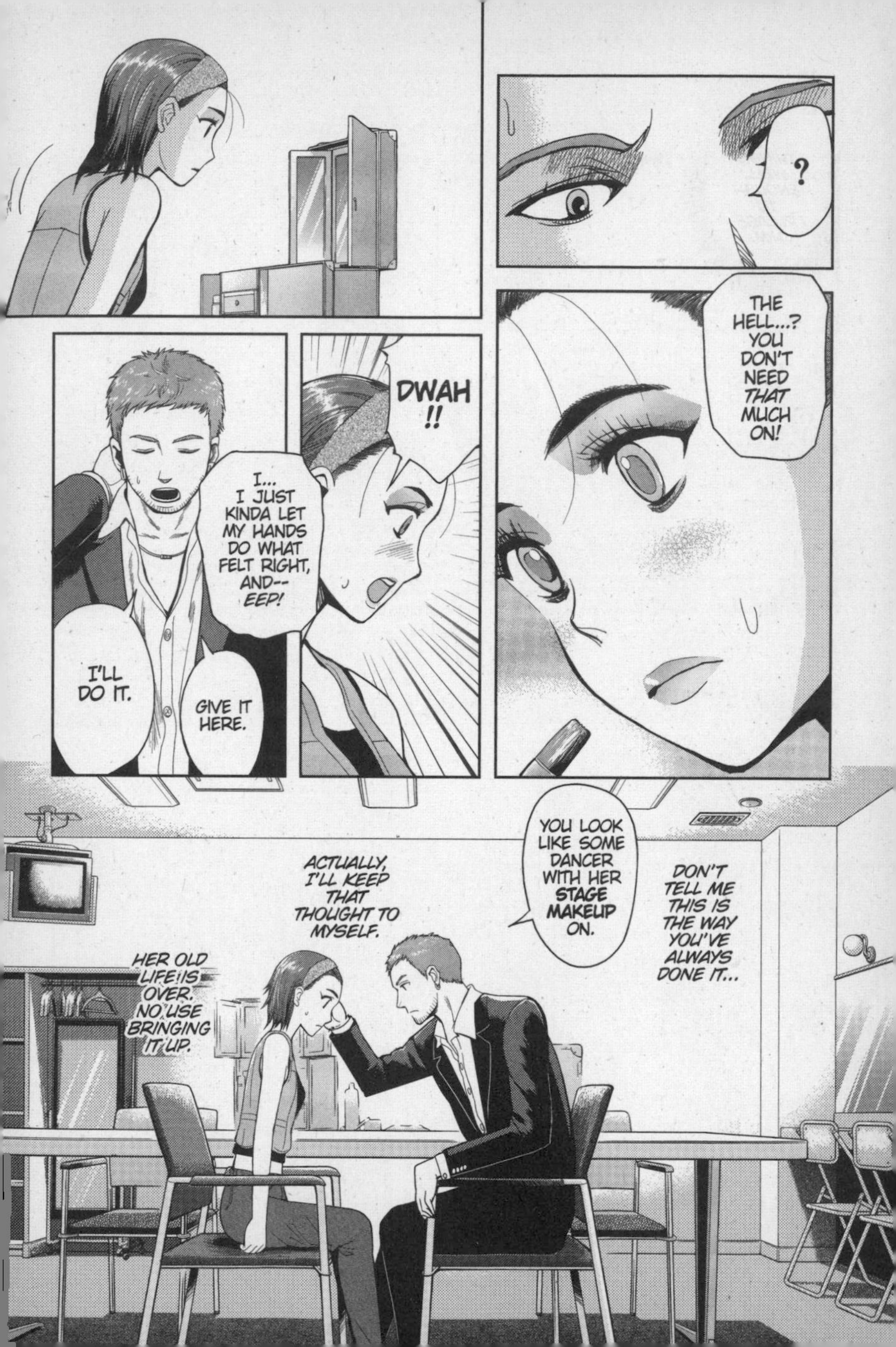
?
THE HELL...? YOU DON'T NEED *THAT* MUCH ON!
DWAH !!
I... I JUST KINDA LET MY HANDS DO WHAT FELT RIGHT, AND-- EEP!
GIVE IT HERE.
I'LL DO IT.
DON'T TELL ME THIS IS THE WAY YOU'VE ALWAYS DONE IT...
YOU LOOK LIKE SOME DANCER WITH HER **STAGE MAKEUP** ON.
ACTUALLY, I'LL KEEP THAT THOUGHT TO MYSELF.
HER OLD LIFE IS OVER. NO USE BRINGING IT UP.

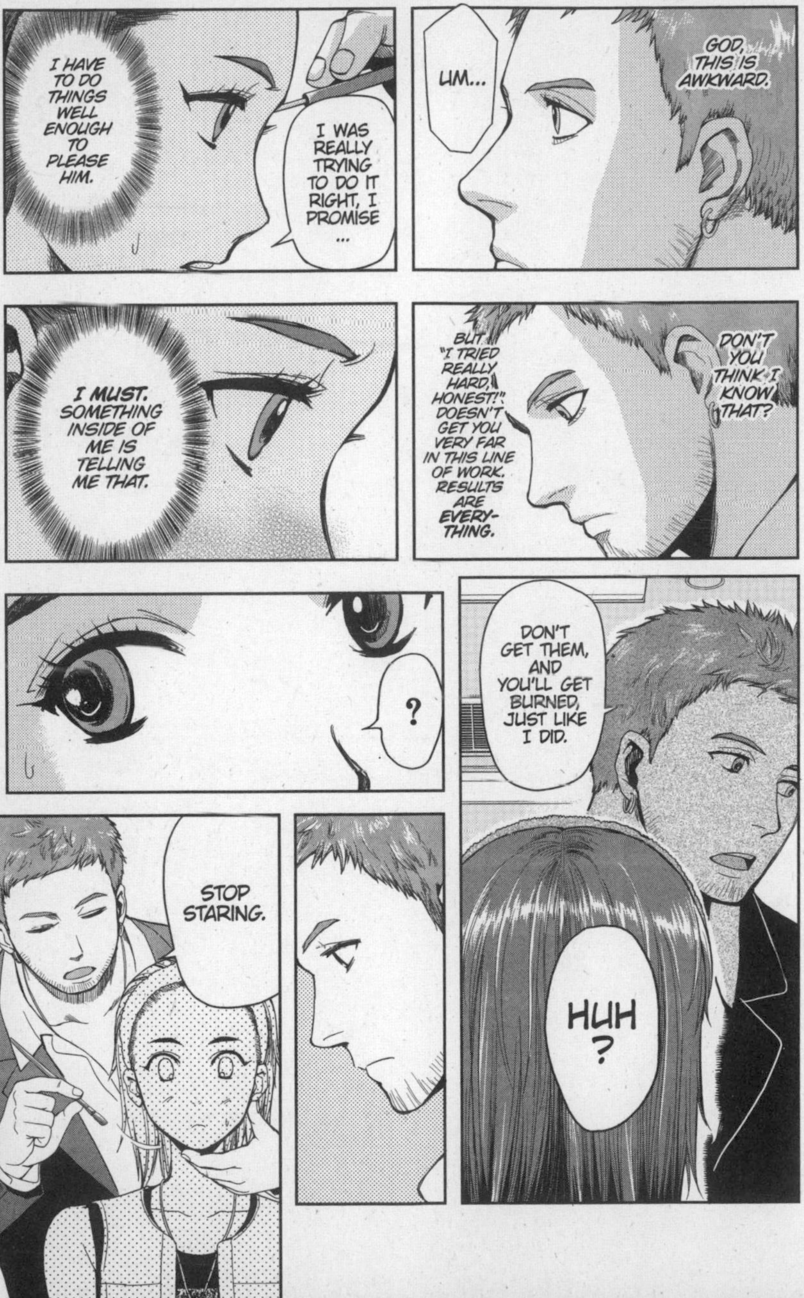
GOD, THIS IS AWKWARD.
UM...
I WAS REALLY TRYING TO DO IT RIGHT, I PROMISE...
I HAVE TO DO THINGS WELL ENOUGH TO PLEASE HIM.
DON'T YOU THINK I KNOW THAT?
BUT "I TRIED REALLY HARD, HONEST!" DOESN'T GET YOU VERY FAR IN THIS LINE OF WORK. RESULTS ARE EVERYTHING.
I MUST. SOMETHING INSIDE OF ME IS TELLING ME THAT.
DON'T GET THEM, AND YOU'LL GET BURNED, JUST LIKE I DID.
HUH?
?
STOP STARING.

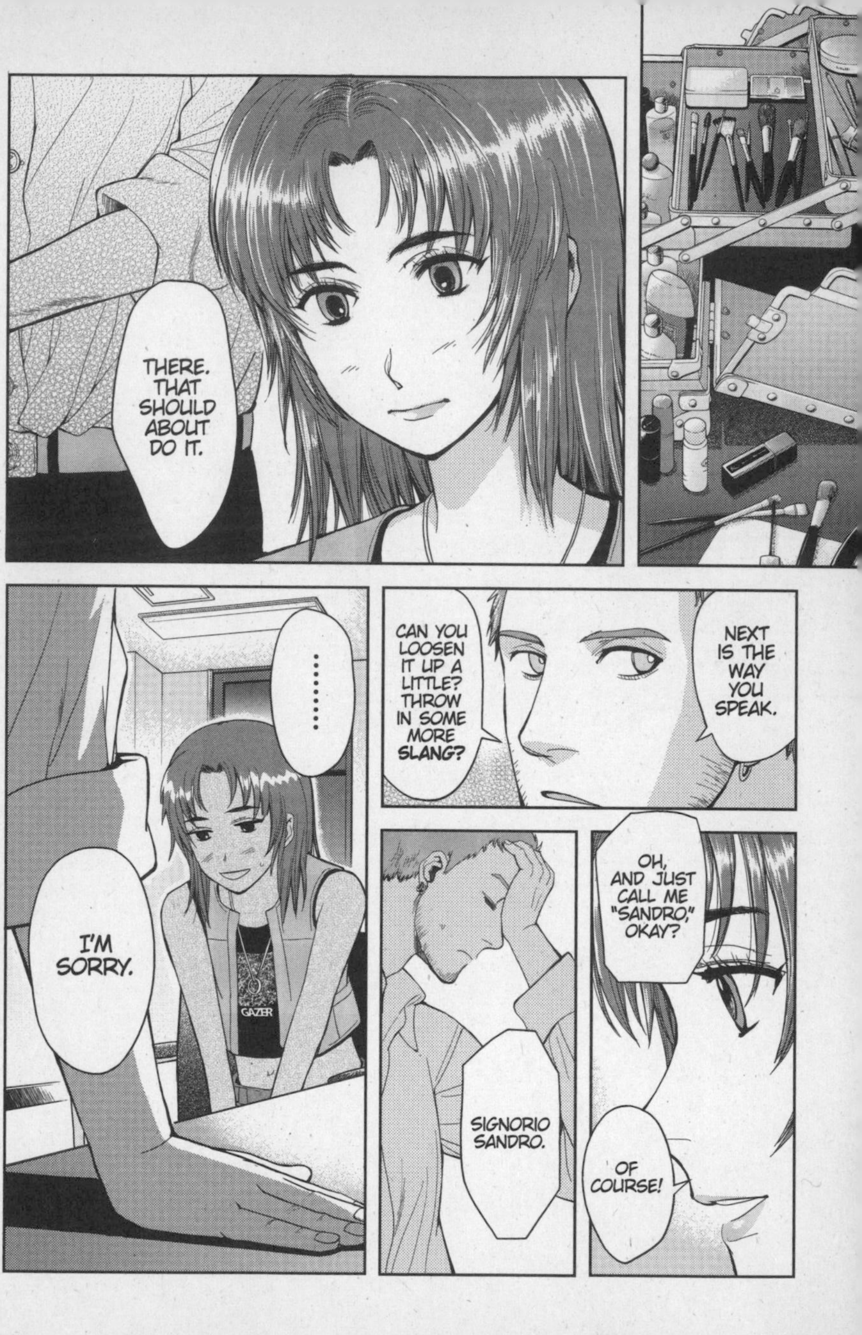
THERE. THAT SHOULD ABOUT DO IT.
NEXT IS THE WAY YOU SPEAK.
CAN YOU LOOSEN IT UP A LITTLE? THROW IN SOME MORE SLANG?
OH, AND JUST CALL ME "SANDRO," OKAY?
OF COURSE!
SIGNORIO SANDRO.
....
I'M SORRY.

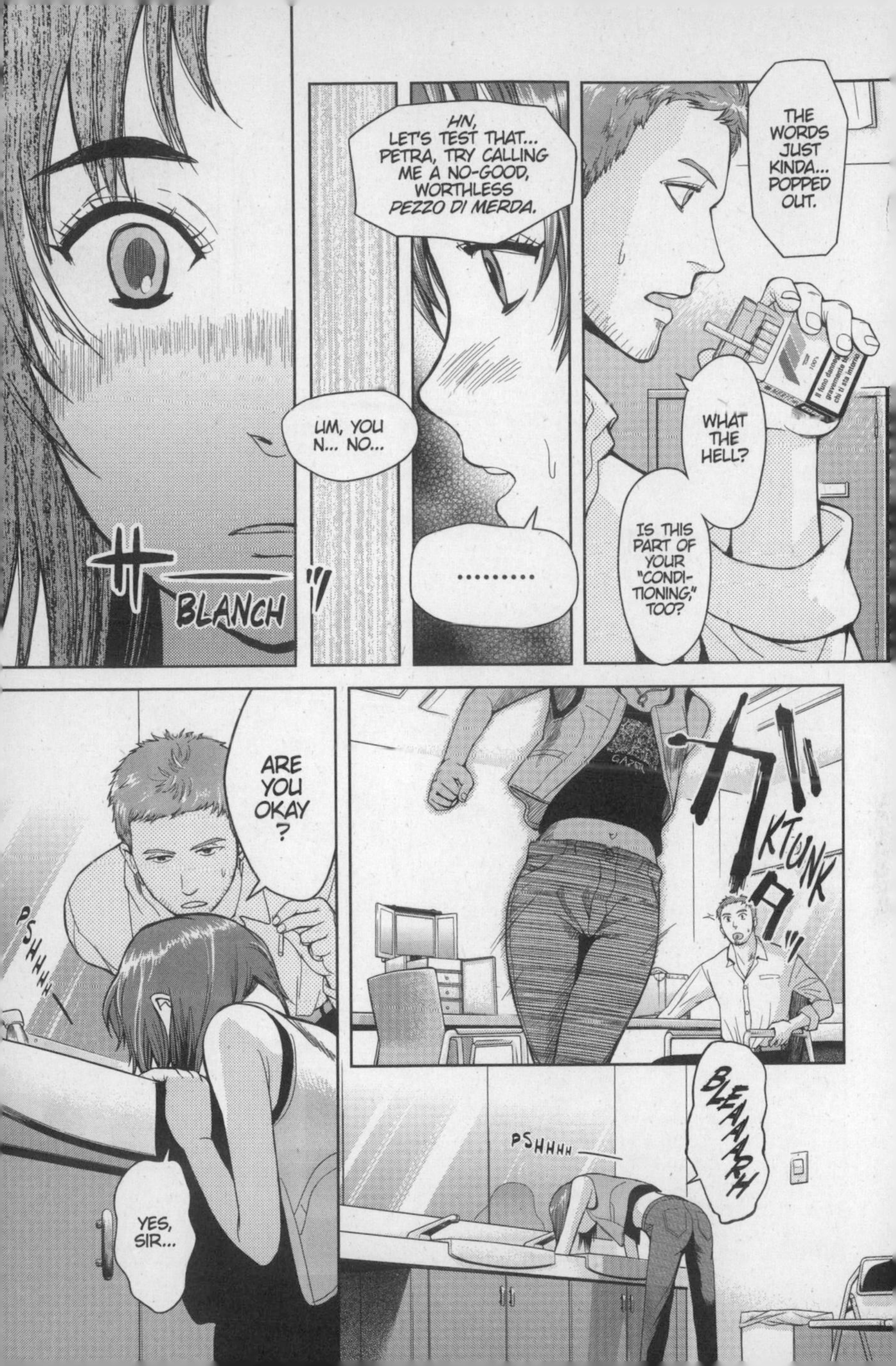
THE WORDS JUST KINDA... POPPED OUT.
WHAT THE HELL?
IS THIS PART OF YOUR "CONDITIONING," TOO?
HN, LET'S TEST THAT... PETRA, TRY CALLING ME A NO-GOOD, WORTHLESS PEZZO DI MERDA.
....
UM, YOU N... NO...
BLANCH
KTUNK
BLEAAARGH
PSHHHH
ARE YOU OKAY?
PSHHH
YES, SIR...

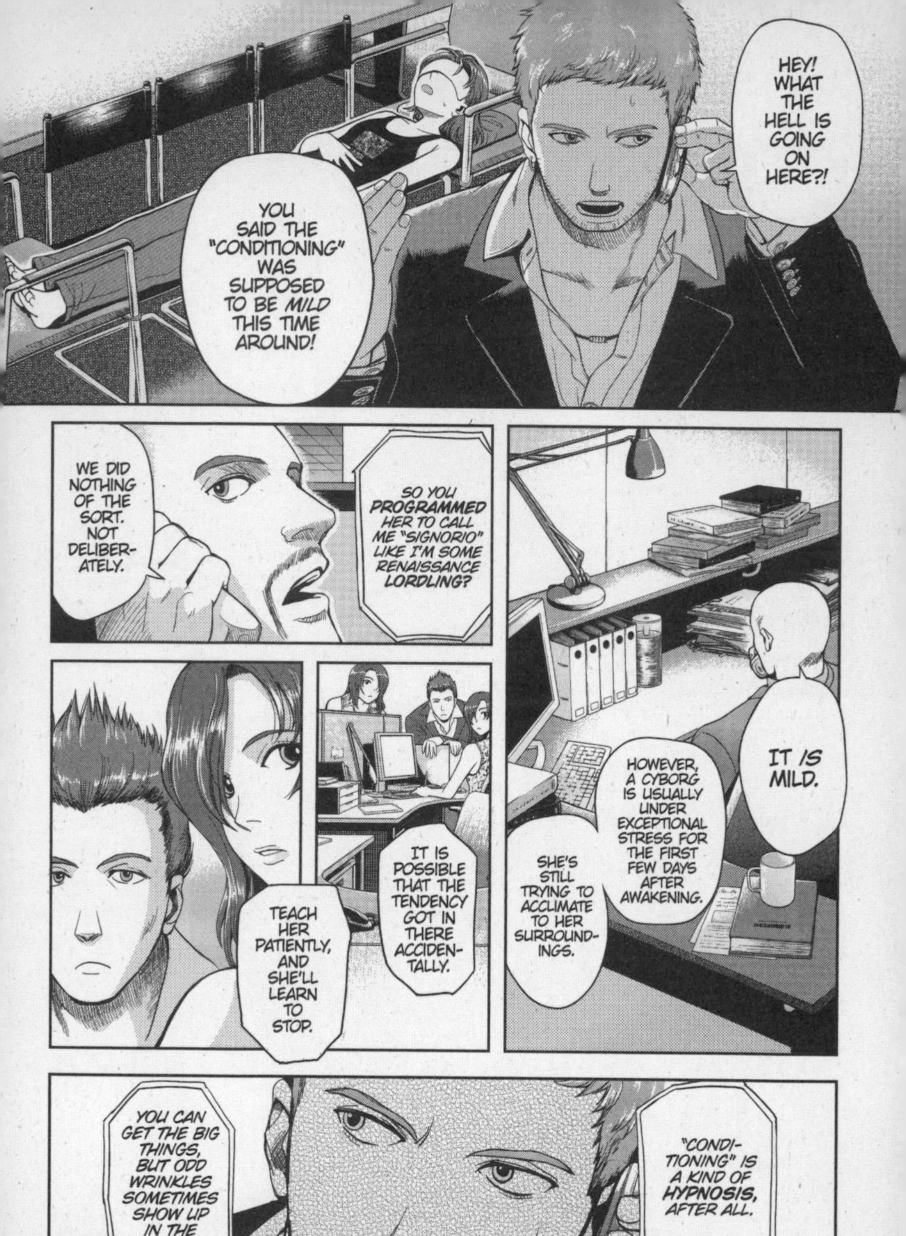
HEY! WHAT THE HELL IS GOING ON HERE?!
YOU SAID THE "CONDITIONING" WAS SUPPOSED TO BE MILD THIS TIME AROUND!
IT IS MILD.
HOWEVER, A CYBORG IS USUALLY UNDER EXCEPTIONAL STRESS FOR THE FIRST FEW DAYS AFTER AWAKENING.
SHE'S STILL TRYING TO ACCLIMATE TO HER SURROUND-INGS.
SO YOU PROGRAMMED HER TO CALL ME "SIGNORIO" LIKE I'M SOME RENAISSANCE LORDLING?
WE DID NOTHING OF THE SORT. NOT DELIBER-ATELY.
IT IS POSSIBLE THAT THE TENDENCY GOT IN THERE ACCIDEN-TALLY.
TEACH HER PATIENTLY, AND SHE'LL LEARN TO STOP.
"CONDI-TIONING" IS A KIND OF HYPNOSIS, AFTER ALL.
YOU CAN GET THE BIG THINGS, BUT ODD WRINKLES SOMETIMES SHOW UP IN THE DETAILS.

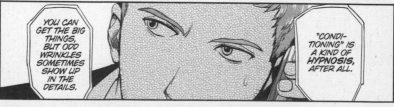

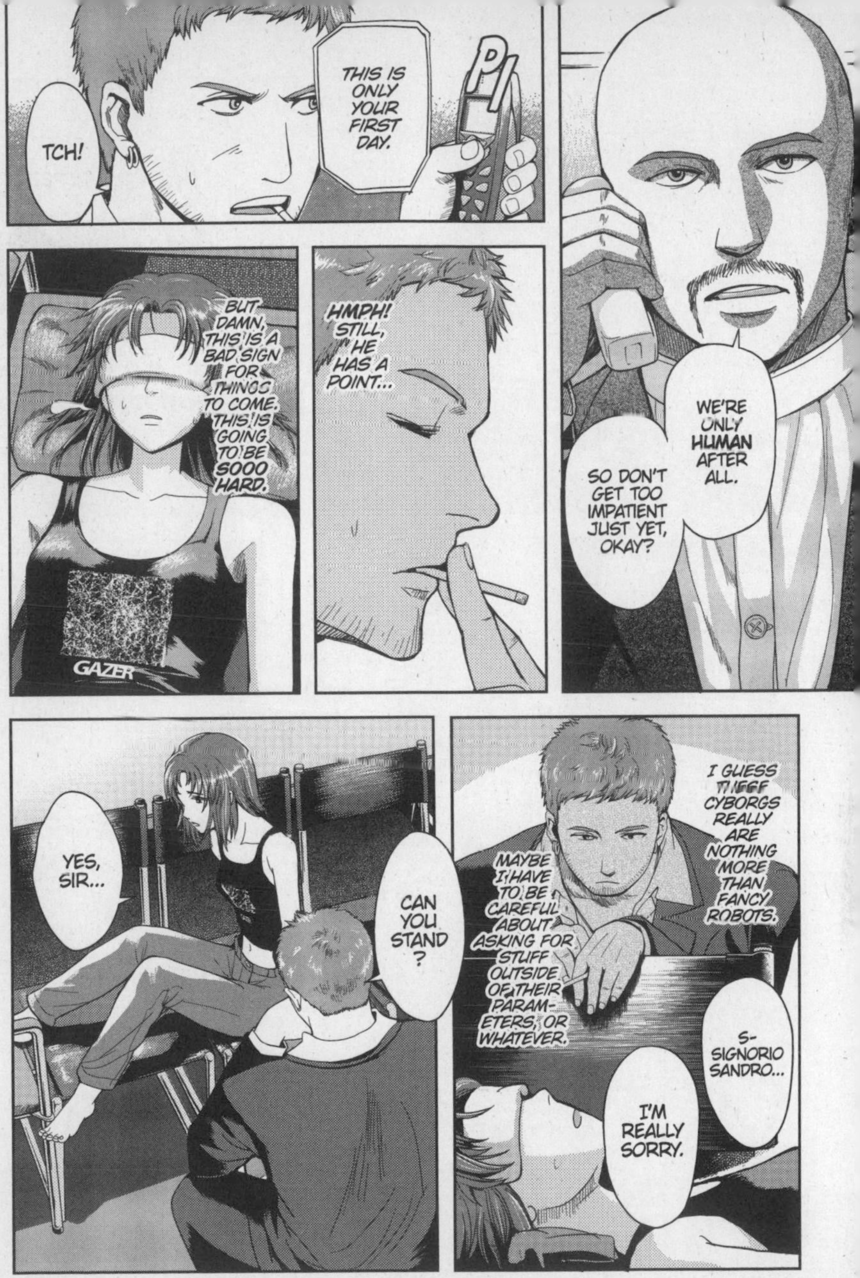
WE'RE ONLY HUMAN AFTER ALL.
SO DON'T GET TOO IMPATIENT JUST YET, OKAY?
P!
THIS IS ONLY YOUR FIRST DAY.
TCH!
HMPH! STILL, HE HAS A POINT...
BUT DAMN, THIS IS A BAD SIGN FOR THINGS TO COME. THIS IS GOING TO BE SOOO HARD.
GAZER
I GUESS THESE CYBORGS REALLY ARE NOTHING MORE THAN FANCY ROBOTS.
MAYBE I HAVE TO BE CAREFUL ABOUT ASKING FOR STUFF OUTSIDE OF THEIR PARAMETERS, OR WHATEVER.
S-SIGNORIO SANDRO...
I'M REALLY SORRY.
CAN YOU STAND?
YES, SIR...

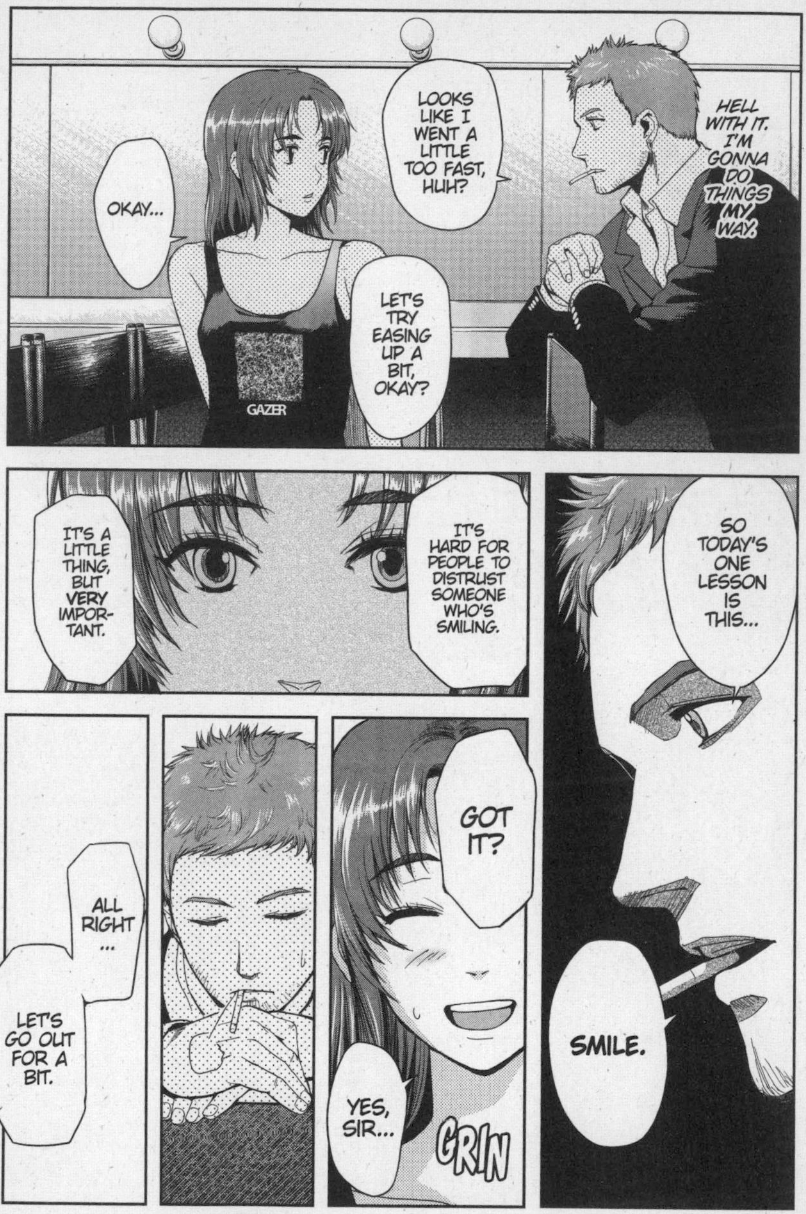
HELL WITH IT. I'M GONNA DO THINGS MY WAY.
LOOKS LIKE I WENT A LITTLE TOO FAST, HUH?
LET'S TRY EASING UP A BIT, OKAY?
OKAY...
GAZER
SO TODAY'S ONE LESSON IS THIS...
SMILE.
IT'S HARD FOR PEOPLE TO DISTRUST SOMEONE WHO'S SMILING.
IT'S A LITTLE THING, BUT VERY IMPORTANT.
GOT IT?
YES, SIR...
GRIN
ALL RIGHT...
LET'S GO OUT FOR A BIT.

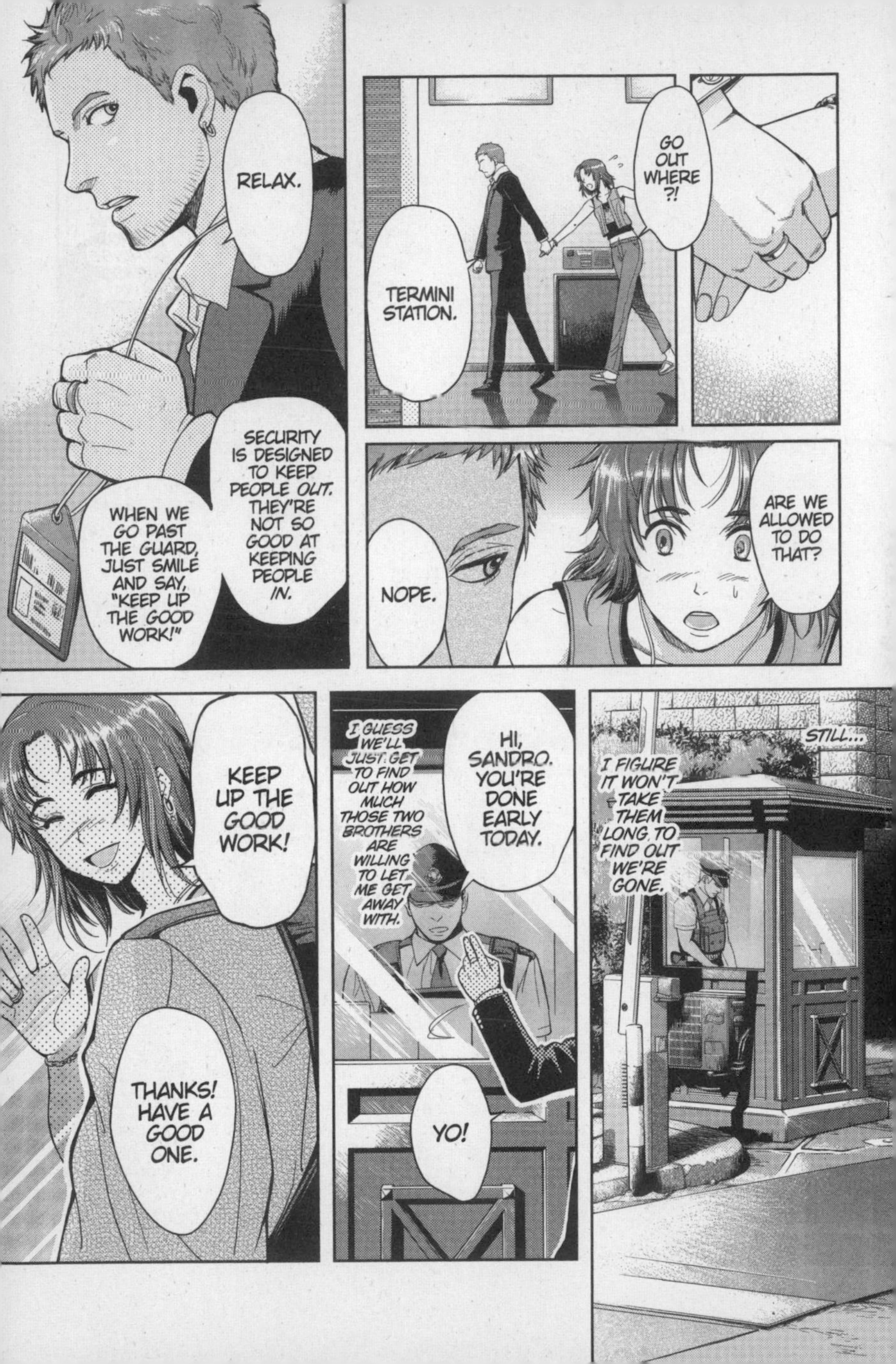
GO OUT WHERE?!
TERMINI STATION.
ARE WE ALLOWED TO DO THAT?
NOPE.
RELAX.
SECURITY IS DESIGNED TO KEEP PEOPLE OUT. THEY'RE NOT SO GOOD AT KEEPING PEOPLE IN.
WHEN WE GO PAST THE GUARD, JUST SMILE AND SAY, "KEEP UP THE GOOD WORK!"
STILL...
I FIGURE IT WON'T TAKE THEM LONG TO FIND OUT WE'RE GONE.
HI, SANDRO. YOU'RE DONE EARLY TODAY.
I GUESS WE'LL JUST GET TO FIND OUT HOW MUCH THOSE TWO BROTHERS ARE WILLING TO LET ME GET AWAY WITH.
YO!
KEEP UP THE GOOD WORK!
THANKS! HAVE A GOOD ONE.

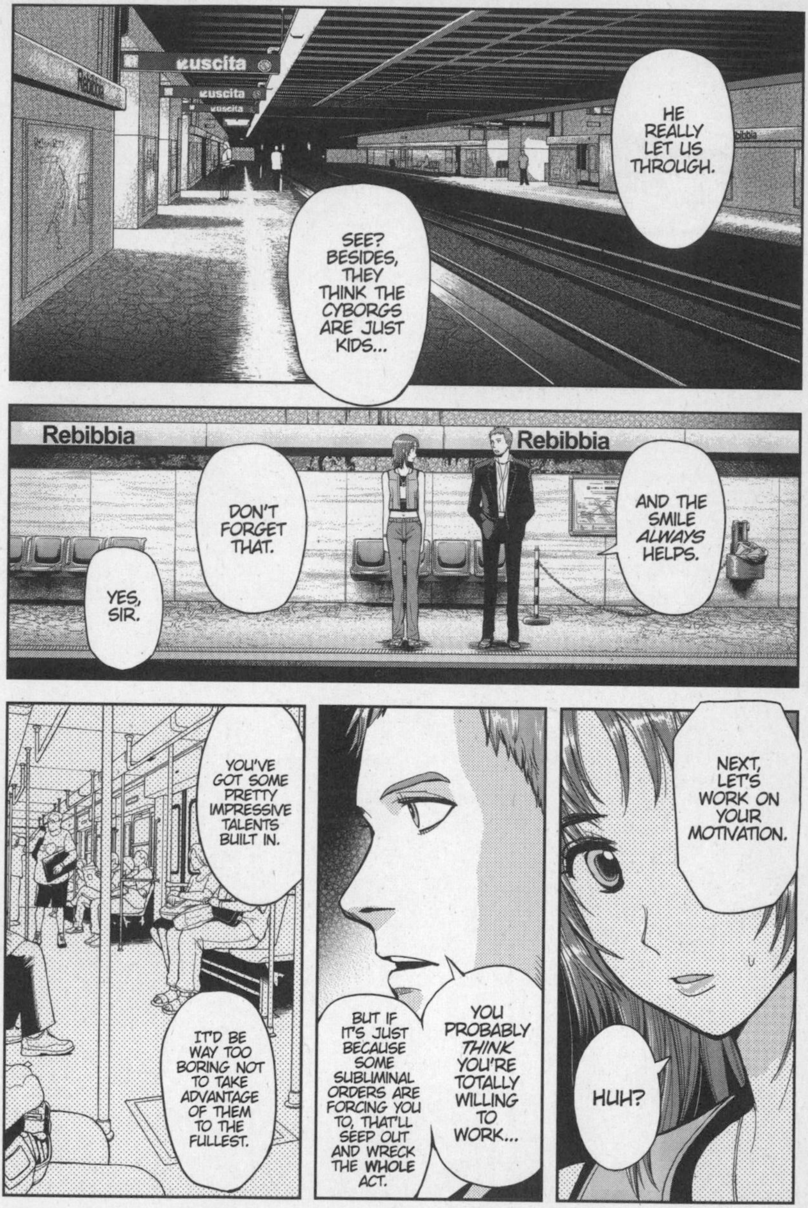
uscita
uscita
uscita
Rebibbia
HE REALLY LET US THROUGH.
SEE? BESIDES, THEY THINK THE CYBORGS ARE JUST KIDS...
Rebibbia
Rebibbia
AND THE SMILE *ALWAYS* HELPS.
DON'T FORGET THAT.
YES, SIR.
NEXT, LET'S WORK ON YOUR MOTIVATION.
HUH?
YOU PROBABLY *THINK* YOU'RE TOTALLY WILLING TO WORK...
BUT IF IT'S JUST BECAUSE SOME SUBLIMINAL ORDERS ARE FORCING YOU TO, THAT'LL SEEP OUT AND WRECK THE WHOLE ACT.
YOU'VE GOT SOME PRETTY IMPRESSIVE TALENTS BUILT IN.
IT'D BE WAY TOO BORING NOT TO TAKE ADVANTAGE OF THEM TO THE FULLEST.

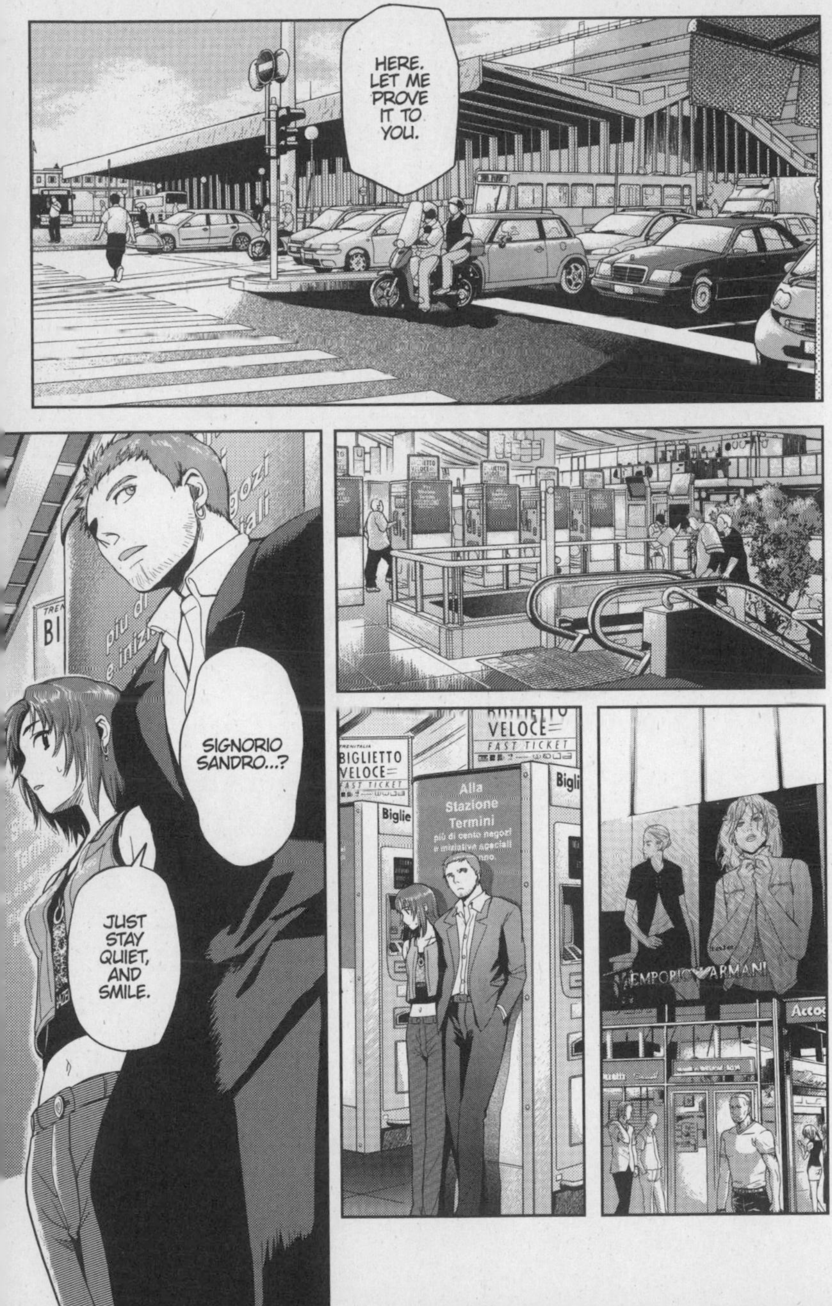
HERE. LET ME PROVE IT TO YOU.
EMPORIO ARMANI
BIGLIETTO VELOCE
FAST TICKET
TRENITALIA
BIGLIETTO VELOCE
FAST TICKET
Alla Stazione Termini
SIGNORIO SANDRO...?
JUST STAY QUIET, AND SMILE.

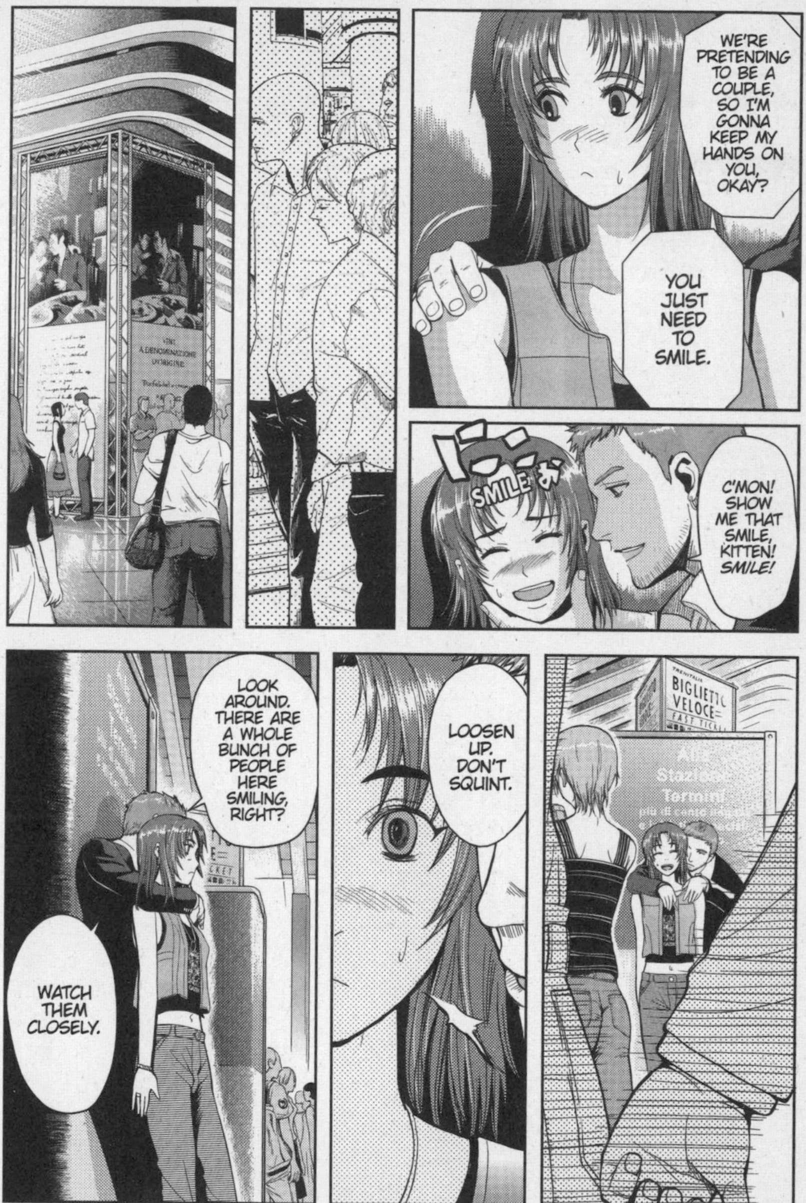
WE'RE PRETENDING TO BE A COUPLE, SO I'M GONNA KEEP MY HANDS ON YOU, OKAY?
YOU JUST NEED TO SMILE.
C'MON! SHOW ME THAT SMILE, KITTEN! SMILE!
SMILE
LOOSEN UP. DON'T SQUINT.
LOOK AROUND. THERE ARE A WHOLE BUNCH OF PEOPLE HERE SMILING, RIGHT?
WATCH THEM CLOSELY.

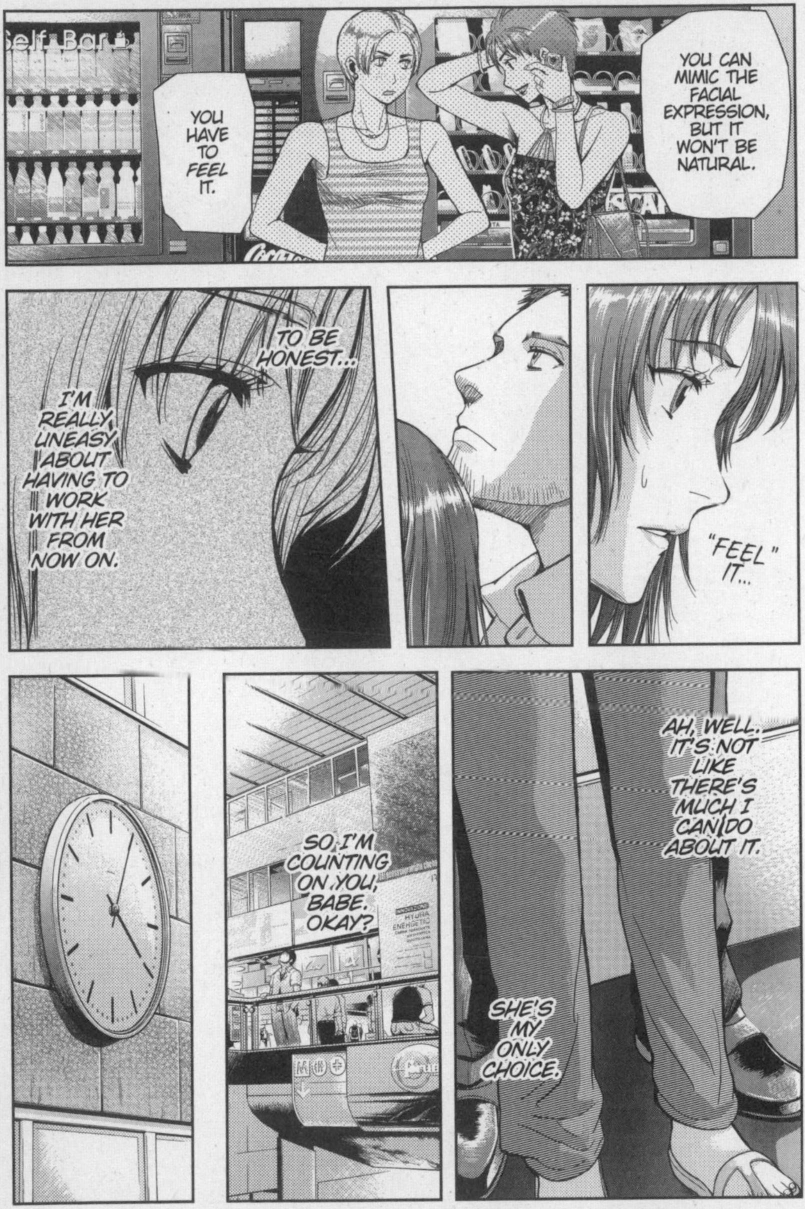
YOU CAN MIMIC THE FACIAL EXPRESSION, BUT IT WON'T BE NATURAL.
YOU HAVE TO FEEL IT.
Self Bar
"FEEL" IT...
TO BE HONEST...
I'M REALLY UNEASY ABOUT HAVING TO WORK WITH HER FROM NOW ON.
AH, WELL. IT'S NOT LIKE THERE'S MUCH I CAN DO ABOUT IT.
SHE'S MY ONLY CHOICE.
SO I'M COUNTING ON YOU, BABE. OKAY?

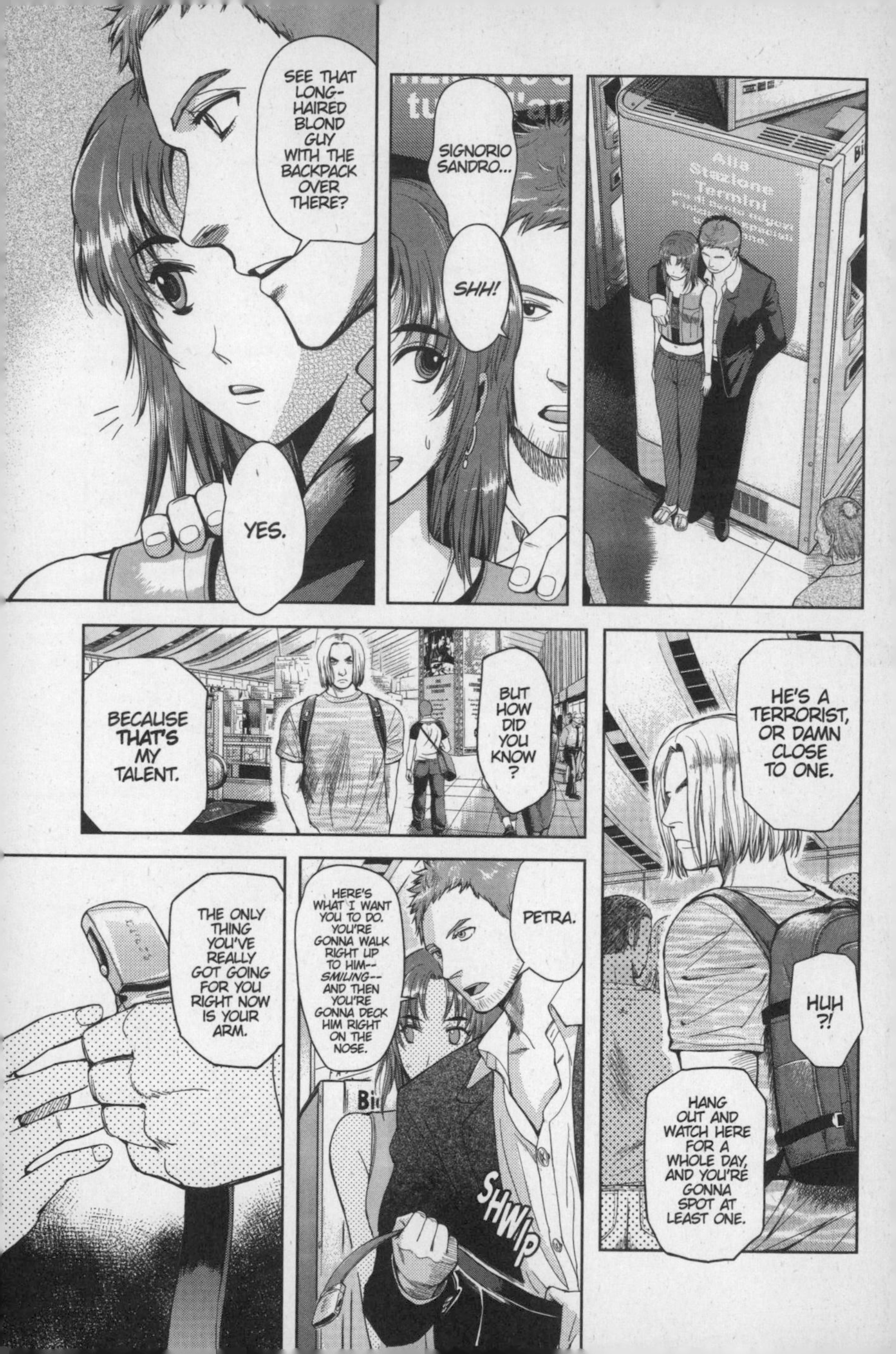

Alla Stazione Termini
SIGNORIO SANDRO...
SHH!
SEE THAT LONG-HAIRED BLOND GUY WITH THE BACKPACK OVER THERE?
YES.
HE'S A TERRORIST, OR DAMN CLOSE TO ONE.
HUH?!
HANG OUT AND WATCH HERE FOR A WHOLE DAY, AND YOU'RE GONNA SPOT AT LEAST ONE.
BUT HOW DID YOU KNOW?
BECAUSE THAT'S MY TALENT.
PETRA.
HERE'S WHAT I WANT YOU TO DO. YOU'RE GONNA WALK RIGHT UP TO HIM--SMILING--AND THEN YOU'RE GONNA DECK HIM RIGHT ON THE NOSE.
SHWIP
THE ONLY THING YOU'VE REALLY GOT GOING FOR YOU RIGHT NOW IS YOUR ARM.

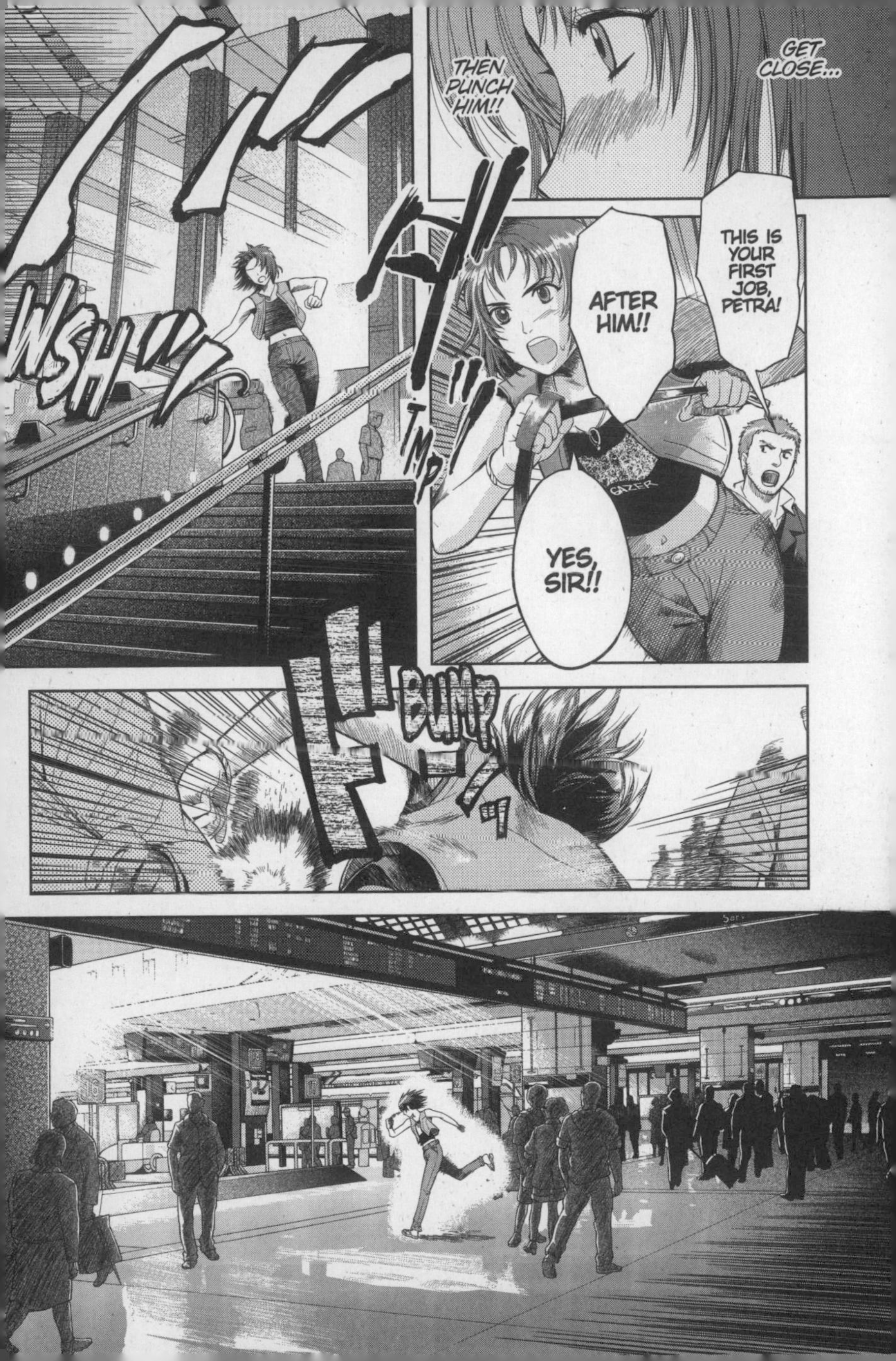

GET CLOSE...
THEN PUNCH HIM!!
THIS IS YOUR FIRST JOB, PETRA!
AFTER HIM!!
YES, SIR!!
GAZER
WSH
TMP
BUMP

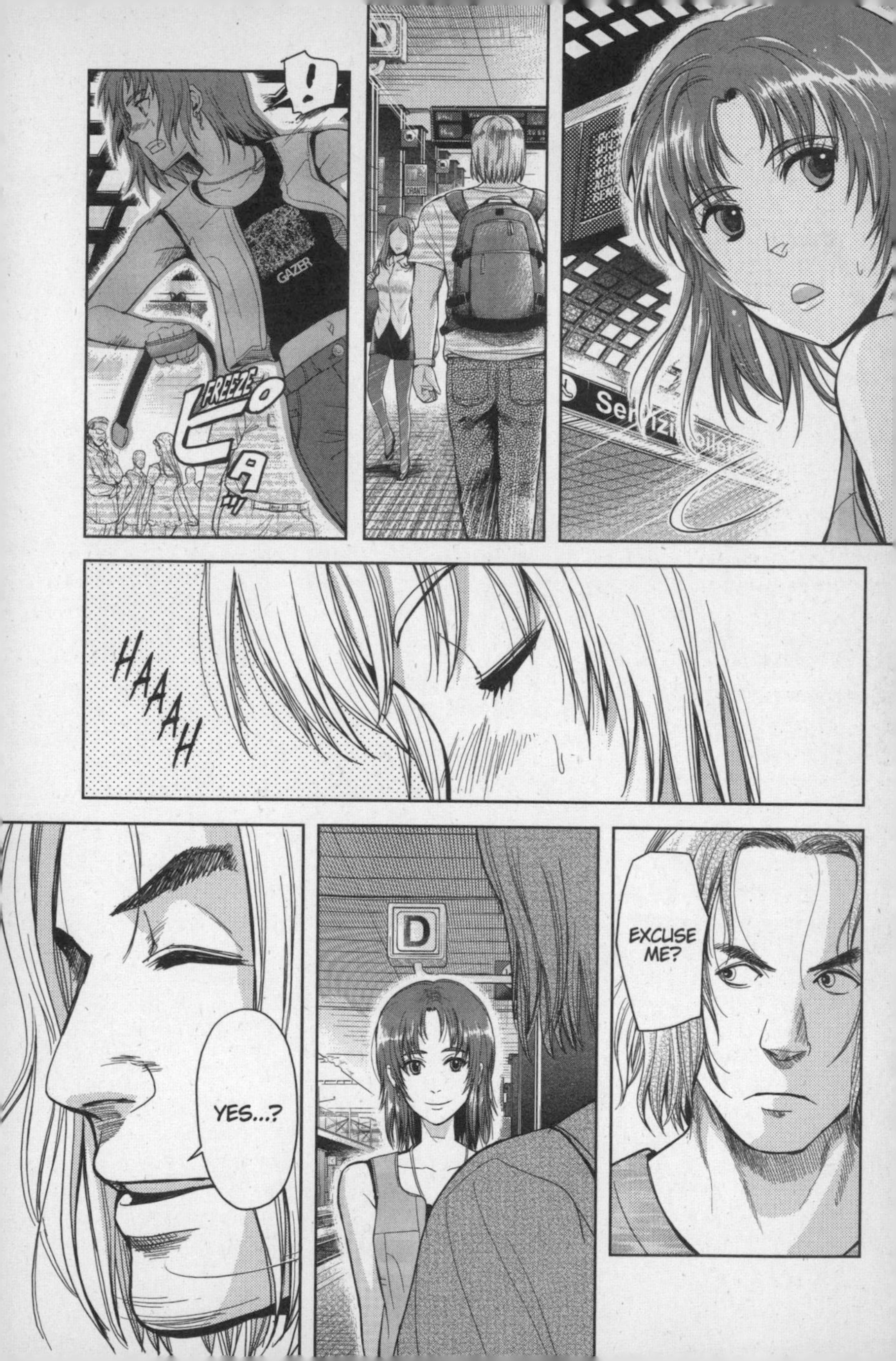

!
GAZER
FREEZE
HAAAAH
EXCUSE ME?
D
YES...?

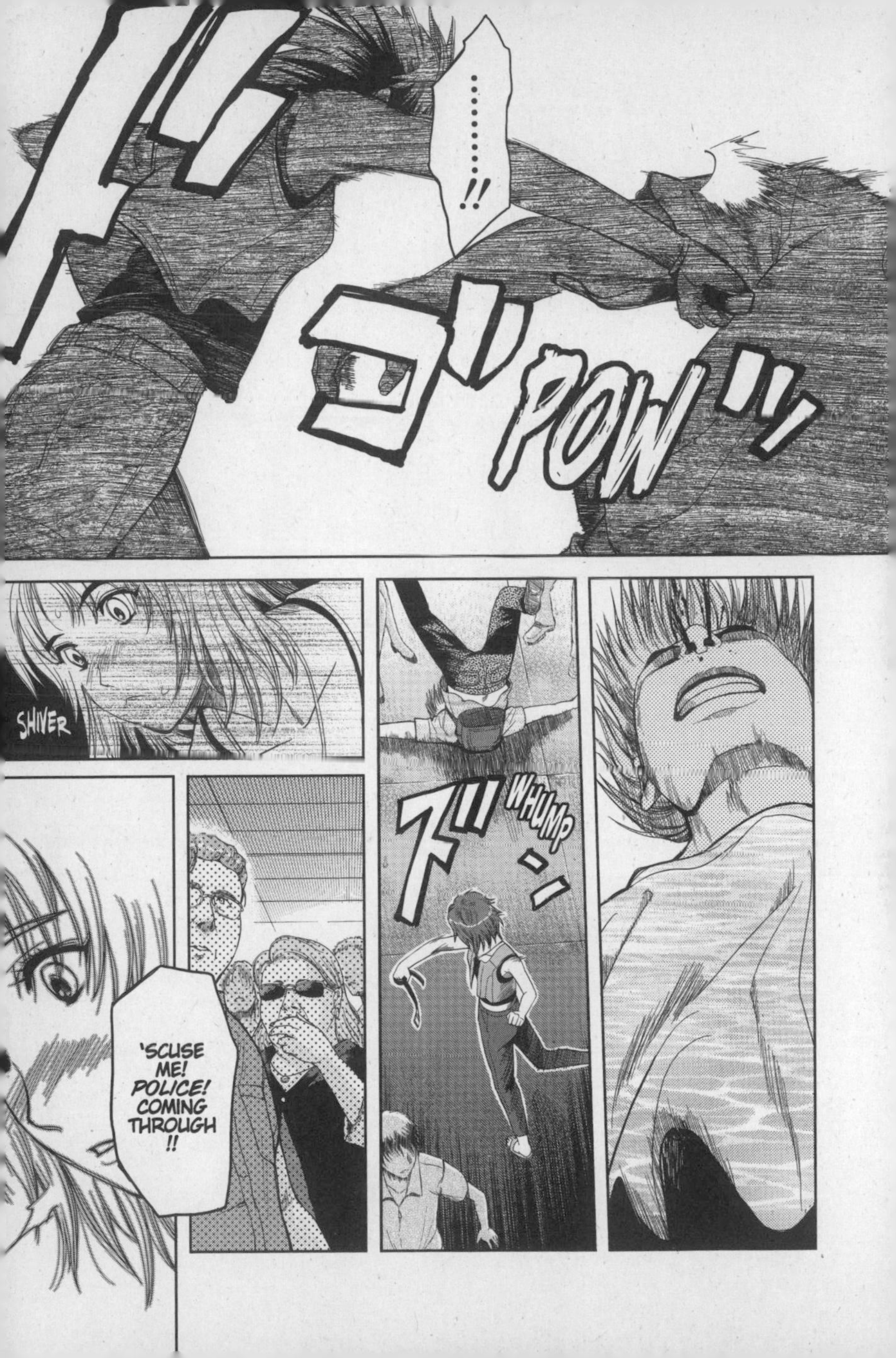
......!!
POW
WHUMP
SHIVER
'SCUSE ME! POLICE! COMING THROUGH !!

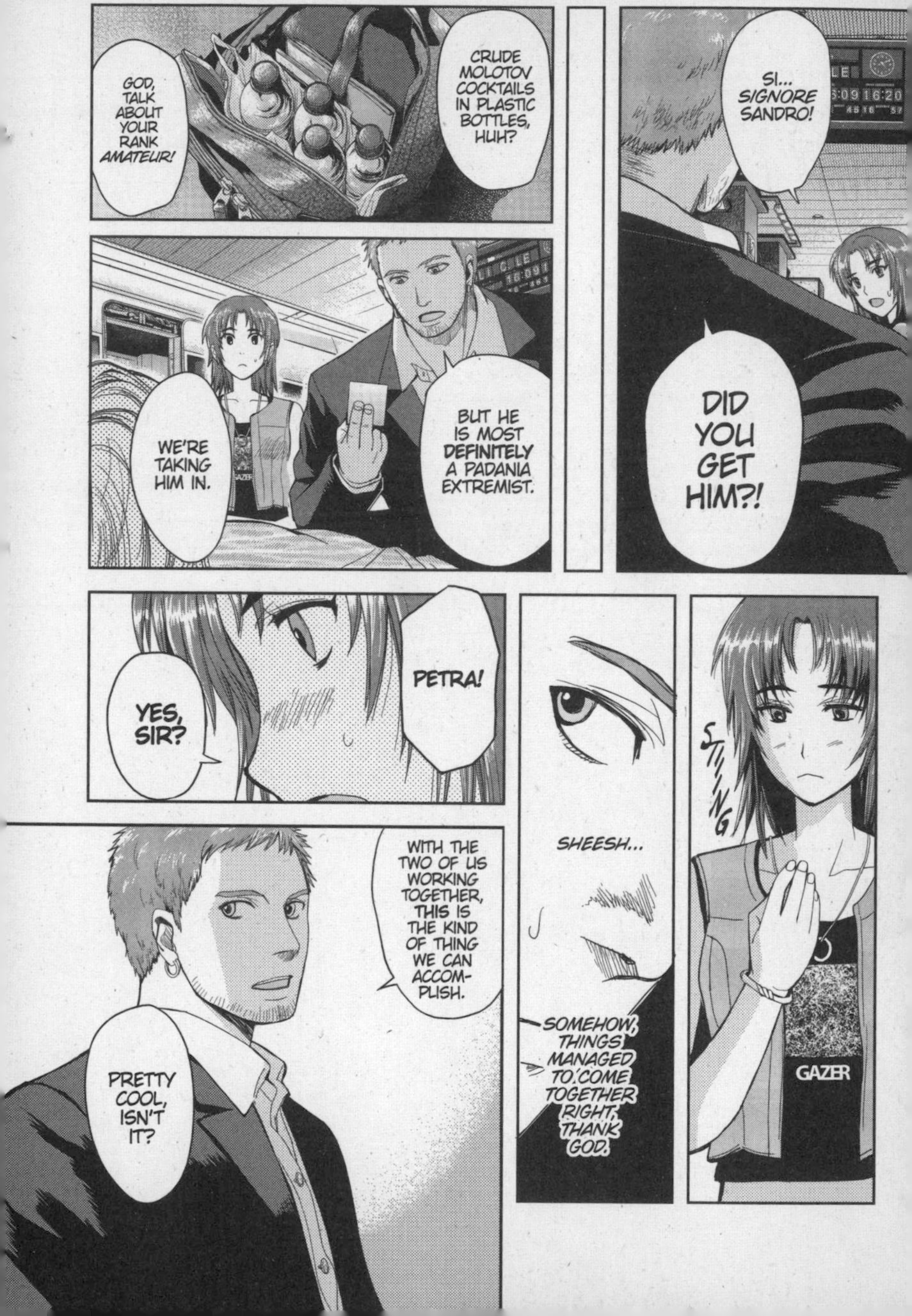
SI... SIGNORE SANDRO!
DID YOU GET HIM?!
CRUDE MOLOTOV COCKTAILS IN PLASTIC BOTTLES, HUH?
GOD, TALK ABOUT YOUR RANK AMATEUR!
BUT HE IS MOST DEFINITELY A PADANIA EXTREMIST.
WE'RE TAKING HIM IN.
STIIING
GAZER
SHEESH...
SOMEHOW, THINGS MANAGED TO COME TOGETHER RIGHT, THANK GOD.
PETRA!
YES, SIR?
WITH THE TWO OF US WORKING TOGETHER, THIS IS THE KIND OF THING WE CAN ACCOMPLISH.
PRETTY COOL, ISN'T IT?

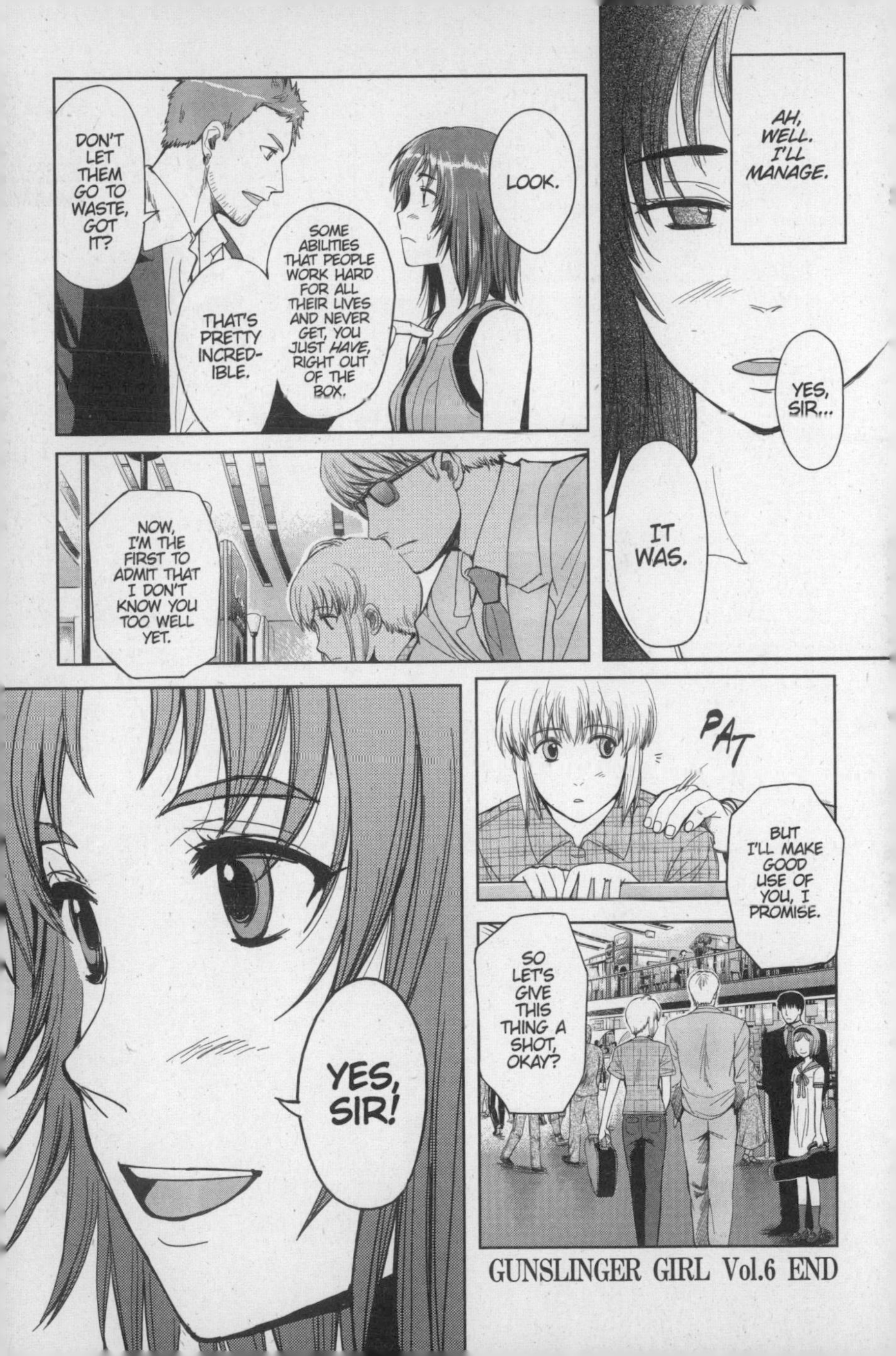
AH, WELL. I'LL MANAGE.
YES, SIR...
IT WAS.
LOOK.
SOME ABILITIES THAT PEOPLE WORK HARD FOR ALL THEIR LIVES AND NEVER GET, YOU JUST *HAVE*, RIGHT OUT OF THE BOX.
THAT'S PRETTY INCREDIBLE.
DON'T LET THEM GO TO WASTE, GOT IT?
NOW, I'M THE FIRST TO ADMIT THAT I DON'T KNOW YOU TOO WELL YET.
PAT
BUT I'LL MAKE GOOD USE OF YOU, I PROMISE.
SO LET'S GIVE THIS THING A SHOT, OKAY?
YES, SIR!

GUNSLINGER GIRL Vol.6 END

GUNSLINGER GIRL vol.6

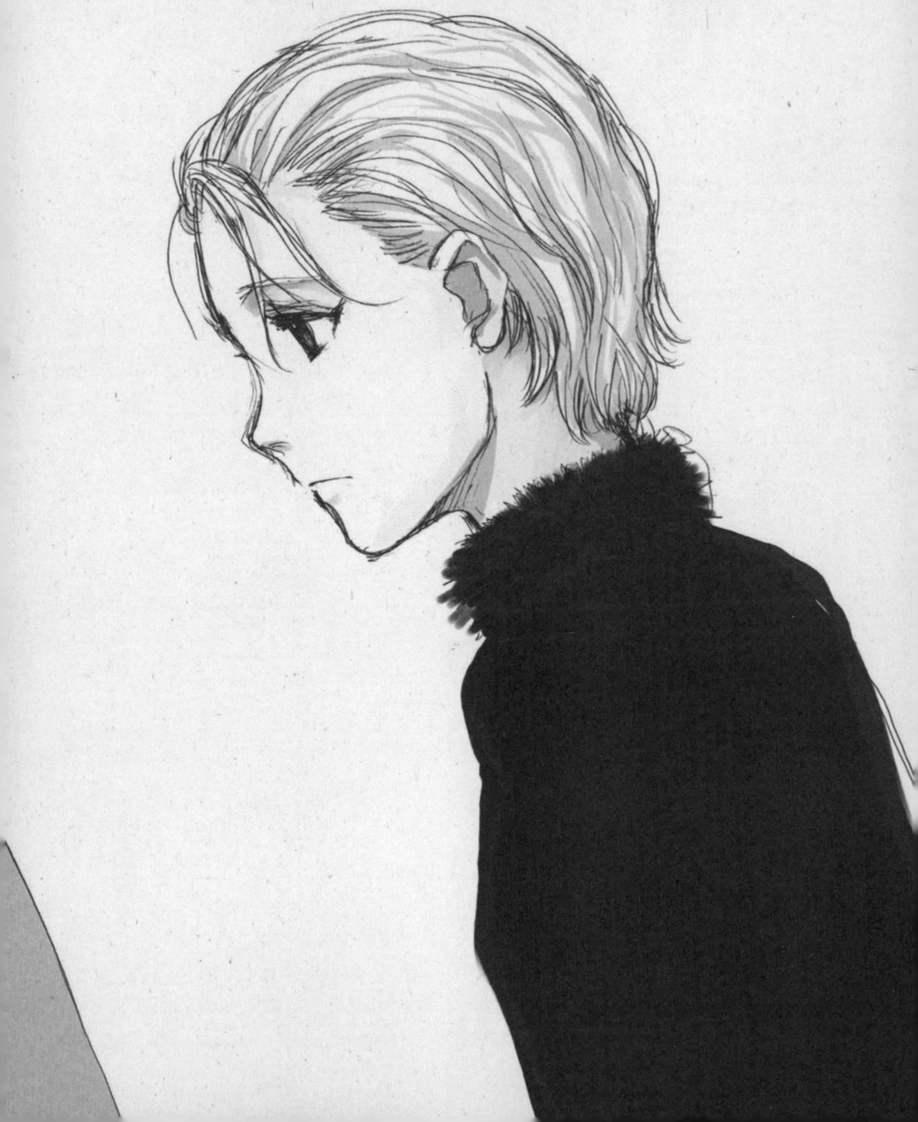

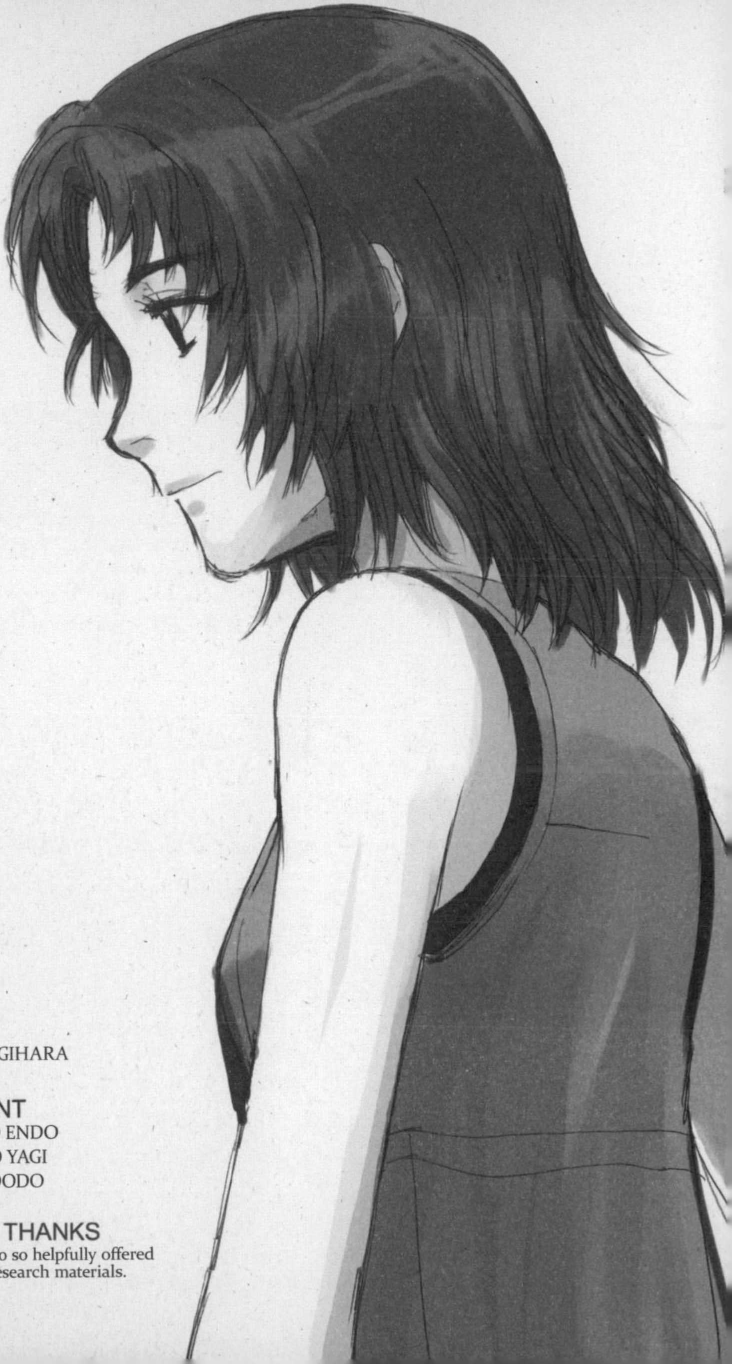

EDITOR
CHIAKI SUGIHARA

ASSISTANT
TAKAHIRO ENDO
JUNICHIRO YAGI
DAISUKE DODO

SPECIAL THANKS
Everyone who so helpfully offered
advice and research materials.

TRANSLATION NOTES

CHAPTER 18
GIS stands for *Gruppo di Intervento Speciale* (or "Special Intervention Group" in English). Along with NOCS, the GIS is an elite tactical response unit of the Carabinieri that specializes in high-risk operations. While NOCS is restricted to working only inside Italy, the GIS has conducted international operations.

CHAPTER 19
Niccolo Machiavelli (1469-1527) was an Italian philosopher during the Renaissance. He is most well-known for his treatise on politics, "The Prince," which outlines a very cynical approach to the exercise of power and politics.

CHAPTER 20
"Tosca" is an Italian opera based off of a French play, which premiered in 1900. A tragedy set during Napoleon's invasion of Italy, it features many grisly scenes of torture, murder and suicide.

Princess Ann – Henrietta is referring to a scene in the 1953 American film *Roman Holiday*. Audrey Hepburn plays Princess Ann, who sneaks away from her official duties to enjoy some private time in Rome. Once there, she meets the reporter Joe, who gives her a tour. Along the way, they are spotted by Ann's guards near Castel Sant'Angelo, who immediately try to detain Ann. She retaliates by smashing a guitar over one of their heads, and both she and Joe jump into the river to swim away.

CHAPTER 21
A barzelletta is a type of short comical verse, much like a limerick. The Carabinieri is a popular topic of ridicule in barzellettas. The one Jose's sister is referring to was actually told to the press by Berlusconi, Italy's Prime Minister, and involves a Carabiniere bringing a lost penguin to the office instead of taking it to the zoo where it belongs.

The Hermes 450 is an unmanned military aircraft designed for long-distance reconnaissance and surveillance missions.

Salsiccia is a type of pork sausage that isn't smoked or cured.

CHAPTER 24
"Padrona" roughly translates as "lady" or "boss." In this case, Dominico and Paola address Franca as their employer and the land owner, but also as the "young lady" of the family which has employed them their entire life. It is a title that implies a relationship between a superior and an inferior.

Roads – In Europe, the roads that loop around metropolitan centers, which Americans generally refer to as a "bypass" or "beltway", are called a "ring road."

CHAPTER 25
"Bouncing Betty" is the nickname coined by the U.S. for the German S-mine, a particularly nasty anti-personnel landmine. Used extensively by Germany during World War II, it gets its name because when triggered, it first bounces up approximately 3 feet before exploding.

CHAPTER 26

Portrait – The famous portrait by Fra Bartolomeo is of Girolamo Savonarola, a Dominican friar known for his preaching against immoral art and literature, and against the wide-spread moral corruption of the clergy during the late 15th century. In particular, Savonarola rallied against the excesses of Rodrigo Borgia, who became Pope Alexander VI in 1492. Savonarola was excommunicated in 1497, and executed in 1498. It's no coincidence that Cristiano shares the same last name, as another "activist" against a central authority.

CHAPTER 30

Osteosarcoma is a form of bone cancer that tends to form at the end of long bones like the femur or tibia leg bones. It is the eighth most common form of cancer in children. It also comprises 20% of all cases of bone cancer.

"Petrushka" is a ballet by Russian composer Igor Stravinsky, composed in 1910-11. The story is about a traditional Russian puppet made of straw and sawdust who comes to life and develops emotions.

CHAPTER 31

"Swan Lake" is a ballet by Russian composer Pyotr Ilyich Tchaikovsky, composed in 1875-76. Based on Russian folk tales, it tells the story of Odette, a princess turned into a white swan by an evil sorcerer's curse. The curse can only be broken by a prince who stays faithful to her. The ballet is associated with the Bolshoi Ballet, as the current authoritative theory places the ballet as originally produced for the company, and it was the troupe that premiered the ballet. The main role of Odette and that of Odile, the black swan and sorcerer's daughter who attempts to seduce Prince Siegfried, is usually played by the same prima ballerina. However, in a school setting, it is usual to split the roles between two dancers, as the ballet is very strenuous.

A **"fouetté"** (more precisely, *fouetté rond de jambe en tournant*) is a ballet movement that involves the dancer making a quick spin in place on one leg, while on pointe. The "grand fouetté" that Liza is referring to is a famous section within "Swan Lake," where Odile the Black Swan does 32 continuous fouettés.

"ALP" is short for alkaline phosphatase, an enzyme responsible for removing phosphates from molecules. ALP levels can be an indicator of bone formation, and consequently, of the presence of bone cancer.

Height Conversions:
152 cm = 5'0"
185 cm = 6'1"
173 cm = 5'8"
154 cm = 5'1"
160 cm = 5'3"

CHAPTER 32

Signorio is an archaic address in Italian, similar to calling someone "Master Sandro," as opposed to "Mister Sandro" (Signor Sandro).

Pezzo di merda is Italian for "piece of shit."

GUNSLINGERGIRL

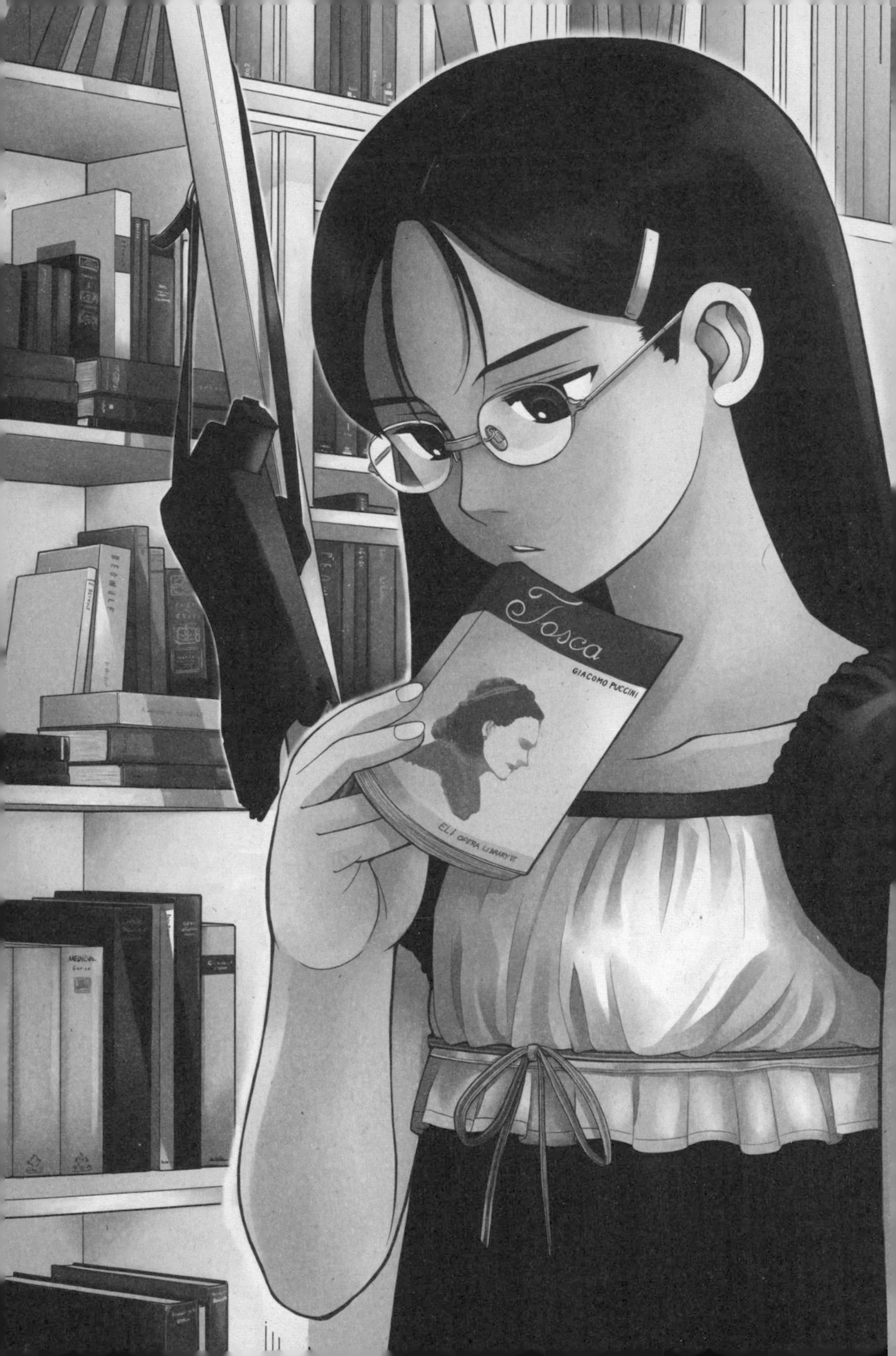
Tosca
GIACOMO PUCCINI
ELI OPERA LIBRARY VI

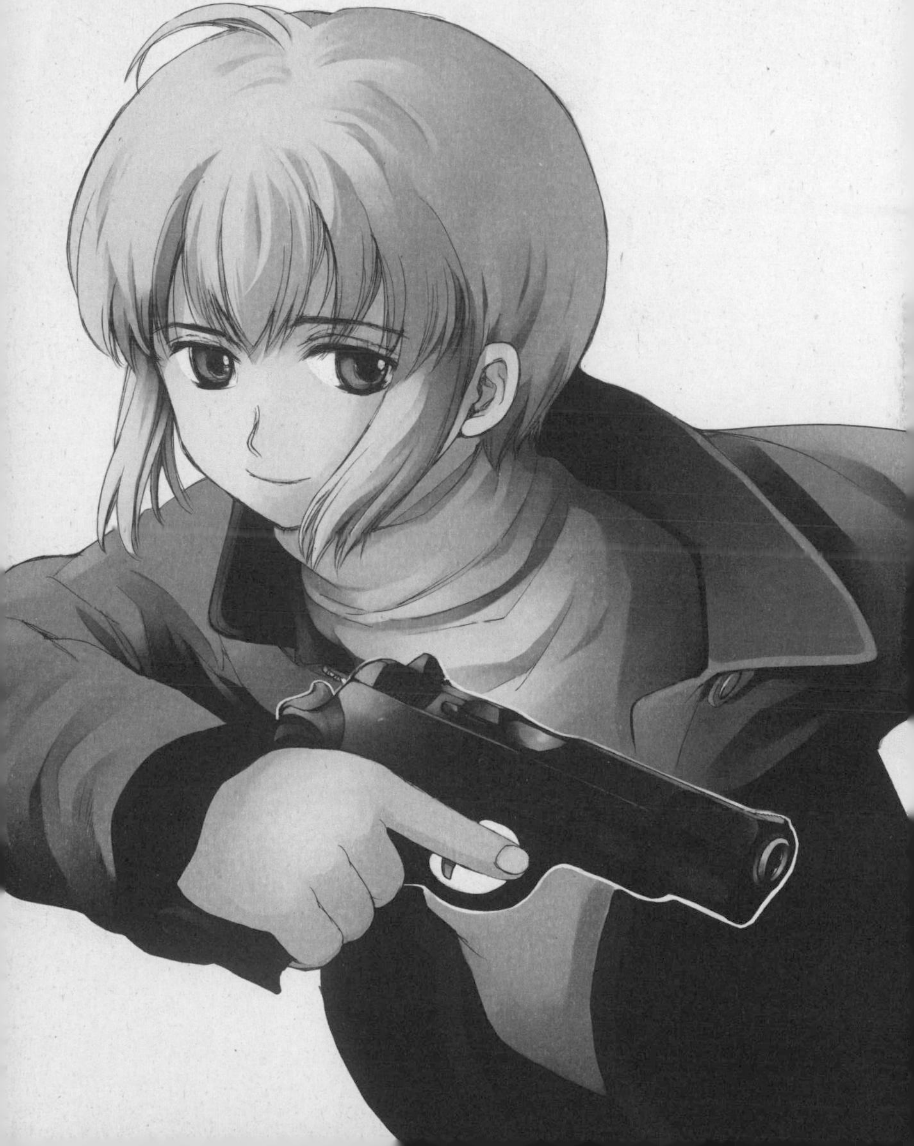

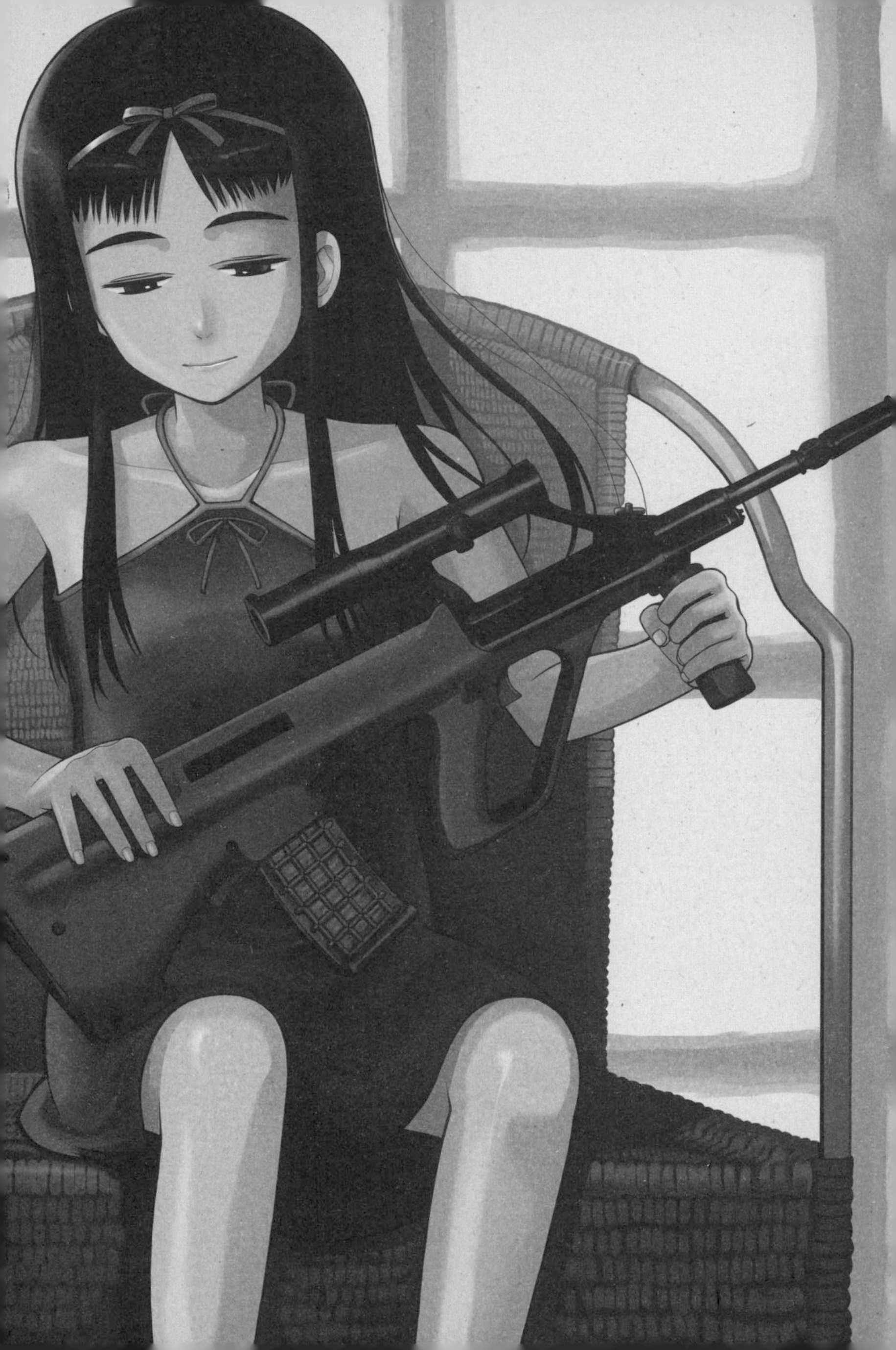

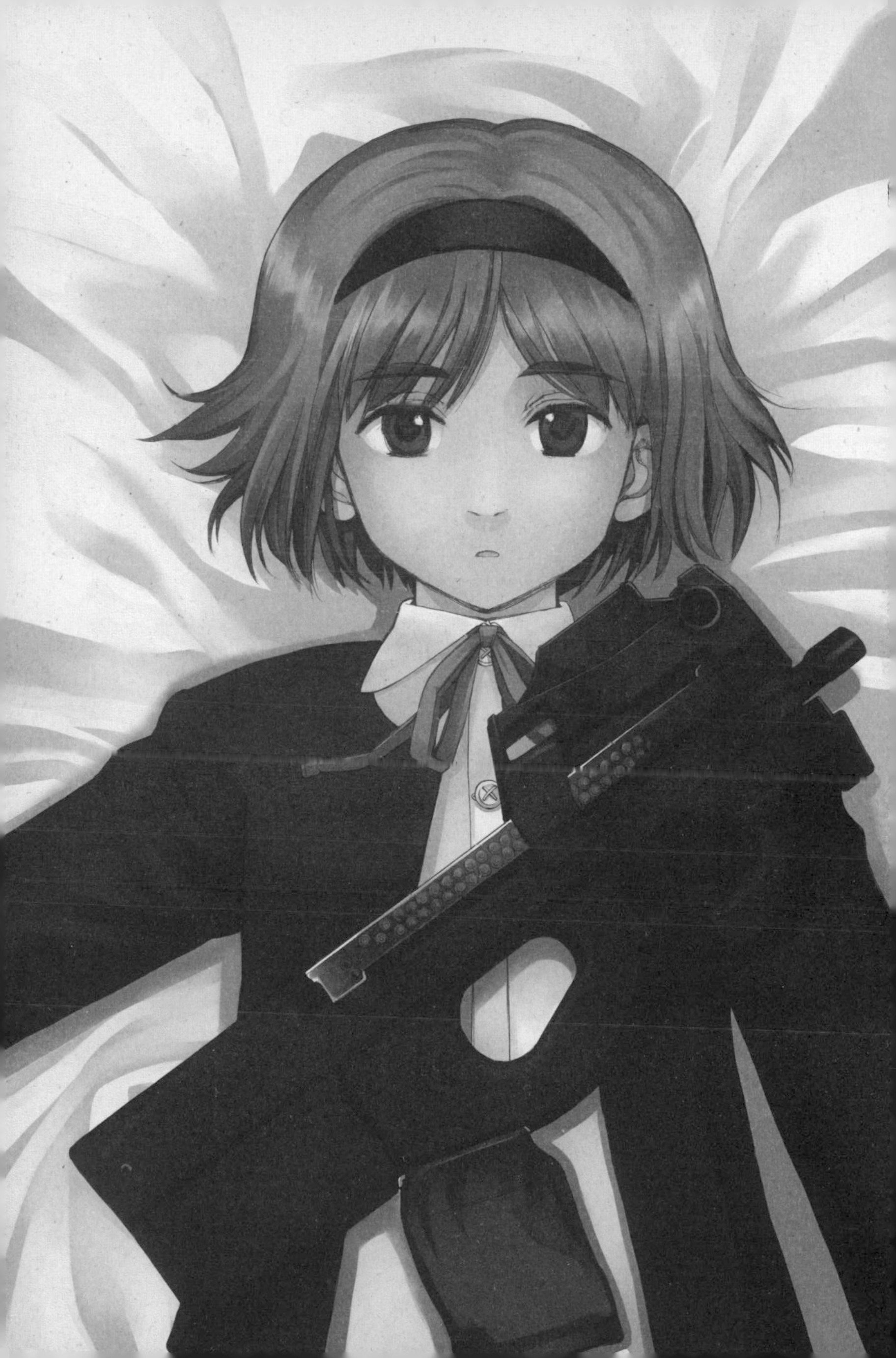

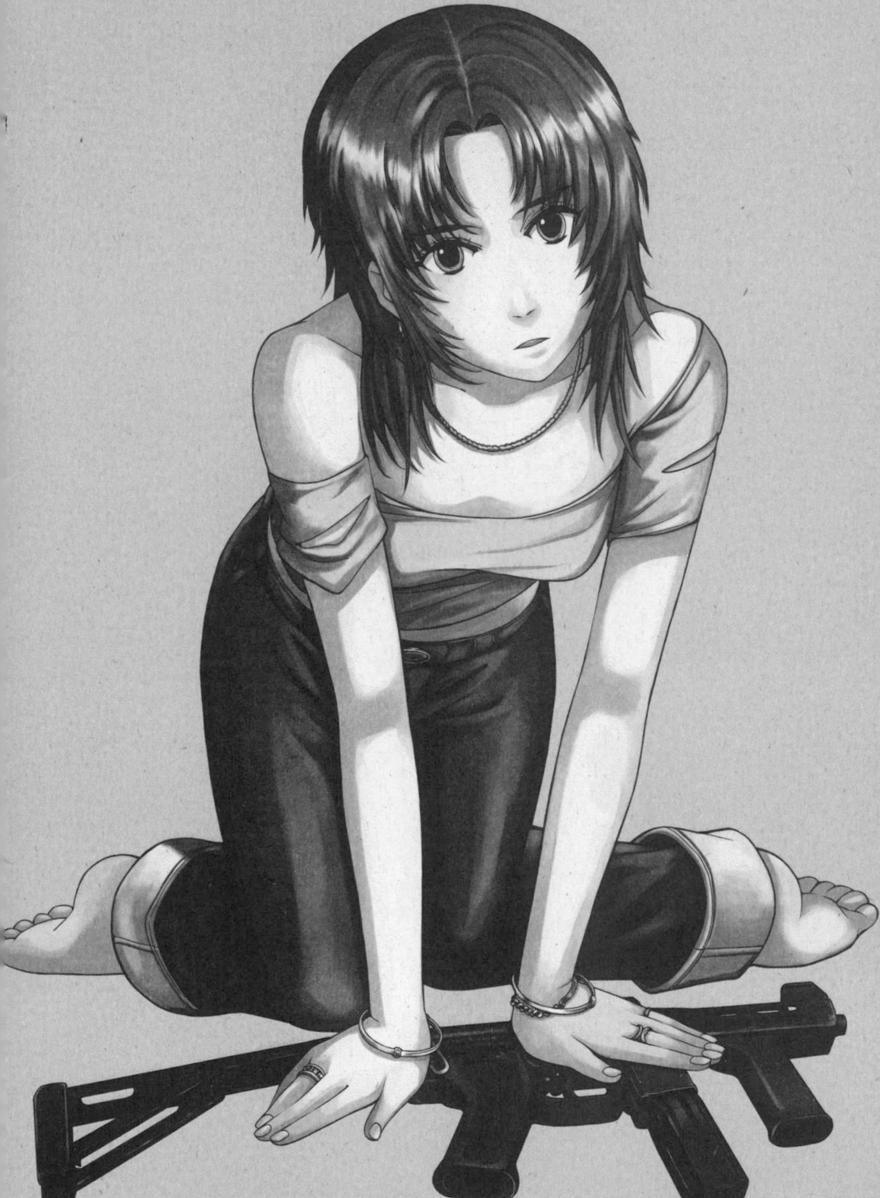

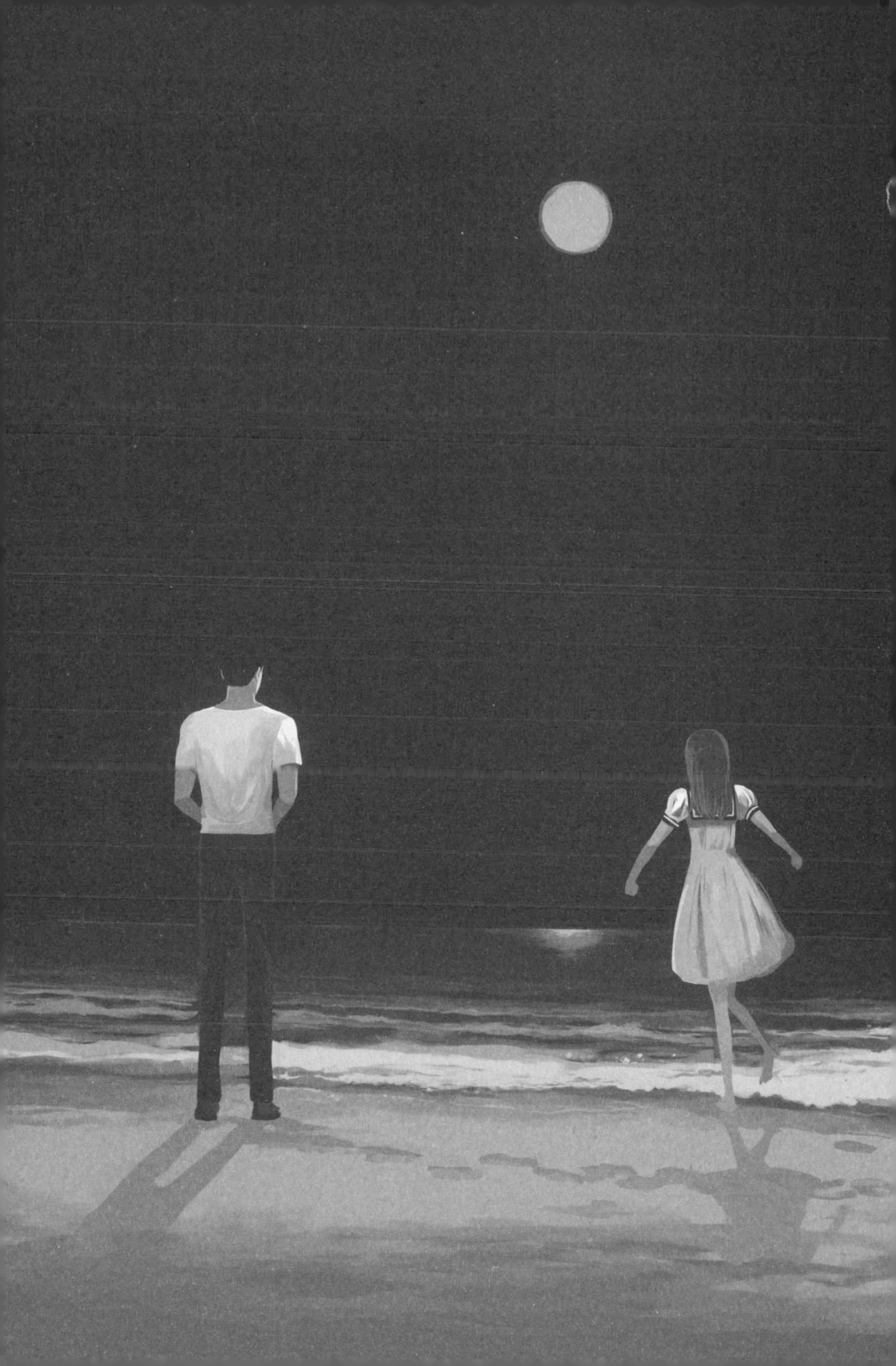

GUNSLINGER GIRL

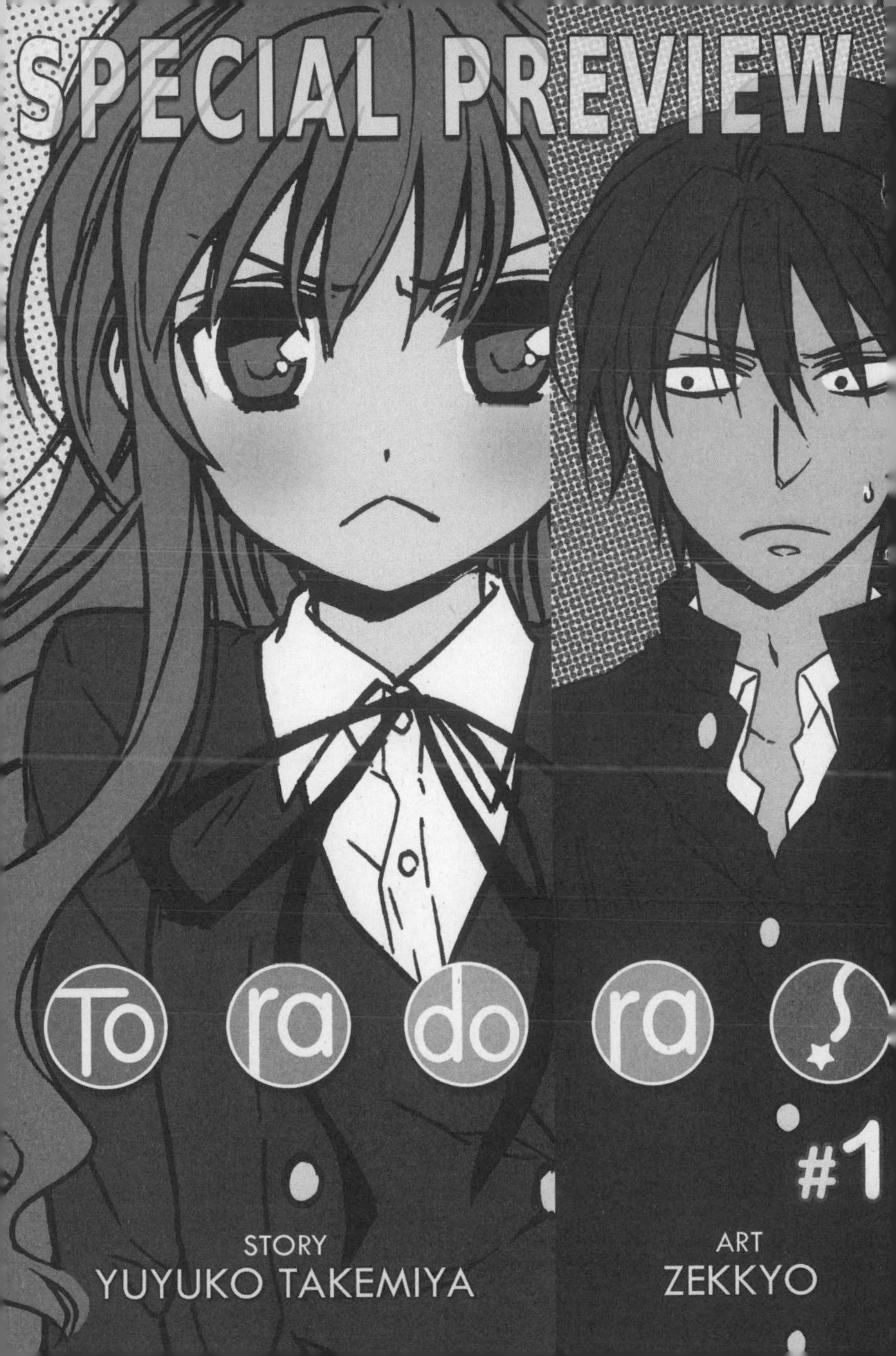
SPECIAL PREVIEW
To ra do ra!
#1
STORY
YUYUKO TAKEMIYA
ART
ZEKKYO

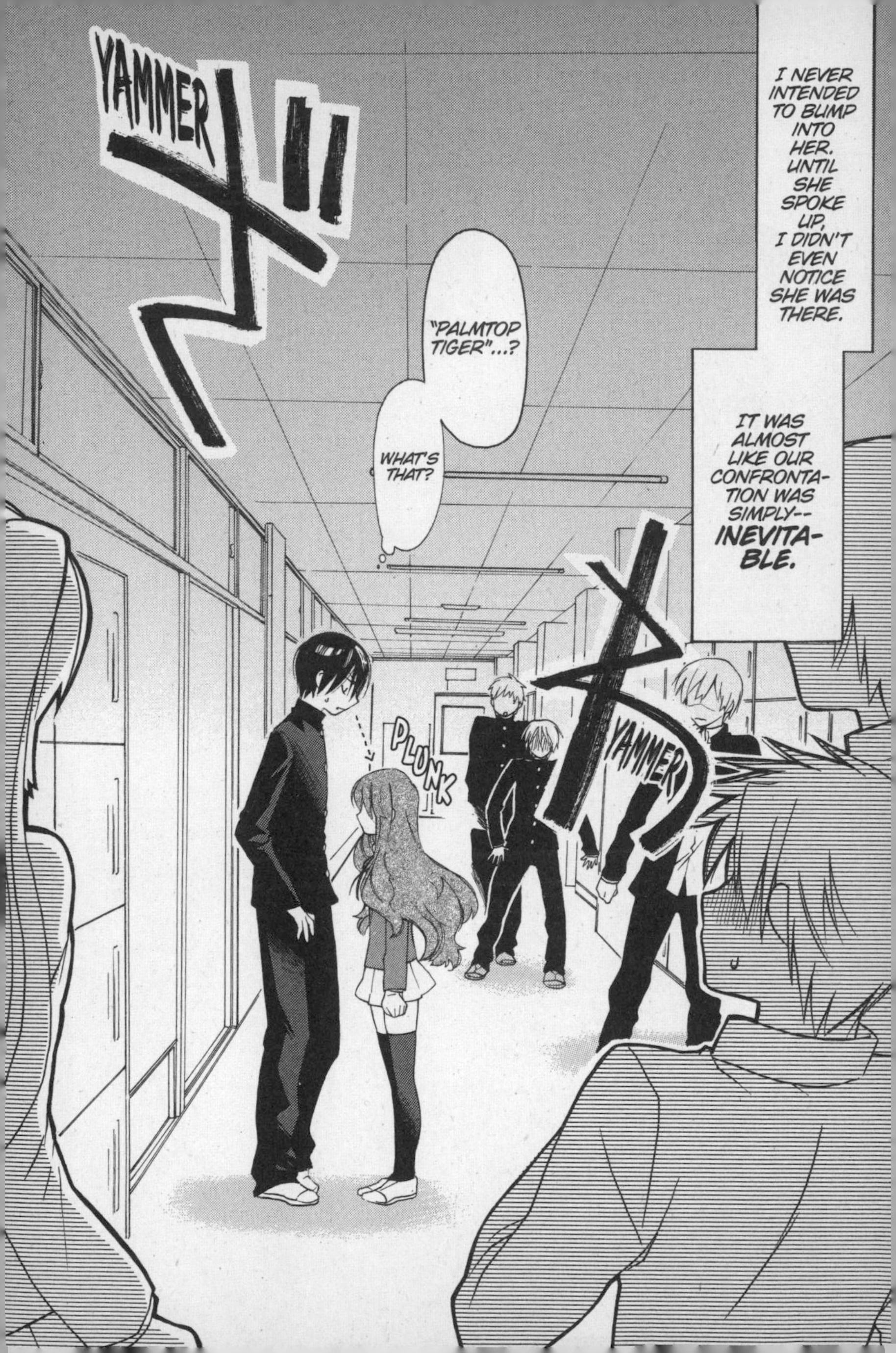
I NEVER INTENDED TO BUMP INTO HER. UNTIL SHE SPOKE UP, I DIDN'T EVEN NOTICE SHE WAS THERE.
YAMMER
"PALMTOP TIGER"...?
WHAT'S THAT?
IT WAS ALMOST LIKE OUR CONFRONTATION WAS SIMPLY-- INEVITABLE.
YAMMER
PLUNK

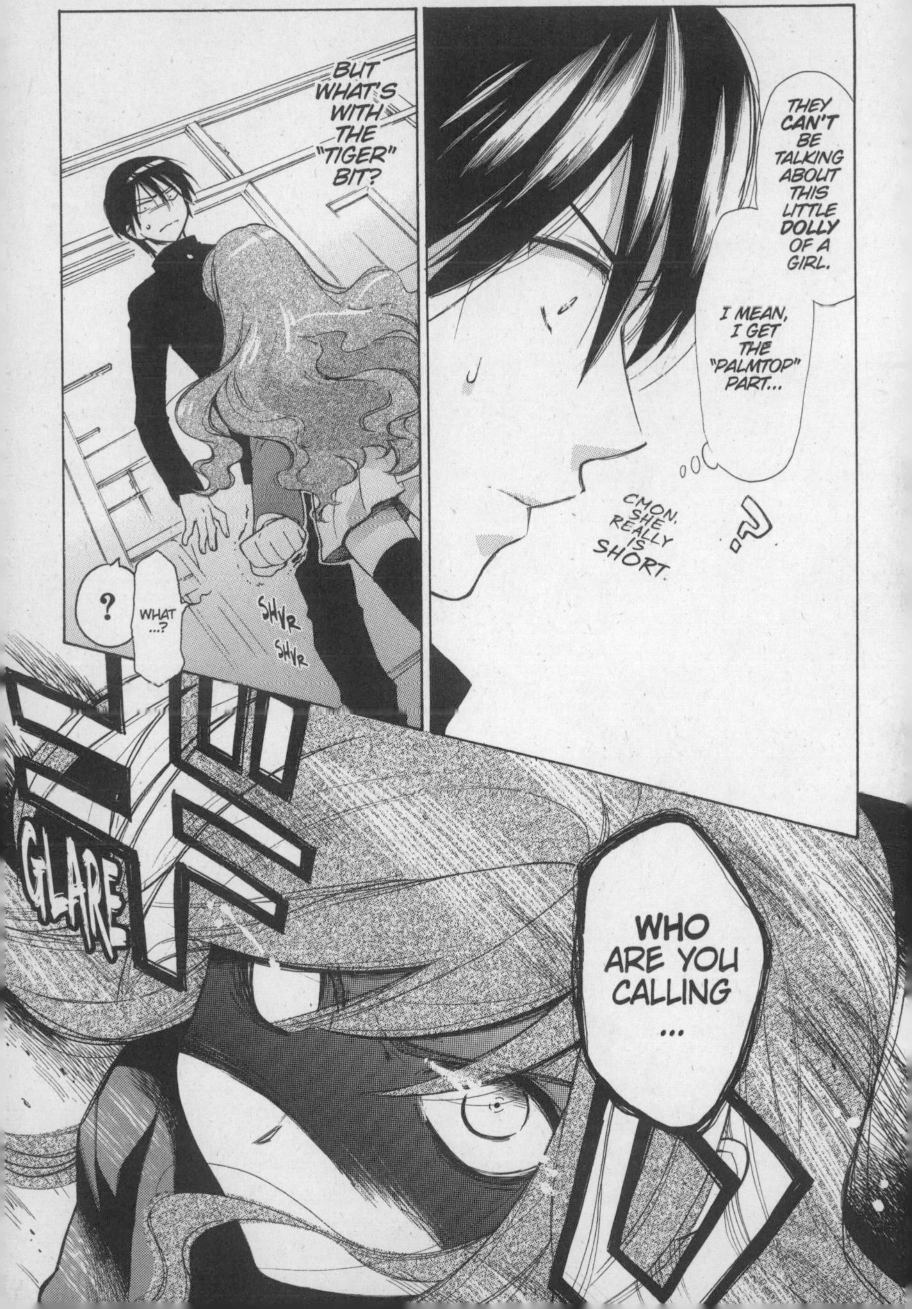
THEY CAN'T BE TALKING ABOUT THIS LITTLE DOLLY OF A GIRL.
I MEAN, I GET THE "PALMTOP" PART...
C'MON, SHE REALLY IS SHORT.
?
BUT WHAT'S WITH THE "TIGER" BIT?
SHVR SHVR
WHAT ...?
?
GLARE
WHO ARE YOU CALLING ...

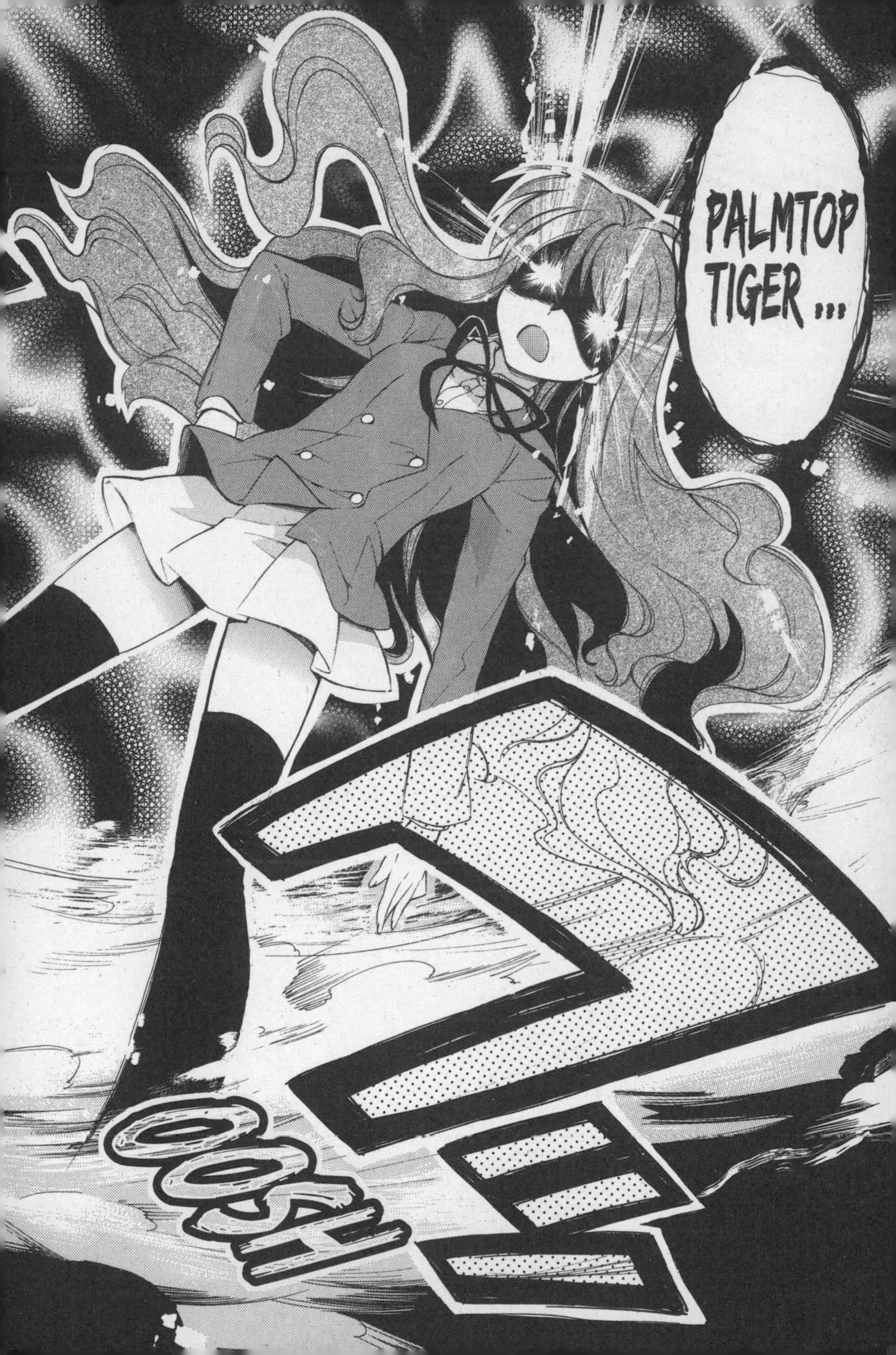
PALMTOP TIGER ...
OOF!!

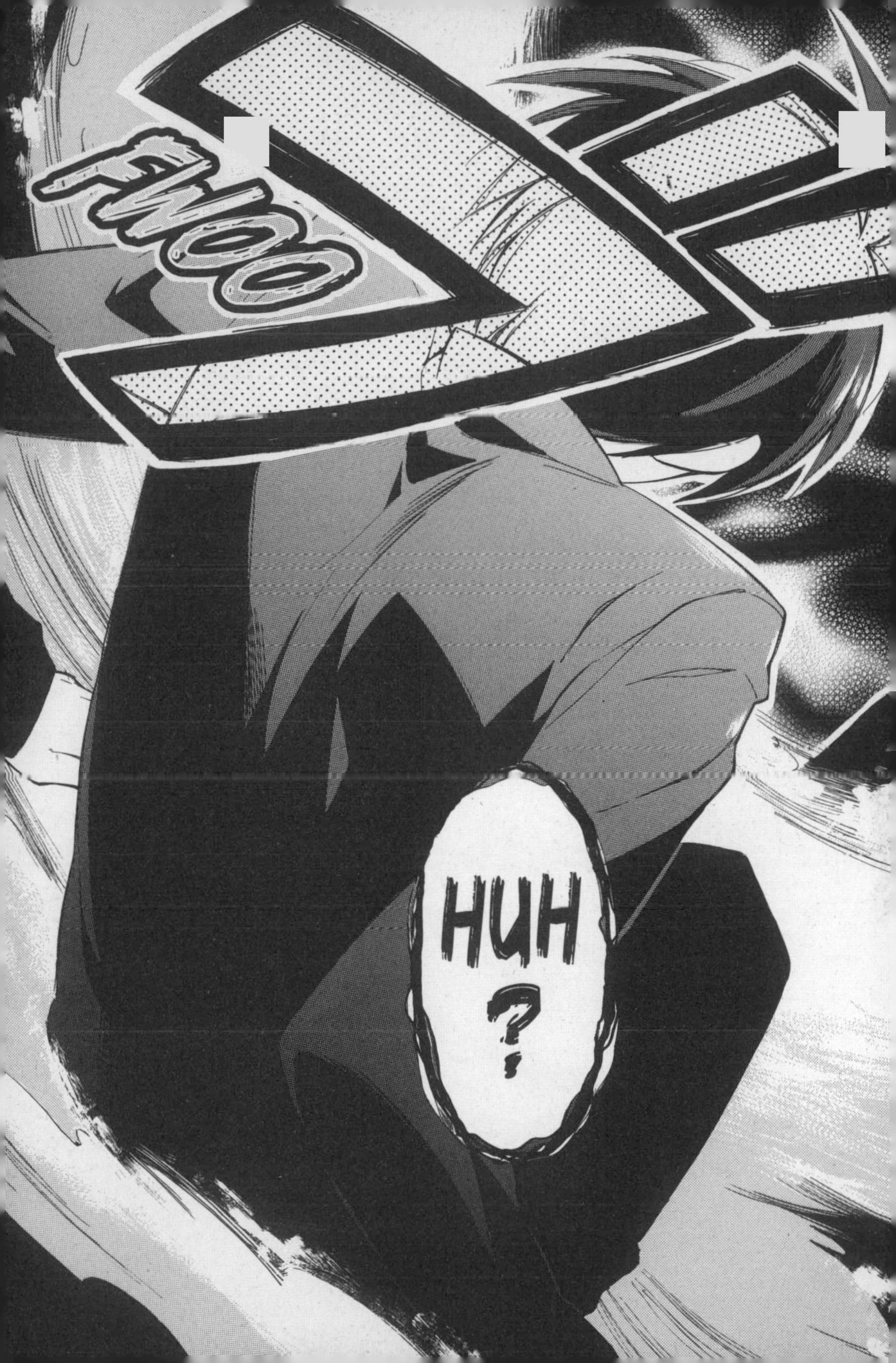
FWOO
HUH?

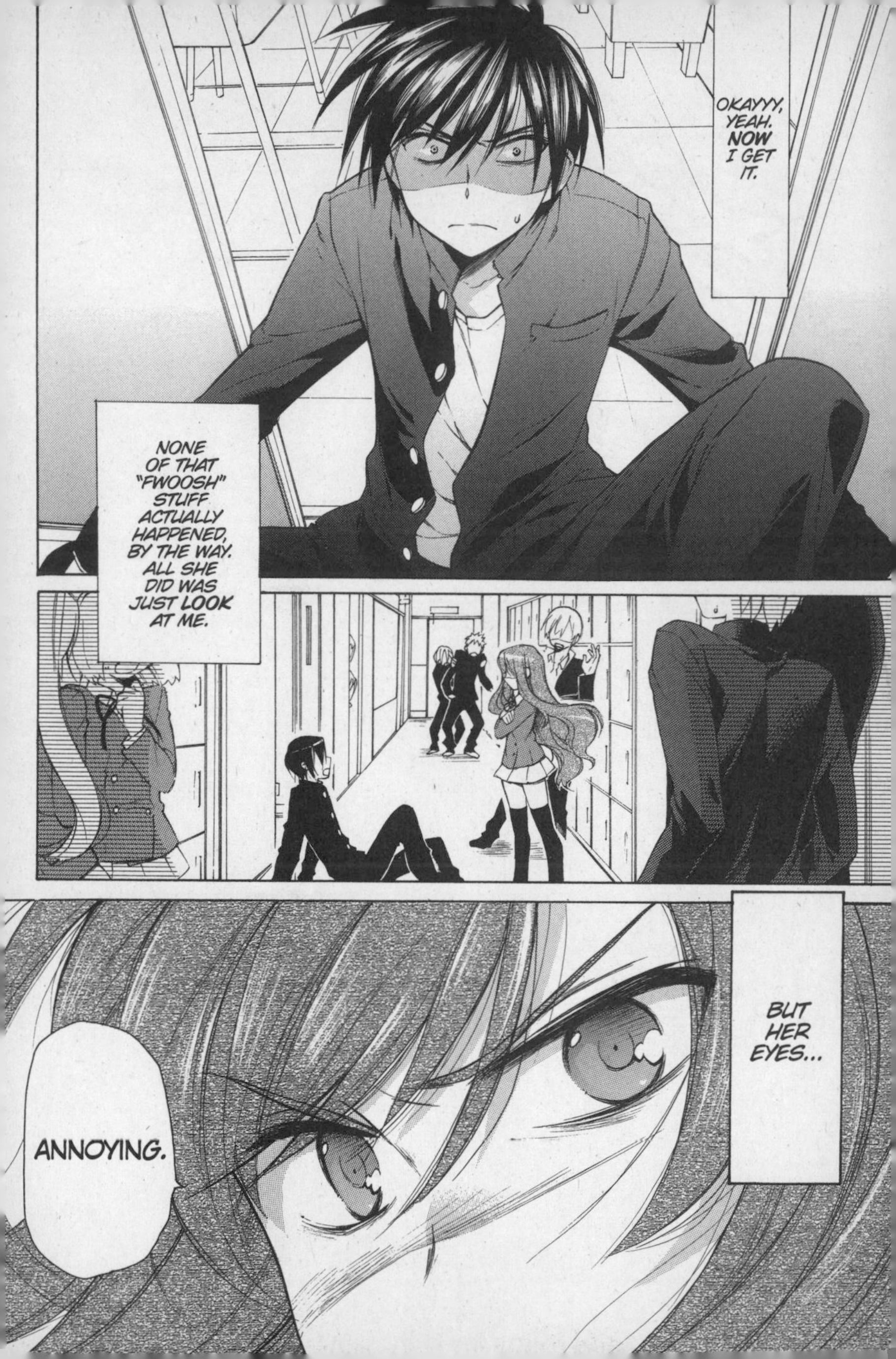
OKAYYY, YEAH. NOW I GET IT.
NONE OF THAT "FWOOSH" STUFF ACTUALLY HAPPENED, BY THE WAY. ALL SHE DID WAS JUST LOOK AT ME.
BUT HER EYES...
ANNOYING.

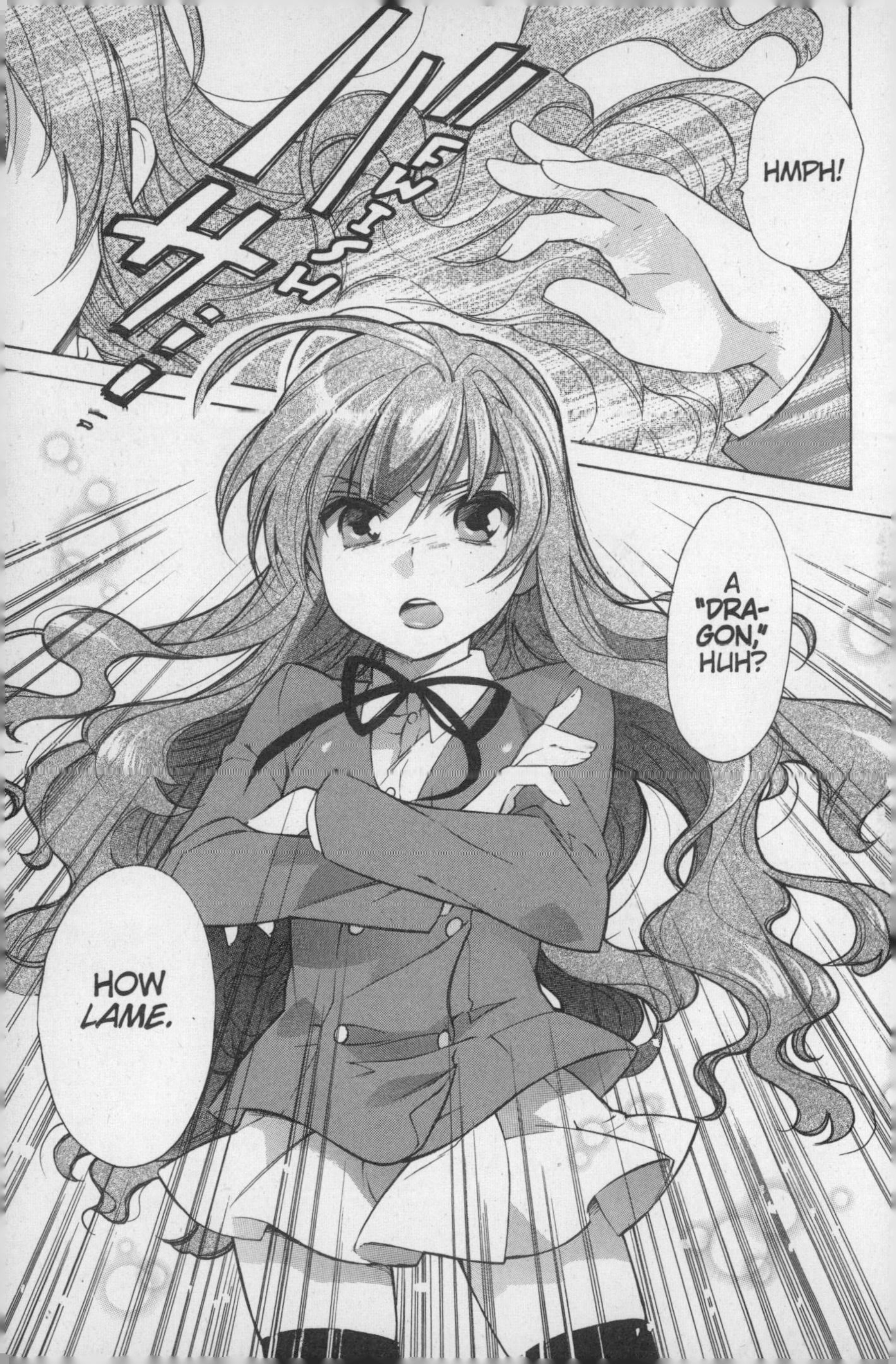
HMPH!
FWISH
A "DRA-GON," HUH?
HOW LAME.

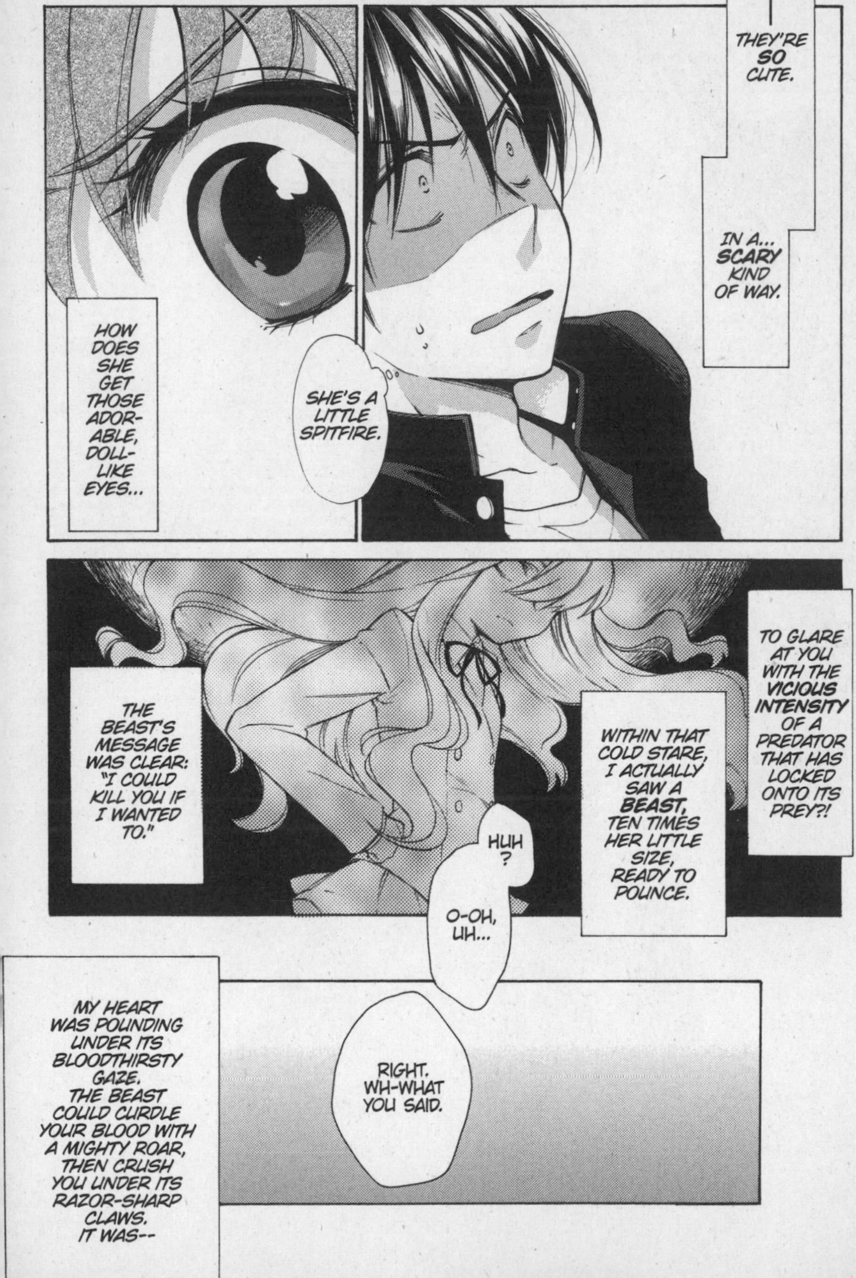
THEY'RE **SO** CUTE.
IN A... **SCARY** KIND OF WAY.
SHE'S A LITTLE SPITFIRE.
HOW DOES SHE GET THOSE ADORABLE, DOLL-LIKE EYES...
TO GLARE AT YOU WITH THE **VICIOUS INTENSITY** OF A PREDATOR THAT HAS LOCKED ONTO ITS PREY?!
WITHIN THAT COLD STARE, I ACTUALLY SAW A **BEAST,** TEN TIMES HER LITTLE SIZE, READY TO POUNCE.
HUH?
THE BEAST'S MESSAGE WAS CLEAR: "I COULD KILL YOU IF I WANTED TO."
O-OH, UH...
RIGHT. WH-WHAT YOU SAID.
MY HEART WAS POUNDING UNDER ITS BLOODTHIRSTY GAZE. THE BEAST COULD CURDLE YOUR BLOOD WITH A MIGHTY ROAR, THEN CRUSH YOU UNDER ITS RAZOR-SHARP CLAWS. IT WAS--

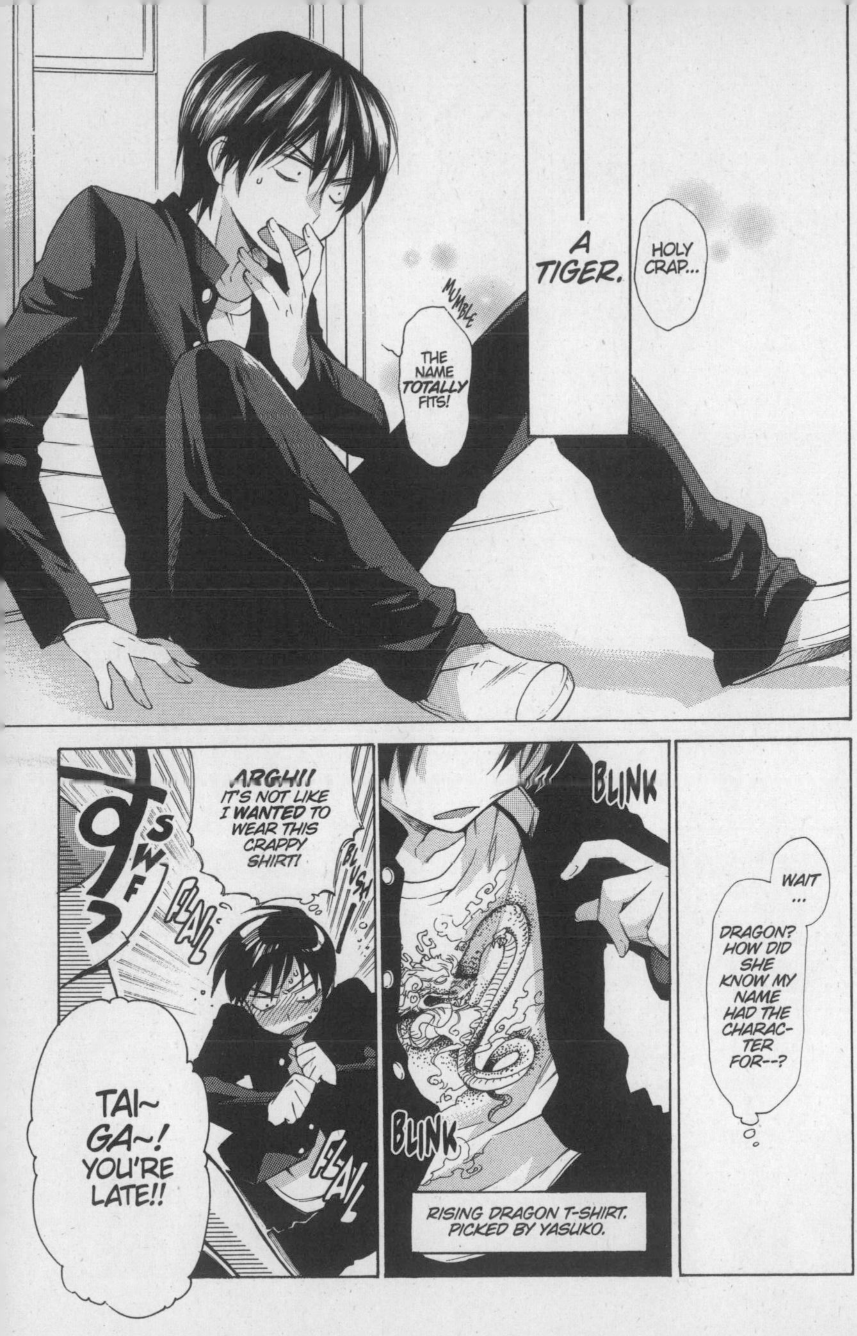
HOLY CRAP...
A TIGER.
MUMBLE
THE NAME TOTALLY FITS!
WAIT ... DRAGON? HOW DID SHE KNOW MY NAME HAD THE CHARACTER FOR--?
BLINK
BLINK
RISING DRAGON T-SHIRT. PICKED BY YASUKO.
ARGH!! IT'S NOT LIKE I WANTED TO WEAR THIS CRAPPY SHIRT!
BLUSH
SWF
FLAIL
FLAIL
TAI~GA~! YOU'RE LATE!!

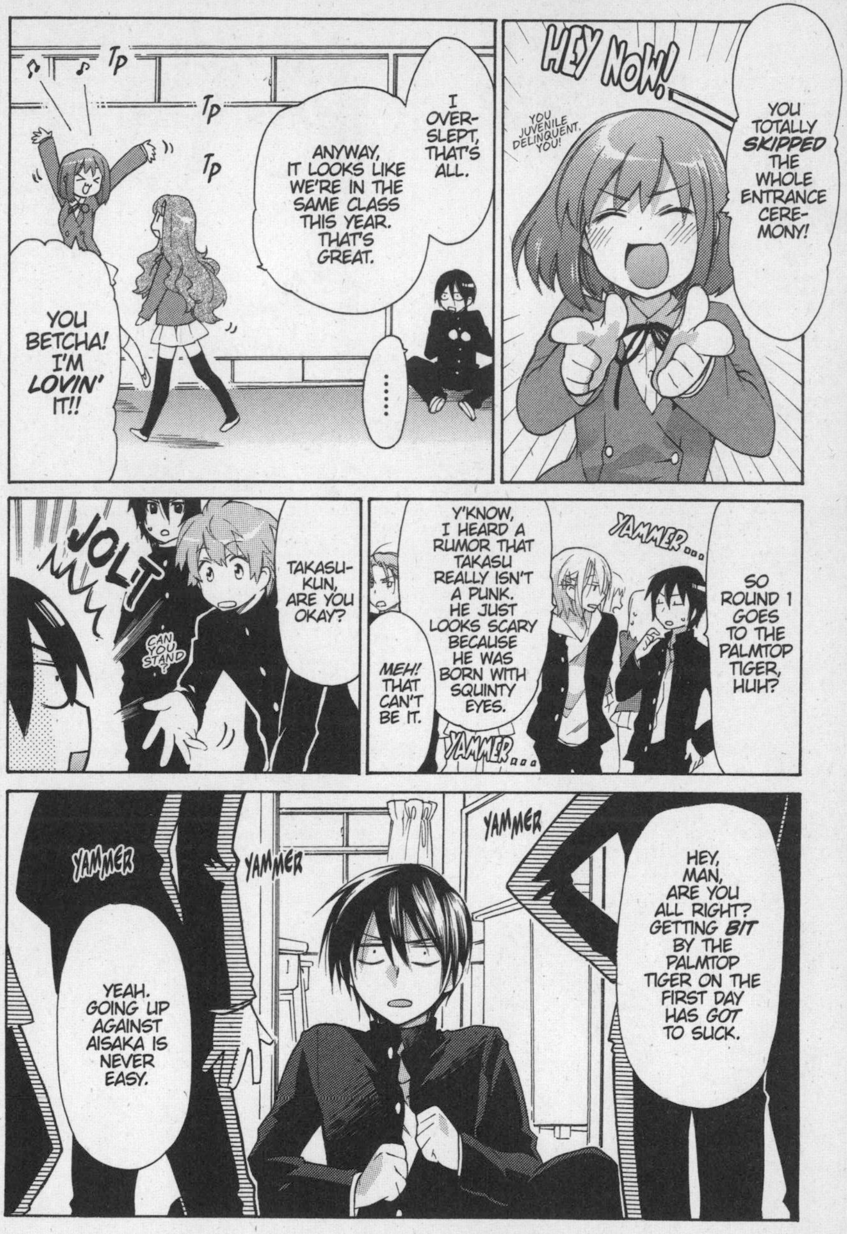
HEY NOW!
YOU TOTALLY SKIPPED THE WHOLE ENTRANCE CEREMONY!
YOU JUVENILE DELINQUENT, YOU!
I OVERSLEPT, THAT'S ALL.
ANYWAY, IT LOOKS LIKE WE'RE IN THE SAME CLASS THIS YEAR. THAT'S GREAT.
Tp
Tp
Tp
......
YOU BETCHA! I'M LOVIN' IT!!
SO ROUND 1 GOES TO THE PALMTOP TIGER, HUH?
YAMMER...
Y'KNOW, I HEARD A RUMOR THAT TAKASU REALLY ISN'T A PUNK. HE JUST LOOKS SCARY BECAUSE HE WAS BORN WITH SQUINTY EYES.
MEH! THAT CAN'T BE IT.
YAMMER...
TAKASU-KUN, ARE YOU OKAY?
JOLT
CAN YOU STAND?
YAMMER
HEY, MAN, ARE YOU ALL RIGHT? GETTING BIT BY THE PALMTOP TIGER ON THE FIRST DAY HAS GOT TO SUCK.
YAMMER
YAMMER
YEAH. GOING UP AGAINST AISAKA IS NEVER EASY.

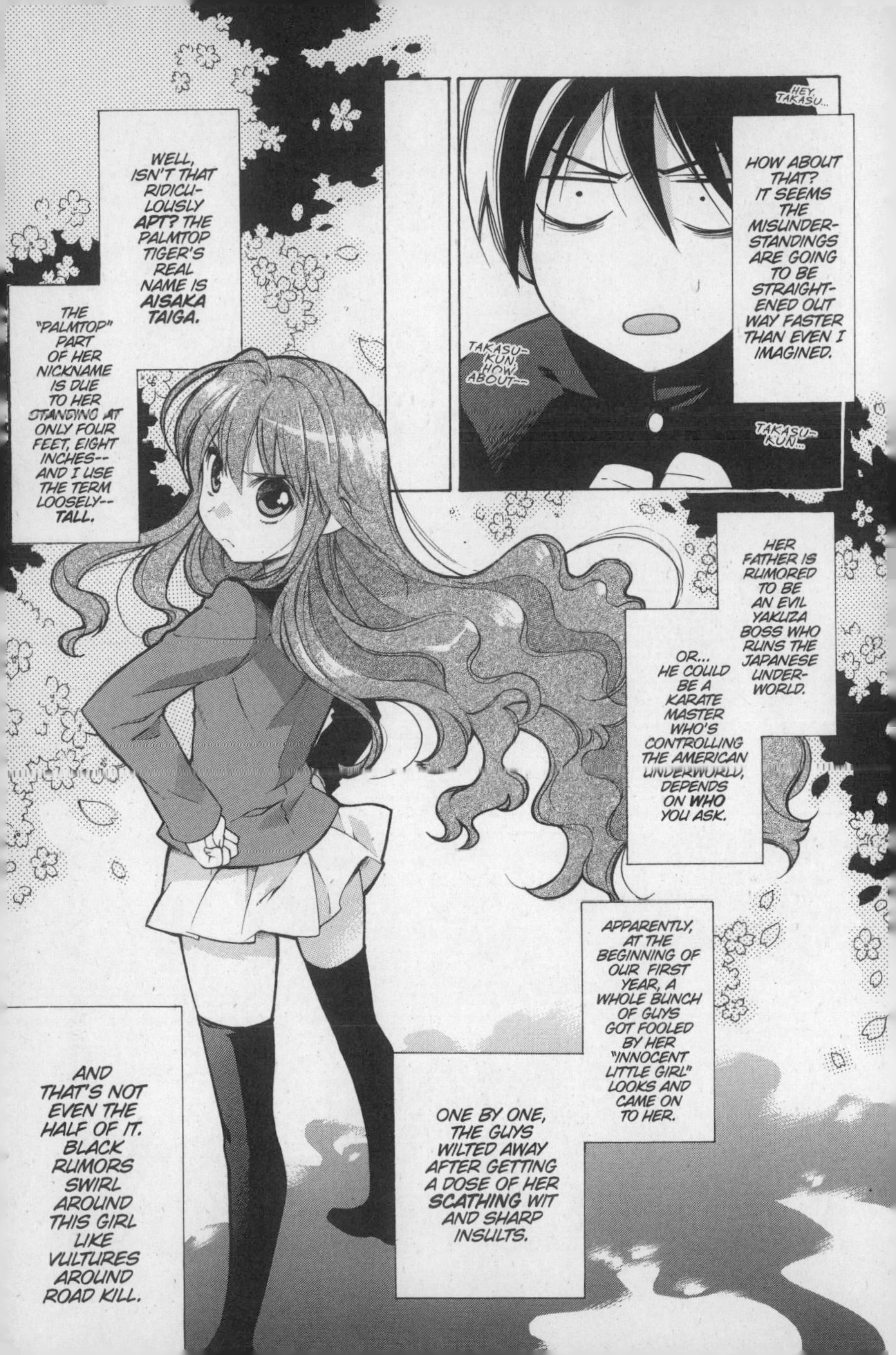
HEY, TAKASU...
HOW ABOUT THAT? IT SEEMS THE MISUNDERSTANDINGS ARE GOING TO BE STRAIGHTENED OUT WAY FASTER THAN EVEN I IMAGINED.
TAKASU-KUN HOW ABOUT--
TAKASU-KUN...
WELL, ISN'T THAT RIDICULOUSLY APT? THE PALMTOP TIGER'S REAL NAME IS AISAKA TAIGA.
THE "PALMTOP" PART OF HER NICKNAME IS DUE TO HER STANDING AT ONLY FOUR FEET, EIGHT INCHES--AND I USE THE TERM LOOSELY--TALL.
HER FATHER IS RUMORED TO BE AN EVIL YAKUZA BOSS WHO RUNS THE JAPANESE UNDERWORLD.
OR... HE COULD BE A KARATE MASTER WHO'S CONTROLLING THE AMERICAN UNDERWORLD, DEPENDS ON WHO YOU ASK.
APPARENTLY, AT THE BEGINNING OF OUR FIRST YEAR, A WHOLE BUNCH OF GUYS GOT FOOLED BY HER "INNOCENT LITTLE GIRL" LOOKS AND CAME ON TO HER.
ONE BY ONE, THE GUYS WILTED AWAY AFTER GETTING A DOSE OF HER SCATHING WIT AND SHARP INSULTS.
AND THAT'S NOT EVEN THE HALF OF IT. BLACK RUMORS SWIRL AROUND THIS GIRL LIKE VULTURES AROUND ROAD KILL.

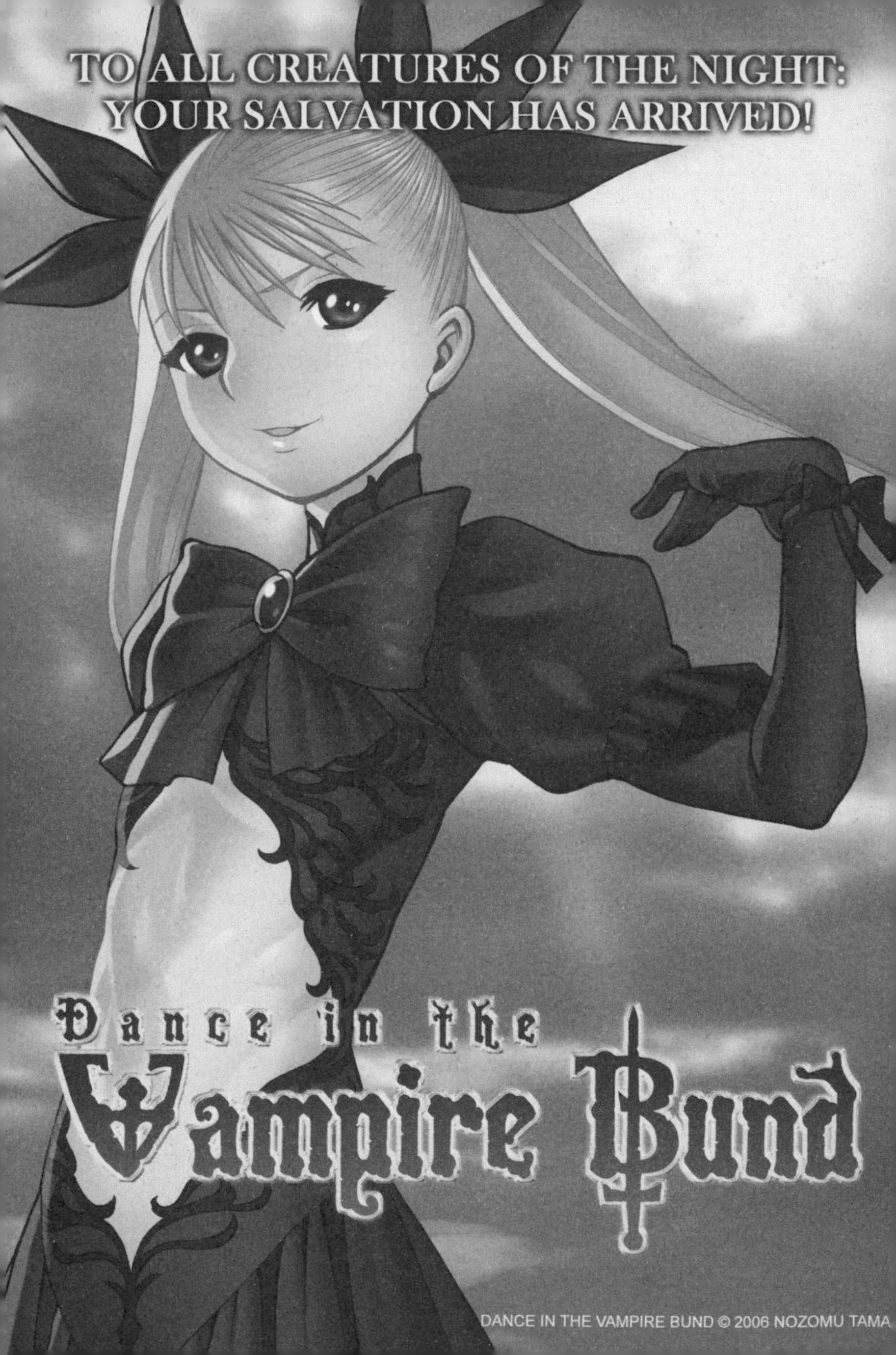
TO ALL CREATURES OF THE NIGHT:
YOUR SALVATION HAS ARRIVED!
Dance in the
Vampire Bund
DANCE IN THE VAMPIRE BUND © 2006 NOZOMU TAMA

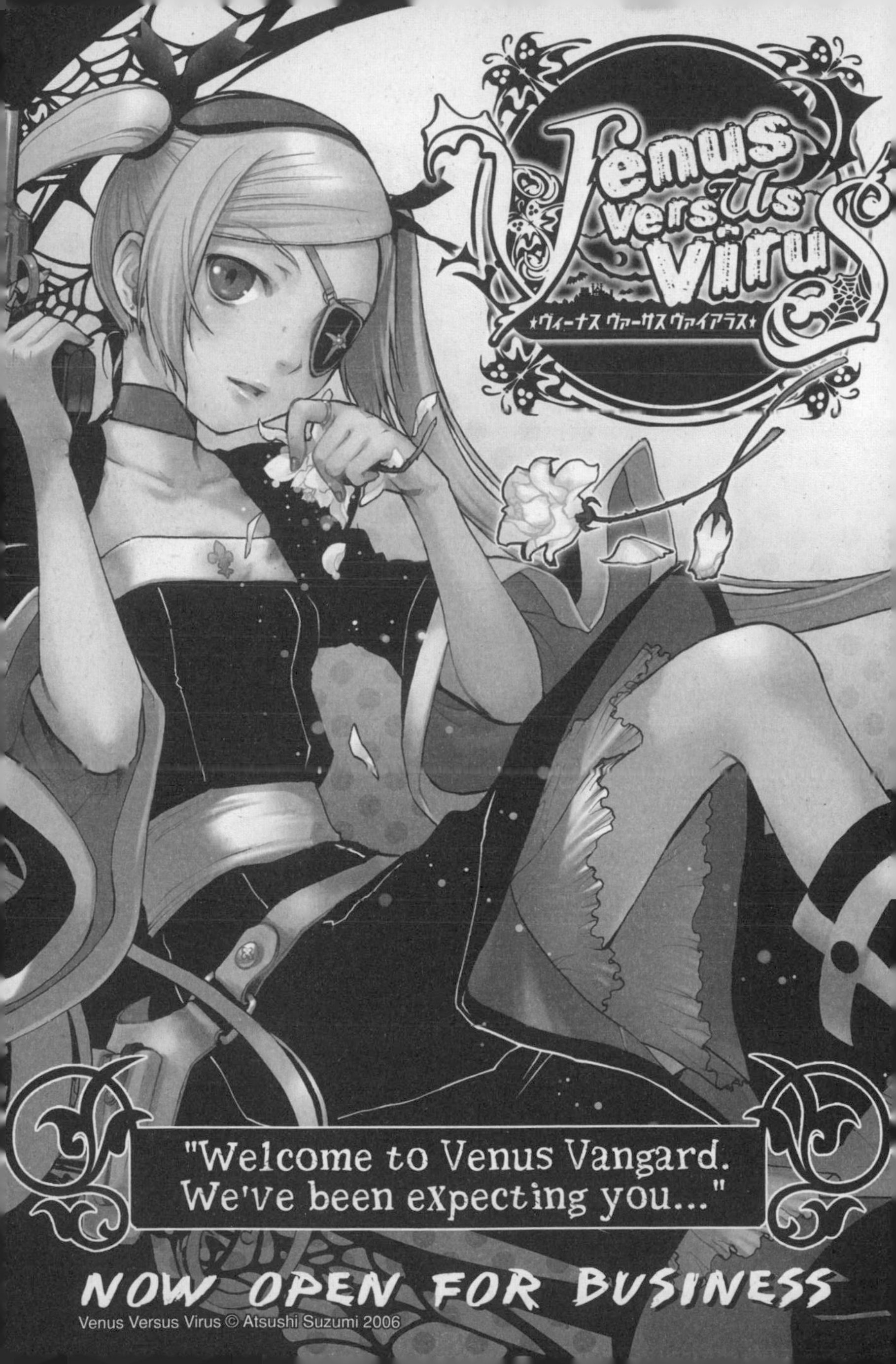
Venus Versus Virus
ヴィーナス ヴァーサス ヴァイアラス
"Welcome to Venus Vangard. We've been expecting you..."
NOW OPEN FOR BUSINESS
Venus Versus Virus © Atsushi Suzumi 2006

YOU'RE READING THE WRONG WAY

This is the last page of
Gunslinger Girl Omnibus Collection 2

This book reads from right to left, Japanese style. To read from the beginning, flip the book over to the other side, start with the top right panel, and take it from there.

If this is your first time reading manga, just follow the diagram. It may seem backwards at first, but you'll get used to it! Have fun!